Bank PO

RBI | SBI | IBPS

20 Sets

Previous Years'
Solved Papers
(2014-2018)

G K Publications (P) Ltd

CL MEDIA (P) LTD.

Edition : 2019

© **PUBLISHER**

No part of this book may be reproduced in a retrieval system or transmitted, in any form or by any means, electronics, mechanical, photocopying, recording, scanning and or without the written permission of the publisher.

ISBN   : **978-81-941144-2-0**
Typeset by : *CL Media DTP Unit*

Administrative and Production Offices

Published by : **CL Media (P) Ltd.**

A-45, Mohan Cooperative Industrial Area, Near Mohan Estate Metro Station, New Delhi - 110044

Marketed by : **G.K. Publications (P) Ltd.**

A-45, Mohan Cooperative Industrial Area, Near Mohan Estate Metro Station, New Delhi - 110044

For product information :

Visit **www.gkpublications.com** or email to **gkp@gkpublications.com**

Contents

2018

ENGLISH ABILITY

Direction (Q. 1-6): Read the passage carefully then answer the questions given below.

People have long circulated news via word-of-mouth, and as language evolved into writing and literacy -and governments played larger roles in people's lives - sharing information became a necessity. However, **disseminating** news and information on paper presented significant challenges. When each copy had to be handwritten, mass distribution was impossible. They were first chiseled in stone or metal; later, they were handwritten and distributed in public forums or read from scrolls by town criers. Though both ancient Romans and Chinese - as well as other ancient civilizations - had early forms of news media, they do not qualify as newspapers because they could not be mass-distributed.

The first true newspapers arrived after Johannes Gutenberg introduced his movable type printing press to the European world around 1440. Though printing presses with movable type had existed in eastern Asia for around two centuries, they never made it to Europe; furthermore, Gutenberg's version made it significantly faster to mass produce documents. By 1500, the printing press had made its way throughout Europe, and news sheets (or news books) were mass-distributed.

The first weekly newspaper was published in Germany by Johann Carolus in 1604. Called Relation aller F ürnemmen und gedenckw ürdigen Historien, the publication satisfied the four tenets of a "true" newspaper: Accessibility by the public , Published at a regular interval (daily, weekly, monthly, etc.) .Information is current ,Covers a variety of topics (politics, events, entertainment, sports, etc.) Despite meeting the requirements for a newspaper, there is some debate as to whether The Relation qualifies as the world's first newspaper since it was printed in quarto, not folio, size. It's worth noting the World Association of Newspapers considers The Relation the first true newspaper.'

Other German newspapers followed, and in 1618 the world's first broadsheet newspaper printed in folio size was published in Amsterdam, called Courante uyt Italien, Duytslandt, &c. The newspaper format soon spread throughout Europe, with newspapers published in Spain, France, and Sweden. The first English newspaper was published in 1665 in Oxford, England. Known as the Oxford Gazette, the newspaper moved to London in 1666 and was renamed the London Gazette. It's still being published today. Soon after, the newspaper became a staple in all major European countries. It then made its way to the New World.

1. Which of the following options is satisfying the condition for being a tenant of a "true newspaper"?

   (a) A newspaper which is accessible to only Asian readers.

   (b) A newspaper which was published once in a month.

   (c) A newspaper which was printed in quarto, not folio, size

   (d) A newspaper which covers historic developments leading to various events.

   (e) A newspaper which is printed in press and is not handwritten.

2. Which of the following options is false according to the passage?

   (a) The relation was not the first newspaper as it did not meet all the required conditions.

   (b) Information on paper was only possible after the introduction of press.

   (c) The concept of newspaper was rejected in Europe earlier.

   (d) London Gazette is the first newspaper to be published in the multiple languages.

   (e) All are incorrect

3. What paved the way for the "true newspapers"?

   (a) The world's first broadsheet newspaper printed in folio size

   (b) The invention of the printing press paved the way for "true" newspapers.

    (c) The technology which allowed it to be printed in multiple languages.

    (d) As the Governments started playing a larger role in people's lives

    (e) None of these.

4. Which of the following statement is true regarding newspapers?

    (a) The first weekly newspaper was published in Germany by Johann Carolus in 1904.

    (b) The Relation qualifies as the world's first newspaper since it was printed in folio, not quarto.

    (c) The first English newspaper was published in 1695 in Oxford, England known as the Oxford Gazette.

    (d) The world's first broadsheet newspaper printed in quarto size was published in Amsterdam, called Courante uyt Italien, Duytslandt, &c.

    (e) The first English newspaper known as the Oxford Gazette, was renamed the London Gazette later.

5. Choose the word which is most nearly the SIMILAR in meaning to the word 'disseminating' printed in bold as used in the passage.

    (a) Agree   (b) Taunt

    (c) Barb   (d) Sneer

    (e) Spread

6. In ancient time what was the biggest challenge that the people had to face while circulating the news?

    (a) The biggest challenge was of printing the news on a paper

    (b) Earlier each copy had to be handwritten; mass distribution was next to impossible.

    (c) It was a herculean task for the editors to get an affirmation by government for printing the news

    (d) Both (a) and (c)

    (e) All are incorrect

Directions (Q. 7-10): In each of the questions given below a part of the sentence is given in bold. It is then followed by three options. Find the alternative that can replace the given bold part to make the sentence grammatically and contextually correct. If none of the alternatives is correct and the sentence is correct as it is then select option (e) as your choice.

7. Economist Deena Khatkhate, **who will pass away** at the age of 92 on September 15 in Bethesda, Maryland, in the US, was an unusual man.

    (i)   who passed away

    (ii) who shall passed away

    (iii) who has passed away

    (a) Only (ii)

    (b) Both (i) and (iii)

    (c) Both (ii) and (iii)

    (d) Only (iii)

    (e) No correction required

8. A misogynist is a person **who is hating** women.

    (i) Who are hating

    (ii) Who have hate

    (iii) Who hates

    (a) Both (i) and (iii)

    (b) Only (i)

    (c) Both (ii) and (iii)

    (d) Only (iii)

    (e) No correction required

9. Samira **is the better of the two girls** when it comes to solving hard mathematic problems,

    (i) is the better of two girls

    (ii) is better of the two girls

    (iii) is better of two girls

    (a) Only (i)

    (b) Only (ii)

    (c) Both (ii) and (iii)

    (d) Both (i) and (iii)

    (e) No correction is required

10. There are two novels on the table which needs to be read before the exams, but **neither one are interesting**.

    (i) neither one has interested

    (ii) neither one is interesting

    (iii) neither one were interesting

    (a) Only (i)

    (b) Both (i) and (ii)

    (c) Only (ii)

    (d) Both (i) and (iii)

    (e) No correction is required

Directions (Q. 11-16): Each question below has one blank, which is indicating that something has been omitted. Find out which option can be used to fill up the blank in the sentence in the same sequence to make it meaningfully complete.

11. Homemade gifts can be completely ______ to what the recipient likes.

    (a) Alters   (b) Firmed

    (c) Tailored   (d) Polite

    (e) Liability

12. After much thought, Ted _____ not to travel abroad this summer.
    (a) Resolved   (b) Concludes
    (c) Resolves   (d) Commence
    (e) Passed

13. Bryan is _____ in his belief that the earth is flat.
    (a) Tentative   (b) Hasten
    (c) Unlikely   (d) Provided
    (e) Confident

14. The noodle maker was _____ in making his noodles and would never let another person take over the task.
    (a) Careless   (b) Negligent
    (c) Cautious   (d) Exciting
    (e) Inattentive

15. If it weren't for the _____ circumstances, he would have certainly lost his job.
    (a) Sharp   (b) Intensify
    (c) Mitigating   (d) Increase
    (e) Aggravate

16. When asked about her father, she lost her outward enthusiasm and became rather _____ .
    (a) Reserved   (b) Expansive
    (c) talkative   (d) Extrovert
    (e) Outgoing

Directions (Q. 17-20): In each of the questions given below four words are given in bold. These four words may or may not be in their correct position. The sentence is then followed by options with the correct combination of words that should replace each other in order to make the sentence grammatically and contextually correct. Find the correct combination of the words that replace each other. If the sentence is correct as it then select option (e) as your choice.

17. Some American officials **lead** (A) to hope that **resumed** (B) sanctions on Iran will **appear** (C) to a popular **uprising** (D).
    (a) A-B
    (b) A-C
    (c) B-D and A-C
    (d) A-D
    (e) The sentence is correct

18. **Tariffs** (A) has **imported** (B) higher **China** (C) on 603 items **imposed** (D) from the US.
    (a) OnlyA-B
    (b) OnlyB-C
    (c) Both A-B and B-D
    (d) Both A-C and B-D.
    (e) The sentence is correct.

19. NATO ally **world** (A) leads the **Turkey** (B) in the **journalists** (C) of **number** (D) jailed.
    (a) A-B and C-D
    (b) Only B-C
    (c) A-C and B-D
    (d) A-D
    (e) The sentence is correct.

20. In 2016, **rising** (A) violence in **Pathankot** (B) by Islamic militants **culminated** (C) in attacks on Indian forces at Uri and **Kashmir** (D).
    (a) Both A-C and B-D
    (b) Both A-D and B-C
    (c) Only B-D.
    (d) C-D
    (e) The sentence is correct.

Direction (Q. 21-24): Read each sentence to find out whether there is any grammatical or idiomatic error in it. The error, if any, will be in one part of the sentence. The number of that part is the answer. If there is 'No error', the answer is (e). (Ignore errors of punctuation, if any.)

21. She held something (a) / at her side which (b) / was totally hiding (c) / by the folds of her sari, (d) / No error, (e)

22. The father forbade his son (a) / to walk in the sun (b) / and play with (c) / his friends on the road (d) / No error (e)

23. The movement, which aims to (a) / raise awareness about climate change, hopes (b) / to bring people together to think about (c) / what they can do for reduce harmful pollution, (d) / No error (e)

24. I declined the invitation (a) / not because I did not (b) / want to go but (c) / because I have no time, (d) / No error (e)

Directions (Q. 25-30): In the following passage, some of the words have been left out, each of which is indicated by a number. Find the suitable word from the options given against each number and fill up the blanks with appropriate words to make the paragraph meaningfully complete.

Stanford economist Nicholas Bloom is a true believer, and like many true believers, he lets his message _(25)_ his evidence. Based on a single study of a Chinese travel agency, he _(26)_ declares working from home a "future-looking technology" with "enormous potential." Not so fast.

Bloom's study comes with serious limitations and is contradicted by a later Gallup report. However, while it is far too soon to draw broad _(27)_ from his findings, savvy business leaders can read between the lines and extract some valuable lessons for working (28) with all employees.

Bloom _(29)_ on China's biggest travel agency, Ctrip, which wanted to expand while controlling office space costs. They __(30)__ a remote work trial, expecting that productivity would slip a little, but not enough to cancel out the savings. Instead, productivity shot up 13%, and attrition dropped 50%. When the work from home option was rolled out to the entire company and employees were given a choice, the productivity gains were 22%.

25. (a) cut   (b) outrun
     (c) exceeded   (d) begin
     (e) choose

26. (a) fast
     (b) enthusiastically
     (c) slowly
     (d) eager
     (e) appropriately

27. (a) resulting
     (b) disappointments
     (c) conclusions
     (d) exercises
     (e) guarantees

28. (a) optimally   (b) extremely
     (c) competitively   (d) abroad
     (e) everywhere

29. (a) emphasising   (b) concentrates
     (c) learned   (d) matched
     (e) focused

30. (a) establishes   (b) appointed
     (c) brought   (d) instituted
     (e) sold

REASONING ABILITY

Directions (Q. 31-35): Study the following information carefully and answer the questions given below:

Nine boxes named P, Q, R, S, T, U, V, W and X are placed one above other but not necessarily in the same order. Only five boxes are placed between P and R. T is placed immediate above R. Only three boxes are placed between T and S. As many boxes placed between P and S as between Q and T. U is placed below Q, but not at bottom. More than four boxes are placed between T and U. One box is placed between U and V. Box X is placed above box W.

31. Which box is placed at bottom?
     (a) P   (b) S
     (c) T   (d) X
     (e) V

32. How many boxes are placed between X and P?
     (a) one   (b) two
     (c) three   (d) four
     (e) more than four

33. If in a certain way S is related to X and P is related to W then by which among the following Q is related?
     (a) P   (b) V
     (c) R   (d) T
     (e) S

34. Which box is placed immediate above and immediate below Q?
     (a) R and W   (b) X and U
     (c) U and S   (d) S and X
     (e) T and R

35. What is the position of W?
     (a) fourth from the top
     (b) fifth from the top
     (c) third from the bottom
     (d) sixth from the bottom
     (e) forth from the bottom

Directions (Q. 36-40): Study the information and answer the following questions:

In a certain code language

Get details for venue --- fe wi mo rs

Venue book required details --- rs gt rd wi

Details required book guest --- wi gt rd ra

Guest get more venue --- ra fe gk rs

36. What is the code for 'details' in the given code language?
     (a) fe   (b) mo
     (c) wi   (d) ra
     (e) None of these

37. What is the code for the word 'guest venue' in the given code language?
     (a) gt gk   (b) fe mo
     (c) rs ra   (d) gt ra
     (e) None of these

38. What is the code for the word 'get' in the given code language?
     (a) gt   (b) fe
     (c) rs   (d) rd
     (e) None of these

39. If the code for the words 'for ______' is coded as 'mo gk' in the coded language then what will be the missing word?
     (a) book   (b) required
     (c) guest   (d) more
     (c) cither (a) or (d)

40. What is the code for 'book' in the given code language?

   (a) rs   (b) gt

   (c) rd   (d) kl

   (e) either (b) or (c)

Directions (Q. 41-45): Study the following information carefully and answer the given questions:

Eight friends A, B, C, D, W, X, Y and Z are sitting around a square table in such a way that four of them sit at four corners of the square while the other four sit in the middle of each sides. The ones who sit at the four corners face outside while those who sit in the middle of the sides face inside.

C is an immediate neighbor of A, who faces center. W sits second to the left of C. Y sits fourth to the left of W. Two persons sit between Y and D (either from left or right). C is not an immediate neighbor of D. B sits second to the right of D. X sits second to the right of B.

41. How many persons sits between Z and C when counted from left of Z?

   (a) None   (b) One

   (c) Two   (d) Three

   (e) More than three

42. What is the position of Y with respect to D?

   (a) Third to the right   (b) Second to the right

   (c) Fourth to the left   (d) Third to the left

   (e) None of these

43. Four of the following five are alike in a certain way and so form a group. Who among the following does not belong to that group?

   (a) Z   (b) W

   (c) D   (d) C

   (e) Y

44. Who sits second to the right of A?

   (a) B   (b) X

   (c) Y   (d) D

   (e) None of these

45. Who among the following sits between B and C, when counted from the right of B?

   (a) Y and Z   (b) W and D

   (c) X and Y   (d) A and W

   (e) A and D

Directions (Q. 46-50): In these questions, a relationship between different elements is shown in the statements. The statements are followed by two conclusions. Give answer

46. **Statement:**

   L ≤ T ≤ I ≥ M < X, W < P ≤ L ≥ B ≥ K

   I.   K < X

   II. W > M

   (a) if only conclusion II is true.

   (b) if only conclusion I is true.

   (c) if neither conclusion I nor II is true.

   (d) if either conclusion I or II is true.

   (e) if both conclusions I and II are true.

47. **Statement:**

   Z < U ≤ D ≤ A ≤ M < S, Q > A ≤ Y < G

   I.   Z < Y

   II. S > Q

   (a) if both conclusion I and II are true.

   (b) if only conclusion I is true.

   (c) if neither conclusion I nor II is true.

   (d) if either conclusion I or II is true.

   (e) if only conclusion II is true.

48. **Statement:**

   L ≤ T ≤ I > M < X, W < P ≤ L ≥ B ≥ K

   I.   K ≥ M

   II. P > M

   (a) if only conclusion II is true.

   (b) if either conclusion I or II is true.

   (c) if neither conclusion I nor II is true.

   (d) if only conclusion I is true.

   (e) if both conclusions I and II are true.

49. **Statement:** Z < U ≤ D ≤ A ≤ M < S, Q > A ≤ Y < G

   I.   M ≥ U

   II. G > Z

   (a) if only conclusion II is true.

   (b) if only conclusion I is true.

   (c) if neither conclusion I nor II is true.

   (d) if either conclusion I or II is true.

   (e) if both conclusions I and II are true.

50. **Statement:** J > K ≥ H = U ≥ B ≤ T < F ≤ R

   I.   J > B

   II. H < R

   (a) if only conclusion II is true.

   (b) if either conclusion I or II is true.

   (c) if neither conclusion I nor II is true.

   (d) if only conclusion I is true.

   (e) if both conclusions I and II are true.

51. How many such pairs of letters are there in the word "Streaming" having same number of letters between them as they have between them according to the alphabetical order.

   (a) Two   (b) More than Three

   (c) Three   (d) One

   (e) None of these

52. Find the odd one out?
    (a) JQK
    (b) BYC
    (c) LRM
    (d) CXD
    (e) OPX

Direction (Q. 53-55): Study the information and answer the following questions:

D is 20m in south of A. C is 5m east of D. E is 10m north of C. F is 10m east of E. G is 15m south of F. X is 15m west of G. B is 10m to the east of A. Z is 10m to the south of B. L is 10m to east of C.

53. In which direction is point A with respect to point G?
    (a) North-west
    (b) South-east
    (c) North
    (d) South-west
    (e) North-east

54. Four of the following are alike in a certain way so form a group, which of the following does not belong to that group?
    (a) EF   (b) EC
    (c) LG   (d) BZ
    (e) CL

55. What is distance between point F and L?
    (a) 10m   (b) 5m
    (c) 15m   (d) 20m
    (e) 25m

Directions (Q. 56-60): Study the information and answer the following questions:

Eight persons K, L, M, N, O, P, Q and R sitting in a row. Some of them are facing north while some are facing south. N sits fifth to the right of M but none of them sits at an extreme end. Q sits third to the right of N. L sits second to the right of Q. Only one person sit between L and P. R sits third to the left of P. K sits second to the left of O. Both the person sitting at extreme ends faces opposite direction to each other. Both the immediate neighbours of M faces same direction. R sits to the left of L and both of them are facing opposite direction to each other. R does not face north direction.

56. Who among the following sits third to the right of R?
    (a) Q   (b) K
    (c) M   (d) N
    (e) None of these

57. Which among the following pair sit at the end of the row?
    (a) Q, L   (b) R, K
    (c) O, P   (d) L, R
    (e) None of these

58. How many persons sits to the right of K?
    (a) Two
    (b) More than Three
    (c) Three
    (d) One
    (e) None of these

59. Who among the following sits second to the right of Q?
    (a) L   (b) N
    (c) M   (d) O
    (e) None of these

60. Four of the following are alike in a certain way so form a group, which of the following does not belong to that group?
    (a) K   (b) N
    (c) R   (d) O
    (e) P

Directions (Q. 61-65): Study the following information carefully and answer the given questions:

Seven persons E, F, G, H, S, T and U buys seven different items viz. Tie, Coat, Ring, Nail paint, Shirt, Diary and Goggles on different days. One person buys one item in a day.

Four person buys items between E and the one who buys Tie. The one who buys coat buys immediately after the one who buys Tie. Two persons buys items between H and the one who buys Tie. T buys immediately after H. F buys his item immediately after the one who buys Diary. Two person buys items between the one who buys coat and the one who buys Shirt. S buys Ring. Goggles was bought immediately after E. Two person buys item between the one who buys Ring and the one who buys Diary. U buys his item before G.

61. Who among the following buys Nail paint?
    (a) U   (b) G
    (c) H   (d) T
    (e) None of These

62. Which item was bought immediately after Shirt?
    (a) Diary   (b) Goggles
    (c) Tie   (d) Coat
    (e) None of These

63. How many persons buys items between S and F?
    (a) One   (b) Two
    (c) Three   (d) Four
    (e) None of These

64. Which of the following combination is true?
    (a) G- Tie   (b) H- Dairy
    (c) T- Goggles   (d) E- Dairy
    (e) None is true

65. Who among the following buys item immediately before Ring?
    (a) U   (b) G
    (c) H   (d) T
    (e) None of These

QUANTITATIVE APTITUDE

Direction (Q. 66-70): Line chart given below shows number of labors (men and women) working in six different years. Study the data carefully and answer the following questions.

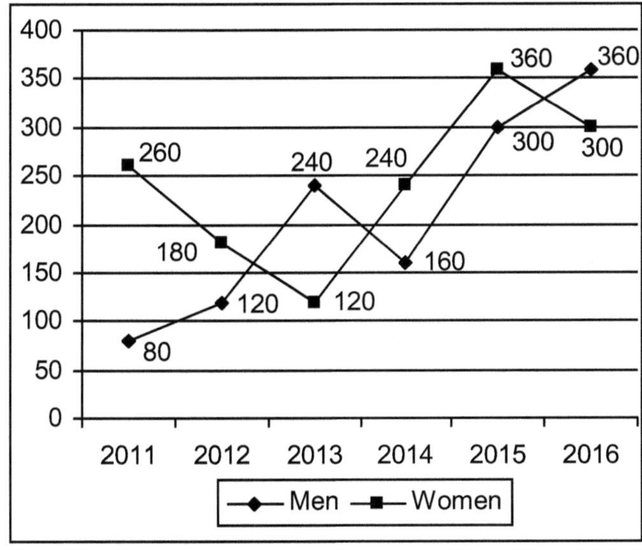

66. Total number of Men working in 2012 and 2013 together is what percent of the total number of labors (Men + Women) working in 2014?
    (a) 60%   (b) 70%
    (c) 80%   (d) 90%
    (e) 40%

67. Average number of Women working in 2014, 2015 and 2016 together is how much more/less than average number of Men working in 2011, 2014 and 2016 together?
    (a) 100   (b) 80
    (c) 90   (d) 70
    (e) None of the given options

68. Number of Men working in 2017 is 15% more than that of 2015 while number of Women working in 2017 is 40% less than that of 2014. Find total number of labors (Men + Women) working in 2017?
    (a) 561   (b) 456
    (c) 489   (d) 594
    (e) 630

69. Find the ratio between total number of Labors working in 2012 and 2013 together to total number of labors working in 2015 and 2016 together?
    (a) 2 : 1   (b) 1 : 2
    (c) 35 : 66   (d) 11 : 10
    (e) None of the given options

70. Total number of Men working in all six years is how much more/less than total number of Women working in all six years together?
    (a) None of the given options
    (b) 140
    (c) 160
    (d) 180
    (e) 200

Directions (Q. 71-76): Find the wrong number in the following number series:

71. 4, 5.1, 7.3, 10.6, 15, 20, 27.1
    (a) 5.1   (b) 4
    (c) 7.3   (d) 20
    (e) 27.1

72. 2, 3, 8, 31, 154, 924, 6460
    (a) 924   (b) 6460
    (c) 154   (d) 8
    (e) 31

73. 251, 252, 254, 227, 243, 118, 154
    (a) 251   (b) 252
    (c) 227   (d) 243
    (e) 154

74. 141, 156, 147, 162, 153, 165, 159
    (a) 156   (b) 153
    (c) 147   (d) 165
    (e) 159

75. 2, 6, 10, 19, 36, 69, 134
    (a) 134   (b) 69
    (c) 6   (d) 2
    (e) 10

76. 0.5, 2, 1, 4, 32, 512, 16384
    (a) 1   (b) 2
    (c) 4   (d) 32
    (e) 512

77. Ratio of present ages of A and B is 16:7. After 12 years, A's age is twice of B's age then find present ages of A and B?
    (a) 64yr; 28yr
    (b) 80yr; 35yr
    (c) None of these
    (d) 96yr; 42 yr
    (e) 102yr;49yr

78. A man invested a certain sum in scheme A at 15% p.a. for 2 years and earned Rs 1950 as simple interest. He increased his sum by Rs. 'x' and invested in another scheme B at 10% p.a. C.I. for 2 years and received Rs. 1680 as compound interest. Find the value of 'x' ?
    (a) Rs. 1750   (b) Rs. 1500
    (c) Rs. 1250   (d) None of these
    (e) Rs. 1850

79. In a class there are 30 girls and 15 boys and total average weight of class is $47\frac{7}{15}$ kg. Total average weight of boys is 58 kg. Find the approximate average weight of girls ?
    (a) 32 kg   (b) 42 kg
    (c) 52 kg   (d) 35 kg
    (e) 50 kg

80. Ram bought a bike at 20% discount on MRP. After 1 year Ram sell the bike to Ramesh at 10% loss. After 1 year more Ramesh sell the bike at 20% profit to Ranjan. If Ranjan paid Rs. 1,29,600, then find the M.R.P. of the bike ?
    (a) 1,50,000   (b) 2,25,000
    (c) 1,40,000   (d) 2,00,000
    (e) 1,80,000

Direction (Q. 81-85): There are 450 coupons which can be used in Pedicure and Hair cutting. Ratio between Males to Females who use their coupons in Hair cutting is 13 : 7 Number of males who use their coupons in Pedicure is 72 more than number of females who use their coupon in Hair cutting. Total number of males who use their coupon in Pedicure and Hair cutting together is 174 more than total number of females who use their coupon in Pedicure and Hair cutting together.

81. Males who use their coupon in Pedicure is what percent of the Males who use their coupons in Hair cutting?
    (a) 200%
    (b) 100%
    (c) None of the given options
    (d) 0%
    (e) 150%

82. Find the ratio between Total number persons who use their coupons in Pedicure to total number of persons who use their coupons in Hair cutting?
    (a) 52 : 23
    (b) None of the given options
    (c) 8 : 9
    (d) 8 : 7
    (e) 7 : 8

83. Females who use their coupon in Hair cutting is how much more than Females who use their coupon in Pedicure?
    (a) 15
    (b) 45
    (c) 30
    (d) None of the given options
    (e) 60

84. Out of males who use their coupons in Hair cutting, 25% belongs to city A, then find number of males who use their coupons in Haircutting which doesn't belongs to city A?
    (a) None of the given options
    (b) 108
    (c) 126
    (d) 117
    (e) 135

85. Ratio between Males who use their coupon in Pedicure to that of in Spa is 4 : 5, while ratio between Females who use their coupon in Hair cutting to that of in Spa is 6 : 11. Find total number of people who use their coupons in Spa?
    (a) 349
    (b) 481
    (c) 300
    (d) 440
    (e) None of the given options

Directions (Q. 86-91): In each of these questions, two equations (i) and (ii) are given, you have to solve both the equations and give answer accordingly.

86. (i) $2x^2 + 9x + 9 = 0$
    (ii) $15y^2 + 16y + 4 = 0$
    (a) x > y
    (b) x < y
    (c) x ≥ y
    (d) x ≤ y
    (e) x = y or no relation can be established between x & y.

87. (i) $2x^3 = \sqrt{256}$

   (ii) $2y^2 - 9y + 10 = 0$

   (a) x = y or no relation can be established between x & y.

   (b) x < y

   (c) x ≤ y

   (d) x ≥ y

   (e) x > y

88. (i) $6x^2 - 11x + 4 = 0$

   (ii) $3y^2 - 5y + 2 = 0$

   (a) x ≤ y

   (b) x < y

   (c) x ≥ y

   (d) x > y

   (e) x = y or no relation can be established between x & y.

89. (i) $3x^2 + 11x + 10 = 0$

   (ii) $2y^2 + 11y + 14 = 0$

   (a) x ≥ y

   (b) x ≤ y

   (c) x > y

   (d) x < y

   (e) x = y or no relation can be established between x & y.

90. (i) $12x^2 + 11x + 2 = 0$

   (ii) $12y^2 + 7y + 1 = 0$

   (a) x ≥ y

   (b) x = y or no relation can be established between x & y.

   (c) x < y

   (d) x ≤ y

   (e) x > y

91. (i) $21x^2 + 10x + 1 = 0$

   (ii) $24y^2 + 26y + 5 = 0$

   (a) x ≤ y

   (b) x = y or no relation can be established between x & y.

   (c) x ≥ y

   (d) x > y

   (e) x < y

92. 'A' can complete a work in 20 days while B is 25% more efficient than 'A'. B worked for 6 days and left, remaining work is completed by 'C in 15 days. Find in how many days 'C can complete the whole work alone?

   (a) 27 days   (b) 21 days

   (c) 18 days   (d) 24 days

   (e) 30 days

93. A man travels from Point P to Q with 90 km/hr and from Q to R with 60 km/hr. Total distance between P to R is 200 km. If his average speed is 75 km/hr then find the distance between P and Q?

   (a) 80 km

   (b) 120 km

   (c) 100 km

   (d) 150 km

   (e) None of the given options

94. A mixture contains wine and water in the ratio 5 : 1. On adding 5 litre of water, the ratio of wine to water becomes 5 : 2. The quantity of wine in the mixture is ?

   (a) 20 l (b) 22 l

   (c) 24 l (d) 26 l

   (e) None of these

95. The average salary of the entire staff in an office is Rs 3200 per month. The average salary of officers is Rs 6800 and that of non-officers is Rs 2000. If the number of officers is 5, then find the number of non-officers in the office?

   (a) 8   (b) 12

   (c) 15   (d) 5

   (e) None of these

Directions (Q. 96-100): Given bar graph shows the number of plain books and lined books (in hundreds) available at three different stores and the table shows the percentage of total books (Plain + lined) that was sold by different stores.

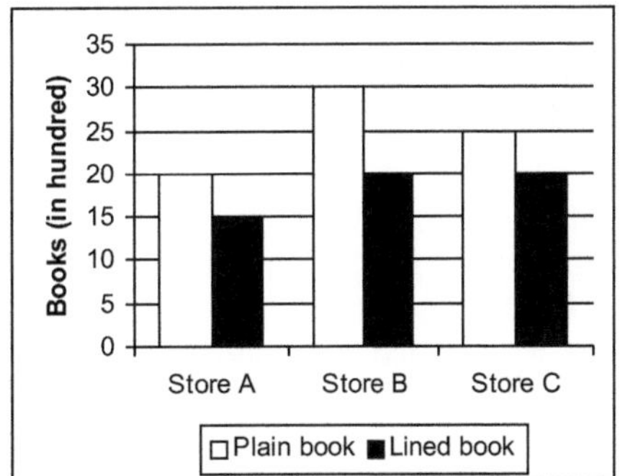

Stores	% of sold books
A	20%
B	40%
C	30%

96. The number of plain books sold by store A and store B was 30% and 40% respectively then find number of lined books sold by store A and store B together is what percent of total books available at store A?

   (a) $22\frac{6}{7}\%$ (b) $23\frac{4}{7}\%$

   (c) $25\frac{5}{7}\%$ (d) 25%

   (e) None of these

97. Average of total books sold by stores B and C together is how much more than total unsold books of store A.
    (a) 1125　　　　(b) 1075
    (c) 1055　　　　(d) 1175
    (e) 1225

98. Ratio of sold plain and lined books for store C is 5 : 4 and for store B is 3 : 2. Then find the total plain books sold by these two stores together ?
    (a) 1750　　　　(b) 1825
    (c) 1850　　　　(d) 1950
    (e) 1975

99. Unsold books of store A is approximately is what percent more or less than total unsold books of store B and C together.
    (a) 48%　　　　(b) 54%
    (c) 59%　　　　(d) 52%
    (e) 57%

100. Selling price of each plain books and lined books sold by store B is Rs. 250 and Rs. 175 respectively. Then, find the total amount earned by store B on selling these books if 60% of lined books are sold by the store ?
    (a) Rs. 2.5 lac　　　　(b) Rs. 3.6 lac
    (c) 3.5 lac　　　　(d) 3.8 lac
    (e) 4.1 lac

ANSWERS

1. (b)	2. (e)	3. (b)	4. (e)	5. (e)	6. (b)	7. (b)	8. (d)	9. (e)	10. (c)
11. (c)	12. (a)	13. (e)	14. (c)	15. (c)	16. (a)	17. (b)	18. (d)	19. (a)	20. (c)
21. (c)	22. (e)	23. (d)	24. (d)	25. (b)	26. (b)	27. (c)	28. (a)	29. (e)	30. (d)
31. (e)	32. (d)	33. (c)	34. (d)	35. (e)	36. (c)	37. (c)	38. (b)	39. (d)	40. (e)
41. (d)	42. (a)	43. (c)	44. (d)	45. (c)	46. (c)	47. (b)	48. (c)	49. (e)	50. (d)
51. (c)	52. (e)	53. (a)	54. (c)	55. (a)	56. (c)	57. (c)	58. (a)	59. (a)	60. (e)
61. (c)	62. (a)	63. (c)	64. (d)	65. (b)	66. (d)	67. (a)	68. (a)	69. (b)	70. (e)
71. (d)	72. (a)	73. (b)	74. (d)	75. (c)	76. (c)	77. (d)	78. (b)	79. (b)	80. (a)
81. (b)	82. (e)	83. (c)	84. (d)	85. (a)	86. (b)	87. (c)	88. (e)	89. (a)	90. (b)
91. (b)	92. (d)	93. (b)	94. (e)	95. (c)	96. (c)	97. (a)	98. (d)	99. (b)	100. (e)

SOLUTIONS

1. (b) There are four tenants of newspaper. One of the tenants is — publishing at regular intervals. In option (b) the newspaper is being published once in a month and hence is a correct choice.

2. (e) All the given options are incorrect. Passage has mentioned that "the relation" follows all the condition but it was still debated therefore it can't be false just because of allegation. Hence (a) was incorrect. Information on paper was distributed earlier too but was just difficult to distribute. Therefore (b) is also incorrect. Option (c) is not mentioned specifically. Option (d) is also inconclusive.

3. (b) Refer to the first few lines of the 2nd paragraph of the passage, "The first true newspapers arrived after Johannes Gutenberg introduced his movable type printing press to the European world around 1440". Earlier mass distribution was impossible but due to the press the distribution became plausible.

4. (e) All the given options are incorrect except (e). Option (e) can be traced from the lines "The first

English newspaper was published in 1665 in Oxford, England. Known as the Oxford Gazette, the newspaper moved to London in 1666 and was renamed the London Gazette."

5. (e) Option (e) is the correct answer choice for the given word. Disseminating- spread (something, especially information) widely. Barb- a sharp projection near the end of an arrow

6. (b) option (b) is the correct answer choice. Option (b) can be traced from the very first paragraph of the passage where it is stated as "However, disseminating news and information on paper presented significant challenges. When each copy had to be handwritten, mass distribution was impossible."

7. (b) The tone of the sentence suggests that something happened in the past. The highlighted phrase has a Future tense which is erroneous.

    Among the given alternatives, the alternative (i) and (iii) imparts the correct grammatical tense to the sentence. Also note that, in this sentence, both Present Perfect tense and Simple Past tense can impart the correct tense to the sentence.

Hence, the option (b) is the correct answer.

'Economist Deena Khatkhate, who passed away at the age of 92 on September 15 in Bethesda, Maryland, in the US, was an unusual man.'

8. (d) 'Who hates' is correct because for universal truth simple present is used.

9. (e) The given sentence is grammatically correct and contextually meaningful and doesn't require any correction.

   Hence, the correct answer is the option (e).

10. (c) The phrase 'neither one' is considered *singular*. So, the usage of 'are' and 'were' is incorrect. The alternative (i) will make a grammatically incorrect and contextually meaningless sentence. Only alternative (ii) is the correct answer. Hence, the correct answer is the option (c).

11. (c) The appropriate word to be used here is 'Tailored'. 'Alters' which is a verb and it means 'change in character or composition, typically in a comparatively small but significant way'. However, the verb required here should be in its plural form, therefore 'alters' is incorrect.

   Tailored- make or adapt for a particular purpose or person.

   All other given options don't fit contextually. Hence, option (c) is the most suitable answer choice.

12. (a) The appropriate word to be used here is 'Resolved'. Here, 'Concludes' 'resolves' are irrelevant as they are in the present tense while the verb required here should be in the past tense. Commence means beginning.

   Resolved- firmly determined to do something. Hence, option (a) is the most viable answer choice.

13. (e) The appropriate word to be used here is 'Confident.'

   Confident- feeling or showing confidence in oneself or one's abilities or qualities.

   All other given options don't fit contextually.

   Tentative means not certain or fixed; provisional.

   Hasten means be quick to do something.

14. (c) The appropriate word to be used here is 'cautious.'

   Cautious means (of a person) careful to avoid potential problems or dangers. Option (a) (b) and (d) are opposite of the correct choice 'meticulous.'

   Negligent means failing to take proper care over something.

15. (c) The appropriate word to be used here is 'Mitigating.'

Mitigating- make (something bad) less severe, serious, or painful, all other options except (c) are the opposite of the correct choice to be filled i.e. 'mitigating'

16. (a) The appropriate word to be used here is 'Reserved'

   Reserved- slow to reveal emotion or opinions, all the other options are either opposite to the correct word 'reserved', or don't frame a contextually correct sentence.

17. (b) To make the sentence meaningful, an interchange between (A) and (C) is required. The phrases 'Some American officials *appear to hope*' and 'sanctions on Iran will lead' are more meaningful.

   (B) and (D) don't require to be interchanged.

   Hence, the correct answer is the A-C, and the option (b) is the correct answer.

   'Some American officials appear to hope that resumed sanctions on Iran will lead to a popular uprising.'

18. (d) 'Tariffs' is a plural noun followed by 'has' which is incorrect. 'China' is also a noun but a singular noun and can be followed by 'has'. So, an interchange between (A) and (C) is required. Moreover, a noun can only be interchanged with a noun, not a finite verb. Similarly, interchanging (B) and (D) would impart better meaning to the sentence.

   Hence, two interchanges are required: A-C and B-D.

   'China has imposed higher tariffs on 603 items imported from the US.'

19. (a) Turkey, which is a nation, could be a NATO ally, not the 'world', 'journalists of number' is a meaningless phrase. The correct phrase should be 'number of journalists'. So, an interchange between (A) and (B), and (C) and (D) is required.

   Hence, the correct answer is A-B and C-D, and the option (a) is the correct answer. *'NATO ally Turkey leads the world in the number of journalists jailed.'*

20. (c) Pathankot is a city inside Kashmir. Kashmir is not inside Pathankot. The given sentence suggests that as if Pathankot is inside Kashmir which is erroneous. An interchange between (B) and (D) is required. (A) and (C) are placed in correct positions.

   Hence, the option (c) is the correct answer.

   'In 2016, rising violence in Kashmir by Islamic militants culminated in attacks on Indian forces at Uri and Pathankot'

21. (c) Use 'hidden' in place of 'hiding' as in passive voice 'To Be + third form of verb' is used.

22. (e) The sentence is grammatically correct.

23. (d) Use 'for reducing' in place of for reduce' because the verb coming after preposition 'for' should always be in fourth form of the verb.

24. (d) 'had' will be used in place of 'have' because words like 'declined' and 'did' infer that the sentence is in past.

25. (b) Outrun [verb]: go beyond or exceed.

Among the given options, only 'outrun' appropriately fills the blank and is the correct answer.

The usage of 'begin', 'choose' and 'cut' would make the sentence meaningless.

Hence, the option (b) is the correct answer.

26. (b) The economist studied a Chinese travel agency and declares working from home a "future-looking technology" with "enormous potential". It seems that the blank would be filled by an adverb.

The tone of the sentence suggests that the economist was enthusiastic with the future-prospect of the Chinese travel agency.

So, the correct adverb which could fill the blank is 'enthusiastically'.

Kindly note that the usage of 'appropriately' would be wrong because whether the assertion of the economist would be true isn't still proved.

Hence, the correct answer is the option (b).

27. (c) The word 'broad' is an adjective. The blank seems to be filled by a noun.

What can be drawn from findings? The word 'Conclusions', among the given options, is the most appropriate choice. Hence, the option (c) is the correct answer.

28. (a) optimally [adverb] means *'in the best or most favourable way'*;

A leader is someone who must manage and work with the employees under her/him. The chances of getting desired result increases when the working or professional relationship between leader and the employees is positive and favourable.

Among the given options, the adverb 'optimally', upon filling the blank, makes the most sense while others don't.

Hence, the option (a) is the correct answer.

29. (e) The blank seems to be filled by a finite verb. What action did (or could) Bloom (Nicholas Bloom) take on China's biggest travel agency, Ctrip? The economist studied the travel agency. Among the given options, the words 'focus' and 'concentrates' are the most relevant, but the option (e) 'focused' also satisfies the grammatical requirement of the sentence. The tense of the sentence should be Simple Past, not Simple Present. Hence, the correct answer is the option (e).

30. (d) 'Instituted' [institute, verb] means *'introduce or establish (a scheme, undertaking, or policy)'*;

The preceding sentence informs us that Ctrip wanted to expand while controlling office space costs. What should be the meaning of 'remote work trial'? The context of the passage suggests that it means that instead of employee coming to office and completing their tasks, they would complete their task remotely, without coming to office, for example, 'work from home' etc. The company should have 'established' such a policy. But the option (a) 'establishes' doesn't satisfy the grammatical requirements imposed on the blank. The tense of the tense should be Simple Past, not Simple Present. The correct word which imparts the correct meaning and satisfies the grammatical requirements imposed on the blank is *'instituted'*. Hence, the correct answer is the option (d).

Solutions (31-35):

T
R
X
Q
S
W
U
P
V

Solutions (36-40):

Words	Code
Venue	rs
Details	wi
Get	fe
For	mo
Guest	ra
book/ required	gt/rd
More	gk

Solutions (41-45):

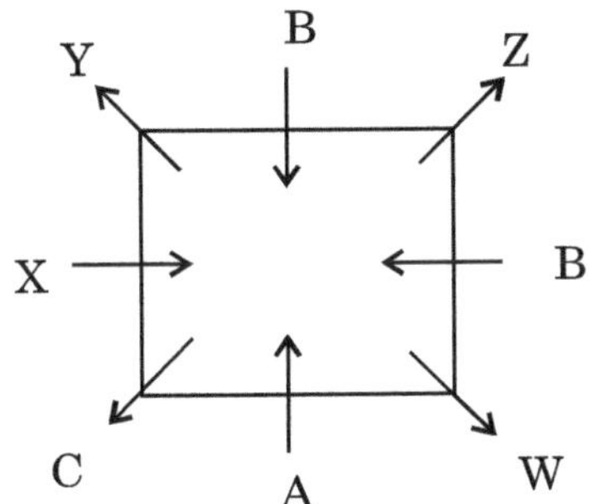

46. (c) I. K < X (false) II. W > M(false)

47. (b) I. Z < Y (True) II. S > Q (false)

48. (c) I. K ≥ M(false) II. P > M(false)

49. (e) I. M ≥ U (True) II. G > Z(True)

50. (d) I. J > B(True) II. H < R(false)

51. (c) 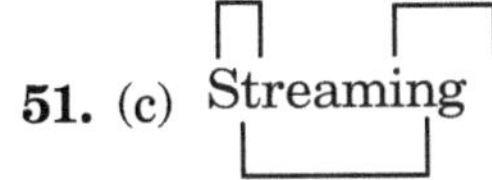

52. (e)

$$\begin{array}{cccccccccc} +7 & +6 & +23 & +22 & +6 & +5 & +21 & +20 & +1 & +5 \end{array}$$

JQK BYC LRM CXD OPU

Solutions (53-55):

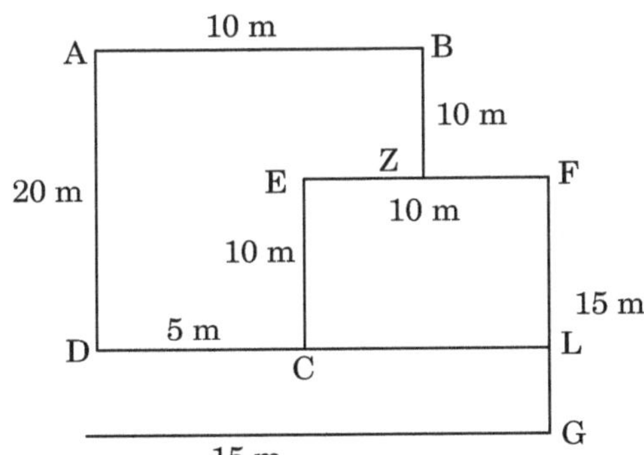

Solutions (56-60):

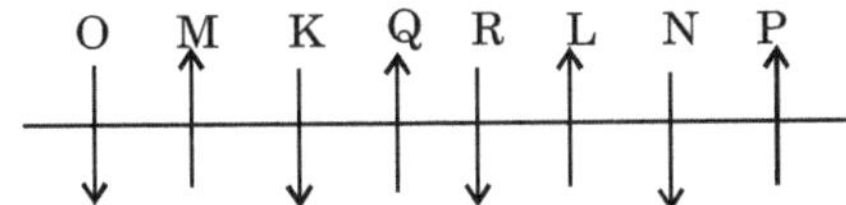

Solutions (61-65):

Person	Items
U	Tie
G	Coat
S	Ring
H	Nail paint
T	Shirt
E	Diary
F	Goggles

66. (d) Required % $= \dfrac{120+240}{160+240} \times 100$

$= \dfrac{360}{400} \times 100 = 90\%$

67. (a) Average number of Women working in 2014, 2015 and 2016 together

$= \dfrac{1}{3}[240+360+300] = \dfrac{900}{3} = 300$

Average number of Men working in 2011, 2014 and 2016 together

$= \dfrac{1}{3}[80+160+360] = \dfrac{600}{3} = 200$

Required difference = 300 – 200 = 100

68. (c) Number of Men working in 2017

$= \dfrac{115}{100} \times 300 = 345$

Number of Women working in 2017

$= \dfrac{60}{100} \times 240 = 144$

Total number of labors working in 2017 = 345 + 144 = 489

69. (b) Required Ratio =

$$\dfrac{(120+180)+(240+120)}{(300+360)+(360+300)}$$

$= \dfrac{300+360}{660+660} = \dfrac{660}{1320} = \dfrac{1}{2}$

70. (e) Total number of Men working in all six years = 80 + 120 + 240 + 160 + 300

+ 360 = 1260

Total number of Women working in all six years = 260 + 180 + 120 + 240 + 360

+ 300 = 1460

Required difference = 1460 – 1260 = 200

71. (d)

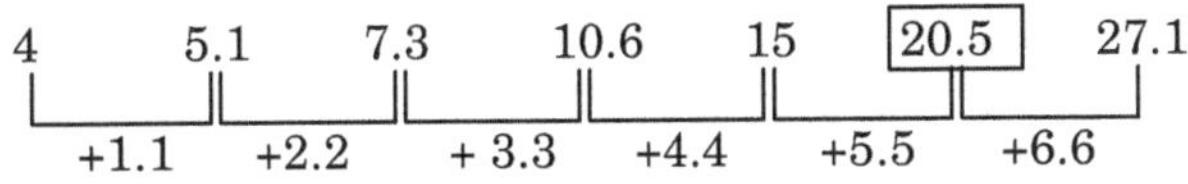

72. (a)

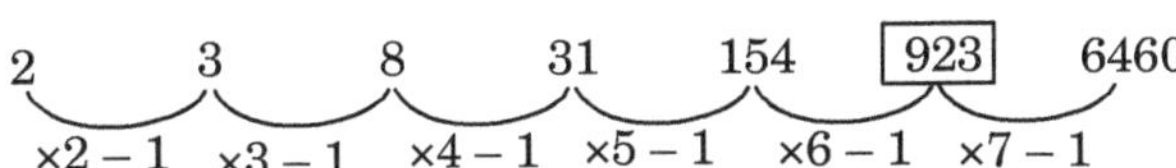

73. (b)

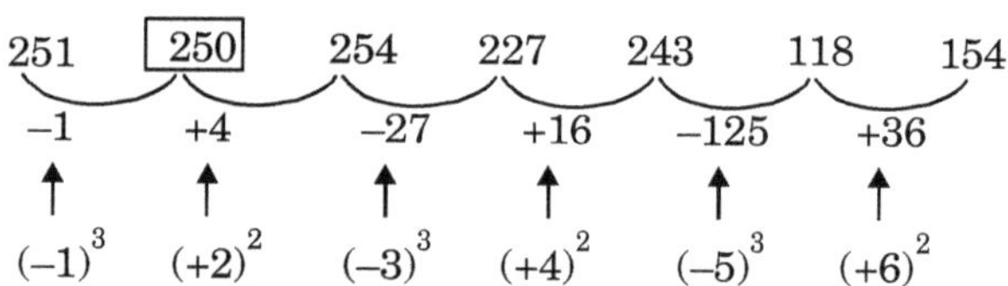

74. (d)

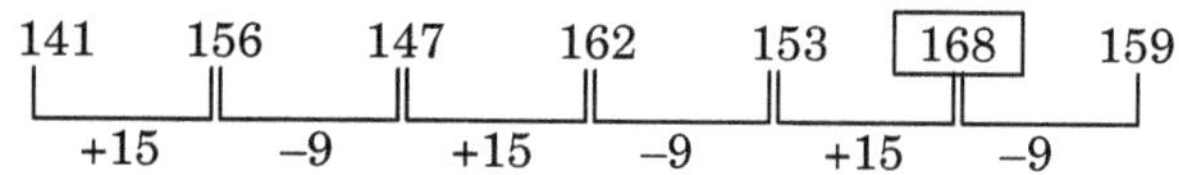

75. (c)

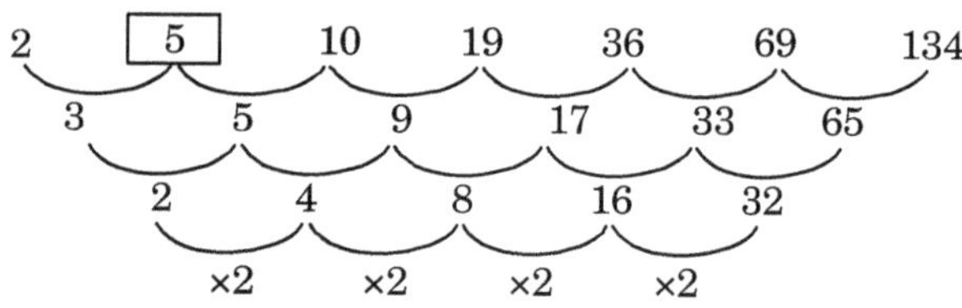

76. (c)

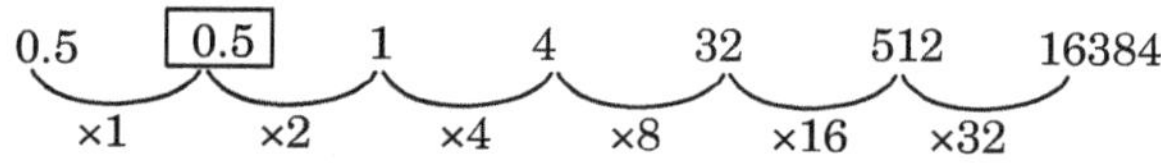

77. (d) Let present age of A and B be 16x yr and 7x yr respectively

ATQ

$$\frac{16x+12}{7x+12}=\frac{2}{1}$$

$\Rightarrow 2x = 12$

$\Rightarrow x = 6$

Present age of A = 96 yr

Present age of B = 42 yr

78. (b) Sum $= \dfrac{1950 \times 100}{2 \times 15} = $ Rs. 6500

CI in 2 years at 10% per annum

$$= 10 + 10 + \frac{10 \times 10}{100} = 21\%$$

ATQ

$$(6500 + x) \times \frac{21}{100} = 1680$$

$\Rightarrow (6500 + x) = 8000$

x = Rs 1500

79. (b) Total weight of students

$$= 47\frac{7}{15}(15 + 30) = 2136 \text{ kg}$$

Total weight of boys = 15× 58 = 870 kg

Average weight of girls

$$= \left(\frac{2136 - 870}{30}\right) \text{kg} = 42.2 \text{ kg} \simeq 42 \text{kg}$$

80. (a) Ram's cost price = M.R.P. $\times \dfrac{80}{100}$

Ramesh C. P. = M. R. P.$\times \dfrac{80}{100} \times \dfrac{90}{100}$

Ranjan C. P.

$= $ M. R. P.$\times \dfrac{80}{100} \times \dfrac{90}{100} \times \dfrac{120}{100} = 1,29,600$

$\Rightarrow$ M.R.P. = Rs. 1,50,000

Solutions (81-85):

Let, Males and females who use their coupons in Haircutting be 13x and 7x respectively.

$\Rightarrow$ Males who use their coupons in Pedicure = 7x+ 72

Then Females who use their coupons in Pedicure = 450 – 13x – 7x – 7x – 72

= 378 – 27x

Pedicure		Haircutting	
Males	Females	Males	Females
7x + 72	378 – 27x	13x	7x

ATQ,

7x+ 72 + 13x – (7x + 378 – 27x) = 174

40x – 306 = 174

40x = 480

x = 12

Pedicure		Haircutting	
Males	Females	Males	Females
156	54	156	84

81. (b) Required % $= \dfrac{156}{156} \times 100 = 100\%$

82. (e) Required Ratio $= \dfrac{156 + 54}{156 + 84} = \dfrac{210}{240} = \dfrac{7}{8}$

83. (c) Required difference = 84 – 54 = 30

84. (d) Number of males who use their coupons in Haircutting which doesn't belongs to city A

$$= 156 \times \frac{75}{100} = 117$$

85. (a) Males who use their coupons in Spa

$$= 156 \times \frac{5}{4} = 195$$

Females who use their coupons in Spa

$$= 84 \times \frac{11}{6} = 154$$

Total number of people who use their coupon in Spa $= 195 + 154 = 349$

86. (b) (i) $2x^2 + 9x + 9 = 0$

$2x^2 + (6 + 3)x + 9 = 0$

$2x(x + 3) + 3(x + 3) = 0$

$$x = \frac{-3}{2}, -3$$

(ii) $15y^2 + 16y + 4 = 0$

$15y^2 + 10y + 6y + 4 = 0$

$5y(3y + 2) + 2(3y + 2) = 0$

$$y = \frac{-2}{5}, \frac{-2}{3}$$

$x < y$

87. (c) (i) $2x^3 = 16$

$x^3 = 8$

$x = 2$

(ii) $2y^2 - 9y + 10 = 0$

$2y^2 - (5 + 4)y + 10 = 0$

$2y^2 - 5y - 4y + 10 = 0$

$y(2y - 5) - 2(2y - 5) = 0$

$$y = 2, \frac{5}{2}$$

$x \leq y$

88. (e) (i) $6x^2 - 11x + 4 = 0$

$6x^2 - (8 + 3)x + 4 = 0$

$6x^2 - 8x - 3x + 4 = 0$

$2x(3x - 4) - 1(3x - 4) = 0$

$$x = \frac{1}{2}, \frac{4}{3}$$

(ii) $3y^2 - 5y + 2 = 0$

$3y^2 - (3 + 2)y + 2 = 0$

$3y^2 - 3y - 2y + 2 = 0$

$3y(y - 1) - 2(y - 1) = 0$

$$y = \frac{2}{3}, 1$$

No relation between x and y

89. (a) (i) $3x^2 + 11x + 10 = 0$

$3x^2 + 6x + 5x + 10 = 0$

$3x(x + 2) + 5(x + 2) = 0$

$$x = -2, \frac{-5}{3}$$

(ii) $2y^2 + 11y + 14 = 0$

$2y^2 + 7y + 4y + 14 = 0$

$y(2y + 7) + 2(2y + 7) = 0$

$$y = -2, -\frac{7}{2}$$

$x \geq y$

90. (b) (i) $12x^2 + 8x + 3x + 2 = 0$

$4x(3x + 2) + 1(3x + 2) = 0$

$$x = \frac{-2}{3}, \frac{-1}{4}$$

(ii) $12y^2 + 7y + 1 = 0$

$12y^2 + 4y + 3y + 1 = 0$

$4y(3y + 1) + 1(3y + 1) = 0$

$$y = \frac{-1}{3}, \frac{-1}{4}$$

No relation between x and y

91. (b) (i) $21x^2 + 10x + 1 = 0$

$21x^2 + 7x + 3x + 1 = 0$

$7x(3x + 1) + 1(3x + 1) = 0$

$$x = \frac{-1}{3}, \frac{-1}{7}$$

(ii) $24y^2 + 26y + 5 = 0$

$24y^2 + (20 + 6)y + 5 = 0$

$24y^2 + 20y + 6y + 5 = 0$

$4y(6y + 5) + 1(6y + 5) = 0$

$$y = \frac{-5}{6}, -\frac{1}{4}$$

No relation between x and y

92. (d) B can complete work alone in

$$= 20 \times \frac{4}{5} = 16 \text{ days}$$

Let C alone can complete work in 'x' days

ATQ,

$$\frac{6}{16} + \frac{15}{x} = 1$$

$$\Rightarrow \frac{15}{x} = \frac{10}{16}$$

$$\Rightarrow x = \frac{15 \times 16}{10} = 24 \text{ days}$$

93. (b) Let distance between P to Q and Q to R be 'x' and 'y' respectively.

ATQ,

$$75 = \frac{200}{\dfrac{x}{90} + \dfrac{y}{60}}$$

$$60x + 90x = 200 \times 90 \times 60 \times \frac{1}{75}$$

$$2x + 3y = 480$$

And $x + y = 200$

$\Rightarrow$ $x = 120$ km and $y = 80$ km

94. (e) Let wine and water are $= 5x : x$

Now, $\dfrac{5x}{x+5} = \dfrac{5}{2} \Rightarrow 10x = 5x + 25$

$x = 5$

$\Rightarrow$ 25 : 5   25 : 10

   Before mixture   After mixture

Quantity of wine $= 25\ell$.

95. (c)

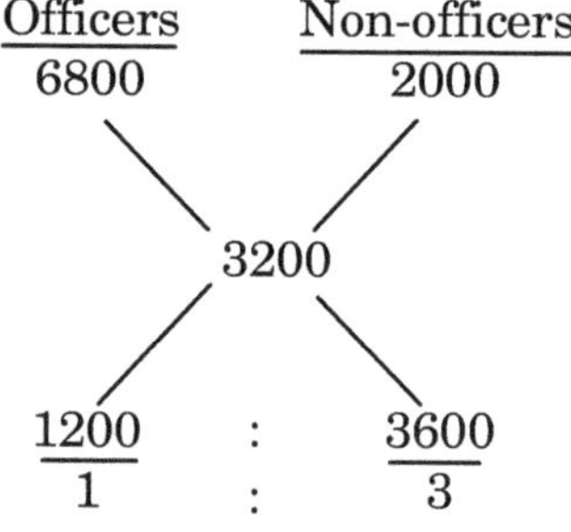

No. of non-officers $= \dfrac{3}{1} \times 5 = 15$

96. (c) Total books sold by store A $= 3500 \times \dfrac{20}{100} = 700$

Total plain books sold by store A

$= 2000 \times \dfrac{30}{100} = 600$

Total lined books sold by store A $= 700 - 600$

$= 100$

Total books sold by store B

$= 5000 \times \dfrac{40}{100} = 2000$

Plain books sold by store B

$= 3000 \times \dfrac{40}{100} = 1200$

Total lined books sold by store B $= 2000 - 1200$

$= 800$

Required % $= \dfrac{900}{3500} \times 100 = \dfrac{180}{7}\% = 25\dfrac{5}{7}\%$

97. (a) Average of total books sold by stores B and C

$= \dfrac{1}{2}\left(50 \times \dfrac{40}{100} \times 100 + 45 \times \dfrac{30}{100} \times 100 \right)$

$= 1675$

Unsold books of store A $= 3500 \times$

$\dfrac{80}{100} = 2800$

Required difference $= 2800 - 1675 = 1125$

98. (d) Total books sold by store C $= 45 \times 100$

$\times \dfrac{30}{100} = 1350$

Plain books sold by C $= 1350 \times \dfrac{5}{9} = 750$

Plain books sold by store

B $= \dfrac{3}{5} \times 5000 \times \dfrac{40}{100} = 1200$

Required number of books $= 1200 + 750$

$= 1950$

99. (b) Unsold books of store A $= 3500 \times$

$\dfrac{80}{100} = 2800$

Unsold books of store B and C together

$= 5000 \times \dfrac{60}{100} + 4500 \times \dfrac{70}{100}$

$= 6150$

Required % $= \dfrac{6150 - 2800}{6150} \times 100 = 54\%$

100. (e) Number of total books sold by store B

$= 5000 \times \dfrac{40}{100} = 2000$

Number of lined books sold

$= 2000 \times \dfrac{60}{100} = 1200$

Total amount earned $= $ Rs. $(800 \times 250 +$
$1200 \times 175)$

$= $ Rs. 4.1 lac

REASONING AND COMPUTER APTITUDE

Directions (Q. 1-3): Study the given information and answer the questions:

When a number arrangement machine is given an input line of numbers, it arranges them following a particular rule. The following is an illustration of an input and its rearrangement.

```
Input-  65  18   41   53   72  34  89  26
Step1- 195  36  123  159  144  68  267  52
         V   V   V    V    V   V   V
Step2-  159 159  36  303   76 335 215
Step3-   45  45  18    0   42  45  10
Step4-  22.5 22.5 9    0   21 22.5  5
```

Step 4, is the last step of the above arrangement as the intended arrangement is obtained. As per the rules followed in the given steps find out the appropriate steps for the given input:

Input: 25 22 93 56 17 74 39

1. What is the sum of the numbers at both the ends in step 3 of the given arrangement?

   (a) 36   (b) 63

   (c) 60   (d) 123

   (e) None of the above

2. Which element is 2nd to the right of the one which is 4th to the left element in step I?

   (a) 112   (b) 44

   (c) 148   (d) 75

   (e) None of these

3. What is the products of the numbers which is 3rd from the right end and 3rd from the left end in final step of the given arrangement?

   (a) 189   (b) 72

   (c) 13.5   (d) 180

   (e) No such step

Directions (Q. 4-8): Study the information carefully and answer the questions given below.

Six people Tarun, charu, Visakha, Monika, Anko and Viraj are born in different years with the current base is taken as 2018. None of them is older than 90 years old. They like different fruits apple, Orange, Grapes, Cherry, Mango, Banana.

Note- The last two digits or reverse of the last two digits of the year in which a person is born can be the age of some other person. (Like A is born in 1943 and age of B is denoted by the last two digits of the birth year of A. Then B's age will be either 34 or 43).

Tarun was born in the year 1983. The difference of age between Tarun and Charu is 21 years. Visakha age is sum of the digits of the year in which Charu was born. The one who likes mango is 5 years elder to Visakha. Anko age is either the last two digits or reverse of the last two digits of the year in which the person who likes mango was born. Only one person is elder to Anko and Visakha likes apple. The one likes cherry is just younger to Anko. The difference between Viraj's and the one who likes cherry is 24 years. The one who likes banana was born in an even year. The one who likes orange is younger to the one who likes grapes both in odd number of years. Monika is younger than Viraj.

4. Who among the following likes Banana?

   (a) Anko   (b) Tarun

   (c) Charu   (d) Visakha

   (e) none of these

5. Who among the following is the eldest?

   (a) Anko   (b) Tarun

   (c) Charu   (d) Visakha

   (e) None of these

6. Which of the following combination is true?

   (a) Anko- 1959-mango

   (b) Viraj- 1983-apple

   (c) Charu-1962-cherry

   (d) Monika-1995- grapes

   (e) none of these

7. Which of the following statement is correct?

   (a) Anko is three years older than the one who likes cherry

   (b) Viraj is the eldest

   (c) Anko born in 1959

   (d) Monika is born before Visakha

   (e) All are correct

8. In which of the following year Monika was born?
   (a) 1995   (b) 2000
   (c) 2012   (d) 2007
   (e) None of these

Directions (Q. 9-10): Study the information carefully and answer the questions given below. Six persons sit around a triangular table such that three of them sits at the corners and the rest on the middle of the side. The one who sits at the corner face away from the center and the one who sit at the middle of the side face towards the center. They also like different animals i.e. fish, dog, rabbit, pigeon, duck and cat. The one who likes fish sits at the corner. The one who likes cat sits immediate right to the one who likes duck. C sits 2nd right to B, who likes rabbit. D faces the center and sits 3rd right to the one who likes pigeon. E sits immediate right to D. F sits at one of the corner but does not like pigeon and cat. A is one of the person. E does not like Duck and Fish.

9. Who among the following likes ducks?
   (a) E   (b) FWC
   (c) C   (d) B   (e) None of these

10. Who among the following sits 2nd to the right of the one who is 3rd left of A?
    (a) E   (b) F
    (c) C   (d) B
    (e) none of these

Directions (Q. 11): Study the following information carefully and answer the question given below:

A certain number of persons sit in a row adjacent to each other. Some of them like different fruits and others like different flowers. Six persons sit between the one who likes mango and the one who likes apple. The one who likes rose sit third to the left of the one who likes apple. Two persons sit between the one who likes rose and the one who likes marigold, who is not a neighbor of the one who likes mango. Only one person sits to the right of the one who likes marigold. No one sits to the right of the one who likes mango.

Note: The one who likes fruits faces South and the one who likes flowers faces North.

11. How many persons sit in the row?
    (a) Fifteen
    (b) Seventeen
    (c) Thirteen
    (d) Eighteen
    (e) Eleven

Direction (Q. 12): Study the following information carefully and answer the question given below:

Five persons A, G, K, L and S purchase some items one after other. Two persons bought between A and the one who bought Chair. G purchase immediately before K but none of them bought Chair. Three persons bought between the one who purchase chair and the one who purchase table. Only two persons bought between the one who purchase wallet and the one who purchase table. Bag is purchased immediately before perfume. Only two persons bought between L and the one who purchase perfume. K does not buy wallet.

12. Who among the following purchase table?
    (a) L   (b) K
    (c) G   (d) S
    (e) A

Directions (Q. 13-15): Study the following information carefully and answer the questions given below:

$ F 3 6 N @ 9 K T Q 5 C % 8 B # 7 D S * H 4 W L

STEP I- The numbers which are immediately preceded by symbol and immediately followed by an alphabet are arranged in the end of the series in increasing order. (Arranged immediate after L)

STEP II- The odd numbers which are immediately preceded by an alphabet interchange their position with respect to the alphabet just before it.

STEP III- The alphabets which are immediately followed by a symbol are arranged in alphabetical order between H and 4 of step II.

Note: (STEP II is applied after STEP I and STEP III is applied after STEP II)

13. What is the sum of number which is sixth from right end in step I and eight from left end in step III?
    (a) 8   (b) 7
    (c) 9   (d) 11
    (e) 13

14. How many alphabets are immediately preceded and immediately followed by numbers in step II?
    (a) one   (b) two
    (c) three   (d) four
    (e) five

15. How many symbols are immediately preceded by alphabets in Step III ?
    (a) one   (b) two
    (c) three   (d) four
    (e) five

Directions (Q.16-20): Study the information carefully and answer the questions given below.

There are three floors in a given building such that floor 2 is above floor 1 and floor 3 is above floor 2. In the building there are two flats in each floor such Flat A is in the west of Flat B. In the building each Flat has an area of 576 ft and each flat has some certain number of room and no two flat has same number of rooms. The area of each rooms of one of the flats on the even number floor is 64 ft. Total rooms on floor number third is seven. The flat which has rooms of area of 72 ft is on odd number floor. Number of rooms in the flat which is exactly below 9 rooms flat is 288 ft. There is only one floor between the flat who's each room area is 192 ft and the flat whose rooms area is 72 ft. There is no flat on the west of the flat having 6 rooms.

16. What is the area of a room in Flat A on floor 2?

    (a) 94　　　　　　　　(b) 92

    (c) 96　　　　　　　　(d) either (a) or (c)

    (e) None of these

17. What is the total number of rooms on floor 2nd?

    (a) 12　　　　　　　　(b) 14

    (c) 13　　　　　　　　(d) 15

    (e) None of these

18. Which of the following statement is true?

    (a) Total number of rooms on floor 2 is 14

    (b) Area of each room is 94 ft of flat A on floor 1

    (c) Total rooms in Flat A of all three floors is 17.

    (d) All are correct

    (e) None is correct

19. What is the area of room of flat B on floor 3rd?

    (a) 144 ft　　　　　　(b) 140.5

    (c) 138.5　　　　　　(d) 142

    (e) None of these

20. How many rooms are there of the west of the flat whose each room area is 288 ft?

    (a) 6　　　　　　　　(b) 4

    (c) 3　　　　　　　　(d) 8

    (e) None of these

Directions for questions 21 to 25: Answer the questions on the basis of the information given below.

Rehan, Rumi, Ritesh, Ramesh, Ravi, Raman and Rita are the seven athletes who run on one of the days of the week that starts on Monday and ends on Sunday but not necessarily in the given order. Distance covered by each of them is - 2 km, 3 km, 4 km, 5 km, 6 km, 7 km and 8 km and each of them takes rest for one of the durations - 10 minutes, 15 minutes, 20 minutes, 25 minutes, 30 minutes, 35 minutes and 40 minutes but not necessarily in the given order. It is also known that:

Distance covered by Rehan was not 3 km and he ran on someday after Ritesh. Rita ran two days after the day on which 3 km run was covered. Distance covered by Rita was less than 5 km. Ramesh took rest for 20 minutes and he ran immediately before Rumi, who ran 7 km. The maximum distance was run at either the start or the end of the week and it was done by either Ravi or Raman. The distance covered by Ritesh was 5 km and he took rest for less than 30 minutes but more than 15 minutes. The distance covered on Thursday was 2 km and the athlete took rest for 35 minutes. Raman took rest for 30 minutes on the day which is either immediately after or before the day on which Rumi ran. Distance covered by Raman was more than that by Rumi and the difference in their rest time was 20 minutes. The distance by Rehan was less than the distance covered by Rita and the difference in their rest duration was 20 minutes.

21. What is the rest time duration of the athlete who ran two days after the athlete who ran 6 km?

    (a) 15 minutes　　　　(b) 20 minutes

    (c) 25 minutes　　　　(d) 30 minutes

    (e) 35 minutes

22. How many athletes took more rest than the athlete who ran immediately after the athlete who ran 2 km?

    (a) One　　　　　　　(b) Two

    (c) Three　　　　　　(d) Four

    (e) Five

23. Four of the following five are alike in a certain way and thus form a group. Find the one that does not belong to it.

    (a) Ritesh, Monday　　(b) Rita, Wednesday

    (c) Rehan, Thursday　　(d) Ramesh, Friday

    (e) Rumi, Saturday

24. Which of the following combinations is correct according to the information given above?

    (a) Ritesh - 15 minutes　(b) Rita - Thursday

    (c) Rehan - 8 km　　　　(d) Ramesh - 40 minutes

    (e) None of these

25. Which of the following athletes took rest for the least time duration among all?

    (a) Ritesh

    (b) Rita

    (c) Rehan

    (d) Ramesh

    (e) Rumi

Directions (Q. 26 to 30): Answer the questions on the basis of the information given below.

The questions are based on following coding formats:

#North

&South

@East

$West

%Either 12 m or 5 m

?Either 5 m or 3 m

+Either 8 m or 3 m

*Either 5 m or 4 m

Above symbols are used in the following manner:

A #% B means 'A is to the North of B at a distance of either 12 m or 5 m'.

A &+ B @* Cmeans 'A is to the South of B, at a distance of either 8 or 3 m, which is to the East of C at a distance of either 5 or 4 m'.

A few points are located as per the information given below using the coded symbols:

   (I) U @+ Q #* M

   (II) O $% V

   (III) R &* N @% U

   (IV)M $? T

   (V) V #? P $+ R

   (VI)O #? T

   (VII)At least three points are collinear

26. As per the given information, which of the following must be true?

   (a) MT = 5 m, OV = 12 m, PR = 8 m

   (b) MT = 3 m, OV = 12 m, PR = 3 m

   (c) MT = 5 m, OV = 5 m, PR = 8 m

   (d) MT = 3 m, OV = 5 m, PR = 8 m

   (e) MT = 5 m, OV = 12 m, PR = 3 m

27. If the distance between points O and T is 5 m, then what can be the shortest distance between points O and P?

   (a) 7 m   (b) 8 m

   (c) 11 m   (d) 13 m

   (e) 15 m

28. What is the distance between points Q and N?

   (a) Either 15 m or 20 m

   (b) Either 20 m or 13 m

   (c) 15 m

   (d) Either 13 m or 15 m

   (e) 20 m

29. Which of the following options shows the correct direction relation between point V and point N?

   (a) V &$ N   (b) V #$ N

   (c) V #@ N   (d) V &@ N

   (e) None of these

30. If the distance between N and R is 4 m, then which of the following statements can hold true?

   (a) P &@ N, the distacen between P and N is 5 m.

   (b) P #$ N, the distance between P and N is 13 m.

   (c) P &$ N, the distance between P and N is 5 m.

   (d) P &@ N, the distance between P and N is 13 m.

   (e) P #@ N, the distance between P and N is 5 m.

Directions (Q. 31 to 35): Answer the questions on the basis of the information given below.

The flowchart shows the various steps involved in filing of Income Tax returns by a salaried person.

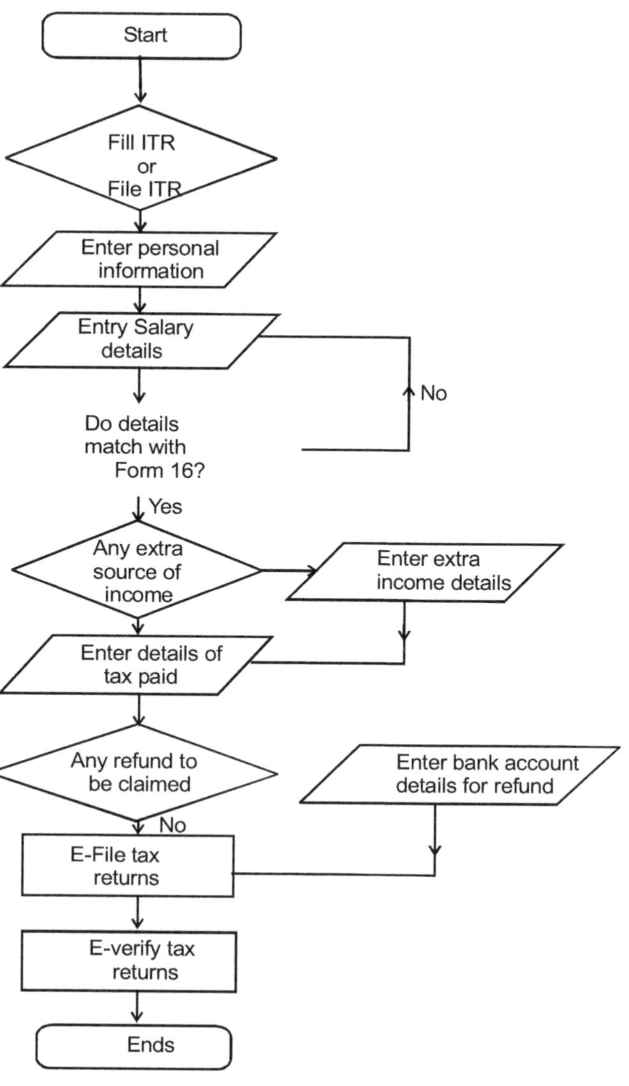

31. Mr.Gupta has already filled the income tax return form and he has saved it in the tax filing website. Which step directs him to the next step?

    (a) Enter salary details

    (b) Enter personal information

    (c) Enter extra income details

    (d) Fill ITR or File ITR

    (e) None of the above

32. Roshni is a salaried person and she also gets a monthly rent for the house that her father willed to her. Where should she enter the details regarding the rent?

    (a) Do details match with Form 16?

    (b) Any refund to be claimed

    (c) Enter extra income details

    (d) Fill ITR or File ITR

    (e) None of the above

33. Harshit has paid an amount of Rs.5,460 as tax through challan, whereas according to the calculation by the income tax department the tax on his income is Rs.4,930. Which step will help him to get back the extra amount that he has paid?

    (a) Do details match with Form 16?

    (b) Enter salary details

    (c) Any extra source of income?

    (d) Fill ITR or File ITR

    (e) Any refund to be claimed?

34. Motilal is reconstructing his house so he is living in a rental accommodation near his house. While filling his address in the ITR he filled the address of the rental house and it showed an error. What should Motilal do?

    (a) Go back to live in his house, which is under construction.

    (b) Fill the rental address again and keep trying till the system accepts it.

    (c) Fill the address that is specified in Form 16.

    (d) Send a request to income tax department regarding his temporary residence.

    (e) None of the above

35. How does the income tax department process the refund claims?

    (a) In cash

    (b) By cheque

    (c) By bank/post office challan

    (d) Direct credit to bank account

    (e) All of the above

Directions (Q. 36 to 40): Answer the questions on the basis of the information given below.

There are 10 shelves numbered 1, 2, …,10. They are arranged in two rows opposite to each other. The shelves 1, 2, …,5 are in row 1 and rest in row 2 which is above row 1. The shelves are arranged in the increasing order of number given to them. Shelf number 1 is placed on extreme left of row 1, then shelf number 2 and so on. Similarly, the shelf number 6 is placed on extreme left end of row 2, and so on. Each shelf contains a certain number of glass slabs and photo frames. There is at least one glass slab in each shelf. The length of each glass slab is 15 cm and that of each photo frame is 6 cm. It is also known that:

The shelf 3 has length 33 cm. There is one shelf between shelf 3 and yellow shelf. The yellow shelf contains 1 glass slab and 6 photo frames more than that in shelf 3. The silver shelf is just above the yellow shelf. The silver shelf contains same number of glass slabs as yellow shelf and 1 photo frame. There are 2 shelves between silver and green shelves. The length of green shelf is 3 cm greater than the silver shelf. The blue shelf is immediate next in number to green shelf. The blue shelf contains 1 glass slab more than that in silver shelf and 1 photo frame less than that in green shelf. There is one shelf between blue and orange shelves. The white shelf is just below the orange shelf. There is one shelf between white and red shelf. Black shelf is in row 2.

The pink shelf is just below the black shelf. The black shelf has same number of photo frames and glass slabs. The orange shelf has 1 glass slab more than black shelf. The length of orange shelf is 24 cm more than the length of pink shelf. The length of violet shelf is half the length of yellow shelf. The red shelf has greater than or equal to four glass slabs. The length of pink shelf is 6 cm less than the shelf immediate next in number. The length of row 1 is 267 cm and that of row 2 is 249 cm.

36. How many more photo frames can row 2 accomodate?

    (a) 1   (b) 2

    (c) 3   (d) None

    (e) 4

37. The color of shelf 2 is:

    (a) Green   (b) Violet

    (c) Red   (d) White

    (e) Pink

38. How many total glass slabs do the silver, black and red shelves contain?

    (a) 7

    (b) 9

    (c) 10

    (d) Other than those given in options

    (e) 12

39. What is the total length of the pink, orange and blue shelves?

    (a) 146 cm   (b) 134 cm

    (c) 141 cm   (d) 133 cm

    (e) 126 cm

40. If all the photo frames of silver and white shelves are removed and added in black shelf, then what will be the length of the black shelf?

    (a) 67 cm   (b) 66 cm

    (c) 61 cm   (d) 69 cm

    (e) 62 cm

Directions for questions 41 to 45: Answer the questions on the basis of the information given below.

Seven persons - A, B, C, D, E, F and G - went to attend an interview each in one of the cities among Delhi, Mumbai, Kolkata, Chennai, Lucknow, Hyderabad and Bangalore (not necessarily in the same order). Each one of them attends that interview in a different day in a week starting from Monday. It is also known that:

Three persons attended the interview between A and the one who attended in Delhi, who did not attend the interview on Monday. D attended the interview in Mumbai and attended the interview immediately before A. The person who attended the interview in Bangalore attended it on Sunday, who is not A. C attended the interview on Thursday and attended the interview before the person who attended in Chennai. Two persons attended the interview between the persons who attended their interviews in Chennai and Kolkata. E, who did not attend the interview in Bangalore, attended the interview three days after the one who attended the interview in Lucknow. B did not attend the interview in Lucknow. Only one person attended the interview between B and F, who did not attend the interview on Sunday. G did not attend the interview on Sunday.

41. How many persons attended the interview before F?

    (a) One   (b) Two

    (c) Three   (d) Four

    (e) More than four

42. Who attended the interview in Hyderabad?

    (a) A   (b) B

    (c) C   (d) E

    (e) None of these

43. How many persons attended the interview between A and B?

    (a) One   (b) Two

    (c) Three   (d) Four

    (e) More than four

44. Who attended the interview on Wednesday?

    (a) The person who attended the interview in Lucknow.

    (c) The person who attended the interview in Hyderabad.

    (c) F

    (d) The person who attended the interview in Delhi.

    (e) B

45. Which of the following statements is true?

    (a) B attended the interview immediately before E.

    (b) F attended the interview immediately before C.

    (c) Two persons attended the interview between G and E.

    (d) F attended the interview before two persons.

    (e) Both (c) and (d)

QUANTITATIVE APTITUDE

46. There is a rectangular path just inside a rectangular park. Width of the path is 2 cm. If length of park is decreased by 4 cm then, it becomes a square. Area of the rectangle is $1\dfrac{1}{3}$ times the area of the path.

    From the above given information which of the following can be found out.   (i) Area of path

    (ii) Length of the park

    (iii) Sum of perimeter of the rectangular park and perimeter of the path (both external and internal perimeter)

    (a) only (ii)

    (b) only (ii) and (iii)

    (c) only (i) and (iii)

    (d) all of the above

    (e) only (iii)

47. A man invest 50% of the amount invested by B. B withdraw whole amount from the business after 4 months. C joins the business with the investment of X Rs in a month after B had withdrawn from the business. At the end of the year A and C share same amount of profit.

    → if investment of B is Rs 2400 then which of the following may be the investment of the C.

    (i)   1800

    (ii) 3600

    (iii) 2400

    (iv) 7200

    (v) 5400

    (a) (i) and (iii)

    (b) only (iii)

    (c) (i), (ii) and (iii)

    (d) (i), (ii), (iii) and (iv)

    (e) (i), (ii) and (iv)

48. A certain number of men can complete a work in six hours less than the time taken by some women.

Work completed by one man in one hour is same as the work completed by one woman in one hour.

→ Which one of the following ratio of number of men to number of women can satisfy the above given condition

(i) 5:6   (ii) 10:3

(iii) 8:5   (iv) 10:7

(a) only (ii)

(b) only (ii) and (iii)

(c) only (i) and (iii)

(d) all of the above

(e) only (ii), (iii) and (iv)

Direction (49-51): Study the given graph given below and answer the following questions

The graph given below shows the percentage of literates in three different villages in three years

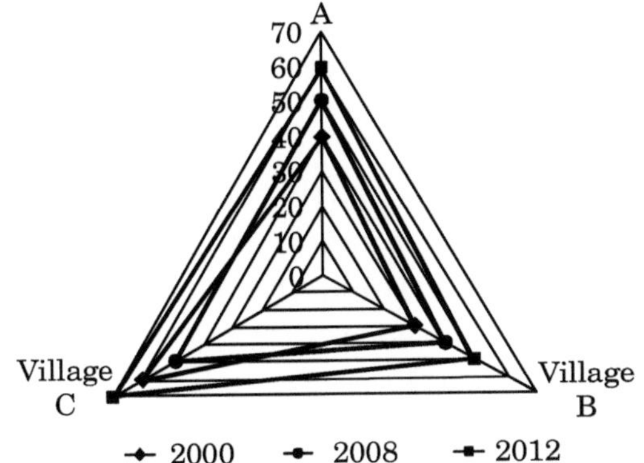

49. If population of A in 2000, 2008 and 2012 is in ratio 2:3:4 and average of literate in 2008, 2012 and 2000 be 1410 then find population of village A in 2000.
(a) 1700   (b) 2000
(c) 2100   (d) 1800
(e) 2200

50. Population of village C continuously decreases from 2000 to 2012 and it decreases by the same number in 2012 from 2008 as it decreased in 2008 from 2000. If literate in C in 2008 and 2012 are same then population of C in 2012 is what percent less than population of C in 2000.

(a) $44\dfrac{2}{7}\%$ (b) $44\dfrac{3}{7}\%$

(c) $41\dfrac{2}{7}\%$ (d) $44\dfrac{4}{9}\%$

(e) $45\dfrac{4}{9}\%$

51. Sum of literate from village B in 2000 and 2008 is 1530 and sum of literates in 2008 and 2012 is 2010 If sum of literates from villages B in all the given years is 2490 then find population of village B in 2008.
(a) 2625   (b) 2200
(c) 2000   (d) 2150
(e) 2050

52. Two numbers A and B are given
What is A + B ?
(i) LCM of A and B is 44 times their HCF
(ii) The sum of LCM of A & B and their HCF is 540.

(iii) $\dfrac{A}{10} + \dfrac{B}{10}$ is an integer

(iv) A + B > 150
Which of the given statements are redundant to find the answer of the question.
(a) statement (ii)
(b) statement (iii)
(c) statement (iv)
(d) statement (i)
(e) Answer cannot be determined even after using all the statements.

53. A vessel has 200 litre of milk and 40 litre of water. If ________ litres of mixture is taken from the vessel and ________ litres of water is added to the remaining mixture, then the final amount of milk in the vessel becomes 125 litre more than the amount of water in it. Which of the following integral values given in the options are possible in the blanks in same order?
(A) (36,11)   (B) (30, 15)
(C) (42,12)   (D) (24, 19)
(E) (18, 24)
(a) only A   (b) only A, B and E
(c) only A and B   (d) only A, B and D
(e) All four are possible

54. A bag has 15 red, green and blue balls. Number of each balls is different in the bag. Difference between red ball and green ball is same as difference between green ball and blue ball. Probability of selecting one blue ball from the bag is greater than 0.2, then number of blue balls in the bag can be
(A) 3   (B) 4
(C) 5   (D) 7
(E) 9
(a) Only B, C, D and E (b) Only B, D, E
(c) All, B, C, D and E (d) Only C, D, E
(e) Only A, B, D, E

55. Marked price of an article is 60% more than the CP of the article. When it is solid at $x\%$ discount then _________ % percent profit is obtained and when it is sold at a discount of $2x\%$, _________ % profit is obtained. Which of the following options are possible for the blanks in same order

A. 60, 30   B. 20, 8
C. 48, 24   D. 36,12
E. 44, 28

(a) A and E   (b) B, D and E
(c) C, D and E   (d) All are possible
(e) A, D and E

56. A set of five two-digit integers numbers is given. Average of first and last number is middle number. Second number is half of first number. Sum of first three numbers is 127. Middle number is (A) and average of five numbers is (B). Fourth number is 62. What can be the values of (A) and (B) respectively?

(a) 64, 50   (b) 62, 55
(c) 62, 50   (d) 64, 55
(e) 60, 55

Directions (57-59): Line chart given below shows expense of five persons (in %) out of total income of two months. Income of persons is same in both months.

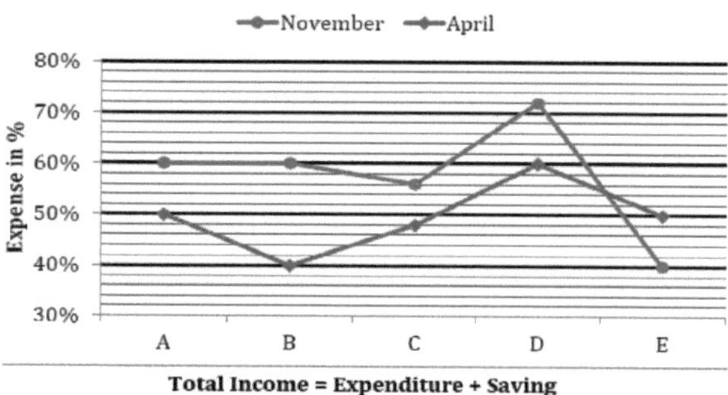

57. Find the difference between income of D and E ?

(I) Difference between expense of 'D' in November and saving of 'E' in April is Rs. 3200.

(II) Difference between Saving of 'D' in April and Expense of 'E' in November is Rs. 8000.

(a) Statement (I) alone is sufficient to answer the question but statement (II) alone is not sufficient to answer the questions.

(b) Statement (II) alone is sufficient to answer the question but statement (I) alone is not sufficient to answer the question.

(c) Both the statements taken together are necessary to answer the questions, but neither of the statements alone is sufficient to answer the question.

(d) Either statement (I) or statement (II) by itself is sufficient to answer the question.

(e) Statements (I) and (II) taken together are not sufficient to answer the question.

58. Average saving of 'C in both months is Rs. 19,200 while A's income is 20% more than C's income. Find expense of 'A' in the month of November.

(a) Rs. 9600   (b) Rs. 19200
(c) Rs. 38400   (d) Rs. 24000
(e) Rs. 28800

59. 'B' invested some amount of his saving in PPF account in November. Find the amount invested by 'B' in PPF account?

(I) Amount invested by 'B' in PPF is 62.5% less than amount expend by 'B' in April while difference between amount expend by 'B' in November and April is Rs. 16,000.

(II) 'B' invested 37.5% of his saving in PPF account while difference between saving of 'B' in November and April is Rs. 16,000.

(a) Statement (I) alone is sufficient to answer the question but statement (II) alone is not sufficient to answer the questions.

(b) Statement (II) alone is sufficient to answer the question but statement (I) alone is not sufficient to answer the question.

(c) Both the statements taken together are necessary to answer the questions, but neither of the statements alone is sufficient to answer the question.

(d) Either statement (I) or statement (II) by itself is sufficient to answer the question.

(e) Statements (I) and (II) taken together are not sufficient to answer the question.

Directions (Q. 60-62): Given below is the information about wind mills in four different villages A, B, C and D. Number of wind mills in villages A, B, C and D are 24, 20, 15 and 12 respectively. Number of electricity units produced in one week by one wind mill when they operate with maximum efficiency in village A, B, C and D is 2 lakh units/week, 80000 units/week, 1 Lakh units/week and 1.5 Lakh units/week respectively. Number of houses in each village A, B, C and D are 540, 240, 150 and 350 respectively. Total units produced are consumed equally by each house in the village.

→ Different number of winds mills are operate in four different weeks

In first week number of wind mills are operative in village A, B, C and D are 75%, 50%, 40% and 75% respectively. In second week it is 50%, 75%, 60% and 50% respectively. In third week it is 75%, 100%, 80% and 50% respectively. In fourth week it is 100%, 50%, 60% and 75% respectively.

→ Given below is the three ranges of efficiency of a wind mills (number of unit produced /Week by one mill)

Efficiency Type	Range
Efficiency 1	60% - 70%
Efficiency 2	45% - 55%
Efficiency 3	30% - 40%

Three wind mills also operate on different levels

→ level 1 : Consider upper limit of range of efficiency

→ level 2 : Consider mid of range of efficiency

→ level 3 : Consider the lower range of efficiency

Eg. If a wind mill is operative at efficiency 2 then its level 2 efficiency will be

$$= \frac{45+55}{2} = 50\%$$

Its level 1 efficiency will be 55%

Its level 3 efficiency will be 45%

60. What is the ratio of total production of village A in First week at level 1 of efficiency 2 to the total production of village B in second week at Level 2 of efficiency 1.

(a) 20 : 13   (b) 33 : 13

(c) 33 : 19   (d) 27 : 19

(e) 27 : 13

61. Total units produced in village C in second and fourth week at level 1 of efficiency range 1 is what percent of total units produced in village A in first and fourth week at level 2 of efficiency range 1?

(a) $25\dfrac{7}{13}\%$

(b) $23\dfrac{21}{273}\%$

(c) $13\dfrac{12}{13}\%$

(d) $22\dfrac{5}{13}\%$

(e) $24\dfrac{5}{13}\%$

62. What is the ratio of units consumed per house in village B in week 4 operating at level 3 of efficiency range 3 to the units consumed per house in second week at level 1 of efficiency range 2 of the village C?

(a) 5 : 6   (b) 13 : 19

(c) 15 : 19   (d) 13 : 33

(e) 10 : 33

Directions (Q. 63-65): There are three quantities provided in the questions. You have to find out the values of the quantities and compare them according to the given codes as follows

@ → >

& → <

* → ≥

\$ → ≤

→ = (or relationship can't be established)

Example :

Quantity I: $3^2 + 5^3$

Quantity II: $5^2 \times 2^2$

Quantity III: 100

(a) @, \$

(b) *, #

(c) S, #

(d) &, *

(e) @, #

Quantity I > Quantity II = Quantity III

So, answer is (e)

63. **Quantity I:** $360\ m^7n^9 \div 120\ m^{-2}\ n^3 \times 24m^{-4}\ n^4$; m>0, n<0

Quantity II: $240\ x^9y^7 \div 60x^4y^3 \div 3x^{-2}y^3$; x<0, y<0

Quantity III: $48\ a^8b^{12} \times 5\ a^3\ b^{-4} \div 6a^6b$, a>0, b<0

(a) (@, &)   (b) (#, @)

(c) (\$, @)   (d) (&, @)

(e) (*, #)

64. 'p', 'q', 'r' and 'n' are positive integers.

Quantity I: 'p': $-\dfrac{(p+n)^2 - (p-n)^2}{8pn(p+n)^2} = 1$

Quantity II: 'p':

$$-\dfrac{(q+n)^3 - (q-n)^3}{(n^2 + 3q^2)^2} = \dfrac{1}{8n}$$

Quantity III: 'p': $-\dfrac{\sqrt{r+n} + \sqrt{r-n}}{\sqrt{r+n} - \sqrt{r-n}} = 2$

(a) (@, &)   (b) (#, @)

(c) (\$, @)   (d) (&, @)

(e) (*, #)

65. **Quantity I-** Coaching teacher asked a question to three students A, B & C and probability of question not being answered by three students is 0.5, 0.4, 0.7 respectively. Find the probability that at most two students will solve the question.

Quantity II - A bag contains 5 green balls & 7 red balls, if three balls drawn at random from bag, then find probability of getting at least 1 green ball.

Quantity III - Arun speaks the truth 4 out of 5 times, and Bhavya speaks the truth 6 out of 7 times. What is the probability that they will contradict each other in stating the same fact?

(a) (@, &)   (b) (#, @)

(c) (@, @)   (d) (&, a)

(e) (*, #)

66. Vijay can cover 'D' distance with 'S' speed in 'T' time. He can cover same distance with 'S + 10' speed in '(T – 2)' time. He can cover same distance 'D' with 'S – 15' speed in (T + 6)' time. What can be found from the given data?

(i) time to cover 200 km with speed 'S + 10'

(ii) distance covered in (T + 6) time with (S + 10) speed

(iii) speed by which a tunnel can be crossed in $\dfrac{T}{2}$ hour

(iv) Ratio between time to cover distance 'D' with speed 'S' to time to cover distance (D – 5) with speed (S + 10)

(a) only (ii)   (b) only (ii) and (iii)

(c) only (i) and (iii) (d) all of the above

(e) only (i), (ii) and (iv)

67. Two trains A and B cross each other in 12 seconds when they move towards each other. Speed of train A and train B is 81 km/hr and 54 km/hr respectively. Length of train A is 150 metre more than length of train B.

→ Which of the following can be obtained from the above given information?

(i) Time taken by train B to cross a man moving in same direction as of train B.

(ii) Time taken by train A to cross a platform of half of its length.

(iii) Length of train A.

(iv) Speed of another train C whose length is equal to average of length of train A and B.

(a) (i) and (iii)

(b) (i), (ii) and (iii)

(c) (ii) and (iii)

(d) All (i), (ii), (iii) and (iv)

(e) (i) and (iv)

68. When the digits of a two digit natural number are interchanged then original number is greater than three times the new number so obtained. How many such natural numbers are

there which satisfy the above given condition? Ignore the numbers which have '0' in its unit place.

(a) 5   (b) 6

(c) 7   (d) 8

(e) 9

69. Veer invested Rs. 10000 at simple interest for 2 years at the rate of R% and gets an interest of Rs. 1400. He invested total amount (Principle + Interest) in a scheme, which offered compound interest at the rate of (R% + x%) for two years.

→ What are the possible integral values of 'x%' so that obtained compound interest is less than Rs. 2400

(i) 1%

(ii) 2%

(iii) 3%

(iv) 4%

(v) 5%

(a) Only (i)

(b) Only (i), (ii)

(c) Only (i), (ii) and (iii)

(d) Only (i), (ii), (iii) and (iv)

(e) All of the above

70. Ratio between marked price of article A to article B is 4 : 5. Shopkeeper allowed d% discount on article 'A' and (d + 18) % discount on article 'B' so selling price of both articles become equal. If shopkeeper made a profit of 20% on article A and 25% on article B and profit made on article B is Rs. 384 more than that of article A, then find the cost price of article 'A' and article 'B' respectively?

(a) Rs. 9000 Rs. 8400

(b) Rs. 9600 Rs. 9216

(c) Rs. 9800 Rs. 9012

(d) Rs. 9600 Rs. 8488

(e) Rs. 9200 Rs. 9216

Direction (Q. 71-74): Study the data given below and answer the following questions

Data is provided for 3 months for a water tank whose capacity is 600000 L to provide continuous water supply to a building. Water tank is first completely filled and then it gets completely emptied to supply water in a building. It supply water continuously to the building and is refilled again and again to provide continuous supply. In the building there are 40 flats in which all flats may or may not be completely occupied in the given three months.

November → Each flat is filled with a tap from which rate of flow of water is 250 L/h and only 50% flats are occupied in November. Water tank provides continuous water supply to these taps in whole month.

December → In this month 30 flats are occupied and tank gets emptied after $4\dfrac{1}{6}$ % days. Rate of flow from one tap in December is <u>A</u>% more or less than rate of flow from one tap in November.

January → Rate of flow of water from the taps is same as of November and gets emptied after supplying water to building for 100 hr. Number of flats occupied in January is <u>B</u>%

71. In November tank has to be filled how many times?

(a) 5   (b) 6

(c) 8   (d) 7

(e) 9

72. What is the value of A%?

(a) 30%   (b) 25%

(c) $33\dfrac{1}{3}$%   (d) 20%

(e) 15%

73. What is the value of B%?

(a) 80%   (b) 40%

(c) 75%   (d) 60%

(e) 70%

74. In October efficiency of each tap decrease by 20% due to leakage as compared to efficiency of November and capacity of tank is reduced to 80%. In how many hours tank will be emptied in October if total occupied flats in October is equal to number of occupied flats in December

(a) 65 hours   (b) 70 hours

(c) 30 hours   (d) 60 hours

(e) 80 hours

Directions (Q. 75-77): Given below is the sequence of series. Analyze the pattern of the series and answer the given following questions.

75. 1, 3, 9, 31,129, 651

2, _, _, _, _, ?

(a) 625

(b) 37

(c) 153

(d) 771

(e) 631

76. 4, 2, 2, 3, 6, 15, 45

If $(2835)^n$ is the term of the sequence where n is the nth term of sequence then find 'n'.

(a) 8th (b) 9th

(c) 10th (d) 11th

(e) 12th

77. A series is 113,170,232,303,399, 556,838. Another series is 93, _, _, _, _, _, <u>m</u>. Which follows same pattern as given number series. Then m = ?

(a) 808   (b) 443

(c) 626   (d) 818

(e) 909

78. A can do a task in 18 days, B can do the same task in 24 days and C can destroy the whole work in 36 days. If A & B work for first x days together after that C also joined them, remaining work is completed in $\left(x+4\dfrac{4}{5}\right)$ days. Find how many days all three worked together?

(a) $6\dfrac{4}{5}$ days

(b) $5\dfrac{4}{5}$ days

(c) $4\dfrac{4}{5}$ days

(d) $7\dfrac{4}{5}$ days

(e) $8\dfrac{4}{5}$ days

79. A boat goes 28 km downstream and while returning covered only 75% of distance that covered in downstream. If boat takes 3 hr more to cover upstream than downstream then find the speed of boat in still water (km/hr) if speed of stream is 5/9m/sec?

(a) 8 km/hr   (b) 2 km/hr

(c) 5 km/hr   (d) 4 km/hr

(e) 3 km/hr

80. A cylindrical vessel with radius and height of 17.5 cm and 18 cm respectively is filled upto 80% of its capacity with milk. If total milk from cylindrical vessel transferred into 30 cuboidal vessels whose length and breadth is 7 cm and 3 cm respectively. Find height of each cuboidal vessel?

(a) 18 cm   (b) 25 cm

(c) 23 cm   (d) 20 cm

(e) 22 cm

ENGLISH LANGUAGE

Directions (81-84): Read the following passage and answer the questions as directed.

Paragraph 1- One of the easiest ways to establish a savings habit is to participate in your employer's 401(k) plan. Funds are withheld from each paycheck and deposited into your account. If your employer matches part of your contribution — and many do! — you will accumulate **yet** more. A second way to consistently save is with an automatic savings transfer program with your financial institution. You decide how much and when you want funds transferred from your checking account into a savings account. You can also use a payroll deduction plan from your employer and get the same results.

Paragraph 2- Along with how much and how often you save, what you earn on your funds will determine how fast your money grows. You cannot control what happens with interest rates or the stock market, but you can consider different types of savings vehicles that provide different returns. The simplest savings vehicle to consider is buying certificates of deposit (CDs) instead of leaving funds in a savings account. CDs usually offer higher interest rates, but they are time deposits and have .... for early withdrawal. If you can accept not having immediate access to your funds, CDs can be an attractive savings vehicle.

81. Which of the following can be inferred as the theme of the passage?
    (a) Certificate of deposits is the best way to establish savings habit.
    (b) Establishing a consistent saving habit and also smart saving with CDs.
    (c) Employer's 401(k) plan provides a convenient way for consistent and smart savings.
    (d) Your savings decide how well you flourish and grow.
    (e) None of the Above

82. Which of the following can replace the word given in bold in the passage?
    (a) though
    (b) even
    (c) quitely
    (d) accrue
    (e) more

83. What is the tone of writing in the passage?
    (a) Satirical
    (b) Critical
    (c) Didactic
    (d) Sarcastic
    (e) Nostalgic

84. Which of the following words can fill in the blank to make it meaningful?
    (a) gifts
    (b) lucrative
    (c) casualities
    (d) penalties
    (e) None of the Above

Directions (85-87): Read the following paragraph and answer the questions as directed.

Budgeting is an important tool for saving. First, you need to segregate all your income and expenses. Now, categorise your expenses as least important, important and very important to prioritise them while settling them through your income, which is limited. Try to figure out ways in which you can **increase** expenses. *Ensure that your income exceeds the expenses with as wider a margin as possible.* The surplus fund after meeting all the expenses would be your saving. It is only after you have assured savings that you can thinking about investment.

85. Which of the followings is the correct chronology of steps as can be inferred from the passage?
    (a) Saving-Budgeting-Investment
    (b) Investment-Budgeting-Saving
    (c) Budgeting-Saving-Investment
    (d) Budgeting-Investment-Saving
    (e) None of the Above

86. Which of the following words, opposite of the word given in bold, should replace the word given in bold in the passage?
    (a) Enhance
    (b) Curtail
    (c) Damage
    (d) Lengthen
    (e) Leverage

87. Which of the following is the best way of writing the line given in italics in the paragraph, without changing its intended meaning?
    (a) Surely, the income will exceed the expenses by a wider margin.
    (b) The income will be greater than the expenses is not a possibility.
    (c) Make sure that the income is greater than the expenses by a margin as wide as possible.
    (d) If the income does not exceed the expenses by a wider margin, it will be useless.
    (e) None of the Above

Directions (88-90): Read the following paragraph and answer the questions as directed.

The way most of us save is to put away whatever is left after all expenses are taken care of, or put away any surplus income. But that is not the best way of saving and there are chances of us falling short. A very stringent savings plan that favours future demands over current aspirations is also likely to fail. Instead, a better approach is where due consideration is given to current and future needs. This will help divide the available income between current consumption and future saving. If an expense or a need is too large to be met out of the regular income, earmark it for the future. So the .... way to buy a coveted watch is not to swipe the credit card and commit yourself to debt, but to set aside money from your current income and buy the watch when you have the required funds.

88. Which of the following can be best inferred from the paragraph?

   (a) The better way to save is to give due consideration to current and future needs and plan accordingly.

   (b) It's better to buy the things that you require at present than to save money and buy them later.

   (c) Buying a watch is more important than saving for the future.

   (d) A stringent savings plan will produce a good result for the future.

   (e) None of the Above

89. Which of the following word should fill in the blank in the paragraph?

   (a) stringent   (b) bad

   (c) unethical   (d) moneywise

   (e) Both (a) and (d)

90. Which of the following can be next line after the last line of the given paragraph?

   (a) Most of us never have enough money for immediate expenses as well as saving.

   (b) There will be a lot of unwanted expenses that can creep in every now and then.

   (c) If we had enough money to meet our current expenses and future goals, there would be no problem.

   (d) Expenses or needs that have to be met at a point of time in the future are called goals.

   (e) Just as we segregate the essential and less important things in our shopping list, do the same with your goals.

Directions (91-93): Read the following passage carefully and answer the questions given below it. Certain words are given in bold to help you locate them while answering some of the questions.

Pakistan's Army and political leadership are on "one page" to take dialogue with India forward, Pakistan's Prime Minister Imran Khan said on Wednesday at the ground-breaking ceremony for the corridor.

Pakistan's Chief of Army Staff General Qamar Bajwa was also present.

The four-kilometre corridor from the border with India will allow pilgrims easy access and will be ready in time for Sikh founder Guru Nanak's 550th birth anniversary on November 23, 2019.

In a speech largely reaching out to the Indian government to "break the shackles of the past" and restart engagement, Mr. Khan also struck a **discordant** note on Kashmir, referring to the dispute as the "single issue" between India and Pakistan. India has maintained that terrorism sponsored by Pakistan is holding back the dialogue process. Asked about the reference, Ms. Badal told The Hindu that the remark didn't change the Indian stand.

91. Which of the following assumptions could be drawn out most appropriately from a clause in the first paragraph 'Pakistan's Army and political leadership are on "one page" to take dialogue with India forward'?

   (I) In Pakistan, to have a dialogue with India, there should be a consensus between Pakistan's Army and the Pakistan's political leadership.

   (II) There is a paper of high strength present in Pakistan where Pakistan's Army and the Pakistan's political leadership could stand together.

   (III) Pakistan's political leadership could independently take forward dialogue with India.

   (a) Only (II) & (III)

   (b) Only (I)

   (c) Only (I) & (II)

   (d) All of (I), (II) and (III)

   (e) None of (I), (II) and (III)

92. What does Mr. Khan mean by referring to the Kashmir dispute as the "single issue" between India and Pakistan?

   (a) According to Mr. Khan, there is only one issue between India and Pakistan which needs to be solved.

   (b) According to Mr. Khan, dispute on Kashmir is an issue among other important unresolved issues between India and Pakistan which has the highest importance.

   (c) According to Mr. Khan, Kashmir is a part of both India and Pakistan.

   (d) According to Mr. Khan, India and Pakistan have failed to resolve the issue between India and Pakistan.

   (e) None of the above

93. Which of the following words has the meaning which is SIMILAR to the meaning 'discordant'?

   (a) Ugly   (b) Concur

   (c) Accord   (d) Clashing

   (e) Endorsement

Directions (94-96): Read the following passage carefully and answer the questions given below it. Certain words are given in bold to help you locate them while answering some of the questions.

The government is of the view that IndiGo and SpiceJet should **withdraw** their web check-in fee, according to a top source in the Ministry of Civil Aviation.

IndiGo and SpiceJet recently revised their web check-in policies to include a levy for air travellers opting for web check-in for any seat in an aircraft. Earlier, passengers would have to pay extra only for certain preferred seats. "We have told the two airlines to remove the new fee," the source told The Hindu. The Ministry had already met the airlines' officials and would be holding another meeting with them. Asked how the government could intervene since airlines were allowed to unbundle fares and charge separately for preferential seating, meal-on-board, check-in baggage and use of airline lounges, a senior official said airlines should incentivise web check-in.

94. Which of the followings, as mentioned in the passage, could create hurdles for the government in its desire to intervene and convince Indigo and SpiceJet to withdraw web check-in fee?

   (a) Ministry of Civil Aviation or government has no authority to give directions to airlines.

   (b) Airlines can unbundle air-fare and charges for services.

   (c) Making airlines to withdraw web check-in fees would invite protest from them and they would stop operating their aircrafts.

   (d) Options (a), (b) & (c)

   (e) None of the above

95. Which of the following statements, if true, would encourage the government to convince Indigo and SpiceJet to withdraw their web check-in fee?

   (I) Keeping web check-in free would encourage passengers to opt for it, would allow the passengers to come to airport not too early and in effect would help in controlling the number of passengers in an airport and would help the security personnel in the security management of an airport.

   (II) Levying fee to web check-in would either make air-travel costly or increase discomfort to the airline passengers. This might discourage people to opt for air travel and would be against the aspiration of the government to increase the overall number of air travel passengers.

   (III) Levying fee to web check-in would discourage the passengers to opt for it and might decrease the usage of internet to avail important services, in contradiction to the objective of the Digital India Initiative.

   (a) Only (II)

   (b) Only (I) & (II)

   (c) Only (II) & (III)

   (d) None of (I), (II) & (III)

   (e) All of (I), (II) & (III)

96. Which of the following words has a meaning which is OPPOSITE in meaning to the word 'withdraw'?

   (a) abolish

   (b) separate

   (c) remove

   (d) rescind

   (e) approve

Directions (97-99): Read the following passage carefully and answer the questions given below it. Certain words are given in bold to help you locate them while answering some of the questions.

Noting that the 1984 anti-Sikh riots were a "dark chapter in the history of independent India," the Delhi High Court on Wednesday upheld the conviction of 70 persons on the charges of rioting, burning houses and violating curfew in the Trilokpuri area in the national capital.

The riots took place after the assassination of Indira Gandhi. Justice R.K. Gauba dismissed the appeals of the convicts against the August 27, 1996, judgment of a sessions court here, sending 89 persons to jail for five years.

The judge said: "Thirty-four years have passed, yet the victims await justice and closure." Of the 89,16 died during the pendency of the trial before the High Court, which dragged on for 22 years. The court dismissed the appeal of three more convicts who absconded during the trial.

"The manner of prosecution of the case at hand would undoubtedly go down in the judicial history of this country as an example of criminal law process that must never be emulated," the High Court said.

97. Why did the Delhi High Court use the phrase 'Dark Chapter in the history of Independent India'?

   (a) The 1984 anti-Sikh riots were not religiously motivated riots.

   (b) The 1984 anti-Sikh riots led to the defense of innocent people belonging to several communities

   (c) The 1984 anti-Sikh riots were shameful events in the history of independent India.

   (d) Options (a) & (b)

   (e) All of (a), (b) & (c)

98. What is the opinion of the Delhi High Court about the manner of prosecution of the 1984 anti-Sikh riots?

   (a) The manner of prosecution of the 1984 anti-Sikh riots has been effective in delivering justice.

   (b) The manner of prosecution of the 1984 anti-Sikh riots has been very pathetic and must not be repeated in the Indian Judiciary.

   (c) The way prosecution of the 1984 anti-Sikh riots was conducted provided timely justice to the victims.

   (d) Options (a) & (c)

   (e) None of the above

99. Which of the following words has a meaning which is SIMILAR in meaning to the word 'absconded'?

   (a) Emulated   (b) Surrendered

   (c) Appointed   (d) Escaped

   (e) Arrested

Directions (100-101): Read the following passage carefully and answer the questions given below it. Certain words are given in bold to help you locate them while answering some of the questions.

Justice Kurian Joseph, one of the senior-most judges of the Supreme Court, on Wednesday said the courts had been imposing the death penalty "arbitrarily and freakishly".

Justice Kurian, in his judgment while heading a three-judge Bench hearing the appeal of a man sentenced to death, said the test of "rarest of rare" had been "inconsistently applied" by courts. The other two judges, Justices Deepak Gupta and Hemant Gupta, disagreed that death penalty was "freakishly" imposed.

100. Which of the followings judges believe that courts have failed to uphold the principle of justice?

   (a) The given passage doesn't talk if courts have failed to uphold the principle of justice.

   (b) Justice Deepak Gupta

   (c) Justice Hemant Gupta

   (d) Options (b) & (c)

   (e) Justice Kurian Joseph

101. Which of the following words has a meaning which is OPPOSITE in meaning to the word 'disagreed'?

   (a) bickered   (b) haggled

   (c) contended   (d) concurred

   (e) feuded

Directions (102-111): Read the given passage carefully and answer the questions.

The system of "local welfare" schemes set up less than five years ago to provide emergency help to England's poorest families, often to help them cope with delays and sanctions to their benefits, is on the (A) of collapse, say poverty campaigners. (B) *A survey of more than 150 council-run schemes by Church Action on Poverty found that nearly a quarter had been shut down since 2013, while a further quarter have reduced spending by 85% or more.* More are expected to close in the next few months. (C) The **destitution** (1) of local welfare would put tens of thousands of **vulnerable** (2) people at increased **risk** (3) of hunger, debt and **demise** (4), the charity said. The system was designed to help people on low incomes deal with unexpected hardship, (D):--------------, or domestic crises such as broken boilers, house fires and flooding. Huge cuts to council budgets have left the system, which replaced the old social fund, struggling to survive. Provision is so uneven that thousands of people cannot access emergency help from the state, Church Action on Poverty said. "Local authority welfare schemes are increasingly (E), leaving families in many areas with nowhere to turn for help," said the bishop of Manchester, David Walker. "It cannot be right for central and local government to (F) **abdicate** responsibility for people in crisis when they need our help most." *In many areas, the most common reason for an application for crisis support is delays or sanctions to benefits, with some councils noting that the five-week minimum wait for a first universal credit payment is an emerging factor in rising demand.* Universal credit claimants facing hardship who contact Department for Work and Pensions (DWP) helplines for help are routinely directed to local welfare schemes in their areas if they do not qualify for official advance loans or hardship funds. Church leaders and anti-poverty charities called on ministers to make local welfare provision a legal duty for top-tier councils, and to provide ringfenced funding to protect crisis services. *The 153 councils that responded to the survey collectively reduced spending on local welfare by an average of 72% between 2013-2014 and 2017-2018.* (G) *Local welfare provision replaced the discretionary social fund, which in its final year spent £240m in crisis loans and community care grants.* (H) It was **going** (1) to councils with DWP **funding** (2) in 2013 but that cash was **stopped** (3) in 2015, with councils left to decide whether to keep the schemes devolved (4). Huge budget pressures faced by councils mean even authorities that have protected local welfare in the past are proposing drastic cuts. West Sussex county council recently unveiled plans for an 80% reduction in its £800,000 crisis fund from next April. (I) *Local welfare has been controversially as most councils refuse to give cash payments to clients in crisis, choosing instead to offer supermarket food vouchers or refer them to food banks.* In one case, Isle of Wight council offered a 62-year-old homeless woman a voucher to buy a tent. Only two English councils - Islington in north London and North Tyneside in the north-east - had higher local welfare budget cash totals year compared with 2013, by 12% and 4% respectively. Niall Cooper, the director of Church Action on Poverty, said: "The (J) ---------- of the social fund was that people could stay afloat and hopefully ride out a crisis, rather than sinking deeper into poverty. A lifeline in times of emergency is a vital part of a compassionate society, but it has been withdrawn in many places and neglected almost everywhere."

102. Which of the following word given in the options should come at the place marked as (A) in the above paragraph to make it grammatically correct and meaningful. Also, the word should fill in the two sentences given below to make them contextually correct and meaningful.

(i) She stood out of his way, barely able to care for a child and at a loss as to what to do with a boy on the .... of becoming a teenager.

(ii) He found the country on the of revolution; but the wisdom of the new monarch saved the situation and won back the Magyars.

(a) middle   (b) edging

(c) verge   (d) resemble

(e) terminate

103. In the passage given, a sentence (B) is given in italics. There may or may not be an error in one part of the sentence. Choose the part which has an error in it as your answer. If there in no error then choose option (e) as your answer.

(a) A survey of more than 150 council-run schemes by

(b) Church Action on Poverty found that nearly a quarter

(c) had been shutted down since 2013, while a further

(d) quarter have reduced spending by 85% or more.

(e) No Error

104. The sentence given in (C) has four words given in bold. Amongst the given bold words which of the following must replace each other to make the sentence contextually correct and meaningful.

(a) 1-4   (b) 1-3

(c) 2-3   (d) 2-4

(e) 1-2

105. Which of the following phrases should fill the blank in (D) to make it contextually correct and meaningful?

(a) facing the severe impacts caused by the crisis

(b) including job programmes and childcare, but also transfers to other state programmes,

(c) which are a cause of severe balance of payments

(d) so some avoid them by limiting how many people are eligible for welfare in the first place.

(e) such as a lack of money caused by benefit payment problems

106. Which of the following word given in the options should come at the place marked as E in the above paragraph to make it grammatically correct and meaningful. Also, the word should fill in the two sentences given below to make them contextually correct and meaningful.

(i) After living in the woods for a week without supplies, my .... clothing was not protecting me from the elements.

(ii) The Defence Department generally defended its existing programs, though the rationale for them was growing ....

(a) flawless

(b) threadbare

(c) pristine

(d) unsullied

(e) Both (b) and (c)

107. A word is given in bold in (F). Choose the word which should replace the word given in bold to make the sentence correct and meaningful. If no change is required, choose option (e) as your answer.

(a) renounce   (b) abjure

(c) surrendering   (d) vacating

(e) No Change

108. Two sentences are given in italics on both sides of (G). Which of the following statements can come in between the two sentences in place of (G) and maintain the continuity of the paragraph?

(a) The dynamic nature of our preferred model allows to estimate the long-term effect of a 1 per cent increase in social spending, which is found to be in the order of a 0.057 points increase in the IHDI.

(b) Continuing investments in the social sectors have been recognized by the international community.

(c) Local authorities are responsible for using their funds to best meet the needs of their residents, and over the next two years we are providing them with £90.7bn to do so.

(d) Together they spent £46m on local welfare last year, compared with a national budget of £172m in 2013-14.

(e) One million people have been lifted out of absolute poverty since 2010 and household incomes have never been higher.

109. The sentence given in (H) has four words given in bold. Amongst the given bold words which of the following must replace each other to make the sentence contextually correct and meaningful.

(a) 1-4   (b) 1-3

(c) 2-3   (d) 2-4

(e) 1-2

110. In the passage given, a sentence (I) is given in italics. There may or may not be an error in one part of the sentence. Choose the part which has an error in it as your answer. If there in no error then choose option (e) as your answer.
    (a) Local welfare has been controversially
    (b) as most councils refuse to give cash payments to clients
    (c) in crisis, choosing instead to offer supermarket
    (d) food vouchers or refer them to food banks.
    (e) No Error

111. Which of the following words should fill the blank given in (J) to make it contextually correct and meaningful?
    (a) caused
    (b) occasion
    (c) desires
    (d) purpose
    (e) reasons

    Directions (112-115): Rearrange the following six sentences (A), (B), (C), (D), (E) and (F) in the proper sequence to form a meaningful paragraph and then answer the questions given below.

(A) With the change from traditional to industrial food processing there has also been a change in the types of product processed.

(B) In the early days of traditional food processing the main aim was preservation to maintain a supply of wholesome, nutritious food during the year and in particular to preserve it for hungry periods, for example when hunting was poor.

(C) Nowadays non-traditional crops are grown all over the world. This together with consumer demand influenced by radio, advertising and television has led to a demand for non-traditional foods that are not appropriate to the local environment.

(D) While food processing still has the main objective of providing a safe nutritious diet in order to maintain health other aspects, particularly the generation of wealth for the producer and seller, have become increasingly important.

(E) Traditional processors worked with foods that grew locally and the methods they developed were in harmony with the climate in which they lived.

(F) Only simple packaging using leaves, animal skins and pottery was possible and necessary to protect the food for its planned storage life.

112. Considering statement (D) "While food processing still has the main objective of providing a safe nutritious diet in order to maintain health other aspects, particularly the generation of wealth for the producer and seller, have become increasingly important." as the second sentence of the rearranged paragraph, then which of the following aptly expresses the theme of the paragraph after rearrangement?
    (a) Benefits of non-traditional food processing
    (b) Reforms in food processing
    (c) Harmful effects of processed foods
    (d) Objective of processing foods
    (e) None of these

113. Considering statement (D) "While food processing still has the main objective of providing a safe nutritious diet in order to maintain health other aspects, particularly the generation of wealth for the producer and seller, have become increasingly important." as the second sentence of the rearranged paragraph, then which among the following should be the FOURTH sentence of the rearranged paragraph?
    (a) A
    (b) B
    (c) E
    (d) F
    (e) C

114. Considering statement (D) "While food processing still has the main objective of providing a safe nutritious diet in order to maintain health other aspects, particularly the generation of wealth for the producer and seller, have become increasingly important." as the second sentence of the rearranged paragraph, then which among the following should follow the last sentence after the rearrangement?
    (a) They need special processing and packaging to protect them for their required storage life.
    (b) The increasing number of women who now work away from home adds additional pressure for such changes.
    (c) Food has been processed and packaged since the earliest days of man's history on earth.
    (d) The small-scale food processing sector is a major source of employment.
    (e) None of these

115. Considering statement (D) "While food processing still has the main objective of providing a safe nutritious diet in order to maintain health other aspects, particularly the generation of wealth for the producer and seller, have become increasingly important." as the second sentence of the rearranged paragraph, then which among the following should coherently link the first and the second sentence of the paragraph, without altering the context of the paragraph?
    (a) The small-scale food processing sector adds value to crops by processing.
    (b) Food and crop processing is generally considered to be the largest industry in most countries.
    (c) The powerful large-scale food sector is also often able to influence government and international policies.
    (d) Food was seldom sold but traded and bartered.
    (e) None of these

GENERAL AWARENESS

116. Which Bank has launched its Multi Option Payment Acceptance Device (MOPAD) for digital payments?
    (a) Axis Bank
    (b) State Bank of India
    (c) Punjab National Bank
    (d) ICICI Bank
    (e) Bank of Baroda

117. The Reserve Bank of India has constituted a 10-member 'High Level Task Force on Public Credit Registry (PCR) for India', which will, among other things, suggest a roadmap for developing a transparent, comprehensive and near-real-time PCR for India. Who is the head of Public Credit Registry?
    (a) Sekar Karnam
    (b) Rashesh Shah
    (c) Vishaka Mulye
    (d) Sriram Kalyanaraman
    (e) YM Deosthalee

118. Kharchi puja is a Hindu festival of which state?
    (a) Tripura
    (b) Manipur
    (c) Assam
    (d) Sikkim
    (e) Meghalaya

119. India's first government run e-waste recycling plant has opened in which city?
    (a) Mumbai
    (b) Hyderabad
    (c) New Delhi
    (d) Bengaluru
    (e) Kolkata

120. Where is the headquarter of Karur Vysya Bank?
    (a) Bengaluru, Karnataka
    (b) Thrissur, Kerala
    (c) Karur, Tamil Nadu
    (d) Jaipur, Rajasthan
    (e) Kochi, Kerala

121. "Sulabh Jal Scheme" has been launched in which state?
    (a) Indore, Madhya Pradesh
    (b) Jodhpur, Rajasthan
    (c) Rajkot, Gujarat
    (d) Guwahati, Assam
    (e) Darbhanga, Bihar

122. Which of the following state has bagged the top position under the Pradhan Mantri Surakshit Matritav Abhiyan (PMSMA)?
    (a) Andhra Pradesh
    (b) Madhya Pradesh
    (c) Uttar Pradesh
    (d) Himachal Pradesh
    (e) Arunachal Pradesh

123. Nelson Mandela Foundation is dedicating this year's (2018) Mandela Day to Action Against-?
    (a) Pollution
    (b) Corruption
    (c) Poverty
    (d) Global Warming
    (e) Polio

124. What is the allocation on Digital India Project under Union budget 2018-19?
    (a) Rs. 1014crore
    (b) Rs. 3073 crore
    (c) Rs. 5054 crore
    (d) Rs. 2315 crore
    (e) Rs. 9432 crore

125. The 10th edition of the Defence Expo was held in-
    (a) Chennai
    (b) Kolkata
    (c) New Delhi
    (d) Mumbai
    (e) Bhopal

126. Which of the following state has launched 'One Person One Car' policy?
    (a) West Bengal
    (b) Kerala
    (c) Madhya Pradesh
    (d) Rajasthan
    (e) Gujarat

127. Who has been named as 'British Indian of the Year'?
    (a) Anoushka Shankar
    (b) Ishwar Sharma
    (c) Shahraan Dutt
    (d) Arhaan Khan
    (e) MC Rama Rao

128. The Government of India has notified the Electoral Bond Scheme 2018. It may be noted that Electoral Bond shall be valid for _______ days from the date of issue.
    (a) 90
    (b) 30
    (c) 15
    (d) 10
    (e) 20

129. Which bank has been ranked as the best PSU bank in the overall digital transaction's category in India?
    (a) Bank of India
    (b) State Bank of India
    (c) Union Bank of India
    (d) Punjab National Bank
    (e) Bank of Baroda

130. India's first engineless rail, Train 18, manufactured by the Integral Coach Factory (ICF) was rolled out in-
    (a) Bhopal
    (b) New Delhi
    (c) Kapurthala
    (d) Madhepura
    (e) Chennai

131. The Union Cabinet has gave its approval to rename the Agartala Airport in Tripura as?
    (a) Om Prakash Gattan, Airport
    (b) Anuradha Devi Thokchom Airport
    (c) Denis P Rayen Airport
    (d) Maharaja Bir Bikram Manikya Kishore Airport
    (e) Pabitra Rabha Dinesh Airport

132. Which state has launched 'I am not afraid of English' initiative to promote English language right from Class 1 in the state"s primary schools?
    (a) Haryana   (b) Bihar
    (c) Uttar Pradesh   (d) Rajasthan
    (e) West Bengal

133. Microdot technology in India to be launched by the Government of India to check-?
    (a) Children thefts   (b) Petrol thefts
    (c) Vehicle thefts   (d) Books thefts
    (e) Girls thefts

134. Under which ministry the Swachh Bharat Mission (Gramin) and the Swachh Bharat Mission (Urban) has launched?
    (a) Ministry of Housing and Urban Affairs
    (b) Ministry of Home Affairs
    (c) Ministry of Human Resource Development
    (d) Ministry of Environment, Forest and Climate Change
    (e) Ministry of Drinking Water and Sanitation

135. The environment ministry re-introduces a scheme 'Medini Puraskar Yojna' which aims at promoting original writing of books in which language?
    (a) Tamil   (b) Hindi
    (c) Urdu   (d) Bengali
    (e) English

136. Petroleum Minister Dharmendra Pradhan has launched which initiative to promote Compressed Bio-Gas as an alternative, green transport fuel?
    (a) SATAT   (b) MOPAD
    (c) WINGS   (d) BHARAT
    (e) NIPAN

137. Indian naval shiph __________ as became the first-ever warship to enter port of Sabang in Indonesia.
    (a) INSArihant
    (b) INS Sumitra
    (c) INSVikrant
    (d) INS Trishul
    (e) INS Garur

138. NABARD has joined hands with which bank to provide collateral-free credit through Joint Liability Groups in Telangana?
    (a) BOB
    (b) ICICI Bank
    (c) SBI
    (d) Axis Bank
    (e) PNB

139. The Government of India has signed a loan deal worth USD 200 million with the World Bank for-
    (a) APY   (b) PMKSY
    (c) NIRVAAN   (d) POSHAN
    (e) ATAL

140. Under project 'SASHAKT' an asset management company/ alternative investment fund (AIF)-led resolution approach to deal with NPA cases of more than-?
    (a) Rs 100 crore   (b) Rs 200 crore
    (c) Rs 300 crore   (d) Rs 400 crore
    (e) Rs 500 crore

141. National Mission for Clean Ganga Organises "Ganga Vriksharopan Abhiyan" in Five Ganga Basin States Intervention in Ganga a Major Components of Namami Gange Programme. These 5 states are Uttarakhand, Uttar Pradesh, Bihar, West Bengal and?
    (a) Assam   (b) Jharkhand
    (c) Himachal Pradesh (d) Haryana
    (e) Odisha

142. Prime Minister Narendra Modi has launched "Rashtriya Gram Swaraj Abhiyan" at Ramnagar, tribal-dominated district of Madhya Pradesh. The scheme aims to strengthen the country's-
    (a) NPA Loss System
    (b) Corruption Based System
    (c) Politics System
    (d) Labour System
    (e) Panchayti Raj System

143. The government was announced a scheme for informants of benami transactions under which an individual can get a reward of up to ______ for providing information to the tax authorities.
    (a) Rs. 1 crore
    (b) Rs. 7 crore
    (c) Rs. 4 crore
    (d) Rs. 10 crore
    (e) Rs. 5 crore

144. NITI Aayog presented India's Voluntary National Review Report on the implementation of the-
    (a) UN Member Countries
    (b) International Review of Progress
    (c) Sustainable development Goals
    (d) All of the above
    (e) None of the given options is true

145. Which Bank has entered into an agreement with CDSL Commodity Repository Limited (CCRL) and it is first Public Sector Bank to become the Repository Participant for Pledge Finance under the Repository Ecosystem for registered/accredited warehouses by WDRA?
    (a) Bank of India
    (b) State Bank of India
    (c) Union Bank of India
    (d) Bank of Baroda
    (e) Punjab National Bank

146. An emerging market economy is highly classified with relatively- one in which the country is becoming a developed nation and is determined through many socio-
    (a) Growth factors
    (b) GDP factors
    (c) commercial factors
    (d) external factors
    (e) economic factors

147. Which High Court has declared the "entire animal kingdom including avian and aquatic" as legal entities with a distinct persona and corresponding rights, duties and liabilities of a living person?
    (a) Kolkata High Court
    (b) Patiala House Courts Complex
    (c) Patna High Court
    (d) Uttarakhand High Court
    (e) Allahabad High Court

148. The Reserve Bank of India has asked banks authorised to deal in foreign exchange (Authorised Dealer-I Banks) to share data with-?
    (a) Ministry of Finance
    (b) Securities and Exchange Board of India
    (c) Directorate of Revenue Intelligence
    (d) Intelligence Bureau
    (e) Comptroller and Auditor General of India

149. Bharat Sanchar Nigam Ltd (BSNL) has launched BSNL ________ a VOIP based service.
    (a) TERMS   (b) WINGS
    (c) NIGAM   (d) WAVES
    (e) NATER

150. Which Airport is the Busiest Airport 2017 by terms of traffic in the world?
    (a) Hartsfield-Jackson Atlanta International Airport, USA
    (b) Beijing Capital International Airport, China
    (c) Indira Gandhi International Airport, New Delhi
    (d) Dubai International Airport, UAE
    (e) London Heathrow Airport, UK

151. Survey points out for the first time in India's history that five States Maharashtra, Gujarat, Karnataka, Tamil Nadu and Telangana account for a whopping ________ of India's exports.
    (a) 50%   (b) 80%
    (c) 70%   (d) 40%
    (e) 60%

152. The government will take steps to boost exports of agriculture commodities which have the potential of reaching ________ billion.
    (a) $100 billion
    (b) $500 billion
    (c) $200 billion
    (d) $700 billion
    (e) $1500 billion

153. A dedicated portal of the ECI'S Systematic Voters Education, pursuit of its mission 'leave no voter behind,' with special focus on-
    (a) Female
    (b) New Voters
    (c) Senior Citizens
    (d) Persons with Disabilities
    (e) None of the given options is true

154. RBI's New Rules To Push Another Rs ________ Loans Into Insolvency stated Credit Suisse.
    (a) Rs 5.5 lakh crore
    (b) Rs 4.5 lakh crore
    (c) Rs 3.5 lakh crore
    (d) Rs 2.5 lakh crore
    (e) Rs 1.5 lakh crore

155. ________ is the value of all finished goods and services produced in a country in one year by its nationals.
    (a) NPA   (b) GNP
    (c) CDS   (d) GDP
    (e) BOP

ANSWERS

1. (b)	**2.** (c)	**3.** (a)	**4.** (e)	**5.** (e)	**6.** (c)	**7.** (e)	**8.** (a)	**9.** (e)	**10.** (d)
11. (a)	**12.** (d)	**13.** (c)	**14.** (c)	**15.** (b)	**16.** (c)	**17.** (d)	**18.** (c)	**19.** (a)	**20.** (d)
21. (d)	**22.** (d)	**23.** (a)	**24.** (e)	**25.** (e)	**26.** (e)	**27.** (d)	**28.** (b)	**29.** (a)	**30.** (c)
31. (d)	**32.** (c)	**33.** (e)	**34.** (c)	**35.** (d)	**36.** (c)	**37.** (e)	**38.** (b)	**39.** (c)	**40.** (b)
41. (d)	**42.** (c)	**43.** (d)	**44.** (a)	**45.** (e)	**46.** (d)	**47.** (d)	**48.** (e)	**49.** (d)	**50.** (d)
51. (a)	**52.** (e)	**53.** (d)	**54.** (b)	**55.** (*)	**56.** (d)	**57.** (b)	**58.** (*)	**59.** (*)	**60.** (b)
61. (b)	**62.** (e)	**63.** (*)	**64.** (d)	**65.** (c)	**66.** (e)	**67.** (c)	**68.** (b)	**69.** (c)	**70.** (b)
71. (b)	**72.** (d)	**73.** (d)	**74.** (e)	**75.** (d)	**76.** (c)	**77.** (d)	**78.** (c)	**79.** (c)	**80.** (*)
81. (b)	**82.** (b)	**83.** (c)	**84.** (d)	**85.** (c)	**86.** (b)	**87.** (c)	**88.** (a)	**89.** (d)	**90.** (d)
91. (b)	**92.** (a)	**93.** (d)	**94.** (b)	**95.** (e)	**96.** (e)	**97.** (c)	**98.** (b)	**99.** (d)	**100.** (e)
101. (d)	**102.** (c)	**103.** (c)	**104.** (a)	**105.** (e)	**106.** (b)	**107.** (e)	**108.** (d)	**109.** (a)	**110.** (a)
111. (d)	**112.** (b)	**113.** (c)	**114.** (a)	**115.** (d)	**116.** (b)	**117.** (e)	**118.** (a)	**119.** (d)	**120.** (c)
121. (e)	**122.** (d)	**123.** (c)	**124.** (b)	**125.** (a)	**126.** (a)	**127.** (b)	**128.** (c)	**129.** (d)	**130.** (e)
131. (d)	**132.** (a)	**133.** (c)	**134.** (e)	**135.** (b)	**136.** (a)	**137.** (b)	**138.** (c)	**139.** (d)	**140.** (e)
141. (b)	**142.** (e)	**143.** (a)	**144.** (c)	**145.** (d)	**146.** (e)	**147.** (d)	**148.** (c)	**149.** (b)	**150.** (a)
151. (c)	**152.** (a)	**153.** (d)	**154.** (e)	**155.** (b)					

SOLUTIONS

Solutions (1-3): In this input output question only numbers is arranged in each step. Let us understand the logic behind it- In each step the numbers are arranged.

In step 1: all the even .0number (input) are multiplied with 2 and all the even numbers are multiplied with 3.

Step 2: Is given in the pattern as firstly the numbers are subtracted and then added respectively.

Step 3: The resultant of the multiplication of its digits in the previous step.

Step 4: The numbers in the previous step is divided by 2.

Input –	25	22	93	56	17	74	39
Step 1 –	75	44	279	112	51	148	117

Step 2 –	31	323	167	163	97	265
Step 3 –	3	18	42	18	63	60
Step 4 –	1.5	9	21	9	31.5	30

Solutions (4-8):

Person	Birth year	Age	Fruit
Viraj	1938	80	Banana
Anko	1959	59	Grapes
Charu	1962	56	Cherry
Tarun	1983	35	Orange
Monika	1995	23	Mango
Vishakha	2000	18	Apple

Solutions (9-10):

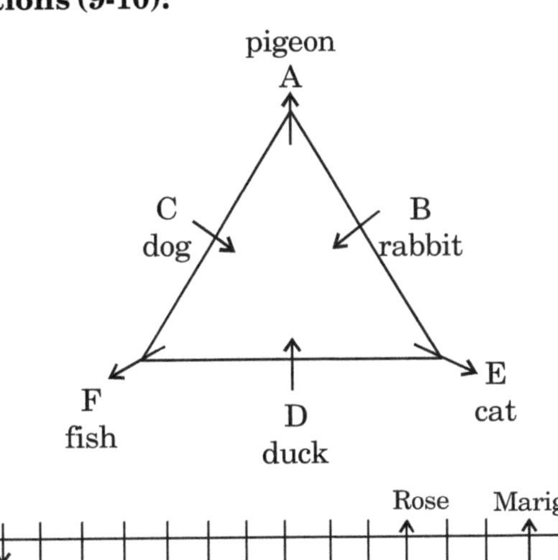

12. (d)

Person	Item
L	Chair
G	Wallet
K	Bag
A	Perfume
S	Table

Solutions (13-15):

Input: $ F 3 6 N @ 9 K T Q 5 C % 8 B # 7 D S * H 4 W L

Step I: $ F 3 6 N @ K T Q 5 C % B # D S * H 4 W L 7 8 9

Step II: $ 3 F 6 N @ K T 5 Q C % B # D S * H 4 W 7 L 8 9

Step III: $ 3 F 6 @ K T 5 Q % # D * H B C N S 4 W 7 L 8 9

Solutions (16-20):

Floor	Flat A	Flat B
3	3 Rooms	4 Rooms
2	6 Rooms	9 Rooms
1	8 Rooms	2 Rooms

For questions 21 to 25:

Day	Monday	Tuesday	Wednesday	Thursday	Friday	Saturday	Sunday
Athlete	Ravi	Ritesh	Rita	Rehan	Ramesh	Rumi	Raman
Distance	3 km	5 km	4 km	2 km	6 km	7 km	8 km
Rest duration	40 minutes	25 minutes	15 minutes	35 minutes	20 minutes	10 minutes	30 minutes

For questions from 26 to 30:

As per the given information, the rough path diagram can be drawn as:

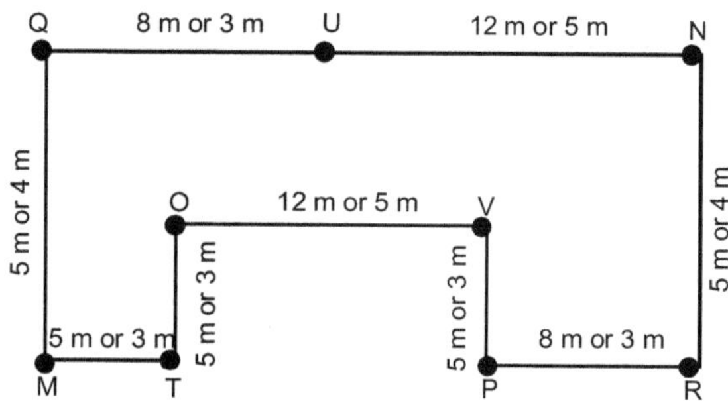

Only points Q, U and N could be collinear.

So, the distance between QN and MR must be the same which could be equal to either 20 m or 13 m and it is possible when

Case I:

QN = QU + UN = 8 + 12 = 20 m

MR = MT + OV + PR = 5 + 12 + 3 = 20 m

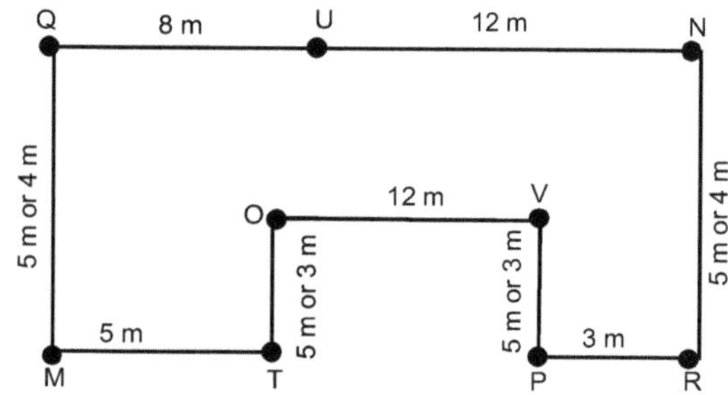

Case II:

QN = QU + UN = 8 + 5 = 13 m

MR = MT + OV + PR = 5 + 5 + 3 = 13 m

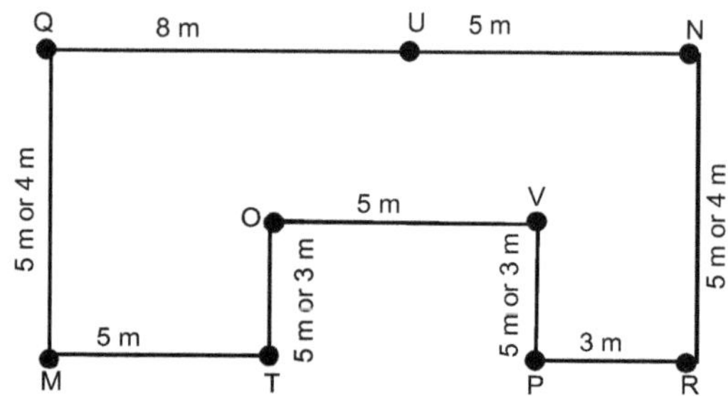

26. Case I satisfies the given option 5.

27. If OT is 5 m, then PV must be 5 m and OV = 12 m or 5 m.

$$\therefore OP = \sqrt{12^2 + 5^2} = 13 \text{ m}$$

Or

$$\therefore OP = \sqrt{5^2 + 5^2} = 5\sqrt{2} \text{ m}$$

29. From the figure, it is clear that V is to the South-West of N i.e. V &$ N.

30. In both the Cases, PR = 3 m and given NR = 4 m.

$$\therefore NP = \sqrt{4^2 + 3^2} = 5 \text{ m}$$

Also, P is to the south west of N i.e. P &$ N.

For questions 36 to 40:

Each glass slab is 15 cm and photo frame is 6 cm. Total length of row-1 is 267 and that of row 2 is 249 cm.

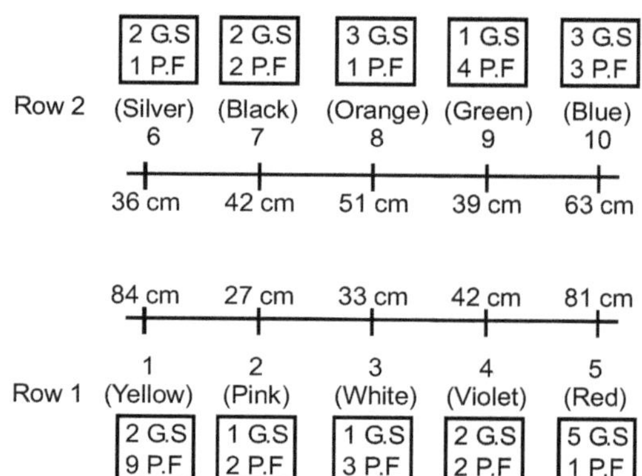

For questions 41 to 45:

Day	Monday	Tuesday	Wednesday	Thursday	Friday	Saturday	Sunday
Person	D	A	G	C	F	E	B
City	Mumbai	Kolkata	Lucknow	Hyderabad	Chennai	Delhi	Bangalore

41. Four persons attended the interview before F.

42. C attended the interview in Hyderabad.

43. Four persons attended the interview between A and B.

44. G, the person who attended the interview in Lucknow, attended the interview on Wednesday.

45. Both (3) and (4) are true.

46. (d)   Let width of the path = x cm

So, length of the park will be = (x + 4) cm

So, $\dfrac{4}{3} \times$ (Area of path) = Area of the park

$$\Rightarrow \frac{4}{3}\,[x(x + 4) - (x - 4)(x + 4 - 4)] = x(x + 4)$$

From this equation we can find out the value of x and hence all value can be find out.

47. (d)   Let C invested for t days

    A   B   C

$1200 \times 12 \;:\; 2400 \times 4 \;:\; xt$

And,

$1200 \times 12 = xt$

Here, x will depend on t and value of t can be maximum 8 month and minimum 1 months

On putting t = 8

X = 1800

Putting t = 6

x = 2400

on putting t = 4

x = 3600

on putting t = 2

x = 7200

48. (e) Let x men do the work in (a – 6) days

And y women do the work in a days

So, x(a – 6) = y(a)

From (i)

Let x = 5p

And y = 6p

5p(a – 6) = 6p(a)

5a – 30 = 6a

a = –30 not possible

From (ii),

10p(a – 6) = 3p(a)

10a – 60 = 3a

7a = 60

$a = \dfrac{60}{7}$ it is possible

From (iii)

8p (a – 6) = 5p(a)

8a – 48 = 5a

3a = 48

a = 16 possible

From (iv)

10p (a – 6) = 7p (a)

10a – 60 = 7a

a = 20 possible

So, (ii), (iii) and (iv) are possible

49. (d) Let total population of village A in 2000, 2008 and 2012 be 200x, 300x and 400x respectively

So,

$$\dfrac{40}{100} \times 200x + \dfrac{50}{100} \times 300x + \dfrac{60}{100} \times 400x$$

$$= 1410 \times 3$$

470x = 1410 × 3

x = 9

Required population = 9 × 200 = 1800

50. (d) Let population of village C in 2000, 2008 and 2012 be (x + 2n), (x + n) and x respectively

So, $\dfrac{50}{100}(x + n) = \dfrac{70}{100}(x)$

5x + 5n = 7x

2x = 5n

$n = \dfrac{2}{5}x$

Required percentage $= \dfrac{x + 2n - x}{x + 2n} \times 100$

$$= \dfrac{2 \times \dfrac{2}{5}}{\dfrac{9}{5}x} \times 100 \quad = 44\dfrac{4}{9}\%$$

51. (a) Sum of literate from B in 2000 and 2008

= 1530

Sum of literate from B in 2008 and 2012

= 2010

And sum of literate from B in all years

= 2490

So, literate in 2008 = (1530 + 2010) – 2490

= 1050

Let population of B in 2008 be x

So,

40% of x = 1050

x = 2625

52. (e) From (i) & (ii),

Let, HCF be x

then LCM is 44x

44x + x = 540

$$x = \dfrac{540}{45} = 12$$

From (iii), A + B = 10K

Let, A = 12a & B = 12b

Then A + B = 12 (a + b), where a & b are coprime.

Also, a × b = 44

Possible values of a and b are (4, 11) or (1, 44)

Sum of A + B = 12 (4 + 11) = 180

Or A + B = 12 (1 + 44) = 540

So, questioned can't be answered even after including all the statements.

53. (d) Let A litres is removed and B litre of water is added to the mixture

Initially, Ratio of milk and water is 5 : 1.

ATQ,

$$200 - \dfrac{5}{6}A = 40 - \dfrac{A}{6} + B + 125$$

$\Rightarrow 105 = 2A + 3B$

Among the options only A, B and D satisfy this eqn.

54. (b) Let number of red, green and blue ball be x, y and z respectively

ATQ,

$x - y = y - z$

$y = \dfrac{x + z}{2}$ or $2y = x + z$

And $\dfrac{z}{x + y + z} > 0.2$

$\dfrac{3}{3y} > \dfrac{1}{5}$

$5z > 3y$

If $y = 5$, then $z > 3$

If $y = 10$, then $z > 6$, but this isn't possible

Hence,

Red	Green	Blue
6	5	4
4	5	6
3	5	7
2	5	8
1	5	9

5, 5, 5 isn't possible as number of balls is different

Hence, from given options only (b), (d) and (e) can be the answers.

So, option, Only (b), (d) and (e) is our correct answer.

55. Let CP = 100 & MP = 160

From A

If profit = 60%

Hence no discount is possible here so, it is not satisfy equation

From B

When profit is 20% then discount will be

$\dfrac{40}{160} \times 100 = 25\%$

When it doubles i.e. discount = 50%

Then, SP $= 160 - \dfrac{50}{100} \times 160 = 80$

So, it gave loss of 20% not possible

From C

When profit = 48%

Then discount $= \dfrac{12}{160} \times 100 = 7.5\%$

When it doubles = 15%

Then SP $= 160 - \dfrac{15}{100} \times 160 = 124$

So, profit is 24%

So, option C is possible

From D

When profit = 36%

Discount $= \dfrac{24}{160} \times 100 = 15\%$

When discount gets doubled = 30%

SP $= 160 - \dfrac{30}{100} \times 160 = 112$

So profit is 12%, hence possible

From E

When profit = 44% = 10%

When discount = 20%

SP $= 160 - \dfrac{20}{100} \times 160 = 128$

Profit is 28%

So, it is possible

Then C, D and E values are possible

56. (d) Let first and fifth numbers be '2x' and '2a' respectively.

Then, third number (A) $= \dfrac{2x + 2a}{2} = x + a$

Second number $= = \dfrac{2x}{2} = x$

| 2x | x | x + a | 62 | 2a |

ATQ,

$2x + x + x + a = 127$

$4x + a = 127$ From option (a)

$x + a = 64$

$\Rightarrow 3x = 63$

$\Rightarrow x = 21$

Average of five numbers

$= \dfrac{42 + 21 + 64 + 62 + 2(64 - 21)}{5} = 55$

According to this, option (d) 64, 55 is our correct answer.

57. (b) Let income of 'D' and 'E' is x and y respectively.

We have to find the value of 'x – y'.

From (I)

$0.72x - 0.5y = 3200$

From (II)

$0.4x - 0.4y = 8000$

$\Rightarrow x - y = \dfrac{8000}{0.4} = 20000$

Hence, only (II) is sufficient to answer the question.

58. Let Rs C's income is Rs x

Atq,

$\dfrac{0.44x + 0.52x}{2} = 19200$

$\Rightarrow x = \dfrac{2 \times 19200}{0.96} = 40,000$

A's income = 1.2 × 40,000 = 48,000

A's expense in the month of November

$= \dfrac{60}{100} \times 48000 = Rs\ 28800$

59. Let, income of B is Rs x

From (I)

$0.6x - 0.4x = 16000$

$\Rightarrow x = \dfrac{16000}{0.2} = 80,000$

Amount invested by 'B' is PPF

$= 80,000 \times \dfrac{40}{100} \times \dfrac{37.5}{100} = Rs.\ 12,000$

From (II)

$0.6x - 0.4x = 16000$

$\Rightarrow x = \dfrac{16000}{0.2} = 80,000$

Amount invested by 'B' in PPF

$= \dfrac{37.5}{100} \times \dfrac{40}{100} \times 80,000 = Rs.\ 12000$

Hence, Either statement (I) or statement (II) by itself is sufficient to answer the question.

Solution (60-62):

Village	No. of wind mills	Maximum units Produced	No. of houses	Wind mills operative			
				Week1	Week2	Week3	Week4
A	24	2 lakh/week	540	75%	50%	75%	100%
B	20	80000/week	240	50%	75%	100%	50%
C	15	1 lakh/week	150	40%	60%	80%	60%
D	12	1.5 lakh/week	350	75%	50%	50%	75%

60. (b) Number of mills operative in week 1 of village

$A = \dfrac{75}{100} \times 24 = 18$

Level 1 (upper limit) of efficiency range 2 means 55%

Total units produced in village A in first week when operated at level 1 of efficiency range 2

$= 18 \times \dfrac{55}{100} \times 2$

Similarly,

Number of mills operative in village B in week 2

$= \dfrac{75}{100} \times 20 = 15$

level 2 (mid limit) of efficiency Range

$1 = \dfrac{60 + 70}{2}\%$

$= 65\%$

Total units produced in village B in week 2 when operated at level 2 of efficiency range 1

$= 15 \times \dfrac{65}{100} \times .8$

Required ratio $= \dfrac{18 \times \dfrac{55}{100} \times 2}{15 \times \dfrac{65}{100} \times .8} = 33 : 13$

61. (b) Mills operating in village C in week second and fourth is

$= \dfrac{3}{5} \times 15$ and $\dfrac{3}{5} \times 15$ respectively.

Total units produced at level 1 of efficiency range 1

$= (9 + 9) \times 100,000 \times \dfrac{70}{100}$

$= 18 \times 1000 \times 70 = 1260000$

Mills operating in village A in first and fourth week is $24 \times \dfrac{3}{4}$ and 24 respectively

Total units produced at level 2 of efficiency range 1

$= (18 + 24) \times 200000 \times \dfrac{65}{100}$

$= 42 \times 2000 \times 65 = 5,460,000$ units

Required percentage $= \dfrac{126}{546} \times 100 = 23\dfrac{21}{273}\%$

62. (e) No. of mills operating in B in fourth week

$$= 20 \times \frac{50}{100} = 10$$

Total units consumed at level 3 of efficiency range 3 per house

$$\frac{10 \times 80000 \times 30}{240 \times 100} = 1000 \text{ units / house}$$

No. of mills operating in C in second week

$$= 15 \times \frac{60}{100} = 9$$

Total units consumed at level 1 of efficiency range 2

$$= \frac{9 \times 1,00000}{150} \times \frac{55}{100} 3300 \text{ unit / house}$$

Required ratio = 10 : 33

63. Quantity I:

$$\frac{360}{120} \times 24.m^{7+2-4}.n^{9-3+4} = 72.m^5.n^{10}$$

If m > 0, n < 0, then Quantity I > 0

Quantity II:

$$\frac{240}{60 \times 3} x^{9-4+2} y^{7-3-3} = \frac{4}{3} x^7 y$$

If x < 0, y < 0, then quantity II > 0

Quantity III:

$$\frac{48 \times 5}{6} a^{8+3-6} . b^{(12-4-1)} = 40a^5 b^7$$

If a > 0, b < 0, then Quantity III < 0.

∴ Relation between Quantity I and Quantity II can't be established but

Quantity II > Quantity III

∴ [#, @] is our correct answer.

Quantity I > Quantity II = Quantity III

64. (d) **Quantity I:** $\dfrac{(p+n)^2 - (p-n)^2}{8pn(p+n)^2} = 1$

$$\frac{p^2 + n^2 + 2pn - (p^2 + n^2 - 2pn)}{8pn(p+n)^2} = 1$$

$$\frac{4pn}{8pn(p+n)^2} = 1$$

$$\frac{1}{2} = (p+n)^2$$

$$p = \frac{1}{\sqrt{2}} - n$$

Quantity II: $\dfrac{(q+n)^3 - (q-n)^3}{\left(n^2 + 3q^2\right)^2} = \dfrac{1}{8n}$

$$\frac{q^3 + n^3 + 3q^2 n + 3n^2 q - (q^3 - n^3 - 3q^2 n + 3n^2 q)}{\left(n^2 + 3q^2\right)^2}$$

$$= \frac{1}{8n}$$

$$\frac{2n^3 + 6q^2 n}{\left(n^2 + 3q^2\right)^2} = \frac{1}{8n}$$

$$\frac{2n\left(n^2 + 3q^2\right)}{\left(n^2 + 3q^2\right)^2} = \frac{1}{8n}$$

$$16n^2 = n^2 + 3q^2.$$

$$q = \sqrt{5}n$$

Quantity III: $\dfrac{\sqrt{r+n} + \sqrt{r-n}}{\sqrt{r+n} - \sqrt{r-n}} = 2$

$$\sqrt{r+n} + \sqrt{r-n} = 2\left(\sqrt{r+n} - \sqrt{r-n}\right)$$

$$3\sqrt{r-n} = \sqrt{r+n}$$

$$9(r-n) = (r+n)$$

$$8r = 10n$$

$$r = \frac{10n}{8} = 1.25n$$

Quantity I < Quantity II > Quantity III

65. (c) **Quantity I –**

Probability of at most two students will solve the question

= 1 – probability of all three students will solve the question

= 1 – (0.5) × (0.6) × (0.3)

= 1 – 0.09

= 0.91

Quantity II –

Total balls = 5 + 7 = 12

Probability of getting at least 1 green ball = 1 – probability of no green

$$= 1 - \frac{7}{44}$$

$$= \frac{37}{44} \approx 0.84$$

Quantity III –

$$P \text{ (Arun speak truth)} = \frac{4}{5}$$

$$P \text{ (Bhavya speak truth)} = \frac{6}{7}$$

Required probability

$$= \frac{4}{5} \times \frac{1}{7} + \frac{1}{5} \times \frac{6}{7}$$

$$= \frac{10}{35} = \frac{2}{7} \approx 0.28$$

Quantity I > Quantity II > Quantity III

66. (e) ATQ,

$$S = \frac{D}{T} \qquad \ldots(i)$$

$$(S + 10) = \frac{D}{T - 2} \qquad \ldots(ii)$$

$$(S + 15) = \frac{D}{T + 6} \qquad \ldots(iii)$$

On solving (i), (ii) & (iii)

D = 400 km, S = 40 km/hr. T = 10 hour

Statement 1, 2 and 4 can be found out from the given data but

statement 3 can't be solved as length of tunnel is not given.

67. (c) Let length of train A be (x + 100) m

So, length of train B be x m

$$(2x + 150) = (54 + 81) \times \frac{5}{18} \times 12m$$

$$= 135 \times 5 \times \frac{2}{3}m = 450m$$

x = 150 m

Length of train A = 250 m

Length of train B = 150 m

(i) Cannot be obtained because speed of man is not given

(ii) Can be obtained

$$t = \frac{(250 + 175)}{81 \times \frac{5}{18}} = \frac{425}{81} \times \frac{81}{5}$$

$$\Rightarrow \frac{170}{9} \text{sec.}$$

(iii) it has already obtained

(iv) can't be obtained because no other condition regarding C has been given

Hence only (ii) and (iii) can be find out.

68. (b) Let the original number by xy

According to given condition

(10x + y) > 3(10y + x)

7x − 29y > 0

On putting y = 1

X has to be more than or equal to 5

So for y = 1,

Possible values for x are 5 , 6, 7, 8 ,9

So, 5 numbers are possible when y is 1

(51), (61), (71), (81), (91) be

On putting y = 2

X has to be 9

So 92 is another number

Values greater than 2 are not possible for y.

If we take y = 3 than x has to be 13 which is not possible

So there are 6 possible numbers.

69. (c) $\frac{2R}{100} \times 10000 = 1400$

R = 7%

Now for x = 1

R = 8% for CI

Equivalent CI at rate of 8% for 2 yrs

$$= 8 + 8 + \frac{64}{100} = 16.64\%$$

CI at 8% for 2 yr

$$= \frac{16.64}{100} \times 11400 = 16.64 \times 114 \text{ Rs}$$

Approximately =

$$\frac{33}{2} \times 114 = 33 \times 57 = 1881$$

For 9%

$$CI = \frac{18.81}{100} \times 11400 = 18.80 \times 114$$

Approx. = 19 × 114 = 2166

For 10% =

$$\frac{21}{100} \times 11400 = 21 \times 114 = 2394$$

So, 3 values of x are possible i.e, 1, 2 and 3.

70. (b) Let marked price of article A and B be 400x and 500x respectively

ATQ—

$$400x \times \frac{(100 - d)}{100} = 500x \times \frac{(100 - d - 18)}{100}$$

400 − 4d = 410 − 5d

d = 10%

Cost price of article A = $\dfrac{400x \times \dfrac{90}{100}}{120} \times 100$

= 300x Rs.

Cost price of article B

$$= \frac{500x \times \dfrac{(100 - 28)}{100}}{125} \times 100$$

= 288x Rs.

ATQ—

$$\left(500x \times \frac{72}{100} - 288x\right) - \left(400x \times \frac{(90)}{100} - 300x\right)$$

= 384

72x – 60x = 384

x = 32

Cost price of article A = 32 × 300 = Rs.9600

Cost price of article B = 32 × 288 = Rs.9216

71. (b) Efficiency of tap = 250 L/h

In November there are total 30 days.

Total flats = 20

Let tank is refilled n times

So,

n × 600000 = 250 × 24 × 30 × 20

n = 6 hours

72. (d) Total time in which tank gets emptied

$$= \frac{25}{6} \times 24 = 100 \text{ hours}$$

So, Rate of flow $= \dfrac{600000}{30 \times 100} = 200 \text{ L/hour}$

$$A\% = \frac{250 - 200}{250} \times 100 = 20\%$$

73. (d) Let n number of flats were occupied

x × 250 × 100 = 600000

x = 24 flats

$$B\% = \frac{24}{40} \times 100 = 60\%$$

74. (e) Efficiency of a tap in October

$$= \frac{4}{5} \times 250 = 200 \, 1/\text{hour}$$

New capacity of the tank $= \dfrac{4}{5} \times 600000 = 480000$

l

Occupied flats in October = 30

Required time $= \dfrac{480000}{200 \times 30} = 80 \text{ hours}$

75. (d) Pattern of the series is,

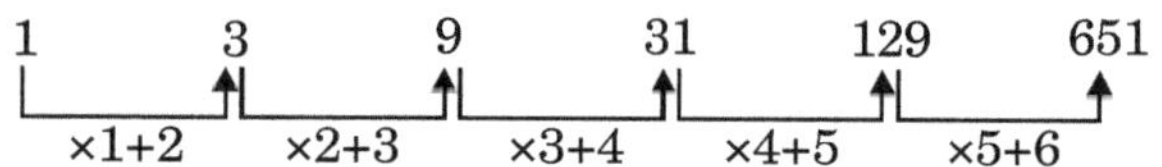

Similarly,

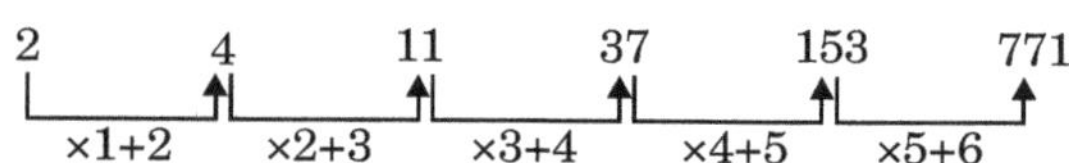

76. (c) Pattern of the series is

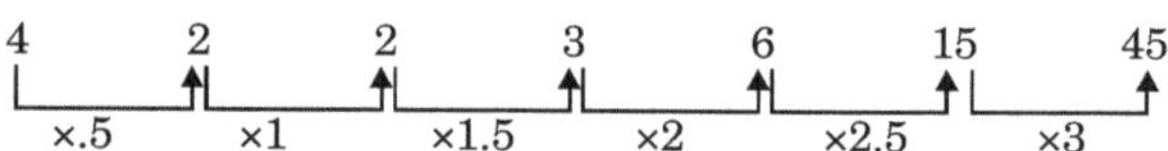

So, next terms will be 45 × 3.5, 45 × 3.5 × 4, 45 × 3.5 × 4, 4.5

Do not calculate exact values. Just calculate approximate values because with increase in values next term

will be for away from 2835

So, 45 × 3.5 is approx. 150

And, 150 × 4 is approx. – 600

600 × 4.5 is approx. × 2700

So, multiplies of 4.5 is nth term which is 10th term.

77. (d)
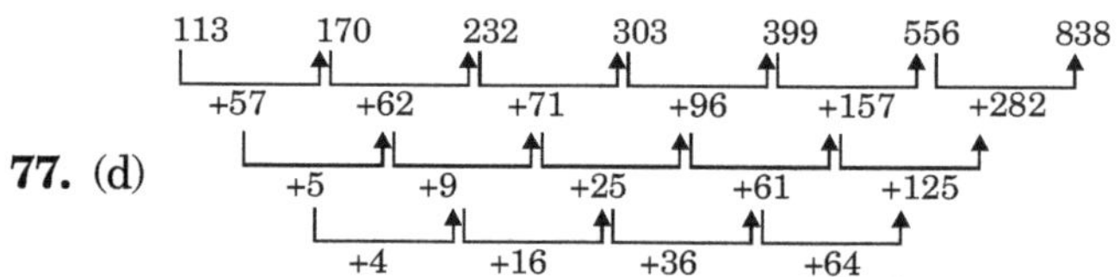

Second series

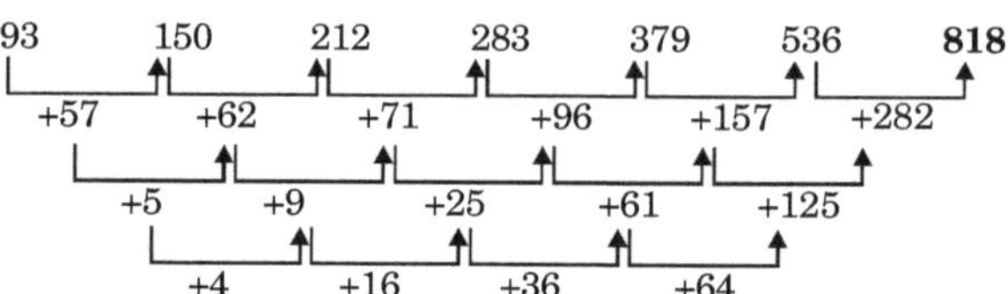

78. (c)
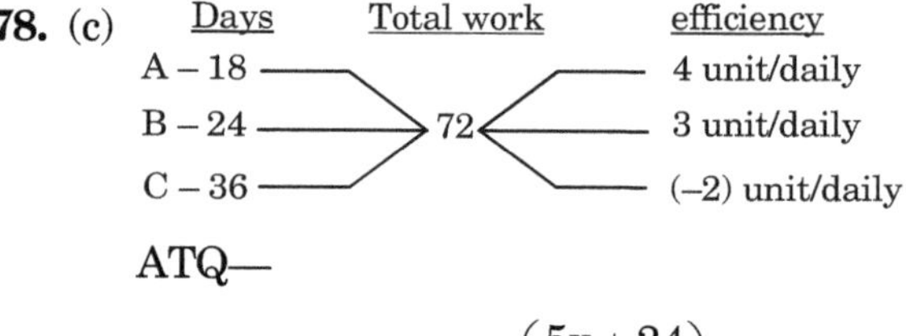

ATQ—

$$(A + B)x + (A + B - C)\left(\frac{5x + 24}{5}\right) = 72$$

$$7x + 5\left(\frac{5x + 24}{5}\right) = 72$$

12x = 48 ⇒ x = 4

(A + B + C) work for

$$= 4 + 4\frac{4}{5} = 8\frac{4}{5} \text{ days}$$

79. (c) Speed of current $= \dfrac{5}{9} \times \dfrac{18}{5} = 2 \text{ km/hr}$

Let's still water speed = x km/hr

ATQ,

$$\frac{28 \times \dfrac{3}{4}}{(x-2)} - \frac{28}{(x+2)} = 3$$

$$21x + 42 - 28x + 56 = 3x^2 - 12$$

$$-7x + 98 = 3x^2 - 12$$

$$3x^2 + 7x - 110 = 0$$

$$x = 5 \text{ km/hr}$$

80. Volume of cylindrical vessel $= \dfrac{22}{7} \times 17.5$

$$\times 17.5 \times 18$$

$$= 17325 \text{ cm}^3$$

Volume of milk $= 17325 \times \dfrac{80}{100} = 13860 \text{ cm}^2$

$$30 \times 7 \times 3 \times h = 13860$$

$$h = \frac{462}{21} \Rightarrow h = 22 \text{ cm}$$

81. (b) The first paragraph of the passage is about the ways to establish a consistent saving habit through various ways and the second paragraph further gives a smarter way to save through the use of certificates of deposit (CDs). Hence, option (b) is the correct theme of the passage.

82. (b) 'Even' will be the correct word to replace 'yet'.

83. (c) The tone of writing in the passage is Didactic because the author tries to teach or instruct through his writing.

84. (d) Before the blank it is given that CDs usually offer higher interest rates, which is a positive phrase. Further, 'but' is used which means that next part of sentence will be something contradictory. Hence, 'penalties' will the correct word.

85. (c) The correct chronology of steps is Budgeting-Saving-Investment.

86. (b) The paragraph deals with improving savings and limiting expenses. 'Curtail' means reduce in extent or quantity; impose a restriction on. So, 'curtail' should replace 'increase'.

87. (c) The correct way of writing the line without changing its intended meaning is 'Make sure that the income is greater than the expenses by a margin as wide as possible.'

88. (a) The paragraph tells about the better ways to save and what all should be considered while spending or maintaining your expenses. So, the statement in option (a) can be the best inference from the passage.

89. (d) 'Money wise' here means in regard of money and so it is the perfect fit for the blank.

90. (d) "Expenses or needs that have to be met at a point of time in the future are called goals." This will be the last line in continuation to the last line of the passage as the last line is an example to set aside money to buy a watch in the future.

91. (b) Let's read the clause *'Pakistan's Army and political leadership are on "one page" to take dialogue with India forward"*. What is the need for mentioning the clause? Could political leadership of Pakistan independently take dialogue with India forward, why had the clause been mentioned?

It means that the statement (III) is a wrong assumption.

In Pakistan, to take dialogue with India forward, there must be consensus between the Pakistan's Army and the political leadership of Pakistan.

Only the statement (I) is the correct assumption to be drawn.

Hence, the option (b) is the correct answer.

92. (a) Option (a) is the correct answer.

Let's re-read the sentence where the given reference was made.

'Mr. Khan also struck a discordant note Kashmir, referring to the dispute as the "single issue" between India and Pakistan.'

Had there been more than one unresolved issue between India and Pakistan, then Mr. Khan wouldn't have referred to the Kashmir dispute as the "single issue" between India and Pakistan.

It means that according to Mr. Khan, there is one and only one unresolved issue between India and Pakistan.

Hence, the option (a) is the correct answer.

93. (d) 'Discordant' [adjective] means *'disagreeing or incongruous'*;

Clashing [adjective] means *'in conflict with each other; incompatible'*;

Concurred means *'be of the same opinion; agree'*;

Accord means *'give or granting someone power'*;

Endorsement means *'the action of endorsing someone or something'*;

Among the given options, the option (d) is the correct answer.

94. (b) The answer to the question can be derived from the last paragraph where it is given that *'airlines were allowed to unbundle fares and charge separately for preferential seating, meal-on-board, check-in baggage and use of airline lounges'*. Only option (b) mentions this.

There is no mention of any information given in the options (a) and (c) in the passage.

So, the option (b) is the correct answer.

95. (e) The statement (I) says that keeping web check-in free would help in keeping the number of passenger in an airport and would help security personnel in the security management. This is a very good motivation for the government to convince the airlines to take back the said fees.

The statement (II) says that levying fee to web check-in would make air-travel costly, might discourage people to opt for air travel and would be in contradiction to the aspiration of the government to increase the overall number of air-travel passengers.

Because the government wants to increase the overall number of air-travel passengers and levying web check-in fees might decrease that number. So, the government would be encouraged to stop this.

In the statement (III), the government wants that people use internet or digital means to avail important services in an increasing number. But levying web-check-in fees would discourage passengers to opt for it and would be against the objective of the Digital India Initiative. So, the government would be encouraged to stop this.

So, the information present in (I), (II) & (III), if true, would encourage the government to stop air lines to levy web check-in fees.

Hence, the option (e) is the correct answer.

96. (e) 'Withdraw' [verb] means *'discontinue or no longer provide (something previously supplied or offered)';* Abolish [verb] means *'do away with or put an end to';*

Rescind [verb] means *'declare null and void';*

From above, it could be understood that the word *'approve',* option (e), has a meaning which is SIMILAR to the meaning of the word *'approve'.*

Hence, the option (e) is the correct answer.

97. (c) The phrase 'dark chapter' usually mean something that shouldn't have happened, meaning the events caused regret, sadness of an extremely high extent.

Among the given options, only option (c) clearly indicate the correct meaning of the phrase.

Hence, the option (c) is the correct answer.

98. (b) The Delhi High Court expressed her opinion about the manner of prosecution of the anti-Sikh riots in the last paragraph.

The meaning of the word 'emulate' is *'Match or surpass (a person or achievement), typically by imitation'; imitation.*

'Not emulate' would mean *'not to imitate'.*

According to the Delhi High Court, the manner in which prosecution of the 1984 anti-Sikh riots has been going on *must never be emulated'.*

The option (b) is saying the same thing and hence, option (b) is the correct answer.

99. (d) Absconded [abscond, verb] means *'leave hurriedly and secretly, typically to escape from custody or avoid arrest';* Emulated [emulate, verb] means *'match or surpass (a person or achievement), typically by imitation'; imitate;*

From above, it could be understood that the word *'escaped'* conveys a meaning which is SIMILAR to the word *'absconded'.*

Hence, the option (d) is the correct answer.

100. (e) Justice Kurian Joseph said that the courts had been imposing the death penalty "arbitrarily and freakishly". If courts are imposing penalty "arbitrarily and freakishly", then it would mean that the courts have failed to uphold the principle of justice.

Among the three judges, Justice Kurian Joseph, Justice Deepak Gupta and Justice Hemant Gupta, Justice Kurian Joseph said that courts had been imposing the death penalty "arbitrarily and freakishly" but the other two judges, Justice Deepak Gupta and Justice Hemant Gupta, disagree that death penalty was "freakishly" imposed.

So, among the three judges mentioned in the passage, only Justice Kurian Joseph believes that courts have failed to uphold the principle of justice.

Hence, the option (e) is the correct answer.

101. (d) Disagreed [disagree, verb] means *'have or express a different opinion';*

Haggled [haggle, verb] means *'dispute or bargain persistently, especially over the cost of something';*

Bickered [bicker, verb] means *'argue about petty and trivial matters';*

Contended [contend, verb] means *'compete with others in a struggle to achieve (something)'; 'assert something as a position in an argument';*

Concurred [concur, verb] means *'be of the same opinion; agree';*

Feuded [feud, verb] means *'a prolonged and bitter quarrel or dispute';*

From above, it could be understood that the word *'concurred'* has a meaning which is SIMILAR to the meaning of the word *'disagreed'.*

Hence, the option (d) is the correct answer.

102. (c) 'Verge' means an extreme limit beyond which something specified will happen. So, 'Verge' is an appropriate choice here.

103. (c) Error is in the part given in option (c). 'shut' is to be used in place of 'shutted'. There is no such word as 'shutted' in English dictionary. Further, 'has been' takes third form of verb and third form of 'shut' is 'shut' itself.

104. (a) 'Destitution' and 'Demise' should replace each other. 'Demise' means the end or failure of an enterprise or institution. 'Destitution' means poverty so extreme that one lacks the means to provide for oneself.

105. (e) 'Such as a lack of money caused by benefit payment problems' is the correct phrase her. The preceding statement talks about hardships and this phrase explains the type of hardship, thus maintaining the continuity of the sentence.

106. (b) 'Threadbare means (of an argument, excuse, idea, etc.) used so often that it is no longer effective. Also, it means poor or shabby in appearance. So, threadbare fits in all the sentences correctly.

107. (e) No Change. 'Abdicate' means fail to fulfill or undertake (a responsibility or duty). Hence, it is correct in context of the sentence.

108. (d) The correct option is (d) 'Together they spent £46m on local welfare last year, compared with a national budget of £172m in 2013-14.' As the previous statement is about the councils spending on local welfare and the statement in (d) also discusses their collective spending. Hence, it is the correct choice.

109. (a) 1 and 4 should replace each other. 'Going' and 'devolved' should replace each other to make the sentence correct. 'Devolve' means transfer or delegate (power) to a lower level, especially from central government to local or regional administration.

110. (a) Error is in the part given in option (a). An adjective is to be used here so 'controversial' should be used in place of 'controversially'

111. (d) 'Purpose' is the most appropriate word here.

112. (b) The logical sequence of the sentences after the rearrangement is *BDAEFC*. Drawing a hint from the second statement, it can be illustrated that the paragraph is providing information on processed foods. If we carefully understand and arrange the other sentences we will articulate that the paragraph is describing about the changes the world has seen from traditional to industrial food processing. However, the paragraph does not mention anything about its benefits, harmful effects or objectives. Hence, option (b) "Reforms in food processing" becomes the most suitable answer choice.

113. (c) Drawing a hint form the second sentence, it can be illustrated that the paragraph is providing information on processed foods. If we carefully understand and arrange the other sentences we will articulate that the paragraph is describing about the changes the world has seen from traditional to industrial food

processing. Thus, sentence (B) perfectly stands as the starter of the rearranged paragraph as it is describing about the objective or aim of food processing in the earlier days. Therefore, it coherently links with the second sentence (D) which states the broaden objectives of food processing. Sentence (A) should take the third position as it is contextually related with the previous statement which indicates a change in the food processing industry. Similarly, sentence (E) and (F) forms a coherent pair as they have mentioned about food processed and practices followed by traditional processors. Next comes, the concluding sentence (C) as it sums up the comparison by providing information on the non-traditional crops grown all over the world and how the demand for these products has increased. Hence, the logical and comprehensive sequence of these sentences after the rearrangement is *BDAEFC*. Therefore, sentence (E) becomes the fourth sentence in the sequence, and option (c) becomes the most viable answer choice.

114. (a) The logical sequence of the sentences after the rearrangement is *BDAEFC*. The last sentence i.e. sentence (C) of the paragraph describes about the changes in the food processing industry. It has also mentioned about the production of the non-traditional crops around the worlds and their rising demand due to mass communication. Thus, it becomes difficult for such products to survive in the local environment. Complying with the given context, option (a) perfectly complements sentence (C) as option (a) has described about the protection of these products to enhance their storage life. All the other options are either irrelevant to the context or fail to adhere to the theme of the paragraph. Hence, option (a) is the most suitable answer choice.

115. (d) The logical sequence of the sentences after the rearrangement is BDAEFC. In order to add a sentence after the first sentence without altering the context of the paragraph, both the sentences should be analyzed. Sentence (B) perfectly stands as the starter of the rearranged paragraph as it is describing about the objective or aim of food processing in the earlier days. Therefore, it coherently links with the second sentence (D) which states the broaden objectives of food processing which is about generation of wealth for the producers as well as sellers. This implies that earlier this wasn't one of the objectives of food processing. Thus, option (d) perfectly links sentences (B) and (A) as it mentions about the trading of processed foods through barter system in the earlier days. Thus, the new sequence would be *B (d) DAEFC*. All the other options are either irrelevant to the context or fail to adhere to the theme of the paragraph. Hence, option (d) is the most suitable answer choice.

116. **(b)** State Bank of India, the largest lender with a fifth of the market share, launched a payments machine that would help merchants eliminate the multiple choices that they keep to facilitate transactions from cards to QR code based payments. The new device titled MOPAD, or Multi Option Payment Acceptance Device, is a Point of Sale (PoS) terminal that would along with cards accept payments through UPI, Bharat QR, and SBI Buddy wallet which till now required different tools to receive payments.

117. **(e)** The Reserve Bank of India has constituted a 10-member 'High Level Task Force on Public Credit Registry (PCR) for India', which will, among other things, suggest a roadmap for developing a transparent, comprehensive and near-real-time PCR for India. Headed by YM Deosthalee, ex-CMD, L&T Finance Holdings, the task force includes Sekar Karnam, DMD & Chief Credit Officer, SBI; Vishaka Mulye, ED, ICICI Bank; Rashesh Shah, Chairman and CEO, Edelweiss Group; and Sriram Kalyanaraman, MD and CEO, National Housing Bank.

118. **(a)** Kharchi puja is a Hindu festival from Tripura, India. Performed in Agartala in July or August, the festival involves the worship of the fourteen gods forming the dynasty deity of the Tripuri people. Kharchi Puja is one of the most popular festivals in Tripura.

119. **(d)** Bengaluru, the IT capital of India, is also the third in terms of e-waste generation in the country. While India produces 18.5 lakh metric tonnes of electronic waste annually,?a whopping 92,000 metric tonnes comes from Bengaluru, according to 2016 figures. And as per the study, computers form 70% of the total e-waste and telecommunication equipment constitutes 12%. The Centre, noting that Bengaluru is one of the topmost e-waste producers nationally, has decided to sanction India's first government run e-waste recycling unit.

120. **(c)** Karur Vysya Bank (Tamil) is an Indian old private-sector bank, headquartered in Karur in Tamil Nadu.

121. **(e)** An innovative cost-effective drinking water project in Bihar promises to lower the price of one-litre bottle to 50 paise (cheapest in the world). The project- "Sulabh Jal" was launched in Darbhanga by Sulabh International.

122. **(d)** Himachal Pradesh has been adjudged first among states for its performance under the Pradhan Mantri Surakshit Matritav Abhiyan (PMSMA) in the country.

Union Health Minister Jagat Prakash Nadda conferred the award upon the state which was received by Additional Chief Secretary, Health, BK Agarwal at a ceremony in New Delhi.

123. **(c)** One hundred years after his birth, Mandela's example of courage and compassion continue to inspire the world. The Nelson Mandela Foundation is dedicating this year's (2018) Mandela Day to Action Against Poverty, honouring Mandela's leadership and devotion to fighting poverty and promoting social justice for all.

124. **(b)** In his address to the Parliament, while presenting the Budget for 2018, Finance Minister Arun Jaitley stated that NITI Aayog will initiate a national program to direct efforts in artificial intelligence. The Budget doubled the allocation on Digital India programme to Rs. 3073 crore in 2018-19.

125. **(a)** Prime Minister Narendra Modi was inaugurated 10th edition of Defence Expo (DefExpo 2018) in Chennai at Tiruvidanthal.

126. **(a)** West Bengal chief minister Mamata Banerjee set a "one person one car" policy for ministers and bureaucrats and mandated economy class for all domestic air travel in a bid to cut costs incurred by the state government.

127. **(b)** An eight-year-old Indian-origin schoolboy who is the under-11 UK national yoga champion has been named the British Indian of the Year for his achievements in the field. Ishwar Sharma has won a string of titles in both individual and artistic yoga, most recently a gold medal representing Great Britain at the World Student Games 2018 in Winnipeg, Canada, in June 2018.

128. **(c)** The Government of India has notified the Electoral Bond Scheme 2018. As per provisions of the Scheme, Electoral Bonds may be purchased by a person, who is a citizen of India or incorporated or established in India. It may be noted that Electoral Bond shall be valid for fifteen days from the date of issue and no payment shall be made to any payee Political Party if the Bond is deposited after expiry of the validity period. The bond deposited by any eligible political party to its account shall be credited on the same day.

129. **(d)** Punjab National Bank (PNB), which was recently hit by a multi billion dollar fraud by manipulation of its financial messaging — Swift — system, has been ranked as the best PSU bank in the overall digital transactions category in India. The bank said in a statement on Saturday: "Based

on the recent findings of DFS (Department of Financial Services), PNB is ranked the number 1 PSU bank in digital transactions in India." A Rs. 13,500-crore fraud came to light in January, when it was found that the financial messaging system SWIFT was manipulated. It was used to issue Letters of Undertakings (LoUs) to conduct the fraud.

130. (e) India's first engineless rail, Train 18, manufactured by the Integral Coach Factory (ICF) was rolled out on October 29 in Chennai.

131. (d) The Union Cabinet chaired by the Prime Minister, Shri Narendra Modi has gave its approval to rename the Agartala Airport in Tripura as 'Maharaja Bir Bikram Manikya Kishore Airport, Agartala. The decision comes in the wake of the long pending demand of people of Tripura as well as the Tripura Government for paying tribute to Maharaja Bir Bikram Manikya Kishore.

132. (a) The Haryana Education Department has launched "I am not afraid of English" initiative to promote English language right from Class 1 in the state"s primary schools. The initiative is aimed at capacity building of teachers to enable them to help the students to learn, read, write and speak English.

133. (c) Microdot technology in India to be launched by the Government of India to check vehicle thefts.

134. (e) Ministry of Drinking Water and Sanitation has launched the Swachh Bharat Mission (Gramin) and the Swachh Bharat Mission (Urban).

135. (b) The environment ministry has decided to re-introduce a scheme "The Medini Puraskar Yojnaa", which aims at promoting original writing of books in Hindi, will have four awards for authors of various environmental topics.

136. (a) Shri Dharmendra Pradhan, Union Minister of Petroleum and Natural Gas & Skill Development and Entrepreneurship has kicked off an innovative initiative in New Delhi on 1st October, 2018, with PSU Oil Marketing Companies (OMCs ,i.e. IOC, BPCL and HPCL) inviting Expression of Interest (Eol) from potential entrepreneurs to set up Compressed Bio-Gas (CBG) production plants and make available CBG in the market for use in automotive fuels. This significant move has the potential to boost availability of more affordable transport fuels, better use of agricultural residue, cattle dung and municipal solid waste, as well as to provide an additional revenue source to farmers. Titled SATAT, the initiative is aimed at providing a Sustainable Alternative Towards Affordable Transportation (SATAT) as a developmental effort that would benefit both vehicle-users as well as farmers and entrepreneurs.

137. (b) Indian naval ship INS Sumitra became the first-ever warship to enter port of Sabang in Indonesia. The Indian Navy said, INS Sumitra was received by traditional dancers and Indonesian traditional band. The ship was welcomed by Indian Ambassador to Indonesia PK Rawat, Indonesian foreign affairs officials, members from Indian embassy, Indian businessmen and Indonesian naval and air force officers onboard. The warship was deployed in Malacca Straits.

138. (c) SBI and Nabard tie-up for credit in Telangana. State Bank of India and National Bank for Agriculture and Rural Development have joined hands to provide collateral-free credit through Joint Liability Groups in Telangana.

139. (d) The Government of India signed a loan deal worth USD 200 million with the World Bank for the National Nutrition Mission (POSHAN Abhiyaan). The POSHAN Abhiyaan, an overarching scheme for holistic nourishment, was launched by Prime Minister Narendra Modi in March this year at Jhunjhunu, Rajasthan.

140. (e) Project "Sashakt" aims to strengthen the credit capacity, credit culture and credit portfolio of public sector banks. The committee has set a five-prong strategy towards resolution of stressed assets. 'SASHAKT' stands for strengthening and the whole objective was to strengthen the credit capacity, credit culture and portfolio of public sector banks. The AMC will be set up by state-run banks for resolution of loans above Rs 500 crore.

141. (b) NMCG Organises "Ganga Vriksharopan Abhiyan" in Five Ganga Basin States Intervention in Ganga a Major Components of Namami Gange Programme. National Mission for Clean Ganga (NMCG) is running "Ganga Vriksharopan Abhiyan" in five main stem Ganga basin states - Uttarakhand, Uttar Pradesh, Bihar, Jharkhand and West Bengal.

142. (e) Prime Minister Narendra Modi has launched a scheme that seeks to strengthen the country's Panchayati Raj system and address critical gaps that hinder its success. He launched the Rashtriya Gram Swaraj Abhiyan at Ramnagar in this tribal-dominated district of Madhya Pradesh on the occasion of National Panchayati Raj Day.

143. (a) The government announced a scheme for informants of benami transactions under which an individual can get a reward of up to ?1 crore for providing information to the tax authorities. "Under the Benami Transactions Informants Reward Scheme 2018, a person can get reward [of] up to ?1 crore for giving specific information in prescribed manner to the Joint or Additional Commissioners of Benami Prohibition Unit (BPU) in Investigation Directorates of Income Tax Department about benami transactions and properties as well as proceeds from such properties which are actionable under Benami Property Transactions Act, 1988, as amended by Benami Transactions (Prohibition) Amendment Act, 2016.

144. (c) As a signatory to the 2030 Agenda for Sustainable Development, India is committed to participate in the international review of progress of Sustainable development Goals (SDGs) on a regular basis. NITI Aayog presented India's Voluntary National Review Report on the implementation of the Sustainable development Goals (SDGs).

145. (d) Bank of Baroda has entered into an agreement in May 2018 with CDSL Commodity Repository Limited (CCRL). Bank of Baroda is the first Public Sector Bank to become the Repository Participant for Pledge Finance under the Repository Ecosystem for registered / accredited warehouses by WDRA.

146. (e) An emerging market economy is highly classified with relatively - one in which the country is becoming a developed nation and is determined through many socio- economic factors.

147. (d) The Uttarakhand High Court on Wednesday declared the "entire animal kingdom including avian and aquatic" as legal entities with a distinct persona and corresponding rights, duties and liabilities of a living person. The Bench comprising Justice Rajiv Sharma and Justice Lok Pal Singh observed, "The Corporations, Hindu idols, holy scriptures, rivers have been declared legal entities and thus, in order to protect and promote greater welfare of animals including avian and aquatic, animals are required to be conferred with the status of legal entity/ legal person. The animals should be healthy, comfortable, well- nourished, safe, able to express innate behaviour without pain, fear and distress. They are entitled to justice.

148. (c) The Reserve Bank of India has asked banks authorised to deal in foreign exchange (Authorised Dealer-I Banks) to share data with the Directorate of Revenue Intelligence (DRI).

149. (b) Aug 16, 2018- Bharat Sanchar Nigam Ltd (BSNL) has launched BSNL WINGS a VOIP based service. In WINGS, there is no SIM or cable wiring as is a VOIP service through an app.

150. (a) Hartsfield-Jackson Atlanta International Airport, USA is the Busiest Airport 2017 by terms of traffic in the world.

151. (c) Survey points out for the first time in India's history that five States Maharashtra, Gujarat, Karnataka, Tamil Nadu and Telangana account for a whopping 70 % of India's exports.

152. (a) The government will take steps to boost exports of agriculture commodities which have the potential of reaching $100 billion. The country's agricultural exports are around $30 billion at present.

153. (d) The Election Commission of India (ECI) has organized a two-day "National Consultation on Accessible Elections," from the 3rd July, 2018 in New Delhi. It inaugurated by the Chief Election Commissioner Shri O.P.Rawat, in presence of the Election Commissioners Shri SunilArora and Shri Ashok Lavasa. The event is a part of the ECI's pursuit of its mission 'leave no voter behind,' with special focus on "Persons with Disabilities" (PwD). During the inaugural session, a dedicated portal for the ECI's 'Systematic Voters Education and Electoral Participation' (SVEEP) initiative will also be launched.

154. (e) Another Rs 1.5 trillion (or Rs 1.5 lakh crore) of non-performing assets are now likely to be with the National Company Law Tribunal in the next six months," according to a Credit Suisse report on RBI's new rules.

155. (b) Gross national product (GNP) is a broad measure of a nation's total economic activity. GNP is the value of all finished goods and services produced in a country in one year by its nationals.

GENERAL AWARENESS

1. Recently, the Pitch Black Military Exercise was held in which of the following countries?
(1) Australia
(2) England
(3) Japan
(4) Sri Lanka
(5) Bhutan

2. Peace Mission military exercise is held by which of the following countries?
(1) India
(2) Russia
(3) Afganistan
(4) China
(5) Uzbekistan

3. Who is the first Chief Financial Officer of RBI?
(1) H R Khan
(2) Somesh Mundra
(3) Arundhati Bhattacharya
(4) Usha Ananthasubramaian
(5) Sudha Balakrishnan

4. Where is the All Prime Minister Museum planned to be built?
(1) Pragati Maidan
(2) Jhandewalan Museum
(3) Kingsway Camp
(4) Teen Murti Premises
(5) Samta Sthal

5. What does the S stand for in BIMSTEC?
(1) South
(2) Section
(3) Sectoral
(4) Significant
(5) System

6. Which is the fifth nation to join the group BRICS?
(1) Brazil
(2) South Africa
(3) India
(4) Russia
(5) China

7. Recently 10th BRICS Summit was held at which of the following places?
(1) St. Petersburg, Russia
(2) Brasilia, Brazil
(3) Mumbai, India
(4) Beijing, China
(5) Johannesburg, South Africa

8. The All India Institute of Ayurveda is a public Ayurveda medicine and research institution in which of the following Indian cities?
(1) New Delhi
(2) Jaipur
(3) Kolkata
(4) Lucknow
(5) Indore

9. Indian PM Narendra Modi unveiled the bust of Sardar Patel at the diaspora event held at which of the following places?
(1) Lusaka
(2) Tel Aviv
(3) Kampala
(4) Rio De Jenerio
(5) Moscow

10. Lusaka is the capital of which of the following countries?
(1) Nigeria
(2) Gambia
(3) Zambia
(4) Djibouti
(5) Eritrea

11. Shanghai Cooperation Organisation (SCO) Leaders Summit was held in the Qingdao, a city located in which of the following countries?
(1) Tajikistan
(2) Turkmenistan
(3) Kazakhstan
(4) Russia
(5) China

12. What is the current repo rate decided by the RBI?
(1) 4.25%
(2) 5.35%
(3) 6.50%
(4) 6.75%
(5) 8.50%

13. At the 2018 FIFA World Cup, who has been awarded the Golden Glove award ?
(1) Thibaut Courtois
(2) Xavier Metres
(3) Miroslav Close
(4) Anwar Ibrahim Musa
(5) Colerter Flistrew

14. Which among the following companies recently launched "PhonePe"?
(1) Amazon
(2) Paytm
(3) Wipro
(4) Adani
(5) Flipkart

15. Which among the following private sector banks launched "Social Pay service" for enabling NRIs to send money to beneficiaries in India?
(1) ICICI Bank
(2) HDFC Bank
(3) RBL Bank
(4) IDFC Bank
(5) Yes Bank

16. "Truncated Cheques" come under which of the following RBI acts?
    (1) Negotiable Instruments Act, 1881
    (2) Negotiable Instruments Act, 1891
    (3) Negotiable Instruments Act, 1911
    (4) Negotiable Instruments Act, 1931
    (5) Negotiable Instruments Act, 1956

17. Under the FRDI Bill, bail-in clause affects whom among the following?
    (1) Creditors
    (2) Lenders
    (3) Depositors
    (4) Bankers
    (5) Mediators

18. In Public Affairs Index 2018, which Indian state topped the list third time in a row?
    (1) Gujarat
    (2) Karnataka
    (3) Tamil Nadu
    (4) Kerala
    (5) Goa

19. Which state attracted 300% FDI in the financial year 2017-18?
    (1) Uttar Pradesh
    (2) Haryana
    (3) Punjab
    (4) Assam
    (5) Karnataka

20. Name the Mascot of Tokyo Olympics 2020?
    (1) Miraitowa
    (2) Grabivova
    (3) Akhonova
    (4) Gabrivola
    (5) Sukhochawa

21. The 2022 Commonwealth Games is scheduled to be held at which of the following places?
    (1) New Delhi, India
    (2) Hamilton, New Zealand
    (3) Birmingham, England
    (4) Ottawa, Canada
    (5) Dublin, Ireland

22. The M. A. Chidambaram Stadium is located in which of the following Indian cities?
    (1) Bengaluru
    (2) Chennai
    (3) Mysuru
    (4) Vizag
    (5) Nagpur

23. In which of the following states is the Hirakud Dam located?
    (1) Andhra Pradesh
    (2) Tamil Nadu
    (3) Odisha
    (4) Telangana
    (5) Karnataka

24. Kunchikall Waterfall is located in which of the following Indian states?
    (1) Goa
    (2) Kerala

    (3) Tamil Nadu
    (4) Goa
    (5) Karnataka

25. In India Haldia Refinery is located in:
    (1) Assam
    (2) Gujarat
    (3) Odisha
    (4) Maharashtra
    (5) West Bengal

26. Under Marginal Standing Facility, banks take the loan from which among the following?
    (1) Finance Ministry
    (2) RBI
    (3) Ministry of Corporate Affairs
    (4) NABARD
    (e) SIDBI

27. Recently Walmart partnered with _________ for Digital Boost in India.
    (1) Paytm
    (2) Google Tez
    (3) Flipkart
    (4) Amazon India
    (5) Recharge it Now

28. In which of the following north eastern Indian states is Nokrek National Park located?
    (1) Arunachal Pradesh
    (2) Manipur
    (3) Mizoram
    (4) Meghalaya
    (5) Sikkim

29. Gangtok is the capital of which among the following states?
    (1) Nagaland
    (2) Tripura
    (3) Manipur
    (4) Mizoram
    (5) Sikkim

30. The "TIES" Scheme is related with which among the following?
    (1) Import
    (2) Export
    (3) Billing
    (4) Manufacturing
    (5) Banking

31. India's fastest supercomputer "Pratyush" is set up at:
    (1) BARC, Mumbai
    (2) IISc, Bengaluru
    (3) BITS Pilani
    (4) IITM Pune
    (5) IGI, New Delhi

32. The term IRAC stands for which among the following?
    (1) Identity, Rule, Approach, and Conclusion
    (2) Issue, Rule, Application, and Conclusion
    (3) Issue, Rupee, Application, and Conduct
    (4) India, Rule, Affordable, and Conclusion
    (5) Issue, Reinforcement, Application, and Character

33. When group lenders provide money to the borrower it is called as:
    (1) Temporary Loan   (2) Fast Track Loan
    (3) Syndicated Loan   (4) Attriculated Loan
    (5) Maturity Loan

34. From India, Ramsay Magsaysay Award 2018 was conferred to whom among the following?
    (1) Samar Mishra and Deepak Rathore
    (2) Adwitya Malahar and Janmejay Das
    (3) Kaushal Bhuchak and Vatsal seth
    (4) Bharat Vatwani and SonamWangchuk
    (5) Bezwada Wilson and Anmol Gupte

35. Sunkanaya Samridhi Yojana was launched in which of the following years?
    (1) 2014   (2) 2015
    (3) 2016   (4) 2017
    (5) 2018

36. The minimum annual deposit requirement for Sukanaya Samridhi Yojana is:
    (1) 250 INR   (2) 500 INR
    (3) 1000 INR   (4) 1500 INR
    (5) 2500 INR

37. The Headquarters of Jena Small Finance Bank is located in which of the following Indian cities?
    (1) Chennai   (2) Bengaluru
    (3) Lucknow   (4) Srinagar
    (5) Dispur

38. The Headquarters of Corporation bank is located in which of the following Indian cities?
    (1) Mangalore   (2) Bengaluru
    (3) Chennai   (4) New Jalpaiguri
    (5) Kolkata

39. The Headquarters of IDFC bank is located in which of the following Indian cities of India?
    (1) Kolkata   (2) New Delhi
    (3) Mumbai   (4) Lucknow
    (5) Gangtok

40. Dada Saheb Phalke Award for best actress was conferred to whom among the following?
    (1) Alia Bhatt   (2) Shraddha Kapoor
    (3) Sonam Kapoor   (4) Kareena Kapoor
    (5) Divya Dutta

41. Who among the following authored the book "Why I am Hindu Book"?
    (1) Manishankar Iyer   (2) Lalji Tandon
    (3) Lal Krishna Advani   (4) Shashi Tharoor
    (5) Murli Manohar Joshi

42. UNESCO's World Heritage Site "Rani kiVav" is located in which of the following Indian states?
    (1) Gujarat   (2) Madhya Pradesh
    (3) Andhra Pradesh   (4) Karnataka
    (5) Kerala

43. Who among the following was made the head of Committee on mob-lynching?
    (1) Rajeev Khandelwal   (2) Rajiv Gauba
    (3) Abhishek Sharma   (4) Deepak Bhatnagar
    (5) Ameesh Gupta

44. A banking outlet which does not provide delivery of service for a minimum of __________ per day and for at least 5 days a week will be considered a 'Part-time Banking Outlet'.
    (1) 2.5 hours   (2) 3 hours
    (3) 3.5 hours   (4) 4 hours
    (5) 6 hours

45. According to the Fugitive Economic Offenders Bill, what is the minimum amount to file a case?
    (1) 25 crore   (2) 50 crore
    (3) 75 crore   (4) 100 crore
    (5) 130 crore

46. Section 22 of Banking Regulation Act deals with which of the following?
    (1) Licensing of banking companies
    (2) Appointment of Deputy Governors of RBI
    (3) Relation between RBI and Finance Ministry
    (4) Penalty imposed on Banks
    (5) Appointment of Governor of RBI

47. Which of the following water bodies connects Mediterranean sea and Red Sea?
    (1) Strait of Gibralter   (2) Suez Canal
    (3) Panama Canal   (4) Strait of Homurz
    (5) Kiel Canal

48. In which of the following states is Sabarimala Sastha Temple Pathanamthitta is located?
    (1) Tamil Nadu   (2) Kerala
    (3) Karnataka   (4) Goa
    (5) Andhra Pradesh

49. Moon Jae-in is the present president of which among the following countries?
    (1) North Korea
    (2) Thailand
    (3) South Korea
    (4) Japan
    (5) Myanmar

50. Which of the following soccer player retired after Football World Cup 2018?
(1) Mohammad Salah   (2) Andres Iniesta
(3) Luka Modric   (4) Leonel Messi
(5) Dipthik Naloo

51. Fakhar Zaman is the opening cricket batsman from which among the following countries?
(1) Bangladesh   (2) Pakistan
(3) Afghanistan   (4) UAE
(5) Hongkong

52. The present Lok Sabha MP Ram Shaqal is from which of the following Indian states?
(1) Madhya Pradesh   (2) Uttar Pradesh
(3) Bihar   (4) Chhattisgarh
(5) Jharkhand

53. Which among the following Indian footballer wins 2017 AIFF Player of the Year award?
(1) Sunil Chhetri
(2) Jeje Lalpekhlua
(3) Jo Paul Ancheri
(4) Eugeneson Lyngdoh
(5) Syed Rahim Nabi

54. Which of the following activities is not performed by the "Payment banks"?
(1) Issue Credit Cards
(2) Issue Debit Cards
(3) Bharti Airtel set up India's first live payments bank
(4) These banks can accept a restricted deposit, which is currently limited to 1 lakh per customer
(5) Payments banks can issue services like net-banking and mobile-banking

55. Every year, September 8 is observed across the world as:
(1) International Literacy Day
(2) International Day of Solidarity with Detained and Missing Staff Members
(3) International Day of Forests
(4) International Red Cross Day
(5) International Day of Families

56. What does W stand for in "WLTS"?
(1) Wire   (2) Wireless
(3) World   (4) Withstand
(5) Withdrawl

57. Shubhankar Sharma is associated with which of the following sports?
(1) Billiards   (2) Golf
(3) Lawn Tennis   (4) Football
(5) Field Hockey

58. Bansagar Dam project is a joint venture between Uttar Pradesh, Madhya Pradesh and which of the following other state?
(1) Jharkhand   (2) Odisha
(3) West Bengal   (4) Uttarakhand
(5) Bihar

59. Which organ in human body regenerates itself?
(1) Small Intestine   (2) Large Intestine
(3) Liver   (4) Kidneys
(5) Heart

60. Where is the headquarters of Arab League located?
(1) Cairo   (2) Riyadh
(3) Tehran   (4) Mosul
(5) Abu Dhabi

61. Who among the following has been appointed as the head of the Committee to tackle NPAs?
(1) Sunil Ambris   (2) Sunil Mehta
(3) Deepak Rathore   (4) Amreesh Tripathi
(5) Rajeev Gauba

62. The Rohingya tribe belongs to which of the following countries?
(1) Maldives   (2) Myanmar
(3) Mauritius   (4) Bhutan
(5) Bangladesh

63. What is the current SLR decided by RBI?
(1) 11.5   (2) 13.75
(3) 14.5   (4) 16.5
(5) 19.5

64. Which among the following countries was fixed as the host of World environment day 2018?
(1) Kenya   (2) Ireland
(3) Iceland   (4) India
(5) Syria

65. The International Micro, Small and Medium-sized Enterprises (MSME) Day is observed every year across the world on:
(1) 17 March   (2) 25 March
(3) 12 April   (4) 23 April
(5) 27 June

66. Who among the following has been appointed as the Head of Committee set up by RBI to make a Public Credit Registry (PCR)?
(1) Shaktikantha Das   (2) Y.M. Deosthalee
(3) Dev Vrat Kanhai   (4) Arun Kumar Roy
(5) H R Khan

67. The Indian athlete Hima Das belongs to which of the following Indian state?
    (1) Tripura   (2) West Bengal
    (3) Assam   (4) Jharkhand
    (5) Chhattisgarh

68. The Headquarters of Asian Infrastructure Investment Bank (AIIB) is located in:
    (1) Beijing, China   (2) Shanghai, China
    (3) Mumbai, India   (4) Tokyo, Japan
    (5) New Delhi, India

69. The Reserve Bank of India launched Financial Literacy Week across the country with customer protection as its main aim which starts:
    (1) 3 May   (2) 17 May
    (3) 23 May   (4) 4 June
    (5) 10 June

70. During Second World War the first nuclear bomb was dropped in:
    (1) Hiroshima, Japan   (2) Nagasaki, Japan
    (3) Chernobyl, Ukraine   (4) Thimphu, Bhutan
    (5) Lahore, Pakistan

71. The headquarters of Interpol is located in which of the following countries?
    (1) Belgium   (2) Switzerland
    (3) France   (4) USA
    (5) UK

72. Which of the following banks was listed as Best bank in private sector in Dun & Bradstreet Corporate Award 2018?
    (1) ICICI Bank   (2) RBL Bank
    (3) Yes Bank   (4) IDFC Bank
    (5) HDFC Bank

73. The bull taming sport Jallikattu is typically practiced in which of the following Indian states?
    (1) Kerala   (2) Karnataka
    (3) Maharashtra   (4) Tamil Nadu
    (5) Andhra Pradesh

74. Which of the following engines has been developed and used by ISRO?
    (1) CE-20 cryogenic rocket engine
    (2) CE-40 cryogenic rocket engine
    (3) CE-60 cryogenic rocket engine
    (4) CE-80 cryogenic rocket engine
    (5) CE-100 cryogenic rocket engine

75. "Banglore Tiger" Book is based on which of the following Indian companies?
    (1) HCL   (2) Tata
    (3) Wipro   (4) Flipkart
    (5) Paytm

76. Who is known as the "Metro man of India"?
    (1) E. Sreedharan   (2) Mangoo Singh
    (3) Dheeraj Sawlani   (4) Lakhim Dorabjee
    (5) Anwar Ibrahim

77. The headquarters of International Campaign to Abolish Nuclear Weapons (ICAN) is located at:
    (1) Lyon   (2) Geneva
    (3) Paris   (4) Amsterdam
    (5) New York

78. What is full form of CVV which credit card companies introduced to protect against fraud?
    (1) Card Verification Value
    (2) Card Virtual Value
    (3) Credit Verification Value
    (4) Centre Virtual Value
    (5) Card Vimplant Value

79. Which of the following banks is to provide Financial and Digital Literacy to farmers across Rajasthan and Haryana?
    (1) RBL Bank   (2) Yes Bank
    (3) IDFC Bank   (4) ICICI Bank
    (5) HDFC Bank

80. As of 2018, the five nations of BRICS have a combined nominal GDP of US.........trillion.
    (1) $11.2   (2) $13.4
    (3) $18.6   (4) $22.4
    (5) $25.6

ENGLISH LANGUAGE

Directions (Q. 81 to 85): In each of the following questions, a sentence has been split into five parts denoted by (1), (A), (B), (C) and (D). Rearrange the parts (A), (B), (C) and (D) to make the sentence both meaningfully and grammatically correct. Of the combination of the parts (A), (B), (C) and (D) given against the sentence, select the combination which makes the sentence both meaningful and grammatically correct as your answer. If the given sentence is correct as it is, select "No rearrangement required" as your answer. Ignore the errors of punctuation, if any.

Please note: Consider Part 1 given in bold as correct and the rearrangement, if any, to make the sentence both meaningful and grammatically correct has to be done with parts (A), (B), (C) and (D).

81. **In the massive new India (1)**/ of aspirational professionals, (A)/ there is a requirement for the collaborative environment of a club (B)/ where people can bond over (C)/ -- if not golf - art, music and philosophy. (D)
    (1) CBDA   (2) ABCD
    (3) BCDA   (4) DCBA
    (5) No rearrangement required

82. **Once you enter Quorum, (1)**/ where paintings by artists such as SH Raza (A)/ and Ram Kumar (B)/ adorn the walls (C)/ it opens up into a huge gallery space, (D)

(1) CBDA   (2) ABCD
(3) BCDA   (4) DABC
(5) No rearrangement required

83. **It's interesting to note, (1)**/ and Singapore, where they first (A)/ came up centuries ago as spaces (B)/ where upper class men could go to network (C)/ the private club culture still flourishes in cities like London (D)

(1) CBDA   (2) ABCD
(3) BCDA   (4) DABC
(5) No rearrangement required

84. **However, The Quorum has tied up (1)**/ around the world, (A)/ reciprocal relationships (B)/ with 40 clubs (C)/ that comes with many privileges. (D)

(1) CBDA   (2) ABCD
(3) BCAD   (4) DABC
(5) No rearrangement required

85. **The image of the leisurely, (1)**/ club-going gentleman (A)/ from an old-boys network (B)/ is about to change, (C)/ dramatically. (D)

(1) CBDA   (2) ABCD
(3) BCAD   (4) DABC
(5) No rearrangement required

Directions (Q. 86 to 90): Match the statements from column 1 with column 2 and find which of the following pair of statements given in the options make contextually and grammatically correct sense.

86.

Column 1		Column 2	
A.	Making things evident	D.	it appears difficult.
B.	Some of his advices might appear to be trivial	E.	so, they went for a toss.
C.	They went for a hunt	F.	but they are important nonetheless.

(1) AE   (2) AD
(3) BF   (4) CD
(5) CF

87.

Column 1		Column 2	
A.	Once upon a time, there was	D.	and very soon, the river was in spate.
B.	He became more garrulous	E.	after drinking a couple of beers.
C.	The vitality of life is contagious	F.	wherever the bikers went.

(1) AD   (2) BE
(3) AF   (4) BD
(5) BF

88.

Column 1		Column 2	
A.	I was literally scared when	D.	for the matter as such.
B.	Diasporic identities	E.	has proved to be a black sheep.
C.	I was very angry with her	F.	but still went to the party nonetheless.

(1) AE   (2) AD
(3) AF   (4) CF
(5) CD

89.

Column 1		Column 2	
A.	I have no time	D.	it is still old wine in a new bottle.
B.	Running out of time	E.	whatsoever for the political leaders, whether they are in the parliament or elsewhere.
C.	Placed in the second division	F.	they are ruined.

(1) AD   (2) AE
(3) CD   (4) CF
(5) Both CE and BE

90.

Column 1		Column 2	
A.	His stance, although widely accepted	D.	proved to be a pain the back.
B.	He has failed	E.	also a humongous task.
C.	This is doubtful	F.	is nevertheless, devoid of logic.

(1) AE   (2) AD
(3) AF   (4) BE
(5) CF

Directions (Q. 91 to 95): Select the phrase/connector (it must be at the start) from the given three options which can be used to form a single sentence from the two sentences given below, implying the same meaning as expressed in the statement sentences.

91. I. The sun was shining.

  II. It wasn't that warm.

  i. whatever

  ii. whenever

  iii. although

  (1) Only i   (2) Only ii

  (3) Only iii   (4) Both I and iii

  (5) None of these

92. I. I checked the facts on the internet a number of times.

  II. I couldn't establish its veracity.

  i. whatever

  ii. although

  iii. elsewhere

  (1) Only i   (2) Only ii

  (3) Only iii   (4) Both I and iii

  (5) None of these

93. I. You look at his attitude.

  II. You can't criticize him.

  i. However

  ii. Nonesoever

  iii. Regardless

  (1) Only i   (2) Only ii

  (3) Only iii   (4) Both I and iii

  (5) None of these

94. I. I change gears.

  II. The pistons in the engine creak.

  i. Wherever

  ii. Whatsoever

  iii. Whenever

  (1) Only i   (2) Only ii

  (3) Only iii   (4) Both I and iii

  (5) None of these

95. I. You know your score.

  II. You need to start immediately.

  i. However it is done, of late

  ii. However it happens, once

  iii. However it is committed,

  (1) Only i   (2) Only ii

  (3) Only iii   (4) Both I and iii

  (5) None of these

Directions (Q. 96 to 100): In each of the questions given below, a sentence is given with three blanks. Choose the correct combination of words that fit in the corresponding blanks. In case all three words fit in the sentence, but are given in incorrect sequence, choose option (4). In case all three words fit in the sentence, in the same sequence as given, i.e., (A), (B), (C), choose (5).

96. Among the ___(A)___ that are out of bounds for traffic due to ___(B)___ are an NH 275 ___(C)___ between Madikeri-Sullia, the NH 75 stretch between Sakleshpur and Gundiya and the NH 234 stretch between Charmadi and Kottigehara.

  A. Highways

  B. Landslides

  C. Stretch

  (1) Only A and B fit

  (2) Only A and C fit

  (3) Only B and C fit

  (4) Sequence can be altered

  (5) All are in correct sequence

97. The rial has ___(A)___ over 50% of its value this year, ___(B)___ prices and ___(C)___ consumers to convert their savings into gold and other assets.

  A. Loose

  B. Pushing up

  C. Compelling

  (1) Only A and B fit

  (2) Only A and C fit

  (3) Only B and C fit

  (4) Sequence can be altered

  (5) All are in correct sequence

98. There is little ___(A)___ in the U.S. for a direct military ___(B)___; Iran too is under no illusion about its military ___(C)___.

  A. Appetite

  B. Missile

  C. Capability

  (1) Only A and B fit

  (2) Only A and C fit

  (3) Only B and C fit

  (4) Sequence can be altered

  (5) All are in correct sequence

99. Iran is ___(A)___ the impact of re-imposed ___(B)___ after the U.S. walked out of the nuclear ___(C)___ in May.

   A. Reeling under

   B. Pranks

   C. Deal

   (1) Only A and B fit

   (2) Only A and C fit

   (3) Only B and C fit

   (4) Sequence can be altered

   (5) All are in correct sequence

100. Recent protests have ____(A)___ a yearning for progress and greater ___(B)___ among ___(C)___ Iranians.

   A. Reflected

   B. Freedom

   C. Domesticated

   (1) Only A and B fit

   (2) Only A and C fit

   (3) Only B and C fit

   (4) Sequence can be altered

   (5) All are in correct sequence

Directions (Q. 101 to 105): Read the passage given below and answer the questions that follow.

Amid rising global trade tensions, there are some signs to hope that all is not lost. The United States and Mexico on Monday reached a breakthrough bilateral trade agreement replacing the decades-old North American Free Trade Agreement (NAFTA) after Mexico agreed to concessions demanded by the Donald Trump administration. According to the new agreement, 75% of all automobile content must be made regionally, which is higher than the current level of 62.5%. Further, 40-45% of such content must be manufactured using labour that costs at least $16 an hour. The U.S. hopes that this will discourage manufacturers from moving their facilities to Mexico, where labour is available at rates lower than in the U.S. It has also invited Canada to join talks for a renegotiation of trade terms in favour of U.S. interests. Notably, the U.S.-Mexico bilateral trade deal comes in the aftermath of President Trump's statement in June that he might enter into separate trade agreements with Canada and Mexico, thus effectively junking the tripartite NAFTA deal. U.S. stocks rallied after news of the deal, with the Nasdaq Composite index moving above the 8,000 level for the first time ever and the Dow Jones index breaking above 26,000. The market reaction was probably a sign of relief, riding on hopes that tit-for-tat tariff wars between the U.S.

and its trade allies could now draw to a close. It is worth noting that Mexico had earlier joined hands with other economies such as Canada, China and the European Union to impose retaliatory tariffs against the U.S.

Mexico's decision could set an example for other countries which have resorted to retaliatory tariffs to deal with Mr. Trump's aggressive trade war against them. China has been at the forefront of this approach, slapping tariffs on several U.S. goods, together worth billions of dollars. There can be no doubt that Mr. Trump's protectionist trade policy, including the current deal which increases restrictions on cross-border trade in order to protect U.S. jobs, is bad for the global economy. However, the best way to win the trade war against the U.S. may simply be to accept "defeat" by refusing to double down on retaliatory tariffs. The reason for such a response is simple. Retaliatory tariffs can only cause further harm to the world economy by increasing the burden of taxes on the private sector, which is crucial to spur growth and create jobs. Further, there is no reason for America's trading partners, in an attempt to protect their domestic producers, to repeat Mr. Trump's mistake of depriving domestic consumers of access to useful foreign goods. The right response to Mr. Trump's trade war will be to abstain from any mutually destructive tit-for-tat tariff regimes while simultaneously pushing for peace talks.

The Trump administration wants to lower the trade deficit between the United States and Mexico. In 2017, Americans bought $71 billion more imports from Mexico than vice versa. The trade deficit with Canada is smaller.

To do this, the administration wants to rewrite the rules on auto manufacturing and trade. Negotiators from each country have agreed to decrease the percentage of a vehicle sourced in Mexico. It also wants stronger protection for U.S. digital trade and intellectual properties.

The Trump administration wants to end the dispute resolution panel. These arbitration panels rule on whether a NAFTA country treated a partner's overseas investments unfairly. The panels make sure U.S. corporations maintain the rights protected by the U.S. Constitution.

But the Trump administration claims it erodes the sovereignty of U.S courts. For example, the U.S. Commerce Department has accused western Canadian provinces of subsidizing their lumber exports. It claims they dump low-cost lumber into the American market. The resolution panel has ruled in favor of Canada. The Commerce Department has threatened to impose a 20 percent tariff on Canadian lumber imports. But U.S. manufacturers want to keep the panel. They agree it protects their foreign investments.

Other measures include making it easier for U.S. telecom companies and banks to operate in the other NAFTA countries. Similarly, the administration wants its trade partners to open up more of their government contracts to U.S. companies. At the same time, it wants to use "Buy American" provisions to limit their firms from winning U.S. government contracts.

The administration had also wanted to eliminate unfair subsidies. It also wanted state-owned companies, such as Mexico's Pemex, to operate more like private corporations. In 2013, Mexican President Enrique Peña Nieto allowed foreign direct investment in Pemex. But the company is a source of national pride, so it's unlikely to be completely privatized.

A draft of the NAFTA proposal wanted to allow "snapback" tariffs if a domestic industry was damaged by imports. But some experts claim those provisions are already in NAFTA.

In the past, Trump said he would like Mexico to end its value-added tax on U.S. companies. Trump claims that the VAT acts as a tax on U.S. exports to Mexico. A VAT tax is like a federal sales tax that's imposed on all companies in the supply chain.

Mexico charges a 16 percent VAT tax on all business sales, whether it's to other firms or the consumer. When companies export the finished product to the United States, Mexico rebates the VAT tax. But U.S. companies that export to Mexico must pay the VAT tax. Trump says that encourages U.S. companies to build factories in Mexico to receive the rebate and avoid the tax.

Trump has asked Mexico to end the maquiladora program. This program allows U.S. companies to set up low-cost factories across the border in Mexico to assemble finished products. They then export the goods back to the United States. As a result, maquiladoras became responsible for 65 percent of Mexico's exports and employ 30 percent of its workforce. That undercut American workers and sent jobs to Mexico. NAFTA expanded the maquiladora program by ending tariffs. The United States would also like Canada to end its tariffs on dairy and poultry products.

101. Out of the following options, which one is an appropriate title of the given passage?

   (1) The increasing American intervention in the internal matters of Mexico

   (2) Easing tensions: On the US-Mexico trade deal

   (3) The US-Mexico political ambience

   (4) The erroneous policies of the Trump government

   (5) The continuous tiff between the Republicans and the Democrats

102. Consider the statements given below:

   a. Labour rates in Mexico are lower than that of US.

   b. The North American Free Trade Agreement (NAFTA) is still in vogue

   c. Automobile manufacturers have a tendency to shift their operations to countries like Mexico.

Out of the above given statements, which one is true in the light of the passage?

   (1) Only a   (2) Only b

   (3) Both a and b   (4) Both a and c

   (5) Both b and c

103. Consider the statements given below:

   a. The trump administration hopes that Mexico's government organisations will operate more like private entities.

   b. The Trump administration wants a direct stake in the energy sector of Mexico.

   c. Successive governments in the US have wanted to stake a claim in the infrastructure industry of Latin America.

Out of the above given statements, which one is true in the light of the passage?

   (1) Only a   (2) Only b

   (3) Both a and b   (4) Both a and c

   (5) Both b and c

104. The author is most likely to agree with which of the following options?

   (1) Trump's present trade policies are aimed at defeating the trade policies of the European Union.

   (2) Trump's present trade policies are not conducive for political stability in the Caribbean region.

   (3) Trump's present trade policies are detrimental to the growth of world trade.

   (4) Trump's present policies can act as a deterrent to world peace.

   (5) Trump's present policies can encourage world trade significantly.

105. What can be inferred about the author's advice to the Trump government's trade policies?

   (1) Mexico's stance towards Trump is nothing but a cul-de-sac.

   (2) A quid pro quo approach is not the need of the hour.

   (3) A sine die approach is the need of the hour.

   (4) A lingua franca approach can be an appropriate for Trump.

   (5) None of the above

Directions (Q. 106 to 110) : Read the following passage carefully and answer the questions given below it. Certain words/phrases are given in **bold** in the passage to help you to locate them while answering some of the questions.

In the past, the richest states often grew the fastest and the poor ones slowest. But India's record GDP growth of 8.49% per year in the five-year period 2004-09 is a case of improved productivity and growth in **customarily** poor states trickling up and aggregating into rapid growth at the national level.

Nobody should call this a success of trickle-down economics. Trickle-down assumes that fast growth can be had simply by changing a few policies that benefit the rich, after which some benefits trickle down to the poor. In fact, miracle growth is globally rare precisely because it is so difficult for countries to improve the productivity of a substantial proportion of the population. Only when productivity improvement is widespread is there enough productivity improvement from all regions and people to **add** up to fast growth. In other words, fast growth does not trickle down, it trickles up.

Once a country grows fast, government revenues will boom, and can be used to accelerate spending in social sectors and welfare. Miracle growth and record revenues enabled the central government to finance social welfare schemes, farm loan waivers and enormous oil subsidies. This can be called the trickling down of part of the revenue bonanza into welfare and workfare. But neither welfare nor workfare could have caused the **sharp** acceleration of economic growth. The growth bonanza itself was **sparked** by state-level political and policy changes that accelerated local growth, which then trickled up to the national level.

106. To which of the following factors does the author attribute India's high growth rate during 2004-09?

    (1) Tremendous growth of the vast majority of richer states

    (2) Change in national level policies to benefit only large well off states

    (3) Gains of richer states have been used to fund social welfare schemes in the larger states

    (4) Improved productivity of traditionally low performing states

    (5) None of the above

107. Which of the following best describes the author's view of trickle down theory?

    (1) It ensures accountability of the government even at the grassroot level

    (2) It has been effective in helping poor states catch up with richer ones

    (3) It promotes inclusive growth over quick growth

    (4) It targets social welfare at the cost of economic growth

    (5) It has largely failed to drive sustained growth

108. Which of the following is TRUE in the context of the passage?

    (1) India's growth was more inclusive in nature during 2004-2009 than it had been in the past

    (2) Developed countries use the same model of development as India

    (3) Widespread growth is best achieved through Central Government monitored schemes

    (4) At present India's traditionally poor states are more prosperous than her socially developed ones

    (5) There should be no government expenditure in social sectors if the current high growth rate is not maintained

109. Why have countries found it difficult to achieve high growth?

    A. Ensuring an increase in the output among a large number of citizens is difficult.

    B. Corruption of politicians at the grassroot level results in the benefits of growth not reaching the poor.

    C. The government's failure to allocate sufficient income to inclusive social welfare schemes.

    (1) Only (A)

    (2) (A) and (B)

    (3) (B) and (C)

    (4) All (A), (B) and (C)

    (5) None of these

110. What is the author's objective in writing this passage?

    (1) Advocating greater autonomy for the richest states in India

    (2) Urging the government to invest in social development to facilitate economic growth

    (3) Criticising traditional economic principles on which the Indian economy is based

    (4) Encouraging larger states to disburse more wealth at the grassroot level

    (5) None of the above

QUANTITATIVE APTITUDE

Directions (Q. 111 to 115): Answer the questions on the basis of the information given below.

A company employs two different processes in its production wing. Both the processes require an initial investment of Rs. 5 lakh each. The bar graph given below shows the running cost for both the production processes. The running cost (in Rs.) for both the processes comprises the maintenance cost, the material cost and the labour cost. The production happens in shifts and one shift is of six hours. Even if the target production is achieved before the end of a shift, the company has to bear the complete maintenance cost and the labour cost for that shift.

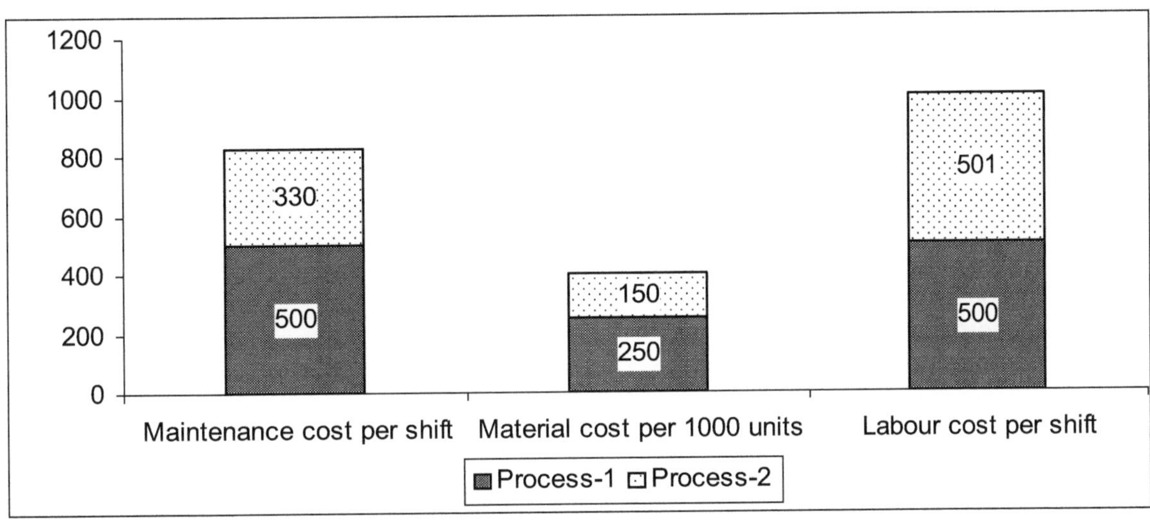

The line graph given below shows the break-up of time taken (in minutes) by each process to complete one cycle resulting in the production of 2 units.

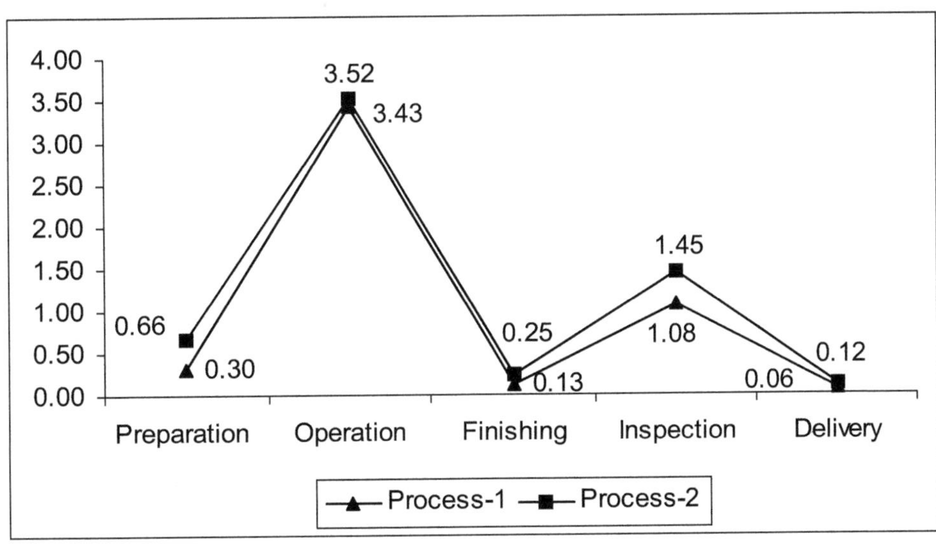

111. For which of the following weekly production targets (in units) would Process-2 be more cost effective?

(1) 288　　　　(2) 400　　　　(3) 500　　　　(4) 450　　　　(5) None of these

112. How much more cost would be incurred by the company if it chooses to use Process-1 over Process-2 to produce 6000 units?

(1) Rs. 1,050　　　　(2) Rs. 1,150　　　　(3) Rs. 1,191　　　　(4) Rs. 1,200　　　　(5) None of these

113. How many hours are required to produce 1800 units using Process-1?

(1) 65　　　　(2) 70　　　　(3) 75　　　　(4) 90　　　　(5) None of these

114. What is the respective ratio of the number of hours required to produce 1200 units using Process–1 and Process–2?

(1) 2 : 3   (2) 6 : 5

(3) 5 : 6   (4) 3 : 2

(5) 4 : 5

115. How much cost would be incurred by the company if it chooses to use Process–1 to produced 20000 units?

(1) Rs. 1,44,000   (2) Rs. 1,54,500

(3) Rs. 1,65,000   (4) Rs. 1,32,000

(5) None of these

Directions (Q. 116 to 120): Answer the questions on the basis of the information given below.

The table given below shows the data related to human resources of a multinational company ABC which has 145 offices across 8 countries.

Country	Offices	Total Number of employees	Respective ratio of male and female employees	Percentage of B.Tech employees
Australia	16	2568	5 : 7	75
Brazil	18	2880	11 : 5	65
China	14	2310	10 : 11	40
Denmark	22	3575	3 : 2	60
Egypt	13	2054	7 : 6	50
France	17	2788	20 : 21	75
Ghana	24	3720	8 : 7	55
Haiti	21	3360	9 : 5	80

116. If the number of male B.Tech employees in Australia is 1275, what percent of female employees in that particular country are B.Tech ?

(1) 25   (2) 29

(3) 28   (4) 31

(5) 35

117. In which of the given countries the percentage of women employees to number of employees (both males and females) in that country is the second lowest?

(1) Ghana   (2) Denmark

(3) Haiti   (4) Egypt

(5) Brazil

118. What is the respective ratio between total number of male employees in Brazil, China, Haiti and Egypt taken together and total number of famale employees in Australia, Denmark, France and Ghana taken together?

(1) 3137 : 3046   (2) 3173 : 3046

(3) 3046 : 3137   (4) 3273 : 3046

(5) None of these

119. What is the difference between average number of B.Tech employees in Australia, Brazil, Egypt and Denmark taken together and average number of B.Tech employees in China, France, Ghana and Haiti taken together?

(1) 185   (2) 199

(3) 195   (4) 179

(5) 180

120. Which of the given countries has the highest number of average employees per office?

(1) Australia   (2) China

(3) France   (4) Denmark

(5) Haiti

Direction (Q. 121 to 125): what should be come in place of question mark (?) in the following number series?"

121. 4, 36, 48, 150, (?), 392

(1) 156   (2) 180

(3) 172   (4) 164

(5) 272

122. 6, 120, (?), 1320, 2730

(1) 376   (2) 484

(3) 504   (4) 512

(5) 444

123. 5, (?), 61, 113, 181, 265

(1) 25   (2) 49

(3) 46   (4) 54

(5) 36

124. 49, 121, (?), 289, 361

(1) 144   (2) 256

(3) 196   (4) 169

(5) 188

125. 9, 73, (?), 561, 1081, 1849

(1) 141   (2) 220

(3) 484   (4) 329

(5) 241

126. A car covers first 39 km of its journey in 45 minutes and the remaining 25 km in 35 minutes. What is the average speed of the car?

(1) 40 km/hr   (2) 64 km/hr

(3) 49 km/hr   (4) 48 km/hr

(5) None of these

127. The average marks in English of a class of 24 students is 56. If the marks of three students were misread as 44, 45 and 61 in lieu of the actual marks 48, 59 and 67respectively, then what would be the correct average?

(1) 56.5   (2) 59

(3) 57.5   (4) 58

(5) None of these

128. A retailer purchases a watch with an offer of 20% + 20% discount on the marked price. He sold it to the customer at a profit of 50%. The price at which the retailer sold the watch was what percent more/less than the marked price?

(1) 32% more

(2) 4% less

(3) 36% less

(4) 4% more

(5) None of these

129. Raman's present age is three times his daughter's and nine-thirteenth of his mother's present age. The sum of the present ages of all three of them is 125 years. What is the difference between the present ages of Raman's daughter and Raman's mother?

(1) 45 years

(2) 40 years

(3) 50 years

(4) Cannot be determined

(5) None of these

130. In a 50 litres sugar solution, the quantity of water is 80% by volume. How much water should be mixed to this solution so that the quantity of water would become 90%?

(1) 5 litres

(2) 40 litres

(3) 50 litres

(4) 6.25 litres

(5) 62.5 litres

Directions (Q. 131 to 135): Answer the questions on the basis of the information given below.

131. Five men and five women are to be arranged in a row while seating in a party.

Quantity I: Number of ways of arranging 5 men and 5 women such that no two men or women are adjacent to each other.

Quantity II: Number of ways of arranging 5 men and 5 women such that all men sit together.

(1) Quantity I > Quantity II

(2) Quantity I < Quantity II

(3) Quantity I ≥ Quantity II

(4) Quantity I ≤ Quantity II

(5) Quantity I = Quantity II or No relation

132. **Quantity I:** Value of 'a' if 's' is an acute angle and PR ∥ QT.

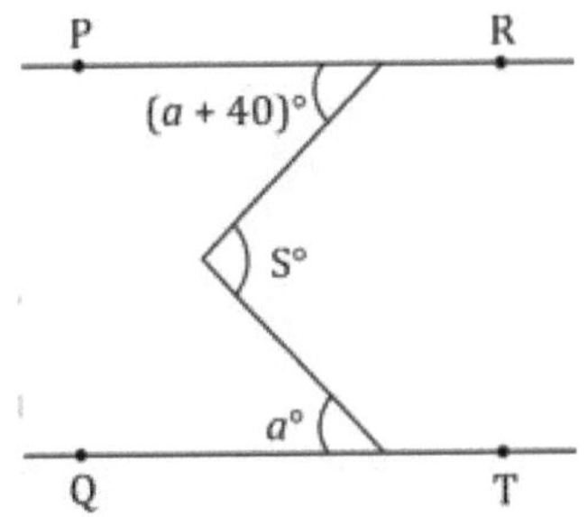

Quantity II: 25°

(1) Quantity I > Quantity II

(2) Quantity I < Quantity II

(3) Quantity I ≥ Quantity II

(4) Quantity I ≤ Quantity II

(5) Quantity I = Quantity II or No relation

133. There are 63 cards in a box numbered from 1 to 63. Every card is numbered with only 1 number.

Quantity I: Probability of picking up a card whose digits, if interchanged, result in a number which is 36 more than the number picked up.

Quantity II: Probability of picking up a card, the number printed on which is a multiple of 8 but not that of 16.

(1) Quantity I > Quantity II

(2) Quantity I < Quantity II

(3) Quantity I ≥ Quantity II

(4) Quantity I ≤ Quantity II

(5) Quantity I = Quantity II or No relation

134. **Quantity I:** Area of quadrilateral BFDE, given ABCD is a rectangle having AB = 10 cm and BC = 12 cm.

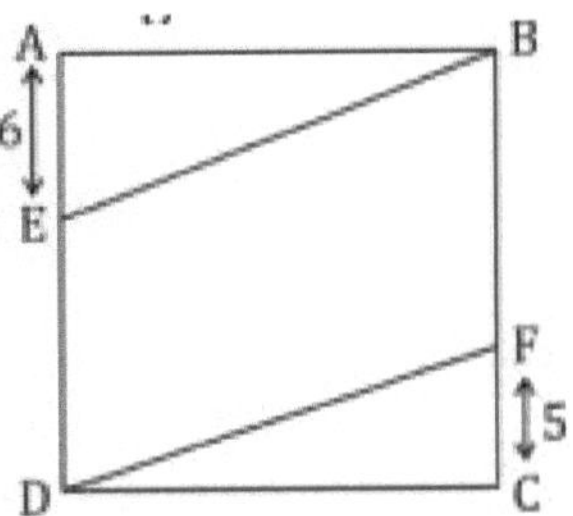

Quantity II: 15 cm²

(1) Quantity I > Quantity II

(2) Quantity I < Quantity II

(3) Quantity I ≥ Quantity II

(4) Quantity I ≤ Quantity II

(5) Quantity I = Quantity II or No relation

135. A, B and C entered into a partnership. A invested Rs. 3,000 at the start. B invested $33\frac{1}{3}\%$ more than that invested by A and C invested the average of the investment made by A and B. After 4 months, A withdrew 40% of his amount, B doubled his amount and C increased his amount by 20%. After another 5 months, B got away from partnership and A doubled his amount while C maintained his amount. Profit at the end of year was Rs. 6,77,000 and profit was shared in the ratio of their investment and time.

Quantity I: Profit earned by C.

Quantity II: Average of profit earned by A, B and C together.

(1) Quantity I > Quantity II

(2) Quantity I < Quantity II

(3) Quantity I ≥ Quantity II

(4) Quantity I ≤ Quantity II

(5) Quantity I = Quantity II or No relation

136. A man buys two cows for Rs. 50,000. He then sold one cow at a loss of 10% and other cow at a profit of 10%, thereby gaining Rs. 500. Find the cost price of each cow.

(1) Rs. 25,000, Rs. 25,000

(2) Rs. 20,000, Rs. 30,000

(3) Rs. 22,500, Rs. 27,500

(4) Rs. 17,500, Rs. 32,500

(5) None of these

137. 3 men and 4 women can do a piece of work in 12 days while 4 men and 3 women can do the same work in 10 days. In how many days 2 men and 3 women can do the work?

(1) 15 days   (2) $17\frac{1}{2}$ days

(3) $20\frac{1}{2}$ days   (4) $18\frac{1}{3}$ days

(5) None of these

138. Sonika invested an amount of ₹5,800 for 2 years. At what rate of compound interest will she get an amount of ₹594·5 at the end of two years ?

(1) 5% per annum   (2) 4% per annum

(3) 6% per annum   (4) 8% per annum

(5) None of these

139. The ratio of the present ages of Anju and Sandhya is 13 : 17 respectively. Four years ago the respective ratio of their ages was 11 : 15. What will be the respective ratio of their ages six years hence ?

(1) 3 : 4   (2) 7 : 8

(3) 5 : 4   (4) 6 : 5

(5) None of these

140. A, B and C enter into a partnership in the ratio 5/3 : 3/2 : 8/5. After 4 months, C increases his share 50%. If the total profit at the end of one year is, Rs. 39,750 then A's share in the profit is

(1) Rs. 11,250   (2) Rs. 12,000

(3) Rs. 12,500   (4) Rs. 13,000

(5) Rs. 16,000

REASONING ABILITY

Directions (Q. 141 to 145) : Answer the questions on the basis of the information given below.

Twelve research scientists from the field of Applied Mathematics meet at a conference and are sitting in two parallel rows in such a way that each person in row 1 faces a person in row 2. There is one scientist each from six different institutions - IIT, ISI, CMI, IISc, TIFR and IISER - in each row.H, I, J, K, L, and M sit in row 1 facing South whereas U, V, W, X, Y and Z sit in row 2 facing North, not necessarily in any particular order.

The two scientists from IISc are at the left end of each row. K from CMI faces V from ISI. M from IIT sits third to the right of L, who is from the same institute as X but not from IISc. H from IISER faces X and he is on the immediate right of I. U from IIT faces I, who is from the same institute as V. Y sits exactly between U and V. The scientist from CMI, Z has only one neighbour, who is from ISI.

141. Who are the two scientists from IISc?

(1) W, K   (2) Y, H

(3) M, U   (4) J, W

(5) H, X

142. Which Instititution does X belong to?

(1) ISI   (2) IISER

(3) IIT   (4) CMI

(5) TIFR

143. Which scientist in Row 2 is from IISER?

(1) Z   (2) Y

(3) X   (4) W

(5) V

144. If M and U form a pair and K and Z form another pair in a particular way, then select a similar pair from the given options.

(1) H, Y   (2) X, I

(3) I, U   (4) J, V

(5) W, L

145. Select the odd one from the given options.

(1) M   (2) W

(3) V   (4) J

(5) Z

Directions (Q. 146 to 150): Answer the questions on the basis of the information given below.

Eight sportsmen - L, M, N, O. P. Q, R and S - go to the Commonwealth Sports Complex on different days of the week, from Monday to Friday. They take part in eight different games - Football, Basketball, Cricket, Badminton, Swimming, Archery, Table Tennis and Hockey, not necessarily in any order. Two of them walk to the complex, two go by cycle, two by bike and two by car.

Q goes by bike on Tuesday along with L who plays Table Tennis.S and M travel by car on different days after the day on which L goes to the complex. P plays Basketball on the day exactly between S and M. L and P go by cycle. N goes for Archery on the day before Q. Football and Cricket practice is held on Friday. S plays Badminton. R, who plays cricket and O, who plays Hockey, walk to the sports complex. O goes to the complex on the same day as P.

146. What sport does Q take part in?

(1) Cricket   (2) Basketball

(3) Hockey   (4) Football

(5) Swimming

147. How does N travel to the sports complex?

(1) Walk   (2) Car

(3) Cycle   (4) Bike

(5) Cannot be determined

148. Which of the following combinations is true about Monday?

(1) Table Tennis, Cycle

(2) Archery, Bike

(3) Cricket, Car

(4) Football, Bike

(5) Hockey, Walk

149. Which of the following pairs of person and game is correct?

(1) Q, Cricket   (2) R, Badminton

(3) N, Basketball   (4) M , Football

(5) L, Swimming

150. Which two people play on Friday?

(1) S, M   (2) L, Q

(3) M, R   (4) S, O

(5) N, P

Directions (Q. 151 to 153: Answer the questions on the basis of the information given below.

There are nine members in a family - N, O, P, Q, R, S, T, U and V - spread across three generations. Each of them has a different profession viz, actor, doctor, lawyer, architect, CA, banker, choreographer, professor and manager. There are three married couples and each couple has at least one child.

R, the lawyer and his wife, Q have an unmarried daughter who is an actor. T is the daughter of V and she is a manager. S is a banker and her husband is an architect. P's wife, U is the daughter-in-law of the doctor. R's grandson is a choreographer. No female is a CA. P's wife is not a doctor. One of R's sons is an architect. N is not a grandchild of Q.

151. Who is the sister of P?

(1) S   (2) T

(3) N   (4) O

(5) U

152. Select the option with the right combination of person and profession.

(1) Q, Lawyer   (2) P, CA

(3) U, Doctor   (4) O, Actor

(5) S, Architect

153. Select the statement that is true regarding the given family.

(1) The choreographer is the daughter of the professor

(2) The banker is the sister of P.

(3) The architect is the son-in-law of Q.

(4) P has a son who is a choreographer.

(5) The granddaughters of R are O and T.

Directions (Q. 154 to 158): Answer the following questions based on the given information.

Seven friends M, N, P, D, E, F and G are working in three different organizations ABC, PQR and JKL and with at least two persons in each organization. Each one of them is in a different department viz. Analysis, HR, Marketing, Research, Design, Production and Administration (not necessarily in same order.) N works in Analysis in organization PQR. F works in Design in organization ABC with only M. Those who work in HR and Administration work in the same organization. P works in organization JKL, but does not work in Research department. G works in Administration in organization PQR. One who works in Production works with organization ABC, D works in organization PQR.

154. Who works in HR?

(1) P

(2) D

(3) E

(4) N

(5) None of these

155. E works in which organization?

(1) ABC   (2) PQR

(3) JKL   (4) ABC or PQR

(5) None of these

156. Three persons work in which organization?

(1) PQR   (2) JKL

(3) ABC   (4) PQR or JKL

(5) ABC or JKL

157. P works in which department?

(1) HR   (2) Design

(3) Research   (4) Marketing

(5) None of these

158. Which of the following combinations is correct?

(1) JKL - E - HR

(2) PQR - P - Marketing

(3) ABC - M - Administration

(4) PQR - G - HR

(5) None of these

Directions (Q. 159 to 163): Answer the questions on the basis of the information given below.

Ten lecturers A, B, C, D, E, F, G, H, I and J teach in the same college. They give lectures in five months (April, May, June, September and December). They give lectures in each month on 8th and 24th date. Only two lectures held in a month. The lectures are attended by different number of students. The total strength of students is 100 in each class and 50% attendance is compulsory for each class. The number of students will be even in the month of 30 days and odd in the month of 31 days. Different number of students attends class on different days. It is also known that:

No lecturer can give the lecture after H. F gives lecture in the month which has 30 days. E and B give lecturers after F on the 8th of different months respectively. Number of studens who attend class on 8th September is a square of a natural number (two digit number). C does not give the lecture in the month in which either J or B gives lecture. The sum of number of students who attend class on the 8th of two month is 152. Only three lecturers give lecture between F and the lecturer whose class is attended by 68 students. The difference of number of students who attend class on 8th September and the sum of number of students who attend class on May, is 58. B gives lecture in the month which has 30 days. The average of number of students who attend class on 24th April and 24th June is 76. A gives lecture in the month which has 31 days. E gives lecture in one of the day before B. Total 55 students attend G's lecture. G does not give lecture in the month in which H gives. There are four persons who give lecturers between G and D. J gives lecture in the month which is after the month in which G gives lecture.

The total number of students who attend class in five months is 714. The sum of number of students who attend

class on 8th may and 8th June is 147. Students who attend class on 8th June is less than 90. The difference of the number of students who attend class of lecturer J and C is 4. I gives lecture after A and the number of students who attend his lecture is greater than 70 and less than 80 and is not divisible by 4. The number of studens who attend class on 8th December is a multiple of 11.

159. Who among the following lecturer gives lecture on 24th June?

(1) E   (2) A

(3) J   (4) G

(5) None of these

160. How many students attend class on 8th December?

(1) 67   (2) 80

(3) 68   (4) 77

(5) 55

161. How many lecturers give lectures between A and B?

(1) Three   (2) Two

(3) Four   (4) One

(5) None

162. Who among the following gives lecture which is attended by 80 students?

(1) D   (2) E

(3) C   (4) F

(5) None of these

163. Four of the following five are alike in a certain way and thus form a group. Which of the following does not belong to that group?

(1) C   (1) 67

(3) G   (4) E

(5) 64

Direction (Q. 164 to 168): Study the following information to answer the given questions:

Six persons - Rahul, Gaur, Rudra, Tej, Vicky and Sam - are sitting around a round table in a restaurant, facing towards the center of the table . They have ordered for different food items and beverages viz. Idili, Dosa, Pizza, Dhokla, Biriyani and Pasta and beverages Coke, Frooti, Fanta, Sprite, Pepsi and Limca - as their lunch. They are wearing shirts of different colors, viz. Green, Black, Red, White, Blue and Yellow. They have mobiles of different brands, viz Samsung, Motorola, Asus, Xiaomi, Oppo and Nokia. Order of food items, beverages for the lunch, and brands of mobiles and colors of shirts are not necessarily according to the order of their names.

It is also known that:

1. The persons who have ordered Idili, Pizza and Biriyani are neither in White shirt nor in Black shirt

also none of them have Motorola or Asus phones.

2. The persons who are in Green and Yellow shirts have neither ordered Idili nor Pizza but they have ordered Frooti and Coke, also they have Asus and Nokia respectively.

3. Rahul is not wearing a White shirt, also he is neither on the immediate left of the person who has ordered Dhokla and Frooti and nor to the left of teh one who has a Samsung phone.

4. The only person who is between Vicky and Sam ordered Dosa and Fanta and has and Oppo phone.

5. The person who is on the left of the person in White shirt does not eat Pasta but drinks Sprite and has a Xiaomi phone.

6. Tej has ordered Dhokla and the color of his shirt is Green. He is facing the person who has ordered Dosa.

7. The person who has ordered Idili is seated opposite to the person wearing a Blue shirt, while the person whose shirt is of Green color is on the left of the person who has ordered Biriyani.

8. Rudra has not ordered Pizza while Sam has not ordered Idili but he drinks Pepsi.

9. The person who has ordered Pasta is on the immediate right of the person in White shirt but on the immediate left of the person who has ordered Pizza , Limca and has a Samsung phone.

164. Who among the following wears a Blue shirt?

(1) Rahul   (2) Vicky

(3) Gaur   (4) Tej

(5) Rudra

165. Which mobile phone does the person, who orders Pizza, have?

(1) Samsung   (2) Oppo

(3) Asus   (4) Xiaomi

(5) Motorola

166. Which beverage was ordered by the person sitting opposite to the person wearing a White shirt?

(1) Coke   (2) Sprite

(3) Limca   (4) Frooti

(5) Pepsi

167. Which among the following is a valid combination?

(1) Tej - Dhokla - Oppo

(2) Sam - Dosa - Pepsi

(3) Blue - Samsung - Sprite

(4) Red - Coke - Gaur

(5) Rahul - Yellow - Nokia

168. Who are the immediate neighbours of Gaur?

(1) Rudra - Sam   (2) Sam - Tej

(3) Sam - Rahul   (4) Tej - Rudra

(5) Vicky - Rudra

Directions (Q. 169 to 173): In the following questions, the symbols #, %, @, $ and © are used with the following meanings illustrated.

'P # Q' means 'P is not smaller than Q'

'P % Q' means 'P is not greater than Q'.

'P @ Q' means 'P is neither smaller than nor equal to Q'.

'P $ Q' means 'P is neither greater than nor equal to Q'.

'P © Q' means 'P is neither smaller than nor greater than Q'.

In each of the following questions assuming the given statements to be true, find out which of the two conclusions I and II given below them is/are **definitely true**.

(1) if only conclusion I is true.

(2) if only conclusion II is true.

(3) if either conclusion I or conclusion II is true.

(4) if neither conclusion I nor conclusion II is true.

(5) if both conclusions I and II are true.

169. **Statement:** R % N,   N # F,   F @ B

     Conclusions: I. F © R

                 II. B $ N

170. **Statement:** H © W,   W % R,   R @ F

     Conclusions: I. R © H

                 II. R @ H

171. **Statement:** M $ T,   T @ K,   K © D

     Conclusions: I. D $ T

                 II. K $ M

172. **Statement:** H @ W,   W $ M,   M # K

     Conclusions: I. K $ W

                 II. H @ M

173. **Statement:** F # K,   K $ B,   B % M

     Conclusions: I. M @ F

                 II. B @ F

Directions (Q. 174 to 178): Each questions is followed by three statements. You have to study the question and all the three statements given and decide whether any information provided in the statement(s) is redundant and can be dispensed with while answering the questions.

174. At what time will the train reach city X from city Y?

    I. The train crosses another train of equal length of 200 metres and running in opposite direction in 15 sec.

    II. The train leaves city Y at 7.15 a.m. for city X situated at a distance at a distance of 560 km.

    III. The 300 metre long train crosses a signal pole in 10 sec.

(1) I Only   (2) II Only

(3) III Only   (4) II and III Only

(5) All I, II and III are required to answer the question.

175. What is the amount saved by Sahil per month from his salary?

   I.   Sahil spends 25% of his salary on food, 35% on medicine and education.

   II.   Sahil spends ₹4,000 per month on food and 15% on entertainment and saves the remaining amount.

   III.   Sahil spends ₹2,500 per month on medicine and education and saves the remaining amount.

(1) II Only

(2) III Only

(3) II and III Both

(4) II or III Only

(5) Question cannot be answered even with information given in all three statements.

176. What is the rate of interest percentage per annum?

   I.   The amount becomes ₹11,025 at compound interest after 2 years.

   II.   The same amount with simple interest becomes ₹11,000 after two years.

   III.   The amount invested is ₹10,000.

(1) I or II or III Only

(2) I or II Only

(3) II and III Only

(4) I or III Only

(5) All I, II and III are required to answer the question.

177. What is the ratio of the present ages of Rohan and his father?

   I.   Five years ago Rohan's age was one-fifth of his father's age that time.

   II.   Two years ago the sum of the ages of Rohan and his father was 36.

   III.   The sum of the ages of Rohan, his mother and his father is 62.

(1) I Only   (2) I and II Only

(3) III Only   (4) II or III Only

(5) I or III only

178. What will be the share of P in the profit earned by P, Q and R together?

   I.   P, Q and R invested total amount of ₹25,000 for a period of two years.

   II.   The profit earned at the end of two years is 30%.

   III.   The amount invested by Q is equal to the amount invested by P and R together.

(1) I Only

(2) II Only

(3) III Only

(4) All I, II and III are required to answer the question.

(5) Question cannot be answered even with information given in all three statements.

Directions (Q. 179 to 181): Answer the questions on the basis of the information given below.

Two boys P and Q start walking from their school. P walks 35 m in the direction of the rising sun and takes a left turn and then walks for 45 m, while Q walks 33 m towards north and then he turns 71° in the clockwise direction and walks for another 37 m before meeting P at a crossing. From there, both start walking towards east. After walking for 2 m, Q takes a right turn and walks 18 m further to reach his home. Whereas after walking for 30 m, P takes a left turn and walks 27 m further to reach his home.

179. How far is P's home from his school?

(1) 85 m   (2) 97 m

(3) 80 m   (4) 77 m

(5) 89 m

180. In which direction is the school from P's home?

(1) North-East   (2) South-East

(3) West   (4) North-west

(5) South-West

181. What is the distance between the homes of P and Q?

(1) 41 m   (2) 45 m

(3) 53 m   (4) 61 m

(5) 65 m

Directions (Q. 182 to 185): Answer the following questions on the basis of the information given below.

In a certain code 'he was dancing on' is written as 'lh aj ey ag', 'he on the floor' is written as 'ag ev aj es', 'he was of dancing' is written as 'ag ib lh ey' and 'his house dancing floor' is written as 'ev md ey oz'.

182. What does 'ib' stand for?

(a) was   (2) dancing

(3) of   (4) he

(5) on

183. 'at ev md' could be a code for which of the following?

(1) floor house party   (2) his house was

(3) the dancing his   (4) floor of house

(5) on his dancing

184. What is the code for 'was'?

(1) ey   (2) ag

(3) ib   (4) aj

(5) lh

185. Which of the following may represent 'he his on'?

(1) aj ib oz   (2) md oz ag

(3) oz ag aj   (4) oz ag ey

(5) md ib aj

Directions (Q. 186 to 191): In each of the questions below, there are four statements followed by four conclusions numbered I, II, III & IV. You have to take the given statements to be true even if they seem to be at variance with commonly known facts. Read all the conclusions and then decide which of the given conclusions logically follow(s) from the given statements disregarding commonly known facts.

186. **Statements:**

All rockets are poles.

Some poles are trams.

Some trams are ropes.

All ropes are tents.

Conclusions:

I.   Some tents are trams.

II. Some ropes are rockets.

III. Some trams are rockets.

IV. Some poles are rockets.

(1) Only I and II follow

(2) Only I, II and III follow

(3) Only I and III follow

(4) Only I and IV follow

(5) None of these

187. **Statements:**

All dials are mirrors.

All mirrors are spoons.

Some spoons are decks.

Some decks are chairs.

Conclusions:

I.   Some decks are mirrors.

II. Some spoons are dials.

III. Some decks are dials.

IV. Some chairs are spoons.

(1) All follow   (2) Only I follows

(3) Only II follows   (4) Only III follows

(5) Only IV follows

188. **Statements:**

Some houses are forests.

All forests are trees.

Some trees are hills.

All hills are buses.

Conclusions:

I.   Some buses are trees.

II. Some trees are houses.

III. Some hills are houses.

IV. Some buses are forests.

(1) Only I and II follow

(2) Only I, II and IV follow

(3) Only I, II and III follow

(4) All I, II, III and IV follow

(5) None of these

189. **Statements:**

Some lakes are rivers.

Some rivers are mountains.

Some mountains are books.

Some books are papers.

Conclusions:

I.   Some books are rivers.

II. Some papers are lakes.

III. Some mountains are lakes.

IV. No paper is a lake.

(1) All follow

(2) Only either II or IV follows

(3) Only II follows

(4) Only IV follows

(5) Only either II or IV and III follow

190. **Statements:**

Some tigers are horses.

All horses are goats.

All goats are dogs.

Some dogs are cats.

Conclusions:

I.   Some cats are tigers.

II. Some dogs are horses.

III. Some goats are tigers.

IV. Some cats are horses.

(1) Only I and II follow

(2) Only I, II and III follow

(3) Only II and III follow

(4) Only II, III and IV follow

(5) None of these

191. **Statements:**

All notebooks are pens.

No pen is a table.

Some tables are desks.

All desks are tanks.

Conclusions:

I.   Some tanks are pens.

II. Some desks are notebooks.

III. Some tanks are tables.

IV. No tank is a pen.

(1) Only I follows

(2) Only III follows

(3) Only IV follows

(4) Only either I or IV follows

(5) Only either I or IV and III follow

Directions (Q. 192 to 196): A passage is given below followed by several possible inferences which can be drawn from the facts stated in the passage. You have to examine each inference separately in the context of the passage and decide upon the degree of its truth or falsity.

(1) if the inference is 'definitely true', i.e., it properly follows from the statement of facts given.

(2) if the inference is 'probably true' though not 'definitely true' in the light of the facts given.

(3) if the 'data are inadequate', i.e., from the facts given you cannot say whether the data is likely to be true or false.

(4) if the inference is 'probably false' though not 'definitely false' in the light of the facts.

(5) if the inference is 'definitely false', i.e., it cannot be drawn from the given facts or contradicts the given facts.

The pace of recruitment has unmistakably picked up in the last few months. After two abysmal quarters business sentiment has turned positive. A flurry of hiring activity has been observed across the manufacturing sector and the IT and ITES sector catering to telecom and legal process outsourcing. The advent of new players and an aggressive expansion of telecom giants has seen a bullish outlook for the industry with a promise of exponential growth. But is the worst over for businesses across the spectrum? Firms are going back to the drawing board and dusting off their plans to see if there is scope for at least incremental hiring in specific domains where they want to build expertise. Besides that, there are few signs to show that there is a broad based revival in the market.

192. Many companies in the manufacturing sector have decided to reduce their fresh intake of employees next year.

193. Persons with legal qualifications and expertise will earn more in the future.

194. Most companies across sectors have decided to increase their manpower requirement manifold.

195. The telecom sector has experienced negative growth in the past few years.

196. Companies in various sectors have projected higher business growth in the near future.

Directions (Q. 197 and 198) : In each question below, a statement is followed by two assumptions numbered I and II. An assumption is something supposed or taken for granted You have to consider the statement and the following assumptions and decide which of the assumptions is implicit in the statement.

(1) if only assumption I is implicit

(2) if only assumption II is implicit

(3) if either assumption I or assumption II is implicit

(4) if neither assumption I nor assumption II is implicit

(5) if both assumptions I and II are implicit

197. Statement:

If parking space is not available in office, park your vehicles in the mall and walk to the office.

Assumptions:

I. The mall is at a walkable distance from the office.

II. The office does not allow visitors' vehicles in its premises.

198. Statement:

Farmers must immediately switch-over to organic fertilizers from chemical fertilizers for better yield.

Assumptions:

I. All the farmers use only chemical fertilizers.

II. Organic fertilizers are available for the farmers.

Directions (Q. 199 and 200): In each question below, two statements (A) and (B) are given. These statements may be either independent causes or may be effects of independent causes or of a common cause. One of these statements may be the effect of the other statement. Read both the statements and decide which of the following answer choices correctly depicts the relationship between these two statements.

(1) if statement (A) is the cause and statement (B) is its effect

(2) if statement (B) is the cause and statement (A) is its effect

(3) if both statements (A) and (B) are independent causes

(4) if both statements (A) and (B) are effects of independent causes

(5) if both statements (A) and (B) are effects of some common cause

199. A. State Government has ordered immediate ban on airing of certain movie channels on television.

B. A few social activists have come together and demanded ban on telecasting 'adult' movies on television.

200. A. Employment scenario in the country has remarkably improved recently.

B. The number of prospective job-seekers going abroad has increased recently.

ANSWERS

1. (1)	**2.** (2)	**3.** (5)	**4.** (4)	**5.** (3)	**6.** (2)	**7.** (5)	**8.** (1)	**9.** (3)	**10.** (3)
11. (5)	**12.** (3)	**13.** (1)	**14.** (5)	**15.** (1)	**16.** (1)	**17.** (3)	**18.** (4)	**19.** (5)	**20.** (1)
21. (3)	**22.** (2)	**23.** (3)	**24.** (5)	**25.** (5)	**26.** (2)	**27.** (3)	**28.** (4)	**29.** (5)	**30.** (2)
31. (4)	**32.** (2)	**33.** (3)	**34.** (4)	**35.** (2)	**36.** (1)	**37.** (2)	**38.** (1)	**39.** (3)	**40.** (3)
41. (4)	**42.** (1)	**43.** (2)	**44.** (4)	**45.** (4)	**46.** (1)	**47.** (2)	**48.** (2)	**49.** (3)	**50.** (2)
51. (2)	**52.** (2)	**53.** (1)	**54.** (1)	**55.** (1)	**56.** (2)	**57.** (2)	**58.** (5)	**59.** (3)	**60.** (1)
61. (2)	**62.** (2)	**63.** (5)	**64.** (4)	**65.** (5)	**66.** (2)	**67.** (3)	**68.** (1)	**69.** (4)	**70.** (1)
71. (3)	**72.** (5)	**73.** (4)	**74.** (1)	**75.** (3)	**76.** (1)	**77.** (2)	**78.** (1)	**79.** (2)	**80.** (3)
81. (2)	**82.** (4)	**83.** (4)	**84.** (3)	**85.** (2)	**86.** (3)	**87.** (2)	**88.** (4)	**89.** (2)	**90.** (3)
91. (3)	**92.** (2)	**93.** (1)	**94.** (3)	**95.** (2)	**96.** (5)	**97.** (3)	**98.** (2)	**99.** (2)	**100.** (1)
101. (2)	**102.** (4)	**103.** (1)	**104.** (3)	**105.** (2)	**106.** (4)	**107.** (5)	**108.** (1)	**109.** (1)	**110.** (2)
111. (5)	**112.** (1)	**113.** (3)	**114.** (3)	**115.** (1)	**116.** (1)	**117.** (3)	**118.** (2)	**119.** (3)	**120.** (2)
121. (2)	**122.** (3)	**123.** (1)	**124.** (4)	**125.** (5)	**126.** (4)	**127.** (5)	**128.** (2)	**129.** (3)	**130.** (3)
131. (2)	**132.** (2)	**133.** (1)	**134.** (1)	**135.** (1)	**136.** (3)	**137.** (2)	**138.** (1)	**139.** (5)	**140.** (3)
141. (4)	**142.** (5)	**143.** (2)	**144.** (1)	**145.** (3)	**146.** (5)	**147.** (4)	**148.** (2)	**149.** (4)	**150.** (3)
151. (3)	**152.** (2)	**153.** (4)	**154.** (2)	**155.** (3)	**156.** (1)	**157.** (4)	**158.** (5)	**159.** (3)	**160.** (4)
161. (1)	**162.** (2)	**163.** (3)	**164.** (3)	**165.** (1)	**166.** (4)	**167.** (5)	**168.** (2)	**169.** (2)	**170.** (3)
171. (1)	**172.** (4)	**173.** (4)	**174.** (1)	**175.** (4)	**176.** (1)	**177.** (3)	**178.** (5)	**179.** (2)	**180.** (5)
181. (3)	**182.** (3)	**183.** (1)	**184.** (5)	**185.** (3)	**186.** (4)	**187.** (3)	**188.** (1)	**189.** (2)	**190.** (3)
191. (5)	**192.** (3)	**193.** (3)	**194.** (4)	**195.** (4)	**196.** (2)	**197.** (1)	**198.** (2)	**199.** (2)	**200.** (4)

EXPLANATIONS

81. 2 The sentence is correct in its given form.

82. 4 DABC is the correct sequence.

83. 4 The correct sequence is DABC.

84. 3 The correct sequence is BCAD.

85. 2 The sentence is correct in its given form.

86. 3 The other options don't make any sense.

87. 2 The other options are not making any sense.

88. 4 The other options are not making any sense.

89. 2 The other options don't match and so, the meaning is altered.

90. 3 Only AF is a logically consistent sentence.

91. 3 The other options are not correct.

92. 2 The other options are incorrect.

93. 1 Only "however" can act as a connector.

94. 3 The correct sentence connector is "whenever."

95. 2 The other options are contextually not feasible.

96. 5 All the three words are in correct sequence.

97. 3 For A, a correct word could've been "lost."

98. 2 For B, an appropriate word could've been "confrontation."

99. 2 For B, an appropriate word can be "sanctions."

100. 1 For C, an appropriate word could've been "ordinary."

101. 2 The other options are out of scope.

102. 4 In the light of the first paragraph, both statements a and c are true. NAFTA is not in vogue anymore. Hence, b is incorrect.

103. 1 Refer to the paragraph beginning with, "The administration had also wanted to eliminate unfair subsidies. It also wanted state-owned companies, such as Mexico's Pemex, to operate more like private corporations. In 2013, Mexican President Enrique Peña Nieto allowed foreign direct investment in Pemex. But the company is a source of national pride, so it's unlikely to be completely privatized."

104. 3 Refer to the sentence, "There can be no doubt that Mr. Trump's protectionist trade policy, including the current deal which increases restrictions on cross-border trade in order to protect U.S. jobs, is bad for the global economy."

105. 2 Refer to the sentence beginning with, "The right response to Mr. Trump's trade war will be to abstain from any mutually destructive tit-for-tat tariff regimes while simultaneously pushing for peace talks."

106. 4 Refer to the second sentence of the first paragraph. The other options are out of scope.

107. 5 Refer to the third sentence of the second paragraph. Other options are either narrow or out of scope.

108. 1 Refer to the first paragraph. The author mentions that in the past only the richer states contributed to the GDP but during 2004-2009, even traditionally poorer states have contributed to the GDP. Hence, it can be said that the growth has been more inclusive in nature during the said period. The other options are out of scope.

109. 1 Refer to the second sentence of the second paragraph. The other options are out of scope.

110. 2 Refer to the first sentence of the third paragraph. The other options are out of scope.

For questions 111 to 115:

Time taken to produce two units by Process-1 = 5 minutes
Time taken to produce two units by Process-2 = 6 minutes
The number of units produced by Process-1 in one shift

$$= \frac{360}{5} \times 2 = 144$$

The number of units produced by Process-2 in one shift

$$= \frac{360}{6} \times 2 = 120$$

Cost for Process-1 per shift, when running at its full capacity

$$= 500 + \frac{250}{1000} \times 144 + 500 = \text{Rs. } 1,036$$

Cost for Process-2 per shift, when running at its full capacity

$$= 330 + \frac{150}{1000} \times 120 + 501 = \text{Rs. } 849.$$

111. 5 To produce 288, 400, 450 or 500 units, Process-1 would be more cost effective than Process-2.

112. 1 Cost of producing 6000 units using Process-1

$$= 42 \times 500 + \frac{250}{1000} \times 6000 + 42 \times 500 = \text{Rs. } 43,500$$

Cost of producing 6000 units using Process-2
$= 50 \times 849 = \text{Rs. } 42,450$
Hence, the difference = Rs. 1,050.

113. 3 Required time $= \frac{5}{2} \times 1800 \times \frac{1}{60} = 75$ hours.

114. 3 Time taken by process $-1 = \frac{5}{2} \times 1200 \times \frac{1}{60}$

$$= 2.5 \times 1200 \times \frac{1}{60} \text{ hours}$$

Time taken by process$-2 = \frac{6}{2} \times 1200 \times \frac{1}{60}$

$$= 3 \times 1200 \times \frac{1}{60} \text{ hours}$$

Hence, required ratio $= \frac{2.5}{3} = 5 : 6$.

115. 1 Cost of producing 20000 units using process-1

$$= 139 \times 500 + \frac{250}{1000} \times 20000 + 139 \times 500$$

$$= \text{Rs. } 1,44,000.$$

116. 1 Total number of B. Tech employees

$$= 2568 \times \frac{75}{100} = 1926$$

Male B.Tech employees = 1275
Female B.Tech employees = 1926 – 1275 = 651

Hence, required percentage $= \frac{651}{2568} \times 100 \approx 25\%$

117. 3 Percentage of women employees:

Ghana $= \frac{7}{15} \times 100 \approx 46.7\%$

Denmark $= \frac{2}{5} \times 100 = 40\%$

Haiti $= \frac{5}{14} \times 100 \approx 35.7\%$

Egypt $= \frac{6}{13} \times 100 \approx 46\%$

Brazil $= \frac{5}{16} \times 100 = 31.25\%$

118. 2 Male employees in:

Brazil $= 2880 \times \frac{11}{16} = 1990$

China $= \frac{2310 \times 10}{21} = 1100$

Haiti $= \frac{3360 \times 9}{14} = 2160$

Egypt $= \frac{2054 \times 7}{13} = 1106$

Total male employees = 1980 + 1100 + 2160 + 1106 = 6346

Female employees in:

Australia = $\dfrac{2568 \times 7}{12} = 1498$

Denmark = $\dfrac{3575 \times 2}{5} = 1430$

France = $\dfrac{2788 \times 21}{41} = 1428$

Ghana = $\dfrac{3720 \times 7}{15} = 1736$

Total female employees = 1498 + 1430 + 1428 + 1736

= 6092

Hence, required ratio = 6346 : 6092 = 3173 : 3046.

119. 3 B.Tech employees in:

Australia = $\dfrac{2568 \times 75}{100} = 1926$

Brazil = $\dfrac{2880 \times 65}{100} = 1872$

Denmark = $\dfrac{3575 \times 60}{100} = 2145$

Egypt = $\dfrac{2054 \times 50}{100} = 1027$

Total B.Tech employees

= 1926 + 1872 + 2145 + 1027 = 6970

China = $\dfrac{2310 \times 40}{100} = 924$

France = $\dfrac{2788 \times 75}{100} = 2091$

Ghana = $\dfrac{3720 \times 55}{100} = 2046$

Haiti = $\dfrac{3360 \times 80}{100} = 2688$

Total B.Tech employees

= 924 + 2091 + 2046 + 2688 = 7749

Hence, required difference

$= \dfrac{7749}{4} - \dfrac{6970}{4} = \dfrac{1}{4}(7749 - 6970) = \dfrac{1}{4} \times 779 \approx 195.$

120. 2 Average employees per office in:

Australia = $\dfrac{2568}{16} = 160.5$

Brazil = $\dfrac{2880}{18} = 160$

China = $\dfrac{2310}{14} = 165$

Denmark = $\dfrac{3575}{22} = 162.5$

Egypt = $\dfrac{2054}{13} = 158$

France = $\dfrac{2788}{17} = 164$

Ghana = $\dfrac{3720}{24} = 155$

Haiti = $\dfrac{3360}{21} = 160$

121. 2 The series is moving as $2^3 - 2^2$, $3^3 + 3^2$, $4^3 - 4^2$, $5^3 + 5^2$, $6^3 - 6^2$, $7^3 + 7^2$. Hence, the correct answer would be option (2).

122. 3 The series is moving as $1 \times 2 \times 3$, $4 \times 5 \times 6$, $7 \times 8 \times 9$, $10 \times 11 \times 12$, $13 \times 14 \times 15$. Hence, the correct answer would be option (3).

123. 1 The series is moving as $1^2 + 2^2$, $3^2 + 4^2$, $5^2 + 6^2$,.... and so on.

Hence, the correct answer would be option (1).

124. 4 The series is moving as the squares of the prime numbers in increasing order.

Hence, the correct answer would be option (4).

125. 5 The series is moving as $1^2 + 2^3$, $3^2 + 4^3$, $5^2 + 6^3$.... and so on.

Hence, the correct answer would be option (5).

126. 4 Average speed $= \dfrac{\text{Total distance covered}}{\text{Total time taken}}$

$= \dfrac{39 + 25}{\dfrac{45 + 35}{60}} = \dfrac{64 \times 60}{80} = 48 \ \text{km/hr}$

127. 5 Total marks = 24 × 56 = 1344

Total of actual marks

$= 1344 - (44 + 45 + 61) + (48 + 59 + 67) = 1368$

Actual Average $= \dfrac{1368}{24} = 57$

128. 2 Let the marked price of the watch be x.

Cost price for the retailer $= x \times 0.8 \times 0.8 = 0.64x$

Selling price of the retailer $= 0.64x \times 1.5 = 0.96x$

Hence, required percentage

$= \dfrac{x - 0.96x}{x} \times 100 = 4\% \ \text{less.}$

129. 3 Let Raman's present age be x years.

$\therefore$ his daughter's present age $= \dfrac{x}{3}$ years

His mother's present age $= \dfrac{13x}{9}$ years

Now, according to the question,

$x + \dfrac{x}{3} + \dfrac{13x}{9} = 125$

$\Rightarrow \dfrac{9x + 3x + 13x}{9} = 125$

$\Rightarrow 25x = 125 \times 9$

$\Rightarrow x = \dfrac{125 \times 9}{25} = 45$

$\therefore$ required difference $= \dfrac{13x}{9} - \dfrac{x}{3} = \dfrac{13x - 3x}{9} = \dfrac{10x}{9}$

$= \dfrac{10}{9} \times 45 = 50$ years.

130. 3 Initial quantity of water in solution $= 50 \times \dfrac{80}{100}$

$= 40$ L

Let x litres water should be mixed.

According to question, we have

$\dfrac{40 + x}{50 + x} = \dfrac{90}{100}$

$\therefore x = 50$

131. 2 **Quantity I :**

Different number of ways of arranging 5 men or 5 women = 5!

Number of ways of arranging 5 men and 5 women such that no two men or women sit together = 2 × 5! × 5!

Quantity II :

Number of ways of arranging 5 men and 5 women such that all men sit together = 6! × 5!

Therefore, 2 × 5! × 5! < 6! × 5!

Hence, Quantity I < Quantity II

132. 2 $\because$ S is an acute angle.

$\therefore$ (a + 40) + a < 90

or, (2a + 40) < 90

or, 2a < 50

or, a < 25°

Hence, Quantity I < Quantity II

133. 1 **Quantity I :**

Let required number be 10x + y.

$\therefore$ 10y + x = 10x + y + 36

$\Rightarrow$ 9y – 9x = 36

$\Rightarrow$ y – x = 4

Thus, unit's place digit of the number should be 4 more than the ten's place digit of the number.

$\therefore$ Such possible numbers from 1 to 63 are = 15, 26, 37, 48, 59

Hence, required probability $= \dfrac{5}{63}$

Quantity II :

Possible numbers from 1 to 63 = 8, 24, 40, 56

Therefore, required probability $= \dfrac{4}{63}$

Hence, Quantity I > Quantity II.

134. 1 **Quantity I :**

Area of quadrilateral BFDE

= Area of rectangle ABCD – Area of $\triangle$ABE – Area of $\triangle$DCF

= 120 – 30 – 25 = 65 cm²

Quantity II :

15 cm²

Hence, Quantity I > Quantity II.

135. 1 **Quantity I :**

Ratio of investment of A, B and C

= (3000 × 4 + 1800 × 5 + 3600 × 3) : (4000 × 4 + 8000 × 5) : (14000 + 33600)

= 31800 : 56000 : 47600 = 159 : 280 : 238

Profit of C $= \dfrac{238}{677} \times 6770000 = $ Rs. 2,38,000

Quantity II :

Average of profit earned by (A + B + C) $\approx$ Rs. 2,25,666

Hence, Quantity I > Quantity II.

136. 3 Let the cost price of one cow be Rs. x.

So, cost price of other cow = Rs. (50000 – x)

Now, 0.9x + 1.1(50000 – x) = 50500

$\Rightarrow$ x = 22500

Hence, cost price of the cows are Rs.22,500 and Rs. 27,500.

137. 2 Let the work done by a man and a woman be 'm' and 'n' units respectively. Then,

12(3m + 4w) = 10(4m + 3w)

$\Rightarrow$ 2m = 9w

Total work = 10(4m + 3w) = 210 w

Hence, required number of days

$= \dfrac{210w}{2m + 3w} = \dfrac{210}{12} = 17\dfrac{1}{2}.$

138. 1 $\quad CI = \left[\left(1+\dfrac{r}{100}\right)^{t} - 1\right]$

$$594.5 = 5800\left[\left(1+\dfrac{r}{100}\right)^{2} - 1\right]$$

$$\Rightarrow \dfrac{594.5}{5800} + 1 = \left(1+\dfrac{r}{100}\right)^{2}$$

$$\Rightarrow \dfrac{6394.5}{5800} = \left(1+\dfrac{r}{100}\right)^{2} \Rightarrow \dfrac{r}{100} = 1.05 - 1$$

$$\Rightarrow \dfrac{r}{100} = 0.05 \Rightarrow r = 5\%.$$

139. 5 Let their present ages be 13x and 17x.

Then, $\dfrac{13x - 4}{17x - 4} = \dfrac{11}{15}$

Solving this, we get

x = 2

$\therefore$ Required ratio $= \dfrac{13 \times 2 + 6}{17 \times 2 + 6} = \dfrac{32}{40} = \dfrac{4}{5}.$

140. 3 Ratio of initial investments $= \left(\dfrac{5}{3}, \dfrac{3}{2}, \dfrac{8}{5}\right) \Rightarrow 50 : 45 : 48$

	A		B		C
Initial investment	50	:	45	:	48
Investment	50×12	:	45×12	:	(48×4) + (48×1.5×8)
Final investment	50	:	45	:	64

Hence, A's share $= \dfrac{50}{159} \times$ Rs. 39,750 = Rs. 12,500.

For questions 141 to 145:

M	H	I	L	K	J	↓
IIT	IISER	ISI	TIFR	CMI	IISc	
IISc	TIFR	IIT	IISER	ISI	CMI	↑
W	X	U	Y	V	Z	

141. 4   **142.** 5   **143.** 2
144. 1   **145.** 3

For questions 146 to 150:

Person	Sport	Day	Mode of transport
L	Table Tennis	Tuesday	Cycle
M	Football	Friday	Car
N	Archery	Monday	Bike
O	Hockey	Thursday	Walk
P	Basketball	Thursday	Cycle
Q	Swimming	Tuesday	Bike
R	Cricket	Friday	Walk
S	Badminton	Wednesday	Car

146. 5   **147.** 4   **148.** 2
149. 4   **150.** 3

For questions 151 to 153:

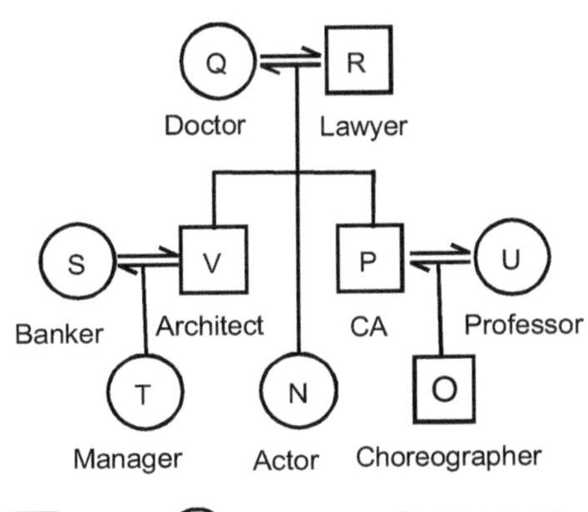

151. 3   **152.** 2   **153.** 4

For questions 154 to 158: All of the given information can be tabulated as:

Friend	Department	Organisation		
		ABC	PQR	JKL
M	Production	✔		
N	Analysis		✔	
P	Marketing			✔
D	HR		✔	
E	Research			✔
F	Design	✔		
G	Admin		✔	

154. 2   **155.** 3   **156.** 1
157. 4   **158.** 5

For questions 159 to 163 :

Month	Date	Lecturer	No. of students
April	8	C	72
April	24	F	84
May	8	A	67
May	24	G	55
June	8	E	80
June	24	J	68
September	8	B	64
September	24	I	78
December	8	D	77
December	24	H	69

159. 3   **160.** 4   **161.** 1
162. 2   **163.** 3

For questions 164 to 168:

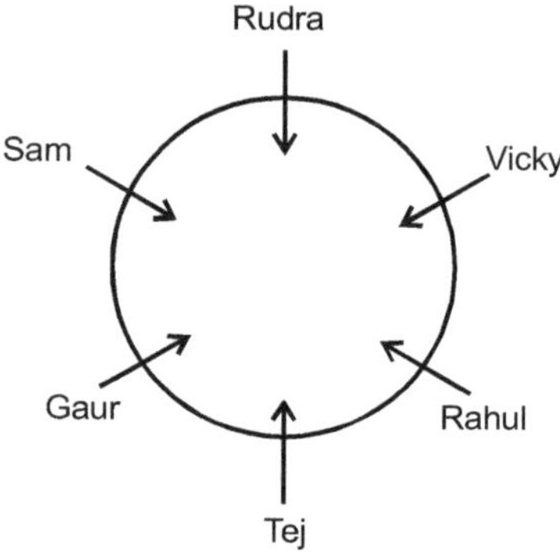

	Positions			Opposite Positions		
	1/4	2/5	3/6	4/1	5/2	6/3
Person	Tej	Rahul	Vicky	Rudra	Sam	Gaur
Food	Dhokla	Biriyani	Idili	Dosa	Pasta	Pizza
Colour	Green	Yellow	Red	White	Black	Blue
Beverage	Frooti	Coke	Sprite	Fanta	Pepsi	Limca
Phone	Asus	Nokia	Xiaomi	Oppo	Motorola	Samsung

164. 3 **165.** 1 **166.** 4

167. 5 **168.** 2

169. 2 $R \le N$ …(i)

$N \ge F$ …(ii)

$F > B$ …(iii)

From (i) and (ii), F and R can't be compared. Hence I does not follow.

Combining (ii) and (iii), we get $N \ge F > B$ or $N > B$ or $B < N$. Hence II follows.

170. 3 $H = W$ …(i)

$W \le R$ …(ii)

$R > F$ …(iii)

From (i) and (ii), $H = W \le R$ or $R \ge H$.

Hence, either I (R = H) or II (R > H) follows.

171. 1 $M < T$ …(i)

$T > K$ …(ii)

$K = D$ …(iii)

From (ii) and (iii), $T > K = D$ or $D < T$.

Hence I follows

From (i) and (ii), K and M can't be compared. Hence II does not follow.

172. 4 $H > W$ …(i)

$W < M$ …(ii)

$M \ge K$ …(iii)

From (ii) and (iii), K and W can't be compared. Hence I does not follow.

From (i) and (ii), H and M cannot be compared. Hence II does not follow.

173. 4 $F \ge K$ …(i)

$K < B$ …(ii)

$B \le M$ …(iii)

From (i) and (ii), F can't be compared with B and consequently with M. Hence neither II nor I follows.

174. 1 (III) gives speed of the train. (II) gives the distance between x and y and also the starting time. Hence (II) and (III) are sufficient to answer the question. Therefore (I) is redundant and can be dispensed with.

175. 4 From (I) and (II) together or (I) and (III) together we can answer the question. Statement I is necessary so we can dispense either (II) or (III) only.

176. 1 We can answer the question from statement I and II both together or II and III together or I and III together.

So, at a time we can dispense either I or II or III only.

177. 3 Information given in (I) includes the age of his mother. So, (III) is useless. Only with the help of (I) and (II) we can get the answer.

178. 5 Even after using all the statements we cannot separate the combined profit of P and R.

179. 2

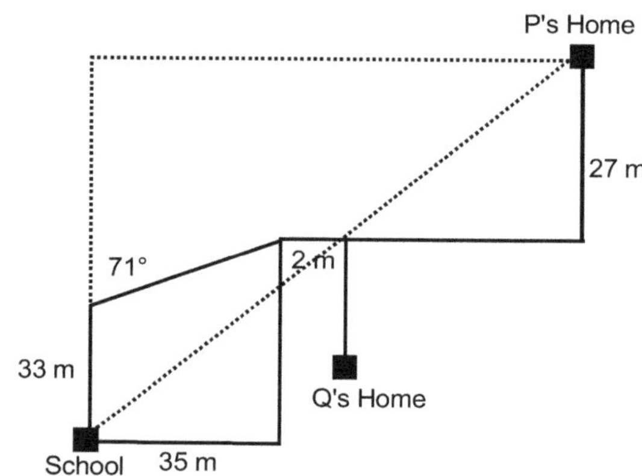

Distance between P's home and school

$$= \sqrt{72^2 + 65^2}$$

$$= \sqrt{5184 + 4225} = \sqrt{9409} = 97 \text{ m.}$$

180. 5

181. 3

Distance between boys' home

$$= \sqrt{28^2 + 45^2} = \sqrt{784 + 2025}$$

$$= \sqrt{2809} = 53 \text{ m.}$$

For questions 182 to 185:

Word	he	w as	dancing	on	the	floor	of	his	house
Code	ag	lh	ey	aj	es	ev	ib	md/oz	oz/md

182. 3   **183.** 1   **184.** 5   **185.** 3

186. 4 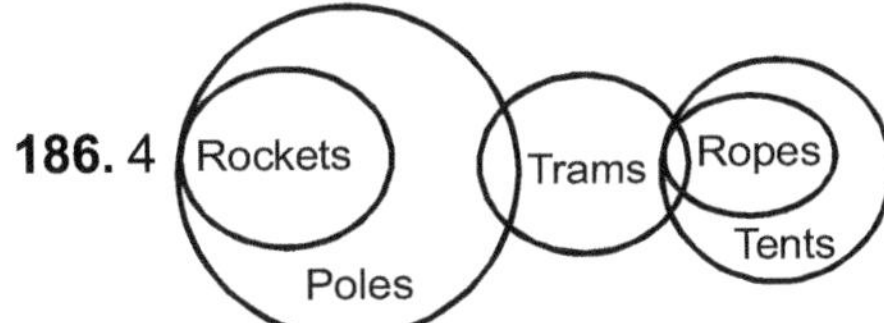

187. 3 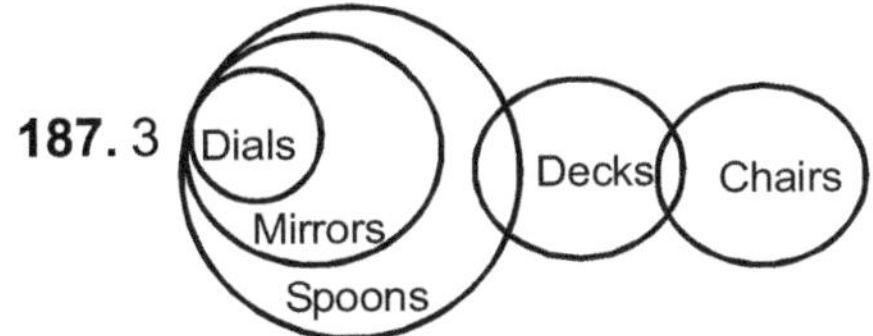

188. 1 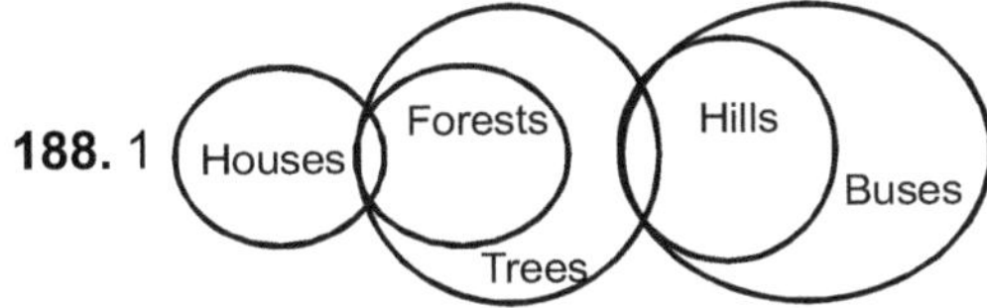

189. 2

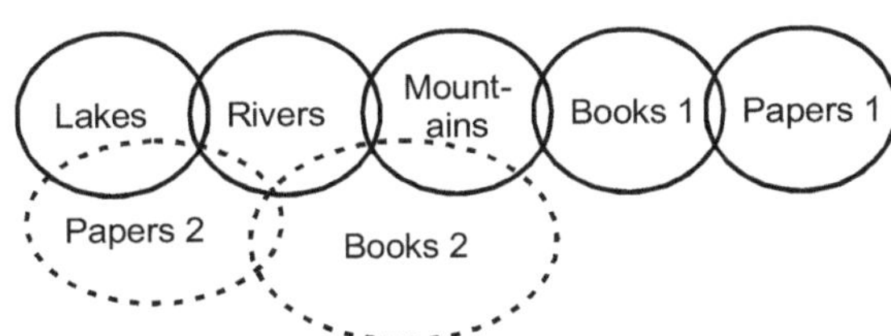

190. 3 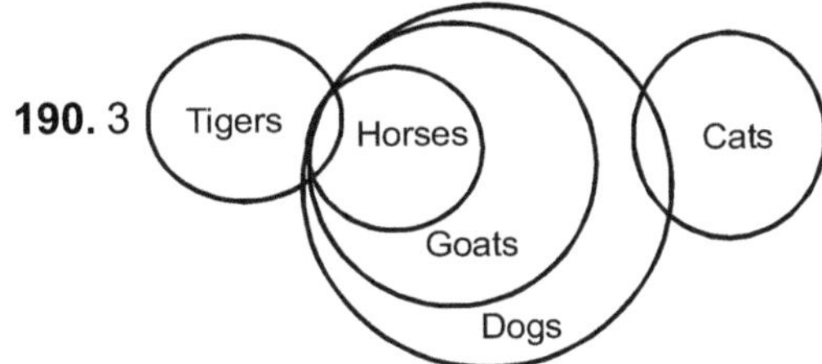

191. 5 Case 1

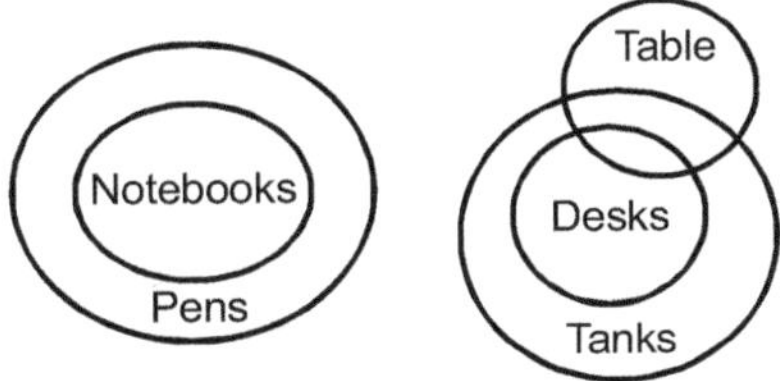

Case 2

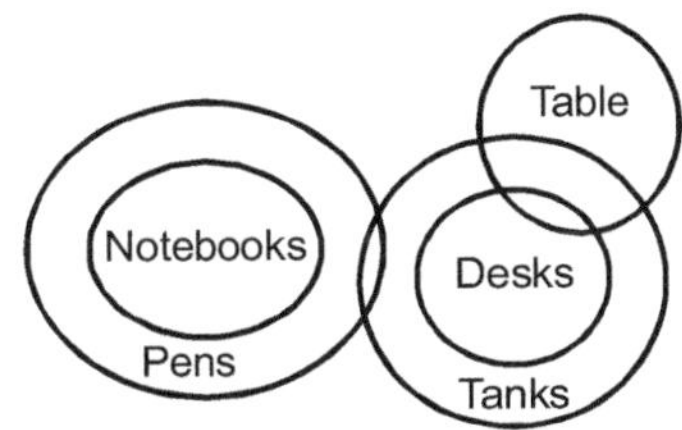

192. 3 The passage does not talk about the recruitment decision of manufacturing sector.

193. 3 The passage does not state whether the people with legal qualifications and expertise will earn more in future.

194. 4 Refer to the line "A flurry of hiring activity…….legal process outsourcing." This statement does not clearly talk about companies across various sectors.

195. 4 Refer to the line "The advent of new……across the spectrum?"

196. 2 Refer to the line "Firms are going back….revival in the market." Therefore, we can infer that companies in various sectors have projected higher business growth in the near future.

197. 1 If one has been asked to park one's vehicle in the mall and walk to office from there, then it can be safely assumed that the office is at a walk able distance. Assumption II is not implicit because it is possible that parking space is not available because it is full.

198. 2 Farmers in general have been asked to switch-over to organic fertilizers from chemical fertilizers. This does not mean that all farmers use chemical fertilizers. It is possible that a few farmers were already using organic fertilizers. So, assumption I is not implicit in the statement. Assumption II is implicit because farmers would not have been asked to switch if organic fertilizers were not available.

199. 2 Government has put a ban on airing of certain movie channels on television because social activists have demanded a ban on telecasting 'adult' movies on television.

200. 4 If job seekers go abroad, it can only marginally improve job scenario in India. There has to be some other cause behind 'remarkable' improvement of job scenario.

REASONING APTITUDE

Directions (1-5): Study the following information carefully and answer the questions given below:

Seven boxes A, B, C, D, E, F and G are kept one above the other containing different number of chocolates ranging from 10-90. Not more than Four boxes are kept above A. Two boxes are kept between A and the box containing 41 chocolates, which is kept below Box A. D contains thrice number of chocolates than box B. Box C contains 50 number of chocolates and is not kept at the top. The number of chocolates in box G is a cube of a number. Only one box is kept between box containing 41 chocolates and 39 chocolates. Box D has less number of chocolates than box A. One of the boxes contain 78 chocolates. Five boxes are kept between box containing 64 chocolates and Box C. Box G is immediately above box E. Box D is not kept immediately above or below box B. Three boxes are kept between box D and box F. Box D is above box F.

1. Which among the following box/boxes is kept exactly between Box D and Box B ?

   (a) G, E   (b) B, C

   (c) B, A   (d) F, C

   (e) none of these

2. How many chocolates are kept in box E?

   (a) 50   (b) 13

   (c) 78   (d) 41

   (e) none of these

3. Which among the following boxes contains the maximum and minimum number of chocolates respectively?

   (a) G, E   (b) B, D

   (c) C, A   (d) F, B

   (e) none of these

4. Which of the following combination is not true?

   (a) 50-D   (b) 13-B

   (c) 41-E   (d) 64-A

   (e) none of these

5. Which among the following boxes is kept immediately below box B?

   (a) G

   (b) C

   (c) A

   (d) F

   (e) none of these

Direction (6-10): Study the following information carefully to answer the given questions.

Number arrangement machine when given an input line of numbers rearranges them following a particular rule in each step. The following is an illustration of input and rearrangement.

Input: 91 53 72 14 39 24 85 76 61 67

Step I: 15 91 53 72 39 85 76 61 67 25

Step II: 40 15 91 72 85 76 61 67 25 54

Step III: 62 40 15 91 72 85 76 25 54 68

Step IV: 73 62 40 15 91 85 25 54 68 77

Step V: 86 73 62 40 15 25 54 68 77 92

Step V, is the last step

Input:- 58 40 99 28 63 84 16 34 71 87

6. How many numbers are there between 59 and the one which 3rd to left of 85 in step V?

   (a) One

   (b) More than three

   (c) Three

   (d) None

   (e) Two

7. How many numbers are there between the one which is 2nd from the left end and 99 in step II?

(a) One   (b) More than three

(c) Three   (d) None

(e) Two

8. What is the position of 35 from the left end in second last step?

(a) First   (b) Fifth

(c) Second   (d) Third

(e) Sixth

9. Which of the following number is 6th to the left of 29 in the III step?

(a) 35   (b) 59

(c) 17   (d) 99

(e) None of these

10. Which of the following number is 5th from the right end in step V?

(a) 35   (b) 59

(c) 17   (d) 29

(e) None of these

Direction (11-12): Study the following information carefully and answer the given question. Point Q is 15m south of point P. Point R is 10m east of point Q. Points S is 5m north of point R. Point T is 5m west of point S.

11. If Point U is 10m east of Point P, then Point S is how far and in which direction from point U?

(a) 10 m, north   (b) 5 m, south

(c) 15 m, north   (d) 10 m, south

(e) 5 m, north

12. Point P is in which direction from Point T?

(a) North-west

(b) South-east

(c) North

(d) South-west

(e) North-east

13. V is married to W. R is the only sister of W. A is the mother of R. A has three children. G is the niece of R and P. V has no sibling. R is unmarried. Then how is P related to V?

(a) Mother-in-law

(b) Sister

(c) Brother-in-law

(d) Brother

(e) None of these

Direction (14-16): Each of the questions below consists of a question and two statements numbered I and II given below it. You have to decide whether the data provided in the statements are sufficient to answer the question. Read both the statements and give answer

(a) if the data in statement I alone are sufficient to answer the question, while the data in statement II alone are not sufficient to answer the question.

(b) if the data in statement II alone are sufficient to answer the question, while the data in statement I alone are not sufficient to answer the question.

(c) if the data either in statement I alone or in statement II alone are sufficient to answer the question.

(d) if the data in both statements I and II together are not sufficient to answer the question.

(e) if the data in both statements I and II together are necessary to answer the question.

14. Statement: Six boys J, K, L, M, N, O are there in a classroom each of them is of different heights. Who among the following is the tallest?

I. M is taller than N and K. J is taller than M but not as tall as O. L is taller than K.

II. M is taller than only three boys. J is taller than K.

15. Statement: Six persons R, S, T, U, V, W lives on a six storey building such as ground floor is numbered as 1 and above it 2 floor and so on ... upto top floor numbered as 7. How many persons live between R and T?

I. T lives on an even numbered floor but not on top floor. Only two persons live between W and T. R lives below W.

II. Four persons live between S and U. No one lives between S and T. V lives immediately above R.

16. Statement: Six persons A, B, C, D, E, F are sitting in row. All of them are facing north direction. Who among the following sits second from the right end?

I. B sits at end extreme end of the row. A sits second to the right of B. Only one person sits between A and C. E sits immediate right of C.

II. E sits third to the right of D. Only one person sits between E and A. F sits to the right to E. C is an immediate neighbor of E.

17. In the given coding system 'Now they live for' is coded as 'gn mu sy fd' and 'go now run for' is coded as "gn sy mo it". Which of the following statement among the given is required to code 'go there now'?

   I. 'Give it for' is coded as 'la sa sy'.

   II. 'Go there get ready' is coded as 'ht mo ga sx'

   III. 'Now there fall' is coded as ' za ga gn'

   (a) Only I

   (b) Both II and III

   (c) Only II

   (d) Both I and II

   (e) Either I or II

Directions (18-22): In these questions, relationship between different elements is shown in the statements. The statements are followed by conclusions.

Give answer

   (a) If only conclusion I is true

   (b) If only conclusion II is true

   (c) If either conclusion I or II is true

   (d) If neither conclusion I nor II is true

   (e) If both conclusions I and II are true

18. **Statements:** $X \geq G = H; G > J \geq L; J \geq K < Y$
Conclusions:

   I. $X > L$

   II. $K < G$

19. **Statements:** $A > B = R \geq S \geq T; X < J \leq K < T$
Conclusions:

   I. $A > X$

   II. $R \geq T$

20. **Statements:** $M > L \geq K \leq J; N \geq R \geq S = M$
Conclusion:

   I. $R > J$

   II. $J \geq R$

21. **Statements:** $C \geq D = E; A = B \leq S \geq C$
Conclusion:

   I. $C < A$

   II. $D \leq B$

22. **Statements:** $X \geq G > H \geq I; M > H \geq L$
Conclusion:

   I. $X > M$

   II. $X > L$

Directions (23-27): Study the following information carefully and answer the questions given below:

Eight persons B, C, D, E, M, N, O, J were born in different months i.e. January, April, June, October on two different dates 16th or 24th. Only One person was born on one date. They all like different flowers i.e. lily, jasmine, hibiscus, marigold, rose, sunflower, lotus, daffodil but not necessarily in the same order.

B was born in April. Only one person was born between B and the one who like lotus, who was not born in January. One person was born between the ones who like lotus and sunflower. Five persons were born between C and N, who was born after C. N was not the youngest. E was born before O and both of them were born in the same month. No one was born before the one who likes hibiscus. The number of persons born before M is same as the number of persons born after the one who likes lotus. No one is born between B and the one who likes jasmine. D does not like jasmine. D was born before J but not immediately before. Four persons were born between the J, who likes rose and the one who likes marigold. J was born after the one who likes marigold. One of the person born in June likes Lilly.

23. Who among the following likes marigold?

   (a) D   (b) J

   (c) N   (d) B

   (e) none of these

24. Who was born exactly between the one who likes Rose and M?

   (a) D   (b) J

   (c) B   (d) O

   (e) none of these

25. Which of the following flower is liked by D?

   (a) lily   (b) rose

   (c) daffodil   (d) marigold

   (e) none of these

26. Which among the following combination is not true?

   (a) D- April   (b) J- rose

   (c) N- sunflower   (d) O- June

   (e) none of these

27. How many persons were born before O?

   (a) two   (b) six

   (c) five   (d) seven

   (e) none of these

Directions (28-31): Study the information and answer the following questions:

In a certain code language

"Entire Money Board Perfect" is written as "Q7 N5 F6 C5",

"Sleeve Washing World Stories" is written as "X7 T6 T7X5",

"Moving Partly Falls Objects" is written as "N6 P7 G5 Q6",

28. What is the code for 'Radio' in the given code language?

   (a) S5   (b) R5

   (c) S4   (d) R6

   (e) None of these

29. What is the code for the word 'Rising Normal' in the given code language?

   (a) S5 O6   (b) O5 S6

   (c) 06 S6   (d) O5 S5

   (e) None of these

30. If the code for the words 'they forward____' is coded as 'U4 G7 T5' in the coded language then what will be the missing word?

   (a) South   (b) Mount

   (c) Stone   (d) Climb

   (e) Both a and c

31. What is the code for 'Elegant' in the given code language?

   (a) G7   (b) D7

   (c) F6   (d) F7

   (e) None of these

Directions (32-35): Read the following information carefully to answer the questions given below. Fourteen persons i.e. A, B, C, D, E, F, G, M, N, O, P, Q, R and S are sitting in two parallel rows such that A, B, C, D, E, G and F sits in row 1 faces towards south direction and M, N, O, P, Q, R and S sits in the row 2 such that all are facing north direction. Person sitting in the row 1 faces the person sitting in row 2.

A sit third to the right of B. Either B or A sits at the end of the row. N sits third to the right of O. Neither N nor O Faces A and B. The one who faces C sits third to the right of M. None of the immediate neighbour B Faces O. C sits third to the left of F. O does not face F. One of the immediate neighbour of F Faces Q, who does not sit at the end of the row. D is not the immediate neighbour of C. G sits on the left of E but

not on the immediate left. P does not face G and C. S does not face C. R and S are immediate neighbours. E does not sit at the end of the row. D does not face P.

32. Who among the following faces P?

   (a) D   (b) A

   (c) F   (d) G

   (e) None of these

33. Who among the following sits at the end of the row?

   (a) P, C   (b) P, D

   (c) O, G   (d) A, S

   (e) None of these

34. How many persons sits to the right of B?

   (a) Two   (b) More than Three

   (c) Three   (d) One

   (e) None of these

35. Who among the following faces N?

   (a) D   (b) B

   (c) F   (d) G

   (e) None of these

NUMERICAL ABILITY

Directions (36-40): Bar graph given below shows pens sold by a retailer on five different days. Study the data carefully and answer the following questions

Pen sold on different days

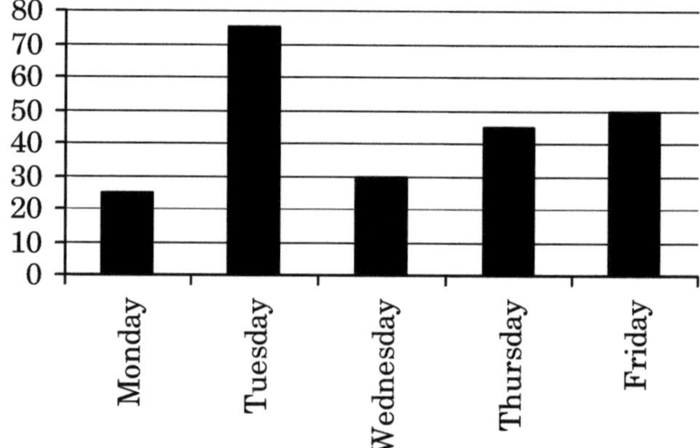

36. Find the difference between total number of pens sold on Monday and Tuesday together to total number of pens sold on Thursday and Friday together?

   (a) 15   (b) 10

   (c) 5   (d) 20

   (e) 0

37. Total number of pens sold on Saturday is 40% more than total number of pens sold on Wednesday. Find total number of pens sold on Friday and Saturday together?

(a) 92   (b) 110

(c) 72   (d) 108

(e) 85

38. Total number of pens sold on Tuesday are 25% more than total number of pens sold on Sunday. Find total number of pens sold on Sunday?

(a) 64   (b) 50

(c) 94   (d) 60

(e) 55

39. Out of total pens sold on Thursday, 20% are blue ink pen. Out of remaining 25% are red ink pen and remaining are black ink pen. Find total number of blue and black ink pen sold on Thursday?

(a) 27   (b) 36

(c) 45   (d) 39

(e) 30

40. Out of total pens sold on Tuesday ratio between total defective pens sold to total pens sold is 7 : 15. Find total number of non-defective pens sold on Tuesday by retailer?

(a) 20   (b) 25

(c) 30   (d) 35

(e) 40

41. Quantity I. 'x' : $x^2 + x - 6 = 0$

Quantity II. 'y' : $y^2 + 7y + 12 = 0$

(a) Quantity I > Quantity II

(b) Quantity I < Quantity II

(c) Quantity I ≥ Quantity II

(d) Quantity I ≤ Quantity II

(e) Quantity I = Quantity II or No relation

42. A's efficiency is 25% more than B

Quantity I – 'x': A can do $\dfrac{5}{6}$ th of total work in 'x' days

Quantity II – 'y': B can do $\dfrac{4}{5}$ th of total work in 'y' days

(a) Quantity I > Quantity II

(b) Quantity I < Quantity II

(c) Quantity I ≥ Quantity II

(d) Quantity I ≤ Quantity II

(e) Quantity I = Quantity II or No relation

43. Sum of 8 consecutive even number is S_1.

Quantity I - Sum of second number and eight number in S_1

Quantity II - Sum of third number and sixth number in S_1

(a) Quantity I > Quantity II

(b) Quantity I < Quantity II

(c) Quantity I ≥ Quantity II

(d) Quantity I ≤ Quantity II

(e) Quantity I = Quantity II or No relation

44. An article is sold at Rs. 1500 after allowing discount of 12.5% on Marked price.

Quantity I – Rs.550

Quantity II – Mark price of article.

(a) Quantity I > Quantity II

(b) Quantity I < Quantity II

(c) Quantity I ≥ Quantity II

(d) Quantity I ≤ Quantity II

(e) Quantity I = Quantity II or No relation

45. If a speed of boat is 500% more than the speed of a current.

Quantity I – 'x' : If boat can travel a distance of 63 km in 3 hr, in downstream then 'x' is the speed of the boat in upstream (km/hr).

Quantity II – 15 km/hr

(a) Quantity I > Quantity II

(b) Quantity I < Quantity II

(c) Quantity I ≥ Quantity II

(d) Quantity I ≤ Quantity II

(e) Quantity I = Quantity II or No relation

Direction (46-50): What number is wrong according to given number series pattern:-

46. 1, 3, 9, 31, 128, 651, 3913

(a) 9   (b) 1

(c) 128   (d) 31

(e) 3913

47. 291, 147, 75, 39, 22, 12, 7.5

(a) 22   (b) 291

(c) 147   (d) 75

(e) 7.5

48. 26, 27, 34, 58, 106, 186, 306

(a) 26   (b) 34

(c) 58   (d) 106

(e) 27

49. 5.9,   6,   6.1,   6.4,   7.9,   18.5,   112.9

(a) 6 (b) 5.9

(c) 6.1 (d) 18.5

(e) 112.9

50. 330,   80,   280,   120,   250,   130,   240

(a) 330 (b) 130

(c) 280 (d) 240

(e) 80

51. Sum of volume of cylinder (S) and volume of cone (C) is 2190π cm² & height of both cylinder and cone is same i.e, 10 cm. If radius of cone is 15 cm then find the ratio of radius of S to radius of C?

(a) 1 : 2 (b) 3 : 4

(c) 2 : 5 (d) 4 : 5

(e) 3 : 5

52. In a box there are 6 blue ball, X red balls & 10 green balls. Probability of choosing one red ball from the given box is $\dfrac{1}{3}$. Then find the sum of red and blue balls in the box?

(a) 20 (b) 12

(c) 14 (d) 18

(e) 16

53. Sum of A's and B's age 6 years ago is 88. A's age 18 yrs ago is equal to B's age 6 years ago. Find the age of A two year hence?

(a) 58 yrs (b) 64 yrs

(c) 42 yrs (d) 52 yrs

(e) 48 yrs

54. Train A of length 120 m can cross a platform of length 240 m in 18 second the ratio of speed of train A and Train B is 4 : 5. Then find the length of Train B if train B can cross a pole in 12 seconds.

(a) 280 m (b) 300 m

(c) 320 m (d) 350 m

(e) 240 m

55. What is the probability of forming word from the letters of word "IMPEACH" such that all vowels come together?

(a) $\dfrac{8}{35}$ (b) $\dfrac{1}{7}$

(c) $\dfrac{3}{35}$ (d) $\dfrac{17}{35}$

(d) $\dfrac{2}{7}$

Direction (56-60): Find the value of (?) in following approximation questions:

56. $2^? = 32.01 \div 128.01 \times 1023.99 \div 7.99$

(a) 7 (b) 3

(c) 4 (d) 5

(e) 8

57. $\dfrac{339.99}{?} = \sqrt{143.99} + \sqrt{64.01}$

(a) 17 (b) 20

(c) 10 (d) 34

(e) 40

58. 34.02% of $550.09 \div ? = 297.07 \div \sqrt{728.95}$

(a) 14 (b) 21

(c) 8 (d) 27

(e) 17

59. $(? \div 9.97) \times 12.08 = 20.12\%$ of 1319.97

(a) 220 (b) 240

(c) 260 (d) 280

(e) 200

60. ? % of 179.99

$$= \sqrt{(24.02)^2 + (17.98)^2 + 60.01\% \text{ of } 659.98}$$

(a) 80 (b) 60

(c) 40 (d) 20

(e) 10

Direction (61-65): Pie chart given below shows total number of workers in three different companies. Table given below shows ratio between officers and workers working in these companies. Study the data carefully and answer the following questions

Total workers = 900

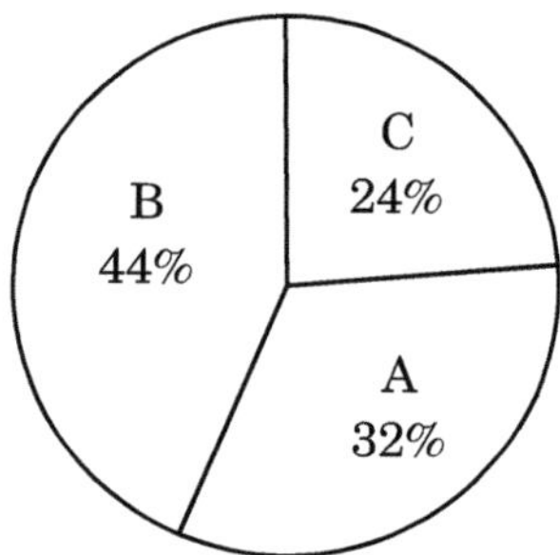

Company	Officers : Workers
A	1:16
B	1:18
C	1:12

Note: Total employees = Officers + Workers

61. Find the ratio between total number of workers in company A and C together to total number of officers in company A and C together?

(a) 16 : 1   (b) 12 : 1

(c) 14 : 1   (d) 18 : 1

(e) 20 : 1

62. Total number of employees in company 'B' is how much more than total number of employees in company 'C.

(a) 174   (b) 194

(c) 204   (d) 214

(e) 184

63. Total number of officers in company 'A' is how much less than total number of officers in company 'B'?

(a) 4   (b) 2

(c) 0   (d) 6

(e) 8

64. Total number of officers and workers in company D is 50% and 25% more than total number of officers and workers in company 'C respectively. Find total number of employees in company 'D'?

(a) 279   (b) 297

(c) 342   (d) 324

(e) 306

65. Find the difference between total number of workers in company 'A' and total number of workers in company 'B' and 'C together?

(a) 432   (b) 396

(c) 360   (d) 324

(e) 288

Direction (66-70): There are three persons A, B and C who each invested in two different scheme S_1 and S_2. A in invested Rs 80,000 for 2 yr in scheme S_1 and 30,000 for 4 years in scheme S_2. B invested Rs 30,000 for 3 year in S_1 and he did not invest in scheme B. B also obtained a profit of 10,000 by selling his car. C invested Rs 50000 for 5 years in scheme S_1 and 10000 for 3 year in scheme S_2. Total profit obtained from scheme S_1 is 2 lakh and scheme S_2 is 90,000.

66. What is the ratio of total profit obtained by B and profit obtained by C from scheme S_1

(a) 23 : 47   (b) 54 : 47

(c) 36 : 43   (d) 23 : 50

(e) 27 : 50

67. Profit obtained by A from scheme S_1 is what percent of profit obtained by C from scheme S_2.

(a) $346\dfrac{7}{9}\%$ (b) $347\dfrac{8}{9}\%$

(c) $356\dfrac{7}{9}\%$ (d) $345\dfrac{4}{9}\%$

(e) $355\dfrac{5}{9}\%$

68. If sum of investment of A in both schemes and total profit obtained by A from both scheme is invested at compound Interest at the rate of 20% p.a. then find the total compound interest obtained in 2 yr

(a) 108240   (b) 104206

(c) 105208   (d) 109280

(e) 106220

69. What is the average of profit attained by A from scheme S_1 and profit of C obtained from scheme S_2.

(a) 41000   (b) 42000

(c) 44000   (d) 55000

(e) 40000

70. If A had invested his sum at Simple Interest for 3 yr at the rate of R% p.a. instead in scheme S_1 and B has invested his sum at compound Interest at (R + 5)% p.a. for 1 year and difference in interest obtained is 30,000 then find value of R%.

(a) 10%   (b) 9%

(c) 15%   (d) 18%

(e) 12%

ENGLISH LANGUAGE

Directions (71-78): In the questions given below, there is a sentence in which one part is given in bold. The part given in bold may or may not be grammatically correct. Choose the best alternative among the four given which can replace the part in bold to make the sentence grammatically correct. If the part given in bold is already correct and does not require any replacement, choose option (e), i.e. "No replacement required" as your answer.

71. Nobody can deny the fact that Indian economy **is very different than** American economy.

    (a) are very different than

    (b) is so much different than

    (c) are very different from

    (d) is very different from

    (e) No replacement required

72. Accurate **statistics with regards to** the area occupied in different forms of cultivation are difficult to obtain.

    (a) statistic with regards to

    (b) statistics with regard to

    (c) statistic with regard to

    (d) statistics in regards to

    (e) No replacement required

73. **Seldom if ever** was there any training or instructions in such tactics for either the tank crews or the infantry formations.

    (a) Seldom or never

    (b) Seldom if never

    (c) Seldom or ever

    (d) Seldom has ever

    (e) No replacement required

74. As soon as I opened the front door of my house, **than I smelled** the distinctive aroma of fresh coffee.

    (a) then I smelled

    (b) that I smelled

    (c) I smelled

    (d) I smell

    (e) No replacement required

75. Although he had fewer supporters among the governing class, **but he was able** to get the popular vote.

    (a) he was able

    (b) and he was able

    (c) else he was able

    (d) or he was able

    (e) No replacement required

76. The party explicitly **denies that they are not** involved in mainstream politics.

    (a) denied that they are not

    (b) denies that they were

    (c) denied that they are

    (d) deny that they are not

    (e) No replacement required

77. I would rather be a poor man in a garret with plenty of good books to read than a king **who did not loved** reading.

    (a) who do not loved

    (b) who did not love

    (c) whom did not loved

    (d) whom did not love

    (e) No replacement required

78. The relatively static lattice in a diamond ensures that the scattering is at a minimum and the thermal conductivity **is exceptional** good.

    (a) are exceptional

    (b) was exceptional

    (c) are exceptionally

    (d) is exceptionally

    (e) No replacement required

Directions (79-83): Select the phrase/connector (it must be at the start) from the given three options which can be used to form a single sentence from the two sentences given below, implying the same meaning as expressed in the statement sentences.

79. We see ourselves repeating our ordinary routine. We realize how much wealth surrounds our life.

    (i) When we see ourselves.............

    (ii) Our ordinary routine.............

    (ii) Realizing how much wealth.............

    (a) Only (i)   (b) Both (ii) and (iii)

    (c) Only (iii)   (d) Only (ii)

    (e) None of these

80. There is a growing influence of the Indian Diaspora on Capitol Hill. Trump will certainly see the advantages of doing business with India.

    (i) As there is a growing influence of...

    (ii) The growing influence of the Indian...

    (iii) With the growing influence of the Indian..

    (a) Only (i) is correct

    (b) Only (iii) is correct

    (c) Both (i) and (ii) are correct

    (d) Both (i) and (iii) are correct

    (e) All are correct

81. There was no democracy in British India. The rulers could take bold decisions fearlessly without bothering about repercussions.

    (i) As there was no democracy in British India...

    (ii) Since there was no democracy in British...

    (iii) With the rulers taking bold decisions...

(a) Only (i) is correct

(b) Only (ii) is correct

(c) Both (i) and (ii) are correct

(d) Both (ii) and (iii) are correct

(e) All are correct

82. Twelve million youth enter the Indian work force every year. Eighty per cent of these youth are unskilled.

(A) While eighty per cent..........

(B) Since twelve million..........

(C) Of the twelve million..........

(a) Only (A)

(b) Only (C)

(c) Only (A) and (C)

(d) All (A), (B) and (C)

(e) None of these

83. Scientists build climate models—computer simulations of the climate system. They are doing this to further explore the causes and effects of global warming

(i) To further explore...

(ii) Scientists are building...

(iii) Predicting effects of global warming...

(a) Only (i) is correct

(b) Only (ii) is correct

(c) Only (iii) is correct

(d) Both (i) and (ii) are correct

(e) All are correct

Directions (84-89): Given below the sentences each of which has been divided into five parts out of which the first part has been marked bold. Each of the questions is then followed by the five options which give the sequence of the rearranged parts. You must choose the option which gives the correct sequence of the parts. If the sentence is already arranged or the correct sequence doesn't match any of the given sequence, mark (e) .i.e. "None of the above" as your answer.

84. **The apex court had ordered that the/** of the biometric scheme and the enabling law(A)/ deadline be extended till the five-judge constitution(B)/ on petitions challenging the validity(C)/ bench delivers its judgment(D)

(a) ACDB   (b) BCAD

(c) BDCA   (d) CADB

(e) None of the above

85. **Repealing the law that safeguards/** the floodgates of poaching(A)/ and it would lead to(B)/ marginalisation of the indigenous people(C)/the indigenous people would open(D)

(a) DCBA   (b) DABC

(c) ACBD   (d) BACD

(e) None of the above

86. **My thoughts are with the families/** in this unfortunate accident(A)/ recovery of the injured(B)/ of those who have lost their loved ones(C)/ I pray for the speedy(D)/

(a) BCAD   (b) DACB

(c) ACBD   (d) CADB

(e) None of the above

87. **Several people became leaders/** remained where they were(A)/ and Ministers after that(B)/ rally but the people(C)/ belonging to the community(D)

(a) ABCD   (b) BCDA

(c) CABD   (d) DACB

(e) None of the above

88. **He also directed the department/** to develop the new schools as model(A)/ completion of construction work(B)/ construction technology for early(C)/ institutions and engage modern(D)

(a) ADCB   (b) ABCD

(c) DACB   (d) CADB

(e) None of the above

89. **The** U.S. **is** a/ to its being an open society(A)/ nation of immigrants(B)/ in the present global order(C)/ and owes its predominant position(D).

(a) ADCB   (b) ABCD

(c) BDCA   (d) CADB

(e) None of the above

Directions (90-95): Read the following passage carefully and answer the questions given below it. Certain words are given in bold to help you locate them while answering some of the questions.

Have you heard that the economy is like a car? It's the most popular **analogy** in financial reporting and political discourse. The American people are repeatedly told by financial pundits and politicians that consumption is an 'engine' that 'drives' economic growth because it makes up 70% of GDP. One notable Nobel-winning economics pundit with a penchant for bizarre growth theories even recently noted that an economy can be 'based on purchases of yachts, luxury cars, and the services of personal trainers and celebrity chefs.' Conversely, other economists including Nobel-winner Joseph Stiglitz claim that our economy is stuck in 'first gear' due to inequality: too much income is concentrated among too few rich people who tend to save larger share of their income and thus have a lower 'marginal propensity to consume'. The Keynesian message is clear: if you want to put the economic pedal to the metal, get out there and consume!

Not so fast, Speed Racer. The systematic failure by Keynesian economists and pundits to distinguish between consuming and producing value is the single most damaging fallacy in popular economic thinking. If the economy were a car, consumer preferences would surely be the steering wheel, but real savings and investment would be the engine that drives it forward.

Economic growth (booms) and declines (bust) have always been led by changes in business and durable goods investment, while final consumer goods spending has been relatively stable through the business cycle. Booms and busts in financial markets, heavy industry and housing have always been leading indicators of recession and recovery.

As John Stuart Mill put it two centuries ago, 'the demand for commodities is not the demand for labor.' Consumer demand does not necessarily translate into increased employment. That's because 'consumers' don't employ people. Businesses do. Since new hires are a risky and costly investment with **unknown** future returns, employers must rely on their expectations about the future and weigh those decision very carefully. As economic historian Robert Higgs' pioneering work on the Great Depression suggests, increased uncertainty can depress job growth even in the face of booming consumption. As recent years have demonstrated, consumer demand that appears to be driven by temporary or unsustainable policies is unlikely to induce businesses to hire.

90. Choose the word which is **MOST SIMILAR** to the word given in passage

   UNKNOWN

   (a) Recognize

   (b) Perceived

   (c) Unpredictable

   (d) Unruly

   (e) Uncanny

91. Which of the following is the most suitable title for the passage above?

   (a) Recession and Recovery

   (b) Consumer: The driving force for Economy

   (c) Economy: a Distant Dream?

   (d) Is Consumption necessary for economic Growth?

   (e) None of the Above

92. In the statement "consumer preferences would surely be the steering wheel, but real savings and investment would be the engine that drives it forward", what can we infer from the line "consumer preferences would surely be the steering wheel"?

   (a) Consumer likings regulate the economy individually.

   (b) If you want to regulate the economy, consumption is the only force.

   (c) The Penchant of the consumers controls the economy.

   (d) The consumer preferences are not at par with savings and economy in driving the economy.

   (e) None of the Above

93. Which of the following statements is/are correct in context with the passage?

   (a) Economists fail to distinguish between consuming and producing value and form a mistaken belief.

   (b) Economic growth and declines have always been led by changes in business and durable goods investment.

   (c) Income distribution is evenly distributed among the rich and is compatible with the tendency to consume.

   (d) Only (a)

   (e) Both (a) and (b)

94. Which of the following is/are likely to induce businesses to hire?

   (a) Consumer Demand

   (b) Consumer Spending

   (c) Increased certainty in future returns.

   (d) Makeshift policies

   (e) Both (b) and (c)

95. Choose the word which is **MOST OPPOSITE** to the word given in passage

ANALOGY

  (a) Similarity   (b) Narrative

  (c) Contrast   (d) Reciprocate

  (e) Variance

Directions (96-100): In the following questions two columns are given containing three sentences/phrases each. In first column, sentences/phrases are *A*, B and C and in the second column the sentences/phrases are D, E and F. A sentence/phrase from the first column may or may not connect with another sentence/phrase from the second column to make a grammatically and contextually correct sentence. Each question has five options, four of which display the sequence(s) in which the sentences/phrases can be joined to form a grammatically and contextually correct sentence. If none of the options given forms a correct sentence after combination, mark (e), i.e. "None of these" as your answer.

96. Column (1):

  (A) As the head of the family, he ensures that

  (B) Ravi is such a disorganized fellow that

  (C) The boy next door nags his parents because

Column (2):

  (D) he runs around like a headless chicken

  (E) he succeeds to make everyone laugh

  (F) he goes out and earns a living for his family

  (a) C-E and B-F   (b) A-F

  (c) B-E   (d) A-D

  (e) None of these

97. Column (1):

  (A) Some rich guy from Boston

  (B) People tend to raise their voices when they

  (C) As soon as the herd heard the gunshots, they

Column (2):

  (D) are losing an argument

  (E) all were fatally injured

  (F) just bought the house next to mine

  (a) C-F   (b) A-D

  (c) B-E   (d) B-D

  (e) None of these

98. Column (1):

  (A) Tom always drinks at least

  (B) If he had taken his doctor's advice

  (C) I can still remember the time when

Column (2):

  (D) he might still be alive.

  (E) went on a picnic together.

  (F) three cups of coffee in the morning,

  (a) C-E   (b) B-F

  (c) A-D   (d) C-F

  (e) None of these

99. Column (1):

  (A) It seems like yesterday, but it's actually

  (B) I can't believe Vijay is still talking about

  (C) The only thing that really matters is

Column (2):

  (D) whether or not you are happy.

  (E) nearly ten years since we first met.

  (F) what happens two years ago.

  (a) A-D   (b) B-E

  (c) C-E   (d) A-F

  (e) None of these

100. Column (1):

  (A) After school, Jack usually sticks around as long as

  (B) We're planning on doing the sights

  (C) Even the repairman couldn't figure out what

Column (2):

  (D) had gone wrong with the microwave.

  (E) he can because he doesn't want to go home.

  (F) of the city tomorrow morning.

  (a) A-F and B-D   (b) B-E and C-F

  (c) B-F and C-D   (d) A-D and C-E

  (e) None of these

ANSWERS

1. (a)	**2.** (d)	**3.** (d)	**4.** (a)	**5.** (d)	**6.** (e)	**7.** (a)	**8.** (d)	**9.** (a)	**10.** (d)
11. (d)	**12.** (a)	**13.** (c)	**14.** (e)	**15.** (e)	**16.** (a)	**17.** (b)	**18.** (e)	**19.** (e)	**20.** (c)
21. (d)	**22.** (b)	**23.** (d)	**24.** (d)	**25.** (c)	**26.** (a)	**27.** (c)	**28.** (a)	**29.** (c)	**30.** (e)
31. (d)	**32.** (b)	**33.** (d)	**34.** (c)	**35.** (e)	**36.** (c)	**37.** (a)	**38.** (d)	**39.** (b)	**40.** (e)
41. (c)	**42.** (b)	**43.** (a)	**44.** (b)	**45.** (e)	**46.** (c)	**47.** (a)	**48.** (e)	**49.** (d)	**50.** (b)
51. (d)	**52.** (c)	**53.** (a)	**54.** (b)	**55.** (b)	**56.** (d)	**57.** (a)	**58.** (e)	**59.** (a)	**60.** (d)
61. (*)	**62.** (e)	**63.** (a)	**64.** (b)	**65.** (d)	**66.** (d)	**67.** (e)	**68.** (a)	**69.** (a)	**70.** (c)
71. (d)	**72.** (b)	**73.** (e)	**74.** (c)	**75.** (a)	**76.** (c)	**77.** (b)	**78.** (d)	**79.** (a)	**80.** (e)
81. (c)	**82.** (b)	**83.** (d)	**84.** (c)	**85.** (b)	**86.** (d)	**87.** (b)	**88.** (a)	**89.** (c)	**90.** (e)
91. (d)	**92.** (c)	**93.** (e)	**94.** (c)	**95.** (e)	**96.** (b)	**97.** (d)	**98.** (a)	**99.** (e)	**100.** (c)

EXPLANATIONS

Directions (1-5):

Boxes	Number of chocolates
A	64
D	39
G	27
E	41
B	13
F	78
C	50

Direction (6-10):

In this input output question numbers are arranged in ascending order from both the ends such as lowest number is first arranged from the left end and the second lowest number is arranged from the right end. And also all the numbers which are getting arranged is added by 1.

Input:- 58 40 99 28 63 84 16 34 71 87

Step I: 17 58 40 99 63 84 34 71 87 29

Step II: 35 17 58 99 63 84 71 87 29 41

Step III: 59 35 17 99 84 71 87 29 41 64

Step IV: 72 59 35 17 99 87 29 41 64 85

Step V: 88 72 59 35 17 29 41 64 85 100

Direction (11-12):

11. (d)

12. (a)

13. (c)

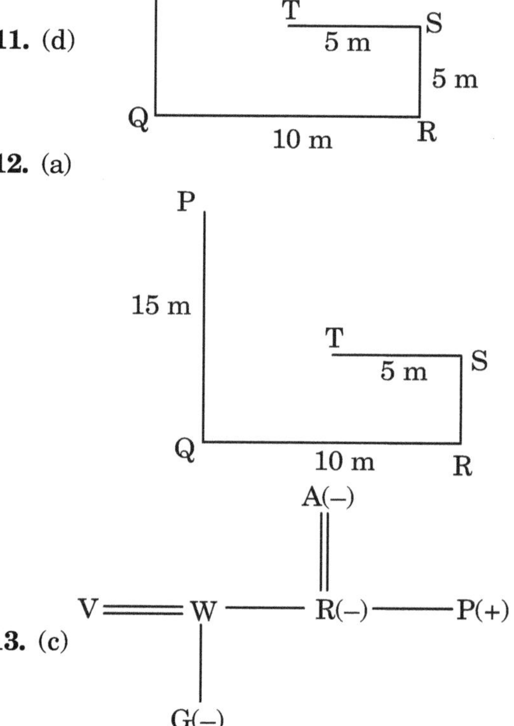

Direction (14-16):

14. (e)

From I - M > N, K, O > J > M and L > K

From II- M >_ >_ >_ and J > K

From both I and II we get that O > J > M > N/K > L/N > K/N

So, O is the tallest boy.

15. (e) **From I,**

Floors	Persons
6	
5	W
4	R/
3	R/
2	T
1	R/

From II,

Floors	Persons
6	S/ U
5	V/T
4	R/V
3	V/R
2	R/T
1	S/U

From both I and II,

Floors	Persons
6	U
5	W
4	V
3	R
2	T
1	S

So, No one lives between R and T.

16. (a) From I,

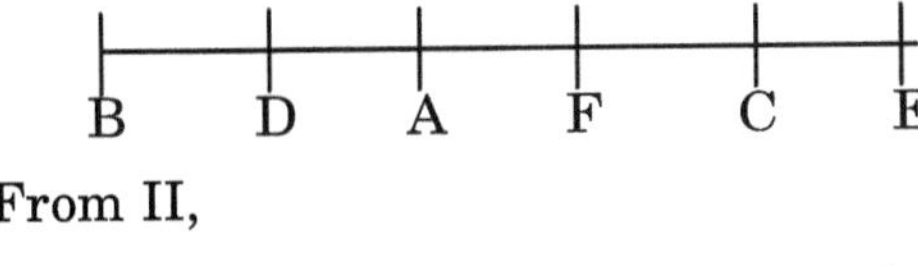

From II,

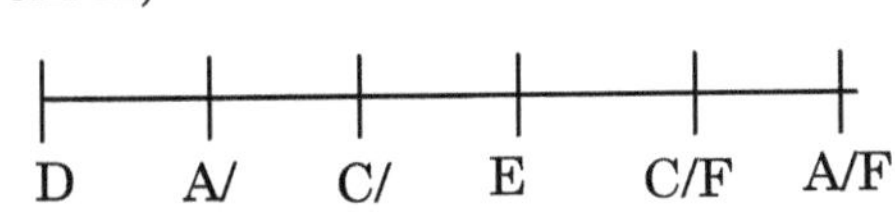

or

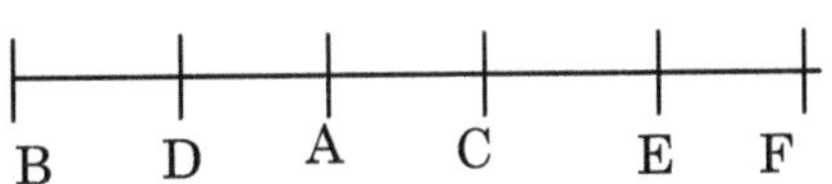

So, from only I we get that C sits second from the right end.

17. (b) From II and III, the code of 'go there now' is gn ga mo.

Directions (18-22):

18. (e) I. X > L (True)   II. K < G (True)

19. (e) I. A > X (True)   II. R = T (True)

20. (c) I. R > J (False)   II. J = R (False)

21. (d) I. C < A (False)   II. D = B (False)

22. (b) I. X > M (False)   II. X > L (True)

Directions (23-27):

Dates / Months	16th	24th
January	C (hibiscus)	D (daffodil)
April	B (marigold)	M (jasmine)
June	E (lotus)	O (Lily)
October	N (sunflower)	J (rose)

Directions (28-31):

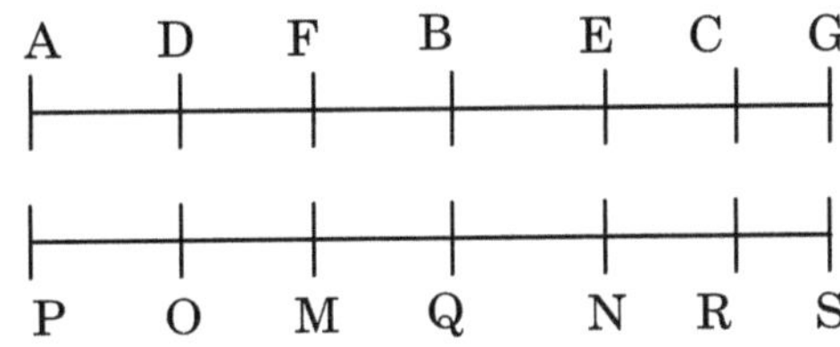

MONEY = N5

Letter immediate after the first letter of the word

Total number of letters in the word.

Directions (32-35):

A D F B E C G

P O M Q N R S

36. (c) Required difference = 25 + 75 − 45 − 50 = 5

37. (a) Total number of pens sold on Saturday = 30 × 1.4 = 42

Total number of pens sold on Friday and Saturday together = 50 + 42 = 92

38. (d) Total number of pens sold on Sunday

$$= \frac{75}{125} \times 100 = 60$$

39. (b) Blue ink pen sold on Thursday

$$= 45 \times \frac{20}{100} = 9$$

Red ink pen sold on Thursday

$$= (45 - 9) \times \frac{25}{100} = 9$$

Black ink pen sold on Thursday

$$= (45 - 9) \times \frac{75}{100} = 27$$

Total number of blue and black ink pen sold on Thursday = 9 + 27 = 36

40. (e) Total number of non-defective pens sold on

Tuesday $= \dfrac{75}{15} \times 8 = 40$

41. (c) Quantity I. $x^2 + x - 6 = 0$

$x^2 + 3x - 2x - 6 = 0$

$x(x + 3) - 2(x + 3) = 0$

$(x + 3)(x - 2) = 0$

$x = -3, 2$

Quantity II. $y^2 + 7y + 12 = 0$

$y^2 + 4y + 3y + 12 = 0$

$(y + 4)(y + 3) = 0$

$y = -4, -3$

Quantity I $\geq$ Quantity II

42. (b) A's efficiency = 5

B's efficiency = 4

Let total work = 60

Quantity I : A can do $\dfrac{5}{6}$ of work in $\rightarrow \dfrac{50}{5} = 10d$

Quantity II : B can do $\dfrac{4}{5}$ of work in $\dfrac{48}{4} = 12d$

Quantity II > Quantity I

43. (a) Let numbers be x, x + 2, x + 4, x + 6, x + 8, x + 10, x + 12, x + 14

Quantity I $\rightarrow$ x + 2 + x + 14 = 2x + 16

Quantity II $\rightarrow$ x + 4 + x + 10 = 2x + 14

Quantity I > Quantity II

44. (b) SP = 1500

Let, MP = x

Quantity I = 550

Quantity II

$$x \times \frac{7}{8} = 1500$$

$$x = \frac{1500 \times 8}{7}$$

$$x = \frac{12000}{7}$$

Quantity II > Quantity I

45. (e) Quantity I :

Let speed of current = x

speed of boat = x + 5x

downstream speed = 7x

$$\frac{63}{7x} = 3$$

$x = 3$

Upstream speed = 6x – x

= 5x = 15 km/hr

Quantity I = Quantity II

46. (c) 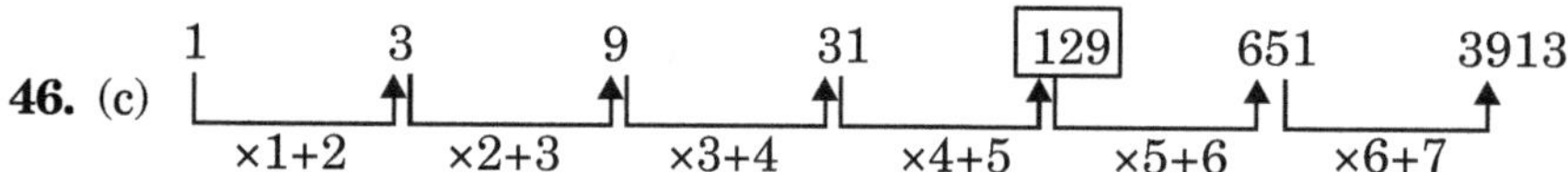

47. (a) 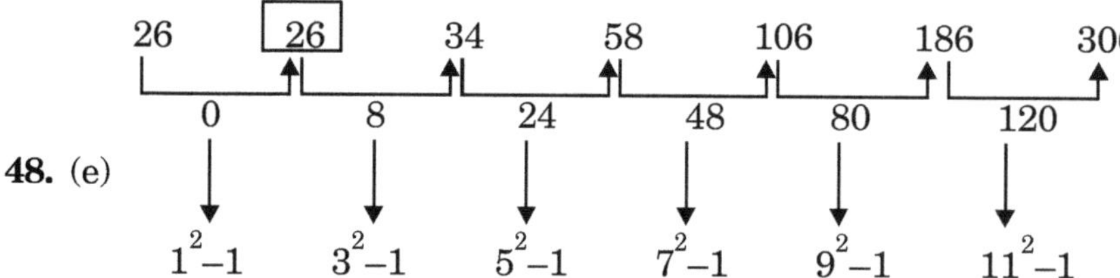

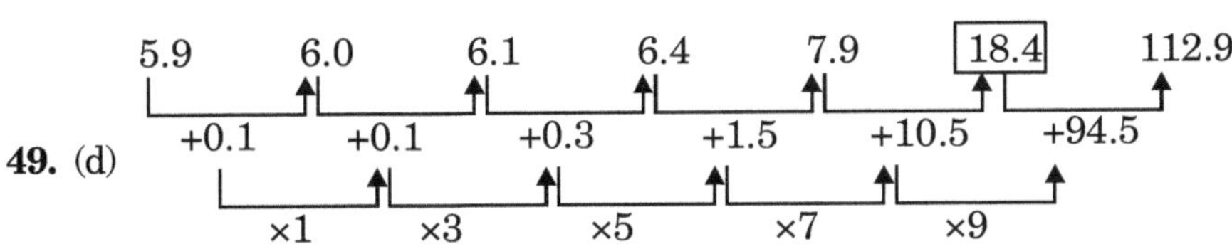

49. (d)

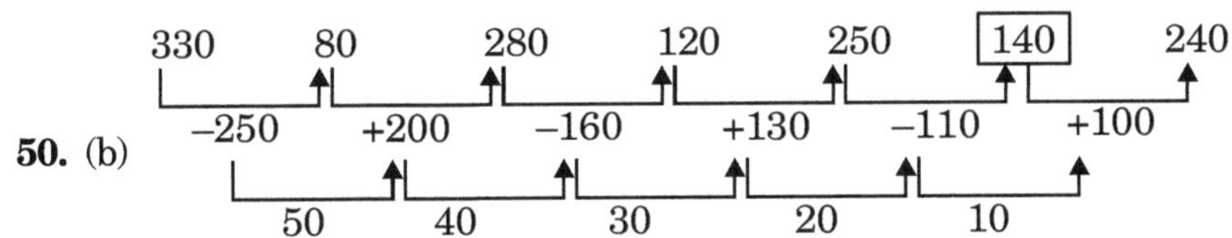

50. (b)

51. (d) Volume of cylinder (s) = $\pi r^2 h$

$(r \rightarrow$ radius$)$ $(h \rightarrow$ height$)$

Volume of cone (c) $= \dfrac{1}{3}\pi R^2 H$

$(R \rightarrow$ radius$)$

$(H \rightarrow$ height$)$

h = H = 10 cm

ATQ,

$$\pi r^2 h + \dfrac{1}{3}\pi R^2 h = 2190\pi$$

$$\pi \times 10\left[r^2 + \dfrac{1}{3} \times 15 \times 15\right] = 219\pi$$

r = 12

$$\therefore \dfrac{r}{R} = \dfrac{12}{15} = 4:5$$

52. (c) Atq,

$$\dfrac{X}{X+16} = \dfrac{1}{3}$$

3X = X + 16

X = 8

$\therefore$ sum of red & blue balls = 8 + 6 = 14

53. (a) Let present age of A be x yrs

& present age of B be y yrs.

ATQ,

x + y = 88 + 12

x + y = 100   ...(i)

x – 18 = y – 6

x – y = 12   ...(ii)

solving (i) & (ii)

x = 56

$\therefore$ age of A 2 year hence = 58 yrs

54. (b) Let speed of train A be S

S × 18 = 360

S = 20 m/s A : B = 4 : 5

A : B = 4 : 5

Speed of B = 25 m/s

Length of train B = 25 × 12 = 300 m

55. (b) Total numbers of ways $\rightarrow$ 7!

Favorable numbers of ways $\rightarrow$ 5! × 3!

Probability $\rightarrow \dfrac{5! \times 3!}{7!} = \dfrac{1}{7}$

56. (d) $2^? = 32.01 \div 128.01 \times 1023.99 \div 7.99$

$$2^? \approx \dfrac{32}{128} \times \dfrac{1024}{8}$$

$2^? \approx 32$

$2^? \approx 2^5$

$? \approx 5$

57. (a) $\dfrac{339.99}{?} = \sqrt{143.99} + \sqrt{64.01}$

$$\dfrac{340}{?} \approx \sqrt{144} + \sqrt{64}$$

$$\dfrac{340}{?} \approx 12 + 8$$

$$\dfrac{340}{20} \approx ?$$

$17 \approx ?$

58. (e) 34.02% of $550.09 \div ? = 297.07 \div \sqrt{728.95}$

$$\dfrac{34 \times 550}{100} \div \approx 297 \div \sqrt{729}$$

$$\dfrac{187}{?} \approx \dfrac{297}{27}$$

$? \approx 17$

59. (a) $(? \div 9.97) \times 12.08 \approx 20.12\%$ of 1319.97

$$(? \div 10) \times 12 \approx \dfrac{20 \times 1320}{100}$$

$$? \approx \dfrac{264}{12} \times 10 \approx 220$$

60. (d) $? \%$ of 179.99

$$= \sqrt{(24.02)^2 + (17.98)^2 + 60.01\% \text{ of } 659.98}$$

$? \%$ of 180

$$\approx \sqrt{(24)^2 + (18)^2 + 60\% \text{ of } 660}$$

$$\frac{?}{100} \times 180 \approx \sqrt{576 + 324 + 396}$$

$$\frac{?}{100} \times 180 \approx \sqrt{1296}$$

$$? \approx \frac{36}{180} \times 100$$

$? = 20$

61. Total number of workers in company A and C together

$$= 900 \times \frac{32}{100} + 900 \times \frac{4}{100}$$

$$= 288 + 216$$

$$= 504$$

Total number of officers in company A and C together

$$= 900 \times \frac{32}{100} \times \frac{1}{16} + 900 \times \frac{4}{100} \times \frac{1}{12}$$

$$= 18 + 18 = 36$$

Required Ratio $= \dfrac{504}{36}$

$$= \frac{14}{1}$$

62. (e) Total number of employees in company B

$$= 900 \times \frac{44}{100} \times \frac{19}{18} = 418$$

Total number of employees in company C

$$= 900 \times \frac{24}{100} \times \frac{13}{12} = 234$$

Required difference $= 418 - 234 = 184$

63. (a) Total number of officers in Company 'A' =

$$= 900 \times \frac{32}{100} \times \frac{1}{16} = 18$$

Total number of officers in Company 'B' =

$$= 900 \times \frac{44}{100} \times \frac{1}{18} = 22$$

Required difference $= 22 - 18 = 4$

64. (b) Total number of officers in company C

$$= 900 \times \frac{24}{100} \times \frac{1}{12} = 18$$

Total number of workers in company C

$$= 900 \times \frac{24}{100} = 216$$

Total number of employees in company D

$$= 216 \times 1.25 + 18 \times 1.5 = 270 + 27 = 297$$

65. (d) Required difference $\dfrac{900}{100} \times (44 + 24 - 32) = 9 \times$

$36 = 324$

Solution (66-70)

Ratio of profit share of A, B and C is scheme S_1

$80000 \times 2 : 30000 \times 3 : 50000 \times 5$

$16 : 9 : 25$

Profit share of A from Scheme

$$S_1 = \frac{16}{50} \times 200,000 = 64000$$

Profit share of B from scheme

$$S_1 = \frac{9}{50} \times 200,000 = 36000$$

Profit share of C from scheme

$$S_1 = \frac{25}{50} \times 20,000 = 100,000$$

Ratio of profit share of A and C in scheme S_2

$30,000 \times 4 : 10,000 \times 3$

$12 : 3$

Profit share of A in scheme

$$S_2 = \frac{12}{15} \times 90000 = 72000$$

Profit share of C in scheme

$$S_2 = \frac{3}{15} \times 90,000$$

66. (d) Required ratio $= (36000 + 10000) : 100,000$

$$= 46 : 100$$

$$= 23 : 50$$

67. (e) Required $\% \dfrac{64000}{18000} \times 100 = \dfrac{3200}{9}\%$

$$= 355\frac{5}{9}\%$$

68. (a) Total investment of A $= 80,000 + 30,000$

$$= 110,000$$

Total profit of A $= 64000 + 72000$

$$= 136000$$

Equivalent rate of Interest for 2 year at CI

$$= 20\% + 20\% + \frac{20 \times 20}{100}$$

$$= 44\%$$

Required CI $= \dfrac{44}{100}(136000 + 110000)$

$= 108240$

69. (a) Required average $= \dfrac{64000 + 18000}{2}$

$= 41000$

70. (c) $\dfrac{80000 \times R \times 3}{100} - 30000 \times \left(\dfrac{R+5}{100}\right) = 30{,}000$

$2400R - 300R - 1500 = 30000$

$8R - R - 5 = 100$

$7R = 105A$

$R = 15\%$

71. (d) The most appropriate phrase to replace the phrase given in bold is "is very different from". In the given sentence, 'than' should be replaced with 'from' because 'different' is followed by 'from'. Also keep in mind that, 'than' is used after 'different', but only in the cases where 'different' is followed by a noun. For example, I read a different novel than this. Since option (d) is in the precise grammatical syntax, it becomes the most suitable answer choice.

72. (b) The most appropriate phrase to replace the phrase given in bold is "statistics with regard to". It is to be noted that 'Statistics', when used as a subject, always takes a singular verb. For example, Statistics is not an easy subject. But, whenever 'statistics' denotes some statistical facts or data, the very following it is always plural, which is the case here. Since option (b) is in the precise grammatical syntax, it becomes the most suitable answer choice.

73. (e) The phrase given in sentence is grammatically correct and does not require any replacement. Hence, option (e) i.e. "No replacement required" is the correct answer.

74. (c) The most appropriate phrase to replace the phrase given in bold is "I smelled". It is to be noted that after 'As soon as, As long as, So long as', we don't use 'than/then'. Since option (c) is in the precise grammatical syntax, it becomes the most suitable answer choice.

75. (a) The most appropriate phrase to replace the phrase given in bold is "he was able". It is to be noted that 'Although/Though' is followed by 'yet' and not 'but/and/or/else'. And in writing, many a times, 'yet' is replaced by a 'comma', which is the case here. Since option (a) is in the precise grammatical syntax, it becomes the most suitable answer choice.

76. (c) The most appropriate phrase to replace the phrase given in bold is "denied that they are". It is to be noted that 'not' will not be used after 'deny' because deny already means refuse to admit. Since option (c) is in the precise grammatical syntax, it becomes the most suitable answer choice.

77. (b) The most appropriate phrase to replace the phrase given in bold is "who did not love". It is to be noted that after 'did' we always use the first form of the verb i.e. VI. Since option (b) is in the precise grammatical syntax, it becomes the most suitable answer choice.

78. (d) The most appropriate phrase to replace the phrase given in bold is "is exceptionally". It is to be noted that 'good' is an adjective, so 'exceptional' should be replaced by 'exceptionally'. 'Exceptional' is itself an adjective and we all know that an adjective never defines another adjective, but an adverb does. Since option (d) is in the precise grammatical syntax, it becomes the most suitable answer choice.

79. (a) (i) When we see ourselves repeating our ordinary routine, we realize how much wealth surrounds our life.

80. (e) (i) As there is a growing influence of the Indian Diaspora on Capitol Hill, Trump will certainly see the advantages of doing business with India.

(ii) The growing influence of the Indian Diaspora on Capitol Hill will certainly allow Trump to see the advantages of doing business with India.

(iii) With the growing influence of the Indian Diaspora on Capitol Hill, Trump will certainly see the advantages of doing business with India.

81. (c) (i) As there was no democracy in British India, the rulers could take bold decisions fearlessly without bothering about repercussions.

(ii) Since there was no democracy in British India, the rulers could take bold decisions fearlessly without bothering about repercussions.

82. (b) Option (b) is correct because while indicates a contrast and because of the given requirement of the statement it cannot start the sentence.

83. (d) Both (i) and (ii) are correct

(i) To further explore the causes and effects of global warming, scientists build climate models—computer simulations of the climate system.

(ii) Scientists are building climate models—computer simulations of the climate system to further explore the causes and effects of global warming and to predict future warming.

84. (c) **BDCA;** (The apex court had ordered that the deadline be extended till the five-judge constitution bench delivers its judgment on petitions challenging the validity of the biometric scheme and the enabling law)

85. (b) **DABC;** (Repealing the law that safeguards the indigenous people would open the floodgates of poaching and it would lead to marginalisation of the indigenous people)

86. (d) **CADB;** (My thoughts are with the families of those who have lost their loved ones in this unfortunate accident. I pray for the speedy recovery of the injured)

87. (b) **BCDA;** (Several people became leaders and Ministers after that rally but the people belonging to the community remained where they were)

88. (a) **ADCB;** (He also directed the department to develop the new schools as model institutions and engage modern construction technology for early completion of construction work)

89. (c) Option (c) **BDCA** is the correct choice for the given question

   The U.S. is a nation of immigrants and owes its predominant position in the present global order to its being an open society.

90. (e) Unknown: not known or familiar. Uncanny: strange or mysterious

91. (d) The most appropriate title for the passage above is "Is Consumption necessary for economic Growth?"

92. (c) The meaning of the line above is that consumer preferences control the economy but savings and investment are the push to drive it forward. Hence option c is the correct choice here.

93. (e) Both statements (a) and (b) are correct. Refer the following lines

   Option(a): The systematic failure by Keynesian economists and pundits to distinguish between consuming and producing value is the single most damaging fallacy in popular economic thinking. Option(b): Economic growth (booms) and declines (bust) have always been led by changes in business and durable goods investment while final consumer goods spending has been relatively stable through the business cycle.

94. (c) Option (c) is the correct choice. Refer last paragraph of the passage, "increased uncertainty can depress job growth even"

95. (e) Option (e) is the correct choice

   Analogy means a comparison between one thing and another, typically for the purpose of explanation or clarification.

   Variance means the fact or quality of being different, divergent, or inconsistent.

96. (b) Out of all the given options, only combination of sentences (A) and (F) makes a grammatically and contextually correct sentence. Hence, option (b) is the correct answer.

97. (d) Out of all the given options, only combination of sentences (B) and (D) makes a grammatically and contextually correct sentence. Hence, option (d) is the correct answer.

98. (a) Out of all the given options, only combination of sentences (C) and (E) makes a grammatically and contextually correct sentence. Hence, option (a) is the correct answer.

99. (e) Out of all the given options, none of the combinations of sentences makes a grammatically and contextually correct sentence. Hence, option (e) is the correct answer.

100. (c) Out of all the given options, combination of sentences (B) and (F) together as well as combination of sentences (C) and (D) together makes a grammatically and contextually correct sentence. Hence, option (c) is the correct answer.

REASONING & COMPUTER APTITUDE

Directions for questions 1 to 4: Answer the questions on the basis of the information given below.

A family consists of twelve members - A, B, C, D, E, F, G, H, I, J, K and L - spread across three generations. Each one has a different profession among doctor, teacher, lawyer, engineer, professor, scientist, architect, banker, businessman, student, singer and housewife. Each of the married couples has at least one child. It is also known that:

F is neither a businessman nor a student. A, the banker, is the sister-in-law of J. G does not have any nephew. The student is the daughter of L, the teacher, who is the sister of J, the scientist. B is neither an engineer nor a professor. The housewife, H, is the mother of the businessman, whose only child is an engineer - who is a male. C, is the mother of I, the female singer. E is an architect and she is the unmarried daughter of the lawyer, who is the grandfather of B. D, the doctor and the husband of L, is the son-in-law of K. One of the daughters- in-law of H is a professor.

1. Select the option having the sons of the lawyer.

    (a) G and the doctor

    (b) The scientist and E

    (c) The businessman and the scientist

    (d) The teacher and the architect

    (e) The banker and the professor.

2. What is the profession of B's father?

    (a) Teacher   (b) Doctor

    (c) Scientist   (d) Businessman

    (e) Engineer

3. Select the odd pair out.

    (a) The lawyer and the housewife

    (b) The doctor and the teacher

    (c) The scientist and the professor

    (d) The engineer and the architect

    (e) The businessman and the banker

4. Which of the following is true regarding the given family?

    (a) The businessman is the son-in-law of the lawyer.

    (b) The scientist is the brother of the banker.

    (c) The housewife has more sons than daughters.

    (d) The lawyer has two daughters and two grand-daughters.

    (e) The teacher and the banker are the two sisters of the scientist.

Directions for questions 5 to 9: Answer the questions on the basis of the information given below.

A, B, C, D, E, F, G and H are eight members of a family who are sitting around a circular table such that some of them are facing towards the center while rest are facing away from the center. Each of them works in a different company-Amul, CL, L&T, HAL, Samsung, Wills, Sahara and LG, but not necessarily in the same order. The given family has four generations. It is also known that:

Only one pair of female members face each other. The woman working in HAL sits second to the right of the person working in Amul. E and G are not immediate neighbors. The great grandmother sits to the immediate right of the son/daughter-in-law. The immediate neighbors of C are of opposite genders with respect to C. The son of A, who works in CL, sits second to the left of H and to the immediate right of the person who works in L & T. H, who is the husband of B, works in LG and is not an immediate neighbor of F's wife. Only one person sits between G, who is the mother of B, and H. F's sister E sits to the immediate right of her father, who works in Sahara. The mother of E sits to the immediate right of the person who works in Wills. B is the mother of D and is not an immediate neighbor of G. C sits second to the right of F's wife, who does not work in either HAL or L & T. Members working in HAL and Samsung face each other. D is a female member of the family.

5. How many members of the family are facing towards the center of the table?
   - (a) Two
   - (b) Three
   - (c) Four
   - (d) Five
   - (e) Cannot be determined

6. Four of the following five are alike in a certain way and thus form a group. Find the one that does not belong to the group.
   - (a) C
   - (b) G
   - (c) B
   - (d) A
   - (e) E

7. If G is related to C in a certain way and E is related to A in the same way, then who will be related to D in the same way?
   - (a) B
   - (b) A
   - (c) G
   - (d) H
   - (e) None of these

8. How many female members are there in the family?
   - (a) Two
   - (b) Three
   - (c) Four
   - (d) Five
   - (e) Either (3) or (4)

9. Who sits third to the right of the daughter of the person who works in CL?
   - (a) D
   - (b) The person working in LG
   - (c) H
   - (d) The person working in Amul
   - (e) C

Directions for questions 10 to 14: Answer the questions on the basis of the information given below.

Twelve persons, from twelve different cities sit in two parallel rows containing six seats in each row facing each other. They all are gathered at a seminar to deliver speeches on twelve different social issues.

A, B, C, D, E and F sit in row 1 and all of them face towards South while P, Q, R, S, T and U sit in row 2 and all of them face towards North but not necessarily in the same order. It is also known that:

I. Q, who is from Nagpur and the persons who speak on Dowry System and Child Marriage always sit together but not necessarily in the given order. Only two persons sit between Q and R, who is from Jaipur. Q speaks neither on Superstition nor on Juvenile Delinquency.

II. B speaks on Beggary and sits second to the right of E. Only two persons sit between B and the person who speaks on Religious conflicts. F, who is neither from Lucknow nor speaks on Alcoholism, faces the one who is from Ahmedabad.

III. A, who speaks on Illiteracy, is the only neighbour of C, who is from Bangalore. The person from Surat sits to the immediate right of the person who speaks on Communalism.

IV. E speaks on Poverty. U speaks on Child marriage and sits to the immediate left of T, who sits opposite to E. The person from Chennai sits third to the left of the person from Lucknow. The one who speaks on Poverty is neither from Mumbai nor from Hyderabad.

V. The person who speaks on Communalism sits opposite to the one who sits to the immediate right of the one who is from Chennai.

VI. P sits between the persons who speak on Child Labour and Dowry system. P and S are from Kolkata and Ahmedabad respectively.

VII. The persons who speak on Unemployment and Alcoholism do not sit in row 2 while the person from Ghaziabad does not sit in row 1. Also, the person from Pune sits at one of the ends of either of the rows.

10. If P's speech is on Superstition, then who speaks on Juvenile delinquency and which city does he belong to?
    - (a) S and he belongs to Pune
    - (b) T and he belongs to Kolkata
    - (c) Q and he belongs to Ahmedabad
    - (d) T and he belongs to Ghaziabad
    - (e) S and he belongs to Surat

11. Who sits to the immediate left of the one who speaks on Communalism?
    - (a) The person who speaks on Child marriage
    - (b) The person who is from Ghaziabad
    - (c) The person speaks on Dowry system
    - (d) The person who is from Surat
    - (e) The person who sits opposite to the one who is from Lucknow

12. Who are the immediate neighbours of the one who is from Chennai?
    (a) The one who speaks on Poverty and the one who is from Lucknow
    (b) The persons who speak on Beggary and Unemployment
    (c) The persons who are from Mumbai and Pune
    (d) The one who speaks on Poverty and the one who is from Hyderabad
    (e) The one who speaks on Beggary and the one who is from Pune

13. Who are the persons sitting between the one who is from Nagpur and the one who speaks on Child labour?
    (a) Those who speak on Juvenile delinquency and Dowry system
    (b) P and the one who is from Ahmedabad
    (c) The persons who speak on Superstition and Dowry system
    (d) The persons who are from Kolkata and Surat
    (e) S and U

14. If R is related to Bangalore in some way and F is related to Ahmedabad in the same way, then following the same condition which of the given options is correct?
    (a) P - Lucknow   (b) S - Mumbai
    (c) Q - Hyderabad   (d) D - Nagpur
    (e) B - Ahmedabad

Directions questions 15 to 19: Answer the questions on the basis of the information given below.

Eight farmers – A, B, C, D, E, F, G and H – are sitting in a row in a vegetable market and selling different vegetables among Brinjal, Capsicum, Cabbage, Mushroom, Onion, Potato, Radish and Tomato, but not necessarily in the given order. Some of them are facing north while some are facing south. They are wearing turbans of different colors among Black, Blue, Brown, Cyan, Gray, Green, Violet and White. It is also known that:

I. The farmer wearing a Black turban, who is a Tomato seller and D, who is a Brinjal seller, sit at the ends of the row facing in directions opposite to each other.

II. A, who is wearing a White turban, is not a Mushroom seller and he sits third to the right of one who is wearing a Gray turban. Also both are in facing directions opposite to each other.

III. The farmer wearing a Green turban, who is a Potato seller, sits adjacent to the farmers wearing Cyan and Gray turbans, also one of them is sitting at the end of the row. The farmer wearing a Cyan turban is a Radish seller.

IV. G, who is wearing a Green turban, and C sit at equidistant positions from A and both face in the same direction.

V. B and C sit adjacent to F, who is neither wearing a Blue nor a Brown turban. Both B and C face in a direction opposite to F, who is a Capsicum seller. C neither sells Mushrooms nor Cabbages.

VI. The one wearing a Brown turban sits on the immediate right of the one wearing a Blue turban. The farmers wearing Brown and Cyan turbans are facing in the same direction.

VII. H, who is not wearing a Brown turban, sits on the immediate left of A, who faces north.

15. Who is sitting third to the right of the Radish seller?
    (a) None
    (b) Farmer wearing Brown turban
    (c) C
    (d) Mushroom seller
    (e) Capsicum seller wearing violet turban

16. How many farmers are sitting facing towards north?
    (a) Three   (b) Six
    (c) Four   (d) Two
    (e) Five

17. Who is the Mushroom seller?
    (a) The one who is sitting third to the left of the farmer wearing a Black turban
    (b) The one who is sitting exactly between C and the farmer wearing a Cyan turban
    (c) C
    (d) The farmer wearing a Blue turban
    (e) The one who is sitting second to the right of the farmer wearing a Cyan turban

18. Which two people are sitting at the ends of the row?
    (a) B and the farmer wearing a Cyan turban
    (b) The Brinjal seller and the farmer wearing a brown turban
    (c) The Tomato seller and the farmer wearing a Gray turban
    (d) The farmers wearing Brown and Gray turbans
    (e) The farmer wearing a Black turban and the Potato seller

19. Four of the following five are alike in a certain way and so form a group. Which one does not belong to that group?
    (a) The farmer wearing a Brown turban
    (b) The Tomato seller
    (c) G
    (d) The Capsicum seller
    (e) The farmer wearing a White turban

Directions for questoins 20 to 24: Answer the questions on the basis of the information given below.

A, B, C, D, E, F, G, H, I, J, K and L are the twelve friends who live in an apartment that comprises seven floors - numbered 1 to 7 - such that each floor consists of two flats. Only one friend lives in one flat and two flats are vacant. Each of them belongs to a different state - UP, MP, Haryana, Punjab, Bihar and Assam such that exactly two friends belong to each state. It is also known that:

The friend from Haryana does not live on the same floor with the friend from UP. C and H, who belongs to Assam, live on the top floor. The two friends from MP and Haryana live together on an even numbered floor. There are only two floors between the vacant flats and only one pair of friends living on the same floor belongs to the same state. D is from Bihar and he lives alone on an even numbered floor. I lives on the lowest floor. B and E are from MP and Haryana respectively and they live on the floor which is immediately below the floor that has one of the vacant flats. The two friends from UP live on two consecutive floors; same is true for the friends from MP. G is from UP and he lives on the floor which is above the floors on which A and B from MP live. F and D belong to the same state; same is true for I and H, and E and L. G lives on the 6th floor.

20. Persons from which state live together on the same floor?

    (a) Haryana   (b) Assam
    (c) Maharashtra   (d) Punjab
    (e) UP

21. Four of the five are alike in a certain way and thus form a group. Find the one that does not belong to the group.

    (a) F   (b) G
    (c) E   (d) D
    (e) L

22. What are the numbers of the floors with the vacant floors?

    (a) 2 and 5   (b) 3 and 6
    (c) 4 and 7   (d) 1 and 4
    (e) Cannot be determined

23. How many floors are there between the floors on which F and K live?

    (a) One   (b) Two
    (c) None   (d) Three
    (e) Four

24. Which of the following pair of friends does not live on the same floor?

    (a) F and G   (b) E and B
    (c) I and L   (d) K and J
    (e) D and A

Directions for questoins 25 to 29: Answer the questions on the basis of the information given below.

Eight colored fruit boxes labelled - A, B, C, D, E, F, G and H contain different fruits in it. At most two boxes contain 1 kg fruits each and out of the remaining six boxes exactly three boxes contain 2 kg and three boxes contain 3 kg fruits each. It is also known that:

(I) The grey box contains 3 kg mangoes while the blue box contains oranges. H is a brown box that contains 1 kg fruits but not papayas.

(II) The black and green boxes contain pears and dates weighing 1 kg and 3 kg respectively.

(III) The red and yellow boxes each contain 2 kg fruits while box A contains 2 kg cherries.

(IV) Box D, which is not a yellow box, contains apples while F is a white box containing 2 kg fruits but not grapes.

(V) Box G, having weight other than 2 kg, neither contains mangoes nor pears.

(VI) C and E each contain 3 kg fruits. C is neither a blue box nor a grey box.

25. Which of the following boxes contains Papaya?

    (a) B   (b) C
    (c) D   (d) E
    (e) F

26. Which of the following combinations of boxes has equal weights?

    (a) A, C, D   (b) C, D, G
    (c) D, F, G   (d) C, E, G
    (e) B, D, G

27. What is the total weight of boxes B, D and G?

    (a) 5 kg   (b) 6 kg
    (c) 7 kg   (d) 8 kg
    (e) 9 kg

28. Which of the following combinations of Box-Weight is definitely false?

    (a) A - 2 kg   (b) B - 1 kg
    (c) D - 3 kg   (d) G - 3 kg
    (e) H - 1 kg

29. Which of the following combinations of Color-Fruits-Weight is definitely true?

    (a) Red - Apple - 3 kg
    (b) Blue - Orange - 1 kg
    (c) Red - Apple - 2 kg
    (d) Yellow - Apple - 3 kg
    (e) Red - Cherry - 2 kg

Directions for questions 30 to 33: Answer the questions on the basis of information given below.

Kintu and Pintu live in a housing complex in which Kintu's house is 18 m to the east of Pintu's. This complex is facilitated with Gym, Clubhouse, Juice Bar, Golf Course, Supermarket and a Temple. Gym is 24 to the west of Club House while Juice Bar is 20 m to the east of Temple which is 22 m south of Kintu's house.

One day, Pintu meets Kintu 4 m away from Kintu's house somewhere between their houses and from there both walk 33 m towards north and reach a T point. From there, Kintu walks 15 m towards north and reaches the Gym while Pintu walks 36 m towards east and reaches Golf Course.

After spending some hours at Golf Course, Pintu visits the Supermarket which is situated somewhere to the south-west of the Golf Course. Here, he purchases some snacks and heads towards the Juice Bar which is situated towards the south at a distance of 39 m from the Supermarket. After using the Gym for some time Kintu heads towards the Club House.

30. How far is the Gym from Pintu's house?
    (a) 48 m   (b) 50 m
    (c) 52 m   (d) 55 m
    (e) None of these

31. How far is the Golf Course from the Supermarket?
    (a) 12 m
    (b) 16 m
    (c) 20 m
    (d) 28 m
    (e) None of these

32. How far is the Juice Bar from the Gym?
    (a) 68 m
    (b) 70 m
    (c) 74 m
    (d) 78 m
    (e) None of these

33. How far and in which direction is the Clubhouse from Kintu's house?
    (a) 50 m, North-East
    (b) 50 m, North
    (c) 52 m, North-West
    (d) 50 m, West
    (e) 52 m, North-East

Directions (Q. 34 to 38): In each question below, there are four statements followed by four conclusions numbered I, II, III and IV. You have to take the four given statements to be true even if they seem to be at variance with commonly known facts and then decide which of the given conclusions logically follows from the four given statements, disregarding commonly known facts. Then decide which of the answers (1), (2), (3), (4) and (5) is the correct answer.

34. **Statements**: Some schools are colleges. Some colleges are hostels. No hostel is office. All offices are institutes.

    Conclusions:
    I.   No hostel is institute.
    II. Some hostels are schools.
    III. Some hostels are institutes.
    IV. Some offices are colleges.
    (a) Only I follows
    (b) Only II and III follows
    (c) Only IV follows
    (d) Only either I or III follows
    (e) None of these

35. **Statements:** Some pins are needles. Some threads are needles. All needles are nails. All nails are hammers.

    Conclusions:
    I.   Some pins are hammers.
    II. Some threads are nails.
    III. Some pins are threads.
    IV. No pin is thread.
    (a) Only I, II and either III or IV follow
    (b) Only III and IV follow
    (c) Only I and II follow
    (d) All follow
    (e) None of these

36. **Statements**: Some chairs are rooms. No room is sofa. All sofas are tables. Some tables are desks.

    Conclusions:
    I.   Some sofas are desks.
    II. No room is table.
    III. Some chairs are tables.
    IV. No desk is room.
    (a) None follows
    (b) Only I follows
    (c) Only either II or III follows
    (d) Only III and IV follow
    (e) All follow

37. **Statements:** Some rings are chains. All chains are bangles. All bracelets are bangles. Some bangles are pendants.

    Conclusions:

    I.   Some rings are bangles.

    II. Some chains are pendants.

    III. Some bracelets are rings.

    V.   No pendant is ring.

    (a) None follows

    (b) Only I follows

    (c) Only II and III follow

    (d) Only IV follows

    (e) None of these

38. **Statements:** Some books are pens. Some pens are pencils. Some pencils are mobiles. Some mobiles are erasers.

    Conclusions:

    I.   Some erasers are pens.

    II. All books are pens.

    III. Some erasers might be books.

    IV. All mobiles are books.

    (a) Only I follows   (b) Only II follows

    (c) Only III follows   (d) Only IV follows

    (e) None of these

Directions (Q. 39): In the question below, a statement is followed by two assumptions numbered I and II. An assumption is something supposed or taken for granted. You have to consider the statement and the following assumptions and decide which of the assumptions is implicit in the statement.

(a) if only assumption I is implicit.

(b) if only assumption II is implicit.

(c) if either assumption I or assumption II is implicit.

(d) if neither assumption I nor assumption II is implicit.

(e) if both assumption I and assumption II are implicit

39. **Statement:**

    The railway authority has announced that it will carry out major repair work for two days beginning Saturday on the main line connecting the two big cities in the state, bringing rail service to a halt.

    Assumptions:

    I.   People may reschedule their journey in view of the railway authority's decision.

    II. People may still plan their travel by train between the two cities even on these two days.

Directions (Q. 40 and 41): Each of the following questions consists of one statement and two assumptions numbered I and II. Examine the statements and select the correct answer using the code given below.

Code:

(a) if only assumption I is implicit

(b) if only assumption II is implicit

(c) if both assumptions I and II are implicit

(d) if neither assumption I nor II is implicit

(e) if either assumption I or II is implicit

40. **Statement:** The pulse polio campaign can now be considered successful since not a single case of polio was reported in the last year.

    Assumptions:

    I.   At least one case of polio was reported in the year before the last.

    II. One year is a long enough period to draw a conclusion about the success of the campaign.

41. **Statement:** "Motivated forgetting" is an especially galling species of ironic effect: when a message makes you feel vulnerable – for example, by reminding you of the ways in which your gender or ethnicity places you at a disadvantage – you're more likely to find ways, conscious or otherwise, to forget it, in order to retain a sense of self-control.

    Assumptions:

    I.   Anything that makes you feel vulnerable affects your sense of self-control.

    II. There are other species or types of ironic effect.

Directions (Q. 42): In the following question, two statements numbered I and II are given. There may or may not be a cause and effect relationship between them. Choose your answer according to the code given below.

Code:

(a) I is the main cause and II is the main effect.

(b) I is an effect but II is not the main cause.

(c) II is the main cause and I is the main effect.

(d) II is an effect but I is not the main cause.

(e) Either Statement I or II can be a cause.

42. **Statement I:** The government does not want smaller parties and independent candidates to be at a disadvantage owing to their limited finance.

    Statement II: The government has decided to put a cap on election expenses of political parties.

43. The government has been building expressways in all the districts of Manipur. Which of the following is a possible effect of the above cause?

(a) Journey time between towns has been considerably reduced.

(b) Insurgency has increased because of the increased connectivity.

(c) Deforestation has taken place because of road construction activities.

(d) A lot of migrant labourers are seen in Manipur nowadays.

(e) The expressways have become very unsafe, especially after sunset.

44. The government has started regulating the activities of different non-governmental organisations (NGOs) across the country.

Which of the following is a possible effect of the above cause?

(a) Foreign donations have stopped coming.

(b) Fake NGOs are finding it extremely difficult to survive.

(c) Celebrities have stopped endorsing NGOs.

(d) People have lost faith in NGOs.

(e) NGOs have stopped operating in rural areas.

45. The government is giving Khel Ratna scholarships to poor but meritorious students.

Which of the following is a possible effect of the above cause?

(a) Poor students will find it easier to pursue extra-curricular activities.

(b) Poor students can now migrate to cities from small villages in order to study.

(c) Poor, yet meritorious students will find it easier to complete their studies and not get themselves engaged in work.

(d) After getting the scholarship, many students have adopted a casual approach to studies.

(e) To get the scholarship, students often have to bribe the officials of the Youth Welfare Ministry.

DATA ANALYSIS & INTERPRETATION

Directions (Q. 46 to 50) : Answer the questions on the basis of the information given below.

The table given below shows the data related to performance of six batsmen in the world cup 2015.

Name of batsman	Number of matches played in the world cup 2015	Average runs scored in the world cup 2015	Total balls faced in the world cup 2015	Strike rate
Kohli	8	-	-	129.6
Rohit	20	81	-	-
Dhoni	-	38	400	114
Suresh	-	-	-	72
Dhawan	28	55	1280	-
Ravindra	-	-	-	66

Note:

(i) Strike rate = (Total runs scored/ Total balls faced) × 100

(ii) All the given batsmen could bat in all the given matches played by them.

(iii) Few values are missing in the table (indicated by —). A candidate is expected to calculate the missing value, if it is required to answer the given question, on the basis of the given data.

46. The respective ratio between total number of balls faced by Suresh and that by Ravindra in the world cup 2015, is 3 : 4. Total number of runs scored by Ravindra in the world cup 2015 is what percent more than the total runs scored by Suresh in the world cup 2015?

(a) $22\frac{2}{9}\%$ (b) $32\frac{4}{9}\%$ (c) $18\frac{8}{9}\%$ (d) $24\frac{4}{9}\%$ (e) $28\frac{2}{9}\%$

47. If the runs scored by Dhawan in last 3 matches of the world cup 2015 are not considered, his average runs scored in the first 25 matches of the world cup 2015 will decrease by 9. If the runs scored by Dhawan in the 26th and 27th match are below 128 and no two scores among these 3 scores are equal, what is the minimum possible score of Dhawan in the 28th match?

    (a) 137   (b) 135
    (c) 141   (d) 133
    (e) 139

48. In the world cup 2015, the total number of balls faced by Kohli is 74 less than the total number of runs scored by him. What is the average score of Kohli in the world cup 2015?

    (a) 42.5   (b) 39.5
    (c) 38   (d) 44
    (e) 40.5

49. Rohit faced an equal number of balls in the first 10 and last 10 matches he played in the world cup 2015. If his strike rate in first 10 matches and last 10 matches are 120 and 150 respectively, what is the total number of balls faced by him in the world cup 2015?

    (a) 1150   (b) 1400
    (c) 1200   (d) 1000
    (e) 1500

50. What is the number of matches played by Dhoni in the world cup 2015?

    (a) 10   (b) 16
    (c) 12   (d) 18
    (e) 8

Directions for questions 51 to 55: In the following questions, two quantities given numbered I and II. Compare these quantities and mark your option as:

(a) if Quantity I > Quantity II

(b) if Quantity I ≥ Quantity II

(c) if Quantity I = Quantity II or relationship can't be established

(d) if Quantity I < Quantity II

(e) if Quantity I ≤ Quantity II

51. **Quantity I:** The cost price of x articles is equal to the selling price of 16 articles and the percentage of profit is 25%. Find the profit/loss percent if the selling price of 'x' articles is equal to the cost price of 25 articles.

    Quantity II: The price of sugar is increased by 20% but the consumption is decreased to two third. Find the percentage change in the expenditure of sugar.

52. **Quantity I:** A, B and C started a business by investing capitals in the ratio of 1 : 2 : 3 respectively. At the end of the first year B invested an additional amount of Rs. 400 while C took out Rs. 600. Due to this, the new ratio of their respective investments became 4 : 10 : 9. Find the amount invested by A at the start of the business.

    Quantity II: A sum of Rs. 4,000 has been divided among P, Q and R in such a way that P receives 2/3rd of the share of Q and R, and R receives 1/4th of the share of P and Q. Find the difference between the amounts received by Q and R.

53. **Quantity I:** Two trains running at 54 km/hr and 72 km/hr respectively in opposite directions cross each other in 12 seconds. If the first train crosses a man running at 18 km/hr in the same direction in 18 seconds, then find the length of the second train.

    Quantity II: A train completely crosses two sprinters running in the same direction at speeds of 18 km/hr and 9 km/hr and in 72 and 48 seconds respectively. What is the length of the train?

54. **Quantity I:** The respective ratio of the numbers p, q and r, are 3 : 4 : 5 and $p + q + r = 12$. If $q = 2p - 2a$ and $r = b - q$, then find the value of $b - 6a$.

    Quantity II: Find the minimum value of the expression: $\dfrac{5x^2 + 1}{(5x^2 - 2)} + 3$

55. **Quantity I:** The volume of a solid sphere is equal to the volume of a cylinder whose height and radius are 8 cm and 6 cm respectively. Find the total surface area of the hemisphere whose radius is equal to half of the radius of the solid sphere.

    Quantity II: What will be the area of a triangle whose three sides are 20 cm, 21 cm and 29 cm.

Directions (Q. 56 to 60): Answer the questions on the basis of the information given below.

7200 students are going for higher studies to three different Universities – Harvard, Stanford and Oxford. $\dfrac{6}{25}$ th of the total students opted for Harvard, 32% opted for Stanford and remaining students opted for Oxford. $\dfrac{5}{18}$ th of the total students who are going to pursue their study from Harvard pay the fees on their own, $\dfrac{1}{3}$ rd of remaining students from this University pay half of their fees on their own and the remaining half would be paid by bank loan, remaining students are solely dependent on bank loan for their fee.

$\frac{2}{9}$th of the total students who are going to pursue higher study from Stanford University pay fees on their own, 50% students from this University pay half of the fees from their side and the remaining half will be paid by bank loan and remaining students are solely dependent on bank loan for their fee. $\frac{13}{36}$th of the total students who are going to pursue their study from Oxford University pay their fees on their own, $\frac{7}{18}$th of total students from this University pay half of the fees on their own and the remaining half would be paid by bank loan and the remaining students are solely dependent on bank loan for their fees.

56. The students from Havard who are solely dependent on bank loan form what percent of the total number of students from all the three Universities who are solely dependent on bank loan for their fees?

(a) 41.24% (b) 36.75%

(c) 30.12% (d) 28.92%

(e) 25.64%

57. If due to some reasons number of students going for their study in Harvard is decreased by 33.33%, then what is the respective ratio between number of remaining students in Harvard to the total number of students of remaining two Universities together?

(a) 19 : 4 (b) 6 : 11

(c) 4 : 19 (d) 6 : 19

(e) 19 : 6

58. What is the difference between the average number of students who pay their total fees on their own in all the three Universities together and total number of students who are solely dependent on bank loan for their fees in all the three Universities together?

(a) 1252 (b) 1562

(c) 1572 (d) 1552

(e) 1592

59. Total number of students going to pursue their studies from Stanford University forms approximately, what percent of those who are going to Harvard and Oxford Universities together?

(a) 49 (b) 45

(c) 47 (d) 46

(e) 43

60. If, X = S + H – O

Y = S + O – H

Z = O + H – S

Then, find the value of X : Y : Z. Where, S represents total number of students going to study in Stanford University. H represents total number of students going to study in Harvard University. O represents total number of students going to study in Oxford University.

(a) 3 : 9 : 13 (b) 13 : 3 : 9

(c) 9 : 3 : 13 (d) 3 : 13 : 9

(e) 9 : 13 : 3

Directions (Q. 61 to 65): Answer the questions on the basis of the information given below.

In a medical college there are 1600 students studying Dentistry and Homeopathy. Each student from each course knows one or more languages out of English, Hindi and Bangla. 45% of the students study Dentistry and remaining students study Homeopathy.

Out of the students studying Dentistry, boys and girls are in the ratio of 5 : 3 respectively.

Out of the boys studying Dentistry, 16% know only English, 10% know only Hindi and 10% know only Bangla. 20% know only English as well as Hindi. 20% know HIndi as well as Bangal. 10% know only English as well as Bangla. Remaining boys know all three languages.

Out of the girls studying Dentistry 10% know only English, 10% know only Hindi and 20% know only Bangla. 10% know only Enlgish as well as Hindi. 20% know only English as well Bangla. 20% know only Hindi as well as Bangla. Remaining girls know all three languages.

Out of the students studying Homeopathy boys and girls are in the ratio of 4 : 7 respectively.

Out of the boys studying Homoepathy, 20% know only English, 15% know only Hindi and 5% know only Bangla, 15% know only English as well as Hindi. 25% know only English as well as Bangla. 10% know only Hindi as well as Bangla. Remaining boys know all three languages.

Out of the girls studing Homeopathy, 15% know only English, 15% know only Hindi and 5% know only Bangla. 20% know only English as well as Hindi, 20% know only English as well as Bangla and 15% know only Hindi as well as Bangla. Remaining girls know all three languages.

61. How many students studying Dentistry and Homeopathy do not know Bangla?

(a) 728 (b) 735

(c) 782 (d) 872

(e) None of these

62. What precent of the total number of girls in the college know both Bangla and English but do not know Hindi?

    (a) 16   (b) 13

    (c) 20   (d) 17

    (e) 21

63. Out of the students studying Homeopathy, what is the ratio between the number of girls knowing only Hindi and Bangla together and the number of boys knowing only English and Bangla together?

    (a) 21 : 20   (b) 19 : 20

    (c) 20 : 19   (d) 20 : 21

    (e) None of these

64. Out of the total number of students studying Homeopathy, what percent knows at least two languages?

    (a) 53   (b) 63

    (c) 68   (d) 70

    (e) 74

65. What percent of the total number of girls in the college do not know Hindi and Bangla together?

    (a) 26.63   (b) 73.37

    (c) 62.27   (d) 43.47

    (e) None of these

Directions (Q. 66 to 70): Each of the questions below consists of a question and three statements numbered I, II and III given below it. You have to decide whether the data provided in the statements are sufficient to answer the question and select the appropriate option.

66. Find the difference in the time taken by A and B to complete a piece of work together and that by B and C to complete it by working together.

    I. A, B and C can complete the same work in 15 days. Also, ratio of the efficiencies of A and B, and B and C is 3 : 4.

    II. A and B together are 25% less efficient than B and C, while, A and C together are 25% more efficient than B and C.

    III. A and C can complete the same work in 18 days while A, B and C can complete the same work in 15 days.

    (a) Only I and II   (b) Only II and III

    (c) Either I or II and III   (d) All three of them

    (e) None of these

67. What will be the ratio of the ages of Suman and Sushil after five years?

    I. Respective ratio of the present ages of Sushil and Sukant is 7 : 6, while the respective ratio of the ages of Suman and Sukant five years ago was 4 : 5.

    II. Respective ratio of the sum of the present ages of Suman and Sushil and that of Suman and Sukant is 12 : 11.

    III. Sushil is ten years elder than Suman who in turn is five years younger than Sukant.

    (a) Only I and II   (b) Either I or III

    (c) Either I or II and III   (d) All three of them

    (e) None of these

68. Find the time taken by Train A to cross a platform whose length is 40% more than the length of the train.

    I. Length of Train B is 250 m and it takes 45 sec to cross stationary Train A whose length is 200 m.

    II. Speed of Train B is 53 m/s and it crosses a platform of length 280 m in 10 sec.

    III. Speed of Train A is 35 m/s and the length of the platform is 267 m.

    (a) Either II or III

    (b) Only III

    (c) Both I and II

    (d) Either III or only I and II

    (e) Only I

69. Find the profit/loss percentage incurred by the shopkeeper while selling a book.

    I. Cost price is 20% less than the mark price of the book and the discount offered is equal to 10% of the cost price.

    II. Ratio of the cost price and the selling price is 9 : 11 after getting a discount of 22.5% of the mark price.

    III. Ratio of the cost price and the mark price is 8 : 13 while the ratio of the selling price and the mark price is 9 : 11.

    (a) Both III and II   (b) Either I or II

    (c) Only I   (d) Either I or II or III

    (e) Only II

70. Find the compound interest received on a sum of Rs. 5,876 after three years if the rate of interest is x%.

    I. The ratio of the simple interest and the principal after five years at x% per annum is 1 : 4.

    II. Simple interest received on Rs. 5,876 after 2.5 years is Rs. 146.75.

    III. The value of 'x' is the average of first nine natural numbers.

    (a) Either I or II

    (b) Either II or III

    (c) Only III

    (d) Either I or II or III

    (e) None of these

Directions (Q. 71 to 75): Answer the questions on the basis of the information given below.

The first bar diagram given below shows the percentage discounts offered by four retail outlets on four different commodities – A, B, C and D. After allowing these discounts, the percentage profits earned by the outlets on selling these commodities are given in the second bar diagram.

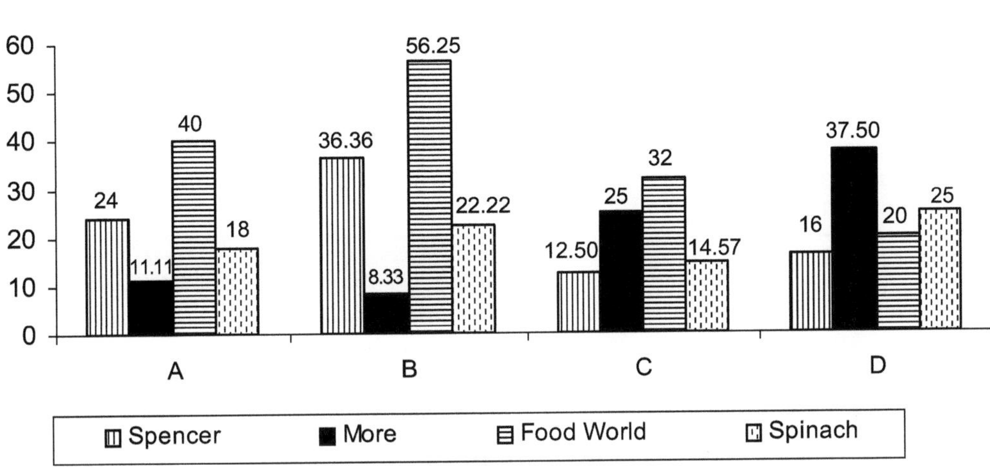

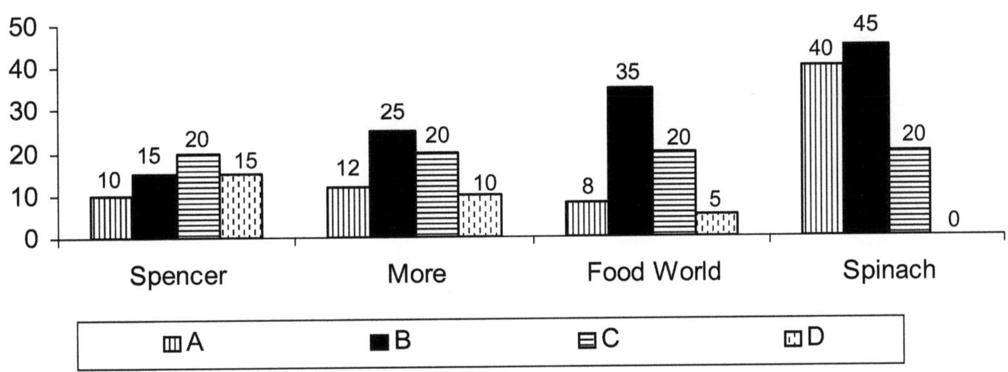

71. If the marked price of A is same at all the four outlets, which outlet must have purchased A at the least price?
    (a) Spencer   (b) More
    (c) Food World   (d) Spinach
    (e) Food World and Spencer

72. If the marked prices of all the four commodities are same at More, which commodity must have been purchased at the highest price by More?
    (a) D   (b) C
    (c) B   (d) A
    (e) A and D

73. What is the mark-up percentage for commodity B at Spencer?
    (a) 84.84   (b) 80.71
    (c) 87.67   (d) 86.73
    (e) 78.63

74. If the marked price of commodity D at Food World is Rs.325, then what is the cost price of commodity D at Food World?
    (a) Rs.247.62   (b) Rs.260
    (c) Rs.145.35   (d) Rs.237.57
    (e) Rs.257.63

75. If the cost price of commodity C at Spinach is Rs.1,050, then what is the marked price of commodity C at Spinach?
    (a) Rs.1,522.50
    (b) Rs.1,474.89
    (c) Rs.1,382.26
    (d) Rs.1,872.16
    (e) Rs.1,657.36

Directions (Q. 76 to 80): Answer the questions on the basis of the information given below.

The multiple bar diagram given below shows the data regarding cost of production and sales revenue of company XYZ in the given years have been given.

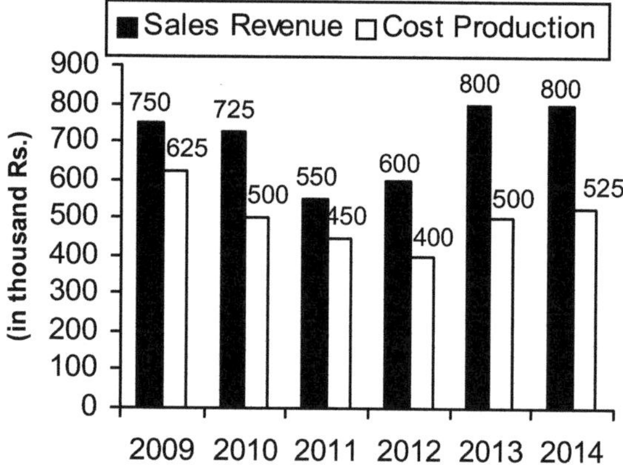

76. In how many years the cost of production is more than the average cost of production of the given years?
    (a) 1   (b) 2
    (c) 3   (d) 4
    (e) None of these

77. In how many years the sales revenue is less than the average sales revenue of the given years?
    (a) 1   (b) 3
    (c) 2   (d) 4
    (e) None of these

78. If the cost of production in 2009 and 2012 be increased by 25% and 30% respectively, then by what percent will the total cost in these two years be more than the sales revenue of the year 2013?
    (a) 62.7%   (b) 65.7%
    (c) 67.7%   (d) 68.5%
    (e) None of these

79. In which year the company had maximum profit percent?
    (a) 2013   (b) 2012
    (c) 2011   (d) 2010
    (e) 2009

80. If the sales revenues in the years 2010, 2011 and 2012 increased by 20%, 25% and 30% respectively and the costs of production in the years 2012, 2013 and 2014 increased by 20%, 25% and 35% respectively, what will be the difference between average sales revenue and average cost of production?
    (a) Rs. 185.59 thousands
    (b) Rs. 188.59 thousands
    (c) Rs. 174.59 thousands
    (d) Rs. 200.59 thousands
    (e) None of these

GENERAL/ECONOMY/ BANKING AWARENESS

81. First CFO of Reserve Bank of India is:
    (a) Sudha Balakrishnan
    (b) Usha Anantasubramaian
    (c) Arundhati Bhattacharya
    (d) Usha Thorat
    (d) Chanda Kochar

82. The winner of Kabaddi Masters Dubai 2018 championship:
    (a) Pakistan
    (b) India
    (c) Iran
    (d) Nepal
    (e) Bangladesh

83. Amangarh Tiger Reserve is located in:
    (a) Madhya Pradesh
    (b) Rajasthan
    (c) Uttar Pradesh
    (d) Haryana
    (e) Uttarakhand

84. Total Fund allocated for "Operation Green" is:
    (a) 100 crore   (b) 200 crore
    (c) 300 crore   (d) 400 crore
    (e) Rs 500 crore

85. The first tri Military Exercise was held between India and:
    (a) Russia   (b) Australia
    (c) UK   (d) France
    (e) Germany

86. Andres Iniesta (Football Playe (r)   belongs to:
    (a) Italy   (b) Spain
    (c) Germany   (d) France
    (e) Portugal

87. The government has identified ___ Regional Rural Banks (RRB   (s) for listing on stock exchanges in line with the Union Budget 2018-19.
   (a) 2   (b) 3
   (c) 4   (d) 6
   (e) 9

88. Which of the following country remains the top export destination for India in 2018:
   (a) Singapore   (b) Russia
   (c) Japan   (d) USA
   (e) France

89. AU Small Finance Bank will raise Rs. 1000 crore from Temasek, a global investment company headquartered in:
   (a) Japan   (b) Germany
   (c) Singapore   (d) Mauritius
   (e) France

90. Artist Anjolie Ela Menon conferred the Kalidas Samman for year:
   (a) 2013   (b) 2014
   (c) 2015   (d) 2017
   (e) 2018

91. Full form of NSFR in economic terms is:
   (a) Net Stable Funding Ratio
   (b) Net Start Fund Ratio
   (c) Near Stable Fund Recurring
   (d) Net Standing Fund Ratio
   (e) None of the above

92. Numaligarh Refinery Limited Public Sector oil Company is located in:
   (a) Gujarat   (b) Assam
   (c) Rajasthan   (d) Arunachal Pradesh
   (e) Andhra Pradesh

93. RBI releases limited edition coins to mark 350th birth anniversary of Sikh Guru:
   (a) Guru Nanak Dev Ji
   (b) Guru Gobind Singh Ji
   (c) Guru Angad Dev Ji
   (d) Guru Ramdas Ji
   (e) Guru Arjan Dev Ji

94. Which of the following banks launched the "Yono App"?
   (a) Punjab National Bank
   (b) Canara Bank
   (c) HDFC Bank
   (d) ICICI Bank
   (e) State Bank of India

95. Asteroid Day is an annual global event which is held on the anniversary of the Siberian Tunguska event that took place on:
   (a) 23rd May   (b) 29th May
   (c) 1st June   (d) 15th June
   (e) 30th June

96. Which of the following is not true regarding a Payment Bank?
   (a) A restricted deposit, which is currently limited to Rs.100,000 per customer
   (b) The bank cannot provide loan
   (c) Both current account and savings accounts can be operated by such banks.
   (d) Bharti Airtel set up India's first live payments bank.
   (e) Payments banks can issue services like ATM cards, debit cards, net-banking and mobile-banking.

97. What percentage of Small Finance Bank's net credits should be in priority sector lending?
   (a) 20%   (b) 35%
   (c) 50%   (d) 75%
   (e) 85%

98. Which of the following Indian city is to get India's first e-waste plant?
   (a) Bengaluru   (b) Chennai
   (c) Mumbai   (d) Lucknow
   (e) Surat

99. Which of the following banks launched 'Social Pay' for Non-Resident Indians (NRI (s) in April 2018?
   (a) HDFC Bank
   (b) ICICI Bank
   (c) State Bank of India
   (d) Yes Bank
   (e) IDFC Bank

100. Who among the following is schedule to organise India's First Global Mobility Summit?
   (a) Ministry of Micro, Small and Medium Enterprises
   (b) Ministry of Corporate Affairs
   (c) Ministry of Electronics and Information Technology
   (d) NITI Aayog
   (e) RBI

101. Jayant Ganpat Nadkarni who passed away in July 2018 was:
   (a) 14th Chief of the Naval Staff
   (b) 13th Air Chief Marshal
   (c) 14th General of Indian Army
   (d) 13th Admiral of Indian Navy
   (e) 1st Indian Auditor General

102. National Digital Communications Policy 2018 attracts investments of US Dollar:
   (a) 10 billion
   (b) 100 billion
   (c) 250 billion
   (d) 500 billion
   (e) 1000 billion

103. Government forms panel to upgrade norms for state, district level economic data collection- .

104. The Government formed the Ravindra Dholakia committee for RRBs to maintain the minimum prescribed Capital to Risk Weighted Assets Ratio (CRA (R) of:.
   (a) 4%
   (b) 5%
   (c) 8%
   (d) 9%
   (e) 12%

105. Commerce and Industry Minister Smt. Nirmala Sitharaman has launched the TIES. What is the meaning of "E" in TIES?
   (a) Education
   (b) Eligibility
   (c) Employment
   (d) Expansion
   (e) Export

106. Atal Pension Yojana (AP(Y)was launched in May 2015 and current number of subscriber stands at:
   (a) 45 lakhs
   (b) 72 lakhs
   (c) 88 lakhs
   (d) 1.10 crore
   (e) 1.45 crore

107. As per the UNCTAD, the foreign inflows to India decreased from USD 44 billion in 2016 to USD ……………..in 2017.
   (a) 40 billion
   (b) 38 billion
   (c) 35 billion
   (d) 30 billion
   (e) 25 billion

108. The new 50Rs denomination has motif of ……….. on the reverse, depicting the country's cultural heritage:
   (a) Sanchi Stupa
   (b) Mount Harriet, Port Blair
   (c) Hampi with Chariot
   (d) Red Fort
   (e) Mangalyaan

109. IBC had strictly mandated that within 180 days (…………………….as extension from the NCL (T) the resolution process of an insolvent company had to be completed.
   (a) 45 days
   (b) 60 days
   (c) 90 days
   (d) 120 days
   (e) 180 days

110. In July 2018 Reserve Bank of India granted license to ……………… to set up its first branch in India.
   (a) Industrial and Commercial Bank of China
   (b) Agricultural Bank of China
   (c) China Construction Bank
   (d) Bank of China
   (e) Bank of Communications

111. Paramparagat Krishi Vikas Yojana (PKV (Y) is the Central government plan for free certification programme for:
   (a) Paddy farmers
   (b) Sugarcane farmers
   (c) Wheat farmers
   (d) Organic farmers
   (e) Grape farmers

112. In June 2018 RBL Bank buys 100% stake in:
   (a) Bajaj Finserv
   (b) Swadhaar FinServe
   (c) Nesam Finserve
   (d) India Finserve
   (e) ICICI FinServe

113. "Project Sashakt" has the five-pronged strategy to deal with :
   (a) Training introduced by BCCI for Indian cricket players
   (b) Power Shortage
   (c) Water Storage in dams
   (d) Nuclear Capability
   (e) Non-performing assets (NPA(s)

114. "Behdienkhlam festival" is celebrated in the month of July for good health, property and bumper harvest in which of the following Indian state?
   (a) Meghalaya
   (b) Telangana
   (c) Tripura
   (d) Manipur
   (e) Kerala

115. In line with the Prime Minister's 'per drop more crop' initiative, the government approved a corpus of …………………….for the setting up of a dedicated micro irrigation fund (MI(F) under the National Bank for Agriculture and Rural Development (NABAR(D).
   (a) Rs 2,000 crore
   (b) Rs 3,000 crore
   (c) Rs 4,000 crore
   (d) Rs 5,000 crore
   (e) Rs 10,000 crore

116. Name India's fastest and the fourth fastest supercomputer in the world dedicated to weather and climate research recently?
   (a) Kaustubh
   (b) Parakram
   (c) Atulya
   (d) Praveen
   (e) Pratyush

117. Name the Bollywood singer, nominated as the Green Ambassador of Sikkim in May 2018?
     (a) Arijit Singh   (b) Ankit Tiwari
     (c) Mohit Chauhan   (d) Sonu Nigam
     (e) Vishal Dadlani

118. The finance ministry reconstituted the Banks Board Bureau (BB (B)and appointed ....as the new chairman.
     (a) Vedika Bhandarkar
     (b) P. Pradeep Kumar
     (c) Bhanu Pratap Sharma
     (d) Pradip Shah
     (e) Chanda Kocchar

119. Which of the following countries is set to host the fourth BIMSTEC Summit in August 2018?
     (a) Sri Lanka   (b) Thailand
     (c) Nepal   (d) Bhutan
     (e) India

120. Prime Minister Narendra Modi launched India's first wellness centre under Ayushman Bharat in:
     (a) Uttar Pradesh   (b) Haryana
     (c) Chhattisgarh   (d) Karnataka
     (e) Punjab

ENGLISH LANGUAGE

Directions (121-128): Read the following passage carefully and answer the questions given below it. Certain parts are given in bold to answer some of the questions based on the passage.

We all are aware of the fact that nothing is permanent in this world, neither products nor technology. As day by day, improvements and updations are made in technology, leading to new inventions and innovations in every sphere of life. Invention refers to the creation of a brand new product or device. Conversely, innovation is an act of making changes to the existing product or the process by introducing new ways or ideas. At first sight, the two terms sound alike, but if you dig deeper, you will find that there is a fine line of difference between invention and innovation that lies in their connotations. While invention is all about creating or designing something, innovation is the process of turning a creative idea into reality. **[A] There is often a fine line between genius and insanity.** Innovation is not only important on the individual level, but can make or break a business as well.

Innovative businesses create dynamic products, adjust existing services, and/or implement new ideas. **[B] They are not afraid to color outside the lines and try something new, even if it is risky.** If a business is not innovative, they risk losing work to competitors. Lack of innovation also has indirect results such as losing staff and decreasing engagement. Therefore, innovation cannot be an afterthought, but rather a crucial element that is included in part of your strategy. It should be a cultural outlook that impacts thinking and improves problem solving. Many successful companies attribute their success to their innovative practices. That said, inventing and innovation are not one in the same. Invention focuses on creating new items or new ways to produce existing items. Very often, invention is a result of innovation, but it is not a requirement. Although invention can be beneficial to a business, the level of importance and necessity can vary according to the industry.

[C] The era of invention is not over, but they have definitely been pushed aside for an era of innovation. While many people are still out there trying to come up with the next "big invention" that is going to improve humanity, businesses have discovered that innovation seems to not only trump invention in furthering a company's brand and profitability, but it can be far cheaper when all the framework is already completed. This can be seen from many major businesses that choose to innovate rather than invent, such as Apple and Sony. First, we must distinguish the difference between invention and innovation. Invention is the creation of a product or introduction of a new process, for example the Alternating Current induction motor is an invention created in 1888. An innovation occurs when someone improves on or makes a significant contribution to an item or process that has already been invented; the Apple iPhone is an innovation of the cell phone. It seems that great inventors are smaller in number - perhaps business models are leaning towards enabling innovation.

Sony's influence in the technology market started with the invention of the first tape recorder and through years of creativity and perseverance, became innovators of a variety of categories, from computing and electronics to entertainment. Sony shows corporations that for a business to thrive in today's market, a company cannot stay stagnant with on particular item - innovations are essential. Innovation drives economic growth. Five combination patterns are what create innovation. These are, the production of a new good, a new method of production, a new market, acquiring a new source of raw minerals and the emergence of a new organization. **[D] A company does not need to invent to have a competitive edge in the market, but need to innovate and create a product that is based on the needs and desires of the consumer.**

121. With what example has the author described 'innovation' as a change that can even prove to be economically lucrative?

(a) Since innovation is coming up with a fresh idea, it leads to research and development department of the organization.

(b) Innovation is a result of invention and hence is economically feasible too.

(c) It focuses on creating new items or new ways to produce existing items.

(d) Innovation can make or break a business as well.

(e) Innovation results in boosting up of economy as an idea for a product or process that has never been made before is highlighted.

122. How is innovation a crucial element that its absence impacts business strategy?

(a) As the companies are destined to fail in its absence because of the stagnant growth.

(b) Competitors could avail benefits over not so innovative businesses.

(c) The lack of innovation has secondary impacts such as losing staff and decreasing engagement.

(d) Both (a) and (b)

(e) Both (b) and (c)

123. Which of the following statements infers that an era of invention has not been dissipated but instead pushed aside by that of innovation?

(a) Innovation outclasses invention in enhancing a company's brand's name and profit.

(b) Innovation is far cheaper than invention when all the framework is completed.

(c) As business models are leading towards enabling new inventions which require scientific skills.

(d) Both (a) and (b)

(e) Both (b) and (c)

124. "Sony chose to innovate rather than invent". How has this helped its business to grow?

(a) Sony made a significant contribution to the item by inventing products according to the needs of the consumer.

(b) Sony needs to invent to have a competitive edge in the market.

(c) Innovation helped Sony against staying stagnant with one item.

(d) Business models like Sony are leaning towards enabling invention which has helped businesses to grow.

(e) All of these.

125. What can be illustrated from statement [A] "There is often a fine line between genius and insanity."

(a) One should be careful while innovating as a successful innovation can build a business while a failure can destabilize the business.

(b) Genius and insane innovations cannot be separated through a thin line of difference.

(c) Genius innovations can turn into insane outcomes if they fall within the line.

(d) Insane innovations provide a line to develop genius innovations.

(e) None of these

126. What can be inferred from statement [B] "They are not afraid to color outside the lines and try something new, even if it is risky"?

(a) Businessmen innovates every colorful product even though it is risky for their enterprise.

(b) Businessmen do not analysis the pros and cons while developing the new innovation.

(c) Businessmen are ready to think or act in a way that does not conform to set rules even though it is quite risky for the business.

(d) Businessmen set their minds to break the rules required to introduce a new innovation.

(e) None of these

127. Statement [C] "The era of invention is not over, but they have definitely been pushed aside for an era of innovation" in the passage may not be grammatically or contextually correct. Choose the most suitable alternative that will replace the statement to adhere to the grammatical syntax of the paragraph.

(a) The era of invention is not over, but it has definitely been pushed aside to an era of innovation.

(b) The era of invention is not over, but it has definitely been pushed aside for an era of innovation.

(c) The eras of invention is not over, but they have definitely been pushed aside for an eras of innovation.

(d) The era of invention is not over, but they had definitely been pushed aside for an era of innovation.

(e) None of these

128. According to the author, in reference with the statement **[D] "A company does not need to invent to have a competitive edge in the market, but need to innovate and create a product that is based on the needs and desires of the** consumer", what should be the criteria for innovation?

(a) Profits   (b) Market trends

(c) Competition   (d) Customer satisfaction

(e) None of these

Directions (129-135): Read the following passage carefully and answer the questions given below it. Certain words are given in bold to help you locate them while answering some of the questions.

Compounding the **woes** for the solar power industry Maharashtra's appellate authority for advance ruling (AAAR) has held that solar power projects are liable to 18% goods and services tax (GST) and not at the lower rate of 5% as claimed by power producers. With the appellate authority reinforcing similar rulings by some other state level authority for advance ruling including of Rajasthan and Maharashtra, this issue seems to be headed for a **prolonged** legal battle unless the government decides to step in and issue clarifications on the taxability of solar power projects. **[A] A rise in project cost could get reflected in the power tariffs that solar power developers offer in auctions to win projects.** With electricity out of the goods and services tax (GST), the higher tax rate becomes an outright cost for the producers thus inflating the final price of the solar power. A government proposal to levy safeguard duty on imported solar panels that is meant to support domestic panel manufacturers is another factor that has brought some uncertainty to solar power project developers.

Solar power generation panels, which constitute around 60-70% of the cost of the solar power projects, are taxed at 5% GST. However, the AAARs have held that setting up of solar projects are covered under the classification of works contract as they consist of supply of goods and services packaged into an immovable property. They held that because of this, these projects are **liable** to be taxed at 18% that applies to works contracts. In the pre-GST era, only a small part of the total project cost, nearly a tenth of it, was covered by a service tax of 15%. The net tax effect on the solar power industry in a pre-GST regime was less than 5%, a reflection of the tax breaks it enjoyed across excise and value added tax.

The higher tax rates being levied on solar power projects is despite the NDA government's focused approach to promote solar power. The industry has sought government intervention to lower the tax burden on such projects.

[B] The solar industry may be about to face what imported coal-based power projects saw some years back — an increase in production cost due to changes in law and the imposition of new tariffs. Due to a safeguards duty recently announced by the government, close to 7,000 MW of under-construction and recently bid solar projects will see their cost go up and would have to revise their tariff accordingly. Over the years, coal power projects have seen massive fluctuations in price and availability of coal. This led to high litigation cost and increase in the power rate, landing several projects in debt trap. Industry executives fear that the same could happen in the solar sector if there is no stability on tariff and clarity on regulations. "A general consensus among various GST advance ruling authorities of 18% rate of GST on solar power projects is quite an aspect of worry for the solar industry players who believe that a 5% tax should be applicable," said Abhishek Jain, tax partner, EY." To end **apprehensions,** the government should consider issuing an explicit clarification on the rate of tax applicable to such projects," he said. India is pursuing a goal of having 100 giga watt (GW) of solar power capacity by 2022, up from 23 GW at present.

India has a renewable power generation capacity of over 70 GW currently, half of which conies from wind power. Intense competition in recent years have drove down solar power tariff discovered in project auctions. The factors that helped producers to bid projects aggressively include lower price of imported solar panels and efficient financial structuring of projects. Industry observers said that global developments like China limiting solar capacity addition making more panels available for imports are helping to counter-balance cost pressures building up in the country. "The solar industry is facing upward cost pressure locally from taxes and financing, but that is getting balanced by lower equipment costs due to global developments. So, for now, project profitability is secure," said Kameswara Rao, Partner, Grid, PwC India.

129. Why does the solar power project issue seems to be heading for a prolonged legal battle?

(a) Because intense competition in recent years have drove down solar power tariff.

(b) As India is pursuing a goal of having 100 giga watt (GW) of solar power capacity by 2022 and it is not getting enough support to do so.

(c) As AAAR's has held that solar power projects are liable to 18% goods and services tax (GST) and not at the lower rate of 5%.

(d) Since the government has issued explicit clarifications on the rate of tax applicable to solar projects.

(e) All of these.

130. What is the factor among **the given options that has brought uncertainty to solar power project developers?**

(a) Lower equipment costs due to global developments.

(b) Unsecure project profitability of solar power projects.

(c) Lowering down of solar power capacity from 23 GW.

(d) Government's proposal to levy safeguard duty on imported solar panels.

(e) High litigation cost.

131. How have AAAR's justified the liability of solar power projects withstanding under 18 % GST?

(a) As under the previous regime, there were issues in tax treatment of works contract.

(b) As an abatement has been prescribed for works contract under the GST law.

(c) Setting up of solar projects are covered under the classification of works contract as they consist of supply of goods and services packaged into an immovable property.

(d) Both (b) and (c)

(e) Both (a) and (b)

132. What was the consequence of massive fluctuations in price and availability of coal?

(a) As coal is not easier to transport than oil or natural gas, the mining industry got impacted.

(b) Cost of extracting coal decreased.

(c) Decreased economic activity and demand for steel.

(d) High litigation cost and increase in the power rate.

(e) None of these.

133. What are the factors highlighted that helped solar power producers in aggressive bidding?

(a) Lower cost pressure from taxes and financing.

(b) Lower price of imported solar panels and efficient financial structuring of projects.

(c) Safeguards duty embedded in the imported solar panels helped solar power project developers.

(d) Dis-balance in equipment costs due to global developments.

(e) 5% tax reflection effect that it enjoyed across excise and value added tax.

134. Statement [A] "A rise in project cost could get reflected in the power tariffs that solar power developers offer in auctions to win projects" in the passage may not be grammatically or contextually correct. Choose the most suitable alternative that will replace the statement to adhere to the grammatical syntax of the paragraph.

(a) A rise for project cost could get reflected in the power tariffs that solar power developers offer in auctions to win projects.

(b) A rise with the project cost could get reflected in the power tariffs that solar power developers offer in auctions to win projects.

(c) A rise with the project cost could reflects in the power tariffs that solar power developers offer in auctions to win projects.

(d) A rise for the project cost could get reflected on the power tariffs that solar power developers offer in auctions for winning projects.

(e) None of these

135. Which of the following options is strengthening the statement **[B] "The solar industry may be about to face what imported coal-based power projects saw** some **years back — an increase in the production cost due to changes in law and the imposition of new tariffs."** of the passage?

(a) The tariff and litigation cost are highly instable in solar industry.

(b) High litigation cost and increase in the power rate, landed several coal power projects in debt trap.

(c) Electricity cost is not covered under GST, therefore the project costs increases.

(d) India is pursuing a goal of having 100 giga watt of solar power capacity.

(e) None of these

Direction (136-140): In the following questions, a paragraph is divided into five parts with one of the parts been omitted. You must choose the most suitable alternative among the five that should fill the omitted part making the paragraph grammatically correct and contextually meaningful. If none of the given alternatives are appropriate to fill the blank, choose option (e) i.e. "none of these" as your answer choice.

136. The new possibility would be thwarted by the Supreme Court directive (a) /to make new car and two-wheeler owners purchase insurance covers (b) /___________, (c) / and

the insurance regulator's fiat to general insurers (d) /to sell long-term third-party motor insurance covers for new cars and two-wheelers from September 1. (e)

(a) to set prices just as they do on own-damage covers

(b) accident-proneness of routine travel regions, distance driven per month and so on

(c) to acquire the capacity to enforce the law and the stipulated penalty for its violation

(d) for at least three years and five years respectively, against the existing norm of one year,

(e) None of these

137. Recently, the National Human Rights Commission (NHRC) conducted the first-ever nationwide survey (a) / of the transgender community in India and found that (b) /___________. (c) / It is profoundly absurd that we think of ourselves as inhabiting a "modem" world, (d) / and yet there exists a sizeable community of people who are structurally ostracized and denied the fundamental right to a livelihood. (e)

(a) as someone who is not of an established and accepted gender.

(b) 92% of the people belonging to the community are subjected to economic exclusion.

(c) it defined a transgender person: as neither a man nor a woman.

(d) what counts as discrimination against a transgender person.

(e) None of these

138. A backlog of 0.24 million unfilled posts in the public sector, (a) /____(b) / surrounding the National Democratic Alliance government's claim on job creation, (c) /With the public sector being the major contributor in formal sector employment in the country, (d) / historically, this backlog of vacancies speaks volumes about the nature of the jobs that the government claims to have created. (e)

(a) as reported by the media recently, has escalated the contention

(b) seems to be in denial that this contemporary trend of informalisation

(c) with presumably higher level of education and skill, is perplexing

(d) finds it difficult to match up to the central government pay-packages

(e) None of these

139. ___________(a) / as their currencies resume their prolonged slide against the U.S. dollar, (b) / The Indian rupee weakened past the 71 mark for the first time ever on Friday, (c) / registering a loss of about 10% of its value against the dollar since the beginning of the year, (d) / This makes the rupee the worst-performing currency in Asia. (e)

(a) Investors who earlier put their money in emerging markets

(b) Emerging market currencies, most notably the Turkish lira have suffered much larger losses owing

(c) Emerging market economies continue to be in the spotlight for the wrong reasons

(d) Emerging market countries, which earlier benefited from the easing of monetary conditions,

(e) None of these

140. Kerala's unique topography of coastal plains (a) / and rolling hills between the Arabian Sea and the Western Ghats (b) /_______, (c) / landslides, flooding and coastal erosion being the most common, (d) / Incidents of flooding have become frequent, aided by human intervention. (e)

(a) 70% of its coastal areas are prone to tsunamis and cyclones

(b) is vulnerable to several natural hazards

(c) 60% of its landmass vulnerable to earthquakes

(d) 12% of its land to floods

(e) None of these

Direction (141-143): Select the phrase/connector (STARTERS) from the given three options which can be used to form a single sentence from the two sentences given below, implying the same meaning as expressed in the statement sentences.

141. (I) Unmanned or remotely piloted aircraft commonly known as drones, hold immense promise for various commercial applications,

(II) The government has done well to set up a regulatory framework for drone operations, including commercial use.

(i) Given how unmanned...

(ii) Since unmanned or...

(iii) Provided that unmanned...

(a) Only (ii) (b) Only (iii)

(c) Both (ii) and (iii) (d) Both (i) and (ii)

(e) All of these

142. (I) People have to be convinced to buy insurance for the expected life of the vehicle at the time of purchase, as in the case of road tax.

(II) This process of convincing interferes with the need to set premium based on data relating to safety and diligence of the driver, which would change over time.

(i) Convincing people to buy...

(ii) People are convinced to buy...

(iii) The convincing process interferes...

(a) Only (i)

(b) Only (iii)

(c) Both (ii) and (iii)

(d) Both (i) and (ii)

(e) All of these

143. (I) The country should find viable and sustainable replacements for its energy needs.

(II) International oil price movements will continue to be an important fault line in India's political economy without sustainable replacements for energy needs.

(i) Unless the country finds...

(ii) Except that the country finds...

(iii) Considering the country finds...

(a) Only (i)

(b) Only (iii)

(c) Both (ii) and (iii)

(d) Both (i) and (ii)

(e) All of these

Directions (144-147): In the following questions, a paragraph is given with three blanks, followed by six words. You have to choose the most suitable combination of words among the five four alternative options, that will fill the blank coherently, forming a grammatically correct and contextually meaningful paragraph. If none of the given combination is appropriate to fill the blank, mark option (e) i.e. "none of these" as your answer choice.

144. The term 'secularism' has meaning only if it assures the expression of any form of difference. This__________, both religious and regional, should not get under the louder voice of the majority, the Commission said. At the same time, it said, discriminatory practices within a religion should not hide behind the cloak of that faith to gain __________ .

(i) Subsumed

(ii) Socialism

(iii) Invigorated

(iv) Diversity

(v) Legitimacy

(vi) Astuteness

(a) ii, iii, vi   (b) iv, i, v

(c) v, i, ii   (d) ii, iv, v

(e) None of these

145. The Directorate General of Civil Aviation (DGCA) has made public its inquiry report into an incident involving a plane__________Congress president Rahul Gandhi from Delhi to Karnataka in April. The__________ has revealed that there was a technical __________ in the plane, and as the response of the two pilots to the situation was delayed, the aircraft tilted sharply on one side and began to fall rapidly.

(i) Gremlin

(ii) Ferrying

(iii) Advocacy

(iv) Glitch

(v) Barging

(vi) Probe

(a) ii, iii, i   (b) iv, i, v

(c) v, i, ii   (d) ii, vi, iv

(e) None of these

146. The government seems to be in denial that this__________ trend of informalisation of labour in India is policy-induced. By __________ the traditionally used National Sample Survey Office's (NSSO) employment-unemployment estimates, with the Employees' Provident Fund Organisation (EPFO) database of inconsistent quality, the government is trying to sweep some __________evidences under the carpet.

(i) Disconcerting

(ii) Posterior

(iii) Superseding

(iv) Contemporary

(v) Bewildering

(vi) Supplanting

(a) ii, iii, i

(b) iv, i, v

(c) iv, vi, i

(d) ii, vi, iv

(e) None of these

147. While the Supreme Court has __________ the detention of the accused in jail, their house arrest is only a limited __________. The truth is that the accused will have to face a never-ending oppressive __________ process which, once initiated, consumes life and is destructive of one's pride and dignity.

  (i) disdain

  (ii) legitimate

  (iii) interdicted

  (iv) consolation

  (v) prosecutorial

  (vi) suppressed

  (a) ii, i, vi   (b) iv, i, v

  (c) v, vi, i   (d) iii, iv, v

  (e) None of these

Directions (148-150): Given below are six sentences (A) (B) (C) (D) (E) and (F). Answer the following questions after rearranging the following sentences into a coherent paragraph.

  (A) Tests of Ganga water indicate it has fared better in Uttar Pradesh; but then, the clean-up plan for the river has received dedicated Central funding of Rs. 3,696 crore over three and a half years, compared to Rs.351 crore given to 14 States to conserve 32 rivers.

  (B) The finding of the Central Pollution Control Board that the number of critically polluted segments of India's rivers has risen to 351 from 302 two years ago is a strong indictment of the departments responsible for environmental protection.

  (C) Their problems are worsened by the poor infrastructure available in a large number of cities and towns located near rivers. It is notable that these results come from a CPCB audit that was carried out at the instance of the National Green Tribunal.

  (D) The data show that the plethora of laws enacted to regulate waste management and protect water quality are simply not working.

  (E) The failed efforts to control pollution are all too evident in Maharashtra, Gujarat and Assam, which account for a third of the degraded river segments.

  (F) The study also underscores the failure of many national programmes run by the Centre for river conservation, preservation of wetlands, and water quality monitoring.

148. Considering statement (a) **"Tests of Ganga water indicate it has fared better in Uttar Pradesh; but then, the clean-up plan for the river has received dedicated Central funding of Rs.3,696 crore over three and a half years, compared to Rs.351 crore given to 14 States to conserve 32 rivers"** as the fourth sentence of the rearranged paragraph, then which among the following becomes the SECOND sentence after rearrangement?

  (a) F   (b) C

  (c) E   (d) D

  (e) B

149. Considering statement (a) **"Tests of Ganga water indicate it has fared better in Uttar Pradesh; but then, the clean-up plan for the river has received dedicated Central funding of Rs.3,696 crore over three and a half years, compared to Rs.351 crore given to 14 States to conserve 32 rivers"** as the fourth sentence of the rearranged paragraph, then which among the following becomes the LAST sentence after rearrangement?

  (a) F   (b) C

  (c) E   (d) D

  (e) B

150. Among the following pairs which one of them is formed with two consecutive statements after the rearrangement?

  (a) D–E   (b) F–C

  (c) B–F   (d) A–D

  (e) B–D

151. Choose the word which is most nearly the **SAME** in the meaning to **SALUBURIOUS.**

  (a) Exorbitant   (b) Quandary

  (c) Enigma   (d) Salutary

  (e) Outrageous

152. Choose the word which is most nearly the **OPPOSITE** of **CAMOUFLAGE.**

  (a) Debunk

  (b) Indignant

  (c) Vapid

  (d) Anemic

  (e) Candid

Directions (153-155): In each of the following questions, a sentence is written in four different ways conveying the same meaning and following the correct grammar structure. Choose the sentence among the four options which is grammatically incorrect or carrying a grammatical/idiomatic error in it as the answer. If there is no error in any of the sentences, choose (e), i.e. " All are correct" as the answer.

153. (a) Two months ahead of the State Assembly elections, widespread discrepancies have been detected in the electoral rolls of Rajasthan with doubts that the names of many legitimate voters have been struck off the lists.

(b) Extensive inconsistencies have been found in the electoral register of Rajasthan with the doubts that the names of many legitimate voters have been removed from the voter lists when two months are left for the State Legislative Assembly.

(c) The doubts that the names of many legitimate voters have been struck off the lists have been precipitated due to the detection of widespread discrepancies in the electoral rolls of Rajasthan just two months ahead of the State Assembly elections.

(d) Removal of names of a few legitimate voters from the voter lists have raised doubts about the widespread consistencies in the electoral rolls of Rajasthan.

(e) All are correct

154. (a) At the time as Punjab Chief Minister Amarinder Singh emphasized on Monday that nobody involved in sacrilege cases would be spared, the Shiromani Akali Dal-BJP combine has decided to meet the Governor over the 'deteriorating law and order' situation in the State of Punjab.

(b) The Shiromani Akali Dal-BJP combine has decided to meet the Governor over the 'deteriorating law and order' situation in the state of Punjab because Punjab Chief Minister Amarinder Singh emphasized on Monday that nobody involved in sacrilege cases would be spared.

(c) While Punjab Chief Minister Amarinder Singh insisted on Monday that nobody involved in sacrilege cases would be spared, the Shiromani Akali Dal-BJP combine has decided to meet the Governor over the 'deteriorating law and order' situation in the State of Punjab.

(d) During the time that Punjab Chief Minister Amarinder Singh insisted on Monday that nobody involved in sacrilege cases would be spared, the Shiromani Akali Dal-BJP combine has decided to meet the Governor over the deteriorating law and order' situation in the State of Punjab.

(e) All are correct

155. (a) The AAP, having made efforts to make peace with "rebels" and "former leaders", has reached out to ex-Punjab convener Sucha Singh Chootepur, two years after he was sacked on charges of taking bribe for allotting party tickets.

(b) The AAP, as part of its efforts to make peace with "rebels" and "former leaders", has reached out to ex-Punjab convener Sucha Singh Chhotepur, two years after he was sacked on charges of taking bribe for allotting party tickets.

(c) The AAP, with an intent to reconciliate with "rebels" and "former leaders", has approached ex-Punjab convener Sucha Singh Chhotepur, two years after he was discharged on charges of taking suborn for allotting party tickets.

(d) The AAP, to reconciliate with "rebels" and "former leaders", has approached ex-Punjab convener Sucha Singh Chhotepur, two years after he was dismissed against taking bribe for allotting party tickets.

(e) All are error

ANSWERS

1. (c)	**2.** (b)	**3.** (d)	**4.** (d)	**5.** (e)	**6.** (a)	**7.** (a)	**8.** (d)	**9.** (e)	**10.** (d)
11. (c)	**12.** (e)	**13.** (b)	**14.** (a)	**15.** (a)	**16.** (e)	**17.** (d)	**18.** (c)	**19.** (d)	**20.** (d)
21. (e)	**22.** (a)	**23.** (b)	**24.** (e)	**25.** (e)	**26.** (d)	**27.** (b)	**28.** (c)	**29.** (c)	**30.** (b)
31. (c)	**32.** (c)	**33.** (e)	**34.** (d)	**35.** (a)	**36.** (a)	**37.** (b)	**38.** (c)	**39.** (a)	**40.** (c)
41. (a)	**42.** (a)	**43.** (a)	**44.** (b)	**45.** (c)	**46.** (a)	**47.** (a)	**48.** (e)	**49.** (c)	**50.** (c)
51. (a)	**52.** (c)	**53.** (d)	**54.** (a)	**55.** (d)	**56.** (b)	**57.** (c)	**58.** (d)	**59.** (c)	**60.** (d)
61. (a)	**62.** (c)	**63.** (a)	**64.** (b)	**65.** (b)	**66.** (b)	**67.** (c)	**68.** (b)	**69.** (d)	**70.** (e)
71. (c)	**72.** (d)	**73.** (b)	**74.** (a)	**75.** (b)	**76.** (b)	**77.** (c)	**78.** (a)	**79.** (a)	**80.** (e)
81. (a)	**82.** (b)	**83.** (c)	**84.** (e)	**85.** (a)	**86.** (b)	**87.** (c)	**88.** (d)	**89.** (c)	**90.** (e)
91. (a)	**92.** (b)	**93.** (b)	**94.** (e)	**95.** (e)	**96.** (b)	**97.** (d)	**98.** (a)	**99.** (b)	**100.** (d)
101. (a)	**102.** (b)	**103.** (*)	**104.** (d)	**105.** (e)	**106.** (d)	**107.** (a)	**108.** (c)	**109.** (c)	**110.** (d)
111. (d)	**112.** (b)	**113.** (a)	**114.** (a)	**115.** (d)	**116.** (e)	**117.** (c)	**118.** (c)	**119.** (c)	**120.** (c)
121. (d)	**122.** (e)	**123.** (d)	**124.** (c)	**125.** (a)	**126.** (c)	**127.** (b)	**128.** (d)	**129.** (c)	**130.** (d)
131. (c)	**132.** (d)	**133.** (b)	**134.** (e)	**135.** (a)	**136.** (d)	**137.** (b)	**138.** (a)	**139.** (c)	**140.** (b)
141. (e)	**142.** (a)	**143.** (d)	**144.** (b)	**145.** (d)	**146.** (c)	**147.** (d)	**148.** (d)	**149.** (b)	**150.** (e)
151. (d)	**152.** (e)	**153.** (d)	**154.** (b)	**155.** (a)					

EXPLANATIONS

For questions 1 to 4:

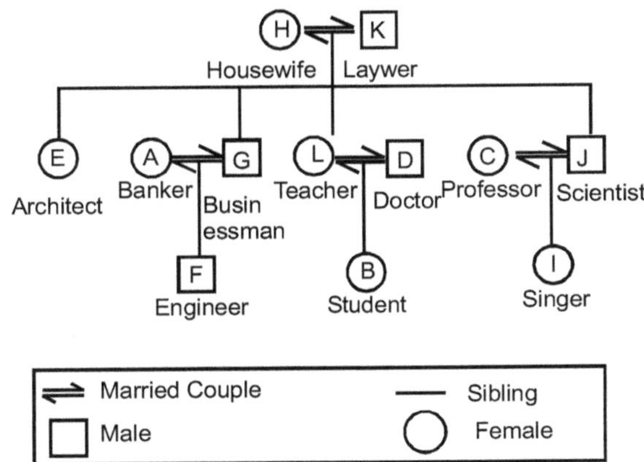

For questions 5 to 9:

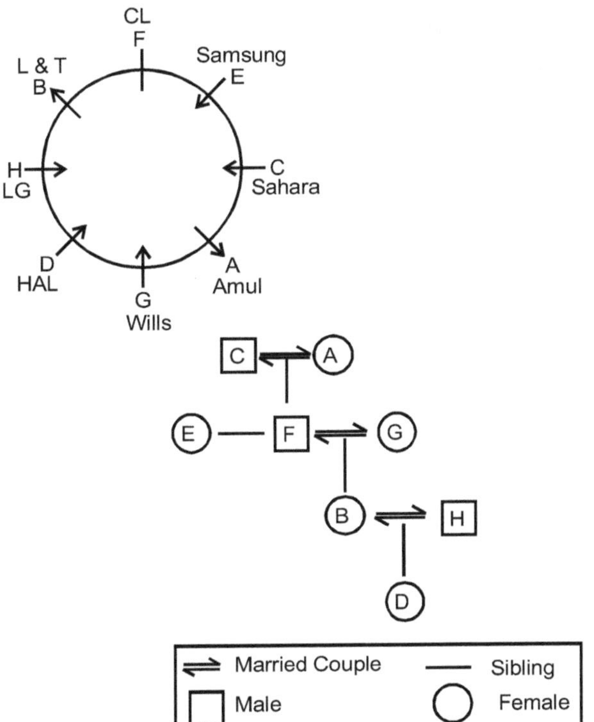

For questions 10 to 14: The given information can be shown as:

Row–1 ↓South	Bangalore	Lucknow	Mumbai /Hyderabad	Hyderabad/ Mumbai	Chennai	Pune
	Religious Conflicts	Illiteracy	Unemployment	Beggary	Alcoholism	Poverty
	C	A	F	B	D	E
↑North Row–2	R	P	S	Q	U	T
	Child Labour	Juvenile Delinquency/ Superstition	Dowry system	Communalism	Child Marriage	Superstition / Juvenile Delinquency
	Jaipur	Kolkata	Ahmedabad	Nagpur	Surat	Ghaziabad

For questions 15 to 19:

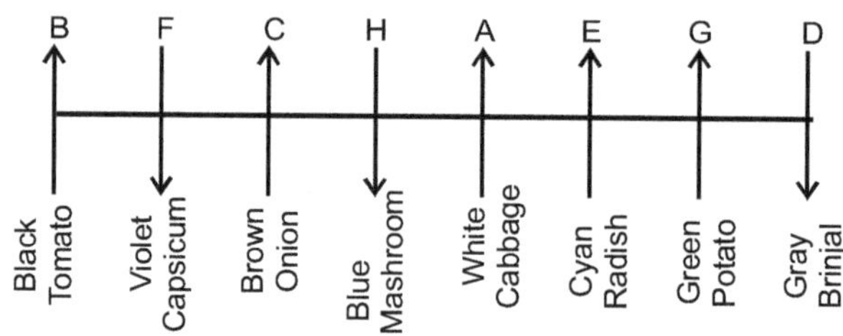

For questions 20 to 24:

Floor number	Friend / State		Friend / State	
7	C	UP	H	Assam
6	F	Bihar	G	UP
5	A	MP	VACANT FLAT	
4	E	Haryana	B	MP
3	K	Punjab	J	Punjab
2	D	Bihar	VACANT FLAT	
1	I	Assam	L	Haryana

For questions 25 to 29:

Box	Color	Fruit	Weight(kg)
A	Yellow	Cherry	2
B	Black	Pear	1
C	Green	Date	3
D	Red	Apple	2
E	Grey	Mango	3
F	White	Papaya	2
G	Blue	Orange	3
H	Brown	Grape	1

For questions 30 to 33:

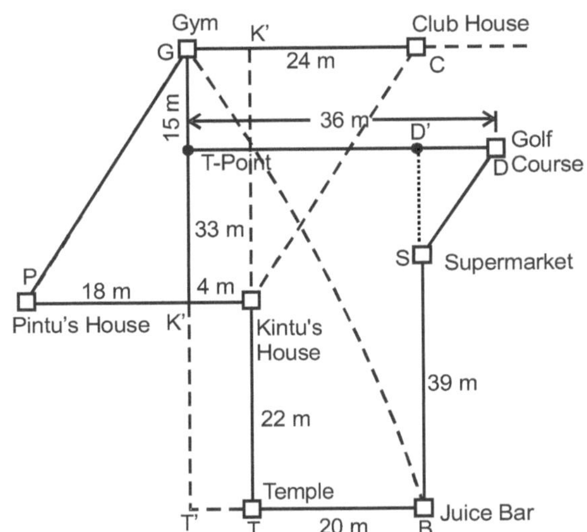

30. Distance between Pintu's house to Gym,

$$PG = \sqrt{14^2 + 48^2} = 50 \text{ m}.$$

31. D'S = (33 + 22) − 39 = 16 m

    D'D = 36 − 24 = 12 m

    So, distance between Golf Course and Supermarket,

$$SD = \sqrt{12^2 + 16^2} = 20 \text{ m}.$$

32. Distance between Juice Bar and Gym

$$BG = \sqrt{70^2 + 24^2} = 74 \text{ m}.$$

33. K'C = TB = 20 m

    So, distance between Clubhouse and Kintu's house

$$KC = \sqrt{48^2 + 20^2} = 52 \text{ m}$$

    Hence, Clubhouse is to the north-east of Kintu's house.

34. 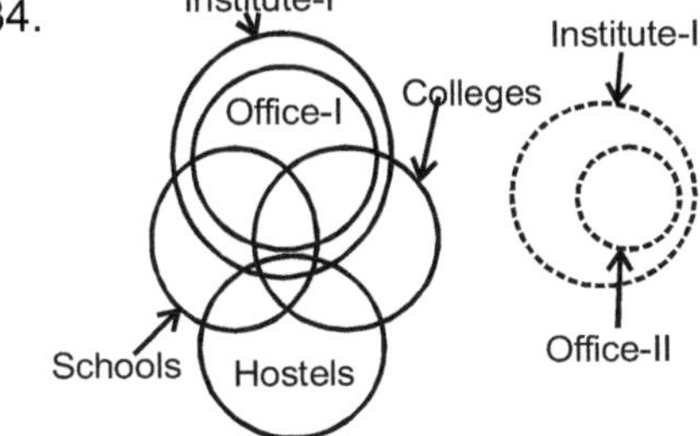

35. 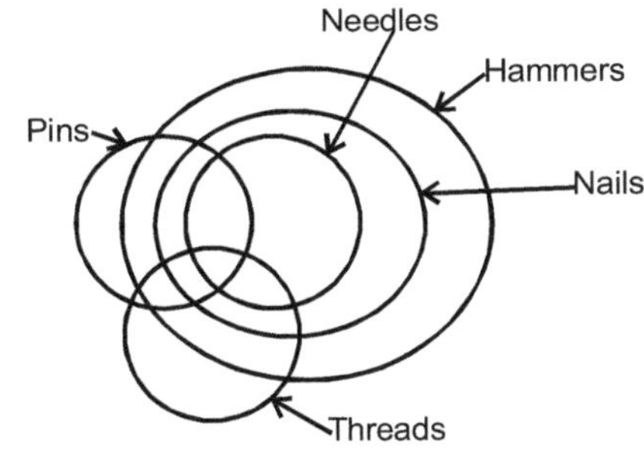

36. 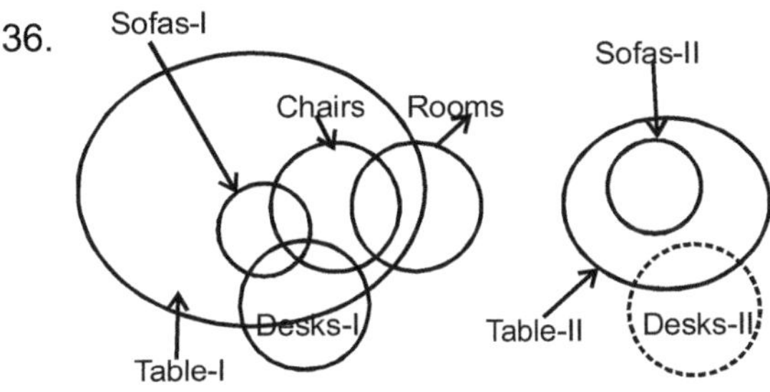

37. 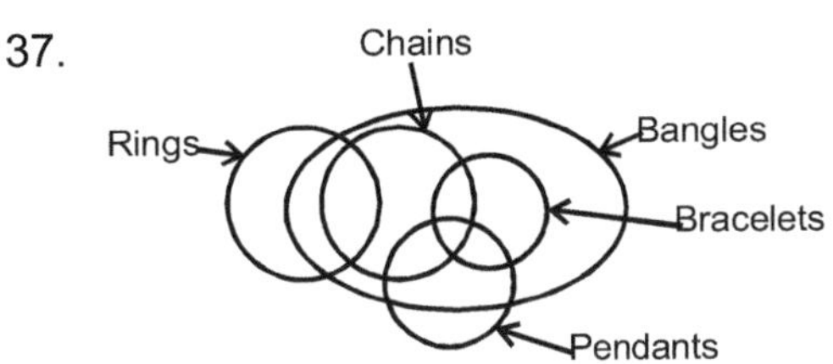

38. Case I:

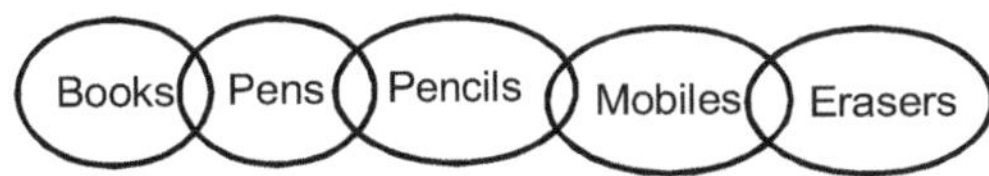

Case II:

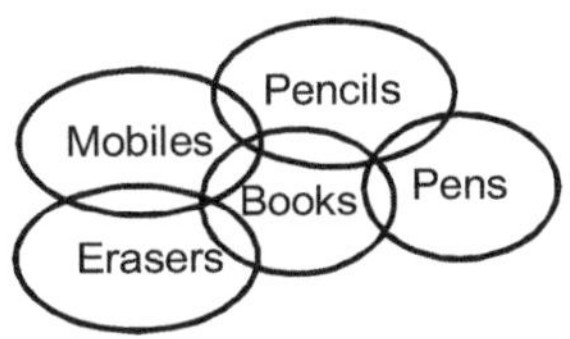

39. Assumption I is implicit because this announcement is made with a hope that people will heed to it and reschedule their journey.

40. The campaign has now been called successful because the last year saw no cases of polio being reported. This means that in the year before the last, at least one case of polio must have been reported. Had this assumption not been valid, that is, no case was reported in the year before the last too, the campaign would have been called successful even a year ago, or the reason for it being a success would then have been that no case of polio has been reported in the last 'two' years. Thus, assumption I is implicit. Assumption II is implicit as the conclusion rests on this unstated premise that one year is a long enough period to judge the success or failure of the campaign. Option (3) is correct.

41. Assumption I can be considered implicit because the statement states that one will try to forget the message that makes you feel vulnerable in order to retain a sense of self-control. Assumption II does not follow because the statement talks about only a

galling species of ironic effect and does not suggest any comparison, for us to assume the existence of other types of ironic effect. So, option (1) is the correct answer.

42. Statement I is the cause and Statement II is its effect. The government has decided to limit the election expenses of political parties so that independent candidates and smaller parties do not remain at a disadvantage with respect to bigger ones due to lack of money. Therefore, option (1) is the correct answer.

43. Options (2), (3), (4) and (5) are too far fetched. Option (1) is certainly one of the probable effects of the aforementioned statement.

44. Only option (2) is a logical effect of the statement. The other options cannot be justified as an effect of the given statement.

45. Only option (3) is a logical effect of the aforementioned statement.

46. Let the total number of balls faced by Suresh and Ravindra be 3x and 4x respectively.

$$\Rightarrow \text{Total number of runs scored by Suresh} = \frac{3x \times 72}{100}$$

and that by Ravindra $= \frac{4x \times 66}{100}$

Thus, ratio of the runs scored by Ravindra and Suresh = 11 : 9

Hence,

$$\text{required percentage} = \frac{11-9}{9} \times 100 = 22\frac{2}{9}\%.$$

47. Total runs scored by Dhawan in the last three matches = 55 × 3 + 9 × 25 = 390

Thus, in order to get the minimum runs for the last match the runs scored by Dhawan in the 26th and the 27th match has to be 127 and 126.

Hence, minimum runs that Dhawan would have scored in the last match will be 390 – (127 + 126) = 137.

48. Let the average runs scored by Kohli be 'x' such that the number of balls faced by him is 8x – 74.

$$\Rightarrow \frac{8x}{8x-74} \times 100 = 129.6$$

Hence, average runs scored by Kohli = 40.5.

49. Let the total number of balls faced by Rohit in the entire 20 matches be 2x.

$$\Rightarrow (20 \times 81) \times 100 = 120x + 150x$$

Hence, x = 600 and total number of balls faced by him is 1200.

50. Let the number of matches played by Dhoni be x.

$$\Rightarrow \frac{38x}{400} \times 100 = 114$$

Hence, x = 12

51. **Quantity I:** CP × x = SP × 16

and SP = 1.25CP

$\Rightarrow x = 20$

Hence, there would be a profit of $\frac{(25-20)}{20} \times 100$

= 25%

Quantity II: Price × Quantity = Expenditure

$$\Rightarrow \frac{6}{5} \text{Price} \times \frac{2}{3} \text{Quantity} = \text{Expenditure}$$

$$\Rightarrow \frac{4}{5} (\text{Price} \times \text{Quantity}) = \text{Expenditure}$$

Hence, the expenditure would have been decreased by 20%.

Therefore, Quantity I > Quantity II.

52. **Quantity I:** Let the amount invested by A, B and C be x, 2x and 3x respectively.

$$\Rightarrow \frac{(2x+400)}{(6x-200)} = \frac{10}{23} \text{ or } x = 800$$

Hence, amount invested by A = Rs. 800.

Quantity II: Let p, q and r be the share of P, Q and R.

$$p = \frac{2}{3}(q+r)...(i)$$

$$\frac{1}{4}(p+q) = r...(ii)$$

Ratio of p : q : r = 2 : 2 : 1

Hence, $p = \frac{2}{5} \times 4000 = $ Rs. 1,600 and

$r = \frac{1}{5} \times 4000 = $ Rs. 800

and q = Rs. 1,600

Hence, required amount = 1600 – 800

= Rs. 800

Therefore, Quantity I = Quantity II.

53. **Quantity I:** Let the lengths (in meter) of the first and the second train be L1 and L2.

Thus, L1 + L2 $= (54 + 72) \times \frac{5}{18} \times 12 = 420$ m.

Again, L1 $= (54 - 18) \times \frac{5}{18} \times 18 = 180$ m and thus L2

= 240 m.

Quantity II: Let the speed of the train be S km/hr.

$\Rightarrow (S - 18) \times \dfrac{5}{18} \times 72 = (S - 9) \times \dfrac{5}{18} \times 48$

$\Rightarrow$ S = 36 km/hr and thus length of the train = 360 m.

Therefore, Quantity I < Quantity II.

54. **Quantity I:** Let the values of p, q and r be 3k, 4k and 5k respectively.

$\Rightarrow$ 3k + 4k + 5k = 12 or k = 1

Thus, p = 3, q = 4 and r = 5

Given that, q = 2p – 2a and r = b – q

$\Rightarrow$ a = 1 and b = 9

Hence, b – 6a = 3.

Quantity II: The minimum value of the expression

will be $-\dfrac{1}{2} + 3 = 2.5$ at x = 0

Hence, Quantity I > Quantity II.

55. **Quantity I:** Let the radius of the metal-sphere be 'r' cm.

$\Rightarrow \dfrac{4}{3}\pi r^2 = \pi \times 6 \times 6 \times 8$

$\Rightarrow$ Radius of the metal sphere = 6 cm and that of the solid hemi-sphere = 3 cm

Therefore, area of the hemi-sphere

= $3\pi \times 3 \times 3 \approx 85$ cm^2.

Quantity II: In order to find the area of the triangle we can use Hero's formula, but the given triangle is a right angled triangle.

Therefore, area of the triangle = $\dfrac{1}{2} \times 20 \times 21$

= 210 cm^2.

Hence, Quantity I < Quantity II.

For questions 56 to 60:

Total students = 7200

HARVARD:

Students going to Harvard = 1728

    Students paying their fees on their own = 480

Students paying half fees on their own = 416

Students paying fees by bank loan = 832

STANFORD:

Students going to Stanford = 2304

    Students paying their fees on their own = 512

Students paying half fees on their own = 1152

Students paying fees by bank loan = 640

OXFORD:

Students going to Oxford = 3168

    Students paying their fees on their own = 1144

Students paying half fees on their own= 1232

Students paying fees by bank loan = 792

56. Required percentage

$= \dfrac{832}{832 + 640 + 792} \times 100 = 36.75\%.$

57. New number of students going to Harvard $\approx$ 1152

    Ratio = 1152 : (2304 + 3168) = 1152 : 5472 = 4 : 19

58. Reuired difference

$= (832 + 640 + 792) - \dfrac{1}{3}(480 + 512 + 1144)$

= 1552

59.

Required percentage $= \dfrac{2304}{1728 + 3168} \times 100 \approx 47\%.$

25. 4   X = S + H – O = 2304 + 1728 – 3168

     = 864

Y = S + O – H = 2304 + 3168 – 1728 = 3744

Z = O + H – S = 3168 + 1728 – 2304 = 2592

X : Y : Z = 864 : 3744 : 2592 = 3 : 13 : 9

For questions 61 to 65:

The students study Dentistry = 1600 × 0.45

              = 720

Therefore, the students study Homeopathy

        = 1600 – 720 = 880

The boys study Dentistry $= 720 \times \dfrac{5}{8} = 450$

Therefore, the girls study Dentistry = 720 – 450

           = 270

The boys study Homeopathy $= 880 \times \dfrac{4}{11} = 320$

Therefore, the girls study Homeopathy = 880 – 320

           = 560

Dentistry : Boys

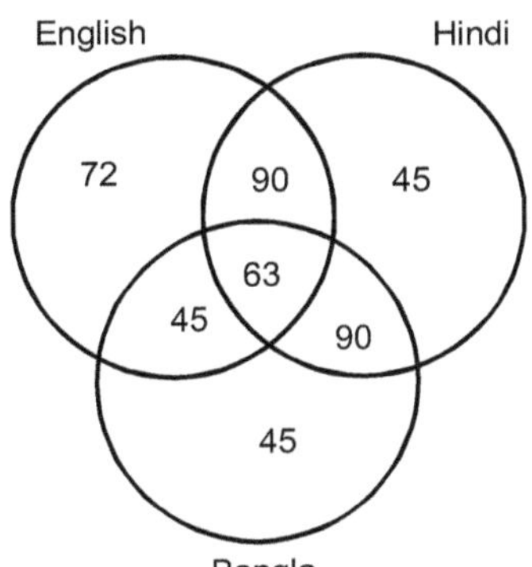

Dentistry : Girls

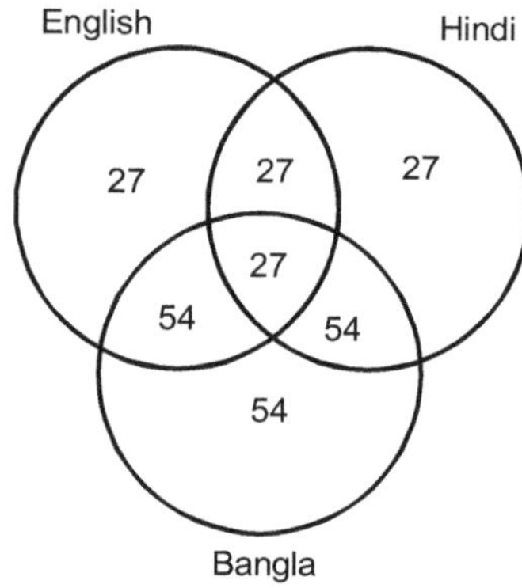

Homeopathy : Boys

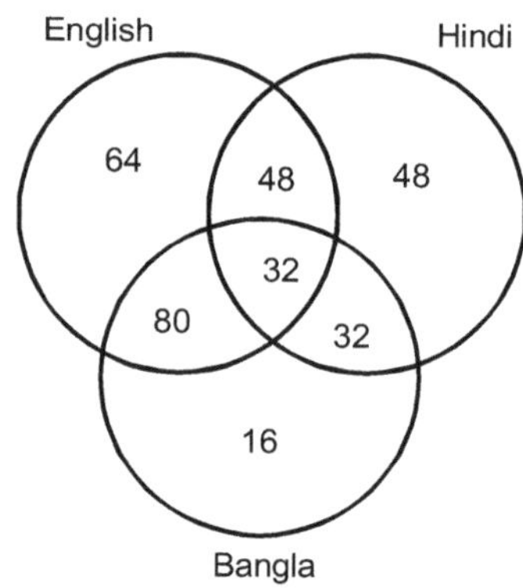

Homeopathy : Girls

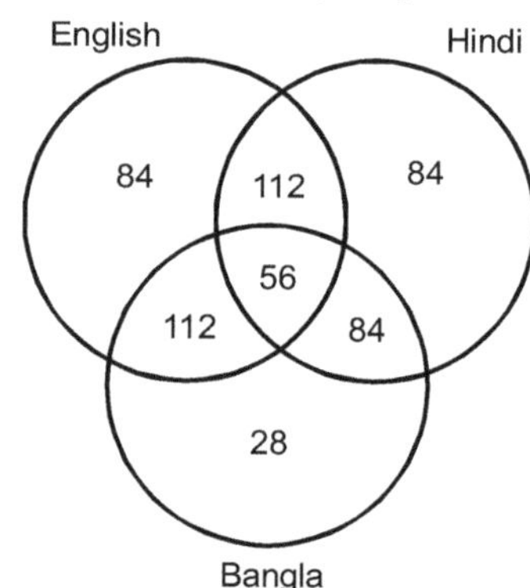

61. Required number of students = 72 + 90 + 45 + 27 + 27 + 27 + 64 + 48 + 48 + 84 + 112 + 84 = 728.

62. Required percentage $= \dfrac{54 + 112}{830} \times 100 = 20\%$.

63. Required ratio = 84 : 80 = 21 : 20.

64. The students of Homeopathy who knows at least 2 languages

$= 48 + 32 + 80 + 32 + 112 + 112 + 84 + 56$

$= 556$

Hence, required percentage $= \dfrac{556}{880} \times 100 \approx 63\%$.

65. The girls who know Hindi and Bangla both

$= 54 + 27 + 84 + 56 = 221$

Hence, required percentage $= \dfrac{830 - 221}{830} \times 100$

$\approx 73.37\%$.

66. Statement I alone does not provide much information. But from statement II, we get the ratio of the efficiencies of A, B and C as 2 : 1 : 3.

Now, combining statement II with III we get the required difference as 7.5 days.

67. The question can be answered by combining the information of statement III with that of either statement I or statement II.

68. Statement III alone is sufficient to answer the question. However, we cannot combine statements I and II because we get different speeds for Train B which contradicts each other.

69. We can determine the ratio of the cost price and the selling price by using either of the statements alone which would be sufficient to get the percentage of profit in the entire transaction.

70. We cannot determine the exact answer even after determining the value of 'x' because it is not mention in the question if the compounding is done semi-annually or annually.

71. Let the Marked Price (MP) of A be Rs. 100 at each of the four outlets. Selling price (SP) and cost price (CP) of A at each of the four outlets can be calculated as shown in the table below.

	MP (in Rs.)	SP (in Rs.)	CP (in Rs.)
Spencer	100	76	69.09
More	100	88.89	79.37
Food World	100	60	55.56
Spinach	100	82	58.57

Hence, it can be concluded that Food World must have purchased A at the least price.

72. Let the Marked Price (MP) of each of the four commodities at More be Rs. 100. Selling prices (SP) and cost prices (CP) of all the four commodities at More can be calculated as shown in the table below.

	MP (in Rs.)	SP (in Rs.)	CP (in Rs.)
A	100	88.89	79.37
B	100	91.67	73.34
C	100	75	62.50
D	100	62.5	56.82

Hence, it can be concluded that A must have been purchased at the highest price by More.

73. Let the marked price of commodity B at Spencer be x.

$\therefore$ Selling price = x $-$ 36.36% of x $= x - \dfrac{4}{11}x = \dfrac{7}{11}x$

Again, profit percentage = 15%

$\therefore$ Selling price = 1.15 C.P.

$\therefore \dfrac{7}{11}x = 1.15$ C.P.

$\Rightarrow x = \dfrac{115 \times 11}{100 \times 7}$ C.P. = 1.8071 C.P.

Hence, the mark-up percentage for commodity B at Spencer is 80.71%.

74. Selling price of commodity D at Food World = 325 × 0.8 = 260

Let cost price of commodity D at Food World be Rs.x. Then,

Selling price = 1.05x

According to problem,

1.05x = 260

$\Rightarrow x \approx$ Rs.247.62.

75. Selling price of commodity C at Spinach

= 1050 × 0.2

= Rs.1,260

Let marked price of commodity C at Spinach be Rs.x. Then,

Selling price = 0.8543x

According to problem,

0.8543x = 1260

$\Rightarrow x \approx$ Rs.1,474.89.

76. Average cost of production (in thousand Rs.)

$= \dfrac{625 + 500 + 450 + 400 + 500 + 525}{6} = 500$

The cost of production is more than the average cost in 2 years.

77. Average sales revenue (in thousand Rs.)

$= \dfrac{750 + 725 + 550 + 600 + 800 + 800}{6} \approx 704$

The sales revenue is less than the average in two years.

78. New cost of production in 2009 (in thousand Rs.) = 1.25 × 625 = 781.25

New cost of production in 2012 (in thousand Rs.) = 1.3 × 400 = 520

Total cost of production in both the years (in thousand Rs.) = 781.25 + 520 = 1301.25

$\therefore$ Required percentage $= \dfrac{1301.25 - 800}{800} \times 100$

= 62.7%.

79. Profit % in year 2009 $= \dfrac{750 - 625}{625} \times 100 = 20\%$

Profit % in year 2010 $= \dfrac{725 - 500}{500} \times 100 = 45\%$

Profit % in year 2011 $= \dfrac{550 - 450}{450} \times 100$

= 22.2%

Profit % in year 2012 $= \dfrac{600 - 400}{400} \times 100 = 50\%$

Profit % in year 2013 $= \dfrac{800 - 500}{500} \times 100 = 60\%$

Profit % in year 2014 $= \dfrac{800 - 525}{525} \times 100$

= 52.3%

80. New sales revenue in 2010 (in thousand Rs.)

= 1.2 × 725 = 870

New sales revenue in 2011 (in thousand Rs.)

= 1.25 × 550 = 687.5

New sales revenue in 2012 (in thousand Rs.)

= 1.3 × 600 = 780

New cost of production in 2012 (in thousand Rs.)

= 1.2 × 400 = 480

New cost of production in 2013 (in thousand Rs.)

= 1.25 × 500 = 625

New cost of production in 2014 (in thousand Rs.)

= 1.35 × 525 = 708.75

New average sales revenue (in thousand Rs.)

$= \dfrac{870 + 687.5 + 780 + 750 + 800 + 800}{6} = 781.25$

New average cost of production (in thousand Rs.)

$= \dfrac{625 + 500 + 450 + 480 + 625 + 708.75}{6} = 565$

$\therefore$ Difference (in thousand Rs.) = 781 – 565 = 216.

121. Though the economic lucrativeness of innovation is described in the whole passage through the idea of success of business but being specific the answer can be derived from the first paragraph of the passage where it is mentioned that innovation is a process of turning a creative idea into reality. Innovation drives economic growth. ". Innovation is not only important on the individual level, but can make or break a business as well."

122. Both the options (b) and (c) are correct. Refer to paragraph 2 where it is given that if a business is not innovative, companies risk losing work to competitors. Furthermore the text is also quoted as, *"Lack of innovation also has indirect results such as losing staff and decreasing engagement."* Thus innovation cannot be an afterthought but rather a crucial element that is included in part of your strategy. Hence option (e) is the correct choice.

123. Options (a) and (b) are the statements which infer the meaning that has been asked in the given question. Refer to the third paragraph where the starting line of the paragraph itself is, *"The era of invention is not over, hut it has definitely been pushed aside for an era of innovation!"* It is also given that *businesses have discovered that innovation seems to not only trump invention in furthering a company's brand and profitability, but it can be far cheaper when all the framework is already completed.*

124. The most appropriate answer here is option (c). Refer to the last paragraph of the passage where it is given Sony's influence in the technology market is through creativity and perseverance. Furthermore in the third paragraph it is mentioned that businesses like Apple and Sony choose to innovate rather than invent. The text is quoted as, *"Sony shows corporations that for a business to thrive in today's market, a company cannot stay stagnant with on particular item - innovations are essential. Innovation drives economic growth."*

125. Option (a) articulates statement (a) in the most precise manner. To understand the given statement, hint from the following statement can be drawn "Innovation is not only important on the individual level, but can make or break a business as well" which explains the importance of innovations in a business. Therefore, one should be careful enough while developing a successful and worthy innovation. Thus, option (a) is the most suitable answer choice.

126. Option (c) can be aptly inferred from the sentence [B] as the idiom "to color outside the lines" means to think or act in a way that does not conform to set rules. Therefore, in context to the passage it can be understood that innovations play a vital role in surviving the business in the dynamic market. Therefore, the businessmen try to introduce new innovations even though it bears risks for the business. Hence, option (c) is the most suitable answer choice.

127. Option (b) is the most appropriate sentence to replace the grammatically incorrect statement [C]. It is to be noted that determiners are words placed in front of a noun to make it clear what the noun refers to. Here, since the associated noun is singular [The *era*], the determiner [it] and the verb [has] should be in their singular form as well. Moreover option (a) stands incorrect due to improper usage of the preposition "to". Hence, option (b) becomes the most suitable answer choice.

128. The statement clearly mentions the driving factor for innovation i.e. customer satisfaction [**...based on the needs and desires of the** consumer]. All the other options are irrelevant. Hence, option (d) is the most suitable answer choice.

129. The only correct answer here is option (c). Refer to paragraph 1 where it is mentioned that *Maharashtra's appellate authority for advance ruling (AAAR) has held that solar power projects are liable to 18% goods and services tax (GST) and not at the lower rate of 5% as claimed by power producers.* Thus, this issue seems to be headed for a prolonged legal battle unless the government decides to step in and issue clarity on the taxability on solar power projects. This statement also makes option (a) wrong making suitability of option (c) correct.

130. Only option (d) is the most suitable choice. Refer to paragraph 1 *where it is given that government proposal to levy safeguard duty on imported solar panels that is meant to support domestic panel manufacturers is another factor that has brought some **uncertainty** to solar power project developers.*

131. Option (c) is the correct choice here. The answer can be deduced from the paragraph 2 where the text is quoted directly as, *"The AAARs have held that setting up of solar projects are covered under the classification of works contract as they consist of supply of goods and services packaged into an immovable property."* They held that because of this, these projects are liable to be taxed at 18% that applies to works contracts.

132. The appropriate answer here is option (d). Refer to the third paragraph where it is given that over years, massive fluctuations have been observed in the prices and availability of coal which led to high litigation cost and increase in the power rate due to which several projects were landed in debt trap.

Hence industry executives fear that the same could happen in the solar sector if there is no stability on tariff and clarity on regulations.

133. Refer to the last paragraph where it is given that the intense competition in recent years has driven down the solar power tariff as discovered in the solar project auctions. Furthermore, the text is highlighted as, *"The factors that helped producers to bid projects aggressively include the lower price of imported solar panels and efficient financial structuring of projects/'*

134. The given statement [A] is grammatically correct and contextually meaningful. Hence, it does not require any corrections. Therefore, option (e) is the most suitable answer choice.

135. The given statement [B] judges the future of the solar project industry by finding its similarities with the coal power industry in the policy formulation. Since, option (a) provides information on the instability of the tariff and cost in solar industry just like coal power industry, it strengthens the given statement. All the options are irrelevant in context of statement [B]. Hence, option (a) is the most suitable answer choice.

136. The most appropriate clause that will complete the sentence to frame it in a correct contextual and grammatical manner is *"for at least three years and five years respectively, against the existing norm of one year"*. The sentence is describing about the Supreme Court directive to make the owners of new car and two wheeler purchase insurance covers. Since, it's a new directive, option (d) perfectly fits the blank as it describes the earlier as well as the improvised time period for which the insurance must be covered. All the other options are incoherent to the context of the sentence. Hence, option (d) is the most suitable answer choice.

137. The most appropriate clause that will complete the paragraph is *"92% of the people belonging to the community are subjected to economic exclusion."* The paragraph is describing about a survey conducted of the transgender community by the NHRC. Since the previous clause mentions"...found that", the latter part must express the outcome or the findings of the survey. This rationale is satisfied by only option (b). Options (a) and (c) are contextually incorrect while option (d) is grammatically incorrect. Therefore, option (b) is the most suitable answer choice.

138. The most appropriate clause that will complete the paragraph is option (a) *"as reported by the media recently, has escalated the contention"* as the initial part of the paragraph has mentioned about the accumulated unfilled jobs in the public sector. Part (a) of the paragraph acts as a cause

for the effect mentioned in option (a). All the other options are either grammatically incorrect or contextually meaningless. Hence, option (a) is the most suitable answer choice.

139. The most appropriate clause that fills the blank of the paragraph is option (c) *"Emerging market economies continue to be in the spotlight for the wrong reasons"* as it acts as a perfect introduction for the paragraph. The paragraph is pointing out the devaluation of the rupee against the dollar; therefore, option (c) will aptly introduce the paragraph stating the fall of emerging market economies. However, option (a) and (d) are contextually meaningless, while, option (b) is grammatically incorrect. Hence, option (c) is the most suitable answer choice.

140. The most appropriate phrase that completes the paragraph coherently is *"is vulnerable to several natural hazards"*, as the paragraph is describing about the about the geographical characteristics of Kerala which makes it vulnerable foe several natural hazards. The latter part of the paragraph already states the hazards that are prone to Kerala, therefore, the phrase "is vulnerable to several natural hazards" aptly fits in the blank. All the other phrases are irrelevant to the context of the sentence. Hence, option (b) is the most suitable answer choice.

141. All the three starters can be used to frame a meaningful sentence without altering the intended meaning of the given sentences. Hence option (e) is the correct choice.

(i) Given how unmanned or remotely piloted aircraft commonly known as drones, hold immense promise for various commercial applications, the government has done well to set up a regulatory framework for drone operations, including commercial use.

(ii) Since unmanned or remotely piloted aircraft commonly known as drones, hold immense promise for various commercial applications, the government has done well to set up a regulatory framework for drone operations, including commercial use.

(iii) Provided that unmanned or remotely piloted aircraft commonly known as drones, hold immense promise for various commercial applications, the government has done well to set up a regulatory framework for drone operations, including commercial use.

142. Only starter (i) can be used to frame a meaningful sentence without altering the exact meaning of the given sentences. However, it is not possible to construct a contextual sentence using the third and second starter as they would alter the intended meaning. Hence option (a) is the correct choice, (i) Convincing people to buy insurance for the expected life of the vehicle at the time of purchase, as in the case of road tax, interferes with the need to set premium based on data relating to safety and diligence of the driver, which would change over time.

143. Both the starters (i) and (ii) can be used to frame a meaningful sentence without altering the exact meaning of the given sentences. However, it is not possible to construct a contextual sentence using the third starter as it would alter the intended meaning. Hence option (d) is the correct choice.

(i) Unless the country finds viable and sustainable replacements for its energy needs, international oil price movements will continue to be an important fault line in India's political economy, (ii) Except that the country finds viable and sustainable replacements for its energy needs, international oil price movements will continue to be an important fault line in India's political economy.

144. The most appropriate set of words that fills the blanks of the paragraph is "diversity, subsumed, legitimacy", "diversity" provides the precise context as it means a range of different things. Moreover 'subsumed' means include or absorb (something) in something else; while 'legitimacy' means conformity to the law or to rules. All the other words are incoherent and fail to make the paragraph comprehensive. Hence, option (b) is the most suitable answer choice.

Socialism means a political and economic theory of social organization which advocates that the means of production distribution, and exchange should be owned or regulated by the community as a whole.

Invigorated means give strength or energy to.

Astuteness means of keen penetration or discernment; sagacious: an astute analysis, clever; cunning; ingenious; shrewd

145. The most appropriate set of words that fills the blanks of the paragraph is "ferrying, probe, glitch". "Ferrying" provides the precise context as it means transport from one place to another on short or regular trips. Moreover, 'probe' means a thorough investigation into a crime or other matter; while 'Glitch' means a sudden, usually temporary malfunction or fault of equipment. All the other words are incoherent and fail to make

the paragraph comprehensive. Hence, option (d) is the most suitable answer choice.

Gremlin means an imaginary mischievous sprite regarded as responsible for an unexplained mechanical or electronic problem or fault. Barging means move forcefully or roughly.

146. The most appropriate set of words that fills the blanks of the paragraph is "contemporary, supplanting, "disconcerting". "Contemporary" provides the precise context as it means belonging to or occurring in the present. Moreover, 'supplanting' means supersede and replace; while 'Disconcerting' means causing one to feel unsettled. All the other words are incoherent and fail to make the paragraph comprehensive. Hence, option (c) is the most suitable answer choice. Posterior means coming after in time or order; later

Superseding means take the place of (a person or thing previously in authority or use); supplant. Bewildering means confusing or perplexing.

147. The most appropriate set of words that fills the blanks of the paragraph is "interdicted, consolation prosecutorial". "interdicted" provides the precise context as it means prohibit or forbid (something). Moreover 'consolation' means the comfort received by a person after a loss or disappointment; while 'prosecutorial' means relating to the institution and conducting of legal proceedings against someone in respect of a criminal charge. All the other words are incoherent and fail to make the paragraph comprehensive. Hence, option (d) is the most suitable answer choice.

Disdain means the feeling that someone or something is unworthy of one's consideration or respect. Legitimate means conforming to the law or to rules. Suppressed means forcibly put an end to.

148. Drawing a hint from the fourth sentence of the rearranged paragraph it can be understood that it is describing about a study which reveals the data reflecting the increased pollution in the rivers in the entire nation. It further mentions about the problems associated in controlling pollution. It should be noted that statement (b) appropriately introduces the paragraph by providing the data about the increase in the segments of river pollution. Statement (d) follows statement (b) as it mentions about the data mentioned in the previous statement indicating that the laws have not been implemented properly. Sentence (F) begins with the phrase "The study also..." which indicates that in the previous sentence the study has been mentioned. Hence it should follow sentence (d). Sentence (a) is the fourth sentence of the rearranged paragraph. Next is sentence (E) as it logically connects with sentence (a). Sentence (c) stands as the concluding part of the rearranged paragraph. The phrase in the statement (c) "It is notable that these results..." provides a clue for the conclusion of the paragraph. Hence, the logical sequence thus formed is, BDFAEC. Since, statement (d) is the second sentence in the rearranged paragraph option (d) becomes the most suitable answer choice.

149. Drawing a hint from the fourth sentence of the rearranged paragraph it can be understood that it is describing about a study which reveals the data reflecting the increased pollution in the rivers in the entire nation. It further mentions about the problems associated in controlling pollution. It should be noted that statement (b) appropriately introduces the paragraph by providing the data about the increase in the segments of river pollution. Statement (d) follows statement (b) as it mentions about the data mentioned in the previous statement indicating that the laws have not been implemented properly. Sentence (F) begins with the phrase "The study also..." which indicates that in the previous sentence the study has been mentioned. Hence it should follow sentence (d). Sentence (a) is the fourth sentence of the rearranged paragraph. Next is sentence (E) as it logically connects with sentence (a). Sentence (c) stands as the concluding part of the rearranged paragraph. The phrase in the statement (c) "It is notable that these results..." provides a clue for the conclusion of the paragraph. Hence, the logical sequence thus formed is, BDFAEC. Since, statement (c) is the last sentence in the rearranged paragraph option (b) becomes the most suitable answer choice.

150. Drawing a hint from the fourth sentence of the rearranged paragraph it can be understood that it is describing about a study which reveals the data reflecting the increased pollution in the rivers in the entire nation. It further mentions about the problems associated in controlling pollution. It should be noted that statement (b) appropriately introduces the paragraph by providing the data about the increase in the segments of river pollution. Statement (d) follows statement (b) as it mentions about the data mentioned in the previous statement indicating that the laws have not been implemented

properly. Since, statements (b) and (d) forms a perfect pair, option (e) becomes the most suitable answer choice.

151. Salubrious means (of a place) pleasant; not run-down while Salutary means (especially with reference to something unwelcome or unpleasant) producing good effects; beneficial. Since they both are synonyms of each other, option (d) becomes the most suitable answer choice. Exorbitant means (of a price or amount charged) unreasonably high.

Quandary means a state of perplexity or uncertainty over what to do in a difficult situation.

Enigma means a person or thing that is mysterious or difficult to understand.

152. CAMOUFLAGE means hide or disguise the presence of (a person, animal, or object) by means of camouflage while CANDID means truthful and straightforward; frank. Since, they both are antonyms of each other; option (e) is the most suitable answer choice.

Debunk means expose the falseness or hollowness of (an idea or belief).

Indignant means feeling or showing anger or annoyance at what is perceived as unfair treatment.

Vapid means offering nothing that is stimulating or challenging; bland.

153. Statements (a), (b) and (c) imply the following:

(i) Two months are left for the State Assembly elections;

(ii) Extensive inconsistencies or widespread discrepancies have been detected in the electoral rolls of Rajasthan.

(iii) There are doubts that the names of *many* legitimate voters have been struck off the lists.

But first of all, there is a grammatical error in the statement (d) which is the following:

The subject of the sentence of the statement (d) is 'removal of names of a few legitimate voters from the voter lists' which is *Singular*. The subject, having **singular noun,** of the sentence is *followed* by **the auxiliary verb** 'have', which is used for a subject having **plural noun.**

Also, there are following contextual errors in the statement (d):

(i) Removal of the names of a few legitimate voters;

(ii) widespread **consistencies** in the electoral rolls of Rajasthan.

(iii) No mention of the phrase 'two months ahead of the State Assembly elections' or an equivalent to convey when would the Assembly elections would be held in Rajasthan.

Hence, option (d) is the correct answer because it is the only **incorrect** sentence.

154. The two events happening are:

(i) The Shiromani Akali Dal-BJP combine has decided to meet the Governor over the 'deteriorating law and order' situation in the state of Punjab.

(ii) Punjab Chief Minister Amarinder Singh emphasized on Monday that nobody involved in sacrilege cases would be spared.

The statements (a), (c) and (d) starts with a conjunction or conjunction-phrase which are synonyms i.e, While, 'At the time as' and 'During the time that' are synonyms. They convey the same meaning that two events are occurring simultaneously.

But, the usage of the conjunction 'because' in the statement (b) implies that one event is causing another event to occur.

So, while the statements (a), (c) and (d) suggest that the events (i) and (ii) are occurring simultaneously and a sort of independently, the statement (b) suggests that the event (ii) has caused the event (i) to occur. So, contextually, statement (b) conveys a different meaning as compared to that conveyed by the statements *(a),* (c) and (d).

Hence, option (b) is the correct answer.

155. The sentences (b), (c) and (d) are conveying the following:

(i) The AAP has reached out to ex-Punjab convener Sucha Singh Chhotepur.

(ii) The AAP wishes to make peace with "rebels" and "former leaders".

(iii) Mr. Sucha Singh Chhotepur was being approached by AAP two years after he was sacked on charges of taking bribe for allotting party tickets.

The above sentences (sentences (b), (c) and (d)) are suggesting that meeting with Sucha Singh Chhotepur was a part of an effort to make peace with "rebels" and "former leaders", but the sentence (a) suggests that AAP has already made (and completed) efforts to make peace with "rebels" and "former leaders", or the AAP has reached out to ex-Punjab convener Sucha Singh Chootepur after making (all) the efforts to make peace with "rebels" and "former leaders".

The meaning conveyed by the statement (a) is different from that conveyed by the statements (b), (c) and (d).

Moreover, the sentence (a) has a grammatical error. The subject of the sentence is a singular noun 'The AAP' which is followed by an auxiliary verb 'have' which is used for plural noun.

Hence, the correct answer is the option (a).

2017

ENGLISH LANGUAGE

Directions (Q. 1 to 10) : Read the following passage carefully and answer the questions given below it. Certain words/phrases are given in **bold** in the passage to help you to locate them while answering some of the questions.

In the past, the richest states often grew the fastest and the poor ones slowest. But India's record GDP growth of 8.49% per year in the five-year period 2004-09 is a case of improved productivity and growth in **customarily** poor states trickling up and aggregating into rapid growth at the national level.

Nobody should call this a success of trickle-down economics. Trickle-down assumes that fast growth can be had simply by changing a few policies that benefit the rich, after which some benefits trickle down to the poor. In fact, miracle growth is globally rare precisely because it is so difficult for countries to improve the productivity of a substantial proportion of the population. Only when productivity improvement is widespread is there enough productivity improvement from all regions and people to **add** up to fast growth. In other words, fast growth does not trickle down, it trickles up.

Once a country grows fast, government revenues will boom, and can be used to accelerate spending in social sectors and welfare. Miracle growth and record revenues enabled the central government to finance social welfare schemes, farm loan waivers and enormous oil subsidies. This can be called the trickling down of part of the revenue bonanza into welfare and workfare. But neither welfare nor workfare could have caused the **sharp** acceleration of economic growth. The growth bonanza itself was **sparked** by state-level political and policy changes that accelerated local growth, which then trickled up to the national level.

1. To which of the following factors does the author attribute India's high growth rate during 2004-09?

  (1) Tremendous growth of the vast majority of richer states

  (2) Change in national level policies to benefit only large well off states

  (3) Gains of richer states have been used to fund social welfare schemes in the larger states

  (4) Improved productivity of traditionally low performing states

  (5) None of the above

2. Which of the following best describes the author's view of trickle down theory?

  (1) It ensures accountability of the government even at the grassroot level

  (2) It has been effective in helping poor states catch up with richer ones

  (3) It promotes inclusive growth over quick growth

  (4) It targets social welfare at the cost of economic growth

  (5) It has largely failed to drive sustained growth

3. Which of the following is TRUE in the context of the passage?

  (1) India's growth was more inclusive in nature during 2004-2009 than it had been in the past

  (2) Developed countries use the same model of development as India

  (3) Widespread growth is best achieved through Central Government monitored schemes

  (4) At present India's traditionally poor states are more prosperous than her socially developed ones

  (5) There should be no government expenditure in social sectors if the current high growth rate is not maintained

4. Why have countries found it difficult to achieve high growth?

  A. Ensuring an increase in the output among a large number of citizens is difficult.

  B. Corruption of politicians at the grassroot level results in the benefits of growth not reaching the poor.

  C. The government's failure to allocate sufficient income to inclusive social welfare schemes.

  (1) Only (A)   (2) (A) and (B)

  (3) (B) and (C)   (4) All (A), (B) and (C)

  (5) None of these

5. What is the author's objective in writing this passage?

  (1) Advocating greater autonomy for the richest states in India

  (2) Urging the government to invest in social development to facilitate economic growth

  (3) Criticising traditional economic principles on which the Indian economy is based

(4) Encouraging larger states to disburse more wealth at the grassroot level

(5) None of the above

6. Which of the following is similar in meaning to the word 'ADD' as used in the context of the passage?

(1) Aggravate

(2) Result

(3) Include

(4) Compute

(5) Intensify

7. Which of the following is opposite in meaning to the word 'SHARP' as used in the context of the passage?

(1) Blunt

(2) Expected

(3) Late

(4) Gradual

(5) Indistinct

8. Which of the following is true according to the author?

(1) Trickle down effect is what makes a country grow faster.

(2) Fast growth trickles up.

(3) Government revenues increase when a country starts to grow.

(4) Welfare causes an economy to grow.

(5) Poor states grow slower than the developing states.

9. Which of the following is same in meaning to the word 'spark', is used in the passage.

(1) Activate

(2) Precipitate

(3) Alleviate

(4) Violate

(5) Adulate

10. Which of the following is opposite in meaning to the word 'customary', as used in the passage?

(1) Standard

(2) Popular

(3) Usual

(4) Exceptional

(5) Revolutionary

Directions (Q. 11 to 15): Fill in the blanks by choosing the most appropriate options.

11. He lost his balance _____ fell _____ the bicycle.

(1) or, of

(2) when, of

(3) that, from

(4) where, from

(5) and, off

12. I am _____ tired _____ I cannot go on.

(1) too, or

(2) so, that

(3) much, that

(4) not, so

(5) very, why

13. He was _____ fatigued that he _____ scarcely stand.

(1) so, could

(2) not, cannot

(3) much, was

(4) so, will

(5) very, would

14. Passengers are warned _____ it is dangerous to lean out of the window _____ the train is in motion.

(1) when, and

(2) so, because

(3) where, for

(4) when, that

(5) that, while

15. One great reason _____ we are insensible to the goodness of the Creator is the fact _______ His bounty is so extensive.

(1) of, when

(2) why, that

(3) since, from

(4) than, when

(5) because, for

Directions (Q. 16 to 20): Rearrange the following six sentences (A), (B), (C), (D), (E) and (F) in the proper sequence to form a meaningful paragraph; then answer the questions given below them.

A. However, many people may not be aware of the numerous other areas where it has been applied.

B. Today, even, those who have little knowledge about the production of virtual reality are now most likely aware of its use in video games.

C. Similarly medical, students have substituted a cadaver for a fiberglass mould of a body and a headset when training to perform surgery.

D. Virtual reality was an unfamiliar concept to many people till the early 90's.

E. Introducing virtual reality to the real world, thus, has already proven to be beneficial for every industry it encounters.

F. For example, astronaut trainees have recently used virtual reality to simulate a trip to space.

16. Which of the following should be the FOURTH sentence after rearrangement?

(1) E

(2) F

(3) A

(4) D

(5) B

17. Which of the following should be the FIRST sentence after rearrangement?

(1) A

(2) B

(3) C

(4) D

(5) E

18. Which of the following should be the LAST (SIXTH) sentence after rearrangement?

(1) A

(2) B

(3) C

(4) D

(5) E

19. Which of the following should be the SECOND sentence after rearrangement?

(1) B

(2) C

(3) D

(4) E

(5) F

20. Which of the following should be the FIFTH sentence after rearrangement?

(1) A   (2) B

(3) C   (4) D

(5) E

Directions (Q. 21 to 25): In each question below, a sentence with four words in bold type is given. These are lettered as (1), (2), (3) and (4). One of these four words in bold may be either wrongly spelt or inappropriate in the context of the sentence. Find out the word which is wrongly spelt or inappropriate, if any. The letter of that word is your answer. If all the words in bold are correctly spelt and also appropriate in the context of the sentence, mark (5) i.e., 'All correct' as your answer.

21. In just one year Beena has **gained** (1) around eight **kilograms** (2) and doctors fear she might be **prune** (3) to heart-related **ailments** (4). All correct (5)

22. The clever **disciple** (1) had decided **to proved** (2) his skills by **reciting** (3) the holy **verse** (4) from the book. All correct (5)

23. Even though the state has been **witnessing** (1) deaths on a daily **basis** (2), it has not **hindered** (3) the **festivity** (4) spirit of the people. All correct (5)

24. On being **threatened** (1) by the king's servants, the poor **gardener** (2) **blurted** (3) out that he had stolen the **jewels** (4). All correct (5)

25. The player was **arrestted** (1) for **kicking** (2) and **punching** (3) a driver outside a fast-food **outlet** (4) in the city. All correct (5)

Directions (Q. 26 to 30): In the following passage there are blanks, each of which has been numbered. These numbers are printed below the passage and against each, five words are suggested, one of which fits the blank appropriately. Find out the appropriate word in each case.

__(26)__ a child, the first trip I ever made outside my village was to the library in the next village with my grandfather. A big banyan tree stood near the building with a cement platform under it. My grandfather would go and sit on the platform after __(27)__ me at the first floor. Other village elders would also join him there. I would read the children's books and be __(28)__ in them, until my grandfather called me to go home.

One day after we reached home my grandfather said, "I have noticed how much you love books. Have you heard of a man named Andrew Carnegie? He was an American billionaire __(29)__ willed most of his wealth not to his children but to a foundation, which built libraries. __(30)__ me, when you grow up, if you have more money than you need, you will buy books for at least one library."

26. (1) When   (2) Like

    (3) Still   (4) As

    (5) Being

27. (1) Seated   (2) Dropping

    (3) Place   (4) Sending

    (5) Abandoned

28. (1) Busy   (2) Engrossed

    (3) Occupied   (4) Distracted

    (5) Absorb

29. (1) Who   (2) That

    (3) Though   (4) Whom

    (5) Himself

30. (1) Remind   (2) Allow

    (3) Commit   (4) Thank

    (5) Promise

QUANTITATIVE APTITUDE

Directions (Q. 31 to 35): Answer the following questions based on the given information.

The bar graph shows the number of persons applied for LC/MC/HC flats in 5 different cities.

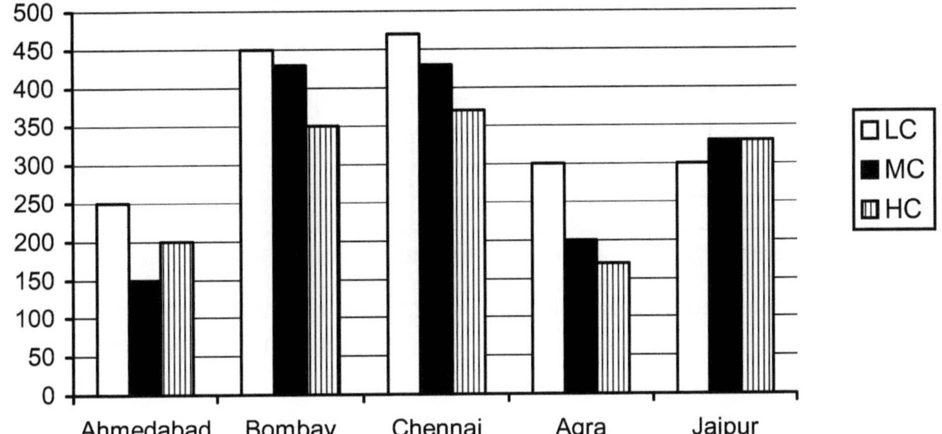

31. What is the total number of people applied for MC flats in all the cities together?
(1) 1775   (2) 1425
(3) 1625   (4) 1575
(5) None of these

32. What is the respective ratio of the total number of people applied for LC, MC and HC flats in all the cities together?
(1) 24 : 21 : 19   (2) 8 : 7 : 6
(3) 71 : 63 : 57   (4) 48 : 42 : 37
(5) None of these

33. Number of people applied for MC flats in Chennai forms approximately what percent of the total number of people applied for MC flats from all the cities together?
(1) 34 %   (2) 48%
(3) 51%   (4) 18%
(5) 27%

34. Number of people applied for LC flats in Ahmedabad forms what percent of total number of people applied from all the categories in Ahmedabad (Rounded off to 2 decimal places)?
(1) 41.67%   (2) 54.16%
(3) 35.34%   (4) 44.44%
(5) None of these

35. What is the total number of people applied for all the categories in Jaipur?
(1) 950   (2) 875
(3) 675   (4) 1050
(5) 1000

36. A motorboat whose speed is 15 km/hr in still water goes 30 km downstream and comes back in a total of 4 hours and 3 minutes. The speed of the stream (in km/hr) is
(1) 4   (2) 5
(3) 6   (4) 10
(5) None of these

37. A and B can do a piece of work in 45 days and 40 days respectively. They began to do the work together but A left after some days and then B completed the remaining work in 23 days. The number of days after which A left the work was
(1) 6   (2) 8
(3) 9   (4) 12
(5) None of these

38. The perimeter of square is equal to twice the perimeter of a rectangle of length 8 cm and breadth 7 cm. What is the semi-circumference of a circle whose diameter is equal to the side of the square? (Rounded off to two decimal places)
(1) 38.57 cm   (2) 23.57 cm
(3) 42.46 cm   (4) 47.47 cm
(5) 28.39 cm

39. A basket contains 4 red, 5 blue and 3 green marbles. If three marbles are picked at random, what is the probability that either all are green or all are red?
(1) $\dfrac{7}{44}$ (2) $\dfrac{7}{12}$
(3) $\dfrac{5}{12}$ (4) $\dfrac{1}{44}$
(5) None of these

40. A sum of money is divided among A, B, C and D in the ratio of 5 : 8 : 9 : 11. If the share of B is Rs. 2,475 more than the share of A, then what is the total amount of money of A & C together?
(1) Rs. 9, 000   (2) Rs. 11,550
(3) Rs. 10, 725   (4) Rs. 9, 075
(5) None of these

Directions (Q. 41 to 45): Answer the questions on the basis of the information given below.

In the following table percentage of marks obtained by seven students in six subjects has been given.

Student	English (60)	History (40)	Computers (130)	Maths (150)	Science (120)	Economics (80)
Meera	100	80	50	90	90	60
Subodh	80	70	80	100	80	40
Kunal	90	70	60	90	70	70
Soni	60	60	65	80	80	80
Richu	50	90	62	80	85	95
Irene	40	60	64	70	65	85
Vijay	80	80	35	65	50	75

***Marks shown in brackets represent maximum marks.**

41. What are the total marks obtained by Meera in all the subjects?
(1) 448   (2) 580
(3) 470   (4) 74.67
(5) None of these

42. What are the average marks obtained by these seven students in History? (rounded off to two digits)
(1) 72.86   (2) 27.32
(3) 24.86   (4) 29.14
(5) None of these

43. How many students have got 60% or more marks in all the subjects?
    (1) One   (2) Two
    (3) Three   (4) None
    (5) None of these

44. What is the overall percentage of Kunal?
    (1) 64   (2) 65
    (3) 75   (4) 64.24
    (5) None of these

45. In which subject is overall percentage the best?
    (1) Maths   (2) Economics
    (3) History   (4) Science
    (5) None of these

46. Mr. Punit invests an amount of Rs. 24,200 at the rate of 4% p.a. for 6 years to obtain a simple interest. Later he invests the principal amount as well as the amount obtained as simple interest for another 4 years at the same rate of interest. What amount of simple interest will he obtain at the end of the last 4 years?
    (1) Rs. 4,800   (2) Rs. 4,801.28
    (3) Rs. 4,850.32   (4) Rs. 4,700
    (5) None of these

47. A car travels a certain distance from A to town B at speed of 42 km/hr and from B to town A at the speed of 48 km/hr. What is the average speed of the car?
    (1) 45 km/hr   (2) 46 km/hr
    (3) 44 km/hr   (4) 44.8 km/hr
    (5) None of these

48. Present ages of Sudha and Neeta are in the ratio of 6 : 7 respectively. Five years ago their ages were in the ratio of 5 : 6 respectively. What is Sudha's present age?
    (1) 30 years   (2) 35 years
    (3) 40 years   (4) Cannot be determined
    (5) None of these

49. A sample of 'p' litre from a container having 112 litre mixture of milk and water containing milk and water in the ratio of 3 : 5 respectively is replaced with pure milk so that the container will have milk and water in the ratio of 3 : 1. What is the value of 'p'?
    (1) 112 litre   (2) 100.8 litre
    (3) 77.4 litre   (4) 67.2 litre
    (5) None of these

50. Vikas purchased a TV set for Rs. 11250 after getting discount of 10% on the labeled price. He spent Rs. 150 on transport and Rs. 800 on installation. At what price should it be sold so that the profit earned would be 15% if no discount was offered?
    (1) Rs. 12937.50   (2) Rs. 14030.00
    (3) Rs. 13450.00   (4) Rs. 15467.50
    (5) None of these

Directions (Q. 51 to 55): In the following number series only one number is wrong. Find out the wrong number.

51. 529, 841, 961, 1296, 1681, 1849, 2209
    (1) 1296   (2) 841
    (3) 961   (4) 1681
    (5) None of these

52. 13, 14, 27, 45, 68, 109, 177
    (1) 27   (2) 109
    (3) 45   (4) 68
    (5) None of these

53. 2, 5, 10, 17, 27, 37
    (1) 10   (2) 5
    (3) 17   (4) 37
    (5) 27

54. 274, 301, 426, 769, 1498, 2824, 5026
    (1) 301   (2) 426
    (3) 769   (4) 2824
    (5) None of these

55. 4, 28, 160, 990, 6970, 55832, 502560
    (1) 160   (2) 990
    (3) 55832   (4) 6970
    (5) None of these

Directions (Q. 56 to 60): Two equations I and II are given in each question. On the basis of these equations you have to decide the relation between p and q and give the answer.
(1) if $p \leq q$
(2) if $p > q$
(3) if $q > p$
(4) if p = q or if relationship cannot be established.
(5) if $p \geq q$

56. I. $p^2 - p - 6 = 0$
    II. $q^2 - 7q + 12 = 0$

57. I. $12p^2 - 17p + 6 = 0$
    II. $8q^2 - 6q + 1 = 0$

58. I. $4p^2 + 12p - 7 = 0$
    II. $8q^2 - 30q - 27 = 0$

59. I. $p^2 = 196$
    II. $q^2 - 15q + 14 = 0$

60. I. $3p + 2q = 3$
    II. $4q - 5p = -27$

Directions (Q. 61 to 65): What will come in place of question mark (?) in the following questions?

61. $[(3024 \div 189)^{1/2} + (684 \div 19)^2] = (?)^2 + 459$
    (1) –27   (2) –29
    (3) 31   (4) 841
    (5) 1089

62. $4.4 \times 5/16$ of 30% of 216 =?

    (1) 81.9   (2) 83.7

    (3) 87.3   (4) 89.1

    (5) None of these

63. $(0.0729 \div 0.1)^3 \div (0.081 \times 10)^5 \times (0.3 \times 3)^5 = (0.9)^{?+3}$

    (1) 1   (2) 2

    (3) 4   (4) 7

    (5) None of these

64. $\left(\sqrt{?\%} \text{ of } \sqrt{1764} \times 5\right) = 149.8 - 112$

    (1) $\sqrt{18}$ (2) 18

    (3) 324   (4) 24

    (5) None of these

65. $(27)^2 \times 6 \div 9 + (7)^3 + 71 = (?)^3 - 431$

    (1) 11   (2) $(13)^3$

    (3) 13   (4) $(11)^2$

    (5) None of these

REASONING

Directions (Q. 66 to 68): Answer the following questions based on the given information.

M, N, O, P, Q, R, S and T are eight friends of different heights. It is also known that:

Q is taller than I but shorter than O. N is shorter than P but taller than R. P is shorter than M but taller than S. O is shorter than S who is not as tall as R.

66. Who is the third shortest among all?

    (1) R   (2) N

    (3) O   (4) S

    (5) None of these

67. How many friends are younger than N?

    (1) Four   (2) Two

    (3) Three   (4) Five

    (5) None of these

68. Who is the eldest among all?

    (1) Q   (2) N

    (3) O   (4) M

    (5) None of these

Directions (Q. 69 and 70) : Answer the following questions on the basis of the information given below.

P, Q, R, S, T, U, V, W and X are nine members of a family of three generations and there are three married couples in the family. W is a male member whose paternal grandfather is P who is the maternal grandfather of T. Q is the daughter of S who is the sister-in-law of U. U is the mother of W. T is the nephew of R. There are five males and four females in the family. X is the spouse of S.

69. How is Q related to W?

    (1) Mother   (2) Aunt

    (3) Niece   (4) Cousin

    (5) Sister

70. How is R related to V?

    (1) Brother   (2) Cousin

    (3) Son   (4) Son-in-law

    (5) Daughter

Directions (Q. 71 to 75): Answer the following questions based on the given information.

Seven friends M, N, P, D, E, F and G are working in three different organizations ABC, PQR and JKL and with at least two persons in each organization. Each one of them is in a different department viz. Analysis, HR, Marketing, Research, Design, Production and Administration (not necessarily in same order.) N works in Analysis in organization PQR. F works in Design in organization ABC with only M. Those who work in HR and Administration work in the same organization. P works in organization JKL, but does not work in Research department. G works in Administration in organization PQR. One who works in Production works with organization ABC, D works in organization PQR.

71. Who works in HR?

    (1) P   (2) D

    (3) E   (4) N

    (5) None of these

72. E works in which organization?

    (1) ABC   (2) PQR

    (3) JKL   (4) ABC or PQR

    (5) None of these

73. Three persons work in which organization?

    (1) PQR   (2) JKL

    (3) ABC   (4) PQR or JKL

    (5) ABC or JKL

74. P works in which department?

    (1) HR   (2) Design

    (3) Research   (4) Marketing

    (5) None of these

75. Which of the following combinations is correct?

    (1) JKL - E - HR

    (2) PQR - P - Marketing

    (3) ABC - M - Administration

    (4) PQR - G - HR

    (5) None of these

Directions (Q. 76 to 80): Answer the following questions on the basis of the information given below.

In a certain code 'he was dancing on' is written as 'lh aj ey ag', 'he on the floor' is written as 'ag ev aj es', 'he was of dancing' is written as 'ag ib lh ey' and 'his house dancing floor' is written as 'ev md ey oz'.

76. What does 'ib' stand for?

    (a) was   (2) dancing

    (3) of   (4) he

    (5) on

77. 'at ev md' could be a code for which of the following?

    (1) floor house party   (2) his house was

    (3) the dancing his   (4) floor of house

    (5) on his dancing

78. What is the code for 'was'?

    (1) ey   (2) ag

    (3) ib   (4) aj

    (5) lh

79. Which of the following may represent 'he his on'?

    (1) aj ib oz   (2) md oz ag

    (3) oz ag aj   (4) oz ag ey

    (5) md ib aj

80. What is the code for 'dancing'?

    (1) ey   (2) ag

    (3) ib   (4) aj

    (5) lh

Directions (Q. 81 to 85): Read the information carefully and answer the questions based on it.

Twelve people are sitting in two parallel rows containing six people each, in such a way that there is an equal distance between adjacent persons. P, Q, R, S, T and U are sitting in the first row and all of them are facing North. A, B, C, D, E and F are sitting in the second row and all of them are facing South. Also, each member in a row is facing a member of the other row. It is also known that: P is sitting third to the left of T. A is sitting second to the right of E. B is sitting third to the right of C and same is true for Q and U. Only one person is sitting between F and D and same is true for S and Q. F is not an immediate neighbour of E and E is not facing Q or R. None among the P, B or U is sitting at an extreme end of the row.

81. Who is sitting between T and U?

    (1) Q   (2) P

    (3) R   (4) S

    (5) None of these

82. Who is sitting third to the right of the one facing the one sitting second to the left of Q?

    (1) F   (2) D

    (3) A   (4) C

    (5) None of these

83. Four of the following five are alike in a certain way and thus form a group. Find the one that does not belong to this group.

    (1) R – E   (2) C – U

    (3) C – S   (4) S – B

    (5) Q – D

84. Which two people are sitting at the extreme ends of the row?

    (1) R – F   (2) A – U

    (3) C – Q   (4) S – A

    (5) Q – T

85. Who are the immediate neighbors of E?

    (1) C and B   (2) D and B

    (3) C and D   (4) F and A

    (5) None of these

Directions (Q. 86 to 90): Answer the following questions based on the given information.

Eight family members – I, J, K, L, M, N, O and P are sitting around a circular table facing the centre at equidistant positions but not necessarily in the same order. It is also known that:

N, who is the sister of O, sits second to the left of the daughter of L. N is not an immediate neighbour of P's husband I. Only one person sits between I and N. I is the father of O. L, who is the brother of P, sits to the immediate left of his mother. Only one person sits between P's mother and M and same is true for P and O. I is sitting second to the right of J who is not an immediate neighbour of any female. O is the mother of K and is not an immediate neighbour of M.

86. How is K related to I?

    (1) Grandson   (2) Nephew

    (3) Granddaughter   (4) Niece

    (5) Cannot be determined

87. Who is sitting opposite to P?

    (1) L   (2) I

    (3) N   (4) K

    (5) None of these

88. How many grandchildren does J have?

    (1) None   (2) Two

    (3) Three   (4) One

    (5) None of these

89. Who is sitting third to the left of M?

    (1) O   (2) K

    (3) I   (4) J

    (5) None of these

90. How many persons are sitting between the grandchild of P and the father of O?

    (1) None   (2) Two

    (3) Three   (4) One

    (5) None of these

Directions (Q. 91 to 95): In the following questions the symbols ×, @, +, ∗ and $ are used with following meaning as illustrated below:

P × Q means 'P is neither less than nor greater than Q'.

P @ Q means 'P is neither greater than nor equal to Q'.

P + Q means 'P is neither less than nor equal to Q'.

P ∗ Q means 'P is not greater than Q'.

P $ Q means 'P is not less than Q'.

Based on the statements given in each of the questions below, find out which of the conclusion follows.

Mark the answer as:

(1) If only conclusion I follows.

(2) If only conclusion II follows.

(3) If conclusion I as well as conclusion II follow.

(4) If either conclusion I or conclusion II follows.

(5) If neither conclusion I nor conclusion II follows.

91. Statement : D ∗ F, M $ F, M @ K

Conclusion:

I.   K $ F

II. K + D

92. Statement: K + M, M @ R, R × T

Conclusion:

I.   M @ T

II. K × T

93. Statement: T @ M, M ∗ R, R × N

Conclusion:

I.   M × N

II. M @ N

94. Statement: B $ N, N × R, R + T

Conclusion:

I.   B $ R

II. T @ N

95. Statement: N × P, K + P, Q @ K

Conclusion

I.   K ∗ N

II. Q + N

Directions (Q. 96 to 100): In each of the questions below are given three statements followed by two conclusions numbered I and II. You have to take the given statements to be true even if they seem to be at variance from commonly known facts. Read all the conclusions and then decide which of the given conclusions logically follows from the given statements disregarding commonly known facts.

Give answer —

(1) if only Conclusion I follows.

(2) if only Conclusion II follows.

(3) if either Conclusion I or II follows.

(4) if neither Conclusion I nor II follows.

(5) if both Conclusions I and II follow.

96. Statements:

All schools are buildings.

Al buildings are towers.

All towers are rooms.

Conclusions:

I.   Some rooms are schools,

II. All towers are schools,

97. Statements:

All pins are hammers.

Some hammers are spoons.

All spoons are plates.

Conclusions:

I.   Some spoons are pins,

II. Some plates are pins.

98. Statements:

Some chairs are doors.

Some doors are walls.

Some walls are pins.

Conclusions:

I.   Some pins are doors.

II. No pin is door.

99. Statements:

All dogs are monkeys.

No monkey is goat.

Some goats are horses.

Conclusions:

I.   Some horses are dogs.

II. Some goats are dogs.

100. Statements:

Some books are rods.

Some rods are desks.

All desks are tables.

Conclusions:

I.   Some desks are books.

II. Some tables are rods.

ANSWERS

1. (4)	**2.** (5)	**3.** (1)	**4.** (1)	**5.** (2)	**6.** (2)	**7.** (4)	**8.** (2)	**9.** (1)	**10.** (4)
11. (5)	**12.** (2)	**13.** (1)	**14.** (5)	**15.** (2)	**16.** (2)	**17.** (4)	**18.** (5)	**19.** (1)	**20.** (3)
21. (3)	**22.** (2)	**23.** (4)	**24.** (5)	**25.** (1)	**26.** (4)	**27.** (2)	**28.** (2)	**29.** (1)	**30.** (5)
31. (5)	**32.** (5)	**33.** (5)	**34.** (1)	**35.** (1)	**36.** (5)	**37.** (3)	**38.** (2)	**39.** (4)	**40.** (2)
41. (1)	**42.** (4)	**43.** (2)	**44.** (3)	**45.** (1)	**46.** (2)	**47.** (4)	**48.** (1)	**49.** (4)	**50.** (2)
51. (1)	**52.** (3)	**53.** (5)	**54.** (4)	**55.** (4)	**56.** (1)	**57.** (2)	**58.** (4)	**59.** (4)	**60.** (2)
61. (2)	**62.** (4)	**63.** (1)	**64.** (5)	**65.** (1)	**66.** (3)	**67.** (4)	**68.** (4)	**69.** (4)	**70.** (3)
71. (2)	**72.** (3)	**73.** (1)	**74.** (4)	**75.** (5)	**76.** (3)	**77.** (1)	**78.** (5)	**79.** (3)	**80.** (1)
81. (4)	**82.** (3)	**83.** (3)	**84.** (1)	**85.** (2)	**86.** (1)	**87.** (4)	**88.** (3)	**89.** (1)	**90.** (1)
91. (2)	**92.** (1)	**93.** (4)	**94.** (3)	**95.** (5)	**96.** (1)	**97.** (4)	**98.** (3)	**99.** (4)	**100.** (2)

EXPLANATIONS

1. 4 Refer to the second sentence of the first paragraph. The other options are out of scope.

2. 5 Refer to the third sentence of the second paragraph. Other options are either narrow or out of scope.

3. 1 Refer to the first paragraph. The author mentions that in the past only the richer states contributed to the GDP but during 2004-2009, even traditionally poorer states have contributed to the GDP. Hence, it can be said that the growth has been more inclusive in nature during the said period. The other options are out of scope.

4. 1 Refer to the second sentence of the second paragraph. The other options are out of scope.

5. 2 Refer to the first sentence of the third paragraph. The other options are out of scope.

6. 2 The word "add" is found in the second last sentence of the second paragraph. In the context of the sentence, the author means to say that improvement in productivity will eventually result in fast growth.

7. 4 The word "sharp" can be found in the third paragraph. "Sharp acceleration" means meteoric acceleration. The opposite of "sharp" in the context of the sentence is "gradual."

8. 2 Refer to the last sentence of the second paragraph.

9. 1 Refer to the last sentence of the passage. "Spark" in the context of the passage means "to start" or "initiate."

10. 4 "Customary" means "traditional" or something which is expected. "Exceptional" is the opposite of "customary."

11. 5 'And, 'off' are the correct words for the blanks.

12. 2 'So', 'that' correctly fills the blanks.

13. 1 'So, 'could' correctly fill the blanks.

14. 5 'That', 'while' are the right options.

15. 2 'Why', 'that' are the right words.

16. 2 Option F is the fourth sentence. The sentence is an example about astronaut trainees. Now refer to the third sentence (option A) which talks about different other areas where virtual reality has been used. The fourth sentence or option F talks about the way in which virtual reality has been used by the astronaut trainees to simulate a trip to space.

17. 4 Statement D is the first sentence of the passage because it initiates the discussion regarding virtual reality.

18. 5 It is the last sentence of the passage. The previous two sentences (options F and C) list the use of virtual reality in real life situations. Statement E offers the perfectconclusion after the two cited examples.

19. 1 The first sentence (statement D) introduces virtual reality to the readers. The second sentence (statement B) offers a continuation and explains how virtual reality is commonly used in video games.

20. 3 The hint word is "similarly." It means something similar has been said in the previous sentence. So, it we look at the fourth sentence (statement 4), we find an example. Similarly, another example has been given in the fifth sentence (statement C).

21. 3 There should be 'prone' in place of 'prune'.

22. 2 There should be 'to prove' in place of 'to proved'.

23. 4 'Festivity' spirit is wrong. Spirit of festivity or festive spirit is correct.

24. 5 The sentence is grammatically correct.

25. 1 The correct spelling is 'arrested' and not 'arrestted.'

26. 4 'As' is the correct option for the blank space.

27. 2 Only 'dropping' is appropriate.

28. 2 The preposition 'in' indicates that 'engrossed' is the correct answer.

29. 1 'Who' refers to the American billionaire Andrew Carnegie.

30. 5 Only 'promise' can correctly fill the blank.

31. 5 Total number of people applied for MC flats
= 150 + 425 + 425 + 200 + 325 = 1525.

32. 5 Total number of people applied for LC flats
= 250 + 450 + 475 + 300 + 300 = 1775.
Total number of people applied for MC flats = 1525.
Total number of people applied for HC flats
= 200 + 350 + 375 + 175 + 325 = 1425.
∴ Respective ratio = 1775 : 1525 : 1425
i.e. 71 : 61 : 57.

33. 5 Number of people applied for MC flats in Chennai
= 425.
Total number of people applied for MC flats = 1525.

∴ Required percentage = $\dfrac{425}{1525} \times 100 \approx 27.86\%$.

34. 1 Number of people applied for LC flats in Ahmedabad
= 250.
Total number of people applied for all flats in Ahmedabad
= 250 + 150 + 200 = 600.

∴ Required percentage = $\dfrac{250}{600} \times 100 \approx 41.67\%$.

35. 1 Total number of people from Jaipur = 300 + 325 + 325 = 950.

36. 5 Let the speed of the stream be x km/hr.

Now, $\dfrac{30}{15+x} + \dfrac{30}{15-x} = 4 + \dfrac{3}{60}$

$\Rightarrow 60(450 - 30x + 450 + 30x) = 243(225 - x^2)$

$\Rightarrow \dfrac{2000}{9} = 225 - x^2$

$\Rightarrow 9x^2 = 25$

$\Rightarrow x = \dfrac{5}{3}$ km/hr

37. 3 Let the amount of work be 360 units (LCM of 45 and 40)
A does 8 units per day and B does 9 units per day.
Let the number of days for which A worked be x
Now, (8 + 9)x + 23 × 9 = 360
$\Rightarrow$ 17x = 153
$\Rightarrow$ x = 9 days

38. 2 Perimeter of rectangle = 2(8 + 7) = 30 cm
Perimeter of square = 60 cm
∴ Side of square = Diameter of circle(d) = 15 cm

Semi circumference of the circle = $\dfrac{\pi d}{2} = \dfrac{22 \times 15}{7 \times 2}$
= 23.57 cm.

39. 4 Number of ways of picking 3 marbles out of 12

$=^{12}C_3 = \dfrac{12 \times 11 \times 10}{3 \times 2 \times 1} = 220$

Favourable number of cases $=^3C_3 +^4C_3 = 1 + 4 = 5$

Required probability $= \dfrac{5}{220} = \dfrac{1}{44}$.

40. 2 Let the amount of A, B, C and D are Rs. 5x, Rs. 8x, Rs. 9x and 11x respectively.
According to the questions,
8x – 5x = 2475
3x = 2475
x = Rs. 825
Total amount of money of (A + C)
= (5 × 825) + (9 × 825)
= 825 × 14 = Rs. 11,550.

41. 1 Marks obtained by Meera in :
English = 60

History $= 40 \times \dfrac{80}{100} = 32$

Computers $= 50 \times \dfrac{130}{100} = 65$

Maths $= \dfrac{90 \times 150}{100} = 135$

Science $= 90 \times \dfrac{120}{100} = 108$

Economics $= \dfrac{60 \times 80}{100} = 48$

∴ Total marks
= 60 + 32 + 65 + 135 + 108 + 48 = 448

42. 4 Marks obtained in History by :

Meera $= \dfrac{40 \times 80}{100} = 32$

Subodh $= \dfrac{70 \times 40}{100} = 28$

Kunal $= \dfrac{70 \times 40}{100} = 28$

Soni $= \dfrac{60 \times 40}{100} = 24$

Richu $= \dfrac{90 \times 40}{100} = 36$

Irene $= \dfrac{60 \times 40}{100} = 24$

Vijay $= \dfrac{80 \times 40}{100} = 32$

∴ Required average

$= \dfrac{32 + 28 + 28 + 24 + 36 + 24 + 32}{7}$

$= \dfrac{204}{7} = 29.14$

44. 3 Total marks obtained by Kunal
= 54 + 28 + 78 + 135 + 84 + 56
= 435

Total marks
= 60 + 40 + 130 + 150 + 120 + 80 = 580

∴ Required percentage $= \dfrac{435}{580} \times 100 = 75$

46. 2 Simple Interest after 6 years $= \dfrac{24200 \times 4 \times 6}{100}$

= Rs. 5808

Total principal for next 4 years = Rs. 24200 + 5808
= Rs. 30,008

SI after 4 years $= \dfrac{30008 \times 4 \times 4}{100}$ = Rs. 4,801.28

47. 4 Let the distance between town A and town B be x km.

Average speed $= \dfrac{2x}{\dfrac{x}{48} + \dfrac{x}{42}} = \dfrac{2 \times 42 \times 48}{90}$

$= 44.8$ km/hr

48. 1 Let the present ages of Sudha and Neeta be 6x and 7x respectively.

Now, $\dfrac{6x - 5}{7x - 5} = \dfrac{5}{6}$

$\Rightarrow$ 36x – 30 = 35x – 25

$\Rightarrow$ x = 5.

∴ Sudha's present age = 6 × 5 = 30 years.

49. 4 In 112 litre mixture, milk $= 112 \times \dfrac{3}{8} = 42$ litre and

water = 112 – 42 = 70 litre

In 'p' litre mixture, milk $= p \times \dfrac{3}{8} = 0.375p$ litre and

water $= p \times \dfrac{5}{8} = 0.625p$ litre

According to problem,

$\dfrac{42 - 0.375p + p}{70 - 0.625p} = \dfrac{3}{1}$

$\Rightarrow$ 42 – 0.375p + p = 210 – 1.875p

$\Rightarrow$ 2.5p = 168

$\Rightarrow$ p = 67.2 litre.

50. 2 CP of the TV = Rs. 11250 + 150 + 800 = Rs. 12200

SP of the TV $= \dfrac{12200 \times 115}{100}$ = Rs. 14030

51. 1 All numbers in the given series are squares of odd numbers, except 1296.

52. 3 13 + 14 = 27
14 + 27 = 41
27 + 41 = 68
41 + 68 = 109
68 + 109 = 177
So, 45 is the wrong number in this series.

53. 5 2 = 1 × 1 + 1
5 = 2 × 2 + 1
10 = 3 × 3 + 1
17 = 4 × 4 + 1
26 = 5 × 5 + 1 ≠ **27**
37 = 6 × 6 + 1

54. 4 The series is
$+3^3, +5^3, +7^3, +9^3, +11^3, +13^3, \ldots$

55. 4 4 × 4 + (4 × 3) = 28
28 × 5 + (5 × 4) = 160
160 × 6 + (6 × 5) = 990
990 × 7 + (7 × 6) = **6972**
6972 × 8 + (8 × 7) = 55832
55832 × 9 + (9 × 8) = 502560.

56. 1   I. $p^2 - p - 6 = 0$
$\Rightarrow p = 3, -2$
II. $q^2 - 7q + 12 = 0$
$\Rightarrow q = 4, 3$
$\therefore p \le q$

57. 2   I. $12p^2 - 17p + 6 = 0$
$\Rightarrow p = 2/3, 3/4$
II. $8q^2 - 6q + 1 = 0$
$\Rightarrow q = 1/4, 1/2$
$\therefore q < p$

58. 4   I. $4p^2 + 12p - 7 = 0$
$\Rightarrow p = 1/2, -7/2$
II. $8q^2 - 30q - 27 = 0$
$\Rightarrow q = -3/4, 9/2$
$\therefore$ Relationship cannot be established.

59. 4   I. $p^2 = 196$
$\Rightarrow p = -14, 14$
II. $q^2 - 15q + 14 = 0$
$\Rightarrow q = 1, 14$
$\therefore$ Relationship cannot be established.

60. 2   I. $3p + 2q = 3$
II. $4q - 5p = -27$
Solving for p and q we get p = 3 and q = –3
$\therefore p > q$

61. 2 $(16)^{1/2} + (36)^2 = ?^2 + 459$
$\Rightarrow ?^2 = 4 + 1296 - 459 = 841$
$\Rightarrow ? = \pm 29.$

62. 4 $? = 4.4 \times \dfrac{5}{16} \times \dfrac{30}{100} \times 216$

$= 4.4 \times \dfrac{5}{16} \times 64.8 = 89.1.$

63. 1 $(0.729)^3 \div (0.81)^5 \times (0.9)^5 = (0.9)^{?+3}$
$\Rightarrow [(0.9)^3]^3 \div [(0.9)^2]^5 \times (0.9)^5 = (0.9)^{?+3}$
$\Rightarrow (0.9)^9 \div (0.9)^{10} \times (0.9)^5 = (0.9)^{?+3}$
$\Rightarrow (0.9)^{9-10+5} = (0.9)^{?+3}$
$\Rightarrow (0.9)^4 = (0.9)^{?+3}$
$\therefore ? = 1.$

64. 5 $\left(\sqrt{\dfrac{?}{100}} \text{ of } 42 \times 5 \right) = 37.8$

$\Rightarrow \left(\dfrac{\sqrt{?}}{10} \text{ of } 42 \times 5 \right) = 37.8$

$\Rightarrow 4.2\sqrt{?} \times 5 = 37.8$
$\Rightarrow 21\sqrt{?} = 37.8$
$\Rightarrow ? = 3.24.$

65. 1 $(729 \times 6 \div 9) + 343 + 71 + 431 = ?^3$
$\Rightarrow 486 + 343 + 71 + 431 = ?^3$
$\Rightarrow ?^3 = 1331 = (11)^3$
$\therefore ? = 11.$

For questions 66 to 68:
$I < Q < O < S < R < N < P < M$

For questions 69 and 70:

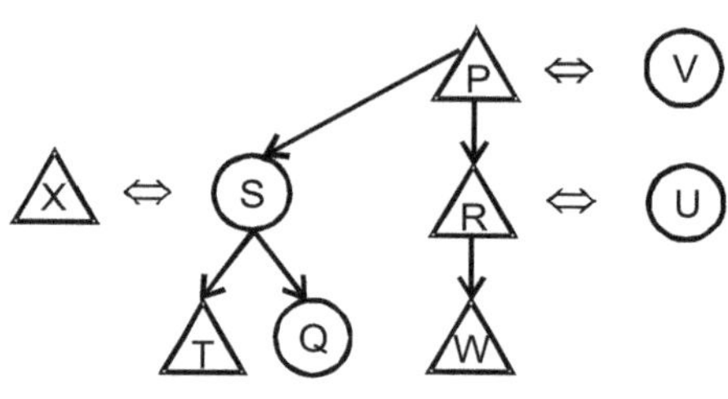

△ = Male members

○ = Female members

X ⇔ Y = X and Y are spouse

Clearly R has to be male and V has to be female. R belongs to generation 2 so, V belongs to generation 1. Therefore T is a male and should be the son of S.

For questions 71 to 75: All of the given information can be tabulated as:

Friend	Department	Organisation		
		ABC	PQR	JKL
M	Production	✔		
N	Analysis		✔	
P	Marketing			✔
D	HR		✔	
E	Research			✔
F	Design	✔		
G	Admin		✔	

For questions 76 to 80:

Word	he	w as	dancing	on	the	floor	of	his	house
Code	ag	lh	ey	aj	es	ev	ib	md/oz	oz/md

For questions 81 to 85:

Row – 2	A	B	E	D	C	F
Row – 1	R	P	U	S	T	Q

For questions 86 to 90:

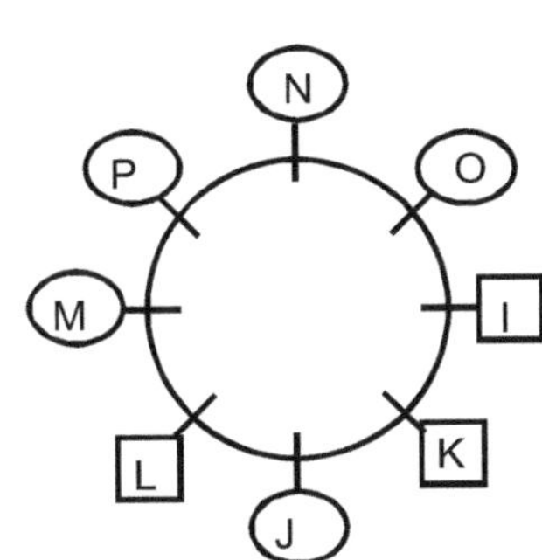

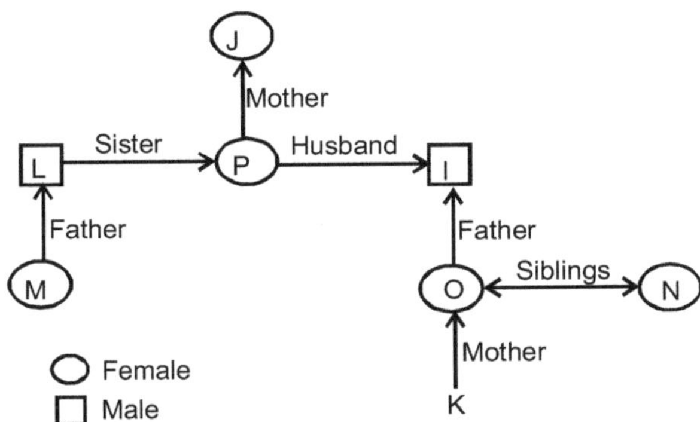

91. 2 $D \le F, M \ge F, M < K$

$\Rightarrow D \le F \le M < K$

Conclusion I: $K \ge F$ does not follow.

Conclusion II: $K > D$ follows.

∴ Conclusion II follows.

92. 1 $K > M, M < R, R = T$

$\Rightarrow K > M$ and $M < R = T$

Conclusion I: $M < T$ follows.

Conclusion II: $K = T$ does not follow.

∴ Conclusion I follows.

93. 4 $T < M, M \le R, R = N$

$\Rightarrow T < M \le R = N$

Conclusion I: $M = N$ may or not follow.

Conclusion II: $M < N$ may or may not follow.

∴ Either conclusion I or conclusion II follows.

94. 3 $B \ge N, N = R, R > T$

$\Rightarrow B \ge N = R > T$

Conclusion I: $B \ge R$ follows.

Conclusion II: $T < N$ follows.

∴ Both conclusions follow.

95. 5 $N = P, K > P, Q < K$

$\Rightarrow N = P < K$ and $Q < K$

Conclusion I: $K \ge N$ does not follow

Conclusion II: $Q > N$ does not follow.

∴ Neither conclusion I nor conclusion II follows.

96. 1

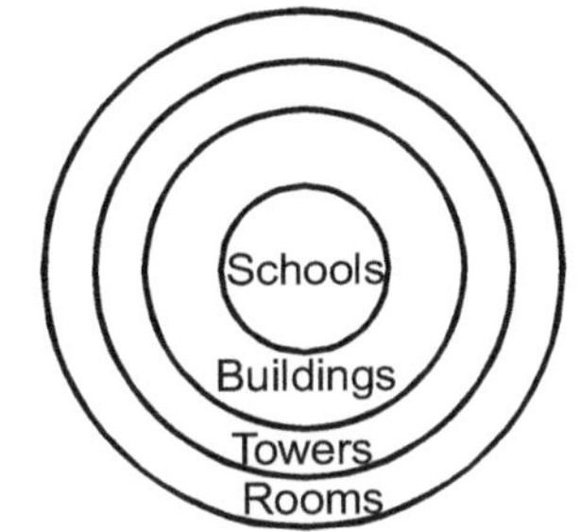

97. 4

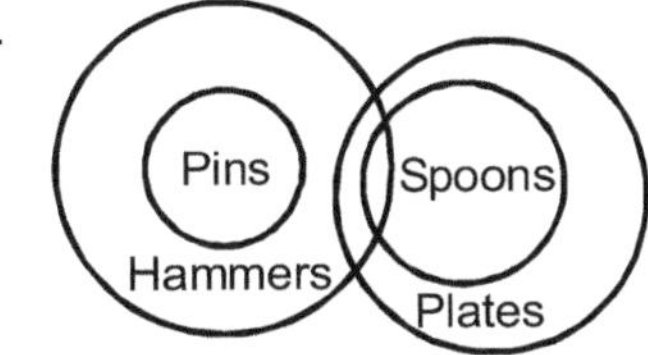

98. 3

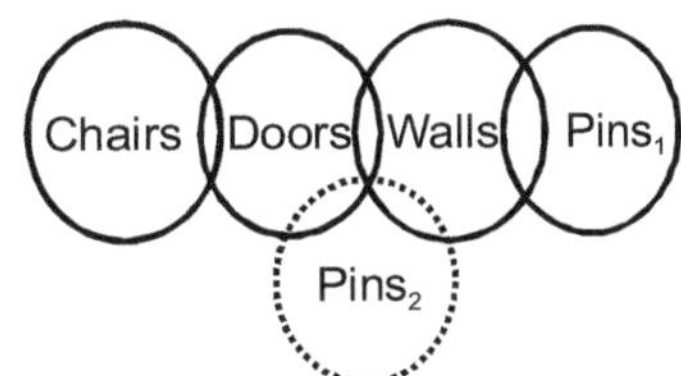

99. 4

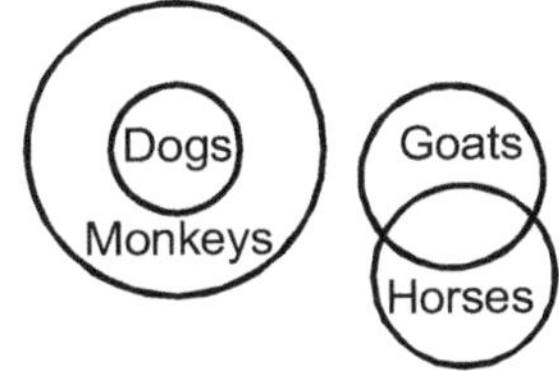

100. 2

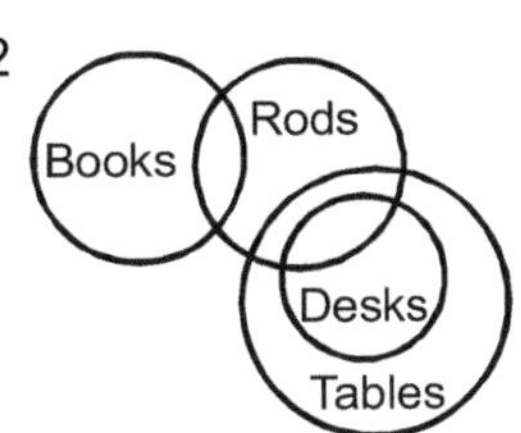

REASONING & COMPUTER APTITUDE

Directions (Q. 1 to 5): Answer the following questions on the basis of the information given below.

Six friends – A, B, C, D, E and F – live in an eight- storey building, numbered from 1 to 8 from ground to top; each friend lives on a different floor. There are two floors between the floors on which D and B live. The topmost floor is not vacant. A lives on the floor which is below the floor of C and above the floor of E. Two of the floors in the building are vacant. Only three friends live between the floors of D and F. There are only two floors between the two vacant floors. The floor numbers of B and E are consecuive natural numbers. Also, equal number of floors are there between the floors of A and E and A and C.

1. Which are the two vacant floors?
  - (1) 1st and 4th
  - (2) 3rd and 6th
  - (3) 7th and 4th
  - (4) 2nd and 5th
  - (5) None of these

2. How many floors are there between the floors on which F and A live?
  - (1) None
  - (2) One
  - (3) Two
  - (4) Three
  - (5) Four

3. Who lives on the 5th floor?
  - (1) A
  - (2) B
  - (3) C
  - (4) D
  - (5) Eithere A or B

4. Who lives on the floor that is immediately above the floor on which F lives?
  - (1) B
  - (2) D
  - (3) E
  - (4) A
  - (5) Cannot be determined

5. How many friends live between the floors on which C and A live?
  - (1) None
  - (2) One
  - (3) Two
  - (4) Three
  - (5) Four

Directions (Q. 6 to 10): Answer the questions on the basis of the information given below.

Ten friends are sitting in two parallel rows in such a way that there are five persons in each row and at equidistant positions. Aman, Billu, Chintu, Dinky and Ekta are sitting in row-1 and are facing towards North. Pammy, Qutub, Supriya, Tanu and Utkarsh are sitting in row-2 and are facing towards South. Each person of a particular row is facing a person of the other row. Pammy, who is sitting at one of the ends of the row, is second to the right of Tanu. Aman is third to the left of Dinky. There are two persons between Qutub and Utkarsh. Only one person is sitting between Chintu and Aman. Ekta is not facing Pammy. Billu is an immediate neighbour of Chintu. Supriya is not an immediate neighbour of Qutub.

6. Who is sitting third to the left of the one facing Aman?
  - (1) Utkarsh
  - (2) Pammy
  - (3) Tanu
  - (4) Supriya
  - (5) Data Inadequate

7. Which of the following persons are sitting opposite to each other?
  - (1) Qutub - Aman
  - (2) Billu - Utkarsh
  - (3) Chintu - Tanu
  - (4) Dinky - Pammy
  - (5) Supriya - Ekta

8. Who is sitting between Billu and Dinky?
  - (1) Aman
  - (2) Chintu
  - (3) Ekta
  - (4) No one
  - (5) Cannot be determined

9. If Supriya is related to Aman and Ekta is related to Qutub, then who will be related to Dinky?
  - (1) Pammy
  - (2) Qutub
  - (3) Supriya
  - (4) Tanu
  - (5) Utkarsh

10. Who is sitting at one of the extreme ends of the row?
  - (1) Qutub
  - (2) Dinky
  - (3) Billu
  - (4) Tanu
  - (5) Ekta

Directions (Q. 11 to 15): Answer the questions on the basis of the information given below.

Amit, Bony, Champak, Dolly and Eram are the five friends who wear five different caps of brands – Nike, Adidas, Puma, Ferrari and Reebok. Each of them owns a different bike – Honda, Passion, Activa, Bullet and Pulsar. Also, each of them has a tie of different colour – Red, Blue, Yellow, White and Orange. The owner of Nike or Adidas does not have a Red tie. Eram owns Honda but is not the owner of Blue tie or Red tie. Dolly wears Puma and owns passion. Bony owns Pulsar. Amit owns Activa and Yellow tie but not the Adidas cap. The owner of Honda also owns Reebok cap. One of the friends owns Orange tie, Ferrari cap and Bullet.

11. Who is the owner of Bullet?
  - (1) Amit
  - (2) Bony
  - (3) Champak
  - (4) Dolly
  - (5) Eram

12. What is the colour of the tie owned by Eram?

   (1) Red

   (2) Blue

   (3) Yellow

   (4) White

   (5) Orange

13. Which of the following combinations is incorrect?

   (1) Amit – Nike

   (2) White – Honda

   (3) Bullet – Adidas

   (4) Eram – Reebok

   (5) None of these

14. What is colour of the tie owned by the owner of the cap of brand Nike?

   (1) Red   (2) White

   (3) Yellow   (4) Blue

   (5) None of these

15. Who is the owner of Nike cap?

   (1) Amit   (2) Bony

   (3) Champak   (4) Dolly

   (5) Eram

Directions (Q. 16 to 20): Each of the questions below consists of a question and three statements numbered I, II and III given below it. You have to decide whether the data provided in the statements are sufficient to answer the question.

16. How many daughters does W have?

   I.   B and D are the sisters of M.

   II. M's father T is the husband of W.

   III. Out of the three children which T has, only one is a boy.

   (1) Only I and III are sufficient to answer the question.

   (2) All I, II and III are required to answer the question.

   (3) Only II and III are sufficient to answer the question.

   (4) Question cannot be answered even with all I, II and III

   (5) Only I and II are sufficient to answer the question.

17. Who among A, B, C, D, E and F, each having a different height, is the tallest?

   I.   B is taller than A but shorter than E.

   II. Only two of them are shorter than C.

   III. D is taller than only F.

   (1) Only I and II are sufficient to answer the question.

   (2) Only I and III are sufficient to answer the question.

   (3) Only II and III are sufficient to answer the question.

   (4) All I, II and III are required to answer the question.

   (5) All I, II and III even together are not sufficient to answer the question.

18. Towards which direction is Village J from Village W?

   I.   Village R is to the west of Village W and to the north of Village T.

   II. Village Z is to the east of Village J and to the south of Village T.

   III. Village M is to the north-east of Village J and to the north of Village Z.

   (1) Only III is sufficient to answer the question.

   (2) Only II and III sufficient to answer the question.

   (3) All I, II and III are required to answer the question.

   (4) Question cannot be answered even with all I, II and III.

   (5) None of these

19. On which day of the week did Suresh visit Chennai? (Assume that the week starts from Monday.)

   I.   Suresh did not visit Chennai on Wednesday.

   II. Suresh visited Chennai the day after his mother's visit to his house.

   III. Suresh's mother visited his house on neither Monday nor Thursday.

   (1) Only II and III are sufficient to answer the question.

   (2) Only I and II are sufficient to answer the question.

   (3) Only I and III are sufficient to answer the question.

   (4) All I, II and III are required to answer the question.

   (5) Question cannot be answered even with all I, II and III.

20. How is 'go' written in a code language?

   I.   'now or never again' is written as 'torn ka na sa' in that code language.

   II. 'you come again now' is written as 'ja ka ta sa' in that code language.

   III. 'again go now or never' is written as 'na ha ka sa torn' in that code language.

   (1) Only I and III are sufficient to answer the question.

   (2) Only II and III are sufficient to answer the question.

   (3) Only I and II are sufficient to answer the question.

   (4) All I, II and III are required to answer the question.

   (5) None of these

Directions (Q. 21 to 25): Answer the following questions on the basis of the information given below.

P, Q, R, S, T, V, W and X are captains of eight different cricket teams, namely Australia, New Zealand, India, Pakistan, Sri Lanka, England, West Indies and South Africa, but not necessarily in the same order. All of them are seated around a circular table and are facing the centre.

P sits third to the left of the Sri Lankan captain. Only two people sit between T and W. Neither T nor W is an immediate neighbour of P. Neither T nor W is the captain of Sri Lanka. The captain of South Africa sits second to the right of S. S is not an immediate neighbour of P. S is not the Sri Lankan captain and P is not the captain of South Africa. The Australian captain sits third to the left of V. The Australian and Sri Lankan captains are not immediate neighbours. Only one person sits between S and the Indian captain. Captains of Pakistan and New Zealand are immediate neighbours. S is not the captain of New Zealand's team. Only one person sits between Q and the captain of England. The captain of England is an immediate neighbour of X. W and Q are not immediate neighbours.

21. How many people sit between T and the captain of England when counted in clockwise direction from T?
    (1) None   (2) One
    (3) Two   (4) Four
    (5) Five

22. Who is the captain of the Australian team?
    (1) P   (2) V
    (3) W   (4) T
    (5) Q

23. Which of the following is true with respect to the given seating arrangement?
    (1) R is the captain of South Africa.
    (2) W is an immediate neighbour of V.
    (3) The captains of Australia and England are immediate neighbours.
    (4) Four people sit between W and Q.
    (5) X sits second to the left of S.

24. Who is the Indian captain?
    (1) Q   (2) V
    (3) X   (4) T
    (5) Cannot be determined

25. What is the position of the captain of West Indies with respect to R?
    (1) Immediate left   (2) Second to the left
    (3) Third to the right   (4) Second to the right
    (5) Third to the left

Directions (Q. 26 to 30): Answer the following questions on the basis of the information given below.

Seven dog owners - T, U, V, W, X, Y and Z from different places in Delhi namely Om Vihar, Prem Nagar, Rajouri Garden, Sangam Vihar, Tilak Nagar, Uttam Nagar and Vikas Puri had gathered in a seminar hall in a dog show with their dogs having breeds viz Australian Shepherd, Boxer, Cane Corso, Dachshund, English Mastiff, French Bulldog and German Shepherd but not necessary in the same order.

Y has German Shepherd and he is neither from Uttam Nagar nor Vikas Puri. The one who is from Tilak Nagar is the owner of Boxer. T is from Sangam Vihar and his dog is neither from Cane Corso nor French Bulldog breed. The one who is form Rajouri Garden has a Australian Shepherd. U has English Mastiff. The one who is from Vikas Puri does not have English Mastiff. W is from Om Vihar. Z is not from Vikas Puri and does not have Boxer. X is not from Vikas Puri.

26. Which of the following dogs does X have?
    (1) Boxer   (2) Cane Corso
    (3) Dachshund   (4) French Bulldog
    (5) None of these

27. Which of the following combination is definitely correct?
    (1) Cane Corso - Uttam Nagar
    (2) English Mastiff - Om Vihar
    (3) French Bulldog - Prem Nagar
    (4) Dachshund - Sangam Vihar
    (5) German Shepherd - Tilak Nagar

28. From which of the following place does V belong?
    (1) Prem Nagar   (2) Rajouri Garden
    (3) Sangam Vihar   (4) Uttam Nagar
    (5) Vikas Puri

29. Which of the following combination of Place and breed is definitely correct with respect to Z?
    (1) Rajouri Garden- Australian Shepherd
    (2) Prem Nagar- Boxer
    (3) Om Vihar- Cane Corso
    (4) VikasPuri- Dachshund
    (5) Tilak Nagar - French Bulldog

30. Four of the following five are alike in a certain way and thus form a group as per the given arrangement. Which of the following does not belong to that group?
    (1) Boxer - Tilak Nagar
    (2) English Mastiff - Uttam Nagar
    (3) Cane Corso - Sangam Vihar
    (4) Dachshund - Om Vihar
    (5) German Shepherd - Prem Nagar

Directions (Q. 31 to 35): Answer the following questions on the basis of the information given below.

A word and number arrangement machine when given an input line of words and numbers rearranges them following a particular rule in each step. The following is an illustration of input and rearrangement.

Input: 96 gain 63 forest 38 78 deep house

Step I: deep 96 gain 63 forest 38 78 house

Step II: deep 38 96 gain 63 forest 78 house

Step III: deep 38 forest gain 96 63 78 house

Step IV: deep 38 forest 63 gain 96 78 house

Step V: deep 38 forest 63 gain 78 96 house

Step VI: deep 38 forest 63 gain 78 house 96

and Step VI is the last step of the rearrangement of the above input.

As per the rules followed in the above steps, find out in each of the following questions the appropriate step for the given input.

31. **Input:** train 59 47 25 over burden 63 sky
    Which of the following steps will be the last but one?
    (1) VI   (2) V
    (3) IV   (4) VII
    (5) None of these

32. **Input:** service 46 58 96 over there desk 15
    Which of the following will be step VI?
    (1) desk 15 over service 46 58 96 there
    (2) desk 15 over 46 service there 58 96
    (3) desk 15 over 46 service 58 there 96
    (4) desk 15 over 46 service 58 96 there
    (5) There will be no such step

33. **Step II of an input is:** below 12 93 house floor 69 57 task
    Which of the following will definitely be the input ?
    (1) 93 house 69 57 below task floor 12
    (2) 93 house below 69 57 task floor 12
    (3) 93 house floor 69 57 task below 12
    (4) Cannot be determined
    (5) None of these

34. **Step III of an input is:** art 24 day 83 71 54 star power
    Which of the following steps will be the last?
    (1) V   (2) VIII
    (3) IX   (4) VII
    (5) None of these

35. **Step II of an input is:** cold 17 wave 69 never desk 52 43
    How many more steps will be required to complete the rearrangement?
    (1) Six   (2) Five
    (3) Four   (4) Three
    (5) None of these

Directions (36 to 40): In each of the questions below, four statements are followed by four conclusions numbered I, II, III and IV. You have to take the given statements to be true even if they seem to be at variance with commonly known facts. Read all the conclusions and then decide which of the given conclusions logically follow(s) from the given statements disregarding commonly known facts.

36. **Statements:**
    Some stoves are ovens.
    All ovens are cylinders.
    Some engines are stoves.
    Some metals are cylinders.
    Conclusions:
    I.   Some ovens are metals
    II. Some cylinders are stoves.
    III. Some ovens are engines.
    IV. No engine is a cylinder.
    (1) None follows
    (2) Only II and IV follow
    (3) Only II and III follow
    (4) Only III follows
    (5) Only II follows

37. **Statements:**
    Some cars are buses.
    Some buses are trains.
    All aeroplanes are trains.
    All trucks are buses.
    Conclusions:
    I.   Some aeroplanes are trucks.
    II. Some cars are trains.
    III. Some trucks are aeroplanes.
    IV. No truck is a train.
    (1) All follow
    (2) Only II and IV follow
    (3) Only III and IV follow
    (4) Only I and III follow
    (5) None of these

38. **Statements:**
    Some tools are hammers.
    All tools are trees.
    Some trees are flowers.
    No hammer is a flower.
    Conclusions:
    I.   All hammers are tools
    II. No tool is a flower.
    III. Some hammers are trees.
    IV. Some flowers are tools
    (1) All follow
    (2) Only I and either II or IV follow
    (3) Only II and IV follow
    (4) Only III follows
    (5) None of these

39. Statements:

Some bags are pockets.

Some pockets are trousers

All skirts are pockets.

Some belts are bags.

Conclusions:

I.   Some trousers are belts.

II. Some skirts are bags.

III. No trouser is a belt.

IV. Some skirts are trousers.

(1) All follow

(2) Only II and IV follow

(3) Only III follows

(4) Only either I or III follows

(5) None of these

40. Statements:

Some cats are tigers.

All lions are cats.

Some horses are lions.

All horses are animals.

Conclusions:

I.   Some lions are tigers.

II. No horse is a tiger.

III. Some horses are cats.

IV. Some horses are tigers.

(1) All follow

(2) Only III follows

(3) Only I and IV follow

(4) Only III and either II or IV follow

(5) None of these

Directions (Q. 41 to 43): In making decisions about important questions, it is desirable to be able to distinguish between 'strong' and 'weak' arguments. 'Strong' arguments are those which are both important and directly related to the question. 'Weak' arguments are those which are of minor importance and also may not be directly related to the question or may be related to a trivial aspect of the question.

Each question below is followed by two arguments numbered I and II. You have to decide which of the arguments is a 'strong' argument and which is a 'weak' argument. Give Answer:

(1)   if only argument I is strong.

(2)   if only argument II is strong.

(3)   if either argument I or II is strong.

(4)   if neither argument I nor II is strong.

(5)   if both arguments I and II are strong.

41. Statement: Should the Research funding in India be increased?

Arguments:

I.   No, there are great scientists in India.

II. Yes, science in India needs a push.

42. Statement: Is Indian football a lost cause?

Arguments:

I.   No, India has recently made a great jump in the FIFA rankings and thus is showing great promises.

II. No, TV ratings show increase in football viewership.

43. Statement: Should the newly formed Southern Sudan shift from democracy to communism for attaining stability?

Arguments:

I.   Yes, the country is the youngest country in the world.

II. No, it is relatively easy to manage a smaller country.

Directions (Q. 44 and 45): In each question below, a statement is followed by two assumptions numbered I and II. An assumption is something supposed or taken for granted. You have to consider the statement and the following assumptions and decide which of the assumptions is implicit in the statement.

Mark:

(1)   if only assumption I is implicit.

(2)   if only assumption II is implicit

(3)   if either assumption I or II is implicit,

(4)   if neither assumption I nor II is implicit.

(5)   if both assumptions I and II are implicit.

44. Statement:

Even though the number of sugar factories is increasing at a fast rate in India, we still continue to import it from other countries.

Assumptions:

I.   Even the increased number of factories may not be able to meet the demand of sugar in India.

II. The demand for sugar may increase substantially in future.

45. Statement:

The government announced a heavy compensation package for all the victims of the terrorist attacks.

Assumptions:

I.   Such incidents of terror may not occur in near future.

II. Compensation may mitigate the anger among the citizens against the current government.

ENGLISH LANGUAGE

Directions (Q. 46 to 50): Read the following passage carefully and answer the questions given below it. Certain words/phrases are given in **bold** to help you to locate them while answering some of the questions.

John Maynard Keynes, the trendiest dead economist of this **apocalyptic** moment, was the godfather of government stimulus. Keynes had the radical idea that throwing money at recessions through aggressive deficit spending would resuscitate flat lined economies - and he wasn't too particular about where the money was thrown, in the depths of the Depression, he suggested that the Treasury could "fill old bottles with banknotes, bury them at suitable depths in disused coal mines" then sit back and watch a money-mining boom create jobs and prosperity. "It would, indeed, be more sensible to build houses and the like," he wrote, but "the above would be better than nothing."

As President-elect <u>Barack Obama</u> prepares to throw money at the current downturn - a stimulus package starting at about $800 billion, plus the second $350 billion chunk of the financial bailout – we all really do seem to be Keynesians now. Just about every expert agrees that pumping $1 trillion into a **moribund** economy will rev up the ethereal goods-and-services engine that Keynes called "aggregate demand" and stimulate at least some short-term activity, even if it is all wasted on money pits.But Keynes was also right that there would be more sensible ways to spend it. There would also be less sensible ways to spend it. A trillion dollars' worth of bad ideas-sprawl-inducing highways and bridges to nowhere, ethanol plants and pipelines that accelerate global warming, tax breaks for overleveraged McMansion builders and burdensome new long-term federal entitlements - would be worse than mere waste. It would be smarter to buy every American an iPod, a set of Ginsu knives and 600 Subway foot-longs.

It would be smarter still to throw all that money at things we need to do anyway, which is the goal of Obama's upcoming American Recovery and Reinvestment Plan. It will include a mix of tax cuts, aid to **beleaguered** state and local governments, and spending to address needs ranging from food stamps to computerized health records to bridge repairs to broadband networks to energy-efficiency retrofits, all designed to save or create 3 million to 4 million jobs by the end of 2010. Obama has said speed is his top priority because the faster Washington injects cash into the financial bloodstream, the better it stands to help avert a multi-year slump with double-digit unemployment and deflation. But he also wants to use the stimulus to advance his long-term priorities: reducing energy use and carbon missions, cutting middle-class taxes, upgrading neglected infrastructure, reining in health-care costs and eventually reducing the budget deficits that exploded under <u>George W. Bush</u>. Obama's goal is

to exploit this crisis in the best sense of the word, to start pursuing his vision of a greener, fairer, more competitive, more sustainable economy.

Unfortunately, while 21st century Washington has demonstrated an impressive ability to spend money quickly, it has yet to prove that it can spend money wisely. And the chum of a 1 with 12 zeros is already creating a feeding **frenzy** for the ages. Lobbyists for shoe companies, zoos, catfish farmers, mall owners, airlines, public broadcasters, car dealers and everyone else who can afford their retainers are lining up for a piece of the stimulus. States that embarked on **raucous** spending and tax-cutting sprees when they were flush are begging for bailouts now that they're broke. And politicians are dusting off their unfunded mobster museums, water slides and other pet projects for rebranding as shovel-ready infrastructure investments. As Obama's aides scramble to assemble something effective and transformative as well as politically achievable, they acknowledge the tension between his desires for speed and reform.

46. John M. Keynes advocated which of the following?
   (1) Spending money recklessly during recessions is suicidal
   (2) Exorbitant spending during recessions is likely to boost economy
   (3) Aggressive deficit spending is likely to be fatal for economic meltdown.
   (4) Government stimulus to economy may not help because of red-tapism
   (5) None of these

47. Which of the following is TRUE about Keynes' philosophy?
   (1) Actual spending of money during meltdown is more important than where and on what it is spent
   (2) Government should be selective in approach for spending money during recession
   (3) Filling old bottles with banknotes and burying them is an atrocious proposal
   (4) Creating jobs and prosperity during recessions is almost an impracticable proposal
   (5) None of these

48. The author of the passage calls Barack Obama and his team as "Keynesians" because
   (1) Barack Obama has been reluctant to follow Keynes philosophy.
   (2) his team is advising Barack to refrain from Keynes philosophy.
   (3) Barack Obama and his team have decided to fill old bottles with banknotes.
   (4) building houses has been under the active consideration of Barack Obama and his team.
   (5) None of these

49. What, according to Keynes, is the **"aggregate demand"**?
(1) Goods and Services Sector
(2) Stimulation of a short-term activity
(3) Attempting to rev up the sluggish economy
(4) Pumping one trillion dollars into economy
(5) None of these

50. Highways, bridges, ethanol plants, etc. are considered by the author as
(1) reasonably appropriate propositions to spend money on.
(2) measures that affect the environment adversely.
(3) imprudent proposals to waste money on.
(4) tax saving schemes bestowed on builders.
(5) None of these

Choose the word which is OPPOSITE in meaning to the word given in bold as used in the passage.

51. Moribund
(1) Declining   (2) Waning
(3) Thriving   (4) Pessimistic
(5) Glorifying

52. Beleaguered
(1) Carefree   (2) Harassed
(3) Stressful   (4) Uneventful
(5) Evaporating

Choose the word which is most nearly the same in meaning to the word given in bold as used in the passage.

53. Apocalyptic
(1) Unwelcome   (2) Disastrous
(3) Risk-free   (4) Joyous
(5) Ceremonious

54. Resuscitate
(1) Melt down   (2) Devastate
(3) Mislead   (4) Save
(5) Deactivate

55. Frenzy
(1) Passion   (2) Expression
(3) Succession   (4) Habit
(5) Manifestation

Directions (Q. 56 to 60): Rearrange the following sentences (A), (B), (C), (D), (E) and (F) to make a meaingful paragraph and then answer the questions given below.

A. Had it been not for them, Indian banks would have had their hands tied down.

B. Today, almost all the countries are facing the heat of recession.

C. One of these is the strict RBI and SEBI rules which regulated banking sector very efficiently.

D. This could have led to massive losses to them, which could have percolated to other sectors as well.

E. However, there are a few things which help India in bouncing back from the state of recession.

F. Like others, India too has not remained immune to the epidemic.

56. Which of the following sentences should be the **third** after rearrangement?
(1) A   (2) E
(3) D   (4) F
(5) C

57. Which of the following sentences should be the **first** after rearrangement?
(1) A   (2) B
(3) C   (4) D
(5) E

58. Which of the following sentence should be the **second** after are arrangement?
(1) A   (2) B
(3) D   (4) E
(5) F

59. Which of the following sentences should be the **sixth (last)** after rearrangement?
(1) A   (2) E
(3) D   (4) B
(5) F

60. Which of the following sentences should be the **fifth** after rearrangement?
(1) B   (2) C
(3) A   (4) E
(5) F

Directions (Q. 61 to 65): In the following passage there are blanks, each of which has been numbered. These numbers are given below the passage and against each, five words are suggested, one of which fits the blank appropriately. Find out the appropriate word in each case.

Technology __(61)__ lives. But only if people want it to. This qualification is important, and __(62)__ to understanding progress. Akio Morita, the founder of Sony, used to make inventions not by writing code but by making minute, detailed studies of how people lived their lives. It is observable that when he relinquished direct involvement in product development at the company in the 1980s, Sony seemed to lose its __(63)__ of developing a truly radical invention like the Walkman that the world takes to en masse.

However much it seems that machines are in control they are not, yet the belief that the technology alone holds the key to __(64)__ the way people work, buy, and do business is strong. The rise of dotcoms in the late 1990s was accompanied by a belief that technology was changing the rules of marketing and employee relationships. This is not to say there have been no changes in the new economy; but that they __(65)__ to appear where technology makes it easier for people to communicate with each other, or have been unrelated to the technology. The dynamic is still a human one.

61. (1) ruins   (2) changes
(3) makes   (4) explains
(5) shakes

62. (1) key   (2) primarily
    (3) encouraging   (4) supported
    (5) disastrous

63. (1) share   (2) profit
    (3) knack   (4) business
    (5) plant

64. (1) determining   (2) highlighting
    (3) informing   (4) encroaching
    (5) accomplishing

65. (1) tend   (2) cease
    (3) fail   (4) refuse
    (5) avoid

Directions (Q. 66 to 70): In each of the questions given below, there might be error(s) in one or more than one section. Your task is to find out the error(s) and accordingly, choose the appropriate option.

66. A significance part (A)/ of my life (B)/ have been (C)/ inspired by my teachers. (D)/ No error (E)
    (1) Both A and B   (2) Both B and C
    (3) Only A.   (4) Both A and C
    (5) No error

67. Its high time (A)/ that you should tendered (B)/ an apology (C)/ to the customer. (D)/ No error (E)
    (1) Both A and B   (2) Both B and C
    (3) Both C and D   (4) Only C
    (5) No error

68. While walking in (A)/ the sidewalk, (B)/ Rahul saw (C)/ a sinking man. (D)/ No error (E)
    (1) Only B   (2) Both A and B
    (3) Both A and D   (4) Both C and D
    (5) No error

69. She went (A)/ to Australia (B)/ where she breathd (C)/ her last. (D)/ No error (5)
    (1) Both B and C   (2) Both C and D
    (3) Only B   (4) Only C
    (5) No error

70. She wanted to (A)/ buy an iPhone she (B)/ couldn't (C)/ afforded one. (D)/ No error (5)
    (1) Both A and B   (2) Both B and D
    (3) Both A and C   (4) Only D
    (5) No error

Directions (Q. 71 and 72): Out of the following options, which one is a synonym of the word given in **bold**?

71. Ethereal
    (1) Filial   (2) Helical
    (3) Celestial   (4) Cereal
    (5) Balliol

72. Weird
    (1) Clandestine   (2) Philistine
    (3) Laterite   (4) Tryst
    (5) Outlandish

Directions (Q. 73 and 74): Out of the following options, which one is anantonymof the word given in **bold**?

73. Zany
    (1) Seizure   (2) Wonted
    (3) Queer   (4) Ledger
    (5) Bizarre

74. Savant
    (1) Academic   (2) Arboreal
    (3) Jovial   (4) Astronomical
    (5) Cretin

Directions (Q. 75: In the following question, a small paragraph is given. You have to read the paragraph and find out which of the answer choices addresses the question at the end of the paragraph. Mark your answer accordingly.

75. You are the engineer of a construction company. Your company has been constructing a flyover in Kolkata. The project is already running behind schedule. Your boss wants you to take steps so that the project can be completed before the deadline ends. Your boss has even asked you to compromise on safety standards, if required, so that the deadline is met. What should you do?
    (1) You should do as your boss says.
    (2) You should convince your boss that the project has to be completed within the deadline but only after meeting the standard safety guidelines.
    (3) You should report the matter to the police.
    (4) You should report the matter to the media.
    (5) You should stop going to the office.

Directions (Q. 76 and 77: In each of the following questions, two sentences are given. Your task is to find out which of the three answer choices can be used to join the two sentences to make them grammatically correct and thematically coherent. Mark your answer choice accordingly.

76. The central food safety regulator on Tuesday warned that hotels and restaurants operating without its licence will be sealed. They cannot renew the permit within the next three months.
    A. and loitered if
    B. and squandered if
    C. and closed if
    (1) Only A   (2) Only B
    (3) Only C   (4) Either A or B
    (5) Either A or C

77. The regulator is working on ratings for cleanliness in restaurants. These would be issued soon.

   A. such as hygiene, safe drinking water and

   B. such as employment, skill and

   C. such as insurance, banking and

(1) Only A   (2) Only B

(3) Only C   (4) Both A and B

(5) Either A or B

Directions (Q. 78 to 80): In question given below there are two statements, each statement consists of two blanks. You have to choose the option which provides the correct set of words that fits both the blanks in both the statements appropriately and in the same order making them meaningful and grammatically correct.

78. (1) Despite the fact that cancerous ovarian stem cells are __________ to chemoresistance, they are the __________ targets for therapy.

   (2) How quickly the __________ branch of Homo heidelbergensis turned into something that could be called Homo sapiens was therefore __________.

   (1) Feigned, indeterminate

   (2) Pertinent, inane

   (3) Relevant, obscure

   (4) affiliated, fatuous

   (5) analogous, insignificant

79. (1) The molecular targeting of CSCs may improve the __________ of current chemotherapeutic __________ needed for the management of this disease.

   (2) __________ and safety of once-daily __________ in the treatment of HIV infection is currently under inspection.

   (1) Germaneness, medication

   (2) Efficacy, regimens

   (3) Emasculation, nutriments

   (4) Potency, sustenance

   (5) Sufficiency, subsistence

80. (1) The six-day war was the last unalloyed military victory for Israel, and the start of a __________ from existential wars against Arab states, which it always won, to __________ campaigns against non-state militias which it could never wipe out.

   (2) He sees these dualities as having been maintained through the __________ by a deliberate and __________ general amnesia.

   (1) Transition, enervating

   (2) Progression, invigorating

   (3) Concatenation, exhilarating

(4) Juncture, frivolous

(5) Movement, enfeeble

DATA ANALYSIS & INTERPRETATION

Directions (Q. 81 to 85): Answer the questions on the basis of the information given below.

The pie chart given below shows the percentage distribution of players who play five different sports.

Total players = 4200

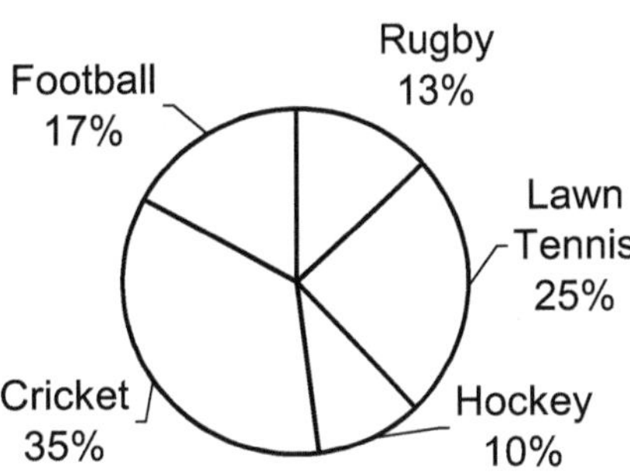

The pie chart given below shows the percentage distribution of female players who play five different sports.

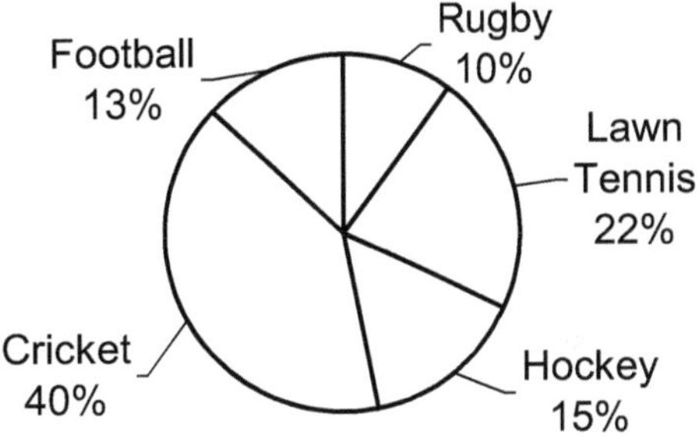

81. What is the average number of players (both male and female) who play football and rugby together?

   (1) 620   (2) 357

   (3) 230   (4) 630

   (5) None of these

82. What is the difference between the number of the female players who play lawn tennis and that of male players who play rugby?

   (1) 94   (2) 84

   (3) 220   (4) 240

   (5) None of these

83. What is the ratio of the number of female players who play cricket to that of male players who play hockey?

   (1) 20 : 7   (2) 4 : 21

   (3) 3 : 20   (4) 20 : 3

   (5) None of these

84. What is the total number of male players who play football, cricket and lawn tennis together?
(1) 1,724 (2) 1,734
(3) 1,824 (4) 1,964
(5) None of these

85. Number of male players who play rugby is approximately what percent of the total number of players who play lawn tennis?
(1) 33 (2) 39
(3) 26 (4) 21
(5) 43

Directions (86 to 90): Study the following information carefully and answer the questions that follow:

An office consists of 520 employees working in different departments, viz. HR, IT, Production and Marketing. The ratio of men to women in the organization is 5 : 3 respectively. 20 percent of the men work in the IT department. 40 percent of the women work in the HR department. The total number of employees in the Production department is 135. Two-fifth of the women work in the IT department. 40 percent of the men work in the Production department. Four percent of the men work in the HR department.

86. Number of men working in the Marketing department forms what percent of the total number of employees in the organization?
(1) 22.5 (2) 34.5
(3) 19.5 (4) 38.5
(5) None of these

87. What is the respective ratio of the number of men working in the HR department to the women working in the same?
(1) 1:5 (2) 2:3
(3) 4:7 (4) 9:11
(5) None of these

88. What is the number of women working in the Marketing department?
(1) 41 (2) 34
(3) 46 (4) 39
(5) None of these

89. Total number of employees working in the Production department forms approximately what percent of the total number of employees working in the organization?
(1) 12 (2) 17
(3) 21 (4) 26
(5) 38

90. What is the total number of employees working in the IT department?
(1) 130 (2) 124
(3) 143 (4) 101
(5) None of these

91. A shokeeper sells two watches for Rs. 308 each. On one he gets 12% profit and on the other 12% loss. His profit or loss in the entire transaction was
(1) $1\dfrac{11}{25}\%$ loss (2) $1\dfrac{11}{25}\%$ gain
(3) $3\dfrac{2}{25}\%$ loss (4) $3\dfrac{2}{25}\%$ gain
(5) None of these

92. Two men alone or three women alone can complete a piece of work in 4 days. In how many days can one woman and one man together complete the same piece of work?
(1) 6 days (2) $\dfrac{24}{5}$ days
(3) $\dfrac{12}{1.75}$ days (4) Cannot be determined
(5) None of these

93. The simple interest accrued on an amount of Rs. 22,500 at the end of four years is Rs.10,800. What would be the compound interest accrued on the same amount at the same rate of interest at the end of two years?
(1) Rs. 16, 908 (2) Rs. 5, 724
(3) Rs. 28, 224 (4) Rs. 8, 586
(5) None of these

94. Mr. Pandit owned 950 gold coins all of which he distributed amongst his three daughters Lalita, Amita and Neeta. Lalita gave 25 gold coins to her husband, Amita donated 15 gold coins and Neeta made jewellery out of 30 gold coins. The new respective ratio of the coins left with them was 20 : 73 : 83. How many gold coins did Amita receive from Mr. Pandit?
(1) 380 (2) 415
(3) 400 (4) 350
(5) None of these

95. Three men A, B and C start a business together. They invest Rs. 30,000, Rs. 24,000 and Rs. 42,000 respectively in the beginning. After 4 months. B took out Rs. 6,000 and C took out Rs. 10,000. They get a profit of Rs. 11,960 at the end of the year. B's approximate share in the profit is
(1) Rs. 2,700 (2) Rs. 2,803
(3) Rs. 2,900 (4) Rs. 2,785
(5) None of these

Directions (Q. 96 to 100) Each question below is followed by two statements I and II. You are to determine whether the data given in the statement is sufficient for answering the question. You should use the data and your knowledge of Mathematics to choose between the possible answers.

(1) if the statement I alone is sufficient to answer the question, but the statement II alone is not sufficient.

(2) if the statement II alone is sufficient to answer the question, but the statement I alone is not sufficient.

(3) if both statements I and II together are needed to answer the question.

(4) if either the statement I alone or statement II alone is sufficient to answer the question.

(5) if you cannot get the answer from the statement I and II together, but need even more data.

96. Is X an even number?

   I.   X is divisible by 2

   II. (X + an odd number) is an odd number.

97. What is the three digit number?

   I.   One-third of that number is less by 27 of the half of that number.

   II. One-fifth of that number is 20% of that number.

98. The ages of Tanish and Shivay are in the ratio of 6 : 5. What is the age of Shivay?

   I.   The ages of Tanish and Danish are in the ratio of 3 : 2.

   II. After 6 years the ratio of Danish's and Shivay's ages will be 7 : 6.

99. In how many days can 15 men complete a piece of work?

   I.   16 children can complete the same piece of work in 48 days.

   II. 9 men can complete the same piece of work in 27 days.

100. What is the salary of C, in a group of A, B, C, D, E and F in which their average salary is Rs. 60,600?

   I.   Total of the salary of A and E is Rs. 64,500.

   II. Total of the salary of B and F is Rs. 52,600.

Directions (Q. 101 to 105): Answer the questions on the basis of the information given below.

The table given below represents the percentage marks obtained by six students in five different subjects in a school examination.

Student \ Subject	English (50)	Maths (100)	Science (150)	Hindi (50)	Social Studies (75)
P	66	89	80	78	84
Q	58	79	64	82	60
R	62	77	74	84	88
S	72	67	84	74	68
T	70	81	70	76	64
U	64	83	60	88	70

Note: Figures in brackets indicates maximum marks for each subject.

101. What is the approximate percentage of marks obtained by U in all the subjects together?

(1) 75   (2) 71

(3) 79   (4) 82

(5) 87

102. If in order to pass the examination a minimum of 109.5 marks are required in Science, how many students pass in the examination?

(1) None   (2) Two

(3) One   (4) Three

(5) None of these

103. What is the average marks obtained by all the students together in Hindi?

(1) $39\dfrac{1}{6}$ (2) $40\dfrac{1}{6}$

(3) $41\dfrac{1}{3}$ (4) $44\dfrac{1}{3}$

(5) None of these

104. What is the approximate average percentage of marks obtained by all the students together in English?

(1) 61   (2) 63

(3) 65   (4) 68

(5) 59

105. What are the total marks obtained by S in all the subjects together?

    (1) 317   (2) 309

    (3) 323   (4) 348

    (5) None of these

Directions (Q. 106 to 110): What will come in place of question mark (?) in the following number series?

106. 8, 11, 20, 47, 128, (?)

    (1) 483   (2) 488

    (3) 397   (4) 371

    (5) None of these

107. 71, 78, 99, 134, 183, (?)

    (1) 253   (2) 239

    (3) 246   (4) 253

    (5) None of these

108. 342, 337.5, 328.5, 315, 297, (?)

    (1) 265.5   (2) 274.5

    (3) 270   (4) 260

    (5) None of these

109. 161, 164, 179, 242, 497, (?)

    (1) 1540   (2) 1480

    (3) 1520   (4) 1440

    (5) None of these

110. 239, 254, 284, 344, 464, (?)

    (1) 726   (2) 716

    (3) 724   (4) 714

    (5) None of these

Directions (Q. 111 to 115): Answer the questions on the basis of the information given below.

Each question given below consists of a statement followed by two quantities i.e. I and II. Solve both of them and mark your answer accordingly.

(1)   Quantity I > Quantity II

(2)   Quantity I < Quantity II

(3)   Quantity I ≥ Quantity II

(4)   Quantity I ≤ Quantity II

(5)   Quantity I = Quantity II or relationship can be established

111. Quantity I: Four years ago, the average age of a group of five members was 16 years. The present average age of the group increases by 2 years after the inclusion of a new member. Find the present age the new member.

Quantity II: A person's present age is two-fifth of the age of his mother. After eight years, he will be half as old as his mother then. Find the present age of the mother.

112. Quantity I: Find the rate percent per annum, if Rs.4,500 amounts to Rs.5,209.3125 in 1.5 years and the interest is compounded semi-annually.

Quantity II: Q's salary is 20% more than that of R and R's salary is 25% more than that of S. By what percent is the salary of S less than that of Q?

113. Quantity I: A can complete a certain work in the same time in which B and C can complete it together. If A and B together can complete the work in 15 days and C alone can do it in 24 days then find the time taken by A, B and C to complete half the work while working together.

Quantity II: A and B can complete a certain piece of work alone in 20/3 days and 5 days respectively. They work together for 2 days and then A quits. How much extra time would B take to complete the work alone?

114. Quantity I: A dishonest shopkeeper uses a weight of 800 gm instead of 1 kg and sells sugar at the price which is 16% less than the cost price. Find the percentage of profit made by him during the entire transaction.

Quantity II: Mohan bought six dozen eggs at Rs. 24 per dozen and three dozen eggs at Rs. 32 per dozen. He mixed the two and sold them after giving a discount of 20%. Find the percentage profit made by him if the mark price of one dozen eggs is Rs. 35.

115. Quantity I: Amit purchased two T.V sets for Rs. 72,720. Later on he sold one of them at a profit of 15% and other at a loss of 9% but ended up in making neither profit nor loss in the entire transaction. Find the difference in the cost prices of the two T.V sets.

Quantity II: Raj spends 15% of her monthly income on rent, 10% on food and Rs. 1,873 on the education of his son. If he invests 24% of her monthly income in mutual investments and ends up in saving Rs. 8,429, then find the half yearly expenditure of Raj on rent.

GENERAL /ECONOMY/ BANKING AWARENESS

116. India's Sivalingam Sathish Kumar and Ragala Venkat Rahul qualified for next year's Commonwealth Games after winning a gold medal each in their respective divisions. These are related to which sports?

    (1) Boxing   (2) Swimming

    (3) Badminton   (4) Weightlifting

    (5) Wrestling

117. Paolo Gentiloni is the current Prime Minister of

(1) Estonia   (2) Italy

(3) Kenya   (4) Canada

(5) Israel

118. The Group of 7 (G7) is a group consisting of 7 countries, with the 7 largest advanced economies in the world, and represents more than 62% of the global net wealth. G7 summit 2018 will be held in

(1) France   (2) Japan

(3) USA   (4) Italy

(5) Canada

119. SWIFT provides a network that enables financial institutions worldwide to send and receive information about financial transactions in a secure, standardized and reliable environment. What is the meaning of "S" in SWIFT?

(1) Society   (2) Service

(3) System   (4) Solution

(5) Sending

120. The Union government has unveiled an ambitious plan to infuse Rs 2.11 lakh crore capital over the next two years into public sector banks (PSBs) that are saddled with high NPAs. These recapitalization bonds are worth Rs. _________ crore.

(1) 1.75 lakh   (2) 1.55 lakh

(3) 1.35 lakh   (4) 1.15 lakh

(5) 1.25 lakh

121. Bandhan Bank Limited is an Indian banking and financial services company headquartered in Kolkata, West Bengal. Bandhan, which started as a _________ company in 2001.

(1) micro-finance   (2) small-finance

(3) medium-finance   (4) industry-finance

(5) rural-finance

122. The SEAC's function on the principle of 7collective responsibility. What is the meaning of "A" in SEAC?

(1) Agriculture   (2) Appraisal

(3) Appeared   (4) Authority

(5) Approval

123. Panna National Park is a national park located in-

(1) Maharashtra   (2) Gujarat

(3) Madhya Pradesh   (4) Rajasthan

(5) Tamil Nadu

124. The City Union Bank Limited is an Indian bank. Where is the headquarters of City Union Bank?

(1) Uttar Pradesh   (2) West Bengal

(3) Kerala   (4) Tamil Nadu

(5) Maharashtra

125. The LTV ratio is a lending risk assessment ratio that financial institutions and others lenders examine before approving a mortgage. What is the meaning of "V" in LTV?

(1) Voucher   (2) Vacuum

(3) Vendor   (4) Vehicles

(5) Value

126. Dudhawa Dam is located in Dhamtari district of Chhattisgarh. It is built across the _________ river in the   village of Dudhawa.

(1) Kanhar   (2) Shivnath

(3) Indravati   (4) Mahanadi

(5) Sabari

127. The World Economic Outlook (WEO) database contains selected macroeconomic data series from the statistical appendix of the World Economic Outlook report. It is published by

(1) IMF   (2) World Bank

(3) UNCTAD   (4) WTO

(5) United Nations

128. Which among the following countries has come back from a two-goal deficit to crush Spain 5-2 and win the FIFA U-17 World Cup final in Kolkata, India?

(1) Austria   (2) Brazil

(3) England   (4) Germany

(5) France

129. 12th November is celebrated as

(1) International Day of Peace

(2) World Animal Day

(3) World Coffee Day

(4) National Food Day

(5) World Pneumonia Day

130. Fugdi is a famous folk dance in

(1) Bihar   (2) Goa

(3) Kerala   (4) Assam

(5) Manipur

131. How much fund for MNREGA is allocated in the Budget 2017-18?

(1) Rs 27,000 crore

(2) Rs 20,000 crore

(3) Rs 10,000 crore

(4) Rs 98,000 crore

(5) Rs 48,000 crore

132. Tallinn is the capital city of

(1) Ethiopia   (2) Algeria

(3) Uruguay   (4) Estonia

(5) Peru

133. MV Sridhar has recently died at the age of 51. He was a
(1) Writer   (2) Actor
(3) Cricketer   (4) Singer
(5) Director

134. Who is the committee head of merger of public sector banks?
(1) Raghuram Rajan   (2) Arun Jaitley
(3) Urjit Patel   (4) Vinod Rai
(5) Arvind Mayaram

135. The Kisan Credit Card (KCC) scheme is a credit scheme introduced in August 1998 by Indian banks. This model scheme was prepared by
(1) NABARD   (2) RBI
(3) SEBI   (4) FICCI
(5) SIDBI

136. Name the author of the book "India 2017 Yearbook"?
(1) Shaktikanta Das
(2) Hasmukh Adhia
(3) Rajiv Mehrishi
(4) Arvind Subramanian
(5) Ratan P Watal

137. For the first time ever, India has jumped 30 positions to become the top 100th country in terms of ease of doing business ranking this year. This was announced by
(1) IMF
(2) World Bank
(3) UNCTAD
(4) WTO
(5) United Nations

138. The Government of India has launched the AMRUT with the aim of providing basic civic amenities. What is the meaning of "U" in AMRUT?
(1) Useful   (2) Universal
(3) Unique   (4) Urban
(5) Uniform

139. Where is the headquarters of Amnesty International?
(1) London, UK
(2) Paris, France
(3) New York, USA
(4) Vienna, Austria
(5) Geneva, Switzerland

140. India Post Payments Bank (IPPB) is the second payments bank to start operations after Airtel Payments Banks. What is maximum limit for saving accounts in IPPB?
(1) Rs 5 lakh   (2) Rs 4 lakh
(3) Rs 3 lakh   (4) Rs 2 lakh
(5) Rs 1 lakh

141. Where is the Headquarters of International Weightlifting Federation (IWF)?
(1) Budapest, Hungary
(2) Nairobi, Kenya
(3) Madrid, Spain
(4) Bern, Switzerland
(5) Helsinki, Finland

142. The 2018 Commonwealth Games 2018 will be held in
(1) India   (2) Australia
(3) Scotland   (4) Norway
(5) Canada

143. The union budget (2017-18) provided NABARD with an additional budget of ________________ under Long Term.
(1) Rs. 30,000 crore   (2) Rs. 90,000 crore
(3) Rs. 20,000 crore   (4) Rs. 50,000 crore
(5) Rs. 80,000 crore

144. According to Price Waterhouse Coopers (PWC) report, which country will be the world's largest economy by 2050?
(1) Japan   (2) Germany
(3) USA   (4) China
(5) India

145. Which among the following is taxable event under new GST regime?
(1) Subject to the other provisions contained in USA
(2) Sale of goods in the course of union territory
(3) Service provided or agreed to be provided by small vendor
(4) Manufacture or production of goods from another country
(5) Goods imported into, or exported from, India

146. Banking Correspondents (BCs) are individuals/ entities engaged by a bank in India (commercial banks, Regional Rural Banks (RRBs) and Local Area Banks (LABs)) for providing banking services in unbanked/under-banked geographical territories. BCs are paid by-
(1) Third Party
(2) Bank which appoints BCs
(3) RBI
(4) NABARD
(5) RRBs

147. RBI has constituted a 10-member 'High Level Task Force on Public Credit Registry (PCR) for India', which will, among other things, suggest a roadmap for developing a transparent, comprehensive and near-real-time PCR for India. Who is the head of Public Credit Registry (PCR) committee?

(1) Sekar Karnam

(2) Sriram Kalyanaraman

(3) Rashesh Shah

(4) Vishaka Mulye

(5) YM Deosthalee

148. Taxpayers who are earning between ___________________ have to pay an additional surcharge of 10% on their total income which was not the case earlier.

(1) Rs.50 lacs to Rs.1 crore

(2) Rs.60 lacs to Rs.3 crore

(3) Rs.40 lacs to Rs.5 crore

(4) Rs.05 lacs to Rs.1 crore

(5) Rs.10 lacs to Rs.2 crore

149. _________ is a written commitment by a bank issued after a request by an importer (foreign buyer) that payment will be made to the beneficiary (exporter) provided that the terms and conditions.

(1) Buyers Products

(2) Shares and debentures

(3) Letter of Credit

(4) Working Capital

(5) None of the given options is true

150. The government stated anti-dumping duty is in force on 93 products including chemicals and machinery items imported from China. Anti-dumping duty notification issued by

(1) Food Processing Minstry

(2) Road and Tranport Ministry

(3) Environment Ministry

(4) Revenue department

(5) Home Ministry

151. ___________ is a market form wherein a market or industry is dominated by a small number of sellers.

(1) Capitalization   (2) Vendor

(3) Group   (4) Cartel

(5) Oligopoly

152. Slowdown in the rate of increase of price of goods and service in national GDP over a time is known as

(1) Deflation   (2) Reflection

(3) Stagflation   (4) Disinflation

(5) Recession

153. Which among the following is NOT a function of RBI?

(1) To work as monetary authority and implement its Monetary Policy

(2) To serve as issuer of bank notes

(3) Working to foster global monetary cooperation, secure financial stability for member countries

(4) Serve as banker to central and state governments

(5) None of the given options is true

154. To make the payments process easier the Government of India has launched the __________ payments transfer mechanism for cashless electronics payments.

(1) UPI

(2) Bharat QR Code

(3) IMPS

(4) Quick Pay

(5) Bhim app

155. __________ is a trade and economic policy which advocates replacing foreign imports with domestic production.

(1) Import substitution

(2) Reduction in import

(3) Decrease in export

(4) Boost of Economy

(5) Increase in trade

ANSWERS

1. (3)	**2.** (4)	**3.** (1)	**4.** (3)	**5.** (2)	**6.** (4)	**7.** (3)	**8.** (2)	**9.** (1)	**10.** (5)
11. (3)	**12.** (4)	**13.** (3)	**14.** (3)	**15.** (1)	**16.** (3)	**17.** (4)	**18.** (5)	**19.** (5)	**20.** (1)
21. (3)	**22.** (1)	**23.** (3)	**24.** (4)	**25.** (4)	**26.** (1)	**27.** (4)	**28.** (5)	**29.** (1)	**30.** (3)
31. (2)	**32.** (5)	**33.** (4)	**34.** (4)	**35.** (3)	**36.** (5)	**37.** (5)	**38.** (4)	**39.** (5)	**40.** (4)
41. (4)	**42.** (1)	**43.** (4)	**44.** (1)	**45.** (4)	**46.** (2)	**47.** (1)	**48.** (5)	**49.** (1)	**50.** (3)
51. (3)	**52.** (1)	**53.** (2)	**54.** (4)	**55.** (1)	**56.** (2)	**57.** (2)	**58.** (5)	**59.** (3)	**60.** (3)
61. (2)	**62.** (1)	**63.** (3)	**64.** (1)	**65.** (1)	**66.** (4)	**67.** (1)	**68.** (3)	**69.** (4)	**70.** (2)
71. (3)	**72.** (5)	**73.** (2)	**74.** (5)	**75.** (2)	**76.** (3)	**77.** (1)	**78.** (3)	**79.** (2)	**80.** (1)
81. (4)	**82.** (1)	**83.** (4)	**84.** (2)	**85.** (1)	**86.** (1)	**87.** (5)	**88.** (2)	**89.** (4)	**90.** (3)
91. (1)	**92.** (2)	**93.** (2)	**94.** (1)	**95.** (2)	**96.** (4)	**97.** (1)	**98.** (5)	**99.** (2)	**100.** (5)
101. (2)	**102.** (4)	**103.** (2)	**104.** (3)	**105.** (1)	**106.** (4)	**107.** (3)	**108.** (2)	**109.** (3)	**110.** (5)
111. (2)	**112.** (2)	**113.** (1)	**114.** (5)	**115.** (5)	**116.** (4)	**117.** (2)	**118.** (5)	**119.** (1)	**120.** (3)
121. (1)	**122.** (2)	**123.** (3)	**124.** (4)	**125.** (5)	**126.** (4)	**127.** (1)	**128.** (3)	**129.** (5)	**130.** (2)
131. (5)	**132.** (4)	**133.** (3)	**134.** (2)	**135.** (1)	**136.** (3)	**137.** (2)	**138.** (5)	**139.** (1)	**140.** (5)
141. (1)	**142.** (2)	**143.** (3)	**144.** (4)	**145.** (5)	**146.** (2)	**147.** (5)	**148.** (1)	**149.** (3)	**150.** (4)
151. (5)	**152.** (4)	**153.** (3)	**154.** (2)	**155.** (1)					

EXPLANATIONS

For questions 1 to 5:

Top Floor	8th	C
	7th	Vacant
	6th	D
	5th	A
	4th	Vacant
	3rd	B
	2nd	E
Ground Floor	1st	F

For questions 6 to 10:

South	Pammy	Qutub	Tanu	Supriya	Utkarsh
North	Aman	Billu	Chintu	Dinky	Ekta

For questions 11 to 15:

Ties	Yellow	Blue	Orange	Red	White
Friends	Amit	Bony	Chapak	Dolly	Eram
Bikes	Activa	Pulsar	Bullet	Passion	Honda
Caps	Nike	Adidas	Ferrari	Puma	Reebok

16. 3 From the statements II and III:

```
    T    ⇔    W
   (+)   /\   (–)
         M
```

Though, sex of M is not known, it is given in statement III, that T has three children and only one of them is boy. Therefore, we may conclude that W has two daughters.

17. 4 From statement I:

E > B > A

From statement II:

— > — > — > C > — > —

From statement III:

— > — > — > — > D > F

Now combining all the above statements, we have

E > B > A > C > D > F

18. 5 From statement II:

```
R        W        N
•        •        ↑
              W←──┼──→E
                  ↓
•        •        S
T                 
```

From statement III:

```
         T
         •

•        •
J        Z
```

Now combining statements I and II:

```
    R        W
    •        •

         •
         T
•        •
J        Z
```

J is in south-west direction from W.

19. 5 Even by combining all the statements, we cannot find the day of the week on which Suresh visited Chennai.

20. 1 From statements I and III:

now or never again ⇒ torn ka na sa   … (i)

again go now or never ⇒ na ho ka sa torn … (ii)

From (i) and (ii), code for 'go' is 'ho'.

For questions 21 to 25

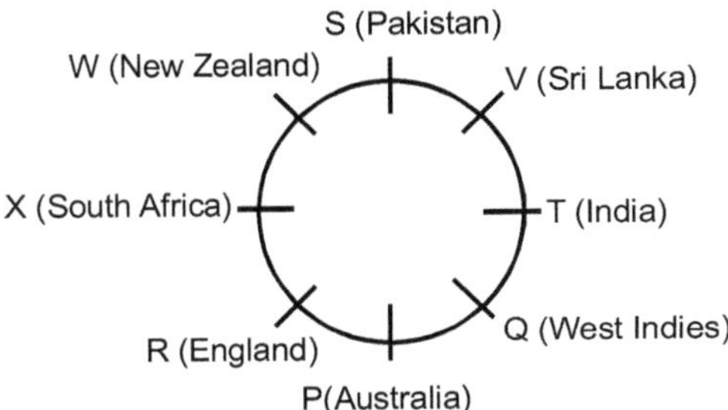

For questions 26 to 30:

Owners	Place	Dog breed
T	Sangam Viahr	Dachshund
U	Uttam Nagar	English Mastiff
V	Vikas Puri	Cane Corso/ French Bulldog
W	Om Vihar	French Bulldog/ Cane Corso
X	Tilak Nagar	Boxer
Y	Prem Nagar	German Shepherd
Z	Rajouri Garden	Australian Shepherd

31. 2 **Input:** train 59 47 25 over burden 63 sky
Step I: burden train 59 47 25 over 63 sky
Step II: burden 25 train 59 47 over 63 sky
Step III: burden 25 over train 59 47 63 sky
Step IV: burden 25 over 47 train 59 63 sky
Step V: burden 25 over 47 sky train 59 63
Step VI: burden 25 over 47 sky 59 train 63
Hence step V is the last but one.

32. 5 **Input:** service 46 58 96 over there desk 15
Step I: desk service 46 58 96 over there 15
Step II: desk 15 service 46 58 96 over there
Step III: desk 15 over service 46 58 96 there
Step IV: desk 15 over 46 service 58 96 there
Step V: desk 15 over 46 service 58 there 96
Since the input is already arranged, there will be no step VI.

33. 4 We can't proceed backward.

34. 4 **Step III:** art 24 day 83 71 54 star power
Step IV: art 24 day 54 83 71 star power
Step V: art 24 day 54 power 83 71 star
Step VI: art 24 day 54 power 71 83 star
Step VII: art 24 day 54 power 71 star 83

35. 3 **Step II:** cold 17 wave 69 never desk 52 43
Step III: cold 17 desk wave 69 never 52 43
Step IV: cold 17 desk 43 wave 69 never 52
Step V: cold 17 desk 43 never wave 69 52
Step VI: cold 17 desk 43 never 52 wave 69
Hence, 6 − 2 = 4 more steps will be required.

36. 5
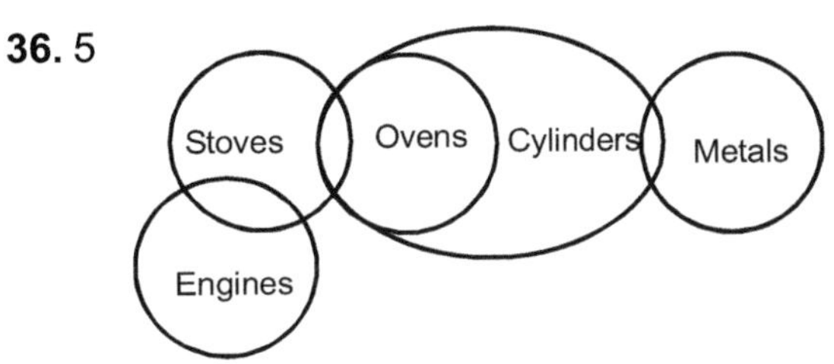

37. 5
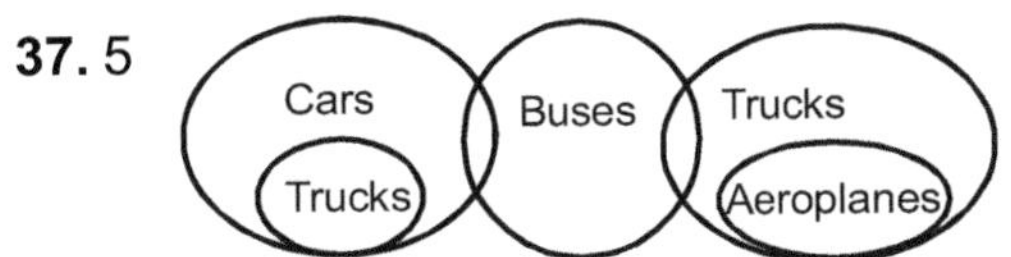

38. 4
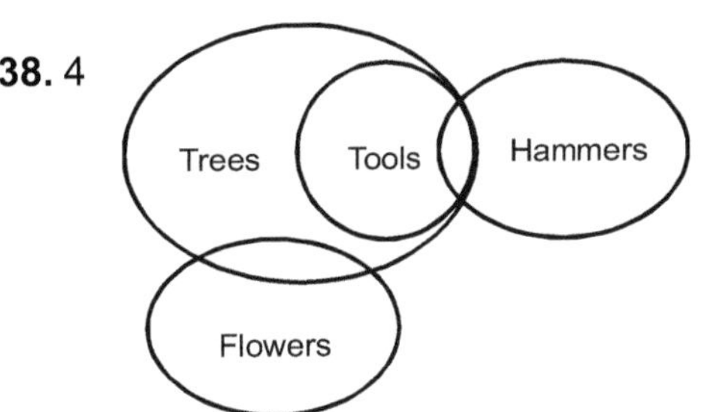

39. 5
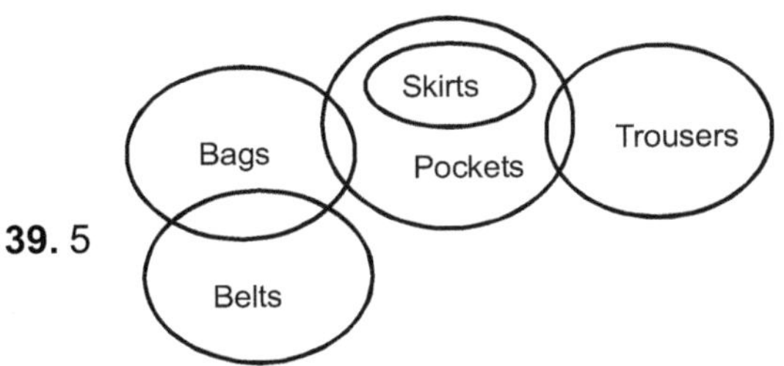

40. 4
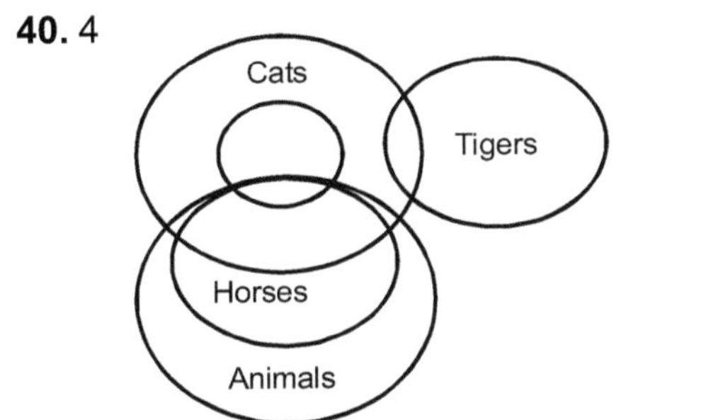

41. 4 None of the given arguments are strong enough to account for the statement. Hence, the answer is option (4).

42. 1 Only the first argument gives a good argument. It clearly says that Indian football is making great promises.

43. 4 For such an important shift in the system of a country, the reasons given are very weak.

44. 1 Assumption I is implicit because it is this that makes us import sugar in spite of the increase in the number of sugar factories. But II is not implicit because 'future' is beyond the scope of the statement.

45. 4   Compensation is a way of sympathising with the victims, not a deterrent to terrorism. Hence II is implicit but I is not.

46. 2   The first paragraph of the passage states that John Maynard Keynes had the radical idea that excessive spending during recession is likely to boost economy.

47. 1   John Maynard Keynes believed that spending money during recession holds more value as compared to where and on what the money is spent.

48. 5   The author of the passage calls Barack Obama and his team as "Keynesians" because Barack Obama prepared to throw money at the current meltdown. None of the given options express this idea.

49. 1   The second paragraph of the passage suggests that 'aggregate demand' refers to goods and services sector. Refer to the line, "moribund economy will....aggregate demand."

50. 3   The second paragraph of the passage states that highways, bridges, ethanol plants, etc. are considered as inappropriate proposals to waste money on. Refer to the line, "A trillion dollars' worth of bad idea....mere waste."

56. 2   The correct sequence is BFECAD. Sentence B fits in the beginning as it introduces the subject-recession in many countries. BF can be established as a mandatory pair because 'almost all countries' in B creates a link with 'like others, India too' in F. ECA is a mandatory sequence because E talks about 'few things which help India in bouncing back from recession' and C further discusses one of the measures to overcome the heat of recession. 'Them' in A refers to RBI and SEBI mentioned in C. AD is another mandatory pair because D states the consequence (massive losses to the banks) if the hands of Indian banks were tied down.

61. 2   'Changes' is the correct answer because the sentence implies that technology transforms our life.

62. 1   'This' refers to technology in the given context and it facilitates the understanding process.

63. 3   'Knack' is the correct answer because the sentence indicates that Sony lost interest in the walkman.

64. 1   The word 'key' in this context is used to explain the way people work, buy or do business. Therefore, determining is synonymous to deciding the way people work.

65. 1   'Tend' is the correct answer because the technological advancements are evident in field of technology.

66. 4   "Significance" should be replaced by "significant". "Have" should be replaced by "has" because the subject is singular.

67. 1   The correct form is "It's". In section B, it should be "you should tender ...."

68. 3   The correct preposition should be "on". "Sinking man" is wrong. It should be "drowning man."

69. 4   It should be "breathed".

70. 2   There should be a "but" between "iPhone" and "she". Furthermore, "afforded" should be replaced by "afford".

75. 2   The other options are not feasible. Reporting the matter to the police or the media sounds too premature.

76. 3   Only option C makes sense in the context of the sentence.

77. 1   The other options do not make any sense in the context of the sentence.

78. 3   Relevant' and 'obscure' fits the two blank most appropriately. Relevant means closely connected or appropriate to what is being done or considered while obscure means not discovered or known about.

79. 2   'Efficacy' and 'regimens' fits the two blank correctly. Efficacy means the ability to produce a desired or intended result. Regimen means a prescribed course of medical treatment, diet, or exercise for the promotion or restoration of health.

80. 1   Option (1) is the best answer choice as, transition means the process or a period of changing from one state or condition to another and enervating means make (someone) feel drained of energy or vitality.

81. 4   Average number of players who play football and

$$\text{rugby} = \frac{1}{2}[(17+13)\% \text{ of } 4200]$$

$$= \frac{1}{2} \times 4200 \times \frac{30}{100} = 630.$$

82. 1   Number of players who play rugby

$$= 4200 \times \frac{13}{100} = 546$$

Number of females players who play rugby

$$= 2000 \times \frac{10}{100} = 200$$

$\therefore$ Number of male players who play rugby
= 546 − 200 = 346

Number of female players who play lawn tennis

$$= 2000 \times \frac{22}{100} = 440$$

$\therefore$ Required difference = 440 − 346 = 94.

83. 4   Number of female cricketers $= 2000 \times \dfrac{40}{100} = 800$

Number of male hockey players

$$= \frac{4200 \times 10}{100} - \frac{2000 \times 15}{100} = 420 - 300 = 120$$

Required ratio = 800 : 120 = 20 : 3.

84. 2 Number of male players who play football, cricket and lawn tennis

= (17 + 35 + 25)% of 4200 − (13 + 40 + 22)% of 2000

$$= 4200 \times \frac{77}{100} - 2000 \times \frac{75}{100}$$

= 3234 − 1500 = 1734.

85. 1 Number of male players who play rugby

$$= 4200 \times \frac{13}{100} - 200 = 346$$

Number of players who play lawn tennis

$$= 4200 \times \frac{25}{100} = 1050$$

$$\therefore \text{Required percentage} = \frac{346}{1050} \times 100 \approx 33\%.$$

For questions 86 to 90:

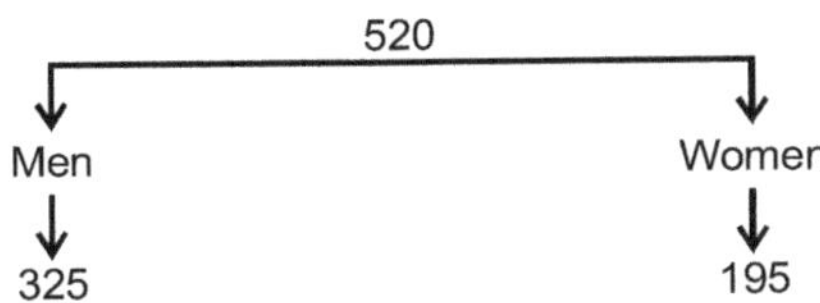

Gender	HR	IT	Production	Marketing
M	13	65	130	117
W	78	78	5	34

86. 1 Required % $= \dfrac{117}{520} \times 100 = 22.5\%$

87. 5 Required ratio = 13 : 78 = 1 : 6

89. 4 Required % $= \dfrac{135}{520} \times 100 = 25.96 \approx 26\%$

91. 1 Loss per cent

$$= \left(\frac{\text{Common gain or loss}}{10} \right)^2 \%$$

$$= \left(\frac{12}{10} \right)^2 \% = \frac{36}{25} \% = 1\frac{11}{25}\%$$

92. 2 2 men = 3 women

$$= \left(\frac{3}{2} + 1 \right) \text{women} = \frac{5}{2} \text{women}$$

$$\therefore M_1 D_1 = M_2 D_2$$

$$\Rightarrow 3 \times 4 = \frac{5}{2} \times D_2$$

$$\Rightarrow D_2 = \frac{3 \times 4 \times 2}{5} = \frac{24}{5} \text{ days.}$$

93. 2 $r = \dfrac{10800 \times 100}{22500 \times 4} = 12\%$

$$CI = 22500 \left(1 + \frac{12}{100} \right)^2 - 22500$$

$$= 22500 \times \frac{112}{100} \times \frac{112}{100} - 22500 = 28224 - 22500$$

= 5724

94. 1 Let the number of coins left with Lalita, Amita and Neeta be 20x, 73x and 83x respectively.

According to question,

20x + 73x + 83x = 950 − 25 − 15 − 30

$\Rightarrow$ 176x = 880

$$\Rightarrow x = \frac{880}{176} = 5$$

$\therefore$ Number of coins received by Amita

= 73x + 15 = 73 × 5 + 15 = 380.

95. 2 Ratio of equivalent capitals for 1 month

= 30000 × 12 : (24000 × 4 + 18000 × 8)

: (42000 × 4 + 32000 × 8)

= 360000 : 240000 : 424000

= 90 : 60 : 106

= 45 : 30 : 53

Sum of ratios = 45 + 30 + 53 = 128

∴ B's share

$$= \frac{30}{128} \times 11960 = ₹2803$$

96. 4 Statement I: X is an even number.

Statement II: X is an even number.

So, either of the statements is sufficient.

97. 1 From I: $\dfrac{x}{3} = \dfrac{x}{2} - 27$

$$\Rightarrow \frac{x}{6} = 27 \quad \therefore x = 162$$

I is sufficient.

From II: $\dfrac{x}{5} = 20\%$ of $x = \dfrac{x}{5}$

II is not sufficient.

98. 5 After combining the two statements, we cannot solve the problem.

99. 2 Only II alone gives, the answer as $27 \left(\dfrac{9}{15} \right)$ days.

100. 5 A + B + C + D + E + F = 60600 × 6 = 363600 ... (i)

Statement I: A + E = 64,500

Statement II: B + F = 52,600

Combining both the statements I and II, we can find C + D, not the value of C.

101. 2 Total marks obtained by U

$$= \frac{64 \times 50}{100} + 83 + \frac{60}{100} \times 150 + \frac{88 \times 50}{100} + \frac{70 \times 75}{100}$$

= 32 + 83 + 90 + 44 + 52.5 = 301.5

$$\therefore \text{Required percentage} = \frac{301.5}{425} \times 100 \approx 71\%.$$

102. 4 Equivalent percentage of 109.5 marks in science

$$= \frac{109.5 \times 100}{150} = 73\%$$

Hence, only three students P, R and S passed in science.

103. 2 Required average $= \dfrac{39 + 41 + 42 + 37 + 38 + 44}{6}$

$$= \frac{241}{3} = 40\frac{1}{6}.$$

104. 3 Average percentage marks in English

$$= \frac{66 + 58 + 62 + 72 + 70 + 64}{6} = \frac{392}{6} \approx 65\%.$$

105. 1 Total marks obtained by S

$$= \frac{72 \times 50}{100} + 67 + \frac{84 \times 150}{100} + \frac{74 \times 50}{100} + \frac{68 \times 75}{100}$$

$$= 36 + 67 + 126 + 37 + 51 = 317.$$

106. 4

8	11	20	47	128	371

$+(3)^1 \quad +(3)^2 \quad +(3)^3 \quad +(3)^4 \quad +(3)^5$

107. 3

71	78	99	134	183	246

$+(7\times1) \quad +(7\times3) \quad +(7\times5) \quad +(7\times7) \quad +(7\times9)$

108. 2

342	337.5	328.5	315	297	274.5

$-(4.5\times1) \quad -(4.5\times2) \quad -(4.5\times3) \quad -(4.5\times4) \quad -(4.5\times5)$

109. 3

161	164	179	242	497	1520

$+3 \quad +15 \quad +63 \quad +255 \quad +1023$

$(3\times4)+3 \quad (15\times4)+3 \quad (63\times4)+3 \quad (255\times4)+3$

110. 5

239	254	284	344	464	704

$+15 \quad +30 \quad +60 \quad +120 \quad +240$

111. 2 Quantity I: Let the present age of the new member be 'x' years.

$$\Rightarrow \frac{(100 + x)}{6} = 20 + 2 \text{ or } x = 32 \text{ years.}$$

Quantity II: Let the present ages (in years) of the person and the mother be 2x and 5x respectively.

$$\Rightarrow (2x + 8) = \frac{(5x + 8)}{2}$$

$\Rightarrow x = 8$ and the age of the mother = 40 years.
Therefore, Quantity I < Quantity II.

112. 2 Quantity I: According to the given condition,

$$4500 \times \left(1 + \frac{r}{100}\right)^3 = 5209.3125$$

$$\Rightarrow \left(1 + \frac{r}{100}\right)^3 = \frac{5209.3125}{4500} = \left(\frac{21}{20}\right)^3$$

Hence, r = 5% and required rate of interest = 10%.
Quantity II: Q = 1.2R and R = 1.25S
$\Rightarrow$ Q = 1.2 × 1.25 × S or Q = 1.5S
Hence, S is 33.33% less than Q.
Therefore, Quantity I < Quantity II.

113. 1 Quantity I: Let the total work be 120 units i.e. LCM of 15 and 24.

$\Rightarrow$ Work done by A and B in one day will be 8 units and that by C in one day will be 5 units

Hence, required time $= \dfrac{60}{13} = 4.6$ days.

Quantity II: Let the total work be 20 units i.e. LCM of 20/3 and 5 such that the work done by A and B in one day is 3 units and 4 units respectively.

Hence, required time $= \dfrac{20 - 14}{4} = 1.5$ days.

Therefore, Quantity I > Quantity II.

114. 5 Quantity I: Let the CP of 1 kg of sugar be Rs. 100
$\Rightarrow$ CP of 800 gm of sugar = Rs. 80 and SP of 800 gm of sugar = 100 × 0.84 = Rs. 84.

Hence, required profit percent $= \dfrac{84 - 80}{80} \times 100$

$$= 5\%.$$

Quantity II: CP of 9 dozen eggs = 24 × 6 + 32 × 3 = Rs. 240

$$\Rightarrow SP = 315 \times \frac{4}{5} = Rs. 252$$

Hence, required profit $= \dfrac{252 - 240}{240} \times 100 = 5\%.$

Therefore, Quantity I = Quantity II.

115. 5 Quantity I: Let the cost prices of the two T.V sets be P and Q
$\Rightarrow$ P × 0.15 = Q × 0.09 or P : Q = 3 : 5

Hence, required difference $= \dfrac{2}{8} \times 72720$

$$= Rs. 18180.$$

Quantity II: Let the monthly income of Raj be Rs. x

$\Rightarrow$ x ×{ 100 − (15 + 10 + 24)} = 1873 + 8429
$\Rightarrow$ x = Rs. 20,200
Hence, required amount = 0.15 × 20200 × 6 = Rs. 18180.

Therefore, Quantity I = Quantity II.

GENERAL AWARENESS

1. India's very own Global Positioning System (GPS) which is set to hit the market for public use in early 2018 is known as the 'Indian Regional Navigation Satellite System' (IRNSS). Its operational name is______.

(1) NASIK   (2) NASIC

(3) NAVIC   (4) NAVIK

(5) NAVIS

2. The 'Dalong Village' covering an area of 11.35 sq. km. has recently (May 2017) been declared as Biodiversity of Heritage Site under Section 37 (I) of Biological Diversity Act, 2002. The village is situated in the Indian State of ___.

(1) Manipur   (2) Madhya Pradesh

(3) Mizoram   (4) Maharashtra

(5) Assam

3. The 'Almatti Dam' is a hydroelectric project on the Krishna River in the Indian State of

(1) Andhra Pradesh   (2) Maharashtra

(3) West Bengal   (4) Karnataka

(5) Telangana

4. The first Indian State which has recently launched its official, T-wallet' offering anytime anywhere platform for digital payments with an additional charge for the citizens is

(1) Chhattisgarh   (2) Telangana

(3) Kerala   (4) Maharashtra

(5) Andhra Pradesh

5. Which of the following categories of banks are not allowed to accept deposits under 'Pradhan Mantri Garib Kalyan Deposit Scheme' (PMGKDS), 2016 ?

(1) Private Sector Banks

(2) Public Sector Banks

(3) Regional Rural Banks

(4) Cooperative Banks

(5) State Bank of India

6. A 'banking outlet' is one which opens for at least five days a week for at least.

(1) two hours a day

(2) five hours a day

(3) three hours a day

(4) four hours a day

(5) six hours a day

7. Which of the following instruments is 'not' a debt instrument ?

(1) Stocks   (2) Debentures

(3) Bonds   (4) Mortgages

(5) Promissory Note

8. The working and activity of NBFCs are registered by the Reserve Bank of India within the framework of the____________.

(1) Reserve Bank of India Act, 1934 (Chapter 10-12)

(2) Banking Regulation Act, 1949

(3) Companies Act, 1956

(4) Banking Companies Act, 1970 (Chapter No. 4)

(5) Corporate Act, 2001

9. The Union Home Minister, Shri Rajnath Singh has recently (May 2017) released the book 'India 2017; Yearbook'. The book is authored by ________.

(1) Dr. Arvind Panagariya

(2) Shri Rajiv Malhotra

(3) Shri Kamal Kishore

(4) Shri Tanay Pant

(5) Shri Rajiv Mehrishi

10. The 'Sonal Rupai Wildlife Sanctuary' is situated in the Indian State of________.

(1) Arunachal Pradesh

(2) Tripura

(3) Meghalaya

(4) Sikkim

(5) Assam

11. The 2017 'North Atlantic Treaty Organisation' (NATO) Summit was recently (May 2017) held in________.

(1) New York, United States of America

(2) London, United Kingdom

(3) Paris, France

(4) Brussels, Belgium

(5) Rome, Italy

12. The 'CGFMU' is a Credit Guarantee Fund established for guaranteeing loans sacrificed under the

(1) PMRY Scheme

(2) PMMY Scheme

(3) PMGSY Scheme

(4) PMAY Scheme

(5) PMUY Scheme

13. The 'Federation of Indian Chamber of Commerce and Industries' (FICCI) Smart Policing Award for the year 2017 has recently (May 2017) been conferred upon__________.

(1) Jammu City Police

(2) Pune City Police

(3) Kolkata City Police

(4) Delhi City Police

(5) Mumbai City Police

14. Which of the following is an integrated payment system which uses the customer's Smart or Credit Card by scanning a code of the merchant's place?

(1) Aadhaar Pay

(2) UPI

(3) Bharat QR

(4) Paytm

(5) Immediate Payment Service

15. Disha Microfin Private Limited has recently (May 2017) received the final approval from the Reserve Bank of India to commence______.

(1) Local Area Bank Operations

(2) Universal Banking Operations

(3) White Label ATM

(4) Payments Bank

(5) Small Finance Bank

16. With an intention of increasing Digital transactions, the Reserve Bank of India has recently permitted cooperative banks to deploy their own or third party point of sale terminals only if their net assets are more than

(1) Rs. 15 crore   (2) Rs. 25 crore

(3) Rs. 50 crore   (4) Rs. 10 crore

(5) Rs. 35 crore

17. 'Kanwar Pal Singh Gill' who recently (May 2017) passed away at the   age of 82 was a former ______.

(1) Indian Civil Rights Activist

(2) Indian Police Officer

(3) Indian Intelligence Officer

(4) Indian Football Player

(5) Indian Civil Servant

18. The currency of the 'Republic of Maldives' is____.

(1) Riyal   (2) Rupee

(3) Ringgit   (4) Rufiyaa

(5) Rupiah

19. A new cheaper, quicker and pollution-free 'soil-to-soil technology to manufacture 'biofuel' has recently (June 2017) been developed by researchers at________.

(1) IIT-Gandhinagar (2) IIT-Jamshedpur

(3) IIT-Kanpur   (4) IIT-Kharagpur

(5) IIT-Bhubaneswar

20. The 'European Extremely Large Telescope' which when completed will be the world's largest optical telescope is being set up on a 3,000 meter high mountain in________.

(1) Arctic Desert in Canada

(2) Gobi Desert in China

(3) Taklimakan Desert

(4) Sahara Desert in Chad

(5) Atacama Desert in Chile

21. Asian Infrastructure Investment Bank (AAIB) has recently approved a loan of USO iGO million for a power project in the Indian State of

(1) Maharashtra   (2) Madhya Pradesh

(3) Andhra Pradesh   (4) Himachal Pradesh

(5) Odisha

22. Payment solutions providers 'Oxigen Services' and 'PayU India' have been granted in principle approval from Reserve Bank of India (RBI) to operate as________.
   (1) Payments Bank
   (2) Small Finance Bank
   (3) White Label ATM
   (4) Universal Bank
   (5) Bharat Bill Payments Operating Unit

23. The archaeological site of the Paleolithic period, the 'Bhim- betka rock shelters' is situated in the Indian State of
   (1) Andhra Pradesh
   (2) Chhattisgarh
   (3) Madhya Pradesh
   (4) Himachal Pradesh
   (5) Odisha

24. The 'Shri Shiv Chhatrapati Sports Complex' also known as Balewadi Stadium, is situated in.
   (1) Nashik, Maharashtra
   (2) Mumbai, Maharashtra
   (3) Aurangabad, Maharashtra
   (4) Nagpur, Maharashtra
   (5) Pune, Maharashtra

25. The 'Cash and ATM Management Companies' are now not required to comply with the Private Security Agencies (Regulation) Act (PSARA). As a result, they may not be allowed to attract Foreign Direct Investment (FOI) up to
   (1) 33 per cent   (2) 51 percent
   (3) 28 per cent   (4) 66 per cent
   (5) 100 per cent

26. At any one time, the maximum balance in a BSBDA small Account should not exceed
   (1) Rs. 40,000   (2) Rs. 50,000
   (3) Rs. 30,000   (4) Rs. 20,000
   (5) Rs. 1,000

27. The Union Cabinet has recently approved the public testing of five state owned general inssurance companies and making the government's stake in them from 100% to
   (1) 75 per cent   (2) 49 per cent
   (3) 51 per cent   (4) 61 per cent

28. In India the Credit rating agencies are regulated by __________
   (1) SEBI   (2) RBI
   (3) FIMMDA   (4) PFRDA
   (5) IRDA

29. The Dadasaheb Phalke Academy Award in the newly introduced 'Internationally Acclaimed Actress' Category has recently been awarded to film actress________.
   (1) Aishwarya Rai Bachchan
   (2) Mallika Sherawat
   (3) Priyanka Chopra
   (4) Deepika Padukone
   (5) Freida Pinto

30. The HCL Asian junior Tennis Championship 2017 was recently (27th May 2017 - 3rd June 2017) held in ______.
   (1) Jakarta, Indonesia
   (2) Pune, India
   (3) Kuala Lumpur, Malaysia
   (4) Mumbai, India

31. The Reserve Bank of India has advised banks to adhere to timelines prescribed for formulation and implementation of the 'CAP' by resolution of stressed loans. The alphabet C in abbreviation 'CAP' stands for
   (1) Convertible   (2) Corporate
   (3) Company   (4) Corrective
   (5) Currency

32. The 1,980 MW 'Ghatampur Thermal Power Project' is proposed to be set up at an estimated cost of Rs. 17,237 crore in the Indian State of ______ .
   (1) Uttar Pradesh   (2) Chhattisgarh
   (3) Bihar   (4) Odisha
   (5) Uttarakhand

33. The city of 'Abu Dhabi, is the capital of ______.
   (1) Republic of Turkey
   (2) Lebanese Republic
   (3) The Hashemite Kingdom of Jordan
   (4) Kingdom of Saudi Arabia
   (5) United Arab Emirates

34. The 'Singareni Collieries Company Limited' (SCCL) is a government-owned coal mining company in India. The company is jointly owned by the Government of India and the

(1) Government of Madhya Pradesh

(2) Government of Andhra Pradesh

(3) Government of Uttar Pradesh

(4) Government of Telangana

(5) Government of Tamil Nadu

35. The 'IRS' is a liquid financial derivative instrument which can be used to hedge against charges in_______.

(1) Income streams

(2) Interest rates

(3) Stock notices

(4) Exchange Rates

36. Punjab National Bank (PNB) has recently (May 2017) received USD 100 million as the first tranche of the USD 500 million multi-tranche finance facility for Solar Rooftop Investment Programme (SRIP) approved in 2016 by ______.

(1) Asian Development Bank

(2) New Development Bank

(3) International Monetary Fund

(4) International Development Association

(5) International Finance Corporation

37. According to the 2011 Census data, the sex ratio of the population in the country in 2011 stood at __________

(1) 931 females to 1000 males

(2) 967 females to 1000 males

(3) 940 females to 1000 males

(4) 94 females to 1000 males

(5) 970 females to 1000 males

38. During the recent (May 2017) six-day four nation tour Prime Minister Narendra Modi visited "Madrid" the capital city of

(1) Slovakia

(2) Spain

(3) Switzerland

(4) Sweden

(5) Swaziland

39. According to RBI guidelines, a scheduled commercial bank can own stake in a payments bank to the extent permitted under Section 19(2) of the

(1) Public Financial Institutions Act, 1956

(2) Banking Regulation Act, 1949

(3) State Bank of India Act, 1955

(4) Reserve Bank of India Act, 1934

(5) Reserve Bank of India Act, 1953

40. July 11, every year is observed as the_______.

(1) World Population Day

(2) World Literacy Day

(3) World Heart Day

(4) Malala Day

(5) World Hepatitis Day

41. The 'Ease of Doing Business Index' is an index proposed by the________.

(1) World Trade Organisation

(2) New Development Bank

(3) World Economic Forum

(4) Asian Development Bank

(5) World Bank Group

42. The Reserve Bank of India has been opening the bank license window only periodically. Under the 'un-top' mechanism, however an application can be made________.

(1) as and when RBI notifies

(2) only for specified corporations

(3) at any time subject to conditions

(4) only for specified branches

(5) None of these

43. In a breakthrough in military aviation technology, its largest indigenously built transport aircraft Y-20, was inducted by________.

(1) Russia　　(2) Pakistan

(3) China　　(4) France

(5) None of these

44. The two-day 'G7 Summit 2017' was recently (May 2017) held in_______.

(1) Italy　　(2) United Kingdom

(3) Japan　　(4) France

(5) Germany

45. In order to move towards a cashless economy, the RBI has recently prohibited non-banking finance companies (NBFCs) from disbursing loans against gold for an amount over______.
    (1) Rs. 20,000　　(2) Rs. 99,000
    (3) Rs. 50,000　　(4) Rs. 15,000
    (5) Rs. 40,000

46. India's largest bridge, the 'Dhola-Sadiya Bridge' has recently (May 2017) been inaugurated by PM Shri Narendra Modi. The bridge in the Indian State of Assam is built over the______.
    (1) Manasa River　　(2) Dhansiri River
    (3) Lohit River　　(4) Teesta River
    (5) Dining River

47. The largest of White Label ATM Kiosks under the brand name 'Indicash' is owned and operated by________.
    (1) BTI Payments
    (2) Tata Communications Payment Solutions
    (3) Muthoot Finance Limited
    (4) Prize Payments Solutions Limited
    (5) Sun Infra Finance

48. The only Indian cricketer of the country to feature in the top 10 of the ICC Player Rankings for ODI in May 2017?
    (1) Virat Kohli　　(2) Amit Mishra
    (3) Shikhar Dhawan　(4) M.S. Dhoni

49. Based on the UN Habitual Data, the World Economic Forum has recently named two Indian cities as the world's most crowded cities. The cities are Mumbai and______.
    (1) New Delhi　　(2) Kolkata
    (3) Surat　　(4) Kota
    (5) Bengaluru

50. 'LAF is a monetary policy instrument which allows banks to borrow money through repurchase agreements. The alphabet 'L' in the abbreviation 'LAF' stands for______.
    (1) Leverage　　(2) Legitimate
    (3) Liquidity　　(4) Liability
    (5) Local

51. 'Aparna Popat' is a famous Indian______.
    (1) Hockey player　　(2) Tennis Player
    (3) Cricket Player　　(4) Badminton Player
    (5) Volleyball Player

52. A nationwide campaign 'Darwaza Band' to promote use and freedom from open defecation across the villages of the country has recently (May 2017) been launched by the______.
    (1) Ministry of Water Resources and River Development
    (2) Ministry of AAYUSH
    (3) Ministry of Drinking Water and Sanitation
    (4) Ministry of Health and Family Welfare
    (5) Ministry of Human Resource Development

53. The Tarun Ramadorai panel set up by the Reserve Bank of India (RBI) has been tasked to look at the variousfacets of the______.
    (1) Household finance in India
    (2) Digital Banking initiatives
    (3) Demonetisation
    (4) Promotion of financial inclusion
    (5) Feasibility of Islamic banking in India

54. The 'Bandodkar Gold Trophy' is associated with the game of
    (1) Basketball
    (2) Badminton
    (3) Football
    (4) Cricket
    (5) Tennis

55. Which of the following Indian wrestlers clinched a Gold medal in the 65 kg category in the 2017 Asian Wrestling Championships final recently (May 2017)?
    (1) BajrangPunia
    (2) Kavita Dalal
    (3) Sushil Kumar
    (4) Yogeshwar Dutt
    (5) Geeta Phogat

56. The RBI recently asked banks to follow the instructions of government organisation CERT-In to prevent attack by which ransomware
    (1) CryptoLocker
    (2) Storm Worm
    (3) WannaCry
    (4) Tiny Banker
    (5) Regin

57. The government recently took away the task of selecting candidates to run state-run financial institutions from which body?

(1) Cabinet Committee of Economic Affairs

(2) Monetary Policy Committee

(3) Banks Board Bureau

(4) Indian Banking Association

(5) Reserve Bank of India

58. Which of the following is not a money market instrument?

(1) Certificates of Deposit

(2) Commercial Paper

(3) Bills of exchange

(4) Treasury Bills

(5) None of these given as options

59. The '2017 World Table Tennis Championships was recently (29 May- 5 June 2017) held in which of the following country?

(1) Japan   (2) France

(3) Germany   (4) UK

(5) Singapore

60. The statutory base for the Depositor Education and Awareness Fund (DEAF) constituted by the Reserve Bank of India is provided by______

(1) Section 21A of the Reserve Bank of India Act, 1935

(2) Section 21A of the Banking Companies Act, 1976

(3) Section 26 A of the Reserve Bank of India Act, 1935

(4) Section 26A of the Banking Regulation Act, 1949

(5) Section 21A of the Banking Regulation Act, 1949

61. Which of the following mountaineers is the first Indian to summit Mount Everest a record six times?

(1) Loveraj Singh

(2) Mohan Singh Gunjyal

(3) H.P.S. Ahluwalia

(4) Harish Kapadia

(5) Jamling Tenzing Norgay

62. ______ provide liquidity for global financial system and capital markets make up financial market.

(1) Capital Markets

(2) Derivative markets

(3) Money Markets

(4) Stock markets

(5) None of these given as options

63. The India Aspiration Fund (IAF) is a fund of funds that would Invest in venture capital funds for meeting the capital requirement of______?

(1) Agriculture Sector

(2) Housing Sector

(3) Mid Corporates

(4) MSME start-ups

(5) Electronics Sector

64. Which of the following banks recently became the first bank against which the revised PCA was invoked by the RBI?

(1) State Bank of India

(2) IDBI Bank

(3) ICICI Bank

(4) Punjab National Bank

(5) Syndicate Bank

65. A security whose income payments and hence value are derived from and collateralized (or "backed") by a specified pool of underlying assets is known as

(1) Structured security

(2) Asset backed security

(3) Collateral security

(4) Security against value

(5) Derived security

66. 'Equity-linked Savings Scheme' (ELSS) are open-ended diversified equity schemes offered by

(1) Stock exchanges (2) Commercial Banks

(3) Primary Dealer   (4) Mutual Funds

(5) SEBI

67. India's first Small Finance Bank, the 'Capital Small Finance Bank' is headquartered in______.

(1) Chennai   (2) Jaipur

(3) Bengaluru   (4) Mumbai

(5) Jalandhar

68. The alphabet 'D' in the abbreviation 'NSDL' stands for
(1) Derivative
(2) Debt
(3) Dematerlalisation
(4) Depository
(5) Demand

69. The 'LTV ratio' is a financial term commonly used by lenders and building securities to express the ratio of a loan to the value of an asset purchased. The alphabet 'V' in the abbreviation 'LTV' stands for
(1) Virtual (2) Valuation
(3) Voluntary (4) Value
(5) Visual

70. India's first underwater metrorail tunnel has recently (May 2017) been completed under the______.
(1) Yamuna River (2) Gomati River
(3) Hooghly River (4) Krishna River
(5) Narmada River

71. The recently launched 'Paytm Payments Bank' is permitted to open savings accounts wherein customers shall be able to hold maximum amounts of up to________.
(1) Rs. 2,00,000 (2) Rs. 1,00,000
(3) Rs. 50,000 (4) Rs. 5,00,000
(5) Rs. 10,00,000

72. The 'External Commercial Borrowing' (ECB) guidelines and policies are regulated and monitored by the Reserve Bank of India along with________.
(1) Department of Economic Affairs
(2) Department of Revenue
(3) Department of Investment and Asset Management
(4) Department of Expenditure
(5) None of these

73. Which of the following Indian businessman is amongst the Forbes list of annual '25 Global Game Changers' 2017 in transforming their industries and changing the lives of billions of people around the globe?
(1) Gautam Adani
(2) Rakesh Jhunjhunwala
(3) Vijay Shekhar Sharma
(4) Mukesh Ambani
(5) Radhika Prasad

74. Under the NEFT system, fund transfers are presently settled at hourly intervals from 8 am to 7 pm on all working days in periodical batches. The RBI has recently announced to raise the number of hourly batches from 12 to
(1) 22 (2) 23
(3) 24 (4) 25
(5) 26

75. The Reserve Bank of India (RBI) has recently permitted banks to open 'banking outlets' in Tier-1 to Tier-6 centre swithout having the need to take RBI permission. The rationalization is however not applicable to ______.
(1) Private Sector Bank
(2) Public Sector Bank
(3) Payments Bank
(4) Small Finance Bank
(5) Regional Rural Bank

76. The 'International Fertiliser Industry Association' (IFIA) having about 500 members, worldwide including 68 countries is based in______.
(1) Strasbourg, France
(2) Washington DC, USA
(3) Geneva, Switzerland
(4) Paris, France
(5) Frankfurt, Germany

77. The author of the book, 'Mann Ki Baat: A Social Revolution on Radio' is________.
(1) Shri Rajesh Jain (2) Shri Anand Jain
(3) Shri Suresh Jain (4) Shri Kailash Jain
(5) Shri Naveen Jain

78. According to the recent data (May 2017) released by the International Stainless Steel Forum (ISSF), the largest producer of Stainless Steel in the world in 2016 was ________.
(1) Russia
(2) China
(3) India
(4) USA
(5) UK

79. Who amongst the following has recently been elected as one of the members of 'Badminton World Federation' (BWF) Athletes' Commission?

(1) Saina Nehwal

(2) Jwala Gutta

(3) P.C. Thulasi

(4) P.V. Sindhu

(5) Meena Shah

80. Mobile Wallets which do not permit cash withdrawal as redemption, but allows customers to buy goods and services at billed merchants and perform financial services at billed locations are known as________.

(1) Open Wallets

(2) Closed Wallets

(3) Semi-open Wallets

(4) Semi-closed Wallets

(5) Semi-blocked Wallets

ENGLISH LANGUAGE

Directions (81-85) : Read the following passage carefully to answer the given questions.

Paragraph 1: It has been obvious for some time that the creation of the euro was a terrible mistake. Europe never had the preconditions for a successful single currency above all, the kind of fiscal and banking union that, for example, ensures that when a housing bubble in Florida bursts, Washington automatically protects seniors against any threat to their medical care or their bank deposits.

Paragraph 2 : Leaving a currency union is, however, a much harder and more frightening decision than never entering in the first place, and until now even the Continent's most troubled economies have repeatedly stepped back from the brink. Again and again, governments have submitted to creditors' demands for harsh austerity, while the European Central Bank has managed to contain market panic.

Paragraph 3 : But the situation in Greece has now reached what looks like a **point of no return**. Banks are temporarily closed and the government has imposed capital controls limits on the movement of funds out of the country. It seems highly likely that the government will soon have to start paying pensions and wages in scrip, in effect creating a parallel currency. And next week the country will hold a referendum on whether to accept the demands of the "troika" - the institutions representing creditor interests - for yet more austerity.

Paragraph 4 : Greece should vote "no," and the Greek government should be ready, if necessary, to leave the euro. To understand this, we need to realize that most - not all, but most - of what we have heard about Greek profligacy and irresponsibility is false. Yes, the Greek government was spending beyond its means in the late 2000s.

But since then it has repeatedly slashed spending and raised taxes. Government employment has fallen more than 25 per cent, and pensions (which were indeed much too generous) have been cut sharply. If all this is added up, all the austerity measures have been more than enough to eliminate the original deficit and turn it into a large surplus. So why didn't this happen? Because the Greek economy collapsed, largely as a result of those very austerity measures, dragging revenues down with it.

Paragraph 5: And this collapse, in turn, had a lot to do with the euro, which trapped Greece in an economic straitjacket. Cases of successful austerity, in which countries rein in deficits without bringing on a depression, typically involve large currency devaluations that make their exports more competitive. This is what happened, for example, in Canada in the 1990s, and to an important extent it's what happened in Iceland more recently. But Greece, without its own currency, didn't have that option.

Paragraph 6 : So have I just made the case for "Grexit" - Greek exit from the euro? Not necessarily. The problem with Grexit has always been the risk of financial chaos, of a banking system disrupted by panicked withdrawals and of business hobbled both by banking troubles and by uncertainty over the legal status of debts. That is why successive Greek governments have acceded to austerity demands, and why even Syriza, the ruling leftist coalition, was willing to accept the austerity that has already been imposed. All it asked for was, in effect, a standstill on further austerity.

81. Through the examples of other countries, the author is trying to throw light on the fact that ________.

(A) not many countries have been successful at currency's devaluation.

(B) a country has a competitive edge only when it has a currency of its own.

(C) when implemented carefully austerity measures can provide expected results.

(1) None of (A), (B) and (C)

(2) Both (B) and (C)

(3) Only (B)

(4) Only (A)

(5) Other than those given as options

82. Which of the following can replace the idiom 'point of no return' as used in the passage?

(1) Barking up the wrong tree

(2) Be glad to see the back of

(3) Light at the end of the tunnel

(4) Back to the drawing board

(5) None of the given options

83. Which of the following are author's views on Grexit?

(1) Greece's exit from the euro zone will aid in taking the country out of the crisis.

(2) None of the given options

(3) Banks will be compelled to lend more.

(4) Greeks must be unwilling to leave euro

(5) Grexit will lead to political unrest in neighbouring countries.

84. Which of the following best summarises Paragraph 4?

(A) Greece' government failed in anticipating the consequences of its action.

(B) Greece's economy collapsed owing to implementation of austerity measures.

(C) Greece's government intends to introduce measures in order to bring the crisis under control.

(1) Only (A)

(2) None of (A), (B) and (C)

(3) Only (B)

(4) Both (B) and (C)

(5) Both (A) and (B)

85. Which of the following can be the concluding sentence to the passage?

(1) Greece, without its own currency, will lead its neighbouring countries to a downfall.

(2) Grexit is inevitable and will take its economy out of crisis.

(3) The Grexit is unlikely to benefit either the country or global economy.

(4) In order to experience brighter days, austerity measures must be eased.

(5) Syriza will continue to play a critical role in Grexit

86. In this question a sentence is given with three words/ group of words in **bold** type. One or more of them may have a certain error. Below the sentence is given three combinations of words/group of words i.e. (A), (B) and (C). **You have to find out the correct word/group of words** from among (A), (B) and (C) given below each sentence to replace the incorrect words/group of words and make the sentence grammatically correct and meaningful. One, two, all three or none of them may be correct. Decide upon which is/are correct, if any, and select the option which decides you answer. **If the sentence is correct as it is, select 'No correction required'** as your answer.

Much concentration of carbon dioxide in the ocean water is making it more acidic and that **harms to** creatures such as crabs and syllis, whose calcium carbonate shells **impact** as marine chemistry alters.

(A) A higher percentage of - will have- have impact

(B) More- harming- wounded

(C) Greater concentration offends to harm- suffer

(1) All (A), (B) and (C)

(2) Only (A)

(3) Only (C)

(4) Only (B)

(5) None of (A), (B) and (C)

87. In this question, there are two statements which can be combined into a single statement in a number of different ways without changing their meaning. Below there are given three probable starters (A), (B) and (C) of such a combined sentence. One, two, three or none of them may be correct. Decide upon which is/are correct, if any, and select the option which denotes your answer. If none of the three starters is suitable, select 'None' as your answer.

I. Technology is beginning to shake up finance.

II. Moreover, technology is already employed for tasks such as compliance, risk management and fraud prevention.

(A) In the beginning of shaking up finance...

(B) It is unexpected that technology can be...

(C) With already being employed for tasks such as....

(1) None

(2) Only (A)

(3) Only (C)

(4) Both (A) and (B)

(5) Both (A) and (C)

Directions (88-90): In each of the following questions, identify the sentence in which the idiom/idiomatic expression given in **bold**, has been correctly given and select that alternative as the answer.

88. (A) The socialist was suspicious of the businessman's malicious intent as he believed that the latter was **not playing with a full deck.**

(B) The launch of Bitcoins **changed the face of** ciyptocurrency and digital payment system.?

(C) Due to low demand for the product, the manufacturers of the product hold **all the aces**.

(1) All the three (A), (B) and (C)

(2) Only (C)

(3) Both (B) and (C)

(4) Only (B)

(5) Only (A)

89. (A) When the show got cancelled, the organisers **felt a bit under the weather** as they got the news of the approaching storm.

(B) The author's popularity lies in the fact that through her writing she makes the reader believe that **every cloud has silver lining.**

(C) Though she hates to speak in public, but she will get up on a stage to stance **at the drop of a hat.**

(1) All the three (A), (B) and (C)

(2) Only (A) and (B)

(3) Only (B)

(4) Only (A) and (B)

(5) Only (B) and (C)

90. (A) When the ruling government launched their new campaign, they **cut the ground from under** their opposition s feet.

(B) The consultant went **back to the drawing board** to as he felt he is technologically incompetent to operate computers.

(C) Monika's colleagues believe that she gets undue advantage in the office **by virtue of** her beauty.

(1) Both (B) and (C)

(2) All the three (A), (B) and (C)

(3) Only (A)

(4) Only (B)

(5) Only (A) and (C)

Directions (91-95) : Read the following passage carefully and answer the given questions in the context of the passage.

In Britain alone millions of people make formal complaints each year about their banks. For them, new European rules, will open the door to a host of innovative services that analyse transactions, so an app could tell you there's a cheaper mortgage available and start the switching process for you. Apps could warn account-holders if they spend more than a predetermined amount or are about to become overdrawn, or even nudge them to save more. Customers need barely ever interact with their bank.

To date, despite dire warnings, European retail banking has been remarkably unscathed by technology-driven disruption. Customers stay loyal, and banks still do the most of the lending. Financial-technology ("fintech") companies are beginning to mount a challenge, most conspicuously in the online-payments industry in northern Europe : Sofort, iDEAL and other fintech firms conduct over half of online transactions in Germany and the Netherlands, for example. But their reach is more limited elsewhere in Europe. Physical payments are still overwhelmingly made with cash or bank cards.

One reason incumbents have proved so resilient is that fintech firms lack the customer-transaction information they need to provide many financial services. Banks can be slow to respond to requests for access to such data, or may block them altogether for security reasons. It is often either cumbersome or insecure for customers to share their own information. Banks, on the other hand, have easy access to transaction data, which they can use to sell their customers other services. Regulators, however, are about to transform the landscape. The Payments Services Directive 2 (PSD2), due to be implemented by EU members in January 2018, aims to kick- start competition while making payments more secure. Provided the customer has given explicit consent, banks will be forced to share customer-account information with licensed financial-services providers.

This should change the way payment services work. They could become more integrated into the internet-browsing experience- enabling, for example, one-click bank transfers, at least for low-value payments. Security for payments above o30 ($32) will be tightened up, with customers having to provide two pieces of secret information ("strong authentication") to wave through a transaction. With access to account data, meanwhile, fintech firms could offer customers budgeting advice, or guide them towards higher-interest savings accounts or cheaper mortgages. Those with limited credit histories may find it easier to borrow, too, since richer transaction data should mean more sophisticated credit checks.

None of this is good news for established banks. Profitability is already threatened by rock-bottom interest rates. In a survey conducted last year by Strategy &, a professional-services firm, 68% of responding banks believed that PDS2 would leave them in a weaker position. The same proportion feared that they would lose control of interactions with customers. Perhaps predictably, resistance is manifested as a concern about data protection: more than half of respondents to the PwC survey voiced concerns about security and liability. Such concerns are legitimate but also, argue fintech supporters, offer a convenient excuse for banks to block competition. Newcomers will be regulated, after all, and will have to convince the authorities that their data-protection systems are robust. As they are also required to be insured against fosses from fraud, they will need to convince insurers, too. They will not be subject to the same capital and stress-testing requirements banks face: but nor will they be licensed to undertake the riskier business of lending.

So PSD2 is "perfect on paper". But as implementation approaches, the rules will be watered down. Banks could also interpret them subjectively: they might delay sharing data or make them too confusing to be useful. But regulators have already bared their teeth: last year German competition authorities, citing the changes proposed in PSD2, ruled that banks were illegally restricting customers' online banking activities. Banks will have to improve, in other words. Santander's British arm, for instance, has teamed up with Kabbage, an American startup, to offer small companies working-capital loans; BBVA, a Spanish bank, acquired Holvi, a Finnish startup that helps companies track cashflow and invoices. Yet for all their complaints, customers still trust banks with their money. In Britain only 3% of customers move current accounts each year. Familiarity, huge customer bases and low funding costs are all attributes entrants want to gain by association, just as banks want to exploit newcomers technology.

91. Which of the following is/are the impact(s) that fintech firms have had on the banking sector?

    (A) Dissatisfaction among customers and millions of formal complaints each year.

    (B) Fintech firms are sapping the profitability of banks but will not kill these (banks) off.

    (C) Banks have been incentivised to improve their services.

    (1) Only (B) and (C)

    (2) Only (A) and (C)

    (3) Only (A)

    (4) Only (B)

    (5) Only (A) and (B)

92. Which of the following mentioned in passage distract from the author's control view in the passage?

(A) The survey by Strategy&.

(B) The ruling by German competition authorities.

(C) Statistics on Britain.

(1) Only (A)

(2) Only (B) and (C)

(3) Only (A) and (C)

(4) Only (C)

(5) All three (A), (B) and (C)

93. Which of the following can be inferred in the context of the passage?

(A) PSD2 could improve the services available to European bank customers.

(B) The financial sector in Europe is headed for a shake up.

(C) Most European banks are in precarious financial condition.

(1) None of (A), (B) and (C)

(2) Only (A) and (B)

(3) Only (A) and (C)

(4) Only (A)

(5) Only (B)

94. Which of the following is/are a likely step that the author will support?

(A) Banks partnering with fintech firms.

(B) Banks competing with fintech firms and utilising customer transaction data to provide novel services.

(C) Enforcing the same capital and stress-testing requirements banks face for fintech firms.

(1) Only (C)   (2) Only (A)

(3) Only (B) and (C)   (4) Only (A) and (B)

(5) None

95. Which of the following describe(s) the author's views in the passage?

(A) Sharing customer data available with banks with fintech companies is good for consumers and banks.

(B) Fintech firms are not yet a complete substitution for the day-to-day operations of banks.

(C) Banks view PSD2 as a Brexit.

(1) Only (B)

(2) Only (C)

(3) All three (A), (B) and (C)

(4) Only (B) and (C)

(5) None

96. In this question, there are two statements which can be combined into a single statement in a number of different ways without changing their meaning. Below there are given three probable starters (A), (B) and (C) of such a combined sentence. One, two, three or none of them may be correct. Decide upon which is/are correct, if any, and select the option which denotes your answer. If none of the three starters is suitable, select 'None' as your answer.

I.   As investors try to achieve their goal, they draw on the work of academics.

II. In doing so, they are both changing the markets and the way academics understand them.

(A) When investors failed to achieve their goal, …

(B) Not only do they draw on the work of academics …

(C) However, in doing so, they are both …

(1) Both (A) and (B)

(2) Only (A)

(3) Only (B)

(4) All the three (A), (B) and (C)

(5) Both (B) and (C)

97. In this question, two sentences (I) and (II) are given. Each sentence (I) and (II) has a blank in it. Below these sentences (I) & (II) four/five options are suggested. Select the option that fits both the blanks to make the sentence meaningful and grammatically correct. If all the given options fit the blanks, select 'All the given options fit' as your answer.

I.   Finland has become the first country to license and start building a final repository for highly radioactive_____fuel from nuclear reactors.

II. The amount of ______that countries produce tends to grow in tandem with their economies, especially with the rate of urbanisation,

(1) All the given options fit

(2) pollution

(3) dirt

(4) waste

(5) mechanics

98. In this question a sentence is given with three words/ group of words in **bold** type. One or more of them may have a certain error. Below the sentence is given three combinations of words/group of words i.e. (A), (B) and (C). **You have to find out the correct word/group of words** from among (A), (B) and (C) given below each sentence to replace the incorrect words/group of words and make the sentence grammatically correct and meaningful. One, two, all three or none of them may be correct. Decide upon which is/are correct, if any, and select the option which decides you answer. If the sentence is correct as it is. select '**No correction required**' as your answer.

Though the **either option** for Britain is to revert to trading with the EU as America, China and India as, under normal World Trade Organisation rules, next economics say this **would** make economic damage from Brexit **worse**.

(A) only way-would likely-exacer-bate

(B) explore-is likely to-better

(C) alternative-could-worsen

(1) Only (C)

(2) No correction required

(3) All (A), (B) and (C)

(4) Only (A) and (B)

(5) Only (A)

99. In this question, there are two statements which can be combined into a single statement in a number of different ways without changing their meaning. Below there are given three probable starters (A), (B) and (C) of such a combined sentence. One, two, three or none of them may be correct. Decide upon which is/are correct, if any, and select the option which denotes your answer. If none of the three starters is suitable, select 'None' as your answer.

I. The fear that business travellers on transatlantic flights might have to stop working on spreadsheets and read a good book instead had been palpable.

II. It had been expected to announce that all electronic gadgets such as tablets and laptops would henceforth have to be put in check-in luggage.

(A) As a threat to public safety which pilots ensure...

(B) In case travellers in transatlantic flights....

(C) Without the fear...

(1) None   (2) Only (A)

(3) Both (A) and (B)   (4) Only (C)

(5) Only (B)

100. In this question a paragraph with a blank space indicated by (______) is given. The blank space stands for a sentence which fits contextually but is presently hidden. From the given alternatives, find the sentence which is the perfect fit in terms of grammar as well as context in the blank space of the paragraph.

The payment mechanism is simple enough. Newcomers provide details of a credit card or bank account. These are verified with a nominal transaction. Thereafter, a buyer can e-mail a payment directly to a seller. This is immediately debited from the buyer's credit card or bank account, and a credit is made to the seller's 'wallet' account. Money to a wallet account can be withdrawn by cheque or transferred to a bank account. It can take several weeks for cheques to arrive in the post and for payments to clear, but online payments are made instantly. (___). It has improved the velocity of trade.

(1) Security remains the prime concern of internet shoppers.

(2) The company has faced regulatory challenges, not least because it could be used for the illicit transfer of funds.

(3) This means goods can be shipped right away.

(4) To overcome their concerns, payment protection is now offered in America (up to $500) and in Britain (up to £250) on goods sold by eligible traders.

(5) All the given options

101. In this question, two sentences (I) and (II) are given. Each sentence (I) and (II) has a blank in it. Below these sentences (I) and (II) four/five options are suggested. Select the option that fits both the blanks to make the sentence meaningful and grammatically correct. If all the given options fit the blanks, select 'All the given options fit' as your answer.

   I. Translation can be lonely work, which may well be why most translators choose the career out of interest, not because they ________ attention.

   II. Still feeling the effects of the recession's high unemployment. Millennial's ________ economic stability over prosperity, hoping to avoid future downturns.

   (1) crave   (2) pine

   (3) spurn   (4) disliked

   (5) All the given options fit

Directions (102-105): In these questions there are four sentences (A), (B). (C) and (D). You have to determine which of these sentences is/are grammatically corrective/correct based on the question given. Select the appropriate option as your answer.

102. Which of these sentences is/are correct?

   (A) The Government has decided to extend coverage under newly launch schemes which impart training to unemployed youth.

   (B) Being a very diligent and clever lad, he soon distinguished himself.

   (C) Grievances need be readdressed as soon as they are known.

   (D) It is the grasping of power combined with the thrust for fame which constitutes ambition.

   (1) Only (B) and (D)

   (2) Only (A), (B) and (C)

   (3) Only (D)

   (4) Only (A)

   (5) Only (A) and (D)

103. Which of these sentences is/ are correct?

   (A) The idea on which she based her philosophy is difficult to understand.

   (B) Ramesh was reprieved as the prosecution failed to pin him up for the crime.

   (C) The President already with acquaintance with the latest development of the current situation.

   (D) Superstitious fears preys on vulnerable mind, and make one behave non-sensical.

   (1) Only (A) and (D)

   (2) Only (C)

   (3) Only (A)

   (4) Only (B) and (D)

   (5) Only (A) and (C)

104. Which of these sentences is/are correct?

   (A) Manisha says she has not seen neither Abhay nor Bipasha all day.

   (B) The bureaucrats reached and out and established a good base for future relation.

   (C) Kaustabh believed that he was in some parts responsible for his own fate.

   (D) Roshan, quite pale in night, rushed into the room.

   (1) All are correct

   (2) Only (A) and (B)

   (3) Only (B)

   (4) Only (B) and (D)

   (5) None

105. Which of these sentences is/ are correct?

   (A) In a communication since January, the two organisations finally decided to merger.

   (B) The Parliament and the Supreme Court was within stone throw distance of each other.

   (C) His nation can be perfectly well in governance till they are competent to govern itself.

   (D) She impressed above him that he need to commit perjury in order to be acquitted.

   (1) Only (A)

   (2) None

   (3) Only (A) and (C)

   (4) Only (B) and (D)

   (5) All are correct

Directions (106-109): In these questions, a sentence is given with three words/ group of words in **bold** type. One or more of them may have a certain error. Below the sentence is given three combinations of words/group of words i.e. (A), (B) (C). **You have to**

find out the correct word/group of words from among (A), (B) and (C) given below each sentence to replace the incorrect words/group of words and make sentence grammatically correct and meaningful. One, two, all three orone of them may be correct. Decipe upon which is/are correct, if any select the option which decides your answer. If the sentence correct as it is, select '**No correction required**' as your answer.

106. Machine-learning, a subset of artificial intelligence (Al) that excels **finds** patterns and making predictions, in beginning and **shook** finance as much as that from 2019, anyone seeking to because a "chartered financial analyst" **need to be an Al expert**.

   (A) in pinpointing- to change- expertise

   (B) at finding- to stake up- will need Al expertise

   (C) at identifying- and shaking- attains Al expertise

   (1) Only (A) and (B)

   (2) Only (B)

   (3) Only (C)

   (4) Only (A) and (C)

   (5) Only (A)

107. The employment bill, **which past its** first test in the Parliament it **aims to** give most new employees increased, emoluments **potentially** improving their lot.

   (A) has not passed its- and intends to-and so

   (B) that has passed its- aims at- thereby

   (C) which is set to pass its- will- thus

   (1) Only (A) and (C)

   (2) Only (B) and (C)

   (3) No correction required

   (4) Only (C)

   (5) Only (B)

108. Fighting **for** sensations that sought to claim him, he moved **nervous** and the note in his hand rattled **for** a dry and ominous whisper.

   (A) against - nervous - with

   (B) for - nervously - by

   (C) against - nervously - with

   (1) Only (A)   (2) Only (C)

   (3) Only (A) and (B)   (4) Only (B) and (C)

   (5) No correction required

109. **By drawing up** the past two years by a coalition of central bankers, the global code of conduct for the forex market **has been down** international standards on a range of practices, from the **dealing with** confidential information to the pricing and settlement of deals.

   (A) Developed over- is expected to lay out - management of

   (B) Drawn up over- will lay down-processing of

   (C) After being worked on for- has laid down - handling of

   (1) Only (B)

   (2) Only (B) and (C)

   (3) All (A), (B) and (C)

   (4) Only (A) and (B)

   (5) No correction required

110. In this question, two sentences (I) and (II) are given. Each sentence (I) and (II) has a blank in it. Below these sentences (I) and (II) four/five options are suggested. Select the option that fits both the blanks to make the sentence meaningful and grammatically correct. If all the given options fit the blanks, select 'All the given options fit' as your answer.

   I. As an officer he was_____and did never dispute my orders or argue upon them.

   II. A small handful of______peasants, priest-ridden and over-administered, formed the basis of the colony.

   (1) adamant   (2) happy

   (3) obedient   (4) obstinate

   (5) lonely

QUANTITATIVE APTITUDE

111. A can complete a project in 20 days and B can complete the same project in 30 days. If A and B start working on the project together and A quits 10 days before the project is completed, in how many days will the project be completed?

   (1) 18 days

   (2) 27 days

   (3) 26.67 days

   (4) 16 days

   (5) 12 days

112. A runs 25% faster than B and is able to allow B a lead of 7 metres to end a race in dead heat. What is the length of the race?

(1) 10 metres

(2) 25 metres

(3) 45 metres

(4) 15 metres

(5) 35 metres

113. A train travelling at 100 kmph overtakes a motorbike travelling at 64 kmph in 40 seconds. What is the length of the train in meters?

(1) 1777 metres

(2) 1822 metres

(3) 400 metres

(4) 1111 metres

(5) 520 metres

Directions (114-118) : Study the following graph and table to answer the given questions.

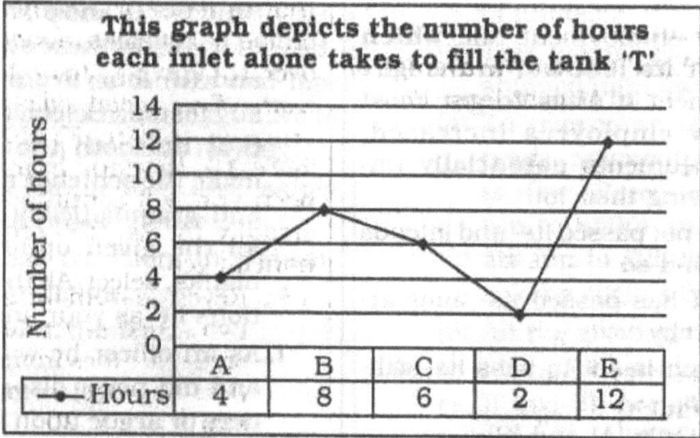

This table depicts the number of hours taken by each outlet alone to empty the full tank T

Outlets	Number of hours
W	—
X	34
Y	-
Z	30

114. The time taken to fill the empty tank completely when inlet A and outlet X were opened together was 6 hours 40 minutes less than that taken by inlet B and outlet W together. How much time will outlet W alone take to completely empty the full tank? (in hours)

(1) 26   (2) 28

(3) 20   (4) 48

(5) 24

115. When the tank was completely full, outlets X and Y were opened together for 8 hours 30 minutes. Both were then closed and inlet A was opened which filled the tank completely in 3 hours 30 minutes. In how much time (in hours) will outlet Y alone empty the full tank?

(1) 15 hours   (2) 13.6 hours

(3) 13 hours   (4) 14 hours

(5) 15.5 hours

116. When the tank was completely full, outlets X and Z were opened together for 'H' hours. Had outlet Z been open alone, it would have taken 'H + 10' hours to empty the same quantity of water from the tank. What is the value of 'H'?

(1) 10   (2) 18

(3) $11\dfrac{1}{3}$ (4) $18\dfrac{1}{3}$

(5) $10\dfrac{2}{3}$

117. Inlet E was open for 2 hours and then closed. If the remaining tank was filled by inlets B and C together, what was the total time (in hours) taken to fill the tank completely?

(1) $5\dfrac{1}{7}$ (2) $5\dfrac{4}{7}$

(3) $4\dfrac{3}{7}$ (4) $4\dfrac{6}{7}$

(5) $5\dfrac{6}{7}$

118. When the tank was completely empty, inlets A, D and E were opened for one hour each and then closed. If after that outlet Z was opened, how much time (in hours) will it take to empty the tank completely?

(1) $15\dfrac{2}{5}$ (2) 18

(3) 17   (4) 20

(5) 25

119. A boat running upstream takes 8 hours 48 minutes to cover a certain distance, while it takes 4 hours to cover the same distance running downstream. What is the ratio between the speed of the boat in still water and speed of the water current respectively?

(1) 2:1   (2) 3 : 2

(3) 8:3   (4) 3 : 5

(5) 8 : 2

120. A, B and C jointly thought of engaging themselves in a business venture. It was agreed that A would invest Rs. 6500 for 6 months, B, Rs. 8400 for 5 months and C, Rs. 10.000 for 3 months. A wants to be the working member for which, he was to receive 5% of the profits. The profit earned was Rs. 7400. What is the share of B in the profit?

(1) Rs. 1900   (2) Rs. 2660

(3) Rs. 2800   (4) Rs. 2840

(5) Rs. 2900

121. How much time will it take for an amount of Rs. 900 to years Rs. 81 as interest at 4.5% PCI annum of simple interest?

(1) 2 years   (2) 3 years

(3) 1 year   (4) 4 years

(5) 5 years

122. Mr. Thomas invested an amount of Rs. 13,900 divided in two different schemes A and B at the simple interest rate of 14% per annum and 11% per annum respectively. If the total amount of simple interest earned in 2 years be Rs. 3508, what was the amount invested in scheme B?

(1) Rs. 6400   (2) Rs. 7200

(3) Rs. 6500   (4) Rs. 7500

(5) Rs. 7000

123. A bag contains 2 red, 3 green and 2 blue balls. Two balls are drawn at random. What is the' probability that none of the balls drawn is blue?

(1) $\dfrac{10}{21}$ (2) $\dfrac{11}{21}$

(3) $\dfrac{2}{7}$ (4) $\dfrac{5}{7}$

(5) $\dfrac{3}{7}$

124. A can contains a mixture of two liquids A and B in the ratio 7 : 5. When 9 litres of mixture is drawn off and the can is filled with B, the ratio of A and B becomes 7: 9. How many litres of liquid A were contained by the can initially?

(1) 10   (2) 20

(3) 21   (4) 25

(5) 29

125. A circular swimming pool is surrounded by a concrete wall 4 ft. wide. If the area of the concrete wall surrounding the pool is $\dfrac{11}{25}$ that of the pool, then the radius of the pool is

(1) 8ft   (2) 16ft

(3) 20ft   (4) 30ft

(5) None of these

Directions (126-130) : In the given questions, two quantities are given, one as Quantity I and another as Quantity II. You have to determine relationship between two quantities and choose the appropriate option.

(1)   If Quantity I > Quantity II

(2)   If Quantity I > Quantity II

(3)   If Quantity I < Quantity II

(4)   If Quantity I = Quantity II

or the relationship cannot be established from the information that is given.

(5)   Quantity I < Quantity II

126. The boat takes total time of 4 hours to travel 14 km upstream and 36 km downstream together. The boat takes total time of 5 hours to travel 20 km up-stream and 24 km downstream together?

Quantity I :

Speed of the boat in still water (in km/h).

Quantity II:

16 km/h

127. M is an integer selected at random from the set.

(7, 14, 25, 27, 33, 29 and 30)

Quantity I :

Probability that the average of 12, 9 and M is at least 17.

Quantity II : $\dfrac{1}{3}$

128. $\left(\dfrac{x^2}{5}\right) + x + \left(\dfrac{4}{5}\right) = 0$

$3\,y^2 + 4y + 1 = 0$

Quantity I : x

Quantity II : y

129. $mn \neq 0$

Quantity I : $m = n$

Quantity II : m/n

130. A and B can together finish a piece of work in 20 days. If B starts working and after 15 days is replaced by A, A can finish the remaining work in 24 days.

Quantity I : Number of days taken by B alone to finish the same piece of work.

Quantity II : Number of days taken by A alone to finish the same piece of work.

Directions (131-135) : Study the given information carefully and answer the given questions.

The revenue of a given railway zone was collected from 4 primary sources- Offline Ticket Sales, Online Ticket Sales, Freight, Fines- during 3 Financial Years (FY 2013- 14, FY 2014-15, FY 2015-16)

FY 2013-14 : Total revenue collected was Rs. 3500 crore. Fines (Rs. x crore) comprised $7\dfrac{6}{7}\%$ of the total revenue and revenue from online ticket sales was Rs. 'x + 300' crore. Revenue from freight was 12% more than that from offline ticket sales.

FY 2014-15 : Revenue from online ticket sales increased by Rs. 25 crore over FY 2013-14. Revenue from Offline ticket sales was 40% of the total revenue in FY 2014-15. Revenue from Freight and Fines was in the respective ratio of 5 : 1.

FY 2015-16 : Revenue from fines in FY 2013-14 was $\dfrac{11}{16}$th of that in FY 2015-16. Revenue from online ticket sales increased by 50% over that in FY 2014-15 and that from offline ticket sales was the average of that in FY 2013-14 and 2014-15. Revenue from freight has been and will continue to increase steadily by Rs. 250 crore every financial year.

131. Revenue from fines comprised two sources- vendors and passengers. Fines from passengers (Rs. y crore) remained constant in FY 2013-14 and FY 2014-15. If the fine from vendors in FY 2013-14 was 55% of that in FY 2014-15, what was the value of y?

(1) 180   (2) 200

(3) 218   (4) 208

(5) 220

132. If the railway profit in FY 2014-15 was 12.5% of the total expense, what was the total expense for FY 2014-15? (in Rs. crore)

(1) 2900

(2) 2400

(3) 3200

(4) 3000

(5) 3822

133. In FY 2017-18, if the revenue from fines increases by 20% over FY 2015-16, what would be the ratio between the revenues from fines and freight in FY 2017-18?

(1) 2 : 3   (2) 1 : 5

(3) 2 : 5   (3) 3 : 4

(5) 4 : 5

134. If the average revenue from online ticket sales in FY 2014-15. FY 2015-16 and FY 2016-17 was Rs. 1150 crore. By what per cent did the revenue from online ticket sales increase in FY 2016-17 as compared to that in 2014-15?

(1) 250

(2) 150

(3) 300

(3) 225

(5) 230

135. If the average cost of a railway ticket was Rs. 300 in FY 2014-15, how many passengers (approx) travelled by railways in FY 2014-15? (in Rs. crore)

(1) 4.8   (2) 6.4

(3) 6.2   (4) 5.4

(5) 7.73

Directions (136-140) : Refer to the pie-charts to answer the given questions.

Data regarding five villages — A, B, C, D and E — in a district in 2015.

Total village population = 18000

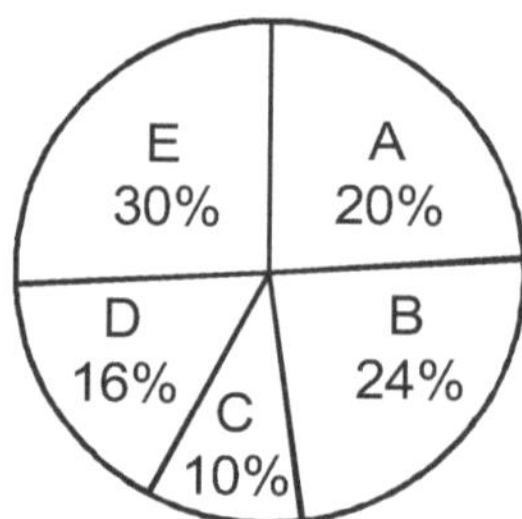

Total number of Illiterates = 40% of Total village population

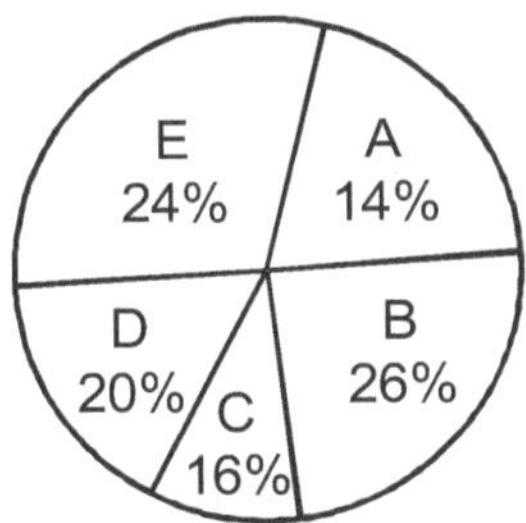

Total village population = Number of literates + Number of Illiterates

136. In 2017, the population of village C remained the same as that in 2015, but the number of literates increased by 'x' As a result, the total number of literates became 70% of that of illiterates. What is the approximate value of 'x'?

(1) 620   (2) 440

(3) 680   (4) 485

(5) 430

137. The difference between the number of illiterates in villages D and E is approximately what per cent of that of literates in village D and E ?

(1) 30%   (2) 20%

(3) 35%   (4) 13%

(5) 15%

138. In village D, the male to female ratio among the illiterates is 5 : 3 respectively, Out of the illiterates, if 'x' females and '1.25x' males work as farmers and the ratio between males and females who do not work as farmers is 5 : 2 respectively, what is the value of 'x'?

(1) 240   (2) 300

(3) 360   (4) 380

(5) 280

139. The average number of illiterates in villages D, F and G is 1910. 40% and 30% of the population of villages F and G respectively are illiterates. If the ratio of the population of villages F and G is 4 : 5 respectively, what is the total population of villages F and G together ?

(1) 10000   (2) 12000

(3) 12456   (4) 13000

(5) 14000

140. In village A, if the respective ratio between number of males and females is 17 : 13 and there are 1000 male literates, what is the number of male illiterates in village A ?

(1) 480   (2) 540

(3) 940   (4) 1040

(5) 1140

Directions (141-146) : Study the following information carefully and answer the questions given below:

When a word and number arrangement machine is given an input line of words and numbers. It arranges them following a particular rule. The following is an illustration of input and rearrangement:

(All the numbers are two-digit numbers before performing the operations)

Input :   tweet 43 also 13 suit 29 money kite 71 59

Step I :   Is tweet 43 13 suit 29 money kite 59 73

Step II :   kt Is tweet 43 13 suit 29 money 73 61

Step III :   mny kt Is tweet 13 suit 29 73 61 47

Step IV :   st mny kt Is tweet 13 73 61 47 31

Step V :   twt st mny kt Is 73 61 47 31 17

Step V is the last step of the above arrangement as the intended output of arrangement is obtained.

As per the rules followed in the given Steps, find the appropriate Steps for the given input.

Input :   neat bites 23 11 piles your 37 79 give 47

141. As per the given arrangement, in Step IV, 'pls' is related to 'gv' following a certain pattern. Following the same pattern, '83' is related to '41' in Step III. In Step V, to which of the following is 'bts' related to following the same pattern?

(1) 29   (2) 41

(3) 53   (4) nt

(5) yr

142. Which is the third element to the left of the seventh element, from the left end in Step V of the given arrangement?

(1) gv   (2) 53

(3) nt   (4) 23

(5) 83

143. How many elements are there between 'your' and '83' in Step III of the given arrangement?

(1) None   (2) Two

(3) Three   (4) One

(5) More than three

144. Which is the fourth element to the right of '11' in the Step IV of the given arrangement?

(1) 29

(2) 41

(3) bts

(4) 83

(5) your

145. In which one of the following Steps is 'bts 11 your' found consecutively in the same order in the given arrangement?

(1) Step II

(2) Step III

(3) There is no such Step

(4) Step V

(5) Step IV

146. In Step II of the given arrangement, which elements appear to the immediate right and immediate left of 'neat' respectively?

(1) '37'and 'piles'   (2) 'give' and '11'

(3) '11' and 'your'   (4) '23' and 'bts'

(5) 'piles' and 'gv'

147. This question consists of a decision and two Statements numbered I and II given below it. You have to decide which of the given Statements weaken/s or strengthen/s the decision and decide the appropriate answer.

Decision : The Government of the State Z decided that no car in the City X shall be allowed to have tinted glasses from next month.

I. Most of the crimes reported in the past few months in City X had an involvement of cars with tinted glasses.

II. Tinted glasses were responsible for a large number of accidents in City X as they affected visibility during night.

(1) Statement I strengthens the decision while Statement II weakens the decision.

(2) Both Statement I and Statement II weaken the decision.

(3) Both Statement I and Statement II strengthen the decision.

(4) Both Statement I and Statement II are neutral statements.

(5) Statement I weakens the decision while Statement II strengthens the decision.

148. This question consists of a Situation and three Statements numbered I, II and III given below it. You have to decide which of the given Statements may be a reason for the given Situation.

Situation : Farmers of State D, who traditionally cultivate crop M, bore considerable losses owing to deficiency of nutrient Z in the soil which is vital for adequate growth of crop M. However, this year the farmers registered a 40% growth in production.

I. The farmers of State D have started producing crop Y only (which does not require nutrient Z for growth) since the past two years.

II. Since the past two years the farmers of State D have been adding a fertiliser to the soil which contains nutrient Z.

III. The nutrition this year was 200% more than the previous year in State D.

(1) Either I or III

(2) Only I

(3) All I, II and III

(4) Only III

(5) Either II or III

149. In this question, there are two Statements (A) and (B). These Statements may either be independent causes or effects of independent causes or a common cause. One of these Statements may be the effect of the other Statement. Read both the Statements carefully and decide which of the following answer choice correctly depicts the relationship between these two Statements.

(A) Around 60% of the computer and software professionals of Country X wish to pursue ethical hacking.

(B) The IT companies in three of the neighbouring countries of Country X recently faced an attack of 'Hacker Virus' in many of their systems.

(1) Both statements (A) and (B) are independent causes.

(2) Both statements (A) and (B) are effects of some common cause.

(3) Statement (B) is the cause and statement (A) is its effect.

(4) Statement (A) is the cause and statement (B) is its effect.

(5) Both the Statement (A) and (B) are effects of independent causes

150. In which of the given expressions does the expression $R \leq T$ definitely holds true?

(1) $T \geq L \geq M; R \geq O \geq M$

(2) $T > L \leq M; R \leq M \leq O$

(3) $T > L > M; R > O > M$

(4) $T \geq L \geq M; R \leq O \leq M$

(5) $T > L = M; R < O \leq M$

Directions (151-155) : Study the following information carefully and answer the questions given below :

Seven people — P, Q, R, S, T, U and V — are related to each other in some or the other way. Each person is of a different age, but not necessarily in the same order.

(**Note :** It is assumed that the husband is older than the wife.)

T is older than V but younger than U. P is the mother of Q. R is the sister-in-law of P. R is unmarried. T is the daughter-in-law of S. S is the eldest member of the family. U is the father of only R and V. U does not have any sibling. V does not have any son. R is older than V. The third eldest member of the family is 54-years old. The youngest member of the family is 4 years old.

151. If in the given arrangement, Q + V = 31, then what is the possible age of R?
   (1) 27   (2) 56
   (3) 23   (4) 59
   (5) 30

152. If P is 24 years old, what will be the sum of ages of P and T?
   (1) 28   (2) 78
   (3) 64   (4) 49
   (5) 75

153. How is T related to Q?
   (1) Grandmother   (2) Granddaughter
   (3) Aunt   (4) Mother-in-law
   (5) Mother

154. If M is married to S, then how is S related to R?
   (1) Grandmother
   (2) Granddaughter
   (3) Grandfather
   (4) Uncle
   (5) Cannot be determined

155. Who amongst the following is/are younger than V?
   (1) Both P and U   (2) Only Q
   (3) Only P   (4) Both P and Q
   (5) No one

Directions (156-160) : Study the following information carefully and answer the questions given below :

Eight people — A, B, C, D, E, F, G and H — live on eight different floors of a building but not necessarily in the same order. The lower most floor of the building is numbered one, the one above that is numbered two and so on till the topmost floor is numbered eight. Eaph one of them ran for a different distance in a marathon — 2300 metre, 3800 metre, 5000 metre, 6400 metre, 7200 metre, 6300 metre, 9100 metre and 10000 metre but not necessarily in the same order.

The one who ran for 5000 metre lives on an even numbered floor above floor number 5. Only three people live between the one who ran for 5000 metre and G. The one who ran for 9100 metre lives immediately above E. Only two people live between the one who ran for 9100 metre and A. A does not live on the topmost floor. The total distance run by people living on floor number 3 and floor number 6 is 11400 metre. The one who ran for 6300 metre, lives immediately above the one who ran for 3800 metre. Neither E nor A ran for 6300 metre, Only two people live between B and the one who ran for 6300 metre. The one who lives immediately below D ran for a distance more than that of B, but not the most. No one lives between H and the one who ran for 7200 metre. E did not ran for 7200 metre. The one who ran for 10000 metre lives immediately above D. C and G together ran for 16,300 metre, C ran more than G.

156. If M ran for 2000 metre more than B, then for how many metres did M run?
   (1) 5200 metre   (2) 5800 metre
   (3) 4900 metre   (4) 7000 metre
   (5) 4300 metre

157. Which of the following statements is true with respect to the given arrangement?
   (1) D lives on the topmost floor.
   (2) Only two people live between G and F.
   (3) None of the given options is true
   (4) The one who ran for 2300 metre lives immediately above F.
   (5) A ran for 9100 metre

158. Who amongst the following lives immediately above the one who ran for 7200 metre?
   (1) The one who ran for 10000 metre
   (2) H
   (3) F
   (4) The one who ran for 3800 metre
   (5) G

159. Which of the given combinations is correct as per the given arrangement?
   (1) Floor number 7-3800 metre
   (2) Floor number 3-E
   (3) C-9100 metre
   (4) D-5000 metre
   (5) Floor number 2-7200 metre

160. How many metres did F and A together run?

   (1) 16200 metre

   (2) 7300 metre

   (3) 12900 metre

   (4) 15300 metre

   (5) 11400 metre

Directions (161-163): In these questions, three statements followed by two Conclusions numbered I and II have been given. You have to take the given statements to be true even if they seem to be at variance from commonly known facts and then decide which of the given Conclusions logically follows from the given statements.

Give answer (1) if both the Conclusion I and Conclusion II follow

Give answer (2) if either Conclusion I or Conclusion II follows

Give answer (3) if neither Conclusion I nor Conclusion II follows

Give answer (4) if only Conclusion I follows

Give answer (5) if only Conclusion II follows

(161-162) : Statements :

Some planets are stars.

All stars are comets.

No comet is an astronaut.

161. Conclusions:

   I. No star is an astronaut.

   II. All astronauts are planets.

162. Conclusions:

   I. Some planets being astronauts is a possibility.

   II. At least some comets are planets.

163. Statements :

   All trains are buses.

   All buses are rickshaws.

   No rickshaw is a plane.

Conclusions:

   I. All trains are rickshaws.

   II. All planes being trains is a possibility.

164. What should come in place of (?) in the expression P ? U = E > J; E ? M < W respectively so that the expression W > P definitely holds true?

   (1) =, <   (2) >, =

   (3) =, =   (4) >, <

   (5) >, <

Directions (165-170) : Study the following information carefully and answer the questions given below:

Twelve people are sitting in two parallel rows containing six people each, in such a way that there is an equal distance between adjacent persons. In row-1 S, T, U, V, W and X are seated and all of them are facing south. In row-2 M, N, O, P, Q and R are seated and all of them are facing north.

Therefore in the given sitting arrangement, each member seated in a row faces another member of the other row.

No two people with names starting with consecutive alphabet is an immediate neighbour of each other. For example, A is not an immediate neighbour of B. B is not an immediate neighbour of either A or C and so on. Each of them also likes a different movies viz. Vertigo, Cinderella, Twilight, Gladiator, Uninhabited, Inception, Frozen, Watchmen, Tangled, Aladdin, Hero and Wanted.

(**Please Note :** None of the information given is necessarily in the same order.)

T sits at an extreme end of the line. Only two people sit between T and the one who likes Frozen. N sits second to the left of the one who faces the one who likes Frozen. The one who likes Twilight sits second to the right of O. T does not face the one who likes Twilight. Only two persons sit between P and R. U does not sit at an extreme end of the line. X is not an immediate neighbour of T. V faces the one who likes Tangled. Only three people sit between the ones who like Tangled and Vertigo. R likes Inception. Only one person sits between R and M. One of the immediate neighbours of M faces the one who likes Hero. The one who likes Cinderella sits to the immediate left of S. P sits second to the right of the one who likes Aladdin. Only one person sits between ones who like Watchmen and Wanted respectively. T does not like Wanted. N does not like Gladiator.

165. Which of the following statements is true as per the given arrangement?

   (1) U likes Watchmen,

   (2) Q faces one of the immediate neighbours of W.

   (3) P is an immediate neighbour of N.

   (4) None of the given statements is true.

   (5) S sits exactly between V and X

166. Who amongst the following likes Uninhabited?

   (1) P   (2) W

   (3) S   (4) X

   (5) N

167. Who amongst the following is facing Q?

(1) X

(2) V

(3) The one who likes Watchmen

(4) S

(5) The one who likes Frozen

168. Four of the following five are alike in a certain way based on the given arrangement and hence they form a group. Which one of them does not belong to that group?

(1) The one who likes Tangled

(2) N

(3) The one who likes Vertigo

(4) The one who likes Gladiator

(5) V

169. W is related to Cinderella and P is related to Inception in a certain way based on the given arrangement. To which of the following is U related, following the same pattern?

(1) The one who faces P

(2) The one who faces O

(3) T

(4) S

(5) The one who likes Uninhabited

170. What is the position of Q with respect to the one who likes Inception?

(1) Third to the right

(2) Second to the right

(3) Third to the left

(4) Second to the left

(5) Fourth to the left

171. Study the following information carefully and answer the question given below :

'If we take a close look at the balance sheets of previous five years, it shows that the amount of loans taken by the company against fixed assets has only increased, the result of which is poor financial health of the company this year',— Financial report of Company B. Which of the following can be inferred from the statement of the financial report of the Company B?

(A) Decreasing the amount of loans against fixed assets will improve the financial health of Company B.

(B) The value of fixed assets of Company B has decreased by taking loans against them.

(C) An analysis of balance sheets of a Company throws light on its financial health.

(D) Company B had not taken any loans in any financial year other than the said five years.

(1) None can be inferred

(2) Both A and D

(3) Both A and C

(4) Only D

(5) Only B

172. Study the following information carefully and answer the question given below :

School X had been, allowing local people to use their basketball court and cricket ground after school hours by charging a fees for the same. This had helped the school generate a significant amount of additional income in the past few years. However, this year the school decided to' discontinue the practice.

Which of the following statements does not strengthen the decision of School X of discontinuing the practice?

(1) The number of people using the basketball court and cricket ground of school is slightly decreased last year as other schools in the vicinity also started following the same practice.

(2) School X could not win even a single trophy in past few years annual inter -school games competition as the participants did not get adequate time for practice due to access of grounds to local people.

(3) Complaints by the nearby residents of School X have increased about the increased disturbance created by the users of the basketball court and cricket ground beyond school hours.

(4) The damage caused to the basketball court and cricket ground of School X has increased significantly due to over-use by the outsiders thus not allowing the students to play.

(5) The governing board of School X denied the access to school premises in any number by the outsiders (other than parents of students) in this year's board meeting for security reasons.

Directions (173-174): In these questions, four statements followed by five Conclusions are given, one of which definitely does not logically follow (or is not a possibility) from the given statements. That Conclusion is your answer.

(**NOTE :** You have to take the four given statements to be true even if they seem to be at variance from commonly known facts and then decide which of the given Conclusions logically does not follow from the given statements.)

173. Statements :

No performance is an experiment.

Some experiments are blueprints.

No blueprint is a table.

All blueprints are chairs.

(1) **Conclusion :** Some experiments are definitely not tables.

(2) **Conclusion :** At least some experiments are chairs.

(3) **Conclusion :** All chairs being performances is a possibility.

(4) **Conclusion :** All tables being experiments is a possibility.

(5) **Conclusion :** All blueprints can never be performances.

174. Statements :

All stations are platforms.

All platforms are dividers.

Some platforms are roads.

No road is a track.

(1) **Conclusion :** All stations are dividers.

(2) **Conclusion :** Some platforms are definitely not tracks.

(3) **Conclusion :** All tracks being stations is a possibility.

(4) **Conclusion :** All dividers being tracks is a possibility

(5) **Conclusion :** Some dividers are roads.

Directions (175-180) : Study the following information carefully and answer the question given below :

Twelve Professors — O, P, Q, R, S, T, U, V, W, X, Y and Z — had lectures in different months of the same year viz., January, March, April, May, June and December but not necessarily in the same order. All the lectures are either on 12th or 25th of these months. No two professors had lectures on the same day. Each professor also likes a different colour namely, Red, Blue, Green, Yellow, Orange, White, Pink, Silver, Maroon, Violet, Brown and Grey but not necessarily in the same order.

(**NOTE :** No lecture was conducted in any other month of the same year).

V had a lecture on 12th April. Only two people had lectures between V and Q. The one who likes red had a lecture in the same month as Q. Q does not like red. The one who likes White had a lecture on an even numbered date of the month which had exactly 30 days. V does not like white. Only three people had a lecture between the one who likes White and the one who likes Violet. As many people had lectures between the one who likes red and O as between Q and the one who likes White. Only two people had lectures between O and the one who likes Blue. U had a lecture on 12th of a month before the one who likes Violet. U likes neither red nor blue. Only two people had lectures between U and the one who likes Orange. Only two people had lectures between the-one who likes Orange and the one who likes Green. X had a lecture in the same month as the one who likes Green. As many people had a lecture after W as before X. Only one person had a lecture between W and Z. Z had a lecture before W. The one who likes Pink had a lecture on an odd numbered day in the same month as Z. P had a lecture on 12th of the same month as R. Only two people had lectures between P and the one who likes Yellow. The one who likes Maroon had a lecture before P. T likes Brown. S does not like Red. W does not like Grey.

175. Which of the following combinations indicates those who had a lecture in March?

(1) The one who likes Maroon and R

(2) U and X

(3) P and R

(4) The one who likes Green and the one who likes Pink

(5) R and V

176. Which of the following combinations is correct?

(1) W-White   (2) X- Pink

(3) U-Grey   (4) V-Violet

(5) O-Red

177. If Y is related to White and P is related to Violet based on the a given arrangement, then which of the following is related too following the same pattern ?

(1) Grey   (2) Pink

(3) Brown   (4) Maroon

(5) Silver

178. How many people have lectures between the lectures by X and Y?

(1) Two   (2) Four

(3) None   (4) One

(5) Three

179. Four of the following five are alike in a certain way based on the given arrangement and hence they form a group. Which one of the following does not belong to that group?

   (1) 12-Y   (2) 25-O

   (3) 12-Green   (4) 25-T

   (5) 12-Pink

180. Who amongst the following had lecture in the same month as S?

   (1) V

   (2) The one who likes Grey

   (3) The one who likes White

   (4) The one who likes Yellow

   (5) W

Directions (181-184): In these questions, relationship between different elements is shown in the statements. The statements are followed by two Conclusions numbered I and II. Study the Conclusions based on the given statements and select appropriate answer.

Give answer (1) if both the Conclusion I and Conclusion II follow

Give answer (2) if either Conclusion I or Conclusion II follows

Give answer (3) if neither Conclusion I nor Conclusion II follows

Give answer (4) if only Conclusion I follows

Give answer (5) if only Conclusion II follows

(181-182) : Statements :

B ≤ R ≤ U ≥ S > H;

Y < O ≤ U ≤ A

181. Conclusions:

   I. B = A

   II. B < A

182. Conclusions:

   I. S ≥ O

   II. R < Y

(183-184) : Statements :

S = H ≥ A ≥ P = E;

P < L ≤ R ≤ E

183. Conclusions:

   I. S ≥ L

   II. E < A

184. Conclusions:

   I. S < P

   II. P < A

185. Study the following information carefully and answer the question given below :

'Goldkart', a leading gold jewellery chain in country 'Rik-maya' is famous for good jewellery with intricate designs. However, it recently chose to import jewellery from Company X for sale besides selling just intricate designs. Which of the following cannot be a reason behind the decisions taken by 'Goldkart'?

   (1) Gold jewellery with intricate designs was a brain child of 'Goldkart' in order to have an edge over other jewellery companies. Since these designs are now overused, they wish to bring a newer concept of designs.

   (2) The new concept of layered gold jewellery recently started by Company X is widely in news worldwide.

   (3) The Jewellery designers of 'Goldkart' haven't updated their skills since 5-6 years making them incompetent as compared to other designers of the country.

   (4) Since Company X has quoted high prices to export gold jewellery to 'Goldkart', the profit gained by 'Goldkart' is just 18% more than the usual profit.

   (5) None of those given as options

186. Study the following information carefully and answer the question given below :

A road construction project has been going on in State Y and was due to be completed two months ago. The government of that time had extended the deadline of the project by three months and also allowed truck carrying the raw material to pass through City Z in order to speed up the process. Yet the construction work is further delayed and is not likely to get over in the extended deadline as well. Which of the following may **NOT** be a reason for the delay of construction work in State Y?

   (1) The workers have started going on strike and off since the past four months as they are demanding higher wages.

   (2) Some part of the land on which the road is to be constructed is owned privately and a dispute is going on in the court regarding the same.

   (3) Monsoon have approached State Y and due to heavy rainfall the construction work is three times slower than the usual pace

   (4) Due to several complaints by the residents living in the vicinity of the construction site, the construction work is done for four hours less than the usual construction hours since past four months

   (5) Most roads of City Z have traffic jam in the morning as well as evening for two hours each as most people in the city travel to work by road.

187. This question consists of two statements numbered I and II. These statements may be either independent causes or effects of independent causes or a common cause. One of these statements may be the effect of the other statement. Read both the statements and decide which of the given answer choices depicts the relationship between these two statements.

Statement I : Unlike last two years, the amount of toxic gases such as carbon monoxide and sulphur dioxide along with volatile organic compounds present in atmosphere crossed the permissible limit in Country X this year.

Statement II : The emissions from stationary sources such as industries and that from mobile sources such as transport have increased substantially this year in Country X.

(1) Both statements I and II are effects of independent causes.

(2) Both statements I and II are effects of some common cause.

(3) Statement I is the cause and statement II is its effect.

(4) Statement II is the cause and statement I is its effect.

(5) Both statements I and II are independent causes.

Directions (188-190): Each of the following questions, consists of a question and two statements numbered I and II given below it. You have to decide whether the data given in the statements are sufficient to answer the question. Read both the statements and choose the most appropriate option.

Give answer (1) if the data in both the Statements I and II together are necessary to answer the question.

Give answer (2) if the data either in Statement I alone or Statement II alone are sufficient to answer the question.

Give answer (3) if the data even in both the Statements I and II together are not sufficient to answer the question.

Give answer (4) if the data in Statement I alone are sufficient to answer the question while the data in Statement II alone are not sufficient to answer the question.

Give answer (5) if the data in Statement II alone are sufficient to answer the question while the data in Statement I alone are not sufficient to answer the question.

188. Six persons A, B, C, D, E and F are sitting around a circular table facing the centre. What is E's position with respect to F?

I. A sits second to the right of D. Only two people sit between A and F. B sits to the immediate right of E,

II. Only two people sit between D and E. E is an immediate neighbour of both B and A. C is not an immediate neighbour of B.

189. How is 'dwarf definitely coded in a language?

I. In a certain code language, 'the dwarf planet' is coded as 'cq sd ap' and 'the solar energy' is coded as 'kb og sd'.

II. In a certain code language, 'only dwarf planet' is coded as 'cq ap st', and 'the coldest planet' is coded as 'sd cq yt'.

190. Fifteen people are standing in a straight row facing north. What is M's position with respect to S?

I. P stands third from the left end of the row. Only two people stand between P and M. N stands third to the right of M. S is an immediate neighbour of N.

II. Q stands second from the right end of the row. Only two people stand between Q and O. O is an immediate neighbour of S. As many people stand to the left of M as to the right of S.

Directions (191-195) : Study the following information carefully and answer the questions given below :

Eight people — A, B, C, D, E, F, G and H — live in eight different cities — Varanasi, Nashik, Chennai, Siliguri, Ujjain, Bhopal, Jaipur and Patna, but not necessarily in the same order. Each one of them also studies in one of the four classes — II, V, VIII and XI. Two people study in each of the given classes.

• A studies in an even numbered class. The one who lives in Ujjain studies with A.

• The one who lives in Varanasi and Jaipur study in the same class, but in a class lower than VIII. D studies in a class lower than that of the one who lives in Varanasi.

• The one who lives in Nashik studies with H in the same class, but not in Class XI. D does not live in Nashik.

• B and G study in different classes. B lives neither in Jaipur nor in Nashik. G is senior to both B and H. Neither B nor the one who lives in Siliguri study in the same class as D. E lives in Siliguri.

- C is junior to F. The one who lives in Patna studies in an odd numbered class.

- Neither H nor D lives in Bhopal. The one who lives in Chennai is senior to the one who lives in Bhopal.

191. In which of the following cities does C live?

(1) Bhopal

(2) Chennai

(3) Jaipur

(4) Nashik

(5) Varanasi

192. Four of the following five are alike in a certain way based on the given arrangement and hence they form a group. Which one of the following does not belong to the group?

(1) G-Siliguri

(2) D-Bhopal

(3) C-Varanasi

(4) F- Chennai

(5) A-Patna

193. In which class does H study?

(1) The one in which A studies

(2) VIII

(3) The one in which E studies

(4) V

(5) II

194. Who amongst the following lives in Bhopal?

(1) A (2) G

(3) C (4) H

(5) Other than those given as options

195. Which one of the following statements is **TRUE** with respect to the given information?

(1) B lives in Nashik

(2) G is senior to E.

(3) B and F study in the same class.

(4) The one who lives in Jaipur studies in Class V.

(5) None of the given statements is true.

196. Study the following information carefully and answer the question given below :

The tourism sector of Country G has emerged out to be the highest contributor to GDP of the economy of Country G for this financial year. The numbers of foreign as well as domestic visitors to various tourist spots of the country were found to be relatively high as compared to last financial year. Which of the following may be a reason for increased tourism in Country G?

(A) The tourism packages offered by various travel agencies for visiting places in Country G were much cheaper and attractive.

(B) The government of Country G had started special buses, trains and flights at highly subsidized rates for passengers during holidays.

(C) The various hotels and travel agencies of City F in Country G started holiday packages of 18% lesser price than any other tourist spot in the country.

(D) Country G was found to be the most preferred tourist destination for the last three years globally

(1) All A, B, C and D

(2) Only A and D

(3) Only B and C

(4) Only A, B and D

(5) Only A and B

Directions (197-200) : Study the following information carefully and answer the questions given below:

Trishaa starts walking from point A, walks 12 metre to the south and reaches Point B. She then takes left turn and walks 7 metre to reach Point C. She then takes a left turn, walks 5 metre and reaches point D. From Point D she turns left, walks 11 metre and stops at point E. Point P is to the west of point B. Rishi who is standing at point P walks for a distance equal to the shortest distance between points B and E and reaches Point Q. From Point Q he takes a left turn, walks for a certain distance and reaches Point E.

197. Mehul starts walking towards south from Point B. He walks for a certain distance to reach Point K. He then takes a left turn and walks for 10 metre, takes another left turn and stops after walking for 9 metre. If his final position is 3 metre to the east of Point D, what is the distance between Point B and Point K?

(1) 4 metre

(2) 6 metre

(3) 5 metre

(4) 2 metre

(5) Cannot be determined

198. Point M is 9 metre to the north of Point Q. From Point M, which of the following walking directions would lead to Point A?

(A) 12 metre towards west, turn right and walk for 2 metre, then turn right and walk for 7 metre.

(B) 4 metre towards east, turn left and walk for 3 metre, then turn right and walk 5 metre.

(C) 3 metre towards north, turn left, walk 19 metre, turn left and walk 5 metre.

(D) 3 metre towards north, turn right and walk for 4 metre.

(1) Both (A) and (D)   (2) Only (D)
(3) Both (B) and (C)   (4) Only (C)
(5) Only (B)

199. In which direction is Point C with respect to Point P?

(1) North-East
(2) West
(3) East
(4) South-East
(5) North-West

200. Point Z is 9 metre to the east of Point A. Arun starts from Point Z, walks towards south, takes a right turn and walks for a certain distance to reach Point D. What is the total distance that Arun has to walk in order to reach Point D?

(1) 20 metre   (2) 11 metre
(3) 19 metre   (4) 9 metre
(5) 15 metre

ANSWERS

1. (3)	**2.** (1)	**3.** (4)	**4.** (2)	**5.** (4)	**6.** (4)	**7.** (1)	**8.** (1)	**9.** (5)	**10.** (5)
11. (4)	**12.** (2)	**13.** (2)	**14.** (3)	**15.** (5)	**16.** (2)	**17.** (2)	**18.** (4)	**19.** (4)	**20.** (5)
21. (3)	**22.** (5)	**23.** (3)	**24.** (5)	**25.** (4)	**26.** (2)	**27.** (1)	**28.** (1)	**29.** (3)	**30.** (2)
31. (4)	**32.** (1)	**33.** (5)	**34.** (4)	**35.** (2)	**36.** (1)	**37.** (3)	**38.** (2)	**39.** (2)	**40.** (1)
41. (5)	**42.** (3)	**43.** (3)	**44.** (1)	**45.** (1)	**46.** (3)	**47.** (2)	**48.** (1)	**49.** (2)	**50.** (3)
51. (4)	**52.** (3)	**53.** (1)	**54.** (3)	**55.** (1)	**56.** (3)	**57.** (3)	**58.** (5)	**59.** (3)	**60.** (4)
61. (1)	**62.** (3)	**63.** (4)	**64.** (2)	**65.** (2)	**66.** (4)	**67.** (5)	**68.** (4)	**69.** (4)	**70.** (3)
71. (2)	**72.** (1)	**73.** (4)	**74.** (2)	**75.** (5)	**76.** (4)	**77.** (1)	**78.** (2)	**79.** (4)	**80.** (4)
81. (2)	**82.** (5)	**83.** (1)	**84.** (3)	**85.** (4)	**86.** (3)	**87.** (3)	**88.** (3)	**89.** (5)	**90.** (2)
91. (1)	**92.** (3)	**93.** (3)	**94.** (4)	**95.** (3)	**96.** (3)	**97.** (4)	**98.** (5)	**99.** (1)	**100.** (3)
101. (1)	**102.** (1)	**103.** (3)	**104.** (5)	**105.** (2)	**106.** (3)	**107.** (1)	**108.** (2)	**109.** (3)	**110.** (3)
111. (1)	**112.** (5)	**113.** (3)	**114.** (2)	**115.** (2)	**116.** (3)	**117.** (4)	**118.** (5)	**119.** (3)	**120.** (2)
121. (1)	**122.** (1)	**123.** (1)	**124.** (3)	**125.** (3)	**126.** (2)	**127.** (3)	**128.** (5)	**129.** (4)	**130.** (2)
131. (4)	**132.** (5)	**133.** (2)	**134.** (4)	**135.** (5)	**136.** (4)	**137.** (4)	**138.** (3)	**139.** (3)	**140.** (4)
141. (3)	**142.** (1)	**143.** (1)	**144.** (2)	**145.** (5)	**146.** (4)	**147.** (3)	**148.** (3)	**149.** (3)	**150.** (4)
151. (5)	**152.** (2)	**153.** (1)	**154.** (3)	**155.** (4)	**156.** (5)	**157.** (4)	**158.** (1)	**159.** (2)	**160.** (3)
161. (4)	**162.** (1)	**163.** (4)	**164.** (3)	**165.** (2)	**166.** (5)	**167.** (3)	**168.** (3)	**169.** (1)	**170.** (4)
171. (3)	**172.** (5)	**173.** (3)	**174.** (4)	**175.** (3)	**176.** (4)	**177.** (1)	**178.** (2)	**179.** (5)	**180.** (3)
181. (2)	**182.** (3)	**183.** (4)	**184.** (5)	**185.** (5)	**186.** (5)	**187.** (4)	**188.** (4)	**189.** (1)	**190.** (1)
191. (3)	**192.** (5)	**193.** (2)	**194.** (1)	**195.** (4)	**196.** (1)	**197.** (1)	**198.** (2)	**199.** (3)	**200.** (4)

Directions (Q.1-5): *Answer the questions on the basis of the information given below.*

In an apartment, 8 persons i.e. D, E, F, G, H, I, J and K live on different floors of 8 storey-building but not necessarily in the same order. The lowermost floor of the building is numbered 1 and the topmost floor of the building is numbered 8. They are of different stream of engineering i.e. Chemical Engineering, Instrumentation Engineering, Software Engineering, Aeronautical Engineering, Mechanical Engineering, Electrical Engineering, Automobile Engineering, and Civil Engineering.

The one who lives on fourth floor is specialized in Mechanical engineering. D lives on odd numbered floor but above 3rd floor. The number of person between D and Electrical engineering specialized person is same as number of person between D and I. The one who is specialized in Instrumentation Engineering lives on lower most floor. K lives on an even numbered floor and he is specialized in Automobile Engineering. There are two floors between E and H and E lives above to H. E is specialized in Aeronautical Engineering. J lives just above the one who is specialized in Aeronautical Engineering. The number of floors between the one who is specialized in Aeronautical Engineering and Mechanical Engineering is two. The one who is specialized in Civil Engineering lives on odd numbered floor. The number of floors between the one who is specialized in Chemical Engineering and J is four. The one who is specialized in Aeronautical Engineering lives on odd numbered floor. The number of floors between the one who is specialized in Civil Engineering and the floor on which F lives is same as the number of floors between F and G. I lives below the floor on which D lives.

1. How many persons live between the person who is specialized in Chemical Engineering and the one who is specialized in Electrical Engineering?
   (*a*) Six   (*b*) One
   (*c*) Four   (*d*) Two
   (*e*) None of these

2. J is specialized in which of the following stream of engineering?
   (*a*) Aeronautical Engineering
   (*b*) Electrical Engineering
   (*c*) Civil Engineering
   (*d*) Instrumentation Engineering
   (*e*) Mechanical Engineering

3. Four of the following five are alike in a certain way and hence they form a group. Which one of the following does not belong to that group?
   (*a*) J   (*b*) K
   (*c*) H   (*d*) I
   (*e*) G

4. D lives on which floor?
   (*a*) 1   (*b*) 3
   (*c*) 4   (*d*) 5
   (*e*) 7

5. G is related to Mechanical Engineering, in the same way as F is related to Automobile Engineering. Then, which of the following is H related to? (Following the same pattern)
   (*a*) Mechanical Engineering
   (*b*) Electrical Engineering
   (*c*) Civil Engineering
   (*d*) Instrumentation Engineering
   (*e*) Aeronautical Engineering

6. Which of the following symbols should replace the sign ($) and (#) in the given expression in order to make the expressions P > C and C ≤ B definitely true?

'A > B ≥ R $ C < R ≤ Z = M # P ≥ X'

(a) ≥, >   (b) ≥, ≤

(c) >, =   (d) =, ≥

(e) <, ≤

7. Five persons namely A, B, C, D and E are going to the school in different days of the week, starting from Monday to Friday. Two persons are going between C and B. C is going before Wednesday. D is going to the school immediate after E. If A is not going on Friday, then who among the following persons is going to school on Wednesday?

(a) B   (b) C

(c) D   (d) E

(e) A

Directions (Q.8-12): *Answer the questions on the basis of the information given below.*

Eight people viz. A, B, C, D, P, Q, R and S are sitting in a straight line. They all are facing north. Each one of them has a different age i.e. 14, 16, 17, 19, 21, 23, 26 and 31 years, but not necessarily in the same order.

B sits at one of the extreme end of the row. There are three persons sitting between C and Q who is neither 14 years nor 19 years old. There are two persons sitting between D and the person who is 23 years old. Neither Q nor D is the oldest person. Age difference of immediate neighbours of D is 5 years. A sits right to the R, but not immediate right. There are three persons sitting between B and the one whose age is 16 years. The one whose age is 19 years sits third to the right of C. R sits to the right of B. Q sits second to the right of the person whose age is 23 years. P sits immediate left of the person whose age is 14 years. Q is not youngest person. The one, whose age is 31 years in not immediate neighbour of the youngest person, C is not the fourth oldest person.

8. Who sits second to the right of D?

(a) A   (b) S

(c) P   (d) R

(e) Nome of these

9. How many persons sit between the person who is 31 years old and S?

(a) Four   (b) Five

(c) Three   (d) One

(e) None of these

10. Who among the following person is 26 years old?

(a) R   (b) D

(c) C   (d) S

(e) None of these

11. If P is related to 16 years in the same way as B is related to 26 years, then which of the following is R related to, following the same pattern?

(a) 19 years   (b) 17 years

(c) 21 years   (d) 31 years

(e) None of these

12. What is the age difference of A's immediate neighbours?

(a) Three   (b) Seven

(c) Five   (d) Six

(e) None of these

13. Q is the daughter of A. J is the brother of Q. J is the son of R. J is the father of S. If it is given that A is mother of Q, then what is the relation of R with respect to S?

(a) Father

(b) Mother-in-law

(c) Mother

(d) Father-in-law

(e) Grand father

Directions (Q.14-18): *Answer the questions on the basis of the information given below.*

There are seven persons P, Q, R, S, T, U and V who were born on the same day of the same month of different year i.e. 1984, 1946, 1967, 1972, 1982, 1989 and 1992 but not necessarily in the same order.

Note: Their age are considered as on the same month and day of 2017 as their date of births.

The difference between the ages of Q and R is twice the square root of the age of one of the any seven persons. Difference between the ages of R and S is 2 years. Age of P is greatest amongst those whose age is a multiple of five. T is older than V who is not the youngest. Q is not youngest person.

14. Who amongst the following is the oldest?

(a) P   (b) V

(c) U   (d) T

(e) None of these

15. What is the age of R?

(a) 33 years   (b) 35 years

(c) 25 years   (d) 45 years

(e) 50 years

16. How many persons are younger than U?

(*a*) One (*b*) Two

(*c*) Three (*d*) Four

(*e*) No one

17. What is the age of S?

(*a*) 45 years

(*b*) 35 years

(*c*) 33 years

(*d*) 50 years

(*e*) 28 years

18. Who was born in 1989?

(*a*) V (*b*) U

(*c*) T (*d*) P

(*e*) Q

19. In a certain code language 'economics growth registered' is written as 've jo qi', 'growth is expected' is written as 'qi lo mn', and 'registered expected number' is written as 'lo ve pr', then what is the code for "economic"?

(*a*) lo (*b*) pr

(*c*) qi (*d*) ve

(*e*) jo

20. If 2 is subtracted from each odd digit in the number 7493652 and 3 is added to each even digit in number then which of the following digit is repeated in the new number so obtained?

(*a*) 9, 4 (*b*) 6, 5

(*c*) 5, 9 (*d*) 5, 4

(*e*) 5, 7

Directions (Q.21-22): *Answer the questions on the basis of the information given below.*

There are four boxes i.e. J, K, L and M in which four types of fruits are stored. Fruits are Litchi, Apple, Grapes and Mango. Boxes are arranged in such a manner from top to bottom.

There are two boxes between K and L. The box in which grapes are stored is above L, but not immediate above. The box in which Apple is stored is immediate below M, but not stored in box L. Litchi box is above the Mango box, but not immediate above Apple box.

21. In which of the following box, Litchi is stored?

(*a*) J (*b*) M

(*c*) K (*d*) L

(*e*) Either (a) or (b)

22. Which of the following fruit is stored in second lowest Box?

(*a*) Grapes (*b*) Apple

(*c*) Mango (*d*) Litchi

(*e*) Can't be determined

Directions (Q.23-27): *Answer the questions on the basis of the information given below.*

Eight persons M, N, O, V, W, X, Y and Z attend seminars on different months of the year viz. March, June, October and November, such that not more than two persons attend their seminars in each of the months. Seminars can be held on either 10th or 27th day of the month. No two seminars can be held on the same day. W and N attend the seminars on the same month. There are three seminars between the seminars of X and O. W does not attend their seminar in November. Z attends his seminar immediately after N. V attends his seminar in the month of November. The number of persons who attend their seminars between the seminars of Y and Z is the same as the number of persons who attend their seminars between the seminars of N and V. X does not attend the seminar on October. W attends his seminar before N.

23. M attends his seminar on which of the following dates?

(*a*) 10th October (*b*) 27th November

(*c*) 10th November (*d*) 10th March

(*e*) None of these

24. Which of the following persons attends his seminar on 27th March?

(*a*) W (*b*) N

(*c*) M (*d*) X

(*e*) None of these

25. How many persons attend the seminar after W?

(*a*) 5 (*b*) 4

(*c*) 6 (*d*) 3

(*e*) None of these

26. Who among the following persons attends the seminar on 10th October?

(*a*) W (*b*) M

(*c*) V (*d*) Z

(*e*) None of these

27. How many persons attended seminar after V?

(*a*) 5 (*b*) 5

(*c*) 7 (*d*) No one

(*e*) None of these

Directions (Q.28-29): *Answer the questions on the basis of the information given below.*

There are six family members A, B, C, D, E and F and all of them are of different age. A is younger than only one person. E is older than B and D but not as old as A. D is older than only one person. F is youngest in the family. The age of D is 25 year and the age of person who is second oldest is 40 year.

28. Who is oldest in the family?

   (*a*) A   (*b*) B

   (*c*) D   (*d*) E

   (*e*) C

29. What is the possible age of B?

   (*a*) 42 year   (*b*) 20 year

   (*c*) 55 year   (*d*) 19 year

   (*e*) 30 year

30. Which of the following statement shows 'A ≥ R' and 'B < C' holds definitely true?

   (a) B ≤ C = A ≥ K = R

   (b) C = K > B < R ≥ A

   (c) C > B > A ≥ K = R

   (d) B = K < C < R = A

   (e) None of these

Directions (Q.31-33): *In the given questions, assuming the given statements to be true. Find which of the given two conclusions numbered I, II is/are definitely true and give your answer accordingly.*

31. Statement: M > U > L = N; L ≥ Y > A

   Conclusions: I. Y < N   II. Y = N

   (*a*) Both I and II are true

   (*b*) Only II

   (*c*) Only I is true

   (*d*) Either I or II is true

   (*e*) None is true

32. Statement: J ≥ A > D = E; L < A < M

   Conclusions: I. M < J   II. J > L

   (*a*) Only II is true

   (*b*) Either I or II are true

   (*c*) Both I and II are true

   (*d*) Only I is true

   (*e*) None is true

33. Statement: M ≤ K > L = Y; P ≤ T > M

   Conclusions: I. P > Y   II. T < L

   (*a*) Only II is true

   (*b*) Only I

   (*c*) Either I or II are true

   (*d*) Both I and II are true

   (*e*) None is true

34. In a vertical row 13 persons are sitting. A is seventh from the beginning and two persons sits between G and A. Persons between A and L is same as persons between G and Q. Then what is the position of Q from the beginning?

   (*a*) Fourth

   (*b*) Eight

   (*c*) Sixth

   (*d*) Ninth

   (*e*) Can't be determined

35. A man walks 12 m east from point A and reaches point B. From point B he takes left turn and walks 4 m and then he takes right turn and walked 6 m and again he takes right turn and walks 7 m and again takes right turn and reaches point M. If it is given that point B is in north from point M, then what is the distance between B and M?

   (*a*) 7 m   (*b*) 6 m

   (*c*) 5 m   (*d*) 4 m

   (*e*) 3 m

NUMERICAL ABILITY

Directions (Q.36–40): *What will come in place of the question mark (?) in each of the following series?*

36. 14, 8, 9, 14.5, 30, ?

   (*a*) 75   (*b*) 76

   (*c*) 60   (*d*) 65

   (*e*) None of these

37. 20, 29, 54, 103, 184, ?,

   (*a*) 310   (*b*) 350

   (*c*) 305   (*d*) 315

   (*e*) None of these

38. 7, 8, 18, 57, ?, 1165

   (*a*) 250   (*b*) 234

   (*c*) 230   (*d*) 232

   (*e*) None of these

39. 5, 7, 18, 47, 103, ?

   (*a*) 195   (*b*) 210

   (*c*) 200   (*d*) 190

   (*e*) None of these

40. 77, 85, 69, 101, 37, ?

   (*a*) 180

   (*b*) 165

   (*c*) 170

   (*d*) 120

   (*e*) None of these

Directions (Q.41-45): *Study the following line graph and answer the following questions given below it.*

There are two car manufacturing companies (Company X and Company Y). The sale of cars by these two different companies is given in different years.

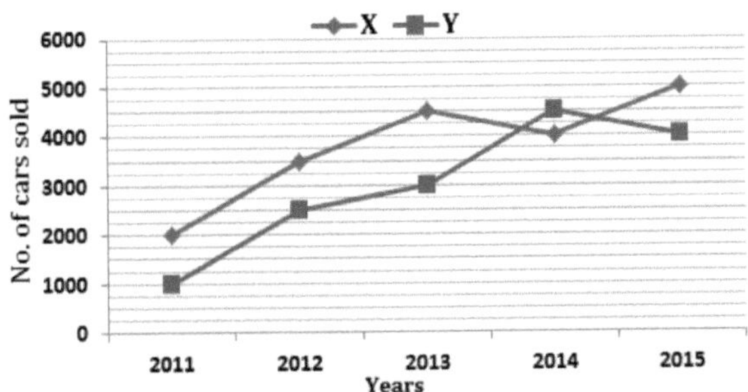

41. If the sale of company X in year 2016 is increased by 20% with respect to year 2015 and the sale of company Y in year 2016 with respect to year 2015 is decreased by 10% then find the total sale of the company X and Y together in year 2016?

(*a*) 7200   (*b*) 9600

(*c*) 8400   (*d*) 5600

(*e*) None of these

42. Find the ratio of the sales of company X in years 2011, 2013 and 2015 together to the total sale of company Y in year 2012 and 2014 together?

(*a*) 23 : 14   (*b*) 14 : 23

(*c*) 11 : 29   (*d*) 29 : 11

(*e*) None of these

43. Total cars sold by both companies in year 2012 are what percent more/less than the total cars sold by both companies in year 2013?

(*a*) 28%   (*b*) 18%

(*c*) 25%   (*d*) 20%

(*e*) None of these

44. Find the difference between the average number of cars sold by company X from 2011 to 2015 and the average number of cars sold by company Y from 2011 to 2015?

(*a*) 750

(*b*) 900

(*c*) 800

(*d*) 850

(*e*) None of these

45. Find the total number of cars sold by both companies from year 2012 to 2014?

(*a*) 23000   (*b*) 21000

(*c*) 22500   (*d*) 21500

(*e*) None of these

Directions (Q.46-50): *Read the following table and answer the following question.*

Total number of visitors and Percentage of male out of these visitors are given.

Districts	Museum	
	Total visitors (Male and Female)	Percentage of male out of total visitors
P	250	40%
Q	350	44%
R	375	60%
S	450	56%
T	300	55%
U	525	32%

46. Total number of female visitors from district Q and R together to see the museum are how much more/less than total number of male visitors from district R and S together to see the museum?

(*a*) 142   (*b*) 126

(*c*) 128   (*d*) 131

(*e*) None of these

47. Average number of visitors from district P, Q and R together to see the museum are approximately what percent of the average number of visitors from district S, T and U together to see the museum.

(*a*) 71%   (*b*) 76%

(*c*) 78%   (*d*) 74%

(*e*) 85%

48. Find the ratio of the male visitors from district T and U together to see the museum to the female visitors form district R and S together to see the museum?

(*a*) 107 : 117

(*b*) 116 : 111

(*c*) 111 : 116

(*d*) 117 : 107

(*e*) None of these

49. Male visitors from district R to see the museum are what percent more/less than the female visitors from district T to see the museum? (Calculate up to two decimal points)

(*a*) $33\dfrac{1}{3}\%$ (*b*) $33\dfrac{2}{3}\%$

(*c*) $66\dfrac{1}{3}\%$ (*d*) $66\dfrac{2}{3}\%$

(*e*) None of these

50. Find the difference between the total number of male visitors from district Q, R and S together to see the museum and the total number of female visitors from district S, T and U together to see the museum?

 (a) 25   (b) 75

 (c) 60   (d) 50

 (e) None of these

Directions (Q.51-55): *Given below are two equations in each question, which you have to solve and give answer*

 (a) if $x > y$

 (b) if $x \geq y$

 (c) if $y > x$

 (d) if $y \geq x$

 (e) if $x = y$ or no relation can be established

51. I. $x^2 - 3x + 2 = 0$ II. $2y^2 - 7y + 6 = 0$

52. I. $3x^2 + 4x + 1 = 0$ II. $y^2 + 5y + 6 = 0$

53. I. $2x^2 + 5x + 2 = 0$ II. $y^2 + 9y + 20 = 0$

54. I. $x^2 - 7x + 10 = 0$ II. $y^2 - 12y + 35 = 0$

55. I. $(x - 12)^2 = 0$ II. $y^2 = 144$

Directions (Q.56-60): *What approximate value should come in place of the question mark (?) in the following questions?*

Note: (You are not expected to calculate the exact value.)

56. $23.001 \times 18.999 \times 7.998 = ?$

 (a) 4200   (b) 3000

 (c) 3500   (d) 4000

 (e) 2500

57. $33.99\sqrt{?} + 42.0032\sqrt{?} = \dfrac{76}{12.998} \times (?)$

 (a) 81   (b) 72

 (c) 169   (d) 121

 (e) 144

58. $94.95 \times 13.03 + \sqrt{35.98} \times 14.99 = 53 \times \sqrt{?}$

 (a) 25   (b) 144

 (c) 225   (d) 625

 (e) 900

59. $1884.88 \div 144.921 + 6.99 + (?)^2 = 69.09$

 (a) 3   (b) 4

 (c) 5   (d) 6

 (e) 7

60. 41% of $601 - 250.17 = ? - 77\%$ of 910

 (a) 800   (b) 500

 (c) 690   (d) 760

 (e) 550

61. An article is marked up 40% higher than CP but it was sold on x% discount. The shopkeeper thus gains 12%. What would be the S.P. of the article with C.P. Rs. 120 and sold on x% profit?

 (a) Rs. 134.50

 (b) Rs. 144

 (c) Rs. 128

 (d) Rs. 148

 (e) None of these

62. There are 27 cards having number 1 to 27. Two cards are picked at random one by one. What is the probability that sum of number on these 2 cards is odd?

 (a) $\dfrac{13}{27}$

 (b) $\dfrac{8}{13}$

 (c) $\dfrac{182}{729}$

 (d) $\dfrac{14}{27}$

 (e) None of these

63. B is 20% more efficient than A. B started the work & do it for x days. And then B is replaced by A. A completed the remaining work in x + 8 days. Ratio of work done by A & B is 3:2. In how many days can A and B working together complete the whole work?

 (a) $13\dfrac{11}{17}$ days   (b) $12\dfrac{7}{11}$ days

 (c) $13\dfrac{7}{11}$ days   (d) $12\dfrac{8}{13}$ days

 (e) None of these

64. A sum of Rs. 91,00 is borrowed at 20% per annum compounded annually. If the amount is to be paid in two years, the amount will be

 (a) Rs. 131,040

 (b) Rs. 132,800

 (c) Rs. 132,500

 (d) Rs. 142,300

 (e) None of these

65. A man spends 28% of his salary on food. From the remaining he spent 1/6 th on rent and sends 3/8 th to his mother. If he left with Rs. 5280, what amount he sends to his mother.

 (a) Rs. 4230   (b) Rs. 4320

 (c) Rs. 4580   (d) Rs. 4420

 (e) None of these

66. The average age of a husband and wife was 23 years when they were married 5 years ago. The average age of the husband, the wife and a child who was born during the interval, is 20 years now. How old is the child now?

    (a) 9 months (b) 1 year

    (c) 3 years (d) 4 years

    (e) None of these

67. The ratio between the ages of a father and a son at present is 5 : 2 respectively. Four year hence the ratio between the ages of the son and his mother will be 1 : 2 respectively. What is the ratio between the present ages of the father and the mother respectively?

    (a) 3 : 4 (b) 5 : 4

    (c) 4 : 3 (d) Cannot be determined

    (e) None of these

68. Total distance between A and B is d kms. The distance travelled along the stream is three time of the total distance and the distance travelled against the stream is two times of the total distance. If the time taken to cover the distance along the stream is 10% less then the time taken to cover the distance against the stream and a person covers a distance of 21 km in 1 hr 24 min along the stream, then find the rate of current.

    (a) 2 km/hr (b) 3 km/hr

    (c) 1 km/hr (d) 4 km/hr

    (e) None of these

69. P and Q started a business by investing Rs. 15,000 and Rs.18,000 respectively. After four months R joined the business with a capital of Rs. 10,000. After two more months Q left the business with his capital. At the end of the year P got a share of Rs. 4,500 in the profit. What is the total profit earned?

    (a) Rs. 6800 (b) Rs. 7600

    (c) Rs. 8600 (d) Rs. 9200

    (e) None of these

70. Inside a square plot a circular garden is developed which exactly fits in the square plot and the diameter of the garden is equal to the side of the square plot which is 28 metre. What is the area of the space left out in the square plot after developing the garden?

    (a) 98 m² (b) 146 m²

    (c) 84 m² (d) 168 m²

    (e) None of these

ENGLISH LANGUAGE

Directions (Q.71-80): *Read the following passage carefully and answer the questions given below it. Certain words are given in bold to help you locate them while answering some of the questions.*

OVER a couple of days in February, hundreds of thousands of point-of-sale printers in restaurants around the world began behaving strangely. Some churned out bizarre pictures of computers and giant robots signed, "with love from the hacker God himself". Some informed their owners that, "YOUR PRINTER HAS BEEN PWND'D". Some told them, "For the love of God, please close this port". When the hacker God gave an interview to Motherboard, a technology website, he claimed to be a British secondary-school pupil by the name of "Stackoverflowin". Annoyed by the **parlous** state of computer security, he had, he claimed, decided to perform a public service by demonstrating just how easy it was to seize control.

Not all hackers are so public-spirited, and 2016 was a bonanza for those who are not. In February of that year cyber-crooks stole $81m directly from the central bank of Bangladesh—and would have got away with more were it not for a crucial **typo**. In August America's National Security Agency (NSA) saw its own hacking tools leaked all over the internet by a group calling themselves the Shadow Brokers. (The CIA suffered a similar indignity this March.) In October a piece of software called Mirai was used to flood Dyn, an internet infrastructure company, with so much meaningless traffic that websites such as Twitter and Reddit were made inaccessible to many users. And the hacking of the Democratic National Committee's e-mail servers and the **subsequent** leaking of embarrassing communications seems to have been part of an attempt to influence the outcome of the American elections.

Away from matters of great scale and grand strategy, most hacking is either show-off vandalism or simply criminal. It is also increasingly easy. Obscure forums oil the trade in stolen credit-card details, sold in batches of housands at a time. Data-dealers hawk "exploits": flaws in code that allow malicious attackers to **subvert** systems. You can also buy "ransomware", with which to encrypt photos and documents on victims' computers before charging them for the key that will unscramble the data. So sophisticated are these facilitating markets that coding skills are now entirely optional. Botnets—flocks of compromised computers created by software like Mirai, which can then be used to flood websites with traffic, knocking them offline until a ransom is paid—can be rented by the hour. Just like a legitimate business, the bot-herders will, for a few dollars extra, provide technical support if anything goes wrong. The total cost of all this hacking is anyone's guess (most small attacks, and many big ones, go unreported). But all agree it is likely to rise, because the scope for **malice** is about to expand remarkably. "We are building a world-sized robot," says Bruce Schneier, a security analyst, in the shape of the "Internet of Things". The IoT is a buzz-phrase used to describe the computerisation of everything from cars and electricity meters to children's toys, medical devices and light bulbs. In 2015 a group of computer-security researchers demonstrated that it was possible to take remote control of certain Jeep cars. When the Mirai malware is used to build a botnet it seeks out devices such as video recorders and webcams; the botnet for fridges is just around the corner.

71. Which is the most appropriate title?

(*a*) Public spirited hackers.

(*b*) Broken Computer security.

(*c*) Hacking: The criminal offence

(*d*) The Internet of Things

(*e*) The Growing Artificial Intelligence

72. According to the paragraph, why did 'the hacker god' decide to perform a public service?

(*a*) To hack the NSA server

(*b*) To show to the people that hacking was very easy

(*c*) To influence the outcome of the American elections

(*d*) To aware the people about the computer security threats

(*e*) None of these

73. Which of the following is false in context of the passage?

(*a*) The IoT is a buzz-phrase used to describe the computerisation of everything from cars and electricity meters to children's toys, medical devices and light bulbs.

(*b*) The hacking of the Democratic National Committee's e-mail servers was performed with the help of a malware named "Mirai".

(*c*) A group called "the Shadow Brokers" leaked hacking tools of America's National Security Agency all over the internet

(*d*) Obscure forums oil the trade in stolen credit-card details, sold in batches of thousands at a time.

(*e*) All of them are true

74. According to the paragraph, what caused the websites like 'twitter and reddit' inaccessible to the users?

(*a*) It was caused due to hacking the security contents of the website.

(*b*) Due to unscramble of the encrypted Data on the websites.

(*c*) Due to Dyn, an internet infrastructure company.

(*d*) Due to surge in the worthless traffic which was forced by the hackers.

(*e*) All are correct.

75. Which of the following statement(s) is/are correct about 'Internet of Things' according to passage?

(i) To take remote control of all digital devices.

(ii) A world sized Robot.

(iii) It means computerization of everything.

(*a*) Only (i) is correct

(*b*) Only (ii) is correct

(*c*) Both (i) and (iii) are correct

(*d*) Both (ii) and (iii) are correct

(*e*) All are correct

Directions (Q.76-77): *Choose the word/group of words which is most opposite in meaning to the word/ group of words printed in bold as used in the passage.*

76. Malice

(*a*) Antipathy (*b*) Malevolence

(*c*) Benignity (*d*) Audacity

(*e*) Valour

77. Parlous

(*a*) Adventurous (*b*) Fatal

(*c*) Terrible (*d*) Innocuous

(*e*) Risky

Directions (Q.78-80): *Choose the word/group of words which is most similar in meaning to the word/ group of words printed in bold as used in the passage.*

78. Subsequent

(*a*) Consequent (*b*) Direct

(*c*) Anterior (*d*) Foregoing

(*e*) Prior

79. Subvert

(*a*) Vitiate (*b*) Comply

(*c*) Undermine (*d*) Betray

(*e*) Overwhelm

80. Typo

(*a*) Advantage (*b*) Defeat

(*c*) Strength (*d*) Bug

(*e*) Stain

Directions (Q.81-90): *Which of the phrases (a), (b), (c) and (d) given below each sentence should replace the phrase printed in **bold** letters to make the sentence grammatically correct? If the sentence is correct as it is, mark (e) i.e., "No correction required" as the answer.*

81. In the modern day, it is common to say you are **bored to death** if someone or something is incredibly uninteresting.
    (a) bored of death
    (b) bored from death
    (c) bored till death
    (d) bored until death
    (e) No correction required

82. We advised them **to going to** a hill station during the summer vacation.
    (a) for going to
    (b) that they go to
    (c) to go to
    (d) that they should have to go to
    (e) No correction required

83. They failed **in their attempt** to repair the demolished portion of the building.
    (a) for their attempt
    (b) in their attempting
    (c) with their attempt
    (d) on their attempt
    (e) No correction required

84. In Indian democracy, it is necessary for the citizens to **beware of** all the political facts about every political party.
    (a) be aware of   (b) be aware for
    (c) beware for   (d) be aware to
    (e) No correction required

85. We're going to have to **put down** our summer vacation until July because of the bad weather conditions.
    (a) put off   (b) put across
    (c) put out   (d) put back
    (e) No correction required

86. We **called on** but we weren't able to find the car part we needed to fix the gear system.
    (a) called off
    (b) called back
    (c) called around
    (d) called up
    (e) No correction required

87. If everyone **chips in** they can get the whole kitchen painted by today afternoon.
    (a) chips on   (b) chips up
    (c) chips off   (d) chips towards
    (e) No correction required

88. **Hang up** there. I'm sure you'll find a better job very soon because you are very sincere.
    (a) hang on   (b) hang back
    (c) hang out   (d) hang in
    (e) No correction required

89. When I **think of** on my youth, I wish I had studied harder and had secured good grades.
    (a) think over   (b) think about
    (c) think out   (d) think back
    (e) No correction required

90. A stranger **cut through** with unsolicited advice on how we could fix our relationship
    (a) cut out   (b) cut about
    (c) cut back   (d) cut in
    (e) No correction required

Directions (Q.91-100): *In the following passage there are blanks, each of which has been numbered and one word has been suggested alongside the blank. These numbers are printed below the passage and against each, five options are given. In four options, one word is suggested in each option. Find out the appropriate word which fits the blank appropriately. if the word written alongside the blank fits the passage, choose option 'e' (No correction required) as the correct choice.*

As a nation, we are in a great dilemma on the financing of public higher educational institutions. Highly subsidised quality higher education, with admissions based strictly on merit, continues to be a great hope for upward socio-economic __(91)__ [alternate]. This public demand has also ensured that there is consensus across the political spectrum on the need for setting up new IITs, IIMs, AIIMSs, NITs, etc. On the other hand, as the number of such institutions increases, the __(92)__ [main] requirements for supporting them will prove to be a challenge.

What are the alternatives? Globally there is a shift towards charging a higher __(93)__ [fraction] of education costs as fees — even in European countries where, traditionally, higher education was completely free. For the purpose of inclusion of students from economically weaker sections, there is the provision of education loans, often at lower-than-commercial rates. This has resulted in education-loan-driven higher education, which has clear __(94)__ [explicit] for blocking the socio-economic mobility of poor people, even in an affluent country like the United States.

In a country like India, public-funded institutions where the full fee is financed through loans are undesirable for many reasons. One, it will make education inaccessible to many who cannot afford to be ____(95)____[casted] with such large loans. Second, heavy debt would result in higher education being seen more as capital investment. It would lead to the clear ___(96)__ [graduation] objective of getting a quick return on investment. The net result would be that graduates would opt for safe career options — even more than they currently do — that provide the "highest package" and not those choices that may be low-paying but have greater social value and impact and which the graduate may ___(97)___ [needlessly] want to pursue. Medical education in India has already fallen into this trap; with high cost of education in private and foreign institutions, the increase in volume is not resulting in ____(98)____ [producing] access for a significant section of the population. Further, in the Indian socio-economic context where, even today, most students pursue academic programmes and careers that are forced on them by family and not out of their own choice, there is another great disadvantage. Just when we were seeing some change — in at least a small fraction of students — the increase in fees or a greater loan burden would put the clock back. The "loan model" is gaining ___(99)___ [attenuations] in the public ___(100)___ [regard] in India primarily driven by the stories of high-paying jobs for IIT graduates.

91. (*a*) structure   (*b*) fabric
    (*c*) good   (*d*) mobility
    (*e*) No correction required

92. (*a*) basic   (*b*) finance
    (*c*) budgetary   (*d*) ordinary
    (*e*) No correction required

93. (*a*) rate   (*b*) part
    (*c*) portions   (*d*) wealth
    (*e*) No correction required

94. (*a*) targets   (*b*) implications
    (*c*) incarnation   (*d*) forms
    (*e*) No correction required

95. (*a*) demanded   (*b*) debited
    (*c*) forced   (*d*) burdened
    (*e*) No correction required

96. (*a*) main   (*b*) achievable
    (*c*) financial   (*d*) accessible
    (*e*) No correction required

97. (*a*) affordably   (*b*) alternatively
    (*c*) not   (*d*) genuinely
    (*e*) No correction required

98. (*a*) cutting   (*b*) providing
    (*c*) enhanced   (*d*) fabricating
    (*e*) No correction required

99. (*a*) focused   (*b*) success
    (*c*) traction   (*d*) force
    (*e*) No correction required

100. (*a*) discourse   (*b*) domain
    (*c*) bodies   (*d*) opinions
    (*e*) No correction required

ANSWERS

1. (*c*)	**2.** (b)	**3.** (e)	**4.** (d)	**5.** (e)	**6.** (b)	**7.** (d)	**8.** (d)	**9.** (a)	**10.** (c)
11. (b)	**12.** (d)	**13.** (e)	**14.** (d)	**15.** (b)	**16.** (e)	**17.** (c)	**18.** (a)	**19.** (e)	**20.** (e)
21. (c)	**22.** (b)	**23.** (c)	**24.** (d)	**25.** (a)	**26.** (d)	**27.** (d)	**28.** (e)	**29.** (e)	**30.** (c)
31. (d)	**32.** (a)	**33.** (e)	**34.** (e)	**35.** (e)	**36.** (b)	**37.** (c)	**38.** (d)	**39.** (a)	**40.** (b)
41. (b)	**42.** (a)	**43.** (d)	**44.** (c)	**45.** (c)	**46.** (d)	**47.** (b)	**48.** (c)	**49.** (d)	**50.** (e)
51. (e)	**52.** (a)	**53.** (a)	**54.** (d)	**55.** (b)	**56.** (c)	**57.** (c)	**58.** (d)	**59.** (e)	**60.** (c)
61. (b)	**62.** (d)	**63.** (c)	**64.** (d)	**65.** (b)	**66.** (d)	**67.** (d)	**68.** (b)	**69.** (d)	**70.** (d)
71. (b)	**72.** (d)	**73.** (b)	**74.** (d)	**75.** (d)	**76.** (c)	**77.** (d)	**78.** (a)	**79.** (c)	**80.** (d)
81. (e)	**82.** (c)	**83.** (e)	**84.** (a)	**85.** (a)	**86.** (c)	**87.** (e)	**88.** (d)	**89.** (d)	**90.** (d)
91. (d)	**92.** (c)	**93.** (e)	**94.** (b)	**95.** (d)	**96.** (e)	**97.** (d)	**98.** (c)	**99.** (c)	**100.** (a)

EXPLANATIONS

For questions 1 to 5:

Floor No.	Person lives	Person's Streams of engineering
8	J	Electrical Engineer
7	E	Aeronautical Engineer
6	K	Automobile Engineer
5	D	Civil Engineer
4	H	Mechanical Engineer
3	F	Chemical Engineer
2	I	Software Engineer
1	G	Instrument Engineer

1. (c) Four

2. (b) Electrical Engineer

3. (e) G

  J, K, H and I live on the even numbered floor.

5. (e) Aeronautical Engineer

6. (b) $A > B \geq R (\geq) C < R \leq Z = M(\leq)P \geq X$

7. (d) E

Mon	Tus.	Wen.	Thu.	Fri.
A	C	E	D	B

For questions 8 to 12:

People	B	P	D	C	R	S	A	Q
Age	31	21	14	26	16	23	19	17

13. (e) A is mother of Q

  Q is the daughter of A= A(Mother), Q(Daughter)

  J is the brother of Q= J(Boy), Q(Girl)

  J is the son of R= R(Father), J(Son)

  J is the father of S, so **R is the Grandfather of S**

For questions 14 to 18:

Person	T	P	Q	R	S	V	U
Born Year	1946	1967	1972	1982	1984	1989	1992
Age	71	50	45	35	33	28	25

19. (e) Economics growth registered = ve jo qi ...(1)

  Growth is expected = qi lo mn   ...(2)

  Registered expected number= lo ve pr ..(3)

  By comparing eq. (1) & (2) we get

  Growth = "qi"...(4)

  By comparing eq. (1) & (3) we get

  Registered = "ve".....(5)

  By eq. (1), (4) & (5) we get

  Economics = 'jo'

20. (e) According to first condition we get

  $7493652 - 2022020 = 5471632$

  According to second condition we get

  $7493652 + 0300303 = 7793955$

  So number 5 & 7 are repeated

For questions 21 and 22:

Box	Fruit
K	Litchi
M	Grapes
J	Apple
L	Mango

For questions 23 to 27:

March		June		October		November	
10th	27th	10th	27th	10th	27th	10th	27th
Y	X	W	N	Z	O	M	V

For questions 28 and 29:

F < D < B < E < A < C

30. (c) $C > B > A \geq K = R$

34. (e) Can't be determined

35. (e)

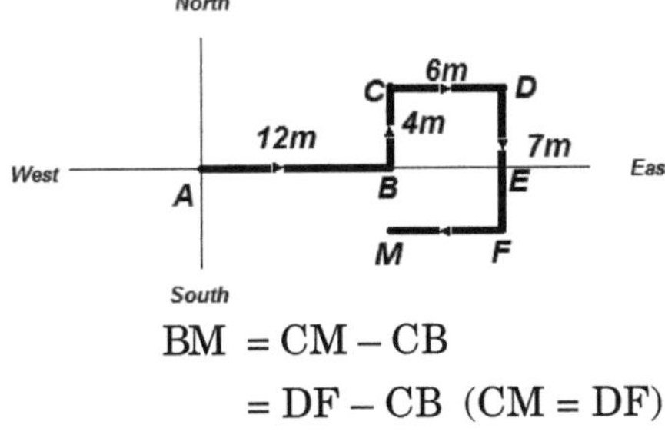

  $BM = CM - CB$

  $= DF - CB$ (CM = DF)

  $= 7 - 4 = 3m$

  Hence the distance B to M is **3m**.

36. (b) 14

  $$14 \times \frac{1}{2} + 1 = 8,$$

  $$8 \times \frac{2}{2} + 1 = 9,$$

  $$9 \times \frac{3}{2} + 1 = 14.5,$$

  $$14.5 \times \frac{4}{2} + 1 = 30,$$

  $$30 \times \frac{5}{2} + 1 = \mathbf{76}$$

37. (c) 20

$20 + 3^2 = 29$

$29 + 5^2 = 54$

$54 + 7^2 = 103$

$103 + 9^2 = 184$

$184 + 11^2 = \mathbf{305}$

38. (d) 7

$7 \times 1 + 1 = 8$

$8 \times 2 + 2 = 18$

$18 \times 3 + 3 = 57$

$57 \times 4 + 4 = \mathbf{232}$

$\mathbf{232} \times 5 + 5 = 1165$

39. (a) 5, 7, 18, 47, 103, **195**

40. (b) 77

$77 + 8 = 85$

$85 - 8 \times 2 = 69$

$69 + 8 \times 2 \times 2 = 101$

$101 - 8 \times 2 \times 2 \times 2 = 37$

$37 + 8 \times 2 \times 2 \times 2 \times 2 = \mathbf{165}$

41. (b) For X company sales of 2015

= 5000 cars

According to question Sales of 2016

$= 5000 \times (100 + 20)/100 = 6000$

For Y company sales of 2015

= 4000 cars

According to question Sales of 2016

$= 4000 \times (100-10)/100 = 3600$

Total sales $= 6000 + 3600 = \mathbf{9600}$ **cars**

42. (a) For X company total sales of 2011, 2013 and 2015 is = 2000+4500+5000=11500

For Y company total sales of 2012 and 2014 is = 2500 + 4500 =7000

Ratio is 11500:7000 = **23:14**

43. (d) Car sold in 2012 = 6000

Car sold in 2013 = 7500

Hence % is $\dfrac{(7500 - 6000) \times 100}{7500} = 20\%$

44. (c) Average no.of car of X company

$= \dfrac{2000+3500+4500+4000+5000}{5}$

$= \dfrac{19000}{5} = 3800$

Average no.of car of Y company

$= \dfrac{1000+2500+3000+4500+4000}{5}$

$= \dfrac{15000}{5} = 3000$

Difference $= 3800 - 3000 = \mathbf{800}$

45. (c) $3500 + 4500 + 4000 + 2500 + 3000 + 4500$

$= \mathbf{22500}$

46. (d) Total number of female visitors from district Q and R

$= (350 \times 56/100) + (375 \times 40/100)$

$= 346$

Total number of male visitors from district R and S

$= (375 \times 60/100) + (450 \times 56/100)$

$= 477$

Difference $= 477 - 346 = \mathbf{131}$

47. (b) Average visitor of P,Q and R district

$= (250 + 350 + 375)/3 = 325$

Average visitor of S,T and U district

$= (450 + 300 + 525)/3 = 425$

$\% = 100 - \dfrac{(425 - 325) \times 100}{425} = 76\%$

48. (c) Total male visitors from district T and U = $(300 \times 55/100) + (325 \times 32/100) = 333$

Total female visitors from district R and S = $(375 \times 40/100) + (450 \times 44/100)$

$= 348$

Ratio $= 333:348 = \mathbf{111:116}$

49. (d) Male visitor from district R

$= 375 \times 60/100 = 225$

Female visitor from district T

$= 300 \times 45/100 = 135$

$\% = (225 - 135) \times 100/135$

$= 66\dfrac{2}{3}\%$

50. (e) Total number of male visitors from district Q, R & S = 154 + 225 + 252 = 631

Total number of female visitors from district S, T & U = 198 + 135 + 375 = 708

Difference $= 708 - 631 = \mathbf{77}$

51. (e) I. $x^2 - 3x + 2 = 0$

$\Rightarrow x^2 - 2x - x + 2 = 0$

$\Rightarrow (x-2)(x-1) = 0$

$\Rightarrow x = \mathbf{2, 1}$

II. $2y^2 - 7y + 6 = 0$

$\Rightarrow 2y^2 - 4y - 3y + 6 = 0$

$\Rightarrow (2y-3)(y-2) = 0$

$\Rightarrow y = 2, \dfrac{3}{2}$

Hence, no relation can be established.

52. (a) I. $3x^2 + 4x + 1 = 0$

$\Rightarrow 3x^2 + 3x + x + 1 = 0$

$\Rightarrow (3x + 1)(x + 1) = 0$

$\Rightarrow x = -1, -\dfrac{1}{3}$

II. $y^2 + 5y + 6 = 0$

$\Rightarrow y^2 + 3y + 2y + 6 = 0$

$\Rightarrow (y + 3)(y + 2) = 0$

$\Rightarrow y = -3, -2$

Hence, $x > y$

53. (a) I. $2x^2 + 5x + 2 = 0$

$\Rightarrow 2x^2 + 4x + x + 2 = 0$

$\Rightarrow (2x + 1)(x + 2) = 0$

$\Rightarrow x = -\dfrac{1}{2}, -2$

II. $y^2 + 9y + 20 = 0$

$\Rightarrow y^2 + 5y + 4y + 20 = 0$

$\Rightarrow (y + 5)(y + 4) = 0$

$\Rightarrow y = -5, -4$

Hence, $x > y$

54. (d) I. $x^2 - 7x + 10 = 0$

$\Rightarrow x^2 - 5x - 2x + 10 = 0$

$\Rightarrow (x - 5)(x - 2) = 0$

$\Rightarrow x = 2, 5$

II. $y^2 - 12y + 35 = 0$

$\Rightarrow y^2 - 5y - 7y + 35 = 0$

$\Rightarrow (y - 5)(y - 7) = 0$

$\Rightarrow y = 5, 7$

Hence, $y \geq x$

55. (b) I. $(x - 12)^2 = 0 \Rightarrow x = 12$

II. $y^2 = 144 \Rightarrow y = \pm 12$

Hence, $x \geq y$

56. (c) $23.001 \times 18.999 \times 7.998 = \mathbf{3500}$

57. (c) $33.99\sqrt{?} + 42.0032\sqrt{?} = \dfrac{76}{12.998} \times (?)$

$\Rightarrow 75.9932\sqrt{?} = \dfrac{76}{12.998} \times (?)$

$\Rightarrow \dfrac{\sqrt{?}}{?} = \dfrac{76}{12.998 \times 75.9932}$

$\Rightarrow \dfrac{1}{\sqrt{?}} = \dfrac{1}{13} \Rightarrow \sqrt{?} = 13 \Rightarrow ? = 169$

58. (d)

$94.95 \times 13.03 + \sqrt{35.98} \times 14.99 = 53 \times \sqrt{?}$

assume that $95 \times 13 + \sqrt{36} \times 15 = 53 \times \sqrt{?}$

$\Rightarrow \dfrac{1235 + 90}{53} = \sqrt{?}$

$\Rightarrow \sqrt{?} = 25 \Rightarrow ? = 625$

59. (e) $1884.88 \div 144.921 + 6.99 + (?)^2 = 69.09$

assume that $1884 \div 144 + 7 + (?)^2 = 69$

$\Rightarrow (?)^2 = 69 - 13 - 7$

$\Rightarrow (?)^2 = 49 \Rightarrow ? = 7$

60. (c) 41% of $601 - 250.17 = ? - 77\%$ of 910

$601 \times \dfrac{41}{100} - 250.17 = ? - 910 \times \dfrac{77}{100}$

Assume that $246 - 250 = ? - 700$

$\Rightarrow ? = 696$ or 690

61. (b) Condition I:

Given that shopkeeper profit = 12% and Prices increased = 40%

So discount = x%

$\Rightarrow 12 = 40 - x - \dfrac{40 \times x}{100}$

$\left(\text{by formula; profit} = r_1 \pm r_2 \pm \dfrac{r_1 \times r_2}{100} \right)$

$\Rightarrow 28 = \dfrac{7x}{5} \Rightarrow x = 20\%$

Condition II:

C.P = Rs. 120 and Profit $x\% = 20\%$

S.P. $= 120 \times \left(\dfrac{100 + 20}{100} \right) = ₹\, 144$

62. (d) In order to get the sum odd, one card should have odd number and the other card should have even number.

Hence, required probability

$= (14 \times 13)/{}^{27}C_2 = 14/17.$

63. (c) Let the work done by A and B in 1 day be 5 units and 6 units respectively.

According to the queston,

$6x : 5(x + 8) = 2 : 3$

Thus, $x = 10$ and total work = 150 units.

Hence, required time = 150/11 days.

64. (d) Given that P = 9100, r% = 20% and t = 2

$A = P(1 + r\%)^t = 9100(1 + 20/100)^2$

$= 9100 \times \dfrac{6}{5} \times \dfrac{6}{5} = 13104$

65. (b) Let the salary of the man be 100x

$\Rightarrow 72x \times (1 - 1/6 - 3/8) = 5280$

$\Rightarrow x = 160$ and required amount

= Rs. 4320.

66. (d) The total age of husband and wife 5 years ago = 23 × 2 = 46 years

In Present total age of husband and wife is = 46 + 5 + 5 = 56 years

Total present age of husband, wife and child is = 20 × 3 = 60 years

So the age of child = 60 − 56 = **4 years**

67. (d) We cannot determine the required answer.

68. (b) Let the speed(in km/hr) of the man and the stream is x and y.

Thus, $(x + y)9t = 3d$ ....(i)

and $(x - y)10t = 2d$ ....(ii)

Solving (i) and (ii) and putting the value of $x + y = 15$ we get,

$15 \times 9 \times 2 = (x - y)10 \times 3$

Hence, $x = 12$ and $y = 3$.

69. (d) Ratio of the investments of P, Q and R = $15000 \times 12 : 18000 \times 6 : 10000 \times 8$

$= 45 : 27 : 20$

Hence, required profit will be Rs.9200.

70. (d) Required area

$= 28^2 - \pi 14^2 = 168 \ m^2$.

71. (b) The entire passage talks about the how the computer security is facing a crisis, allowing hackers an easy control over the computer security system. Hence (b) is the correct answer.

72. (d) Refer to- "Annoyed by the parlous state of computer security, he had, he claimed, decided to perform a public service by demonstrating just how easy it was to seize control". Hence (d) is the correct answer. Option (b) is incorrect as the passage makes it clear that the hacker did a public service. He just didn't want to 'show' anything.

73. (b) Refer to the end of paragraph 2- "In October... the American elections." Only option (b) is factually incorrect.

74. (d) The passage states- ".**with so much meaningless traffic** that websites such as Twitter and Reddit were made inaccessible to many users." This clearly makes (d) correct. Option (c) just mentions the name of the company which used the software Mirai.

75. (d) The passage states- "We are building a world-sized robot," says Bruce Schneier, a security analyst, in the shape of the "Internet of Things". The IoT is a buzz-phrase used to describe the computerisation of everything". This makes statements (ii) and (iii) correct. Statement (i) cannot be verified. Hence (d) is the correct answer.

76. (c) "Malice" refers to "hatred." Option b is a synonym of "malice." "Benignity" refers to "an act of kindness." Hence, it is an antonym of "malice."

77. (d) "Parlous" refers to a "dreadful state." "Innocuous" which means "harmless" is an appropriate antonym of "parlous."

78. (a) "Subsequent" and "consequent" are synonyms. Both mean "ensuing".

79. (c) "Subvert" means "to destabilize." "Undermine" is a synonym. It means "to diminish."

80. (d) "Typo" refers to an error. "Bug" can be a synonym of "typo."

81. (e) "Bored to death" refers to a state of extreme boredom. The sentence is correct.

82. (c) The infinitive form of the verb "go" should be used in the sentence. The principal verb is "advised."

83. (e) The sentence is grammatically correct.

84. (a) "Aware" is followed by the preposition "of."

85. (a) "Put off" refers to delaying a schedule.

86. (c) "Call around" refers to calling several people usually when one is trying to organize something.

87. (e) "Chip in" means "to contribute."

88. (d) "Hang in" refers to being persistent.

89. (d) "Think back" refers to reminiscing something.

90. (d) "Cut in" refers to interrupting someone.

91. (d) The sentence talks about the upward socio-economic 'movement' with respect to better quality of education. The use of the term 'continues' is a clue here. Hence, 'mobility' is the only correct option. Other options will make the sentence illogical.

92. (c) Since the entire passage focuses on the financing of higher educational institutions, therefore 'budgetary' is the correct fit.

93. (e) 'Fraction' best fits in the blank as the sentence is talking about a portion of education cost. 'Portions' however is incorrect because of its plural form.

94. (b) The sentence is talking about the results of something, which has a hidden agenda. Hence 'implications' is the correct fit. Other options do not make any sense.

95. (d) Large loans are bound to 'burden' people. Hence (d) is the correct answer.

96. (e) In the following sentence, it has been mentioned that "graduates would opt for safe career options". This indicates that the objective of the graduate post graduation. Hence (e) is the correct answer.

97. (d) The blank would take in a word with respect to the opening of this sentence. It states that due to large loans graduates would opt for safe options, not what they really or 'genuinely' want to pursue.

98. (c) The given blank requires an adjective and out of the given options only 'enhance' fits the best.

99. (c) Out of the given options only 'traction' best fits in, especially how the remaining passage pans out.

100. (a) Since stories of high paying jobs have been mentioned, public 'discourse' best fits.

REASONING & COMPUTER APTITUDE

Directions (Q. 1 and 2): Study the four diagrams and convert it into other diagrams by implementing the instructions in each of the three steps.

14	RS2	EK3
AC9		MT7
F8	05	UL

Interchange the Alphabets to get step 1 as arrows mention in the above figure.

Step 1 :

UL4	02	F3
MT9		AC7
EK8	RS5	I

Step 2 :

(i) If the alphabets contain one consonant and one vowel and the number with them is greater than 3, then subtract 3 from the given number.

(ii) If the alphabets are two consonant and the number with them is greater than 5, then change the letters with the previous letter in alphabetical series.

UL1	02	F3
LS9		AC4
EK5	RS5	I

Step 3 : In this step elements are coded in a special pattern.

EK5	R2	I
UL1		F3
LS9	WX5	AC4

As per the rules followed in the above step, find out the appropriate steps for the given input.

And answer the following questions.

A5	LM3	FT2
ZU8		BC6
G5	S7	MO

1. Which element will come in the second cell of the third row after step 2?

(a) LM7

(b) KL7

(c) ZU3

(d) AB8

(e) None of these

2. Which element will replace AB8 in step-3?

(a) PQ7

(b) ZU3

(c) FT5

(d) MO2

(e) None of these

Directions (Q. 3 and 4): *Answer the questions on the basis of the information given below.*

The Budget session began on a stormy note as opposition members demanding a debate on the recent hate crimes against Indians living in the USA. Congress blamed the Modi government for remaining silent on the attacks against Indians in US. In his reply, Union Home Minister said that the government has taken a serious note and PM will reply in next week of Parliament session. In recent weeks, at least two Indians have been killed in incidents of hate crime in the US. "Each attack involved a slogan. Go back to your country". America condemned it but is not taking any steps to address the issue.

3. What may be the repercussions after recent attacks on Indians in US?

   I. There may be impact on Indian-US trade policy.

   II. Indian Government will coerce US Government.

   III. American Govt. will give life imprisonment to accused to make a set mark that America is against racism.

  (*a*) Only I   (*b*) Only I and III

  (*c*) Only III   (*d*) Only I and II

  (*e*) None of these

4. Which of the following substantiates the laxity of Indian-American Govt.?

   I. Modi govt. has taken a serious note and ready to reply in next week of parliament session.

   II. Condemning the attack but not taking any steps by American Govt.

   III. Still there is no action as racism slogan "Go back to your country" is spreading.

  (*a*) Only III   (*b*) Only I and II

  (*c*) I, II and III   (*d*) Only II

  (*e*) None of these

Directions (Q. 5 to 7): *Answer the questions on the basis of the information given below.*

A, B, C, D, E, F, G and H are sitting in a row facing north but not necessary in the same order. No two persons whose names are consecutive letters sit next to each other. Each of them have a hobby – Playing game, Watching TV, Singing, Dancing, Online surfing, Chatting, Acting and Cooking, but not necessary in the same order. Either A or H sits at the extreme end of the row. A is sitting third to the left of the person whose hobby is online surfing. B sits second to the right of the person who likes acting. C sits second to the right of F. G who likes watching TV is sitting second from the right end of the row. The

person whose hobby is dancing is immediate neighbor of F who likes Playing Games. The person whose hobby is acting is not sitting adjacent to the person whose hobby is online surfing. C's hobby is neither acting nor online surfing. D and E do not sit any extreme end of the row. One of the immediate neighbors of H likes Cooking and the one whose hobby is singing sits left end of the row. Neither H nor D likes Acting.

5. Which of the following members is sitting second to the right of the sixth person from the right end of the row?

  (*a*) E

  (*b*) The one whose hobby is acting

  (*c*) A

  (*d*) The one whose hobby is cooking

  (*e*) None of these

6. If A is related to B and F is related to E in a particular way, then with whom is the member whose hobby is dancing related to in the same way?

  (*a*) The one whose hobby is acting

  (*b*) G

  (*c*) The one whose hobby is acting

  (*d*) C

  (*e*) B

7. Which of the following combinations is not true?

  (*a*) A-Singing   (*b*) E-Acting

  (*c*) G-Watching TV   (*d*) B-Playing games

  (*e*) D-Dancing

Directions (Q. 8 to 10): *Answer the questions on the basis of the information given below.*

@ means either hour hand or minute hand is at 8

means either hour hand or minute hand is at 5

$ means either hour hand or minute hand is at 4

% means either hour hand or minute hand is at 12

& means either hour hand or minute hand is at 2

£ means either hour hand or minute hand is at 3

Note: if two symbols are given then by default first symbol is considered as hour hand and second one is considered as minute hand. All time are considered as PM.

(For eq. @ # → 8 : 25 pm)

8. If A takes 25 min to reach railway station and his train is scheduled at #& then at what time should he leave to reach the station 5 minute earlier?

  (*a*) $%   (*b*) $&

  (*c*) &$ (*d*) $@

  (*e*) £$

9. If a train departed from a station at &£ and it takes 2 hours to reach the destination, then when will it reach its destination?

(a) $£   (b) $%

(c) #$ (d) $#

(e) £$

10. A person has to catch a train that is scheduled to depart at '@%'. It takes the person 4 hours and 15 minutes to reach the railway station from his home. At what time should he leave from his home for the railway station to arrive at the station at least 25 minutes before the departure of the train?

(a) %@   (b) £$

(c) %+   (d) +@

(e) None of these

Directions (Q. 11 to 15): *Answer the questions on the basis of the information given below.*

There are six cars – A, B, C, D, E, F – parked in a row facing north direction, but not necessarily in the same order. The distances between two adjacent cars are successive multiples of three (i.e., if the distance between the 1st and the 2nd car is 3 m, 1st and the 3rd cars is 6 m and between 1st and 4th cars is 9 m and so on.)

It is also known that:

(i) The distance between 'A' and 'B' is 33 m and car 'A' is to the immediate left of car 'B'.

(ii) The distance between the cars 'E' and 'F' is 99 m. the distance between 'E' and 'D' is a multiple of '2'.

(iii) The car 'B' is 75 m away from car 'C'. Car 'D' is in one position to the left of car 'C'; but not to the immediate left of 'C'.

(iv) Car 'F' starts moving towards north and after going 18 m, it turns right, then it moves 63 m and then it goes another 7 m to its right turn and stops at point 'Z'

(v) Car 'C' moves 33 m towards south direction, and then takes a right turn and goes 75 m straight. Then it turns again to its right direction and moves another 17 m and halts at point 'X'.

(vi) An another car 'M' is parked at 13 m to the west of point 'Z', Now 'M' starts moving towards further west and covers 77 m and reached point 'Y'.

11. How many cars are there between 'D' and 'F'?

(a) Two

(b) None

(c) More than three

(d) One

(e) Three

12. What is the distance between point 'Z' and point 'X'?

(a) 25 m

(b) 18 m

(c) They are not in same line

(d) 32 m

(e) 27 m

13. What is the position of 'M' with respect to 'F'?

(a) $5\sqrt{34}$ m towards north-west

(b) 50 m towards south-east

(c) $10\sqrt{17}$ m towards north-east

(d) $5\sqrt{34}$ m towards south-east

(e) None of these

14. Which car will be met first, if 'M' moves through the shortest distance from point 'Y'?

(a) E   (b) F

(c) C   (d) D

(e) None of these

15. What is the position of 'A' with respect to car 'E'?

(a) 75 m towards right

(b) To the immediate right

(c) 36 m towards left

(d) 69 m towards left

(e) None of the above

16. The mushrooming of business schools in the country is a cause for shortage of faculty with Ph.D qualification. In addition, the higher pay and generous fringe benefits given by industry has encouraged qualified people to not seek academic positions.

Which of the following statements, if true, would tend to STRENGTHEN the argument?

(a) The average salary for industry positions in Gujarat is more than the average salary for faculty positions in some business schools in Ahmedabad by around 30%

(b) The average salary for industry positions in Gujarat is less than the average salary for faculty positions in a top business school in Ahmedabad by around 30%

(c) The average salary for recent Ph.D graduates in the industry is 20% higher than that in academics

(d) The rate of growth of salaries for the industry positions is equal to the rate of growth of salaries for academic positions for the past three years

(e) None of the above

17. The Government has appealed to all citizens to use potable water judiciously as there is an acute shortage in supply.

Excessive use may lead to huge scarcity in future months.

Which of the assumptions is implicit in the above statement?

An assumption is something supposed or taken for granted)

(*a*) People may ignore the appeal and continue using water as per their consideration

(*b*) Government may be able to tap those who do not respond to the appeal

(*c*) Government may be able to put in place alternate sources of water in the event of a crisis situation

(*d*) Large number of people may positively respond to the Government's appeal and help tide over the crisis

(*e*) Only poor are going to suffer from this shortage of water supply.

Directions (Q. 18 to 20): *Answer the questions on the basis of the information given below.*

An input-output is given in different steps. Some mathematical operations are done in each step. No mathematical operation is repeated in next step.

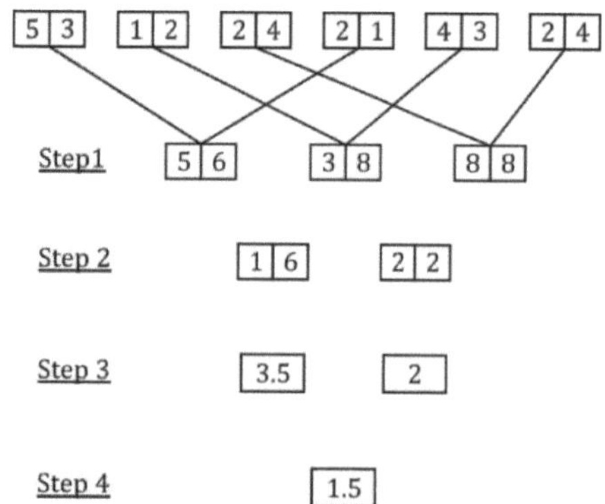

As per the rules followed in the steps given above, find out in each of the following questions the appropriate step for the given input.

4 2   5 1   2 9   3 2   7 1   1 4

18. Find the addition of the two numbers obtained in step III?

(*a*) 1.5

(*b*) 3

(*c*) 7

(*d*) 3.5

(*e*) None of these

19. Find the difference between sum of numbers which obtained in 1st step and sum of numbers obtained in all other steps?

(*a*) 232   (*b*) 185

(*c*) 188   (*d*) 183.5

(*e*) None of these

20. Find the multiplication of the numbers obtained in step II?

(*a*) 426   (*b*) 462

(*c*) 188   (*d*) 98

(*e*) None of these

21. Statement: Science is a sort of news agency comparable in principle to other news agencies. But this news agency gives us information which is reliable to an extraordinary high degree due to elaborate techniques of verification and its capacity to survive centuries. So, science should be read with as much interest as we read news.

Assumptions:

I. Science encourages investigative spirit.

II. People read news out of interest.

(*a*) If only assumption I is implicit

(*b*) If only assumption II is implicit

(*c*) If either I or II is implicit

(*d*) If neither I nor II is implicit

(*e*) Both I and II are implicit

Directions (Q. 22 and 23): *In each of the following questions, a question is followed by three statements numbered I, II and III.*

Read all the statements to find the answer to given question and then answer accordingly that which statement/s can give the answer alone/together.

22. What is the direction of point U with respect to point X?

Statement I : Point R is 7 m to the North of point Q. Point P is 8 m to the West of point Q. Point R is 6 m to the West of point U.

Statement II : Point B is 9 m to the North of point A. Point P is 5 m to the North of point Z. Point Z is 4 m to the West of point A.

Statement III : Point C is 7 m to the East of point A. Point X is 2 m to the East of point F. Point F is 3 m to the North of point C.

(*a*) Both I and III

(*b*) Both II and III

(*c*) All I, II and III

(*d*) II and either I or III

(*e*) Even I, II and III together are not sufficient

23. What does the code 'bp' stand for in the given code language?

    Statement I : In the language, 'black white red' is coded as 'df dc or' and 'green blue grey' is coded as 'st hn wo'

    Statement II : In the language, 'blue pink brown' is coded as 'er bp hn' and 'pink blue white' is coded as 'hn or bp'

    Statement III : In the language, 'green violet orange' is coded as 'pa wo kl' and 'yellow pink brown' is coded as 'bp bi er'

    (a) Both II and III

    (b) I and either II or III

    (c) II and either I or III

    (d) Both I and III

    (e) All I, II and III

24. A very large number of technically qualified young Indians are coming cut of colleges every year though there are not enough opportunities for them to get gainful employment.

    Which of the following contradicts the views expressed in the above statements?

    (a) Technically qualified persons are for superior to those with standard degrees like BA/BSc/ BCom etc.

    (b) The Government has not done effective perspective planning for engaging technically qualified personnal while authorizing the setting up of technical colleges.

    (c) All huge gap exists between the level of competence of technically qualified graduates and requirements of the industry.

    (d) Majority of the technically qualified persons are migrating from India to developed countries for better opportunities.

    (e) None of the above

Directions (Q. 25 and 26): *Answer the questions on the basis of the information given below.*

There are two square fields of different size such that the larger one is surrounding the smaller field. Four gates are there for each field in the middle of the sides. Eight people A, B, C, D, E, F, G and H are standing at different gates but not necessary in the same order. It is also known that:

The persons who are on the sides of larger park facing center while the persons who are at the sides of the smaller park facing outside such that inner sides persons and outer sides persons are facing each other. There is one person standing between B and D. C faces B. A is to the immediate right of C. G is not the immediate neighbor of D. G faces neither D nor F. One person is standing between H and F. E is facing the center

25. Which of the following persons are facing each other?

    (a) BD

    (b) EB

    (c) FH

    (d) DE

    (e) AH

26. Four of the following five are alike in a certain way based from a group which one of the following does not belong to that group?

    (a) EF

    (b) CH

    (c) DA

    (d) FC

    (e) BH

Directions (Q. 27 and 28): *Answer the questions on the basis of the information given below.*

P is the husband of Q. R is the grandchild of P. P has only one child(son) who is married to T's child. T has only two children, one son and one daughter. X is the grandson of T. S is the brother in law of the son of T. U and V are the children of T. W is married to the son of T. X is the son of U's brother.

27. How is T related to R?

    (a) Grandfather

    (b) Grandmother

    (c) Maternal Grandfather

    (d) Maternal Grandmother

    (e) Either (c) or (d)

28. How is X related to V?

    (a) Son

    (b) Daughter

    (c) Son in law

    (d) Daughter in law

    (e) Husband

Directions (Q. 29 and 30): *In each question below are given a statement followed by two courses of action numbered I and II. You have to assume everything in the statement to be true and on the basis of the information given in the statement, decide which of the suggested courses of action logically follow(s) for pursuing.*

Give answer

(a) If only I follows

(b) If only II follows

(c) If either I or II follows

(d) If neither I nor II follows

(e) If both I and II follow

29. Statement : Every year, at the beginning or at the end of the monsoons, we have some cases of conjunctivitis, but this year, it seems to be a major epidemic, witnessed after nearly four years.

Courses of action:

I. Precautionary measures should be taken after every four years to check this epidemic.

II. People should be advised to drink boiled water during rainy season.

30. Statement : Researchers are feeling agitated as libraries are not equipped to provide the right information to the right users at the right time in the required format. Even the users are not aware about the various services available for them.

Courses of action:

I. All the information available to the libraries should be computerized to provide faster services to the users.

II. Library staff should be trained in computer operations.

Directions (Q. 31 to 35): *Answer the questions on the basis of the information given below.*

Ten lecturers P, Q, R, S, T, U, V, W, X and Y teach in the same college. They give lectures in five months (April, May, June, September and December). They give lectures in each month on 7th and 21st date. Only two lectures held in a month. The lectures are attended by different number of students. The total strength of students is 100 in each class and 50% attendance is compulsory for each class. The number of students will be even in the month of 30 days and odd in the month of 31 days. Different number of students attends class on different days. It is also known that:

No lecturer can give the lecture after W. U gives lecture in the month which has 30 days. T and Q give lecturers after U on the 7th of different months respectively. Number of students who attend class on 7th September is a whole square (two digit number).

R does not give the lecture in the month in which either Y or Q gives lecture. The sum of number of students who attend class on the 7th of two month is 152. Only three lecturers give lecture between U and the lecturer whose class is attended by 68 students. The difference of number of students who attend class on 7th September and the sum of number of students who attend class on May, is 58. Q gives lecture in the month which has 30 days. The average of number of students who attend class on 21st April and 21st June is 76. P gives lecture in the month which has 31 days. T gives lecture in one of the day before Q. Total 55 students attend V's lecture. V does not give lecture in the month in which W gives. There are four persons who give lecturers between V and S. Y gives lecture in the month which is after the month in which V gives lecture.

The total number of students who attend class in five months is 714. The sum of number of students who attend class on 7th may and 7th June is 147. Students who attend class on 7th June is less than 90. The difference of the number of students who attend class of lecturer Y and R is 4. X gives lecture after P and the number of students who attend his lecture is greater than 70 and less than 80 and is not divisible by 4. The number of studens who attend class on 7th December is multiple of 11.

31. Who among the following lecturer gives lecture on 21st June?

(a) T   (b) P

(c) Y   (d) V

(e) None of these

32. How many students attend class on 7th December?

(a) 67   (b) 80

(c) 68   (d) 77

(e) 55

33. How many lecturers give lectures between P and Q?

(a) Three   (b) Two

(c) Four   (d) One

(e) None

34. Who among the following gives lecture which is attended by 80 students?

(a) S   (b) T

(c) R   (d) U

(e) None of these

35. Four of the following five are alike in a certain way and thus form a group. Which of the following does not belong to that group?

(a) R   (b) 67

(c) V   (d) T

(e) 64

Directions (Q. 36 and 37): *Answer the questions on the basis of the information given below.*

First 12 even numbers are written from top to bottom. The letters of the word 'SACRED' are written in alphabetical order against each multiple of 4 (One letter against one number). There are 2 letters between N and S. There are as many letters between E and N as between P and D. P is not against number 14. There are 5 letters between U and T such that U is above T. I is written against number 6. (No letter is repeated against any number)

36. Which is the second letter in the word formed by using the letters assigned to the numbers – 6, 12, 14 and 20?

(a) T
(b) D
(c) N
(d) I
(e) R

37. If there are 3 letters of English Alphabet between the letters assigned to 10 and 22, then how many letters in the English alphabet are there between the letters assigned to the numbers 18 and 22?

(a) Three
(b) Five
(c) One
(d) Four
(e) Cannot be determined

38. The rate of violent crime in this state is increased up to 30% from last year. The fault lies entirely in our system of justice. Recently our judge's sentences have been so lenient that criminals can now do almost anything without fear of a long prison term.

The argument above would be weakened if it were true that

(a) 85% of the other States in the nation have lower crime rates than does this state

(b) White-collar crime in this state has also increased by over 25% in the last year

(c) 35% of the police in this state have been laid off in the last year due to budget cuts

(d) Polls show that 65% of the population in this state opposes capital punishment

(e) None of the above

Directions (Q. 39 to 43): *Answer the questions on the basis of the information given below.*

There are 10 shelves numbered 1, 2....10. They are arranged in two rows opposite to each other. The shelves 1, 2...5 are in row 1 and rest in row 2 which is above row 1. The shelves are arranged in the increasing order of number given to them. Shelf number 1 is placed on extreme left of row 1, then shelf number 2 and so on. Similarly the shelf number 6 is placed on extreme left end of row 2, and so on. Each shelf contains a certain number of glass slabs and photo frames. There is at least one glass slab in each shelf. The length of each glass slab is 15 cm and that of each photo frame is 6 cm. It is also known that:

The shelf 3 has length 33 cm. There is one shelf between shelf 3 and yellow shelf. The yellow shelf contains 1 glass slab and 6 photo frames more than that in shelf 3. The silver shelf is just above the yellow shelf. The silver shelf contains same number of glass slabs as yellow shelf and 1 photo frame. There are 2 shelves between silver and green slabs. The length of green shelf is 3 cm greater than the silver shelf. The blue shelf is immediate next in number to green shelf. The blue shelf contains 1 glass slab more than that in silver shelf and 1 photo frame less than that in green shelf. There is one shelf between blue and orange shelves. The white shelf is just below the orange shelf. There is one shelf between white and red shelf. Black shelf is in row 2.

The pink shelf is just below the black shelf. The black shelf has same number of photo frames and glass slabs. The orange shelf has 1 glass slab more than black shelf. The length of orange shelf is 24 cm more than the length of pink shelf. The length of violet shelf is half the length of yellow shelf. The red shelf has greater than or equal to four glass slabs. The length of pink shelf is 6 cm less than the shelf immediate next in number. The length of row 1 is 267 cm and that of row 2 is 249 cm.

39. How many more photo frames can row 2 accomodate?

(a) 1
(b) 2
(c) 3
(d) None
(e) 4

40. The color of shelf 2 is:

(a) Green
(b) Violet
(c) Red
(d) White
(e) Pink

41. How many total glass slabs do the silver, black and red shelves contain?

(a) 7
(b) 9
(c) 10
(d) Other than those given in options
(e) 12

42. What is the total length of the pink, orange and blue shelves?

(a) 146 cm
(b) 134 cm
(c) 141 cm
(d) 133 cm
(e) 126 cm

43. If all the photo frames of silver and white shelves are removed and added in black shelf then what will be the length of the black shelf?

(*a*) 67 cm

(*b*) 66 cm

(*c*) 61 cm

(*d*) 69 cm

(*e*) 62 cm

44. During the SARS days, about 23,500 doctors who had treated SARS sufferers died and about 23,670 doctors who had not engaged in treatment for SARS sufferers died. On the basis of those figures, it can be concluded that it was not much more figures, it can be concluded that it was not much more dangerous to participate in SARS treatment during the SARS day than it was not to participate in SARS treatment.

Which of the following would reveal most clearly the absurdity of the conclusion drawn above?

(*a*) Counting deaths among doctors who had participated in SARS treatment in addition to addition to deaths among doctors who had not participated is SARS treatment

(*b*) Expressing the difference between the numbers of deaths among doctors who had treated SARS sufferers and doctors who had not treated SARS suffers as a percentage of the total number of deaths

(*c*) Separating deaths caused by accidents during the treatment to SARS suffers from deaths caused by infect of SARS suffers

(*d*) Comparing death rates per thousand members of each group rather than comparing total numbers of deaths

(*e*) None of the above

45. Study the following information carefully and answer the questions given below.

Following are the conditions for selecting Marketing Manager in an organization. The Candidate must-

(i) Be a Graduate in any discipline with at least 55% marks.

(ii) Have secured at least 40% marks in the selection interview.

(iii) Have post qualification work experience of at least five years in the Marketing division of an organization.

(iv) Have secured at least 45% marks in the selection examination.

(v) Have a post Graduate degree/diploma in Marketing-Management with at least 60% marks.

Study the following information carefully and find which of the following condition shows candidate is not selected?

(*a*) Candidate is daughter of a renowned freedom fighter from another state.

(*b*) Candidate has a post Graduate degree in Finance with 60% marks.

(*c*) Candidate has completed his graduation with 80% marks.

(*d*) Candidate does not own a house in Noida.

(*e*) Candidate has secured 56% marks in Cap Gemini's interview.

DATA ANALYSIS & INTERPRETATION

46. Five men and five women are to be arranged in a row while seating in a party.

Quantity I: Number of ways of arranging 5 men and 5 women such that no two men or women are adjacent to each other.

Quantity II: Number of ways of arranging 5 men and 5 women such that all men sit together.

(*a*) Quantity I > Quantity II

(*b*) Quantity I < Quantity II

(*c*) Quantity I ≥ Quantity II

(*d*) Quantity I ≤ Quantity II

(*e*) Quantity I = Quantity II or No relation

47. Quantity I: Value of 'a' if 's' is an acute angle and PR I I QT.

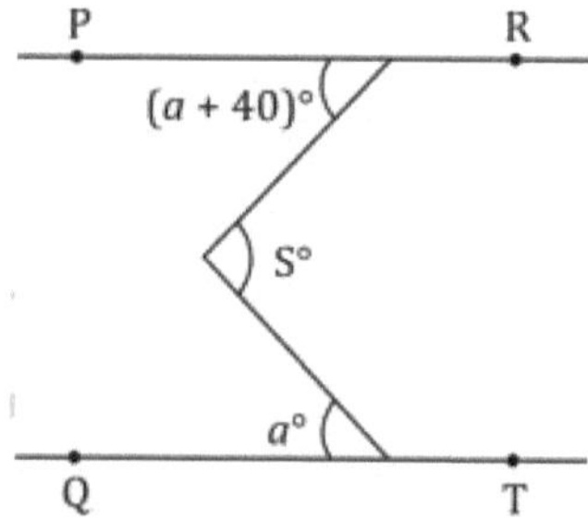

Quantity II: 25°

(*a*) Quantity I > Quantity II

(*b*) Quantity I < Quantity II

(*c*) Quantity I ≥ Quantity II

(*d*) Quantity I ≤ Quantity II

(*e*) Quantity I = Quantity II or No rclation

48. There are 63 cards in a box numbered from 1 to 63. Every card is numbered with only 1 number.

Quantity I: Probability of picking up a card whose digits, if interchanged, result in a number which is 36 more than the number picked up.

Quantity II: Probability of picking up a card, the number printed on which is a multiple of 8 but not that of 16.

(*a*) Quantity I > Quantity II

(*b*) Quantity I < Quantity II

(*c*) Quantity I ≥ Quantity II

(*d*) Quantity I ≤ Quantity II

(*e*) Quantity I = Quantity II or No relation

Direction (Q. 49): *Each of the following questions consists of 3 statements A, B and C. You have to determine that which of the following statement/ statements are necessary to answer the questions:*

49. If m and n are integers then is n completely divisible by 10?

A. The value of $\left(\dfrac{m}{10} + \dfrac{n}{10}\right)$ is an integer value.

B. The value of $\left(\dfrac{m}{7} + \dfrac{n}{10}\right)$ is an integer value.

C. Value of n is greater than m.

(*a*) Any two of them

(*b*) A and B together

(*c*) Any of them

(*d*) All statements are required

(*e*) Data is not sufficient and it requires more information to answer the given question.

Directions (Q. 50 to 54): *Answer the questions on the basis of the information given below.*

The pie charts shown below shows the distance covered by a boat moving upstream and downstream in different days of a week. And the table shows the speed of stream in km/hr. in different days of a week.

Day	Speed of stream (km/hr)
Monday	2
Tuesday	3
Wednesday	—
Thursday	1
Friday	2
Saturday	—
Sunday	4

50. If the time taken by boat to travel upstream on Thursday is equal to the time taken by it to travel downstream on Monday and the speed of boat in still water on Monday is 16 kmph then find the speed of boat in still water on Thursday?

(*a*) 16.2 kmph

(*b*) 17.2 kmph

(*c*) 15.4 kmph

(*d*) 12.5 kmph

(*e*) None of these

51. If the time taken by boat to travel upstream on Monday is $\dfrac{45}{11}$ hrs. more than the time taken by it to travel downstream on the same day, then find the speed of boat in still water on Monday ?

(*a*) 22 kmph

(*b*) 18 kmph

(*c*) 20 kmph

(*d*) 19 kmph

(*e*) None of these

52. If the speed of boat in still water on Tuesday was 15 km/hr and the speed of boat in still water on Wednesday was $66\dfrac{2}{3}\%$ more than that of Tuesday and time taken to travel upstream on Wednesday is $\dfrac{9}{10}$ times than time taken by it to travel downstream on Tuesday, then find the speed of stream (in kmph) on Wednesday?

(*a*) 1.5

(*b*) 2.5

(*c*) 2

(*d*) 1

(*e*) None of these

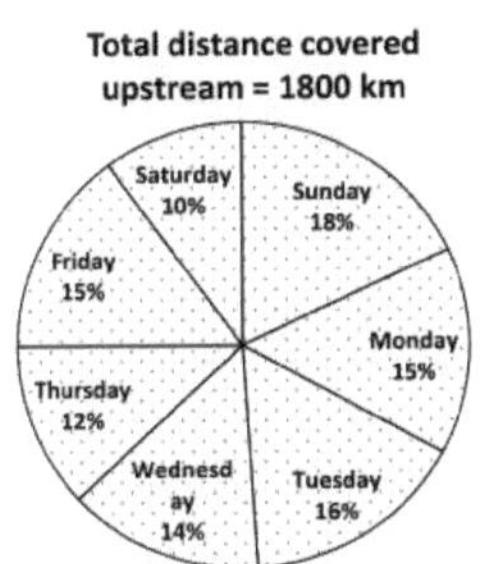

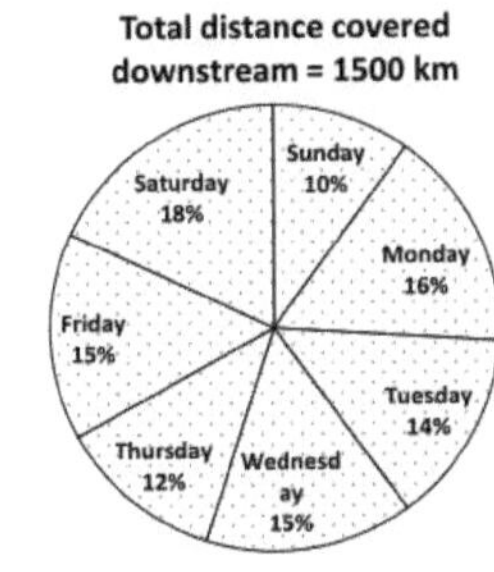

53. The speed of boat in still water on Saturday was 21 km/hr. and that on Sunday was $28\frac{4}{7}\%$ less than that on Saturday, if the time taken by boat to travel upstream on Saturday is $1\frac{3}{16}$ times than taken to travel downstream on Sunday, then find the time taken by the boat to cover a distance of 57.6 km upstream when the speed of stream is same as that of Saturday.

(a) 3 hrs   (b) 2 hrs

(c) 4 hrs   (d) 2.5 hrs

(e) None of these

54. If the time taken by boat to travel upstream on Sunday is 2 hours more than the time taken by it to travel downstream on Thursday and the speed of boat in still water on Thursday is 17 kmph, then find the upstream speed of boat on Sunday?

(a) 27 kmph

(b) 22 kmph

(c) 20 kmph

(d) 25 kmph

(e) None of these

Direction (Q. 55 to 57): *Answer the questions on the basis of the information given below.*

There are three bags A, B and C. In each bag there are three types of colored balls Yellow, Green and Black. In bag A, number of yellow balls are y and number of green balls are g. Also, number of green balls are 4 more than the number of yellow balls. If one ball is picked at random then the probability of getting black color ball is $\frac{5}{13}$. The value of y is $18\frac{2}{11}\%$ less then g.

In bag B, number of yellow is $22\frac{2}{9}\%$ more than that of bag A. If two balls are picked at random from bag B then the probability of getting both green color ball is $\frac{4}{37}$. Total number of balls in bag B is 75.

In bag C, the ratio of number of green balls and number of black balls is 7 : 5. Total number of green and black colored balls is 36. If one ball is picked at random then the probability of getting one yellow ball is $\frac{7}{13}$.

55. If x number of yellow balls from bag B are taken and placed into bag A and 20% of black balls from bag A are taken and placed into in bag B. If we pick one ball from bag B then the probability that the ball is of black color is $\frac{11}{26}$. Then find the value of x?

(a) 5   (b) 6

(c) 3   (d) 2

(e) None of these

56. If one ball picked at random from each of the bag A and bag B then find the probability that both of the balls are of the same color?

(a) $\dfrac{21 \times 47}{65 \times 75}$

(b) $\dfrac{22 \times 43}{65 \times 75}$

(c) $\dfrac{11 \times 17}{65 \times 75}$

(d) Can't be determined

(e) None of these

57. Difference between the number of green balls in bag A and bag C is how much percent more/less than the sum of the number of black balls in bag A and bag C together?

(a) 100%   (b) 95%

(c) 97.5%   (d) 102.5%

(e) None of these

Directions (Q. 58 to 62): *Answer the questions on the basis of the information given below.*

There are five shop owners A, B, C, D and E. They are selling five different items given in the table.

In the table, Discount (as a percentage) is given on mark price of these five products by different sellers. Study the table and answer the following questions:

	Item I	Item II	Item III	Item IV
A	18%	32%	36%	—
B	22%	—	33%	40%
C	—	16%	14%	15%
D	28%	28%	16%	—
E	—	8%	—	7%

Note:

1. Some values are missing. You have to calculate these values as per data given in the questions.

2. Mark price of a particular item is same for all of the shop owners.

58. If the profit percentage of seller A after selling item II is s% and that of seller C for the same item is (2s - 4)% and the ratio of cost price of item II by seller A and seller C is 17 : 21 then find the value of s?

(a) 2   (b) 3

(c) 4   (d) 5

(e) None of these

59. For seller D, between the selling price of item II and that of item III is Rs. 420 if the sum of the mark price of item II and item III by the same seller is Rs. 6000 then the Mark price (in Rs.) of item II is what percent more/less than that of item III by the same seller ? (Selling price of item II is greater than that of item III)

(a) 50%

(b) 40%

(c) 30%

(d) 35%

(e) 45%

60. Average SP of item II by seller A and B is Rs. 3888, by seller B and C is Rs. 4320. Find the SP (in Rs.) of item III by seller C.

(a) 4536   (b) 3656

(c) 5430   (d) 4150

(e) None of these

61. If the selling price of item I and item III by seller E are in the ratio of 5 : 6. If the seller earned a profit of 25% which is Rs. 750 on item I and 20% on item III then find the total profit (in Rs.) by selling item I and item III together by the same seller?

(a) 750   (b) 2000

(c) 1750   (d) 1250

(e) 1500

62. Cost price of item III is 60 Rs. for all of the sellers and all of them marked the same product at $66\frac{2}{3}\%$ higher than the cost price, then to get a total profit of Rs. 80 by all of the five sellers after selling item III, what is the minimum discount should be provided by seller E on item III.

(a) 21%

(b) 19%

(c) 17%

(d) 25%

(e) None of these

Directions (Q. 63 and 64): *Answer the questions on the basis of the information given below.*

A, B and C invested Rs. 900 Rs. 1600 and Rs. 700 respectively in a business venture. After end of the first quarter they invested additional amount in the ratio of 2 : 5 : 3. Then after end of the second quarter A, B and C invested additional amount in the ratio of 4 : 3 : 4.

Again after end of the 3 rd quarter they invested additional amount in the ratio of 7 : 6 : 7.

They invested the whole amount for one year and the profit earned in the business is proportional to the investment and the period of investment

63. If they had invested additional amount at the end of each quarter in same ratio as they had invested after end of the first quarter then find the profit of B at the end of one year if the total profit at the end of the year is Rs. 125000

(a) Rs. 75000   (b) Rs. 62500

(c) Rs. 12500   (d) Rs. 37500

(e) None of these

64. If the sum of the total amount invested by A and B in the year is Rs. 9000 and that of B and C is Rs. 10500, then find the total amount invested by all of them for only second quarter ?

(a) Rs. 16500

(b) Rs. 17000

(c) Rs.17500

(d) Rs. 18500

(e) Can't be determined

Directions (Q. 65 and 66): *Answer the questions on the basis of the information given below.*

Train A and train B are travelling towards each other from stations P and Q. Train A left station P at 9 : 45 am with a speed of 54 kmph. After half an hour train B left station Q with a speed of 66 kmph. Stations P & Q are situated at a distance of x kms and both trains met each other at 2 : 35 pm the same day.

65. Calculate the difference in the original time taken as given above in condition to meet train A and B and the time taken by train B to catch train A if the train A had started in same direction as that of B. Train B had started 2 hrs after train A while going in same direction.

(a) 45 hrs. 40 min.

(b) 24 hrs. 20 min.

(c) 55 hrs. 30 min.

(d) 49 hrs. 45 min.

(e) None of these

66. What is the ratio of relative speed of both the trains while travelling towards the same direction and while travelling towards opposite direction?

(a) 10 : 1

(b) 9 : 2

(c) 1 : 10

(d) 10 : 3

(e) None of these

67. Quantity I: Area of quadrilateral BFDE, given ABCD is a rectangle having AB = 10 cm & BC = 12 cm.

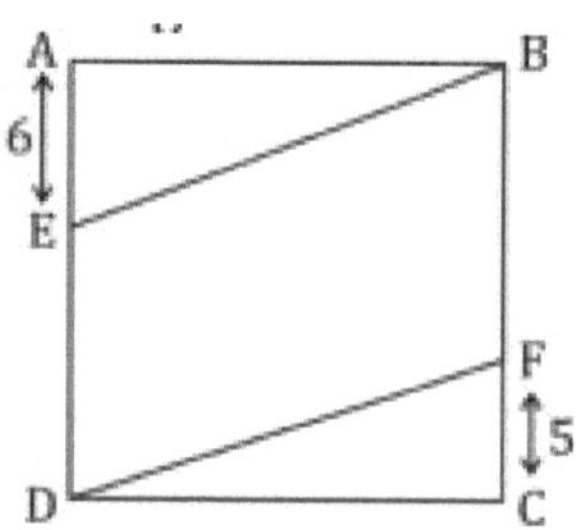

Quantity II: 15 cm^2

(a) Quantity I > Quantity II

(b) Quantity I < Quantity II

(c) Quantity I ≥ Quantity II

(d) Quantity I ≤ Quantity II

(e) Quantity I = Quantity II or No relation

68. A, B and C entered into a partnership. A invested Rs. 3000 at the start. B invested

$33\dfrac{1}{3}\%$ more than that invested by A and

C invested the average of the investment made by A and B. After 4 months, A withdrew 40% of his amount, B doubled his amount and C increased his amount by 20%. After another 5 months, B got away from partnership and A doubled his amount while C maintained his amount. Profit at the end of year was Rs. 677000 and profit was shared in the ratio of their investment and time.

Quantity I: Profit earned by C.

Quantity II: Average of profit earned by A, B and C together.

(a) Quantity I > Quantity II

(b) Quantity I < Quantity II

(c) Quantity I ≥ Quantity II

(d) Quantity I ≤ Quantity II

(e) Quantity I = Quantity II or No relation

Directions (69-70) : Each of A, B, C and D need a unique time to do a certain work. A can do the work in x days and B can do the work in

2x days. A started the work and do it for $22\dfrac{2}{9}$

days then he is replaced by B and B completed remaining work in same time as C and D together can complete the whole work.

The ratio of the efficiency of C and D is 4 : 5. If C and D work for alternative days starting from

C then they can do the total work in $44\dfrac{1}{2}$ days.

69. Find the value of x

(a) $66\dfrac{2}{3}$ (b) $33\dfrac{1}{3}$

(c) $16\dfrac{2}{3}$ (d) $14\dfrac{2}{7}$

(e) None of these

70. If E and F together work for 24 days then they are replaced by A and B respectively then they can do the remaining work in 20 days. If the efficiency of E and F is 5 : 4, If E and F together complete the whole work then find the difference between the work done by E alone and the total work done by F alone?

(a) $\dfrac{1}{9}$ (b) $\dfrac{1}{7}$

(c) $\dfrac{2}{7}$ (d) $\dfrac{1}{3}$

(e) $\dfrac{3}{4}$

Directions (71-75): A, B, C, D and E are five persons employed to complete a job X. Line graph shows the data regarding the time taken by these persons to complete the job X. Table 2 shows the actual time for which everyone of them worked on the job X.

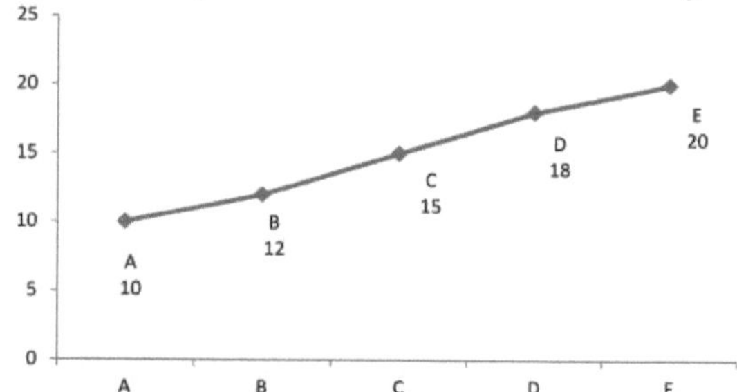

Person	Time (in Days)
A	2
B	—
C	3
D	—
E	2

Note 1: All the persons worked on the job X for 'whole number' days.

Note 2: Two jobs Y and Z are similar to job X and require same effort as required by job X.

71. A and C worked on job Y working alternatively for 10 days. B and D then worked together for 'x' days. If $\dfrac{1}{36}$ of the job was still remained, then find the value of 'x' ?

   (a) 2 days   (b) $1\dfrac{1}{4}$ days

   (c) $1\dfrac{1}{3}$ days   (d) $1\dfrac{1}{7}$ days

   (e) 1 day

72. E worked on job 'Z' for 5 days and the remaining job was completed by A, B and D who worked on alternate days starting with A followed by B and D in that order. Find the number of days B worked for?

   (a) 2   (b) 4

   (c) 9   (d) 3

   (e) None of these

73. If A, C and E worked on job Z for 2 days each and the remaining job was done by B and D. If the ratio of number days for which B and D worked is in ratio 20 : 21, then find the number of days for which B worked?

   (a) 50 days   (b) $4\dfrac{1}{2}$ days

   (c) $5\dfrac{1}{2}$ days   (d) 4 days

   (e) None of these

74. If the ratio of number of days for which B and D worked on job X 4 : 3, then find the difference between number of days for which B and D worked?

   (a) 2   (b) 3

   (c) 1   (d) 4

   (e) None of these

75. If C worked on job Y with $\dfrac{5}{4}$ times his given efficiency and was assisted by B every 3rd day, then find the time taken by C to complete the job Y?

   (a) 13 days   (b) $12\dfrac{1}{6}$ days

   (c) $13\dfrac{1}{2}$ days   (d) 9 days

   (e) 12 days

76. ABCD is a trapezoid. PQRS and MLKJ are two rhombus. Diagonal of PQRS are 6 cm and 8 cm. One of the angles of MLKJ is 120 degree and the diagonal bisecting that angle measures 15 cm. Side   of PQRS = AB, side of MLKJ = CD. Find XY (median of trapezoid)

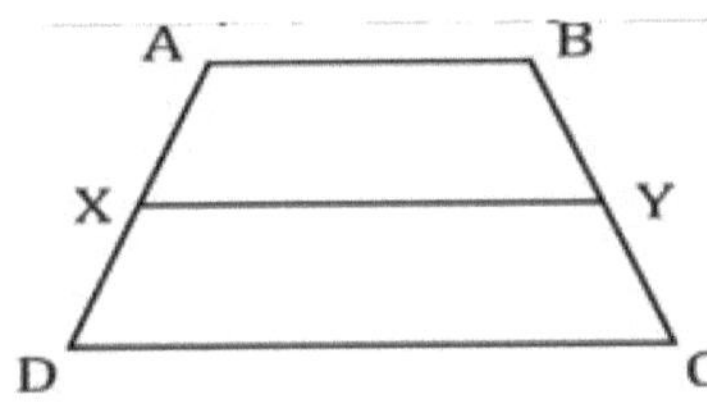

   (a) 5 cm   (b) 10 cm

   (c) 15 cm   (d) 20 cm

   (e) None of these

77. A vessel contains 2.5 liters of water and 10 liters of milk 20% of the contents of the vessel are removed. In the remaining contents, x liters of water is added to reverse the ratio of water and milk. If y liters of milk is added again to reverse the ratio of water and milk, then find the value of y.

   (a) 100   (b) 110

   (c) 120   (d) 130

   (e) None of these

Directions (Q. 78 to 80): *Answer the questions on the basis of the information given below.*

Each of the following questions consist of 3 statements A,B and C. You have to determine that which of the following statement/statements are necessary to answer the questions:

78. A, B and C entered into a partnership. If the profit earned in the business is proportional to the investment and the period of investment, then what is the profit of B if all of them invested the amount for one year and total profit is Rs. x.

   A. A invested Rs. 1500 more than that of C.

   B. A invested 2 times more than that of B while C invested 3 times more than that of A.

   C. B invested 200 percent more than that of A and 100% less than that of C.

   (a) Any two of them

   (b) Either B or C alone

   (c) Any one of them

   (d) All of them are required

   (e) None of these

79. 6 men and 9 women and 5 children can do a work in 14 days. In how many days can 12 men and 3 women and 5 children do the same work?

   A. 20 men and 30 women can do the same work in 5 days.

   B. Work done by 2 men is equal to 3 women.

   C. 6 children can do two-thirds of the same work in 28 days.

   (*a*) Any one of them

   (*b*) Only C

   (*c*) C and either A or B

   (*d*) Any two of them

   (*e*) Either only A or B

80. Rajnish buys 30 books and 65 pens. If price of each book is more than price of each pen then what money does he have to pay for this?

   A. At a profit of 20% he sells all the objects for Rs 3828.

   B. The CP of one book and one pen is Rs 90.

   C. The difference between sum and difference of buying price of one pen and one book is Rs 28.

   (*a*) Only A alone or B alone is sufficient

   (*b*) B and C together are sufficient

   (*c*) A alone or B and C together are sufficient

   (*d*) All together are necessary

   (*e*) All even together are not sufficient

ENGLISH LANGUAGE

Directions (Q. 81-85): *Read the following passage divided into number of paragraphs carefully and answer the questions that follow it.*

Paragraph 1: At a global financial services firm we worked with, a longtime customer accidentally submitted the same application file to two offices. Though the employees who reviewed the file were supposed to follow the same guidelines—and thus arrive at similar outcomes—the separate offices returned very different quotes. Taken aback, the customer gave the business to a competitor. From the point of view of the firm, employees in the same role should have been interchangeable, but in this case they were not. Unfortunately, this is a common problem.

Paragraph 2: Professionals in many organizations are assigned arbitrarily to cases: appraisers in credit-rating agencies, physicians in emergency rooms, underwriters of loans and insurance, and others. Organizations expect consistency from these professionals: Identical cases should be treated similarly, if not identically. The problem is that humans are unreliable decision makers; their judgments are strongly influenced by irrelevant factors, such as their current mood, the time since their last meal, and the weather. We call the chance variability of judgments noise. It is an invisible tax on the bottom line of many companies.

Paragraph 3: Some jobs are noise-free. Clerks at a bank or a post office perform complex tasks, but they must follow strict rules that limit subjective judgment and guarantee, by design, that identical cases will be treated identically. In contrast, medical professionals, loan officers, project managers, judges, and executives all make judgment calls, which are guided by informal experience and general principles rather than by rigid rules. And if they don't reach precisely the same answer that every other person in their role would, that's acceptable; this is what we mean when we say that a decision is "a matter of judgment." A firm whose employees exercise judgment does not expect decisions to be entirely free of noise. But often noise is far above the level that executives would consider tolerable—and they are completely unaware of it.

Paragraph 4: The prevalence of noise has been demonstrated in several studies. Academic researchers have repeatedly confirmed that professionals often contradict their own prior judgments when given the same data on different occasions. For instance, when software developers were asked on two separate days to estimate the completion time for a given task, the hours they projected differed by 71%, on average. When pathologists made two assessments of the severity of biopsy results, the correlation between their ratings was only .61 (out of a perfect 1.0), indicating that they made inconsistent diagnoses quite frequently. Judgments made by different people are even more likely to diverge. Research has confirmed that in many tasks, experts' decisions are highly variable: valuing stocks, appraising real estate, sentencing criminals, evaluating job performance, auditing financial statements, and more. The unavoidable conclusion is that professionals often make decisions that deviate significantly from those of their peers, from their own prior decisions, and from rules that they themselves claim to follow.

Paragraph 5: Noise is often insidious: It causes even successful companies to lose substantial amounts of money without realizing it. How substantial? To get an estimate, we asked executives in one of the organizations we studied the following: "Suppose the optimal assessment of a case is $100,000. What would be the cost to the organization if the professional in charge of the case assessed a value of $115,000? What would be the cost of assessing it at $85,000?" The cost estimates were high. Aggregated over the assessments made every year, the cost of noise was measured in billions—an unacceptable number even for a large global firm. The value of reducing noise even by a few percentage points would be in the tens of millions. Remarkably, the organization had completely ignored the question of consistency until then.

81. What is the opposite of the phrase "***Unfortunately, this is a common problem***" as mentioned in the Paragraph 1?

(*a*) Employees often constitute variable decision-making capability even if they are assigned the same task to perform.

(*b*) Even though employees are expected to come out with fair, positive and noise-free results, organizations find it almost an opposite and contradictory outcome to it.

(*c*) A major problem is that the outcomes of decisions taken by different employees in the organization often aren't known until far in the future, if at all.

(*d*) Employees have to follow the strict norms and rules of the organization which often allow them to take rationale and conventional decisions in the best interest of the organization which hardly go unnoticed.

(*e*) None of the above.

82. What does the author mean by the term "**noise**" as used in Paragraph 2?

I. In an organization where work efficiency decides the potential of its employees, employees find it difficult to cope with their decisions and most of the time they land up in variable outcome to their motive which is termed as Noise.

II. Noise is a problem which is effectively invisible in the business world; it can be observed that audiences get quite surprised when the reliability of professional judgment is mentioned as an issue.

III. Noise is a problem associated with the decision-making process of the employees involved in the corporate world which is invisible as people do not go through life imagining plausible

alternatives to every judgment they make.

(*a*) Only I is correct

(*b*) Only III is correct

(*c*) Both II and III are correct

(*d*) Both I and III are correct

(*e*) All are correct

83. Why according to the author decision is considered as "a matter of judgment" as mentioned in Paragraph 3?

I. In most of the cases, decisions are guided by informal experience and general principles rather than by rigid rules.

II. In certain cases, medical professionals, judges and executives have to take decisions which are beyond the strict rules that control the instinctive judgment which might not be noise-free, yet acceptable to the system.

III. Long experience on a job always increases people's confidence in their judgments, but in the absence of rapid feedback, confidence is no guarantee of either accuracy or consensus.

(*a*) Only I is correct

(*b*) Only III is correct

(*c*) Both I and III are correct

(*d*) Both I and II are correct

(*e*) All are correct

84. Which of the following statements can follow paragraph 4 to form a connection with paragraph 5?

(*a*) The surprising result of much research is that in many contexts reasoned rules are about as accurate as statistical models built with outcome data.

(*b*) Uncomfortable as people may be with the idea, studies have shown that while humans can provide useful input to formulas, algorithms do better in the role of final decision maker.

(*c*) Executives who are concerned with accuracy should also confront the prevalence of inconsistency in professional judgments.

(*d*) Controlling noise is hard, but we expect that an organization that conducts an audit and evaluates the cost of noise in dollars will conclude that reducing random variability is worth the effort.

(*e*) The major puzzle for us was the fact that neither organization had ever considered reliability to be an issue.

85. What is/are the author's viewpoint(s) in accordance with Paragraph 5?

I. The author is skeptical about the credibility of the research works on the measurement of cost of noise.

II. The author is critical about the consequences of the problem of noise as it leads organizations to lose substantial amounts of money that often go unrealized.

III. The author feels that the problem of noise is severe enough to require action.

(*a*) Only I   (*b*) Only II

(*c*) Both I and III   (*d*) Both II and III

(*e*) All I, II and III

Directions (Q. 86-90): *Read the following passage divided into number of paragraphs carefully and answer the questions that follow it.*

Paragraph 1: Deutsche is more leveraged than its peers; it is unusual in lacking a crown jewel around which it can base a business model; and it has a stack of derivatives whose prices are hard to observe in the market. More positively, it is light on the non-performing loans that clog the balance-sheets of banks in places like Italy. But in other ways its problems have a very familiar ring. Deutsche is struggling to make a decent return. It has taken too long to face up to its problems. And the market it operates in is overbanked. Years after American banks were forced to clean themselves up, too many European lenders are still flailing as a result.

Paragraph 2: Europeans prefer to blame others for the turmoil. Deutsche has lashed out at "forces in the market" for its most recent bout of trouble. But its shares had already fallen by 42% this year before news broke last month of a proposed Department of Justice (DoJ) fine of $14 billion for mortgage-related misdeeds. German politicians insinuate that the mooted fine represents revenge for Europe's recent tax case against Apple, an American champion. Yet the DoJ has slapped large fines on American banks, too. Deutsche's vulnerability to shocks is the problem, not the shocks themselves.

Paragraph 3: Fingers also point at global regulators. The boss of Credit Suisse, Tidjane Thiam, says his sector is "not really investible". It is true that the rules have got much stricter in the past few years, particularly for institutions, like Deutsche, that have big investment-banking arms. It is also true that ultra-loose monetary policy, and in particular the negative interest rates that now prevail in much of Europe, eat away at banks' profitability. But some banks cope better than others in this painful environment. The IMF has compared returns on equity before and after the financial crisis.

Those at large European banks fell by 11.4 percentage points, whereas those at American lenders dipped by only three points. Rather than blaming speculators, Americans and regulators, Europe's bankers and policymakers need to put their own house in order.

Paragraph 4: Within institutions, that means cutting costs and raising capital. According to S&P Global Market Intelligence, the average cost-to-income ratio at an American bank in 2015 was 59%; Italy's figure stood at 67% and Germany's at 72%. Scandinavian banks already operate with much lower costs than their peers elsewhere in Europe.

The axe is now swinging: Commerzbank, another struggling German lender, and ING, a Dutch bank, have announced thousands of job cuts in the past few days.

Paragraph 5: But more can be done. Pay is one obvious lever. Deutsche's bankers trousered roughly the same amount in annual compensation between 2011 and 2015, even as the bank's share price dived. And before shareholders complain too loudly about that, recall that in 2007-15 the dividend payments by 90 euro-zone banks amounted to €223 billion ($250 billion). Their retained earnings would have been 64% higher at the end of that period if they had not paid out dividends.

86. Which of the following sentences justifies the statement, "**Deutsche is more leveraged than its peers**" as mentioned in Paragraph 1?

I. Deutsche is scuffling to generate adequate profits to stay afloat in the market.

II. Though the market in which Deutsche operates is overbanked, it has a mound of derivatives whose prices are hard to observe in the market.

III. Though Deutsche has taken a longer time to face up to its problems, it is still airy on the non-performing loans that obstruct the balance-sheets of banks in places like Italy.

(*a*) Only I is correct

(*b*) Only II is correct

(*c*) Both I and II are correct

(*d*) Both II and III are correct

(*e*) All are correct

87. What does the author mean by the statement, "**Deutsche's vulnerability to shocks is the problem, not the shocks themselves**" as mentioned in Paragraph 2?

(*a*) Deutsche is more prone to consistent failures which may have indirect effects on the market in coming years.

(*b*) Deutsche is losing its share values inadvertently due to certain forces in the market which is surprising to German politicians.

(*c*) Despite performing better in certain specific fields than other banks, Deutsche is finding itself in the midst of turbulence which is itself a revelation.

(*d*) The arguable fine of $14 billion for mortgage-related misdeeds by Department of Justice has completely shocked the entire European bureaucrats.

(*e*) None of the above.

88. Which of the following statements cannot be inferred from Paragraph 3?

(*a*) Despite having bigger investment-banking arms, the consistent downfall of European banks is a matter of serious concern.

(*b*) The prevailing negative interest rates in many parts of Europe indicate that there is ultra-loose monetary policy in Europe.

(*c*) The IMF figures on return on equity show that American banks are performing far better than European banks in the existing critical market.

(*d*) European policymakers need to come out with strict and robust policies to safeguard its downgrading existence in the world market than pointing fingers on speculators and regulators.

(*e*) Without pruning, returns on equity of European banks are projected to fall towards zero as a result of ultra-low rates and regulation as compared to American counterpart.

89. Which of the following sentences can be connected with Paragraph 4 to make a connection with Paragraph 5?

(*a*) Some European markets have been clearing away excess capacity.

(*b*) Like Deutsche, Credit Suisse is freer to make plans after a recent settlement with American authorities over misselling mortgage-backed securities before the financial crisis.

(*c*) It expects to wind up a unit in which it has dumped unwanted assets by the end of 2018, a year ahead of schedule.

(*d*) European banks could have done a lot more sooner.

(*e*) The recapitalisation of Europe's banks has been as gradual as that of America's was swift, and in dribs and drabs of tens of billions a year rather than in one big splurge.

90. What could be the possible solutions for the rehabilitation of European banks in the existing system?

I. Proper fiscal stimulus by European governments would cut the chances that central banks have to keep interest rates so low.

II. Using public money to recapitalise the weakest banks in countries like Italy, and requiring them to slim down in return, is the fastest way to return them to health.

III. Significant job cuts of their employees to compensate the losses occurred in last few years could bring everything back to normalcy.

(*a*) Only I   (*b*) Only II

(*c*) Both I and III   (*d*) Both I and II

(*e*) All I, II and III

Direction (Q. 91): *There are sets of four statements in question given below which when connected using the correct sentence structure forms a complete single sentence without altering the meaning of the sentences given in the question. There are four options given below the question, choose the sentence that forms the correct formation of single sentence which is both grammatically correct and contextually meaningful. If none follows, choose (e) as your answer.*

91. There is a statedly contemporary twist of a 360 degree review by peers, seniors and colleagues; it is an equally hush-hush affair; it does not really pass muster as an objective assessment tool for professional capabilities; it is in spite of our unique work environment.

(*a*) The statedly contemporary twist of a 360 degree review by peers, seniors and colleagues, is an equally hush-hush affair and does not really pass muster as an objective assessment tool for professional capabilities, given our unique work environment.

(*b*) Despite our unique work environment, there is a statedly contemporary twisting of a 360 degree review by peers, seniors and colleagues which is an equally hush-hush affair but it has not really passed muster as an objective assessment tool for professional capabilities.

(*c*) Twisting review to 360 degree by peers, seniors and colleagues and making it an equally hush-hush affair, it does not really pass muster as an objective assessment tool for professional capabilities in our unique work environment.

(*d*) Although we have unique work environment, there is a statedly contemporary twist of a 360 degree review by peers, seniors and colleagues and an equally hush-hush affairs which do not pass muster as an objective assessment tool for professional capabilities.

(*e*) None of the above is correct.

Direction (Q. 92): *The following question consists of a sentence which is divided into three parts which contain grammatical errors in one or more than one part of the sentence. If there is an error in any part of the sentence, find the correct alternatives to replace those parts from the three options given below each question to make the sentence grammatically correct. If there is an error in any part of the sentence and none of the alternatives is correct to replace that part, then choose (d) i.e. None of the (I), (II) and (III) as your answer. If the given sentence is grammatically correct or does not require any correction, choose (e) i.e. No correction required as your answer.*

92. The announcement by the Saudi-led coalition to sever (I)/ diplomatic ties with Qatar marks the culmination of a year-long (II)/ dispute over few Gulf Arab states and Qatar. (III)

(I) The announcement by the Saudi-led coalition severing

(II) diplomatic tie with Qatar marked a year-long culmination

(III) dispute between some Gulf Arab states and Qatar

(a) Only (I)

(b) Only (III)

(c) Both (I) and (III)

(d) None of the (I), (II) and (III)

(e) No correction required

Direction (Q. 93): *In the following question a part of the sentence is given in bold, it is then followed by three sentences which try to explain the meaning of the phrase given in bold. Choose the best set of alternatives from the five options given below each question which explains the meaning of the phrase correctly without altering the meaning of the sentence given as question.*

93. The problem of secularism in independent India lies in the fact that the Constitution was essentially a **Western construct** with the sidelining of the Gandhian Influence in the Constituent Assembly.

(I) Secularism in India is highly motivated by the Western pattern of Constitution with hardly any presence of Gandhian Influence.

(II) The Constitution was basically influenced by the culture followed in Western societies and it hardly considered the Gandhian Influence in the Constituent Assembly which depicts the problem of secularism in independent India.

(III) The developmental projects of western countries had such an impact on Indian Constitution that it ignored the Gandhian

Influence and today we are facing the problem of secularism in the country.

(a) Only (I) is correct

(b) Only (II) is correct

(c) Both (I) and (II) are correct

(d) Both (II) and (III) are correct

(e) All are correct

Direction (Q. 94): *In question given below there are two statements, each statement consists of two blanks. You have to choose the option which provides the correct set of words that fits both the blanks in both the statements appropriately and in the same order making them meaningful and grammatically correct.*

94. (1) Despite the fact that cancerous ovarian stem cells are __________ to chemoresistance, they are the ______________ targets for therapy.

(2) How quickly the __________ branch of Homo heidelbergensis turned into something that could be called Homo sapiens was therefore __________.

(a) Feigned, indeterminate

(b) Pertinent, inane

(c) Relevant, obscure

(d) affiliated, fatuous

(e) analogous, insignificant

Direction (Q. 95): *In each of the given questions an inference is given in bold which is then followed by three paragraphs. You have to find the paragraph(s) from where it is inferred. Choose the option with the best possible outcome as your choice.*

95. The major concern is security.

(I) The major dilemma for many security professionals is whether the Brexit will make the UK more or less safe when it comes to cybersecurity. One poll found that most security professionals believed there would not be any major cybersecurity implications; however, another poll offered different conclusions, with most respondents believing that a Brexit would weaken cybersecurity because of additional bureaucratic hurdles to information sharing with the EU.

(II) Most debate over Brexit has been about economics, trade and migration. But when David Cameron called the EU referendum in February he cited a new factor, asserting that membership made Britain safer. This week the prime minister went further, hinting that Brexit might increase the risk related to security—and adding that, every time Britain turned its back on Europe, it had come to regret it.

(III) Prime Minister Shinzo Abe touted the implementation of the legislation as an event of "historic importance that makes peace and security of our country even more secure" and "upgrades our deterrence and enables the nation to proactively contribute more than ever to peace and stability of regional and international communities."

(*a*) Only (I)

(*b*) Both (II) and (III)

(*c*) Only (III)

(*d*) Both (I) and (III)

(*e*) All are correct

Direction (Q. 96): *There are sets of four statements in question given below which when connected using the correct sentence structure forms a complete single sentence without altering the meaning of the sentences given in the question. There are four options given below the question, choose the sentence that forms the correct formation of single sentence which is both grammatically correct and contextually meaningful. If none follows, choose (e) as your answer.*

96. The major thrust of Marx's political philosophy was aimed at human liberation; it is important to consider the significant shift to comprehend it; the shift occurred in the late 17th century; In that period traditional analysis of the political order based on scarcity was replaced by a philosophy of abundance.

(*a*) Comprehending the major thrust of Marx's political philosophy that was aimed at human liberation, it is important to consider the significant shift of late 17 century when the scarcity based on traditional analysis was replaced by a philosophy of abundance.

(*b*) Marx's major thrust was on political philosophy aiming human liberation while it is important to consider the significant shift that occurred in the late 17th century, it was then that traditional analysis of the political order based on scarcity was replaced by a philosophy of abundance.

(*c*) It is important to consider the significant shift in the late 17th century when traditional analysis of the political order based on scarcity replaced philosophy of abundance to comprehend the major thrust of Marx's political philosophy of human liberation.

(*d*) To comprehend the major thrust of Marx's political philosophy that aimed at human liberation, it is important to consider the significant shift that occurred in the late 17th century when traditional analysis of the political order based on scarcity was replaced by a philosophy of abundance.

(*e*) None of the above is correct.

Direction (Q. 97): *The following question consists of a sentence which is divided into three parts which contain grammatical errors in one or more than one part of the sentence. If there is an error in any part of the sentence, find the correct alternatives to replace those parts from the three options given below each question to make the sentence grammatically correct. If there is an error in any part of the sentence and none of the alternatives is correct to replace that part, then choose (d) i.e. None of the (I), (II) and (III) as your answer. If the given sentence is grammatically correct or does not require any correction, choose (e) i.e. No correction required as your answer.*

97. Italian officials have been arguing that (I)/ volatility caused by Britain's vote to leave the European Union (II)/means it could have given greater flexibility to prop up struggling banks. (III)

(I) Italians officials had argued that

(II) volatility that caused Britain's vote to leave the European Union

(III) meant it should be given greater flexibility to prop up struggling banks

(*a*) Only (II)

(*b*) Both (I) and (III)

(*c*) All (I), (II) and (III)

(*d*) None of the (I), (II) and (III)

(*e*) No correction required

Direction (Q. 98): *In the following question a part of the sentence is given in bold, it is then followed by three sentences which try to explain the meaning of the phrase given in bold. Choose the best set of alternatives from the five options given below each question which explains the meaning of the phrase correctly without altering the meaning of the sentence given as question.*

98. The trial began only in 1996 and a couple of years ago all accused were cleared of all charges by a trial court in what activists have called **a grave miscarriage of justice.**

(I) All accused involved in the case were cleared of all charges by a trial court in 1996 and that is what activists have called a complete failure of justice in prevailing the truth.

(II) In 1996, by letting go all accused by clearing all charges against them, the trial court once again proved the incompetence of judicial system in justifying the truth.

(III) Activists have felt that the decision by trial court in 1996 of clearing of all the charges against the accused is a serious negligence of true justice by the system.

(*a*) Only (I) is correct

(*b*) Only (II) is correct

(*c*) Both (I) and (III) are correct

(*d*) None is correct

(*e*) All are correct

Direction (Q. 99): *In question given below there are two statements, each statement consists of two blanks. You have to choose the option which provides the correct set of words that fits both the blanks in both the statements appropriately and in the same order making them meaningful and grammatically correct.*

99. (1) The molecular targeting of CSCs may improve the _______ of current chemotherapeutic _________ needed for the management of this disease.

(2) ______ and safety of once-daily ______ in the treatment of HIV infection is currently under inspection.

(*a*) Germaneness, medication

(*b*) Efficacy, regimens

(*c*) Emasculation, nutriments

(*d*) Potency, sustenance

(*e*) Sufficiency, subsistence

Direction (Q. 100): *In each of the given questions an inference is given in bold which is then followed by three statements. You have to find the statement(s) from where it is inferred. Choose the option with the best possible outcome as your choice.*

100. Country's economic standard can be best adjudged by per capital income.

(I) Exports and imports, a swelling favourable balance of trade, investments and bank-balances, are not an index or a balance sheet of national prosperity. Till the beginning of the Second World War, English exports were noticeably greater than what they are today. And yet England has greater national prosperity today than it ever had. Because the income of average Englishmen, working as field and factory labourers, clerks, policemen, petty shopkeepers and shop assistants, domestic workers and other low-paid workers, has gone up.

(II) It is possible that while per capita real income is increasing per capita consumption of goods and services might be falling. This happens when the Govt. might itself be using up the increased income for massive military buildup necessitating heavy production of arms and ammunitions.

(III) A rise in national income may occur as a result of increased spending on items such as defence. National income often rises in time of war, or the threat of war, because money is spent on weapons. This will push up GNP, but the people may be acutely short of goods to buy.

(*a*) Both (II) and (III)

(*b*) Both (I) and (II)

(*c*) Only (I)

(*d*) Only (II)

(*e*) All are correct

Direction (Q. 101): There are sets of four statements in question given below which when connected using the correct sentence structure forms a complete single sentence without altering the meaning of the sentences given in the question. There are four options given below the question, choose the sentence that forms the correct formation of single sentence which is both grammatically correct and contextually meaningful. If none follows, choose (e) as your answer.

101. There is a giant footprint of the ransomware attack; it leveraged a leaked NSA-created Windows hacking technique; it infected more than 200,000 systems across 150 countries; malware analysts say poor choices on the part of WannaCry's creators have limited both its scope and profit.

(*a*) The giant footprint of the ransomware attack has leveraged a leaked NSA-created Windows hacking technique and infected more than 200,000 systems across 150 countries while malware analysts say poor choices on the part of WannaCry's creators had limited both its scope and profit.

(*b*) Despite the giant footprint of the ransomware attack, which leveraged a leaked NSA-created Windows hacking technique to infect more than 200,000 systems across 150 countries, malware analysts say poor choices on the part of WannaCry's creators have limited both its scope and profit.

(*c*) Malware analysts said that poor choices on the part of WannaCry's creators have limited both its scope and profit, whereas the giant footprint of the ransomware attack leveraged a leaked NSA-created Windows hacking technique infecting more than 200,000 systems across 150 countries.

(*d*) The ransomware attack is a giant footprint as it has leveraged a leaked NSA-created Windows hacking technique and infected more than 200,000 systems across 150 countries which have limited both the scope and profit due to poor choices on the part of WannaCry's creators as malware analysts said.

(*e*) None of the above is correct.

Direction (Q. 102): *The following question consists of a sentence which is divided into three parts which contain grammatical errors in one or more than one part of the sentence. If there is an error in any part of the sentence, find the correct alternatives to replace those parts from the three options given below each question to make the sentence grammatically correct. If there is an error in any part of the sentence and none of the alternatives is correct to replace that part, then choose (d) i.e. None of the (I), (II) and (III) as your answer. If the given sentence is grammatically correct or does not require any correction, choose (e) i.e. No correction required as your answer.*

102. Many environmentalists think that too much interference with (I)/ nature for development projects is gradually destroying that balance and natural (II)/ calamities are happening to forewarn us about a possible doomsday in future. (III)

(I) Many of the environmentalists believe that too much interference in

(II) nature for developing new projects has destroyed the balance and natural

(III) calamities which may happen to forewarn us about doomsday possibly in future

(*a*) Only (II)

(*b*) Both (I) and (II)

(*c*) Both (II) and (III)

(*d*) None of the (I), (II) and (III)

(*e*) No correction required

Direction (Q. 103) : *In question given below there are two statements, each statement consists of two blanks. You have to choose the option which provides the correct set of words that fits both the blanks in both the statements appropriately and in the same order making them meaningful and grammatically correct.*

103. (1) The six-day war was the last unalloyed military victory for Israel, and the start of a __________ from existential wars against Arab states, which it always won, to ____________ campaigns against non-state militias which it could never wipe out.

(2) He sees these dualities as having been maintained through the __________ by a deliberate and __________ general amnesia.

(*a*) Transition, enervating

(*b*) Progression, invigorating

(*c*) Concatenation, exhilarating

(*d*) Juncture, frivolous

(*e*) Movement, enfeeble

Direction (Q. 104): *In this question a small paragraph is given followed by three possible inferences which may or may not be correct. The question is then followed by five options. You have to choose the option which gives the best possible outcome.*

104. Techniques to increase productivity in the performance of discrete tasks, by requiring less human labour in each step of the production process, are widely utilized. Consultants on productivity enhancement point out, however, that although these techniques achieve their specific goal, they are not without drawbacks. They often instill enough resentment in the work force eventually to lead to a slowdown in the production process as a whole.

(I) The fact that productivity enhancement techniques are so widely employed has led to a decline in the ability of American business to complete abroad.

(II) Productivity enhancement techniques do not attain their intended purpose and should not be employed in the workplace.

(III) Ironically, an increase in the productivity of discrete tasks may result in a decrease in the productivity of the whole production process.

(*a*) Only (I) is correct

(*b*) Only (II) is correct

(*c*) Only (III) is correct

(*d*) Both (I) and (III) are correct

(*e*) None of the given inferences is correct.

Direction (Q. 105): *In question given below there are two statements, each statement consists of two blanks. You have to choose the option which provides the correct set of words that fits both the blanks in both the statements appropriately and in the same order making them meaningful and grammatically correct.*

105. (1) The obvious ___________ between China's level of participation and other Asian states' requires some ___________.

(2) For years there has been talk Aldo's lazy performances had more to do with a brutal weight cut than any skill ________. That's always been a pretty probable _______, given the number of horrendous weight cuts MMA sees.

(*a*) Deviation, delineation

(*b*) Discrepancy, explanation

(*c*) Incongruity, cogitation

(*d*) contrast, contemplation

(*e*) Contrariety, rumination

Direction (Q. 106): *There are sets of four statements in question given below which when connected using the correct sentence structure forms a complete single sentence without altering the meaning of the sentences given in the question. There are four options given below the question, choose the sentence that forms the correct formation of single sentence which is both grammatically correct and contextually meaningful. If none follows, choose (e) as your answer.*

106. Pro-Russian hackers bombarded the sites of opposition leaders; it included Garry Kasparov in the midst of his 2007 campaign for president; it started in the late 2000s; it kept Kasparov's site offline or sluggish at key moments during the campaign season.

    (*a*) Bombarding the sites of opposition leaders including Garry Kasparov the midst of his 2007 campaign for president in the late 2000s, Kasparov's site was kept offline or sluggish at key moments during the campaigning season.

    (*b*) In the late 2000s, pro-Russian hackers started bombarding the sites of opposition leaders that included Garry Kasparov in the midst of his 2007 campaign for president and keeping Kasparov's site offline or sluggish at key moments during the campaign season.

    (*c*) Starting in the late 2000s, pro-Russian hackers bombarded the sites of opposition leaders like Garry Kasparov in the midst of his 2007 campaign for president, keeping Kasparov's site offline or sluggish at key moments during the campaign season.

    (*d*) The sites of opposition leaders like Garry Kasparov was kept offline or sluggish at key moments during the campaigning season by pro-Russian hackers who bombarded the sites in the midst of his 2007 campaign for President.

    (*e*) None of the above is correct.

Direction (Q. 107): *The following question consists of a sentence which is divided into three parts which contain grammatical errors in one or more than one part of the sentence. If there is an error in any part of the sentence, find the correct alternatives to replace those parts from the three options given below each question to make the sentence grammatically correct. If there is an error in any part of the sentence and none of the alternatives is correct to replace that part, then choose (d) i.e. None of the (I), (II) and (III) as your answer. If the given sentence is grammatically correct or does not require any correction, choose (c) i.e. No correction required as your answer.*

107. Career diplomats in the State Department are wringing (I)/ the hands of diplomats in despair after seeing their president (II)/ uncorking US policies which had taken decades at maturing. (III)

    (I) Diplomacy in Career in the State Department has wringed

    (II) their hands in despair at seeing their president

    (III) uncorking US policies that have taken decades to mature

    (*a*) Both (II) and (III)

    (*b*) Both (I) and (III)

    (*c*) All (I), (II) and (III)

    (*d*) None of the (I), (II) and (III)

    (*e*) No correction required

Direction (Q. 108): *In each of the given questions an inference is given in bold which is then followed by three statements. You have to find the statement(s) from where it is inferred. Choose the option with the best possible outcome as your choice.*

108. GDP fluctuates because of the business cycle.

    (I) The downturn of a business cycle is called a recession, which is defined as a period in which real GDP declines for at least 2 consecutive quarter-years. The recession begins at a peak and ends at a trough. After the downward phase reaches bottom and economic conditions begin to improve, the economy gradually enters the expansionary phase.

    (II) As interest rates rise, companies and consumers cut back their spending, and the economy slows down. Slowing demand leads companies to lay off employees, which further affects consumer confidence and demand. To break this vicious circle, the central bank eases monetary policy to stimulate economic growth and employment until the economy is booming once again. Rinse and repeat.

    (III) High levels of investment as a share of GDP might be superb for creating extra capacity to produce but at the expense of consumer goods and services for the current generation. This imbalance is one of the reasons why GDP data may give a distorted picture of living standards in a country.

    (*a*) Only (I)

    (*b*) Both (II) and (III)

    (*c*) Both (I) and (II)

    (*d*) Only (II)

    (*e*) All are correct

Direction (Q. 109): *In question given below there are two statements, each statement consists of two blanks. You have to choose the option which provides the correct set of words that fits both the blanks in both the statements appropriately and in the same order making them meaningful and grammatically correct.*

109. (1) Polish environment minister to __________ over COP24 conference, the choice was made __________ by the climate-change committee of the United Nations.

(2) The Labour Party is led by two Marxists: Mr Corbyn and John McDonnell, his shadow chancellor, who believe in the materialist interpretation of history. Yet they now _______ over a coalition of voters defined ______ by their shared values.

(*a*) Debate, diligently

(*b*) Concoct, congruently

(*c*) Supervise, perspicaciously

(*d*) Conduct, unanimously

(*e*) Preside, overwhelmingly

Direction (Q. 110): *In the given question an inference is given in bold which is then followed by three statements. You have to find the statement(s) from where it is inferred. Choose the option with the best possible outcome as your choice.*

110. The calorie count of foods that are high in carbohydrates is significant.

(I) Moderate use of nonnutritive sweeteners like aspartame for low calorie count could have a positive effect on insulin and blood sugar by aiding weight control. It is also important to keep in mind that many foods containing aspartame still provide calories and carbohydrate, even though they may be labeled "sugar-free."

(II) Ironically, people who use aspartame as a sweetener to reduce their calorie intake could wind up defeating their purpose, since studies show that high levels of aspartame may trigger a craving for carbohydrates by depleting the brain of a chemical that registers carbohydrate satiety.

(III) Forty-five to 65 percent of your total calories should come from carbs, recommends the Institute of Medicine. If you consume carbs on a regular basis, glycogen stores stay full and become a normal part of your total body weight. The rise in the popularity of Aspartame is due to its comparatively low calorie count.

(*a*) Only (I)

(*b*) Only (II)

(*c*) Both (I) and (II)

(*d*) Both (II) and (III)

(*e*) All are correct.

Direction (Q. 111): *There are sets of four statements in question given below which when connected using the correct sentence structure forms a complete single sentence without altering the meaning of the sentences given in the question. There are four options given below the question, choose the sentence that forms the correct formation of single sentence which is both grammatically correct and contextually meaningful. if none follows, choose (e) as your answer.*

111. Hong Kong has prospered economically; it is visible from US $177 billion GDP in 1997 to $319 billion; it has risen by 80 per cent; it has been building on her strengths of superior infrastructure, free port and low-tax status, and her superior financial and logistic hubs.

(*a*) Economically, Hong Kong has prospered visibly, from US $177 billion GDP in 1997 to $319 billion, rising by 80 per cent, building on her strengths of superior infrastructure, free port and low-tax status, and her superior financial and logistic hubs.

(*b*) Hong Kong has been prospering economically which is visible from US $177 billion GDP in 1997 to $319 billion that has risen by 80 per cent which has been building on her strengths of superior infrastructure, free port and low-tax status, and her superior financial and logistic hubs.

(*c*) Building on her strengths of superior infrastructure, free port and low-tax status, and her superior financial and logistic hubs, Hong Kong has prospered economically visible from US $177 billion GDP in 1997 to $319 billion that has risen by 80 per cent.

(*d*) Hong Kong has made visibly a prosperous economic condition rising by 80 per cent from US $177 billion GDP in 1997 to $319 billion which shows that it has been building on her strengths of superior infrastructure, free port and low-tax status, and her superior financial and logistic hubs.

(*e*) None of the above is correct.

Direction (Q. 112): *The following question consists of a sentence which is divided into three parts. There are grammatical errors in one or more than one part of the sentence. If there is an error in any part of the sentence, find the correct alternatives to replace those parts from the three options given below each question to make the sentence grammatically correct. If there is an error in any part of the sentence and none of the alternatives is correct to replace that part, then choose (d) i.e. None of the (I), (II) and (III) as your answer. If the given sentence is grammatically correct or does not require any correction, choose (e) i.e. No correction required as your answer.*

112. Around 1960s it was widely assumed about politics which had been (I)/ divided from religions and after societies started becoming more industrialized, religious (II)/ belief and practice were restricted to private thought and action. (III)

(I) Politics was assumed widely till about 1960s that it is

(II) divided out of religion and as societies were becoming more industrialized, religious

(III) beliefs and practices should have restricted to private thoughts and actions.

(a) Only (I)

(b) Both (II) and (III)

(c) Both (I) and (II)

(d) None of the (I), (II) and (III)

(e) No correction required

Direction (Q. 113): *In the following question a part of the sentence is given in bold, it is then followed by three sentences which try to explain the meaning of the phrase given in bold. Choose the best set of alternatives from the five options given below each question which explains the meaning of the phrase correctly without altering the meaning of the sentence given as question.*

113. Having studied the laws of social development and of capitalism, Marx sought to prove that the destruction of capitalism was inevitable, for it had given rise to its **own grave diggers**.

(I) After studying the laws of social development and of capitalism, Marx was assured that there would be complete destruction of capitalism as the ones who constructed it would themselves be responsible for its downfall.

(II) The laws of social development and of capitalism were so deplorable that Marx felt that it would destroy Capitalism and sooner it would give rise to a new destructive method.

(III) Marx's studies suggested that the laws of social development and capitalism were so woeful

that desolation of capitalism was certain and nobody else than these laws themselves would be accountable for its destruction.

(a) Only (I) is correct

(b) Only (II) is correct

(c) Only (III) is correct

(d) Both (I) and (II) are correct

(e) All are correct

114. If Sentence (C), "Presidential contests in India are usually tame and predictable, and 2017 does not promise to be any different" is the first sentence, what is the order of other sentences after rearrangement?

(A) Prime Minister Indira Gandhi called for a "conscience vote" just before the election, and a sizeable number of Congress parliamentarians and legislators voted against the "official" candidate, Reddy, in favour of Giri.

(B) The Bharatiya Janata Party, with its regular allies and new-found friends, should be able to see any non-controversial candidate through.

(C) Presidential contests in India are usually tame and predictable, and 2017 does not promise to be any different.

(D) To date, the election of V.V. Giri over Neelam Sanjiva Reddy in 1969 remains the only notable exception to the long list of humdrum presidential elections.

(E) Before and after that, however, the favourites have carried the day, with opposition-sponsored candidates putting up no more than a symbolic fight to prove no more than a political point.

(F) At present, the numbers are stacked against the opposition for the July 17 election.

(a) AEFBD   (b) FBADE

(c) DAEFB   (d) AFDBE

(e) DBFEA

115. If sentence (C), "The IS immediately claimed responsibility for the attack that killed 12 people" is the last sentence of the paragraph, then which of the following sentences does not fit into the paragraph formed after rearranging other sentences?

(A) The terrorists clearly wanted to send a message to the Iranian state, and they retained the element of surprise.

(B) The attack, the first major terror incident in Iran in many years, suggests that even the formidable security cover put in place by the elite Revolutionary Guards can be breached by terrorists.

(C) The IS immediately claimed responsibility for the attack that killed 12 people.

(D) But the attacks and the Iranian reaction must also be seen in the context of heightened Saudi Arabia-Iran rivalry.

(E) Wednesday's attacks in Tehran targeted the two most significant symbols of the 1979 Revolution — the Parliament and the tomb of Ayatollah Khomeini, the founder of the Islamic Republic.

(F) Though it is involved in the fight against the Islamic State in Iraq and Syria, Iran has so far largely remained insulated from the regional crises.

(*a*) A   (*b*) E

(*c*) F   (*d*) D

(*e*) C

GENERAL/ECONOMY/ BANKING AWARENESS

116. Which of the following countries stood first in Doing Business (DB) Report, 2018 by World Bank?

(*a*) Singapore   (*b*) Denmark

(*c*) New Zealand   (*d*) South Korea

(*e*) Norway

117. Which of the following Indian cities is/are included in the Creative Cities Network of UNESCO for contributions to music till date?

(*a*) Chennai   (*b*) Jaipur

(*c*) Varanasi   (*d*) Only (*a*) and (*b*)

(*e*) (a), (b) and (c)

118. Which of the following countries has issued a commemorative stamp in honour of the world's largest radio telescope in 2017?

(*a*) India   (*b*) USA

(*c*) China   (*d*) Germany

(*e*) Russia

119. Aadiperukku festival is celebrated in which of the following Indian state?

(*a*) Kerala   (*b*) Tamil Nadu

(*c*) Goa   (*d*) Telangana

(*e*) Karnataka

120. "Hopman Cup" is related with which of the following sports?

(*a*) Tennis   (*b*) Table Tennis

(*c*) Badminton   (*d*) Horse Racing

(*e*) Ice Hockey

121. In December 2017, India's first-ever mobile food testing laboratory was launched in:

(*a*) Haryana   (*b*) Punjab

(*c*) Goa   (*d*) Assam

(*e*) Madhya Pradesh

122. The joint military exercise 'Ajeya Warrior' is held between India and:

(*a*) Israel   (*b*) New Zealand

(*c*) UK   (*d*) USA

(*e*) Nepal

123. Which of the following Indian banks has launched non-interest bearing savings account in December 2017?

(*a*) Federal Bank   (*b*) HDFC Bank

(*c*) ICICI Bank   (*d*) IndusInd Bank

(*e*) Axis Bank

124. Who is the first man on the planet to have 20 hundreds in T-20 cricket?

(*a*) Shahid Afridi

(*b*) Chris Gayle

(*c*) Chris Lewis

(*d*) Brendon McCullum

(*e*) Rohit Sharma

125. Name the first Indian state in the country to use the ultramodern "ring architecture technology" to connect village panchayats by optical fiber to ensure better connectivity?

(*a*) Sikkim   (*b*) Haryana

(*c*) Maharashtra   (*d*) Chhattisgarh

(*e*) Nagaland

126. At present how many members are there in ASEAN?

(*a*) Six   (*b*) Ten

(*c*) Twelve   (*d*) Seventeen

(*e*) Twenty

127. Name the first Indian state to get the first draft of its own updated NRC in India?

(*a*) Arunachal Pradesh

(*b*) Assam

(*c*) Meghalaya

(*d*) Sikkim

(*e*) Nagaland

128. Recently UNESCO has accepted the "bird language" in the UNESCO list of Intangible Cultural Heritage. This bird language is used in:

(*a*) Egypt

(*b*) South Sudan

(*c*) Eritrea

(*d*) Turkey

(*e*) Chad

129. Which of the following is the first public sector bank that has introduced a special leave for employees who have suffered bereavement in the family?

(*a*) Punjab National Bank

(*b*) Indian Overseas Bank

(*c*) Union Bank of India

(*d*) Bank of India

(*e*) State Bank of India

130. Which of the following organization publishes the Global Innovation Index?

(*a*) World Economic Forum

(*b*) World Bank

(*c*) International Monetary Fund

(*d*) World Intellectual Property Organization

(*e*) UNESCO

131. The Minimum Support Price for agricultural products is recommended by which of the following?

(*a*) Cabinet Committee on Economic Affairs

(*b*) Commission for Agricultural Costs and Prices

(*c*) Agricultural Produce Market Committee

(*d*) Directorate of Marketing and Inspection

(*e*) All of the above

132. Eminent Hindi writer MamtaKaliawas honoured with literary award VyasSamman for year 2017 for her novel:

(*a*) Kaatnashamikavrikshapadma-pankhurikidhar se

(*b*) VyomkeshDarvesh

(*c*) SukkhamDukkham

(*d*) Na Bhooto Na Bhavishyati

(*e*) InhiHathiyaron Se

133. Which of the following best describes disguised unemployment?

(*a*) Labour force not recognized by the government

(*b*) Labour productivity is low or near zero

(*c*) Labour force consisting mainly of females and children workers at home

(*c*) Labour working predominantly in the unorganized sector

(*e*) None of the above

134. Which of the following Indian cities is to be the country's first Green Field Smart City?

(*a*) Pune

(*b*) Panaji

(*c*) Ranchi

(*d*) Varanasi

(*e*) Hisar

135. In India, one rupee note bear the signature of:

(*a*) Finance Secretary, Ministry of Finance

(*b*) Finance Minister

(*c*) Prime Minister

(*d*) RBI Governor

(*e*) Vice Chairman, NITI Aayog

136. Name the first country in the world to make it illegal to pay men more than women?

(*a*) Ireland

(*b*) Iceland

(*c*) Norway

(*d*) Sweden

(*e*) New Zealand

137. Recently, Union Cabinet approved a proposal that government will bear the merchant discount rate (MDR) charges on transactions up to………made through debit cards, BHIM UPI or Aadhaar-enabled payment systems.

(*a*) Rs 500

(*b*) Rs 1,500

(*c*) Rs 2,000

(*d*) Rs 5,000

(*e*) Rs 10,000

138. Which of the following has been listed as an Intangible Cultural Heritage under UNESCO for year 2017?

(*a*) Kalbelia

(*b*) Buddhist chanting of Ladakh

(*c*) Ramman

(*d*) KumbhMela

(*e*) Koodiyattam

139. Shyama Prasad MukherjiRurban Mission is a reflection of former President, Dr APJ Abdul Kalam's idea of:

(*a*) GURA

(*b*) RURA

(*c*) PURA

(*d*) PERA

(*e*) MEGA

140. Which of the following banks has become the first bank to start using WhatsApp enterprise solution to provide basic banking services to its customers?

(*a*) Kotak Mahindra Bank

(*b*) Yes Bank

(*c*) Bandhan Bank

(*d*) IndusInd Bank

(*e*) IDFC Bank

141. Who became the first woman cricketer to grace Wisden's famous yellow jacket in 2018?

(*a*) Mithali Raj

(*b*) Megan Schutt

(*c*) Anya Shrubsole

(*d*) Chamari Atapattu

(*e*) Bismah Maroof

142. Which of the following is the largest bank in the world in terms of market capitalization (Till January 2018)?

(*a*) Citibank

(*b*) Industrial and Commercial Bank of China

(*c*) HSBC

(*d*) JP Morgan Chase & Co.

(*e*) Standard Chartered Bank

143. Tax on agricultural income is assigned to the state government by:

(*a*) Finance Commission

(*b*) NITI Aayog

(*c*) Inter-state council

(*d*) National Development Council

(*e*) The Constitution of India

144. Infrastructure Finance Company (IFC) is a non-banking finance company. Which among the following is not a key feature of IFC?

(*a*) IFC deploys at least 55 per cent of its total assets in infrastructure loans

(*b*) IFC has a minimum Net Owned Funds of Rs. 300 crore

(*c*) The minimum credit rating of the company should be at 'A' or equivalent of CRISIL, FITCH, CARE, ICRA, BRICKWORK or equivalent rating by any other accrediting rating agencies.

(*d*) The CRAR of the company should be at 15% with Tier I capital at 10%

(*e*) Both (a) and (c)

145. NAV is the price of:

(*a*) The price per unit of a fund is calculated

(*b*) The price calculated Entire fund value

(*c*) Surrender value

(*d*) Average value of shares

(*e*) Normalized average value of a share

146. Recently, India and Nepal launched ....India-Nepal petroleum products pipeline which is the first international cross-country pipeline project in India will connect:

(*a*) Rs 2.73 billion, Gopalganj and Nagarkot

(*b*) Rs 3.24 billion, Motihari to Amlekhgunj

(*c*) Rs 3.98 billion, Narkatiaganj and Bhaktapur

(*d*) Rs 4.26 billion Kathiyar and Pokhara

(*e*) Rs 5.37 billion Araria and Nepalgunj

147. In 2018, Union Budget of India for the financial year 2018-19 was presented on:

(*a*) 1st February

(*b*) 15th February

(*c*) Last working Friday of January

(*d*) Last Saturday of March

(*e*) On 31st March

148. Recently, the Reserve Bank switched back to the ....based measure to offer its growth estimates from the gross value added (GVA) methodology, citing global best practices.

(*a*) Gross National Product (GNP)

(*b*) Gross Domestic Product (GDP)

(*c*) Net Primary Productivity (NPP)

(*d*) National Property Index (NPI)

(*e*) None of the above

149. Which of the following has decided to set up Data Sciences Lab to improve its forecasting, surveillance and early warning detection abilities which will aid policy formulation?

(*a*) Finance Ministry

(*b*) Reserve Bank of India

(*c*) SEBI

(*d*) SBI

(*e*) SIDBI

150. Who launched 'Project Dhoop', an initiative aimed at shifting the school assembly time to noon to ensure maximum absorption of Vitamin D in students through natural sunlight recently?

(*a*) Ministry of Women & Child Development

(*b*) Food Safety and Standards Authority of India (FSSAI)

(*c*) ICSE

(*d*) Delhi Government

(*e*) Bachpan Bachao Andolan

151. Which of the following Indian banks becomes first to get global financial messaging cooperative Swifts new cross-border payment service?

(*a*) RBL Bank

(*b*) ICICI Bank

(*c*) Kotak Mahindra Bank

(*d*) City Union Bank

(*e*) Yes Bank

152. The Cricket World Cup 2019 is scheduled to be held in:

(*a*) India & Sri Lanka

(*b*) Bangladesh & Pakistan

(*c*) Australia & New Zealand

(*d*) England & Wales

(*e*) West Indies

153. Recently, Britain opened its first permanent military base in the Middle East in more than four decades in the Persian Gulf country of:

(*a*) Qatar

(*b*) Oman

(*c*) Bahrain

(*d*) Kuwait

(*e*) Saudi Arabia

154. 'Gobar-dhan Yojana', the central scheme for managing and converting cattle dung into manure and biogas will be launched at the national level from:

(*a*) Ballia

(*b*) Osmanabad

(*c*) Karnal

(*d*) Madhepura

(*e*) Indore

155. In financial term AIRCSC, S stands for:

(*a*) Secondary

(*b*) Stability

(*c*) Static

(*d*) Survey

(*e*) Superior

ANSWERS

1. (b)	**2.** (d)	**3.** (d)	**4.** (c)	**5.** (d)	**6.** (b)	**7.** (d)	**8.** (d)	**9.** (a)	**10.** (b)
11. (b)	**12.** (e)	**13.** (e)	**14.** (d)	**15.** (d)	**16.** (a)	**17.** (d)	**18.** (d)	**19.** (b)	**20.** (b)
21. (d)	**22.** (c)	**23.** (a)	**24.** (d)	**25.** (d)	**26.** (e)	**27.** (e)	**28.** (a)	**29.** (b)	**30.** (e)
31. (c)	**32.** (d)	**33.** (a)	**34.** (b)	**35.** (c)	**36.** (d)	**37.** (c)	**38.** (c)	**39.** (c)	**40.** (e)
41. (b)	**42.** (c)	**43.** (b)	**44.** (d)	**45.** (b)	**46.** (b)	**47.** (b)	**48.** (a)	**49.** (b)	**50.** (b)
51. (c)	**52.** (d)	**53.** (a)	**54.** (a)	**55.** (d)	**56.** (e)	**57.** (c)	**58.** (c)	**59.** (b)	**60.** (a)
61. (e)	**62.** (a)	**63.** (b)	**64.** (b)	**65.** (d)	**66.** (c)	**67.** (a)	**68.** (a)	**69.** (b)	**70.** (a)
71. (e)	**72.** (d)	**73.** (d)	**74.** (c)	**75.** (d)	**76.** (b)	**77.** (c)	**78.** (b)	**79.** (d)	**80.** (c)
81. (d)	**82.** (c)	**83.** (d)	**84.** (a)	**85.** (e)	**86.** (d)	**87.** (c)	**88.** (e)	**89.** (a)	**90.** (d)
91. (a)	**92.** (b)	**93.** (b)	**94.** (c)	**95.** (d)	**96.** (d)	**97.** (b)	**98.** (e)	**99.** (b)	**100.** (c)
101. (b)	**102.** (e)	**103.** (a)	**104.** (c)	**105.** (b)	**106.** (c)	**107.** (a)	**108.** (d)	**109.** (e)	**110.** (b)
111. (a)	**112.** (d)	**113.** (c)	**114.** (c)	**115.** (d)	**116.** (c)	**117.** (e)	**118.** (c)	**119.** (b)	**120.** (a)
121. (c)	**122.** (c)	**123.** (a)	**124.** (b)	**125.** (d)	**126.** (b)	**127.** (b)	**128.** (d)	**129.** (e)	**130.** (d)
131. (b)	**132.** (c)	**133.** (b)	**134.** (c)	**135.** (a)	**136.** (b)	**137.** (c)	**138.** (d)	**139.** (c)	**140.** (d)
141. (c)	**142.** (b)	**143.** (e)	**144.** (a)	**145.** (a)	**146.** (b)	**147.** (a)	**148.** (b)	**149.** (b)	**150.** (b)
151. (b)	**152.** (d)	**153.** (c)	**154.** (c)	**155.** (d)					

EXPLANATIONS

For questions 1 and 2 :

A5	LM3	FT2
ZU8		BC6
G5	S7	MO

The letters are arranged according to the direction of arrows.

Step 1 :

MO5	S3	G2
BC8		ZU6
FT5	LM7	A

Step 2 :

MO2	S3	G2
AB8		ZU3
FT5	KL7	A

In step 3, the elements are arranged in the first and third column in such way that the element in the third row shifted in the first row, that of the first row is shifted in the second row and that of the second row is shifted in the third row. The letter/s of the first cell of the second column is replaced with the letter/s which is/are placed three places after it/then in the english alphabet. The letter/s of third cell of the second column is replaced with the letter/s which is/are placed five places after it/them in the english alphabet.

Step 3 :

FT5	V3	A
MO2		G2
AB8	PQ7	ZU3

3. (d) According to the given statement, America is not taking any step to address the issue, so to calm down the situation Indian Govt. may compel American Govt. stating its impact on India-US trade. Furthermore, America is not taking any action despite racism attack on Indians which results death of two citizens. Thus, it cannot be assumed that American Govt. will give life imprisonment.

4. (c) All the three statements support the negligence of Indian-American Govt. as Modi Govt. denies replying in same week after racial attack. American Govt. is not ready to tackle the issue despite environment of racism is spreading.

For questions 5 to 7 :

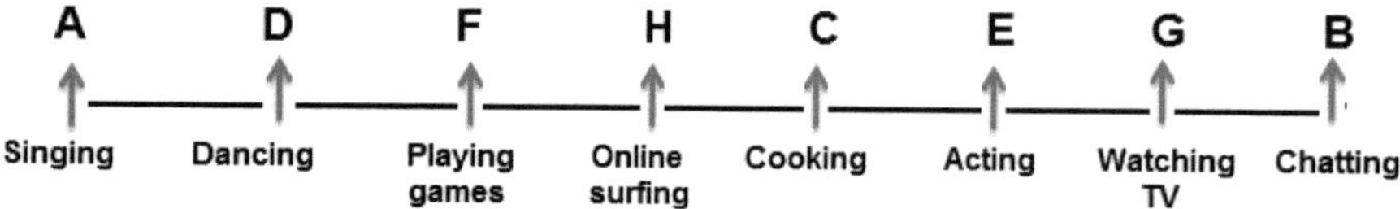

8. (d) Train is scheduled at 5 hour 10 minute (#&).

Hence, required time = 5 hour 10 minute – (25 + 5) minutes

= 4 hour 40 minutes = $@

9. (a) Required time = 4 hour 15 minutes = $£

10. (b) Scheduled departure = @% = 8:00 PM

Hence, required time = 8:00 PM – 4 hour 40 minutes = 3:20 PM = £$

For questions 11 to 15 :

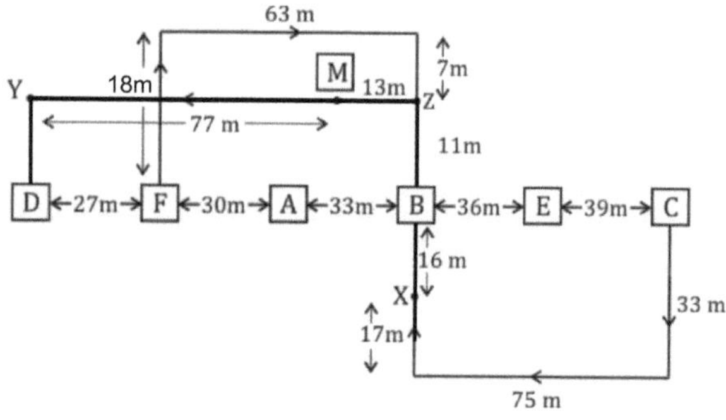

16. (a) Statement (a) is the correct option because it clearly strengthen the argument that persons with sufficient qualification prefer to go to industrial field rather than to go in academics as a faculty in business schools.

17. (d) Option (d) is an assumption. Any appeal has some effects and people generally respond positively to any appeal.

For questions 18 to 20 :

For step-I, both the numbers of 1st block is written as, I^{st} number of block-1 of the Input is multiplied with 2nd no. of block-4 of the Input same as 2nd number of block-1 is multiplied with 1st number of block-4. This process is same for Block-2 and Block-3 in step-1.

For step-II, All 1st digit of each block is added and that sum is written in 1st block and all 2nd digit of each block is added and that sum is written as 2nd block.

For step-III, Half of the addition of 1st and 2nd digit of each block.

For Step- IV, Subtraction of both numbers of Step-3.

So, INPUT: 42 51 29 32 71 14

Step-1: 86 57 89

Step-2: ..21..22...

Step-3: ..1.5..2...

Step-4:.....0.5....

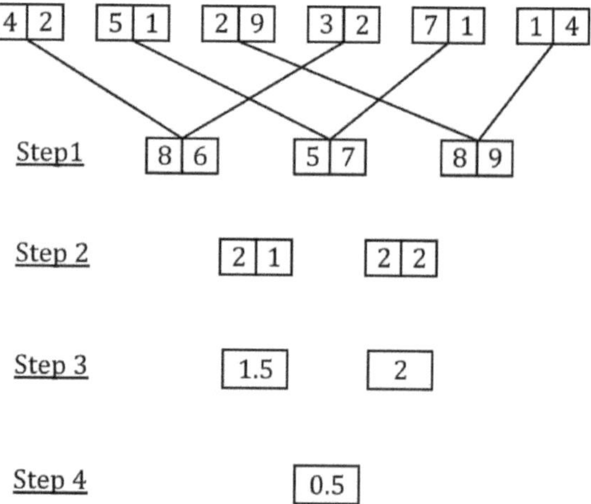

21. (d) Both statements I and II can't be assumed from the given statement as statement I is vague and statement II is also not implicit because it is not clear from the given statement that whether people are interested in such news or not.

22. (c) Combining all the statements together:

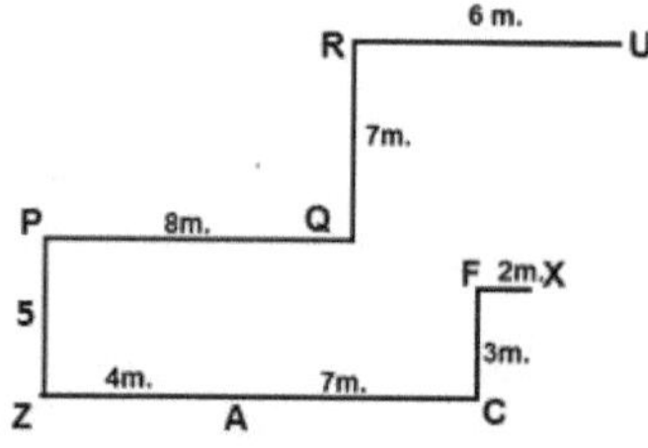

24. (d) Option (d) contradicts the views expressed in the statement.

For questions 25 and 26 :

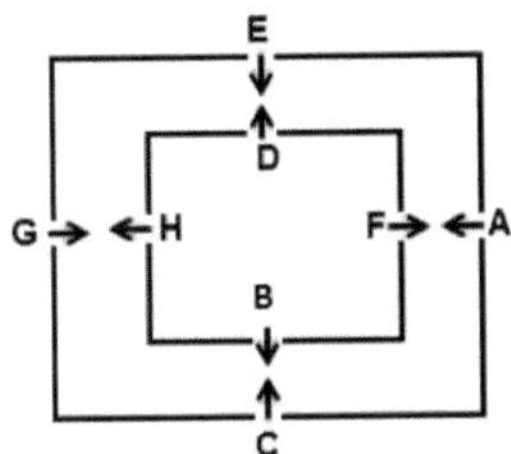

For questions 27 and 28 :

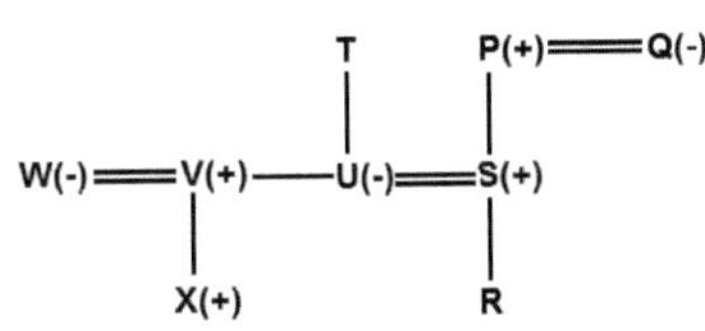

29. (b) The disease occurs at the end of monsoons every year. Therefore, precautionary measures every four years shall not help.

The second course of action shall be a preventive measure.

Hence, only course II follows.

30. (e) Clearly, the library needs to be provided with the essential facilities and trained personnel for better services. So, both the courses follow.

For questions 31 to 35 :

Month	Date	Lecturer	No. of students
April	7	R	72
April	21	U	84
May	7	P	67
May	21	V	55
June	7	T	80
June	21	Y	68
September	7	Q	64
September	21	X	78
December	7	S	77
December	21	W	69

For questions 36 and 37 :

(2 - U), (4 - A), (6 - I), (8 - C), (10 - P), (12 - D), (14 - T), (16 - E), (18 - N), (20 - R), (22), (24 - S)

36. (d) Required word is DIRT.

So second letter – I

37. (c) Given that 10 is P.

For 22, we have P + 3 = T, but T is already written and we cannot repeat any letter. Thus, (22) = P – 3 = L

Hence, required letter will be M.

38. (c) Statement (c) is the correct option because according to this, the increase in crime rate has been contributed by other factors, not leniency in the punishment.so it weakens the given passage.

For questions 39 to 43 :

Each glass slab is 15 cm and photo frame is 6 cm. Total length of row-1 is 267 and that of row 2 is 249 cm.

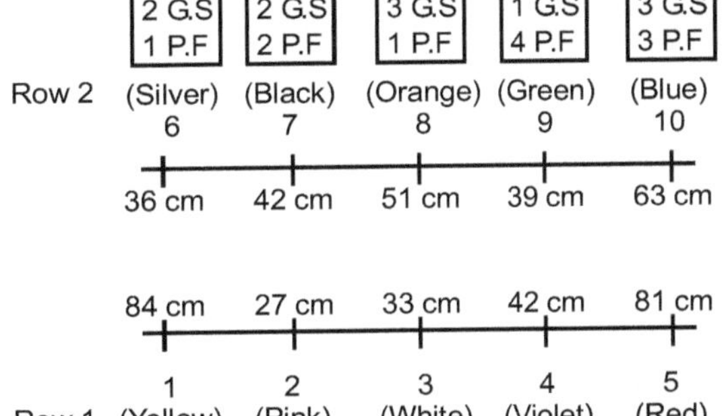

44. (d) Most logically such comparison should reveal mortality rate per thousand doctors indulged in SARS treatment and not indulged in treatment.so statement (d) is the correct option.

46. (b) Quantity I :

Different number of ways of arranging 5 men or 5 women = 5!

Number of ways of arranging 5 men and 5 women such that no two women or men sit together = 2 × 5! × 5!

Quantity II :

Number of ways of arranging 5 men and 5 women such that all men sit together

= 6! × 5!

Hence, 2 × 5! × 5! < 6! × 5!

Therefore, Quantity I < Quantity II

47. (b) Since S is an acute angle

∴ $(a + 40) + a < 90$

$(2a + 40) < 90$

$2a < 50$

$a < 25°$

Therefore, Quantity I < Quantity II

48. (a) Quantity I :

Let required number $= 10x + y$

$\therefore \qquad 10y + x = 10x + y + 36$

$\Rightarrow \qquad 9y - 9x = 36$

$\Rightarrow \qquad y - x = 4$

Thus, unit digit of the number should be 4 more than the ten's digit of the number.

$\therefore$ such possible numbers from 1 to 63 are = 04, 15, 26, 37, 48, 59

Hence, required probability $= \dfrac{6}{63}$

Quantity II :

Possible numbers from 1 to 63 = 8, 24, 40, 56

Hence, required probability $= \dfrac{4}{63}$

Therefore, Quantity I > Quantity II

49. (b) From A : $m + n$

$= 10 \times k$ (Let k is an integer value)

From B : $10m + 7n$

$= 70 \times 1$ (let I is an integer value)

From C : $n > m$

From A and B

$3n = 10 (10k - 71);$

Hence n is divisible by 10. Thus option A and B together are required to solve the question.

50. (b) Let speed of the boat in still water on Thursday $= x$

$$\frac{12 \times 18}{x - 1} = \frac{16 \times 15}{16 + 2}$$

$$= \frac{12 \times 18 \times 18}{16 \times 15} = x - 1$$

$x - 1 = 16.2$

$x = 17.2$ kmph

51. (c) Let speed of boat in still water on Monday $= x$

$$\frac{15 \times 18}{x - 2} = \frac{45}{11} + \frac{16 \times 15}{x + 2}$$

$$15\left(\frac{18}{x - 2} - \frac{16}{x + 2}\right) = \frac{45}{11}$$

$$\frac{18}{x - 2} - \frac{16}{x + 2} = \frac{3}{11}$$

If we put $x = 20$

Then it satisfy the above equation

$\therefore$ $x = 20$ kmph

52. (d) Speed of boat in still water on Tuesday

$= 15$ km/hr

$$66\frac{2}{3}\% = \frac{2}{3}$$

Speed of boat in still water on Wednesday

$$= 15 + \frac{2}{3} \times 15 = 25 \text{ km/hr}$$

$$\frac{14 \times 18}{25 - x} = \frac{14 \times 15}{(15 + 3)} \times \frac{9}{10}$$

$$\frac{6}{25 - x} = \frac{5}{18} \times \frac{9}{10}$$

$$\frac{6}{0.25} = 25 - x$$

$25 - x = 24$

$x = 1$ km/hr

53. (a) Given

Speed of boat in still water on Saturday

$= 21$ km/h

$$28\frac{4}{7}\% = \frac{2}{7}$$

$\therefore$ Speed of boat in still water on Sunday

$$= 21 - \frac{2}{7} \times 21$$

$$= 21 - 6 = 15 \text{ kmph}$$

$$\frac{10 \times 18}{21 - x} = \frac{19}{16} \times \frac{10 \times 15}{15 + 4}$$

$$x = 1.8$$

$$\text{Required time} = \frac{57.6}{21 - 1.8}$$

$$= \frac{57.6}{19.2} = 3 \text{hrs}$$

54. (a)
$$\frac{18 \times 18}{x - 4} = 2 + \frac{12 \times 15}{17 + 1}$$

$18 \times 18 = 12 (x - 4)$

$x - 4 = 27$

$x = 31$ kmph

Required upstream speed

$= 31 - 4 = 27$ kmph

For question 55 to 57 :

Bag A :

Number of yellow balls = 18

Number of green balls = 18 + 4 = 22

Total number of balls in bag A are in multiple of 13.

Thus by hit and trial method

We can assume total number of balls in bag A = 65

Then, number of black balls = 25

It satisfies the give probability.

Bag B :

Number of Yellow balls = 22

Number of Green balls = 25

Number of Black balls = 28

Bag C :

Number of Yellow balls = 42

Number of Green balls = 21

Number of Black balls = 15

55. (d) After replacement :

Yellow number of balls in beg B = 22 – x

Black number of balls in beg B

$$= 28 + 5 = 33$$

Green number of balls in bag B = 25

Then, $\dfrac{33}{22 - x + 33 + 25} = \dfrac{11}{26}$

$$\dfrac{33}{80 - x} = \dfrac{11}{26}$$

$$78 = 80 - x$$

Hence, x = 2

56. (e) Required probability

$$= \dfrac{18}{65} \times \dfrac{22}{75} + \dfrac{22}{65} \times \dfrac{25}{75} + \dfrac{25}{65} \times \dfrac{28}{75} = \dfrac{1646}{65 \times 75}$$

57. (c) Required percentage

$$= \dfrac{40 - 1}{40} \times 100 = \dfrac{39}{40} \times 100 = 97.5\%$$

58. (c) Let MP of item-II by seller A = 100x

$\therefore$ MP of item-II by seller C = 100x

$$\dfrac{\dfrac{100}{100 + s} \times 68x}{\dfrac{100}{100 + 2s - 4} \times 84x} = \dfrac{17}{21}$$

$$\dfrac{68}{84} \times \dfrac{96 + 2s}{100 + s} = \dfrac{17}{21}$$

$$\dfrac{96 + 2s}{100 + s} = \dfrac{1}{1}$$

$$96 + 2s = 100 + s$$

$$s = 4$$

59. (b) Let mark price of item II = 100x

Let mark price of item III = 100y

$\therefore \quad 100x + 100y = 6000$

$$x + y = 60 \qquad \text{....(i)}$$

And, $\quad 72x - 84y = 420$

$$6x - 7y = 35 \qquad \text{....(ii)}$$

From (i) and (ii)

$$y = 25$$

$$x = 35$$

$\therefore$ M.P. of item II = 3500

M.P. of item III = 2500

Hence required % $= \dfrac{3500 - 2500}{2500} \times 100$

$$= \dfrac{1000}{25} = 40\%$$

60. (a) Let M.P. of item II = 100a

$\therefore$ S.P. of item II by seller A = 68a

S.P. of item II by seller B = (100 – x)a

Then (168 – x)a = (3888) × 2

(184 – x)a = 4320 × 2

$\therefore \quad \dfrac{168 - x}{184 - x} = \dfrac{9}{10}$

$(10 \times 168) - 10x = 9 \times 184 - 9x$

$$x = 24$$

$$a = 54$$

Hence, S.P. of item II by seller C

$$= 4536 \text{ Rs.}$$

61. (e) Let S.P. of item I = 500

$\therefore$ S.P. of item III = 600

C.P. of item I $= \dfrac{100}{125} \times 500 = 400$

C.P. of item II $= \dfrac{100}{120} \times 600 = 500$

Profit on item I = 500 – 400 = 100

$\therefore \quad 100 \to 750$

$$1 \to 7.5$$

$$(200) \to (200 \times 7.5) = \text{Rs. } 1500$$

62. (a)   C.P. = Rs. 60

$$\text{M.P.} = \frac{200}{300} \times 60 + 60$$

$$= 40 + 60 = 100$$

Total C.P. = 60 × 5

$$= 300 \text{ Rs.}$$

Total selling price should be = 380 Rs.

S.P. of item III by seller E

$$= (380 - 64 - 67 - 86 - 84) = 79$$

Hence, minimum required discount

$$= (100 - 79) = 21\%$$

63. (b) From question we observe that sum of investment of A and C is equal to B for first quarter.

So, if ratio of investment of B is equal to (A + C) for all quarters of year then B's profit is 50% of total profit.

Hence, profit of B = $\dfrac{125000}{2}$

$$= \text{Rs. } 62500$$

64. (b) Total amount invested by A + B in a year

$$\Rightarrow 2500 + 7x + 7y + 13z = 9000 \quad ....(i)$$

Total amount invested by B and C in a year

$$\Rightarrow 2300 + 8x + 7y + 13z = 10500 ....(ii)$$

From (i) and (ii)

$$200 - x = -1500$$

$$x = 1700$$

Hence, total amount for second quarter

$$= \text{Rs. } 17000$$

65. (d) In $\dfrac{1}{2}$h train A will cover = 27 km

Distance between P and Q (x)

$$= 27 + \frac{13}{3} \times 120$$

$$= 27 + 520$$

$$= 547 \text{ km}$$

Total time taken in given condition

$$= \left(\frac{1}{2} + \frac{13}{3}\right)h = \frac{29}{6}h$$

New time taken according to condition

$$= \frac{547 + 2 \times 54}{(66 - 54)} = \frac{655}{12}h$$

Hence, required difference in time

$$= \frac{655}{12} - \frac{29}{6} = \frac{597}{12}$$

$$= 49 \text{ hour } 45 \text{ min.}$$

66. (c) Required ratio = $\dfrac{66 - 54}{66 + 54} = 1:10$

67. (a) Area of quadrilateral BFDE

$$= \text{Area of rectangle ABCD}$$

$$- \text{Area of } \Delta \text{ABE} - \text{Area of } \Delta \text{DCF}$$

$$= 120 - 30 - 25 = 65 \text{ cm}^2$$

68. (a) Ratio of Investment of A, B and C

$$(3000 \times 4 + 1800 \times 5 + 3600 \times 3) : (4000 \times 4$$

$$+ 8000 \times 5) : (14000 + 33600)$$

$$31800 : 56000 : 47600$$

$$159 : 280 : 238$$

Profit of C $= \dfrac{238}{677} \times 6770000$

$$= 238000$$

Average of profit earned by (A + B + C)

$$\approx 225666$$

69. (b) Let the C do in one day = 4y work

Let the D do in one day = 5y work

2 day work of C + D = 9y

In 44 day they will complete 9y × 22

$$= 198y$$

In another $\dfrac{1}{2}$ days 2y work will be done

C will take $= \dfrac{200y}{4y}$ days

$$= 50 \text{ day}$$

D will take = 40 days.

C and D will complete work together in

$$= \frac{50 \times 40}{90} = \frac{200}{9}$$

According to condition

$$\frac{200}{9x} + \frac{200}{9 \times 2x} = 1$$

$$\frac{400 + 200}{18x} = 1$$

$$\Rightarrow x = 33\frac{1}{3}$$

70. (a) Let E do work in 4x days

Let F do work in 5x days

$$\frac{24}{5x}+\frac{24}{4x}+\frac{200}{\frac{100}{3}}+\frac{20}{\frac{200}{3}}=1$$

$$24\left(\frac{9}{20x}\right)+\frac{60}{100}+\frac{60}{200}=1$$

$$\frac{24\times9}{20x}=1-\frac{180}{200}$$

$$\frac{24\times9}{20x}=\frac{1}{10}$$

x = 108

Together E and F can do work in

$$=\frac{4\times108\times5\times108}{9\times108}=240 \text{ days}$$

$$\text{Required difference} =\frac{240}{4\times108}-\frac{240}{5\times108}$$

$$=\frac{240}{108}\left(\frac{1}{20}\right)=\frac{1}{9}$$

71. (e) As per given condition

$$\frac{5}{10}+\frac{5}{15}+\frac{x}{12}+\frac{x}{18}=\left(1-\frac{1}{36}\right)$$

$$\frac{5x}{36}=\frac{35}{36}-\frac{5}{6}$$

$$x=\frac{36}{5}\left(\frac{35-30}{36}\right)=1 \text{ days.}$$

72. (d) Part of work completed by

$$E=\frac{5}{20}=\frac{1}{4}$$

3 day work by (A + B + D)

$$=\frac{1}{10}+\frac{1}{12}+\frac{1}{18}=\frac{18+15+10}{180}=\frac{43}{180}$$

9 day work = (3A + 3B + 3D) = $\dfrac{129}{1.80}$

$$\text{Remaining work } =\frac{3}{4}-\frac{129}{180}$$

$$=\frac{135-129}{180}=\frac{6}{180}=\frac{1}{30}$$

this will be done by A in

$$=\frac{1}{30}\times10=\frac{1}{3} \text{ days}$$

so B worked for 3 days.

73. (d) Work done by A, C and E on Job Z

$$=\frac{2}{10}+\frac{2}{15}+\frac{2}{20}$$

$$=\frac{12+8+6}{60}$$

$$=\frac{26}{60}=\frac{13}{30}$$

Remaining work done by B and D in 20x and 21x

$$\frac{20x}{12}+\frac{21x}{18}=\frac{17}{30}$$

$$\frac{60x+42x}{36}=\frac{17}{30}$$

$$\Rightarrow 102x=17\times\frac{36}{30}$$

$$x=\frac{6}{30}=\frac{1}{5}$$

$$\text{Required days}=20\times\frac{1}{5}=4 \text{ days}$$

74. (c) According to question

$$\frac{2}{10}+\frac{4x}{12}+\frac{3}{15}+\frac{3x}{18}+\frac{2}{20}=1$$

$$\Rightarrow \frac{1}{5}+\frac{x}{3}+\frac{1}{5}+\frac{x}{6}+\frac{1}{10}=1$$

$$\frac{6+10x+6+5x+3}{30}=1$$

15x + 15 = 30

x = 1

Required difference = 4x – 3x

$$=4-3=1$$

75. (d) With new efficiency C will complete job in = 12 days

3 days work of C and 1 day work of B

$$=1/3$$

Days required = 9 days

76. (b) Rhombus PQRS :

$$\text{Side of PQRS } = \frac{\sqrt{6^2 + 8^2}}{2}$$

$$= \frac{10}{2} = 5 \text{ cm}$$

Rhombus MLKJ

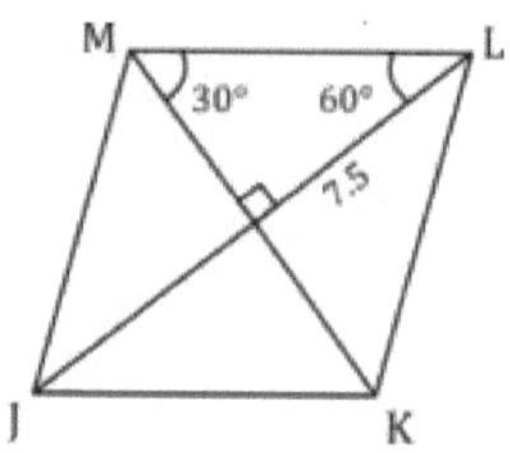

$$\sin 30 = \frac{\text{perpendicular}}{\text{Hypotenuse}}$$

$$\frac{1}{2} = \frac{75}{\text{side of MLJK}}$$

Side of MLJK = 15 cm

Now,   AB = 5 cm

CD = 15 cm

So median XY = $\dfrac{5 + 15}{2}$ = 10 cm

77. (c) After 20% of the content of the vessels is removed,

Remaining content

$$= \frac{80}{100}(12.5) = 10 \text{ litres.}$$

Ratio of water and milk in it = 1 : 4.

∴ It will contain $\dfrac{4}{5}(10) = 8$ litres of milk and 2 litres of water.

Now, reverse the ratio, 2 litres of water must be made 32 litres of water must be added.

To reservse this ratio again 8 litres of milk must be made 4 × (32) = 128 litres,

Therefore, y = 128 − 8 = 120 litres of milk must be added.

78. (b) We can get ratio of investments from either statement B alone or C alone. Hence profit of B can be determined.

79. (d) From A and C we can determine the ratio of efficiencies between men, women and children. From A and B we can determine the value of ratio of men, women and children. We can calculate the answer from B and C.

80. (c) Statement A :

$$\text{Total price } = \frac{3828 \times 100}{120}$$

Statement C :

(x + y) − (x − y) = 28

⇒   y = 14

Hence,   x = 76

81. (d) Paragraph 1 states– "Unfortunately, this is a common problem". The author mentions this to talk about the common problem that every organization is facing nowadays with the changes in the decision-making process by their employees. Options (a), (b) and (c) support the given statement whereas option (d) states that their decisions are often rationale and in the best interest of the organization making it opposite to the problem mentioned in the paragraph. Hence (d) is the correct option.

82. (c) Paragraph 2 states– "We call the chance variability of judgments noise. It is an invisible tax on the bottom line of many companies." Hence both options (II) and (III) define the problem of noise as the author has tried to explain in the passage.

83. (d) Paragraph 3 states–"In contrast, medical professionals, loan officers, project managers, judges, and executives all make judgment calls, which are guided by informal experience and general principles rather than by rigid rules. And if they don't reach precisely the same answer that every other person in their role would, that's acceptable; this is what we mean when we say that a decision is "a matter of judgment." Statements (I) and (II) align with this information. Hence (d) is the correct option.

84. (a) Both paragraphs 4 & 5 state several examples with different statistical figures. They are inconnection to research work. Hence (a) is the best answer that establishes connection between 4 & 5 paragraphs.

85. (e) In the last paragraph, the author expresses his doubt over the research work's measurement of cost of noise. Moreover he states that this will give rise to several huge problems & hence the firms should take action on the issue of noise. This makes all (*i*), (*ii*) and (*iii*) correct.

86. (d) The passage states–"More positively, it is light on the non-performing loans that clog the balance-sheets of banks in places like Italy. But in other ways its problems have a very familiar ring. Deutsche is struggling to make a decent return. It has taken too long to face up to its problems. And the market it operates in is overbanked".

This clearly makes statements II & III correct.

87. (c) Paragraph 2 mentions that Deutsche is piled up with new problems which is shocking European bureaucrats, even though its condition is better than other existing banks in the market. Hence (c) is the correct option in context of the passage.

88. (e) Option (e) talks about the projected fall of returns on equity towards zero, which is not mentioned in the paragraph. Hence (e) is the correct option. All other options are stated in paragraph 3.

89. (a) Amongst all the given options, only option (a) connects paragraphs 4 & 5.

90. (d) After going through the passage, only statements (I) and (II) seem probable solutions to the problem being faced by European banks. Statement (III) is an extreme step. Hence (d) is the correct option.

91. (a) Among the provided options, the sentences, except (a) are either grammatically incorrect or carrot be validated be from the given context. Only sentence (a) forms the correct sentence which follows the sentences given in the question both grammatically and contextually.

92. (b) The use of 'few' is incorrect in the third part of the sentence; it should be replaced with 'some'. "Dispute between some..". is the correct grammatical usage.

93. (b) The phrase "a western construct" in the sentence denotes the cultures and practices prevalent in western societies. Among the given statements, only (II) is able to explain the meaning correctly. Hence (b) is the correct choice.

94. (c) 'Relevant' and 'obscure' fits the two blank most appropriately.

Relevant means closely connected or appropriate to what is being done or considered while obscure means not discovered or known about.

95. (d) Statement (II) is incorrect if we look at, to "Most debate over ..and migration" therefore it is definitely not the major concern but is just a new factor. Statement (I) and (III) both are correct as security is the major concern here. You may get confused with cyber-security but it is also a part of the security system.

96. (d) All the other options except (d) are either grammatically incorrect or contextually invalid here. Hence (d) is the correct option which is both grammatically correct and fits the given context.

97. (b) In the first part of the sentence, 'have been' needs to be replaced by 'had' as the sentence is in Past Tense. In part (III), "meant it should be given" is the correct phrase to make the sentence grammatically correct.

98. (e) The phrase used in the sentence "a grave miscarriage of justice" means a wrong decision made by a court, as a result of which an innocent person is punished. In the given context, it means a wrong decision made by a court which failed in justifying the actual truth, as a result of which innocent person failed to get the justice. Hence all three statements (I), (II) and (III) define the same meaning. So (e) is the correct choice.

99. (b) 'Efficacy' and 'regimens' fits the two blank correctly.

Efficacy means the ability to produce a desired or intended result.

Regimen means a prescribed course of medical treatment, diet, or exercise for the promotion or restoration of health.

100. (c) Per capita income is the ratio of real national income and total income. Statement (III) is talking specifically about the per capita income and therefore is not the parent statement. Statement (II) is incorrect as it goes against the theme of the inference. Only statement (I) is correct and therefore option (c) is the correct choice for the given question.

101. (b) Out of the given answers, only (b) is both grammatically and logically correct. Other options are beyond the scope of the given context.

102. (e) No correction is required as the given sentence is grammatically correct.

103. (a) Option (a) is the best answer choice as, transition means the process or a period of changing from one state or condition to another and enervating means make (someone) feel drained of energy or vitality.

104. (c) Only option (c) is correct. The clue here is "slowdown in the production process as a whole".

105. (b) Option (b) fits the two blank most appropriately.

Discrepancy means an illogical or surprising lack of compatibility or similarity between two or more facts

106. (c) Only (c) is both grammatically and logically correct. Other options therefore can be eliminated.

107. (a) As the given sentence is present tense, option (a) is the only correct answer.

108. (d) Only statement (II) is correct as the given inference talks about the reasons for fluctuation in GDP and is not indicating about the living standard.

109. (e) 'preside, overwhelmingly' fits the two blank correctly.

Other options are logically and grammatically incorrect.

110. (b) Statement II is the answer because there is a direct relation between intake of aspartame and a craving for carbohydrate. Furthermore, the statement says that people who use … defeating their purpose. This directly relates to the fact that the calorie count of foods that are high in carbs is significant. Statement I is incorrect. It says that aspartame provides calories and carbohydrates but we cannot say that carbohydrates contain significant calories.

111. (a) Options b. c and d have many grammatical errors. Only option a is correct and delivers a coherent structure and meaning.

112. (d) The given sentence is grammatically erroneous. However, the options given are incorrect as well. Hence, option (d) is the answer.

113. (c) The given idiom refers to something suicidal. In the light of that, only option III makes sense. The crux of the statement is that Capitalism will cause its own destruction.

114. (c) DA is a mandatory pair. A explains the voting pattern during Indira Gandhi's time. Furthermore, E logically follows A.

115. (d) The correct sequence of the sentences is EAFBC. EA is a mandatory pair. C effectively concludes the paragraph. D is clearly out of context. There is no mention of Saudi Arabia in the other sentences.

117. (e) Chennai, often called as cultural capital of South India, joined the elite club of world cities when it was included in Creative Cities Network of UNESCO for its contributions to music. The city joins two other cities in India - Jaipur and Varanasi - to have figured in the prestigious list for their contributions to music and folk arts.

118. (c) China issued a commemorative stamp in honour of the world's largest radio telescope, the Five-hundred-meter Aperture Spherical radio Telescope (FAST), located in Guizhou province.

119. (b) Aadipirappu is a unique South Indian and specially a Tamil festival celebrated on the 18th day of the Tamil month of Adi (Mid July). It is celebrated near river basins, water tanks, lakes and wells etc. of Tamil Nadu when the water level in the rises significantly heralding the onset of Monsoon

120. (a) The Hopman Cup is an annual international eight-team indoor hardcourt tennis tournament held in Perth, Western Australia in early January (sometimes commencing in late December) each year, which plays mixed-gender teams on a country-by-country basis.

121. (c) Goa Chief Minister ManoharParrikar launched country's first-ever mobile food testing laboratory.

122. (c) The joint Indo-UK military exercise 'Ajeya Warrior' was held at Mahajan Field Firing Range in Rajasthan in December 2017.

123. (a) Federal Bank has launched non-interest bearing savings account targeting those whose beliefs do not permit them to accept interest payment.

124. (b) Chris Gayle became the first man on the planet to have 20 T20 hundreds as the belligerent left-hander smashed an unbeaten 146 off just 69 balls for Rangpur Riders against Dhaka Dynamites in the Bangladesh Premier League final.

125. (d) Chhattisgarh is the first state in the country to use the ultramodern "ring architecture technology" to connect village panchayats by optical fiber to ensure better connectivity.

126. (b) The Association of Southeast Asian Nations is a regional intergovernmental organisation comprising ten Southeast Asian states which promotes Pan-Asianism and intergovernmental cooperation and facilitates economic, political, security, military, educational and socio-cultural integration amongst its members and Asian states.

127. (b) Assam is the only State in the country that prepared an NRC in 1951 following the census of that year and has become the first State to get the first draft of its own updated NRC.

128. (d) The unusual and very efficient whistle language used as a means of communication by villagers in remote northern Turkey entered the UNESCO list of Intangible Cultural Heritage.

129. (e) SBI has introduced a special leave for employees who have suffered bereavement in the family.

130. (d) The Global Innovation Index (GII) is an annual ranking of countries by their capacity for, and success in, innovation. It is published by Cornell University, INSEAD, and the World Intellectual Property Organization, in partnership with other organisations and institutions.

131. (b) The decision to increase MSPs is based on the recommendations of Commission for Agricultural Costs and Prices (CACP) which takes into account the cost of production, overall demand-supply, domestic and international prices, inter-crop price parity, terms of trade between agricultural and non-agricultural sectors, the likely effect of the Price Policy on the rest of economy, besides ensuring rational utilization of production resources like land and water, while recommending MSPs.

132. (c) Eminent Hindi writer MamtaKalia will be honoured with literary award VyasSamman for year 2017 for her novel "DukkhamSukkham".

133. (b) Disguised unemployment exists where part of the labor force is either left without work or is working in a redundant manner where worker productivity is essentially zero. It is unemployment that does not affect aggregate output.

134. (c) Ranchi will be the country's first Green Field Smart City.

135. (a) Printing of one rupee notes was discontinued in 1994 but was relaunched in 2015. The one rupee note will bear signature of Finance Secretary in the Ministry of Finance. The other currency notes bear the signature of the RBI Governor.

136. (b) Iceland has become the first country in the world to enforce equal pay between men and women.

137. (c) Union Cabinet approved a proposal that government will bear the merchant discount rate (MDR) charges on transactions up to Rs 2,000 made through debit cards, BHIM UPI or Aadhaar-enabled payment systems to promote digital transactions.

138. (d) KumbhMela, the largest congregation of pilgrims, has been listed as an Intangible Cultural Heritage under UNESCO.

139. (c) Shyama Prasad MukherjiRurban Mission is a reflection of former President, Dr APJ Abdul Kalam's idea of PURA (Providing Urban Amenities in Rural Areas).

140. (d) IndusInd Bank has become the first lender to start using WhatsApp enterprise solution to provide basic banking services to customers.

141. (c) Anya Shrubsole becomes first woman to grace Wisden's famous yellow jacket.

142. (b) Industrial and Commercial Bank of China Limited is a Chinese multinational banking company. It is the largest bank in the world by total assets and the most valuable bank in the world by market capitalization since February 2017.

144. (a) A minimum of 75 per cent of the total assets of an IFC-NBFC should be deployed in infrastructure loans.

145. (a) If a fund has assets of $50 million and liabilities of $10 million, it would have a NAV of $40 million. This number is important to investors, because it is from NAV that the price per unit of a fund is calculated.

146. (b) Indian Prime Minister Narendra Modi and his Nepal counterpart K P Sharma Oli launched the ground-breaking ceremony of the Rs 3.24 billion India-Nepal petroleum products pipeline from Motihari to Amlekhgunj.

147. (a) The 2018 Union budget of India was the annual financial statement (AFS), demand for grants, appropriation bill and finance bill of India for the financial year 2018-19.It was presented to Parliament on 1 February 2018 by Finance Minister Arun Jaitley.

148. (b) The Reserve Bank switched back to the gross domestic product (GDP)-based measure to offer its growth estimates from the gross value added (GVA) methodology, citing global best practices.

149. (b) Reserve Bank of India has decided to set up Data Sciences Lab to improve its forecasting, surveillance and early warning detection abilities which will aid policy formulation.

150. (b) The Food Safety and Standards Authority of India (FSSAI) launched 'Project Dhoop', an initiative aimed at shifting the school assembly time to noon to ensure maximum absorption of Vitamin D in students through natural sunlight.

151. (b) Global financial messaging cooperative Swift said ICICI Bank has become its first Indian client to go live with an improved cross-border payments service.

152. (*) The 2019 Cricket World Cup is the 12th edition of the Cricket World Cup, scheduled to be hosted by England and Wales, from 30 May to 14 July 2019.

153. (c) Britain opened its first permanent military base in the Middle East in more than four decades in the Persian Gulf country of Bahrain, giving the U.K. an expansive presence along key international shipping routes.

154. (c) 'Gobar-dhan Yojana', the central scheme for managing and converting cattle dung into manure and biogas, will be launched at the national level from Karnal in Haryana on April 30.

155. (d) The All India Rural Credit Survey committee (AIRCS) was appointed to take stock of rural finances in 1951.

■■

2016

GENERAL AWARENESS

1. Recently, the seventh edition of mega seed event- Seed Congress 2017 was organized in:
   (1) Mumbai
   (2) New Delhi
   (3) Kurushetra
   (4) Kolkata
   (5) Karnal

2. In February 2017, a scientific panel on food fortification and nutrition has been set up by which of the following?
   (1) Ministry of Consumers Affairs, Food and Public Distribution
   (2) Ministry of Agriculture and Farmers Welfare
   (3) FAO
   (4) FSSAI
   (5) Ministry of Food Processing Industries

3. Recently, the 11th edition of International Aerospace and Defence Exhibition - Aero India 2017 was held at:
   (1) Chennai
   (2) Madurai
   (3) Bengaluru
   (4) Mysuru
   (5) Kurnool

4. Recently Special Edition of "Atlas for Visually Impaired (India)" in English Braille in New Delhi was released by which of the following Ministry/Ministries?
   (1) Ministry of Social Justice and Welfare
   (2) Ministry of Home Affairs
   (3) Ministry of Finance
   (4) Ministry for Science & Technology and Earth Sciences
   (5) Both (1) & (2)

5. Which is the first Indian state in the country to launch India's first comprehensive 'Crime Criminal Tracking Network System' (CCTNS)?
   (1) Haryana
   (2) Gujarat
   (3) Maharashtra
   (4) Tamil Nadu
   (5) Goa

6. Recently the first Indian Ocean Rim Association (IORA) leaders' summit is held at:
   (1) Singapore
   (2) Kuala Lumpur
   (3) Jakarta
   (4) Hanoi
   (5) Mali

7. How much insurance cover is provided to a person booking a train ticket through the IRCTC website?
   (1) 4 Lakhs
   (2) 6 Lakhs
   (3) 8 Lakhs
   (4) 10 Lakhs
   (5) 20 Lakhs

8. The GST Council Secretariat will have its office at:
   (1) Gurugram
   (2) Greater Noida
   (3) New Delhi
   (4) Jaipur
   (5) Mumbai

9. The world's first daily driverless bus service was started in:
   (1) Germany
   (2) Sweden
   (3) France
   (4) Singapore
   (5) USA

10. According Gramin Swachh Survekshan 2016, which is the cleanest district among 'Hills' category in India?
    (1) Dharamshala
    (2) Srinagar
    (3) Mussorie
    (4) Shimla
    (5) Mandi

11. India's first LIGO (Laser Interferometer Gravitational-Wave Observatory) laboratory is to be set up at:
    (1) Majuli
    (2) Hingoli
    (3) Sholapur
    (4) Dhar
    (5) Mirzapur

12. Which is the First bank to introduce Software Robotics for power banking operations in 2016?
    (1) HDFC Bank
    (2) ICICI Bank
    (3) Yes Bank
    (4) Axis Bank
    (5) Kotak Mahindra

13. The first international conference on LPG was hosted by:
    (1) Cuttack
    (2) Bhubaneswar
    (3) Hyderabad
    (4) Patna
    (5) Kanpur

14. Which is the first state in India to implement Public Fund Management System (PFMS)?
    (1) Odisha
    (2) Jharkhand
    (3) Chhattisgarh
    (4) Madhya Pradesh
    (5) Assam

15. Which of the following city hosted Bharatiya Pravasi Divas 2017?
    (1) Hyderabad   (2) Bengaluru
    (3) Chennai   (4) Rajkot
    (5) Shimla

16. The two cricketers who were conferred with the Arjuna Award 2016 for their contributions to sport of cricket were:
    (1) Shikhar Dhawan and Ravindra Jadeja
    (2) Rohit Sharma and Ajinkya Rahane
    (3) Ravindra Jadeja and Ravichandran Ashwin
    (4) Ravindra Jadeja and Amit Mishra
    (5) Shikhar Dhawan and Murli Vijay

17. Who won the Fellows of Nature (FON) South Asia Short Story Award in Nature writing in 2016?
    (1) Ruby Bhatia   (2) Meghna Pant
    (3) Mamta Nayak   (4) Sukamini Nayyar
    (5) Sushma Bharadwaj

18. Who has been re-appointed as President of World Bank for a second five-year term beginning 1 July 2017?
    (1) Paul Wolfowitz
    (2) Robert Zoellick
    (3) Sir James Wolfensohn
    (4) Jim Yong Kim
    (5) Barber Conable

19. Which Indian Airport has become Asia-Pacific's only and one of the world's few airports to achieve a carbon neutral status?
    (1) Rajiv Gandhi International Airport
    (2) Indira Gandhi International Airport
    (3) Veer Savarkar International Airport
    (4) Sardar Vallabhbhai Patel International Airport
    (5) Kempegowda International Airport

20. Which is the first biosphere reserve of India?
    (1) Nilgiri   (2) Nanda Devi
    (3) Gulf of Mannar   (4) Nokrek
    (5) Simlipal

21. Which is the only country in the world where both tigers and lions are found?
    (1) India   (2) Indonesia
    (3) South Africa   (4) Zimbabwe
    (5) Ethiopia

22. Currency of New Zealand is:
    (1) New Zealand Pound   (2) New Zealand Dollar
    (3) New Zealand Peso   (4) New Zealand Ringgit
    (5) New Zealand Yeric

23. The Capital city of Vietnam is:
    (1) Ho Chi Minh   (2) Hanoi
    (3) Ulaanbaatar   (4) Dili
    (5) Vientiane

24. Former Defence Minister of India Shri Manohar Parrikar is a Rajya Sabhya Member from:
    (1) Goa   (2) Madhya Pradesh
    (3) Uttar Pradesh   (4) Haryana
    (5) Gujarat

25. Headquarters of World Meteorological Organization is at:
    (1) New York   (2) Paris
    (3) Vienna   (4) London
    (5) Geneva

26. Who among the following has been appointed as United Nations Women's Advocate for Gender Equality and Women's Empowerment in India?
    (1) Sania Mirza   (2) Aishwaryaa Dhanush
    (3) Mamta Sharma   (4) Aishwarya Rai
    (5) Rekha

27. The largest private bank in India at present is:
    (1) Yes Bank   (2) Kotak Mahindra Bank
    (3) HDFC Bank   (4) ICICI Bank
    (5) Axis Bank

28. The Indian Space Research Organization (ISRO) for the first time has successfully conducted the Scramjet (or Supersonic Combusting ramjet) engine test, with this India became......nation to have conducted this test.
    (1) First   (2) Second
    (3) Third   (4) Fourth
    (5) Sixth

29. In 2016, which company became the first OEM (original equipment manufacturer) in India to integrate its product line-up onto a cloud-based technology platform?
    (1) Tata Motors   (2) Hero MotoCorp
    (3) Suzuki India   (4) Mahindra
    (5) Bajaj

30. Who is the current Managing Director & CEO of National Payments Corporation of India (NPCI)?
    (1) A.P. Hota
    (2) Anand Gupta
    (3) Ravi Shankar Bhadauria
    (4) Shashank Lamba
    (5) Murli Manohar Tambe

31. What is the current ranking of India among the 171 countries in the 2016 World Risk Index (WRI)?
    (1) 34th (2) 44th
    (3) 68th (4) 77th
    (5) 109th

32. Which country is to create world's largest protected marine reserve area named as Papahanaumokuakea Marine National Monument?
    (1) UK (2) Italy
    (3) USA (4) Canada
    (5) Sri Lanka

33. Every year, the International Literacy Day is observed on:
    (1) 8 March (2) 9 April
    (3) 10 May (4) 8 September
    (5) 10 October

34. The first edition of 'IoT (Internet of Things) India Congress, 2016' was held in:
    (1) Hyderabad (2) Jaipur
    (3) Noida (4) Bengaluru
    (5) Pune

35. Which is the first country in the world with which India has inked an open sky arrangement under its new civil aviation policy in 2016?
    (1) USA (2) Greece
    (3) Finland (4) Sweden
    (5) New Zealand

36. A bilateral military exercise PRABAL DOSTYK-16 was held between India and:
    (1) Afghanistan (2) Kazakhstan
    (3) Armenia (4) Turkmenistan
    (5) Uzbekistan

37. The 2017 G20 summit will be held in:
    (1) France (2) Brazil
    (3) Germany (4) South Africa
    (5) Qatar

38. Who has won prestigious 'Heritage Heroes Award' of the International Union for Conservation of Nature (IUCN) in 2016?
    (1) Ajay Rawat (2) Shiv Kumar Khatri
    (3) Bibhuti Lahkar (4) Rajan Mudgal
    (5) Shyam Girotra

39. Urjit Patel is ….. Governor of Reserve Bank of India.
    (1) 21st (2) 22nd
    (3) 23rd (4) 24th
    (5) 29th

40. Which state has launched the Biju Kanya Ratna Yojana (BKRY) for the development of girls in 2016?
    (1) Telangana (2) Jharkhand
    (3) Chhattisgarh (4) Odisha
    (5) Madhya Pradesh

41. In 2016, The Election Commission of India (ECI) has granted national party status to:
    (1) Samajwadi Party
    (2) Aam Aadmi Party
    (3) All India Trinamool Congress
    (4) Akali Dal
    (5) Shiv Sena

42. What is the maximum flight range of Bramhos Supersonic Cruise Missile?
    (1) 150 Kms (2) 190 Kms
    (3) 200 Kms (4) 290 Kms
    (5) 350 Kms

43. Recently, which of the following Indian state government has declared year 2017 as 'Year of Apple'?
    (1) Jammu & Kashmir (2) Himachal Pradesh
    (3) Uttar Pradesh (4) Arunachal Pradesh
    (5) Uttarakhand

44. Name the first bank which launched India's first internationally-listed certified green bond to finance climate change solutions around the world at London Stock Exchange (LSE)?
    (1) HDFC Bank (2) SBI
    (3) Axis Bank (4) ICICI Bank
    (5) Punjab National Bank

45. Narsingh Pancham Yadav is a:
    (1) Kabaddi Player (2) Footballer
    (3) Badminton Player (4) Wrestler
    (5) Chess Player

46. Kakrapar nuclear power plant is located in which among the following states?
    (1) Gujarat (2) Goa
    (3) Karnataka (4) Maharashtra
    (5) Tamil Nadu

47. Name of the first woman in the world to receive the Award for Exceptional Bravery at Sea for the year 2016 from the International Maritime Organization (IMO)?
    (1) Alexandra Flavoichk (2) Raziya Bibi
    (3) Swetlana Foocki (4) Radhika Menon
    (5) Deepti Talwar

48. Name the first state in India that imposed a "fat tax" on junk food in a bid to counter rising obesity?
    (1) Tamil Nadu
    (2) Goa
    (3) Maharashtra
    (4) Kerala
    (5) Himachal Pradesh

49. Which is the first city in India to have its own city animal?
    (1) Shillong
    (2) Gangtok
    (3) Guwahati
    (4) Jammu
    (5) Kochi

50. According to census 2011, most urbanized state by geographical area and total population was:
    (1) Maharashtra
    (2) Goa
    (3) Sikkim
    (4) Kerala
    (5) Tamil Nadu

51. In a matter of conflict in South China Sea, which country is not involved in it?
    (1) Brunei
    (2) Japan
    (3) Vietnam
    (4) Malaysia
    (5) Fiji

52. Annual inter-governmental security forum Shangri-La Dialogue is not concerned with:
    (1) Vietnam
    (2) Japan
    (3) India
    (4) Singapore
    (5) Maldives

53. Saudi Arabia's Islamic Development Bank (IDB) is to open its first branch in India at:
    (1) Surat
    (2) Lucknow
    (3) New Delhi
    (4) Ahmedabad
    (5) Jodhpur

54. Salarjung Museum is located at:
    (1) New Delhi
    (2) Lucknow
    (3) Mumbai
    (4) Cochin
    (5) Hyderabad

55. Number of banks which were nationalized 2nd time in 1980:
    (1) 5
    (2) 6
    (3) 7
    (4) 9
    (5) 11

56. Author of book "Making India awesome" is:
    (1) Arundhati Roy
    (2) Jhumpa Lahiri
    (3) Shashi Tharoor
    (4) Chetan Bhagat
    (5) Salman Rushdie

57. India's first dedicated multi-wavelength space observatory is:
    (1) Astrosat
    (2) Astrosec
    (3) Astrolac
    (4) Astro Print
    (5) Astro Luna

58. India's first automated Vault Locker was issued by which of the following bank of India?
    (1) HDFC
    (2) ICICI
    (3) Axis
    (4) Kotak Mahindra
    (5) SBI

59. First person to be awarded Bharat Ratna posthumously was:
    (1) Dr. B.R. Ambedkar
    (2) Pt. Lal Bahadur Shastri
    (3) Pt. Jawaharlal Nehru
    (4) C Rajagopalachari
    (5) Netaji Subhash Chandra Bose

60. In MICR, C stands for:
    (1) Character
    (2) Cross
    (3) Currency
    (4) Country
    (5) Charge

61. Rupay card was launched by which among the following?
    (1) RBI
    (2) MasterCard
    (3) Visa
    (4) NPCI
    (5) Maestro

62. India's first island district Majuli is in:
    (1) Nagaland
    (2) Sikkim
    (3) Assam
    (4) Arunachal Pradesh
    (5) Meghalaya

63. Which is the first country in the world to have electric road?
    (1) Norway
    (2) Switzerland
    (3) Canada
    (4) Sweden
    (5) Finland

64. Indigenously developed Airborne Early Warning and Control System (AEW&CS) 'Netra' was inducted into the Indian Air Force. It is developed by:
    (1) BARC
    (2) HAL
    (3) DRDO
    (4) ISRO
    (5) Indian Air Force

65. Who is the current chairperson of the Insolvency and Bankruptcy Board of India?
    (1) Anuj Priyadarshi
    (2) Dr. M. S. Sahoo
    (3) Ram Charan Teja
    (4) Roop Singh Rathore
    5) Radha Raman Agarwal

66. The third National Dam Safety Conference 2017 was held in which of the following city?
    (1) Gurugram   (2) Roorkee
    (3) Dispur   (4) Bengaluru
    (5) Shimla

67. Recently Reserve Bank of India (RBI) has raised the ceiling of gold loans given by regional rural banks (RRB) to:
    (1) Rs 1 Lakh   (2) Rs 2 Lakhs
    (3) Rs 4 Lakhs   (4) Rs 10 Lakhs
    (5) Rs 15 Lakhs

68. Recently World Health Organisation (WHO) has dropped the term 'counterfeit' and retained 'falsified' to describe medicines of:
    (1) Superior quality
    (2) Inferior quality
    (3) Wrong quantity of ingredients medicines
    (4) All of the above
    (5) Both (1) and (3)

69. The 13th World Robot Olympiad was held in:
    (1) USA   (2) Japan
    (3) South Korea   (4) India
    (5) China

70. Currently how many Coastal Economic Zones (CEZ) have been identified along the coastline of the country in the National Perspective Plan of the Sagarmala programme?
    (1) 8   (2) 10
    (3) 14   (4) 18
    (5) 20

71. Which film won the Golden Peacock at the 47th International Film Festival of India (IFFI)?
    (1) Daughter
    (2) Wood
    (3) Gone Through Days
    (4) The Throne
    (5) Game of Throne

72. The Asian Infrastructure Investment Bank (AIIB), conceived and hosted by China is essentially a multilateral development bank. Who is the current President of AIIB?
    (1) Danny Alexander
    (2) Jin Liqun
    (3) K. V Kamath
    (4) DJ Pandian
    (5) Aric C Charech

73. How many banks have joined the NPCI's Unified Payments Interface (UPI), a system that allows money transfer between any two bank accounts by using a mobile phone?
    (1) 22   (2) 24
    (3) 27   (4) 30
    (5) 36

74. India's largest producer state of rice at present is:
    (1) Andhra Pradesh   (2) Telangana
    (3) West Bengal   (4) Uttar Pradesh
    (5) Punjab

75. Name the Indian company that has launched its payments bank services from Rajasthan, becoming the first payments bank in the country to go live?
    (1) Bharati Airtel   (2) Reliance
    (3) Tata   (4) Wipro
    (5) HCL

76. Who has been resigned as chairman of the Central Advisory Board on Minimum Wages in 2016?
    (1) Sandeep Jain   (2) B. Janardhan Reddy
    (3) S. Ashok Reddy   (4) N. Shekar Sharma
    (5) Vitthal Acharya

77. The 'Give Up' campaign of LPG subsidy now stands extended to which of the following schemes of central Government?
    (1) Swacch Bharat Mission
    (2) Urban Rejuvenation Mission
    (3) Bhagyashree scheme
    (4) Ujala Scheme
    (5) None of the above

78. Sardar Vallabhbhai Patel National Police Academy (SVPNPA) is headquartered at:
    (1) Dehradun   (2) Mumbai
    (3) New Delhi   (4) Hyderabad
    (5) Chennai

79. The Centre forms a committee to form a strategy to expedite the process of transforming India into a cashless economy. The committee is headed by:
    (1) Bibek Debroy   (2) Arvind Subramanian
    (3) Arvind Panagariya   (4) Amitabh Kant
    (5) Ratan P Watal

80. Recently Rohingya community was facing threads to ethnic cleansing. Rohingya community belongs to which country?
    (1) Pakistan   (2) Myanmar
    (3) Maldives   (4) Malaysia
    (5) Indonesia

ENGLISH LANGUAGE

Directions (Q. 81 to 85): Read the following passage carefully and answer the questions given below it. Certain words are given in bold to help you locate them while answering some of the questions.

North Korea's provocative action of launching four missiles into the Sea of Japan a few hundred kilometres from the Japanese coastline has triggered fears of renewed tension between nuclear-armed powers. The launch seems timed to test the strategic fortitude and tactical capabilities of new relationships in the broader power balance that reins in Pyongyang's nuclear ambitions. The first test would be of the strength of bilateral U.S.-Japan ties on the watch of U.S. President Donald Trump and Japanese Prime Minister Shinzo Abe. North Korean Supreme Leader Kim Jong-un had already given these two leaders a wake-up call when his regime fired a medium-range missile last month. Mr. Trump has assured both Mr. Abe and South Korea's acting President, Hwang Kyo-Ahn, of his ironclad commitment to stand by them through this crisis. Yet it is likely that Mr. Kim was, in fact, trying to get a measure of Mr. Trump, who had tweeted shortly before assuming office in January, "it won't happen!", on the North being close to testing an ICBM. Experts seem to concur that the missiles launched now did not appear to be of intercontinental range. Yet, the prospect looms of the North miniaturising nuclear warheads to the point where even shorter-range weapons could, if they were nuclear-tipped, pose unprecedented risk to South Korea, Japan and the U.S. military assets in the vicinity.

The continuous **belligerence** of North Korea is only one side of the story. The other is that the international community, led by the U.S. and nations within striking distance of the North's aggression, has hardly managed the conflict consistently. The commendable effort of the Six Party Talks to invest diplomatic currency in bringing Pyongyang back to the negotiating table got derailed early on in President Barack Obama's first term. The cycle of sanctions and international isolation fuelling further bravado by the Kim regime then dominated the **denouement**, as indeed it has since 1992. This time the conflict seems to be following a distinctly more unstable trajectory as Mr. Trump has authorised the deployment in South Korea of the first elements of the U.S.'s advanced anti-missile system, the Terminal High Altitude Area Defence (THAAD), disregarding the possibility that it may be a double-edged sword. On the one hand, the presumed retaliatory move of THAAD deployment glosses over the fact that in the past week the U.S. and South Korea had conducted military drills in the region, war games that Pyongyang views as overt hostility. On the other, Washington has clearly decided to ignore the justifiable fears of Beijing and Moscow that THAAD's nuclear umbrella threatens their interests in the region too, not North Korea's alone. Unless de-escalation becomes a priority for all parties involved, the Korean Peninsula region will remain a flashpoint.

81. Out of the following options, which one closest to the meaning of the word **"denouement"**?
   (1) Annihilation   (2) Culmination
   (3) Fulmination   (4) Detonation
   (5) Ratification

82. What is the perception of the author on the deployment of the Terminal High Altitude Area Defence (THAAD)?
   (1) The deployment of THAADwill escalate tension between the US and Iran.
   (2) The deployment will encourage the hostilities among nations in the Korean Peninsula region?
   (3) The deployment of THAAD will help improve the relations among countries located around the Korean Peninsula.
   (4) The deployment of THAADwill lead to more sanctions against North Korea.
   (5) None of the above

83. Out of the following options, which one would come closest to the word **"belligerence"**?
   (1) Passivity   (2) Felicitous
   (3) Truculence   (4) Coronation
   (5) Ramification

84. What is the tone of the author at the end of the passage?
   (1) Unbiased   (2) Pessimistic
   (3) Circumspect   (4) Vigilant
   (5) Cautionary

85. What is the author's opinion on the Six Party Talks?
   (1) Fretful   (2) Exasperating
   (3) Embarrassing   (4) Admirable
   (5) Doubtful

Directions (Q. 86 to 92): In the following passage, there are blanks, each of which has been numbered. These numbers are printed below the passage and against each, five words are suggested, one of which fits the blank appropriately. Find out the appropriate word in each case.

At the time of Indian __(86)__, there were three important features of the global state of affairs following the end of the Second World War. The long crisis of the capitalist world from 1914 to 1945 – a period during which the world saw two __(87)__ wars caused by inter-imperialist conflicts, the revolutionary overthrow of czarist Russia followed by the emergence of the Union of Soviet Socialist Republics (USSR), and the Great Depression lasting through the 1930s causing great economic __(88)__ throughout the capitalist world even as the USSR made spectacular economic advancement under a regime of socialist central planning had considerably weakened the European imperial powers and Japan. This, and the emergence of a Socialist camp which __(89)__ for around a sixth of the world's territory and a third of its population by the early 1950s, strengthened the national liberation wars against colonial rule.

The global wave of decolonisation that followed __(90)__ 1945 and the early 1960s, taken together with these two developments, made it possible for many newly __(91)__ countries, at least the more populous among them with considerable land and natural resources, to embark upon a relatively autonomous (though essentially capitalist) path of economic development, even while engaging with the international economy in various ways. This was the international context in which independent India embarked on the path of economic development.

The national context was characterised by the presence of several militant movements of workers and peasants in the period between 1945 and 1950. There was the tribal land struggle of Warli in present-day Maharashtra; the Tebhaga movement for an __(92)__ share of produce for the sharecroppers in Bengal; the struggles of agricultural labourers and poor peasants in the Madras Presidency; and the armed resistance of peasants in the Telangana region of what later became Andhra Pradesh.

86. (1) invention   (2) discovery
    (3) independent   (4) proclamation
    (5) independence

87. (1) beautiful   (2) productive
    (3) constructive   (4) devastating
    (5) sweet

88. (1) celebration   (2) literacy
    (3) distress   (4) jubilation
    (5) happiness

89. (1) allowed   (2) collided
    (3) accounted   (4) vexed
    (5) irritated

90. (1) between   (2) among
    (3) in   (4) at
    (5) on

91. (1) prepared   (2) invented
    (3) favoured   (4) independent
    (5) preferred

92. (1) allied   (2) entity
    (3) increased   (4) inclement
    (5) absurd

Directions (Q. 93 to 95): In each of the given sentences, select the sentence which would either follow or precede the given sentence(s) in grammatically and conceptually appropriate manner. The instruction is given at the end of every statement.

93. There has been substantial reduction in cases of piracy on the high seas around the Andaman and Nicobar islands.

Which of the following would precede the above statement?

(1) The government wants to sign an extradition treaty with Myanmar on the piracy issue.

(2) The Indian government wants police reforms to counter law and order problems.

(3) A new Admiral has taken charge of the Indian Navy.

(4) The American government has said that it is against piracy.

(5) The Indian Coast Guard has been asked to step up vigil around the Andaman and Nicobar islands.

94. Veerappan was a dreaded dacoit who used to operate in the sandalwood forests of Karnataka. Although he was cornered many a time by the police, Veerappan always managed to give police the slip. But his luck ran out in 2004.

Which of the following would follow the above statements?

(1) A number of forest officials were killed by Veerappan.

(2) The police had announced a reward of Rupees 10 lakhs on his head.

(3) He had even kidnapped a famous Kannada film director.

(4) The police gunned him down in an encounter.

(5) Veerappan was supported by some political leaders.

95. Recently, Royal Enfield recalled its Himalayan variant of motorcycles because of some teething problems. The company's reputation took a beating because of the problem and the subsequent recall.

Which of the following would follow the above statements?

(1) The Himalayan motorcycle is being endorsed by many Bollywood celebrities.

(2) The Himalayan is available in the market in three different colours.

(3) The problem was due to a piston in the Himalayan series of motorcycles which was a buzzing sound while riding the bike at a speed of more than 60kmph.

(4) Royal Enfield has been manufacturing motorcycles for over 100 years now.

(5) Eicher Motors now owns the brand of Royal Enfield.

Directions (Q. 96 to 100): Read the following passage carefully and answer the questions given below it. Certain words are given in bold to help you locate them while answering some of the questions.

Raghuram Rajan will on Tuesday conduct what will be his last monetary policy update for the Reserve Bank of India (RBI) and also, perhaps, the last that a central bank governor can henceforth undertake independently. The policy update comes against the backdrop of the government fixing on Friday the inflation target for the next five years at plus or minus four per cent - a task which will be entrusted with the soon-to-be-constituted Monetary Policy Committee (MPC) to realise by **mandating** it to fix policy rates. Finance Ministry officials said the committee - which will fashion the contours of the monetary policy once it is in place - would be finalised before the next bi-monthly policy review, due in October. "The MPC would be entrusted with the task of fixing the benchmark policy rate (repurchase rate) required to contain inflation within the specified target level," a Finance Ministry statement said after the inflation target was notified.

The Reserve Bank Governor will be its chair with two more representatives from the central bank, while the other three will be chosen by the government on the basis of the recommendations of a search-cum-selection committee. "Under Sub-Section (1) of Section 45ZA of the RBI Act, the Central Government, in consultation with the RBI, determines the inflation target in terms of the Consumer Price Index (CPI), once in every five years. This target would be notified in the Official Gazette. "Given this backdrop and the fact that India's retail inflation in June stood at 5.77 per cent - and as high as 6.20 per cent in rural India - the possibility of a rate cut has been virtually ruled out, as the current price-line is precariously close to the upper tolerance level of six per cent. "While we continue to factor in another 25 bps rate cut for the rest of 2016-17, we are cautious on the 2017-18 rate cycle. We would factor in further cuts only after clarity on the pace of disinflation in Q4 of 2016-17 and RBI's new policy regime," said a report by Kotak Institutional Equities. "We expect the RBI to pause on August 9," it said.

This is also because the amended law requires the Reserve Bank to also state the reasons if it fails to meet the inflation target, along with the remedial actions the estimate time-period by which it hoped to achieve the same. "The government's commitment to reform continues. The monetary policy framework will provide right environment for investment and growth," said Economic Affairs Secretary Shaktikanta Das. "An announcement on MPC members will be made soon. "Ahead of the policy update, Mr. Rajan met Finance Minister ArunJaitley on Friday, as has been customary, but declined to comment. "We have a policy on Tuesday. So I have to wait till policy. On Tuesday, I'll be able to talk. "Since January 2015, when the central bank started seeing some improvement in the economy and external conditions, the repurchase rate, or the short-term lending rate for commercial banks on borrowings from the Reserve Bank, have been cut by 150

basis points - the last one on April 5 worth 25 basis points. Thus far, since Mr. Rajan took the high office, the policy rate has been raised thrice and and cut five times. Now as his three-year term ends on September 4, he intends to return to academia as professor at the University of Chicago - from where he is on a three-year leave.

96. As per the passage, the Reserve Bank Governor is a person from the
    (1) community of retired bureaucrats.
    (2) community of academicians.
    (3) community of bankers.
    (4) field of social science.
    (5) field of political thinkers.

97. What is one of the objectives of the Monetary Policy Committee?
    (1) Determine the borrowing rate
    (2) Determine the lending rate
    (3) Determine the foreign exchange rate
    (4) Determine the benchmark policy rate
    (5) None of the above

98. The author of the passage is most likely a/an
    (1) bureaucrat   (2) economist
    (3) politician   (4) poll observer
    (5) scientist

99. Acccording to the passage, how many times has the policy rate been revised during Dr. Rajan's tenure as the RBI governor?
    (1) 8 times   (2) 6 times
    (3) 3 times   (4) 9 times
    (5) More than 10 times

100. Choose the option which is **most nearly** the same in meaning to the word in **bold**, as used in the passage.
    MANDATE
    (1) Assert   (2) Livid
    (3) Bellicose   (4) Belligerent
    (5) Commission

Directions (Q. 101 to 105): Read each sentence to find out whether there is any grammatical error in it. The error if any, will be in one part of the sentence, the number of that part is the answer. If there is no error, mark (5). (Ignore errors of punctuation, if any)

101. Sarah Ledecky now looks overwhelmingly like (1)/ to achieve her goal of three individual gold in the 200, 400 and 800 (2)/ - a feat not achieved at a single Games (3)/ since American Debbie Meyer accomplished it in Mexico City in 1968. (4)/ No error (5)

102. The recent developments in (1)/ Uttarakhand and Arunachal Pradesh (2)/ has turned the spotlight (3)/ on the office of the governor. (4)/ No error (5)

103. It has therefore become necessary both in the interests of the federal polity (1)/ and democracy, that the office of the governor (2)/ preserves its constitutional sanctity and morality (3)/ and is used by the incumbent for safeguarding the interests of the country and not those of any political party. (4)/ No error (5)

104. In the last two years, (1)/ the defence ministry has accepted (2)/ the necessity in equipment worth nearly (3)/ Rs 2 lakh crore for the armed forces. (4)/ No error (5)

105. Coolpad is going for a flash sale (1)/ model with this smartphone, (2)/ and registrations will open (3)/ from today at 5 pm in Amazon India. (4)/ No error (5)

Directions (Q. 106 to 110): In each of the following questions, a sentence/passage is given with two blank spaces. Three phrases/sentences are given below, two of which can be placed in blank spaces to make a meaningful sentence/passage. If none of the phrases/sentences is appropriate, mark (5) as the answer.

106. A Hawk advanced jet trainer crashed on Thursday soon after _______ from Air Force Station, Kalaikunda in West Midnapore due to a "technical snag" but both the pilots ______ safely.

(A) take off (B) take of

(C) ejected

(1) A and B (2) A and C

(3) B and C (4) C and B

(5) None of these

107. The island of Mauritius was ______ before its first recorded visit ______ the Middle Ages by Arab sailors, who named it Dina Arobi.

(A) uninhibited (B) uninhabited

(C) during

(1) A and B (2) A and C

(3) B and C (4) C and B

(5) None of these

108. While Rio de Janeiro is set to organise 28______, two more than the 26 held in the London Games, the cricketing world is once again debating why India's favourite sport has not found favour with the International Olympic Committee since its ______ after the Paris Games.

(A) sporting disciplines

(B) first and last

(C) debut and exit

(1) A and B (2) A and C

(3) B and C (4) C and B

(5) None of these

109. The cabinet on Wednesday agreed to bring all app-based taxi-hailing services under the ____ that will allow state governments to fix a fare cap and check ____ charging, the biggest customer grouse.

(A) regulatory network

(B) arbitrary

(C) arbitrarily

(1) A and B (2) A and C

(3) B and C (4) C and B

(5) None of these

110. A new study, _______ by Liuba Belkin of Lehigh University, William Becker of Virginia Tech and Samantha A. Conroy of Colorado State University, found a link between organizational after-hours email expectations and emotional exhaustion, which _______ work-family balance.

(A) authored (B) abstracts

(C) hinders

(1) A and B (2) A and C

(3) B and C (4) C and B

(5) None of these

QUANTITATIVE APTITUDE

Directions (Q. 111 to 115): Answer the questions on the basis of the information given below.

The bar graph given below shows the number of candidates appeared (in '000) in a competitive examination during the period 2008 to 2015.

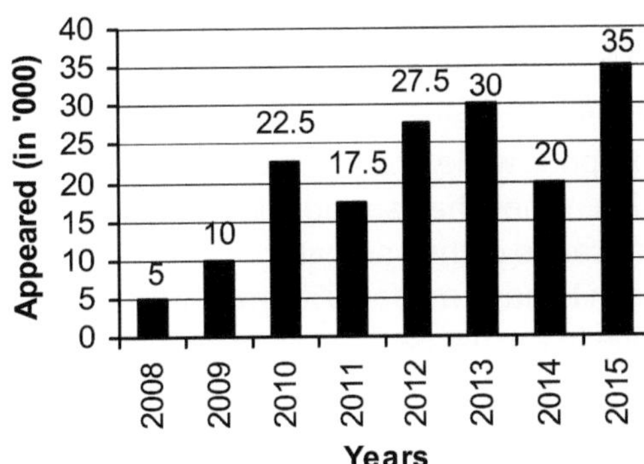

The line graph given below shows the percentage of candidates qualified in the examination during the period 2008 to 2015.

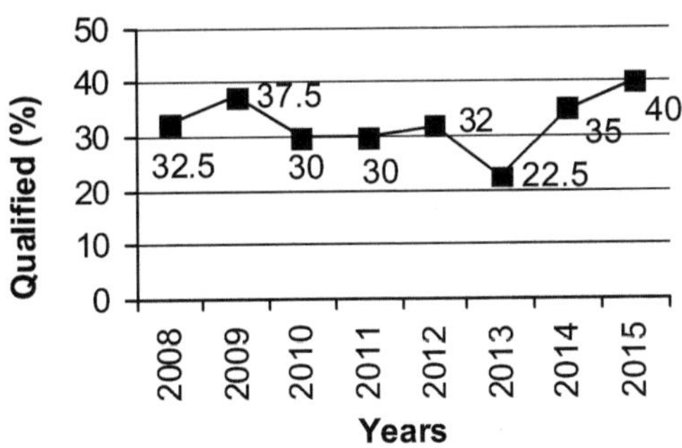

111. What is the respective ratio between the average number of candidates qualified in 2008, 2009 and 2010 and the average number of candidates qualified in 2013, 2014 and 2015?
    (1) 94 : 157
    (2) 97 : 222
    (3) 93 : 173
    (4) 92 : 159
    (5) None of these

112. In which of the following years was the number of candidates qualified in the competitive examination the lowest during the period 2008 to 2015?
    (1) 2008
    (2) 2011
    (3) 2009
    (4) 2014
    (5) None of these

113. Which year witnessed the maximum percentage change in the number of qualified candidates over the previous year?
    (1) 2012
    (2) 2015
    (3) 2014
    (4) 2009
    (5) None of these

114. How many candidates qualified in 2013?
    (1) 6750
    (2) 13500
    (3) 9900
    (4) 5750
    (5) None of these

115. The number of candidates qualified in 2010 was what percentage of the number of candidates appeared in 2009?
    (1) 68.5
    (2) 70
    (3) 32.5
    (4) 67.5
    (5) None of these

116. Aman calculates the percentage of profit on the cost price while Shashank calculates on the selling price. When their selling prices are same, then the difference of their actual profits is Rs. 85 and both claim to have made 20% profit. What is the selling price in each case?
    (1) Rs. 1,980
    (2) Rs. 2,652
    (3) Rs. 2,578
    (4) Rs. 2,550
    (5) Rs. 2,125

117. A contractor undertakes to build a road 15 km long in 250 days and employs 35 men. After 150 days, he finds that only 7 km of the road has been completed. The number of extra men he must employ to finish the work on time is
    (1) 30 men
    (2) 65 men
    (3) 35 men
    (4) 25 men
    (5) 60 men

118. A, B and C enter into a partnership with investments in the ratio $\dfrac{5}{3} : \dfrac{3}{4} : \dfrac{4}{5}$. After 4 months, A increases his investment by 50%. If the total profit at the end of the year was Rs. 81,480, then B's share in the profit will be
    (1) Rs. 17,280
    (2) Rs. 16,200
    (3) Rs. 18,280
    (4) Rs. 15,000
    (5) Rs. 18,200

119. A money lender borrows money at 2.5% per annum and pays the interest at the end of the year. He lends it at 10% per annum compounded half-yearly and receives the interest at the end of the year. In this way he gains Rs. 465. What was the amount that he borrowed?
    (1) Rs. 5,000
    (2) Rs. 6,000
    (3) Rs. 5,400
    (4) Rs. 6,300
    (5) None of these

120. Sujata scored 2240 marks in an examination that is 128 marks more than the minimum passing percentage of 64%. What is the percentage of marks obtained by Meena if she scores 907 marks less than Sujata?
    (1) 35
    (2) 40
    (3) 45
    (4) 36
    (5) 48

Directions (Q. 121 to 125): Each of the questions below consists of a question and three statements numbered I, II and III given below it. You have to decide whether the data provided in the statements are sufficient to answer the question and select the appropriate option.

121. Find the difference in the time taken by A and B to complete a piece of work together and that by B and C to complete it by working together.
    I. A, B and C can complete the same work in 15 days. Also, ratio of the efficiencies of A and B, and B and C is 3 : 4.
    II. A and B together are 25% less efficient than B and C, while, A and C together are 25% more efficient than B and C.
    III. A and C can complete the same work in 18 days while A, B and C can complete the same work in 15 days.
    (1) Only I and II
    (2) Only II and III
    (3) Either I or II and III
    (4) All three of them
    (5) None of these

122. What will be the ratio of the ages of Suman and Sushil after five years?

    I. Respective ratio of the present ages of Sushil and Sukant is 7 : 6, while the respective ratio of the ages of Suman and Sukant five years ago was 4 : 5.

    II. Respective ratio of the sum of the present ages of Suman and Sushil and that of Suman and Sukant is 12 : 11.

    III. Sushil is ten years elder than Suman who in turn is five years younger than Sukant.

    (1) Only I and II   (2) Either I or III

    (3) Either I or II and III   (4) All three of them

    (5) None of these

123. Find the time taken by Train A to pass a platform whose length is 40% more than the length of the train.

    I. Length of Train B is 250 m and it takes 45 sec to pass Train A whose length is 200 m.

    II. Speed of Train B is 53 m/s and it crosses a platform of length 280 m in 10 sec.

    III. Speed of Train A is 35 m/s and the length of the platform is 267 m.

    (1) Either II and III

    (2) Only III

    (3) Both I and II

    (4) Either III or only I and II

    (5) Only I

124. Find the profit/loss percentage incurred by the shopkeeper while selling a book.

    I. Cost price is 20% less than the mark price of the book and the discount offered is equal to 10% of the cost price.

    II. Ratio of the cost price and the selling price is 9 : 11 after getting a discount of 22.5% of the mark price.

    III. Ratio of the cost price and the mark price is 8 : 13 while the ratio of the selling price and the mark price is 9 : 11.

    (1) Both III and II   (2) Either I or II

    (3) Only I   (4) Either I or II or III

    (5) Only II

125. Find the compound interest received on a sum of Rs. 5,876 after three years if the rate of interest is x%.

    I. The ratio of the simple interest and the principal after five years at x% per annum is 1 : 4.

    II. Simple interest received on Rs. 5,876 after 2.5 years is Rs. 146.75.

    III. The value of 'x' is the average of first nine natural numbers.

    (1) Either I and II   (2) Either II or III

    (3) Only III   (4) Either I or II or III

    (5) None of these

Directions (Q. 126 to 130): Answer the questions on the basis of the information given below.

In the following bar graph, the number of passengers carried to different cities in first quarter of a year by four airlines A, B, C and D has been given.

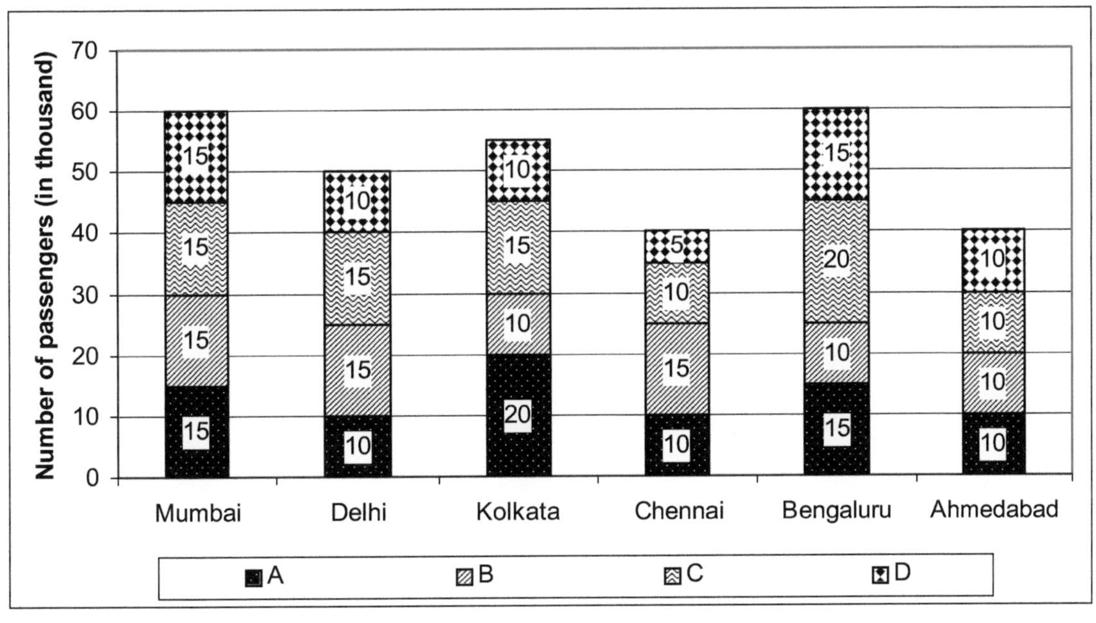

126. By what percent was the number of passengers travelling to all cities by the airline A more or less than those travelling by airline C?

(1) 5.88%   (2) 5.98%

(3) 5.68%   (4) 5.82%

(5) 5.81%

127. For which city was the number of passengers travelling by airline B as a percentage of all the passengers together the maximum?

(1) Delhi   (2) Kolkata

(3) Chennai   (4) Mumbai

(5) Bengaluru

128. What is the respective ratio of the number of passengers who travelled to Chennai and Bengaluru by airline B and that to Mumbai and Ahmedabad by airline D?

(1) 6 : 7   (2) 3 : 4

(3) 1 : 1   (4) 7 : 6

(5) None of these

129. The number of passengers travelling to Chennai by airline A in second quarter is 150% of that in first quarter by the same airline. The number of passengers in the second quarter by the same airline going to the same city is 120% of that in the third quarter. What is the percentage increase in the number of passengers in third quarter from that in first quarter going to Chennai by ariline A?

(1) 15%   (2) 18%

(3) 20%   (4) 25%

(5) 30%

130. The number of passengers going to Bengaluru and Kolkata in first quarter by airline B is what percent of the number of passengers going to the same cities by the same airline. For airline B in second quarter if there be an increase of 30% in the number of passengers going to Bengaluru from first quarter to second quarter and in that going to Kolkata shows a 40% increase from first to second quarter?

(1) 68   (2) 60

(3) 65   (4) 70

(5) 74

131. A man mixes 5 litre of wine worth Rs. 420 per litre with 5 litre of wine worth Rs. 280 per litre. How many litres of water should be added to this mixture so that the resultant mixture become worth Rs. 210 per litre?

(1) $\dfrac{10}{3}$ litre   (2) $\dfrac{14}{3}$ litre

(3) $\dfrac{20}{3}$ litre   (4) $\dfrac{17}{2}$ litre

(5) $\dfrac{16}{3}$ litre

132. The speed of a boat in still water is 12 km/hr. It covers a distance of 54 km in 6 hours. What distance will the boat cover in 5 hours while travelling downstream?

(1) 90 km   (2) 75 km

(3) 60 km   (4) 59 km

(5) None of these

133. A bank offers 10% compound interest calculated on half-yearly basis. A customer deposits Rs. 10,000 each on 1st January and 1st July of a year. At the end of the year, total interest he would have received is

(1) Rs. 1,525   (2) Rs. 1,655

(3) Rs. 2,100   (4) Rs. 3,100

(5) Rs. 3,310

134. The ratio of the ages of Mohana and her daughter Sandhya ten years hence will be 5 : 3. Ten years ago the ratio of their ages was 3 : 1. What is the difference between their ages at present?

(1) 20 years   (2) 40 years

(3) 30 years   (4) 25 years

(5) None of these

135. Three circles of radii 8 cm, 5 cm and 5 cm touch each other externally. The area of the triangle formed, by the line segments joining the centers of the three circles is

(1) 30 cm²   (2) $30\sqrt{2}$ cm²

(3) 60 cm²   (4) $60\sqrt{2}$ cm²

(5) 45 cm²

Directions (Q. 136 to 140): Find out the wrong number in the series.

136. 0, 10, 24, 68, 126, 222, 336

(1) 24   (2) 68

(3) 126   (4) 222

(5) 336

137. 1636, 820, 408, 204, 101, 52.5

(1) 408   (2) 204

(3) 52.5   (4) 820

(5) 101

138. 0, 5, 16, 40, 84, 163, 260

(1) 0   (2) 16

(3) 40   (4) 84

(5) 163

139. 1, 145, 15, 75, 11, 41, 7

(1) 75   (2) 15

(3) 145   (4) 11

(5) None of these

140.   12, 24, 60, 180, 720, 2520, 11340
   (1) 2520   (2) 24
   (3) 180   (4) 720
   (5) None of these

REASONING ABILITY

Directions (Q. 141 to 145): In the questions given below, certain symbols are used with the following meanings:

P # Q means P is not smaller than Q.

P % Q means P is neither greater nor smaller than Q.

P & Q means P is neither greater than nor equal to Q.

P $ Q means P is neither equal to nor smaller than Q.

P @ Q means P is not greater than Q.

Now in each of the following questions, assuming the given statements to be true, find which of the four conclusions I, II, III and IV given below them is/are definitely true and give your answer accordingly.

141.   **Statement:** S $ R, U @ T % R, S @ V

   Conclusions:

   I.   R $ V

   II. S @ T

   III. R % S

   IV. V $ T

   (1) Only I is true.

   (2) Only II is true

   (3) Only II and IIII are true

   (4) All I, II and III are true

   (5) Only IV is true

142.   **Statement :** S $ P, P % Q, Q @ R, R $ T

   Conclusions :

   I.   P @ R

   II. P $ T

   III. S % T

   IV. S $ Q

   (1) Only I and IV is true.

   (2) Only III is true

   (3) Only III and IV are true

   (4) Only I and III

   (5) Conclusion I, III and IV are true

143.   **Statement:** A # C, C % D, F @ E & D

   Conclusions:

   I.   A % E

   II. A # F

   III. C % E

   IV. A # D

   (1) Only III is true

   (2) Only III and IV are true

   (3) Only either I or IV

   (4) Only IV is true.

   (5) None of these

144.   **Statement:** O # P $ T, T # Q, Q % S, R $ S

   Conclusions:

   I.   T & R

   II. S % T

   III. P $ Q

   IV. Q @ O

   (1) Only I and II is true

   (2) Only III is true

   (3) Only III and IV are true

   (4) Only II and III are true

   (5) None of these

145.   **Statement:** M $ O, O # T, T % S, S @ R

   Conclusions:

   I.   R $ T

   II. R % T

   III. M $ S

   IV. O # R

   (1) Only either I or II is true

   (2) Only III is true

   (3) Only III and IV are true

   (4) Only III and either I or II are true

   (5) None of these

Directions (Q. 146 to 151): Answer the questions on the basis of the information given below.

Eight teachers of a government school – Amita, Bela, Cauvery, Devika, Esther, Fathima, Garima and Hira - sit around a circular table at equi-distant positions. Among the eight members there are teachers of the following subjects – Mathematics, History, Physics, English, Hindi, Geography, Biology and Chemistry. Five of them are facing the centre whereas three are facing outside.

i.   The English teacher, Garima, faces the centre and the Chemistry teacher sits opposite to her. The Biology teacher sits to the immediate left of Amita as well as Bela.

ii.   The Hindi teacher and Devika are immediate neighbours of the Chemistry teacher. All three of them face the same direction. Hira and Garima have a common neighbour. Neither Devika nor Cauvery is a Hindi teacher.

iii. Amita, the History teacher, is sitting on the second left of the English teacher as well as on the second left of Bela.

iv. The Geography teacher, Fathima, and the Physics teacher sit on the immediate right and immediate left of the History teacher and the Mathematics teacher respectively.

146. Which of the given sets of people face outside?

(1) Devika, Bela, Esther

(2) Fathima, Garima, Cauvery

(3) Esther, Amita, Hira

(4) Hira, Devika, Esther

(5) None of these

147. Who is the Hindi teacher?

(1) Hira   (2) Fathima

(3) Esther   (4) Cavery

(5) None of these

148. Who sits to the immediate left of the Biology teacher?

(1) Esther   (2) Garima

(3) Cauvery   (4) Amita

(5) None of these

149. Amita, Cauvery, Hira and Fathima are four members of a group of five people. Who is the fifth member?

(1) Bela   (2) Esther

(3) Devika   (4) Garima

(5) None of these

150. What is the subject taught by Bela?

(1) English   (2) Chemistry

(3) Physics   (4) Biology

(5) Geography

151. If all the members are made to sit in alphabetical order of their names in a clockwise manner starting with Amita, then how many places remain unchanged (excluding Amita)?

(1) None

(2) One

(3) Two

(4) Three

(5) None of these

Directions (Q. 152 to 156): Answer the questions on the basis of the information given below.

A word and number arrangement machine when given an input line of words and numbers rearranges them following a particular rule in each step. The following is an illustration of input and various steps of rearrangement. (All the numbers are two digit numbers.)

Input: screen 31 award 93 blind 57 troop 19

Step I: 93 screen 31 award blind 57 troop 19

Step II: 93 award screen 31 blind 57 troop 19

Step III: 93 award 57 screen 31 blind troop 19

Step IV: 93 award 57 blind screen 31 troop 19

Step V: 93 award 57 blind 31 screen troop 19

Step VI: 93 award 57 blind 31 screen 19 troop

And Step VI is the last step of the rearrangement as the desired arrangement is obtained.

As per rules followed in the above steps, find out in each of the questions the appropriate step for the given input.

Input : vital 54 cards 72 help 24 wall 66 lamp 49

152. How many steps would be required to complete the rearrangement?

(1) Eight   (2) Six

(3) Seven   (4) Nine

(5) Cannot be determined

153. How many elements (words/numbers) are there between "lamp" and "66" as they appear in Step V?

(1) Five   (2) Six

(3) Four   (4) Seven

(5) Three

154. Which step number is the following output?

72 cards 66 help 54 lamp vital 24 wall 49

(1) Step III   (2) Step IV

(3) Step V   (4) Step VI

(5) There is no such step

155. Which word / number would be to the immediate right of the fourth element from the right end in Step III?

(1) help   (2) wall

(3) 24   (4) lamp

(5) 54

156. In the final step "66" is related to "lamp" and "72" is related to "help" in a certain way, then "cards" is related to

(1) vital

(2) 66

(3) 49

(4) wall

(5) 54

Directions (Q. 157 to 161): Answer the questions on the basis of the information given below.

Eleven members of a family - Jaya, Hema, Indra, Aruna, Bhushan, Gautam, Ketan, Shankar, Dhruv, Mahesh and Lokesh - live together in a house. There are three married couples and members are spread across four generations in the family. Each member has a different occupation. Shankar's son Bhushan is a retired headmaster and daughter-in-law is a housewife. Bhusan has two sons - Dhruv and Ketan. Dhruv, who is an MLA is married to a singer. Ketan who is a college student is younger than his unmarried sister Hema, who is a teacher.

The housewife, Aruna has a daughter, Indra, who is a doctor. Dhruv's brother-in-law Gautam is a professor and he has a son Mahesh, who goes to pre-school. Mahesh's cousin Lokesh studies in high school and his great grandfather is a retired policeman.

157. What is the occupation of Gautam's younger brother-in-law?

   (1) MLA   (2) Professor
   (3) College student   (4) Teacher
   (5) Doctor

158. How many daughter's-in-law are there in the family?

   (1) four   (2) two
   (3) three   (4) one
   (5) None of these

159. Select the odd pair from the given options.

   (1) Dhruv - Jaya
   (2) Ketan - Lokesh
   (3) Gautam - Indra
   (4) Bhushan - Aruna
   (5) None of these

160. Who are the sons of Aruna?

   (1) Ketan, Lokesh
   (2) Mahesh, Lokesh
   (3) Indra, Hema
   (4) Hema, Ketan
   (5) Dhruv, Ketan

161. Who are the youngest and the eldest members of the family?

   (1) Shankar and Bhushan
   (2) Mahesh and Bhushan
   (3) Lokesh and Shankar
   (4) Mahesh and Shankar
   (5) Ketan and Shankar

Directions (Q. 162 to 166): Answer the questions on the basis of the information given below.

Seven employees of a private sector bank - Ahil, Dhiraj, Kapil, Lokesh, Prem, Tanay and Viraj - will retire during the month of December 2016. They work at seven different locations, viz. Cochin, Cuttack, Delhi, Hyderabad, Kanpur, Mysore and Pune. Their work experience at the bank varies from a minimum of 5 years to a maximum of 13 years. Their retiring bonus is a multiple of their years of service at the bank.

Those employees whose years of service is less than 10 years get a bonus of "Rs. 12,000y" whereas those who have worked for 10 years or more get a bonus of "Rs. 15,000y", where y is the number of years of service.

Lokesh has worked for one year more than Viraj, who is located at Hyderabad. Kapil, who is from Cochin, has worked for three years more than Ahil but four years less than Prem, who is located at Pune.

The person located at Delhi has the minimum work experience.

Dhiraj, who is not from Delhi or Kanpur, has worked for two years more than Ahil and two years less than Viraj.

Tanay is not from Kanpur or Cuttack and he has the maximum work experience.

162. Which city does Tanay live in?

   (1) Cochin   (2) Cuttack
   (3) Hyderabad   (4) Mysore
   (5) Pune

163. Who receives a bonus of more than one lakh but less than 1.2 lakh?

   (1) Kapil   (2) Lokesh
   (3) Viraj   (4) Prem
   (5) Tanay

164. How much bonus does Lokesh receive?

   (1) Rs. 96,000
   (2) Rs.1,08,000
   (3) Rs.1,80,000
   (4) Rs.1,50,000
   (5) Rs.1,95,000

165. Select the correct combination of person and place.

   (1) Ahil - Delhi
   (2) Lokesh - Pune
   (3) Prem - Cochin
   (4) Tanay - Hyderabad
   (5) Viraj - Cuttack

166. The employee from which city receives a retiring bonus that is second highest?

    (1) Cochin   (2) Cuttack

    (3) Hyderabad   (4) Mysore

    (5) Pune

Directions (Q. 167 to 171): Answer the questions on the basis of the information given below.

In a certain code "glass of cold water" is coded as "re eo la lo", "extremely cold water" is coded as "me re lo", "cold wine bottle" is coded as "od lo aw" and "extremely thin glass" is coded as "ni me la".

167. What does the code "me" stand for?

    (1) glass   (2) water

    (3) cold   (4) extremely

    (5) None of these

168. What is the code for "wine bottle" ?

    (1) re ni   (2) od aw

    (3) aw me   (4) od lo

    (5) None of these

169. If "warm sparkling water" is coded as "ti sa re" then what could be the code for "sparkling thin"?

    (1) ti od   (2) aw sa

    (3) re sa   (4) sa od

    (5) ti ni

170. How will "thin glass of water" be coded?

    (1) eo la lo me   (2) me lo la re

    (3) la ni re eo   (4) me la re eo

    (5) aw od ni eo

171. What is the code for "bottle"?

    (1) od   (2) la

    (3) aw   (4) ni

    (5) Either (1) or (3)

Directions (Q. 172 to 176): Each of the questions below consists of a question and three statements numbered I, II and III given below It. You have to decide whether the data provided in the statements are sufficient to answer the question.

172. Who amongst P, Q, R, S, T and V, each securing different marks, secured the second lowest marks?

    I.   R and T secured more marks than P and Q.

    II. V secured the highest marks.

    III. S secured more marks than P but less than Q.

    (1) Only I and III

    (2) All I, II and III are required to answer the question

    (3) Only II and III

    (4) Question cannot be answered even with all I, II and III

    (5) Only I and II

173. Which village is to the North-East of village R?

    I.   Village S is to the South-East of village N which is to the South-West of village P and village P is to the North of village Q.

    II. Village T is to the North-West of village Q which is to the south of village P.

    III. Village R which is to the North of village S, lies between villages N and Q and village N is to the West of village R.

    (1) Only I and II

    (2) Only II and III

    (3) All I, II and III are not sufficient to answer the question

    (4) All I, II and III are required to answer the question

    (5) Only I and III or only II and III are required to answer the question

174. What is the rank of Animesh in a class of 17 students?

    I.   Nirmal who is thirteenth from the bottom is six ranks ahead of Bhumika who is two position below Animesh.

    II. Bhumika is four position ahead of Kamal.

    III. Bhumika is two position below Animesh and Kamal's rank is 15th.

    (1) Only I and III

    (2) Only I and II

    (3) Only I or II and III together are required to answer the question

    (4) Only II is required to answer the question

    (5) All I, II and III are not sufficient to answer the question

175. How is 'them' written in a code language?

    I.   'tell them young' is written as 'se me ye' and 'young sharp tell' is written as 'me na ye' in that code language.

    II. 'clever sharp come tomorrow' is written as 'na ki pa lo' and 'bring clever young them' is written as 'ki po se ye' in that code language.

    III. 'clever sharp come them no' is written as 'pa na se ki te' and 'yellow come sharp run clever no' is written as 'ki ni pa be te na' in that code language.

(1) Only III is required to answer the question

(2) Only I and II are required to answer the question

(3) Only I or II and III together are required to answer the question

(4) Only II is required to answer the question

(5) All I, II and III are not sufficient to answer the question

176. In which year was X born?

   I.   X is three years older than Y.

   II.   Z is five years younger than Y.

   III.   Z was born in 1990.

(1) Only II and III

(2) Only I and III

(3) Only III and either I or II

(4) All I, II and III

(5) None of these

Directions (Q. 177 to 181): Answer the questions on the basis of the information given below.

Nine students Ananya, Bhavya, Chaya, Divya, Jiya, Maya, Priya, Rabiya and Sreya stay on different floors of a hostel building numbered 1 to 9. The ground floor is numbered 1 and the topmost floor is numbered 9. All of them are doing post graduate studies in various subjects namely Histoty, Geography, Commerce, English, Mathematics, Physics, Botany, Zoology and Chemistry but not necessarily in the same order.

Ananya is a student of Physics and she stays on an even numbered floor. Jiya, who does not study Mathematics, stays on an even numbered floor above the floor on which Ananya stays. The one who is studying History stays on the seventh floor. There are three floors between the floors on which the student of Physics and the student of Mathematics stay. There are three floors between the floors on which Divya and Priya stay. There is one floor between the floors on which Priya and Sreya stay. Sreya is not studying Chemistry. Chaya is studying Geography and she stays on the topmost floor. The Zoology student stays on a floor immediately below the student of English. Maya stays on the floor immediately below Rabiya. Divya who is studying Botany stays on the ground floor. The one studying Commerce stays on the second floor.

177. Who among the following studies English?

    (1) Sreya

    (2) Priya

    (3) Jiya

    (4) Maya

    (5) None of these

178. Who among the following stays on the third floor?

    (1) Student of Histoty

    (2) Student of Chemistry

    (3) Student of Zoology

    (4) Student of Mathematics

    (5) None of these

179. How many floors are there between the floor on which the student of Mathematics and the floor on which the student of Chemistry stays?

    (1) Two

    (2) Three

    (3) Four

    (4) Five

    (5) None

180. Which subject does Priya study?

    (1) Chemistry

    (2) History

    (3) Botany

    (4) Zoology

    (5) Physics

181. Which of the following is true as per the given information?

    (1) Divya stays on a floor immediately above the floor on which the student of Commerce stays.

    (2) Ananya stays between the floor on which student of Zoology stays and the Jiya stays.

    (3) Student of Mathematics stays on the seventh floor.

    (4) The girls living immediately above and below the floor on which Rabiya lives are Sreya and the student of Physics.

    (5) The student of Physics stays on a floor immediately below the floor on which Priya stays.

Directions (Q. 182 to 186): Answer the questions on the basis of the information given below.

Ten people are sitting in two parallel rows containing five people each, in such a way that there is an equal distance between adjacent persons. Panchi, Usha, Rakhi, Sanchi and Tanvi are seated in row 1 and all of them are facing South. Ameya, Barkha, Chavi, Drishti and Gauri are seated in row 2 and all of them are facing North. Therefore, in the given seating arrangement each member seated in a row faces another member of the other row. Each person in a row is wearing a different coloured cap, namely red, blue, green, yellow and pink.

Drishti, who wears a red cap, is sitting third to the left of Ameya who wears a pink cap. Panchi, who wears a blue cap faces the immediate neighbour of Drishti. Rakhi, who wears the same coloured cap as Drishti, is sitting second to the right of Panchi. Only one person is sitting between Usha, who wears a green cap and Sanchi, who wears a yellow cap. Barkha, who wears the same coloured cap as Usha and Gauri are immediate neighbours of each other. Gauri does not wear a yellow cap and does not face either Panchi or Usha.

182. How many persons are seated between Usha and Tanvi?

    (1) None   (2) One

    (3) Two   (4) Three

    (5) Cannot be determined

183. Select the correct combination of person and colour.

    (1) Rakhi - green   (2) Sanchi - blue

    (3) Chavi - red   (4) Tanvi - pink

    (5) Ameya - yellow

184. Who amongst the following represent the people sitting exactly in the middle of the rows?

    (1) Panchi, Gauri   (2) Sanchi, Drishti

    (3) Sanchi, Ameya   (4) Ameya, Rakhi

    (5) Panchi, Barkha

185. Select the pair which is odd.

    (1) Ameya - Tanvi   (2) Barkha - Usha

    (3) Drishti - Rakhi   (4) Chavi - Panchi

    (5) Gauri - Panchi

186. What is the colour of the cap of the person who is sitting second to the left of the one facing Sanchi?

    (1) Red   (2) Yellow

    (3) Bluei   (4) Pink

    (5) Green

Directions (Q. 187 to 191): In each question below are three statements followed by two conclusions numbered I and II. You have to take the given statements to be true even if they seem to be at variance with commonly known facts and then decide which of the given conclusions logically follows from the given statements disregarding commonly known facts. Give answer.

(1)   If only conclusion I is true.

(2)   If only conclusion II is true.

(3)   If either conclusion I or II is true

(4)   If neither conclusion I nor II is true

(5)   If both conclusions I and II are true.

187. **Statements:**

    All tubs are basins.

    All basins are mugs.

    Some mugs are white.

    Conclusions:

    I.   Some tubs being white is a possibility.

    II.   Some basins are white.

188. **Statements:**

    Some departments are institutions.

    Some institutions are organisations.

    Some organisations are private.

    Conclusions:

    I.   Some departments are private.

    II.   Some institutions are private.

189. **Statements:**

    Some wallets are purses.

    Some purses are bags.

    Some bags are leather.

    Conclusions:

    I.   Some wallets might be leather.

    II.   Some purses might be leather.

190. **Statements:**

    Some students are workers.

    All workers are women.

    Some women are young.

    Conclusions:

    I.   Some students might be young.

    II.   Some workers being young is a possibility.

191. **Statements:**

    All trains are engines.

    Some engines are beautiful.

    All beautiful are antique.

    Conclusions:

    I.   Some trains are antique.

    II.   Some trains being beautiful is a possibility.

Directions (Q. 192 to 195): Each question given below consists of a statement, followed by two arguments numbered I and II. You have to decide which of the arguments is a 'strong' argument and which is a 'weak' argument.

Give answer:

(1) If only argument I is strong

(2) If only argument II is strong

(3) If either I or II is strong

(4) If neither I nor II is strong

(5) If both I and II are strong.

192. **Statement:** Should women be granted permanent commission in the armed forces?

     Arguments:

     I.   No, women will not be able to bear with the stress that comes with an armed force's job.

     II. Yes, women should be given equal opportunities.

193. **Statement:** Should there be a retirement age in politics?

     Arguments:

     I.   Yes, like any other age, there should be a retirement age in politics as well.

     II. No, age also brings wisdom. Furthermore, politics is not a gainful profession.

194. **Statement:** Should Indian Railways be privatized?

     Arguments:

     I.   Yes, this is the only way to bring an element of transparency and efficiency.

     II. No, If Indian Railways is privatized, many people will lose their jobs.

195. **Statement:** Should social networking sites be banned?

     Arguments:

     I.   Yes, social networking sites spread a lot of rumours and hatred.

     II. No, social networking sites can generate a lot of public opinion on a certain subject.

Directions (Q. 196 to 200): In the following questions a fact or situation is given followed by two suggested courses. A course of action is a step of administrative decision taken for improvement or follow-up action. Read the situation and then decide which of the given courses of action follows.

Give answer:

(1) if only course of action I follows

(2) if only course of action II follows

(3) if both the course of action follow

(4) if neither follows

(5) If the data given is inadequate

196. **Statement:** Since its first flight in 1997, Delta Airlines has so far suffered losses amounting to Rs. 70 crores.

     Courses of Action:

     I.   Delta Airlines should try to reduce unnecessary expenses and increase passenger fares.

     II. An amount of about Rs. 50 crores should be provided to Delta Airlines to make it economically viable.

197. **Statement:** Court cases can drag for years and often, it takes too long a time for a judgement to be delivered.

     Courses of Action:

     I.   The government should appoint more judges so that the cases are disposed of swiftly.

     II. The government can also open mediation centres where minor disputes can be resolved out of the court under the supervision of a government appointed official.

198. **Statement:** A bus has met with an accident while going from Ramgarh to Daman.

     Courses of Action:

     I.   The District administration should immediately dispatch a team of doctors, ambulances and medicines.

     II. The Government should send the army to rescue the injured.

199. **Statement:** India's performance in sports has always been abysmal. Recently, the government spent a few crores in the training of players.

     Courses of Action:

     I.   India should stop sending players to any future international sporting event.

     II. The government should impose heavy penalties on sportspersons if they fail to win any medal in an event.

200. **Statement:** All India Radio is worried about the popularity of their programmes in view of the stiff competition faced from different FM channels.

     Courses of Action:

     I.   In an effort to make the programmes popular, All India Radio has decided to revise the payment structure meant for guest artistes.

     II. The government should stop the operations of all private FM channels, at least for the time being.

ANSWERS

1. (4)	**2.** (4)	**3.** (3)	**4.** (4)	**5.** (3)	**6.** (3)	**7.** (4)	**8.** (3)	**9.** (3)	**10.** (5)
11. (2)	**12.** (2)	**13.** (2)	**14.** (2)	**15.** (2)	**16.** (2)	**17.** (2)	**18.** (4)	**19.** (2)	**20.** (1)
21. (1)	**22.** (2)	**23.** (3)	**24.** (3)	**25.** (5)	**26.** (2)	**27.** (4)	**28.** (4)	**29.** (4)	**30.** (1)
31. (4)	**32.** (3)	**33.** (4)	**34.** (4)	**35.** (2)	**36.** (b)	**37.** (3)	**38.** (3)	**39.** (4)	**40.** (4)
41. (3)	**42.** (4)	**43.** (1)	**44.** (3)	**45.** (4)	**46.** (1)	**47.** (4)	**48.** (4)	**49.** (3)	**50.** (5)
51. (5)	**52.** (5)	**53.** (4)	**54.** (5)	**55.** (2)	**56.** (4)	**57.** (1)	**58.** (2)	**59.** (2)	**60.** (1)
61. (4)	**62.** (3)	**63.** (4)	**64.** (3)	**65.** (2)	**66.** (2)	**67.** (2)	**68.** (2)	**69.** (4)	**70.** (3)
71. (1)	**72.** (2)	**73.** (4)	**74.** (3)	**75.** (1)	**76.** (2)	**77.** (1)	**78.** (4)	**79.** (4)	**80.** (2)
81. (2)	**82.** (2)	**83.** (3)	**84.** (5)	**85.** (4)	**86.** (5)	**87.** (4)	**88.** (3)	**89.** (3)	**90.** (1)
91. (4)	**92.** (3)	**93.** (5)	**94.** (4)	**95.** (3)	**96.** (2)	**97.** (4)	**98.** (2)	**99.** (1)	**100.** (5)
101. (1)	**102.** (3)	**103.** (5)	**104.** (3)	**105.** (4)	**106.** (2)	**107.** (3)	**108.** (2)	**109.** (1)	**110.** (2)
111. (2)	**112.** (1)	**113.** (4)	**114.** (1)	**115.** (4)	**116.** (4)	**117.** (4)	**118.** (2)	**119.** (2)	**120.** (2)
121. (2)	**122.** (3)	**123.** (2)	**124.** (4)	**125.** (5)	**126.** (1)	**127.** (5)	**128.** (3)	**129.** (4)	**130.** (5)
131. (3)	**132.** (2)	**133.** (1)	**134.** (1)	**135.** (3)	**136.** (3)	**137.** (2)	**138.** (5)	**139.** (1)	**140.** (4)
141. (5)	**142.** (1)	**143.** (4)	**144.** (2)	**145.** (4)	**146.** (1)	**147.** (3)	**148.** (4)	**149.** (4)	**150.** (2)
151. (2)	**152.** (3)	**153.** (1)	**154.** (4)	**155.** (2)	**156.** (5)	**157.** (3)	**158.** (2)	**159.** (2)	**160.** (5)
161. (4)	**162.** (4)	**163.** (3)	**164.** (4)	**165.** (1)	**166.** (5)	**167.** (4)	**168.** (2)	**169.** (5)	**170.** (3)
171. (5)	**172.** (2)	**173.** (5)	**174.** (3)	**175.** (3)	**176.** (4)	**177.** (3)	**178.** (2)	**179.** (3)	**180.** (4)
181. (5)	**182.** (3)	**183.** (4)	**184.** (5)	**185.** (4)	**186.** (1)	**187.** (1)	**188.** (4)	**189.** (5)	**190.** (5)
191. (2)	**192.** (2)	**193.** (2)	**194.** (4)	**195.** (2)	**196.** (1)	**197.** (3)	**198.** (1)	**199.** (4)	**200.** (1)

EXPLANATIONS

1. 4   The National Seed Association of India organized the seventh edition of the mega Seed Industry event- Seed Congress 2017 from 12 - 14 February 2017 in Kolkata.

2. 4   Food regulator FSSAI has set up a scientific panel to frame final regulations on fortification of foods and prepare strategies to address malnutrition problem.

3. 3   The 11th edition of International Aerospace and Defence Exhibition - Aero India 2017 was held at the Air Force Station, Yelahanka in Bengaluru from 14th to 18th February 2017.

4. 4   This Braille Atlas has been prepared by National Atlas and Thematic Mapping Organisation (NATMO) under Department of Science & Technology.

5. 3   The Maharashtra Government became first state in the country to launch India's first comprehensive 'Crime Criminal Tracking Network System' (CCTNS) in Mumbai.

6. 3   The first ever Indian Ocean Rim Association (IORA) Leaders' Summit was held in Indonesia's capital city of Jakarta at the Jakarta Convention Center from 5th March to 7th March 2017.

23. 3   From 1954 to 1976, Hanoi was the capital of North Vietnam, and it became the capital of a reunified Vietnam in 1976, after the North's victory in the Vietnam War.

24. 3   Manohar Parrikar is a member of the Rajya Sabha from Uttar Pradesh.

25. 5 Headquarters of World Meteorological Organisation is at Geneva.

26. 2 Aishwaryaa Dhanush has been appointed as United Nations Women's Advocate for Gender Equality and Women's Empowerment in India.

27. 4 In India the largest four banks are
- State Bank of India
- ICICI Bank
- Punjab National Bank
- Bank of Baroda

29. 4 Mahindra became the first OEM (original equipment manufacturer) in India to integrate its product line-up onto a cloud-based technology platform.

30. 1 A.P. Hota is the current Managing Director & CEO of National Payments Corporation of India (NPCI).

31. 4 India ranked 77th among the 171 countries in the 2016 World Risk Index (WRI).

32. 3 World's largest protected marine reserve area named as Papahanaumokuakea Marine National Monument is in USA.

34. 4 The first edition of 'IoT (Internet of Things) India Congress, 2016' began in Bengaluru.

35. 2 Greece is the first country in the world with which India has inked an open sky arrangement under its new civil aviation policy in September 2016.

36. b

37. 3 The 2017 G20 summit is to be held in Germany.

38. 3 Bibhuti Lahkar was awarded won prestigious 'Heritage Heroes Award' of the International Union for Conservation of Nature (IUCN) in 2016.

39. 4 Urjit Patel is 24th Governor of Reserve Bank of India.

40. 4 Odisha launched the Biju Kanya Ratna Yojana (BKRY) for the development of girls in the state.

41. 3 The Election Commission of India (ECI) has granted national party status to All India Trinamool Congress (TMC) Party led by West Bengal Chief Minister Mamata Banerjee. With this recognition, TMC became seventh national party in the country along with Bharatiya Janata Party (BJP), Congress, Bahujan Samaj Party (BSP), Nationalist Congress Party (NCP), Communist Party of India (CPI) and Communist Party of India-Marxist (CPM).

46. 1 Kakrapar Atomic Power Station is a nuclear power station in India, which lies in the proximity of the city of Vyara in the state of Gujarat.

58. 2 ICICI Bank launched the first of its kind fully automated digital locker, which would be available to customers even on weekends and post banking hours.

64. 3 The AEWS & CS was developed by the Centre for Airborne Systems (CABS). The laboratory comes under the Defence Research and Development Organisation and headed by woman scientist J Manjula.

65. 2 Dr. M.S. Sahoo is the current chairperson of Insolvency and Bankruptcy Board of India.

66. 2 The third National Dam Safety Conference was organized at Roorkee, Uttarakhand.

68. 2 World Health Organisation (WHO) has dropped the term 'counterfeit' and retained 'falsified' to describe medicines of inferior quality.

69. 4 The 13th World Robot Olympiad was held in Greater Noida, India. This was the first year that the World Robot Olympiad was held in India.

70. 3 Total fourteen Coastal Economic Zones (CEZ) have been identified along the coastline of the country in the National Perspective Plan of the Sagarmala programme. These CEZs are aimed at promoting development of port-proximate industrial clusters

71. 1 Iranian film Daughter, directed by Reza Mirkarimi, won the coveted Golden Peacock award at the 47th International Film Festival of India (IFFI).

72. 2 Jin Liqun is currently the President of the Asian Infrastructure Investment Bank (AIIB).

73. 4 As many as 30 PSBs, private and foreign banks have joined the NPCI's Unified Payments Interface (UPI), a system that allows money transfer between any two bank accounts by using a mobile phone.

74. 3 West Bengal is India's largest producer of rice at 158 lakh tonnes a year. Of this, nearly 110 lakh tonnes is harvested during the kharif season.

75. 1 Bharti Airtel the country's largest telecom company, launched its payments bank services from Rajasthan, as a pilot, becoming the first payments bank in the country to go live.

76. 2 B. Janardhan Reddy, from Telangana, resigned as chairperson of the Central Advisory Board on Minimum Wages.

77. 1 The 'Give Up' campaign of LPG subsidy now stands extended to another government scheme - "Swacch Bharat". The govt is now appealing to citizens not to take Rs 4000 subsidy to build household toilets in urban centres.

78. 4 The Sardar Vallabhbhai Patel National Police Academy (SVPNPA), trains officers of the Indian Police Service, who have been Selected through an All India, based Civil Services Examination. It is headquartered in Hyderabad, Telanagana State.

79. 4 The Centre announced a new committee, headed by Niti Aayog CEO Amitabh Kant, to form a strategy to expedite the process of transforming India into a cashless economy.

80. 2 The Rohingya people are Muslim Indo-Aryan peoples from the Myanmar.

82. 2 Refer to the last sentence of the passage where the author mentions that the deployment of THAAD will only complicate matters among US, China and Russia.

84. 5 The author is cautioning us that unless de-escalation becomes a priority for all parties involved, the Korean Peninsula region will remain a flashpoint.

85. 4 The author has used the word "commendable" while commenting on the Six Party talks.

93. 5 It is because of the increased vigil of the Indian Coast Guard that piracy has been contained in the area.

94. 4 His luck ran out in 2004 when police gunned him down.

95. 3 Option (3) explains the problem that is mentioned in the given statements.

96. 2 Refer to the last sentence of the passage where the RBI Governor's previous occupation is mentioned.

97. 4 Refer to the last sentence of the first paragraph where the function of the benchmark policy rate is given.

98. 2 The most likely answer is 'economist.'

99. 1 Refer to the second last sentence of the passage for the answer. Since Mr. Rajan took the high office, the policy rate has been raised thrice and cut five times.

101. 1 'Likely' should have been used.

102. 3 The subject is 'developments' and so, 'have' should have been used.

103. 5 The sentence is grammatically correct.

104. 3 The preposition 'in' is wrong. 'For' should have been used.

105. 4 The preposition 'in' is wrong. 'On' should have been used.

111. 2 Numbers of candidates qualified in 2008, 2009 and 2010

$$= 5000 \times \frac{32.5}{100} + 10000 \times \frac{37.5}{100} + 22500 \times \frac{30}{100}$$

$$= 1625 + 3750 + 6750 = 12125$$

Number of candidate qualified in 2013, 2014 and 2015

$$= 30000 \times \frac{22.5}{100} + 20000 \times \frac{35}{100} + 35000 \times \frac{40}{100}$$

$$= 6750 + 7000 + 14000 = 27750$$

Hence, required ratio = 12125 : 27750 = 97 : 222.

112. 1 It is clearly seen from the information given that the number of students who appeared in 2008 is least among all. So, the number of students who qualified will be least in 2008 only.

113. 4 Number of qualified candidates in the given years:

2008 → 1625

2009 → 3750

2010 → 6750

2011 → $17500 \times \dfrac{30}{100} = 5250$

2012 → $27500 \times \dfrac{32}{100} = 8800$

2013 → 6750

2014 → 7000

2015 → 14000

Hence, the required percentage was maximum for 2009.

114. 1 Number of students who qualified in 2013

$$= \frac{22.5}{100} \times 30000 = 6750$$

115. 4 Required percentage $= \dfrac{\dfrac{30}{100} \times 22.5}{10} \times 100 = 67.5\%$

116. 4 Let the CP for the Aman be Rs. 100x, then SP will be Rs. 120x.

Thus SP for the Shashank = Rs. 120x

Now, 24x − 20x = 85

Hence, 120x = Rs. 2,550.

117. 4 Let x men finish the remaining work in 100 days.

Therefore,

$$\frac{M_1 D_1}{W_1} = \frac{M_2 D_2}{W_2}$$

$$\Rightarrow \frac{35 \times 150}{7} = \frac{x \times 100}{8}$$

$$\Rightarrow x = \frac{35 \times 150 \times 8}{7 \times 100}$$

$$\therefore x = 60$$

Thus, number of extra men = 60 − 35 = 25

118. 2 Ratio of A, B and C = $\frac{5}{3} : \frac{3}{4} : \frac{4}{5}$ = 100 : 45 : 48

Investement	A	:	B	:	C
For 1st 4 months	100 × 4	:	45 × 4	:	48 × 4
For last 8 months	150 × 8	:	45 × 8	:	48 × 8
	1600	:	540	:	576

Therefore, ratio of A, B and C = 400 : 135 : 144

Total profit = Rs. 81,480

So, profit of B $= \frac{135}{679} \times$ Rs. 81480 = Rs. 16,200.

119. 2 Let the borrowed amount be x.

According to the question

$$x\left[\left(1+\frac{5}{100}\right)^2 - 1\right] - \frac{x \times 2.5 \times 1}{100} = 465$$

$$\Rightarrow (1.1025 - 1)x - 0.025x = 465$$

$$\Rightarrow x = \frac{465}{0.0775} = \text{Rs.}6{,}000$$

120. 2 Let total maximum marks be *x*. Then,

$$\frac{x \times 64}{100} = 2240 - 128 = 2112$$

$$\Rightarrow x = \frac{2112 \times 100}{64} = 3300$$

Marks obtained by Meena

= 2240 − 907 = 1333

Required percentage $= \frac{1333}{3300} \times 100 \approx 40.$

121. 2 Statement I alone does not provide much information. But from statement II, we get the ratio of the efficiencies of A, B and C as 2 : 1 : 3.

Now, combining statement II with III we get the required difference as 7.5 days.

122. 3 The question can be answered by combining the information of statement III with that of either statement I or statement II.

123. 2 Statement III alone is sufficient to answer the question. However, we cannot combine statements I and II because we get different speeds for Train B which contradicts each other.

124. 4 We can determine the ratio of the cost price and the selling price by using either of the statements alone which would be sufficient to get the percentage of profit in the entire transaction.

125. 5 We cannot determine the exact answer even after determining the value of 'x' because it is not mention in the question if the compounding is done semi-annually or annually.

126. 1 Passengers of airline A

= (15 + 10 + 20 + 10 + 15 + 10) thousands

= 80 thousands

Passengers of airline C

= (15 + 15 + 15 + 10 + 20 + 10) thousands

= 85 thousands

Hence, required percent $= \frac{85 - 80}{85} \times 100 = 5.88\%$

127. 5 Required percent is maximum for Bengaluru.

128. 3 Required ratio = (15 + 10) : (15 + 10)

= 25 : 25 = 1 : 1

129. 4 Passengers to airline A who travelled to Chennai

First quarter ⇒ 10000

Second quarter $\Rightarrow 10000 \times \frac{150}{100} = 15000$

Third quarter $\Rightarrow \frac{15000 \times 100}{120} = 12500$

Percentage increase $= \frac{12500 - 10000}{10000} \times 100 = 25\%.$

130. 5 Passengers of airline B who travelled to Bangaluru.

First quarter ⇒ 10000

Second quarter $\Rightarrow \frac{10000 \times 130}{100} = 13000$

Passengers of airline B who travelled to Kolkata

First quarter ⇒ 10000

Second quarter ⇒ 14000

$\therefore$ Required percentage $= \frac{20000}{27000} \times 100 = 74$

131. 3 Cost of wine per litre when two different varieties of wine is mixed

$$\frac{5 \times 420 + 5 \times 280}{5 + 5} = \frac{3500}{10} = 350$$

Cost of water = Rs. 0 per litre

Applying alligation, we have

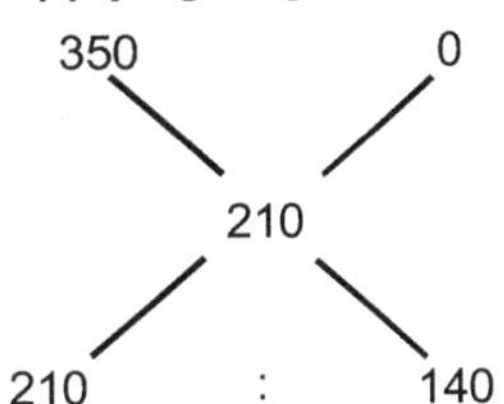

Therefore, ratio of wine to water $= \dfrac{210}{140} = \dfrac{3}{2}$

Which implies that 3 litres of wine should be mixed with 2 litres of water to make the resultant mixture worth Rs. 210 per litre of wine. Hence, 10 litres of wine would required $\dfrac{20}{3}$ litres of water.

132. 2 The speed of the boat while going upstream

$$= \frac{54}{6} = 9 \text{ km/hr}$$

Speed of stream = 12 – 9 = 3 km/hr

Speed of the boat while going down stream

$$= 12 + 3 = 15 \text{ km/hr}$$

∴ Distance covered by the boat in 5 hours

$$= 15 \times 5 = 75 \text{ km.}$$

133. 1 When compound interest is calculated on half-yearly basis

$$\text{Amount}(A) = P\left(1 + \frac{r}{2 \times 100}\right)^{2n}$$

$$A = 10000\left(1 + \frac{10}{2 \times 100}\right)^{2} + 10000\left(1 + \frac{10}{2 \times 100}\right)^{1}$$

= Rs. 21,525.

Therefore, CI = A – P = Rs. (21525 - 20000) = Rs. 1,525

134. 1 Let the ages of Mohana and Sandhya ten years hence be 5x and 3x respectively.

According to the question : $\dfrac{5x - 10 - 10}{3x - 10 - 10} = \dfrac{3}{1} \Rightarrow x = 10$

The ages of Mohana and Sandhya at present are 40 years and 20 years respectively

Required difference = 20 years

135. 3

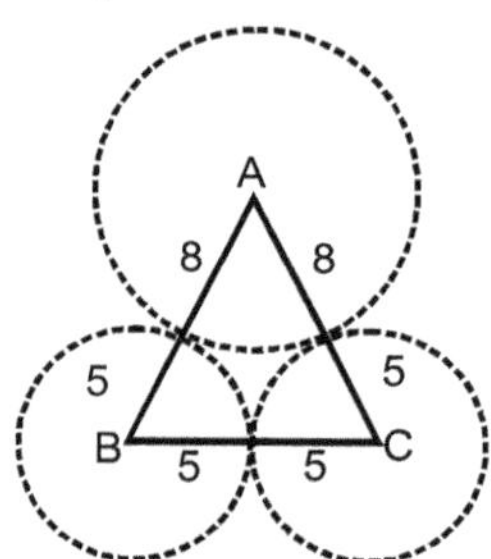

In triangle ABC, draw AD perpendicular to BC.

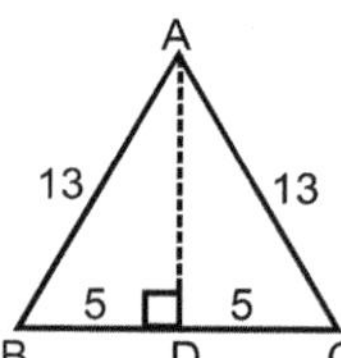

In triangle ADB, Pythagoras theorem we have

$$AD = \sqrt{AB^2 - BD^2} = \sqrt{13^2 - 5^2} = \sqrt{136 - 25} = \sqrt{144} = 12 \text{ cm}$$

Therefore, area of triangle ABC

$$\frac{1}{2}BC \times AD = \frac{1}{2} \times 10 \times 12 = 60 \text{ cm}^2$$

136. 3 $1^3 - 1, 2^3 + 2, 3^3 - 3, 4^3 + 4, \mathbf{5^3 - 5}, 6^3 + 6, 7^3 - 7$

$\quad = 1 - 1, 8 + 2, 27 - 3, 64 + 4, \mathbf{125 - 5}, 216 + 6, 343 - 3$

$\quad = 0, 10, 24, 68, \mathbf{120}, 222, 340.$

137. 2 $1636 \div 2 + 2 = 820$

$\quad 820 \div 2 - 2 = 408$

$\quad 408 \div 2 + 2 = \mathbf{206}$

$\quad 208 \div 2 - 2 = 101$

$\quad 101 \div 2 + 2 = 52.5.$

138. 5

139. 1 $10^2 - 9^2, 9^2 + 8^2, 8^2 - 7^2, 7^2 + 6^2, 6^2 - 5^2, 5^2 + 4^2, 4^2 - 3^2$

$\quad = 100 - 99 , 91 + 64, 64 - 49, 49 + 36, 36 - 25, 25 + 16, 16 - 9$

$\quad = 1, 145, 15, \mathbf{85}, 11, 41, 7$

140. 4 $12 \times 2 = 24$

$\quad 24 \times 2.5 = 60$

$\quad 60 \times 3 = 180$

$\quad 180 \times 3.5 = \mathbf{630}$

$\quad 630 \times 4 = 2520$

$\quad 2520 \times 4.5 = 11340$

For questions 141 to 145:

P # Q means P ≥ Q

P % Q means P = Q

P & Q means P < Q

P $ Q means P > Q.

P @ Q means P ≤ Q

141. 5 V ≥ S > R = T ≥ U

    I.   R $ V ⇒ R > V is false.

    II. S @ T ⇒ S ≤ T is false.

    III. R % S ⇒ R = S is false.

    IV. V $ T ⇒ V > T is true.

142. 1 S > P = Q ≤ R > T

    I.   P @ R ⇒ P ≤ R is true.

    II. P $ T ⇒ P > T is false.

    III. S % T ⇒ S = T is false.

    IV. S $ Q ⇒ S > Q is true.

143. 4 A ≥ C = D > E ≥ F

    I.   A % E ⇒ A = E is false.

    II. A # F ⇒ A ≥ F is false.

    III. C % E ⇒ C = E is false.

    IV. A # D ⇒ A ≥ D is true.

144. 2 O ≥ P > T ≥ Q = S < R

   I.　T & R ⇒ T < R is false.

   II.　S % T ⇒ S = T is false.

   III.　P $ Q ⇒ P > Q is true.

   IV.　Q @ O ⇒ Q ≤ O is false.

145. 4 M > O ≥ T = S ≤ R

   I.　R $ T ⇒ R > T

   II.　R % T ⇒ R = T　　　　Either I or II is true.

   III.　M $ S ⇒ M > S　　　is true.

   IV.　O # R ⇒ O ≥ R is false.

   Hence, either I or II and III are true.

For questions 146 to 151:

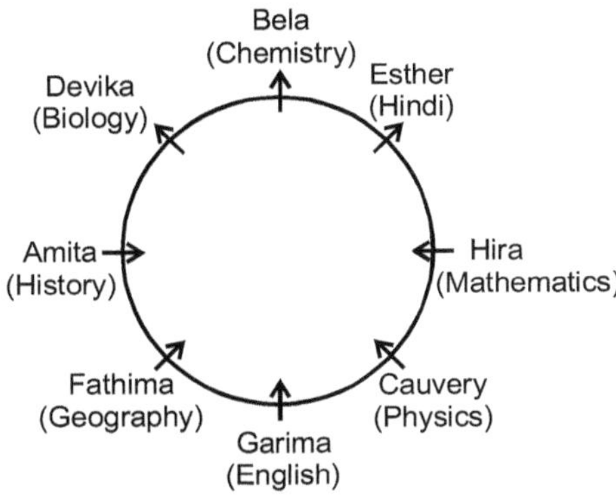

For questions 152 to 156: After careful analysis of the given input and various steps or re-arrangement, it is evident that in each step one number or a word get re-arranged. In the first step, the highest number moves to the extreme left position. In the second step the word which comes first in the dictionary moves to the second position from the left. These two steps are repeated alternately till all the numbers get rearranged in descending order and the words in alphabetical order.

Input: vital 54 cards 72 help 24 wall 66 lamp 49

Step I: 72 vital 54 cards help 24 wall 66 lamp 49

Step II: 72 cards vital 54 help 24 wall 66 lamp 49

Step III: 72 cards 66 vital 54 help 24 wall lamp 49

Step IV: 72 cards 66 help vital 54 24 wall lamp 49

Step V: 72 cards 66 help 54 vital 24 wall lamp 49

Step VI: 72 cards 66 help 54 lamp vital 24 wall 49

Step VII: 72 cards 66 help 54 lamp 49 vital 24 wall

And, Step VII is the last step.

152. 3 Seven steps would be required to complete the rearrangement.

153. 1 There are five elements (help, 54, vital, 24, wall) between "66" and "lamp" in the Step V.

154. 4 This is Step VI.

155. 2 Fourth element from the right end in the Step III ⇒ 24 Immediate to the right of "24" ⇒ wall

156. 5 There are two elements between "6" and "lamp" in the final Step. Similarly, there are two elements between "72" and "help" in the final Step

So, "cards" would be related to "54".

For questions 157 to 161:

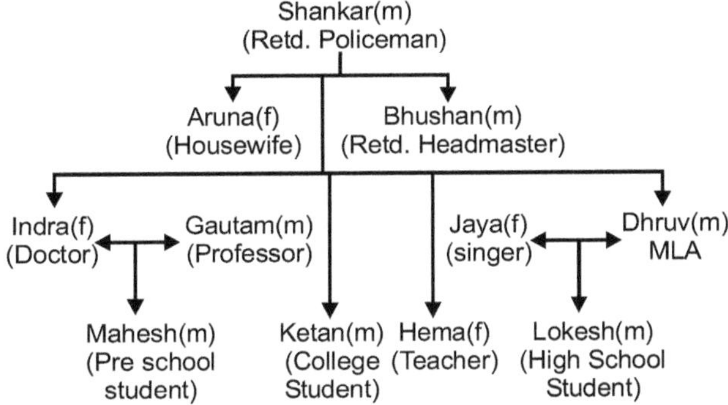

Directions for questions 162 to 166:

Name	Years	Place	Bonus (in Rs.)
Ahil	5	Delhi	60,000
Dhiraj	7	Cuttack	84,000
Kapil	8	Cochin	96,000
Lokesh	10	Kanpur	1,50,000
Prem	12	Pune	1,80,000
Tanay	13	Mysore	1,95,000
Viraj	9	Hyderabad	1,08,000

For questions 167 to 171:

glass	la
of	eo
cold	lo
water	re
extremely	me
thin	ni
wine	od / aw
bottle	aw / od

172. 2 From statement I

   R, T > P, Q

   From statement II

   V > R, T, P, Q, S

   From statement III

   Q > S > P

   From statement I and II

   V > R, T > P, Q

   From all the three statements

   V > R, T > Q > S > P

   Clearly, S secured the second lowest marks.

173. 5 From statement I

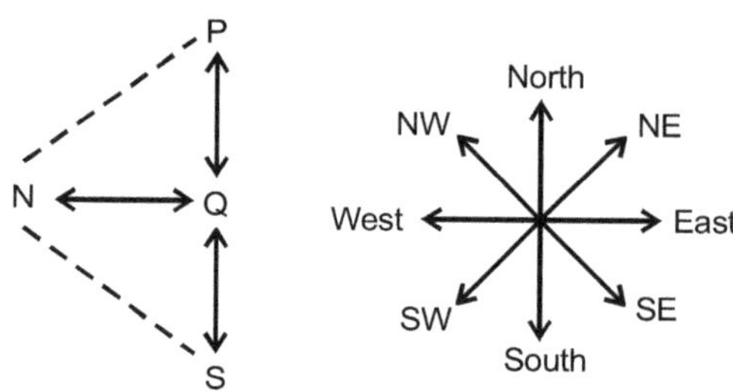

There is no information about the village R in the statement I.

From statement II

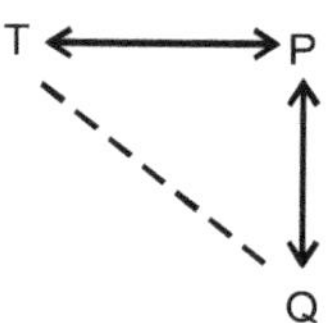

There is no information about the village R in the statement II.

From statement III

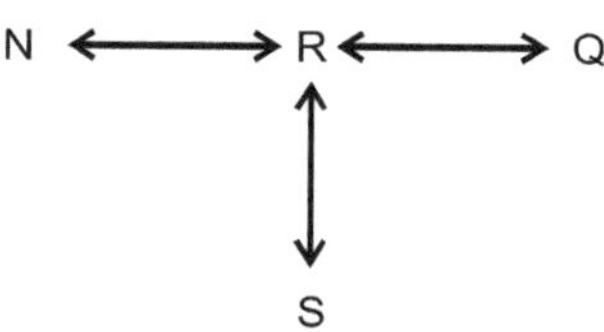

There is no information about the village R in the statements I and II. Therefore, we cannot arrive at the answer even with the statements I and II taken together.

From statements I and III

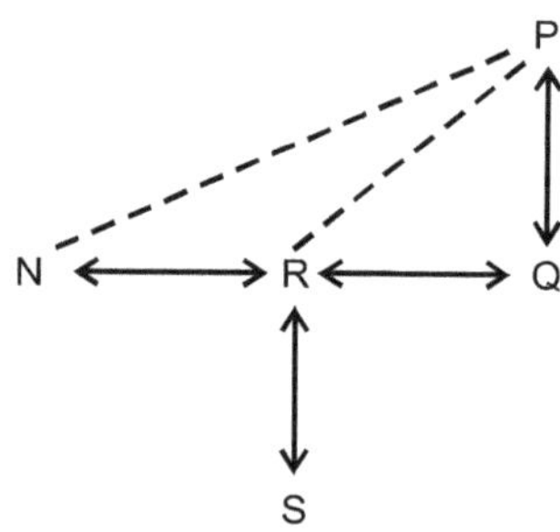

It is clear from the diagram that village P is to the North-East of village R.

From statements II and III

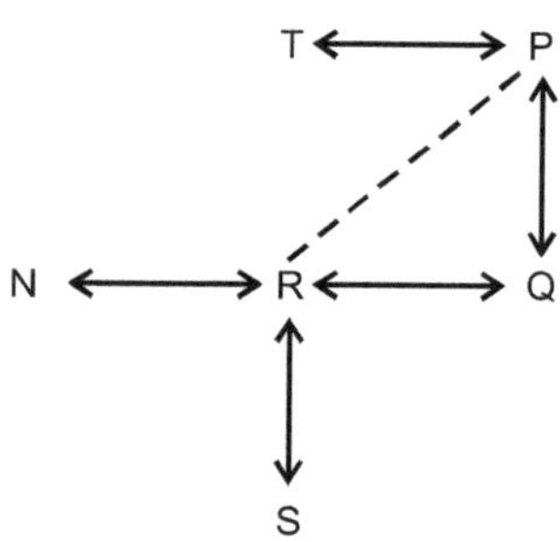

It is clear from the diagram that village P is to the North-East of village R.

174. 3 From statement I

The position of Nirmal from the top

= 17 − 13 + 1 = 5th

The rank of Animesh from the either end is 9th.

From statement II

$$B \;|||\; K$$

From statement III

The rank of Kamal = 15th

Bhumika is two position below Animesh

From statement II and III

$$8 \rightarrow \boxed{A}\; |\; \boxed{B}\; |||\; \boxed{K} \overset{2}{\leftarrow}$$

The rank of Animesh is 9th.

175. 3 From statement I:

'tell them young' = 'se me ye'

'young sharp tell' = 'me na ye'

Hence, the code for 'them' will be 'se'.

From statement II and III:

'clever sharp come tomorrow' = 'na ki pa lo'

'clever sharp come them no' = 'pa na se ki te'

'yellow come sharp run clever no' = 'ki ni pa be te na'

Hence, the code for 'no' will be 'te' and that of 'them' will be 'se'.

Therefore, only I or II and III together are required to answer the question.

176. 4 From III, we know that Z was born in 1990.

From II, we find that Z was 5 years younger to Y, i.e. Y was born in 1985.

From I, we find that X is 3 years older than Y. Thus, X was born in 1982.

For questions 177 to 181

Floor	Student	Subject
9	Chaya	Geography
8	Bhavya	Mathematics
7	Sreya	History
6	Jiya	English
5	Priya	Zoology
4	Ananya	Physics
3	Rabiya	Chemistry
2	Maya	Commerce
1	Divya	Botany

For questions 182 to 186:

Row 1 ↓	red Rakhi	green Usha	blue Panchi	yellow Sanchi	pink Tanvi
Row 2 ↑	Chavi yellow	Drishti red	Barkha green	Gauri blue	Ameya pink

187. 1

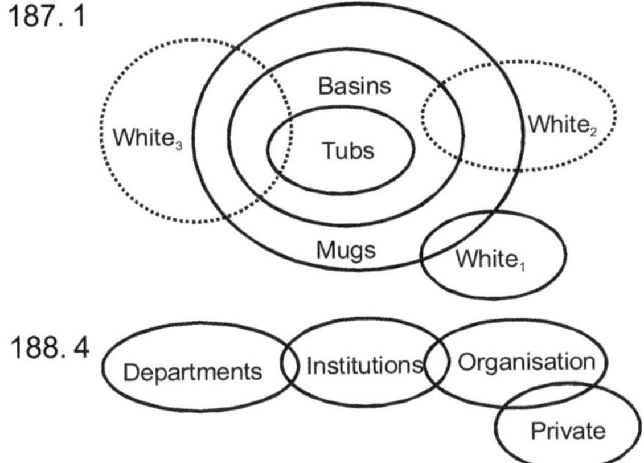

188. 4

189. 5 Case I:

Case II:

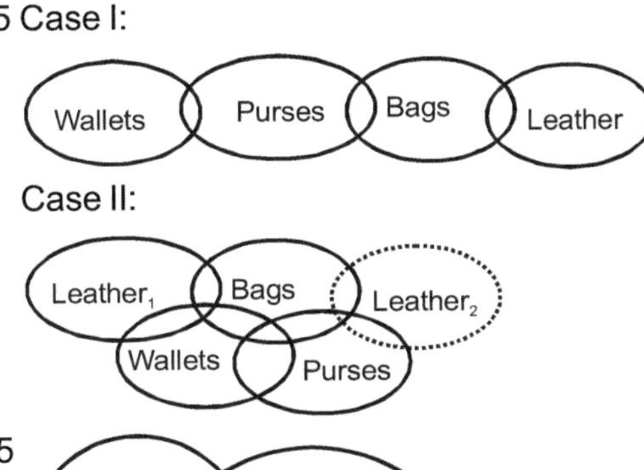

190. 5

191. 2

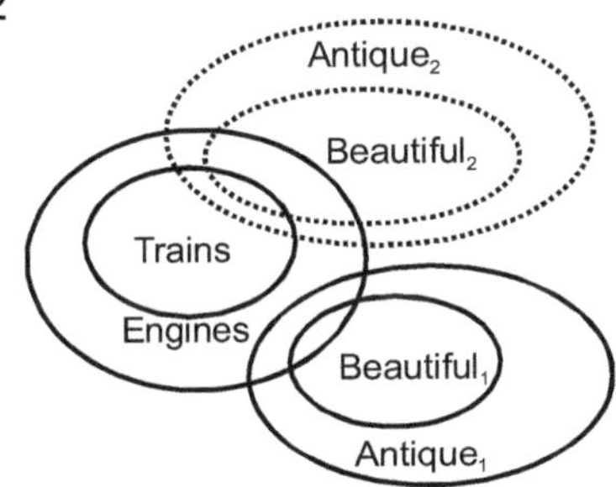

192. 2 Argument II is strong.

193. 2 Argument II is strong.

194. 4 Both arguments are weak. Privatization doesn't lead to loss of jobs. Moreover, there are other ways to bring transparency and efficiency.

195. 2 Argument II is strong.

196. 1 Course I is a logical step that can be implemented to minimize losses and maximize profits. Option (II) can be a short term step but it cannot be a permanent solution.

197. 3 Both the courses of action sound logical.

198. 1 Only course of action I sounds logical.

199. 4 Neither of the two courses of action sound logical.

200. 1 Course of action I follows. It can be an appropriate course of action in the light of the aforementioned problem. Course of action II is not feasible in a democratic set up like India.

ENGLISH ABILITY

Directions (Q. 1 - 10): Read the following passage carefully and answer the questions given below it. Certain words have been printed in bold to help you to locate them while answering some of the questions.

Despite rapid economic growth, the explosion of microcredit programs and self-help groups, and laudable efforts to increase women's political participation, gender disparities have remained deep and **persistent** in India. The UN Gender Inequality Index has ranked India below several sub-Saharan African countries. Gender disparities are even more pronounced in economic participation and women's business conditions in India. Using data from the 2011 Global Gender Gap report shows that while India scores around the average of the gender gap index overall, its score for women's economic participation and opportunity is worse than 95% of all countries in the sample. Despite India being the second fastest growing economy in the world, gender disparities have remained deep and persistent in India.

The good news is that the overall India average female business-ownership share (in manufacturing) has increased over time from 26% in 2000 to 37% in 2005. However, there is wide variation across states and industries in the **prevalence** of women as entrepreneurs. Among the major states of India, those with the highest share of new proprietary businesses in the unorganized manufacturing sector owned by women in 1994 are Karnataka, Tamil Nadu, Andhra Pradesh, and Kerala. Those with the lowest share of female entrepreneurs are Uttar Pradesh, Haryana, Maharashtra, Madhya Pradesh, and Rajasthan. Similar patterns hold across states when comparing overall business ownership rates by gender. All but one state (Sikkim) saw an increase in the share of new businesses owned by women over the period of 1994 to 2005.

Not surprisingly, the same industries in which female entrepreneurship is concentrated relative to male entrepreneurship also comprise the industries in which most women-owned businesses are found. In 1994, more than 90 percent of new female-owned businesses were found in six of 22 2-digit industries. These industries include Textiles, Tobacco, Wood Products, Food Products, Furniture and Chemical Products. By 2005, 90 percent of female entrepreneurs were still concentrated in six largely overlapping 2-digit industries. At the opposite end, female shares of 2% or less are evident in industries related to computers, motor vehicles, fabricated metal products, and machinery and equipment. In services, female ownership rates in major cities tend to be higher than overall state averages and exceed 30% in sanitation and education industries.

Among district-level traits, a higher female-to-male sex ratio, an age profile emphasizing working age population, better quality infrastructure, and more stringent labor regulations appear important. The relative entry rate declines with high population density. Education and female literacy rates are not associated with gender differences in manufacturing. The relationship between infrastructure and the female entry share is the most policy relevant. Inadequate infrastructure affects women more than men, perhaps because women often bear a larger share of the time and responsibility for household activities. It is notable that infrastructure access within a district matters. Women face greater constraints in geographic mobility imposed by safety concerns and/or social norms. Better transport infrastructure may **alleviate** a major constraint for female entrepreneurs accessing markets. Ironically industries related to transportation have the lowest share of women entrepreneurs. Somewhat surprisingly, a higher female entry ratio is not associated with a greater female sex ratio in the district. Stronger female-owned incumbent businesses again predict a greater female entrepreneurship in service industries. Our results support the conclusion that female entrepreneurship in India follows from incumbent female-owned businesses in a district-industry that encourage subsequent entry.

Marshallian channels are important, but they mostly appear to be operating through the district-industry agglomeration for female business owners itself. While our approach does not rule out every potential bias, it does **circumvent** the most worrisome endogeneity or omitted factors.

A central driver of economic growth over the past century is the increased role of women. This growth via the role of women comes in many forms: better education and health, increased female labor force participation generally, reduced discrimination and wage differentials that encourage greater effort, and improved advancement practices that promote talented women into leadership and managerial roles. Simply put, empowering half of the potential workforce has significant economic benefits beyond promoting gender equality. The infrastructure correlation is the most policy relevant. Inadequate infrastructure affects women in particular ways due to responsibilities regarding household and domestic activities. It is notable that while our within-district infrastructure access is important in predicting female entrepreneurship, access to major cities is not found to influence the gender balance of entrepreneurs.

We find evidence of agglomeration economies in both manufacturing and services, where higher female ownership among incumbent businesses within a district-industry predicts a greater share of subsequent entrepreneurs will be female. Moreover, higher female ownership of local businesses in related industries (e.g., similar labor needs, input- output markets) predict greater relative female entry rates even after controlling for the focal district-industry's conditions. Our analysis suggests that gender-based business networks may play a role in encouraging women's entrepreneurship. Our analysis is only suggestive in this respect, and points to the need for future research which develops a better understanding regarding the dynamics of gender-based networks, entrepreneurship and productivity. Linkages and spillovers across firms can depend on common traits of business owners, and interactions between the informal (unorganized) and formal (organized) sectors may not be as strong as interactions within each sector. Further research needs to identify how these forces affect small-scale female entrepreneurs and the welfare of women generally. This will be especially helpful for evaluating the performance of industry concentrations in developing economies and guiding appropriate policy actions.

Much recent work emphasizes the role of women in development. India's economic growth and development depends upon successfully utilizing its workforce. Despite recent economic advances, India's gender balance for entrepreneurship remains among the lowest in the world. Improving this balance is an important step for India's development and its achievement of greater economic growth and gender equality.

1. What is the main reason for huge gender disparities in women's economic participation in India?

   (*a*) Female literacy rate which is very low because of social reasons.

   (*b*) Substandard education among the women because of their social status.

   (*c*) Dearth in infrastructure facilities.

   (*d*) Stringent labour regulation laws.

   (*e*) Lack of physical strength in women which is required in industries.

2. Which of the following is/ are the reason(s) for district-industry with high rate of incumbent female employment?

   (i) High population density.

   (ii) Stringent labour regulation laws which suppresses Indian entrepreneurship.

   (iii) Strong open minded male owned incumbent businesses.

   (*a*) Only (ii).

   (*b*) Both (ii) and (iii).

   (*c*) Both (i) and (ii).

   (*d*) Only (i).

   (*e*) All of these.

3. Share of women entrepreneurs is lowest in which of the following industries?

   (*a*) Wood industries.

   (*b*) Fertilizer industries.

   (*c*) Tobacco industries.

   (*d*) Fabricated metal products.

   (*e*) Transportation industries.

4. Which of the following can help significantly in embolden women entrepreneurs?

   (*a*) Lenient labour laws.

   (*b*) Better education facilities in districts and more importantly in villages.

   (*c*) Giving emphasis to services which are more skill intensive than manufacturing.

   (*d*) Business based on gender.

   (*e*) Efforts in improving female sex ratio as people prefer boys more than girls.

5. Which of the following is false in context of the passage?

   (*a*) Safety concern is one of the reasons for gender disparity.

   (*b*) Incumbent female owned businesses encourage more female entrepreneurs.

   (*c*) Increase in the female connection in input-output markets increases the share of female entrants.

   (*d*) Female literacy rate is not the reasons for gender disparity in manufacturing.

   (*e*) None of these.

6. What is the writing style used by the author in this passage?

   (*a*) Descriptive   (*b*) Analytical

   (*c*) Critical   (*d*) Argumentative

   (*e*) Narrative

Directions (Q. 7 - 8) : *Which of the following is most* **opposite** *in* **meaning** *as word printed in bold letters as used in context of the passage.*

7. PERSISTENT

   (*a*) Tenacious   (*b*) Pertinacious

   (*c*) Intermittent   (*d*) Importunate

   (*e*) Unremitting

8. PREVALENT

   (*a*) Sporadic   (*b*) Extensive

   (*c*) Pervasive   (*d*) Ubiquitous

   (*e*) Omnipresent

Directions (9 - 10): *Which of the following is most similar in* **meaning** *as word printed in bold letters as used in context of the passage.*

9. CIRCUMVENT

   (*a*) Outmanoeuvre   (*b*) Accede

   (*c*) Assent   (*d*) Embrace

   (*e*) Pursue

10. ALLEVIATE

   (*a*) Aggravate   (*b*) Intensify

   (*c*) Escalate   (*d*) Assuage

   (*e*) Augment

Directions (Q. 11 - 15): *Rearrange the following six sentences*

(A), (B), (C), (D) ,(E)and (F) in the proper sequence to form a meaningful paragraph and then answer the questions given below.

   A. Securities and banking firms spend 6% to 8% of their total revenues on IT. Insurance companies in contrast spend around 3.5%.

   B. Wipro has over a dozen insurance companies as customers he said citing Aviva, Friends Provident, and Allianz as examples.

   C. The story with insurance companies, like their counterparts in the other industries is the same - pressure to reduce cost and retain customers.

   D. Echoing Mr Ghosh's view, senior executives of software firms also say that disjointed IT systems, created by wave of consolidation that swept the insurance industry,

   E. Is proving to be opportunistic for Indian companies, for service offerings like consolidation of applications, maintenance and conversion from legacy to newer platforms.

   F. Regulatory pressure combined with need to introduce new products and services are forcing insurance companies to seek external help to drive their business forward, says Soumitro Ghosh, vice president, BFSI, Wipro Technologies.

11. Which of the following would be the **FIRST** sentence after rearrangement?

   (*a*) A   (*b*) B

   (*c*) C   (*d*) D

   (*e*) E

12. Which of the following would be the **LAST (SIXTH)** sentence after rearrangement?

   (*a*) A   (*b*) B

   (*c*) C   (*d*) D

   (*e*) E

13. Which of the following would be the **SECOND** sentence after rearrangement?

   (*a*) A   (*b*) B

   (*c*) C   (*d*) D

   (*e*) F

14. Which of the following would be the **THIRD** sentence after rearrangement?

   (*a*) A   (*b*) B

   (*c*) C   (*d*) D

   (*e*) F

15. Which of the following would be the **FOURTH** sentence after rearrangement?

   (*a*) A   (*b*) B

   (*c*) C   (*d*) D

   (*e*) E

Directions (Q. 16 - 20) : *In each of the following sentences there are two blank spaces. Below each sentences there are five pairs of words denoted by numbers* (*a*), (*b*), (*c*), (*d*) *and* (*e*). *Find out which pair of words can be filled up in the blanks in the sentences in the same sequence to make the sentence meaningfully complete.*

16. He was ________of playing ________and loose with the sentiments of his dearest friends.

   (*a*) Innocent; false   (*b*) Guilty; fast

   (*c*) Accused; tight   (*d*) Complained; thick

   (*e*) Proper; right

17. Raising _________ over the funding to media houses, Zee group chairman sought of media licences before they are issued.
    (*a*) burden, opinion　(*b*) concern, scrutiny
    (*c*) matter, opinion　(*d*) charges, regulation
    (*e*) worry, security

18. Everyone even ________ familiar with serious theater is familiar with the effort that it takes to process Shakespearean language ________ live.
    (*a*) remotely; performed
    (*b*) comically; restrained
    (*c*) hardly; directing
    (*d*) so; bring
    (*e*) similarly; spoked

19. The government has decided not to make any ________ changes in the country's tax________
    (*a*) Sweeping; regime
    (*b*) Transparent; hike
    (*c*) Drastically; net
    (*d*) Constitutional; revenue
    (*e*) Existing; structure

20. If criminals are ________to join electoral fray,________is likely to increase.
    (*a*) Compelled, brotherhood
    (*b*) encouraged, harmony
    (*c*) Allowed, extortion
    (*d*) deterred, corruption
    (*e*) Invited, voting

Directions (Q. 21 - 25): *Read each sentence to find out whether there is any grammatical error in it. The error, if any, will be one part of the sentence. The number of that part is the answer. If there is no error, the answer is (e). (Ignore the errors of punctuation, if any.)*

21. Hectic schedules can (*a*)/ take a toll on anybody and (*b*)/ the solutions to this is (*c*)/ a quick holiday to some exotic location. (*d*)/ No error (*e*).

22. (*a*) If Rajeshwari would have come/(*b*) to me I would have/(*c*) given her the/(*d*) help she needed./(*e*) No error.

23. The court has asked the authorities (*a*)/to take appropriate steps to restore natural water resources (*b*)/ so that the water shortage problem (*c*)/ in the state can be solved. (*d*)/ No error (*e*)

24. District police arrested (*a*)/a gang of notorious robbers, (*b*)/who were planning to strike at (*c*)/a house in the vicinity. (*d*)/No error(*e*)

25. Households across the state are either opting for (*a*)/a more modest lifestyle or compromising on (*b*)/the nutritional value of their food in efforts to negate (*c*)/the price rise of essential commodities, cereals, vegetable and fruits. (*d*)/No error (*e*)

Directions (Q. 26-30): *In the following passage, some of the words have been left out, each of which is indicated by a number. Find the suitable word from the options given against each number and fill up the blanks with appropriate words to make the paragraph meaningful.*

Without science there is no future for any society. Even with science, ...(26)... it is controlled by some spiritual impulses, there is no future. One great thing about science is that it does not accept anything on mere ...(27)... everything has to be proved beyond any doubt. All acceptance comes after experiment which has no room for any ...(28)... This is the reason why development of science and technology has revolutionised human life all over the world. There are very few spheres of human activity which have not experienced the impact of such development. However, despite its manifold ...(29)...science has not been able to solve any of man's moral or spiritual problems. Society is still groping in the dark to find out what its future will be. The need, therefore, is to make science ...(30)... for the ultimate truth.

26. (*a*) unless　　　　(*b*) without
    (*c*) if　　　　　　(*d*) before
    (*e*) because

27. (*a*) principles　　(*b*) conjecture
    (*c*) experiment　　(*d*) research
    (*e*) experience

28. (*a*) accepted　　　(*b*) demonstrated
    (*c*) proved　　　　(*d*) performed
    (*e*) understood

29. (*a*) limitations　　(*b*) benefits
    (*c*) shortcomings　(*d*) researches
    (*e*) inventions

30. (*a*) useful　　　　(*b*) worthy
    (*c*) ready　　　　 (*d*) search
    (*e*) Fit

QUANTITATIVE APTITUDE

Directions (Q. 31 – 35) : *In the Bar-chart, total members enrolled in different years from 1990 to 1994 in two gymnasium A and B. Based on this Bar chart solve the following questions-*

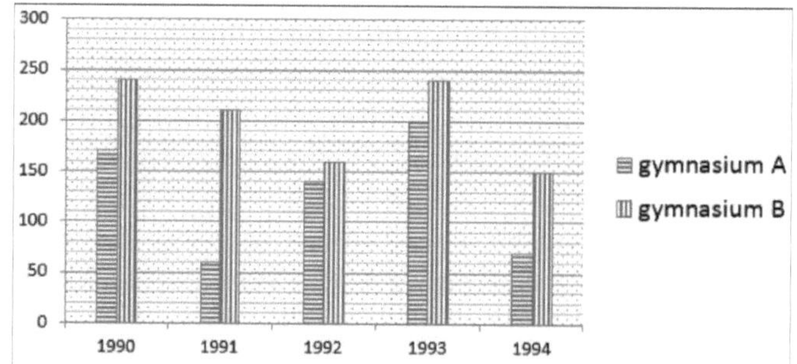

31. In the year 1995, 30% increase in total number of members enrolled in 1994 of both gymnasium, then find the total no. of members enrolled in 1995?

  (*a*) 282　　　　　(*b*) 296

  (*c*) 292　　　　　(*d*) 286

  (*e*) none of these

32. The ratio between total members of both gymnasium in 1991 to total members in 1994 of both gymnasium is-

  (*a*) 22:27　　　　(*b*) 21:11

  (*c*) 11:21　　　　(*d*) 25:13

  (*e*) 27:22

33. The number of members of gymnasium A in 1991 is what % of the no. of members of gymnasium B in 1994.

  (*a*) 60%　　　　(*b*) 55%

  (*c*) 58%　　　　(*d*) 62%

  (*e*) none of these

34. The average of members enrolled in gymnasium A from 1991 to 1994 together is what percent more then the average of members enrolled in gymnasium B in 1993 and 1994 together?(Rounded off to 2 decimal places)

  (*a*) 10.51%　　　　(*b*) 20.51%

  (*c*) 15.51%　　　　(*d*) 17.51%

  (*e*) none of these

35. Total member enrolled in gymnasium B in 1993 and 1994 together is what % more then members enrolled in gymnasium A in 1990 and 1994 together?

  (*a*) 60%

  (*b*) 65%

  (*c*) 62.5%

  (*d*) 61.5%

  (*e*) none of these

Directions (Q. 36 – 40): *What should come in place of question mark (?) in the following number series?*

36. 4, 3, 4, 7, 15, ?

  (*a*) 38.5　　　　(*b*) 40

  (*c*) 45　　　　　(*d*) 37.5

  (*e*) none of these

37. 7, 5, 7, 17, 63, ?

  (*a*) 321　　　　(*b*) 309

  (*c*) 305　　　　(*d*) 301

  (*e*) none of these

38. 11, 14, 19, 28, 43, ?

  (*a*) 60　　　　(*b*) 63

  (*c*) 66　　　　(*d*) 70

  (*e*) none of these

39. 2　60　10　120　30　?

  (*a*) 222　　　　(*b*) 216

  (*c*) 208　　　　(*d*) 230

  (*e*) None of these

40. 23　50　108　232　492　?

  (*a*) 1028　　　　(*b*) 1024

  (*c*) 1020　　　　(*d*) 1032

  (*e*) None of these

Directions (Q. 41 – 45): *There are five companies and we have given the no. of employee working in different companies. In the table we have also given the percentage of male and female employees of HR and Marketing department.*

Company	Employees	HR		Marketing	
		Male	Female	Male	Female
P	400	12	14	9	7
Q	650	19	10	11	13
R	500	28	14	4	7
S	550	31	9	6	4
T	300	12	18	3	7

41. If 60% of the employees of company T in HR department have MBA degree and 40% of the employees of the same company in the Marketing dept. have MBA degree, then how many employees have MBA degree in company T in both dept. together.

  (*a*) 98　　　　(*b*) 108

  (*c*) 106　　　　(*d*) 92

  (*e*) 66

42. The ratio of female employee of company Q in HR dept. to male employee of company R in Marketing dept. ?

  (*a*) 4:13　　　　(*b*) 5:22

  (*c*) 22:5　　　　(*d*) 13:4

  (*e*) none of these

43. Total number of HR employees of company P is what % more then the total no. of marketing employee in company T?

  (*a*) 236.76%　　　　(*b*) 226.67%

  (*c*) 276.76%　　　　(*d*) 246.67%

  (*e*) none of these

44. The ratio of male employee in HR dept. of company P and R together to female employee of Marketing department in company S and T together?

  (*a*) 187:27

  (*b*) 43:188

  (*c*) 188:43

  (*d*) 27:187

  (*e*) none of these

45. Difference between female employees of HR dept. in all companies together (excluding company S) and the female employees of Marketing dept. in all companies together (excluding company Q)?

  (*a*) 139   (*b*) 129

  (*c*) 135   (*d*) 141

  (*e*) none of these

46. A mixture contains wine and water in the ratio 3 : 2 and another mixture contains them in the ratio 4 : 5. How many litres of the latter must be mixed with 3 litres of the former so that the resultant mixture may contain equal quantities of wine and water ?

  (*a*) $1\dfrac{2}{3}$ litre   (*b*) $5\dfrac{2}{5}$ littre

  (*c*) $4\dfrac{1}{2}$ litre   (*d*) $3\dfrac{3}{4}$ litre

  (*e*) None of these

47. A trader sells two bullocks for Rs. 8,400 each, neither losing nor gaining in total. If he sold one of the bullocks at a gain of 20%, the other is sold at a loss of

  (*a*) 20%   (*b*) $18\dfrac{2}{9}\%$

  (*c*) $14\dfrac{2}{7}\%$ (*d*) 21%

  (*e*) None of these

48. Two trains, A and B, start from stations X and Y towards each other, they take 4 hours 48 minutes and 3 hours 20 minutes to reach Y and X respectively after they meet if train A is moving at 45 km/hr., then the speed of the train B is

  (*a*) 60 km/hr   (*b*) 64.8 km/hr

  (*c*) 54 km/hr   (*d*) 37.5 km/hr

  (*e*) None of these

49. Out of his total income, Mr. Kapoor spends 20% on house rent and 70% of the rest on house hold expenses. If he saves Rs 1,800 what is his total income (in rupees)?

  (*a*) Rs 7,800   (*b*) Rs 7,000

  (*c*) Rs 8,000   (*d*) Rs 7,500

  (*e*) None of these

50. A can do a piece of work in 8 days which B can destroy in 3 days. A has worked for 6 days, during the last 2 days of which B has been destroying. How many days must A now work alone to complete the work?

  (*a*) 7 days   (*b*) $7\dfrac{1}{3}$ days

  (*c*) $7\dfrac{2}{3}$ days   (*d*) 8 days

  (*e*) None of these

Directions (Q. 51 – 55): *What approximate value should come in place of the question mark (?) in the following questions? (You are not expected to calculate the exact value.)*

51. 57% of 394 – 2.5% of 996 = ?

  (*a*) 215   (*b*) 175

  (*c*) 200   (*d*) 180

  (*e*) 205

52. 96.996 × 9.669 + 0.96 = ?

  (*a*) 860   (*b*) 870

  (*c*) 1020   (*d*) 940

  (*e*) 1100

53. $\dfrac{3}{5} \times \dfrac{1125}{1228} \times 7 = ?$

  (*a*) 7   (*b*) 12

  (*c*) 9   (*d*) 4

  (*e*) 15

54. $\left(\sqrt{339} \times 25\right) \div 30 = ?$

  (*a*) 12   (*b*) 15

  (*c*) 24   (*d*) 21

  (*e*) 9

55. (638 + 9709 – 216) ÷ 26 = ?

  (*a*) 275   (*b*) 365

  (*c*) 420   (*d*) 300

  (*e*) 390

Directions (Q. 56 – 60): *Solve the equations given below and answer*

  (*a*) if $x > y$ (*b*) if $x < y$

  (*c*) if $x \geq y$ (*d*) if $x \leq y$

  (*e*) $x = y$ or no relation can be established

56. $6x^2 + 31x + 35 = 0$

  $2y^2 + 3y + 1 = 0$

57. $2x^2 - (4 + \sqrt{13})x + 2\sqrt{13} = 0$

  $10y^2 - (18 + 5\sqrt{13})y + 9\sqrt{13} = 0$

58. $2x^2 + 9x + 10 = 0$

  $4y^2 + 28y + 45 = 0$

59. $15x^2 - 11x - 12 = 0$

  $20y^2 - 49y + 30 = 0$

60. $2x^2 - 15 = 7x$

  $17y = -7 - 6y^2$

61. A and B are partners in a business. They invest in the ratio 5 : 6, at the end of 8 months A withdraws. If they receive profits in the ratio of 5 : 9, find how long B's investment was used?

  (*a*) 12 months   (*b*) 10 months

  (*c*) 15 months   (*d*) 14 months

  (*e*) 18 months

62. There are 3 red balls, 4 blue balls and 5 white balls. 2 balls are chosen randomly. Find probability that 1 is red and the other is white.

(a) 5/22
(b) 5/23
(c) 7/22
(d) 4/9
(e) None of these

63. According to a new plan rolled out by HISP Bank, the rate of simple interest on a sum of money is 8% p.a. for the first two years, 10% p.a. for the next three years and 6% p.a. for the period beyond the first five years. Simple interest accrued on a sum for a period of eight years is Rs. 12,800. Find the sum.

(a) Rs. 24, 000
(b) Rs. 16, 000
(c) Rs. 15, 000
(d) Rs. 13,500
(e) None of these

64. Three Science classes A, B and C take a Life Science test. The average score of students of class A is 83. The average score of students class B is 76. The average score of class C is 85. The average score of class A and B is 79 and average score of class B and C is 81. Then the average score. Of classes A, B and C is

(a) 80
(b) 80.5
(c) 81
(d) 81.5
(e) None of these

65. A hemispherical bowl of internal diameter 54 cm contains a liquid. The liquid is to be filled in cylindrical bottles of radius 3 cm and height 9 cm. How many bottles are required to empty the bowl?

(a) 221
(b) 343
(c) 81
(d) 243
(e) None of these

REASONING ABILITY

Directions (Q. 66 – 70): *In these questions, relationship between different elements is shown in the statements. These statements are followed by two conclusions. Mark answer*

(a) If only conclusion I follows.

(b) If only conclusion II follows.

(c) If either conclusion I or II follows.

(d) If neither conclusion I nor II follows.

(e) If both conclusions I and II follow.

66. Statements: $A > B \le C = D \le E, C \ge F = G > H$
Conclusions: I. $G \le E$ II. $A > H$

67. Statements: $H \ge T > S \le Q, T \ge U = V > B$
Conclusions: I. $V > S$ II. $B \le H$

68. Statements: $F < K \le L, H \ge R > K$
Conclusions: I. $H > L$ II. $R > F$

69. Statements: $N \ge P > K = L, P \le Q < Z, T > K$
Conclusions: I. $N > Q$ II. $Z < T$

70. Statements: $P < H = O \ge N, E \ge H < S$
Conclusions: I. $N \le E$ II. $S > P$

Directions (Q. 71-75): *Study the given information carefully to answer the given question.*

J, K, L, M, N, O and P are seven different boxes of different colours i.e. Brown, Orange, Silver, Pink, Yellow, White and Green but not necessarily in the same order.

Box which is of Brown colour is immediately above J. There are only two box between M and the box which is of Brown colour. Box which is of Silver colour is above M but not immediately above M. Only three box are between L and the box which is of Silver colour. The box which is of Green colour is immediately above L. The box which is of Pink colour is immediately above the box G. Only one box is there between K and N. Box K is above N. Neither box K nor J is of Yellow colour. J is not of orange colour.

71. How many box is/are there between M and G?

(a) One
(b) Two
(c) Three
(d) Four
(e) None

72. What is the colour of 'O'?

(a) Green
(b) Brown
(c) Silver
(d) Pink
(e) Can't be determined.

73. Find the pair of colour and boxes which is not correct?

(a) K-Pink
(b) O-Silver
(c) J-white
(d) G-Brown
(e) None of these

74. Which of the following condition is correct regarding yellow colour with respect to N?

(a) There are one person between N and Yellow colour

(b) N is immediately above of yellow colour

(c) Yellow colour related to the person immediately above N

(d) All of the above is true

(e) None of the above is true.

75. Which of the following colour is belong to 'J'?

(a) Brown
(b) Pink
(c) Yellow
(d) Orange
(e) None of these.

Direction (Q. 76 – 78): *Study the following information and answer the given question.*

- T is the sister of D. D is married to P. P is the son of M.
- T is the mother of J. Y is the father of U.
- Y has only one son and only one daughter.
- U is the daughter of T. Q is the son of D.

76. How is P related to T ?

   (*a*) Brother

   (*b*) cannot be determined

   (*c*) Brother-in-law

   (*d*) Cousin brother

   (*e*) Uncle

77. How is J related to D ?

   (*a*) Son   (*b*) Niece

   (*c*) Son-in-law   (*d*) Nephew

   (*e*) Daughter

78. If M is wife of W then how is Q related to W ?

   (*a*) Son-in-law   (*b*) Grandson

   (*c*) Nephew   (*d*) Son

   (*e*) cannot be determined

Directions (Q. 79 – 80) : *Read the given information carefully and answer the given question*

P is 9 m to the south of K. K is 5 m to the east of H. H is 4 m to the north of B. L is 3 m west of B. D is 7 m south of L. G is 8 m east of D.

79. If Point Z is 5 m to the west of point P, then what is the distance between B and Z?

   (*a*) 8 m   (*b*) 9 m

   (*c*) 5 m   (*d*) 2 m

   (*e*) 6 m

80. How far and in which direction is point K from Point G?

   (*a*) 11 m to the south   (*b*) 7 m to the north

   (*c*) 11 m to the north   (*d*) 7 m to the south

   (*e*) 11 m to the west

Directions (Q. 81 - 85): *Study the lowing information to answer the given questions*

S, T, U, V, W, X, Y and Z are sitting in a straight line equidistant from each other (but not necessarily in the same order). Some of them are facing south while some are facing north.

(**Note :** Facing the same direction means, if one is facing north then the other also faces north and vice-versa. Facing the opposite directions means, if one is facing north then the other faces south and vice-versa)

S faces north. Only two people sit to the right of S. T sits third to the left of S. Only one person sits between T and X. X sits to the immediate right of W. Only one person sits between W and Z. Both the immediate neighbors of T face the same direction. U sits third to the left of X. T faces the opposite direction as S. Y does not sit at any of the extremes ends of the line. V faces the same direction as W. Both Y and U face the opposite direction of Z.

81. How many persons in the given arrangement are facing North?

   (*a*) More than four   (*b*) Four

   (*c*) One   (*d*) Three

   (*e*) Two

82. Four of the following five are alike in a certain way, and so form a group. Which of the following does not belong to the group?

   (*a*) W, X   (*b*) Z, Y

   (*c*) T, S   (*d*) T, Y

   (*e*) V, U

83. What is the position of X with respect to Z?

   (*a*) Second to the left

   (*b*) Third to the right

   (*c*) Third to the left

   (*d*) Fifth to the right

   (*e*) Second to the right

84. Who amongst the following sits exactly between Z and W?

   (*a*) T   (*b*) Y

   (*c*) X   (*d*) W

   (*e*) U

85. Who is sitting 2nd to the right of T?

   (*a*) Z   (*b*) V

   (*c*) X   (*d*) W

   (*e*) None of these.

Directions (Q. 86 – 92): *Study the following information carefully to answer the given questions*

W, X, Y, Z, M, N and O are belongs to three different department R&D , Marketing and HR with at least 2 of them in any of these department. Each of them has a favourite Colour such viz. Green, Blue, Red, Pink, Black, Violet and Purple.

X works in departmet Marketing with M. M's favourite Colour is Purple. Those who work in department R&D do not like Green and Pink. The one who likes Blue works only with O in department HR. The one whose favourite Colour is Black does not works in the same department with either M or O. W does not works in department Marketing. W likes Violet. Z and N are work in the same department. N does not like Red. The one whose favourite Colour is Pink does not works in department Marketing.

86. In which department W, Z and N work?

 (*a*) Cannot be determines

 (*b*) R&D

 (*c*) Marketing

 (*d*) HR

 (*e*) None of these

87. Whose favourite Colour is Green ?

 (*a*) X   (*b*) W

 (*c*) Y   (*d*) Z

 (*e*) None of these

88. What is M's favourite Colour?

 (*a*) Violet   (*b*) Pink

 (*c*) Purple   (*d*) Black

 (*e*) None of these

89. Which of the following combination is right ?

 (*a*) W – HR : Blue   (*b*) O – R&D : Black

 (*c*) N – HR : Pink   (*d*) Z – R&D : Red

 (*e*) None of these

90. Y works in which department ?

 (*a*) R & D   (*b*) Marketing

 (*c*) HR   (*d*) Cannot be determined

 (*e*) None of these

91. Whose favourite Colour is Pink ?

 (*a*) X   (*b*) W

 (*c*) O   (*d*) Z

 (*e*) None of these

92. In which department M works?

 (*a*) Cannot be determines

 (*b*) R&D

 (*c*) Marketing

 (*d*) HR

 (*e*) None of these

Directions(Q. 93–97): *Study the following information carefully and answer the questions given below:*

Seven persons, P, Q, R, S, T, U and V are going to attend marriage ceremony but not necessarily in the same order, in seven different months (of the same year) namely January, February, March, June, August, October and December, Each of them also likes a different fruit namely Banana, Grapes, Papaya, Orange, Mango, Litchi and Apple but not necessarily in the same order. R is going to attend marriage in a month which has less than 31 days. Only two persons are going to attend marriage ceremony between the month in which R and S attends marriage ceremony. The one who likes Banana is going to attend marriage ceremony immediately before T. Only one person attends ceremony before the one who likes Papaya.

Q attends ceremony immediately after the one who likes Papaya. Only three persons attends marriage ceremony between Q and the one who likes Mango. T likes neither Mango nor Papaya. P attends ceremony immediately before T. V likes Apple. The one who likes Grapes attends ceremony in the month, which has less than 31 days. The one who attends ceremony in March does not like Orange.

93. Which of the following represents the month in which S attends marriage ceremony ?

 (*a*) January   (*b*) Cannot be determined

 (*c*) October   (*d*) December

 (*e*) June

94. Which of the following represents the people who attends ceremony in January and June respectively ?

 (*a*) V, S   (*b*) U, S

 (*c*) Q, T   (*d*) U, R

 (*e*) V, R

95. How many persons attends ceremony between the months in which V and R attend ceremony ?

 (*a*) None   (*b*) Three

 (*c*) Two   (*d*) One

 (*e*) More than three

96. As per the given arrangement, R is related to Banana and P is related to Orange following a certain pattern, which of the following is U related to following the same pattern ?

 (*a*) Mango   (*b*) Litchi

 (*c*) Apple   (*d*) Papaya

 (*e*) Grapes

97. Which of the following fruits, does U like ?

 (*a*) Papaya   (*b*) Mango

 (*c*) Banana   (*d*) Grapes

 (*e*) Orange

Directions (Q. 98–100): *Study the given information carefully and answer the given questions.*

Among six books i.e. - A, B, C, D, E and F kept in library shelf of different size. Book A is kept at that shelf which is only less in size than shelf in which book D is kept. Only three shelfs are less in size than shelf in which book C is kept. Shelf in which F is kept is less in size than shelf in which book E is kept. Book F is not kept at the lowest shelf.

98. Who amongst the following book is kept at lowest shelf?

 (*a*) B   (*b*) A

 (*c*) E   (*d*) C

 (*e*) None of these

99. If size of shelf in which book E is kept is 16 cm2, then which of the following may be the size of shelf in which book B is kept?

(*a*) 19 cm^2

(*b*) 22 cm^2

(*c*) 18 cm^2

(*d*) 17 cm^2

(*e*) 12 cm^2

100. How many shelf are less in size than shelf in which book E is kept?

(*a*) One

(*b*) Two

(*c*) Three

(*d*) Four

(*e*) More than four

ANSWERS

1. (*c*)	**2.** (*a*)	**3.** (*e*)	**4.** (*d*)	**5.** (*e*)	**6.** (*b*)	**7.** (*c*)	**8.** (*a*)	**9.** (*a*)	**10.** (*d*)
11. (*c*)	**12.** (*a*)	**13.** (*e*)	**14.** (*b*)	**15.** (*d*)	**16.** (*b*)	**17.** (*b*)	**18.** (*a*)	**19.** (*a*)	**20.** (*c*)
21. (*c*)	**22.** (*a*)	**23.** (*e*)	**24.** (*c*)	**25.** (*c*)	**26.** (*a*)	**27.** (*b*)	**28.** (*c*)	**29.** (*b*)	**30.** (*e*)
31. (*d*)	**32.** (*e*)	**33.** (*e*)	**34.** (*b*)	**35.** (*c*)	**36.** (*a*)	**37.** (*b*)	**38.** (*c*)	**39.** (*e*)	**40.** (*a*)
41. (*e*)	**42.** (*d*)	**43.** (*d*)	**44.** (*c*)	**45.** (*a*)	**46.** (*b*)	**47.** (*c*)	**48.** (*c*)	**49.** (*d*)	**50.** (*b*)
51. (*c*)	**52.** (*d*)	**53.** (*d*)	**54.** (*b*)	**55.** (*e*)	**56.** (*b*)	**57.** (*c*)	**58.** (*c*)	**59.** (*e*)	**60.** (*e*)
61. (*a*)	**62.** (*a*)	**63.** (*e*)	**64.** (*d*)	**65.** (*e*)	**66.** (*a*)	**67.** (*d*)	**68.** (*b*)	**69.** (*d*)	**70.** (*e*)
71. (*b*)	**72.** (*c*)	**73.** (*a*)	**74.** (*c*)	**75.** (*e*)	**76.** (*c*)	**77.** (*d*)	**78.** (*b*)	**79.** (*c*)	**80.** (*c*)
81. (*b*)	**82.** (*d*)	**83.** (*b*)	**84.** (*a*)	**85.** (*b*)	**86.** (*b*)	**87.** (*a*)	**88.** (*c*)	**89.** (*d*)	**90.** (*c*)
91. (*c*)	**92.** (*c*)	**93.** (*d*)	**94.** (**e**)	**95.** (*c*)	**96.** (*b*)	**97.** (*a*)	**98.** (*a*)	**99.** (*e*)	**100.** (*b*)

SOLUTIONS

For questions (11-15)- the correct sequence is: CFBDEA

16. 'Guilty, fast' is the correct use. Here, Guilty will be most appropriate word because he didn't play well, where Fast and lose means to treat something without enough care or attention.

18. remotely; performed is the correct option waning; precipitously

19. For the second blank, the suitable words are 'regime' and 'structure' but for the first blank 'existing' is not suitable.

20. The correct use is 'allowed, extortion' where 'extortion' means the practice of obtaining something, especially money, through force or threats.

21. 'Solutions' should be replaced by 'solution' so that the sentence becomes correct.

22. Change 'if Rajeshwari would have' into 'If Rajeshwari had'.

23. No error.

24. Remove 'at' from the expression. With 'at' the meaning comes as 'to' attack someone.

25. Efforts' should be replaced by 'an effort' because this is singularly related here.

31. Required members = $\dfrac{130}{100} \times 220 = 286$

32. Required Ratio = $\dfrac{60 + 210}{70 + 150} = \dfrac{270}{220} = 27 : 22$

33. Required % = $\dfrac{60}{150} \times 100 = 20 \times 2 = 40\%$

34. Required %

$$= \dfrac{(60 + 140 + 200 + 70) - (240 + 150)}{(240 + 150)} \times 100$$

$$= \dfrac{470 - 390}{390} \times 100$$

$$= \dfrac{80}{390} \times 100$$

$$= 20.51\%$$

35. Required % = $\dfrac{(240 + 150) - (170 + 70)}{(170 + 70)} \times 100$

$$= \dfrac{150}{240} \times 100 = 62.5\%$$

38. +3,   + 5,   +9,   + 15........
+2,   +4,   +6........
15 + 8 = 23,   43 + 23 = 66.

39. $1^3 + 1$, $4^3 - 4$, $2^3 + 2$, $5^3 - 5$, $3^3 + 3$, $6^3 - 6$

$$6^3 - 6 = 210$$

41. Required no. of employees

$$= \dfrac{60}{100} \times \dfrac{30}{100} \times 300 + \dfrac{40}{100} \times \dfrac{10}{100} \times 300$$

$$= 54 + 12 = 66$$

42. Required Ratio = $65 : 20 = 13 : 4$

43. HR employees in company P = $26 \times 4 = 104$
Marketing employee in company T = $10 \times 3 = 30$

$$\text{Required \%} = \dfrac{104 - 30}{30} \times 100 = 246.67\%$$

44. Required Ratio = $\dfrac{48 + 140}{22 + 21} = \dfrac{188}{43} = 188 : 43$

45. Required difference

$$= (56 + 65 + 70 + 54) - (28 + 35 + 22 + 21)$$

$$= 245 - 106 = 139$$

46.

$$\dfrac{3}{5} \qquad \dfrac{4}{9}$$

$$\dfrac{1}{2}$$

$$\left(\dfrac{1}{2} - \dfrac{4}{9} = \dfrac{1}{18}\right) \quad \left(\dfrac{3}{5} - \dfrac{1}{2} = \dfrac{1}{10}\right)$$

$$\text{Ratio} = \dfrac{1}{18} : \dfrac{1}{10} = 10 : 18 = 5 : 9$$

$$\text{Required Quantity} = \dfrac{3}{5} \times 9 = \dfrac{27}{5} = 5\dfrac{2}{4} \text{ litre}$$

47. S.P. of two bullock = $8400 + 8400$

$$= \text{Rs. } 16800$$

CP of first bullock = $\dfrac{100}{120} \times 8400 = 7000$

CP of second bullock = $16800 - 7000$

$$\text{Required \% loss} = \dfrac{9800 - 8400}{9800} \times 100$$

$$= \dfrac{1400}{9800} \times 100$$

$$= \dfrac{7}{49} \times 100$$

$$= \dfrac{100}{7} = 14\dfrac{2}{7}\%$$

48.
$$\frac{s_2}{s_1} = \sqrt{\frac{\frac{24}{5}}{\frac{10}{3}}} = \sqrt{\frac{72}{50}}$$

$$\frac{s_2}{s_1} = \sqrt{\frac{36}{25}} = \frac{6}{5}$$

$$s_2 = \frac{45 \times 6}{5}$$

$$= 54 \text{ km/hr}$$

49.   Saving % $= 100 - (20 + 56) = 24\%$

$\therefore \qquad 24\% = 1800$

$\therefore \qquad 100\% = \dfrac{1800}{24} \times 100$

$$= \text{Rs. } 7500$$

50. In 6 days part of the work done by

$$A = \frac{6}{8} = \frac{3}{4}$$

during 2 days, part of the work destroyed by

$$B = \frac{2}{3}$$

$$\text{work done} = \frac{3}{4} - \frac{2}{3} = \frac{9-8}{12} = \frac{1}{12}$$

$$\text{Remaining work} = 1 - \frac{1}{12} = \frac{11}{12}$$

$\therefore$ Required no of days $= \dfrac{11}{12} \times 8 = 7\dfrac{1}{3}$ days.

51.
$$? = \frac{394 \times 57}{100} - \frac{996 \times 2.5}{100}$$

$$= \frac{400 \times 57}{100} - \frac{1000 \times 2.5}{100}$$

$$= 228 - 25 = 203$$

$\therefore$ Required answer $= 200$

52. $\qquad ? = 97 \times 10 + 1 = 971$

$\therefore$ Required answer $= 940$

53. $\qquad ? = \dfrac{3}{5} \times \dfrac{1125}{1228} \times 7 = 4$

54. $\qquad ? = \dfrac{\sqrt{339} \times 25}{30} = 15$

55. $\qquad ? = \dfrac{638 + 9709 - 216}{26} = 390$

56. $6x^2 + 21x + 12x + 35 = 0$

$3x(2x + 7) + 5(2x + 7) = 0$

$\qquad (3x + 5)(2x + 7) = 0$

$$x = \frac{-5}{3}, \frac{-7}{2}$$

$2y^2 + 2y + y + 1 = 0$

$2y(y + 1) + 1(y + 1) = 0$

$\qquad (2y + 1)(y + 1) = 0$

$$y = \frac{-1}{2}, -1$$

$$x < y$$

57. $2x^2 - 4x - \sqrt{13}x + 2\sqrt{13} = 0$

$2x(x - 2) - \sqrt{13}(x - 2) = 0$

$$x = 2, \frac{\sqrt{13}}{2}$$

$10y^2 - 18y - 5\sqrt{13}y + 9\sqrt{13} = 0$

$2y(5y - 9) - \sqrt{13}(5y - 9) = 0$

$$y = \frac{9}{5}, \frac{\sqrt{13}}{2}$$

$$x \geq y$$

58. $2x^2 + 4x + 5x + 10 = 0$

$2x(x + 2) + 5(x + 2) = 0$

$$x = -2, \frac{-5}{2}$$

$4y^2 + 28y + 45 = 0$

$4y^2 + 18y + 10y + 45 = 0$

$2y(2y + 9) + 5(2y + 9) = 0$

$$y = \frac{-5}{2}, \frac{-9}{2}$$

$$x \geq y$$

59. $15x^2 - 20x + 9x - 12 = 0$

$5x(3x - 4) + 3(3x - 4) = 0$

$$x = \frac{-3}{5}, \frac{4}{3}$$

$20y^2 - 25y - 24y - 30 = 0$

$5y(4y - 5) - 6(4y - 5) = 0$

$$y = \frac{6}{5}, \frac{5}{4}$$

No relation can be established

60. $2x^2 - 10x + 3x - 15 = 0$

$2x(x - 5) + 3(x - 5) = 0$

$$x = -\frac{3}{5}, 5$$

$6y^2 + 14y + 3y + 7 = 0$

$2y(3y + 7) + 1(3y - 7) = 0$

$$y = -\frac{1}{2}, \frac{-7}{3},$$

No relation can be established

61. $5x : 6x$,

Let B investment was used for y months

$$8 \times 5x : 6x \times y = 5 : 9$$

$$\frac{40x}{6xy} = \frac{5}{9}$$

$$y = 12$$

62. $P = \dfrac{{}^3C_1 \times {}^5C_1}{{}^{12}C_2} = \dfrac{5}{22}$

63. Let the sum be 'x' Rs.

$$\frac{x \times 8 \times 2}{100} + \frac{x \times 10 \times 3}{100} + \frac{x \times 6 \times 3}{100} = 12800$$

$$\frac{64x}{100} = 12800$$

$$\text{Sum} = 12800 \times \frac{100}{64}$$

$$= 20000 \text{ Rs.}$$

64. Let number of students in class A, B and C be x, y and z

$\therefore$

$$A = 83x$$
$$B = 76y$$
$$C = 85z$$

Now,

$$A + B = 79x + 79y$$
$$B + C = 81(y + z)$$
$$= 81y + 81z$$

$\therefore$

$$83x + 76y = 79x + 79y$$
$$4x = 3y$$
$$\frac{x}{y} = \frac{3}{4}$$

And,

$$76y + 85z = 81y + 81z$$
$$5y = 4z$$
$$\frac{y}{z} = \frac{4}{5}$$

$\therefore$

$$x : y : z = 3 : 4 : 5$$

$\therefore$ Required average

$$= \frac{83 \times 3 + 76 \times 4 + 85 \times 5}{12}$$

$$= \frac{249 + 304 + 425}{12}$$

$$= \frac{978}{12} = 81.5$$

65. Volume of hemi-sphere $= \dfrac{2}{3} \times \pi \times (27)^3 \text{ cm}^3$

Volume of cylindrical bottle $= \pi r^2 h$

$$= \pi \times (3)^2 \times 9$$

$\therefore$ Required number of bottles

$$= \frac{\dfrac{2}{3} \pi \times (27)^3}{\pi \times (3)^2 \times 9}$$

$$= 2 \times 3 \times 27$$

$$= 162 \text{ bottles}$$

Questions (66 – 70):

66. I. G = F ≤ C = D ≤ E (TRUE)

II. A > B ≤ C = D ≤ E (FALSE)

67. I. V = U ≤ T > S (FALSE)

II. B < V = U ≤ T ≤ H (FALSE)

68. I. H ≥ R > K ≤ L (FALSE)

II. R > K > F (TRUE)

69. I. N ≥ P ≤ Q (FALSE)

II. Z > Q ≥ P > K < T (FALSE)

70. I. N ≤ O = H ≤ E (TRUE)

II. S > H > P (TRUE)

Questions (71-75):

Boxes	Colours
O	Silver
K	Orange
M	Yellow
N	Green
L	Pink
G	Brown
J	White

Questions (76 – 78):

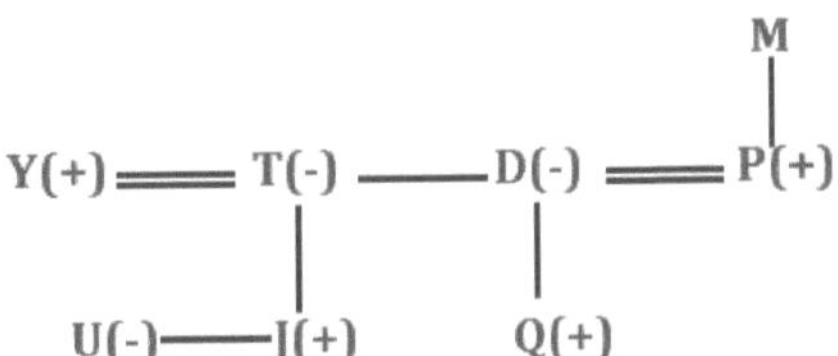

Questions (79 – 80) :

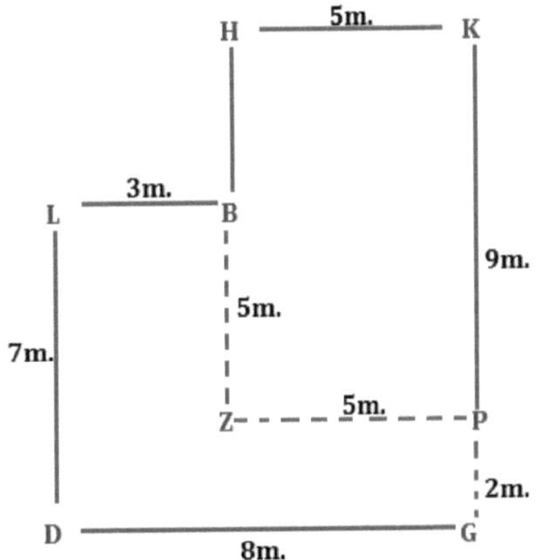

Questions (81 – 85) :

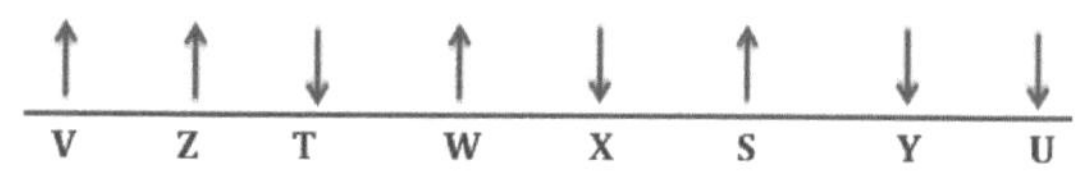

Questions (86 – 92):

Persons	Department	Colour
W	R&D	Violet
X	Marketing	Green
Y	HR	Blue
Z	R&D	Red
M	Marketing	Purple
N	R&D	Black
O	HR	Pink

Questions (93 – 97):

Months in which persons are attending ceremony	Different Persons	Fruits
January	V	Apple
February	U	Papaya
March	Q	Litchi
June	R	Grapes
August	P	Banana
October	T	Orange
December	S	Mango

Questions (98 – 100):

Size of shelf in which different books are kept:

D's shelf >A's shelf >C's shelf >E's shelf >F's shelf >B's shelf

Directions (Q. 1-5): *Read the passage given below and answer the questions that follow based on the information given in the passage.*

Right through history, imperial powers have clung to their possessions to death. Why, then, did Britain in 1947 give up the jewel in its crown, India? For many reasons. The independence struggle exposed the hollowness of the white man's burden. Provincial self-rule since 1935 paved the way for full self-rule. Churchill resisted independence, but the Labour Government of Atlee was anti-imperialist by ideology. Finally, the Royal Indian Navy Mutiny in 1946 raised fears of a second Sepoy Mutiny, and convinced British waverers that it was safer to withdraw gracefully. But politico-military explanations are not enough. The basis of empire was always money. The end of empire had much to do with the fact that British imperialism had ceased to be profitable. World War II left Britain victorious but deeply indebted, needing Marshall Aid and loans from the World Bank. This constituted a strong financial case for ending the no longer-profitable empire.

Empire building is expensive. The US is spending one billion dollar a day in operations in Iraq that fall well short of fullscale imperialism. Through the centuries, empire building was costly, yet constantly undertaken because it promised high returns. The investment was in armies and conquest. The returns came through plunder and taxes from the conquered. No immorality was attached to imperial loot and plunder. The biggest conquerors were typically revered (hence titles like Alexander the Great, Akbar the Great, and Peter the Great). The bigger and richer the empire, the more the plunderer was admired. This mindset gradually changed with the rise of new ideas about equality and governing for the public good, ideas that culminated in the French and the American Revolutions. Robert Clive was impeached for making a little money on the side, and so was Warren Hastings. The white man's burden came up as a new moral rationale for conquest. It was supposedly for the The Princeton Review CAT sample paper 12 good of the conquered. This led to much muddled hypocrisy. On the one hand, the empire needed to be profitable. On the other hand, the white man's burden made brazen loot impossible.

An additional factor deterring loot was the 1857 Sepoy Mutiny. Though crushed, it reminded the British vividly that they were a tiny ethnic group who could not rule a gigantic subcontinent without the support of important locals. After 1857, the British stopped annexing one princely state after another, and instead treated the princes as allies. Land revenue was fixed in absolute terms, partly to prevent local unrest and partly to promote the notion of the white man's burden. The empire proclaimed itself to be a protector of the Indian peasant against exploitation by Indian elites. This was denounced as hypocrisy by nationalists like Dadabhai Naoroji in the 19th century, who complained that land taxes led to an enormous drain from India to Britain. Objective calculations by historians like Angus Maddison suggest a drain of perhaps 1.6 percent of Indian Gross National Product in the 19th century.

But land revenue was more or less fixed by the Raj in absolute terms, and so its real value diminished rapidly with inflation in the 20th century. By World War II, India had ceased to be a profit centre for the British Empire. Historically, conquered nations paid taxes to finance fresh wars of the conqueror. India itself was asked to pay a large sum at the end of World War I to help repair Britain's finances.

But, as shown by historian Indivar Kamtekar, the independence movement led by Gandhiji changed the political landscape, and made mass-taxation of India increasingly difficult. By World War II, this had become politically impossible. Far from taxing India to pay for World War II, Britain actually began paying India for its contribution of men and goods. Troops from white dominions like Australia, Canada and New Zealand were paid for entirely by these countries, but Indian costs were shared by the British government. Britain paid in the form of non-convertible sterling balances, which mounted swiftly. The conqueror was paying the conquered, undercutting the profitability on which all empire is founded. Churchill opposed this, and wanted to tax India rather than owe it money.

But he was overruled by Indian hands, who said India would resist payment, and paralyze the war effort. Leo Amery, Secretary of State for India, said that when you are driving in a taxi to the station to catch a life-or-death train, you do not loudly announce that you have doubts whether to pay the fare. Thus, World War II converted India from a debtor to a creditor with over one billion pound in sterling balances. Britain, meanwhile, became the biggest debtor in the world. It's not worth ruling over people who are afraid to tax.

(The topic of the Passage asked in the exam was based on African banks)

1. Which of the following was NOT a reason for the emergence of the 'white man's burden' as a new rationale for empire building in India?

(*a*) The emergence of the idea of the public good as an element of governance.

(*b*) The decreasing returns from imperial loot and increasing costs of conquest.

(*c*) The weakening of the immorality attached to an emperor's looting behaviour.

(*d*) A growing awareness of the idea of equality among peoples.

(*e*) None of these

2. Which of the following best expresses the main purpose of the author?

(*a*) To present the various reasons that can lead to the collapse of an empire and the granting of independence to the subjects of an empire.

(*b*) To point out the critical role played by the 'white man's burden' in making a colonizing power give up its claims to native possessions.

(*c*) To highlight the contradictory impulse underpinning empire building which is a costly business but very attractive at the same time.

(*d*) To illustrate how erosion of the financial basis of an empire supports the granting of independence to an empire's constituents.

(*e*) None of these

3. What was the main lesson the British learned from the Sepoy Mutiny of 1857?

(*a*) That the local princes were allies, not foes.

(*b*) That the land revenue from India would decline dramatically.

(*c*) That the British were a small ethnic group.

(*d*) That India would be increasingly difficult to rule. The Princeton Review CAT sample paper 13

(*e*) None of these

4. Which of the following best captures the meaning of the 'white man's burden', as it is used by the author?

(*a*) The British claim to a civilizing mission directed at ensuring the good of the natives.

(*b*) The inspiration for the French and the American Revolutions.

(*c*) The resource drain that had to be borne by the home country's white population.

(*d*) An imperative that made open looting of resources impossible.

(*e*) None of these

5. Why didn't Britain tax India to finance its World War II efforts?

(*a*) Australia, Canada and New Zealand had offered to pay for the Indian troops.

(*b*) India had already paid a sufficiently large sum during World War I.

(*c*) It was afraid that if India refused to pay, Britain's war efforts would be jeopardised.

(*d*) The British empire was built on the premise that the conqueror pays the conquered.

(*e*) None of these

Directions (6-13): *Read the following passage carefully and answer the given questions.*

Today emerging markets account for more than half of world GDP on the basis of purchasing power according to the International Monetary Fund (IMF). In the1990s it was about a third and in the late 1990s 30% of countries in the developing world managed to increase their output per person faster than America did, thus achieving what is called 'catch-up growth'. That catching up was somewhat lackadaisical. The gap closed at just 1.5% a year. Some of this was due to slower grower in America, most was not. The most impressive growth was in four of the biggest emerging economies Brazil, Russia, India and China (BRICS). These economies have grown in different ways and for different reasons. The remarkable growth of emerging markets in general and the BRICS in particular transformed the global economy in many ways. Some wrenching commodity prices soared and the cost of manufacturers and labour sank. A growing and vastly more accessible pool of labour in emerging economies played a part in both wage stagnation and rising income inequality in rich ones. Global poverty rates tumbled. Gaping economic imbalances fuelled an era of financial vulnerability and laid the ground work for global crisis. The shift towards the emerging economies will continue. But its most tumultuous phase seems to have more or less reached its end.

Growth rates have dropped, the nature of their growth is in the process of changing too and its new mode will have lesser direct effects on the rest of the world. The likelihood of growth in other emerging economies having an effect in the near future comparable to that of the BRICS in the recent past is low. The emerging giants will grow larger and their ranks will swell but their tread will no longer shake the Earth as it once did.

After the 1990s there followed 'convergence with a vengeance'. China's pivot towards liberalization and global markets came at a propitious time in terms of politics, business and technology. Rich economies were feeling relatively relaxed about globalization and current account deficits. America's booming and confident was little troubled by the growth of Chinese industry or by off-shoring jobs to India. And the technology etc., necessary to assemble and maintain complex supply chains were coming into their own, allowing firms to spread their operations between countries and across oceans. The tumbling costs of shipping and communication sparked 'globalization's second unbounding' (the fiat was the simple ability to provide consumers in one place with goods from another). As longer supply chains infiltrated and connected places with large and fast growing working-age populations, enormous quantities of cheap new labour became accessible. In 2007 China's economy expanded by an eye-popping 14.2%. India managed 10.1% growth, Russia 8.5% and Brazil 6.1%. The IMF now reckons there will be a slowdown in growth. China will grow by just 7.6% in 2013 India by 5.6% and Russia and Brazil by 2.5%. Other countries have impressive growth potential. 'Next 11' (N 11) which includes Bangladesh, Indonesia, Mexico, Nigeria and Turkey. But there are various reasons to think that this N11 cannot have an impact on the same scale as that of the BRICS. The first is that these economies are smaller. The N11 has a population of just over 1.3 billion, less than half that of the BRICS. The second is that the N11 is richer now than the BRICS were back in the day. The third reason that the performance of the BRICS cannot be repeated is the very success of that performance. The world economy is much larger than it used to be twice as in real terms as it was in 1992 according to IMF figures. But whether or not the world can build remarkable era of growth will depend in large part on whether new giants tread a path towards greater global co-operation or stumble in times of tumult and in the worst case fight.

(The topic of the Passage asked in the exam was based on Brain drain in China)

6. According to the passage which of the following is a reason for the author's prediction regarding N11 countries?

(*a*) N11 countries are poorer, have less resources than BRICS countries and do not have much scope to grow

(*b*) The size of these countries is too great to fuel a high rate of growth as expected by BRICS countries

(*c*) The world economy is so large that the magnitude of growth from these countries will have to be huge to equal the growth of BRICS

(*d*) These economies are agricultural and have not opened up their economies yet so their scope of growth is greater than that of BRICS

(*e*) Other than those given as options

7. What is the author's view of globalization's second unbounding?

(*a*) It proved beneficial since it created a large number of jobs and tremendous growth in crossborder trade

(*b*) It disturbed the fragile balance of power among BRICS nations and caused internal strife

(*c*) It caused untold damage to America's economy since it restricted the spread of American firms off-shore

(*d*) It proved most beneficial for the agricultural sector creating huge employment opportunities

(*e*) Citizens in advanced countries became much better off than those in emerging economies

8. What do the comparative statistics of 2007 and 2013 for BRICS countries published by the IMF as cited in the passage indicate?

(*a*) BRICS economies are contributing less to global growth

(*b*) As the population of these countries grows its growth rate is falling

(*c*) The financial practices followed by these countries will continue to pay rich dividends

(*d*) These countries are creating global financial imbalances to the detriment of smaller developing economies like Africa

(*e*) IMF forecasts of growth rate for these countries have not been fulfilled

9. What effect did rise in economies of BRICS have on the global economy?

  (*a*) It helped stabilize the globle economy and insulate it from the fall out of the global financial crisis

  (*b*) Labour became more highly skilled and wages rose alarmingly reducing the off-shoring of jobs to developing countries

  (*c*) Though worldwide poverty rates tumbled, the gap between the rich and the poor in rich economies increased

  (*d*) The cost of living and level of inflation in these countries were maintained at low levels

  (*e*) All the given options are effects of the rise in BRICS economies

10. What does the phrase "their ranks will swell but their tread will no longer shake the Earth as it once did" convey in the context of the passage?

  (*a*) While many countries will try and achieve the same rate of growth as BRICS they will not succeed

  (*b*) The growth of BRICS countries has changed the world's economy in ways that any further growth will not have such a disruptive effect on the world economy

  (*c*) Developing countries have strengthened their fiscal systems in such a way that they will not be shaken to such an extent again

  (*d*) Poverty may increase as the gap between the rich the poor increase but it will never reach the same levels as prior to the crisis

  (*e*) Citizens in advanced countries became much better off than those in emerging economies

11. Which of the following best describes 'catch up growth'?

  (*a*) Emerging economies tried but failed to catch up with America which always grew at a higher growth rate

  (*b*) The size of emerging economies and their purchasing power has caught up with and now exceeds as rich countries together

  (*c*) The growth of the America economy determines the growth of emerging economies

  (*d*) In the latter half of the 1990s some emerging economies out did America in terms of output per person

  (*e*) None of the given statements describes catch up growth

12. Which of the following can be said about 'convergence with a vengeance'?

  A. After the 1990s advanced economies like America were open to the idea of free trade and globalization.

  B. There were huge technological advances which were conducive to allowing business to spread their area of operations.

  C. Rich economies felt threatened by the competition from China.

  (*a*) Only A   (*b*) Only B

  (*c*) Only C   (*d*) A and B

  (*e*) B and C

13. What is the author's main objective in writing this passage?

  A. To urge emerging economies to deal with growth which can be disruptive maturely and without conflict.

  B. To point out that while the period of growth of BRICS was disruptive this disruption has almost come to a close.

  C. To criticize advanced economies for their handling of growth and promoting competition and conflict in certain regions.

  (*a*) A and B   (*b*) Only A

  (*c*) Only C   (*d*) All A, B and C

  (*e*) B and C

Directions (Q. 14-20): *In each of the following questions five options are given, of which one word is most nearly the same or opposite in meaning to the given word in the question. Find the correct option having either same or opposite meaning.*

14. Snitch

  (*a*) Bode   (*b*) Stitch

  (*c*) Suffix   (*d*) Sneak

  (*e*) Parity

15. Porch

  (*a*) Peek   (*b*) Demur

  (*c*) Verandah   (*d*) Capitulate

  (*e*) Bigotry

16. Vituperate

  (*a*) Examine   (*b*) Variegate

  (*c*) Belittle   (*d*) Compliment

  (*e*) Baleful

17. Conundrum

  (*a*) Abjure   (*b*) Quash

  (*c*) Riddle   (*d*) Thrill

  (*e*) Vendetta

18. Praise

   (*a*) Portend   (*b*) Lash

   (*c*) Fidget   (*d*) Creak

   (*e*) Visage

19. Notional

   (*a*) Quixotic   (*b*) Unworldly

   (*c*) Ethereal   (*d*) Impalpable

   (*e*) Cosmic

20. Vacillate

   (*a*) Dally   (*b*) Hem

   (*c*) Dither   (*d*) Sway

   (*e*) Waffle

Directions (Q.21-30): *In each of the following questions a short passage is given with one of the lines in the passage missing and represented by a blank. Select the best out of the five answer choices given, to make the passage complete and coherent (coherent means logically complete and sound).*

21. Business is instead moving to digital-native insurers, many of which are offering low premiums to those willing to collect and share their data. Yet the biggest winners could be tech companies rather than the firms that now dominate the industry. Insurance is increasingly reliant on the use of technology to change behaviour; firms act as helicopter parents to policyholders, warning of impending harm—slow down; reduce your sugar intake; call the plumber—the better to reduce unnecessary payouts. Yet this sort of relationship relies on trust, and the Googles and Apples of the world, on which consumers rely day-by-day and hour-by-hour, may be best placed to win this business.

   (*a*) The growing mountain of personal data available to individuals and, crucially, to firms is giving those with the necessary processing power the ability to distinguish between low-risk and high-risk individuals.

   (*b*) Cheap sensors and the tsunami of data they generate can improve our lives; blackboxes in cars can tell us how to drive more carefully and wearable devices will nudge us toward healthier lifestyles.

   (*c*) The better behaviour resulting from smart devices is just one threat to the insurance industry. Conventional risk pools (for home or car insurance, for example) are shrinking as preventable accidents decline, leaving the slow-footed giants of the industry at risk.

   (*d*) The uncertainty that underpins the need for insurance is now shrinking thanks to better insights into individual risks.

   (*e*) The data has enabled insurance companies to gauge the situation and plan accordingly.

22. By calling for exempting unionized businesses from the minimum wage, unions are creating more incentives for employers to favor unionized workers over the non-unionized sort. Such exemptions strengthen their power. Once employers are obliged to pay the same minimum wage to both unionized and non-unionized labor, workers often see less reason to pay the dues to join a union.

   (*a*) High rates of unionization make minimum-wage rules unnecessary as collaborative wage setting achieves the flexibility goals of a low minimum wage and the fairness goals of a high one.

   (*b*) Workers who have no real alternative to employment in the unregulated shadows of the labor market are even more vulnerable to exploitation and abuse than workers with the legal right to take low wages.

   (*c*) The labor ethos of worker solidarity seems hollow if non-union workers are underpriced by union workers and left unemployed or scrambling for unauthorized work.

   (*d*) This is useful because for all the effort unions throw at raising the minimum wage, laws for better pay have an awkward habit of undermining union clout.

   (*e*) Unions have been demanding democratic vaues in the work cluture but on the contrary they have been practicing dictatorial ways.

23. The premise that the choice of major amounts to choosing a career path rests on the faulty notion that the major is important for its content, and that the acquisition of that content is valuable to employers. But information is fairly easy to acquire and what is acquired in 2015 will be obsolete by 2020. What employers want are basic but difficult-to-acquire skills.

Theycare about a potential employee's abilities: writing, researching, quantitative, and analytical skills. A vocational approach to education eviscerates precisely the qualities that are most valuable about it: intellectual curiosity, creativity and critical thinking.

   (*a*) As students flock to the two or three majors they see as good investments, professors who teach in those majors are overburdened, and the majors themselves become more formulaic and less individualized.

(*b*) Often it is the art historians and anthropology majors, for example, who, having marshaled the abilities of perspective, breadth, creativity, and analysis, have moved a company or project or vision forward.

(*c*) Furthermore, the link between education and earnings is notoriously fraught, with cause and effect often difficult to disentangle.

(*d*) Ideas such as education is necessary to be successful in corporate life are unacceptable because education isn't that much relevant into day's society.

(*e*) When they ask students about their majors, it is usually not because they want to assess the applicants' mastery of the content, but rather because they want to know if the students can talk about what they learned.

24. What happens to our brains as we age is of crucial importance not just to science but to public policy. However,this demographic time- bomb would be much less threatening if the elderly were looked upon as intelligent contributors to society rather than as dependants in long-term decline. It is time we rethink what we mean by the ageing mind before our false assumptions result in decisions and policies that marginalize the old or waste precious public resources to re-mediate problems that do not exist.

(*a*) The idea that we get dumber as we grow older is just a myth, according to brain research that will encourage anyone old enough to know better.

(*b*) By 2030, for example, 72 million people in the US will be over 65, double the figure in 2000 and their average life expectancy will likely have edged above 20 years

(*c*) Many of the assumptions scientists currently make about 'cognitive decline' are seriously flawed and, for the most part, formally invalid.

(*d*) Using computer models to simulate young and old brains, Ramscar and his colleagues found they could account for the decline in test scores simply by factoring in experience

(*e*) The reason it becomes harder to recall an acquaintance's name as you grow older is that there are so many more of them.

25. The expenditure of time, money and sparse judicial and prosecutorial resources is often justified by claims of a powerful deterrent message embodied in the ultimate punishment- the death penalty.

In 2010, the average time between sentencing and execution in the United States averaged nearly 15 years. A much more effective deterrent would be a sentence of life imprisonment imposed close in time to the crime.

(*a*) A single federal death penalty case in Philadelphia was found to cost upwards of $10 million — eight times higher than the cost of trying a death eligible case where prosecutors seek only life imprisonment.

(*b*) The ethics of the issue aside, it is questionable whether seeking the death penalty is ever worth the time and resources that it takes to sentence someone to death.

(*c*) Apart from delaying justice, the death penalty diverts resources that could be used to help the victims' families heal.

(*d*) But studies repeatedly suggest that there is no meaningful deterrent effect associated with the death penalty and further, any deterrent impact is no doubt greatly diluted by the amount of time that inevitably passes between the time of the conduct and the punishment.

(*e*) While some victims and their families supported and some opposed the decision, any expectation that Tsarnaev will be put to death might be misplaced.

26. Five statements are given below, labelled a, b, c, d and e. Among these, four statements are in logical order and form a coherent paragraph/ passage. From the given options, choose the option that does not fit into the theme of the passage.

(*a*) Dinets first observed the behaviour in 2007 when he spotted crocodiles lying in shallow water along the edge of a pond in India with small sticks or twigs positioned across their snouts.

(*b*) The behaviour potentially fooled nest-building birds wading in the water for sticks into thinking the sticks were floating on the water.

(*c*) The crocodiles remained still for hours and if a bird neared the stick, they would lunge.

(*d*) Crocodiles are way clever than thought about generally.

(*e*) To see if the stick-displaying was a form of clever predation, Dinets and his colleagues performed systematic observations of the reptiles for one year at four sites in Louisiana, including two rookery and two non-rookery sites.

27. Five statements are given below, labelled a, b, c, d and e. Among these, four statements are in logical order and form a coherent paragraph/passage. From the given options, choose the option that does not fit into the theme of the passage.

    (*a*) The competitive pressures in the environment have radically altered the context in which human Resource services are delivered in Indian organizations.

    (*b*) The HR competencies, in other words, differentiate outstanding performers from average performers in the HR function.

    (*c*) The traditional role of HR, based on the image of a transaction and administrative oriented HR practitioner providing services to a set of customers, is undergoing change.

    (*d*) With the focus moving towards integrating HR into strategic planning of the organization, another dimension is added to the picture of HR service deliver.

    (*e*) This change in focus calls for HR professionals taking up the emerging roles of advocate, business partner, and change agent in new organizational structures that are radically different from the past.

28. Five statements are given below, labelled a, b, c, d and e. Among these, four statements are in logical order and form a coherent paragraph/passage. From the given options, choose the option that does not fit into the theme of the passage..

    (*a*) Every campaign leader known how to pick up and kiss a child in the crowds, how to hug an old widow, how to chant with the pundits, and show abeyance to the Mullahs.

    (*b*) Did anyone hit at "quality" for infrastructure amenities, education, health and finally governance.

    (*c*) Politics is still a game of money, mind and manipulations.

    (*d*) False promise are not entirely a sin, but let these be redeemed by true, professional, and quality governance, that shows at the end of the tenure.

    (*e*) Many Asian countries have transformed their work culture, and up-scaled their economies.

29. Five statements are given below, labelled a, b, c, d and e. Among these, four statements are in logical order and form a coherent paragraph/passage. From the given options, choose the option that does not fit into the theme of the passage..

    (*a*) The emerging web services paradigm offers the promise of new efficiencies and improve integration designed to enhance collaboration between internal and external applications.

    (*b*) For example web services can serve as a bridge between an e-procurement application and an internal inventory system.

    (*c*) Although, web services are relatively nascent and adoption rates currently low, it is critical for ERP vendors to begin taking steps to prepare for their rapidly maturing initiative.

    (*d*) As items are purchased through e-procurement application, a web service specific to inventory reduction can be invoked to adjust inventory levels.

    (*e*) As soon as re-order points are hit, a Web services, the cycle time between buying and replenishment can be greatly reduced and the potential for errors virtually eliminated.

30. Five statements are given below, labelled a, b, c, d and e. Among these, four statements are in logical order and form a coherent paragraph/passage. From the given options, choose the option that does not fit into the theme of the passage..

    (*a*) Much of the modern use of metals happens behind closed doors of corporations, under the veil of trade secrets.

    (*b*) He chooses to restrict his analysis to metals and metalloids, which could face more critical constraints because many of them are relatively rare.

    (*c*) Even if we can find out how certain metals are used, it may not always be possible to determine theproportions they are used in.

    (*d*) The authors compromise was to account for the use of 80% of the material that is made available each year through extraction and recycling.

    (*e*) Their compromise was to account for the use of 80% of the material that is made available each year through extraction and recycling.

Direction (31-35): *Select the phrase/connector from the given three options which can be used to form a single sentence from the two sentences given below, implying the same meaning as expressed in the statement sentences.*

31. If the issuer issues masala bond in rupees, then he gets rid of the risk in the form of currency fluctuation which he passes on to the investor. This bond brings a new and diversified set of investors for Indian companies and more liquidity in foreign exchange.

(*a*) Risk gets passed on the investor

(*b*) More liquidity in foreign exchange

(*c*) Masala bonds bring a new set of investors

Pick out the option which when used to start a sentence combines both the above sentences in one.

(*a*) Only a

(*b*) Only b

(*c*) Only c

(*d*) Only a and b

(*e*) None of the above

32. Captain Michael allowed his men to make important decisions in a democratic manner. This democratic attitude fostered a spirit of togetherness and commitment on the part of Michael's fellow explorers.

(*a*) As soon as

(*b*) In accordance with

(*c*) Allowing

Pick out the option which when used to start a sentence combines both the above sentences in one.

(*a*) Only a

(*b*) Only b

(*c*) Only c

(*d*) Only a and b

(*e*) None of the above

33. High interest rates on the loan the business procured consumed so much of their revenue that they were forced to liquidate some of their holdings. All this happened when its refinancing attempts failed.

(*a*) The high interest rates of the loan

(*b*) The business was forced to liquidate

(*c*) The high interest rate of the loan

Pick out the option which when used to start a sentence combines both the above sentences in one.

(*a*) Only a

(*b*) Only b

(*c*) Only c

(*d*) Only a and c

(*e*) None of the above

34. Reporting a 90 percent drop in net income during the second quarter, dragged down by restructuring charges and weak sales, the earnings guidance for the year was withdrawn by Best Buy Co.

(*a*) Report of a 90 percent drop in net income

(*b*) Best Buy Co. is reporting a 90 percent drop in net income

(*c*) Best Buy Co. has reported a 90 percent drop in net income

Pick out the option which when used to start a sentence combines both the above sentences in one.

(*a*) Only a

(*b*) Only b

(*c*) Only c

(*d*) Only a and b

(*e*) None of the above

35. Percival Lowell was interested in astronomy due to his belief in canals on Mars. However, modern astronomers dismiss this belief as material for pop science fiction.

(*a*) Percival Lowell was interested in astronomy

(*b*) Percival Lowell's interest in astronomy was due to

(*c*) Percival Lowell was interested in astronomy

Pick out the option which when used to start a sentence combines both the above sentences in one.

(*a*) Only a

(*b*) Only b

(*c*) Only c

(*d*) Only a and c

(*e*) None of the above

DATA ANALYSIS & INTERPRETATION

Direction (36-37): *In a bag there are three types of colored balls of red, white and Bluecolors. The probability of selecting one red ball out of the total ball is* $\frac{1}{2}$ *and the probability of selecting one blue ball out of the total ball is* $\frac{2}{7}$ *.The number of white balls in the bag is 6.*

36. If all the ball are numbered starting from *1, 2, 3,* and so onthen what is the probability of selecting one ball which is numbered as a multiple of 3 or 7 out of the total balls.

(*a*) $\dfrac{3}{7}$

(*b*) $\dfrac{5}{14}$

(*c*) $\dfrac{1}{12}$

(*d*) $\dfrac{6}{11}$

(*e*) none of these

37. What are the total number of balls in the bag?

(a) 28

(b) 30

(c) 35

(d) 40

(e) none of these

38. Given that D is the midpoint of AC and BC is diameter of circle, and circumference of circle is 44cm. quantity1- area of shaded region quantity 2-7π cm²

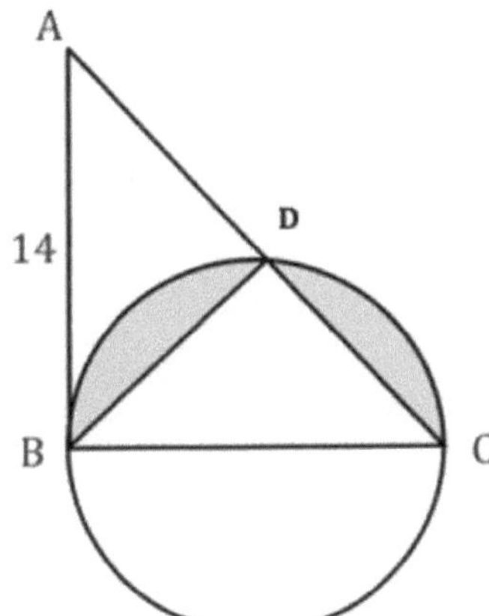

(a) quantity I > *quantityll*

(b) quantity I < *quantityll*

(c) quantityl > quantityll

(d) quantityl < quantityll

(e) quantity I=quantity II or No relation

39. Quantity I = 18x³ y³, Quantity II = 12 x⁴y⁴ ,if x>0 & *y* <0

(a) Quantity I >Quntity II

(b) Quantity I < Quantity II

(c) Quantity I < Quantity II

(d) Quantity I=quantity II or No relation

(e) Quantity I > Quantity II

40. Speed of a boat in still water and speed of current is in ratio 6 : 1. If the difference between distance covered by boat in 2 hours upstream and in 2 hours downstream is 8 km.

Quantity-1- Speed of boat in still water Quantity-2-speed of cyclist who goes 28 km in 2 hrs.

(a) quantity1 > *quantity2*

(b) quantity1 < *quantity2*

(c) quantity1 > quantity2

(d) quantity1 < quantity2

(e) quanity1 = quantity2

Directions (41-45): *Study the following information to answer the given questions.*

Percentage of students in various courses (A, B, C, D, E, F) in pie chart I and percentage of girls in pie chart II.

Total students: 1200 (800 girls + 400 boys)

Chart I

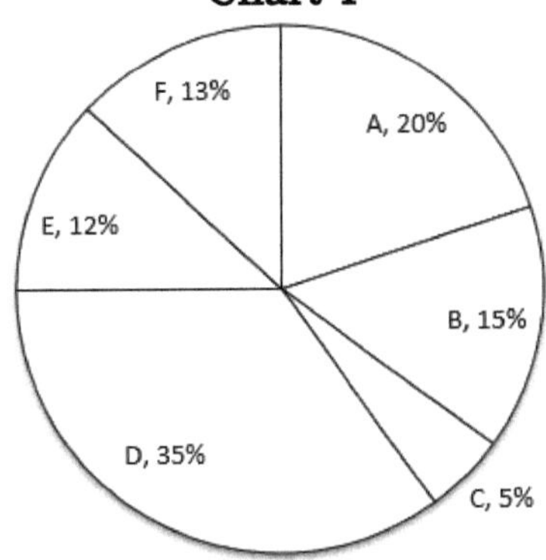

Chart II

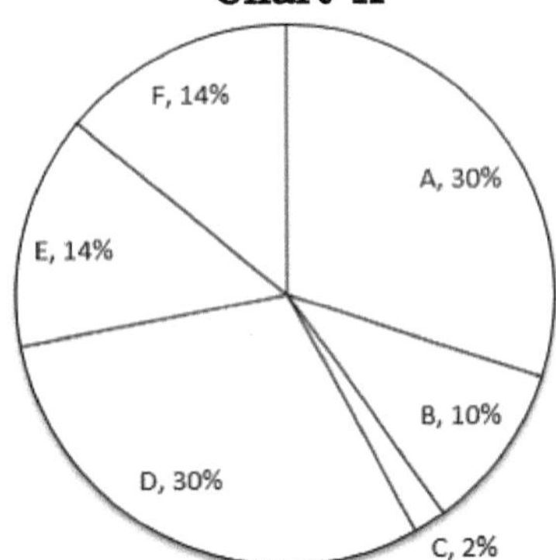

41. For course D, what is the respective ratio of boys and girls?

(a) 3:4   (b) 4:5

(c) 3:5   (d) 5:6

(e) None of these

42. For which pair of courses is the number of boys the same?

(a) E and F   (b) A and D

(c) C and F   (d) B and D

(e) None of these

43. For course E, the number of girls is how much percent more than the number of boys for course E?

(a) 250   (b) 350

(c) 150   (d) 80

(e) None of these

44. For which course is the number of boys the minimum?

(a) E   (b) F

(c) C   (d) A

(e) None of these

45. How many girls are there in course C?

  (*a*) 44   (*b*) 16

  (*c*) 40   (*d*) 160

  (*e*) None of these

Directions (Q. 46 - 50): *Following line graph shows the percentage growth in population of six cities A, B, C, D, E and F from 2011 to 2012 and 2012 to 2013.*

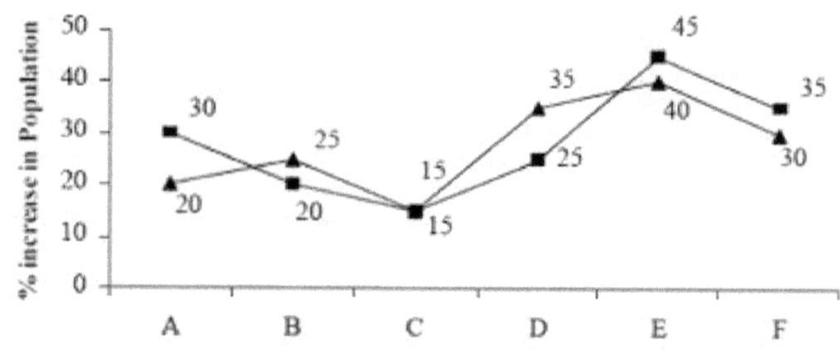

46. If the population of City A is 5.4 lakh in year 2011 then what will be its population in year 2013.

  (*a*) 7.842 lakh   (*b*) 8.424 lakh

  (*c*) 8.765 lakh   (*d*) 9.168 lakh

  (*e*) None of these

47. What is the percentage increase in population of city C from year 2011 to year 2013.

  (*a*) 15%   (*b*) 22.5%

  (*c*) 30%   (*d*) 32.25%

  (*e*) 33.5%

48. If the population of city E and City D are equal in year 2012 then the population of city E is approximately what percentage of population of city D in 2013.

  (*a*) 86.2%   (*b*) 96%

  (*c*) 104%   (*d*) 116%

  (*e*) 124%

49. If the population of city-F in year 2013, is 16.848 lakh then what was its population in year 2011 ?

  (*a*) 7.8 lakh   (*b*) 8.4 lakh

  (*c*) 9.6 lakh   (*d*) 10.2 lakh

  (*e*) 11.4 lakh

50. If the population of city-B and city-D in year 2011 are equal to 6 lakh then what will be the difference between population of city-D in 2013 and population of city-B in 2013 ?

  (*a*) 75500

  (*b*) 97400

  (*c*) 112500

  (*d*) 137600

  (*e*) 148500

Directions(51-52): *Ritu'sexpense out of her total expenditure in a trip is in between travel expenses, Accommodation expenses and shopping expenses are in the ratio of 5 : 4 : 3. Out of the travel expenses he spent 25% on bus tickets, 60% on air tickets and remaining travel expenses are saved. All of the accommodation expenses are spent on hotels. And out of the total expenses on shopping expenses 50% spent on tax free products,$47\frac{2}{9}$ % spent on footpath shopping and remaining are saved.*

The total amount saved is 17500.

51. From the above information, what is the total amount on accommodation expense?

  (*a*) Rs75000   (*b*) Rs84000

  (*c*) Rs90000   (*d*) Rs95000

  (*e*) none of these

52. Ritu's total amount on the trip is.

  (*a*) Rs242000   (*b*) Rs252000

  (*c*) Rs262000   (*d*) Rs275000

  (*e*) none of these

Directions (53 - 57): *Each question below is followed by two statements I and II. You are to determine whether the data given in the statement is sufficient to answer the question. You should use the data and your knowledge of Mathematics to choose between the possible answers.*

Give answer (a) if the statement I alone is sufficient to answer the question, but the statement II alone is not sufficient.

Give answer (b) if the statement II alone is sufficient to answer the question, but the statement I alone is not sufficient.

Give answer (c) if both statements I and II together are needed to answer the question.

Give answer (d) if either the statement I alone or the statement II alone is sufficient to answer the question.

Give answer (e) if you cannot get the answer from the statements I and II together, but need even more data.

53. Tower 'P' is in which direction with respect to tower 'Q'?

  I. P is to the West of H, which is to the South of Q.

  II. F is to the West of Q and to the North of P.

54. How is K related to N?

  I. N is the brother of M, who is the daughter of K.

  II. F is the husband of K

55. In a row of girls facing North, what is D's position from the left end?

   I. D is twentieth from the right end.

   II. There are ten girls between B and D.

56. In a row of 40 students facing North, how many students are there between R and S?

   I. S's position in the row is 15th from the right end.

   II. R's position in the row is 4th from the left end.

57. How far is A from the starting point?

   I. A moves 5 km. towards East, then 2 km. towards left, 10 km, towards right and finally. 2 km, towards right and stops

   II. A moves 2 km. towards East, then 2 km. towards right, 13 km, towards left and finally, 2 km. towards left and stops.

Directions (58-62): *Study the following graph to answer the given questions.*

Percent profit earned by two companies over the given years

$$\% \ \textbf{profit} = \frac{\text{Income} - \text{Expenditure}}{\text{Expenditure}} \times 100$$

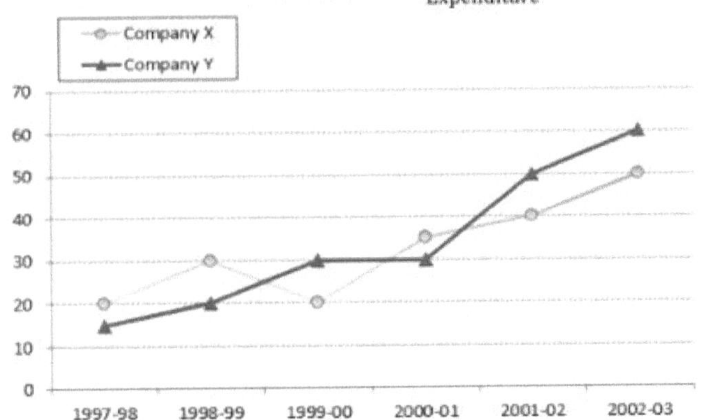

58. If the income of Company X in 1998-99 was equal to the expenditure of Company Y in 2001-2002, what was the ratio of their respective profits?

   (*a*) 13:15

   (*b*) 15:26

   (*c*) 13:26

   (*d*) Cannot be determined

   (*e*) None of

59. For Company X, its income in 2001-2002 was equal to its expenditure in 2002-2003, what was the ratio of its respective incomes in these two years?

   (*a*) 4:5

   (*b*) 3:4

   (*c*) 2:3

   (*d*) Cannot be determined

   (*e*) None of these

60. For Company Y, in which year is the percent of increase in percent profit over that of previous year the highest?

   (*a*) 2002-03

   (*b*) 1999-2000

   (*c*) 2001-02

   (*d*) Cannot be determined

   (*e*) None of these

61. In 1997-98, the expenditure of Company X was Rs. 40 crores. What was its income in that year?

   (*a*) Rs. 50 crore

   (*b*) Rs. 48 crore

   (*c*) Rs. 46 crore

   (*d*) Cannot be determined

   (*e*) None of these

62. What was the difference in the expenditures of the two companies in 1999-2000?

   (*a*) 10

   (*b*) 100

   (*c*) 1000

   (*d*) Cannot be determined

   (*e*) None of these

Direction(63-64): *24 men can do a work in X days and 32 women can do the same work in (X + 8) days. The ratio of work done by 15 men and 12 women in the same time is 3 : 1.*

63. Find the value of X ?

   (*a*) 8

   (*b*) 10

   (*c*) 12

   (*d*) 11

   (*e*) 5

64. 10 men and 24 women works for 6 days on the same work and the remaining work is done by 18 boys in 18 days. Then find the number of days in which 12 boys completed the whole work.

   (*a*) 54

   (*b*) 48

   (*c*) 45

   (*d*) 58

   (*e*) None of the above

Directions (65-70): *Study the following table carefully to answer the questions that follow.*

Number (N) of six type of Electronic Products sold by Six different stores in a month and the price per product (P) (price in Rs '000) charged by each Store

Store	A		B		C		D		E		F	
Product	N	P	N	P	N	P	N	P	N	P	N	P
L	54	135	48	112	60	104	61	124	40	136	48	126
M	71	4.5	53	3.8	57	5.6	49	4.9	57	5.5	45	4.7
N	48	12	47	18	52	15	54	11.5	62	10.5	56	11
O	52	53	55	48	48	50	54	49	59	47	58	51
P	60	75	61	68	56	92	44	84	46	76	59	78
Q	43	16	44	15	45	14.5	48	15.6	55	18.2	55	14.9

65. What is the total amount earned by Store C through the sale of M and O type products together?

(*a*) Rs 2719.2 lakh

(*b*) Rs 271.92 lakh

(*c*) Rs 2.7192 lakh

(*d*) Rs 27.192 lakh

(*e*) None of these

66. Number of L type product sold by Store F is what percent of the number same type of products sold by Store E?

(*a*) 76.33 (*b*) 124

(*c*) 83.33 (*d*) 115

(*e*) None of these

67. What is the difference in the amount earned by Store A through the sale of P type products and that earned by Store B through the sale of Q type products?

(*a*) Rs 38.4 lakh (*b*) Rs 0.384 lakh

(*c*) Rs 3.84 lakh (*d*) Rs 384 lakh

(*e*) None of these

68. What is the respective ratio of total number of N and L type products together sold by Store D and the same products sold by Store A?

(*a*) 119 : 104 (*b*) 102 : 115

(*c*) 104 : 115 (*d*) 117 : 103

(*e*) None of these

69. A milkman buys some milk contained in 10 vessels of equal size. If he sells his milk at Rs 5 a litre, he loses Rs 200; while selling it at Rs6 a litre, he would gain Rs150 on the whole. Find the numberof litres contained in each vessel.

(*a*) 30 (*b*) 35

(*c*) 40 (*d*) 45

(*e*) None of these

70. A watch passes through three hands and each gains 25%. If the third sells it for Rs250, what did the first pay for it?

(*a*) 128 (*b*) 130

(*c*) 145 (*d*) 150

REASONING & COMPUTER APTITUDE

Directions (Q. 71 – 75): *Study the following information to answer the given questions. (each question is worth 1 mark)*

In a certain code language, 'chi na le ba pi' means 'Messi and Ronaldo are rivals', 'ki ba lo tha' means 'both rivals play football', 'da ki chi' means 'Messi plays excellent', 'tha na da' means 'excellent and football' and 'mu ki' means 'children plays'.

71. What is the code for 'Ronaldo'?

(*a*) le (*b*) pi

(*c*) ba (*d*) Either le or pi

(*e*) None of these

72. What is the code for 'both'?

(*a*) ba (*b*) ki

(*c*) lo (*d*) Can't be determined

(*e*) None of these

73. Which of the following is the code for 'Ronaldo and rivals are children'?

(*a*) chi na ki le pi

(*b*) pi le na ba mu

(*c*) ba mu le ki pi

(*d*) chi pi le ba mu

(*e*) None of these

74. Which of the following may be the code for 'some rivals plays excellent'?

(*a*) ba da fi ki (*b*) lo da no ki

(*c*) ki fi ba le (*d*) da ba ha fi

(*e*) None of these

75. What is the code for 'plays'?

   (*a*) ba   (*b*) ki

   (*c*) lo   (*d*) Can't be determined

   (*e*) None of these

Directions (Q. 76 – 78): *Study the following information to answer the given questions.* (*each question is worth 1 mark*)

  i. 'P   Q' means 'P is brother of Q'

 ii. 'P – Q' means 'P is sister of Q'

iii. 'P + Q' means 'P is father of Q'

iv. 'P   Q' means 'P is mother of Q'

76. Which of the following represents V is daughter of C?

   (*a*) $C \div R + V$ (*b*) $C \times R \times V$

   (*c*) $C + R \times V - P$ (*d*) $C + R - V + P$

   (*e*) None of these

77. Which of the following represents 'D is nephew of X'?

   (*a*) $X - P + D$ (*b*) $X \times P \div D$

   (*c*) $X \div P \times D$ (*d*) $X - P + D \times T$

   (*e*) None of these

78. How is S related to G in the expression:

   $M + S \div R - G$?

   (*a*) Father   (*b*) Mother

   (*c*) Brother   (*d*) Data inadequate

   (*e*) None of these

Directions (Q. 79 – 80): *Read the following information to answer these questions:*

Consider a group comprising of 4 students – Reetika, Babita, Meena and Nisha, who stand in a row. Reetika and Babita stand in sixth and seventh positions respectively from the left. Meena and Nisha stand in the fourth and fifth positions respectively from the right. When Babita and Meena exchange their positions, then Babita will be fifteenth from the left.

79. If Nisha and Reetika also exchange their positions between themselves, then after the exchange, Nisha's position from the left will be?

   (*a*) 13   (*b*) 5

   (*c*) 6   (*d*) 9

   (*e*) None of these

80. After exchange of positions between Babita and Meena, Meena's position from the right is

   (*a*) 15   (*b*) 10

   (*c*) 12   (*d*) 16

   (*e*) None of these

Directions (Q. 81 – 85): *In the following questions, the symbols @, #, $, % and © are used with the following meaning as illustrated below:*

'P $ Q' means 'P is not greater than Q'.

'P @ Q' means 'P is neither smaller than nor equal to Q'.

'P % Q' means 'P is neither greater than nor equal to Q'.

'P © Q' means 'P is not smaller than Q'.

'P # Q' means 'P is neither greater than nor smaller than Q'.

Now in each of the following questions assuming the given statements to be true, find which of the three conclusions I, II and III given below them is/are definitely true?

81. Statements: S © M, N % S, K @ N

   Conclusions: I. K @ M

                    II. M @ N

                    III. S @ K

   (*a*) None follows

   (*b*) Only I follows

   (*c*) Only either I or II follows

   (*d*) Only III follows

   (*e*) All follow

82. Statements: M @ R, R © K, J % K

   Conclusions: I. M @ J

                    II. J @ R

                    III. K % M

   (*a*) None follows

   (*b*) Only I and II follow

   (*c*) Only II and III follow

   (*d*) Only I and III follow

   (*e*) All follow

83. Statements: F © N, N # P, W $ P

   Conclusions: I. F # W

                    II. W % F

                    III. P # F

   (*a*) None follows

   (*b*) Only either I or II follows

   (*c*) Only either II or III follows

   (*d*) Only either I or II and III follows

   (*e*) All follow

84. Statements: Z % D, M © D, Q # M

   Conclusions: I. Q @ Z

                    II. D # Q

                    III. Q @ D

(*a*) All follow

(*b*) Only I follow

(*c*) Either II or III follows

(*d*) Either II or III and I follows

(*e*) None of these

85. Statements: T # X, X $ W, W % G

Conclusions: I. G @ X

II. G @ T

III. G © T

(*a*) Only I follows (*b*) Only II follows

(*c*) Only III follows (*d*) Only I and II follow

(*e*) All follow

86. Directions: In the question below are given four statements followed by three conclusions I, II and III. You have to take the given statements to be true even if they seem to be at variance from commonly known facts. Read all the conclusions and then decide which of the given conclusion logically follows from the given statement disregarding commonly known facts.

Statements:

Some shoes are socks.

All socks are towels

All towels are bed sheets.

No bed sheet is blanket

Conclusions:

I. No towel is blanket

II. At least some shoes are towels

III. All shoes are bed sheets

(*a*) I and II follow

(*b*) II and III follow

(*c*) I and III follow

(*d*) All follow

(*e*) None of these

87. Directions: In the question below are given four statements followed by four conclusions I, II, III and IV. You have to take the given statements to be true even if they seem to be at variance from commonly known facts. Read all the conclusions and then decide which of the given conclusion logically follows from the given statement disregarding commonly known facts.

Statements:

All kites are buses

All buses are trains

Some trains are roads.

Some roads are stones

Conclusions:

I. Some stones are kites.

II. Some roads are buses.

III. Some stones being buses is a possibility.

IV. All kites are trains.

(*a*) None follows

(*b*) Only I follows

(*c*) Only II follows

(*d*) III and IV follow

(*e*) None of these

88. Directions: In the question below are given four statements followed by four conclusions I, II, III and IV. You have to take the given statements to be true even if they seem to be at variance from commonly known facts. Read all the conclusions and then decide which of the given conclusion logically follows from the given statement disregarding commonly known facts.

Statements:

Some chairs are pencils.

Some pencils are bottles.

Some bottles are bags.

Some bags are books

Conclusions:

I. At least some books are pencils

II. Some bottles are definitely chairs

III. No book is pencil

IV. All bags being chairs is a possibility

(*a*) Only I follow

(*b*) Either I or III and IV follow

(*c*) III and IV follows

(*d*) Only IV follows

(*e*) None of these

89. Directions: In the question below are given four statements followed by four conclusions I, II, III and IV. You have to take the given statements to be true even if they seem to be at variance from commonly known facts. Read all the conclusions and then decide which of the given conclusion logically follows from the given statement disregarding commonly known facts.

Statements:

All chairs are pockets

No pocket is table

Some tables are boys

All boys are puppets

Conclusions:

I.   Some puppets are chairs.

II. Some puppets are tables.

III. Some puppets being pockets is a possibility

IV. Some chairs are not tables

(*a*) I and III follow

(*b*) II, III and IV follow

(*c*) I and II follow

(*d*) III and IV follow

(*e*) None of these

90. Directions: In the question below are given four statements followed by four conclusions I, II, III and IV. You have to take the given statements to be true even if they seem to be at variance from commonly known facts. Read all the conclusions and then decide which of the given conclusion logically follows from the given statement disregarding commonly known facts.

Statements:

Some Pies are lanes.

Some lanes are Races.

Some Races are rivers.

Some rivers are Jugs

Conclusions:

I.   Some Jugs are not Races

II. All Races being lanes is a possibility

III. Atleast some Jugs are Pies

IV. No Jug is Race

(*a*) Only I follows

(*b*) Only II follows

(*c*) Either I or IV follows

(*d*) Only IV follows

(*e*) Either I or IV and II follow

Directions (Q. 91 – 94): *A letters/letter combination arrangement machine when given an input of letters/ letter combinations rearranges them following a particular rule in each step. The following is an illustration of the input and the steps of rearrangement.*

Input: Get blessings fat car the let sit

Step I: blessings get fat car the let sit

Step II: car blessings get fat the let sit

Step III: fat car blessings get the let sit

Step IV: get fat car blessings let the sit

Step V: let get fat car blessings sit the

Step VI: sit let get fat car blessings the

Step VII: the sit let get fat car blessings

(Step VII is the last step for this input.)

91. Input: test if call at hash might mom

Which of the following will be the third step for this input?

(*a*) hash if call at test might mom

(*b*) call at test if hash might mom

(*c*) might hash if call at test mom

(*d*) hash call at test if might mom

(*e*) None of the above

92. If the second step of an input is 'curl bat rest west set tin nest' which of the following steps would be last step of that input?

(*a*) IV   (*b*) V

(*c*) VI   (*d*) VII

(*e*) None of the above

93. If the input is 'trivia soul van being nut mat love', which of the following will be the IVth step?

(*a*) van trivia nut love soul being mat

(*b*) being mat soul love trivia van nut

(*c*) love nut trivia van being soul mat

(*d*) being mat love soul trivia van nut

(*e*) None of the above

94. Input: 'dog cat vat list',

Which of the following steps would be the last step for this input?

(*a*) IV   (*b*) V

(*c*) VI   (*d*) VII

(*e*) None of the above

95. Below a question is given with two statements (I) and (II). These statements may be either independent causes or may be effects of independent causes or a common cause. One of these statements may be the effect of the other statement. Read both the statements and decide which of the following answer choice correctly depicts the relationship between these two statements.

I.   He had not paid the rent.

II. He has not arrived yet.

(*a*) Statement (I) is the cause and statement (II) is the effect.

(*b*) Statement (II) is the cause and statement (I) is the effect.

(*c*) Both the statements (I) and (II) are independent causes.

(*d*) Both the statements (I) and (II) are effects of independent causes.

(*e*) Both the statements (I) and (II) are effects of some common cause.

96. Effect – There has been unprecedented increase in the number of institutions training spoken phonetic English in all the major cities of India during the last few years.

Which of the following can be a probable cause of the above effect?

(*a*) Many parents want their children to speak fluent English.

(*b*) Various activities are being outsourced to India by many European and North American countries.

(*c*) English is no longer being taught in the school and colleges in India.

(*d*) India has highest number of English speaking educated youth compared to any other country.

(*e*) None of these

97. Cause – All the major rivers in the state have been flowing way over the danger level for the past few weeks.

Which of the following is / are possible effects(s) of the above cause? (2 marks)

1. Many villages situated near the riverbanks are submerged forcing residents to flee.

2. Government has decided to provide alternate shelter to all the affected villagers residing near the river banks.

3. The entire state has been put on high flood alert.

(*a*) Only 1

(*b*) Only 1 and 2

(*c*) Only 2 and 3

(*d*) All 1, 2, and 3

(*e*) None of these

Directions (Q. 98 – 102): *These questions are based on the information given below.*

Six persons – A, B, C, D, E and F – are sitting around a circular table facing center. They are studying one of the courses among Engineering, Medical, B.Sc. and Polytechnic. Two of them are studying medical and two Engineering one B.Sc and one polytechnic. Each of these persons are studying in a different college among P, Q, R, S, T and U. Further it is known that:

1. If E does not take admission in Engineering, then A takes admission in Medical.

2. If D takes admission in P, then B takes admission in R and C sits between A and E.

3. If E takes admission in U, then B takes admission polytechnic and A takes admission in B.Sc.

4. If E does not take admission in U, then C takes admission in P.

5. If F takes admission in Engineering then D takes admission in Engineering.

6. Two of them, who neither want to take admission in B.Sc nor in polytechnic take admission in college P and Q.

7. F does not want to take admission in Engineering but sits neither opposite nor adjacent to B.

8. D does not take admission in college Q and B sits adjacent to A, who is two places to the left of E.

9. C takes admission in college S. (each question is worth 2 marks)

98. Who wants to take admission in college P?

(*a*) A   (*b*) B

(*c*) D   (*d*) E

(*e*) F

99. Who is sitting opposite D?

(*a*) A   (*b*) B

(*c*) C   (*d*) E

(*e*) F

100. In which college does F want to take admission?

(*a*) P   (*b*) Q

(*c*) R   (*d*) T

(*e*) S

101. Who among the following want(s) to take admission in Engineering?

(*a*) A   (*b*) B

(*c*) C   (*d*) D

(*e*) F

102. Which of the following statements is / are true?

I. F sits adjacent to C

II. F and D take admission in medical course

III. A takes admission in college T

(*a*) Only I   (*b*) Only II

(*c*) Only I and II   (*d*) Only II and III

(*e*) Only III

Directions (Q. 103 – 107): *Read the following information carefully and answer the questions given below:*

P, Q, R, S, T, V and Z are seven employees of call center. They work in three shifts – I, II and III. There is at least one and not more than three among them in any of these shifts. Each of them get one day off in every week from Monday to Sunday. Q works with only T in shift II and his weekly off is immediate to the next of the off day of P. S has weekly off on Sunday and he is not in the same shift with either R or Q. P is in shift I with R whose off day is immediately after

Q and immediately before T. V's off day is immediately after T but not on Saturday. The employee having off day on Friday works in shift III and that on a Saturday does not work with T. Z does not work either in shift II or in shift III. (each question is worth 2 marks)

103. Who among them has off day immediately on the next of V's off day?

(*a*) P

(*b*) P or Z

(*c*) Z

(*d*) Data inadequate

(*e*) None of these

104. In which shift do three of them work?

(*a*) I

(*b*) I or II

(*c*) II or III

(*d*) III and I

(*e*) None of these

105. On which day of the week does Q have off day?

(*a*) Thursday

(*b*) Wednesday

(*c*) Saturday

(*d*) Tuesday

(*e*) None of these

106. Which of the following combinations of employee-off-shift day is not correct?

(*a*) P – Wednesday – I

(*b*) T – Thursday – II

(*c*) V – Friday – III

(*d*) Z – Saturday – I

(*e*) All are correct

107. In which shift does V work?

(*a*) II

(*b*) II or III

(*c*) III

(*d*) Data inadequate

(*e*) None of these

108. Directions: The question below consists of a question and two statements numbered I and II given below it. You have to decide whether the data provided in the statements are sufficient to answer the question. Read both the statements and give answer.

How is Ram related to Nitin?

I. Revati, Nitin's mother, is cousin of Sukesh, the uncle of Ram

II. Pravin, Ram's father-in-law, is the grandfather of Sachin, the nephew of Nitin

(*a*) Data in statement I alone are sufficient to answer the question, while the data in statement II alone are not sufficient to answer the question.

(*b*) Data in statement II alone are sufficient to answer the question, while the data in statement I alone are not sufficient to answer the question.

(*c*) Data in statement I alone or in statement II alone are sufficient to answer the question.

(*d*) Data in both the statements I and II together are not sufficient to answer the question.

(*e*) Data in both the statements I and II together are necessary to answer the question.

109. Directions: The question below consists of a question and two statements numbered I and II given below it. You have to decide whether the data provided in the statements are sufficient to answer the question. Read both the statements and give answer.

Who among M, N, O, P and Q is the youngest?

I. N, the 2nd youngest, is younger than Q, O and M

II. O, the 2nd oldest is older than N,

(*a*) Data in statement I alone are sufficient to answer the question, while the data in statement II alone are not sufficient to answer the question.

(*b*) Data in statement II alone are sufficient to answer the question, while the data in statement I alone are not sufficient to answer the question.

(*c*) Data in statement I alone or in statement II alone are sufficient to answer the question.

(*d*) Data in both the statements I and II together are not sufficient to answer the question.

(*e*) Data in both the statements I and II together are necessary to answer the question.

110. Directions: The question below consists of a question and two Statements I and II given below it. You have to decide whether the data provided in the statements are sufficient or not sufficient to answer the question. Read both the statements and give answer.

Which company's bike was driven by Vinay Sachdeva while going to Dimana, a tourist place at Jamshedpur, with his friends?

I. There were four bikes – Suzuki Samurai, Hero Honda, Kawasaki-4s Champion and Yamaha among six friends. And not more than two persons can sit on a bike.

II. Suresh and Deepali were on Suzuki Samurai, Vinay was not on Hero Honda and Aneesh was alone on Yamaha.

(a) Data in statement I alone are sufficient to answer the question, while the data in statement II alone are not sufficient to answer the question.

(b) Data in statement II alone are sufficient to answer the question, while the data in statement I alone are not sufficient to answer the question.

(c) Data in statement I alone or in statement II alone are sufficient to answer the question.

(d) Data in both the statements I and II together are not sufficient to answer the question.

(e) Data in both the statements I and II together are necessary to answer the question.

111. To get all capital letters while typing we have to ________.

(a) Keep Ctrl button pressed

(b) Keep caps lock on

(c) Keep caps lock off

(d) Keep Alt button pressed

(e) None of the above

112. The most commonly used standard data code to represent alphabetical, numerical and punctuation characters used in electronic data processing system is called.

(a) ASCII   (b) EBCDIC

(c) BCD   (d) All of above

(e) None of these

113. To go to the end of the document ______ command can be used. (1 mark)

(a) Ctrl+Home   (b) Alt+Home

(c) Ctrl+End   (d) Ctrl+Delete

(e) None of these

114. What is necessary to understand the XML documents for a user? (1 mark)

(a) Use standardized tags

(b) Have a document type definition which defines the tags

(c) Define the tags separately

(d) Specify tag filename

(e) None of these

115. Borders can be applied to (1 mark)

(a) Cells

(b) Paragraph

(c) Text

(d) All of above

(e) None of the above

116. Expand the term 'EMI' as used in banking/finance sector? 1. Easy Monthly Investment

(b) Equal Monthly Investment

(c) Equated Monthly Installment

(d) Equated Mortgage Investment

(e) None of the above

117. What does 'S' in NSEL stand for?

(a) Standard   (b) Stock

(c) Securities   (d) Spot

(e) None of the above

118. Which of the following rates is closest to Marginal standing facility rate?

(a) Liquid adjustment facility rate

(b) Repo rate

(c) SLR

(d) Reverse repo rate

(e) Call money rate

119. Which of the following does not describe Indian Economy?

(a) Fixed Exchange rate

(b) Liberalized

(c) Managed exchange rate

(d) Mixed Economy

(e) None, all of them describe Indian economy

120. Where is the headquarters of Forward Markets Commission located?

(a) Hyderabad

(b) Mumbai

(c) New Delhi

(d) Bengaluru

(e) Chennai

121. What do the growth related figures of '7.5%' or '8%' discussed w.r.t the economy signify?

(a) Gross National Product growth rate

(b) Grand Domestic Product value

(c) Gross Domestic Product growth rate

(d) Gross National Product absolute value

(e) Per Capita Income growth rate

122. MUDRA Bank is a wholly owned subsidiary of

(a) RBI   (b) SIDBI

(c) NABARD   (d) SBI

(e) Govt. of India

123. Before a loan account turns into an NPA, NBFCs are required to identify incipient stress in the account by creating a sub-asset category called
   (a) Bad Debt Account
   (b) Special Mention Account
   (c) Post-Loan Account
   (d) Extraction Account
   (e) None of the above

124. FINO Paytech has entered into a partnership with which of the following bank?
   (a) HDFC Bank   (b) AXIS Bank
   (c) SBI   (d) ICICI Bank
   (e) None of the above

125. If RBI decreases the CRR, what will happen to the credit creation process?
   (a) It will decrease
   (b) It will stop
   (c) It will increase
   (d) It will first decrease then increase
   (e) None of the above

126. Which of the following is not an example of current asset?
   (a) Cash   (b) Inventory
   (c) Bills receivable   (d) Building
   (e) None of the above

127. In which of the following cities, the Head Office of Reserve Bank of India is located?
   (a) Mumbai   (b) New Delhi
   (c) Kolkata   (d) Dehradun
   (e) Hyderabad

128. Which of the following companies was amongst the first e-commerce companies in India?
   (a) Flipkart   (b) Snapdeal
   (c) Amazon   (d) Alibaba
   (e) Indiaplaza

129. The first Finance Commission was constituted in
   (a) 1950   (b) 1951
   (c) 1952   (d) 1954
   (e) 1968

130. 'Relationship Beyond Banking' is the tagline of
   (a) CITI Bank
   (b) Allahabad Bank
   (c) Central Bank of India
   (d) Bank of Baroda
   (e) Bank of India

131. What percentage of Indian adult population has Aadhar number?
   (a) 74%   (b) 87%
   (c) 93%   (d) 97%
   (e) 95%

132. Who is the current Finance Secretary?
   (a) Hasmukh Adia   (b) Ashok Lavasa
   (c) Rajiv Mehrishi   (d) Punit Sinha
   (e) None of the above

133. Federal Bank is headquartered in
   (a) Kochi   (b) Mumbai
   (c) Mangalore   (d) Nagpur
   (e) None of the above

134. The total amount disbursed by banks under Pradhan Mantri Mudra Yojana is
   (a) 50000 crore
   (b) 1.25 lakh crore
   (c) 1.50 Lakh crore
   (d) 95000 crore
   (e) 1.15 Lakh crore

135. BRICS Friendship Cities Conclave was recently hosted by
   (a) New Delhi
   (b) Shanghai
   (c) Johannesburg
   (d) Mumbai
   (e) None of the above

136. What was the pen name of the famous Hindi novelist and critique Subhash Chandra who passed away on June 14?
   (a) Mudrarakshas   (b) Suraj
   (c) Deshpremi   (d) Guruji
   (e) Baaghi

137. Which country has awarded President Pranab Mukherjee the 'National Grand Crois', the highest civilian award?
   (a) Chile   (b) Portugal
   (c) Israel   (d) Ivory Coast
   (e) France

138. Who has been appointed as Union Law Secretary on June 14?
   (a) Kashinath Ghanekar
   (b) Mukut Mithi
   (c) Suresh Chandra
   (d) A. J. John, Anaparambil
   (e) Paidi Jairaj

139. Who is the Chairman of the Appointments Committee of the Cabinet (ACC)?
- (a) President
- (b) Prime Minister
- (c) Chief Justice of India
- (d) Law Minister
- (e) Speaker

140. In which city is the United Breweries Group headquartered?
- (a) Delhi
- (b) Ludhiana
- (c) Chennai
- (d) Bengaluru
- (e) Mumbai

141. Which country became the first country to stop clear-cutting of trees to curb global deforestation?
- (a) Poland
- (b) Norway
- (c) USA
- (d) Canada
- (e) Brazil

142. Who is the chief executive officer (CEO) of LinkedIn?
- (a) Martin S. Ackerman
- (b) Rex Adams
- (c) Latta Malette Autrey
- (d) Jeff Weiner
- (e) Kevin Cushing

143. What is the theme for the 2016 World Blood Donor Day?
- (a) Blood connects us all
- (b) Thank you for saving my life
- (c) Every blood donor is a hero
- (d) Give the gift of life
- (e) Save blood for saving mothers

144. Famous cricketer Donald Carr, who passed away recently, made his Test debut against which country?
- (a) Australia
- (b) South Africa
- (c) India
- (d) New Zealand
- (e) Sri Lanka

145. Who is the Lieutenant Governor of Delhi?
- (a) Bhagwan Sahay
- (b) Najeeb Jung
- (c) Mohan M.K. Wali
- (d) Markandey Singh
- (e) Tejendra Khanna

146. Which of the following states recently became the first state to have its own data center?
- (a) Gujarat
- (b) Maharashtra
- (c) Himachal Pradesh
- (d) Delhi
- (e) Telangana

147. Which of the following states has launched Asia's first vulture breeding program?
- (a) Chattisgarh
- (b) Tripura
- (c) Meghalaya
- (d) Assam
- (e) None of the above

148. India Post has released a stamp dedicated to which of the following?
- (a) TATA Steel
- (b) Flipkart
- (c) Amazon
- (d) Snapdeal
- (e) None of the above

149. River Seine is located in
- (a) Germany
- (b) Portugal
- (c) Netherlands
- (d) Italy
- (e) France

150. In which city is the Directorate General of Civil Aviation headquartered?
- (a) Mumbai
- (b) Chennai
- (c) Delhi
- (d) Bengaluru
- (e) Ahmedabad

151. For 2016-17, the government aims to further bring down the fiscal deficit to __%.
- (a) 3.6
- (b) 3.1
- (c) 3.5
- (d) 2.9
- (e) 1.82

152. What is the tagline of State Bank of India (SBI)?
- (a) A tradition of Trust
- (b) Your Faithful and Friendly Financial Partner
- (c) We understand your world
- (d) Pure Banking, Nothing Else
- (e) Much more to do with you in Focus

153. Who has been appointed as the new Chief of the Naval Staff?
- (a) KK Sharma
- (b) R.K. Dhowan
- (c) Radhakrishna Hariram Tahiliani
- (d) Durga Shanker Mishra
- (e) Sunil Lanba

154. In which year did the Foreign Account Tax Compliance Act (FATCA) come into effect?

    (*a*) 2007

    (*b*) 2008

    (*c*) 2010

    (*d*) 2013

    (*e*) 2015

155. Which ministry has launched ASMITA, a student tracking system programme?

    (*a*) Education

    (*b*) Skill Development and Entrepreneurship

    (*c*) Social Justice and Empowerment

    (*d*) Women and Child Development

    (*e*) Ministry of Human Resource Development

ANSWERS

1. (*b*)	**2.** (*d*)	**3.** (*c*)	**4.** (*a*)	**5.** (*c*)	**6.** (*e*)	**7.** (*a*)	**8.** (*a*)	**9.** (*c*)	**10.** (*b*)
11. (*d*)	**12.** (*b*)	**13.** (*b*)	**14.** (*d*)	**15.** (*c*)	**16.** (*d*)	**17.** (*c*)	**18.** (*b*)	**19.** (*a*)	**20.** (*c*)
21. (*c*)	**22.** (*d*)	**23.** (*e*)	**24.** (*b*)	**25.** (*d*)	**26.** (*d*)	**27.** (*b*)	**28.** (*b*)	**29.** (*c*)	**30.** (*b*)
31. (*e*)	**32.** (*c*)	**33.** (*b*)	**34.** (*c*)	**35.** (*c*)	**36.** (*a*)	**37.** (*a*)	**38.** (*a*)	**39.** (*b*)	**40.** (*b*)
41. (*a*)	**42.** (*c*)	**43.** (*a*)	**44.** (*d*)	**45.** (*b*)	**46.** (*d*)	**47.** (*d*)	**48.** (*d*)	**49.** (*c*)	**50.** (*c*)
51. (*b*)	**52.** (*b*)	**53.** (*c*)	**54.** (*a*)	**55.** (*b*)	**56.** (*e*)	**57.** (*d*)	**58.** (*e*)	**59.** (*c*)	**60.** (*c*)
61. (*b*)	**62.** (*d*)	**63.** (*b*)	**64.** (*a*)	**65.** (*d*)	**66.** (*e*)	**67.** (*a*)	**68.** (*e*)	**69.** (*b*)	**70.** (*a*)
71. (*d*)	**72.** (*c*)	**73.** (*b*)	**74.** (*a*)	**75.** (*b*)	**76.** (*c*)	**77.** (*d*)	**78.** (*b*)	**79.** (*c*)	**80.** (*c*)
81. (*a*)	**82.** (*d*)	**83.** (*b*)	**84.** (*d*)	**85.** (*d*)	**86.** (*a*)	**87.** (*d*)	**88.** (*b*)	**89.** (*b*)	**90.** (*b*)
91. (*d*)	**92.** (*d*)	**93.** (*e*)	**94.** (*a*)	**95.** (*d*)	**96.** (*b*)	**97.** (*d*)	**98.** (*c*)	**99.** (*c*)	**100.** (*b*)
101. (*c*)	**102.** (*d*)	**103.** (*c*)	**104.** (*a*)	**105.** (*d*)	**106.** (*a*)	**107.** (*c*)	**108.** (*d*)	**109.** (*a*)	**110.** (*e*)
111. (*b*)	**112.** (*a*)	**113.** (*c*)	**114.** (*b*)	**115.** (*d*)	**116.** (*c*)	**117.** (*d*)	**118.** (*a*)	**119.** (*a*)	**120.** (*b*)
121. (*c*)	**122.** (*b*)	**123.** (*b*)	**124.** (*d*)	**125.** (*c*)	**126.** (*d*)	**127.** (*a*)	**128.** (*e*)	**129.** (*b*)	**130.** (*e*)
131. (*c*)	**132.** (*b*)	**133.** (*a*)	**134.** (*e*)	**135.** (*d*)	**136.** (*a*)	**137.** (*d*)	**138.** (*c*)	**139.** (*b*)	**140.** (*d*)
141. (*b*)	**142.** (*d*)	**143.** (*a*)	**144.** (*c*)	**145.** (*b*)	**146.** (*c*)	**147.** (*e*)	**148.** (*c*)	**149.** (*e*)	**150.** (*c*)
151. (*c*)	**152.** (*d*)	**153.** (*e*)	**154.** (*c*)	**155.** (*e*)					

EXPLANATIONS

1. a, c and d are stated in the third paragraph.

2. Refer to the last line of the first paragraph, the second paragraph and the last line of the passage.

3. Refer to the part it reminded the British vividly.

4. Refer to the part it was supposedly for the good of the conquered.

5. Refer to the part India would resist payment, and paralyze the war effort.

6. The reasons are clearly given in the last paragraph of the passage.

7. proved beneficial since it created a large number of jobs and tremendous growth in cross-border trade.

8. BRICS economies are contributing less to global growth.

9. Though worldwide poverty rates tumbled, the gap between the rich and the poor in rich economies increased

10. The growth of BRICS countries has changed the world's economy in ways that any further growth will not have such a disruptive effect on the world economy

11. In the latter half of the 1990s some emerging economies out did America in terms of output per person

12. Only B

13. Only A

36. Required probability = $\dfrac{3}{7}$

38. Radius of circle = $\dfrac{44}{2\pi}$ = 7 cm

Quantity I – Area of shaded region

$$= \frac{1}{2\pi}(7)^2 - \frac{1}{2} \times \frac{1}{2} \times 14 \times 14$$

$$= 25 \text{ cm}^2$$

Quantity II = 22 cm²

Quantity I > quantity II

39. as Y < 0, so quantity I will always be less than zero.

40. quantity I, speed of boat = 12 km/h

Quantity II, speed of cyclist = 14 km/h

Quantity I < quantity II

41. Total number of students for course D = 35% of 1200 = 420

Number of girl students for course D = 30% of 800 = 240

Number of boy students for course D = 420 – 240 = 180

Required ratio = 180 : 240 = 3 : 4.

42. Number of boys for different courses are

A = 0; B = 100; C = 44; D = 180; E = 32; F = 44.

44. Number of boys for different courses are

A = 0; B = 100; C = 44; D = 180; E = 32; F = 44.

45. Number of girls in course C = 2% of 800 = 16

46. A2013 = 540000 × 120/100 × 130/100 = 842400

47. Let its population in 2011 = 100

Population (2013) = 100 × 115/100 × 115/100

$$= 132.25$$

%Increase = 32.25%

48. Let the population of D & E are 'X' in year 2012

D2013 = x × 125/100 = 1.25x

E2013 = x × 145/100 = 1.45x

Req% = 1.45x/1.25x × 100 = 116%

49. F2011 = 1684800 × 100/130 × 100/130 = 960000

50. D2013 = 600000 × 135/100 × 125/100 = 1012500

B2013 = 600000 × 125/100 × 120/100 = 900000

Diff = 1012500 – 900000 = 112500

51. Let expenses, accommodation 500, 400 and 300 respectively

Money saved = $\dfrac{15}{100} \times 500 + \dfrac{25}{900} \times 300 = \dfrac{250}{3}$

Actual amount saved = Rs. 17500

So total amount = $17500 \times \dfrac{3}{250} \times 1200$

$$= \text{Rs. } 252000$$

Accommodation expense = $\dfrac{400}{1200} \times 252000$

$$= \text{Rs. } 84000$$

61. Required income

$$= 120\% \text{ of Rs. } 40 \text{ Crore}$$

$$= \text{Rs. } 48 \text{ Crore}$$

62. The given graph depicts only the percent profit earned by the two companies over the given years. Hence, these information are insufficient to answer the question.

63.
$$\frac{M}{W} = \frac{3}{1} \times \frac{12}{15}$$

$$= \frac{12}{5}$$

$$\therefore \quad 24 \times x \times 12 = 32 \times 5(x + 8)$$

$$288x = 160x + 160 \times 8$$

$$128x = 160 \times 8$$

$$\Rightarrow \quad x = 10$$

64. M → 240 days

W → 32 × 18 = 576 days

Remaining work after 6 days

$$= 1 - 6\left(\frac{10}{240} + \frac{24}{576}\right)$$

$$= 1 - \frac{6}{12}$$

$$= 1 - \frac{1}{2} = \frac{1}{2}$$

$$\therefore \quad \text{Boy} \to 2 \times 18 \times 18 \to 648 \text{ days}$$

$$\therefore \quad \text{Required No. of days} = \frac{648}{12}$$

$$= 54 \text{ days}$$

65. Total amount earned by store C through the sales of M and O type products together

$$= (57 \times 5.6 + 48 \times 50) \text{ thousand}$$

$$= (319.2 + 2400) \text{ thousand}$$

$$= 27.192 \text{ lakh}$$

66. Number of L type product sold by store F = 48

Number of L type product sold by store E = 40

Required percentage = 48/40 × 100 = 120

67. Required difference

$$= (60 \times 75 - 44 \times 15) \text{ thousand}$$

$$= (4500 - 660) \text{ thousand}$$

$$= 38.4 \text{ lakh}$$

68. Required ratio = (61 + 54) : (54 + 48) = 115 : 102

69. Suppose he has x litre of milk in total.

Thus, we have $5x + 200 = 6x - 150$

or, $\quad x(6 - 5) = 200 + 150$

$$x = 350 \text{ litres.}$$

each vessel contains = 35 litres

70. First Purchased $= 250 \times \dfrac{100}{125} \times \dfrac{100}{125} \times \dfrac{100}{125} = 128$

(Solutions 71-75)

The given codes are written by

Messi (and) Ronaldo are △rivals△ : chi (na) Le △ba△ pi

both △rivals△ play football : ki △ba△ lo tha

Messi play excellent : da ki chi

excellent (and) football : tha (na) da children play : mu ki

From the given code, we have

mess	→ chi
and	→ na
Ronaldo / are	→ le/pi
both	→ lo
rivals	→ ba
plays	→ ki
football	→ tha
excellent	→ da
children	→ mu

71. From the given question the code for Ronaldo is either le or pi

72. The code for both is 'lo'

73. The code for Ronaldo and rivals are children is 'pi le na ba mu'.

74. The code for 'some rivals plays excellent is 'ba da fi ki'.

75. The code for plays is 'ki'

(Q. 76 to 78)

when

$\times$ → Brother

$-$ → Sister

$+$ → Father

$\div$ → Mother

76. C + R → C is Father of R

R × V → R is Brother of V

V – P → V is Sister of P

Hence option (*c*) is correct.

77. X – P → X is Sister of P

P + D → P is Father of D

O × T → D is Brother of T

Hence X – P + D × T is correct.

(*d*) option currect.

79. According to statement

$$1 \quad 2 \quad 3 \quad 4 \quad 5 \quad 6 \quad 7 \quad 8 \quad 9 \quad 10 \quad 11 \quad 12 \quad 13 \quad 14 \quad 15 \quad 16 \quad 17 \quad 18$$
$$\downarrow \qquad \downarrow \qquad\qquad\qquad\qquad\qquad\qquad \downarrow \qquad \downarrow$$

Left→   Ritika   Babita   Nisha   Meena   ←Right
$$\uparrow \qquad \uparrow$$
$$18 \quad 17 \quad 16 \quad 15 \quad 14 \quad 13 \quad 12 \quad 11 \quad 10 \quad 9 \quad 8 \quad 7 \quad 6 \quad 5 \quad 4 \quad 3 \quad 2 \quad 1$$

When Babita Meena exchange thier position

6	7	....	14	15
Ritika	Meena		Nisha	Babita

Now Nisha and Reetika also exchange thier position

6	7	....	14	15
Nisha	Meena		Ritika	Babita

Nisha position is 6.

Option (*c*) is correct

80. 12th position of Meena from Right.

Q.81-85 :

From the given questions

P $ Q   :   P ≤ Q

P @ Q   :   P > Q

P % Q   :   P < Q

P © Q   :   P ≥ Q

P # Q   :   P = Q

81. From the statements

S © M   :   S ≥ M

N % S   :   N < S

K @ N   :   K > N

Combine the above statements

    K > N < S ≥ M

Conclusion

I   K @ M   :   K > M → ×

II   M @ N   :   M > N → ×

III   S @ K   :   S > K → ×

so from the given statement none follows.

78. M × S ÷ R – G

M + S → M Father of S

S ÷ R → S Mother of R

R – G → R Sister of G

S ÷ G → Six the Mother of G

Option (*b*) is correct.

82. From the statements

M @ R   :   M > R

R © K   :   R ≥ K

J % K   :   J < K

Combine the above statements we get

    M > R ≥ K > J

Conclusions:

I.   M @ J : M > J → ✓

II.   J @ R   :   J > R → ×

III. K % M : K < M → ✓

So from the given statement only conclusion I and II follow.

83. From the statements

F © N   :   F ≥ N

N # P   :   N = P

W $ P   :   W ≤ P

combine above statements, we get

    F ≥ N = P ≥ W

Conclusions:

I.　F # W　:　F = W → ✓

II.　W % F　:　W < F → ✓

III. P # F　:　P = F → ✗

So from the above statements only either conclusion I or II follows.

84. From the statements

Z % D　:　Z < D

M © D　:　M ≥ D

Q # M　:　Q = M

combine above statements, we get

　Q = M ≥ D > Z

Conclusions:

I.　Q @ Z　:Q > Z → ✓

II.　D # Q : D = Q

III.　Q @ D : Q > D $\Big\}$ Q ≥ D → ✓

So from the given statements conclusion I and either II or III follows.

85. From the statements

T # X　:　T = X

X $ W　:　X ≤ W

W % G　:　W < G

Combine above statements, we get

　T = X ≤ W < G

Conclusions:

I.　G @ X : G > X → ✓

II.　G @ T : G > T → ✓

III. G © T : G ≥ T → ✗

So from the given statements only conclusions I and II follow .

86. From the given statement

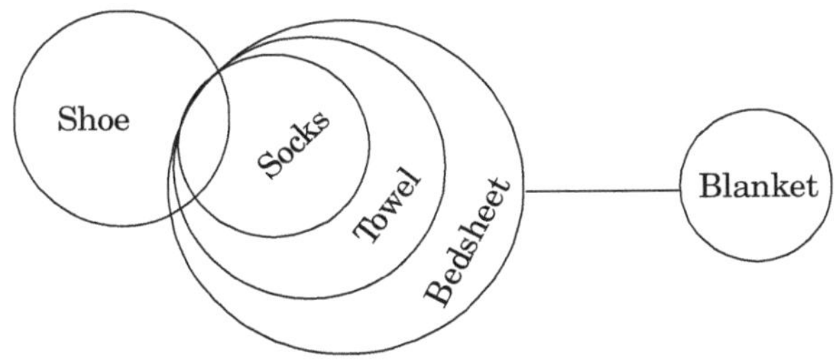

Conclusions:

I. ✓

II. ✓

III. ✗

So from the above statements only conclusions I and II follow.

87. From the given statement

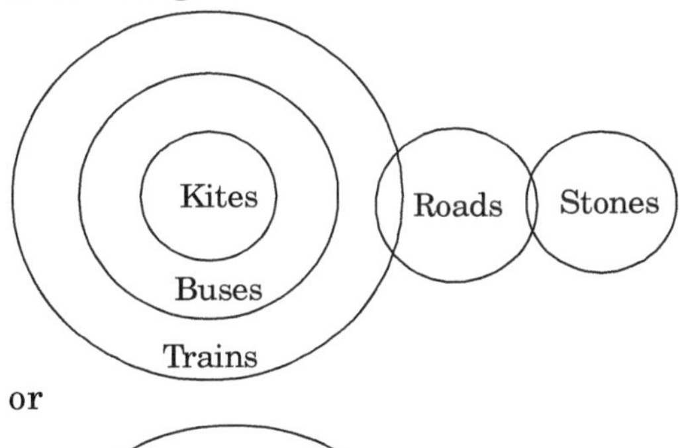

or

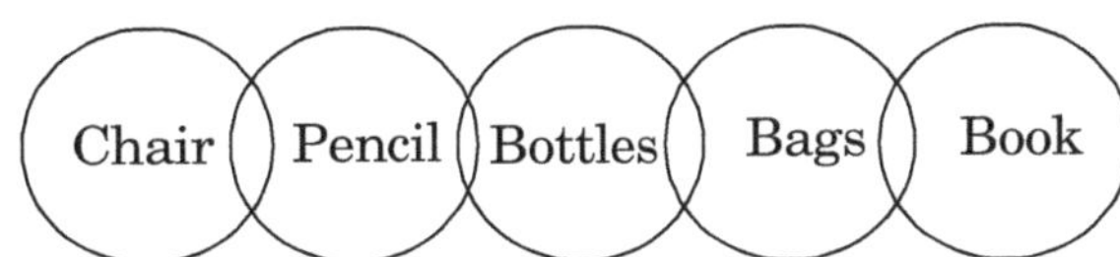

Conclusions:

I.　✗

II.　✗

III. ✓

IV. ✓

So from the above statements only conclusions III and IV follows.

88. Statements

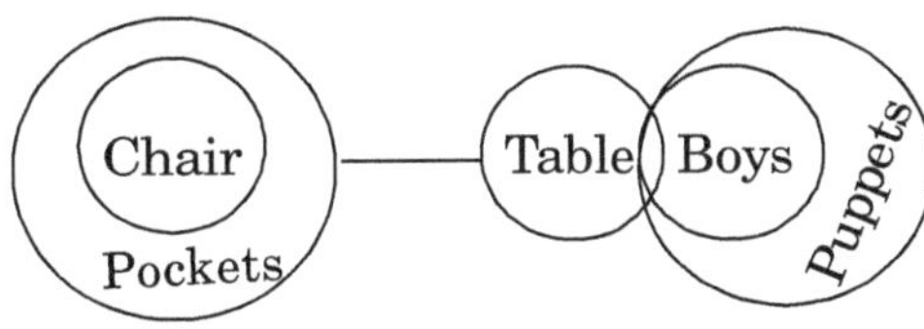

Conclusions:

I.　✗

II.　✗

III. ✗

IV. ✓

So from above statements only conclusions IV follows

89. Statements:

Conclusions:

I.　✗

II. ✓

III. ✓

IV. ✓

From the above statements only conclusions II, III and IV follows.

90. Statements

Pie — Lanes — Races — River — Jug

Conclusions:
I. ×
II. ✓
III. ×
IV. ×

From the above statements only conclusion II follows.

91. Input – test if call at hash might mons

Step 1 : At test if call hash might mons

Step 2 : Call at test if hast might mons

Step 3 : hash call at test if might mons

∴ Option (d) is correct

93. Input – trivia soul van bring nut mat love

Step 1: being trivia soul van nut mat love

Step 2: Love being trivia soul van nut mat

Step 3 : mat love being trival soul van nut

Step 4 : nut mat love being trival soul van

∴ Option (e) is correct

94. Input – dog cat vat list

Step 1 : cat dog vat list

Step 2 : dog cat vat list

Step 3 : list dog cat vat

Step 4 : vat list dog cat

∴ Option (a) is correct

(Q. 103–107):

Employee	**Shift**			Holiday
	I	II	III	
P	✓	✗	✗	Monday
Q	✗	✓	✗	Tuesday
R	✓	✗	✗	Wednesday
S	✗	✗	✓	Sunday
T	✗	✓	✗	Thursday
V	✗	✗	✓	Friday
Z	✓	✗	✗	Saturday

103. 'Z' has off day immediately on the next of V's off day.

104. Three of them work in shift I

105. 'Q' has off day on Tuesday

107. V works in shift III

2015

REASONING

Directions (Q. 1– 5) : *In these questions, symbols @, #, $, % and © are used with different meanings as follows :*

'P @ Q' means 'P is smaller than Q'

'P # Q' means 'P is either smaller than or equal to Q'

'P $ Q' means 'P is greater than Q'

'P % Q' means 'P is either greater than or equal to Q'

'P © Q' means 'P is neither greater than nor smaller than Q'

Now in each of the following questions assuming the given statements to be true, find which of the two conclusions I and II given below is/are definitely true?

Give Answer :

(a) If only Conclusion I is true

(b) If Conclusion II is true

(c) If either Conclusion I or Conclusion II is true

(d) If neither Conclusion I nor Conclusion II is true

(e) If both Conclusions I and II are true.

1. Statements :
   M @ R, R © F, F # L

   Conclusions :

   I. M @ L

   II. R @ L

2. Statements :
   T $ J, J @ V, V # W

   Conclusions :

   I. T © W

   II. T@W

3. Statements :
   J @ 0, 0 $ L, L # N

   Conclusions :

   I. J # L

   II. J $ L

4. Statements :
   R $ M, M % H, H $ F

   Conclusions :

   I. R % F

   II. M$F

5. Statements :
   K $ H, H % I, I © F

   Conclusions :

   I. K $ I

   II. H%F

Directions (Q. 6 – 10) : *Study the following information carefully and answer the questions given below:*

Ten persons A, B, C, D, E, F, G, H, I and J are sitting in two rows with five persons in each row in such a way that one person in the first row sits exactly opposite and facing a person in the second row. Members of the first row are facing North.

B sits in the first row to the immediate right of H who sits exactly opposite of D. C is at the extreme end of the second row and is second to the left of D. A is to the immediate right of D and exactly opposite to F. G sits exactly opposite to E who is at one of the ends of the second row. J does not sit at the end.

6. Which of the following pairs of persons are sitting at the two ends of the first row?

   (a) GJ   (b) EI

   (c) GI   (d) EJ

   (e) None of these

7. Who is second to the left of B?

   (a) I   (b) ti

   (c) H   (d) F

   (e) None of these

8. Who is third to the left of E?

   (a) D   (b) I

   (c) H   (d) C

   (e) None of these

9. A sits between which of the following persons?

   (a) DJ   (b) ED

   (c) FB   (d) BI

   (e) None of these

10. Who sits exactly opposite of B?

   (a) J   (b) I

   (c) G   (d) A

   (e) None of these

Directions (Q. 11 – 15) : *In each of the questions below are given three statements followed by two conclusions numbered I and II. You have to take the given statements to be true even if they seem to be at variance from commonly known facts. Read all the conclusions and then decide which of the given conclusions logically follows from the given statements disregarding commonly known facts.*

Give Answer :

(*a*) If only Conclusion I follows

(*b*) If only Conclusion II follows

(*c*) If either Conclusion I or Conclusion II follows

(*d*) If neither Conclusion I nor Conclusion II follows

(*e*) If both Conclusions I and II follow.

11. Statements :

Some doors are rooms.

All rooms are halls.

All halls are auditoriums.

Conclusions :

I. Some auditoriums are doors.

II. All rooms are auditoriums.

12. Statements :

Some hats are gloves.

Some gloves are socks.

All socks are shoes

Conclusions :

I. Some shoes are gloves.

II. Some socks are hats.

13. Statements :

All guavas are mangoes.

Some mangoes are apples.

No apple is pineapple.

Conclusions :

I. Some pineapples are guavas.

II. No pineapple is guava.

14. Statements :

Some roads are rails.

Some rails are rivers.

Some rivers are oceans.

Conclusions :

I. Some roads are rivers.

II. Some rails are oceans.

15. Statements :

Some pens are sharpeners.

All sharpeners are erasers.

No eraser is ink.

Conclusions :

I. Some pens are ink.

II. Some erasers are pens.

16. Harihar starts walking straight facing South. After walking 30 metres he turned to his right, walked 25 metres and turned to his left. Again after walking a distance of 10 metres he turned to his left. Which direction is he facing now?

(*a*) West   (*b*) East

(*c*) North-East   (*d*) South-West

(*e*) None of these

17. How many pairs of letters are there in the word DISASTER each of which has as many letters between them in the word as in the English alphabet ?

(*a*) None   (*b*) One

(*c*) Two   (*d*) Three

(*e*) More than one

18. B is only child of C's grandfather's only daughter. How is C's father related to B?

(*a*) Maternal Uncle

(*b*) Paternal Uncle

(*c*) Father

(*d*) Cannot be determined

(*e*) None of these

19. What will come next in the following letter series?

A A C A C E A C E G A C E G I A C E G I

(*a*) K   (*b*) L

(*c*) A   (*d*) B

(*e*) None of these

20. If it possible to make only one meaningful English word with the first, the fifth, the sixth, the tenth and the eleventh letters of the word EXCEPTIONAL using each letter only once, first letter of that word is your answer. If no such word can be formed, your answer is 'X' and if more than one such word can be formed, your answer is 'Y'.

(*a*) P   (*b*) L

(*c*) T   (*d*) X

(*e*) Y

Directions (Q. 21 – 22) : *These questions are based on the following information.*

(*i*) 'A × B' means 'A is mother of B'

(*ii*) 'A ÷ B' means 'A is brother of B'

(*iii*) 'A + B' means 'A is son of B'

(*iv*) 'A – B' means 'A is wife of B'

21. In J – T ÷ K + F, how is F related to J?

(*a*) Daughter-in-law

(*b*) Daughter

(*c*) Mother-in-law

(*d*) Cannot be determined

(*e*) None of these

22. In R × H + D, how is R related to D?

(*a*) Mother

(*b*) Uncle

(*c*) Wife

(*d*) Cannot be determined

(*e*) None of these

23. In the number 3276158, if the digits were arranged in ascending order, how many digits will remain far away from the beginning of the number as they are in the number?

(*a*) None   (*b*) One

(*c*) Two   (*d*) Three

(*e*) More than three

24. In a certain code RELATION is written as BMFSOPJU. How is ADVISORY written in that code?

(*a*) JWEBTPZS   (*b*) JWEBZSPT

(*c*) BEWJZSPT   (*d*) BEWJTPSZ

(*e*) None of these

25. If 'Red' means 'Blue', 'Blue' means 'Green', 'Green' means 'Orange', 'Orange' means 'Pink' and 'Pink' means 'Black', then what is the colour of the clear sky?

(*a*) Orange   (*b*) Green

(*c*) Blue   (*d*) Red

(*e*) None of these

Directions (Q. 26 – 30) : *Each of the questions below consists of a question and two statements numbered I and II given below it. You have to decide whether the data provided in the statements are sufficient to answer the question. Read both the statements and —*

Give Answer as

(*a*) if the data in statement I alone are sufficient to answer the question, while the data in statement II alone are not sufficient to answer the question

(*b*) if the data in statement II alone are sufficient to answer the question, while the data in statement I alone are not sufficient to answer the question

(*c*) if the data either in statement I alone or in statement II alone are sufficient to answer the question

(*d*) if the data given in both statements I and II together are not sufficient to answer the question and

(*e*) if the data in both statements I and II together are necessary to answer the question

26. What is the code for TAIL in a code language?

   I. In the code language DELAY is written as 57382.

   II. In the code language TIDE is written as 6457.

27. Village 'P' is in which direction with respect to Village 'Q'?

   I. Village H is to the East of Village P and to the South of Viliager

   II. Village F is to the North of Village P and to the West of Village Q.

28. How many students are there in the class?

   I. In the class, Nisha ranks tenth form the top and twenty-third from the bottom.

   II. Nandita is ten ranks above Shama who is eighteenth form the top.

29. How many sons does 'X' have?

   I. D is brother of A who is son of X.

   II D's sister is M's wife.

30. Among P, T, J, Land F each having different height, who is the tallest one?

   I. P is taller than J and F only.

   II. T is not the tallest.

Directions (Q. 31 – 35) : *Study the following arrangement carefully and answer the questions given below:*

7 6 1 7 9 2 4 1 5 6 4 9 2 3 4 1 2 5 8 5 8 4 8 3 1 2 7 5 2 6 7 2 9 5 3

31. How many 2s are there in the above arrangement, each of which is immediately followed by a digit which has a numerical value of more than four?

(*a*) None   (*b*) One

(*c*) Two   (*d*) Three

(*e*) More than three

32. How many such 1s are there in the above arrangement, each of which is immediately preceded by a perfect square?

(*a*) None   (*b*) One

(*c*) Two   (*d*) Three

(*e*) More than three

33. How many such 5s are there in the above arrangement each of which is immediately preceded and followed by an odd digit?

(*a*) None   (*b*) One

(*c*) Two   (*d*) Three

(*e*) More than three

34. Which of the following is third to the left of the eighteenth digit from the left end of the above arrangement?

(*a*) 8   (*b*) 3

(*c*) 4   (*d*) 5

(*e*) 1

35. If all the even digits are deleted from the above arrangement, which of the following will be ninth from the right end of the arrangement?

(*a*) 9   (*b*) 3

(*c*) 1   (*d*) 5

(*e*) 7

Directions (Q. 36 – 40) : *Study the following information carefully and answer the questions given below:*

A, B, C, D, E, F, G and H are sitting around a circle facing at the centre. F is third to the right of B who is third to the right of H. A is third to the left of H. C is fourth to the left of A. E is third to the right of D who is not a neighbour of A.

36. In which of the following pairs the second person is to the immediate right of the first person?

   (*a*) HC   (*b*) BE

   (*c*) GB   (*d*) FA

   (*e*) None of these

37. Who is second to the right of D?

   (*a*) F   (*b*) G

   (*c*) A   (*d*) Data inadequate

   (*e*) None of these

38. Who is third to the left of G?

   (*a*) H   (*b*) D

   (*c*) C   (*d*) F

   (*e*) None of these

39. Who is fourth to the left of C?

   (*a*) F   (*b*) A

   (*c*) E   (*d*) Data inadequate

   (*e*) None of these

40. What is B's position with respect to D?

   (A) Fourth to the right

   (B) Fourth to the left

   (C) Fifth to the left

   (D) Fifth to the right

   (*a*) (A) Only   (*b*) (B) Only

   (*c*) (A) and (B) only   (*d*) (C) and (D) only

   (*e*) None of these

NUMERICAL ABILITY

Directions (Q. 41 – 50) : *What should come in place of the question mark (?) in the following questions?*

41. $(58)^5 \times (58)^7 \div (58)^2 = (58)^?$

   (*a*) 12   (*b*) 6

   (*c*) 8   (*d*) 17.5

   (*e*) None of these

42. $(37685 + 29452 - 41897) \div 250 = ?$

   (*a*) 72.11   (*b*) 112.56

   (*c*) 100.96   (*d*) 98.96

   (*e*) None of these

43. 65% of 480 = ?% of 750

   (*a*) 40.4   (*b*) 41.6

   (*c*) 46   (*d*) 42.5

   (*e*) None of these

44. $\sqrt{3136} + \sqrt{4096} = ?$

   (*a*) 120   (*b*) 3584

   (*c*) 105   (*d*) 2744

   (*e*) None of these

45. $560 \div ? \times 500 = 400$

   (*a*) 440   (*b*) 550

   (*c*) 600   (*d*) 750

   (*e*) None of these

46. $[(12)^2 + (6)^2] \div (7)^2 = 7.2$

   (*a*) 6   (*b*) 8

   (*c*) 3   (*d*) 4

   (*e*) None of these

47. $774 \times 326 = ?$

   (*a*) 244584   (*b*) 253224

   (*c*) 244854   (*d*) 252324

   (*e*) None of these

48. $\sqrt[3]{13824} = ?$

   (*a*) 22   (*b*) 28

   (*c*) 24   (*d*) 32

   (*e*) None of these

49. $7480 \times \dfrac{2}{3} \times \dfrac{3}{4} \times \dfrac{5}{8} = ?$

   (*a*) 2330   (*b*) 2337.8

   (*c*) 2530   (*d*) 2373.5

   (*e*) None of these

50. $\dfrac{0.5 \times 6 \div 2.5}{4.5 + 0.6 + 0.9} = ?$

   (*a*) 0.6   (*b*) 6

   (*c*) 0.2   (*d*) 4

   (*e*) None of these

Directions (Q. 51 – 55) : *Answer the questions on the basis of the information given below.*

The pie chart given below shows the percentage wise distribution of students in six different schools.

Total number of students = 6000

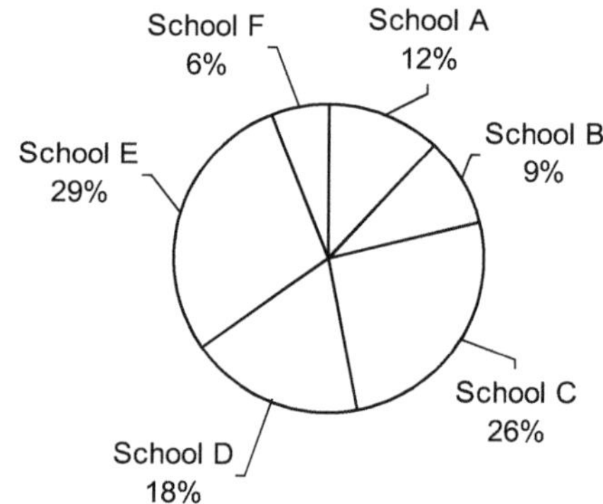

The bar graph given below shows the number of boys out of 6000 students in each school separately.

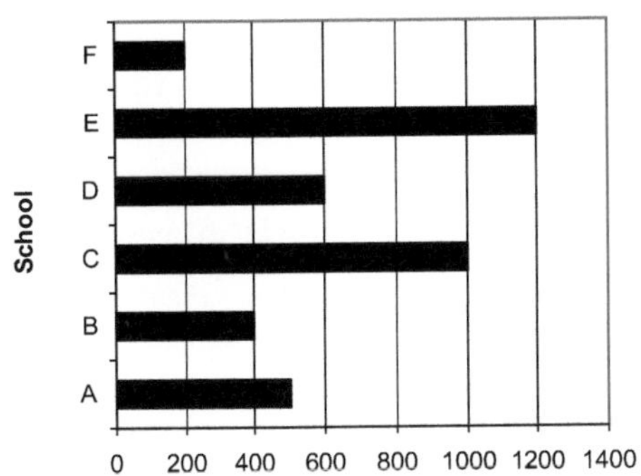

51. What is the sum of the number of girls in School-C, number of girls in School-E and the number of boys in School-D together?

(a) 1700
(b) 1900
(c) 1600
(d) 1800
(e) None of these

52. What is the respective ratio between the number of boys in School-C, number of girls in School-B and total number of students in School-E?

(a) 45 : 7 : 97
(b) 43 : 9 : 97
(c) 50 : 7 : 87
(d) 43 : 9 : 87
(e) None of these

53. What is the difference between the total number of students in School-F and the number of boys in School-E?

(a) 820
(b) 860
(c) 880
(d) 900
(e) None of these

54. In which school the total number of students (both boys and girls together) is equal to the number of girls in School-E?

(a) A
(b) B
(c) C
(d) D
(e) F

55. Number of girls in School-A is approximately what percent of total number of students in School-B?

(a) 55
(b) 50
(c) 35
(d) 45
(e) 41

Directions (Q. 56 – 60) : *Answer the questions on the basis of the information given below.*

The bar graph given below shows the number of candidates (in thousands) who qualified in an exam in three different states during the period 2004 to 2009.

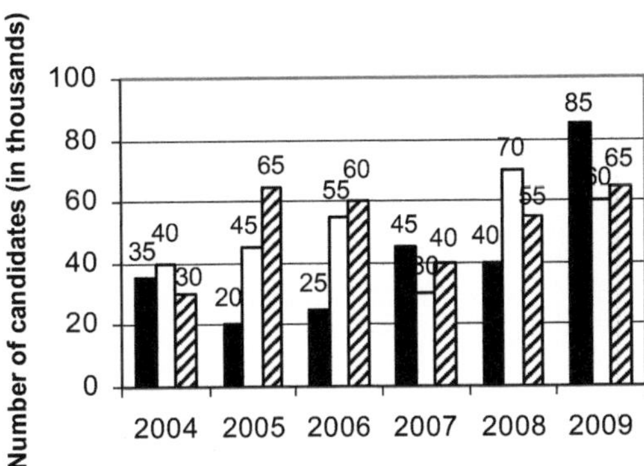

56. If 40% of the candidates who qualified in the exam from state-P in 2009 were females, then what was the sum of the number of male candidates who qualified from State-P in 2009 and the total number of candidates who qualified in the exam from state-R in 2007?

(a) 91,000
(b) 9.1 lacs
(c) 93,000
(d) 9.3 lacs
(e) None of these

57. What was the respective ratio between the number of candidates who qualified in the exam from state-R in 2008 and the number of candidates who qualified in the exam from state-P in 2004?

(a) 11 : 10
(b) 9 : 11
(c) 11 : 7
(d) 11 : 9
(e) None of these

58. Total number of candidates who qualified in the exam in 2004 and 2005 together from state-Q was approximately what percentage of total number of candidates who qualified in the exam from all the states together in 2007?

(a) 61
(b) 65
(c) 79
(d) 69
(e) 74

59. What was the difference between the total number of candidates who qualified in the exam from all the states together in 2006 and the total number of candidates who qualified in the exam from State-P over all the years together?

(a) 1.2 lacs
(b) 11,000
(c) 1.1 lacs
(d) 12,000
(e) None of these

60. What was approximate percentage decrease in the number of candidates who qualified in the exam from State-Q in 2007 as compared to the previous year ?

(a) 45　　　　　　　(b) 55

(c) 50　　　　　　　(d) 60

(e) 30

Direction (Q. 61 – 65) : *Answer the questions on the basis of the information given below.*

The pie chart given below shows the percentage wise distribution of passengers in six different trains.

Total number of passengers in six different trains = 4800

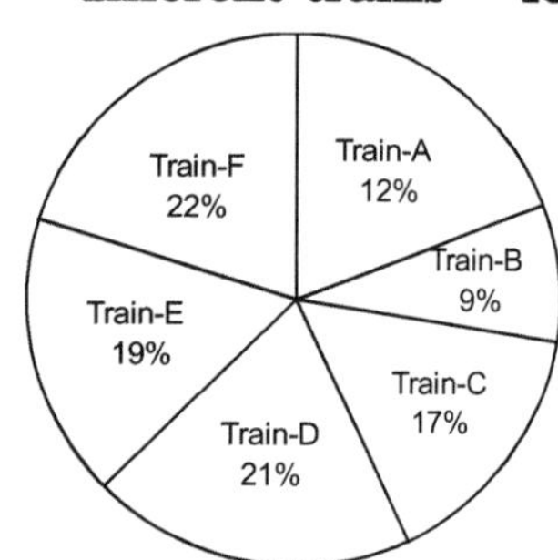

61. What was the average number of passengers travelling in Train-A, Train-C and Train-F together ?

(a) 816　　　　　　　(b) 826

(c) 824　　　　　　　(d) 812

(e) None of these

62. If cost of one ticket is ₹ 124, what is the total amount paid by passengers of Train-B? (Assuming all the passengers purchased ticket and cost of each ticket is equal.)

(a) ₹ 53, 658　　　　(b) ₹ 53,568

(c) ₹ 53,558　　　　(d) ₹ 53,468

(e) None of these

63. Number of passengers in Train-E is approximately what percent of the total number of passengers in Train-B and Train-D together?

(a) 63　　　　　　　(b) 69

(c) 75　　　　　　　(d) 54

(e) 79

64. What is the difference between the number of passengers in Train-C and that of in Train-A?

(a) 280　　　　　　　(b) 250

(c) 230　　　　　　　(d) 260

(e) None of these

65. What is the total number of passengers in Train-D, Train-E and Train-F together?

(a) 2796　　　　　　(b) 3225

(c) 2976　　　　　　(d) 3125

(e) None of these

66. Raman's present age is three times his daughter's present age and nine-thirteenth of his mother's present age. The sum of the present ages of all of them is 125 years. What is the difference between the Raman's daughter's present age and Raman's mother's present age?

(a) 45 years　　　　(b) 40 years

(c) 50 years　　　　(d) Cannot be determined

(e) None of these

67. The difference between the amount of compound interest and simple interest obtained on an amount of ₹ 26,000 at the end of 3 years is ₹ 2,994.134. What is the rate of interest per annum?

(a) 22　　　　　　　(b) 17

(c) 19　　　　　　　(d) Cannot be determined

(e) None of these

68. On a shelf there are 4 books on Economics, 3 books on Management and 4 books on Statistics. In how many different ways can the books be arranged so that the books on Economics are kept together?

(a) 967680　　　　　(b) 120960

(c) 5040　　　　　　(d) 40320

(e) None of these

69. Average score of Rahul, Manish and Suresh is 63. Rahul's score is 15 less than Ajay and 10 more than Manish. If Ajay scored 30 marks more than the average score of Rahul, Manish and Suresh, what is the sum of Manish's and Suresh's scores?

(a) 120　　　　　　　(b) 111

(c) 117　　　　　　　(d) Cannot be determined

(e) None of these

70. Philip, Tom and Brad start jogging around a circular field and complete a single round in 18, 22 and 30 seconds respectively. In how much time will they meet again at the starting point?

(a) 8 min 15 sec　　(b) 12 min 30 sec

(c) 16 min 30 sec　　(d) 12 min

(e) None of these

71. A water tank has three taps– A, B and C. Tap A, when opened, can fill the water tank alone in 4 hours. Tap B, when opened can fill the water tank alone in 6 hours and tap C, when opened, can empty the water tank alone in 3 hours. If taps A, B and C are opened simultaneously, how long will it take to fill the tank completely?

(a) 10 hours　　　　(b) 8 hours

(c) 18 hours　　　　(d) 12 hours

(e) None of these

72. What total amount would Mithilesh get at the end of three years if he invests an amount of ₹ 11,200 in a scheme which offers simple interest at the rate of 8.5% per annum for three years?

(a) ₹ 14,056　　　　(b) ₹ 14,348

(c) ₹ 13,852　　　　(d) ₹ 15,064

(e) None of these

73. The ratio between the adjacent angles of a parallelogram is 2 : 3 respectively. Half the smaller angle of the parallelogram is equal to the smallest angle of a quadrilateral. Largest angle of the quadrilateral is four times its smallest angle. What is the sum of the largest angle of the quadrilateral and the smaller angle of the parallelogram?

(a) 252°　　　　(b) 226°

(c) 144°　　　　(d) 180°

(e) None of these

Directions (Q. 74 – 78) : *In the following questions two equations numbered I and II are given. You have to solve both equations and*

Give answer If

(a) $x > y$　　　　(b) $x \geq y$

(c) $x < y$　　　　(d) $x \leq y$

(e) $x = y$

or the relationship cannot be established

74. I.　$x^2 - 7x + 10 = 0$

　　II.　$y^2 + 11y + 10 = 0$

75. I.　$x^2 + 28x + 192 = 0$

　　II.　$y^2 + 16y + 48 = 0$

76. I.　$2x - 3x = -3.5$

　　II.　$3x + 2y = -6.5$

77. I.　$x^2 + 8x + 15 = 0$

　　II.　$y^2 + 11y + 30 = 0$

78. I.　$x = \sqrt{3136}$

　　II.　$y^2 = 3136$

79. If the numerator of a fraction is increased by 500% and the denominator is increased by 300%, the resultant fraction is $1\frac{1}{17}$. What was the original fraction?

(a) $\dfrac{12}{17}$　　　　(b) $\dfrac{13}{17}$

(c) $\dfrac{3}{7}$　　　　(d) $\dfrac{4}{11}$

(e) None of these

80. In a class of 50 students and 5 teachers, each student got sweets that are 12% of the total number of students and each teacher got sweets that are 20% of the total number of students. How many sweets were there?

(a) 345　　　　(b) 365

(c) 330　　　　(d) 350

(e) None of these

GENERAL AWARENESS

81. Which non-banking organisation recently announced plans to set up 1000 ATMs and an entry into the banking sector ?

(a) BSE　　　　(b) LIC

(c) BSNL　　　　(d) Railways

(e) Department of Post

82. Rating agency DBRS stands for :

(a) Debt Banking Rating Service

(b) Direct Bonafide Rating Service

(c) Dominion Bond Rating Service

(d) Devolution Bond Rating Service

(e) Development Banking Rating Service

83. Rating agency DBRS stands for :

(a) Debt Banking Rating Service

(b) Direct Bonafide Rating Service

(c) Dominion Bond Rating Service

(d) Devolution Bond Rating Service

(e) Development Banking Rating Service

84. Which of the following hears petitions against decisions of Indian Patents Office?

(a) Competition Appellate Tribunal

(b) Indian Patents Appellate Board

(c) National Patents Appellate Authority

(d) Intellectual Property Appellate Board

(e) National Consumer Disputes Redressal Commission

85. Which public sector bank has entered recently in the mutual fund business in a joint venture with AXA Investment Managers ?

(a) Bank of India　　　(b) Bank of Baroda

(c) State Bank of India　(d) Union Bank of India

(e) Punjab National Bank

86. Name the government's project of setting up subsidised medicine stores for the poor, under which 348-odd drugs mentioned in the National List of Essential Medicines were distributed at affordable rates.

(a) Jan Swasthya　　　(b) Jan Chikitsa

(c) Jan Aushadhi　　　(d) Jan Suraksha

(e) Jan Chetna

87. Which retail major of India has entered into a partnership with Tihar Jail in Delhi to sell bakery and confectionery products made by the prisoners?

(*a*) Trent   (*b*) Pantaloon

(*c*) Barista   (*d*) Reliance Retail

(*e*) Escada

88. The government has withdrawn the permission granted to Indian oil companies to import crude oil from which country on CIF (cost, insurance and freight) basis ?

(*a*) Saudi Arabia

(*b*) Iran

(*c*) Nigeria

(*d*) United Arab Emirates

(*e*) Russia

89. The governments of which two states of India have signed a Memorandum of Understanding (MoU) for the execution of the Shri Naina Devi-Anandpur Sahib Ropeway project to link the two shrines ?

(*a*) Uttarakhand and Uttar Pradesh

(*b*) Uttarakhand and Himachal Pradesh

(*c*) Himachal Pradesh and Punjab

(*d*) Punjab and Haryana

(*e*) Rajasthan and Punjab

90. To which country is India sending a team to learn from its experiences in erecting security barriers and to assess technologies that India could implement at its fences with Pakistan and Bangladesh ?

(*a*) Russia   (*b*) Britain

(*c*) Israel   (*d*) Poland

(*e*) US

91. Which state recently came in confrontation with the Election Commission (EC) of India, when the state legislature reinstated two expelled MLAs, soon after the EC had declared those seats vacant?

(*a*) Odisha   (*b*) Assam

(*c*) Karnataka   (*d*) Madhya Pradesh

(*e*) Rajasthan

92. "Core industries witness lower growth in last few months" - was the news in some major economic newspapers recently. This means the performance of which of the following is NOT taken into account for the same?

(*a*) Cement   (*b*) Steel

(*c*) Coal   (*d*) Gems and Jewellery

(*e*) Crude Oil

93. Who among the following can be called a 'pawnbroker'?

(*a*) A stock broker who is similar to a 'bull'

(*b*) A stock broker who is similar to a 'bear'

(*c*) A person who lends money against a pledged article which he is free to sell if the loan is not repaid with interest

(*d*) A person who lends money against gold

(*e*) None of these

94. In the context of the banking industry, what is the correct full form of PCR?

(*a*) Profit Credit Ratio

(*b*) Provision Credit Ratio

(*c*) Provisioning Coverage Ratio

(*d*) Profit Coverage Ratio

(*e*) Performance Credit Ratio

95. The foundation for induction of computer technology in the Indian banking system was laid with the recommendations of which of the following committees?

(*a*) Abid Hussain Committee

(*b*) Deepak Parekh Committee

(*c*) Rangarajan Committee

(*d*) Narsimham Committee

(*e*) Tarapore Committee

96. Which bank has launched "Bank on Wheels" vehicles that travel to villages which don't have banking facilities, to help people in rural areas open bank accounts?

(*a*) State Bank of India

(*b*) Punjab National Bank

(*c*) HDFC Bank

(*d*) Union Bank of India

(*e*) ICICI Bank

97. 'Business Correspondents' (BCs) working for banks can work from

A. Their retail outlets

B. Bank premises

C. Bank ATMs

Select the right option.

(*a*) Only A

(*b*) Only A and B

(*c*) Only B and C

(*d*) Only A and C

(*e*) All A, B and C

98. In the context of various financial systems, which of the following is not related to India?

(*a*) RTGS   (*b*) NEFT

(*c*) CHAPS   (*d*) IFSC

(*e*) KYC

99. Name the budget carrier airline which has recently received government's approval for directly importing fuel from overseas market.

(*a*) Spice Jet   (*b*) Go Air

(*c*) IndiGo   (*d*) Kingfisher Red

(*e*) JetLite

100. Poll Monitoring System was recently implemented for the first time in which of the following states of India?

(*a*) Punjab   (*b*) Manipur

(*c*) Uttar Pradesh   (*d*) Uttarakhand

(*e*) Goa

101. Which of the following companies is planning to bring to India a unique railway track-laying technology called 'SilentTrack', which will reduce noise in the vicinity of tracks by up to 50 per cent?

(*a*) IRCON

(*b*) TELCO

(*c*) Bharat Earth Movers

(*d*) Tata Steel

(*e*) Delhi Metro

102. Which of the following private banks of India has not stipulated a minimum monthly balance of ₹ 10,000 in saving accounts, instead of the earlier practice of such requirement on a quarterly basis?

(*a*) ICICI Bank   (*b*) HDFC Bank

(*c*) Axis Bank   (*d*) IDBI Bank

(*e*) All of these

103. When a customer opens a deposit account with the bank, which of the following is the status of the bank?

(*a*) Debtor   (*b*) Creditor

(*c*) Trustee   (*d*) Beneficiary

(*e*) None of these

104. With which country is India under negotiations for signing the Mutual Legal Assistance Treaty (MLAT)?

(*a*) China

(*b*) US

(*c*) Pakistan

(*d*) Sri Lanka

(*e*) Bangladesh

105. A bank normally does not have to deal with an issue related to

(*a*) payments and settlement system

(*b*) contractual rights of creditors

(*c*) intellectual property rights

(*d*) cases of insolvency

(*e*) coordination bètween regulators active in banking/ finance

106. When a loan is granted by a bank for purchase of electronic goods, it is called

(*a*) Priority sector loan

(*b*) White goods loan

(*c*) Consumer durable loan

(*d*) All the above

(*e*) None of these

107. Bank branches which can undertake foreign exchange business directly are known as

(*a*) Authorized dealers

(*b*) Foreign dealers

(*c*) Overseas branches

(*d*) Approved dealers

(*e*) Exchange branches

108. JM Lyngdoh Committee report is related to which of the following?

(*a*) Code of conduct for students' union elections

(*b*) Centre-State relations

(*c*) Electoral reforms

(*d*) Bicameral legislatures in all states

(*e*) Division of executive and legislature

109. Which of the following states decided to give Khatedhari Rights to about 30,000 farmers occupying the custodian lands?

(*a*) Gujarat

(*b*) Rajasthan

(*c*) Madhya Pradesh

(*d*) Uttar Pradesh

(*e*) Uttarakhand

110. Which of the following functions are not being performed by the Reserve Bank of India?

(*a*) Regulation of banks in India

(*b*) Regulation of foreign direct investment in India

(*c*) Foreign currency management in India

(*d*) Control & supervision of money supply

(*e*) Currency management in India

111. A bank is called as 'Scheduled Bank' when

(*a*) its business has crossed ₹1000-crore mark.

(*b*) its branch network is over 100.

(*c*) it is included in the second schedule of the RBI Act.

(*d*) when it complies with all the three conditions above.

(*e*) None of these

112. April 22 is celebrated every year as which of the following days?

(*a*) World Earth Day

(*b*) World Health Day

(*c*) National Stress Awareness Day

(*d*) World Green Day

(*e*) Dental Health Day

113. The central government will soon take up a study on 100-odd dams that will soon come up in which of the following states?

(*a*) Arunachal Pradesh   (*b*) Assam

(*c*) West Bengal   (*d*) Kerala

(*e*) Andhra Pradesh

114. For allowing the foreign direct investment (FDI) from which country to India has the Finance Ministry decided to amend the Foreign Exchange Management Act (FEMA)?

(*a*) North Korea   (*b*) Cuba

(*c*) Myanmar   (*d*) Pakistan

(*e*) South Sudan

115. Which body has recently issued broad guidelines on Algorithmic Trading based on recommendations of technical advisory committee (TAC) and secondary market advisory committee (SMAC)?

(*a*) IRDA   (*b*) RBI

(*c*) ASSOCHAM   (*d*) SEBI

(*e*) CII

116. The army chief of Pakistan, Gen Ashfaq Kayani, has recently called for the resolution of which of the following contentious issues between India and Pakistan?

(*a*) Sir Creek issue

(*b*) Kashmir issue

(*c*) Pak-occupied Kashmir

(*d*) Siachen issue

(*e*) Tulbul river barrage

117. Name the human disease about which scientists at Washington University School of Medicine in St Louis found that other than diet and not drinking enough water, a gene called Claudin-14 is responsible substantially for it.

(*a*) Jaundice   (*b*) Typhoid

(*c*) Kidney stone   (*d*) Cancer

(*e*) Malaria

118. Who among the following has recently taken over as the chairman of the Confederation of Indian Industry (CII) for 2015?

(*a*) Rahul Thakkar   (*b*) Sumit Mazumder

(*c*) Ajay S Shriram   (*d*) S Gopalakrishnan

(*e*) None of these

119. Under the mentorship of which Indian Institute of Technology (IIT), an extension IIT centre is being made operational in Chhattisgarh?

(*a*) IIT-Delhi

(*b*) IIT-Kanpur

(*c*) IIT-Kharagpur

(*d*) IIT- Kolkata

(*e*) IIT-Mumbai

120. A short-term credit investment created by a non-financial firm and guaranteed by a bank to make payment is called

(*a*) banker's acceptance

(*b*) collateral loan

(*c*) repo

(*d*) treasury bill

(*e*) call money

ENGLISH LANGUAGE

Directions (Q. 121 – 135) : *Read the following passage carefully and answer the questions given below it. Certain words are printed in bold to help you locate them while answering some of the questions.*

A goat was struggling violently and injured many people, as it was being led away by a dozen men through the street. It was being taken away for a sacrificial offering. But it became calm the moment it saw a saint. The saint bent down and said something in its ear and **patted** it on its back. He then **withdrew,** covering his face and muttering "How sad! My poor friend".

The animal now **tame** allowed itself to be led away. The onlookers **flocked** around the saint and asked him what he had whispered to the goat?

The saint explained that the goat was a reincarnation of his good friend, a wealthy man who **instituted** the sacrifice as a ritual in the village and that he had told the goat that the game was started by it in its previous birth so why was it complaining now when it was its time to be **in the same boat.** He continued "As one sows, so shall he reap".

The story spread and eventually brought an **end** to the ritual of animal slaughter in the name of sacrificial offering in the village.

121. Which of the following can be inferred from the passage?

   (a) Reincarnation is a phenomenon which occurs.

   (b) One receives as one propagates

   (c) Animal slaughter is now banned by law

   (d) Saints do have magical powers

   (e) Such stories do not have any effect

122. Why was the goat being led away by the people ?

   (A) It had helped many people

   (B) To be slaughtered as a sacrificial offering

   (C) To avoid panic in the town

   (a) Only (A)

   (b) Only (B)

   (c) Only (C)

   (d) Both (A) and (B)

   (e) None of these

123. Which of the following is **true** in the context of the passage ?

   (a) The goat was not sacrificed

   (b) The ritual of sacrifice gradully stopped in the village

   (c) The saint did not believe in reincanation

   (d) The onlookers were ashamed of themselves and avoided the saint

   (e) The goat was afraid of the saint

124. Why did the goat recognise the saint?

   (a) It was the saint who had asked people to sacrifice it

   (b) The saint was wearing a robe unlike the other onlookers

   (c) The saint had a peculiar look

   (d) The saint had been a good friend of the goat in its previous birth

   (e) None of these

125. Why did the saint mutter "How sad! My poor friend"?

   (a) He was against the lifestyle of his friend

   (b) The goat had been injured while it was being led way

   (c) The goat was dying from its wounds

   (d) He was sad because his friend was going to be killed

   (e) None of these

126. Why did the animal become docile after the saint talked to it?

   (a) It was keen to be sacrificed

   (b) It had already injured many people and was tired

   (c) The priest promised that it wouldn't be sacrificed

   (d) The goat was familiar to the priest

   (e) It had accepted that it deserved its fate

127. What was the goat in its previous birth?

   (a) A saint

   (b) A poor man

   (c) A rich man

   (d) A poor friend of the saint

   (e) A priest who slaughtered animals as an offering to God

128. The saint did not stop the sacrifice of the goat because he ________.

   (a) was incapable of doing so

   (b) feared that the onlookers may harm him

   (c) thought that it was a result of the goat's own past deeds

   (d) wanted to kill the goat himself

   (e) wanted to please goat

129. What does **"in the same boat"** mean in the context of the passage?

   (a) The goat and the saint were being sacrificed together

   (b) The goat was undergoing a ritual it had initiated in its previous life

   (c) The sain could sense how the goat must have been feeling

   (d) Animal sacrifice is as unacceptable as human sacrifice

   (e) Going to the same direction

Directions (Q. 130 – 133) : *Chooose the word that is most nearly the SAME in meaning to the word printed in bold as used in the passage.*

130. Patted

    (*a*) stroked   (*b*) flatttened

    (*c*) hit   (*d*) hurt

    (*e*) beaten

131. Flocked

    (*a*) herd   (*b*) together

    (*c*) gathered   (*d*) accompanied

    (*e*) group

132. Instituted

    (*a*) ereced   (*b*) found

    (*c*) appointed   (*d*) educated

    (*e*) established

133. Withdrew

    (*a*) resigned   (*b*) removed

    (*c*) absent   (*d*) detached

    (*e*) departed

Directions (Q. 134 – 135) : *Choose the word which is most OPPOSITE in the meaning to the word pinted in bold as used in the passage.*

134. Tame

    (*a*) spirited   (*b*) disciplined

    (*c*) cruel   (*d*) insane

    (*e*) extravagant

135. End

    (*a*) life

    (*b*) begin

    (*c*) middle

    (*d*) continue

    (*e*) start

Directions (Q. 136 – 140) : *Which of the phrases* (*a*), (*b*), (*c*) *and* (*d*) *given below should replace the phrase given in bold in the following sentence to make the sentence grammatically meaningful and correct. If the sentence is correct as it is and no correction is required, mark* (*e*) *as the answer.*

136. Many animals **had been using** for experimentation.

    (*a*) have been using

    (*b*) are being used

    (*c*) are using

    (*d*) have being used

    (*e*) No correction required

137. Most of the basic facilities **in the hospital being** quite poor.

    (*a*) in these hospitals are

    (*b*) in this hospital is

    (*c*) off these hospitals are

    (*d*) with this hospital being

    (*e*) No correction required

138. He was detained **over the airport for** possessing illegal documents.

    (*a*) into the airport

    (*b*) by the airports in

    (*c*) at the airport for

    (*d*) near the airport by

    (*e*) No correction required

139. It **was a disappointed end to** a historic match.

    (*a*) disappointment end to

    (*b*) disappointing end

    (*c*) disappointment to

    (*d*) disappointing end to

    (*e*) No correction required

140. Being injured, one of the migratory birds **have not flown** south.

    (*a*) have not flew

    (*b*) does not flew

    (*c*) have not flown

    (*d*) has not flown

    (*e*) No correction required

Directions. (Q. 141 – 145) : *Read each sentence to find out whether there is any error in it. The error, if any, will be in one part of the sentence. The letter of that part is the answer. If there is no error, the answer is* (*e*)*. (Ignore errors of punctuation, if any)*

141. Many multinational companies (*a*)/ have not been as (*b*)/ successful in India (*c*)/than we expected. (*d*) No error (*e*)

142. He has ruined (*a*)/ his eyesight (*b*)/ by not using (*c*)/ his spectacles regularly. (*d*) No error (*e*)

143. Mostly of the (*a*)/ newly recruited officers (*b*)/ have no experience (*c*)/ in the banking sector. (*d*) No error (*e*)

144. The resignation of (*a*)/ one of our directors (*b*)/ have caused the price (*c*)/ of shares to fall. (*d*) No error (*e*)

145. There are many (*a*)/ ways of which (*b*)/ inflation can (*c*)/ be measured. (*d*) No error (*e*)

Directions. (Q. 146 – 150) : *Rearrange the following six sentences (1), (2), (3), (4), (5) and (6) in the proper sequence to form a meaningful paragraph; then answer the questions given below.*

A. The able bodied men of the tribe gathered to discuss how to climb the mountain.

B. As part of their plundering they kidnapped a baby of one of the families.

C. One day the mountain tribe invaded those living in the valley.

D. "We couldn't climb the mountain. How could you?", they asked, "It wasn't your baby !" she replied.

E. There were two tribes in the Andes—one lived in the valley and the other high up in the mountains.

F. Two days later they noticed the child's mother coming down the mountain that they hadn't yet figured out how to climb.

146. Which of the following should be the SECOND sentence after rearrangement ?

(a) A   (b) B

(c) C   (d) D

(e) E

147. Which of the following should be the FIFTH sentence after rearrangement ?

(a) F   (b) E

(c) D   (d) C

(e) B

148. Which of the following should be the FIRST sentence after rearrangement ?

(a) A   (b) B

(c) C   (d) D

(e) E

149. Which of the following should be the SIXTH (LAST) sentence after rearrangement ?

(a) A

(b) B

(c) C

(d) D

(e) E

150. Which of the following should be the THIRD sentence after rearrangement ?

(a) A

(b) B

(c) C

(d) D

(e) E

Directions (Q. 151 – 160) : *In the following passage there are blanks each of which has been numbered. These numbers are printed below the passage and against each five words/phrases are suggested one of which fits the blank appropriately. Find out the appropriate word in each case.*

I used to look...(**151**)... to the holidays. I was usually ...(**152**)... to my uncle's house where I ...(**153**)... his children. I did not get paid a salary for ...(**154**)... What I received in return however, was far more ...(**155**)... My uncle was an avid reader. During the time I spent with his family I had an ...(**156**)... to read the vast amount of books and magazines that he possessed. This improved my English to some ...(**157**)... Reading became my new ...(**158–159**)... spending my pocket money on a ticket to the cinema I began to ...(**160**)... books. This has benefited me greatly.

151. (a) forward   (b) towards

(c) backward   (d) up

(e) around

152. (a) went   (b) sent

(c) visited   (d) travelled

(e) gone

153. (a) cared   (b) occupy

(c) guarded   (d) taught

(e) played

154. (a) them   (b) whom

(c) this   (d) now

(e) which

155. (a) expensive   (b) deserving

(c) helping   (d) demanding

(e) valuable

156. (a) opportunity   (b) ability

(c) use   (d) encouragement

(e) achievement

157. (a) distance   (b) extent

(c) time   (d) limits

(e) degrees

158. (a) activity   (b) hope

(c) hobby   (d) duty

(e) worship

159. (a) despite   (b) though

(c) by   (d) instead of

(e) while

160. (a) sell   (b) read

(c) exchange   (d) invest

(e) buy

COMPUTER KNOWLEDGE

161. The most commonly used standard data code to represent alphabetical, numerical and punctuation characters used in electronic data processing system is called—
(a) ASCII
(b) EBDIC
(c) BCD
(d) EDIAC
(e) All of these

162. A compiler is a translating program which—
(a) Translates instruction of a high language into machine language
(b) Translates entire source program into machine language program
(c) It is not involved in program's execution
(d) All of these
(e) None of these

163. Microprocessors can be used to make—
(a) Digital systems
(b) Computers
(c) Calculator
(d) All of these
(e) None of these

164. Storage capacity of magnetic disk depends on—
(a) Tracks per inch of surface
(b) Bits per inch of tracks
(c) Disk pack in disk surface
(d) All of these
(e) None of these

165. Who invented the microprocessor?
(a) Marcian E. Huff
(b) Herman H. Goldstein
(c) Joseph Jacquard
(d) Johnson Swift
(e) All of these

166. Computer instructions written with the use of English words instead of binary machine code is called—
(a) Mnemonics
(b) Symbolic code
(c) Gray code
(d) Opcode
(e) Logic code

167. Which part of the computer is used for calculating and comparing ?
(a) Disk unit
(b) Control unit
(c) ALU
(d) Modem
(e) Compiler

168. As compared to the secondary memory, the primary memory of a computer is—
(a) Large
(b) Cheap
(c) Fast
(d) Slow
(e) Small

169. An application program that helps the user to change any number and immediately see the result of that change to—
(a) Desktop publishing program
(b) Database
(c) Spreadsheet
(d) Both (b) and (c)
(e) None of these

170. The system unit of a personal computer contains all of the following except—
(a) Microprocessor
(b) Disk controller
(c) Serial interface
(d) Modem
(e) None of these

171. A program used to browse the web is called—
(a) Browser
(b) Modem
(c) Bootstrap
(d) Processor
(e) Converter

172. The device which sends computer data using a phone line is called—
(a) Repeater
(b) Bridge
(c) Modem
(d) Router
(e) Browser

173. The processing of eliminating programming faults is known as—
(a) Correcting
(b) Debugging
(c) Deleting
(d) Shorting
(e) None of these

174. The unwanted or non-requested e-mails are called—
(a) Spam
(b) Blog
(c) Popup
(d) Both (a) and (b)
(e) None of these

175. A collection of 8 bits is called—
(a) Nibble
(b) Byte
(c) Word
(d) Assembler
(e) None of these

176. The component that process data are located in the—
(a) Input devices
(b) Output devices
(c) System unit
(d) Storage component
(e) None of these

177. The operating system manages—
(*a*) Memory　(*b*) Processes
(*c*) Disk and I/O devices　(*d*) All of these
(*e*) None of these

178. Servers are computers that provide resources to other computers connected to a—
(*a*) Mainframe　(*b*) Network
(*c*) Super computer　(*d*) Client
(*e*) Converter

179. A software used to convert source program instructions to object instruction is known as—
(*a*) Compiler　(*b*) Assembler
(*c*) Interpretor　(*d*) Language processor
(*e*) Router

180. DSL is an example of which connection—
(*a*) Network　(*b*) Wireless
(*c*) LAN　(*d*) Broadband
(*e*) None of these

181. One thousand bytes is a—
(*a*) Kilobyte　(*b*) Megabyte
(*c*) Gigabyte　(*d*) Terabyte
(*e*) None of these

182. The fastest memory is—
(*a*) Hard disk　(*b*) Virtual memory
(*c*) Cache memory　(*d*) Magnetic tape
(*e*) Floppy disk

183. 'CRAY X-MP' is name of—
(*a*) Vector computer　(*b*) Super computer
(*c*) Array computer　(*d*) Mainframe computer
(*e*) None of these

184. Output printed through a printer is referred to as—
(*a*) Soft copy output　(*b*) Hard copy output
(*c*) Temporary output　(*d*) Volatile output
(*e*) None of these

185. The section of the CPU that selects interprets and sees to the execution of program—
(*a*) Memory　(*b*) Register unit
(*c*) Control unit　(*d*) ALU
(*e*) All of these

186. Routers are often used to implement FIRWALLS—
(*a*) True
(*b*) False
(*c*) Depends on the network
(*d*) Depends on the System
(*e*) None of these

187. Fibre optic cable is often used to—
(*a*) Replace UTP because it is cheaper
(*b*) Overcome distance limitation
(*c*) Connect PC's to wall outlets
(*d*) Both (*b*) and (*c*)
(*e*) None of these

188. Which of the following is a database administrator's function ?
(*a*) Database design
(*b*) Backing up the database
(*c*) Performance monitoring
(*d*) All of these
(*e*) None of these

189. What is the name given to the database management system which is able to handle full text data, image data, audio and video ?
(*a*) Full media　(*b*) Graphics media
(*c*) Multimedia　(*d*) Hyper text
(*e*) Animation

190. Updating a database means—
(*a*) revising the file structure
(*b*) reorganizing the database
(*c*) modifying or adding record occurrence
(*d*) Both (*a*) and (*b*)
(*e*) None of these

191. In the DBM approach, application program perform the
(*a*) Storage function　(*b*) Processing function
(*c*) Access control　(*d*) All of these
(*e*) None of these

192. The distinguishable parts of a record are called—
(*a*) Files　(*b*) Data
(*c*) Fields　(*d*) Database
(*e*) Memory

193. A relational database management (RDMS) package manages data in more than one file at once. How does it organize these files ? As—
(*a*) Tables　(*b*) Relation
(*c*) Tuple　(*d*) Both (*a*) and (*b*)
(*e*) None of these

194. Which peripheral port provides the FASTEST throughput to laser printer ?
(*a*) RS-232　(*b*) SCSI
(*c*) Parallel　(*d*) Serial
(*e*) CS-480

195. A modem could be attached to which port ?

    (*a*) Parallel port   (*b*) ASYNC port

    (*c*) Keyboard connector   (*d*) Video port

    (*e*) None of these

196. What is a common language that computers used to talk with one other on a network ?

    (*a*) Client   (*b*) Adapter

    (*c*) Protocol   (*d*) Operating system

    (*e*) Compiler

197. A parity error usually indicates a problem with—

    (*a*) Memory

    (*b*) Hard drive

    (*c*) Hard drive controller

    (*d*) I/O controller

    (*e*) Data

198. Every video card must have—

    (*a*) CMOS   (*b*) RAM

    (*c*) CPU   (*d*) All of these

    (*e*) None of these

199. Which is the easiest component to environmentally recycle ?

    (*a*) Motherboards

    (*b*) CMOS batteries

    (*c*) Toner cartridges

    (*d*) Cathode ray tube

    (*e*) All of these

200. What are the IRQ's for sound card?

    (*a*) IRQ8   (*b*) IRQ4

    (*c*) IRQ5   (*d*) IRQ7

    (*e*) IRQ2

ANSWERS

1. (*a*)	**2.** (*d*)	**3.** (*c*)	**4.** (*b*)	**5.** (*e*)	**6.** (*c*)	**7.** (*d*)	**8.** (*e*)	**9.** (*b*)	**10.** (*a*)
11. (*e*)	**12.** (*a*)	**13.** (*c*)	**14.** (*d*)	**15.** (*b*)	**16.** (*b*)	**17.** (*d*)	**18.** (*a*)	**19.** (*a*)	**20.** (*e*)
21. (*d*)	**22.** (*c*)	**23.** (*c*)	**24.** (*b*)	**25.** (*b*)	**26.** (*e*)	**27.** (*c*)	**28.** (*a*)	**29.** (*d*)	**30.** (*e*)
31. (*e*)	**32.** (*c*)	**33.** (*b*)	**34.** (*c*)	**35.** (*d*)	**36.** (*a*)	**37.** (*e*)	**38.** (*c*)	**39.** (*b*)	**40.** (*c*)
41. (*e*)	**42.** (*c*)	**43.** (*b*)	**44.** (*a*)	**45.** (*e*)	**46.** (*e*)	**47.** (*d*)	**48.** (*c*)	**49.** (*b*)	**50.** (*c*)
51. (*a*)	**52.** (*c*)	**53.** (*e*)	**54.** (*b*)	**55.** (*e*)	**56.** (*a*)	**57.** (*c*)	**58.** (*e*)	**59.** (*c*)	**60.** (*a*)
61. (*a*)	**62.** (*b*)	**63.** (*a*)	**64.** (*e*)	**65.** (*c*)	**66.** (*c*)	**67.** (*c*)	**68.** (*a*)	**69.** (*b*)	**70.** (*c*)
71. (*d*)	**72.** (*a*)	**73.** (*e*)	**74.** (*a*)	**75.** (*d*)	**76.** (*c*)	**77.** (*b*)	**78.** (*e*)	**79.** (*a*)	**80.** (*d*)
81. (*e*)	**82.** (*c*)	**83.** (*c*)	**84.** (*d*)	**85.** (*a*)	**86.** (*c*)	**87.** (*d*)	**88.** (*b*)	**89.** (*c*)	**90.** (*c*)
91. (*d*)	**92.** (*d*)	**93.** (*c*)	**94.** (*c*)	**95.** (*c*)	**96.** (*a*)	**97.** (*a*)	**98.** (*c*)	**99.** (*a*)	**100.** (*e*)
101. (*d*)	**102.** (*d*)	**103.** (*b*)	**104.** (*c*)	**105.** (*c*)	**106.** (*c*)	**107.** (*a*)	**108.** (*a*)	**109.** (*b*)	**110.** (*b*)
111. (*c*)	**112.** (*a*)	**113.** (*a*)	**114.** (*d*)	**115.** (*d*)	**116.** (*d*)	**117.** (*c*)	**118.** (*b*)	**119.** (*c*)	**120.** (*a*)
121. (*b*)	**122.** (*b*)	**123.** (*b*)	**124.** (*d*)	**125.** (*d*)	**126.** (*e*)	**127.** (*c*)	**128.** (*c*)	**129.** (*b*)	**130.** (*a*)
131. (*c*)	**132.** (*e*)	**133.** (*b*)	**134.** (*a*)	**135.** (*e*)	**136.** (*b*)	**137.** (*a*)	**138.** (*c*)	**139.** (*d*)	**140.** (*d*)
141. (*d*)	**142.** (*e*)	**143.** (*a*)	**144.** (*c*)	**145.** (*b*)	**146.** (*c*)	**147.** (*a*)	**148.** (*e*)	**149.** (*d*)	**150.** (*b*)
151. (*a*)	**152.** (*b*)	**153.** (*d*)	**154.** (*c*)	**155.** (*e*)	**156.** (*a*)	**157.** (*b*)	**158.** (*c*)	**159.** (*d*)	**160.** (*e*)
161. (*a*)	**162.** (*d*)	**163.** (*d*)	**164.** (*d*)	**165.** (*a*)	**166.** (*b*)	**167.** (*c*)	**168.** (*c*)	**169.** (*c*)	**170.** (*d*)
171. (*a*)	**172.** (*c*)	**173.** (*b*)	**174.** (*a*)	**175.** (*b*)	**176.** (*c*)	**177.** (*d*)	**178.** (*b*)	**179.** (*d*)	**180.** (*d*)
181. (*a*)	**182.** (*c*)	**183.** (*b*)	**184.** (*b*)	**185.** (*c*)	**186.** (*a*)	**187.** (*b*)	**188.** (*d*)	**189.** (*c*)	**190.** (*c*)
191. (*b*)	**192.** (*c*)	**193.** (*d*)	**194.** (*c*)	**195.** (*a*)	**196.** (*c*)	**197.** (*a*)	**198.** (*b*)	**199.** (*c*)	**200.** (*c*)

EXPLANATIONS

1-5.

(*i*) P @ Q → P < Q

(*ii*) P # Q → P ≤ Q

(*iii*) P $ Q → P > Q

(*iv*) P % Q → P ≥ Q

(*v*) P © Q → P = Q

1. M @ R ⇒ M < R

R © F ⇒ R = F

F # L ⇒ F ≤ L

Hence, M < R = F ≤ L

Conclusions :

I. M @ L ⇒ M < L ; True

II. R @ L ⇒ R < L ; Not True

2. T $ J ⇒ T > J

J@V ⇒ J < V

V # W ⇒ V ≤ W

Hence, T > J < V ≤ W

Conclusions :

I. T © W ⇒ T = W : Not True

II. T @ W ⇒ T < W : Not True

3. J @ D ⇒ J < D

D $ L ⇒ D > L

L # N ⇒ L ≤ N

Hence, J < D > L ≤ N

Conclusions :

I. J # L ⇒ J ≤ L : Not True

II. J $ L ⇒ J > L : Not True

But, either I or II is true.

4. R $ M ⇒ R > M

M % H ⇒ M ≥ H

H $ F ⇒ H > F

Hence, R > M ≥ H > F

Conclusions :

I. R % F ⇒ R ≥ F : Not True

II. M $ F ⇒ M > F : True

5. K $ H ⇒ K > H

H % I ⇒ H ≥ I

I © F ⇒ I = F

Hence, K > H ≥ I = F

Conclusions :

I. K $ I ⇒ K > I : True

II. H % F ⇒ H ≥ F : True

6-10.

11-15.

(*i*) All rooms are halls

⇒ Universal Affirmative (A-type)

(*ii*) Some doors are rooms

⇒ Particular Affirmative (I-type).

(*iii*) No apple is pineapple

⇒ Universal Negative (E-type).

(*iv*) Some apples are not pine apples

⇒ Particular Negative (O-type).

11. Some doors are rooms.

All rooms are halls.

I + A ⇒ I-type of Conclusion

"Some doors are halls:'

Some doors are halls.

All halls are auditoriums.

I + A ⇒ I-type of Conclusion

"Some doors are auditoriums."

Conclusion I is Converse of this Conclusion.

All rooms are halls.

All halls are auditoriums.

A + A ⇒ A-type of Conclusion

"All rooms are auditoriums."

This is Conclusion II.

12. Some gloves are socks.

All socks are shoes.

I+ A ⇒ I-type of Conclusion

"Some gloves are shoes:"

Conclusion I is Converse of this Conclusion.

13. Some mangoes are apples.

No apple is pineapple.

I + E ⇒ O-type of Conclusion

"Some mangoes are not pineapples."

Conclusions I and II form Complementary Pair. Therefore, either Conclusion I or II follows.

14. All the three Premises are Particular Affirmative. No Conclusion follows from Particular Premises.

15. Some pens are sharpeners.

All sharpeners are erasers.

I + A ⇒ I-type of Conclusion

"Some pens are erasers."

Conclusion II is Converse of this Conclusion.

Some pens are erasers.

No eraser is ink.

I + E ⇒ O-type of Conclusion

"Some pens are not ink."

All sharpeners are erasers.

No eraser is ink.

A + E ⇒ E-type of Conclusion

"No sharpener is ink."

16.

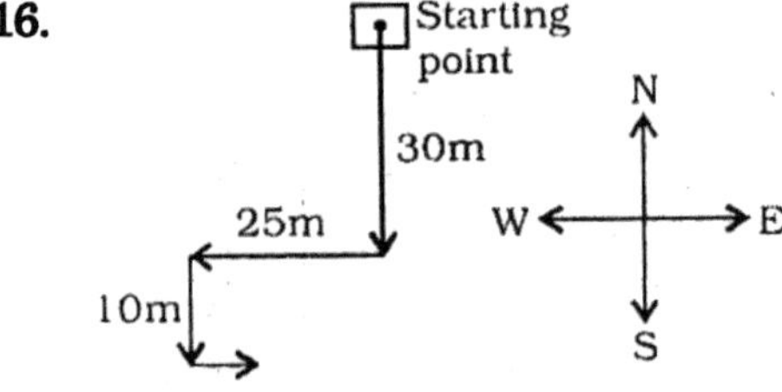

17.

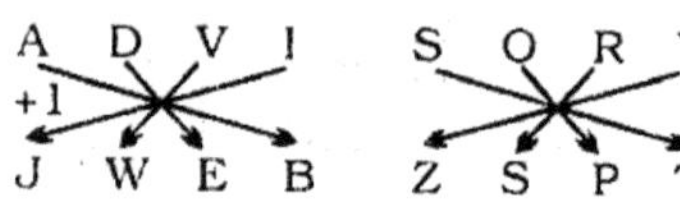

18. C's grandfather's only daughter is mother of B. C is cousin of B. Therefore, C's father is maternal uncle of B.

19. A, AC, ACE, ACEG, ACEGI, ACEGI $\boxed{K}$

20. $\boxed{1}$ 2 3 4 $\boxed{5}$ $\boxed{6}$ 7 8 9 $\boxed{10}$ 11
$\boxed{E}$ X C E $\boxed{P}$ $\boxed{T}$ I O N $\boxed{A}$ L

Meaningful words are :

      PEAT, TAPE

21. J − T → J is wife of T.

T ÷ K → T is brother of K.

K + F → K is son of F.

T and K are sons of F.

Hence, F is either Father-in-law or Mother-in-law of J.

22. R × H → R is mother of H.

H + D → H is son of D.

Hence, R is wife of D.

23. 3 $\boxed{2}$ 7 6 1 5 $\boxed{8}$
  1 $\boxed{2}$ 3 5 6 7 $\boxed{8}$

24. 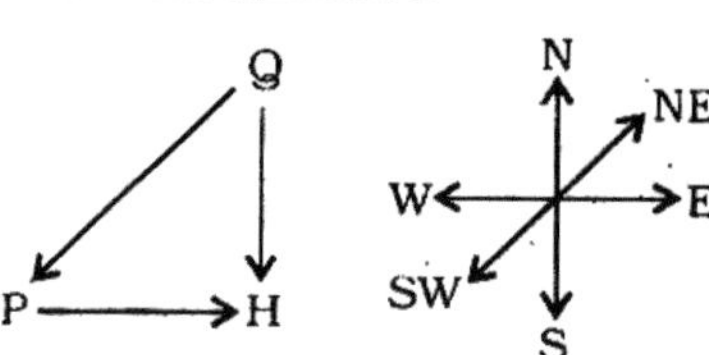

Similarly,

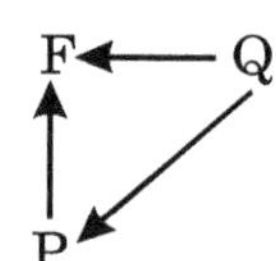

25. Colour of clear sky is blue.

But here blue is called green.

26. *From both the statements*

D E L A Y   T I D E
↓ ↓ ↓ ↓ ↓   ↓ ↓ ↓ ↓
5 7 3 8 2   6 4 5 7

Hence

T A I L
↓ ↓ ↓ ↓
6 8 4 3

27. *From statement I*

P is in south-west direction of Q.

From statement II

P is in south-west direction of Q.

28. *From statement I*

Total number of students in the class

$$= 10 + 23 - 1 = 22$$

From statement II

The rank of Nandita is eighth in the class.

29. *From both the statements*

D and A are sons of X.

A and D are brothers-in-law of M.

30. *From both the statements*

      L > T > P > J, F

31. 7 6 1 7 9 2 4 1 5 6 4 9 2 3 4 1 2 5 8 5 8 4 8 3 1 2 7 5
2 6 7 2 9 5 3

32. 7 6 1 7 9 2 4 1̲ 5 6 4 9 2 3 4 1̲ 2 5 8 5 8 4 8 3 1 2 7 5
2 6 7 2 9 5 3

33. 7 6 1 7 9 2 4 1 5 6 4 9 2 3 4 1 2 5 8 5 8 4 8 3 1 2
7 5 2 6 7 2 9 5̲ 3

34. 3rd to the left of 18th from the left

$$= (18 - 3 =)15\text{th from the left}$$

$$= 4$$

36–40.

37. C is second to the right of D.

38. C is third to the left of G.

39. A is fourth to the left of C.

40. B's position with respect to D is Fourth to the right and Fourth to the left.

41.
$$(58)^? = \frac{(58)^5 \times (58)^7}{(58)^2} \; (58)^{5+7-2}$$

$$\Rightarrow \quad (58)^? = (58)^{10}$$

$$\Rightarrow \quad\quad ? = 10$$

42. $? = (37685 + 29452 - 41897) \div 250$

$$= \frac{(67137 - 41897)}{250}$$

$$= \frac{25240}{250} = 100.96$$

43.
$$480 \times \frac{65}{100} = \frac{750 \times ?}{100}$$

$$\Rightarrow \quad 750 \times ? = 480 \times 65$$

$$\Rightarrow \quad ? = \frac{480 \times 65}{750} = 41.6$$

44. $? = \sqrt{3136} + \sqrt{4096}$

$$= 56 + 64 = 120$$

45.
$$\frac{560 \times 500}{?} = 400$$

$$\Rightarrow ? = \frac{560 \times 500}{400} = 700$$

46.
$$\frac{[144 + 36]}{(?)^2} = 7.2$$

$$\Rightarrow 7.2 \times (?)^2 = 180$$

$$\Rightarrow (?)^2 = \frac{180}{7.2} = 25$$

$$\Rightarrow ? = \sqrt{25} = 5$$

47. $? = 774 \times 326 = 252324$

48. $? = \sqrt[3]{13824} = \sqrt[3]{24 \times 24 \times 24} = 24$

49. $? = 7480 \times \dfrac{2}{3} \times \dfrac{3}{4} \times \dfrac{5}{8} = 2337.5$

50. $? = \dfrac{0.5 \times 6 \div 2.5}{4.5 + 0.6 + 0.9}$

$$= \frac{3 \div 2.5}{6} = \frac{3}{6 \times 2.5} = 0.2$$

51. Number of girls in :

School-C

$$\Rightarrow \frac{6000 \times 26}{100} - 1000 = 1560 - 1000 = 560$$

School – E

$$\Rightarrow \frac{6000 \times 29}{100} - 1200 = 1740 - 1200 = 540$$

Required answer

$$= 560 + 540 + 600 = 1700.$$

52. Number of girls in School-B

$$= \frac{6000 \times 9}{100} - 400$$

$$= 540 - 400 = 140$$

Number of students in School-E

$$= \frac{6000 \times 29}{100} = 1740$$

∴ Required ratio $= 1000 : 140 : 1740$

$$= 50 : 7 : 87.$$

53. Required difference

$$= 1200 - \frac{6000 \times 6}{100}$$

$$= 1200 - 360 = 840.$$

54. Number of students in School-B

$$= \frac{6000 \times 9}{100} = 540$$

$$= \text{Number of girls in School-E}$$

55. Number of girls in School-A

$$= \frac{6000 \times 12}{100} - 500$$

$$= 720 - 500 = 220$$

∴ Required percentage

$$= \frac{220}{540} \times 100 \approx 41.$$

56. Number of male candidates who qualified from state P in 2009

$$= \frac{85000 \times 60}{100} = 51000$$

∴ Required sum $= 51000 + 40000 = 91000.$

57. Required ratio $= 55 : 35 = 11 : 7.$

58. Number of candidates who qualified in 2004 and 2005 together from state Q = (40 + 45) thousand = 85 thousand

Total number of candidates who qualified from all the states in 2007

= (45 + 30 + 40) thousand = 115 thousand

Required percentage = $\dfrac{85}{115} \times 100 \approx 74$.

59. Number of qualified candidates from state P over the

years = (35 + 20 + 25 + 45 + 40 + 85) thousand

$\quad\quad$ = 250 thousand

Total number of qualified candidates in 2006

$\quad\quad$ = (25 + 55 + 60) thousand = 140 thousand

Difference = (250 – 140) thousand

$\quad\quad$ = 110 thousand = 1.10 lacs.

60. Percentage decrease = $\dfrac{55 - 30}{55} \times 100$

$\quad\quad = \dfrac{25}{55} \times 100 \approx 45\%$.

61. Required average number of passengers

$\quad\quad = \dfrac{1}{3}\left(\dfrac{4800 \times 51}{100}\right) = 816$.

62. Total amount paid by passengers of train-B

$\quad\quad = \dfrac{124 \times 4800 \times 9}{100} = ₹\,53{,}568$.

63. Required percentage = $\dfrac{19}{30} \times 100 \approx 63\%$.

64. Required difference = (17 – 12)% of 4800

$\quad\quad = \dfrac{4800 \times 5}{100} = 240$.

65. Required number of passengers

$\quad\quad = \dfrac{4800 \times 62}{100} = 2976$.

66. Let Raman's present age be x years.

$\therefore$ His daughter's present age = $\dfrac{x}{3}$ years

His mother's present age = $\dfrac{13x}{9}$ years

$\therefore\quad x + \dfrac{x}{3} + \dfrac{13x}{9} = 125$

$\Rightarrow\quad \dfrac{9x + 3x + 13x}{9} = 125$

$\Rightarrow\quad\quad\quad 25x = 125 \times 9$

$\Rightarrow\quad\quad\quad x = \dfrac{125 \times 9}{25} = 45$

$\therefore$ Required difference = $\dfrac{13x}{9} - \dfrac{x}{3}$

$\quad\quad = \dfrac{13x - 3x}{9} = \dfrac{10x}{9}$

$\quad\quad = \dfrac{10}{9} \times 45 = 50$ years.

67. Let 'r' be the rate of interest per annum.

$\therefore\quad$ Principal = $\dfrac{\text{Difference} \times (100)^3}{r^2(r + 300)}$

$\Rightarrow\quad 26000 = \dfrac{294.134 \times (100)^3}{r^2(r + 300)}$

$\Rightarrow\quad r^2(r + 300) = \dfrac{2994134000}{26000} = 115159$

$\Rightarrow\quad r^2(r + 300) = 19 \times 19\,(300 + 19)$

$\therefore\quad\quad\quad r = 19\%$ per annum.

68. Books on Economics are to be kept together. Hence, we have to arrange 3 books on management, 4 books on Statistics and one book on Economics.

These can be arranged in 8! ways.

Again, 4 books on Economics can be arranged together in 4! ways.

$\therefore\quad$ Total number of arrangements

$\quad\quad = 8! \times 4! = 967680$.

69. $\quad\quad$ Ajay's score = 63 + 30 = 93

$\therefore\quad$ Rahul's score = 93 – 15 = 78

$\therefore\quad$ Sum of Manish's and Suresh's scores

$\quad\quad = 3 \times 63 - 78 = 189 - 78 = 111$.

70. $\quad\quad$ Required time = LCM of 16, 22 and 30 seconds

$\quad\quad = 990$ seconds = $\dfrac{990}{60}$ minutes

$\quad\quad = 16$ minutes 30 seconds.

71. Part of the tank filled in 1 hour when all the taps are opened

$\quad\quad = \dfrac{1}{4} + \dfrac{1}{6} - \dfrac{1}{3}$

$\quad\quad = \dfrac{3 + 2 - 4}{12} = \dfrac{1}{12}$

Hence, the tank will be filled in 12 hours.

72. $\quad\quad$ S.I. = $\dfrac{\text{Principal} \times \text{Time} \times \text{Rate}}{100}$

$\quad\quad = \dfrac{11200 \times 3 \times 8.5}{100} = ₹\,2856$

$\therefore\quad$ Required amount = 11200 + 2856 = ₹14,056.

73. Let the adjacent angles of the parallelogram be $2x$ and $3x$ respectively, then

$$2x + 3x = 180°$$

$$\Rightarrow \quad 5x = 180$$

$$\Rightarrow \quad x = 36°$$

$\therefore$ Smaller angle of the parallelogram $= 2x = 72°$

$\therefore$ Smallest angle of the quadrilateral $= 36°$

$\therefore$ Largest angle of the quadrilateral $= 4 \times 36$

$$= 144°$$

$\therefore$ Required sum $= 144 + 72 = 216°$.

74. From statement I

$$x^2 - 7x + 10 = 0$$

$$x^2 - 5x - 2x + 10 = 0$$

$$x(x - 5) - 2(x - 5) = 0$$

$$(x - 2)(x - 5) = 0$$

$\therefore \qquad x = 2 \text{ or } 5$

From statements II

$$= y^2 + 11y + 10$$

$$= y^2 + 10y + y + 10$$

$$= y(y + 10) + 1(y + 10)$$

$$= (y + 1)(y + 10)$$

$\therefore \qquad y = -1 \text{ or } -10$

So, $\qquad x > y$

75. From the statement I

$$x^2 + 28x + 192 = 0$$

$$\therefore \quad x = \frac{-28 \pm \sqrt{(28)^2 - 4 \times 192}}{2}$$

$$= \frac{-28 \pm \sqrt{784 - 768}}{2}$$

$$= \frac{-28 \pm \sqrt{16}}{2}$$

$$= \frac{-28 \pm 4}{2} = -16, -12$$

From the statement II

$$y^2 + 16y + 48 = 0$$

$$\therefore \qquad y = \frac{-16 \pm \sqrt{256 - 192}}{2}$$

$$= \frac{-16 \pm \sqrt{64}}{2}$$

$$= \frac{-16 \pm 8}{2} = -12, -4$$

From statement I and II, we have

$$x \leq y$$

76. From the statement I

$$2x - 3y = -3.5 \qquad \text{...(i)}$$

$$3x + 2y = -6.5 \qquad \text{...(ii)}$$

equation $[(i) \times 2 + (ii) \times 3]$

$$13x = -\frac{53}{2}$$

$$\therefore \qquad x = -\frac{53}{26}$$

From equation (i),

$$-\frac{53}{13} - 3y = -\frac{7}{2}$$

$$3y = -\frac{15}{13}$$

$$\therefore \qquad y = -\frac{5}{13}$$

So, from above it is clear that

$$x < y$$

77. From statement I

$$x^2 + 8x + 15 = 0$$

$$x^2 + 5x + 3x + 15 = 0$$

$$x(x + 5) + 3(x + 5) = 0$$

$$(x + 3)(x + 5) = 0$$

$$x = -3 \text{ or } -5$$

From statement II

$$y^2 + 11y + 30 = 0$$

$$y^2 + 6y + 5y + 30 = 0$$

$$y(y + 6) + 5(y + 6) = 0$$

$$(y + 5)(y + 6) = 0$$

$\therefore \qquad y = -5 \text{ or } -6$

From statement I and II, we have

$$x = y \text{ or } x > y$$

Hence $\qquad x \geq y$

78. From statement I

$$x = \sqrt{3136} = 56$$

From statement II

$$y^2 = 3136$$

$$\therefore \qquad y = \sqrt{3136} = 56$$

So, it is clear that $x = y$

79.

$$\frac{x + 5x}{y + 3y} = \frac{18}{17}$$

$$\Rightarrow \qquad \frac{6x}{4y} = \frac{18}{17}$$

$$\Rightarrow \qquad \frac{x}{y} = \frac{18 \times 4}{17 \times 6} = \frac{12}{17}$$

80. Total number of sweets

$$= 50 \times 6 + 5 \times 10$$
$$= 300 + 50$$
$$= 350$$

130. Meaning of the word 'pat' as used in the passage is 'to touch somebody/something several times with your hand flat, especially as sign of affection'.

Of the given alternatives, the word 'stroke' means 'to move your hand gently and slowly over an animal's fur or hair'.

Hence, words 'patted' and 'stroked' are synonymous.

131. Meaning of the word 'flock' as used in the passage is 'to go or gather together somewhere in large numbers'.

Hence, words 'flocked' and 'gathered' are synonyous.

132. Meaning of the word 'institute' as used in the passage is 'to introduce a system, policy, etc. or start a process'.

Hence, words 'instituted' and 'established' are synonymous.

133. Meaning of the word 'withdraw' as used in the passage is 'to move back or away from a place or situation'.

Hence, words 'withrew' and removed' are synonynons.

134. Meaning of the word 'tame' as used in the passage is 'not aftraid of people, and used to living with them'; 'not fierce, domesticated', 'submissive, spiritless'.

Hence, words 'tame' and 'spirited' are antonymous.

135. Meaning of the word 'end' as used in the passage is 'the final part of a period of time, an event, an activity or a story'.

Hence, words 'end' and 'start' are antonymous.

■■

ENGLISH ABILITY

Directions (1 – 15) : *Read the following passage carefully and answer the questions given below it. Certain words have been printed in* **bold** *to help you locate them while answering some of the questions.*

Rocketing food prices have **sparked** riots in numerous countries recently. Millions are **reeling** from the price rise and goverments are scrambling to halt a fast – moving crisis before it spins out of control. From Mexico to Pakistan, Senegal and Mauritania protest have turned violent. In many poor countries, the protests have been fuelled by pent-up anger against authoritarian or corrupt officials, some of whom have earned fortunes from oil and minerals while locals are struggling to buy food. Protesters burned hundreds of food - ration stores government-subsidised food on the lucrative accusing the owners of selling black market. 'This is a serious security issue, "says Joachim von Braun, Director General of the International Food Policy Research Institute (IFPRI), in Washington. He has been bombarded by calls from officials around the world, all asking one question : How long will the crisis last?

The forecast is **grim.** Governments might **quell** the protests, but bringing down food prices could take at least a decade, food analysts say. One reason : billions of people are buying ever - greater quantities of foodespecially in booming China and India, where many have stopped growing their own food and now have the cash to buy a lot more of it. Increasing meat consumption, for example, has helped drive up demand for grain, and with it the price. There are other problems too. The spike in oil prices, an unbelievable (\$ 109 per barrel), has pushed up fertiliser prices, as well as the cost of trucking food from farms to local markets and shipping it abroad. In China, where food prices have soared 23% in a year, officials have frozen the pritce of fertiliser and boosted farm subsidies, in an effort to lower pork and wheat prices and avert possible protests. But the problems do not end there. Harvests have been seriously disrupted by freak weather, including prolonged droughts in Australia and Southern Africa, floods in West Africa, deep frost in China and record-breaking warmth in Northern Europe. The **push** to produce biofuel as an anternative to hydrocarbons is further straining food supplies, especially in the U.S., where generous subsidies for ethanol have lured thousands of farmers aways from growing crops for food and increasing the area used for biofuel cultivation. As always in a crisis, there are winners. The creeping fear that the world might actually run short of food has led speculators to pour billions into commodities accelerating price rises.

For the world's poorest people, the price spikes are disastrous. Aid officials say that millions who previously eked out enough to feed their families can no longer afford the food in their local stores, and are seeking help from relief organisations. "We are seeing a new face of hunger" says the Executive Director of the U.N's World Food Program, "People who were not in urgent category are now moving into that category. "Despite the widespread demonstrations, the food crisis has been largely ignored by North American and European officials - who pay for much of the world's food aid "because no one is starving in rich countries."

Several African countries have begun planting high - protein, pest-resistant rice crops, and aid organisations are beginning to recruit locals for new job programs to help people pay their food bills. In the poorest parts of Asia and Africa, officials hope that sky-high food prices might lift out of poverty small farmers who have barely scraped by on low crop prices - a hope that would get a big boost if the rich world agreed to cut agricultural subsidies in the current round of trade talks.

1. What have experts predicted about the current food crisis?

    (A) They believe it will pose a severe security risk.

    (B) China and India will reduce their food exports drastically to feed their own population.

    (C) It is likely that food prices will be reduced in at leat a decade.

    (*a*) only A   (*b*) both A and C

    (*c*) only B   (*d*) all A, B and C

    (*e*) none of these

2. Which of the following cannot be considered as a cause of rising foodgrain prices?

    (*a*) Increased meat consumption

    (*b*) Manipulation of commodities markets

    (*c*) Recommendation of International Food Policy Research Institutes

    (*d*) Drastic shifts in existing weather patterns

    (*e*) Exorbitant oil prices

3. What does the phrase "new face of hun-ger" imply in the context of the passage?

  (A) In some countries a large section of the middle class cannot afford food.

  (B) Aild organisations themselves cannot afford local food prices in some countries and require increased aid.

  (C) The number of people below the poverty line has drastically grown.

    (*a*) none　　　　　(*b*) only A

    (*c*) only B　　　　(*d*) both B and C

    (*e*) all A, B and C

4. Why has the area being utilised for biofuel cultivation increased ?

  (*a*) Low hydrocarbon levels have forced farmers to grow biofuels.

  (*b*) Prices of ethanol have soared resul-ting in higher profits for farmers.

  (*c*) Governments have provided a high subsidy for biofuels like ethanol.

  (*d*) Rise in prices of fertilisers required for the cultivation of traditional crops.

  (*e*) none of these

5. Why have U.S. officials not paid attention to the food crisis ?

  (*a*) Relief organisations have been handling the crisis well.

  (*b*) Crops grown for food are highly subsidised in America.

  (*c*) The U.S. has a huge surplus stock of food.

  (*d*) The percentage of those affected by the crisis in America is low

  (*e*) No one is starving in rich countries

6. What measures have relief organisations taken to help people in poorer countries to cope with the food crisis ?

  (*a*) Creating awareness among rich and develped nations about the severity of the food shortage

  (*b*) Hiring local labour to help implement new programmes

  (*c*) Providing knowledge to local farmers on the latest farming technology such as pest resistant crops

  (*d*) Threatening to wind up their operations in afflicted countries if Western countries don't increase aid

  (*e*) Campaigning to reduce fuel prices

7. How can small farmers benefit from high food prices?

  (A) If their governments increase the subsidies offered on their agricultural produce

  (B) If rich countries participate in trade talks to set fixed export duties

  (C) If all governments agree to subsidise oil prices

    (*a*) none　　　　　(*b*) only A

    (*c*) both A and B　(*d*) only C

    (*e*) all A, B and C

8. Which of the following is **not** an impact of high food prices?

  (A) Riots and destruction of property in many parts of the world

  (B) IFPRI has been boycotted by several governments

  (C) Officials have become rich by capitalising on high prices

    (*a*) only A　　　　(*b*) only B

    (*c*) both B and C　(*d*) both A and C

    (*e*) none of these

9. Which of the following is a measure that governments have taken to deal with the food crisis?

  (*a*) Placed the blame for the crisis on the International Food Policy Research Institute

  (*b*) Uniformly decided to cut export duties

  (*c*) Reduced subsidies on biofuels

  (*d*) Set a fixed price on fertilisers

  (*e*) none of these

10. What is the author's main objective in writing the passage ?

  (*a*) Criticising subsidy policy of rich countries

  (*b*) Urging governments to control pollution and reduce its impact on the climate

  (*c*) Berating citizens for using violent means of protest

  (*d*) Cautioning governments against speculators

  (*e*) Drawing our attention to the global and severe nature of the food crisis

Directions (Q. 11 – 13) : *Choose the word which is* ***most similar*** *in meaning to the word printed in* **bold** *as used in the passage.........*

11. SPARKED

  (*a*) Flickered　　　(*b*) Flashed

  (*c*) Enlivened　　　(*d*) Provoked

  (*e*) Energised

12. PUSH

  (*a*) Incite　　　　(*b*) Promote

  (*c*) Drive　　　　(*d*) Assault

  (*e*) Encouragement

13. REELING

    (*a*) Stumbling   (*b*) Wavering

    (*c*) Shivering   (*d*) Falling

    (*e*) Shocked

Directions (14 – 15) : *Choose the word which is most opposite in meaning of the word printed in bold as used in the passage.*

14. QUELL

    (*a*) Agitate   (*b*) Focus

    (*c*) Rebel   (*d*) Allay

    (*e*) Oppose

15. GRIM

    (*a*) Flexible   (*b*) Pleasant

    (*c*) Amiable   (*d*) Gentle

    (*e*) Friendly

Directions (16 – 20) : *Read each sentence to find out whether there is any grammatical error or idiomatic error in it. The error, if any, will be in one part of the sentence. The number of that part is the answer. If there is no error, the answer is 'e'. (Ignore errors of punctuation, if any.)*

16. Western investors are /
                  (*a*)

reluctant to invest in /
               (*b*)

Asian countries because of the /
                  (*c*)

lack in law and order.   No error.
       (*d*)   (*e*)

17. Though the country
          (*a*)

has got independent
          (*b*)

in 1947, many districts
          (*c*)

still have no electricity   No error.
       (*d*)   (*e*)

18. After retirement many employees
                (*a*)

usually spent time with
          (*b*)

their families and
          (*c*)

engage in social work.   No error.
       (*d*)   (*e*)

19. The bank has
        (*a*)

designated an executive
          (*b*)

whom will guide customers
          (*c*)

during online transactions.   No error.
       (*d*)   (*e*)

20. Rising prices have forced
          (*a*)

consumers either to reduce
          (*b*)

their consumption else to
          (*c*)

opt for less costly products.   No error.
       (*d*)   (*e*)

Directions (Q. 21 – 25) : *Which of the phrases* (*a*), (*b*), (*c*) *and* (*d*) *given below each sentence should replace the phrase printed in* **bold** *in the sentence to make it grammatically correct? If the sentence is correct as it is given and no correction is required, mark* (*e*) *as the answer.*

21. **Improving from** the quality of new recruits, the company is planning to devote greater resources to training.

    (*a*) By improving

    (*b*) In order to improve in

    (*c*) To improve

    (*d*) An improvement of

    (*e*) No correction required

22. Your plan sounds easy in theory but it will be quite difficult **putting in practice.**

    (*a*) While in practice

    (*b*) In practice

    (*c*) When putting to practising

    (*d*) To put up for practice

    (*e*) No correction required

23. The volume of exports of goods and services from the U.S. is **all times highest.**

    (*a*) At its highest of all time

    (*b*) Higher all the time

    (*c*) Higher than all time

    (*d*) At an all time high

    (*e*) No correction required

24. **Much of the money allotted** by the State for primary education goes unspent every year.

    (*a*) Lot of the money allotted

    (*b*) Mostly of the money allotment

    (*c*) More the allotted money

    (*d*) So much of the money been allotted

    (*e*) No correction required

25. Collaboration of world leaders **has helped addressed** some of the most pressing problems the world is currently facing

(a) can help address

(b) is helping the address of

(c) will be addressed to

(d) is a help to addressing

(e) no correction required

Directions (Q. 26 – 30) : *In the following passage there are blanks, each of which has been numbered. These numbers are printed below the passage and against each, five words are suggested, one of which fits the blank appropriately. Find out the appropriate word in each case.*

Kenya is one of the few African countries which has held elections regularly **(26)** independence. Its economy **(27)** 6.4% in 2007 and it has been relatively stable till **(28)**. The sudden outbreak of violence and unrest in Kenya last month **(29)** from three root causes. The first is poverty. Despite an overall economic growth, 58% of the population are still poor - **(30)** as living on $ 2 a day or less.

26. (a) by (b) with

(c) getting (d) prior

(e) since

27. (a) achieved (b) grew

(c) expand (d) growth

(e) advanced

28. (a) presently (b) current

(c) nowadays (d) date

(e) recent

29. (a) attributes (b) traces

(c) stems (d) result

(e) ensue

30. (a) defined (b) condemned

(c) confined (d) record

(e) primarily

REASONING ABILITY

31. "Mustard" is related to 'Seed' in the same way as 'Carrot' is related to

(a) Fruit (b) Stem

(c) Flower (d) Root

(e) None of these

32. How many meaningful English words can be formed made with the letters ESTR using each letter only once in each word?

(a) None (b) One

(c) Two (d) Three

(e) More than three

33. Four of the following five are alike in certain way and so form a group. Which is the one that does not belong to that group?

(a) Cup (b) Jug

(c) Tumbler (d) Plate

(e) Pitcher

34. Four of the following five are alike in a certain way and so form a group. Which is the one that does not belong to that group?

(a) Copper (b) Mercury

(c) Iron (d) Aluminium

(e) Zinc

35. 'FI' is related to 'LO' in the same way as 'PS' is related to

(a) VY (b) VZ

(c) WZ (d) UX

(e) None of these

36. Four of the following five are alike in certain way and so form a group. Which is the one that does not belong to that group?

(a) 217 (b) 143

(c) 241 (d) 157

(e) 181

37. K is brother of T. M is mother of K. W is brother of M. How is related to T?

(a) Maternal uncle (b) Paternal uncle

(c) Grandfather (d) Data inadequate

(e) None of these

38. 'Gram' is related to 'Mass' in the same way as 'Centimeter' is related to

(a) Area (b) Volume

(c) Length (d) Sound

(e) Energy

39. Four of the following five are alike in a certain way and so form a group. Which is the one that does not belong to that group?

(a) 12 (b) 28

(c) 52 (d) 68

(e) 96

40. If 'white' means 'black', 'black' means 'red', 'red' means 'blue', blue' means 'yellow' and 'yellow' means 'grey', then which of the following represents the colour of clear sky?

(a) blue (b) red

(c) yellow (d) cannot be determined

(e) none of these

Directions (Q. 41 – 45) : *In each question below is given a group of letters followed by four combinations of digits/symbols numbered (a), (b), (c) and (d). You have to find out which of the combinations correctly represents group of letters based on the following coding system and the conditions and mark the number of that combination as your answer. If none of the four combinations correctly represents the group of letters, give (e) i.e 'None of these' as the answer.*

Letters : M D R P A T W E I F H U K Z
Digit/Symbol
Code : 5 6 # 7 8 1 @ $ 2 % 3 © 4 9

Conditions:

(*i*) If the first letter is a consonant and the last letter is a vowel, their codes are to be interchanged.

(*ii*) If both the first and the last letters are vowels, both are to be coded as ★.

(*iii*) If the first letter is a vowel and the last letter is a consonant, both are to be coded as the codes for the consonant.

41. TUKDIP
  (*a*) 1©4627   (*b*) 1©4621
  (*c*) 7©4621   (*d*) 1©6427
  (*e*) None of these

42. EFDMKA
  (*a*) $%6548   (*b*) $%654$
  (*c*) ★%654★   (*d*) 8%6548
  (*e*) None of these

43. APWTUH
  (*a*) ★7@1©★   (*b*) 87@1©3
  (*c*) 37@1©8   (*d*) 87@1©8
  (*e*) None of these

44. MARTWE
  (*a*) 58#1@$ (*b*) 58#1@5
  (*c*) $8#1@5   (*d*) $8#1@$
  (*e*) None of these

45. HEMKZI
  (*a*) 2$5493   (*b*) 3$5492
  (*c*) 3$5493   (*d*) 2$5492
  (*e*) None of these

Directions (Q. 46 – 50) : *In each of the question below are given three statements followed by two conclusions numbered I and II. You have to take the given statements to be true even if they seem to be at variance with commonly known facts. Read all the conclusions and then decide which of the given conclusions logically from the given statements disregarding commonly known facts.*

Give answer as

 (*a*) if only Conclusion I follows.
 (*b*) if only Conclusion II follows.
 (*c*) if either Conclusion I or II follows.
 (*d*) if neither Conclusion I nor II follows.
 (*e*) if both Conclusions I and II follow.

46. Statements :
  All benches are cots.
  No cot is lamp.
  Some lamps are candles.
  Conclusions :
  I. Some cots are benches.
  II. Some candles are cots.

47. Statements :
  Some cats are dogs.
  All dogs are goats.
  All goats are walls.
  Conclusions :
  I. Some walls are dogs.
  II. Some walls are cats.

48. Statements :
  Some buildings are sofas.
  Some sofas are benches.
  Some benches are tables.
  Conclusions :
  I. Some benches are sofas.
  II. No table is sofa.

49. Statements :
  All rats are bats.
  Some bats are desks.
  All desks are chairs.
  Conclusions :
  I. Some desks are rats.
  II. Some chairs are rats.

50. Statements :
  Some roads are ponds.
  All ponds are stores.
  Some stores are bags.
  Conclusions :
  I. Some bages are ponds.
  II. Some stores are roads.

Directions (Q. 51 – 55) : *In the follow questions, the symbols @, ©, $, % and★ are used with the following meanings as illustrated below :*

'P © Q' means 'P is not greater than Q'.

'P%Q' means 'P is not smaller than Q'.

'P ★ Q' means 'P is neither smaller than nor equal to Q'.

'P @ Q' means 'P is neither greater than nor equal to Q'.

'P $ Q' means 'P is neither greater than nor smaller than Q'.

Now in each of the following questions, assuming the given statements to be true, find which of the conclusions I and II given below them is/are **definitely true**.

Give answer as

(*a*) if only Conclusion I is true.

(*b*) if only Conclusion II is true.

(*c*) if either Conclusion I or II is true.

(*d*) If neither Conclusion I or II is true.

(*e*) if both Conclusions I and II are true.

51. Statements :

K @ V,   V © N,   N% F

Conclusions :

I. F @ V

II. K @ N

52. Statements :

H © W, W $ M, M @ B

Conclusions :

I. B ★ H

II. M % H

53. Statements :

D % B, B ★ T, T $ M

Conclusions :

I. T © D

II. M © D

54. Statements :

M ★ T, T @ K, K © N

Conclusions :

I. N ★ T

II. N ★ M

55. Statements :

R $ J,   J % D, D ★ f

Conclusions :

I. D $ R

II. D @ R

Directions (Q. 56 – 60): *Study the following information carefully and answer the questions given below :*

P, Q, R, S, T and M are six students of a school, one each studies in Class I-VI. Each of them has a favourite colour from red, black, blue, yellow, pink and green, not necessarily in the same order.

Q likes black and does not study in Class IV or V. The one who studies in Class IV does not like green. P studies in Class II. M likes blue and does not study in Class IV. The one who likes yellow studies in Class VI. S likes pink and studies in Class I. R does not study in Class VI.

56. In which class does R study?

  (*a*) V

  (*b*) III

  (*c*) IV

  (*d*) Data inadequate

  (*e*) None of these

57. Which colour does R like?

  (*a*) Black

  (*b*) Yellow

  (*c*) Green

  (*d*) Blue

  (*e*) None of these

58. Which colour does P like?

  (*a*) Green

  (*b*) Yellow

  (*c*) Red

  (*d*) Data inadequate

  (*e*) None of these

59. Which of the following combinations is correct?

  (*a*) P - II - Yellow

  (*b*) Q - III - Green

  (*c*) S - I - Black

  (*d*) T - V - Yellow

  (*e*) None of these

60. In which class does M study?

  (*a*) IV

  (*b*) III

  (*c*) II

  (*d*) V

  (*e*) None of these

Directions (Q. 61 – 65) : *Below in each question are given two statements (A) and (B). These statements may be either independent causes or may be effects of independent causes or a common cause. One of these statements may be the effect of the other statement. Read both the statements and decide which of the following answer choices correctly depicts the relationship between these two statements.*

Mark answer as

(*a*) if statement (A) is the cause and statement (B) is its effect.

(*b*) if statement (B) is the cause and statement (A) is its effect.

(*c*) if both the statements (A) and (B) are independent causes.

(*d*) if both the statements (A) and (B) are effects of independent causes.

(*e*) if both the statements (A) and (B) are effects of some common cause.

61. A. Many elderly people are continuously harassed by the youngsters in the locality.

  B. Many children living in the locality play till late in the evening.

62. A. The state govt has decided to change the syllabus of mathematics for Std IX from the next academic year.

  B. Many students from the state could not secure admission to the colleges of their choice.

63. A. Majority of the employees of the manufacturing company received a hefty bonus at the end of the current financial year.

  B. The manufacturing company has made considerable profit in the current financial year.

64. A. The municipal authority decided to carry out repair work of the pipeline under the main arterial road of the city.

B. Vehicular movement has been diverted through alternate roads for a period of fifteen days.

65. A. There is a significant drop in the number of people travelling by air during the last quarter.

B. There is a significant drop in the number of people travelling by long-distance trains during the last quarter.

QUANTITATIVE APTITUDE

Directions (66 – 75) : *What should come in place of the question mark (?) in the following questions ?*

66. $\dfrac{5.4 \div 3 \times 16 \div 2}{18 \div 5 \times 6 \div 3} = ?$

(a) 2   (b) 4
(c) 6   (d) 8
(e) none of these

67. $6.66 \times 66.6 \times 66 = ?$

(a) 27274.696   (b) 29274.696
(c) 31274.696   (d) 33274.696
(e) none of these

68. $1\dfrac{3}{5} + 1\dfrac{2}{7} + 1\dfrac{1}{4} = ?$

(a) $5\dfrac{9}{35}$ (b) $6\dfrac{1}{7}$
(c) $3\dfrac{2}{9}$ (d) $4\dfrac{19}{140}$
(e) none of these

69. $\sqrt{\sqrt{3969} + \sqrt{3364}} = ?$

(a) 169   (b) 121
(c) 141   (d) 15
(e) none of these

70. $\{(\sqrt{729} \times 32) \div 45\} \times ? = 10502.4$

(a) 383   (b) 476
(c) 547   (d) 651
(e) none of these

71. $?\%$ of $225 + 22\%$ of $555 = 203.1$

(a) 23   (b) 44
(c) 36   (d) 58
(e) none of these

72. $\{(35)^2 + (38)^2\} \div ? = 5$

(a) 503   (b) 543.6
(c) 567.8   (d) 592
(e) none of these

73. $(18.92)^2 - \sqrt{121} = ?$

(a) 386.9466   (b) 346.9664
(c) 366.9646   (d) 356.6964
(e) none of these

74. $1000^{12} \div 10^{30} = ?$

(a) 1000^2 (b) 10
(c) 100^2 (d) 100
(e) none of these

75. 64% of $562.8 = 25\%$ of?

(a) 678.909   (b) 1134.564
(c) 360.192   (d) 1440.768
(e) none of these

76. Out of 5 women and 4 men, a committee of three members is to be formed in such a way that at least one member is a woman. In how many different ways can this be done?

(a) 80   (b) 84
(c) 76   (d) 96
(e) None of these

77. The present ages of Amit and his father are in the ratio of 2 : 5 respectively. Four years hence the ratio of their ages will become 5 : 11 respectively. What was the father's age five years ago?

(a) 40 years   (b) 45 years
(c) 30 years   (d) 35 years
(e) None of these

78. Twice the square of a number is six times the other number. What is the ratio of the first number to the second?

(a) 1 : 4   (b) 2 : 5
(c) 1 : 3   (d) Cannot be determined
(e) None of these

79. Manoj sold an article for Rs 15,000. Had he offered a discount of 10% on the selling price, he would have earned a profit of 8%. What is the cost price?

(a) Rs. 12,500   (b) Rs.13,500
(c) Rs. 12,250   (d) Rs. 13,250
(e) None of these

80. The cost of 8 pens and 4 pencils is Rs. 176 and the cost of 2 pens and 2 pencils is Rs.48. What is the cost of one pen?

(a) Rs. 16   (b) Rs. 14
(c) Rs. 12   (d) Rs. 18
(e) None of these

Directions (Q. 81 – 85): *Study the following table carefully to answer these questions.*

Table showing number (in lakhs) of instruments manufactured by six companies over the years

Company→ Year ↓	A	B	C	D	E	F
2002	45	35	48	42	50	49
2003	40	32	52	46	48	45
2004	48	36	50	43	56	48
2005	49	37	45	48	52	44
2006	46	30	55	50	54	50
2007	52	38	47	40	51	52

81. What is the average number of instruments manufactured by Company C for all the given years?

  (*a*) 49,00,000   (*b*) 49,50,000

  (*c*) 48,50,000   (*d*) 48,00,000

  (*e*) None of these

82. The no. of instruments manufactured by Company E in 2004 is approximately what per cent of the total no. of instruments manufactured by all the companies together in 2004?

  (*a*) 23   (*b*) 25

  (*c*) 20   (*d*) 16

  (*e*) 18

83. The total number of instruments manufactured by Company A is **approximately** what per cent of the total no. of instruments manufactured by Company F for all the given years together?

  (*a*) 97   (*b*) 87

  (*c*) 92   (*d*) 90

  (*e*) 85

84. The number of instruments manufactured by Company B in 2005 is approximately what per cent of the total no. of instruments manufactured by Company B in all the years together?

  (*a*) 20   (*b*) 16

  (*c*) 14   (*d*) 18

  (*e*) 22

85. What is the ratio of the total no. of instruments manufactured by all the companies together in 2007 to that in 2006?

  (*a*) 56 : 57   (*b*) 57 : 56

  (*c*) 29 : 28   (*d*) 28 : 29

  (*e*) None of these

Directions (Q. 86 – 90) : *Study the following graph carefully to answer these questions.*

Population of two states (in lakhs) over the years.

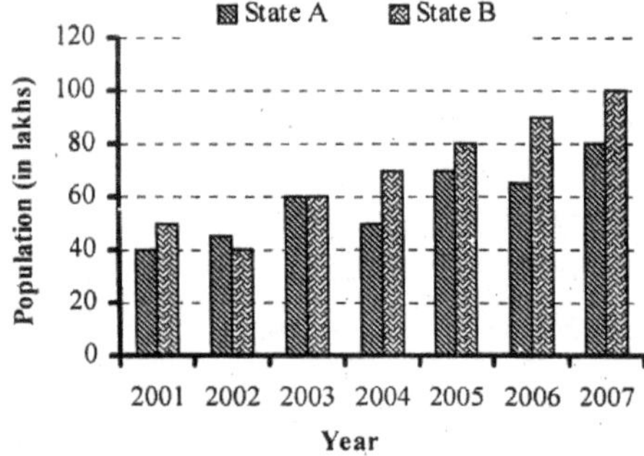

86. The population of State B in 2002 is what per cent of the total population of State B in all the years together? (Rounded off to two digits after decimal)

  (*a*) 8.26   (*b*) 7.26

  (*c*) 8.32   (*d*) 7.82

  (*e*) None of these

87. What is the ratio of the total population of State A for the years 2001, 2002 and 2003 together to the total population of state B for the years 2005, 2006 and 2007 together?

  (*a*) 27 : 53   (*b*) 54 : 29

  (*c*) 29 : 54   (*d*) 53 : 27

  (*e*) None of these

88. For which State and in which year was the per cent rise in population from the previous year was the highest?

  (*a*) State B-2003   (*b*) State B-2002

  (*c*) State A-2004   (*d*) State A-2005

  (*e*) None of these

89. What is the per cent rise in the population of State B from 2003 to 2004?

  (*a*) $16\dfrac{1}{3}$ (*b*) $16\dfrac{2}{3}$

  (*c*) $18\dfrac{2}{3}$ (*d*) $18\dfrac{1}{3}$

  (*e*) None of these

90. Approximately what is the average population of State A for all the given years?

  (*a*) 65 lakhs   (*b*) 50 lakhs

  (*c*) 48 lakhs   (*d*) 58 lakhs

  (*e*) 52 lakhs

Directions (Q. 91 – 95) : *Study the following information carefully to answer these questions.*

Percentage of employees in various departments of an organization and the male-female ratio

Total No. of Employees = 2500

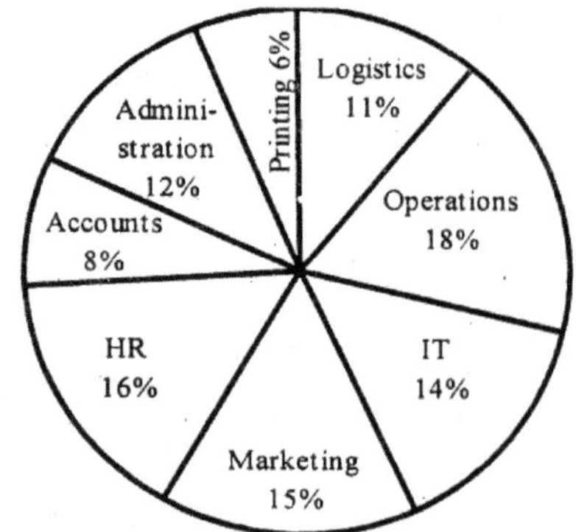

Male : Female Ratio

Department	Male : Female
Administration	7 : 5
Accounts	2 : 3
HR	5 : 3
Marketing	7 : 8
IT	3 : 4
Operations	5 : 4
Logistics	6 : 5
Printing	2 : 1

91. What is the ratio of male employees in Administration to those in Printing Department?

(a) 7 : 4

(b) 4 : 7

(c) 3 : 4

(d) 7 : 3

(e) None of these

92. What is the difference between the total number of employees in IT and that in Operations Department?

(a) 75

(b) 150

(c) 100

(d) 50

(e) None of these

93. What is the ratio of the total number of males in HR and Marketing to the total number of females in these two departments?

(a) 13 : 15

(b) 15 : 13

(c) 13 : 17

(d) 17 : 14

(e) None of these

94. How many female employees are there in the HR Department?

(a) 250

(b) 120

(c) 125

(d) 150

(e) None of these

95. What is the difference between the numbers of male and female employees in Logistics Department?

(a) 50

(b) 25

(c) 75

(d) 100

(e) None of these

Directions (Q. 96 – 100) : *What will come in place of the question mark (?) in each of the following number series?*

96. 2   8   26   ?   242

(a) 78

(b) 72

(c) 82

(d) 84

(e) None of these

97. 3   4   12   ?   196

(a) 45

(b) 40

(c) 41

(d) 49

(e) None of these

98. 9   17   ?   65   129

(a) 32

(b) 24

(c) 35

(d) 33

(e) None of these

99. 7   13   ?   49   97

(a) 27

(b) 25

(c) 23

(d) 29

(e) None of these

100. 5   3   6   ?   64.75

(a) 15

(b) 15.5

(c) 17.5

(d) 17.25

(e) None of these

ANSWERS

1. (b)	2. (c)	3. (b)	4. (c)	5. (e)	6. (c)	7. (a)	8. (b)	9. (e)	10. (e)
11. (d)	12. (e)	13. (e)	14. (a)	15. (b)	16. (d)	17. (b)	18. (b)	19. (c)	20. (c)
21. (c)	22. (b)	23. (d)	24. (e)	25. (a)	26. (e)	27. (b)	28. (d)	29. (c)	30. (a)
31. (d)	32. (b)	33. (d)	34. (b)	35. (a)	36. (b)	37. (a)	38. (c)	39. (d)	40. (b)
41. (a)	42. (c)	43. (e)	44. (c)	45. (a)	46. (a)	47. (e)	48. (c)	49. (d)	50. (b)
51. (b)	52. (e)	53. (d)	54. (a)	55. (c)	56. (c)	57. (e)	58. (a)	59. (e)	60. (d)
61. (d)	62. (c)	63. (b)	64. (a)	65. (e)	66. (a)	67. (b)	68. (d)	69. (e)	70. (c)
71. (c)	72. (e)	73. (b)	74. (a)	75. (d)	76. (a)	77. (d)	78. (d)	79. (a)	80. (e)
81. (b)	82. (e)	83. (a)	84. (d)	85. (a)	86. (e)	87. (c)	88. (a)	89. (b)	90. (d)
91. (a)	92. (c)	93. (d)	94. (d)	95. (b)	96. (e)	97. (a)	98. (d)	99. (b)	100. (c)

EXPLANATIONS

31. The first is found in the form of the second.

32. REST

33. All others are used to contain liquid.

34. All other metals are solid.

35. Corresponding letters are obtained by moving six places forward in the alphabet.

36. All others are of the form $12n + 1$, but 143 is of the form $12n - 1$, where n is a natural number

37. 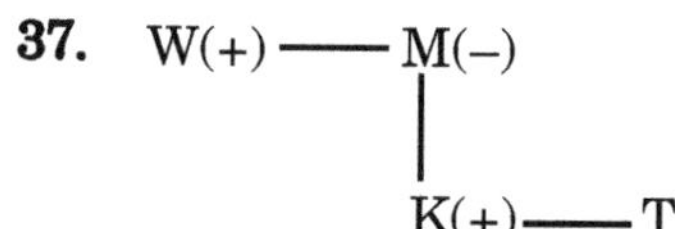

38. The first is a unit of the second.

39. All others are prime multiples of 4.

40. The colour of sky is blue, but here 'red' means 'blue'.

41. No condition applies

42. Condition (*ii*) applies

43. Condition (*iii*) applies and we get 37@1©3

44. Condition (*i*) applies.

45. Condition (*i*) applies.

46. All benches are cots (A) → conversion
→ Some cots are benches.
Hence I follows.
No cot is lamp + some lamps are candles
= E + I = O*
= Some candles are not cots.
Hence II does not follow.

47. All dogs are goats + All goats are walls
= A + A = A
= All dogs are walls
→ conversion
→ Some walls are dogs (I).
Hence I follows.
Some cats are dogs
+ all dogs are walls
= 1 + A = I
= Some cats are walls
→ conversion
→ Some walls are cats (I).
Hence II follows.

48. Some sofas are benches
+ Some benches are tables
= I + I = No conclusion.
Hence I and II do not follow by combination. However, since they make a complementary) I-E pair, either I or II follows.

49. All rats are bats + Some bats are desks
= A + I = No conclusion.
Hence I and subsequently II do not follow.

50. All ponds are stores
+ Some stores are bags
= A + I = No conculusion.
Hence I does not follow.
Some roads are ponds
+ All ponds are stores
= I + A = I
= Some roads are stores
→ conversion
→ Some stores are roads (I).
Hence II follows.

51.
$$K < V \quad ....(i)$$
$$V \le N \quad ....(ii)$$
$$N \ge F \quad ....(iii)$$
From (*ii*) and (*iii*), F and V can't be compared. Hence I does not follow.
From (*i*) and (*ii*),
$$K < V \le N \text{ or } K < N.$$
Hence II follows.

52.
$$H \le W \quad ....(i)$$
$$W = M \quad ....(ii)$$
$$M < B \quad ....(iii)$$
Combining these, we get
$$H \le W = M < B.$$
Hence, B > H and I follows.
Also, $M \ge H$ and II follows.

53.
$$D \ge B \quad ....(i)$$
$$B > T \quad ....(ii)$$
$$T = M \quad ....(iii)$$
Combining these, we get
$$D \ge B > T = M.$$
Hence, $T < D$ and I ($T \le D$) does not follow.
Also, $M < D$ and II ($M \le D$) does not follow.

54.
$$M > T \quad ....(i)$$
$$T < K \quad ....(ii)$$
$$K \le N \quad ....(iii)$$

From (ii) and (iii), we get

$$T < K \le N \text{ or } T < N \text{ or } N > T$$

Hence I follows.

But, from (i) and I, we get no relationship between M and N. Hence II does not follow.

55.
$$R = J \quad ....(i)$$
$$J \ge D \quad ....(ii)$$
$$D > F \quad ....(iii)$$

Combining these, we get $R = J \ge D > F$.

Hence $D \le R$. So either I (D = R) or II (D < R) follows.

56-60.

Student	Class	Colour
P	II	Green
Q	III	Black
R	IV	Red
S	I	Pink
T	VI	Yellow
M	V	Blue

57. Red

61-65. (A) is the effect of the presence of some wicked youngsters living in the locality while (B) is the effect of a rather peaceful atmosphere.

62. There seems to be no connection between the syllabus of Std IX and admission to colleges.

63. The "considerable profit" has led to the "hefty bonus".

64. The repair work has led to the diversion.

65. Both are the effects of a recession in the economy.

66.
$$? = \frac{5.4 \div 3 \times 16 \div 2}{18 \div 5 \times 6 \div 3}$$

$$= \frac{\dfrac{5.4}{3} \times \dfrac{16}{2}}{\dfrac{18}{5} \times \dfrac{6}{3}} = \frac{1.8 \times 8}{3.6 \times 2} = 2$$

67.
$$? = 6.66 \times 66.6 \times 66$$
$$= 29274.696$$

68.
$$? = 1 + \frac{3}{5} + 1 + \frac{2}{7} + 1 + \frac{1}{4}$$
$$= 3 + \left(\frac{3}{5} + \frac{2}{7} + \frac{1}{4}\right)$$

$$= 3 + \left(\frac{84 + 40 + 35}{140}\right) = 3 + \frac{159}{140}$$

$$= 3 + 1\frac{19}{140} = 4\frac{19}{140}$$

69.
$$? = \sqrt{\sqrt{3969} + \sqrt{3364}}$$
$$= \sqrt{63 + 58} = \sqrt{121} = 11$$

70.
$$\{(\sqrt{729} \times 32) \div 45\} \times ? = 10502.4$$
$$\Rightarrow \quad (27 \times 32) \div 45 \times ? = 10502.4$$
$$\Rightarrow \quad 19.2 \times ? = 10502.4$$
$$\Rightarrow \quad ? = \frac{10502.4}{19.2} = 547$$

71.
$$\frac{225 \times ?}{100} + \frac{555 \times 22}{100} = 203.1$$
$$\Rightarrow \quad 225 \times ? + 12210 = 20310$$
$$\Rightarrow \quad 225 \times ? = 20310 - 12210 = 8100$$
$$\Rightarrow \quad ? = \frac{8100}{225} = 36$$

72.
$$\left\{\frac{(35)^2 + (38)^2}{?}\right\} = 5$$
$$\Rightarrow \quad 5 \times ? = 1225 + 1444 = 2669$$
$$\Rightarrow \quad ? = \frac{2669}{5} = 533.8$$

73.
$$? = (18.92)^2 - \sqrt{121}$$
$$= 357.9664 - 11$$
$$= 346.9664$$

74.
$$? = \frac{(10^3)^{12}}{10^{30}} = \frac{10^{3 \times 12}}{10^{30}}$$
$$= (10)^{36-30} = (10)^6 = (1000)^2$$

75.
$$? \times \frac{25}{100} = \frac{562.8 \times 64}{100}$$
$$\Rightarrow \quad ? = \frac{562.8 \times 64}{25} = 1440.768$$

81. We assume 50 as average check deviation. From 50, we get –3 as deviation. Then

$$\text{Actual average} = \left(50 - \frac{3}{6}\right) \times 10^5$$
$$= 49,50,000$$

82.
$$\frac{560}{311} \times 100 \approx 18\%$$

83.
$$\frac{280}{288} \times 100 \approx 97\%$$

84. $\dfrac{37}{208} \times 100 \approx 18\%$

85. $280 : 285 = 56 : 57$

86. $\dfrac{40}{490} \times 100 \approx 8.16$

87. $145 : 270 = 29 : 54$

88. $B_{03} = 50\%$

$B_{03} \rightarrow$ Percentage rise of B in 2003.

$A_{05} \rightarrow$ Percentage rise of A in 2005.

89. $\dfrac{10}{60} \times 100 = 16\dfrac{2}{3}$

90. Average $= \dfrac{410}{7} \approx 58$ lakh

$[40 + 45 + 60 + 50 + 70 + 65 + 80 = 410]$

91. Ratio $= 12 \times \dfrac{7}{12} : 6 \times \dfrac{2}{3} = 7 : 4$

92. 4% of $2500 = 100$

93. Ratio $= \left(16 \times \dfrac{5}{8} + 15 \times \dfrac{7}{15}\right) : \left(16 \times \dfrac{3}{8} + 15 \times \dfrac{8}{15}\right)$

$\qquad = 17 : 14$

94. $\dfrac{3}{8} \times 16 \times 25 = 150$

96. Series is $\times 3 + 2$.

97. Series is $\times 1+1$, $\times 2 + 4$, $\times 3+9$, $\times 4 + 16$.

98. Series is $\times 2 - 1$.

99. Series is $\times 2 - 1$.

100. The series is $\times \dfrac{1}{2} + \dfrac{1}{2}, \times \dfrac{3}{2} + \dfrac{3}{2}, \times \dfrac{5}{2} + \dfrac{5}{2}, \times \dfrac{7}{2} + \dfrac{7}{2}$

REASONING

1. In a class of 60 students the numbers of boys and girls participating in the annual sports are in the ratio of 3 : 2. The number of girls from the class not participating in the sports in 5 more than the number of boys from the class who are not participating in the sports. If the number of boys participating in the sports in 15, how many girls are there in the class?
   - (a) Date inadequate
   - (b) 20
   - (c) 25
   - (d) 30
   - (e) None of these

Directions (Q. 2 – 5) : *Read the following information and answer the questions given below:*

i. P, Q, R, S and T finished the work, working from Monday to Saturday, one of the days being a holiday, each working overtime only on one of the days,

ii. R and T did not work overtime on the first days.

iii. Q worked overtime the next day after the holiday.

iv. The overtime work done on the previous day of the holiday was by R.

v. There was a two days' gap between the days on which P and Q worked overtime.

vi. P worked overtime the next day of overtime day of S.

2. When did T work overtime?
   - (a) On the days previous of that on which S worked overtime
   - (b) On the next day of the day on which Q worked overtime
   - (c) Two days after the day on which S worked overtime
   - (d) Cannot be determined
   - (e) None of these

3. How many days' gap was there between the days on which P and T worked overtime?
   - (a) Three
   - (b) Two
   - (c) One
   - (d) Cannot be determined
   - (e) None of these

4. On what day did R work overtime?
   - (a) Monday
   - (b) Tuesday
   - (c) Thursday
   - (d) Friday
   - (e) None of these

5. Which of the following is a correct statement?
   - (a) P worked overtime, last among them.
   - (b) P worked overtime earlier than S.
   - (c) The holiday was on Friday.
   - (d) S worked overtime earlier than Q.
   - (e) None of these

6. In a certain code 'acquisition or construction should be completed within three years' is written as 'three be or within should years construction completed acquisition'. How will 'interest paid on loan will be allowed for deduction' be written in that code?
   - (a) for will paid allowed loan on deduction be interest
   - (b) for will allowed paid loan deduction on be interest
   - (c) for will paid allowed loan deduction on be interest
   - (d) for will paid allowed loan deduction be on interest
   - (e) None of these

7. Which of the following will be the changed from of the word OBLIQUE when the word is written again by substituting each vowel by the 2nd letter following it in the English alphabet and each consonant is substituted by the 3rd letter following in the English alphabet?
   - (a) MEDGTSD
   - (b) RDNLSXH
   - (c) QEOKTXG
   - (d) QEOKTWG
   - (e) None of these

8. If a meaningful word can be formed using the five letters NWROD, each only once, then the fourth letter of that word is your answer.If more than one such word can be formed then Y is your answer and if no such word can be formed then 'Z' is your answer
   - (a) D
   - (b) W
   - (c) R
   - (d) Y
   - (e) Z

9. Pointing towards a girl in the picture, Sunita said, 'She is the mother of Renu, whose father is my son." How is Sunita related to that girl in the picture?
   - (a) Mother
   - (b) Aunt
   - (c) Cousin
   - (d) Data inadequate
   - (e) None of these

10. P's father is Q's son. M is the paternal uncle of P and N is the brother of Q. How is N related to M?

   (*a*) Brother   (*b*) Nephew

   (*c*) Cousin   (*d*) Data inadequate

   (*e*) None of these

Directions (Q. 11 – 15) : *Read the following information and answer the questions given below:*

  i. A, B, C, D, E, F and G are sitting along a circle facing at the centre and are playing cards.

 ii. E is the neighbour of A and (*d*)

iii. G is not between F and C

 iv. F is on the immediate right of (*a*)

11. Who are the neighbours of B?

   (*a*) C and D   (*b*) F and C

   (*c*) A and F   (*d*) Data inadequate

   (*e*) None of these

12. Which pair given below has the second person sitting immediately to the right of the first?

   (*a*) CB   (*b*) DG

   (*c*) EA   (*d*) AB

   (*e*) None of these

13. Which of the following has the persons sitting adjacent to each other from left to right in order as given?

   (*a*) CDG   (*b*) EDG

   (*c*) BGC   (*d*) FBC

   (*e*) None of these

14. What is the position of F?

   (*a*) To the immediate left of A

   (*b*) To the immediate right of B

   (*c*) 2nd to the right of C

   (*d*) 3rd to the left of D

   (*e*) None of these

15. Which of the following **does not** have the pair sitting adjacent to each other?

   (*a*) BA   (*b*) CB

   (*c*) DE   (*d*) GD

   (*e*) All are sitting adjacent to each other.

Directions (Q. 16 – 20) : *To answer these questions study the following arrangement :*

JY2 = S £ δ E G M ★ 7 $ H P 9 K L β @ W Q 1 3 # C D ©

16. How many such symbol are there in the above arrangement each of which is either immediately followed by a number or immediately preceded by a letter, but not both?

   (*a*) Nil   (*b*) 1

   (*c*) 2   (*d*) 3

   (*e*) None of these

17. How many such letters are there each of which is either immediately followed by a number of immediately preceded by a symbol, but not both?

   (*a*) 4   (*b*) 5

   (*c*) 6   (*d*) 7

   (*e*) None of these

18. How many such numbers are there each of which is either immediately followed by a symbol or immediately preceded by a letter, but not both?

   (*a*) 2   (*b*) 4

   (*c*) 3   (*d*) 5

   (*e*) None of these

19. '2YS' is to 'EG£' in the same way as 'PHK' is to

   (*a*) @WL   (*b*) WQβ

   (*c*) @3Q   (*d*) @WK

   (*e*) None of these

20. Four of the following five are alike in certain way based on the positions of the elements in the above arrangement and hence from a group. Which one **does not** belong to the group?

   (*a*) 2YCD   (*b*) £S13

   (*c*) JS©3   (*d*) £E1W

   (*e*) =#2C

Directions (Q. 21 – 25) : *Below in each question are given two statements (A) and (B). These statements may be either independent causes or may be effects of independent causes or a common cause. One of these statements may be the effect of the other statement. Read both the statements and decide which of the following answer choices correctly depicts the relationship between these two statements.*

Mark answer as

  (*a*) if statement (A) is the cause and statement (B) is its effect.

  (*b*) if statement (B) is the cause/and statement (A) is its effect.

  (*c*) if both the statements (A) and (B) are inde-pendent causes.

  (*d*) if both the statements (A) and (B) are effects of independent causes.

  (*e*) if both the statements (A) and (B) are effects of some common cause.

21. (*a*) Huge tidal waves wrecked the vast coastline early in the morning killing thousands of people.

    (*b*) Large number of people gathered along the coastline to enjoy the spectacular view of sunrise.

22. (*a*) The Govt: has suspended several police officers in the city.

(*b*) Five persons carrying huge quantity of illicit liquor were apprehended by police.

23. (*a*) The traffic police removed the signal post at the intersection of two roads in a quiet locality.

(*b*) There have been many accidents at the intersection involving vehicles moving at high speed.

24. (*a*) The local steel company has taken over the task of development and maintenance of the civic roads in the town.

(*b*) The local civic body requested the corporate bodies to help them maintain the civic facilities.

25. (*a*) Majority of the students in the college expressed their opinion against the college authority's decision to break away from the university and become autonomous.

(*b*) The university authority has expressed it inability to provide grants to its constituent colleges.

Directions (Q. 26 – 30) : *In each question below is given a statement followed by two assumptions numbered I and II. An assumption is something supposed or taken for granted. You have to consider the statement and the following assumptions and decide which of the assumptions is implicit in the statement.*

Give answer as

(*a*) if only Assumption I is implicit.

(*b*) if only Assumption II is implict.

(*c*) if either I or II is implicit.

(*d*) if neither I nor II is implicit.

(*e*) if both I and II are implicit.

26. Statements :

The General Administration Departement has issued a circular to all the employees informing them that hence forth the employees can avail their lunch break at any of the half-hour slots between 1.00 pm and 2.30 pm.

Assumptions :

I. The employees may welcome the decision and avail lunch break at different time slots.

II. There may not be any break in the work of the organisation as the employees will have their lunch break at different time slots.

27. Statement :

The Government has decided against reduction of prices of petroleum products though there is a singnificant drop in the crude oil prices in the international market.

Assumptions :

I. The prices of crude oil in the international market may again increase in the near futur(*e*)

II. The present price difference of petroleum products will help the government to withstand any possible price rise in futur(*e*)

28. Statement :

The Govt has made an appeal to all the citizens to honestly pay income tax and file returns reflecting the true income level to help the Government to carry out developmental activities.

Assumptions :

I. People may now start paying more taxes in response to the appeal.

II. The total income tax collection may considerably increase in the near futur(*e*)

29. Statement :

The state government has decided to appoint four thousand primary school teachers during the next financial year.

Assumptions :

I. There are enough schools in the state to accommodate four thousand additional primary school teachers.

II. The eligible candidates may not be interested to apply as the Government may not finally appoint such a large number of primary school teachers.

30. Statement :

The school authority has decided to increase the number of students in each classroom to seventy form the next academic session to bridge the gap between income and expenditure to a large extent.

Assumptions :

I. The income generated by way of fees of the additional students will be sufficient enough to bridge the gap.

II. The school will get all the additional students in each class from the next academic session.

Directions (Q. 31 – 35) : *In making decisions about important questions, it is desirable to be able to distinguish between 'strong' arguments and 'week' arguments. 'Strong' arguments are those which are both important and directly related to the quesiton. 'Weak' arguments are those which are of minor importance and also may not be directly related to the question or may be related to a trivial aspect of the question.*

Each question below is followed by two arguments numbered I and II. You have to decide which of the arguments is 'strong' argument and which is a 'weak' argument.

Give answer as

(*a*) if only argument I is strong.

(*b*) if only argument II is strong.

(*c*) if eigher I and II is strong.

(*d*) if neither I nor II is strong.

(*e*) if both I and II are strong.

31. Should the parents in India in future be forced to opt for only one child as against two or many at present?

Arguments :

I. Yes, this is the only way to check the ever-increasing population of India.

II. No, this type of pressure tactic is not adopted by any other country in the world.

32. Should the sex determination test during pregnacny be completely banned?

Arguments :

I. Yes, this leads to indiscriminate female foeticide and eventually will lead to social imbalance.

II. No, people have a right to know about their unborn child.

33. Should all the slums in big cities be demolished and the people living in such slums be relocated outside the city limits?

Arguments :

I. No, all these people will lose their home and livelihood and hence they should not be relocated.

II. Yes, the big cities need more and more spaces to carry out development activities and hence these slums should be removed.

34. Should there be a complete ban on mining coal in India?

Arguments :

I. Yes, the present stock of coal will not last long if we continue mining at the present rat(*e*)

II. No, we do not have alternate energy source of sufficient quanitity.

35. Should there be uniforms for students in the colleges in India as in the schools ?

Arguments :

I. Yes, this will improve the ambience of the colleges as all the students will be decently dressed.

II. No, college students should not be regimented and they should be left to choose their clothes for coming to college.

Directions (Q. 36 – 40) : *In the following questions, the symbols @, #, % ✶ and $ are used with the following meaning as illustrated below.*

'P @ Q' means 'P is not smaller than Q'.

'P # Q' means 'P is not greater than Q'.

'P % Q' means 'P is neither greater than nor equal to Q'.

'P ✶ Q' means 'P is neither smaller than nor greater than Q'.

'P $ Q' means 'P is neither smaller than nor equal to Q'.

Now in each of the following quesitons assuming the given statements to be true, find which of the three conclusions, I, II and III given below them is/are **definitely true** and give your answer accordingly.

36. Statements :

M % R,   R # T,   T ✶ N

Conclusions :

I. N ✶ R

II. N $ R

III. N$M

(*a*) All follow

(*b*) Only either I or II follows

(*c*) Only either I or II and III follow

(*d*) Only either I or III and II follow

(*e*) None of these

37. Statements :

J # N,   K @ N,   T $ K

Conclusions :

I. J % T

II. T $ N

III. N @ J

(*a*) None follows

(*b*) Only I and II follow

(*c*) Only I and III follow

(*d*) Only II and III follow

(*e*) All follow

38. Statements :

B ✶ D,   D @ H,   H % F

Conclusions :

I. B ✶ F

II. B $ F

III. D $ F

(*a*) None follows

(*b*) Only either I or II follows

(*c*) Only either I or II and III follow

(*d*) Only III follows

(*e*) All follow

39. Statements :

T $ K, K # R, R ✷ M

Conclusions :

I. M ✷ K

II. M % T

III. M $ K

(a) All follow

(b) Only either I or III follows

(c) Only either I or II follows

(d) Only either II or III follows

(e) None of these

40. Statements :

V @ M, A $ M, R # V

Conclusions :

I. R # A

II. V @ A

III. R $ M

(a) Only follows   (b) Only II follows

(c) Only III follows   (d) None follows

(e) All follow

Directions (Q. 41 – 45) : *Each of the question below contains three elements. These three elements may or may not have some linkage. Each group of the elements may fit into one of the diagrams at (1), (2), (3), (4) and (5). You have to indicate the groups of elements in each of the questions fit into which of the diagrams given below. The number of the diagram is the answer.*

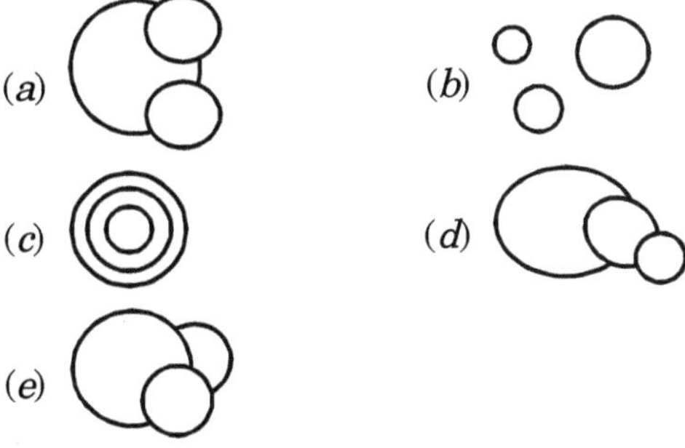

41. Cloth, Cotton, Shirt

42. Paper, Stationery, Ink

43. Iron, Lead, Nitrogen

44. Classroom, Blackboard, School

45. Hockey, Football, Cricket

Directions (Q. 46 – 50) : *Below is given a passage followed by several possible inferences which can be drawn from the facts stated in the passage. You have to examine each inference separately in the context of the passage and decide upon its degree of truth or falsity.*

Mark answer as

(a) if the inference is **'definitely true'**, ie it properly follows from the statment of facts given.

(b) if the inference is **'probably true'** though not 'definitely true' in the light of the facts given.

(c) if the **'data are inadequate'**, ie from the facts given you cannot say whether the inference is like to be ture or fals(e)

(d) if the inference is **'probably false'** though not **'definitely false'** in the light of the facts given.

(e) if the inference is 'definitely false', i.(e) it cannot possibly be drawn from the facts given or it contradicts the given facts.

Economic liberalisation and globalisation have put pressures on Indian industry, particularly on the service sector, to offer quality products and services at low costs and with high speed. Organisations have to compete with unequal partners from abroad. It is well recognised that develping countries like India are already behind other countries technologically, in many areas although **some** of them, particularly India, boast of huge scientific and technical manpower. In addition to this, if an entrepreneur or industrialist has to spend a lot of his time, money and energy in dealing with unpredictable services and in negotiating with the local bureaucracy, if can have a significant dampening effect on business.

46. No other developing country except India claims that they have highly trained technical manpower.

47. Foreign companies are more equipped than domestic companies to provide quality service in good tim(e)

48. Official formalities are less cumbersome in almost all the countries except India.

49. Indian service industry was more comfortable before economic liberalisation.

50. India at present is to some extent on par with develped countries in terms of technological development.

QUANTITATIVE APTITUDE

51. 724.998 ÷ 24.048 ÷ 14.954 = ?

(a) 8   (b) 13

(c) 2   (d) 10

(e) 16

52. (848.999 + 274.05(b) ÷ 3.0054 = ?

(a) 940   (b) 836

(c) 184   (d) 298

(e) 374

53. $3\sqrt{84900}$ = ?

   (a) 56   (b) 44

   (c) 67   (d) 33

   (e) 21

54. 18.5% of 425 + 16.2% of 388 = ?

   (a) 114   (b) 224

   (c) 116   (d) 183

   (e) 215

55. 18.345 × 19.068 × ? = 11538.93375

   (a) 46   (b) 61

   (c) 27   (d) 33

   (e) 55

Directions (Q. 56 – 60) : *Study the followin pie-chart carefully and answer the question given below:*

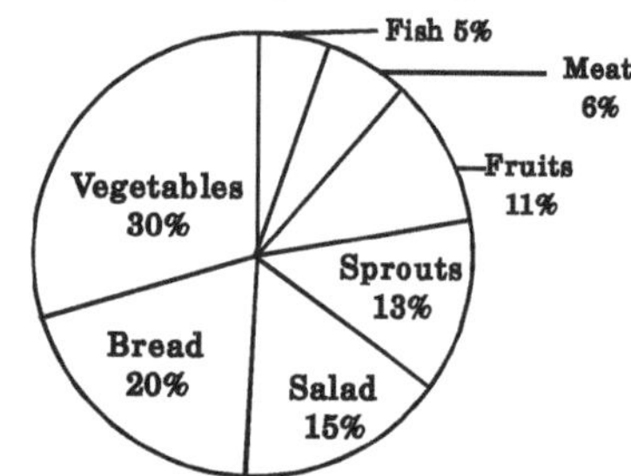

56. What is the total number of people preferring vegetables and those preferring sprouts?

   (a) 11,990   (b) 12,300

   (c) 12,500   (d) 11,500

   (e) None of these

57. What is the difference between the total number of people prefreeing meat to the total number of people prefrring fish?

   (a) 150   (b) 200

   (c) 300   (d) 350

   (e) None of these

58. People preferring fruits are approximately what per cent of the people preferring vegetables?

   (a) 48   (b) 35

   (c) 46   (d) 37

   (e) 30

59. Out of the total sample population, how many people have given preference for fish?

   (a) 1600   (b) 1800

   (c) 1500   (d) 1400

   (e) None of these

60. What is the ratio of the number of people preferring meat to the number of people preferring salad?

   (a) 2 : 5   (b) 3 : 5

   (c) 2 : 3   (d) 4 : 3

   (e) None of these

Directions (Q. 61 – 65) : *In the following number series only one number is wrong. Find out the wrong number.*

61. 529 841 961 1296 1681 1849 2209

   (a) 1296   (b) 841

   (c) 961   (d) 1681

   (e) None of these

62. 13 14 27 45 68 109 177

   (a) 27   (b) 109

   (c) 45   (d) 68

   (e) None of these

63. 14 22 34.5 55.5 87.25 1 35.875 209.125

   (a) 55.5   (b) 34.5

   (c) 135.875   (d) 87.25

   (e) None of these

64. 274 301 426 769 1498 2824 5026

   (a) 301   (b) 426

   (c) 769   (d) 2824

   (e) None of these

65. 4 28 160 990 6970 55832 502560

   (a) 160   (b) 990

   (c) 55832   (d) 6970

   (e) None of these

Directions (Q. 66 – 70) : *What should come in place of the question mark (?) in the following questions?*

66. $8^{9.4} \times 4^{12.8} \times 64^{8.1} = 16^?$

   (a) 41.8   (b) 16.2

   (c) 18.4   (d) 25.6

   (e) None of these

67. $\dfrac{8 \div ? \times 3.5}{4 \times 5 \div 2} = 0.7$

   (a) 2   (b) 6

   (c) 10   (d) 3

   (e) None of these

68. $4\dfrac{16}{17} \times 1\dfrac{11}{16} \div \dfrac{7}{38}$ = ?

   (a) $12\dfrac{3}{17}$ (b) $45\dfrac{9}{34}$

   (c) $12\dfrac{21}{34}$ (d) $36\dfrac{8}{17}$

   (e) None of these

69. $(e)^2 + (10)^2 + (6)^2 = (?)^2$

   (a) 130321   (b) 361

   (c) 103041   (d) 17

   (e) None of these

70. 12% of 840 × 0.25% of 148 = ?
 (*a*) 37.296   (*b*) 101.17
 (*c*) 68.432   (*d*) 97.046
 (*e*) None of these

71. A shopkeeper sells 200 metres of cloth for Rs 9,000 at a profit of Rs 5 per metre. What is the cost price of 1 meter of cloth?
 (*a*) Rs 45   (*b*) Rs 40
 (*c*) Rs 35   (*d*) Rs 30
 (*e*) None of these

72. The area of a circle is 1386 sq cm. What is the circumference of the circle?
 (*a*) 142 cm   (*b*) 160 cm
 (*c*) 130 cm   (*d*) 132 cm
 (*e*) None of these

73. In a college a total number of 27 professors are appointed for all the faculties, viz Arts, Commerce and Science. If equal number of professors are appointed for each of the faculties, how many professors are assigned to each faculty?
 (*a*) 9   (*b*) 12
 (*c*) 6   (*d*) 3
 (*e*) None of these

74. If $(1(a)^2$ is subtracted from the square of a number, the answer so obtained is 135. What is the number?
 (*a*) 12   (*b*) 18
 (*c*) 17   (*d*) 13
 (*e*) None of these

75. If the cost of 7 kg of rice is Rs 168, what is the cost of 105 kg of rice?
 (*a*) Rs 2,580   (*b*) Rs 2,630
 (*c*) Rs 2,520   (*d*) Rs 2,500
 (*e*) None of these

76. Seema and Meena divide a sum of Rs 2,500 in the ratio of 3 : 2 respectively. If Rs 500 is added to each of their share, what would be the new ratio formed?
 (*a*) 2 : 3   (*b*) 3 : 4
 (*c*) 5 : 4   (*d*) 4 : 3
 (*e*) None of these

77. Sridhar invests Rs. 3,750 in shares, which is 25% of his monthly income. What is his monthly income?
 (*a*) Rs 12,000   (*b*) Rs 15,000
 (*c*) Rs 10,000   (*d*) Rs 16,000
 (*e*) None of these

78. Find the average of the following set of scores.
 302, 152, 132, 122, 112
 (*a*) 184   (*b*) 165
 (*c*) 152   (*d*) 176
 (*e*) None of these

79. A bus covers a distance of 172 kms in 4 hours. What is the speed of the bus?
 (*a*) 52 km/hr   (*b*) 47 km/hr
 (*c*) 43 km/hr   (*d*) 38 km/hr
 (*e*) None of these

80. The total number of students in a school is 4800, out of which 60% are girls. What is the total number of boys in this school?
 (*a*) 1920   (*b*) 1934
 (*c*) 1980   (*d*) 1910
 (*e*) None of these

Directions (Q. 81 – 85): *Each of the questions below consists of a question and two statements numbered I and II. You have to decide whether the data provided in the statements are sufficient to answer the question. Read both the statements and*

Give answer as :

 (*a*) if the data in Satement I alone are sufficient to answer the quesiton, while the data in statement II alone are not sufficient to answer the question.
 (*b*) if the data in statement II alone are sufficient to answer the quesiton, while the data in statement I alone are not sufficient to answer the question.
 (*c*) if the data either in statement I alone or in statement II alone are sufficient to answer the question.
 (*d*) if the data in both the statement I and II together are not sufficient to answer the question.
 (*e*) if the data in both the statements I and II together are necessary to answer the question.

81. What is Niddi's age?
 I. Niddi is 3 times younger than Rani.
 II. Surekha is twice the age of Rani and the sum of their ages is 72.

82. What is the ratio of the total number of girls to the total number of boys in a school?
 I. The ratio of the total number of boys to the total number of girls last year was 4 : 5.
 II. There are 3500 students in the school, out of which 60% are boys.

83. What is the speed of a bus?
 I. The bus covers a distance of 80 km in 5 hrs.
 II. The bus covers a distance of 160 km in 10 hrs.

84. What is the ratio of the number of freshers to the number of seniors in a college?

   I.   The ratio of males and females in the college is 2 : 3.

   II. There are 1125 female freshers in the colleg(e)

85. What if Mr. Mehta's present income?

   I.   Mr Mehta's income increases by 10% every year.

   II. His income will increase by Rs 2,500 this year.

Directions (Q. 86 – 90) : *Study the following graph carefully to answer these questions.*

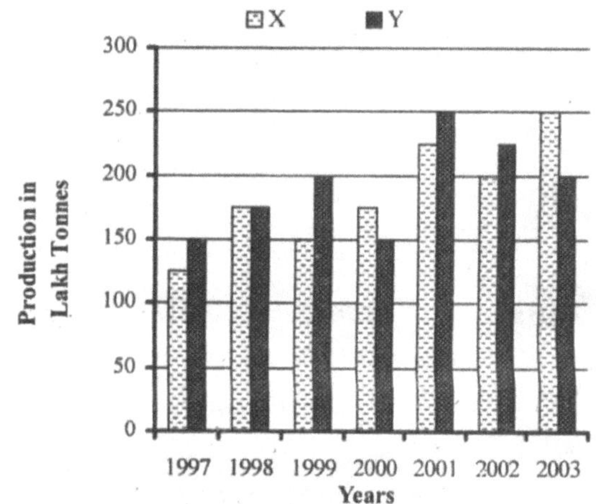

86. For which of the following pairs of years the total production of the two commodities together is equal?

   (*a*) 1997 & 2000   (*b*) 2002 & 2003

   (*c*) 2001 & 2003   (*d*) 1998 & 1999

   (*e*) None of these

87. What is the ratio between the total production of commodities X and Y for all the seven years together?

   (*a*) 26 : 27   (*b*) 13 : 14

   (*c*) 27 : 26   (*d*) 14 : 13

   (*e*) None of these

88. During which year the percentage increase/ decrease in production of commodity 'X' from the previous year was the **maximum**?

   (*a*) 1998   (*b*) 2000

   (*c*) 2003   (*d*) 2002

   (*e*) None of these

89. Approximately, what was the average production (in lakh tonnes) of commodity 'Y' ?

   (*a*) 225   (*b*) 216

   (*c*) 195   (*d*) 185

   (*e*) 205

90. What is the ratio between total production of the two commodities together for years 1997, 1998 & 1999 and the total production of the two commodities together for years 2001, 2002 & 2003?

   (*a*) 9 : 13   (*b*) 13 : 18

   (*c*) 18 : 13   (*d*) 10 : 13

   (*e*) None of these

91. The owner of a furniture shop charges his customers 12% more than the cost price. If a customer paid Rs 14,056 for a dining table, what is the cost price of the dining table?

   (*a*) Rs 14,000   (*b*) Rs 12,500

   (*c*) Rs 13,540   (*d*) Rs 11,550

   (*e*) None of these

92. The difference between 55% of a number and 25% of the same number is 11.10. What is 75% of that number?

   (*a*) 27.75   (*b*) 37

   (*c*) 21.25   (*d*) 45

   (*e*) None of these

93. The product of two successive numbers is 1980. Which is the smaller number?

   (*a*) 34   (*b*) 44

   (*c*) 35   (*d*) 45

   (*e*) None of these

94. Which of the following smallest number should be added to 41116 to make it exactly divisible by 8?

   (*a*) 8

   (*b*) 5

   (*c*) 4

   (*d*) 12

   (*e*) None of these

95. The difference between of $\dfrac{3}{4}$ of $\dfrac{2}{5}$ of a number and $\dfrac{4}{5}$ of $\dfrac{1}{4}$ of the same number is 5. What is the number?

   (*a*) 25

   (*b*) 40

   (*c*) 45

   (*d*) 50

   (*e*) None of these

Directions (Q. 96 – 100) : *Study the following table carefully to answer these questions.*

MARKS OBTAINED OUT OF

Subject → Student ↓	History (75)	Geography (75)	Science (120)	Maths(150)	English (80)	Hindi (60)
P	45	53	100	117	50	45
Q	56	58	96	132	46	50
T	48	60	112	120	52	42
D	62	67	88	108	48	34
G	66	55	92	140	60	32
F	54	64	108	116	53	40

96. What is the average percentage of marks obtained by all the students in Science? (rounded off to two digits after decimal)

(a) 99 (b) 82.78

(c) 88.72 (d) 78.88

(e) None of these

97. What is the overall percentage of marks obtained by D in all subjects? (rounded off to two ditits after decimal)

(a) 72.88 (b) 76.28

(c) 73.17 (d) 72.68

(e) None of these

98. What are the average marks obtained by all students in English?

(a) 52.5 (b) 64.38

(c) 56.38 (d) 60.5

(e) None of these

99. What is the ratio between total marks obtained in all subjects by F and G respectively?

(a) 87 : 89 (b) 89 : 87

(c) 67 : 69 (d) 69 : 67

(e) None of these

100. Which student has scored in Maths closets to the average marks in Maths?

(a) P (b) Q

(c) T (d) F

(e) None of these

ENGLISH LANGUAGE

Directions (Q. 101 – 110): *Read each sentence to find out if there is any error in it. The error, if any, will be in one part of the sentence. The number of that part is the answer. If there is no error the answer is (5). (Ignore errors in punctuation, if any).*

101. In spite of the extreme cold / she insisted
    (a)   (b)

on / taking a trip to Shimla / where is her
    (c)   (d)

birthplace / No Error
    (e)

102. The government decision
    (a)

will benefit all/the software companies
    (b)   (c)

registered/under the scheme. No error
    (d)   (e)

103. The trustee has agreed/not to fund the
    (a)   (b)

construction of the auditorium/
    (c)

but also the new research/No Error
    (d)   (e)

104. Keeping in mind the rivalry
    (a)

/between Vinod and Sachin
    (b)

/the manager has assigned him
    (c)

/to different teams./No error
    (d)   (e)

105. In recent times companies have found
    (a)

/the internet to be ideal place
    (b)

/to hire personnel/and form business
    (c)   (d)

partnerships./ No error
    (e)

106. These rules were created
(a)
/to protect the interests of the student
(b)
/who live away from home
(c)
/and have no local guardian. No error
(d)   (e)

107. Concerned over/the loss of revenue
(a)   (b)
/the Government plan/to review the
(c)   (d)
policy immediately. No error
(e)

108. Having heard all the evidence
(a)
/the Chairman should now/be able to
(b)   (c)
arrive/to a fair decision. No error
(d)   (e)

109. There are very fewer hotels
(a)
/providing facilities for/
(b)
guests who want to bring their pets
(c)
/along with them. No error
(d)   (e)

110. The report states that/in several parts
(a)   (b)
of the country/ there has not been
(c)
/adequately rain this year. No error
(d)   (e)

Directions (Q. 111 – 125) : *Which of the phrases (a), (b), (c), (d) given below each sentence should replace the phrase printed in bold type to make the sentence grammatically correct? If the sentence is correct as it is, mark (e), ie 'No correction required', as the answer.*

111. The meeting is **attempted to mend** the strained relations between the management and the employees.
(a) was attempted for mending
(b) is an attempt to mend
(c) is attempted at mending of
(d) will be attempted by mending
(e) No correction required

112. He arrived at the hotel, **which a reception** was held in his honour.
(a) in which a reception is
(b) while a reception being
(c) where a reception was
(d) since a reception going on
(e) No correction required

113. Since his college days he has been **standing up with** the rights of the weak and the oppressed.
(a) stood up along with
(b) standing in for
(c) for standing beside
(d) standing up for
(e) No correction required

114. **Unless a man with** plenty of money can afford a house in this locality.
(a) Until a man has
(b) When a man possesses
(c) Except a man of
(d) Only a man with
(e) No correction required

115. They lost the vote because they could not **express clearly.**
(a) express themselves clearly
(b) express each other clearly
(c) clearly express
(d) be clearly expressed
(e) No correction required

116. Ramesh must be punished for acting **in opposite to my** wishes.
(a) opposing to   (b) in opposite with
(c) opposite against   (d) in opposition to
(e) No correction required

117. India is a diverse and breathtaking country with many places **worthwhile to see.**
(a) worth sight   (b) worth seeing
(c) worth while scene   (d) worthy seeing
(e) No correction required

118. The sales conference **cannot be began** till the festive season in over.
(a) cannot have beginning
(b) unable to begin
(c) cannot begin
(d) has no beginning
(e) No correction required

119. It was surprising to note that she enjoyed the game of cricket **same as** her brother did.

(*a*) as much as

(*b*) with the same liking as

(*c*) alike

(*d*) same like

(*e*) No correction required

120. They are **very much enterprising of** all the other students I have taught

(*a*) so much enterprising like

(*b*) more enterprising than

(*c*) very much enterprising than

(*d*) much enterprising of

(*e*) No correction required

121. **Taken everything into consideration,** we feel that the principal was justified in suspending the student.

(*a*) Taking all things into considering

(*b*) To take everything with consideration

(*c*) Taking everything into consideration

(*d*) While taking everything for consideration

(*e*) No correction required

122. He succeeded in getting the promotion as he **performed well** than the other candidates in the written test.

(*a*) performed best of

(*b*) performed better

(*c*) performance was better

(*d*) performing very well

(*e*) No correction required

123. The inquiry found that both the secretary and the treasurer had been **negligent in their duties.**

(*a*) neglecting his duty

(*b*) neglected by their duties

(*c*) neglecting in their duty

(*d*) neglignece for their duties

(*e*) No correction required

124. **I with my family have** resided in a small village near the sea for the past two decades.

(*a*) My family along with I has

(*b*) My family and me have

(*c*) My family and I have

(*d*) I together with my family has

(*e*) No correction required

125. The channel has **brought the rights to the** cricket series for a huge sum of money.

(*a*) paid the rights for

(*b*) bought the rights for

(*c*) been paid the rites to

(*d*) bought off the rights

(*e*) No correction required

Directions (Q. 126 – 135) : *Read the following passage carefully and answer the questions given below it. Certain words/phrases are given in bold to help you locate them while answering some of the questions.*

Aviation is an essential link for travel, trade and connectivity. While full-service carriers attract passengers with the overall quality of their services, low-cost airlines compete on cost. They offer bare-bone services, fly more sectors a day and operate from smaller secondary airports that have lower charges. These may be very far from the city centres costing passengers more time and money to get into town. Some services like London's Luton are aimed at eliminating the problems of connecting flights. They tend to avoid head-on competition with each other and prey on full-services airlines. Staff are usually less well paid, more **intensively** used and in shorter supply as compared to full-service airlines! There are numerous exceptions though in other countries. Easy jet operates from major airports and J(*e*) Blue offers live programmes for fre(*e*)

In India 70% of the operating costs of low-cost airlines are the same as that of full-service carriers, leaving just 30% to juggle with to gain an overall advantage over full-service carriers. Many of these costs like fuel are above global levels. Exorbitant State and Central government taxes and duties are the main culprits. Air Deccan envisions that their airline fares will match rail fares — unattainable because of the economies of scale that the railways enjoy. Few secondary airports and fares falling faster than their costs have hurt low-cost airlines more than others, as they have to achieve higher fleet utilization. Allowing low cost airlines to utilize non-metro airports at lower charges during off-peak hours while providing full-service airlines peak-hour slots but a higher rates could help.

Low-cost airlines can aid economic development and the current economic boom has been the right times to launch India's low-cost revolution though in their efforts to achieve economies of scale and greater market share they have been reckless and have gone deep into the red. India has to await second-generation low-cost airlines to deliver the goods.

126. The primary purpose of low-cost airlines is to
  (a) provide connectivity at low rates
  (b) enhance economic development
  (c) do away with the inconevenience of connecting flights
  (d) reduce congestion at crowded city airports
  (e) reduce the passanger pressure on the railways

127. The author's view of Indian low-cost airlines is that
  (a) they are based on global models allowing them to compete with railways.
  (b) they benefit from certain exemptions on tax and duties.
  (c) with only 70% of the operating cost being the same as full-service airlines they have a major advantage.
  (d) they are loss-making enterprises as their efforts to expand have been hasty.
  (e) None of these

128. Which of the following is/are TRUE in the context of the passage?
  A. Indian lows-cost carriers though launched at the right time have been mismanaged.
  B. Jet Blue is one of the premier full-service air carriers in the world.
  C. Business for low-cost carriers is good enough to allow them to compete with railways.
  (a) Only A   (b) Both A & C
  (c) Only B   (d) Both B & C
  (e) None of these

129. Which of the following measures can boost the low-cost carrier business?
  (a) Increasing rail fares to allow low-cost carriers a chance to compete
  (b) Government should own a stake in low-cost airlines.
  (c) Preference for low-cost carriers during peak hours at major airports
  (d) Developing adequate secondary airports
  (e) Equivalent charges for full services and low-cost airlines at metro airports

130. The growth of low-cost airlines in India has been hampered by
  A. inadequate airport infrastructur(e)
  B. attracting and retaining staff in spite of higher pay packages.
  C. costs of providing additional quality services.
  (a) Only C   (b) Both A & B
  (c) Only A   (d) Both A & C
  (e) All A, B & C

131. Which of the following is NOT TRUE in the context of the passage?
  (a) The low-cost airline industry has recently come to India.
  (b) Full-service airlines operate from secondary airports to meet the costs of free services.
  (c) Indian low-cost airlines have not been able to make even a marginal profit
  (d) Staff of low-cost airlines has longer working hours as compared to full-service airlines.
  (e) None of these

132. A benefit of low-cost airlines is
  (a) they operate away form crowded cities.
  (b) their fares are more reasonable than rail fares.
  (c) decrease in fares despite a rise in costs.
  (d) efficient bare minimum services at affordable rates
  (e) utilising secondary airports despite their higher charges.

133. Why are low-cost airlines India currently experiencing difficulties?
  (a) Over-ambitious plans for expansion
  (b) Recession in global airline industry
  (c) Monopoly of govt-ownedfull-service airlines
  (d) Lack of favourable economic conditions
  (e) None of these

134. Choose the word/phrase which is most nearly the same in meaning as the word **intensively** as used in the passage.
  (a) severely   (b) excessively
  (c) powerfully   (d) strongly
  (e) harshly

135. Choose the word/phrase which is the most opposite in meaning to the word **aid** as used in the passage
  (a) ignore   (b) disregard
  (c) protect   (d) obstruct
  (e) conceal

Directions (Q. 136 – 140) : *Pick out the most effective word from the given words to fill in the blank to make the sentence meaningfully complete.*

136. You must ensure the correctness of the information before .... to conclusion.
  (a) drawing   (b) enabling
  (c) leaning   (d) jumping
  (e) examining

137. The rocket .... the target and did not cause any casually.

(*a*) sensed   (*b*) reached

(*c*) missed   (*d*) exploded

(*e*) aimed

138. It is desirable to take .... in any business if you want to make profit.

(*a*) advice   (*b*) risk

(*c*) loan   (*d*) recourse

(*e*) perseverance

139. They wasted all the money on purchase of some .... items.

(*a*) excellent   (*b*) important

(*c*) significant   (*d*) quality

(*e*) trivial

140. When he found the wallet his face glowed but soon it faded as the wallet was ....

(*a*) empty   (*b*) vacant

(*c*) recovered   (*d*) stolen

(*e*) expensive

GENERAL AWARENESS

141. Section 9 of the Banking Regulation Act prohibits the banking Companies from holding any immovable property except for its own use for a period of not more property. The RBI may extend this period for a further period of ______:

(*a*) 2 years   (*b*) 4 years

(*c*) 5 years   (*d*) 6 years

(*e*) None of the above

142. Which of the following stock exchange is derecognized by SEBI on 19.11.2014 on the allegations of serious irregularities in its functioning?

(*a*) Bombay Stock Exchange

(*b*) Delhi Stock Exchange

(*c*) Calcutta Stock Exchange

(*d*) Bangalore Stock Exchange

(*e*) None of the above

143. Which of the following is not a function of General Insurance?

(*a*) Cattle Insurance

(*b*) Crop Insurance

(*c*) Marine Insurance

(*d*) Fire Insurance

(*e*) Medical Insurance

144. Liability- side of the balance-sheet comprises:

(*a*) Capital and reserve

(*b*) Long-term liabilities

(*c*) Current liabilities

(*d*) All of the above

(*e*) None of the above

145. Minimum cash reserves fixed by law constitute ___

(*a*) A percentage of aggregate deposits of the bank

(*b*) A percentage of aggregate loans and advances of the bank

(*c*) A percentage of capital & reserves of the bank

(*d*) All of the above

(*e*) None of these

146. Which of the following organizations/ agencies has sought an emergency fund of Rs.1000 crore from banks to tackle acute liquidity crisis, which is coming in the way to give loans to micro borrowers?

(*a*) Regional Rural & Cooperative Banks

(*b*) RBI

(*c*) Micro Finance Institutions

(*d*) NABARD

(*e*) None of the above

147. Which of the following types of accounts are known as "Demat Accounts"?

(*a*) Zero Balance Accounts

(*b*) Accounts which are opened to facilitate repayment of a loan taken from the bank. No other business can be conducted from there

(*c*) Accounts in which shares of various companies are traded in electronic form

(*d*) Accounts which are operated through internet banking facility

(*e*) None of the above

148. Mortgage is a :

(*a*) Security on movable property for a loan

(*b*) Security on immovable property for a loan

(*c*) Concession on immovable property

(*d*) Facility on immovable property

(*e*) Security on loan sanctioned against fixed deposits

149. ___ assumed charge as the Minister of State for Micro, Small & Medium Enterprises (MSME) on 11th November 2014.

(*a*) Gopal Singh   (*b*) Veerabhadra Singh

(*c*) Manoj Tiwari   (*d*) Giriraj Singh

(*e*) Raju Bhai Gandhi

150. Identify the well known person related to Banking field in India from the following?

(a) Mrs. Meira Kumar   (b) Mrs. Kiran Shaw

(c) Mr. Arun Jaitley   (d) Dr. D subbarao

(e) All of the above

151. Currency notes deposited in the currency chest are the property of ____?

(a) Respective bank

(b) RBI

(c) SBI

(d) Government of India

(e) Respective state Government

152. A fixed deposit receipt is kept with the bank for its safety, is known as ___?

(a) Safe custody   (b) Safe deposit

(c) Locker   (d) Valid safe deposit

(e) None of the above

153. Which Institute has developed training modules to fill the gaps in rural infrastructure and provide training to elected public representatives under the Prime Minister Sansad Aadarsh Gram Yojana (PMSAGY)?

(a) IIM   (b) FMS

(c) IIT   (d) NIRDPR

(e) None of these

154. Name the space agency whose probe has gone into orbit around Ceres, the largest object in the Solar System between Mars and Jupiter?

(a) NASA   (b) ISRO

(c) DAWN   (d) All of these

(e) None of these

155. Name the Member of Parliament who tabled a motion in House of Commons to mark the unveiling of a new statue of Mahatma Gandhi at Parliament Square in London?

(a) David Cameron   (b) Bobby Jindal

(c) Keith Vaz   (d) Bobby dowley

(e) None of these

156. Which state government is contemplating on framing a law under which registration of pregnancy would be made compulsory within first three months of pregnancy?

(a) Haryana   (b) Karnataka

(c) Uttar Pradesh   (d) Maharashtra

(e) Punjab

157. Name the country's umbrella body for all retail payments system that has reached a new milestone with successful linking of 15 crore bank accounts with the Aadhaar numbers?

(a) National Retail Corporation

(b) Reserve bank of India

(c) National Securities Depository Ltd.

(d) National Payments Corporation

(e) None of these

158. Name the project which will be the first transit oriented development (TOD) smart city in Delhi?

(a) South Delhi Hub Project

(b) Combine Delhi Hub Project

(c) East Delhi Hub Project

(d) Unique Delhi Hub Project

(e) None of these

159. Which day would be celebrated as Safe Motherhood Day as announced by Health Ministry of India?

(a) 7th March   (b) 8th March

(c) 9th March   (d) 10th March

(e) 11th March

160. As per the Mercer's Quality of Living Report 2015, which city has the world's best quality of living?

(a) New York   (b) Tokyo

(c) Vienna   (d) Canberra

(e) sydney

161. As per the Mercer's Quality of Living Report 2015, which Indian City has the best quality of living?

(a) Mumbai   (b) New Delhi

(c) Pune   (d) Hyderabad

(e) Chennai

162. Name the person re-nominated as the Alternate Executive Director of International Monetary Fund?

(a) Kewal Sharma   (b) Sunil Sabhrawal

(c) Rahul Jindal   (d) All of these

(e) None of these

163. Indian captain Mahendra Singh Dhoni becomes the most successful captain in terms of ODI victories on foreign shores. He surpassed the record of _____.

(a) Kapil Dev

(b) Mohd. Azharudeen

(c) Sunil Gavaskar

(d) Sourav Ganguly

(e) None of these

164. In which state, the Prime Minister Narendra Modi will inaugurate the first phase of Shri Singaji Thermal Power Project on 5th Mar'15?

(*a*) Uttar Pradesh (*b*) Madhya Pradesh

(*c*) Arunachal Pradesh (*d*) Himachal Pradesh

(*e*) Haryana

165. Name the fourth among the seven of the IRNSS constellation of satellites designed to provide accurate position information service to users in the country as well as the region extending up to 1,500 km from its boundary?

(*a*) IRNSS-1B (*b*) IRNSS-1F

(*c*) IRNSS-1D (*d*) IRNSS-2A

(*e*) None of these

166. Name the mission replaced by Jawahalal Nehru National Urban Renewal Mission (JNNRUM)?

(*a*) National Urban Renewal Mission

(*b*) Mahatma Gandhi National Urban Renewal Mission

(*c*) Sardar Patel National Urban Renewal Mission

(*d*) India Renewal Mission

(*e*) None of these

167. How many points were cut in Repo Rate by the Reserve Bank of India on 4th Mar'15?

(*a*) 50 Basis Point (*b*) 80 Basis Point

(*c*) 35 Basis Point (*d*) 25 Basis Point

(*e*) 75 Basis point

168. The govt has decided to go for third phase of coal auction. Which of the following is NOT correct in this regard?

(*a*) 10 mines, 8 producing and 2 about to produce, to be on sale.

(*b*) In this phase of auction, there will be no coal mine for power generators.

(*c*) The bidding will run from Aug 11 to 17.

(*d*) The ministry of coal will auction linkages to Coal India's production for five years.

(*e*) None of these

169. The FMC will have to complete all pending investigations before its merger with the securities market regulator, Securities and Exchange Board of India (Sebi). The term FMC stands for

(*a*) Future Markets Commission

(*b*) Food Markets Commission

(*c*) Foreign Markets Commission

(*d*) Forward Markets Commission

(*e*) None of these

170. Mark Rutte, who visited India, recently, is the present Prime Minster of which of the following countries?

(*a*) Netherlands (*b*) Hungry

(*c*) Sweden (*d*) Norway

(*e*) None of these

171. India and which of the following countries have agreed on a 17-point road map aimed at strengthening mutual trust and confidence during President Pranab Mukherjee visit to this country recently?

(*a*) Belarus (*b*) Sweden

(*c*) Lithuania (*d*) Latvia

(*e*) None of these

172. Who among the following has been appointed by the govt as the PM's 'Special Envoy on Countering Terrorism and Extremism' recently?

(*a*) Ajit Doval (*b*) Asif Ibrahim

(*c*) Alok Joshi (*d*) Dineshwar Sharma

(*e*) None of these

173. The govt has launched IAP HealthPhone programme, world's largest digital mass education programme to address malnutrition in women and children. The brand ambassador of the programme is

(*a*) Anushka Sharma (*b*) Salman Khan

(*c*) Aamir Khan (*d*) Shah Rukh Khan

(*e*) None of these

174. Bangladesh has granted permission to which of the following Indian insurance firms, recently, to do business in the country which will start its operations as a joint venture (JV) entity?

(*a*) LIC of India (*b*) SBI Life

(*c*) ICICI Prudential (*d*) HDFC Life

(*e*) None of these

175. Who among the following will lead the events at the United Nations on the International Yoga Day on Jun 21?

(*a*) Sushma Swaraj (*b*) Narendra Modi

(*c*) Rajnath Singh (*d*) VK Singh

(*e*) None of these

176. The WTO, recently, ruled that the Indian ban on import of poultry meat, eggs and live pigs from _________ is inconsistent with the international norms and now India will have to allow these products.

(*a*) Pakistan (*b*) Bangladesh

(*c*) US (*d*) China

(*e*) None of these

177. The employees of five associate banks of State Bank of India (SBI) went on a strike on 4 Jun to protest against their merger with it. Which of the following is NOT an associate bank of the SBI as of now?

(*a*) State Bank of Bikaner & Jaipur

(*b*) State Bank of Travancore

(*c*) State Bank of Mysore

(*d*) State Bank of Hyderabad

(*e*) State Bank of Surastra

178. RBI Provides ____ for meeting day - to - day receipt and expenditure mismatch to both Central and State Governments.

(*a*) Treasury bills

(*b*) Ways and Means advance

(*c*) Date and securities

(*d*) All the above

(*e*) None of these

179. RBI known as lender of last resort because:

(*a*) It has to meet the credit need of citizens to whom no one else is willing to lend

(*b*) Banks lend to go to RBI as a last resort

(*c*) It comes to help banks in times of crisis

(*d*) All of the above

(*e*) None of these

180. These days RBI uses Selective credit control measures rather infrequently because of:

(*a*) Deregulation of functions

(*b*) Autonomy given to banks

(*c*) Comfortable liquidity

(*d*) Reasonable inflation level

(*e*) All the above

COMPUTER KNOWLEDGE

181. Computer program

(*a*) A accurate notation used to express algorithms understand by computers

(*b*) Instructions written in natural language

(*c*) An algorithm expressed in a graphical form

(*d*) An algorithm expressed in a programming language

(*e*) An instruction

182. Device used to store the Programs and data is

(*a*) Memory Unit

(*b*) Control Unit

(*c*) Arithmetic and Logic Unit (ALU)

(*d*) Motherboard

(*e*) None of these

183. Input/output unit with secondary storage are known as

(*a*) Peripheral devices

(*b*) Processing devices

(*c*) Programs

(*d*) All of these

(*e*) None of these

184. An ASCII code is:

(*a*) The codes used to represent each character.

(*b*) It includes codes for English alphabets both capitals and small alphabets and also decimal digits

(*c*) It includes codes for, 32 special characters, and symbols used to control operation which are non-printable

(*d*) All of these

(*e*) None of these

185. The base of binary numbers is

(*a*) One   (*b*) Two

(*c*) Eight   (*d*) Sixteen

(*e*) Four

186. The quality of the display is better if

(*a*) resolution is higher

(*b*) resolution the moderate

(*c*) resolution is least

(*d*) no change in resolution

(*e*) none of these

187. It consists of a print head, with number of nozzles. An individual nozzle is heated very rapidly by integrated circuit resistor. When resistor heats up, ink near it vaporizes and is ejected through nozzle to makes a dot on paper placed near head. Name printer.

(*a*) Dot matrix printers

(*b*) Ink jet printers

(*c*) Laser printer

(*d*) Both (*a*) and (*b*)

(*d*) None of these

188. A RAM is the memory that is

(*a*) Permanent   (*b*) Erasable

(*c*) Non erasable   (*d*) External

(*e*) None of these

189. 1 KB is equivalent to

(*a*) 2560 bytes   (*b*) 210 bytes

(*c*) 220 bytes   (*d*) 1024 bytes

(*e*) None of these

190. A memory cell, which does not loose the bit stored in it when no power is supplied to the cell, is known as
(a) non-volatile cell
(b) volatile cell
(c) permanent cell
(d) both (b) and (c)
(e) None of these

191. The electronic circuits/devices used in building the computer that executes the software is known as
(a) Hardware
(b) Software
(c) Live ware
(d) both (a) and (b)
(e) None of these

192. Machine language programs are
(a) Machine dependent
(b) Machine independent
(c) Users friendly
(d) both (a) and (c)
(e) None of these

193. Which of the following is a high level language?
(a) FORTRAN
(b) BASIC
(c) COBOL
(d) All of these
(e) None of these

194. Mark I was the first computer that used
(a) Vacuum tubes
(b) Mechanical switches
(c) Transistors
(d) Integrated circuits
(e) Micoprocessor

195. The following generates more energy and consumes more electricity
(a) Vacuum tube
(b) Transistors
(c) Integrated Circuit
(d) Micoprocessor
(e) None of these

196. Most electronic devices today use some form of integrated circuits placed on printed circuit boards-thin pieces of bakelite or fiberglass that have electrical connections etched onto them is called
(a) Mother board
(b) Sister board
(c) Father board
(d) Switch board
(e) None of these

197. The following generation computers saw the development of GUIs, the mouse and handheld devices
(a) First generation computers
(b) Second generation computers
(c) Third generation computers
(d) Fourth generation computer
(e) None of these

198. The micro processor was introduced in
(a) First generation computers
(b) Second generation computers
(c) Third generation computers
(d) Fourth generation computer
(e) None of these

199. Assembly language is
(a) A low-level programming language
(b) High level programming language
(c) Machine Language
(d) Both (a) and (b)
(e) None of these

200. Following is true for Bandwidth?
(a) The narrow the bandwidth of a communications system the less data it can transmit in a given period of time.
(b) The narrow the bandwidth of a communications system the more data it can transmit in a given period of time.
(c) The wider the bandwidth of a communications system the less data it can transmit in a given period of time.
(d) Both (a) and (c)
(e) None is true

ANSWERS

1. (d)	**2.** (b)	**3.** (a)	**4.** (e)	**5.** (d)	**6.** (c)	**7.** (d)	**8.** (b)	**9.** (e)	**10.** (e)
11. (b)	**12.** (c)	**13.** (d)	**14.** (e)	**15.** (a)	**16.** (d)	**17.** (e)	**18.** (b)	**19.** (a)	**20.** (d)
21. (e)	**22.** (d)	**23.** (a)	**24.** (b)	**25.** (c)	**26.** (e)	**27.** (d)	**28.** (e)	**29.** (a)	**30.** (e)
31. (d)	**32.** (a)	**33.** (e)	**34.** (b)	**35.** (e)	**36.** (c)	**37.** (e)	**38.** (a)	**39.** (b)	**40.** (d)
41. (e)	**42.** (a)	**43.** (b)	**44.** (c)	**45.** (b)	**46.** (e)	**47.** (a)	**48.** (d)	**49.** (b)	**50.** (e)
51. (c)	**52.** (e)	**53.** (b)	**54.** (a)	**55.** (d)	**56.** (e)	**57.** (c)	**58.** (d)	**59.** (c)	**60.** (a)
61. (a)	**62.** (c)	**63.** (e)	**64.** (d)	**65.** (d)	**66.** (d)	**67.** (e)	**68.** (b)	**69.** (e)	**70.** (a)
71. (b)	**72.** (d)	**73.** (d)	**74.** (e)	**75.** (c)	**76.** (d)	**77.** (b)	**78.** (e)	**79.** (c)	**80.** (a)
81. (e)	**82.** (b)	**83.** (c)	**84.** (d)	**85.** (e)	**86.** (d)	**87.** (a)	**88.** (a)	**89.** (c)	**90.** (b)
91. (e)	**92.** (a)	**93.** (a)	**94.** (c)	**95.** (d)	**96.** (b)	**97.** (e)	**98.** (b)	**99.** (a)	**100.** (c)
101. (d)	**102.** (e)	**103.** (b)	**104.** (c)	**105.** (b)	**106.** (b)	**107.** (c)	**108.** (d)	**109.** (a)	**110.** (d)
111. (b)	**112.** (c)	**113.** (d)	**114.** (d)	**115.** (a)	**116.** (d)	**117.** (b)	**118.** (c)	**119.** (a)	**120.** (b)
121. (c)	**122.** (b)	**123.** (e)	**124.** (c)	**125.** (b)	**126.** (a)	**127.** (d)	**128.** (a)	**129.** (d)	**130.** (c)
131. (b)	**132.** (d)	**133.** (a)	**134.** (a)	**135.** (d)	**136.** (d)	**137.** (c)	**138.** (b)	**139.** (e)	**140.** (a)
141. (c)	**142.** (b)	**143.** (e)	**144.** (d)	**145.** (a)	**146.** (d)	**147.** (c)	**148.** (b)	**149.** (d)	**150.** (d)
151. (b)	**152.** (a)	**153.** (d)	**154.** (c)	**155.** (c)	**156.** (a)	**157.** (d)	**158.** (d)	**159.** (b)	**160.** (c)
161. (d)	**162.** (b)	**163.** (d)	**164.** (b)	**165.** (c)	**166.** (a)	**167.** (d)	**168.** (e)	**169.** (d)	**170.** (a)
171. (a)	**172.** (b)	**173.** (c)	**174.** (a)	**175.** (a)	**176.** (c)	**177.** (e)	**178.** (b)	**179.** (c)	**180.** (e)
181. (d)	**182.** (c)	**183.** (a)	**184.** (d)	**185.** (b)	**186.** (a)	**187.** (b)	**188.** (b)	**189.** (b)	**190.** (a)
191. (a)	**192.** (a)	**193.** (d)	**194.** (b)	**195.** (a)	**196.** (a)	**197.** (d)	**198.** (d)	**199.** (a)	**200.** (a)

EXPLANATIONS

1. No. of boys participating = 15

∴ No. of girls participating

$$= \frac{15}{3} \times 2 = 10 \qquad \text{...(i)}$$

∴ Total students participating

$$= 15 + 10 = 25$$

∴ Total students not participating

$$= 60 - 25 = 35$$

Suppose x boys do not participate. Then there are x + 5 girls who do not participate. And,

$$x + x + 5 = 35$$

or $\quad\quad 2x = 30$

∴ $\quad\quad\quad x = 15$

Hence no. of girls not participating

$$= x + 5$$

$$= 15 + 5 = 20 \qquad \text{...(ii)}$$

From (i) and (ii), no. of girls in the class

$$= 10 + 20 = 30$$

2-5 :

Person	Overtime
S	Monday
P	Tuesday
R	Wednesday
Holiday	Thursday
Q	Friday
T	Saturday

4. Wednesday

6. The positions of the words shift as follows:

$$1 \rightarrow 9$$
$$2 \rightarrow 3$$
$$3 \rightarrow 7$$
$$4 \rightarrow 5$$
$$5 \rightarrow 2$$

$$6 \to 8$$
$$7 \to 4$$
$$8 \to 1$$
and $$9 \to 6$$

7.

O	B	L	I	Q	U	E
+2	+3	+3	+2	+3	+2	+2
Q	E	O	K	T	W	G

8. D R O <u>W</u> N

9. Sunita's son = Renu's father

Hence Renu = Sunita's granddaughter

Now, girl = mother of Renu

= mother of Sunita's granddaughter

= Sunita's daughter-in-law.

Hence Sunita is the girl's mother-in-law

10.

Q —— N (+)
|
P's father (+) —— M
|
P

Hence N is M's uncle.

11-15:

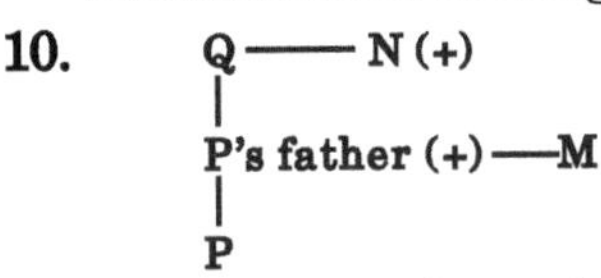

16. J Y 2 = S £ δ E G M ✹ 7 $ H P 9 K L β @ W Q 1 3 # C D ©

17. J <u>Y</u> 2 = <u>S</u> £ δ <u>E</u> G M ✹ $ <u>H</u> <u>P</u> 9 K L β @ <u>W</u> Q 1 3 # <u>C</u> D ©

There are eight such letters.

18. J Y 2 = S £ δ E G M ✹ <u>7</u> $ H P <u>9</u> K L β @ W Q <u>1</u> <u>3</u> # C D ©

19. If you put a mirror after the third element of the first term, the points of reflection constitute the second term.

20. In all others, the first element occupies the same position from the left as the thrid does from the right. And a similar relationship exists between the second and fourth elements.

21. It appears some special cosmic phenomenon has led to both A and B.

22. A certainly can't be the effect of B if we believe in an ethical world. A is the effect of bad policing and B of good policing.

23. The removal of the signal post has led to the accidents.

24. A has been done in response to B.

26. A decision is taken when it is felt that it would be accepted by most of the people concerned. Hence I is implicit. II is also implicit as the reason behind the need.

27. It is not necessary that price rise be there on the mind of the govt while taking the decision. Hence neither I nor II is implicity. In fact, the truth is that our petroleum companies are running losses even after the drop in international prices.

28. Both are imminent positive outcomes assumed.

29. I is implicit because teachers can't be appointed in a vacuum. II is more of a presumption.

30. When a move is made, it is assumed to be effective. Hence I is implicit. It is also assumed that the stipulated target will be met. Hence II is implicit.

31. I is weak because it is superfluous; it does not go into the reason for population control. II is an argument by example and hence weak.

32. I is strong because female foeticide is undesirable. II is weak; which right are we talking about? Right to know the *sex* of the unborn child? No. Parents can wait till the child's birth.

33. I is strong on humanitarian grounds.

II is strong on economic grounds.

34. I is weak because it is not relevant to "complete ban".

II is a strong argument because banning mining in such a scenario will lead us into great trouble.

35. I is strong as improved ambience is desirable.

II is strong because regimentation of adults is undesirable.

36.

$$M < R \qquad \text{... (i)}$$
$$R \leq T \qquad \text{... (ii)}$$
$$T = N \qquad \text{... (iii)}$$

Combining these, we get

$$M < R \leq T = N.$$

Hence N ≥ R.

Which means either I (N = R) or II (N > R) follows.

37.

$$J \leq N \qquad \text{... (i)}$$
$$K \geq N \qquad \text{... (ii)}$$
$$T > K \qquad \text{...(iii)}$$

Combining these, we get

$$T > K \geq N \geq J.$$

Hence J < T and I follows

Also, T > N and II follows

Besides, N ≥ J and III follows

38.

$$B = D \qquad \text{... (i)}$$
$$D \geq H \qquad \text{...(ii)}$$
$$H < F \qquad \text{...(iii)}$$

D and F cant be compared from (ii) and (iii). And for the same reason, if we bear (i) in mind, B and F also can't be compared. Hence none follows.

39.
$$T > K \quad \text{...(i)}$$
$$K \le R \quad \text{...(ii)}$$
$$R = M \quad \text{...(iii)}$$

From (ii) and (iii), $M \ge K$ ...(iv).

Hence either I (M = K) or III (M > K) follows.

But M and T can't be compared from (i) and (iv). Hence II does not follow.

40.
$$V \ge M \quad \text{...(i)}$$
$$A > M \quad \text{...(ii)}$$
$$R \le V \quad \text{...(iii)}$$

These lead us to no relationship by combination.

41. Some cloths are cotton and *vice versa*. A shirt may be made of cotton or some other cloth.

42. Paper and ink are generally stationary items.

43. They are three distinct elements.

44. A blackboard is found in a classroom and the latter is found in a school.

45. They are three distinct sports.

46. The passage clearly says that *some* of the developing countries boast of huge scientific and technical manpower.

47. This is what the entire passage deals with.

48. Official formalities appear to be cumbersome in developing countries in general.

49. Probably true from the fact that liberalisation has "put pressures on Indian industry".

50. The passage clearly says: "It is well recognised that developing countries like India are already behind other countries technologically..."

51.
$$? = 724.998 \div 24.048 \div 14.954$$
$$= 724.998 \times \frac{1}{24.048} \times \frac{1}{14.954}$$
$$= 2.0160461589 \approx 2$$

52.
$$? = (848.999 + 274.05(2) \div 3.0054$$
$$= 1123.051 \div 3.0054$$
$$= 373.67 \approx 374$$

53.
$$? = 3\sqrt{84900} \approx 44$$

54.
$$? = 18.5\% \text{ of } 425 + 16.2\% \text{ of } 388.$$
$$= 78.625 + 62.856$$
$$= 141.481 \approx 141$$

55.
$$? = \frac{11538.93375}{18.345 \times 19.068} = \frac{11538.93375}{349.80246}$$
$$= 32.986 \approx 33$$

56. Number of people preferring vegetables
$$= 30,000 \times 30\% = 9000$$

Number of people preferring **sprouts**
$$= 30,000 \times 13\% = 3900$$

Required total number
$$= 9000 + 3900 = 12,900.$$

57. Difference between the total number of people preferring meat to the total number of people preferring fish
$$= 30,000 \times (6\% - 5\%) = 300.$$

58. Number of people preferring fruits
$$= 30,000 \times 11\% = 3300$$

Number of people preferring vegetables = 9000.

$$\text{Required } \% = \frac{3300}{9000} \times 100 = 36.66 = 37 \text{ (Approx)}$$

59. Number of people preferring fish
$$= 30,000 \times 5\% = 1500.$$

60. Number of people preferring meat
$$= 30,000 \times 6\% = 1800.$$

Number of people preferring salad
$$= 30,000 \times 15\% = 4500$$

$$\text{Required ratio} = \frac{1800}{4500} = 2 : 5$$

61. All no. in the given series are squares of odd nos., except 1296.
$$1296 = (36)^2$$

62.
$$13 + 14 = 27$$
$$14 + 27 = 41$$
$$27 + 41 + 68$$
$$41 + 68 = 109$$
$$68 + 109 = 177$$

So, 45 is the wrong number in this series.

64. The series is:
$$+ 3^3, +5^3, + 7^3, 9^3, + 11^3 + 13^3, ...$$

65.
$$4 \times 4 + (4 \times (3) = 28$$
$$28 \times 5 + (5 \times (4) = 160$$
$$160 \times 6 + (6 \times (5) = 990$$
$$990 \times 7 + (7 \times 6) = 6972$$
$$6972 \times 8 + (8 \times 7) = 55832$$
$$55832 \times 9 + (9 \times 8) = 502560$$

66.
$$8^{9.4} \times 4^{12.8} \times 64^{8.1} = 16^?$$
$$8^{2 \times 4.7} \times 4^{12.8} \times 64^{8.1} = 16^?$$
$$64^{4.7} \times 4^{12.8} \times 64^{8.1} = 16^?$$
$$64^{4.7+8.1} \times 4^{12.8} = 16^?$$
$$(64 \times (4)^{12.8} = 16^?$$
$$(256)^{12.8} = 16^?$$
$$16^{2 \times 12.8} = 16^?$$
$$? = 25.6$$

67.
$$\frac{8 \div ? \times 3.5}{4 \times 5 \div 2} = 0.7$$
$$? = \frac{8 \times 3.5 \times 2}{0.7 \times 4 \times 5} = 4$$

68.
$$? = \frac{84}{17} \times \frac{27}{16} \times \frac{38}{7} = \frac{1539}{34} = 45\frac{9}{34}$$

69.
$$? = \sqrt{(15)^2 + (10)^2 + (16)^2}$$
$$= \sqrt{225 + 100 + 36} = \sqrt{361}$$
$$= 19$$

70.
$$? = 12\% \text{ of } 840 \times 0.25\% \text{ of } 148$$
$$= 100.8 \times 0.37 = 37.296.$$

71. Profit on 200 metres of cloth
$$= 200 \times 5 = \text{Rs } 1000.$$
Cost price of 200 m of cloth
$$= 9000 - 1000 = \text{Rs } 8000.$$
Cost price of 1 m of cloth
$$= \frac{8000}{200} = \text{Rs } 40.$$

72. Area of a circle = 1386 sq cm
$$\pi r^2 = 1386$$
$$r^2 = \frac{1386 \times 7}{22}$$
$$\therefore \quad r = \sqrt{63 \times 7} = 21 \text{ cms}$$
Circumference $= 2\pi r = 2 \times \dfrac{22}{7} \times 21 = 132 \text{ cm}$

73. Number of professors are assigned to each faculty
$$27 \div 3 = 9$$

74.
$$x^2 - (1(1)^2 = 135$$
$$x^2 = 135 + 121 = 256$$
$$x = \sqrt{256} = 16.$$
Required number = 16.

75. Cost of 105 kg of rice
$$= \frac{168}{7} \times 105$$
$$= 168 \times 15 = \text{Rs } 2520$$

76. Share of Seema $= 2500 \times \dfrac{3}{5} = \text{Rs} 1500$

Share of Meena $= 2500 \times \dfrac{2}{5} = \text{Rs} 1000$

New ratio $= \dfrac{1500 + 500}{1000 + 500} = \dfrac{2000}{1500}$
$$= \frac{4}{3} = 4 : 3$$

77. Monthly income $= 3750 \times 4$
$$= \text{Rs } 15,000$$

78. Average of set of scores
$$= \frac{302 + 152 + 132 + 122 + 112}{5}$$
$$= \frac{820}{5} = 164$$

79. Speed of the bus
$$= \frac{172 \text{ kms}}{4 \text{hr}} = 43 \text{km/h}$$

80. Total number of boys in this school
$$= 4800 \times 40\% = 1920.$$

81. Statement II:
Let the age of Rani = x years
$\therefore$ Age of Surekha = 2x years
Sum of their ages = 72
$$x + 2x = 72$$
$$3x = 72$$
$$x = 24 \text{ years}$$

Statement I:
Niddi's age = 3 times younger than Rani
$$= \frac{24}{3} = 8 \text{ years.}$$

82. Statement II:
Required ratio
$$= \frac{\text{Number of girls}}{\text{Number of boys}} = \frac{1400}{2100} = \frac{2}{3} = 2 : 3$$

83. From either of the statements,
$$\text{Speed of bus} = \frac{80 \text{km}}{5 \text{hr}} = \frac{160 \text{km}}{10 \text{hr}} = 16 \text{ km/h}$$

84. Both statements are not sufficient to give the required ratio.

85. Let the present income of Mehta = Rs. x.
Income increase by 10% every year
$$= \frac{x \times 10}{100} = \text{Rs} \frac{x}{10}$$
$$\frac{x}{10} = 2500$$
$$\therefore \quad x = \text{Rs } 25000.$$

86. Total production of two commodities together in 1998
$$= 175 + 175 = 350.$$
Total production of two commodities together in 1999
$$= 150 + 200 = 350.$$

87. Total production of 'X' for all the seven years together
$$= 125 + 175 + 150 + 175 + 225 + 200 + 250$$
$$= 1300$$
Total production of 'Y' for all the seven years together
$$= 150 + 175 + 200 + 150 + 250 + 225 + 200$$
$$= 1350$$
Required ratio $= \dfrac{1300}{1350} = \dfrac{26}{27} = 26 : 27$

88. In 1998, % increase in production of commodity X

$$= \frac{(175 - 125)}{125} \times 100 = \frac{50 \times 100}{125} = 40\%$$

Which is maximum.

89. Average production (in lakh tonnes) of commodity 'Y'

$$= \frac{1350}{7} = 192.85 = 195 \text{ (approx)}$$

90. Total production of the two commodities together for years 1997, 1998 & 1999

$$= 125 + 150 + 350 + 350 = 975$$

Total production of the two commodities together for years 2001, 2002 & 2003

$$= 225 + 250 + 200 + 225 + 250 + 200$$
$$= 450 + 500 + 400 = 1350$$

Required ratio $= \dfrac{975}{1350} = 13 : 18$

91. Cost of the dining table

$$= \frac{14056 \times 100}{112} = \text{Rs } 12,550$$

92. $(55\% - 25\%) = 11.10$

$$30\% = 11.10, \; 1\% = \frac{11.10}{30}$$

$$75\% = \frac{11.10}{30} \times 75 = 27.75$$

93. $x(x + (1) = 1980$

$$x^2 + x - 1980 = 0$$
$$x = 44, 45$$

Required smallest number = 44

94. Required smallest number to be added is

$$= (8 - 4) = 4$$

95. $\dfrac{3}{4} \times \dfrac{2}{5} \times x - \dfrac{4}{5} \times \dfrac{1}{4} \times x = 5$

or $\dfrac{3x}{10} - \dfrac{x}{5} = 5,$

or $\dfrac{3x - 2x}{10} = 5$

or $x = 5 \times 10 = 50$

96. Total marks obtained by all the students in Science

$$= \frac{100}{120} \times (100 + 96 + 112 + 88 + 92 + 108)$$

$$= \frac{100}{120} \times 596 = 82.77 = 82.78 \text{ (approx.)}$$

97. Total marks obtained by D in all subjects

$$\frac{62 \times 4}{3} + \frac{67 \times 4}{3} + \frac{88 \times 10}{12}$$

$$+ \frac{108 \times 24}{3} + \frac{48 \times 5}{4} + \frac{34 \times 5}{3}$$

$$= 82.66 + 89.11 + 73.30 + 72 + 60 + 56.66$$

$$= \frac{4333.73}{6} = 72.28\%$$

98. Average marks obtained by all students in English

$$= \frac{\dfrac{100}{80} \times (50 + 46 + 52 + 48 + 60 + 53)}{6}$$

$$= \frac{386.25}{6} = 64.375 = 64.38 \text{ (approx.)}$$

99. Total marks obtained in all subjects by F
$$= 54 + 64 + 108 + 116 + 53 + 40 = 435$$

total marks obtained in all subjects by G
$$= 66 + 55 + 92 + 140 + 60 + 32 = 445$$

Required ratio $= \dfrac{435}{445} = 87 : 89$

100. Average marks in Maths

$$= \frac{733}{6} = 122 \text{ (approx)}$$

101. Substitute which for where

103. Rearrange as to fund not only

104. Substitute them.

105. Insert the before ideal.

106. Substitute students.

107. Substitute plans.

108. Substitute at for to.

109. Substitute few.

110. Substitute adequate.

126. Read the first two sentences of the passage.

127. Read the last para.

128. (A) follows from the last para.

129. The fact that there are few secondary airports has hurt low-cost airlines.

130. Among the given choices, this is the only one talked about in the passage.

133. Read the last para.

ENGLISH ABILITY

Directions (1-5): *Each sentence given below has two blanks. Each blank indicates that something has been omitted. Choose the word that best fits in the meaning of the sentence as a whole.*

1. Realistically, however this, disconnect cannot _______ itself very long, sooner rather than _______ the whole will no doubt converge.
   - (*a*) sustain, later
   - (*b*) sustained, later
   - (*c*) submerge, latter
   - (*d*) harmonize, lately
   - (*e*) mend, lately

2. Digitisation will _______ a couple of billion, dollars in pay revenues, bring more taxes choice and clean out black money_______ cable.
   - (*a*) realise, from
   - (*b*) replenish, off
   - (*c*) release, from
   - (*d*) revive, with
   - (*e*) supply, with

3. Public sector infrastructure financing companies could _______ of the ambitious 'smart cities' citing _______ of guaranteed returns on investments.
   - (*a*) opt for, crisis
   - (*b*) opt out, lack
   - (*c*) prefer, excess
   - (*d*) select, lack
   - (*e*) opt, cause

4. Looks like the oil markets are not only showing _______ between the physical and the financial perspectives from .time to time but also _______ between the short term view and the long term realities.
   - (*a*) disconnect, convergence
   - (*b*) disconnect, divergence
   - (*c*) connection, difference
   - (*d*) supply, demand
   - (*e*) similarity, contrast

5. Top global oil exporter Saudi Arabia _______ its crude production in April to a record high, _______ its flourishing Asian market share.
   - (*a*) rose, feed
   - (*b*) risen, collecting
   - (*c*) raised, lead
   - (*d*) raised, feeding
   - (*e*) increased, healing

Directions (6 -15): *Read the following passage carefully and answer the questions given below it, Certain words/phrases are given in **bold** to help you locate them while answering some of the questions.*

Core competencies and focus are now the mantras of corporate strategists in Western economies. But while managers in the West have **dismantled** many conglomerates assembled in the 1960s and 1970s, the large, diversified business group remains the dominant form of enterprise throughout most emerging markets. Some groups operate as holding companies with full ownership in many enterprises, others are collections of publicly traded companies, but all have some degree of central control.

As emerging markets open up to global competition, consultants and foreign investors are increasingly pressuring these groups to **conform to** Western practice by scaling back the scope of their business activities. The conglomerate is the dinosaur of organizational design, they argue, too unwieldy and slow to compete in today's fast paced markets. Already a number of executives have decided to break up their groups in order to show that they are focusing on only a few core businesses.

There are reasons to worry about this trend. Focus is good advice in New York or London, but something important gets lost in translation when that advice is given to groups in emerging markets. Western companies take for granted a range of institutions that support their business activities, but many of these institutions are absent in other regions of the world. Without effective securities regulation and venture capital firms, for example, focused companies may be unable to raise adequate financing; and without strong educational Institutions, they will struggle to hire skilled employees. Communicating with customers is difficult when the local infrastructure is poor, and unpredictable government behavior can stymie any operation. Although a focused strategy may enable a company to perform a few activities well, companies in emerging markets must take responsibility for a wide range or functions in order to do business effectively.

In the case of product markets, buyers and sellers usually suffer from a severe **dearth**, of information for three reasons. First, the communications infrastructure in emerging markets is often underdeveloped. Even as wireless communication spreads throughout the West, vast stretches in countries such as China and India remain without telephones. Power shortages often render the modes of communication that do exist Ineffective, The postal service is typically inefficient, slow, or unreliable; and the private sector rarely provides efficient courier services. High rates of illiteracy make it difficult for marketers to communicate effectively with customers.

Second, even when information about products does get around, there are no mechanisms to corroborate the claims made by sellers. Independent consumer information organizations are rare, and government watchdog agencies are of tittle use. The few analysts who rate products are generally less sophisticated than their counter parts in advanced economies.

Third, consumers have no redress mechanisms, if a product does not deliver on its promise. Law enforcement is often **capricious** and so. slow that few who 'assign any value to time would resort.to it. Unlike in advanced markets, there are few extrajudicial arbitration mechanisms to which, one can appeal.

As a result of this lack of information, companies in emerging markets face much higher costs in building credible brands than their counterparts in advanced economies. In turn, established brands wield tremendous power. A conglomerate with a reputation for quality products and services can use its group name to enter new businesses, even if those businesses are completely unrelated to its current lines. Groups also have an advantage when they do try to build up a brand because they can spread the cost of maintaining it across multiples lines of business. Such groups then have a greater incentive not to damage brand quality in any one business because they will pay the price in their other businesses as well.

6. Which of the following sentence(s) is/are correct in the context of the given passage ?

 I. Consultants and foreign Investors argue that the conglomerate is the dinosaur of organisational design too unwieldly and slow to compete in today's- fast-paced markets.

 II. Core competencies and focus are now the mantras of corporate strategists in western economies.

III. Due to lack of information required, companies in emerging markets face much higher costs in building credible brands in comparison to their counterparts in advanced economies.

(a) Only I   (b) Only II and III
(c) Only I and III   (d) Only I and II
(e) All I, II and III

7. What suggestions have been cited by the writer in regard to raising adequate financing and hiring skilled employees ?

(a) Effective securities regulation

(b) Effective securities regulation and venture capital firms

(c) Effective securities regulation and venture capital firms and strong educational institutions

(d) Both (a) and (c)

(e) None of these

8. The writer has cited some hurdles in the case of product markets regarding shortage of information which of the following statement(s) in this regard is/are true ?

 I. Communications infrastructure to emerging markets is often underdeveloped.

 II. Postal service is typically inefficient, slow or unreliable.

III. High rates of illiteracy make it difficult for marketers to communicate effectively with customers.

(a) Only I   (b) Only III
(c) Only II and III   (d) Only I and II
(e) All I, II and III

9. Which of the following statements is correct in regard to the given passsge?

(a) The few analysts in emerging markets who rate products are generally less sophisticated than their counterparts in advanced economies.

(b) Unlike in advanced markets there are few extrajudicial arbitration mechanisms in emerging markets to which one can appeal.

(c) Even as wireless communication spreads throughout the West, vast regions of China and India remain without telephones.

(d) Unpredictable government behaviour can stymie any operation.

(e) All are correct

10. Established brands can wield tremendous power in emerging markets because

(a) a conglomerate with a reputation for quality products and services can use its group name to enter new businesses.

(b) they have much political nexus and strongman power

(c) they have excess of money and customers

(d) they have greater incentive to damage brand quality in any one business

(e) None of these

11. What should be the most appropriate title of this passage ?

    (*a*) Hurdles in Emerging markets

    (*b*) What is an Emerging market

    (*c*) Lack of Information in Emerging Markets

    (*d*) Advanced Markets Eat Emerging Markets

    (*e*) None of these

Directions (12-13): *Choose the word/group of words which is **most similar** in meaning to the word/group of words printed in **bold** as used in the passage.*

12. CONFORM TO

    (*a*) comply   (*b*) conflict between

    (*c*) confirm   (*d*) confiscate

    (*e*) confine to

13. DISMANTLE

    (*a*) take together   (*b*) hold

    (*c*) take apart   (*d*) disorder

    (*e*) dismount

Directions (14 - 15): *Choose the word which is **MOST OPPOSITE** in meaning to the word printed in **bold** as used in the passage.*

14. CAPRICIOUS

    (*a*) unpredictable   (*b*) predictable

    (*c*) changeable   (*d*) captive

    (*e*) reasonable

15. DEARTH

    (*a*) scarcity   (*b*) Shortage

    (*c*) paucity   (*d*) abundance

    (*e*) debility

Directions (16 - 20): *Rearrange the fallowing six sentences (A), (B), (C), (D), (E) and (F) in the proper sequence to form meaningful paragraph; then answer the questions given below them.*

(A) Colony losses last year weren't as dramatic as the declines associated with Colony Collapse Disorder (CCD), which was first identified in October 2006.

(B) Beekeepers tapped for the survey manage a total of 400,000 colonies, representing about 14.5 percent of the United States honeybee colonies.

(C) Overall, colony losses during the 12-month period that ended in April reached 42.1 percent the second- highest annual loss to date.

(D) Summcr colony losses reached 27.4 percent, exceeding winter losses that came in at 23.7 percent.

(E) For the first time, beekeepers watched more of their colonies disappear during the summer than in winter.

(F) A new survey outlining honeybee colony losses in the U.S. has scientists scratching their heads.

16. Which of the following should be the **FIRST** sentence after rearrangement ?

    (*a*) A

    (*b*) B

    (*c*) F

    (*d*) E

    (*e*) D

17. Which of the following should be the **SECOND** sentence after rearrangement ?

    (*a*) E   (*b*) F

    (*c*) A   (*d*) B

    (*e*) C

18. Which of the following should be the **SIXTH** sentence after rearrangement.

    (*a*) A   (*b*) B

    (*c*) C   (*d*) D

    (*e*) E

19. Which of the following should be the **FOURTH** sentence after rearrangement?

    (*a*) A   (*b*) B

    (*c*) C   (*d*) D

    (*e*) E

20. Which of the following should be the **FIFTH** sentence after rearrangement?

    (*a*) A   (*b*) B

    (*c*) C   (*d*) D

    (*e*) E

Directions (21-25): *Read each sentence to find out whether there is any grammatical error or idiomatic error in it. The error, if any, will be in one part of the sentence. The number of that part is the answer. If there is no error, the answer is (e). (Ignore errors of punctuation, if any.)*

21. Profitability of fleet operators (*a*) / have improved due to a decline (*b*) / in fuel prices during (*c*) / the last two months (*d*)/No error (*e*).

22. We are a young country, (*a*) / a brash country, a forward (*b*)/ looking country, and (*c*) / true history interest us a lot (*d*)/ No error (*e*).

23. The joint statement included (*a*) / just three lines on military (*b*) / cooperation, restriction itself for (*c*) / exercise and ship visits (*d*) / No error (*e*).

24. In a counfay currently there is (*a*)/absolute no shortage in fact (*b*)/ there is an abundance of pilots holding (*c*)/ a valid licence but unable to find a job (*d*)/No error (*e*).

25. WPI might have turned negative primarily (*a*)/due to a steep decline in the prices (*b*)/of non-food articles (*c*)/raising vegetable prices keep food articles firm during this month (*d*)/No error (*e*).

Directions (26 - 30): *In the following passage there are blanks, each of which has been numbered. These numbers are printed below the passage and against each, five words are suggested, one of which fits the blank appropriately. Find out the appropriate word in each case.*

There is plenty written about the wealth divide in the U.S. economy. But there is another important divide the one between consumers and corporations. If you look at how U.S. households have been behaving **(26)** you'd think it was all blue skies. Consumer confidence is at a five-year high, thanks to higher stock prices and a **(27)** in the housing market. Home prices have had their biggest jump since 2005. Consumers, finally feeling more **(28)** are buying that new car or electronic gadget and bolstering GDP growth a bit. The wealth gap between America's high income group and everyone else has **(29)** record high levels since the economic recovery from the Great Recession of 2007-09. with a clear **(30)** of increasing wealth for the upper- income families and no wealth growth for the middle and lower- income families.

28. (*a*) late
(*b*) lately
(*c*) uniformly
(*d*) eager
(*e*) earnestly

27. (*a*) discovery   (*b*) growing
(*c*) recovery   (*d*) delivery
(*e*) depletion

28. (*a*) flush   (*b*) happy
(*c*) satisfied   (*d*) flung
(*e*) flunk

29. (*a*) reach   (*b*) reached
(*c*) delivered   (*d*) targeted
(*e*) subjugated

30. (*a*) target   (*b*) projection
(*c*) trajectory   (*d*) tarnation
(*e*) temptation

QUANTITATIVE APTITUDE

Directions (31-35): *Study the following table carefully and answer the questions given below it.*

Number of students enrolled in 4 different courses at a college during the given years

Years	2010		2011		2012	
Courses	Total No. of Students	Total Female Students	Total No. of Students	Total Female Students	Total No. of Students	Total Female Students
A	840	378	820	553	800	432
B	1200	660	1200	660	1250	750
C	952	342	900	360	980	441
D	900	540	860	602	700	525

31. What was the average number of boys studying in all four courses of the college in the year 2010?
(*a*) 493
(*b*) 480
(*c*) 439
(*d*) 468
(*e*) None of these

32. What was the average number of female students studying in all four courses of the college in the year 2012?
(*a*) 573
(*b*) 537
(*c*) 437
(*d*) 473
(*e*) None of these

33. By what percent **approximately** is the number of boys studying in all four courses of the college in the year 2011 less than that of the girl students studying in all four courses in the same year?
(*a*) 32   (*b*) 30
(*c*) 26   (*d*) 22
(*e*) None of these

34. What is the difference between the number of girls studying in all four courses in the year 2010 and that of boys studying in all four courses in the year 2011?
(*a*) 205   (*b*) 215
(*c*) 305   (*d*) 315
(*e*) None of these

35. What is the respective ratio between the total number of boys in courses B and D together to 2010 and that of all students to courses A and D to 2012?
(*a*) 3 : 5
(*b*) 1 : 3
(*c*) 3 : 7
(*d*) 4 : 5
(*e*) None of these

36. A dealer allowed a discount of 25% on the marked price of Rs. 12000 on an article and incurred a loss of 10%. What discount should he allow on the marked price so that he gains Rs. 440 on the article ?
(*a*) 11%
(*b*) 13%
(*c*) 19%
(*d*) 15%
(*e*) None of these

Directions (37-41): *Study the following line graph carefully to answer the given questions.*

Number of projects handled by 6 companies during years

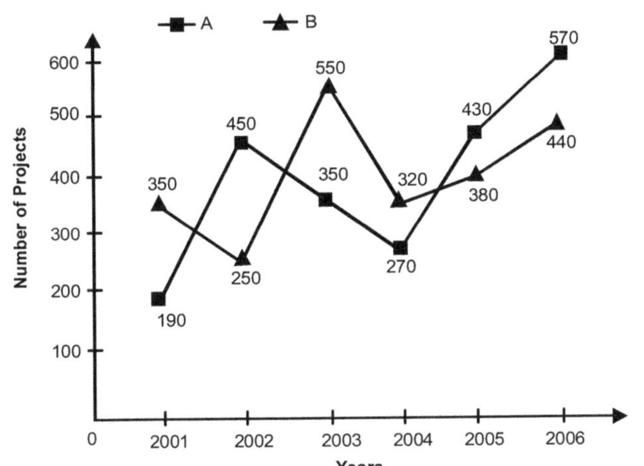

37. What is the average number of projects handled by company A during all the given years?

(a) $370\dfrac{2}{3}$

(b) $376\dfrac{2}{3}$

(c) $376\dfrac{1}{3}$

(d) $367\dfrac{2}{3}$

(e) None of these

38. What is the respective ratio between the total number of projects handled by both companies in the years 2002 and 2003?

(a) 4 : 5

(b) 5 : 9

(c) 7 : 9

(d) 5 : 7

(e) None of these

39. By what per cent is the number of projects handled by company B in the year 2006 more than that handled in the year 2002 by the same company ?

(a) 84%

(b) 86%

(c) 72%

(d) 76%

(e) None of these

40. What is the average number of projects handled by company B during all the given years ?

(a) $381\dfrac{2}{3}$

(b) $381\dfrac{1}{3}$

(c) $381\dfrac{2}{3}$

(d) $376\dfrac{1}{3}$

(e) None of these

41. What is the difference between the total number of projects handled by company A and company B in the years 2001, 2003 and 2006 taken together ?

(a) 250

(b) 230

(c) 260

(d) 240

(e) None of these

42. A man gave 20% of his salary to his only son and only daughter. The ratio of amount given to son and daughter is 3 : 2 respectively. Twice the amount what he gave to his daughter, he invested in LIC. Out of the remaining amount he gave one-fourth to his wife. After that he was left with Rs. 16800. Find out the amount invested in LIC.

(a) Rs. 5600

(b) Rs. 5400

(c) Rs. 5800

(d) Rs. 6200

(e) None of these

43. In a vessel there is 40 litres mixture of milk and water, There is 15% water in the mixture. The milkman sells 10 litres of mixture to a customer and thereafter adds 12.5 litres of water to the remaining mixture. What Is the respective ratio of milk and water in the new mixture ?

(a) 2:3

(b) 3:2

(c) 3:4

(d) 4:3

(e) None of these

44. A boat covers a distance of 2.75 km upstream in 11 minutes. The ratio between speed of current and that of boat downstream is 1 :7 respectively. The boat covers distance between A and B downstream in 52 minutes. What is the distance between point A and point B ?

(a) 19.2 km.

(b) 17.2 km.

(c) 18.2 km.

(d) 16.5 km.

(e) None of these

Directions (45-49): *What will come in place of the question mark (?) in each of the following number series ?*

45. 125 128 119 146 65 ?

(a) 308

(b) 316

(c) 298

(d) 294

(e) 264

46. 8 17 30 47 68

(a) 83

(b) 93

(c) 98

(d) 95

(e) 96

47. 24 12 12 18 ? 90

(a) 40

(b) 38

(c) 36

(d) 45

(e) None of these

48. 5 16 49 104 ? 280
   (*a*) 165   (*b*) 160
   (*c*) 171   (*d*) 181
   (*e*) 175

49. 13 19 30 48 75 ?
   (*a*) 107   (*b*) 108
   (*c*) 116   (*d*) 112
   (*e*) 113

50. A and B together can complete a piece of work in $10\frac{2}{7}$ days white B and C together can complete the same work in $13\frac{1}{3}$ days. B is 25% more efficient than C. In how many days will A and C together complete the same work ?

   (*a*) $11\frac{1}{4}$ (*b*) $12\frac{1}{4}$

   (*c*) $11\frac{1}{3}$ (*d*) $12\frac{1}{3}$

   (*e*) None of these

51. The sum of present ages of Ria and Abby is 48 years. Today Abby is 4 years older than Shweta. The respective ratio of the present ages of Ria and Shweta is 4 : 7. What was Abby's age two years ago ?
   (*a*) 32 years   (*b*) 30 years
   (*c*) 28 years   (*d*) 34 years
   (*e*) None of these

Directions (52-56): What **approximate** value will come in place of the question mark (?) in the following questions ? (You are not expected to calculate the exact value)

52. 52.02% of 749 + 45% of 419.98 – ? = 15^2
   (*a*) 354   (*b*) 364
   (*c*) 370   (*d*) 368
   (*e*) None of these

53. 349.98 × 19.99 + ?² × 180.16 =11500
   (*a*) 3   (*b*) 5
   (*c*) 4   (*d*) 9
   (*e*) 25

54. $(1800 \div \sqrt{?} \times 29.99) \div 15.02 = 144$
   (*a*) 12
   (*b*) 25
   (*c*) 625
   (*d*) 144
   (*e*) 169

55. $(52.02^2 - 34.01^2) \div 17.99 \times \sqrt{?} = 1720$
   (*a*) 400   (*b*) 20
   (*c*) 25   (*d*) 625
   (*e*) None of these

56. (340 × 9.98) ÷ 6.4001 + 1245.15 = ?
   (*a*) 1766   (*b*) 1776
   (*c*) 1676   (*d*) 1876
   (*e*) 1806

57. A, B and C together start a business. The ratio of the investments of A, B and C is 0. 125 : 0.70 : 0.25, After 8 months A adds thrice amount of his earlier investment and C withdraws half of his earlier investment. At the end of the year, they earn a total profit of Rs. 5800. What is B's share in the profit ?
   (*a*) Rs. 3400   (*b*) Rs. 3200
   (*c*) Rs. 3600   (*d*) Rs. 3800
   (*e*) None of these

58. In a bag there are 4 white, 4 red and 1 green balls. Two balls are drawn at random. What is the probability that at least one ball is of green colour ?

   (*a*) $\frac{4}{5}$ (*b*) $\frac{3}{5}$

   (*c*) $\frac{1}{5}$ (*d*) $\frac{2}{5}$

   (*e*) None of these

59. Equal amounts are Invested in two schemes A and B for 6 years and 8 years respectively. Scheme A offers interest at the rate of 12% per annum and scheme B offers Interest at the rate of 8% per annum. The difference between the interests earned is Rs. 1280. What is the amount invested in each scheme?
   (*a*) Rs. 16000
   (*b*) Rs. 16500
   (*c*) Rs. 17000
   (*d*) Rs. 18000
   (*e*) None of these

60. The area of a rectangle is equal to the area of a square whose diagonal is $12\sqrt{6}$ metre. The difference between the length and the breadth of the rectangle is 6 metre. What is the perimeter of rectangle ? (in metre)   .
   (*a*) 160 metre
   (*b*) 80 metre
   (*c*) 82 metre
   (*d*) 84 metre
   (*e*) None of these

Directions (61-65) : *In the following questions two equations numbered I and II are given. You have to solve both the equations and –*

Give answer (a) if x > y

Give answer (b) if x ≥ y

Give answer (c) if x < y

Give answer (d) if x ≤ y

Give answer (e) if x = y or the relationship cannot be established.

61. I. $3x^2 + 14x + 15 = 0$
    II. $6y^2 + 17y + 12 = 0$

62. I. $3x^2 - 17x + 24 = 0$
    II. $4y^2 - 15y + 14 = 0$

63. I. $2x^2 + 11x + 14 = 0$
    II. $2y^2 - 17y + 33 = 0$

64. I. $3x^2 + 13x + 12 = 0$
    II. $2y^2 + 15y + 27 = 0$

65. I. $x^2 - 22x + 121 = 0$
    II. $y^2 = 121$

REASONING ABILITY

Directions (66-70): *Study the following information carefully and answer the questions given below:*

Eight friends - C, D, E, F, N, O, P and Q – are sitting in a straight line facing north but not necessarily in the same order. O is sitting second to the right of P, E is sitting third to the left of Q, F is sitting fourth to the left of P, E does not sit on the extreme end of the line. D is immediate neighbour of neither F nor P, C is not an immediate neighbour of P.

66. Which of the following pairs represents the two persons sitting at the extreme ends of the line ?
    (a) F, C
    (b) D, F
    (c) C, Q
    (d) N, D
    (e) O, F

67. Which of the following statements is 'definitely' true as per the given arrangement ?
    (a) F and E are immediate neighbours of P.
    (b) C is sitting third to the right of Q.
    (c) There are only three persons between D and E.
    (d) N is sitting to the immediate left of P.
    (e) All the given statements are true

68. Who among the following is sitting third to the right of N ?
    (a) O   (b) D
    (c) C   (d) E
    (e) Q

69. What is the position of C with respect to Q ?
    (a) Fourth to the right
    (b) Third to the right
    (c) Fourth to the left
    (d) Third to the left
    (e) Second to the right

70. Four of the following five are alike in a certain way based on the given arrangement and hence they form a group. Which one of the following does not belong to that group ?
    (a) FN   (b) PD
    (c) EQ   (d) CP
    (e) NQ

Directions (71-73): Study the following information carefully and answer the questions given below :

S is the daughter of U, V has only two children S and Y, Y is married to D, P is the brother of B, V has only two daughters. J is the mother of U, J is married to L, P is married to S, V is the son of T.

71. Who among the following is the sister-in-law of B ?
    (a) Y   (b) S
    (c) U   (d) J
    (e) T

72. Who among the following is the father of U ?
    (a) J   (b) T
    (c) V   (d) L
    (e) None of these

73. How is V related to P ?
    (a) Father-in-law
    (b) Mother-in-law
    (c) Father
    (d) Mother
    (e) Brother

74. Point A is 30 metres to the east of point B. Point C is 10 metres to the south of Point A. Point D is 15 metres to the west of Point C. Point E is exactly in the middle of the Points D and F. Points D, E and F lie in a straight line. The length of the line DEF is 20 metres. Point F is to the north of Point D. Point G is 15 metres to the east of Point F. How far and in which direction is Point G from Point A ?
    (a) 10 metres, South
    (b) 15 metres, North
    (c) 10 metres, North
    (d) 5 metres, South
    (e) 10 metres, East

75. A person starts from his house and moves towards the market. He walks 40 metres towards south and takes a right turn. After walking 30 metres he takes a left turn and walks 20 metres. Finally he takes a left turn and reach the market after walking 30 metres. How far and in which direction is his house from the market?

(*a*) 60 metres, South

(*b*) 60 metres, North

(*c*) 70 metres, North

(*d*) 70 metres, South

(*e*) 90 metres, North

Directions (76-80) : *In each question given below two or three statements followed by two Conclusions numbered I and II have been given. You have to take the given statements to be true even if they seem to be at variance from the commonly known facts and then decide which of the following Conclusions logically follows from the given statements, disregarding commonly known facts.*

Give answer (*a*) if only Conclusion I follows

Give answer (*b*) if only Conclusion II follows

Give answer (*c*) if either Conclusion I or Conclusion II follows

Give answer (*d*) if neither Conclusion I nor Conclusion II follows

Give answer (*e*) if both the Conclusions I and II follow

(76-77) : Statements

All magazines are journals. Some journals are periodicals. All periodicals are bulleteins.

76. Conclusions

I. Some periodicals are definitely not journals.

II. All periodicals being magazines is a possibility.

77. Conclusions

I. At least some bulleteins are journals.

II. No bulletein is a magazine.

78. Statements

All turns are loops.

No loop is a bend.

Some bends are curves.

Conclusions

I. At least some curves are loops.

II. No bend is a turn.

79. Statements

No country is a village.

All villages are districts.

Conclusions

I. All countries are districts.

II. All districts are villages.

80. Statements

All progress are growth.

All developments are growth. No growth is an evolution.

Conclusions

I. All developments being progress is a possibility.

II. No evolution is a progress.

Directions (81-85): *In each of the following questions, relationship between different elements is shown in the statements. The statements are followed by two Conclusions numbered I and II. Study the Conclusions based on the given statements and select the appropriate answer:*

Give answer (*a*) if only Conclusion I is true.

Give answer (*b*) if only Conclusion II is true

Give answer (*c*) if either Conclusion I or Conclusion II is true

Give answer (*d*) if neither Conclusion I nor Conclusion II is true

Give answer (*e*) if both the Conclusions I and II are true.

(81-82) : Statements

$Y \leq K < D = S \; ; \; D < V < O \; ; \; G \geq D < Q$

81. Conclusions

I. $G > V$

II. $Y < Q$

82. Conclusions

I. $K < O$

II. $G = V$

83. Statements

$D < L \leq F = N : L = A$

Conclusions

I. $N > D$

II. $A \leq F$

(84-85) : Statements

$B > Z = R \geq M < J \leq H : J > P : K < Z$

84. Conclusions

I. $H < P$

II. $B > M$

85. Conclusions

I. $K < J$

II. $R \geq H$

Directions (86-90): Study the following information carefully and answer the questions given below:

In a certain code language.

'good time to buy' is written as 'sy bo nj kw'.

'invest money and time' is written as 'sy ta ge mr'.

'only work and money' is written as 'ta fp mr ux'.

'buy good stuff only' is written as 'kw bo rd fp'.

86. What Is the code for "to" in the given code language ?
  (*a*) ge   (*b*) kw
  (*c*) nj   (*d*) sy
  (*e*) bo

87. What is the code for "buy good" in the given code language?
  (*a*) bo kw   (*b*) kw nj
  (*c*) rd bo   (*d*) rd nj
  (*e*) Cannot be determined

88. What is the code for "only-time and money" in the given code language ?
  (*a*) sy bo ux fp
  (*b*) fp ta rd kw
  (*c*) ge fp ta bo
  (*d*) mr ta sy fp
  (*e*) bo nj ta ge

89. What is the code for "stuff" in the given code language ?
  (*a*) fp
  (*b*) rd
  (*c*) kw
  (*d*) bo
  (*e*) Either 'bo' or rd'

90. What is the code for "Invest time to work" in the given code language ?
  (*a*) sy bo mr fp
  (*b*) ta nj kw rd
  (*c*) ta fp ux nj
  (*d*) mr sy bo ta
  (*e*) ux ge nj sy

Directions (91-95): *Study the following information carefully and answer the questions given below:*

Eight persons - M, N, O, P, Q, R, S and T - are sitting around a circular table at equal distance between each other, but not necessarily in the same order. Some of them are facing the centre while some others are facing outside (i.e., in a direction opposite to the centre)

Note : Facing the same direction means if one faces the centre then the other also faces the centre and vice-versa. Facing opposite directions means if one person faces the centre then the other person faces outside and vice-versa.

R is sitting second to the right of Q. Only three persons are sitting between R and S. T is sitting second to the right of R, T faces the centre. R and S face opposite directions. P and S face opposite directions. N is sitting second to the left of P. P is not an immediate neighbour of Q. Only one person is sitting between P and O. O is not an immediate neighbour of Q. M is sitting third to the left of T. The immediate neighbours of T face opposite directions. M and R face opposite directions. N faces the same direction as that of O.

91. Which of the following statements is true regarding T according to the given seating arrangement ?
  (*a*) T is sitting second to the left of S.
  (*b*) T is sitting exactly between O and P.
  (*c*) T is sitting just opposite to N.
  (*d*) There are four persons between T and Q.
  (*e*) T faces the opposite direction as that of M,

92. How many persons in the given seating arrangement face outside ?
  (*a*) Three   (*b*) Four
  (*c*) Five   (*d*) Six
  (*e*) Two

93. Four of the following five are alike in a certain way based on the given seating arrangement and hence they form a group. Which is the one that does not belong to that group ?
  (*a*) O   (*b*) S
  (*c*) M   (*d*) Q
  (*e*) N

94. Who among the following sits exactly between S and Q when counted from the left of S ?
  (*a*) None   (*b*) O
  (*c*) M   (*d*) N
  (*e*) T

95. What is the position of M with respect to R ?
  (*a*) Other than those given as options
  (*b*) Third to the right
  (*c*) Second to. the left
  (*d*) Second to the right
  (*e*) Third to the left

Directions (96-100) : Study the following information carefully and answer the questions given below:

Seven persons - M, N, O, P, Q, R and S - live on separate floors of a seven-storeyed building, but not necessarily in the same order. The ground floor of the building is numbered 1, the floor above it 2 and so on until the topmost floor is numbered 7. Each person likes different cartoon characters, viz. Chipmnuk, Flinstone, Jetson, Popeye, Scooby Doo, Simpson and Tweety, but not necessarily in the same order.

The person who likes Popeye lives on floor numbered 4. Only two persons live between P and the one who likes Popeye. M does not live on the lowermost floor. M lives on any odd numbered floor below the one who likes Popeye. S lives on an even numbered floor but neither immediately above nor immediately below the floor of M. Only two persons live between M and the person who likes Tweety. Only one person lives between N and R. R lives on an even numbered floor and does not like Popeye. Only three persons live between the persons who like Chipmnuk and Jetson respectively. The person who likes Chipmnuk live on any floor above the N's floor. The person who likes Chipmnuk does not live on the topmost floor. O does not like Chipmnuk or Jetson. The person who likes Scooby Doo lives on the floor immediately above the floor or the person who likes Simpson.

96. How many persons live between the floors on which S and P live?

   (*a*) Three   (*b*) Two

   (*c*) Four   (*d*) Five

   (*e*) No One

97. Which of the following statements is/are true according to the given information?

   (*a*) Q lives on floor numbered 5 and he does not like Popeye

   (*b*) M likes Scooby Doo and he does not live on floor numbered 4.

   (*c*) O Likes Flinstone and he lives on the topmost floor.

   (*d*) Only two persons live between the floors of Q and R ?

   (*e*) All the statements are true

98. Who among the following lives on the floor immediately above the floor of M ?

   (*a*) N

   (*b*) R

   (*c*) S

   (*d*) O

   (*e*) No One

99. Who among the following lives exactly between the floors on which S and N live ?

   (*a*) P

   (*b*) R

   (*c*) M

   (*d*) Q

   (*e*) No one

100. Who among the following does like cartoon character Jetson ?

   (*a*) R

   (*b*) P

   (*c*) N

   (*d*) Q

   (*e*) S

ANSWERS

1. (*a*)	**2.** (*c*)	**3.** (*b*)	**4.** (*b*)	**5.** (*d*)	**6.** (*e*)	**7.** (*c*)	**8.** (*e*)	**9.** (*e*)	**10.** (*a*)
11. (*a*)	**12.** (*a*)	**13.** (*c*)	**14.** (*b*)	**15.** (*d*)	**16.** (*c*)	**17.** (*a*)	**18.** (*a*)	**19.** (*c*)	**20.** (*b*)
21. (*b*)	**22.** (*e*)	**23.** (*d*)	**24.** (*b*)	**25.** (*d*)	**26.** (*b*)	**27.** (*c*)	**28.** (*a*)	**29.** (*b*)	**30.** (*c*)
31. (*a*)	**32.** (*b*)	**33.** (*c*)	**34.** (*d*)	**35.** (*a*)	**36.** (*b*)	**37.** (*b*)	**38.** (*c*)	**39.** (*d*)	**40.** (*a*)
41. (*b*)	**42.** (*a*)	**43.** (*b*)	**44.** (*b*)	**45.** (*a*)	**46.** (*b*)	**47.** (*c*)	**48.** (*d*)	**49.** (*e*)	**50.** (*a*)
51. (*b*)	**52.** (*a*)	**53.** (*b*)	**54.** (*c*)	**55.** (*a*)	**56.** (*b*)	**57.** (*c*)	**58.** (*d*)	**59.** (*a*)	**60.** (*d*)
61. (*c*)	**62.** (*a*)	**63.** (*e*)	**64.** (*b*)	**65.** (*e*)	**66.** (*b*)	**67.** (*d*)	**68.** (*a*)	**69.** (*c*)	**70.** (*e*)
71. (*b*)	**72.** (*d*)	**73.** (*a*)	**74.** (*c*)	**75.** (*b*)	**76.** (*b*)	**77.** (*a*)	**78.** (*b*)	**79.** (*d*)	**80.** (*e*)
81. (*c*)	**82.** (*a*)	**83.** (*e*)	**84.** (*b*)	**85.** (*d*)	**86.** (*c*)	**87.** (*a*)	**88.** (*d*)	**89.** (*b*)	**90.** (*e*)
91. (*b*)	**92.** (*a*)	**93.** (*d*)	**94.** (*c*)	**95.** (*e*)	**96.** (*c*)	**97.** (*e*)	**98.** (*a*)	**99.** (*d*)	**100.** (*b*)

EXPLANATIONS

31. For 2010

Number of boys studying in course A
$$= 840 - 378 = 462$$

Number of boys studying in course B
$$= 1200 - 660 = 540$$

Number of boys studying in course C
$$= 952 - 342 = 610$$

and number of boys studying in course O
$$= 900 - 540 = 360$$

Average number of boys $= \dfrac{462 + 540 + 610 + 360}{4}$

$$= \dfrac{1972}{4} = 493$$

∴ Option (a) is correct.

32. For 2012

Average number of female student

$$= \dfrac{432 + 750 + 441 + 525}{4}$$

$$= 537$$

∴ Option (b) is correct.

33. Total number of boys in all four courses in 2011
$$= (820 - 553) + (1200 - 660)$$
$$+ (900 - 360) + (860 - 602)$$
$$= 267 + 540 + 540 + 258$$
$$= 1605$$

and total number of girls in all four courses in 2011

$$= 553 + 660 + 360 + 602$$
$$= 2175$$

Required percent $= \left[\left(\dfrac{2175 - 1605}{2175}\right) \times 100\right]\%$

$$\approx 26\%$$

∴ Option (c) is correct.

34. Number of girls studying in all four courses in 2010

$$= 378 + 660 + 342 + 540$$
$$= 1920$$

and number of boys studying in all four courses in 2011

$$= 1605 \quad (\because \text{ for question 33})$$

∴ Required difference $= 1920 - 1605 = 315$

∴ Option (d) is correct.

35. Total number of boys in courses 'B' and 'D' in 2010
$$= (1200 - 660) + (900 - 540)$$
$$= 540 + 360 = 900$$

and total number of student in courses A and D in 2012
$$= 800 + 700 = 1500$$

Required ratio $= 900 : 1500$

$$= 9 : 15$$

$$= 3 : 5$$

∴ Option (a) is correct.

36. A dealer allowed discount of 25% on the market price of Rs. 12000

∴ S.P of article $= $ Rs. $\left(\dfrac{12000 \times 75}{100}\right) = 9000$

Now by giving discount of 25%, he increased loss of 10%

∴ C.P of article $= $ Rs. $\left(\dfrac{9000 \times 100}{90}\right)$

$$= \text{Rs. } 10{,}000$$

Now in order to gain Rs. 440 on article

∴ S.P of article $= 10440$

∴ Discount percent $= \left[\left(\dfrac{12000 - 10440}{12000}\right) \times 100\right]\%$

$$= 13\%$$

∴ Option (b) is correct.

37. Average number of projects handled by Company 'A' during all the given years

$$= \dfrac{190 + 450 + 350 + 270 + 430 + 570}{6}$$

$$= \dfrac{2260}{6}$$

$$= 376\dfrac{2}{3}$$

∴ Option (b) is correct.

38. Total number of project handled by both Company in 2002
$$= 250 + 450 = 700$$

and total number of project handled by both Company in 2003
$$= 350 + 550 = 900$$

Required ratio $= 700 : 900 = 7 : 9$

∴ Option (c) is correct.

39. Number of projects handled by Company 'B' in 2006 $= 440$

and project handled by Company 'B' in 2002 $= 250$

Required percent $= \left[\dfrac{440 - 250}{250} \times 100\right]\% = 76\%$

∴ Option (d) is correct.

40. Average number of project handled by Company 'B' for all given years

$$= \frac{350 + 250 + 550 + 320 + 380 + 440}{6}$$

$$= \frac{2290}{6} = 381\frac{2}{3}$$

∴ Option (a) is correct.

41. Total number of project handled by Company 'A' in 2001, 2003 and 2006

$$= 190 + 350 + 570 = 1110$$

and total number of project handled by Company 'B' in 2001, 2003 and 2006

$$= 350 + 550 + 440 = 1340$$

Required difference = $1340 - 1110 = 230$

∴ Option (b) is correct.

42. Let the salary be Rs. 'x'

Now he gave 20% salary to his only son and only daughter in ratio 3 : 2

Amount given to son $= \dfrac{3}{5} \times \dfrac{20x}{100} = \dfrac{3x}{25}$

Amount given to daughter $= \dfrac{2}{5} \times \dfrac{20x}{100} = \dfrac{2}{25}x$

Now amount invested in LIC $= 2 \times \left(\dfrac{2}{25}x\right) = \dfrac{4}{25}x$

Remaining amount $= x - \left(\dfrac{3x}{25} + \dfrac{2x}{25} + \dfrac{4x}{25}\right)$

$$= \frac{25x - 9x}{25} = \frac{16x}{25}$$

Amount given to wife $= \dfrac{1}{4} \times \dfrac{16x}{25} = \dfrac{4x}{25}$

Now according to question $= \dfrac{16x}{25} - \dfrac{4x}{25} = 16800$

∴ $\dfrac{12x}{25} = 16800$

∴ $x = \dfrac{16800 \times 25}{12} = 35000$

Hence amount invested in LIC

$$= \frac{4}{25}x = \text{Rs.}\left(\frac{4}{25} \times 35000\right)$$

$$= \text{Rs. } 5600$$

∴ Option (a) is correct.

43. Amount of milk in mixture

$$= \left(\frac{85}{100} \times 40\right) \text{litre} = 34 \text{ litre}$$

and amount of water in mixture

$$= (40 - 34) \text{ litre} = 6 \text{ litre}$$

44. Let the speed of boat be x km/hr.

and speed of stream be y km/hr.

Now boat covers a distance of 2.75 km upstream in 11 minutes

∴ $x - y = \dfrac{2.75 \times 60}{11}$

∴ $x - y = 15$ km/hr. ...(i)

and $\dfrac{y}{x} = \dfrac{1}{7}$ ...(ii)

Solving equations (i) and (ii)

$$\frac{x}{x} - \frac{y}{x} = \frac{15}{x}$$

∴ $1 - \dfrac{1}{7} = \dfrac{15}{x}$

∴ $\dfrac{6}{7} = \dfrac{15}{x}$

∴ $x = \dfrac{15 \times 7}{6}$

∴ $x = 17.5$

and $y = \dfrac{17.5}{7} = 2.5$

Now $x + y = 17.5 + 2.5 = 20$ km/hrs.

Hence in down stream boat covers 20 km in 1 hr.

∴ Distance cover in 52 min = 17.2 km

∴ Option (b) is correct.

45. The given series follows the following pattern

$$125 + 3 = 128$$
$$128 - (3)^2 = 128 - 9 = 119$$
$$119 + (3)^3 = 119 + 27 = 146$$

and $146 - (3)^4 = 146 - 81 = 65$

∴ $65 + (3)^5 = 65 + 243 = 308$

∴ Option (a) is correct.

46. The given series follow the following pattern

$$8 + 9 = 17$$
$$17 + 13(= 9 + 4) = 30$$
$$30 + 17(= 13 + 4) = 47$$
$$47 + 210(= 17 + 4) = 68$$

∴ $68 + 25(= 21 + 4) = 93$

∴ Option (b) is correct.

47. The given series follow the following pattern

$$24 \times \frac{1}{2} = 12$$
$$12 \times 1 = 12$$
$$12 \times \frac{3}{2} = 18$$
$$18 \times 2 = 36$$

and $36 \times \dfrac{5}{2} = 90$

∴ Option (c) is correct.

48. The given series follow the following pattern

$$5 + 11(= 11 \times 1) = 16$$
$$16 + 33(= 11 \times 3) = 49$$
$$49 + 55(= 11 \times 5) = 104$$
$$104 + 77(= 11 \times 7) = 181$$
$$181 + 99(= 11 \times 9) = 280$$

$\therefore$ Option (d) is correct.

49.
$$13 + 6 = 19$$
$$19 + 11(= 6 + 5) = 30$$
$$30 + 18(= 11 + 7) = 48$$
$$48 + 27(= 18 + 9) = 75$$
$$75 + 38(= 27 + 11) = 113$$

51. According to question

$$\text{Rita} + \text{Abby} = 48 \qquad ...(i)$$
$$\text{Abby} - \text{Shweta} = 4 \qquad ...(ii)$$
$$\frac{\text{Rita}}{\text{Shweta}} = \frac{4}{7} \qquad ...(iii)$$

Solving equations (i) and (ii)

$$\text{Rita} + \text{Shweta} = 44$$
$$4\left(\frac{\text{Shweta}}{7}\right) + \text{Shweta} = 44$$

$\therefore \qquad 11 \text{ Shweta} = 44 \times 7$

$\therefore \qquad \text{Shweta} = 28$ years

$\therefore \qquad \text{Abby} = 4 + \text{Shweta}$
$$= 32 \text{ years}$$

Hence age of Abby's two years ago
$$= 32 - 2 = 30 \text{ years}$$

$\therefore$ Option (b) is correct.

52. $\dfrac{52}{100} \times 749 + \left(\dfrac{45}{100} \times 420\right) - x = 225$

$\therefore \quad \dfrac{52 \times 749}{100} + \dfrac{45 \times 420}{100} - 225 = x$

$\therefore \quad 389.48 + 189 - 225 = x$

$\therefore \quad x = 353.48$

$\therefore \quad x \approx 354$

$\therefore$ Option (a) is correct.

53. $\qquad 350 \times 20 + x^2 \times 180 = 11500$

$\therefore \qquad 700 + x^2 \times 180 = 11500$

$\therefore \qquad x^2 \times 180 = 11500 - 7000$

$\therefore \qquad x^2 = 25$

$\therefore \qquad x = 5$

$\therefore$ Option (b) is correct.

54. $\left(180 \div \sqrt{x} \times 30\right) \div 15 = 144$

$\therefore \qquad \dfrac{1800}{\sqrt{x}} \times \dfrac{30}{15} = 144$

$\therefore \qquad \dfrac{3600}{\sqrt{x}} = 144$

$\therefore \qquad \sqrt{x} = \dfrac{3600}{144}$

$\therefore \qquad \sqrt{x} = 25$

$\therefore \qquad x = 625$

$\therefore$ Option (c) is correct.

55. $\dfrac{(52)^2 - (34)^2}{18} \times \sqrt{x} = 1720$

$$1548 \times \sqrt{x} = 1720 \times 18$$

$\therefore \qquad \sqrt{x} = 20$

$\therefore \qquad x = 400$

$\therefore$ Option (a) is correct.

59.

$$A \qquad\qquad\qquad B$$

A: Principal = x, time = 6 years, Rate = 2%

B: Principal = x, time = 8 years, Rate = 8%

$$\text{Difference of S.I} = \left(\frac{x \times 6 \times 12}{100} - \frac{x \times 8 \times 8}{100}\right)$$

$$1280 = \frac{72x}{100} - \frac{64x}{100}$$

$\therefore \qquad \dfrac{128000}{8} = x$

$\therefore \qquad x = 16000$

$\therefore$ Option (a) is correct.

60. According to question,

$$\text{Area of rectangle} = \text{Area of square}$$

Now diagonal of square $= 12\sqrt{6} = \sqrt{2}a$

$\therefore \quad$ Side of square (a) $= \dfrac{12\sqrt{6}}{\sqrt{2}} = 12\sqrt{3}$

$\therefore \quad$ Area of rectangle $= \left(12\sqrt{3}\right)^2 = 144 \times 3$

$\therefore \qquad l \times b = 432 \text{ m}^2 \qquad ...(i)$

and $\qquad\qquad l - b = 6 \qquad\qquad ...(ii)$

Solving equations (i) and (ii)

$\therefore \qquad \dfrac{432}{b} - b = 6$

$\therefore \qquad 432 - b^2 = 6b$

$\therefore \qquad b^2 + 6b = 432$

$\therefore \qquad b^2 + 6b - 432 = 0$

$\therefore \quad b^2 + 24b - 18b - 432 = 0$

$\therefore \quad b(b + 24) - 18(b + 24) = 0$

$\therefore \qquad \boxed{b = 18\text{m}}$

$\Rightarrow \qquad l = 6 + b = 6 + 18 = 24\text{m}$

Hence perimeter of rectangle

$$= 2(l + b)$$
$$= 2(24 + 18)$$
$$= 2(42) = 84 \text{ m}$$

∴ Option (d) is correct.

61. I. $\qquad 3x^2 + 14x + 15 = 0$

∴ $\quad 3x^2 + 9x + 5x + 15 = 0$

∴ $\quad 3x(x + 3) + 5(x + 3) = 0$

∴ $\qquad x = -\dfrac{5}{3}$ and $x = -3$

$\qquad\qquad x = -1.66$ and $x = -3$

II. $\qquad 6y^2 + 17y + 12 = 0$

∴ $\quad 6y^2 + 9y + 8y + 12 = 0$

∴ $3y(2y + 3) + 4(2y + 3) = 0$

∴ $\qquad y = -\dfrac{4}{3}$ and $y = -\dfrac{3}{2}$

∴ $\qquad\qquad y = -1.33, y = -1.5$

$\qquad\qquad y > x$

∴ Option (c) is correct.

62. I. $\qquad 3x^2 - 17x + 24 = 0$

∴ $\quad 3x^2 - 8x - 9x + 24 = 0$

∴ $\quad x(3x - 8) - 3(3x - 8) = 0$

∴ $\qquad x = 3$ and $x = \dfrac{8}{3} = 2.66$

II. $\qquad 4y^2 - 15y + 14 = 0$

∴ $\quad 4y^2 - 8y - 7y + 14 = 0$

∴ $\quad 4y(y - 2) - 7(y - 2) = 0$

∴ $\qquad y = \dfrac{7}{4}$ and $y = 2$

∴ $\qquad y = 1.75$ and $y = 2$

Hence $x > y$

∴ Option (a) is correct.

63. I. $\qquad 2x^2 + 11x + 14 = 0$

∴ $\quad 2x^2 + 7x + 4x + 14 = 0$

∴ $\quad x(2x + 7) + 2(2x + 7) = 0$

∴ $\qquad x = -2$ and $x = -\dfrac{7}{2} = -3.5$

II. $\qquad 2y^2 + 17y + 33 = 0$

∴ $\quad 2y^2 + 11y + 6y + 33 = 0$

∴ $y(2y + 11) + 3(2y + 11) = 0$

∴ $\qquad y = -3$ and $y = -5.5$

Hence option (e) is correct

64. I. $\qquad 3x^2 + 13x + 12 = 0$

∴ $\quad 3x^2 + 9x + 4x + 12 = 0$

∴ $\quad 3x(x + 3) + 4(x + 3) = 0$

∴ $\qquad x = -\dfrac{4}{3}$ and $x = -3$

$\qquad\qquad x = -1.33$ and $x = -3$

II. $\qquad 2y^2 + 15y + 27 = 0$

∴ $\quad 2y^2 + 9y + 6y + 27 = 0$

∴ $\quad y(2y + 9) + 3(2y + 9) = 0$

∴ $\qquad y = -3$ and $y = -\dfrac{9}{2} = -4.5$

Hence $\qquad x \geq y$

∴ Option (b) is correct.

65. I. $\qquad x^2 - 22x + 121 = 0$

∴ $\qquad (x - 11)^2 = 0$

∴ $\qquad x = 11$

II. $\qquad y^2 = 121$

∴ $\qquad y \pm 11$

∴ $\qquad x \geq y$

Hence option (b) is correct.

(Q. 66-70) : From the given information

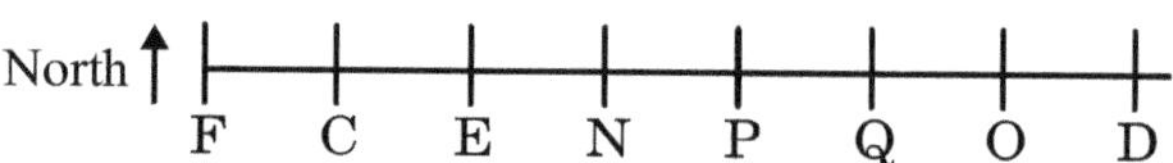

66. D and F are at the extreme end of the line

∴ Option (b) is correct.

67. Among the given statement only 4th statement is true i.e. 'N' is sitting to the immediate left of 'P'.

∴ Option (d) is correct.

68. 'O' is sitting third to the right of 'N'

∴ Option (a) is correct.

69. 'C' is fourth to the left of 'Q'

∴ Option (c) is correct.

70. All the pair given in option has two element in between except in option (e) i.e. 'NQ' pair has only single element in between i.e. 'P'

∴ Option (e) does not belong to the group.

(Q. 71-73) : From the given information

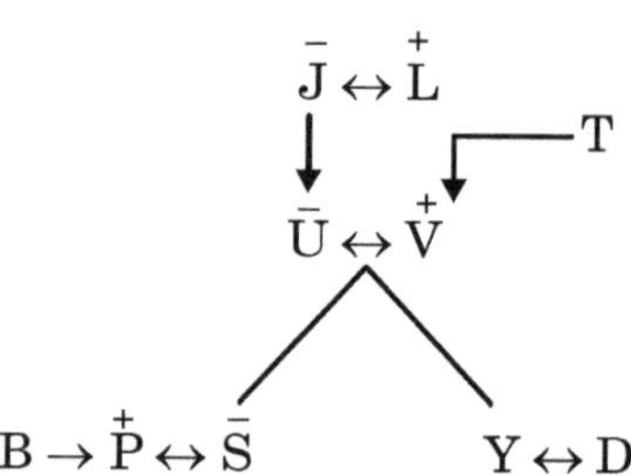

71. 'S' is Sister-in-law of 'B'

∴ Option (b) is correct.

72. 'L' is the father of 'U'

∴ Option (d) is correct.

73. 'V' is father-in-law of 'P'

∴ Option (a) is correct.

74. From the given information

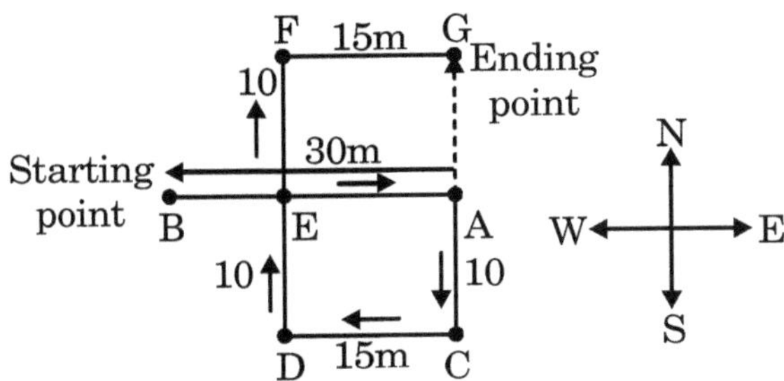

Hence point 'G' is 10 m away in North direction from point 'A'.

∴ Option (c) is correct.

75.

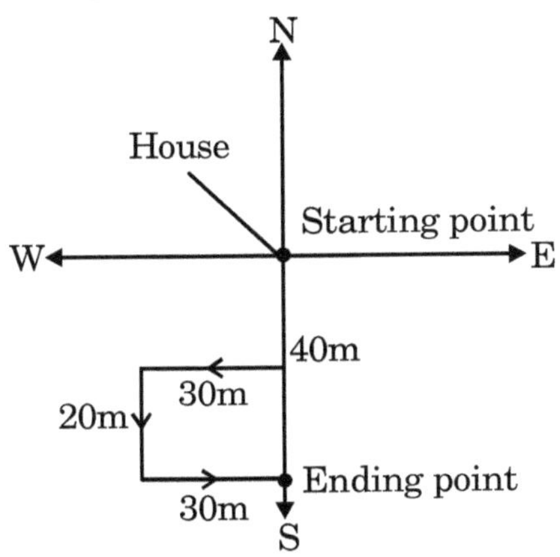

From figure it is clear that market is 60m from starting point and in North direction from market.

∴ Option (b) is correct

(Q. 76-77):

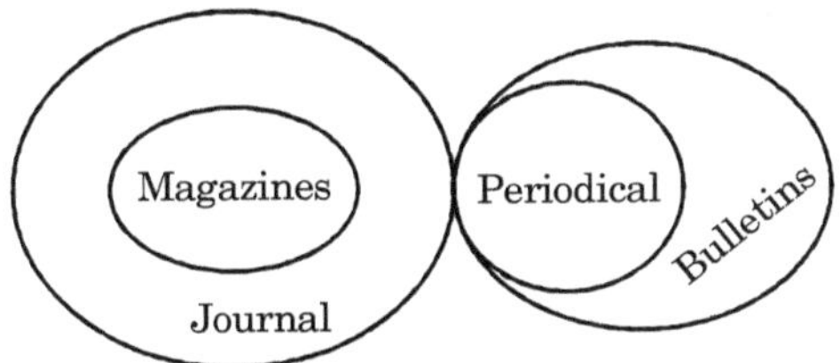

76. All periodicals being magazines is a possibility is the conclusion which follows

∴ Hence only conclusion II follows

∴ Option (b) is correct.

77. Only conclusion I follows

78.

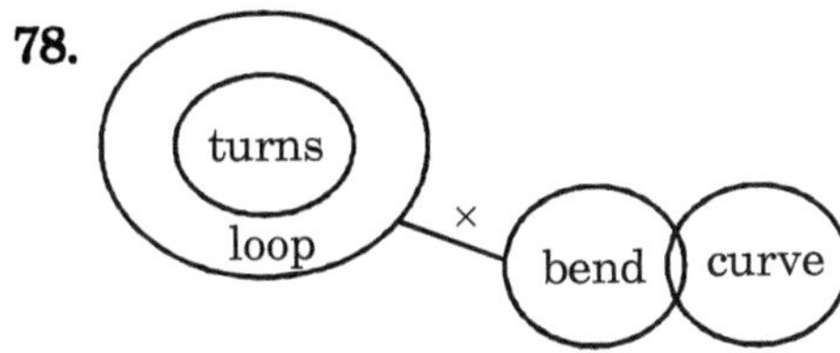

Only conclusion II follows

79.

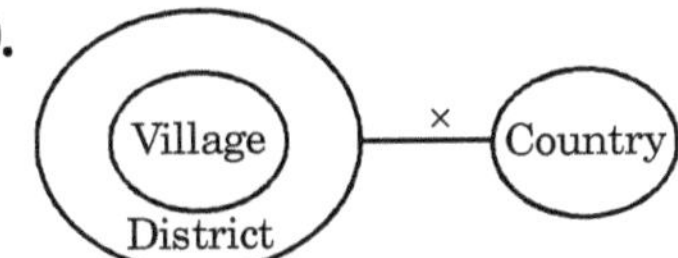

Neither conclusion I nor conclusion II follows

80.

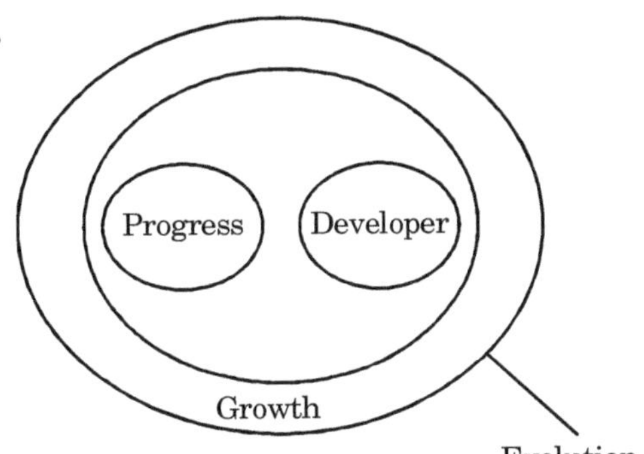

Both conclusion I and II follows

(Q. 86-90):

Statement-1 :	"good time to buy"
Code :	"sy bo jn kw"
Statement-2 :	"invest money and time"
Code :	"sy ta ge mr"
Statement-3 :	"Only work and money"
Code :	"ta fp mr ux"
Statement-4 :	"buy good stuff only"
Code :	"kw bo rd fp"

From Statement-I and II

$$\boxed{\text{time} \rightarrow \text{sy}}$$

From Statement-I and IV

$$\boxed{\text{good / by} \rightarrow \text{bo / kw}}$$

From Statement-II and III

$$\boxed{\text{and / money} \rightarrow \text{ta / mr}}$$

$$\boxed{\text{invest} \rightarrow \text{ge}}$$

From Statement-III and IV

$$\boxed{\text{only} \rightarrow \text{fp}}$$

$$\boxed{\text{stuff} \rightarrow \text{rd}}$$

86. From the above conclusion

Code for 'to' is 'ry'

∴ Option (c) is correct.

87. From the above conclusion

Code for "buy good" is 'bo kw'

∴ Option (a) is correct

88. From the above conclusion

Code for "Only time and money" is "mr ta sy fp"

∴ Option (d) is correct.

89. From the above conclusion

The code for "stuff" is 'rd'

∴ Option (b) is correct.

90. From the above conclusion,

Code for " invest time to work" is "ux ge nj sy"

∴ Option (e) is correct

(Q. 91-95) : From the given information

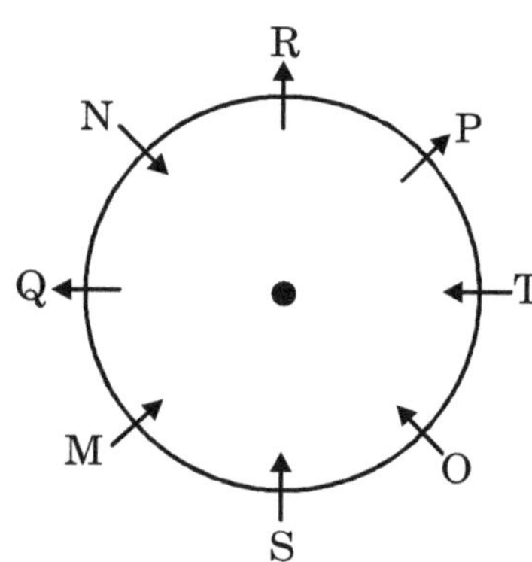

91. 'T' is sitting exactly between 'O' and 'P'.

∴   Option (*b*) is correct.

92. In the given arrangement three person faces outside

∴   Option (*a*) is correct.

93. O, S, M and N faces inside while 'Q' faces outside. Hence 'Q' does not belong to that group.

∴   Option (*d*) is correct

94. 'M' sits exactly between S and Q when counted from the left of S.

∴   Option (*c*) is correct.

95. 'M' is third to the left of 'R'

∴   Option (*e*) is correct.

(Q. 96-100) :

Floor	Person	Cartoon Character
7	O	Flin stone
6	S	Tweety
5	Q	Chipmnuk
4	N	Popeye
3	M	Scoobydo
2	R	Simpson
1	P	Jetson

96. Fout person lives between floor 'S' and 'P'

∴   Option (*c*) is correct.

97. All the given statement are true

∴   Option (*e*) is correct

98. 'N' lives on the floor immediately above the floor 'M'

∴   Option (*a*) is correct.

99. 'Q' live exactly between the floors on which S and N live.

∴   Option (*d*) is correct.

100. 'P' likes cartoon character jetson

∴   Option (*b*) is correct.

REASONING ABILITY

Directions (Q. 1-4) : *Study the following information carefully and answer the given questions :*

A word and number arrangement machine when given an input line of words and numbers rearranges them following a particular rule in each step. The following is an illustration of input and rearrangement. (All the numbers are two digits numbers)

Input:	tall 4813 rise alt 99 76 32 wise jar high 28 56 bam
Step I:	13 tall 48 rise 99 76 32 wise jar high 28 56 bam alt
Step II:	28 13 tall 48 rise 99 76 32 wise jar high 56 alt bam
Step III:	32 28 13 tall 48 rise 99 76 wise jar 56 alt bam high
Step IV:	48 32 28 13 tall rise 99 76 wise 56 alt bam high jar
Step V:	56 48 32 28 13 tall 99 76 wise alt bam high jar rise
Step VI:	76 56 48 32 28 13 99 wise alt bam high jar rise tall
Step VII:	99 76 56 48 32 28 13 alt bam high jar rise tall wise

and Step VII is the last step of the above input, as the desired arrangement is obtained.

As per the rules followed in the above steps, find out in each of the following questions the appropriate step for the given input.

Input: 84 why sit 14 32 not best ink feet 51 27 vain 68 92

(All the numbers are two digits numbers

1. Which step number is the following output ?

32 27 14 84 why sit not 51 vain 92 68 feet best ink

(*a*) Step V

(*b*) Step VI

(*c*) Step IV

(*d*) Step III

(*e*) There is no such step

2. Which word/number would be at 5th position from the right in Step V?

(*a*) 14   (*b*) 92

(*c*) feet   (*d*) best

(*e*) why

3. How many elements (words or numbers) are there between 'feet' and '32' as they appear in the last step of the output?

(*a*) One   (*b*) Three

(*c*) Four   (*d*) Five

(*e*) Seven

4. Which of the following represents the position of 'why' in the fourth step?

(*a*) Eighth from the left

(*b*) Fifth from the right

(*c*) Sixth from the left

(*d*) Fifth from the left

(*e*) Seventh from the left

Directions (Q. 5-11) : *Study the following information carefully and answer the given questions :*

A, B, C, D, E, F, G and H are sitting around a circle facing the centre but not necessarily in the same order.

- B sits second to left of H's husband. No female is an immediate neighbour of B.

- D's daughter sits second to right of F. F is the sister of G. F is not an immediate neighbour of H's husband

- Only one person sits between A and F, A is the father of G, H's brother D sits to the immediate left of H's mother. Only one person sits between H's mother and E.

- Only one person sits between H and G, G is the mother of C, G is not an immediate neighbour of E.

5. What is position of A with respect to his mother-in-law?

(*a*) Immediate left

(*b*) Third to the right

(*c*) Third to the left

(*d*) Second to the right

(*e*) Fourth to the left

6. Who amongst the following is D's daughter?

(*a*) B   (*b*) C

(*c*) E   (*d*) G

(*e*) H

7. What is the position of A with respect to his grandchild?

(*a*) Immediate right   (*b*) Third to the right

(*c*) Third to the left   (*d*) Second to the left

(*e*) Fourth to the left

8. How many people sit between G and her uncle?

(*a*) One   (*b*) Two

(*c*) Three   (*d*) Four

(*e*) More than four

9. Four of the following five are alike in a certain way based on the given information and so form a group. Which is the one that does not belong to that group ?

(*a*) F   (*b*) C

(*c*) E   (*d*) H

(*e*) G

10. Which of the following is true with respect to the given seating arrangement?

(*a*) C is the cousin of E

(*b*) H and H's husband are immediate neighbours of each other

(*c*) No female is an immediate neighbour of C

(*d*) H sits third to left of her daughter

(*e*) B is the mother of H

11. Who sits to the immediate left of C?

(*a*) F's grandmother   (*b*) G's son

(*c*) D's mother-in-law   (*d*) A

(*e*) G

Directions (Q. 12-18) : *In each group of questions below are two/three statements followed by two conclusions numbered I and II. You have to take the given statements to be true even if they seem to be at variance from commonly known facts and then decide which of the given conclusions logically follows from the two/three statements disregarding commonly known facts.*

Give answer

(*a*) if only conclusion I follows;

(*b*) if only conclusion II follows;

(*c*) if either conclusion I or conclusion II follows;

(*d*) if neither conclusion I nor conclusion II follows;

(*e*) if both conclusion I and conclusion II follow.

12. Statements: Some exams are tests.

No exam is a question.

Conclusions:

I. No question is a test

II. Some tests are definitely not exams.

Directions (Q. 13-14) : Statements: *All forces are energies. All energies are powers. No power is heat.*

13. Conclusions:

I. Some forces are definitely not powers.

II. NO heat is force,

14. Conclusions:

I. No energy is heat.

II. Some forces being heat is a possibility.

Directions (Q. 15-16) : Statements: *No note is a coin. Some coins are metals. All plastics are notes.*

15. Conclusions:

I. No coin is plastic.

II. All plastics being metals is a possibility.

16. Conclusions:

I. No metal is plastic.

II. All notes are plastics

17. Statements: Some symbols are figures.

All symbols are graphics.

No graphic is a picture.

Conclusions:

I. Some graphics are figures.

II. No symbol is a picture.

18. Statements: All vacancies are jobs.

Some jobs are occupations.

Conclusions:

I. All vacancies are occupations.

II. All occupations being vacancies is a possibility.

Directions (Q. 19-21) : *Study the following information carefully to answer the given questions:*
Each of the six friends, A, B, C, D, E and F scored different marks in an examination. C scored more than only. A and E. D scored less than only B. E did not score the least. The one who scored the third highest marks scored 81 marks. E scored 62 marks.

19. Which of the following could possibly be C's score?

(*a*) 70   (*b*) 94

(*c*) 86   (*d*) 61

(*e*) 81

20. Which of the following is true with respect to the given information?

(*a*) D's score was definitely less than 60

(*b*) F scored the maximum marks

(*c*) Only two people scored more than C

(*d*) There is a possibility that B scored 79 marks.

(*e*) None is true

21. The person who scored the maximum, scored 13 marks more than F's marks. Which of the following can be D's score?

(*a*) 94   (*b*) 60

(*c*) 89   (*d*) 78

(*e*) 81

Directions (Q. 22-29) : *Study the following information carefully to answer the given questions:*

Eight persons from different banks viz. UCO bank, Syndicate bank, Canara bank, PNB, Dena Bank, Oriental Bank of Commerce, Indian bank and Bank of Maharashtra are sitting in two parallel rows containing four people each, in such a way that there is an equal distance between adjacent persons. In row-1 A, B, C and D are seated and all of them are facing south. In row-2 P, Q, R and S are seated and all of them are facing north. Therefore, in the given seating arrangement each member seated in a row faces another member of the other row. (All the information given above does not necessarily represent the order of seating as in the final arrangement)

- C sits second to right of the person from Bank of Maharashtra. R is an immediate neighbour of the person who faces the person from Bank of Maharashtra.

- Only one person sits between R and the person for PNB, Immediate neighbour of the person from PNB faces the person from Canara Bank.

- The person from UCO bank faces the person from Oriental Bank of Commerce. R is not from Oriental Bank of Commerce P is not from PNB. P does not face the person from Bank of Maharashtra.

- Q faces the person from Dena bank. The one who faces S sits to the immediate left of A.

- B does not sit at any of the extreme ends of the line. The person from Bank of Maharashtra does not face the person from Syndicate bank.

22. Which of the following is true regarding A?

(*a*) The person from UCO bank faces A

(*b*) The person from Bank of Maharashtra is an immediate neighbour of A

(*c*) A faces the person who sits second to right of R

(*d*) A is from Oriental Bank of Commerce

(*e*) A sits at one of the extreme ends of the line

23. Who is seated between R and the person from PNB?

(*a*) The person from Oriental Bank of Commerce

(*b*) P

(*c*) Q

(*d*) The person from Syndicate bank

(*e*) S

24. Who amongst the following sit at extreme ends of the rows?

(*a*) D and the person from PNB

(*b*) The person from Indian bank and UCO bank

(*c*) The person from Dena bank and P

(*d*) The persons from Syndicate bank and D.

(*e*) C, Q

25. Who amongst the following faces the person from Bank of Maharashtra?

(*a*) The person from Indian bank

(*b*) P

(*c*) R

(*d*) The person from Syndicate bank

(*e*) The person from Canara bank

26. P is related to Dena bank in the same way as B is related to PNB based on the given arrangement. To who amongst the following is D related to, following the same pattern?

(*a*) Syndicate bank

(*b*) Canara bank

(*c*) Bank of Maharashtra

(*d*) Indian bank

(*e*) Oriental Bank of Commerce

27. Four of the following five are alike in a certain way based on the given seating arrangement and thus form a group. Which is the one that does not belong to that group?

(*a*) Canara bank   (*b*) R

(*c*) Syndicate bank   (*d*) Q

(*e*) Oriental Bank of Commerce

28. Who amongst the following is from Syndicate bank?

(*a*) C   (*b*) R

(*c*) P   (*d*) D

(*e*) A

29. C is from which of the following banks?

(*a*) Dena bank

(*b*) Oriental Bank of Commerce

(*c*) UCO bank

(*d*) Syndicate bank

(*e*) Canara bank

30. Directions : *Read the following information carefully and answer the questions which follow :*

Small brands are now looking beyond local grocery stores and are typing up with Supermarkets such as Big Bazaar to pull their business out of troubled waters.

Which of the following can be inferred from the given information ?

(An inference is something that is not directly stated but can be inferred from the given information)

(*a*) Merchandise of smaller brands would not be available at local grocery stores in the near future.

(*b*) Smaller brands cannot compete with bigger ones in a supermarket set-up.

(*c*) There is a perception among small brands that sale in a supermarket is higher than that of small grocery stores.

(*d*) Supermarkets generate more revenue by selling products of bigger brands as compared to the smaller ones.

(*e*) Smaller brands have always had more tie-ups with supermarkets as compared to small grocery stores.

Directions (Q. 31-34) : *These questions are based on the information given above and the sentences labeled (A), (B), (C), (D), (E) and (F) as given below.*

(A) A smaller brand manufacturing a certain product of quality comparable with that of a bigger brand makes much more profit from the local grocery stores than from the supermarkets.

(B) As the supermarkets have been set up only in bigger cities at present, this step would fail to deliver results in the smaller cities.

(C) Supermarkets help the smaller brands to break into newer markets without investing substantially in distribution.

(D) Supermarkets charge the smaller brands 10% higher than the amount charged to the bigger brands.

(E) Being outnumbered by the bigger brands, visibility of the smaller brands at local grocery stores is much tower as compared to the supermarkets.

(F) Smaller brands are currently making substantial losses in their businesses.

31. Which of the statements numbered (A), (B), (C), (D), (E) and (F) can be assumed from the facts/information given in the statement ?

(An assumption is something supposed or taken for granted)

(*a*) Only (A)   (*b*) Only (B)

(*c*) Both (B) and (C)   (*d*) Both (D) and (E)

(*e*) Only (F)

32. Which of the statements numbered (A), (B), (C), (E) and (F) represents a disadvantage of the small grocery stores over the supermarkets from the perspective of a smaller brand ?

(*a*) Only (A)   (*b*) Only (C)

(*c*) Only (E)   (*d*) Only (F)

(*e*) Both (B) and (C)

33. Which of the statements (A), (B), (C), (D) and (E) mentioned above represents a reason for the shift from local grocery stores to supermarkets by the smaller brands?

(*a*) Only (A)   (*b*) Only (B)

(*c*) Only (D)   (*d*) Both (A) and (D)

(*e*) Both (C) and (E)

34. Which of the statements numbered (A), (B), (C), (E) and (F) mentioned above would prove that the step taken by the smaller brands (of moving to supermarkets) may not necessarily be correct?

(*a*) Only (A)   (*b*) Only (C)

(*c*) Only (E)   (*d*) Only (F)

(*e*) Both (B) and (E)

35. Read the following information carefully and answer the question which follows:

Farmers found using chemical fertilizers in the organic-farming area of their farms would be heavily fined.

Which of the following statements is an assumption implicit in the given statement?

(An assumption is something supposed or taken for granted.)

(*a*) Chemical fertilizers harm the crop.

(*b*) A farm's area for organic and chemical farming is different.

(*c*) Farmers who do not use chemical fertilizers in the chemical farming area would be penalized as well.

(*d*) All farmers undertake both these kinds of farming (chemical as well as organic) in their farms.

(*e*) Organic fertilizers are banned in the area for chemical farming.

Directions (Q. 36 – 40) : *Study the following information carefully and answer the questions given below:*

P, Q, R, S, T, V, W and Z are eight friends studying in three different engineering colleges- A, B and C in three disciplines- Mechanical, Electrical and Electronics with not less than two and not more than three in any college. Not more than three of them study in any of the three disciplines. W studies Electrical in college B with only T who studies Mechanical. P and Z do not study in college C and study in same discipline but not Electrical. R studies Mechanical in college C with V who studies Electrical. S studies Mechanical and does not study in the same college where R studies. Q does not study Electronics.

36. Which of the following combinations of college-students-specialization is correct ?

(*a*) C-R-Electronics   (*b*) A-Z-Electrical

(*c*) B-W- Electronics   (*d*) B-W-Electrical

(*e*) B-Z- Electronics

37. In which of the following colleges two students study in electrical discipline ?

(*a*) A only

(*b*) B only

(*c*) C only

(*d*) Can not be determined

(*e*) None of these

38. In which discipline does Q study ?

(*a*) Electrical

(*b*) Mechanical

(*c*) Electrical or Mechanical

(*d*) Data inadequate

(*e*) None of these

39. In which of the college at least one students in mechanical discipline ?

(*a*) A only   (*b*) B only

(*c*) C only   (*d*) Both A and B

(*e*) All A , B and C

40. S studies in which college ?

(*a*) A   (*b*) B

(*c*) A or B   (*d*) Data inadequate

(*e*) None of these

Directions (Q. 41 – 45) : *In each question below is given a group of letters followed by four combinations of digits/symbols numbered (a), (b), (c) and (d). You have to find out which of the combinations correctly represents the group of letters based on the following coding system and mark the number of that combination as the answer.*

Letter   : P M A K T I J E R N D F U W B

Digit/Symbol : 7 # 8 % 1 9 2 @ 3 © $ 4 * 5 6

Conditions :

(*i*) If both the first and the last letters of the group are consonants, both are to be coded as the code for the last letter.

(*ii*) If the first letter is a consonant and the last letter is a vowel, the codes are to be interchanged.

41. BDATFE

(*a*) 6$8146   (*b*) 6$814@

(*c*) @$814@   (*d*) @$8146

(*e*) None of these

42. AWBRND

(*a*) $563©8   (*b*) 8563©$

(*c*) 8365©$ (*d*) 8536©$

(*e*) None of these

43. EMNTKU

(*a*) *#©1%@

(*b*) @#©14*

(*c*) @#©1%*

(*d*) #@©1%*

(*e*) None of these

44. MDEAJI

(*a*) 1$@82#

(*b*) #$@821

(*c*) 1$@821

(*d*) None of these

(*e*) All of these

45. RKUMFP

(*a*) 7%*#43

(*b*) 3*%#47

(*c*) 3%*#43

(*d*) 3%*#47

(*e*) None of these

46. Statements :

R # J, J $ D, D @ K, K % T

Conclusions :

I. T # D

II. T @ D

III.R # K

IV. J $ T

(*a*) Only either I or II is true

(*b*) Only III is true

(*c*) Only III and IV are true

(*d*) Only either I or II and III are true.

(*e*) None of these

47. Statements :

T % R, R $ M, M @ D, D © H

Conclusions :

I. D % R

II. H # R

III.T © M

IV. T % D

(*a*) Only I is true

(*b*) Only I and IV are true

(*c*) Only I and II are true

(*d*) Only II and IV are true

(*e*) None of these

48. Statements :

M @ B, B # N, N $ R, R © K

Conclusions :

I. K # B

II. R © B

III.M $ R

IV. N © M

(*a*) Only I and III are true

(*b*) Only I and II are true

(*c*) Only II and IV are true

(*d*) Only II, III and IV are true

(*e*) None of these

49. Statements :

F # H, H @ M, M © E, E $ J

Conclusions :

I. J © M

II. E # H

III.M © F

IV. F # E

(*a*) Only I and II are true

(*b*) Only II and III are true

(*c*) Only I, II and III are true

(*d*) Only II, III and IV are true

(*e*) None of these

50. Statements :

D % A, A @ B, B © K, K % M

Conclusions :

I. B $ D

II. K # A

III.M # B

IV. A © M

(*a*) Only I, II and IV are true

(*b*) Only I, II and III are true

(*c*) Only II, III and IV are true

(*d*) Only I, III and IV are true

(*e*) All I, II, III and IV are true

ENGLISH ABILITY

Directions (Q. 51-65) : *Read the follwoing passage carefully and answer the questions given below it. Certain words/phrases have been printed in **bold** to help you locate them while answering some of the questions.*

When times are hard, doomsayers are aplenty. The problem is that if you listen to them too carefully, you tend to overlook the most obvious signs of change.

2011 was a bad year. Can 2012 be any worse? Doomsday forecasts are these easiest to make these days. So let's try a contrarian's forecast instead.

Let's start with the global economy. We have seen a steady flow of good news from the US. The employment situation seems to be improving rapidly and consumer sentiment, reflected in retail expenditures on discretionary items like electronics and clothes, has picked up. If these frends sustain, the US might post better growth numbers for 2012 than the 1.5-1.8 per cent being forecast currently.

Japan is likely to pull out of recession in 2012 as post-earthquake reconstruction efforts gather momentum and the fiscal stimulus announced in 2011 begins to pay off. He consensus estimate for growth in Japan is a respectable 2 per cent for 2012.

Europe is certainly in a spot of trouble. It is perhaps already in recession and for 2012 it is likely to post mildly negative growth. The risk of implosion has dwindled over the last few months peripheral economies like Greece, italy and Spain have new governments in place and have made progress towarss genuine economic reform.

Even with some of these positive factors in place, we have to accept the fact that global growth in 2012 will be **tepid.** But there is a flipside to this. Softer growth means lower demand for commodities and this is likely to drive a corection in commodity prices. Lower commodity inflation will enable emerging market central banks to reverse their monetary stance. China, for instance, has already reversed its stance and has pared its reserve ratio twice. The RBI also seems poised for a reversal in its rate cycle as headline inflation seems well on its way to its target of 7 per cent for March 2012.

That said, oil might be an exception to the general trend in commodities. rising geopolitical tensions, particularly the continuing face-off between Iran and the US, might lead to a spurt in prices. It might make sense for our oil companies to hedge this risk instead of buying oil in the spot market.

As inflation fears abate and emerging market central banks begin to cut rates, two things could happen. Lower commodity iflation would mean lower interest rates and better credit availability. This could set a floor to growth and slowly reverse the business cycle within these economies. Second, as the fear of untamed, runaway inflation in these economies abates, the global investors's comfort levels with their markets will increase.

Which of the emergin markets will outperform and who will get left behind? In an environment in which global growth is likely to be weak, economies like India that have a powerful domestic consumption dynamic should lead; those dependent on exports should, prima facie, fall behind Specifically for India, a fall in the exchange rate could not have come at a better time. It will help Indian exporters gain market share even if global trade remains depressed. More importantly, it could lead to massive import susbtitution that favours domestic producers.

Let's now focus on India and start with a caveat. It is important not to confuse a short-run cyclical dip with a permanent de-rating of its long-term structural potential. The arithmetic is simple. Our growth rate can be in the range of 7-10 per cent depending on policy action. Ten per cent if we get everything right, 7 per cent if we get it all wrong. Which policies and reforms are critical to taking us to our 10 per cent potential? In judging this, let's again be careful. Let's not go by the laundry list of reforms that FIIs like to wave: increase in foreign equity limits in foreign shareholding, greater voting rights for institutional shareholders in banks, FDI in retail, etc. These can have an impact only at the margin. We need not bend over backwards to appease the FIIs through these reforms-they will invest in our markets when momentum picks up and will be the first to exit when the momentum flags, reforms or not.

The reforms that we need are the ones that can actually raise out sustainable long-term growth rate. These have to come in areas like better targeting of subsidies, making projects in infrastructure viable so that they draw capital, raising the productivity of agriculture, improving healthcare and education, bringing the parallel economy under the tax net, implementing fundamental reforms in taxation like GST and the direct tax code and finally easing the myriad rules and regulations that make doing business in India such a nightmare. A number of these things do not require new legislation and can be done through executive order.

51. Which of the following is NOT TRUE according to the passage?

(*a*) China's economic growth may decline in the year 2012 as compared to the year 2011

(*b*) The European economy is not doing very well

(*c*) Greece is on the verge of bringing about economic reforms

(*d*) In the year 2012, Japan may post a positive growth and thus pull out of recession

(*e*) All are true

52. Which of the following will possibly be a result of softer growth estimated for the year 2012?

(A) Prices of oil will not icrease

(B) Credit availability would be lesser

(C) Commodity inflation would be lesser

(*a*) Only (B)   (*b*) Only (A) and (B)

(*c*) Only (A) and (C)   (*d*) Only (C)

(*e*) All (A), (B) and (C)

53. Which of the following can be said about the present status of the US economy?

(*a*) There is not much improvement in the economic scenario of the country from the year 2011

(*b*) The growth in the economy of the country, in the year 2012, would definitely be lesser that 1.8 percent

(*c*) The expenditure on clothese and electronic commodities, by consumers, is lesser than that in the year 2011

(*d*) There is a chance that in 2012 the economy would do better than what has been forecast

(*e*) The pace of change in the employment scenario of the country is very slow.

54. Which of the following is possibly the most appropriate title for the passage?

(*a*) The Economic Disorder

(*b*) Indian Economy Versus the European Economy

(*c*) Global Trade

(*d*) The Current Economic Scenario

(*e*) Characteristics of the Indian Economy

55. According to the author, which of the following would characterise Indian growth scenario in 2012?

(A) Domestic producers will take a hit because of depressed global trade scenario.

(B) On account of its high domestic consumption, India will lead.

(C) Indian exporters will have a hard time in gaining market share.

(*a*) Only (B)

(*b*) Only (A) and (B)

(*c*) Only (B) and (C)

(*d*) Only (A)

(*e*) All (A), (B) and (C)

56. Why does the author not recommend taking up the reforms suggested by FIIs?

(*a*) These will bring about only minor growth

(*b*) The reforms suggested will have no effect on the economy of our country, whereas will benefit the FIIs significantly

(*c*) The previous such recommendations had backfired

(*d*) These reforms will be the sole reason for our country's economic downfall

(*e*) The reforms suggested by them are not to be trusted as they will not bring about any positive growth in India.

57. Which of the following is TRUE as per the scenario presented in the passage?

   (*a*) The highest growth rate that India can expect is 7 per cent

   (*b*) The fall in the exchange rate will prove beneficial to India.

   (*c*) Increased FDI in retail as suggested by FIIs would benefit India tremendously

   (*d*) The reforms suggested by the author require new legislation in India

   (*e*) None is true.

58. According to the author, which of the following reform(s) is/are needed to ensure long term growth in the India?

   (A) Improving healthcare and educational facilities.

   (B) Bringing about reforms in taxation.

   (C) Improving agricultural productivity.

   (*a*) Only (B)   (*b*) Only (A) and (B)

   (*c*) Only (B) and (C)   (*d*) Only (A)

   (*e*) All (A), (B) and (C)

Directions (Q. 59-62) : *Choose the word/group of words which is* **most similar** *in meaning to the word/group of words printed in* **bold** *as used in the passage.*

59. DRAW

   (*a*) entice   (*b*) push

   (*c*) decoy   (*d*) attract

   (*e*) persuade

60. CLOCK

   (*a*) watch   (*b*) achieve

   (*c*) time   (*d*) second

   (*e*) regulate

61. ABATE

   (*a*) rise   (*b*) gear

   (*c*) hurl   (*d*) lessen

   (*e*) retreat

62. EMERGING

   (*a*) raising

   (*b*) developing

   (*c*) noticeable

   (*d*) conspicuous

   (*e*) uproaring

Directions (Q. 63-65) : *Choose the word/group of words which is* **most opposite** *in meaning to the word/group of words printed in* **bold** *as used in the passage.*

63. MYRIAD

   (*a*) trival   (*b*) difficult

   (*c*) few   (*d*) effortless

   (*e*) countless

64. TEPID

   (*a*) moderate   (*b*) high

   (*c*) warm   (*d*) irregular

   (*e*) little

65. MYTH

   (*a*) reality   (*b*) belief

   (*c*) contrast   (*d*) idealism

   (*e*) falsehood

Directions (Q. 66-70) : *Rearrange the following six sentences (A), (B), (C), (D), (E) and (F) in the proper sequence to form a meaningful paragraph; then answer the questions given below them.*

(A) If China is the world's factory, India has become the world's outsourcing centre - keeping in line with this image.

(B) But India's future depends crucially on its ability to compete fully in the Creative Economy - not just in tech and software, but across design and entrepreneurship; arts, culture and entertainment; and the knowledge-based professions of medicine, finance and law.

(C) While its crative assets outstrip those of other emerging competitors, India must address several challenges to increase its international competitiveness as the world is in the midst of a sweeping transformation.

(D) This transformation is evident in the fact that the world is moving from an industrial economy to a Creative Economy that generates wealth by harnessing intellectual labour, intangible goods and human creative capabilities.

(E) Its software industry is the world's second-largest its tech outsourcing accounts for more than half of the $300 billion global industry, according to a technology expert.

(F) If the meeting of world leaders at Davos is any indication, India is rapidly becoming an economic 'rock star'.

66. Which of the following should be the SIXTH (LAST) sentence after the rearrangement?

   (*a*) A   (*b*) B

   (*c*) C   (*d*) D

   (*e*) E

67. Which of the following should be the THIRD sentence after rearrangement?

   (*a*) A   (*b*) B

   (*c*) C   (*d*) D

   (*e*) E

68. Which of the following should be the FIFTH sentence after the rearrangement?

   (*a*) A   (*b*) B

   (*c*) C   (*d*) F

   (*e*) E

69. Which of the following should be the FIRST sentence after the rearrangement?

(*a*) F   (*b*) B

(*c*) C   (*d*) A

(*e*) E

70. Which of the following should be the SECOND sentence after the rearrangement?

(*a*) A   (*b*) B

(*c*) C   (*d*) D

(*e*) F

Directions (Q. 71-75) : *The following questions consist of a single sentence with one blank only. You are given six words denoted by A, B, C D, E & F as answer choices and from the six choices you have to pick two correct answers, either of which will make the sentence meaningfully complete.*

71. ____ before the clock struck 8 on Saturday night, India Gate was swamped with people wearing black tee-shirts and holding candles.

(A) Minutes   (B) Time

(C) Later   (D) Quickly

(E) Since   (F) Seconds

(*a*) (B) and (E)   (*b*) (A) and (C)

(*c*) (A) and (F)   (*d*) (B) and (D)

(*e*) (C) and (E)

72. The States should take steps to ____ the process of teachers appointments as the Centre has already sanctioned six lakh posts.

(A) fasten   (B) move

(C) hasten   (D) speed

(E) Early   (F) Quicken

(*a*) (D) and (F)   (*b*) (A) and (C)

(*c*) (C) and (F)   (*d*) (D) and (E)

(*e*) (B) and (D)

73. A senior citizen's son ____ threatened her every day and physically harmed her, forcing her to transfer her property to him.

(A) superficially   (B) mistakenly

(C) allegedly   (D) miserably

(E) doubtfully   (F) purportedly

(*a*) (C) and (F)   (*b*) (A) and (E)

(*c*) (C) and (E)   (*d*) (D) and (F)

(*e*) (A) and (C)

74. Medical teachers said that the management had continued to remain ____ to their cause leading to the stretching of their strike.

(A) unmoved   (B) lethargic

(C) unconcerned   (D) apathetic

(E) indifferent   (F) bored

(*a*) (B) and (C)   (*b*) (C) and (F)

(*c*) (A) and (E)   (*d*) (A) and (D)

(*e*) (D) and (E)

75. The parents had approached the high court to ____ the government order after their children, who passed UKG, were denied admission by a school.

(A) void   (B) quash

(C) annul   (D) stay

(E) lift   (F) post

(*a*) (A) and (D)   (*b*) (B) and (C)

(*c*) (C) and (E)   (*d*) (E) and (F)

(*e*) (C) and (E)

Directions (Q. 76-80) : *In the following passage there are blanks, each of which has been numbered. These numbers are printed below the passage and against each, five words/phrases are suggested, one of which fits the blank appropriately. Find out the appropriate word/phrase in each case.*

Greenhouse gases are only (**76**) of the story when it comes to global warming. Changes to one part of the climate system can (**77**) additional changes to the way the planet absorbs or reflects energy. These secondary changes are (**78**) climate feedbacks, and they could more than double the amount of warming caused by carbon dioxide alone. The primary feedback are (**79**) to snow and ice, water vapour, clouds, and the carbon cycle.

Perhaps the most well (**80**) feedback comes from melting snow and ice in the Northern Hemisphere.

76. (*a*) whole   (*b*) part

    (*c*) material   (*d*) issue

    (*e*) most

77. (*a*) raise   (*b*) brings

    (*c*) refer   (*d*) stop

    (*e*) cause

78. (*a*) sensed   (*b*) called

    (*c*) nothing   (*d*) but

    (*e*) term

79. (*a*) due   (*b*) results

    (*c*) reason   (*d*) those

    (*e*) because

80. (*a*) done   (*b*) known

    (*c*) ruled   (*d*) bestowed

    (*e*) said

Directions (Q. 81–85) : *Each question below has two blanks, each blank indicating that something has been omitted. Choose the set of words for each blank that best fits the meaning of the sentence as a whole.*

81. A plethora of cultural talent ____ the spectators busy at a talent hunt programme where students from various colleges get together to ____ their mettle in various contests.

(*a*) tried, show   (*b*) kept, prove

(*c*) caught, puzzle   (*d*) held, learn

(*e*) helped, mention

82. The _____ of Chinese plastic thread should be banned as it _____ thousands of birds every year during the kite flying season.

(a) sale, cripples

(b) sell, kills

(c) sale, disturbs

(d) sell, disables

(e) sale, saves

83. Harish _____ with me some basic techniques that one can _____ at home without even owning a drumset.

(a) made, shred

(b) imparted, try

(c) learned, balance

(d) fits, rechearses

(e) shared, practise

84. In the present case, the facts clearly _____ that the required reasonable degree of care and caution was not _____ by hospital in the treatment of the patient.

(a) reflect, compressed

(b) fix, advancement

(c) show, proceeded

(d) observe, considered

(e) indicate, taken

85. Students from the Middle East and the African countries have _____ been _____ contributors to the pool of foreign students in the university.

(a) traditionally, major

(b) conservatively, crucial

(c) suprisingly, most

(d) intutively, salient

(e) annually, lucid

Directions (Q. 86–90) : *Read each sentence to find out whether there is any grammatical error or idiomatic error in it. The error, if any, will be in one part of the sentence. The number of that part is the answer. If there is "No Error" the answer is '5'. (Ignore errors of punctuation if any.)*

86. The couple's work in (a) / upgrading rural technicians (b)/ has set a benchmarking (c)/ for future generations. (d)/ No Error (e)

87. It has taking almost (a)/ a year for India (b)/ to let its pessimism (c)/ translate into fewer Jobs. (d)/ No Error (e)

88. The city needs an airport (a)/ that can efficiently manage (b)/ a constantly flow of (c)/ passengers and flights. (d)/ No Error (e)

89. This group of (a)/ rural achievers is very (b)/ different than the (c)/ ones in the past. (d)/ No Error (e)

90. The government has announced (a)/ plans to creating (b)/ one million new (c)/ training places. (d)/ No Error (e)

Directions (Q. 91–100) : *Read the following passage carefully and answer the questions given below it. Certain words have been printed in **bold** to help you locate them while answering some of the questions.*

Indeed the western recession is really the beginning of good news for India! But to understand that we will have to move away for a while from the topic of western recession .... to the Japanese recession! For years the Japanese style of management has been admired. However, over the last decade or so, one **key** question has sprung up 'if Japanese management style is as wonderful as described then why has Japan been in a recession for more than a decade?'

The answer to this question is very simple. Culture plays a very Important part in shaping up economies. What succeeds in one culture fails in another. Japanese are basically non materialistic. And however rich they become, unlike others, they cannot Just keep throwing and buying endlessly. And once they have everything they need; there is a saturation point. It was only when companies like Toyota realized that they cannot keep selling cars endlessly to their home market that they went really **aggressive** in the western markets and the rest is history. Japanese companies grew bigger by **catering** to the world markets when their home markets shrunk.

And the markets have to shrink finally after attaining a level of affluence! And that's great for the world because earth needs sustainable development. It does not need monstrous consumers who keep consuming at the cost of the environment and the earth. There should be limits to growth so that consumers are not converted into material dustbins for the profit of a handful of corporations.

Owing to the materialistic culture elsewhere, it was possible to keep selling newer products to the consumers despite having existing ones which served equally well. They were lured through advertising and marketing techniques of 'dustbinisation' of the customer; and then finally, once they became ready customers, they were given loans and credits to help them buy more and more. When all the creditworthy people were given loans to a logical limit, they ceased to be a part of the market. Even this would have been understandable if it could work as an eye opener. Instead of taking the 'Right Step' as Toyota did, they preferred to take a 'shortcut'. Now banks went to the non creditworthy people and gave them loans. The people expectedly defaulted and the entire system collapsed.

Now like Toyota western companies will learn to find new markets. They will now lean towards India because of its common man! The billion plus population in the next 25 years will become, a **consuming** middle-class. Finally, the world's attention will, shift to the developing world. Finally, there will be a real **surge** in income of these people and in the next fifty odd years, one can really hope to see an equal world in terms of material plenty, with poverty being almost nonexistent! And this will happen not by selling more cars to Americans and Europeans. It will happen by creating markets in India, China, Latin America and Africa, by giving their people purchasing power and by making products for them.

The recession has made us realize that it is not because of worse management techniques, but because of limits to growth. And they will realize that it is great for planet earth. After all, how many cars and houses must the rich own before calling it enough? It's time for them to look at others as well. Many years back, to increase his own profits. Henry Ford had started paying his workers more, so that they could buy his cars. In similar fashion, now the developed world will pay the developing world people so that they can buy their cars and washing machines.

The recession will kick-start the process of making the entire world more **prosperous,** and lay the foundation of limits to growth in the west and the foundation of real globalization in the world - of the globalization of prosperity. And one of its first beneficiaries will be India.

91. What does the author mean by the "Right Step" in the passage ?

(*a*) Giving loans to creditworthy people only

(*b*) Considering market growth along with environment protection.

(*c*) Restricting people to buy only such products which are needed by them.

(*d*) To start looking at newer avenues and markets.

(*e*) None of these

92. Although admired since years, why did the scepticism over the Japanese management style start since the last decade?

(*a*) Japanese companies have been moving out of their home markets since the last decade.

(*b*) Japanese banks have provided loans indiscriminately to the creditworthy as well as non creditworthy people.

(*c*) Because Japanese markets have been going through a period of continuous recession since the last decade.

(*d*) The unlimited growth of the Japanese markets has come at the cost of the western market.

(*e*) None of these

93. Why does the author foresee the markets being created in the developing countries instead of America and Europe ?

(*a*) All developing countries have materialistic culture.

(*b*) Developed countries are willing to make an effort to achieve globalization.

(*c*) American and European markets have had a large number of credit defaulters.

(*d*) Recession has not hit the markets of developing countries yet.

(*e*) None of these

94. According to the author, what is the main cause of Japanese recession ?

(*a*) Only a handful of corporations earned profits and not the people in general.

(*b*) Non creditworthy people defaulted which led to a collapse of the entire system.

(*c*) Consumers were sold newer products which were similar in quality to the existing ones.

(*d*) Japanese do not purchase endlessly and thus when products had been sold to every customer, the markets slowed down.

(*e*) None of these

95. How does the author foresee the future globalization as an analogy to Henry Ford's example ?

(A) Car companies would start selling cars in developing countries as well.

(B) By paying the developing world the developed world would increase its own profit, in turn bringing affluence to developing world as well.

(C) To earn profit, the companies in developing countries would move to foreign land.

(*a*) Only A (*b*) Only B

(*c*) Only C (*d*) Only A and C

(*e*) None of these

Directions (Q. 96 – 98) : *Choose the word which is* **most similar** *in meaning to the word printed in* **bold** *as used in the passage.*

96. CATERING

    (*a*) Considering   (*b*) Lending

    (*c*) Supplying   (*d*) Working

    (*e*) Indulging

97. KEY

    (*a*) Foundation   (*b*) Solution

    (*c*) Requisite   (*d*) Difficult

    (*e*) Important

98. AGGRESSIVE

    (*a*) Violent   (*b*) Determined

    (*c*) Demanding   (*d*) Offensive

    (*e*) Brutish

Directions (Q. 99 – 100) : *Choose the word/phrase which is* **most opposite** *in meaning to the word printed in* **bold** *as used in the passage.*

99. PROSPEROUS

    (*a*) Distressed   (*b*) Helpless

    (*c*) Worse   (*d*) Worthless

    (*e*) Underprivileged

100. CONSUMING

    (*a*) Destroying   (*b*) Exhausting

    (*c*) Greedy   (*d*) Curtailing

    (*e*) Spending

QUANTITATIVE APTITUDE

Directions (Q. 101-105) : *What will come in place of the question mark (?) in the following questions?*

101. $4003 \times 77 - 21015 = ? \times 116$

    (*a*) 2477   (*b*) 2478

    (*c*) 2467   (*d*) 2476

    (*e*) None of these

102. $[(5\sqrt{7} + \sqrt{7}) \times (4\sqrt{7} + 8\sqrt{7})] - (19)^2 = ?$

    (*a*) 143   (*b*) $72\sqrt{7}$

    (*c*) 134   (*d*) $70\sqrt{7}$

    (*e*) None of these

103. $(4444 \div 40) + (645 \div 2(e) + (3991 \div 26) = ?$

    (*a*) 280.4   (*b*) 290.4

    (*c*) 295.4   (*d*) 285.4

    (*e*) None of these

104. $\sqrt{33124} \times \sqrt{2601} - (83)^2 = (?)^2 + (37)^2$

    (*a*) 37   (*b*) 33

    (*c*) 34   (*d*) 28

    (*e*) None of these

105. $5\dfrac{17}{37} \times 4\dfrac{51}{52} \times 11\dfrac{1}{7} + 2\dfrac{3}{4} = ?$

    (*a*) 303.75   (*b*) 305.75

    (*c*) $303\dfrac{3}{4}$ (*d*) $305\dfrac{1}{4}$

    (*e*) None of these

Directions (Q. 106-110) : *What approximate value should come in place of the question mark (?) in the following questions? (Note: You are not expected to calculate the exact value.)*

106. $8787 \div 343 \times \sqrt{50} = ?$

    (*a*) 250   (*b*) 140

    (*c*) 180   (*d*) 100

    (*e*) 280

107. $\sqrt[3]{54821} \times (303 \div 8) = (?)^2$

    (*a*) 48   (*b*) 38

    (*c*) 28   (*d*) 18

    (*e*) 58

108. $\dfrac{5}{8}$ of $4011.33 + \dfrac{7}{10}$ of $3411.22 = ?$

    (*a*) 4810   (*b*) 4980

    (*c*) 4890   (*d*) 4930

    (*e*) 4850

109. 23% of $6783 + 57\%$ of $8431 = ?$

    (*a*) 6460   (*b*) 6420

    (*c*) 6320   (*d*) 6630

    (*e*) 6360

110. $335.01 \times 244.99 \div 55 = ?$

    (*a*) 1490   (*b*) 1550

    (*c*) 1420   (*d*) 1590

    (*e*) 1400

Directions (Q. 111-115) : *In each of these questions a number series is given. In each series only one number is wrong. Find out the wrong number.*

111. 5531 5506 5425 5304 5135 4910 4621

    (*a*) 5531   (*b*) 5425

    (*c*) 4621   (*d*) 5135

    (*e*) 5506

112. 6 7 9 13 26 37 69

    (*a*) 7   (*b*) 26

    (*c*) 69   (*d*) 37

    (*e*) 9

113. 1 3 10 36 152 760 4632

    (*a*) 3   (*b*) 36

    (*c*) 4632   (*d*) 760

    (*e*) 152

114. 4 3 9 34 96 219 435

    (*a*) 4   (*b*) 9

    (*c*) 34   (*d*) 435

    (*e*) 219

115. 157.5 45 15 6 3 2 1

(*a*) 1   (*b*) 2

(*c*) 6   (*d*) 157.5

(*e*) 45

Directions (Q. 116-120) : *Study the following graph and table carefully and answer the questions given below:*

TIME TAKEN TO TRAVEL (IN HOURS) BY SIX VEHICLES ON TWO DIFFERENT DAYS

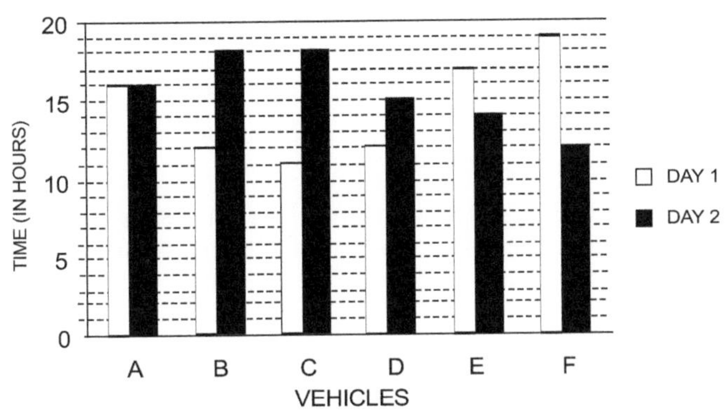

DISTANCE COVERED (IN KILOMETERS BY SIX VEHICLES ON EACH DAY)

Vehicle	Day 1	Day 2
A	832	864
B	516	774
C	693	810
D	552	765
E	935	546
F	703	636

116. Which of the following vehicles travelled at the same speed on both the days ?

(*a*) Vehicle A   (*b*) Vehicle C

(*c*) Vehicle F   (*d*) Vehicle B

(*e*) None of these

117. What was the difference between the speed of vehicle A on day 1 and the speed of vehicle C on the same day ?

(*a*) 7 km/hr

(*b*) 12km/hr

(*c*) 11 km/hr

(*d*) 8km/hr

(*e*) None of these

118. What was the speed of vehicle C on day 2 in terms of meters per second ?

(*a*) 15.3   (*b*) 12.8

(*c*) 11.5   (*d*) 13.8

(*e*) None of these

119. The distance travelled by vehicle F on day 2 was approximately what percent of the distance travelled by it on day 1?

(*a*) 80   (*b*) 65

(*c*) 85   (*d*) 35

(*e*) 90

120. What is the respective ratio between the speeds of vehicle D and vehicle E on day 2 ?

(*a*) 15 : 13   (*b*) 17 : 13

(*c*) 13 : 11   (*d*) 17 : 14

(*e*) None of these

121. An article was purchased for ₹ 78,350/-. Its price was marked up by 30%. It was sold at a discount of 20% on the marked up price. What was the profit percent on the cost price ?

(*a*) 4   (*b*) 7

(*c*) 5   (*d*) 3

(*e*) 6

122. When X is subtracted from the numbers 9, 15 and 27, the remainders are in continued proportion. What is the value of X?

(*a*) 8   (*b*) 6

(*c*) 4   (*d*) 5

(*e*) None of these

123. What is the difference between the simple and compound interest on ₹ 7,300/- at the rate of 6 p.c.p.a. in 2 years ?

(*a*) ₹ 29.37/-   (*b*) ₹ 26.28/-

(*c*) ₹ 31.41/-   (*d*) ₹ 23.22/-

(*e*) ₹ 21.34/-

124. Sum of three consecutive numbers is 2262. What is 41% of the highest number?

(*a*) 301.51   (*b*) 303.14

(*c*) 308.73   (*d*) 306.35

(*e*) 309.55

125. In how many different ways can the letters of the word 'THERAPY' be arranged so that the vowels never come together ?

(*a*) 720   (*b*) 1440

(*c*) 5040   (*d*) 3600

(*e*) 4800

126. A certain amount was to be distributed among A, B and C in the ratio 2 : 3 : 4 respectively, but was erroneously distributed in the ratio 7 : 2 : 5 respectively. As a result of this, B got ₹ 40 less. What is the amount ?

(*a*) ₹ 210/-   (*b*) ₹ 270/-

(*c*) ₹ 230/-   (*d*) ₹ 280/-

(*e*) None of these

127. Rachita enters a shop to buy ice-creams, cookies and pastries. She has to buy at least 9 units of each. She buys more cookies than ice-creams and more pastries than cookies. She picks up a total of 32 items. How many cookies does she buy ?
(*a*) Either 12 or 13
(*b*) Either 11 or 12
(*c*) Either 10 or 11
(*d*) Either 9 or 11
(*e*) Either 9 or 10

128. The fare of a bus is ₹ X for the first five kilometers and ₹ 13/- per kilometer thereafter. If a passenger pays ₹ 2402/- for a journey of 187 kilometers, what is the value of X ?
(*a*) ₹ 29/-   (*b*) ₹ 39/-
(*c*) ₹ 36/-   (*d*) ₹ 31/-
(*e*) None of these

129. The product of three consecutive even numbers is 4032. The product of the first and the third number is 252. What is five times the second number ?
(*a*) 80   (*b*) 100
(*c*) 60   (*d*) 70
(*e*) 90

130. The sum of the ages of 4 members of a family 5 years ago was 94 years. Today, when the daughter has been married off and replaced by a daughter-in-law, the sum of their ages is 92. Assuming that there has been no other change in the family structure and all the people are alive, what is the difference in the age of the daughter and the daughter-in-law?
(*a*) 22 years   (*b*) 11 years
(*c*) 25 years   (*d*) 19 years
(*e*) 15 years

131. A bag contains 13 white and 7 black balls. Two balls are drawn at random. What is the probability that they are of the same colour ?
(*a*) $\dfrac{41}{190}$ (*b*) $\dfrac{21}{190}$
(*c*) $\dfrac{59}{190}$ (*d*) $\dfrac{99}{190}$
(*e*) $\dfrac{77}{190}$

132. Akash scored 73 marks in subject A. He scored 56% marks in subject B and X marks in subject C. Maximum marks in each subject were 150. The overall percentage marks obtained by Akash in all the three subjects together were 54%. How many marks did he score in subject C ?
(*a*) 84   (*b*) 86
(*c*) 79   (*d*) 73
(*e*) None of these

133. The area of a square is 1444 square meters. The breadth of a rectangle is 1/4th the side of the square and the length of the rectangle is thrice the breadth. What is the difference between the area of the square and the area of the rectangle ?
(*a*) 1152.38 sq.mtr.   (*b*) 1169.33 sq.mtr.
(*c*) 1181.21 sq.mtr.   (*d*) 1173.25 sq.mtr.
(*e*) None of these

134. ₹ 73,689/- are divided between A and B in the ratio 4 : 7. What is the difference between thrice the share of A and twice the share of B ?
(*a*) ₹ 36,699/-   (*b*) ₹ 46,893/-
(*c*) ₹ 20,097/-   (*d*) ₹ 26.796/-
(*e*) ₹ 13,398/-

135. A and B together can complete a task in 20 days. B and C together can complete the same task in 30 days. A and C together can complete the same task in 40 days. What is the respective ratio of the number of days taken by A when completing the same task alone to the number of days taken by C when completing the same task alone ?
(*a*) 2 : 5   (*b*) 2 : 7
(*c*) 3 : 7   (*d*) 1 : 5
(*e*) 3 : 5

136. One man, 3 woman and 4 boys can do a piece of work in 96 hrs, 2 men and 8 Boys can do it in 80 hrs, 2 men and 3 women can do it in 120 hrs. 5 Men and 12 Boys can do it in?

(*a*) $39\dfrac{1}{11}$ hrs   (*b*) $42\dfrac{7}{11}$ hrs

(*c*) $43\dfrac{7}{11}$ days   (*d*) 44 hrs

(*e*) None of these

137. A Man borrowed ₹ 24000 from two money lenders. For one loan, he paid 15% per annum and for other 18% per annum. At the end of one year, he paid ₹ 4050. How much did he borrowed at 18% rate?
(*a*) 14000   (*b*) 15000
(*c*) 18000   (*d*) 12000
(*e*) None of these

Directions (Q. 138 – 142) : *In each of these questions two equations numbered I and II are given. You have to solve both the equations and give answer.*
(*a*) if a < b
(*b*) if a > b
(*c*) if relationship between a and b cannot be established
(*d*) if a ≥ b
(*e*) if a ≤ b

138. I. $a^2 + 5a + 6 = 0$
      II. $b^2 + 3b + 2 = 0$

139. I. $2a^2 + 3a + 1 = 0$
  II. $12b^2 + 7b + 1 = 0$

140. I. $a^2 = 4$
  II. $a^2 = 9$

141. I. $6a^2 - 25a + 25 = 0$
  II. $15b^2 - 16b + 4 = 0$

142. I. $4a^2 - 20a + 21 = 0$
  II. $2b^2 - 5b + 3 = 0$

Directions (Q. 143 – 145) : *Study the graphs carefully to answer the questions that follow:*

Total number of children in 6 different schools and the percentage of girls in them.

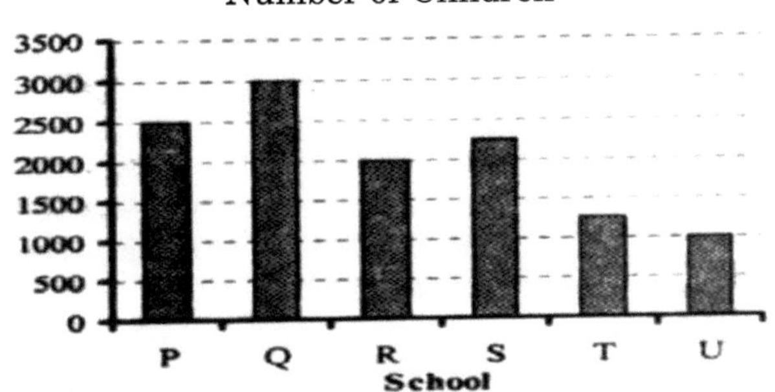

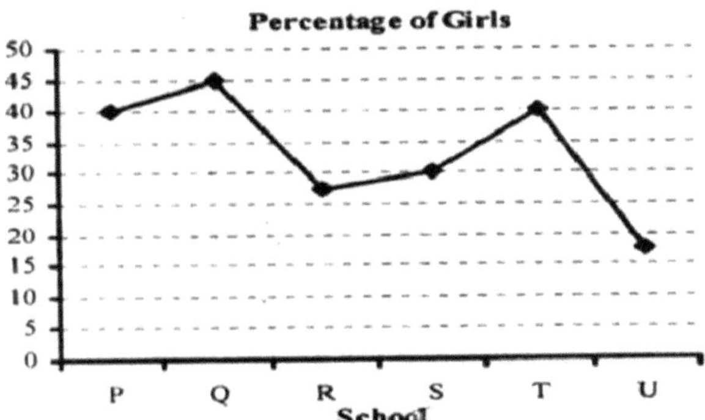

143. The total number of students in school R is **approximately**. What percent of the total number of students in school S?
  (a) 89
  (b) 75
  (c) 78
  (d) 82
  (e) 94

144. What is the average number of boys in schools P and Q together?
  (a) 1425
  (b) 1575
  (c) 1450
  (d) 1625
  (e) None of these

145. What is the ratio of the number of girls in school P to the number of girls in school Q?
  (a) 27 : 20
  (b) 17 : 21
  (c) 20 : 27
  (d) 21 : 17
  (e) None of these

Directions (Q. 146 – 148): *In each of the following questions a number series is given. After the series a number is given followed by (a), (b), (c), (d) and (e). You have to complete the series starting with the given number, following the sequence of original series and answer the questions that follow the series.*

146. 3   19   103   439   1381   2887
  5   (a)   (b)   (c)   (d)   (e)
  What will come in place of (b)?
  (a) 139
  (b) 163
  (c) 161
  (d) 157
  (e) None of these

147. 4   13   40   135   552   2765
  2   (a)   (b)   (c)   (d)   (e)
  What will come in place of (c)?
  (a) 123
  (b) 133
  (c) 127
  (d) 131
  (e) None of these

148. 5   12   4   10   3   8
  6   (a) (b) (c) (d) (e)
  What will come in place of (d)?
  (a) 3
  (b) 5
  (c) 4
  (d) 7
  (e) None of these

149. The speed of a train A, 100m long is 40% more than the speed of another train B, 180m long running in opposite direction. To find out the speed of B, which of the information given in statements P and Q is sufficient

  P : The two trains crossed each other in 6 seconds

  Q : The difference between the speed of the trains is 26 kmph

  (a) Only P is sufficient
  (b) Only Q is sufficient
  (c) Both P and Q are needed
  (d) Both P and Q are not suficient
  (e) None of these

150. What is the average weight of girls in the class?
  I. Average weight of all the 60 students is 42 kg.
  II. Average weight of boys is 43 kg.
  III. Total weight of all girls together is 1144 kg.
  (a) Any two of three
  (b) All I, II and III
  (c) I and II only
  (d) II and III only
  (e) Question cannot be answered even with information in all three statements.

GENERAL AWARENESS, MARKETING AND COMPUTERS

151. Narendra Modi launches which bank in China?

(*a*) HDFC
(*b*) ICICI Bank
(*c*) SBI
(*d*) Yes Bank
(*e*) None of these

152. A Basic Savings Bank Deposit Account facility is available ______.

(*a*) to all individuals irrespective to their background
(*b*) all individuals from below poverty-line-families only
(*c*) only to individuals from the SC/ST only
(*d*) only to individuals from the minority communities only
(*e*) only to individuals from weaker sections of the society

153. Which of the following is an example of an input device ?

(*a*) Monitor
(*b*) Scanner
(*c*) Printer
(*d*) CD
(*e*) Speaker

154. The Reserve Bank of India has been critical of home loan with comparatively low interest rates in the initial year but higher in the subsequent years, which are properly known as the ______.

(*a*) Teaser Rates
(*b*) Cheater Rates
(*c*) Twister Rates
(*d*) Cheaper Rates
(*e*) Trickster Rates

155. Relationship marketing is also know as ______.

(*a*) Loyalty marketing
(*b*) Experiential marketing
(*c*) Value marketing
(*d*) Promotional marketing
(*e*) Brand marketing

156. PCs are considered fourth-generation and contain ______.

(*a*) information
(*b*) data
(*c*) vacuum tube
(*d*) microprocessors
(*e*) transistors

157. Which of the following is not an aggressiveness strategy ?

(*a*) All the given options are aggressivenes strategies
(*b*) Building
(*c*) Harvesting
(*d*) Holding
(*e*) Intensification

158. Which of the following nations is 'not' a member of SAARC ?

(*a*) Nepal
(*b*) Mauritius
(*c*) Bhutan
(*d*) Afghanistan
(*e*) Maldives

159. Market Price is also known as ______.

(*a*) List price
(*b*) Value price
(*c*) Effective price
(*d*) Retail price
(*e*) Wholesaler price

160. The phenomenon when a customer dislikes a product and talks against the product

(*a*) Misinformation
(*b*) Unfavorable environment
(*c*) Propaganda
(*d*) Bad impression
(*e*) Bad mouth

161. The RBI policy rate which is purely an indicative rate used by the Reserve Bank of India to signal long-term outlook on interest rate is ______.

(*a*) Bank Rate
(*b*) Repo rate
(*c*) Call Money Rate
(*d*) Notice Money Rate
(*e*) Reserve Repo Rate

162. Which country agreed to lend 1165cr for odissa transmission system improvement project?

(*a*) America
(*b*) Japan
(*c*) Russia
(*d*) China
(*e*) None of these

163. The amount specified as the Cash Reserve Ratio (CRR) is held in cash and cash equivalents and is stored in bank vaults or parked with ______.

(*a*) Small industries Development Bank of India (SIDBI)
(*b*) Government of India (Gol)
(*c*) Reserve Bank of India (RBI)
(*d*) State Bank of India (SBI)
(*e*) Rural Infrastructure Development Fund (RIDF)

164. As consumer banking frauds are on the rise, a Reserve Bank of India (RBI) group has suggested the use of PKI in order to improve payment system in the country.

The abbreviation PKI stands for ______.

(*a*) Public key infrastructure
(*b*) Personal key infrastructure
(*c*) Private key infrastructure
(*d*) Permanent key infrastructure
(*e*) Proprietary key infrastructure

165. The Reserve Bank of India recently issued guidelines allowing minors over 10 years of age to operate bank accounts independently with a view to ______.
   (a) Promoting financial inclusion
   (b) Increasing low-cost deposits of banks
   (c) Improving CASA percentage of banks
   (d) Mobilising Savings Bank Deposits of banks
   (e) Putting ATMs and other infrastructure to optimum use

166. Java is referred to as a ______.
   (a) high-level language
   (b) complex language
   (c) hardware device driver
   (d) low-level language
   (e) programming mid-level language

167. 'Kepler-78b' is the name of ______.
   (a) an American nuclear missile
   (b) Russian armoured vehicle
   (c) a precision-measuring instrument
   (d) a Spanish sea vessel
   (e) an earth-sized planet far beyond our solar system

168. The Depositor Education and Awareness Fund (DEAF) has been set up with
   (a) Public Sector Banks
   (b) Indian Banks' Association
   (c) State Bank of India
   (d) Reserve Bank of India
   (e) Government of India

169. The operating system is the most common type of ______ software.
   (a) application
   (b) antivirus
   (c) communication
   (d) system
   (e) word-processing software

170. Hindustan Motors, India's oldest car maker, recently shut down its factory at Uttarpara in West Bengal and suspended the production of the iconic
   (a) Utility Vehicle Pushpak
   (b) Ambassador Car
   (c) Bedford Truck
   (d) Contessa Car
   (e) Morris Oxford Car

171. Jim Corbett National Park is located in which state?
   (a) Jharkhand
   (b) Bihar
   (c) Uttar Pradesh
   (d) Uttarakhand
   (e) None of these

172. In Trade Finance, a financial transaction involving the purchase of receivables from exporters by a third party who takes all the risks associated with the receivables is known as ______.
   (a) Forfaiting
   (b) Securitisation
   (c) Negotiation
   (d) Factoring
   (e) Assignment

173. Which is not a storage device ?
   (a) A floppy disk
   (b) A printer
   (c) A DVD
   (d) A Hard Disk
   (e) A CD

174. ______ is a written description of a computer programme functions.
   (a) Explanatory instructions
   (b) Graphical user interface
   (c) Plug and Play
   (d) README files
   (e) Documentation

175. The term 'pre-shipment finance' relates to ______.
   (a) Export Credit
   (b) Farm Credit
   (c) Consumer Credit
   (d) Investment Credit
   (e) Industrial Credit

176. The Government of India has undertaken a programme of recapitalisation of Public Sector Banks to help them enhance business growth and ______.
   (a) Captial Adequacy Norms
   (b) Ratio of Non Performing Assets
   (c) Per Employee Business Ratio
   (d) CASA Ratio
   (e) Credit to Deposit Ratio

177. Which of the following keys is used to delete characters to the left of the cursor ?

(*a*) Alt + Delete (*b*) Shift

(*c*) Esc (*d*) Delete

(*e*) Backspace

178. Products that are usually purchased due to adversity and high promotional back-up rather than desire are called ______.

(*a*) regular goods

(*b*) unsought goods

(*c*) preferred goods

(*d*) sought goods

(*e*) unique goods

179. The amount of memory (RAM or ROM) is measured in ______.

(*a*) Bites

(*b*) Bits

(*c*) Mega Bytes

(*d*) Mega Bits

(*e*) Hertz

180. Nobel laureate and recipient of the US Presidential Medal and also the US Congressional Medal Muhammad Yunus is well known for his contribution to Bangladesh's ______.

(*a*) Consumer Credit Sector

(*b*) Agro-Credit Sector

(*c*) Housing Finance sector

(*d*) Micro-Credit Sector

(*e*) Retail Credit Sector

181. Which of the following is NOT a technique of measuring customer satisfaction and monitoring customer's complaint ?

(*a*) Exit interviews

(*b*) Web information hotlines

(*c*) Business analysis

(*d*) Customer complaints database

(*e*) Telephone information hotlines

182. Underpriced products sell very well, but they produce less revenue than they would have if prices were raised to the ______.

(*a*) variable level

(*b*) demand-curve level

(*c*) price-floor level

(*d*) perceived-value level

(*e*) value-based level

183. A customer's requirement about any product in which he/she needs to avail core features in that product, is called

(*a*) Real need

(*b*) No need

(*c*) Stated need

(*d*) Unstated need

(*e*) Delighted need

184. Which of the following is a mode for creating charge on Life Insurance Policies ?

(*a*) Pledge (*b*) Lien

(*c*) Assignment (*d*) Hypothecation

(*e*) Equitable Mortgage

185. Bankers generally do not allow opening of accounts in the name of ______.

(*a*) executors and trustees

(*b*) persons of unsound mind

(*c*) illiterate persons

(*d*) pardanashin ladies

(*e*) visually impaired persons

186. Omkareshwar dam is situated in which state?

(*a*) Bihar (*b*) Gujarat

(*c*) Madhya Pradesh (*d*) Rajasthan

(*e*) None of these

187. The hard drive is normally located ______.

(*a*) next to the printer

(*b*) plugged into the back of the computer

(*c*) underneath the monitor

(*d*) on top of the CD-ROM

(*e*) inside the system base unit

188. The winner of the 51st Femina Miss India 2014 pageant is ______.

(*a*) Jhatalckha Malhotra

(*b*) Navneet Kaur Dhillon

(*c*) Koyal Rana

(*d*) Gail Nicole da Silva

(*e*) Megan Young

189. Virtual memory allocates hard disk space to supplement the immediate, functional memory capacity of what ?

(*a*) ROM (*b*) EPROM

(*c*) The registers (*d*) Extended memory

(*e*) RAM

190. 3/10 net 30 is an example of which of the following?

   (*a*) Cash discount   (*b*) Quantity discount

   (*c*) Seasonal discount   (*d*) Bulk discount

   (*e*) Trade discount

191. Which of the following refers to restarting the system when it is already powered on ?

   (*a*) a strong boot   (*b*) hibernation

   (*c*) a cold boot   (*d*) standby mode

   (*e*) a warm boot

192. ______ is having more memory addresses than are physically available.

   (*a*) Virtual Memory

   (*b*) System software

   (*c*) Applications software

   (*d*) RAM

   (*e*) Vertical Memory

193. Which of the following refers to dangerous programs that can be 'caught' be opening e-mail attachments and downloading software from the internet ?

   (*a*) utiliy   (*b*) virus

   (*c*) honeypot   (*d*) spam

   (*e*) app

194. What is the premium of PM Suraksha Bima Yojana?

   (*a*) Rs. 12   (*b*) Rs. 21

   (*c*) Rs. 49   (*d*) Rs. 79

   (*e*) None of these

195. Commercial Paper (CP) is an unsecured money market instrument issued in the form of a promissory note. Commercial Paper can be issued in denominations of ______.

   (*a*) ₹ 1 lakh or multiples thereof

   (*b*) ₹ 2 lakh or multiples thereof

   (*c*) ₹ 3 lakh or multiples thereof

   (*d*) ₹ 5 lakh or multiples thereof

   (*e*) ₹ 10 lakh or multiples thereof

196. A company is providing warehousing facility to its channel members. The company is using which of the following ?

   (*a*) Seasonal discount

   (*b*) Cash discount

   (*c*) Quantity discount

   (*d*) Trade discount

   (*e*) Quality discount

197. Aggressive pricing is associated with which of the following stage of product life cycle ?

   (*a*) Not Associated

   (*b*) Introduction

   (*c*) Growth

   (*d*) Maturity

   (*e*) Decline

198. The United nations (UN) and the International Olympic Committee (IOC) have recently signed a historic agreement to use the power of sports to promote ______.

   (*a*) Literacy and awareness

   (*b*) Peace and economic development

   (*c*) World amity and Friendship

   (*d*) Peaceful use to nuclear technology

   (*e*) World trade and commerce

199. Which of the following is NOT an objective of discounts ?

   (*a*) All the given options are objectives of discounts

   (*b*) Reward competitors

   (*c*) Reward valuable customers

   (*d*) Move out-of-date stock

   (*e*) Increase short-term sales

200. The abbreviation ASBA stands for ______.

   (*a*) Applications Supported by Blocked Account

   (*b*) Applications Supported by Bank Account

   (*c*) Applications Sustained by Blocked Amount

   (*d*) Applications Serviced by Blocked Account

   (*e*) Applications Supported by Blocked Amount

ANSWERS

1. (d)	**2.** (b)	**3.** (b)	**4.** (c)	**5.** (d)	**6.** (c)	**7.** (a)	**8.** (c)	**9.** (b)	**10.** (e)
11. (a)	**12.** (d)	**13.** (b)	**14.** (a)	**15.** (e)	**16.** (d)	**17.** (e)	**18.** (b)	**19.** (a)	**20.** (e)
21. (c)	**22.** (b)	**23.** (e)	**24.** (d)	**25.** (a)	**26.** (d)	**27.** (d)	**28.** (c)	**29.** (e)	**30.** (c)
31. (a)	**32.** (c)	**33.** (a)	**34.** (e)	**35.** (d)	**36.** (d)	**37.** (c)	**38.** (a)	**39.** (e)	**40.** (a)
41. (d)	**42.** (b)	**43.** (c)	**44.** (e)	**45.** (a)	**46.** (d)	**47.** (a)	**48.** (c)	**49.** (b)	**50.** (e)
51. (e)	**52.** (c)	**53.** (d)	**54.** (d)	**55.** (a)	**56.** (a)	**57.** (e)	**58.** (e)	**59.** (b)	**60.** (e)
61. (d)	**62.** (b)	**63.** (c)	**64.** (a)	**65.** (a)	**66.** (d)	**67.** (c)	**68.** (a)	**69.** (d)	**70.** (b)
71. (c)	**72.** (a)	**73.** (c)	**74.** (b)	**75.** (a)	**76.** (d)	**77.** (e)	**78.** (b)	**79.** (a)	**80.** (b)
81. (c)	**82.** (a)	**83.** (e)	**84.** (e)	**85.** (a)	**86.** (c)	**87.** (a)	**88.** (c)	**89.** (c)	**90.** (b)
91. (d)	**92.** (c)	**93.** (e)	**94.** (d)	**95.** (b)	**96.** (c)	**97.** (e)	**98.** (b)	**99.** (e)	**100.** (a)
101. (d)	**102.** (a)	**103.** (b)	**104.** (e)	**105.** (b)	**106.** (c)	**107.** (b)	**108.** (c)	**109.** (e)	**110.** (a)
111. (a)	**112.** (b)	**113.** (d)	**114.** (d)	**115.** (a)	**116.** (d)	**117.** (c)	**118.** (e)	**119.** (e)	**120.** (a)
121. (a)	**122.** (e)	**123.** (b)	**124.** (e)	**125.** (c)	**126.** (a)	**127.** (c)	**128.** (c)	**129.** (a)	**130.** (a)
131. (d)	**132.** (b)	**133.** (d)	**134.** (e)	**135.** (d)	**136.** (c)	**137.** (b)	**138.** (e)	**139.** (a)	**140.** (c)
141. (b)	**142.** (d)	**143.** (a)	**144.** (b)	**145.** (c)	**146.** (b)	**147.** (a)	**148.** (c)	**149.** (a)	**150.** (b)
151. (b)	**152.** (a)	**153.** (b)	**154.** (a)	**155.** (a)	**156.** (d)	**157.** (e)	**158.** (b)	**159.** (d)	**160.** (e)
161. (a)	**162.** (b)	**163.** (c)	**164.** (a)	**165.** (a)	**166.** (a)	**167.** (e)	**168.** (d)	**169.** (d)	**170.** (b)
171. (d)	**172.** (a)	**173.** (b)	**174.** (d)	**175.** (a)	**176.** (a)	**177.** (d)	**178.** (b)	**179.** (b)	**180.** (d)
181. (a)	**182.** (d)	**183.** (a)	**184.** (c)	**185.** (b)	**186.** (c)	**187.** (e)	**188.** (c)	**189.** (e)	**190.** (a)
191. (c)	**192.** (a)	**193.** (b)	**194.** (a)	**195.** (d)	**196.** (d)	**197.** (b)	**198.** (b)	**199.** (b)	**200.** (e)

EXPLANATIONS

Input   : 84 why sit 14 32 not best inR feet 51 27 va in 68 92

Step 1 : 14 84 why sit 32 not inR feet 51 va in 68 92 best

Step 2 : 27 14 84 why sit 32 not inR 51 va in 68 92 best feet

Step 3 : 32 27 14 84 why sit not 51 va in 68 92 best feet inR

Step 4 : 51 32 27 14 84 why sit va in 68 92 best feet inR not

Step 5 : 68 51 32 27 14 84 why va in 92 best feet inR not sit

Step 6 : 84 68 51 32 27 84 va in 92 best feet inR not sit why

Step 7 : 92 84 68 51 32 27 14 best feet inR not sit why va in

(5-11)

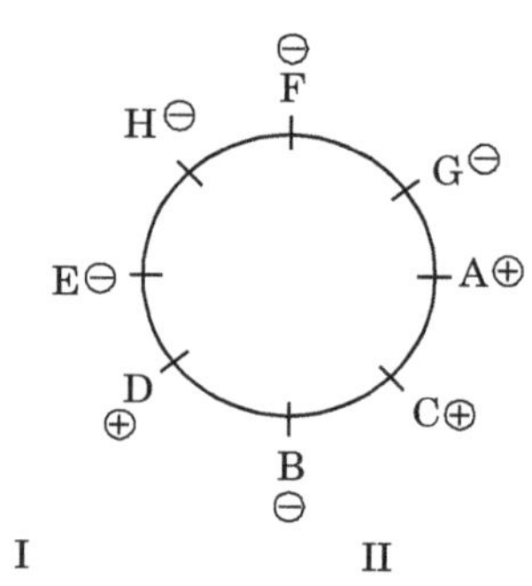

12.

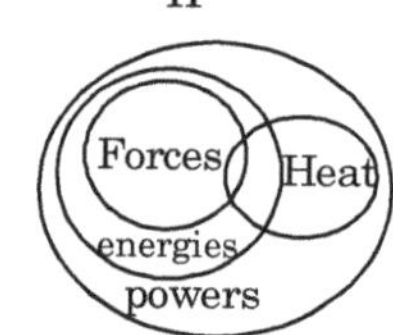

13.

19-21 Right sequence of student according to marks in decreasing order is

$$B > D > F > C > E > A$$

∴ Score of F = 81

Score of E = 62

22-29 The correct sequence of sitting arrangement is

CANARA	DENA	Maharastra	Oriental	
C	A	B	D	Facing South ↓

P	Q	R	S	
Syndicate	PNB	Indian	UCO	Facing North ↑

36.

	Disciplines		College
Mechanical	Electronic	Electrical	
S	P + Z	X	A
T	X	W	B
R	X	V + Q	C

W study in college B doing specilization in electrical

∴ Option (*d*) is correct.

37. In college 'C' two student study in electrical discipline.

38. Q study in electrical discipline.

39. In all colleges i.e., A, B and C, at least one student is in mechanical discipline.

40. S studies in college A.

41.

B	D	A	T	F	E
@	$	8	1	4	6

Condition (*ii*) applies.

42.

A	W	B	R	N	D
8	5	6	3	©	$

43.

E	M	N	T	K	U
@	#	©	1	%	*

44.

M	D	E	A	J	I
9	$	@	8	2	#

Condition (*ii*) applies

45.

R	K	U	M	F	P
7	%	*	#	4	3

46.

$$R \# J \Rightarrow R > J$$
$$J \$ D \Rightarrow J \geq D$$
$$D @ K \Rightarrow D = K$$
$$K \% T \Rightarrow K \leq T$$

Therefore, $R > J \geq D = K \leq T$

Conclusions :

I. $T \# D \Rightarrow T > D$: Not True

II. $T @ D \Rightarrow T = D$: Not True

Either I or II is true.

III. $R \# K \Rightarrow R > K$: True

IV. $J \$ T \Rightarrow J \geq T$: Not True

47.

$$T \% R \Rightarrow T \leq R$$
$$R \$ M \Rightarrow R \geq M$$
$$M @ D \Rightarrow M = D$$
$$D © H \Rightarrow D < H$$

Therefore, $T \leq R \geq M = D < H$

Conclusions :

I. $D \% R \Rightarrow D \leq R$: True

II. $H \# R \Rightarrow H > R$: Not True

III. $T © M \Rightarrow T < M$: Not True

IV. $T \% D \Rightarrow T \leq D$: Not True

48.

$$M @ B \Rightarrow M = B$$
$$B \# N \Rightarrow B > N$$
$$N \$ R \Rightarrow N \geq R$$
$$R © K \Rightarrow R < K$$

Therefore, $M = B > N \geq R < K$

Conclusions :

I. $K \# B \Rightarrow K > B$: Not True

II. $R © B \Rightarrow R < B$: True

III. $M \$ R \Rightarrow M \geq R$: Not True

IV. $N © M \Rightarrow N < M$: True

49.

$$F \# H \Rightarrow F > H$$
$$H © M \Rightarrow H = M$$
$$M © E \Rightarrow M < E$$
$$E \$ J \Rightarrow E \geq J$$

Therefore, $F > H = M < E \geq J$

Conclusions :

I. $J © M \Rightarrow J < M$: Not True

II. $E \# H \Rightarrow E > H$: True

III. $M © F \Rightarrow M < F$: True

IV. $F \# E \Rightarrow F > E$: Not True

50.

$$D \% A \Rightarrow D \leq A$$
$$A @ B \Rightarrow A = B$$
$$B © K \Rightarrow B < K$$
$$K \% M \Rightarrow K \leq M$$

Therefore, $D \leq A = B < K \leq M$

Conclusions :

I. $B \$ D \Rightarrow B \geq D$: True

II. $K \# A \Rightarrow K > A$: True

III. $M \# B \Rightarrow M > B$: True

IV. $A © M \Rightarrow A < M$: True

96. The meaning of the word **Cater (Verb)** as used in the passage is : to provide the things that a particular type of person wants.

Look at the sentence :

They only publish novels which cater to the massmarket.

Hence, the word **catering** and **supplying** are synonymous.

97. The meaning of the word **Key (Adjective)** as used in the passage is : most important; essential; critical; vital.

Look at the sentence :

He played a key role in the dispute.

Hence, the words **key** and **important** are synonymous.

98. The meaning of the word **Aggressive (Adjective)** as used in the passage is : acting with force and determination in order to succeed.

Look at the sentence :

A good sales person has to be aggressive in today's competitive market.

Hence, the words **aggressive** and **determined** are synonymous.

99. The meaning of the word **Prosperous (Adjective)** as used in the passage is : rich and successful; affluent.

The word **Underprivileged (Adjective)** means : having less money and fewer opportunities than others; disadvantaged.

Hence, the words **prosperous** and **underprivileged** are antonymous.

100. The meaning of the word **Consume (Verb)** as used in the passage is : to use somthing.

Hence, the words **consuming** and **destroying** are antonymous.

101. $400 \ 3 \times 77 - 21015 = ? \times 116$

$$\frac{308231 - 21015}{116} = 2476$$

102. $[(5\sqrt{7} + \sqrt{7}) \times (4\sqrt{7} + 8\sqrt{7})] - (19)^2$

$(6\sqrt{7}) \times (12\sqrt{7}) - (19)^2$

$72 \times 7 - 19^2 = 143$

103. $(4444 \div 40) + (645 \div 25) + (3991 \div 26)$

$111.1 + 25.8 + 153.5 = 290.4$

104. $\sqrt{33124} \times \sqrt{2601} - (83)^2 = (?)^2 + 37^2$

$\Rightarrow 182 \times 51 - 6889 = (?)^2 + 1369$

$\Rightarrow 9282 - 6889 - 1369 = (?)^2$

$\Rightarrow 1024 = (?)^2$

$? = 32$

105. $5\dfrac{17}{37} \times 4\dfrac{51}{52} \times 11\dfrac{1}{7} + 2\dfrac{3}{4} = \dfrac{202}{37} \times \dfrac{259}{52} \times \dfrac{78}{7} + \dfrac{11}{4}$

$$= 303 + 2.75 = 305.75$$

106. $8787 \times \dfrac{1}{7 \times 7 \times 7} \times \sqrt{50} = 180 \text{ (approx)}$

107. $\sqrt[3]{54821} \simeq 38 \ (\because 38^3 = 54872)$

and $\dfrac{303}{8} \simeq 38 \, (37.875)$

$\therefore \sqrt[3]{54821} \times (303 \div 8) = (38) \times 38 = 38^2$

108. $\dfrac{5}{8}$ of $4011.33 + \dfrac{7}{10}$ of 3411.22

$\dfrac{5}{8} \times 4000 + \dfrac{7}{10} \times 3400 = 4880 \ \begin{pmatrix} 4011.33 \simeq 4000 \\ 3411.22 \simeq 3400 \end{pmatrix}$

Nearest option is 4890.

110. $335.01 \times 244.99 \div 55 = 335 \times \dfrac{245}{55} \simeq 1490.$

111.

5531		5506		5425		5304		5135		4910		4621
	25		81		121		169		225		289	
	$(5)^2$		$(9)^2$		$(11)^2$		$(13)^2$		$(15)^2$		$(17)^2$	

Hence wrong number is 5425.

112.

6	+1	7	+2	9	+4	13	+13	26	+16	37

Hence wrong number is 26. It should be 21 instead of 26.

113. 1 3 10 36 152 760 4632

$3 \ \to 1 \times 1 + 2$ $152 \to 36 \times 4 + 8$

$10 \to 3 \times 2 + 4$ $770 \to 152 \times 5 + 10$

$36 \to 10 \times 3 + 6$ $4632 \to 770 \times 6 + 12$

Hence wrong number is 760. It should be 770 instead of 760.

115. 157.5 45 15 6 3 2 1

$$\frac{157.5}{3.5} = 45; \qquad \frac{6}{2} = 3; \qquad \frac{45}{3} = 15$$

$$\frac{3}{1.5} = 2; \qquad \frac{15}{2.5} = 6; \qquad \frac{2}{1} = 2$$

Hence wrong number is 1

116. Vehicle B speed on day $1 \to \dfrac{516}{12} = 43$

on day $2 \to \dfrac{774}{18} = 43$

117. Speed of vehicle A on day $1 = \dfrac{832}{16} = 52$ km/hrs

Speed of vehicle C on day $1 = \dfrac{693}{11} = 63$ km/hrs

difference between the speed = $63 - 52 = 11$ km/hrs

118. Speed of C on day $2 = \dfrac{810}{18} = 45$ km/hr

45 km/hr $= 45 \times \dfrac{5}{18} = 12.5$ m/s

119. Distance travelled by F on day 2 = 636 km

Distance travelled by F on day 1 = 703 km

$$\% = \frac{636}{703} \times 100 = 90\%$$

120. Speed of D on day $2 = \dfrac{765}{15} = 51$ km/hr

Speed of E on day $2 = \dfrac{546}{14} = 39$ km/hr

Now, Ratio of speed $= \dfrac{51}{39} = \dfrac{17}{13}$

121. Cost Price = ₹ 78, 350

Mark Price $= 78350 \times \dfrac{730}{100} = $ ₹ 101855

Selling price after 20% discount $= 101855 \times \dfrac{80}{100}$

$= $ ₹ 81484

Profit = 81484 − 78350 = ₹ 3134

$\%$ Profit $= \dfrac{3134}{78350} \times 100 = 4\%$

122. $\dfrac{9-x}{15-x} = \dfrac{15-x}{27-x}$

$\Rightarrow 243 - 36x + x^2 = 225 - 30x + x^2$

$\Rightarrow 18 = 6x \Rightarrow x = 3$

123. Sum = difference $\left[\dfrac{100}{\text{Rate}}\right]^2$ (for two years)

$\therefore$ difference $= $ sum $\left[\dfrac{\text{Rate}}{100}\right]^2 = 7300 \times \left(\dfrac{6}{100}\right)^2$

$= $ ₹ 26.28

124. Let numbers are x, $x + 1$, $x + 2$

$3x + 3 = 2262; \qquad x + 1 = 754$

$x = 753; \qquad 7500 \times \dfrac{41}{100} = 309.55$

126. $\dfrac{3}{9}x - \dfrac{2}{14}x = 40; \qquad \dfrac{42x - 18x}{126} = 40$

$\Rightarrow \dfrac{24x}{126} = 40 \Rightarrow x = 210$

128. $187 - 5 = 182$ km at the rate of ₹ 13/km

$182 \times 13 = 2366$

Remaining amount = 2402 − 2366 = ₹ 36

129. Let three consecutive No. = x, $x + 2$, $x + 4$

Product of there three numbers = $x(x+2)(x+4)$
= 4032

and $x(x+4) = 252$ given

$\therefore$ Second number i.e. $(x+2) = \dfrac{4032}{252} = 16$

5 times the second number = $16 \times 5 = 80$

130. Let ages of 4 members are w, x, y, z

5 years ago total age = $(w + x + y + z) = 94$ ....(1)

Today their ages are $(w + 5 + x + y + 5 + a) = 92$

$w + x + y + a = 77$ ....(2)

Subtracting (*ii*) from (*i*)

$\begin{pmatrix} z \to daughter'\ age \\ a \to daughter\ in\ law\ age \end{pmatrix}$

we get $z - a = 15$

136. 1 man, 3 women and 4 boys can do a piece of work is 96 hrs.

$\therefore \qquad \dfrac{1}{M} + \dfrac{3}{W} + \dfrac{4}{B} = \dfrac{1}{96}$ ... (*i*)

2 men and 8 Boys can do it in 80 hrs.

$\therefore \qquad \dfrac{2}{M} + \dfrac{8}{B} = \dfrac{1}{80}$ ... (*ii*)

and 2 men and 3 women can do it in 120 hr.

$\therefore \qquad \dfrac{2}{M} + \dfrac{3}{W} = \dfrac{1}{120}$ ... (*iii*)

Solving equation (*i*), (*ii*) and (*iii*), we get

$$W = 720 \text{ hr,}$$
$$B = 960 \text{ hr}$$

and $\qquad$ M = 480 hr.

$\therefore$ 5 men and 12 boys, one day work

$$= \frac{5}{M} + \frac{12}{B} = \frac{5}{480} + \frac{12}{960}$$

$$= \frac{1}{96} + \frac{12}{960} = \frac{10+12}{960}$$

$$= \frac{22}{960} \text{ hr.}$$

$\therefore$ 5 men and 12 boys will complete the work in $\dfrac{960}{22}$ hr.

$$= \frac{480}{11} \text{ hrs.} = 43\frac{7}{11} \text{ days}$$

Hence option (*c*) is correct.

137.

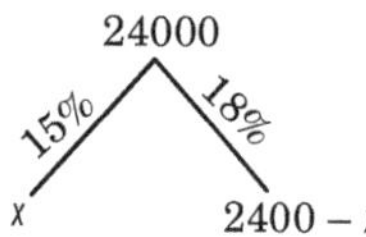

$$\therefore \qquad 4050 = \frac{x \times 15}{100} + \frac{(24000 - x)}{100} 18$$

$$\therefore \qquad 40500 = 15x + 432000 - 18x$$

$$\therefore \qquad 432000 - 405000 = 3x$$

$$27000 = 3x$$

$$\therefore \qquad \boxed{x = 9000}$$

$\therefore$ Amount borrowed at 18% = 24000 − *x*

$$= 24000 - 9000$$
$$= 15000$$

138. For I

$$a^2 + 5a + 6 = 0$$
$$(a + 3)(a + 2) = 0$$
$$\therefore \qquad a = -3 \text{ or } -2.$$

For II

$$b^2 + 3b + 2 = 0$$
$$\therefore \qquad (b + 2)(b + 1) = 0$$
$$\therefore \qquad b = -2 \text{ or } -1$$

Here $a \le b$ relation is established between values of *a* and *b*.

$\therefore$ Option (*e*) is correct.

139. For I

$$2a^2 + 3a + 1 = 0$$
$$\therefore \qquad (a + 1)(2a + 1) = 0$$

$$\therefore \qquad a = -1 \text{ or } a = \frac{-1}{2}$$

For II

$$12b^2 + 7b + 1 = 0$$
$$12b^2 + 4b + 3b + 1 = 0$$
$$\therefore \quad 4b(3b + 1) + 1(3b + 1) = 0$$
$$\therefore \qquad (4b + 1)(3b + 1) = 0$$

$$\therefore \qquad b = \frac{-1}{4} \text{ or } \frac{-1}{3}$$

$$\therefore \qquad a < b$$

Here $a < b$ relation is established between values of *a* and *b*.

$\therefore$ Option (*a*) is correct.

140. For 1

$$a^2 = 4$$
$$\Rightarrow \qquad a = -2 \text{ or } 2.$$

For II

$$b^2 = 9$$
$$\Rightarrow \qquad b = -3 \text{ or } 3$$

$\therefore$ Relation between *a* and *b* cannot be established

$\therefore$ Option (*c*) is correct.

141. For I

$$6a^2 - 25a + 25 = 0$$
$$\therefore \quad 6a^2 - 15a - 10a + 25 = 0$$
$$\therefore \quad 3a(2a - 5) - 5(2a - 5) = 0$$
$$\therefore \qquad (3a - 5)(2a - 5) = 0$$

$$\therefore \qquad a = \frac{5}{3} \text{ or } a = \frac{5}{2}$$

For 2

$$15b^2 - 16b + 4 = 0$$
$$\therefore \quad 15b^2 - 10b - 6b + 4 = 0$$
$$\therefore \quad 5b(3b - 2) - 2(3b - 2) = 0$$
$$\therefore \qquad (5b - 2)(3b - 2) = 0$$

$$\therefore \qquad b = \frac{2}{5}, b = \frac{2}{3}$$

From (1) and (2), $a > b$

$\therefore$ Option (*b*) is correct.

142. For I

$$4a^2 - 20a + 21 = 0$$
$$\therefore \quad 4a^2 - 14a - 6a + 21 = 0$$
$$\therefore \quad 2a(2a - 7) - 3(2a - 7) = 0$$
$$\therefore \quad (2a - 3)(2a - 7) = 0$$
$$\therefore \quad a = \frac{3}{2} \text{ or } a = \frac{7}{2}$$

For II

$$2b^2 - 5b + 3 = 0$$
$$\therefore \quad 2b^2 - 3b - 2b + 3 = 0$$
$$\therefore \quad b(2b - 3) - 1(2b - 3) = 0$$
$$\therefore \quad (b - 1)(2b - 3) = 0$$
$$\therefore \quad b = 1 \text{ or } b = \frac{3}{2}$$

∴ Here $a \geq b$ relation is established between vlaues of a and b.

∴ Option (d) is correct.

143. Total number of student in school R

$$= 2000$$

and total number of student in school S

$$= 2250$$

$$\therefore \quad \text{required percent} = \left[\frac{2000}{2250} \times 100\right]\%$$

$$= 88.88\% \approx 89\%$$

144. 40% are girls in school P

∴ 60% are boys in school P

∴ Number of boys in school P

$$= 60\% \text{ of } 2500$$

$$= \frac{60}{100} \times 2500 = 1500$$

Now,

45% are girls in school Q

∴ 55% are boys in school Q

∴ Number of boys in school Q

$$= 55\% \text{ of } 3000$$

$$= \frac{55}{100} \times 3000$$

$$= 1650$$

∴ Average number of boys in school P and Q together

$$= \frac{1500 + 1650}{2} = 1575$$

145. Number of girls in school P

$$= 40\% \text{ of } 2500$$

$$= \frac{40}{100} \times 2500$$

$$= 1000.$$

and number of girls in school Q

$$= 45\% \text{ of } 3000$$

$$= \frac{45}{100} \times 3000$$

$$= 1350.$$

∴ Ratio of number of girls in school P to the number of girls in school Q

$$= \frac{1000}{1350}$$

$$= \frac{100}{135}$$

$$= \frac{20}{27}$$

∴ Option (c) is correct.

146. The given series is 3, 19, 103, 439, 1381, 2887.

The given series follow the following pattern

$$3 \times 6 + (1)^3 = 19$$
$$19 \times 5 + (2)^3 = 103$$
$$103 \times 4 + (3)^3 = 439$$
$$439 \times 3 + (4)^3 = 1381$$
$$2887 \times 2 + (5)^3 = 2887$$

Similarly,

$$5 \times 6 + (1)^3 = 31$$
$$31 \times 5 + (2)^3 = 163$$
$$163 \times 4 + (3)^3 = 679$$
$$679 \times 3 + (4)^3 = 2101$$
$$2101 \times 2 + (5)^3 = 4327$$

Hence the series is 5, 31, 163, 679, 2101, 4327.

Hence 163 will come in place of (b)

∴ Option (b) is correct.

147. The given series is

4, 13, 40, 135, 552, 2765

$$4 \times 1 + 1 \times 9 = 13$$
$$13 \times 2 + 2 \times 7 = 40$$
$$40 \times 3 + 3 \times 5 = 135$$
$$135 \times 4 + 4 \times 3 = 552$$
$$552 \times 5 + 5 \times 1 = 2765$$

Similarly,

$$2 \times 1 + 1 \times 9 = 11 \text{ will come in place of } (a)$$
$$11 \times 2 + 2 \times 7 = 36 \text{ will come in place of } (b)$$
$$36 \times 3 + 3 \times 5 = 123 \text{ will come in place of } (c)$$

Hence, option (a) is correct.

148. The given series is

5, 12, 4, 10, 3, 8

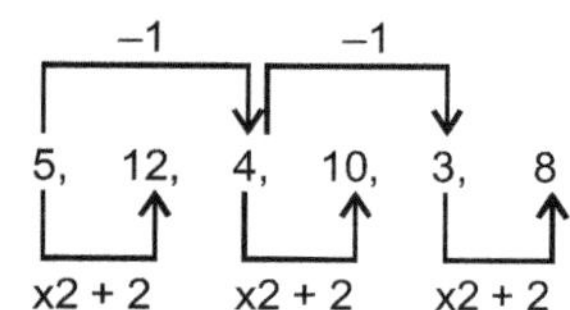

Similarly,

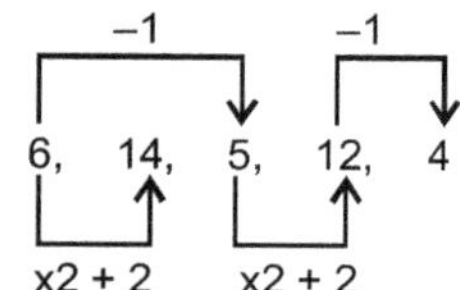

Hence 4 will come in place of (d)

∴ Option (c) is correct.

149. Let speed of B be x km/hr

then, speed of A $= \dfrac{140\,x}{100}$ km/hr $= \dfrac{7x}{5}$ km/hr

relative speed $= x + \dfrac{7x}{5} = \dfrac{2x}{3}$ m/s

time taken to cross each other $= \dfrac{(100 + 180) \times 3}{2x}$

$$6 = \dfrac{420}{x}$$

∴ $\quad x = 70$ m/hrs

150. Total student $= 60$

Let x be number of boys,

then $(60 - x)$ will be number of girls.

Now, **from statement - 1**

Average weight of all 60 student is 42 kg

∴ Total weight of 60 student

$$= 60 \times 42$$
$$= 2520 \text{ kg}$$

From statement - 2

Average weight of boys = 43 kg

∴ Total weight of boys $= (43 \times x)$ kg

$$= 43x \text{ kg}$$

From statement - 3

Total weight of girls $= 1144$ kg.

∴ From all the three statement

$$43x + 1144 = 2520$$
∴ $\qquad 43x = 1376$
∴ $\qquad x = 32$

Hence, number of girls $= 60 - x$

$$= 60 - 32 = 28$$

∴ Average weight of girls in the class

$$= \dfrac{1144}{28} = 40.85$$

Hence all the three statement are required to give the answer

∴ Option (b) is correct.

∎∎

2014

QUANTITATIVE APTITUDE

1. From a container of milk, 5 litres of milk is replaced with 5 litres of water. This process is repeated again.Thus in two attempts the ratio of milk and water became 81 : 19. The initial amount of milk in the container was

   (1) 50 litres   (2) 45 litres

   (3) 40 litres   (4) 25 litres

   (5) None of these

2. A bag A contains 4 green and 6 red balls. Another bag B contains 3 green and 4 red balls. If one ball is drawn from each bag. find the probability that both are green.

   (1) $\dfrac{13}{70}$ (2) $\dfrac{1}{4}$

   (3) $\dfrac{6}{35}$ (4) $\dfrac{8}{35}$

   (5) None of these

3. The sum of the radius and height of a cylinder is 42 cm. Its total surface area is 3696 cm^2. What is the volume of cylinder ?

   (1) 17428 cubic cm

   (2) 17248 cubic cm

   (3) 17244 cubic cm

   (4) 17444 cubic cm

   (5) None of these

Directions (4-8) : *Study the pie-charts given below carefully and answer the questions.*

Percentagewise Distribution of laptops (Dell & Lenovo) sold by six stores A, B, C, D, E and F in March 2014.

Total Number of Laptops (Dell & Lenovo) sold = 48000

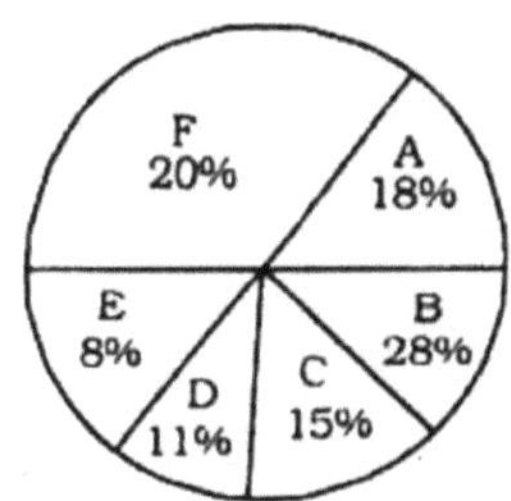

Number of Dell Laptops sold = 28000
Percentage of Dell Laptops sold

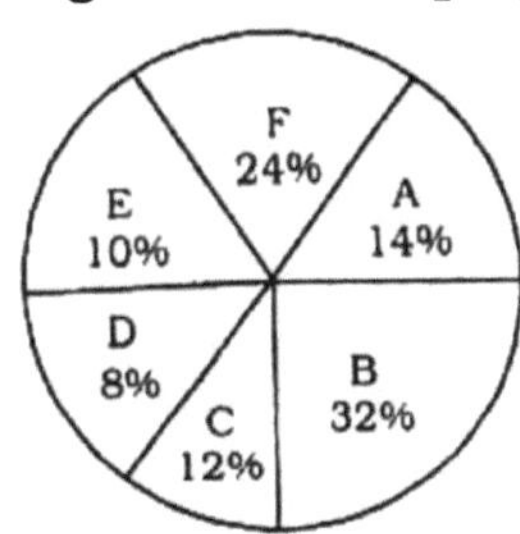

4. The number of laptops of both types sold by stores A and C is more than that sold by stores E and F by

   (1) 2500   (2) 2600

   (3) 2000   (4) 2400

   (5) None of these

5. What is the ratio between the number of Dell and Lenovo laptops sold by store A ?

   (1) 49 : 59   (2) 47 : 49

   (3) 49 : 53   (4) 49 : 47

   (5) None of these

6. What is the respective ratio between the average number of Dell laptops sold by stores A, C and E and that sold by stores B, D and F ?

   (1) 3:4   (2) 4:9

   (3) 9: 16   (4) 5: 12

   (5) None of these

7. By what per cent is the number of Lenovo laptops sold by store B is more than that of Dell laptops sold by store E ?

   (1) 40%   (2) 60%

   (3) 55%   (4) 45%

   (5) None of these

8. What will be the central angle corresponding to number of laptops of both kinds sold by stores C and F ?

   (1) 126°   (2) 115°

   (3) 90°   (4) 80°

   (5) 120°

Directions (Q. 9-13) : *Study the following table carefully and answer the questions that follow :*

Description of Literate and Illiterate population of six villages

Villages	Percentage of Literate population	Male : Female	Ratio of Literate Males and Females
A	48%	7 : 5	13:7
B	60%	8 : 7	3:5
C	72%	4 : 5	3 : 4
D	60%	5 : 4	6:5
E	50%	7 : 3	14 : 11
F	64%	5 : 3	7 : 5

9. The number of literate women in village B is 39760 and that of Illiterate women in village C is 25600. By what per cent is the population of village B less than that of village C ?

  (1) 11.25%   (2) 13.25%

  (3) 14.25%   (4) 9.75%

  (5) None of these

10. If the population of village F is 168000, what is the number of literate males ?

  (1) 67200   (2) 68200

  (3) 86200   (4) 76200

  (5) None of these

11. If the number of literate women in village D is 32200, what is the number of illiterate population in the same village?

  (1) 48500   (2) 48300

  (3) 46300   (4) 46500

  (5) None of these

12. If the number of literate males in village A be 35840 the number of illiterate males in the same village is

  (1) 43224   (2) 43284

  (3) 43264   (4) 45264

  (5) None of these

13. If the illiterate female population of village E be 77000, What is the total population of that village?

  (1) 350000   (2) 360000

  (3) 400000   (4) 320000

  (5) None of these

14. Three typists P, Q and R have to type 368 pages. P types one page in 8 minutes, Q in 18 minutes and R in 24 minutes. In what time will these pages be typed if they work together?

  (1) 25 hours   (2) 27.6 hours

  (3) 27 hours   (4) 28 hours

  (4) None of these

15. The distance between two points is 36 km. A boat rows in still water at 6 kmph. It takes 8 hours less to cover this distance in downstream in comparison to that in upstream. The rate of stream is

  (1) 3 kmph

  (2) 2 kmph

  (3) 2.5 kmph

  (4) 4 kmph

  (5) None of these

Directions (Q. 16-20) : *In each of the following questions, two equations I and II have been given. Solve these questions and answer*

(1) if $x < y$

(2) if $x \le y$

(3) if $x = y$ or the relation cannot be established

(4) if $x \ge y$

16. I. $30x^2 + 11x + 1 = 0$

    II. $42y^2 + 13y + 1 = 0$

17. I. $x^2 - x - \sqrt{2}x + \sqrt{2} = 0$

    II. $y^2 - 3y + 2 = 0$

18. I. $x^2 - 2x - \sqrt{5}x + 2\sqrt{5} = 0$

    II. $y^2 - \sqrt{3}y - \sqrt{2}y + \sqrt{6} = 0$

19. I. $x^2 + 12x + 36 = 0$

    II. $y^2 = 16$

20. I. $9x^2 + 3x - 2 = 0$

    II. $8y^2 + 6y + 1 = 0$

Directions (Q. 21-25) : *Each of the questions given below consists of a question and two statements numbered I and II given below it. You have to decide whether the data provided in the statements is sufficient to answer the question. Read both the statements.*

Give answer

(1) if the data in statement I alone is sufficient to answer the question, while the data in statement II alone is not sufficient to answer the question.

(2) if the data in statement II alone is sufficient to answer the question, while the data in statement I alone is not sufficient to answer the question.

(3) if the data in statement I alone or in statement II alone is sufficient to answer the question.

(4) if the data in both the statements I and II is not sufficient to answer the question.

(5) if the data in both the statements I and II together is necessary to answer the question.

21. What is the annual salary of Mr. X.

    I.   The ratio of monthly salaries of X and Y is 9 : 7.

    II. The monthly salary of X is more than that of Y by Rs. 16000.

22. What is the cost price of article?

    I.   A man earns a profit of 20% on selling the article.

    II. The selling price of article is ₹ 5016

23. What will be the total cost of fencing a rectangular plot ?

    I.   The area of plot is 1134 sq. metre. The length of plot is 15 metre more than its breadth.

    II. The cost of fencing is Rs. 180 per metre.

24. How many marks did Subodh obtain in Physics?

    I.   The average marks of Subodh in History, Geography and Chemistry are 75.

    II. His average marks in History, Geography and Physics are 78.

25. What is the population of the city A?

    I.   The ratio of the population of males and females in city A is 27 : 23 and the difference between their population is 100000.

    II. The population of city A is 80% of that of city B. The difference of population of city A and city B is 312500.

Directions (Q. 26-30) : *In the following number series, a wrong number is given. Identify the wrong number that does not follow the given pattern.*

26. 3 10 33 111 349 1072 3252

    (1) 33   (2) 111

    (3) 349   (4) 1072

    (5) 10

27. 1 2 12 63 316 1704 10446

    (1) 63   (2) 1704

    (3) 316   (4) 10446

    (5) 2

28. 2 6 24 96 285 568 567

    (1) 6   (2) 96

    (3) 24   (4) 568

    (5) 567

29. 15 28 43 60 79 101 123

    (1) 28   (2) 43

    (3) 60   (4) 101

    (5) 123

30. 9 10 18 45 109 235 450

    (1) 10   (2) 9

    (3) 18   (4) 109

    (5) 235

Directions (Q. 31-35) : *Study the following information carefully and answer the questions given below :*

In a certain code language, 'economy receiving very fast' is written as 'va jo ni pa'.

'very essence of economy' is written as 'su pa lo jo'.

'fast money in banks' is written as 'gy bt ks va'.

'of banks in industry' is written as 'ks dm bt su'.

31. What does 'su' stand for ?

    (1) economy

    (2) banks

    (3) of

    (4) Cannot be determined

    (5) None of these

32. What would be the code for 'essence'?

    (1) lo   (2) pa

    (3) ni   (4) jo

    (5) va

33. What would be the code for 'essence of money' ?

    (1) lo pa su   (2) su gy jo

    (3) bt va gy   (4) gy lo su

    (5) Cannot be determined

34. What would be the code for 'economy in industry'?

    (1) jo bt dm

    (2) dm ks pa

    (3) pa ks dm

    (4) pa bt dm

    (5) Cannot be determined

35. What is the code for 'fast' in that code ?

    (1) va   (2) gy

    (3) ni   (4) jo

    (5) lo

Directions (Q. 36-40) : *Study the following information carefully to answer the questions given below:*

A building has seven floors numbered one to seven, in such a way that the ground floor is numbered one, the floor above it, number two and so on such that the topmost floor is numbered seven. One of the seven people, viz. A, B, C, D, E, F and G lives on each floor. A lives on fourth floor. C lives on the floor immediately below B's floor. Two people live between the floors of D and G. One people lives between the floors of G and A. Four people live between the floors of C and F.

36. Who among the following lives on the topmost floor?

(1) F   (2) B

(3) G   (4) D

(5) E

37. Who among the following lives immediately above D's floor?

(1) G   (2) E

(3) F   (4) A

(5) C

38. Four of the following five are alike in a certain way and hence form a group. Which one of the following does not belong to that group?

(1) B   (2) D

(3) G   (4) E

(5) F

39. Who among the following lives on third numbered floor?

(1) E   (2) F

(3) G   (4) C

(5) D

40. Who among the following lives exactly between the floors of E and F?

(1) C   (2) A

(3) D   (4) G

(5) None

Directions (Q. 41-45) : *Study the following information carefully and answer the questions given below :*

A word and number arrangement machine when given an input line of words and numbers rearranges them following a particular rule in each step. The following is an illustration of input and various steps of rearrangement. (All the numbers are two digit numbers) .

Input :   10 sea 25 57 41 rose giraffe 85 hot 32 lost 77 99 beard cost palm

Step I :   10 beard 25 57 41 rose giraffe 85 hot 32 lost 77 cost palm sea 99

Step D :   10 25 beard cost 57 41 giraffe hot 32 lost 77 palm rose sea 85 99

Step III :   10 25 32 beard cost giraffe 57 41 hot lost palm rose sea 77 85 99

Step IV :   10 25 32 41 beard cost giraffe hot lost palm rose sea 57 77 85 99

And Step IV is the last step of the rearrangement as the desired arrangement is obtained. As per rules followed in the above steps, find out in each of the questions the appropriate step for the given input.

Input :   31 11 win arm blanket zebra 24 81 chip team slip 62 55 dawn 91 78

41. Which of the following represents the position of "slip" in the Step III?

(1) Ninth from right   (2) Eighth from left

(3) Eighth from right   (4) Seventh from left

(5) Sixth from left

42. How many elements (words/ numbers) are there between "dawn" and "81" as they appear in Step IV?

(1) Five   (2) Six

(3) Seven   (4) Four

(5) Eight

43. Which element (word/number) would be at the ninth position from the left in the Step II?

(1) 62   (2) slip

(3) 55   (4) team

(5) dawn

44. At which of the following position "dawn" would appear from the right in the Step III?

(1) Tenth

(2) Ninth

(3) Seventh

(4) Fifth

(5) Eighth

45. Which word/number would be third to the left of the sixth element from the right in the Step III?

(1) dawn   (2) 55

(3) chip   (4) slip

(5) 62

Directions (Q. 46-50) : *In these questions, relationship between different elements is shown in the statements.*

The statements are followed by two conclusions.

Give answer

(1) if only Conclusion I is true.

(2) if only Conclusion II is true.

(3) if either Conclusion I or II is true.

(4) if neither Conclusion I nor II is true.

(5) if both Conclusions I and II are true.

46. Statement :

$V = I \le T < A = L \ge Z > E$

Conclusions :

I.   A > E   II.   L > V

(Q. 47-48) :

Statements :

P ≥ H = J ≥ R; H ≤ I < T

47. Conclusions:

I. J > T   II. P ≥ T

48. Conclusions:

I. R < T   II. T > H

(Q. 49-50) :

Statements :

C ≥ H < M < R = A ; Z ≥ M ≥ Y

49. Conclusions :

I. Z ≥ C   II. Y < A

50. Conclusions :

I. Y ≥ C   II. Z > A

Directions (Q. 51-56) : *In each question below are three statements followed by two conclusions numbered I and II. You have to take the given statements to be true even if they seem to be at variance from commonly known facts and then decide which of the given conclusions logically follows from the given statements disregarding commonly known facts.*

Give answer

(1) if only conclusion I follows.

(2) if only conclusion II follows.

(3) if either conclusion I or II follows.

(4) if neither conclusion I or II follows.

(5) if both conclusions I and II follow.

(Q. 51-52) :

Statements :

All triangles are squares.

No square is rectangle.

Some rectangles are cones.

51. Conclusions:

I. Some cones are rectangles.

II. All cones are rectangles.

52. Conclusions:

I. No triangle is rectangle.

II. Some cones being triangles is a possibility.

(Q. 53-54) :

Statements :

No aim is vision.

All visions are objectives.

No objective is goal.

53. Conclusions:

I. All goals being aim is a possibility.

II. All aims being objective is a possibility.

54. Conclusions:

I. No goal is vision.

II. All objectives are visions.

(Q. 55-56) :

Statements :

All years are ages.

Some years are eras.

All eras are distances.

55. Conclusions:

I. At least some distances are ages.

II. Some eras are definitely not years.

56. Conclusions:

I. At least some eras are ages.

II. All distances being years is a possibility.

Directions (Q. 57-64) : *Study the following information carefully and answer the questions given below :*

Eight persons - A, B, C, D, E, F, G and H - are sitting around a circular table facing the centre. Each one of them has a different profession viz.. Doctor, Lawyer, Painter, Librarian, Architect, Engineer, Teacher and Accountant, but not necessarily in the same order.

A sits third to the right of F. Only one person sits between A and C. Accountant is sitting third to the right of C. Accountant is sitting to the immediate left of Engineer. B is sitting to the immediate left of H. Three persons sit between B and Architect. D is an immediate neighbour of G. D is neither an Engineer nor an Architect. Only one person sits beween Librarian and Architect. Painter is to the immediate left of Teacher. D is not a Doctor. G is neither a Librarian nor a Lawyer. Lawyer is an immediate neighbour of Architect.

57. What is the profession of D ?

(1) Teacher

(2) Architect

(3) Painter

(4) Engineer

(5) Accountant

58. Who amongst the following is a Doctor ?

(1) C   (2) B

(3) G   (4) A

(5) H

59. What is the position of Lawyer with respect to G?

(1) Third to the left

(2) Third to the right

(3) Fourth to the left

(4) Fourth to the right

(5) Second to the right

60. Who sit(s) exactly between the Engineer and Teacher ?

(1) Architect and E

(2) Doctor and Librarian

(3) Painter and H

(4) Accountant

(5) C and Doctor

61. Which of the following is **Not True** with respect to the given seating arrangement ?

(1) E is an immediate neighbour of Librarian

(2) G is a Doctor

(3) Accountant is an immediate neighbour of Teacher

(4) Lawyer sits third to the left of G

(5) Doctor is sitting exactly between B and A

62. Starting from A, if all the persons are made to sit in the alphabetical order in anticlockwise direction, the position of how many (excluding A) will remain unchanged?

(1) Three　　　　(2) Two

(3) One　　　　(4) Five

(5) Four

63. Four of the following five are alike in a certain way based on the above seating arrangement and hence form a group. Which one of the following **does not** belong to that group?

(1) AC　　　　(2) DH

(3) GE　　　　(4) EF

(5) BC

64. Who among the following is third to the left of Librarian?

(1) Engineer　　　　(2) Teacher

(3) Painter　　　　(4) Accountant

(5) Architect

Directions (Q. 65-71): *Study the following information carefully and answer the questions given below :*

Eight persons are sitting in two parallel rows containing four persons each, in such a way that there is an equal distance between adjacent persons. In row-1, P, Q, R and S are seated and all of them are facing south. In row-2, A, B, C and D are seated and all of them are facing north. Therefore, in the given seating arrangement each person seated in a row faces another person of the other row. Each of them belongs to different places, viz., Delhi. Jaipur, Patna, Pune, Mumbai, Chennai, Shillong and Surat, but not necessarily in the same order.

The person from Delhi is second to the right of the person who faces C. The immediate neighbour of person from Delhi faces the person from Patna. Only one person sits between person from Patna and B. One who faces B is second to the left of P. One who is immediate neighbour of B faces person from Jaipur. A person facing the person from Jaipur is second to the right of the person from Pune. There is only one person between the person from Jaipur and S. R faces the person from Surat. R is neither from Jaipur nor Mumbai. The person who is immediate neighbour of D is from Shillong. D is not an immediate neighbour of B.

65. Who among the following belongs to Jaipur ?

(1) S　　　　　　(2) D

(3) B　　　　　　(4) Q

(5) R

66. Who amongst the following faces S ?

(1) C　　　　　　(2) A

(3) B　　　　　　(4) D

(5) Cannot be determined

67. Which of the following pairs of persons is seated at the at extreme ends in any of the two rows?

(1) SQ　　　　　　(2) PR

(3) AC　　　　　　(4) BD

(5) RS

68. Which of the following statements is not true regarding R?

(1) R is at the extreme right end of the row

(2) R faces the person from Surat

(3) R is second to the left of P.

(4) There are two persons between R and S

(5) R is an immediate neighbour of Q

69. Four of the following five are alike in a certain way based on the above seating arrangement and hence they form a group. Which one of the following **does not** belong to that group?

(1) R　　　　　　(2) S

(3) C　　　　　　(4) A

(5) B

70. Which of the following combinations of person and place is not true ?

   (1) P — Mumbai   (2) R — Delhi

   (3) D — Patna   (4) B — Surat

   (5) C — Shillong

71. Who amongst the following belongs to Pune ?

   (1) S   (2) Q

   (3) R   (4) A

   (5) B

Directions (Q. 72-74) : *Study the following information carefully and answer the questions given below :*

Among the six persons - P, Q, R, S, T and U - each has different weight. P is heavier than three persons. R is lighter than T. S is lighter than only Q. R is not the lightest. The second heaviest person is of 68 kg and the second lightest person is of 35 kg.

72. Which of the following represents the descending order of weights of the six persons?

   (1) S, Q, P, T, R, U   (2) Q, S, P, U, T, R

   (3) Q, S, P, T, R, U   (4) Q, S, P, T, U, R

   (5) S, Q, P, U, R, T

73. Who among the following is heavier than only U?

   (1) R   (2) P

   (3) T   (4) S

   (5) Q

74. Who among the following may weigh 67 kg?

   (1) Q   (2) P

   (3) T   (4) S

   (5) Can not be determined

Directions (Q. 75-77) : *Study the following Information carefully and answer the questions given below :*

In a certain code language 'work is important today' is written as 'tx ne zu ka'

'is work there now' is written as 'ne ht ka mu'

'work for joy only' is written as 'oj un ft ne'

'for money only joy' is written as 'oj ft ds un'

75. What is the code for 'money'?

   (1) ds   (2) un

   (3) oj   (4) ft

   (5) ft or ds

76. Which of the following may represent 'money is important today'?

   (1) ne ds zu ft   (2) tx oj ka ne

   (3) zu ds ka tx   (4) ht ds ka mu

   (5) ka tx un oj

77. Which of the following may represent 'now there is work'?

   (1) mu ka tx zu   (2) ht ne ds ft

   (3) ht ft oj un   (4) ka ht zu ft

   (5) ne mu ka ht

Directions (Q. 78-80) : *Each of the questions below consists of a question and two statements numbered I and II given below it. You have to decide whether the data provided in the statements are sufficient to answer the question. Read both the statements and—*

Give answer

(1) if the data in Statement I alone are sufficient to answer the question, while the data in Statement II alone are not sufficient to answer the question.

(2) if the data in Statement II alone are sufficient to answer the question, while the data in Statement I alone are not sufficient to answer the question.

(3) if the data either in Statement I alone or in Statement II alone are sufficient to answer the question.

(4) if the data even in both Statements I and II together are not sufficient to answer the question.

(5) if the data in both Statements I and II together are necessary to answer the question.

78. Seven different exams - P, Q, R, S, T, U and V - are conducted on different days of the same week, i.e., from Monday to Sunday. Which exam was conducted on Wednesday?

   I. Two exams were conducted after exam P. Exam Q took place immediately after exam U. Exam Q was not conducted on Sunday or on Thursday. Exam T was not conducted immediately after exam P.

   II. Three exams were conducted before exam R. Exam S was conducted after exam P but before exam V. Exam Q was conducted after exam U and before exam T. Exam P was not conducted on Monday.

79. What is the position O among 20 persons standing in a straight line ?

   I. There are five persons between Y and L. L is at one of the extreme ends. T is sixth to the left of Y. There are three persons between O and T.

   II. R is at one of the extreme ends of the line. There are two persons between O and J. There are nine persons between R and U. J is fourth to the left of U.

80. How is 'X' related to 'R' ?

I. The brother of 'X' is married to 'D'. The father-in-law of D is the grandfather of R. R is the only daughter of D. X is brother-in-law of D.

II. R is the only daughter of P. D is the daughter-in-law of M. P and X are two sons of M. X is not married to D.

Directions (Q. 81-85) : *Study the following information carefully and answer the questions given below :*

'P © Q' means 'Q is the brother of P'.

'P # Q' means 'P is the daughter of Q'.

'P = Q' means 'Q is the sister of P'

'P £ Q' means 'P is the son of Q'

'P ★ Q' means 'P is the father of Q'.

'P @ Q' means 'P is the mother of Q'.

81. What does the expression 'P @ R = S © T £ V' ?

(1) V is the husband of P

(2) R is the son of V

(3) R is the daughter of V

(4) V is the wife of P

(5) None of these

82. Which of the following indicates that 'C is the paternal uncle of D'?

(1) C £ V # N @ L © D

(2) C £ V £ L @ N © D

(3) D £ L £ N @ V © C

(4) D £ N # V @ L © C

(5) None of these

83. Which of the following can be the correct conclusion drawn from the expression

'L = M # N © P ★ Q' ?

(1) Q is the grandson of M

(2) L is the uncle of N

(3) N is the uncle of Q

(4) Q is the niece of N

(5) None of these

84. Which of the following can be correct conclusion drawn from the expression

'Q £ N @ S © M = P' ?

(1) S is the brother of P

(2) N has two sons and two daughters

(3) S is the sister of Q

(4) P is the sister of Q

(5) None of these

85. Which of the following indicates that 'Q is the daughter of N' ?

(1) Q ★ P # C @ N @ V

(2) N ★ P # C @ Q @ V

(3) M @ N # R ★ Q

(4) M © Q = V # N

(5) None of these

86. Expert A says that dinosaurs became extinct due to climatic changes occurred on the Earth due to volcanic eruptions some 65 million years ago. Expert B does not agree with the volcanic eruption theory. According to him dinosaurs became extinct due to the impact of asteroid.

Which of the following statements may provide support to the theory propounded by Expert B?

A. The frigid and sweltering climatic extremes caused the extinction of dinosaurs.

B. A wide crater lying just off the Yucatan peninsula was created due to the impact of asteroid.

C. Scientists have discovered levels of iridium 30 times greater than average in the Cretaceous/Tertiary boundary, the layer of sedimentary rock laid down at the time of the dinosaur extinction.

D. Some palaeontologists after analysing the fossil record believe that dinosaurs were doing quite well prior to the end of Cretaceous, when the dinosaurs became extinct.

(1) Only (A)   (2) Only (A) and (C)

(3) Only (C) and (D)   (4) Only (A) and (B)

(5) Only (B), (C) and (D)

Directions (Q. 87) : *In making decisions about important questions, it is desirable to be able to distinguish between 'strong' arguments and 'weak' arguments so far as they relate to the question. 'Strong' arguments are those which are both important and directly related to the questions. 'Weak' arguments are those which are of minor importance and also may not be directly related to the questions or may be related to a trivial aspect of the question.*

The question below is followed by two arguments numbered I and II. You have to decide which of the arguments is a 'strong' argument and which is a 'weak' argument.

Give answer

(1) if only argument I is strong

(2) if only argument II is strong

(3) if either I or II is strong.

(4) if neither I nor II strong.

(5) if both I and II are strong.

87. Should all the power generation and distribution units in the State Y be handed over to the private sector ?

Arguments :

I. Yes, the State Government are not equipped to handle generation and distribution of electricity efficiently and it is not beneficial too.

II. Yes, The private companies handle generation and distribution of electricity efficiently.

Directions (Q. 88-90) : Below in each question are given two statements (A) and (B). These statements may be either independent causes or may be effects of independent causes or a common cause. One of these statements may be the effect of the other statement. Read both the statements and decide which of the following answer choice correctly depicts the relationship between these two statements.

Mark answer

(1) if statement (A) is the cause and statement (B) is its effect.

(2) if statement (B) is the cause and statement (A) is its effect.

(3) if both the statements (A) and (B) are independent causes.

(4) if both the statements (A) and (B) are effects of independent causes.

(5) if both the statements (A) and (B) are effects of some common cause.

88. (A) Company A sales shampoo in urban areas. It has launched small sachets for penetration into the rural areas.

   (B) Company A wants to expand its business to rural areas as rural people cannot afford larger packets.

89. (A) Railway Minister has increased fare by 14 per cent but he has slashed the fare of second class.

   (B) Second class travellers have sent letters to the Railway Ministry for rolling back the hike in fare.

90. (A) Lung cancer is the most hazardous disease in India. It is not necessarily caused due to smoking rather passive smoking is more dangerous.

   (B) Government has banned smoking in public and it has been made a punishable offence.

ENGLISH LANGUAGE

Directions (Q. 1-10) : *Read the following passage carefully and answer the questions based on it. Some words have been printed in **bold** to help you locate them while answering some of the questions.*

Gross Domestic Savings (GDS) play a vital role in the economic growth of a country since it facilitates to provide requisite financial resources to undertake various developmental and welfare programs. A high level of savings helps the economy to progress on a continuous growth path as investment is mainly financed out of savings. GDS is one of the important economic indicators to measure financial regulation and soundness of the country. Absence of required savings rate may lead to external dependence, which may **jeopardize** the interests of the Nation.

Savings habit is an in-built culture of the Indian system and it has been growing consistently over the years. The GDS percentage to GDP has shown considerable improvement from 10% in 1950 to 33.70% in 2010. which is one of the highest globally. It is interesting to note that while the share of corporate sector increased from 10% to 24% during 1950 to 2010. the share of public sector has come down to 6% from 18% during the said period. The buoyancy of corporate sector in post reform era could be one of the reasons for increased share of cor-porates in GDS. While there is increasing trend in saving rate, marginal decline is observed under household sector i.e. 72% to 70%.

Notwithstanding the fact that the share of household savings to GDS is showing decline, still this segment is the significant contributor to GDS with 70% share. Indian households are among the most frugal in the world. However, **commensurate** capital formation has not been taking place as a lion's share of household savings are being parked in physical assets compared to financial assets.

The pattern of disposition of saving is an important factor in determining how the saved amount is utilized for productive purposes. The proportion of household saving in financial assets determines the channelisation of saving for investment in other sectors of the economy. However, the volume of Investment of saving in physical assets determines the productivity and generation of income in that sector itself.

Post-Independence era has witnessed a significant shift in deployment of household savings especially the share of financial assets increased from 26.39% in 1950 to 54.05% in 1990 may be on account of increased bank branch network across the country coupled with improved awareness of investors on various financial/banking products. However, contrast to common expectations, the share of financial assets in total household savings has come down from 54.05% to 50.21% especially in post reform period i.e. 1990 to 2010 despite providing easy access and availability of banking facilities compared to earlier years. The increased share of physical assets over financial assets (around 4%) during the last two decades is a cause of concern requires focused attention to arrest the trend.

Traditionally, the Indians are risk-averse and prefer to invest surplus funds in physical assets such as Gold, Silver and lands. Nevertheless, considerable share of savings also flowing to financial assets, which includes, Currency, Bank Deposits, Claims on Government, **Contractual** Savings, Equities.

The composition of household financial savings shows that the bank deposits (44%) continue to remain the major contributor along with the rise in the Contractual Savings. Claims on Government and Currency.

Though there was gradual decline in currency holdings by the households i.e. 13.79% in 1970s to 9.30% in 2007, still the present currency holding level with households appears to be on high side compared to other countries. The primary reasons for higher currency holdings could be absence of banking facilities in majority villages (5.70 lakh villages) as well as hoarding of unaccounted money in the form of cash to circumvent tax laws. Though, cash is treated as financial asset, in reality, a major portion of currency is blocked and become unproductive.

Bank deposits seemed to be the preferred choice mainly on account of its inbuilt features such as Safety, Security and Liquidity. Traditionally, the Household sector has been playing a leading role in the landscape of bank deposits followed by the Government sector. However, the last two decades has witnessed significant shift in ownership of Bank deposits. While there was improvement in Corporate and Government sectors' share by 8.30% and 7.20% respectively during the period 1999 to 2009, household sector lost a share of 13.30% in the post reform period.

In the post independence era, Indian financial system was characterized by poor infrastructure and low level of financial deepening. Savings in physical assets constituted the largest portion of the savings compared to the financial assets in the initial years of the planning periods. While rural households were keen on acquiring farm assets, the portfolio of urban households constituted consumer durables, gold, Jewellery and house property.

Despite the fact that the household savings have been gradually moving from physical assets to financial assets over the years, still **49.79%** of household savings are wrapped in unproductive physical assets, which is a cause of concern as the share of physical assets to total savings are very high in the recent years compared to emerging economies. This trend needs to be arrested as scarce funds are being diverted into unproductive segments.

Of course, investment in Real estate sector can be treated as productive provided construction activity is commenced within reasonable time, but it is regrettably note that many investors just buy and hold it for speculation leading to unproductive investments.

India has probably the largest fascination with gold than any other country in the world with a share of 9.50% of the world's total gold holdings. The World Gold Council believes that they are over 18000 tonnes of gold holding in the country. More impressive is the fact that current demand from India alone consumes 25% of the world's annual gold output. Large amount of capital is blocked in gold which resides in bank lockers and remain unproductive.

Indian economy would grow faster if the capital markets could attract more of the nation's savings and channel them into more productive areas, especially infrastructure. If the Indian market can develop and evolve into a more mature financial system, which persuades the middle class to put more of its money into equities, the potential is **mind-boggling**.

1. Which of the following statement(s) is/are correct in the context of the given passage?

    I. The GDS percentage to GDP has shown considerable improvement from 10% in 1950 to 33.7% in 2010. which is one of the highest globally.

    II. The saving rate however shows an increasing trend, marginal decline is observed under household sector.

    III. The share of financial assets in total household savings have come down from 54.05% to 50.21% especially in post reform era.

    (1) Only I

    (2) Only I and II

    (3) Only II and III

    (4) All I, II and III

    (5) None of these

2. Post independence era has witnessed a significant shift in deployment of household savings especially the share of financial assets increased to 54.05% in 1990. Which of the following is/are supposed to be the prime cause of this shift?

(1) It is due to bank branch network across the country.

(2) Government has made arrangements to aware the people.

(3) It is due to increase in bank branch network and awareness among investors on various banking products.

(4) Indian economy is growing at 8% and people are saving more than earlier

(5) None of these

3. India has probably the largest fascination with gold than any other country in the world. Which of the following is incorrect in regard to this fascination as mentioned in the passage?

(1) India shares 9.50% of the total gold holdings

(2) According to the World Gold Council estimates, there are over 18000 tonnes of gold holding in India

(3) The current demand from India alone consumes 25% of the world's annual gold output.

(4) A small amount of capital is blocked in gold in banks but is however productive.

(5) None of these

4. Which of the following are the primary reasons, cited in the passage, for higher currency holdings?

(1) It is due to large banking network that stashes money.

(2) It is due to absence of banking facilities in majority of villages and tendency to circumvent tax laws for unaccounted money.

(3) People do not believe in banks and fear that government may take their money.

(4) There is lack of awareness among people about savings in banks

(5) None of these

5. Despite the fact that the household savings have been gradually moving from physical assets to financial assets over the years. What percentage of household savings is wrapped in unproductive physical assets?

(1) 45%   (2) 46.79%

(3) 58%   (4) 49.79%

(5) None of these

6. Which of the following should be a suitable title

of the passage?

(1) Importance of Gross Domestic Savings

(2) Growth of Indian economy

(3) Fascination for Gold

(4) Physical assets versus financial assets

(5) None of these

Directions (Q. 7-8) : *Choose the word/group of words which is* ***most nearly the same*** *in meaning to the word/group of words printed in bold.*

7. Contractual

(1) promising   (2) agreeing

(3) promissory   (4) agreeable

(5) concord

8. Commensurate

(1) matching   (2) commesal

(3) commemorative   (4) unmatching

(5) comfortable

Directions (Q. 9-10) : *Choose the word(s) which is most opposite in meaning of the word printed in bold, as used in the passage.*

9. Jeopardize

(1) severe   (2) endanger

(3) saddle   (4) safeguard

(5) saturate

10. Mind-boggling

(1) conscious   (2) inclined

(3) very difficult   (4) surprising

(5) unsurprising

Directions (Q. 11-15) : *In the following questions, a passage is given with a blank space in the beginning. Three statements are given following the passage. You are required to select which of the statement(s) may be the starter?*

11. ___ it is so pleasant a profession that it is not surprising if a vast number of persons adopt it who have no qualifications for it. The writer is free to work in what he believes.

A. I am a writer

B. I am a writer as I might have been a doctor or a lawyer.

C. I was a writer as I might have been a doctor.

(1) Only A

(2) Only B

(3) Only C

(4) Both A and B

(5) Both B and C

12. ___ it grew faster in year 2010. The conditions

were favourable which helped in economic boom. The agriculture, tourism, export and mining helped in the growth of the economy.

A. Indian economy is not growing well.

B. The Indian economy grew fast at 10 per cent in 2008.

C. Due to economic reforms, economic growth of India was 8 per cent in 2009.

(1) Only A

(2) Only B

(3) Only C

(4) Both A and B

(5) Both B and C

13. ___ So, Anti Corruption campaign occupied centre stage during election season. Corruption prevailing in the high and mighty adversely impacts our nation, and its global image.

A. Corruption is a big evil in India.

B. Corruption is not a big evil in India as propagated.

C. Anti corruption is a big challenge in India.

(1) Only A

(2) Only B

(3) Only C

(4) Both A & B

(3) Both B & C

14. Roads are unsafe because of shortcomings in road and traffic engineer, old and non standard codes of traffic control devices, poor driver training and assessment, out dated legislations and a poor enforcement system.

A. Road safety is not a standalone phenomenon.

B. Indian roads are unsafe not due to a single factor.

C. Road safety is a standalone phenomenon.

(1) Only A

(2) Only B

(3) Only C

(4) Both A and B

(5) Both B and C

15. ___ Such an initiative was long overdue. India has been characterized as one of the most over regulated countries in the world .No central database of all laws and regulations exists in the country.

A. The government was considering to prepare database.

B. The government is considering to prepare a database of all laws and regulations.

C. The government has considered to prepare a database.

(1) Only A

(2) Only B

(3) Only C

(4) Both A and B

(5) Both B and C

Directions (Q. 16-20) : Rearrange the following six sentences (A), (B), (C), (D), (E) and (F) in the proper sequence to form a meaningful paragraph: then answer the questions given below them.

(A) Arctic sea ice has been melting at break-neck speeds in the past few decades, driven by warming air temperature, warming ocean water temperature, all of which are caused by or accelerated by man-made climate change.

(B) But there are other factors at play in the decline of ice in the Arctic Ocean.

(C) Sea ice is generally moderated by sunlight.

(D) Warm ocean currents travel north from the equator and usher in warmer and warmer water, making sea ice growth difficult.

(E) It grows in the winter and melts in the summer.

(F) Weather patterns over the high mid-latitudes and the Arctic can also affect sea ice growth.

16. Which of the following should be the **FOURTH** sentence alter rearrangement ?

(1) E

(2) D

(3) C

(4) B

(5) A

17. Which of the following should be the **SIXTH** sentence alter rearrangement ?

(1) A

(2) B

(3) C

(4) D

(5) E

18. Which of the following should be the **SECOND** sentence after rearrangement ?

(1) E

(2) D

(3) C

(4) B

(5) A

19. Which of the following should be the **FIRST** sentence after rearrangement ?

(1) A

(2) B

(3) C

(4) D

(5) E

20. Which of the following should be the **THIRD** sentence after rearrangement ?

(1) A

(2) B

(3) C

(4) D

(5) F

Directions (Q. 21-30) : In the following passage there are blanks, each of which has been numbered. These numbers are printed below the passage and against each, five words are suggested, one of which fits the blank appropriately. Find out the appropriate word in each case.

The rise of Asian manufacturers in the 1990s hit African firms hard: many were wiped out. Northern Nigeria, which once had a **(21)** garments industry, was unable to **(22)** with low-cost imports. South Africa has similar problems: its manufacturing failed to grow last year **(23)** the continental boom.

This is partly the **(24)** of governments. Buoyed by commodity income, they have neglected industry's needs, **(25)** for roads and electricity. But that, too, may at last be changing. Wolfgang Fengler, a World Bank economist, says, "Africa is now in a good position to industrialise with the right mix of ingredients." This includes **(26)** demography, urbanisation, an emerging middle class and strong services. "For this to happen," he adds, "the continent will need to scale up its infrastructure **(27)** and improve the business climate and many (African) countries have started to **(28)** these challenges in recent years."

Kenya is not about to become **(29)** next South Korea. African countries are likely to follow a more diverse path, benefiting from the growth of countless small and medium-sized businesses, as well as some big ones. For the next decade or so, services will still generate more jobs and wealth in Africa than manufacturing, which is fine. India has **(30)** for more than two decades on the back of services, while steadily building a manufacturing sector from a very low base. Do not bet against Africa doing the same.

21. (1) thriving   (2) flourish
     (3) detractive   (4) dooming
     (5) repulsive

22. (1) competed   (2) compete
     (3) complete   (4) surrender
     (5) commensurate

23. (1) inspite   (2) additional
     (3) in addition   (4) despite
     (5) despite of

24. (1) fact   (2) quality
     (3) fault   (4) default
     (5) fiction

25. (1) specific   (2) especially
     (3) particular   (4) partially
     (5) generally

26. (1) favourable   (2) favourably
     (3) ferrocious   (4) special
     (5) contrast

27. (1) expenditures   (2) disinvestment
     (3) investments   (4) development
     (5) developing

28. (1) tackle   (2) tackling
     (3) decrease   (4) increase
     (5) improve

29. (1) a   (2) an
     (3) the   (4) such
     (5) for

30. (1) boomed   (2) booming
     (3) boom   (4) expand
     (5) plummeted

GENERAL AWARENESS

The following questions are based on the memory of candidates and have been obtained from various forums-mrunal.org, Pagalguy.com, rbi.vze.corn's forum on FB etc..

RBI organized the paper online in 2013 for the first time. These questions were asked in phase I test conducted in 2014 in various shifts. The questions do not include all the options as they were asked. There can be grammatical mistakes and incomplete sentences in the paper but the intent of the question will remain clear. The objective of presenting these questions is to acquaint the aspirants to the kind of questions that can be expected in future phase I exams.

1. International women day is celebrated on which date?
     (1) 5 June   (2) 12 March
     (3) 8 March   (4) 20 June
     (5) 5 March

2. What is FDI limit in private sector banks?
     (1) 74%   (2) 71%
     (3) 73%   (4) 78%
     (5) 79%

3. Who is IMF MD and CEO?
     (1) Dominique strauss kahn
     (2) Rodrigo Rato
     (3) Horst Kohler
     (4) Michel Camdessus
     (5) Christine Lagarde

4. WMA - stands for
   (1) Windows Media Audio
   (2) Win Media Audio
   (3) Win Media Audit
   (4) Windows Mass Audio
   (5) None of these

5. Who is CEO of infosys?
   (1) Vishal Sikka
   (2) N.R. Narayan Murthy
   (3) Nandan Nilekani
   (4) S. Gopalakrishnan
   (5) S.D. Shibulal

6. Who is chairman of Apple ?
   (1) Tim Cook   (2) Arthur D. Levinson
   (3) Jonathan Ive   (4) Luca Maestri
   (5) Ronald Wayne

7. What is name of the actor playing Mr. Bean?
   (1) Mel Smith   (2) Peter Bennet-Jones
   (3) Eric Fellner   (4) Powan Atkinson
   (5) Rebecca O'Brien

8. Who played the lead in Booby Jasoos?
   (1) Sahil Sangha   (2) Samar Shaikh
   (3) Vidya Balan   (4) Ali Fazal
   (5) Hemal Kothari

9. Who was lead actor in movie kochidaiyyan?
   (1) K.S. Ravi Kumar   (2) Rajnikanth
   (3) R. Sarath Kumar   (4) Sunil Lulla
   (5) Soundarya R. Ashwin

10. FIFA organized Footbal world cup in which country recently?
   (1) Russia   (2) Brazil
   (3) Germany   (4) France
   (5) Qatar

11. Which country has "Rupee" NOT as its currency?
   (1) India   (2) Indonesia
   (3) Nepal   (4) Pakistan
   (5) Myanmar

12. Tamil Nadu opposed whom in Mr. Narendra Modi's oath ceremony?
   (1) Mahinda Rajapaksa (Sri Lankan President)
   (2) Nawaz Sharef (Pakistani Prime Minister)
   (3) U. Thein Sein (Myanmar President)
   (4) Mohammad Ashrof Ghani (Afghanistan)
   (5) None of these

13. Who is the CM of andhra pradesh?
   (1) N. Kiran Kumar Reddy
   (2) K. Rosaiah
   (3) Y. S. Rajasekhara Reddy
   (4) N. T. Rama Rao
   (5) N. Chandrababu Naidu

14. Credit information is maintained by?
   (1) RBI   (2) ICICI Bank
   (3) HSBC Bank   (4) UCO Bank
   (5) Bank of India

15. What is full form of BIS?
   (1) Bureau of Indian Standards
   (2) Black Berry Internet Service
   (3) Bank of International Settlements
   (4) Business, Innovation and Skills
   (5) Bureau of Industry and Security

16. What is used to control liquidity in market?
   (1) Cash Reserve Ratio (CRR)
   (2) Repo Rate
   (3) Bank Rate
   (4) Statutory Liquidity Ratio (SLR)
   (5) Marginal Standing Facility (MSF)

17. What is balance of payment?
   (1) The rate at which the RBI lends short-term money to the banks against securities.
   (2) It summarizes an economy's transactions with the rest of the world for a specified time period.
   (3) The payment at which central bank (RBI) lends money to other banks or financial institutions.
   (4) The ratio of cash and some other approved securities to liabilities (deposits).
   (5) The payment at which central bank of the country allows finance to commercial banks.

18. Which of the following country's capital is not correctly matched?
   (1) France – Paris
   (2) Germany – Berlin
   (3) Indonesia – Jakarta
   (4) Australia – Canberra
   (5) Denmark – Oslo

19. Who is the oldest member in the Modi cabinet?
   (1) Rajnath Singh   (2) Suresh Prabhu
   (3) Najma Heptullah   (4) Arun Jaitley
   (5) Manohar Parrikar

20. What is the Address of Website of prime minister modi where you can contact him?
    (1) http://pm.india.gov.in/en/interact-with-honble-pm/
    (2) http://pmIndia.gov.com/en/interact-in-honble-pm/
    (3) http:/pm.gov.com/en/interact-with-honble-pm/
    (4) http://pm.gov.in/interact-with-honble-pm/
    (5) None of these

21. Who is Secretory department of economic affairs, finance ministry?
    (1) Shri S. Selvakumar
    (2) Shri Udai Singh Kumawal
    (3) Shri Ashok Kumar Singh
    (4) Shri Shaktikanta Das
    (5) Shri Ashutosh Singh

22. Which out of the following five is not an organ of World Bank?
    (1) International Bank of Reconstruction and Development (IBRD)
    (2) International Development Association (IDA)
    (3) International Finance Corporation (IFC)
    (4) World Trade Organization (WTO)
    (5) Multilateral Investment Guarantee Agency (MIGA)

23. Which of the following five is not correct regarding WTO?
    (1) Negotiating the reduction or elimination of obstacles to trade (import tariffs, other barriers to trade)
    (2) Settling disputes among our members regarding the interpretation and application of the agreements
    (3) Building capacity of developing country government officials in international trade matters.
    (4) Assisting the process of accession of some 30 countries who are not yet members of the organization
    (5) Its purpose is to contribute to peace and security by promoting international collaboration through education, science and culture.

24. Which of the following statements is/are correct about SLR?
    (1) The rate at which central bank of the country allows finance to commercial banks.
    (2) The term is used by bankers and indicates the minimum percentage of deposits that the bank has to maintain in form of gold, cash or other approved securities.
    (3) The rate at which the RBI lends short-term money to the banks against securities.
    (4) It regulates the credit growth in India
    (5) Both options (b) and (d)

25. Which of the following can be used for tighten the liquidity by RBI?
    (1) Cash Reserve Ratio (CRR)
    (2) Bank Rate
    (3) Repo Rate
    (4) Reverse Repo Rate
    (5) Statutory Liquidity Ratio (SLR)

26. Which of the following is not a function of RBI?
    (1) Issue of Bank Notes
    (2) Banker to Government
    (3) Custodian of Cash Reserves of Commerical Banks
    (4) Central clearance and Account settlement
    (5) It is the part of insurance regulatory and development authority of India.

27. Capital market is also known as — option money, equity, cash and spot, futures?
    (1) Financial markets for buying and selling of long-term debt or equity-backed securities
    (2) Investment market
    (3) Insurance market
    (4) Trading market
    (5) Electronic market

28. A science related Indian award was given to whom?
    (1) S. Ramakrishnan
    (2) C.R. Rao
    (3) Narender K. Sehgal
    (4) D. Balasubramanian
    (5) Yash Pal

29. Who wrote the tales of two cities?
    (1) Charles Dickens
    (2) William Shakeshpeare
    (3) Harold Robbins
    (4) Danielle Steel
    (5) Leo Tolstoy

30. Which is the largest thermal power plant in India?
   (1) Vindhyachal Thermal Power Station
   (2) Talcher Super Thermal Power Station
   (3) Rihand Thermal Power Station
   (4) Korba Super Thermal Power Plant
   (5) Mundra Thermal Power Station.

31. After increasing the height of Narmada dam, what has become its rank in the world?
   (1) 109   (2) 111
   (3) 105   (4) 103
   (5) 100

32. Most costly city in the world according to some world livelihood index report?
   (1) Sydney   (2) Paris
   (3) Singapore   (4) Zurich
   (5) Melbourne

33. Air Asia alliance is with which Indian company?
   (1) Tata
   (2) Kingfisher Air lines
   (3) Air Indian Cargo
   (4) Air Deccan
   (5) Air Sahara

34. Recently banking license given to which company?
   (1) HDFC
   (2) IDFC
   (3) HSBC
   (4) Gramin Bank of Aryavrat
   (5) Tripura Gramin Bank

35. Which among the following not a PSU bank?
   (1) Indian Bank   (2) Canara Bank
   (3) UCO Bank   (4) Bandhan Bank
   (5) Dena Bank

36. Highest number of ministers in the cabinet from which state?
   (1) Uttar Pradesh   (2) Karnataka
   (3) Rajasthan   (4) Madhya Pradesh
   (5) Gujarat

37. Ajit doval recently appointed as
   (1) National security advisor to Prime Minister
   (2) Law enforcement officer
   (3) CBI director
   (4) UPSC Chairman
   (5) Auditor and Comptroller General

38. What is the number of females in Lok Sabha currently?
   (1) 64   (2) 61
   (3) 58   (4) 60
   (5) 66

39. Who is present Attorney General of India ?
   (1) Soli Sorabjee
   (2) Ashok Desai
   (3) L.N. Sinha
   (4) Goolam Essaji Vahanvati
   (5) Mukul Rohatgi

40. Who is present Chancellor of Germany?
   (1) Helmut Schmidt   (2) Willy Brandt
   (3) Angela Merkel   (4) Gerhard Schroder
   (5) Ludwig Erhard

41. Who will be the new chairman of FICCI from January 2008?
   (1) M.Damodaran
   (2) Rajiv Chandrashekharan
   (3) Kiran Karnik
   (4) Ratan Tata
   (5) None of these

42. At which place are the Headquarter of International Monetary Fund (IMF) located?
   (1) Vienna
   (2) The Hague
   (3) Washington
   (4) Denmark
   (5) None of these

43. In which of the following cities, 'World Economic Summit' will be held in January 2008?
   (1) Davos   (2) Geneva
   (3) Berlin   (4) London
   (5) None of these

44. Who has written the book, 'India's Century'?
   (1) P.Chidambaram
   (2) Kamalnath
   (3) Amartya Sen
   (4) Pranav Mukherjee
   (5) None of these

45. At which place was the meeting of 'The Commonwealth Heads of Government (CHOGM)' held?
   (1) Dhaka   (2) Uganda
   (3) Canberra   (4) Suva
   (5) None of these

46. India and ASEAN agreed to enhance bilateral trade upto howmany billion dollar, in the next three years?
   (1) $ 50 ab　　　　(2) $ 60 ab
   (3) $ 65 ab　　　　(4) $ 55 ab
   (5) None of these

47. Which of the following statements is/are TRUE about the Red Ribbon Express?
   (A) The Red Ribbon Express carrying the message of HIV/AIDS awareness has been flagged off in New Delhi on December 1 marking theWorld AIDS Day.
   (B) The special train with seven coaches will stopped at 180 railway stations during its 9000 km long journey.
   (C) It is launched jointly by National AIDS Control Organization and the Union Railway Ministry.
   (D) It is expected to increase accurate knowledge levels about AIDS.
   (1) A, B and C
   (2) B, C and D
   (3) All are true
   (4) A, C and D
   (5) None of these

48. Which of the following bank has started the first biometric ATM in India?
   (1) Punjab National Bank
   (2) State Bank of India
   (3) Bank of Baroda
   (4) Oriental Bank of Commerce
   (5) None of these

49. Which of the following statements is/are TRUE according to the Organization for Economic Co-operation and Development?
   (A) Total Property and Infrastructure exposure is forecast to rise to $ 35 trillion 9% of projected global GDP.
   (B) Guangzhou in China will be second most exposed city in terms of assets in 2070.
   (C) The report analyzed the vulnerability now and in the future of 130 part cities to a major flood ona scale likely to occur once in 100 years.
   (1) Only A
   (2) Only B
   (3) Only C
   (4) A and B
   (5) All of the above

50. According to UN study on climate change that net investment of $ 200-210 billion by which year were needed in cleaner areas, such as renewable energies in a gigantic shift from dirtier fossil fuels?
   (1) 2015　　　　(2) 2020
   (3) 2030　　　　(4) 2040
   (5) None of these

51. According to a report, at present the contribution of urban sector to India's GDP is about 62-63 percent. By which year will it be 75 percent?
   (1) 2012　　　　(2) 2015
   (3) 2020　　　　(4) 2021
   (5) None of these

52. In which country will the National Bank of Pakistan (NBP) open its first branch?
   (1) India　　　　(2) China
   (3) Bhutan　　　　(4) Bangladesh
   (5) None of these

53. The Hindu Rights Action Force (Hindraf) , the Organization of the Hindus was recently in the news. It belongs to which of the following countries?
   (1) Malaysia　　　　(2) Nepal
   (3) Myanmar　　　　(4) Canada
   (5) None of these

54. Upto howmany low budget hotels will be set up by the Indian Railways with private participation?
   (1) 100　　　　(2) 170
   (3) 248　　　　(4) 525
   (5) None of these

55. International Conference on T.B. held on?
   (1) Geneva　　　　(2) Vienna
   (3) Singapore　　　　(4) Cape Town
   (5) None of these

56. Which of the following statements is/are TRUE about the report of National Rural Health Mission?
   (A) According to it nearly 8% primary health centres do not have a doctor.
   (B) According to it about 39%were running without a lab technician and about 17.7% without a pharmacist.
   (C) The country's 22669 primary health centres were facing acute shortage of trained medical personals.

(D) The condition of 3910 community health centres supposed to provide specialized medical care.

(1) A, B and C

(2) B and D

(3) All are true

(4) A, C and D

(5) None of these

57. According to the current report of Inter Government Panel on Climate change (IPCC), the average temperature of our earth is currently 15.80 Celsius what would be its average temperature in the year 2100?

(1) 280 C   (2) 250C

(3) 210 C   (4) 260 C

(5) None of these

58. Which of the following statements is/are TRUE about the mid-term review of the annual policy announced by the RBI?

(1) The Reserve Bank of India has hiked the Cash Reserve Ratio (CRR) by 50 bases points to 7.5% with effect from November 10.

(2) Hike of 50 bases points in CRR will suck out Rs. 16000 cr. from the system.

(3) The RBI left the key rates such as repo, reserve repo and bank rate unchanged

(4) The Policy said that inflation would be contained close to 5 percent during 2007-08.

(5) All are true.

59. Which of the following statements is/are TRUE about the Ministry of New and Renewable Energy?

(A) It has celebrated its Silver Jubilee Year.

(B) Under this ministry about 40 lakh biogas plants are under operation.

(C) The different wind power plants are producing 75000 MW wind power under the ministry, which is at fourth position globally.

(1) Only A   (2) A and B

(3) All are true   (4) B and C

(5) None of these

60. Who has sworn in as the caretaker Prime Minister of Pakistan?

(1) Nawaz Sharif

(2) Soomro Muhummed mian

(3) Benzir Bhutto

(4) Chaudhry Shujaat Hussain

(5) None of these

61. Which of the following statement is/are TRUE about ASEAN declaration on greening the region by 2020?

(1) The main aim of ASEAN declaration is to reduce the emission of greenhouse gases.

(2) More than 10 million hectares of trees will be planted by the members of ASEAN.

(3) The declaration will also urge the member countries to promote coral reef protection.

(4) 1, 2 and 3

(5) None of these

62. Which of the following statements is/are TRUE about the Prime Minister Manmohan Singh's Russia visit?

(A) During this visit India and Russia will be ready to launch an ambitious Chandrayaan-2, a joint unmanned lunar exploration programme.

(B) Both sides have decided to jointly develop and build multi-role transport aircraft.

(C) They also signed an agreement on drug trafficking and on the rupee-rouble debt.

(1) A and B   (2) Only B

(3) B and C   (4) All are true

(5) None of these

63. "World Energy Conference" was held in which of the following city?

(1) Rome

(2) Bali

(3) Beijing

(4) Mumbai

(5) None of these

64. Which of the following bank has entered into an agreement with UK based legal and General Group to set up a Life Insurance Venture?

(1) Punjab National Bank

(2) Bank of Baroda

(3) Allahabad Bank

(4) SBI

(5) None of these

65. About how much railway station has been used as the "Krishi Outlet" according to the Railway Ministry?

(1) 800

(2) 1375

(3) 7500

(4) 10000

(5) None of these

66. How much many billion dollars have been attracted as FDI in India in the first half of 2007-08?

(1) $ 37 bn.   (2) $ 49 bn.

(3) $ 56 bn.   (4) $ 28 bn.

(5) None of these

67. Which of the following statements is/are TRUE about the Aravali Super Thermal Power Plant?

(A) It is a joint venture of NTPC, Delhi and Haryana Government.

(B) This is a coal based power plant, which will provide electricity to Delhi and Haryana.

(C) This power plant will have three units of 500 MW each.

(D) It will set up in Jhajjar with the 50:50 share of Delhi and Haryana Government.

(1) A and B   (2) All are true

(3) B,C and D   (4) A,C and D

(5) None of these

68. Which of the following statements is/are TRUE about the Aam Admi Bima Yojana?

(A) This scheme has been launched on Gandhi Jayanti for the benefit of rural landless households.

(B) The Centre, State Union Territory Governments present this scheme administered by LIC for rural landless house holds.

(C) The member should be aged between 18 to 59 years.

(D) The premium under the scheme shall be Rs. 200 out of which 50% shall be subsidized from the fund created by the Central Government and the remaining 50% shall be contributed by the State Government.

(E) It provides a cover of Rs. 30000 to the member for Natural death while Rs. 75000 on death due to an accident.

(1) A,B and C   (2) B,C and D

(3) All are true   (4) B,D and E

(5) None of these

69. At which place a two day summit of SAARC countries on the support of United Nations Office on Drug and Crime to reduce women and child trafficking held?

(1) Hyderabad   (2) New Delhi

(3) Lucknow   (4) Nagpur

(5) None of these

70. Which of the following statements is/are TRUE about the participatory notes (PNs) by Foreign Institutional Investors?

(A) SEBI has proposed an immediate ban on issue of PN with underlying derivatives.

(B) It has also proposed a restriction on issue of PN with underlying shares.

(C) FIIs are required to wind up outstanding PNs over 18 months.

(1) Only A

(2) Only B

(3) Only C

(4) All are true

(5) None of these

71. Which of the following statements is/are TRUE about the National Family and Health Survey-3(NFHS-3) ?

(A) It has put the HIV prevalence rate in the country at 0.28 percent compared to 0.36 percent claimed by the National AIDS Control Organization (NACO) .

(B) The prevalence rate among men is 0.36 percent which is higher than the rate among women i.e. 0.22 percent.

(C) For both men and women the prevalence is highest in the 30-34 age groups and the rate is 40 percent higher in cities than in rural areas.

(1) Only A   (2) A and B

(3) All are true   (4) A and C

(5) None of these

72. Which of the following statements is/are TRUE about the recommendation of Deepak Parekh Committee on Infrastructure Financial estimates?

(A) According to it about Rs. 1900000 crore needed for the infrastructure sector over next five years.

(B) For Power sector Rs. 800000 crore is needed over next 7 years.

(C) For Roads Rs. 200000 crore is needed over next five year.

(D) For telecom sector Rs. 88000 crore is needed.

(1) A and B

(2) A, C and D

(3) All are true

(4) B and D

(5) None of these

73. What is the National Birth Rate, according to NSSO?

   (1) 16.25%   (2) 31.46%

   (3) 23.80%   (4) 28.54%

   (5) None of these

74. By which years have India, Brazil and South Africa committed themselves to increasing tradeamong themselves to $15 bn.?

   (1) 2010   (2) 2009

   (3) 2012   (4) 2015

   (5) None of these

75. Upto which years will Revenue Deficit is totally phased out, according to Central Government?

   (1) 2007-08   (2) 2009-10

   (3) 2008-09   (4) 2010-11

   (5) None of these

76. Which of the following leading industrialist families of India got the 'Carnegie Medal of Philanthropy' ?

   (1) Sahara Group   (2) Ambani Group

   (3) Tata Group   (4) Bharti Group

   (5) None of these

77. The International Monetary Fund has warned that the continued expansion of Global Economy will slow down due to the recent-----.

   (1) Terrorist attacks on different places

   (2) Increasing level of Global Warming

   (3) Financial Turmoil

   (4) Indo-US Nuclear Deal

   (5) None of these

78. Who has been selected for Gandhi Global Non-Violence Award?

   (1) Desmond Tutu   (2) Nelson Mandela

   (3) Bill Clinton   (4) Shirin Ebadi

   (5) None of these

79. GSLV-F04 satellite launch vehicle has successfully put------satellite INSAT-4CR in orbit.

   (1) Defence   (2) Communication

   (3) Agricultural   (4) Weather

   (5) None of these

80. How many Central Public Sector Enterprises have got SCOPE Meritorious Awards for 2005-06?

   (1) 6   (2) 8

   (3) 15   (4) 12

   (5) None of these

ANSWERS

QUANTITATIVE APTITUDE

1. (1)	**2.** (3)	**3.** (2)	**4.** (4)	**5.** (1)	**6.** (3)	**7.** (2)	**8.** (1)	**9.** (1)	**10.** (1)
11. (2)	**12.** (3)	**13.** (1)	**14.** (2)	**15.** (1)	**16.** (2)	**17.** (2)	**18.** (4)	**19.** (1)	**20.** (3)
21. (5)	**22.** (5)	**23.** (5)	**24.** (4)	**25.** (3)	**26.** (1)	**27.** (2)	**28.** (3)	**29.** (4)	**30.** (5)

REASONING

31. (3)	**32.** (1)	**33.** (4)	**34.** (5)	**35.** (1)	**36.** (2)	**37.** (5)	**38.** (3)	**39.** (1)	**40.** (4)
41. (4)	**42.** (2)	**43.** (1)	**44.** (3)	**45.** (5)	**46.** (5)	**47.** (4)	**48.** (5)	**49.** (2)	**50.** (4)
51. (1)	**52.** (5)	**53.** (4)	**54.** (1)	**55.** (1)	**56.** (5)	**57.** (3)	**58.** (5)	**59.** (1)	**60.** (4)
61. (2)	**62.** (5)	**63.** (3)	**64.** (4)	**65.** (4)	**66.** (2)	**67.** (5)	**68.** (1)	**69.** (3)	**70.** (2)
71. (4)	**72.** (3)	**73.** (1)	**74.** (2)	**75.** (1)	**76.** (3)	**77.** (5)	**78.** (2)	**79.** (4)	**80.** (3)
81. (1)	**82.** (3)	**83.** (5)	**84.** (4)	**85.** (2)	**86.** (5)	**87.** (4)	**88.** (2)	**89.** (2)	**90.** (1)

ENGLISH LANGUAGE

1. (4)	**2.** (3)	**3.** (4)	**4.** (2)	**5.** (4)	**6.** (1)	**7.** (3)	**8.** (1)	**9.** (4)	**10.** (5)
11. (4)	**12.** (5)	**13.** (1)	**14.** (4)	**15.** (2)	**16.** (2)	**17.** (1)	**18.** (1)	**19.** (3)	**20.** (2)
21. (1)	**22.** (2)	**23.** (4)	**24.** (3)	**25.** (2)	**26.** (1)	**27.** (3)	**28.** (1)	**29.** (3)	**30.** (1)

GENERAL AWARENESS

1. (3)	**2.** (1)	**3.** (5)	**4.** (1)	**5.** (1)	**6.** (2)	**7.** (4)	**8.** (3)	**9.** (2)	**10.** (2)
11. (5)	**12.** (1)	**13.** (5)	**14.** (1)	**15.** (3)	**16.** (4)	**17.** (2)	**18.** (*)	**19.** (3)	**20.** (1)
21. (4)	**22.** (4)	**23.** (*)	**24.** (5)	**25.** (1)	**26.** (5)	**27.** (1)	**28.** (2)	**29.** (1)	**30.** (5)
31. (2)	**32.** (3)	**33.** (1)	**34.** (2)	**35.** (4)	**36.** (1)	**37.** (1)	**38.** (5)	**39.** (5)	**40.** (3)
41. (2)	**42.** (3)	**43.** (1)	**44.** (2)	**45.** (2)	**46.** (1)	**47.** (3)	**48.** (1)	**49.** (5)	**50.** (3)
51. (4)	**52.** (1)	**53.** (1)	**54.** (1)	**55.** (2)	**56.** (3)	**57.** (3)	**58.** (5)	**59.** (3)	**60.** (2)
61. (4)	**62.** (4)	**63.** (1)	**64.** (2)	**65.** (3)	**66.** (2)	**67.** (2)	**68.** (3)	**69.** (3)	**70.** (3)
71. (2)	**72.** (3)	**73.** (3)	**74.** (1)	**75.** (3)	**76.** (3)	**77.** (3)	**78.** (1)	**79.** (2)	**80.** (1)

EXPLANATIONS

QUANTITATIVE APTITUDE

1. Let the initial amount of milk in container be 'x' litre

Hence after two attempts,

Amount of milk in container = $x - 10$

and amount of water in container = 10

Now according to question,

$$\frac{x-10}{10} = \frac{81}{19}$$

$\therefore$ $19x - 190 = 810$

$\therefore$ $19x = 810 + 190$

$\therefore$ $x \approx 50$ litre

$\therefore$ Option (1) is correct.

2.

Bag A	Bag B
4 – green 6 – red	3 – green 4 – red

Now one ball is drawn randomly from each bag.

The probability that both are green

$$= \left(\frac{4}{4+6}\right) \times \left(\frac{3}{3+4}\right)$$

$$= \frac{4}{10} \times \frac{3}{7} = \frac{6}{35}$$

$\therefore$ Option (3) is correct.

3. Let the radius and height of cylinder be 'r' and 'h' respectively.

Now according to question,

$$r + h = 42 \qquad \ldots(i)$$

Now, total surface area of cylinder

$$= 2\pi r(r + h)$$

$\therefore$ $3696 = 2\pi r(42)$ ($\because$ from equation (i))

$\therefore$ $\dfrac{3696}{2\pi \times 42} = r$

$\therefore$ $\boxed{\dfrac{44}{\pi} = r}$

$\therefore$ $r = 14$ cm

$\Rightarrow$ $h = (42 - 14)$ cm

$= 28$ cm

Now volume of cylinder $= \pi r^2 h$

$$= \frac{22}{7} \times (14)^2 \times 28$$

$$= 22 \times (14)^2 \times 4$$

$$= 88 \times 196$$

$$= 17248 \text{ cubic cm}$$

$\therefore$ Option (2) is correct.

4. Total number of laptop sold by store A and C together

$$= \frac{48000 \times (18 + 15)}{100}$$

$$= \frac{48000 \times 33}{100}$$

$$= 480 \times 33$$

$$= 15840$$

and total number of laptop sold by store E and F together

$$= \frac{48000 \times (20 + 8)}{100}$$

$$= 480 \times 28$$

$$= 13440$$

Difference $= 15840 - 13440$

$$= 2400$$

$\therefore$ Option (4) is correct.

5. Number of Dell Laptop sold by store A

$$= \frac{28000 \times 14}{100}$$

$$= 3920$$

and Number of Lenovo Laptop sold by store A

$$= \frac{48000 \times 18}{100} - 3920$$

$$= 4720$$

Required ratio $= \dfrac{3920}{4720}$

$$= \frac{49}{59}$$

$\therefore$ Option (1) is correct.

6. Average Dell Laptop sold by store A, C and E

$$= \frac{28000}{3} \times \left(\frac{14 + 12 + 10}{100}\right)$$

$$= \frac{28000}{3} \times \frac{36}{100}$$

$$= 280 \times 12 = 3360$$

and Average Dell Laptop sold by stores B, D and F

$$= \frac{28000}{3} \times \left(\frac{32 + 8 + 24}{100}\right)$$

$$= \frac{280}{3} \times (64)$$

$$= \frac{17920}{3}$$

Now, required ratio $= \dfrac{3360 \times 3}{17920}$

$$= \dfrac{9}{16}$$

∴ Option (3) is correct.

7. Number of Lenovo Laptop sold by store B

$$= \dfrac{48000 \times 28}{100} - \dfrac{28000 \times 32}{100}$$

$$= 13440 - 8960$$

$$= 4480$$

and number of Dell Laptop sold by store (E)

$$= \dfrac{28000 \times 10}{100}$$

$$= 2800$$

∴ Required percent $= \left[\dfrac{4480 - 2800}{2800} \times 100 \right]\%$

$$= 60\%$$

∴ Option (2) is correct.

8. Central angle of Laptop sold by store C and F

$$= \dfrac{35}{100} \times 360°$$

$$= 126°$$

∴ Option (1) is correct.

10. Population of village 'F' is 168000

∴ Number of literate person in village 'F'

$$= \dfrac{16800 \times 64}{100}$$

$$= 107520$$

Number of literate males

$$= \dfrac{7}{12} \times 107520$$

$$= 62720$$

∴ Option (5) is correct.

14. Time taken by P to type 368 pages

$$= \left(368 \times 8 \right) \text{min}$$

$$= 2944 \text{ min}$$

and time taken by Q to type 368 pages

$$= (368 \times 18) \text{ min}$$

$$= 6624 \text{ min}$$

and time taken by R to type 368 pages

$$= (368 \times 24) \text{ min}$$

$$= 8832 \text{ min}$$

If all of them work together,

$$= \dfrac{1}{2944} + \dfrac{1}{6624} + \dfrac{1}{8832}$$

$$= \dfrac{9 + 4 + 3}{26496}$$

$$= \dfrac{16}{26496}$$

Hence work will be completed in $\dfrac{26496}{16}$ min

$$= 1656 \text{ min}$$

$$= 27.6 \text{ hours}$$

∴ Option (2) is correct.

15.   A •⟵—— 36 km ——⟶• B

Let the speed of boat = 6 km/hrs

and speed of stream be y km/hrs

Now according to question,

$$\dfrac{36}{6 - y} - \dfrac{36}{6 + y} = 8$$

∴ $36\,(6 + y) - 36\,(6 - y) = 8\,(36 - y^2)$

∴ $36\,[6 + y - 6 + y] = 8\,(36 - y^2)$

∴ $36\,(2y) = 8\,(36 - y^2)$

∴ $72\,y = 36 \times 8 - 8y^2$

∴ $8y^2 + 72y - 36 \times 8 = 0$

∴ $8y^2 + 72y - 288 = 0$

∴ $y = 3$ Or $y = -12$

Hence rate of stream is 3 km/hrs

∴ Option (1) is correct.

16. From I

$$30x^2 + 11x + 1 = 0$$

∴ $30x^2 + 6x + 5x + 1 = 0$

∴ $6x\,(5x + 1) + 1\,(5x + 1) = 0$

∴ $x = -\dfrac{1}{6}$ Or $x = -\dfrac{1}{5}$

From II

$$42y^2 + 13y + 1 = 0$$

∴ $42y^2 + 7y + 6y + 1 = 0$

∴ $7y\,(6y + 1) + 1\,(6y + 1) = 0$

∴ $y = -\dfrac{1}{7}$ Or $y = -\dfrac{1}{6}$

From I and II

$$\boxed{x \le y}$$

∴ Option (2) is correct.

17. From I

$$x^2 - x - \sqrt{2}\,x + \sqrt{2} = 0$$

$$\therefore \quad x(x-1) - \sqrt{2}\,(x-1) = 0$$

$$\therefore \quad \left(x - \sqrt{2}\right) = 0 \qquad \text{Or} \quad x - 1 = 0$$

$$\therefore \qquad x = \sqrt{2} \quad \text{Or} \qquad x = 1$$

From II

$$y^2 - 3y + 2 = 0$$

$$\therefore \qquad y^2 - 2y - y + 2 = 0$$

$$\therefore \qquad y(y-2) - 1\,(y-2) = 0$$

$$\therefore \quad y - 1 = 0 \quad \text{Or} \quad y - 2 = 0$$

$$\therefore \qquad y = 1 \quad \text{Or} \qquad y = 2$$

From statement I and II we get

$$\therefore \qquad \boxed{x \leq y}$$

$\therefore$ Option (2) is correct.

18. From I

$$x^2 - 2x - \sqrt{5}\,x + 2\sqrt{5} = 0$$

$$\therefore \quad x(x-2) - \sqrt{5}(x-2) = 0$$

$$\therefore \quad x - \sqrt{5} = 0 \qquad \text{Or} \quad x - 2 = 0$$

$$\therefore \qquad x = \sqrt{5} \quad \text{Or} \qquad x = 2$$

From II

$$y^2 - \sqrt{3}\,y - \sqrt{2}\,y + \sqrt{6} = 0$$

$$\therefore \quad y\left(y - \sqrt{3}\right) - \sqrt{2}\left(y - \sqrt{3}\right) = 0$$

$$\therefore \quad y - \sqrt{2} = 0 \qquad \text{Or} \quad y - \sqrt{3} = 0$$

$$\therefore \qquad y = \sqrt{2} \quad \text{Or} \qquad y = \sqrt{3}$$

From statement I and II

$$\boxed{x > y}$$

$\therefore$ None of the answer are true.

19. From I

$$x^2 + 12x + 36 = 0$$

$$\therefore \qquad x^2 + 6x + 6x + 36 = 0$$

$$\therefore \qquad x(x+6) + 6\,(x+6) = 0$$

$$\therefore \qquad x = -6$$

From II

$$y^2 = 16$$

$$\therefore \qquad y = \pm 4$$

From statement I and II we get

$$\boxed{x < y}$$

$\therefore$ Option (1) is correct.

20. From I

$$9x^2 + 3x - 2 = 0$$

$$\therefore \qquad 9x^2 + 6x - 3x - 2 = 0$$

$$\therefore \qquad 3x(3x + 2) - 1(3x + 2) = 0$$

$$\therefore \quad 3x - 1 = 0 \qquad \text{Or} \quad 3x + 2 = 0$$

$$\therefore \qquad x = \frac{1}{3} \quad \text{Or} \qquad x = -\frac{2}{3}$$

From II

$$\therefore \qquad 8y^2 + 6y + 1 = 0$$

$\therefore$ The given equation has imaginary roots.

$\therefore$ Option (3) is correct.

21. From statement I

The ratio of monthly salaries of x and y is $9 : 7$

Let the monthly salary of x is $9x$

and monthly salary of y is $7x$

Now from statement II,

$$9x - 7x = 16000$$

$$\therefore \qquad 2x = 16000$$

$$\therefore \qquad x = 8000$$

$\therefore$ Monthly salary of x is 72000 and y is 56000

Hence annual salary of Mr. $x = 72000 \times 12$

$$= ₹\ 864000$$

Hence both the statement I and II are required to answer the question.

$\therefore$ Option (5) is correct.

22. From statement I and II

$$\text{Cost price of article} = ₹\left(\frac{5016 \times 100}{120}\right)$$

$$= ₹\ 4180$$

Hence, both the statement I and II are required

$\therefore$ Option (5) is correct.

23. From I

$$l - b = 15 \qquad\qquad ...(i)$$

and **From II**

The cost of fencing is ₹ 180 per metre

As from statement I and II data is insufficient to find the perimeter.

$\therefore$ Option (4) is correct.

24. From statement I

History + Geography + Chemistry = 75×3

$$= 225$$

From statement II

History + Geography + Physics = 78×3

$$= 234$$

As from statement I and II marks of chemistry is not known, and hence marks of physics cannot be guessed.

∴   Option (4) is correct.

25. From statement I

Let the male population of city A is $27\,x$

and female population of city B is $23\,x$

and $27x - 23x = 100000$

∴ $x = \dfrac{100000}{4}$

            $= 25000$

Hence total population of city A

         $= 50\,x$

         $= 50 \times 25000$

         $= 1250000$

From statement II

Population of city A

        $= \dfrac{80}{100} \times$ Population of city B   ...(*i*)

and population of city B – population of city A

         $= 312500$ ...(*ii*)

∴   From solving equations (*i*) and (*ii*) we will get the population of city A

∴   Option (3) is correct.

26. $3 \times 3 + (1)^2 = 10$

     $10 \times 3 + (2)^2 = \boxed{34}$ odd one

     $34 \times 3 + (3)^2 = 111$

     $111 \times 3 + (4)^2 = 349$

     $349 \times 3 + (5)^2 = 1072$

    $1072 \times 3 + (6)^2 = 3252$

Hence instead of '33' it should be '34'

∴   Option (1) is correct.

28. 2, 6, 24, 96, 285, 568, 567

       $2 \times \underline{6} - \underline{6} = 6$

      $6 \times \underline{5} - \underline{5} = \boxed{25}$ odd one

      $25 \times \underline{4} - \underline{4} = 96$

      $96 \times \underline{3} - \underline{3} = 285$

    $285 \times \underline{2} - \underline{2} = 568$

    $568 \times \underline{1} - \underline{1} = 567$

∴ Option (3) is correct.

29. 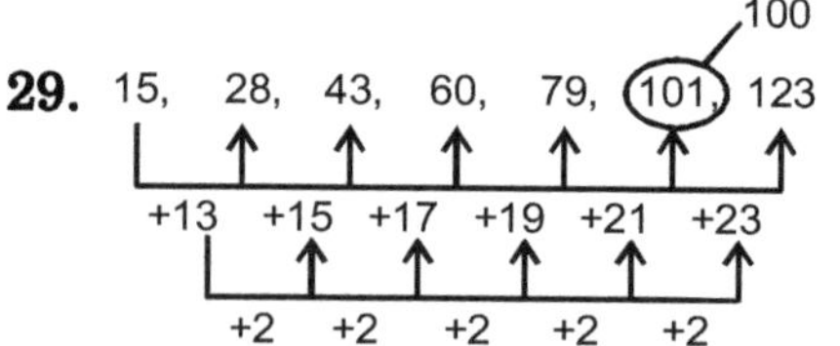

Hence odd one out is '101'.

∴   Option (4) is correct.

30. 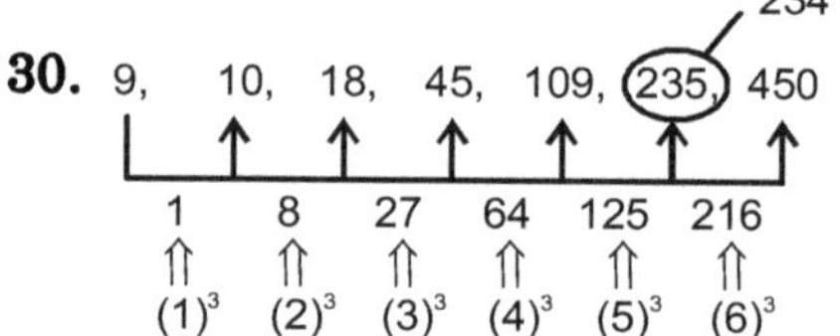

Hence 235 is odd one out.

∴   Option (5) is correct.

REASONING

(Q. 31 – 35) :

→ "Economy	receiving	very	fast"	(1-sentence)
va	jo	ni	pa	(Code)
→ "Very	essence	of	economy"	(2-sentence)
sa	Pa	lo	jo	(Code)
→ "fast	money	in	banks"	(3-sentence)
gy	let	ks	va	(Code)
→ "of	banks	in	industry"	(4-sentence)
ks	dm	bt	su	(Code)

From Statement-1 and 2,

         Economy/very → jo/pa

From Statement-1 and 3,

          fast → va

From Statement-2 and 4,

           of → su

From Statement-3 and 4,

        in/banks → bt/ks

31. Hence 'Su' stands for 'of'

   ∴   Option (3) is correct

32. As code of "very/economy and of" is "jo/pa, su"

Hence code of 'Essence' is 'lo'

   ∴   Option (1) is correct

33. The code of 'money' from statement – 3 is 'gy'

Hence code of "essence of money" is 'lo, su, gy'

Option (4) is correct.

34. The code of "industry" from statement – 4 is 'dm'

Hence code of "economy in industry" cannot be determined as code of economy is either jo or pa

   ∴   Option (5) is correct.

35. Hence code for 'fast' is 'va'.

   ∴   Option (1) is correct.

(Q. 36 – 40) :

According to the given information, following table is formed –

Floor	Name of Person
7th	B
6th	C
5th	D
4th	A
3rd	E
2nd	G
1st	F

36. From the above table, 'B' lives on topmost floor.

∴   Option (2) is correct.

37. From the above table 'C' lives immediately above D's floor.

∴   Option (5) is correct.

38. All the given options i.e., B, D, E and F stays on odd number floor. Only 'G' lives on an even number floor.

∴   Option (3) is correct.

39. From the above table, 'E' lives on third number floor.

∴   Option (1) is correct.

40. From the above table, 'G' lives exactly between the floors of E and F.

∴   Option (4) is correct.

(Q. 41 – 45) :

For the given input

Input

31, 11, win, arm, blanket, zebra, 24, 81, chip, team, slip, 62, 55, dawn, 91, 78

Output

Step-I

11, arm, 31, win, blanket, 24, 81, chip, team, slip, 62, 55, dawn, 78, zebra, 91

Step-II

11, 24, arm, blanket, 31, chip, team, slip, 62, 55, dawn, 78, win, zebra, 81, 91

Step-III

11, 24, 31, arm, blanket, chip, slip, 62, 55, dawn, team, win, zebra, 78, 81, 91

Step-IV

11, 24, 31, 55, arm, blanket, chip, dawn, slip, team, win, zebra, 62, 78, 81, 91

41. In Step III position of "slip" is seventh from left.

∴   Option (4) is correct.

42. In Step IV, number of 'words/number' present between "dawn" and '81' is six

∴   Option (2) is correct.

43. In Step II, the word/number present at the ninth position from the left is '62'.

∴   Option (1) is correct.

44. In Step III, "dawn" word is seventh from the right.

∴   Option (3) is correct.

45. In Step III, 62 is the number from the third to the left of the sixth element from the right.

∴   Option (5) is correct.

46. Statements :

$$V = I \le T < A = L \ge Z > E$$

Conclusion :

I.   A > E ✓

II. L > V ✓

Both conclusion I and II are true

∴   Option (5) is correct.

(Q. 47 – 48) :

Statements :

$$P \ge H = J \ge R;$$
$$H \le I < T$$
$$\Rightarrow P \ge H = J \ge R$$

$$\begin{array}{c} \wedge\!| \\ I \\ \wedge \\ T \end{array}$$

47. Conclusion :

I.   J > T (×)

II. P ≥ T (×)

Both conclusion I and II are false

∴   Option (4) is correct.

48. Conclusion :

I.   R < T (✓)

II. T > H (✓)

Both conclusion I and II are true.

∴   Option (5) is correct.

(Q. 49 – 50) :

Statements :

$$C \ge H < M < R = A;$$
$$Z \ge M \ge Y$$
$$\Rightarrow C \ge H < M < R = A$$

$$\begin{array}{c} \wedge\!| \\ Z \\ \wedge\!| \\ Y \end{array}$$

49. Conclusion :

    I. Z ≥ C (×)

    II. Y < A (×)

  Both conclusion I and II are false

  ∴ Option (4) is correct.

50. Conclusion :

    I. Y ≥ C (×)

    II. Z > A (×)

  Both conclusion I and II are false.

  ∴ Option (4) is correct.

(Q. 51 – 52) :

  According to given statements

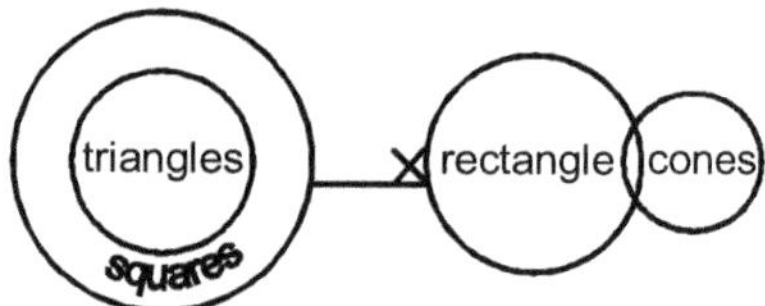

51. Conclusions :

    I. Some cones are rectangle (✓)

    II. All cones are rectangle (×)

  Hence only conclusion I follows

  ∴ Option (1) is correct.

52. Conclusions :

    I. No triangle is rectangle (✓)

    II. Some cones being triangles is a possibility (✓)

  Hence both conclusion I and II follows

  ∴ Option (5) is correct.

(Q. 53 – 54) :

  According to given statement

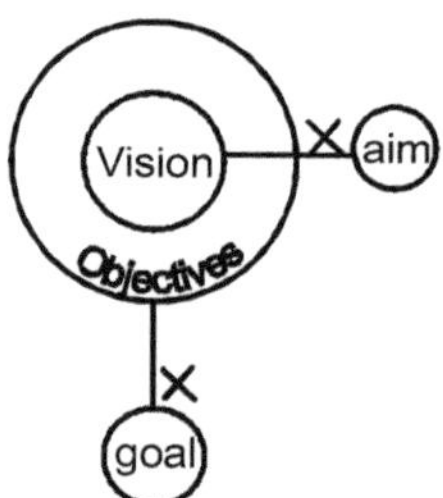

53. Conclusion :

    I. All goals being aim is a possibility (×)

    II. All aims being objective is a possibility (×)

  Here both conclusion I and II do not follows

  ∴ Option (4) is correct

54. Conclusions :

    I. No goal is vision. (✓)

    II. All objectives are visions. (×)

  Here only conclusion I follows.

  ∴ Option (1) is correct.

(Q. 55 – 56) :

  According to given statements –

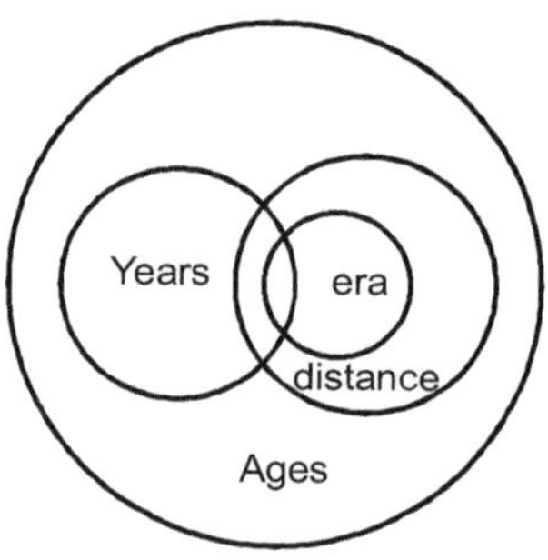

55. Conclusions :

    I. At least some distances are ages (✓)

    II. Some eras are definitely not years (×)

  Here only conclusion I follows

  ∴ Option (1) is correct.

56. Conclusions :

    I. At least some eras are ages (✓)

    II. All distances being years is a possibility (✓)

  Here both the conclusion I and II follows

  ∴ Option (5) is correct.

(Q. 57 – 64) :

  According to given information –

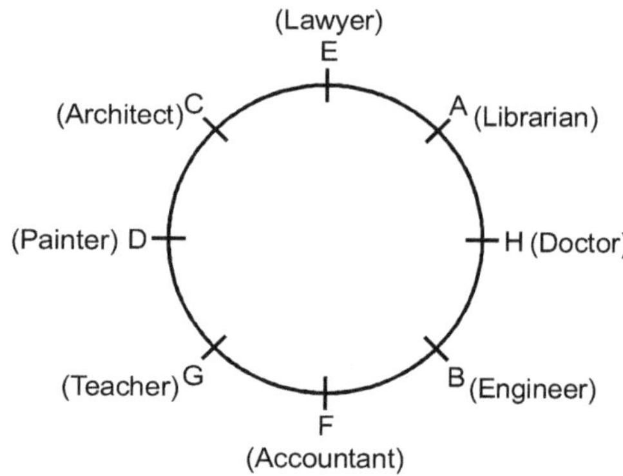

57. From the above diagram, 'D' is a Painter.

  ∴ Option (3) is correct.

58. From the above diagram, 'H' is a Doctor.

  ∴ Option (5) is correct.

59. From the above diagram, Lawyer is third to the left of 'G'

  ∴ Option (1) is correct.

60. From the above diagram, Accountant sit exactly between Engineer and Teacher

  ∴ Option (4) is correct.

61. According to given sitting arrangement all the options are true except option (2) i.e. 'G' is not a Doctor as 'G' is a Teacher

  ∴ Option (2) is correct.

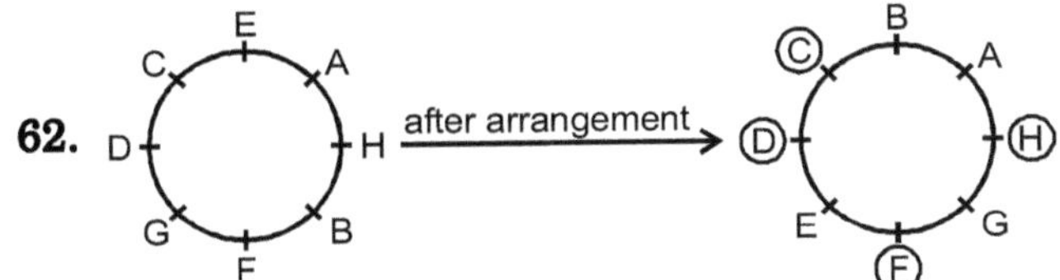

62.

After rearrangement position of C, D, F and H remains unchanged

∴ Option (5) is correct.

63. In all of the options, three persons sits between each group but in option (3) between 'G' and 'E' only two person sits.

∴ Option (3) is correct.

64. From the above diagram, Accountant sit third to the left of Librarian.

∴ Option (4) is correct.

(Q. 65 – 71) :

According to given information–

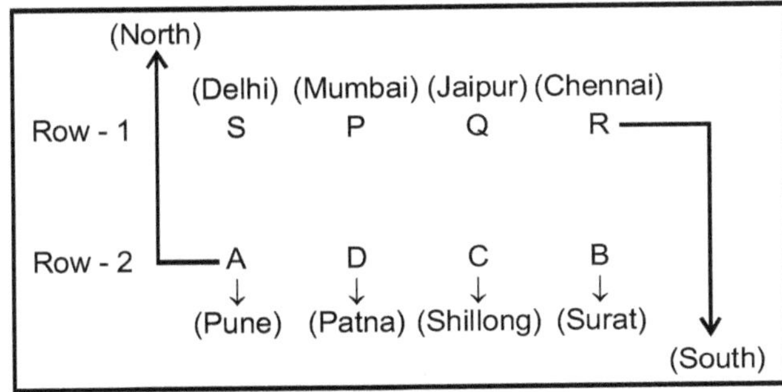

65. 'Q' belongs to Jaipur

∴ Option (4) is correct.

66. 'A' faces 'S'

∴ Option (2) is correct.

67. Among the given option only in option (4), R and S are extreme points of row - 1

∴ Option (5) is correct.

68. All of the given statements are true except in option (1) i.e., "R is at the extreme right end of the row" as "R is at the extreme left end of the row".

∴ Option (1) is correct.

69. All of the given options are extreme points of row, except 'C'

∴ Option (3) is correct.

70. All of the given options are related correctly except option (2) i.e., R is from Chennai not from Delhi.

∴ Option (2) is correct.

71. 'A' belongs to pune

∴ Option (4) is correct.

(Q. 72 – 74) :

From the given information

$$Q > S > P > T > R > U$$

$$\downarrow \qquad\qquad \downarrow$$

$$68\ kg \qquad 35\ kg$$

72. The descending order of weight of the six person is

Q, S, P, T, R, U

∴ Option (3) is correct.

73. 'R' is heavier than only U

∴ Option (1) is correct.

74. As the weight of 'S' is 68 kg, hence the weight of 'P' will be 67 kg.

∴ Option (2) is correct.

(Q. 75 – 77) :

→ "work	is	important	today"	→ (Statement-1)
tx	ne	zu	ka	→ (Code)
→ "is	work	there	now"	→ (Statement-2)
ne	ht	ka	mu	→ (Code)
→ "work	for	joy	only"	→ (Statment-3)
oj	un	ft	ne	→ (Code)
→ "For	money	only	joy"	→ (Statement-4)
oj	ft	ds	un	→ (Code)

From statement – 1 and – 2

work/is → ne/ka

From statement – 1 and – 3

work → ne ⇒ is → ka

From statement – 3 and – 4

For/Joy/only → oj/ft/un ⇒ money → ds

75. The code for 'money' is 'ds'

∴ Option (1) is correct.

76. The code for "is important today" is "tx zu ka" and code for "money" is 'ds'.

∴ Code for "money is important today" is

"ds tx zu ka"

∴ Option (3) is correct.

77. From statement – 2, code for "now there is work" is "ne ht ka mu"

∴ Option (5) is correct.

(Q. 78 – 80) :

From statement–1, we can't guess which exam was conducted on wednesday.

From statement– 2, we get the following sequence

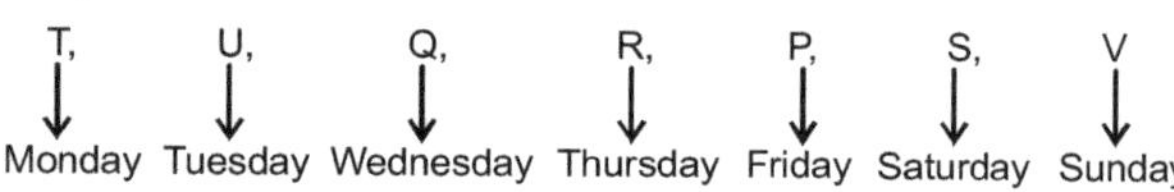

Hence 'Q' exam was conducted on Wednesday.

Hence statement-II alone is sufficient to answer the question.

∴ Option (2) is correct.

79. **From statement-I** and **statement-II,** we are not able to know the position of 'O' among 20 persons standing in a straight line.

∴ Option (4) is correct.

80. From each statement, conclusion is dervied

∴ Option (3) is correct.

(Q. 81 – 85) :

81. P @ R → 'P' is the mother of 'R'

R = S → 'R' is the sister of 'S'

S © T → 'S' is the brother of 'T'

T £ V → 'T' is the son of 'V'

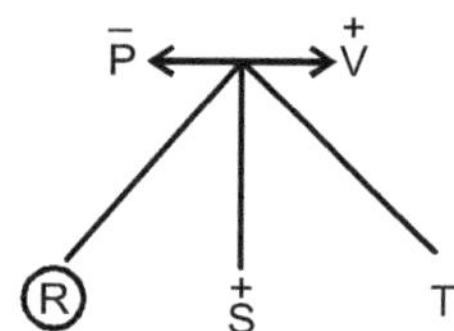

Here 'V' is the husband of 'P'

∴ Option (1) is correct.

82. From option (3),

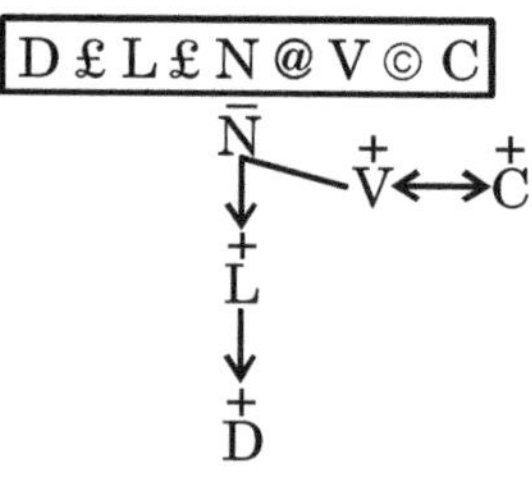

Hence 'C' is the paternal uncle of 'D'

∴ Option (3) is correct.

84. Q £ N @ S © M = P

Q £ N → 'Q' is the son of 'N'

N @ S → 'N' is the mother of 'S'

S © M → 'S' is the brother of 'M'

M = P → 'M' is the sister of 'P'

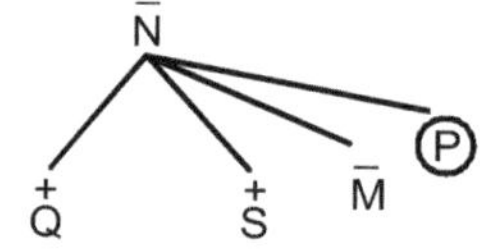

"S" is brother of 'P'

∴ Option (1) is correct.

85. **From option (2),**

N ★ P # C @ Q @ V

N ★ P → 'N' is the father of 'P'

P # C → 'P' is the daughter of 'C'

C @ Q → 'C' is the mother of 'Q'

Q @ V → 'Q' is the mother of 'V'

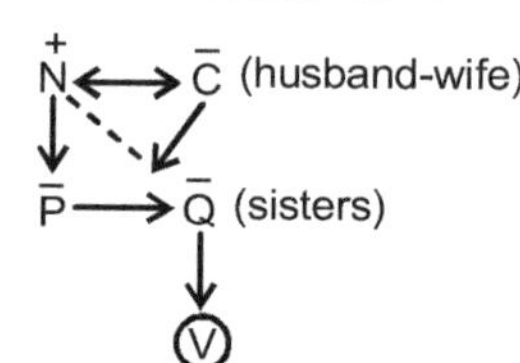

Here 'Q' is daughter of 'N'.

∴ Option (2) is correct.

TEST–I : ENGLISH LANGUAGE

Directions (Q. 1 – 10) : *Read the following passage carefully and answer the given questions. Certain words have been given in bold to help you locate them while answering some of the questions.*

On attending a conference which focused on the role of the service sector in Indian economy, I was amazed. The conference gave a very interesting **perspective** on the role of the service sector in the growth of the indian economy in relation to growth rate in agriculture and industry. The current situation in India is that the growth rate of services has overtaken both agriculture and industry and is now contributing to more than fifty per cent of GDP. The services sector has the highest growth rate and is the least **volatile** sector. Growth is particularly marked in public services, IT and financial services. In some areas the growth rate of services sector is forty to fifty per cent due to increased use of mobile technologies. India, therefore, has a services oriented economy. It hasn't followed traditional growth models as in China. However, in the process of doing so it has skipped the manufacturing stage and has jumped straight from the agricultural stage to service stage, which is also the main reason for the expansion of the service sector. In fact, the situation now is such that the growth in the service sector can and will support the growth in the agricultural and industrial sectors. However, the only setback for Indian economy is the lack of growth in the manufacturing sector, which causes dependence on other countries, which is not so desirable in terms of job creation and increase in prosperity. Population is also a major concern of the Indian economy. As the population of India grows so also does the number of dependents in the population both in the lower and higher age groups. In such a scenario of increasing population, especially in an economy which is still recovering from crisis, growth becomes difficult. For such an economy to grow it has to invest. Currently, the public sector invests more than it saves. The household sector saves in surplus but it is not increasing, so it cannot continue to support private and public sectors. There is a **massive** need to spend on agriculture and infrastructure development of the country. A part from health, education should also be the priority of the government, particularly the education of women, in order to reduce the birth rate.

However, all said and done, we cannot deny the fact that growing population of the country can also benefit the economy if considered as a resource and used efficiently. In fact, it is said that in the next two decades a 'growth window' for India will open, which may not come again because the working population to total population ratio will rise up to mid 2030s only. It is important for India to maximise its economic growth in this period. For doing so, it will be important for Indian to absorb the growing labour force. This would mean that most people in the country would be employed (with a steady income), the number of dependents in the population would reduce and with effect the economy would prosper. Absorbing the labour force is also very important if the service sector is to play a key role in the growing Indian economy. Today, to address the issue of poverty in India, there is a need **to change the bad sectors into good sectors** and in turn to move people from unemployment to employment. Only the service sector can help in doing so and thus can have major impact on poverty. Although service-intensive sectors such as hotels, restaurants and IT are booming with growth in human skills, there are geographical, labour unions and human skills restrictions on labour movement. The key question here, I suppose, is that – can service sector lead the economy? For example, can service such as IT be taken to rural areas? Experts in the conference have suggested that it seems that services could lead the economy. However, there are certain **prerequisites** for the same. In other words, there needs to be greater equality between the different states and better gender balance. There is also the need for additional fiscal equality, tax reforms to fund education, reducation in goverment debt, and the revenue account must be kept in balance. Progress is good but still the initial conditions for growth have not yet been achieved.

Directions (Q. 1) : *Choose the word which is most opposite in meaning of the word given inbold as used in the passage.*

1. VOLATILE

   (*a*) erratic   (*b*) impatient

   (*c*) stable   (*d*) solid

   (*e*) strained

2. According to the passage, which of the following is/are true about the impact of the increasing population on Indian economy ?

   (A) If India attempts to absorb all the labour force, it will impact the growth of service sector negatively and, in turn, hamper the economic growth of the country.

   (B) As the population of the country increases, the number of dependents in the country also increase, which, in turn, increases the pressure on the economy.

   (C) An increasing population can never lead the economy of the country towards prosperity. In fact, it can only put strain on the economy of a country.

   (*a*) All (A), (B) and (C)   (*b*) Only (C)

   (*c*) Both (B) and (C)   (*d*) Both (A) and (C)

   (*e*) Only (B)

3. According to the passage, which of the following can be said about the agriculture and industry sectors in India ?

   (A) Looking at the growth of the service sector in India, it can be safely said that the service sector will soon be in a position to support both agriculture and industry sector.

   (B) The agriculture and the industry sector of the country have reached their threshold and there would be no use of further investment in these sectors.

   (C) Currently, the agriculture and industry sectors contribute less as compared to service sector to the GDP of the country.

   (*a*) Only (A)   (*b*) Only (C)

   (*c*) Both (A) and (C)   (*d*) Both (B) and (C)

   (*e*) All (A), (B) and (C)

4. What does the author mean by the statement, ".... a 'growth window' for India will open." ?

   (*a*) In the coming years the Indian economy will grow as the service sector of the country would be booming due to the focus of the government in that sector.

   (*b*) In the next two decades Indian economy will have an opportunity to grow as the working population of India will be high as compared to the dependent population.

   (*c*) There would be only a small period of time in which the economy of India has to grow and if it fails to do so it will never be able to recover from the economic downfall.

   (*d*) Only up to the next two decades would Indian people be interested in finding jobs in the country, beyond which they would search for jobs abroad, thus hampering the growth of Indian economy.

   (*e*) The growth of Indian economy is like a small window and in order to substantiate the growth it is important to increase the size of the window by improving trade relations with other countries.

Directions (Q. 5) : *Choose the word which is most similar in meaning to the word given in bold as used in the passage.*

5. PREREQUISITES

   (*a*) requirements   (*b*) instincts

   (*c*) acknowledgments   (*d*) prohibitions

   (*e*) problems

6. What does the author mean by the statement "to change the bad sectors into good sector" ?

   (*a*) In order to deal with the problem of poverty, it is important to distinguish between good and bad sectors and encourage people to start searching for jobs in the good sectors.

   (*b*) The government should make efforts to improve the sectors that are not functioning well in order to create greater job opportunities in those sectors and in turn eradicate poverty.

   (*c*) Poverty alleviation is possible only if the government understands the importance of good sectors and provides them with necessary opportunities.

   (*d*) The bad sectors of the country should be identified and such jobs should be outsourced to other underprivileged countries in order to eradicate poverty from those countries.

   (*e*) People should be educated to ensure that they work only in the good sectors and, in turn, the issue of poverty in the country is resolved.

Directions (Q. 7) : *Choose the word which is most similar in meaning to the word given in bold as used in the passage.*

7. PERSPECTIVE

   (*a*) viewpoint   (*b*) prospect

   (*c*) attitude   (*d*) agreement

   (*e*) proportion

8. Which of the following is true as per the passage ?

   (*a*) India has not followed the conventional model of growth and has moved directly from the agriculture sector to th service sector.

   (*b*) The service sector of the country is yet to make a mark on the IT and financial sectors of the country.

   (*c*) With availability of labour and growth in human skills, the service sector of Indian economy is booming limitlessly as there is no restriction on the movement of labour.

   (*d*) India has become self-reliant and does not have to depend on other countries because of the development in the manufacturing sector.

   (*e*) All the given statements are true.

9. According to the author, which of the following can be said about the growth of service sector in India ?

   (*a*) India is essentially an agrarian economy and is not yet ready to shift focus from agriculture sector to service sector.

   (*b*) The expansion of service sector in India has been mainly because of the growth in the agricultural sector.

   (*c*) Indian economy cannot run only on the basis of service sector, i.e. without further development in the agriculture and the industrial sector.

   (*d*) The growth of service sector in India is facilitated by the improvement in technology.

   (*e*) It will take the service sector at least around two decades before it can overtake the agriculture and industry sector.

Directions (Q. 10) : *Choose the word which is most opposite in meaning of the word given in bold as used in the passage.*

10. MASSIVE

   (*a*) prominent   (*b*) proactive

   (*c*) short   (*d*) little

   (*e*) vast

Directions (Q. 11-20) : *Read the following passage carefully and answer the given questions. Certain words/phrases are given in bold to help you locate them while answering some of the questions.*

We should never confuse education with training or the 'tools' that educators use. Education is no more a computer or an online class than it is chalkboard – those are simple tools. Additionally, precious few new and relevant findings have been added to our insights into the learning process. Much of what many proclaim to be insightful turns out to be faddish and misguided. What we need for learning to occur is well-prepared and motivated teachers, students who are willing and able to learn and a social system that values education attainment. Many might take exception to these assertions, raining a host of ancillary social, economic, nutritional and sociological issues. However, decades of data from failed public experiments aimed at **mitigating** these problems argue to the contrary.

What are we to do? Create a wave of educational entrepreneurship? Despite all of the hype and media attention, no one currently knows the best way forward. We must incentivise educationalists, technologists and classroom teachers to experiment and innovate. Such partnerships should freely explore alternatives as we seek to define the blended face-to-face and online classrooms of the future. Some approaches will fail, but that is part of the change process. There will be no one-size-fits-all experience; success will vary by discipline and educational objectives. Unless everyone involved in this process is inspired to take risks, we will not enjoy the full potential these new approaches represent. Also, we should not forget the extent to which those who most benefit from the current system will attempt to hijack this change process for their own purposes.

With these issues in mind, consider the following vision of the change process to the classroom of tomorrow – a vision that leverages technology to create a more personalised learning experience. With the onset of this vision, the professor-student relationship will change. What is not likely to survive is the large class in which everyone progresses at the same pace. That paradigm will be replaced by a more customised and collaborative learning process. The reality of a technology-enabled **personalised** learning environment is still evolving. What seems clear is that at its heart is a more collaborate and student-mapped and paced process. The function of the professor, aided by educationalist, will also change. Student-professor collaboration will then determine both what content can be assigned to practice methods and how the student demonstrates mastery of that content. In such cases, timing issues will most likely be left entirely in the student's hands while technology specialists recommend the best hardware and software solutions. Critical thinking or application ideas will involve more specialised, face-to-face and interactive online approaches geared to the real-time needs and progress the student is making. Thus the professor, with the student's help, will vigilantly mix and blend the learning ingredients to produce a new learning environment. How this process plays out in reality will be the result of educational entrepreneurship, but it will surely **entail** both successes and some failures. The administration and accreditation of education will also have to change. As more education occurs outside the brick-and-mortar framework and is more centred on the student-professor interaction, the role of all non-teaching staff will need to be reassessed. As students and faculty increase their use of technology to **personalise** their formal and informal learning, educational technologist must be on hand to facilitate the effective use of that technology. Also the current hierarchical and standardised outcome formulas for administration and accreditation of colleges and universities are no longer tenable. Realistically, they are an **impediment** to the change needed.

Finally, we must address one of the most serious challenges facing online education – cheating. Simply put, cheating is rampant and we are turning a blind eye to the problem. Cheating threatens the integrity of the educational process and the value-added of the degree. Solutions must be found and implemented – or all changes **will be for naught**.

11. Which of the following is most nearly the **SAME** in meaning as the word given in bold as used in the passage

   Entail

   (*a*) limit   (*b*) occasion

   (*c*) involve   (*d*) subject

   (*e*) end

12. Which of the following can be the most suitable title for the passage ?

   (*a*) Educating Through Technology – What the Future can Be

   (*b*) Teachers – An Obsolete Future

   (*c*) The Hype Around Technology-Aided Education

   (*d*) Limitations of Technology

   (*e*) Evolution of Technology – The Way Forward for Tech Giants

13. Which of the following is/are **true** according to the author ?

   (A) The way the colleges are granted certification will have to change to accommodate the changes in imparting education through technology.

   (B) With the onset of technology-enabled education, the school/college premises or building will lose its importance slightly.

   (C) With onset of the desired level of technology-enabled education, learning will become a joint effort of students as well as teachers.

   (*a*) Only (A)

   (*b*) All the three (A), (B) and (C)

   (*c*) Only (B) and (C)

   (*d*) Only (C)

   (*e*) Only (A) and (B)

14. Choose the word which is most **OPPOSITE** in meaning of the word given in bold as used in the passage.

   Mitigating

   (*a*) aggravating   (*b*) irritating

   (*c*) annoying   (*d*) frustrating

   (*e*) infuriating

15. Which of the following is most nearly the **SAME** in meaning as the word given in bold as used in the passage ?

   Personalise

   (*a*) customise   (*b*) cause

   (*c*) sensitise   (*d*) own

   (*e*) preside

16. According to the author, which of the following changes will occur with the onset of the desired level of technology-aided education ?

   (A) The pace of learning for each student will be different.

   (B) The decision of how much time a student needs to learn will be left to the student's disposal.

   (C) The role of the teacher will change and become one of being the provider of tailored learning content to the student.

   (*a*) Only (C)

   (*b*) Only (B) and (C)

   (*c*) Only (A)

   (*d*) All the three (A), (B) and (C)

   (*e*) Only (A) and (C)

17. Which of the following is most **OPPOSITE** in meaning of the word given in bold as used in the passage ?

   Impediment

   (*a*) freedom

   (*b*) advantage

   (*c*) extravagance

   (*d*) luxury

   (*e*) autonomy

18. What does the author mean when he uses the word 'will be for naught' ?

(*a*) will be trouble

(*b*) will face complications

(*c*) will not be allowed

(*d*) will come together

(*e*) will amount to nothing

19. According to the author, which of the following is **NOT TRUE** about cheating ?

(*a*) It is one of the gravest problems faced in education.

(*b*) it undermines the value of the credential obtained through education.

(*c*) Not much is being done to curtail it at present.

(*d*) It is quite prevalent at present.

(*e*) All the given options are true.

20. According to the author, which of the following should be done to effectively integrate technology into education ?

(A) Risk taking should be kept to a bare minimum to mitigate adverse effects.

(B) Innovation amongst stakeholders of education and technology should be encouraged.

(C) We should be alert about people who may not allow certain changes for their own benefits.

(*a*) Only (A) and (C)

(*b*) Only (C)

(*c*) Only (B) and (C)

(*d*) Only (A)

(*e*) All the three (A), (B) and (C)

Directions (Q. 21-25) : *In this question four words are given of which two are most nearly the same or opposite in meaning. Find the two words which are either most nearly the same or opposite in meaning and indicate your answer by marking the option which represents the correct letter combination.*

21. (A) Tormented   (B) Agonised

(C) Aroused   (D) Removed

(*a*) A – C   (*b*) A – B

(*c*) A – D   (*d*) C – D

(*e*) B – D

22. (A) Striking   (B) Unimpressive

(C) Striving   (D) Unwilling

(*a*) A – C   (*b*) B – D

(*c*) A – B   (*d*) C – D

(*e*) B – C

23. (A) Patent   (B) Stylish

(C) Wasted   (D) Fashionable

(*a*) A – C   (*b*) C – D

(*c*) A – D   (*d*) B – D

(*e*) B – C

24. (A) Disclose   (B) Withstand

(C) Withhold   (D) Decide

(*a*) A – C   (*b*) B – C

(*c*) A – D   (*d*) C – D

(*e*) B – D

25. (A) Fathomed   (B) Devastated

(C) Ruined   (D) Abrupt

(*a*) B – D   (*b*) B – C

(*c*) C – D   (*d*) A – C

(*e*) A – D

Directions (Q. 26-30) : *Each question below has two blanks. Each blank indicates that something has been omitted. Choose the words that best fit the meaning of the sentence as a whole.*

26. As per the present definition, the factory inspector _____ all factories located in an area to _____ a day other than Sunday as the weekly holiday.

(*a*) permits, attend   (*b*) allows, observe

(*c*) assures, believe   (*d*) admits, accept

(*e*) grants, adhere

27. The family members of the victim said that the victim was being _____ into _____ her complaint.

(*a*) protected, accepting

(*b*) disturbed, locating

(*c*) allowed, maintaining

(*d*) forced, preparing

(*e*) threatened, withdrawing

28. The new management is pro-cleanliness and will _____ all the employees who spit or smoke in the office _____.

(*a*) penalise, hours

(*b*) punish, environment

(*c*) warn, surrounding

(*d*) fine, premises

(*e*) pardon, area

29. Sixty-six years after India attained Independence, the government has finally _____ to change the measure to estimate the output of a steam-engine horsepower that is being _____ since the British Raj.

(*a*) thought, operated   (*b*) decided, used

(*c*) planned, provided   (*d*) caused, handled

(*e*) reasoned, postponed

30. With women participation _____ sharply in the labour force over the past decade, there is a need to improve _____ for them.

   (*a*) dipping, opportunities

   (*b*) reducing, ways

   (*c*) withdrawing, convenience

   (*d*) stressing, circumstances

   (*e*) steeping, excuses

Directions (Q. 31-35) : *Rearrange the given six sentences (A), (B), (C), (D), (E) and (F) in a proper sequence so as to form a meaningful paragraph and then answer the given questions.*

(A) But it is normal for rates to vary somewhat.

(B) The rate at which these actions emerge is sometimes a worry for parent.

(C) As a child grows, his or her nervous system becomes more mature.

(D) Having said that variation is normal, nearly all children begin to exhibit certain motor skills at a fairly consistent rate unless some type of disability is present.

(E) As this happens, the child becomes more and more capable of performing increasingly complex actions.

(F) Hence, they frequently fret about whether or not their children are developing these skills at a normal rate.

31. Which of the following should be the **THIRD** sentence after the rearrangement ?

   (*a*) A   (*b*) B

   (*c*) C   (*d*) E

   (*e*) F

32. Which of the following should be the **SIXTH** (last) sentence after the rearrangement ?

   (*a*) A   (*b*) B

   (*c*) C   (*d*) D

   (*e*) E

33. Which of the following should be the **FIRST** sentence after the rearrangement ?

   (*a*) A   (*b*) B

   (*c*) C   (*d*) D

   (*e*) E

34. Which of the following should be the **SECOND** sentence after the rearrangement ?

   (*a*) A   (*b*) B

   (*c*) F   (*d*) D

   (*e*) E

35. Which of the following should be the **FOURTH** sentence after the rearrangement ?

   (*a*) A   (*b*) D

   (*c*) B   (*d*) F

   (*e*) E

Directions (Q. 36-40) : *Read each sentence to find out whether there is any grammatical error in it. The error, if any, will be in one part of the sentence. Mark the part with the error as your answer. If there is no error, mark 'No error' as your answer. (Ignore the errors of punctuations, if any.)*

36. Attributing rise in inflation partly for withholding of food stock by traders,/the minister said that/he was committed/to easing this supply side bottleneck.

   (*a*) Attributing rise inflation partly for withholding of food stocks by traders

   (*b*) the minister said that

   (*c*) he was committed

   (*d*) to easing this supply side bottleneck

   (*e*) No error

37. India's largest utility vehicle and tractor maker/ is again in the race of acquire/for stake in Swedish company/which is a premium car maker.

   (*a*) India's largest utility vehicle and tractor maker

   (*b*) is again in the race of acquire

   (*c*) for stake in Swedish company

   (*d*) which is a premium car maker

   (*e*) No error

38. With sale of branded or premium petrol becoming almost nil/due to high duties,/a government appointed panel has recommended/slashing excise duty to make them at par with regular fuel.

   (*a*) With sale of branded or premium petrol becoming almost nil

   (*b*) due to high duties

   (*c*) a government appointed panel has recommended

   (*d*) slashing excise duty to make them at par with regular fuel.

   (*e*) No error

39. Keeping in mind/that power cuts are on different days in different areas/the change in the factory law would enable individual factories within an area/to determining their own weekly holidays.

   (*a*) Keeping in mind

   (*b*) that power cuts are on different days in different areas

   (*c*) the change in the factory law would enable individual factories within an area

   (*d*) to determining their own weekly holidays.

   (*e*) No error

40. Police officers have refused on identify the bystander,/who is the only eyewitness to the crime,/but have said that the investigating team would explore/if he could be a witness in the case.

   (*a*) Police officers have refused on identify the bystander

   (*b*) who is the only eyewitness to the crime

   (*c*) but have said that the investigating team would explore

   (*d*) if he could be a witness in the case

   (*e*) No error

Directions (Q. 41 – 50) : *In the given passage there are blanks, each of which has been numbered. Against each, five words are suggested, one of which fits the blank appropriately. Find out the appropriate word in each case.*

Generally a disaster (**41**) in significant loss in social, psychological and economic aspects. It not only (**42**) to structural damages, but also leaves families torn apart, children orphaned, livelihoods destroyed and communities traumatised.

Non-structural factors such as lack of responsiveness of government officials and ineffective leadership are mainly (**43**) for any disaster mismanagements. India is (**44**) to a variety of natural and man-made disasters. Strong and effective emergency management has been a felt (**45**) in all corners of the world. Effective policies play a (**46**) role in mitigating the impact of disasters and reducing likely losses of life and property. Economic resources are important for any disaster management. Yet, it has been (**47**) that economic resources did not necessarily translate into greater investment in this domain as there is no (**48**) of issues that demand governments attention and resources. Disaster management has (**49**) acquired importance in the agenda of governance, unless there is a major natural or man-made disaster. The major shortcomings observed in Indian disaster management, along with their probable solutions, need to be discussed on an (**50**) basis.

41. (*a*) prepares   (*b*) results

   (*c*) affects   (*d*) entails

   (*e*) promotes

42. (*a*) causes   (*b*) creates

   (*c*) results   (*d*) imparts

   (*e*) leads

43. (*a*) reasons   (*b*) responsible

   (*c*) accounts   (*d*) amounts

   (*e*) factors

44. (*a*) subjected   (*b*) susceptibility

   (*c*) available   (*d*) vulnerable

   (*e*) centre

45. (*a*) relation   (*b*) abstract

   (*c*) evolution   (*d*) creation

   (*e*) need

46. (*a*) enormous   (*b*) tough

   (*c*) vital   (*d*) single

   (*e*) important

47. (*a*) recognised   (*b*) routed

   (*c*) placed   (*d*) collected

   (*e*) seeing

48. (*a*) much   (*b*) amount

   (*c*) collection   (*d*) dearth

   (*e*) failure

49. (*a*) seldom   (*b*) forever

   (*c*) great   (*d*) much

   (*e*) always

50. (*a*) important   (*b*) understanding

   (*c*) urgent   (*d*) priority

   (*e*) upright

TEST–II : GENERAL AWARENESS, MARKETING AND COMPUTERS

51. A Basic Savings Bank Deposit Account facility is available ______ .

   (*a*) to all individuals irrespective to their background

   (*b*) all individuals from below poverty-line-families only

   (*c*) only to individuals from the SC/ST only

   (*d*) only to individuals from the minority communities only

   (*e*) only to individuals from weaker sections of the society

52. Which of the following is an example of an input device ?

   (*a*) Monitor   (*b*) Scanner

   (*c*) Printer   (*d*) CD

   (*e*) Speaker

53. The Reserve Bank of India has been critical of home loan with comparatively low interest rates in the initial year but higher in the subsequent years, which are properly known as the ______ .

   (*a*) Teaser Rates   (*b*) Cheater Rates

   (*c*) Twister Rates   (*d*) Cheaper Rates

   (*e*) Trickster Rates

54. Relationship marketing is also know as _____.

  (*a*) Loyalty marketing

  (*b*) Experiential marketing

  (*c*) Value marketing

  (*d*) Promotional marketing

  (*e*) Brand marketing

55. PCs are considered fourth-generation and contain _____.

  (*a*) information   (*b*) data

  (*c*) vacuum tube   (*d*) microprocessors

  (*e*) transistors

56. Which of the following is not an aggressiveness strategy ?

  (*a*) All the given options are aggressivenes strategies

  (*b*) Building

  (*c*) Harvesting

  (*d*) Holding

  (*e*) Intensification

57. Which of the following nations is 'not' a member of SAARC ?

  (*a*) Nepal   (*b*) Mauritius

  (*c*) Bhutan   (*d*) Afghanistan

  (*e*) Maldives

58. Market Price is also known as _____.

  (*a*) List price   (*b*) Value price

  (*c*) Effective price   (*d*) Retail price

  (*e*) Wholesaler price

59. The phenomenon when a customer dislikes a product and talks against the product

  (*a*) Misinformation   (*b*) Unfavorable environment

  (*c*) Propaganda   (*d*) Bad impression

  (*e*) Bad mouth

60. The RBI policy rate which is purely an indicative rate used by the Reserve Bank of India to signal long-term outlook on interest rate is _____.

  (*a*) Bank Rate   (*b*) Repo rate

  (*c*) Call Money Rate   (*d*) Notice Money Rate

  (*e*) Reserve Repo Rate

61. The amount specified as the Cash Reserve Ratio (CRR) is held in cash and cash equivalents and is stored in bank vaults or parked with _____.

  (*a*) Small industries Development Bank of India (SIDBI)

  (*b*) Government of India (GoI)

  (*c*) Reserve Bank of India (RBI)

  (*d*) State Bank of India (SBI)

  (*e*) Rural Infrastructure Development Fund (RIDF)

62. As consumer banking frauds are on the rise, a Reserve Bank of India (RBI) group has suggested the use of PKI in order to improve payment system in the country.

The abbreviation PKI stands for _____.

  (*a*) Public key infrastructure

  (*b*) Personal key infrastructure

  (*c*) Private key infrastructure

  (*d*) Permanent key infrastructure

  (*e*) Proprietary key infrastructure

63. The Reserve Bank of India recently issued guidelines allowing minors over 10 years of age to operate bank accounts independently with a view to _____.

  (*a*) Promoting financial inclusion

  (*b*) Increasing low-cost deposits of banks

  (*c*) Improving CASA percentage of banks

  (*d*) Mobilising Savings Bank Deposits of banks

  (*e*) Putting ATMs and other infrastructure to optimum use

64. Java is referred to as a _____.

  (*a*) high-level language

  (*b*) complex language

  (*c*) hardware device driver

  (*d*) low-level language

  (*e*) programming mid-level language

65. 'Kepler-78b' is the name of _____.

  (*a*) an American nuclear missile

  (*b*) Russian armoured vehicle

  (*c*) a precision-measuring instrument

  (*d*) a Spanish sea vessel

  (*e*) an earth-sized planet far beyond our solar system

66. The Depositor Education and Awareness Fund (DEAF) has been set up with

  (*a*) Public Sector Banks

  (*b*) Indian Banks' Association

  (*c*) State Bank of India

  (*d*) Reserve Bank of India

  (*e*) Government of India

67. The operating system is the most common type of _____ software.

  (*a*) application

  (*b*) antivirus

  (*c*) communication

  (*d*) system

  (*e*) word-processing software

68. Hindustan Motors, India's oldest car maker, recently shut down its factory at Uttarpara in West Bengal and suspended the production of the iconic

   (*a*) Utility Vehicle Pushpak

   (*b*) Ambassador Car

   (*c*) Bedford Truck

   (*d*) Contessa Car

   (*e*) Morris Oxford Car

69. In Trade Finance, a financial transaction involving the purchase of receivables from exporters by a third party who takes all the risks associated with the receivables is known as ______.

   (*a*) Forfaiting   (*b*) Securitisation

   (*c*) Negotiation   (*d*) Factoring

   (*e*) Assignment

70. Which is not a storage device ?

   (*a*) A floppy disk   (*b*) A printer

   (*c*) A DVD   (*d*) A Hard Disk

   (*e*) A CD

71. ______ is a written description of a computer programme functions.

   (*a*) Explanatory instructions

   (*b*) Graphical user interface

   (*c*) Plug and Play

   (*d*) README files

   (*e*) Documentation

72. The term 'pre-shipment finance' relates to ______.

   (*a*) Export Credit

   (*b*) Farm Credit

   (*c*) Consumer Credit

   (*d*) Investment Credit

   (*e*) Industrial Credit

73. The Government of India has undertaken a programme of recapitalisation of Public Sector Banks to help them enhance business growth and ______.

   (*a*) Captial Adequacy Norms

   (*b*) Ratio of Non Performing Assets

   (*c*) Per Employee Business Ratio

   (*d*) CASA Ratio

   (*e*) Credit to Deposit Ratio

74. Which of the following keys is used to delete characters to the left of the cursor ?

   (*a*) Alt + Delete   (*b*) Shift

   (*c*) Esc   (*d*) Delete

   (*e*) Backspace

75. Senior Supreme Court advocate Mukul Rohatgi has recently been appointed as the new

   (*a*) Principal Secretary to the PM

   (*b*) Director of Public Prosecutions

   (*c*) Advocate General of India

   (*d*) Solicitor General of India

   (*e*) Attorney General of India

76. Products that are usually purchased due to adversity and high promotional back-up rather than desire are called ______.

   (*a*) regular goods   (*b*) unsought goods

   (*c*) preferred goods   (*d*) sought goods

   (*e*) unique goods

77. The amount of memory (RAM or ROM) is measured in ______.

   (*a*) Bites   (*b*) Bits

   (*c*) Mega Bytes   (*d*) Mega Bits

   (*e*) Hertz

78. Who amongst the following has recently been sworn in as the first female judge at Pakistan's National Sharia court, which hears cases under the Islamic legislation ?

   (*a*) Ashraf Jilani   (*b*) Ashraf Jabber

   (*c*) Ashraf Jana   (*d*) Ashraf Jahangir

   (*e*) Ashraf Jehan

79. The Canadian Government has announced the suspension of funding to the Common wealth Secretariat for two years over the issue of human rights abuse by ______.

   (*a*) United Kingdom   (*b*) New Zealand

   (*c*) South Africa   (*d*) Australia

   (*e*) Sri Lanka

80. Nobel laureate and recipient of the US Presidential Medal and also the US Congressional Medal Muhammad Yunus is well known for his contribution to Bangladesh's ______.

   (*a*) Consumer Credit Sector

   (*b*) Agro-Credit Sector

   (*c*) Housing Finance sector

   (*d*) Micro-Credit Sector

   (*e*) Retail Credit Sector

81. Which of the following is NOT a technique of measuring customer satisfaction and monitoring customer's complaint ?

   (*a*) Exit interviews

   (*b*) Web information hotlines

   (*c*) Business analysis

   (*d*) Customer complaints database

   (*e*) Telephone information hotlines

82. Who amongst the following has been named as the goodwill ambassador for the 35th National Games to be held in Kerala in early 2015 ?

(*a*) S Sreesanth   (*b*) Sachin Tendulkar

(*c*) Mary Kom   (*d*) PT Usha

(*e*) Mahendra Singh Dhoni

83. The official football of the Brazil 2014 FIFA World Cup is named as 'Brazuca', which means ______.

(*a*) The spirit of sportsmanship

(*b*) The spirit of the game is in playing

(*c*) The Brazilian way of life

(*d*) May the best team win

(*e*) We play to win

84. Underpriced products sell very well, but they produce less revenue than they would have if prices were raised to the ______.

(*a*) variable level

(*b*) demand-curve level

(*c*) price-floor level

(*d*) perceived-value level

(*e*) value-based level

85. A customer's requirement about any product in which he/she needs to avail core features in that product, is called

(*a*) Real need   (*b*) No need

(*c*) Stated need   (*d*) Unstated need

(*e*) Delighted need

86. Which of the following is a mode for creating charge on Life Insurance Policies ?

(*a*) Pledge

(*b*) Lien

(*c*) Assignment

(*d*) Hypothecation

(*e*) Equitable Mortgage

87. Bankers generally do not allow opening of accounts in the name of ______.

(*a*) executors and trustees

(*b*) persons of unsound mind

(*c*) illiterate persons

(*d*) pardanashin ladies

(*e*) visually impaired persons

88. The hard drive is normally located ______.

(*a*) next to the printer

(*b*) plugged into the back of the computer

(*c*) underneath the monitor

(*d*) on top of the CD-ROM

(*e*) inside the system base unit

89. The winner of the 51st Femina Miss India 2014 pageant is ______.

(*a*) Jhatalckha Malhotra (*b*) Navneet Kaur Dhillon

(*c*) Koyal Rana   (*d*) Gail Nicole da Silva

(*e*) Megan Young

90. Virtual memory allocates hard disk space to supplement the immediate, functional memory capacity of what ?

(*a*) ROM   (*b*) EPROM

(*c*) The registers   (*d*) Extended memory

(*e*) RAM

91. 3/10 net 30 is an example of which of the following?

(*a*) Cash discount   (*b*) Quantity discount

(*c*) Seasonal discount   (*d*) Bulk discount

(*e*) Trade discount

92. Which of the following refers to restarting the system when it is already powered on ?

(*a*) a strong boot   (*b*) hibernation

(*c*) a cold boot   (*d*) standby mode

(*e*) a warm boot

93. ______ is having more memory addresses than are physically available.

(*a*) Virtual Memory

(*b*) System software

(*c*) Applications software

(*d*) RAM

(*e*) Vertical Memory

94. Which of the following refers to dangerous programs that can be 'caught' be opening e-mail attachments and downloading software from the internet ?

(*a*) utiliy   (*b*) virus

(*c*) honeypot   (*d*) spam

(*e*) app

95. Commercial Paper (CP) is an unsecured money market instrument issued in the form of a promissory note. Commercial Paper can be issued in denominations of ______.

(*a*) ₹ 1 lakh or multiples thereof

(*b*) ₹ 2 lakh or multiples thereof

(*c*) ₹ 3 lakh or multiples thereof

(*d*) ₹ 5 lakh or multiples thereof

(*e*) ₹ 10 lakh or multiples thereof

96. A company is providing warehousing facility to its channel members. The company is using which of the following ?

(*a*) Seasonal discount   (*b*) Cash discount

(*c*) Quantity discount   (*d*) Trade discount

(*e*) Quality discount

97. Aggressive pricing is associated with which of the following stage of product life cycle ?

(*a*) Not Associated   (*b*) Introduction

(*c*) Growth   (*d*) Maturity

(*e*) Decline

98. The United nations (UN) and the International Olympic Committee (IOC) have recently signed a historic agreement to use the power of sports to promote ______.

(*a*) Literacy and awareness

(*b*) Peace and economic development

(*c*) World amity and Friendship

(*d*) Peaceful use to nuclear technology

(*e*) World trade and commerce

99. Which of the following is NOT an objective of discounts ?

(*a*) All the given options are objectives of discounts

(*b*) Reward competitors

(*c*) Reward valuable customers

(*d*) Move out-of-date stock

(*e*) Increase short-term sales

100. The abbreviation ASBA stands for ______.

(*a*) Applications Supported by Blocked Account

(*b*) Applications Supported by Bank Account

(*c*) Applications Sustained by Blocked Amount

(*d*) Applications Serviced by Blocked Account

(*e*) Applications Supported by Blocked Amount

TEST–III : DATA ANALYSIS AND INTERPRETATION

Directions (Q. 101 – 106) : *Study the following graph carefully to answer the given questions.*

Strength of seven technology institutes with specialisation in IT, Electronics and Mechanical in 2012

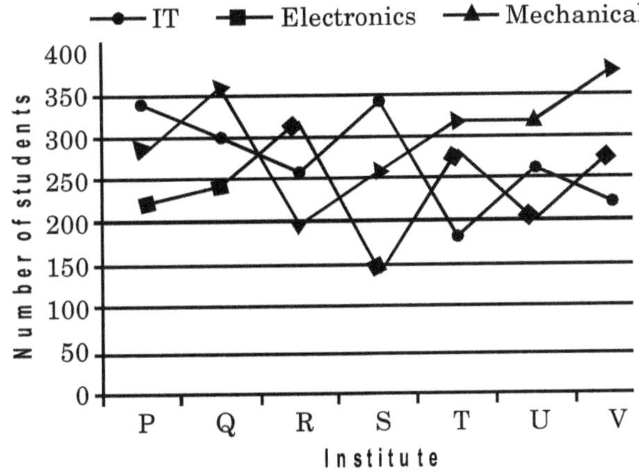

101. If the no. of students with Mechanical specialisation in each institute increased by 20% and the no. of students with Electronics specialisation in each institute decreased by 15% from 2012 to 2013, the total no. of students with Mechanical from all the institutes in 2013 is approximately what per cent of the total no. of students with Electronics specialisation from all the institutes in 2013 ?

(*a*) 122   (*b*) 116

(*c*) 162   (*d*) 132

(*e*) 178

102. What is the ratio of the total no. of students in institute R to that in V ?

(*a*) 39 : 43   (*b*) 39 : 44

(*c*) 37 : 44   (*d*) 39 : 45

(*e*) 38 : 43

103. What is the difference between the total no. of students with IT specialisation from all the institutes together and the total no. of students with Mechanical specialisation from all the institutes together ?

(*a*) 260   (*b*) 240

(*c*) 280   (*d*) 220

(*e*) 250

104. If the no. of students in institutes P, Q and R with IT specialisation increased by 15%, 22% and 10% respectively from 2012 to 2013, what was the total no. of students with IT specialisation in the three institutes together in 2013 ?

(*a*) 1028   (*b*) 1056

(*c*) 1043   (*d*) 1142

(*e*) 1145

105. If out of the total no. of students for all three specialisations together in Institute Q, the no. of students having liking for Music, Painting and Cricket are in the ratio of 5 : 6 : 7, then what is the no. of students having liking for Music from this institute ?

(*a*) 250   (*b*) 300

(*c*) 350   (*d*) 360

(*e*) 280

106. In institutes P, T and U the percentage of girls out of total no. of students with Electronics specialisation in the respective institutes is 50%, 55% and 48% respectively, what is the total no. boys in these three institutes with Electronics specialisation ?

(*a*) 340   (*b*) 386

(*c*) 356   (*d*) 360

(*e*) 314

Directions (Q. 107 – 112) : *Study the table and answer the given questions :*

Advertisement revenues (in ₹ thousand) generated from Printed Version (PV) and Online Version (OV) of 6 magazines during 6 months

Month	Magazine P		Magazine Q		Magazine R		Magazine S		Magazine T		Magazine U	
	PV	OV	PV	OV	PV	OV	PV	OV	PV	OV	PV	OV
Jan	169	163	201	145	136	141	209	168	152	209	131	184
Feb	144	171	157	139	156	149	132	223	186	217	98	190
Mar	129	148	204	144	152	174	174	164	116	185	118	219
Apr	163	139	232	139	168	207	148	172	129	156	174	236
May	113	152	128	151	196	209	132	211	187	139	168	111
June	172	141	142	163	178	243	211	177	154	144	151	194

107. Which of the given statement is /are true ?

(A) Total advertisement revenue generated from online version by magazine T in all the given months together is exactly 44% less than the total advertisement revenue generated from printed version by the same magazine in all the given months together.

(B) The difference between advertisement revenue generated (from both online and printed version) by all the given magazines in January and advertisement revenue generated (from both Online and Printed version) by all the given magazines in June is ₹ 62000.

(C) Only for one magazine the advertisement revenue generated from printed version displayed a constant increase from the previous month during the given 6-month period.

(*a*) Only (B) and (C)   (*b*) Only (A) and (B)

(*c*) Only (A)   (*d*) Only (B)

(*e*) All (A), (B) and (C)

108. Total advertisement revenue generated from online version by Magazine U in all the given months together is by what per cent more than the total advertisement revenue generated from printed version by the same magazine in all the given months together ?

(*a*) 25   (*b*) 27.5

(*c*) 35   (*d*) 30

(*e*) 32.5

109. In case of Magazine R, between which two given months was there approximately 15% rise in advertisement revenues generated (from both Printed and Online version together) ?

(*a*) January-February   (*b*) February-March

(*c*) May-June   (*d*) March-April

(*e*) April-May

110. The ratio of advertisement revenue generated from printed version by Magazine P to advertisement revenue generated from online version by the same magazine in July is the same as the ratio of advertisement revenue generated from printed version by Magazine Q to advertisement revenue generated from online version by the same magazine in March. If the advertisement revenue generated from online version by Magazine P in July was ₹ 1,08,000, what was the advertisement revenue generated from the printed version by the same magazine in July?

(*a*) ₹ 1,87,000

(*b*) ₹ 1,53,000

(*c*) ₹ 1,36,000

(*d*) ₹ 1,70,000

(*e*) ₹ 1,19,000

111. What is the ratio of the total advertisement revenue generated from online version of all the given magazines together in February to the total advertisement revenue generated from printed version of all the given magazines together in May ?

(*a*) 33 : 28   (*b*) 39 : 28

(*c*) 27 : 16   (*d*) 33 : 20

(*e*) 27 : 22

112. The total advertisement revenue generated from printed version by Magazine P in January and April together is what per cent less than the total advertisement revenue generated from online version by magazine S in February and June together ?

(*a*) 22   (*b*) 14

(*c*) 27   (*d*) 19

(*e*) 17

Directions (Q. 113 – 117) : *Study the table and answer the given questions :*

Data related to human resource of a multinational company (X) which has 145 offices across 8 countries

Country	Offices	Total number of employees	Ratio of male to female employees	Percentage of post-graduate employees
A	16	2568	5 : 7	75
B	18	2880	11 : 5	65
C	14	2310	10 : 11	40
D	22	3575	3 : 2	60
E	13	2054	7 : 6	50
F	17	2788	20 : 21	75
G	24	3720	8 : 7	55
H	21	3360	9 : 5	80

113. If the number of male postgraduate employees in Country H is 1800, what per cent of the female employees in that particular country are postgraduate ?

(*a*) 76　　　　　　(*b*) 74

(*c*) 72　　　　　　(*d*) 64

(*e*) 68

114. In which of the given countries is the percentage of women employees with respect to the total number of employees (both males and females in that country the second lowest ?

(*a*) G　　　　　　(*b*) B

(*c*) E　　　　　　(*d*) H

(*e*) D

115. What is the ratio of the total number of male employees in countries B and H together to the total number of female employees in countries C and D together ?

(*a*) 63 : 52　　　　(*b*) 51 : 38

(*c*) 77 : 64　　　　(*d*) 69 : 44

(*e*) 57 : 40

116. What is the difference between the average number of postgraduate employees in countries A, B and D together and the average number of postgraduate employees in countries F, G and H ?

(*a*) 282　　　　　(*b*) 276

(*c*) 316　　　　　(*d*) 342

(*e*) 294

117. Which of the given countries has the highest number of average employees per office ?

(*a*) F　　　　　　(*b*) H

(*c*) B　　　　　　(*d*) C

(*e*) D

Directions (Q. 118 – 122) : *Study the following graph carefully to answer the given questions.*

Number of students playing Carrom, Cricket and Hockey from different schools

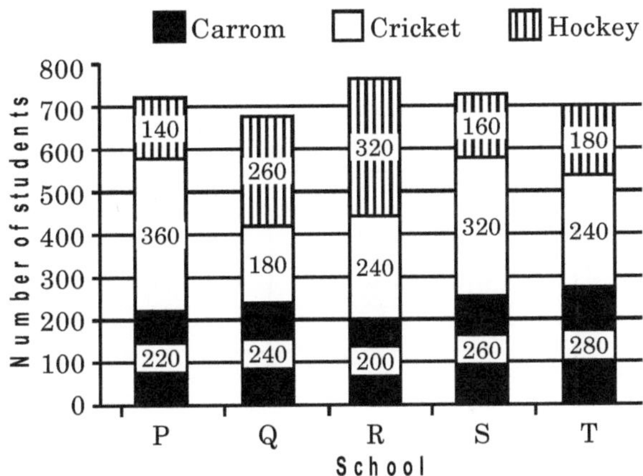

118. The total number of students playing Carrom and Hockey together from school P is what per cent of the total no. of students playing these two games together from school R ?

(*a*) $68\dfrac{3}{16}$　　　　(*b*) $62\dfrac{3}{13}$

(*c*) $69\dfrac{3}{13}$　　　　(*d*) $63\dfrac{3}{13}$

(*e*) $62\dfrac{3}{16}$

119. If the no. of students playing each game in school S is increased by 15% and the no. of students playing each game in school Q is decreased by 5%, what will be the difference between the no. of students in school S and Q ?

(*a*) 54　　　　　　(*b*) 218

(*c*) 356　　　　　(*d*) 224

(*e*) 205

120. If out of the students playing Cricket from schools Q, S and T, 40%, 35% and 45% respectively got selected for State level competition, what is the total no. of students who got selected for State level competition from these three schools together ?

   (*a*) 346   (*b*) 241

   (*c*) 292   (*d*) 284

   (*e*) 268

121. The total number of students playing Hockey from all schools together is approximately what per cent of the total number of students playing Cricket from all schools together ?

   (*a*) 84   (*b*) 74

   (*c*) 72   (*d*) 79

   (*e*) 70

122. From school P, out of the students playing Carrom, 40% got selected for State level competition, out of which 25% further got selected for National level competition. From school T, out of the students playing Carrom, 45% got selected for State level competition, out of which two-thirds further got selected for National level competition. What is the total no. of students playing Carrom from these two schools who got selected for National level competition ?

   (*a*) 106

   (*b*) 98

   (*c*) 112

   (*d*) 108

   (*e*) 96

Directions (Q. 123 – 128) : *Study the following table carefully and answer the given questions.*

Population Abstract of country 'X'

State	Total population	Rural : Urban	Male : Female	Literate : Illiterate	% Graduate out of Literates
Maharashtra	22,50,000	28 : 17	23 : 22	5 : 3	48
Madhya Pradesh	16,42,000	5 : 3	5 : 3	3 : 1	35
Odisha	11,36,000	11 : 5	9 : 7	11 : 5	38
West Bengal	24,80,000	18 : 13	21 : 19	20 : 11	42
Tamil Nadu	20,50,000	16 : 9	13 : 12	3 : 2	56
Uttaranchal	2,48,000	5 : 3	9 : 7	3 : 1	44
Jharkhand	9,60,000	17 : 7	11 : 9	4 : 1	32

Note : All the figures are fictitious and not actual.

123. The urban population of Maharashtra and Odisha together is what per cent of the total population of these two states ? (rounded off to two digits after decimal)

   (*a*) 32.49   (*b*) 35.59

   (*c*) 38.55   (*d*) 32.85

   (*e*) 36.57

124. Approximately, by what per cent is the urban population of Maharashtra less than its rural population ?

   (*a*) 33   (*b*) 39

   (*c*) 49   (*d*) 45

   (*e*) 34

125. What per cent of the total population of West Bengal, Odisha and Madhya Pradesh together is illiterate ? (rounded off to nearest integer)

   (*a*) 28   (*b*) 34

   (*c*) 29   (*d*) 33

   (*e*) 31

126. What is the difference between the number of graduates from Madhya Pradesh and Uttaranchal ?

   (*a*) 3,66,340   (*b*) 3,49,185

   (*c*) 3,88,185   (*d*) 3,82,340

   (*e*) 3,55,840

127. What is the total no. of graduates from Odisha, West Bengal and Maharashtra together ?

   (*a*) 15,09,695

   (*b*) 15,29,559

   (*c*) 16,43,780

   (*d*) 16,19,455

   (*e*) 16,29,095

128. What is the ratio of the total female population of Tamil Nadu and Jharkhand together to the total male population of these two states together ?

   (*a*) 697 : 798   (*b*) 715 : 797

   (*c*) 708 : 797   (*d*) 698 : 797

   (*e*) 696 : 797

Directions (Q. 129 – 135) : *Study the following information carefully to answer the questions.*

In a medical college there are 1600 students studying Dentistry and Homeopathy. Each student from each course knows one or more languages out of English, Hindi and Bengali. 45% of the students study Dentistry and the remaining students study Homeopathy.

Out of the students studying Dentistry, boys and girls are in the ratio of 5 : 3.

Out of the boys studying Dentistry, 16% know only English, 10% know only Hindi and 4% know only Bengali. 24% know English as well as Hindi, 20% know English as well as Bengali and 14% know Hindi as well as Bengali. The remaining boys know all three languages.

Out of the girls studying Dentistry, 20% know only English, 10% know only Hindi and 10% know only Bengali, 20% know English as well as Hindi. 20% know English as well as bengali. 10% know Hindi as well as Bengali. The remaining girls know all the three languages.

Out of the students studying Homeopathy, boys and girls are in the ratio of 4 : 7.

Out of the boys studying Homeopathy, 20% know only English, 15% know only Hindi and 5% know only Bengali. 15% know English as well as Hindi, 25% know English as well as Bengali, and 10% know Hindi as well as Bengali. The remaining boys know all three languages.

Out of the girls studying Homeopathy, 15% know only English, 15% know only Hindi and 5% know only Bengali. 20% know English as well as Hindi, 20% know English as well as Bengali, and 15% know Hindi as well as Bengali. The remaining girls know all three languages.

129. How many students studying Dentistry know only either English or Hindi ?

  (*a*) 166   (*b*) 162

  (*c*) 308   (*d*) 198

  (*e*) 248

130. How many students in the college know all three languages ?

  (*a*) 108   (*b*) 132

  (*c*) 169   (*d*) 137

  (*e*) 142

131. What per cent of the total no. of girls in the college know Bengali ?

  (*a*) 45   (*b*) 40

  (*c*) 48   (*d*) 42

  (*e*) 50

132. How many students studying Homeopathy do not know English ?

  (*a*) 292   (*b*) 232

  (*c*) 228   (*d*) 298

  (*e*) 207

133. Out of the students studying Homeopathy, what is the ratio of the no. of boys knowing English to the no. of girls knowing Hindi ?

  (*a*) 3 : 5   (*b*) 2 : 3

  (*c*) 9 : 11   (*d*) 9 : 13

  (*e*) 1 : 3

134. Out of the total no. of students studying Dentistry, what per cent knows at least two languages ?

  (*a*) $61\dfrac{12}{13}$ (*b*) $57\dfrac{13}{16}$

  (*c*) $59\dfrac{13}{17}$ (*d*) $66\dfrac{1}{4}$

  (*e*) $62\dfrac{12}{19}$

135. What per cent of the total no. of girls in the college do not know Hindi ? (rounded off to nearest integer)

  (*a*) 38   (*b*) 46

  (*c*) 48   (*d*) 36

  (*e*) 43

Directions (Q. 136 – 143) : *Study the following pie-charts carefully to answer the questions.*

Distribution of number of watches (Sports watches & Luxury watches) sold by 8 stores in 2004 :

Total number = 56000

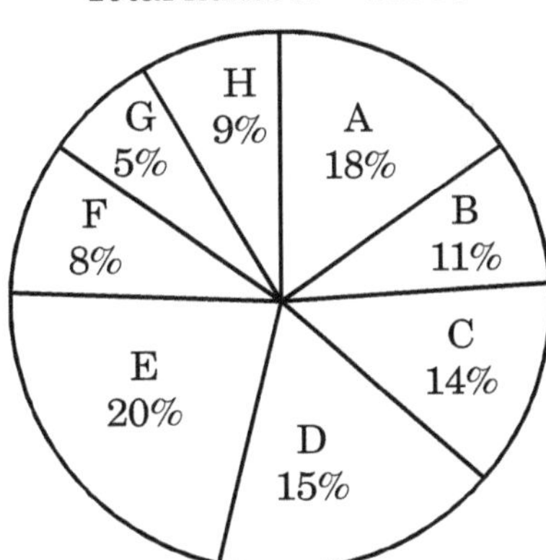

Distribution of Sports watches sold by 8 stores in 2004:

Total number = 32000

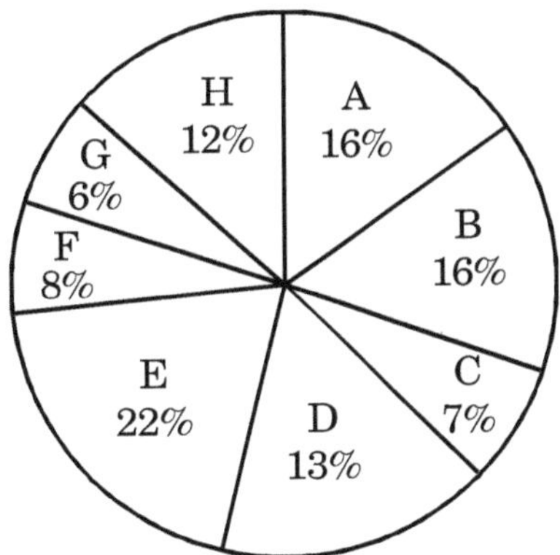

136. Total no. of luxury watches sold by Stores C and H together is by what per cent less than the total number of watches (Sports watches and Luxury watches) sold by Stores F and H together ?

(a) $29\frac{5}{6}$ (b) $27\frac{3}{7}$

(c) $31\frac{3}{5}$ (d) $28\frac{4}{7}$

(e) $26\frac{5}{9}$

137. The number of watches (Sports watches and Luxury watches) sold by Store D is by what per cent more than the total number of Sports watches sold by Stores C, F and G together ?

(a) 22.5   (b) 25

(c) 27.5   (d) 35

(e) 30

138. What is the ratio of the total number of Sports watches sold by Stores A and B together to that of the total number of watches (Sports and Luxury) sold by Stores C and F together ?

(a) 64 : 77   (b) 48 : 61

(c) 56 : 77   (d) 64 : 81

(e) 48 : 73

139. What is the average number of Luxury watches sold by Stores A, D, E, F and H together ?

(a) 3152   (b) 3296

(c) 3548   (d) 3186

(e) 3428

140. If the number of watches sold by stores A, D and E increased by 10%, 35% and 15% respectively and so did Sports watches sold by these stores from 2004 to 2005 what was the total no. of Luxury watches sold by these three stores in 2005 ?

(a) 16172   (b) 14966

(c) 15848   (d) 15964

(e) 16392

141. What is the central angle corresponding to the number of watches (Sports watches and Luxury watches) sold by Store B ?

(a) 39.6°   (b) 36.6°

(c) 44.2°   (d) 42.2°

(e) 45.4°

142. The total number of Sports watches sold by Store E and F together is what per cent of the total number of watches (Sports watches and Luxury watches) sold by Store E ?

(a) $78\frac{7}{11}$ (b) $83\frac{3}{7}$

(c) $82\frac{5}{14}$ (d) $65\frac{9}{14}$

(e) $85\frac{5}{7}$

143. What is the difference between the average number of Sports watches sold by Stores B, C, G and H together and the average number of Luxury watches sold by the same stores together ?

(a) 1100   (b) 12000

(c) 900   (d) 800

(e) 1300

Directions (Q. 144 – 150) : *Study the following graph carefully to answer the given questions.*

Total investment (in ₹ thousand) of Gautam and Rudra in 6 schemes (M, N, O, P, Q and R)

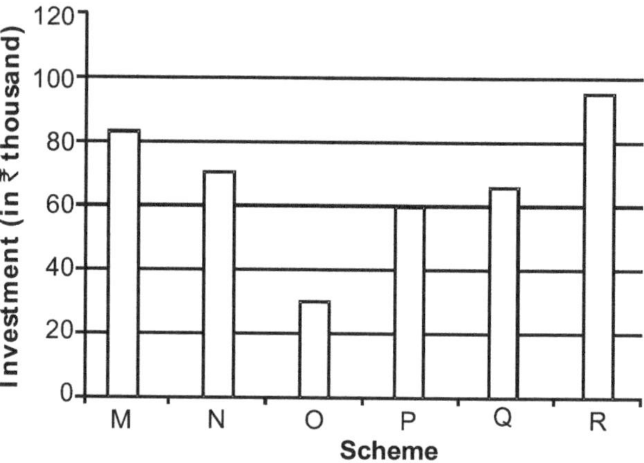

Percentage of Gautam's investment out of total investment :

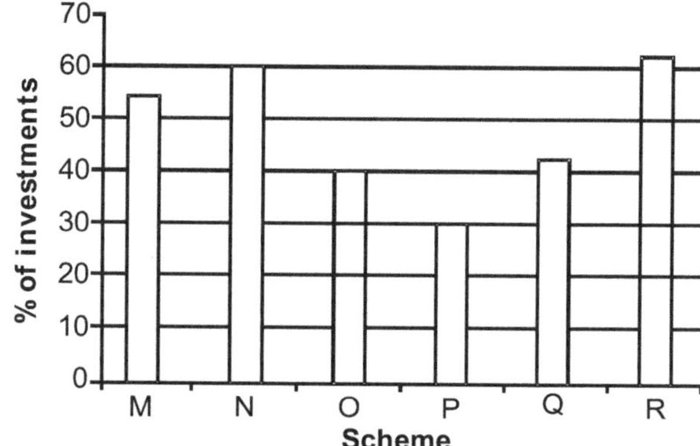

144. Scheme M offers simple interest at a certain rate of interest (pcpa). If the difference between the interest earned by Gautam and Rudra from scheme M after 4 years is ₹ 4436.520, what is the rate of interest (pcpa) ?

(a) 17.8   (b) 18

(c) 16.5   (d) 20

(e) 15

145. What is the ratio of the total amount invested by Gautam in schemes O and Q together to the total amount invested by Rudra in the same schemes together ?

(a) 31 : 44   (b) 31 : 42

(c) 27 : 44   (d) 35 : 48

(e) 29 : 38

146. If scheme P offers compound interest (compounded half-yearly) @ 16 pcpa what would be sum of interest earned by Gautam and Rudra from scheme P after one year ?

(a) ₹ 10,244　　　　(b) ₹ 10,464

(c) ₹ 9,872　　　　(d) ₹ 9,984

(e) ₹ 9,442

147. The scheme O offers compound interest (compounded annually) @ 12 pcpa. What is difference between the interests earned by Gautam and Rudra from scheme O after 2 years ?

(a) ₹ 1628.16　　　　(b) ₹ 1584.38

(c) ₹ 1672.74　　　　(d) ₹ 1536.58

(e) ₹ 1722.96

148. What is the average amount invested by Gautam in schemes M, N, O, P and Q together ?

(a) ₹ 29,248　　　　(b) ₹ 30,562

(c) ₹ 31,126　　　　(d) ₹ 29,688

(e) ₹ 28,848

149. Rudra invested in scheme R for 4 years. If scheme R offers simple interest @ 7 pcpa for the first two years and then compound interest @ 10 pcpa (compounded annually) for the 3rd and 4th year, what will be the interest earned (in ₹) by Rudra after 4 years ?

(a) 13,112　　　　(b) 12,096

(c) 12,242　　　　(d) 12,364

(e) 11,886

150. The amount invested by Gautam in scheme S is equal to the amount invested by him in scheme N. The rate of interest (pcpa) of scheme S and N are the same. The only difference is that scheme S offers compound interest (compounded annually) while the scheme N offers simple interest. If the difference between the interest earned by Gautam from both the schemes after 2 years is ₹ 349.92, what is the rate of interest (in %) ?

(a) 9　　　　(b) 5

(c) 13　　　　(d) 11

(e) 7

TEST–IV : REASONING

Directions (Q. 151 – 154) : *Study the following information and answer the questions given below :*

J, K, L, M, N, O, P and R are sitting around a circular table, facing the centre. Each of them was born in a different year – 1971, 1975, 1979, 1980, 1981, 1984, 1985 and 1990, but not necessarily in the same order.

M is sitting second to the right to K. L is sitting third to the right of J. L and J were born before 1980. Only the one born in 1984 is sitting exactly between J and K. N, who is the eldest, is not an immediate neighbour of J or M. R is older than only M. R is sitting second to the left of P. P is not an immediate neighbour of N. J is younger than L. K was born before O.

151. Who is the second oldest in the group ?

(a) J　　　　(b) L

(c) K　　　　(d) P

(e) None of these

152. Who is sitting third to the right of O ?

(a) The one born in 1979

(b) The one born in 1980

(c) The one born in 1985

(d) The one born in 1984

(e) None of these

153. In which year was R born ?

(a) 1979　　　　(b) 1975

(c) 1980　　　　(d) 1985

(e) None of these

154. Which of the following statements is true regarding K ?

(a) K is sitting fourth to the right of R.

(b) The one who was born in 1975 is on the immediate left of K.

(c) K is younger than R.

(d) There are four persons sitting between N and K.

(e) None of these

Directions (Q. 155 – 160) : *In each of the questions below, three statements are given followed by conclusions/group of conclusions numbered I and II. You have to assume all the statements to be true even if they seem to be at variance with the commonly known facts and then decide which of the given two conclusions logically follows from the information given in the statements.*

Give answer

(a) if only conclusion I follows.

(b) if only conclusion II follows.

(c) if either conclusion I or conclusion II follows.

(d) if neither conclusion I nor conclusion II follows.

(e) if both conclusions I and II follow.

(155- 156) :

Statements :　All pens are books

　　　　　　　Some books are pages.

　　　　　　　All pages are papers.

155. Conclusions :　I.　No paper is a pen.

　　　　　　　　　II.　At least some pages are pens.

156. Conclusions :　I.　All books are papers.

　　　　　　　　　II.　Some books are papers.

(157- 158) :

Statements : Some Ds are Gs.

All Gs are Ks.

All Ks are Ls.

157. Conclusions : I. At least some Ds are Ls.

II. All Gs are Ls.

158. Conclusions : I. At least some Ks are Ds.

II. All Ds are Ls.

(159- 160) :

Statements : Some files are folders.

All folders are pockets.

No pocket is a bag.

159. Conclusions : I. All pockets are files.

II. All files are bags.

160. Conclusions : I. At least some bags are folders.

II. All folders are files.

Directions (Q. 161 – 162) : *Study the following information carefully and answer the question given below :*

There are five statues –L, M, N, O and P each of them having different height. Statue L is smaller than only statue M, Statue O is smaller than statue N. Statue O is longer than statue P. The height of the tallest stature is 20 feet. The height of the second smallest statue is 11 feet.

161. What will be the height of statue P ?

    (*a*) 13 feet   (*b*) 15 feet

    (*c*) 9 feet   (*d*) 12 feet

    (*e*) 14 feet

162. What will be the height of the third tallest statue?

    (*a*) 13 feet   (*b*) 10 feet

    (*c*) 19 feet   (*d*) 9 feet

    (*e*) 11 feet

Directions (Q. 163 – 164) : *Four of the following five are alike in a certain way and so form a group. Which is the one that does not belong to the group ?*

163. (*a*) Stem   (*b*) Branch

    (*c*) Leaf   (*d*) Web

    (*e*) Fruit

164. (*a*) Clone   (*b*) Replica

    (*c*) Duplicate   (*d*) Copy

    (*e*) Fake

Directions (Q. 165 – 169) : *Study the following information and answer the questions that follow :*

In a certain code language, 'hope to see you' is coded as 're so na di', 'please come to see the party' is coded as 'fi ge na di ke zo', 'hope to come' is coded as 'di so ge' and 'see you the party' is coded as 're fi zo na'.

165. How is 'please' coded in the given code language ?

    (*a*) di   (*b*) ke

    (*c*) fi   (*d*) na

    (*e*) None of these

166. What does the code 'so' stand for in the given code language ?

    (*a*) hope   (*b*) come

    (*c*) see   (*d*) to

    (*e*) None of these

167. How is 'party' coded in the given code language ?

    (*a*) Either 're' or 'fi'   (*b*) Either 'zo' or 'na'

    (*c*) Either 'zo' or 'fi'   (*d*) Either 'zo' or 'ge'

    (*e*) Either 'ke' or 'fi'

168. How will 'please see you' be coded in the given code language ?

    (*a*) re na ke   (*b*) so re na

    (*c*) zo re na   (*d*) na di ke

    (*e*) ke re ge

169. Which of the following will be coded as 'so di re' in the given code language ?

    (*a*) you see hope   (*b*) hope you please

    (*c*) hope you come   (*d*) the hope to

    (*e*) you hope to

Directions (Q. 170 – 173) : *In these questions, relationship between different elements is shown in the statements. The statements are followed by two conclusions.*

Give answer

(*a*) if only conclusion I is true.

(*b*) if only conclusion II is true.

(*c*) if either conclusion I or II true.

(*d*) if neither conclusion I nor II is true.

(*e*) if both conclusions I and II are true.

170. Statements : $A \geq B = C, B < D \leq E$

    Conclusions : I. $D > A$

II. $E > C$

171. Statements : $L > U \geq K; Z < U < R$

    Conclusions : I. $L > Z$

II. $K < R$

172. Statements : $Y < J = P \geq R > I$

    Conclusions : I. $J > I$

II. $Y < R$

173. Statements : $V \geq K > M = N; M > S; T < K$

    Conclusions : I. $T < N$

II. $V = S$

Directions (Q. 174 – 178) : *Each of the questions below consists of a questions and two statements numbered I and II given below it. You have to decide whether the data given in the statements are sufficient to answer the questions. Read both the statements.*

Give answer

(*a*) if the data in statement I alone are sufficient to answer the question, while the data in statement II alone are not sufficient to answer the question.

(*b*) if the data in statement II alone are sufficient to answer the question, while the data in statement I alone are not sufficient to answer the question.

(*c*) if the data either in statement I alone or in statement II alone are sufficient to answer the question.

(*d*) if the data given in both statements I and II together are not sufficient to answer the question.

(*e*) if the data in both statements I and II together are necessary to answer the question.

174. How is J related to K ?

    I. J's father P is brother of N. N is K's wife.

    II. J is son of P. P is brother of N. N is K's wife.

175. On which floor of the building does G stay ? (The building has five floors 1, 2, 3, 4, 5)

    I. Only the even-numbered floors are occupied and G does not stay on the second floor.

    II. G does not stay on an odd-numbered floor.

176. How many days did Raju take to complete his assignment ?

    I. Mohit correctly remembers that Raju took more than 3 days but less than 9 days to complete his assignment.

    II. Mina corrrectly remembers that Raju took more than 7 days but less than 11 days to complete his assignment.

177. How is the word 'GATES' coded in the code language ?

    I. 'BRICK' is coded as "LDJSC" and 'PIN' is coded as 'OJQ'.

    II. 'WATER' is coded as 'SFUBX' and 'DISH' is coded as 'ITJE'.

178. Among A, B, C, D which school has the highest number of students ?

    I. School A has fewer students than school D.

    II. School C has fewer students than school D.

Directions (Q. 179 – 183) : *Study the following information to answer the given questions :*

Six persons C, D, E, F, G and H are standing in a straight line facing north but not necessarily in the same order. D is standing second to the right of F. C is standing fourth to the left of H and H is not standing on the extreme end of the line. E is standing second to the right of D.

179. What is the position of G with respect to E ?

    (*a*) Immediate left   (*b*) Second to the left

    (*c*) Third to the left   (*d*) Third to the right

    (*e*) None of these

180. Which of the following pairs represents the people standing at the extreme ends of the line ?

    (*a*) F, H   (*b*) C, E

    (*c*) D, E   (*d*) C, H

    (*e*) None of these

181. Who is standing second to the right of C ?

    (*a*) F   (*b*) D

    (*c*) G   (*d*) E

    (*e*) None of these

182. Four of the following five are alike in a certain way based on their positions in the above arrangement and so form a group. Which of the following does not belong to that group ?

    (*a*) C, G   (*b*) G, E

    (*c*) G, H   (*d*) D, E

    (*e*) F, D

183. If all the persons are asked to stand in alphabetical order from left to right, the positions of how many will remain unchanged ?

    (*a*) One

    (*b*) Two

    (*c*) Three

    (*d*) None

    (*e*) None of these

Directions (Q. 184 – 188) : *In each question below is given a statement followed by three courses of action numbered A, B and C. A course of action is a step or administrative decision to be taken for improvement, follow-up or further action with regard to the problem, policy, etc. On the basis of the information given in the statement, you have to assume everything in the statement to be true, then decide which of the suggested courses of action logically follows for pursuing.*

184. Statement : There has been a continuous increase in the number of dropout students of Govt-run primary schools in the state.

Courses of action :

(A) Govt should immediately set up a committee to review the situation and suggest measures to reverse the trend.

(B) Govt should conduct orientation programmes for parents of the students, emphasising on the need for educating their children.

(C) Govt should close down such state-run primary schools where dropout rates are more than fifty per cent.

(*a*) Only (A) follows

(*b*) Only (B) follows

(*c*) Only (C) follows

(*d*) Only (A) and (B) follows

(*e*) None of these

185. Statement : Every year during monsoon, the condition of most of the roads in the city deteriorates causing immense problem to the commuters.

Courses of action :

(A) The civic body should include a heavy penalty clause while awarding future contracts for road repairs.

(B) The civic officials in charge of maintenance of city roads should be asked to explain why the condition of the roads worsens every year.

(C) General public should avoid taking their vehicles out during monsoon.

(*a*) Only (A) follows

(*b*) Only (B) follows

(*c*) Only (A) and (B) follow

(*d*) Only (B) and (C) follow

(*e*) None of these

186. Statement : During the past few days more and more number of indoor patients of the local Govt hospital have been diagnosed to be suffering from malaria.

Courses of Action :

(A) All such patients as are suffering from malaria should immediately be discharged from the hospital.

(B) The hospital authority should immediately put a ban on admitting new patients into the hospital.

(C) All such patients as are suffering from malaria should be kept in an isolated ward.

(*a*) Only (A) follows

(*b*) Only (B) follows

(*c*) Only (C) follows

(*d*) None follows

(*e*) None of these

187. Statement : Many public sector undertakings have been making losses for the past few years and the situation is equally bad in the current year.

Courses of action :

(A) These loss-making public sector companies should immediately be closed down.

(B) The Govt should scout for potential buyers in the private sector to sell these companies to get back part of the investments made by the Govt.

(C) All the employees of these companies should be retrenched with adequate compensation and the fixed assets may be put up for sale.

(*a*) None follows

(*b*) Only (A) and (B) follow

(*c*) Only (B) and (C) follow

(*d*) All (A), (B) and (C) follow

(*e*) None of these

188. Statement : Many shops in the local market have extended their shops and occupied most part of the footpath in front of their shops.

Courses of action :

(A) The civic authority should immediately activate a task force to clear all the footpaths encroached by the shop owners.

(B) The civic authority sould charge hefty penalty to the shop owners for occupying the footpath.

(C) The civic authority should set up a monitoring system so that such encroachments do not recur in future.

(*a*) None follows

(*b*) Only (A) and (B) follow

(*c*) Only (B) and (C) follow

(*d*) All (A), (B) and (C) follow

(*e*) None of these

189. In which of the following expressions will the expression 'P < F' be definitely false ?

(*a*) $F = B > P \leq M$ (*b*) $P > B \geq M = F$

(*c*) $P \leq B < F \leq M$ (*d*) $B < P \leq M < F$

(*e*) None of these

Directions (Q. 190 – 191) : *Read the following information carefully and answer the questions which follow :*

'A × B' means A is son of B.

'A + B' means A is father of B.

'A > B' means A is daughter of B.

'A < B' means A is wife of B.

190. Which of the following pairs of persons represent first cousins with regard to the relations given in the expressions, if it is provided that A is the sister of J, 'L > V < J + P' and 'S × A < D + F < E + K' ?

(*a*) LP   (*b*) SP

(*c*) SK   (*d*) SF

(*e*) Can't be determined

191. What will come in place of question mark (?), if it is provided that M is grandmother of F in the expression 'F × R < S ? M' ?

(*a*) >

(*b*) <

(*c*) +

(*d*) ×

(*e*) Can't be determined

192. In which of the following expressions will the expression P < M be definitely true ?

(a) M < R > P ≥ S   (b) M ≥ S = P < F

(c) Q < M < F = P   (d) P = A < R < M

(e) None of these

193. In a class of 42 children, Joseph's rank is sixteenth from the top. Kevin is seven ranks below joseph. What is Kevin's rank from the bottom ?

(a) 22nd   (b) 20th

(c) 19th   (d) 23rd

(e) 25th

Directions (Q. 194 – 200) : *Study the following information carefully and answer the questions given below :*

A word and number arrangement machine when given an input line of words and numbers rearranges them following a particular rule in each step. The following is an illustration of input and various steps of rearrangement. (All the numbers are two digit numbers).

sInput	Sweet	46	Nice	36	Friend	26	Help	96	Bright	76	Kind	66
Step I	Sweet	46	Nice	36	Friend	26	Help	Bright	76	Kind	66	96
Step II	Sweet	Nice	46	36	Friend	26	Help	Bright	Kind	66	76	96
Step III	Sweet	Nice	Kind	46	36	Friend	26	Help	Bright	66	76	96
Step IV	Sweet	Nice	Kind	Help	36	Friend	26	Bright	46	66	76	96
Step V	Sweet	Nice	Kind	Help	Friend	26	Bright	36	46	66	76	96
Step V	Sweet	Nice	Kind	Help	Friend	Bright	26	36	46	66	76	96

And Step VI is the last step of the rearrangement as the desired arrangement is obtained.

As per rules follow in the above steps, find out in each of the questions the appropriate step for the given input.

Input : arrow 98 paint 58 lamb 38 each 78 great 18 most 48 rent 88

194. Which word/number would be fifith to the left of the sixth element from the right in the Step V ?

(a) great

(b) arrow

(c) lamb

(d) 38

(e) 48

195. Which of the following represents the position of "58" in the step IV ?

(a) Eighth from left

(b) Third from right

(c) Ninth from left

(d) Eleventh from left

(e) Fifth from right

196. How many elements (words/ numbers) are there between "most" and "78" as they appear in the Step VI ?

(a) Eight

(b) Seven

(c) Nine

(d) Five

(e) Four

197. Which step number is the following output? rent paint most arrow 58 lamb 38 each great 18 48 78 88 98

(a) There is no such step

(b) Step II

(c) Step V

(d) Step VI

(e) Step III

198. Which element (word/number) would be at the elevent position from the right in the Step III ?

(a) lamb   (b) arrow

(c) 58   (d) 38

(e) each

199. Which element (word/number) would be at the sixth position from the left in the Step VI?

(a) 18   (b) arrow

(c) great   (d) each

(e) 38

200. At which of the following positions "great" would appear from the left in the Step V ?

(a) Fifth   (b) Sixth

(c) Fourth   (d) Second

(e) Third

ANSWERS

1. (c)	2. (e)	3. (c)	4. (b)	5. (a)	6. (b)	7. (a)	8. (a)	9. (d)	10. (e)
11. (c)	12. (a)	13. (d)	14. (a)	15. (a)	16. (d)	17. (a)	18. (e)	19. (e)	20. (c)
21. (b)	22. (c)	23. (d)	24. (a)	25. (b)	26. (b)	27. (e)	28. (d)	29. (b)	30. (a)
31. (b)	32. (d)	33. (c)	34. (e)	35. (d)	36. (a,d)	37. (b,c)	38. (e)	39. (d)	40. (a)
41. (b)	42. (e)	43. (b)	44. (d)	45. (e)	46. (c)	47. (a)	48. (d)	49. (a)	50. (c)
51. (a)	52. (b)	53. (a)	54. (a)	55. (d)	56. (e)	57. (b)	58. (d)	59. (e)	60. (a)
61. (c)	62. (a)	63. (a)	64. (a)	65. (e)	66. (d)	67. (d)	68. (b)	69. (a)	70. (b)
71. (d)	72. (a)	73. (a)	74. (d)	75. (e)	76. (b)	77. (b)	78. (e)	79. (e)	80. (d)
81. (a)	82. (b)	83. (c)	84. (d)	85. (a)	86. (c)	87. (b)	88. (e)	89. (c)	90. (e)
91. (a)	92. (c)	93. (a)	94. (b)	95. (d)	96. (d)	97. (b)	98. (b)	99. (b)	100. (e)
101. (e)	102. (b)	103. (d)	104. (c)	105. (a)	106. (b)	107. (d)	108. (c)	109. (d)	110. (b)
111. (a)	112. (e)	113. (b)	114. (d)	115. (d)	116. (e)	117. (d)	118. (c)	119. (e)	120. (c)
121. (d)	122. (a)	123. (b)	124. (b)	125. (e)	126. (b)	127. (c)	128. (c)	129. (b)	130. (c)
131. (e)	132. (a)	133. (b)	134. (d)	135. (e)	136. (d)	137. (b)	138. (a)	139. (b)	140. (d)
141. (a)	142. (e)	143. (e)	144. (c)	145. (a)	146. (d)	147. (a)	148. (a)	149. (a)	150. (e)
151. (b)	152. (a)	153. (d)	154. (e)	155. (d)	156. (c)	157. (e)	158. (a)	159. (d)	160. (d)
161. (c)	162. (a)	163. (d)	164. (e)	165. (b)	166. (a)	167. (c)	168. (a)	169. (e)	170. (b)
171. (e)	172. (a)	173. (d)	174. (b)	175. (a)	176. (e)	177. (c)	178. (d)	179. (c)	180. (b)
181. (c)	182. (b)	183. (a)	184. (d)	185. (d)	186. (d)	187. (a)	188. (c)	189. (b)	190. (b)
191. (e)	192. (d)	193. (b)	194. (c)	195. (d)	196. (a)	197. (a)	198. (b)	199. (d)	200. (a)

EXPLANATIONS

1. 'Volatile' refers to something that is likely to change in a very sudden or extreme way. Therefore, its antonym is option (c), stable.

2. The passage states that the number of dependents grow with an increase in population and in such a scenario, growth becomes difficult. Hence, option (e) is the correct answer.

3. Both (a) and (c) can be said about the agriculture and industry sectors in India. Refer to the lines "The current situation in India…overtaken both agriculture and industry… " and "… growth in service sector can and will support the growth in the agricultural and industrial sectors." Hence, option (c) is the correct answer.

4. The passage says that a growth window will open in the next two decades. This will happen because the ratio between the working population and the total population will rise. This means that that working population will be more than the dependent population. Hence, option (b) is the correct answer.

5. 'Prerequisite' means something that you officially must have or do before you can have or do something else. Hence, option (a) is the correct answer.

6. The latter part of the sentence says that people should be moved from unemployment to employment, which means that job opportunities should be created in these sectors. The given phrase means that efforts should be made to improve the sectors that are not working properly. This meaning has been brought about in option (b), rendering it the correct answer.

7. 'Perspective' means viewpoint. Hence, option (*a*) is the correct answer.

8. Only option (*a*) is true as per the passage. Refer to the lines "It hasn't followed traditional growth…skipped the manufacturing stage and has jumped from the agricultural stage to service stage…". Hence, option (*a*) is the correct answer. Option (*b*) is incorrect since the passage says that the IT sector is booming. Option (*c*) is incorrect since the passage clearly says that there is restriction on the movement of labour. Option (*d*) is incorrect since the passage says that there is lack of growth in manufacturing sector, which causes dependence on other countries.

9. Option (*a*) is incorrect since the passage clearly says that India is a service oriented economy. Option (*b*) is incorrect since the passage states that India has jumped straight from agriculture sector to service stage and has skipped manufacturing stage, which is the main reason for India's growth in service sector. Option (*c*) is also incorrect since it is nowhere stated in the passage. Only option (*d*) can be inferred from the passage and hence, is the correct answer.

10. 'Massive' here means vast. Hence, option (*e*) is the correct answer.

11. 'Entail' means to have (something) as a part, step, or result. Hence, option (*c*), involve, is the correct answer.

12. The passage talks about how education can be imparted through technology. Hence, option (*a*) is the correct answer.

13. (*a*) is incorrect because the passage says that the criteria should be changed. Nothing is said about the way certification is granted. (*b*) is incorrect because nothing is said about the school/college premises loosing importance. (*c*) is correct as the third paragraph of the passage clearly says that student-professor collaboration will determine what content is to be assigned and how student will attain mastery of it. Hence, option (*d*) is the correct answer.

14. 'Mitigating' means making something less severe, harmful or painful. Hence, its opposite will be option (*a*), 'aggravating'.

15. 'Personalise' means customize. Hence, option (*a*) is the correct answer.

16. The third paragraph says that with the onset of technology driven education, large classrooms, in which everyone learned at the same pace, will not survive. This means that the pace of learning for each student will be different. Therefore, (*a*) is correct. Refer to the line "In such cases, timing issues…   students hands… ". Therefore, (*b*) also follows. From the third paragraph we can infer that the role of teachers will change and become one of being the provider of tailored learning content. It says that the onset of technology-aided education will lead to customized and collaborative learning process. It further says that both students and teachers will determine what content will be assigned to practice methods. Therefore, (*c*) is also correct. Hence, option (*d*) is the correct answer.

17. 'Impediment' means bar or hindrance. Hence, option (*a*), freedom, is the correct answer.

18. 'Naught' means nothing. 'Will be for naught' means will amount to nothing.

19. Refer to the last paragraph of the passage. All the options can be said to be true about cheating. Hence, option (*e*) is the correct answer.

20. (*a*) is incorrect as the second paragraph clearly says that full potential can only be enjoyed if everyone involved in the process takes risks. The author in the second paragraph says that educationalists, technologists and classroom teachers must be encouraged to experiment and innovate. Therefore, (*b*) follows. The author in the last sentence of the second paragraph warns the readers of the people who may not allow certain changes for their own benefits. Therefore, (*c*) follows. Hence, option (*c*) is the correct answer.

21. 'Torment' means to cause to feel extreme physical or mental pain. 'Agonize' also means to cause to suffer torture or anguish. Hence, option (*b*) is the correct answer.

22. Something is referred to as 'striking' when it is unusual or extreme in a way that attracts attention. So, its antonym is 'unimpressive'. Hence, option (*c*) is the correct answer.

23. Something that is fashionable can be called stylish. Hence, option (*d*) is the correct answer.

24. 'Disclose' means to make something known to the public. 'Withhold' means to hold something back. Hence, option (*a*) is the correct answer.

25. 'Devastated' is the same as 'ruined'. Hence, option (*b*) is the correct answer.

26. A holiday is 'observed' and not 'attended', 'believed', 'accepted' or 'adhered'. Hence, option (*b*) is the correct answer.

27. Only 'forced' or 'threatened' can fit in the first blank. A victim will not be 'forced' into preparing her complaint. She can be encouraged into filling a complaint. Therefore, option (*d*) is incorrect. Option (*e*) correctly brings about the meaning of the sentence that the victim was threatened to take back her complain. Hence, option (*e*) is the correct answer.

28. The sentence says that the management is pro-cleanliness. Therefore, pardoning employees who spit and smoke in the office does not make sense. Also, warning can be given to all the employees, warning only the specific people do not make sense. Therefore, options (*c*) and (*e*) are incorrect. Option (*a*) is incorrect since it suggests that the management does not care if an employee spits or smokes after or before the office hours. 'Office environment' refers to the kind of atmosphere there is at office. It does not go with the meaning of the sentence. Therefore, option (*b*) is also incorrect. Only option (*d*) fits in the meaning of the sentence and is hence, the answer.

29. The sentence means that government is willing to change the method of estimating the output of steam engine. The only word that fits in the second blank is 'used'. Hence, option (*b*) is the correct answer.

30. 'There is a need to' suggests that the women participation in labour force is reducing. To overcome the problem, the best thing to do is to improve opportunities for them. Hence, option (*a*) is the correct answer.

For questions 31-35:
The correct sequence is CEBFAD. 'As this happens' in E refers to the fact that a child's nervous system becomes mature, which is mentioned in C.EBF is a mandatory sequence. 'These actions' in B refers to 'increasingly complex actions' in E and 'they' in F refers to 'parents' in B. AD again is a mandatory pair. A says that variation is normal. D adds a condition to it and says that unless some kind of disability exists, all children begin to exhibit certain motor skills.

31. The third sentence after rearrangement is B.

32. The sixth sentence after rearrangement is D.

33. The first sentence after rearrangement is C.

34. The second sentence after rearrangement is E.

35. The fourth sentence after rearrangement is F.

36. The sentence has two errors. In option (*a*), 'for' should be replaced by 'to', 'Attributing' means regarding something as being caused by. It takes the preposition 'to' and not 'for' after it. 'Easing', in part (*d*), should be replaced by 'ease'. 'To easing' is incorrect grammar. The correct phrase should be 'was committed to ease this supply side bottleneck.'

37. The sentence has two errors. In option (*b*), 'of' should be replaced with 'to' and in option (*c*), 'for' should be replaced with 'a'.

38. The sentence is correct in its given form. Hence, option (*e*) is the correct answer.

39. The error is in option (*d*). 'To determining' is grammatically incorrect. It should be replaced by 'to determine'.

40. 'On' has been incorrectly used in option (*a*). The correct usage is 'to identify'.

41. Disasters lead to significant loss or in other words, they result in significant loss. Hence, option (*b*) is the correct answer.

42. Disasters lead to or result in structural damages. Hence, option (*e*) is the correct answer.

43. Disaster mismanagements happen because of non-structural factors and ineffective leadership, i.e., non-structural factors and ineffective leadership are responsible for disaster managements. Hence, option (*b*) is the correct answer.

44. 'Vulnerable' means open to attack. The sentence means that India is susceptible to disasters. Hence, option (*d*) is the correct answer. Option (*b*) is incorrect as the blank does not require a noun here. Had it been 'susceptible', it would have been correct.

45. The correct answer is option (*e*). The sentence means that emergency management is required in all parts of the world.

46. The sentence says that effective policies help in mitigating the impact of disaster. Therefore, the best option that fits in the blank is 'vital', rendering option (*c*) the correct answer.

47. 'Recognize' means to acknowledge or to accept that something is true or exists. Hence, option (*a*) is the correct answer.

48. 'Dearth' refers to the state or condition of not having enough of something. The sentence means that there isn't any shortage of issues that demand government attention.

49. 'Unless' suggests that the blank will take a word that suggests that disaster management rarely acquires importance in the agenda of governance.

50. The correct phrase is 'on an urgent basis'. Hence, option (*c*) is the correct answer.

101. Number of students with mechanical specialization after increase = 2544
Number of students with electronics specialization after decrease = 1436.5

Percentage = 177.09 ≈ 178

102. Total number of students in institute R = 780
Total number of students in institute V = 880
Required Ratio = 39 : 44

103. Total number of students from IT specialization = 1900

Total number of students from mechanical specialisation = 2120

Difference = 220

104. Total number of students in institute P after increase = $1.15 \times 340 = 391$

Total number of students in institute Q after increase = $1.22 \times 300 = 366$

Total number of students in institute R after increase = $1.10 \times 260 = 286$

Total number of students = 1043

105. Let the number of students be 5x, 6x and 7x respectively

So, $\qquad 18x = 900$

$\qquad\qquad x = 50$

$\therefore$ Students having liking towards music
$$= 50 \times 5 = 250$$

106. Number of boys in institute
$$P = 0.5 \times 220 = 110$$

Number of boys in institute
$$T = 0.45 \times 280 = 126$$

Number of boys in institute
$$U = 0.52 \times 280 = 145.6$$

Total number of boys
$$= 381.6 \approx 386$$

107. (*a*) Total advertisement revenue generated from online version by magazine T in all the months = ₹1050 Thousand

Total advertisement revenue generated from printed version by magazine T in all the months = ₹924 Thousand

So, clearly the online version generated more revenue than printed version.

(*b*) The advertisement revenue in January
$$= ₹ 20,08,000$$

The advertisement revenue in June
$$= ₹ 20,70,000$$

Difference between revenue in January and June $\quad = ₹ 62,000$

(c) There is no such magazine which has its revenue of printed version in increasing fashion.

108. Total revenue generated from printed version of Magazine U = ₹ 840 Thousand

Total revenue generated from online version of Magazine U = ₹1134

Difference = ₹ 294

$$\text{Percentage} = \frac{294}{1134} = 35\%$$

109. Total sum of the revenues of Magazine R in March = ₹ 3,26,000

Total sum of the revenues of Magazine R in April = ₹ 3,75,000

Difference = ₹ 49,000

$$\text{Percentage increase} = \frac{49000}{326000} \times 100 \approx 15$$

110. The ratio of advertisement revenue generated from printed version by Magazine P to advertisement revenue generated from online version by the same magazine in July
$$= \frac{204}{144} = \frac{17}{12}$$

$$\text{Required revenue} = \frac{108000}{12} \times 17 = ₹\, 1,53,000\,.$$

111. Total revenue in February from online version
$$= 171 + 139 + 149 + 223 + 217 + 190 = 1089$$

Total revenue in May from printed version
$$= 113 + 128 + 196 + 132 + 187 + 168 = 924$$

$$\text{Ratio} = \frac{1089}{924} = \frac{33}{28}$$

112. Total revenue generated by magazine P from printed version in January and April
$$= 169 + 163 = ₹ 332 \text{ thousand}$$

Total revenue generated by magazine S from printed version in February and June
$$= 223 + 177 = ₹ 400 \text{ thousand}$$

Difference = ₹ 68 thousand

$$\text{Percentage} = \frac{68}{400} \times 100 = 17\,\%$$

113. Total number of postgraduates
$$= \frac{80}{100} \times 3360 = 2688$$

Total number of female postgraduates
$$= 2688 - 1800 = 888$$

$$\text{Percentage} = \frac{888 \times 100}{\dfrac{5}{14} \times 3360} = 74\,\%$$

114. The second lowest is in H i.e 35.7%

115. Total number of male employees in B and H
$$= 1980 + 2160 = 4140$$

Total number of female employees in C and D
$$= 1210 + 2560 = 2640$$

$$\text{Ratio} = \frac{4140}{2640} = \frac{69}{44}$$

116. Average number of postgraduates in A, B and D =
$$\frac{1926 + 1872 + 2145}{3} = 1981$$

Average number of postgraduates in F, G and
$$H = \frac{2091 + 2046 + 2688}{3} = 2275$$

Difference = 294

117. Average number of employees is highest in Country C i.e. 165

118. Number of students playing carom and hockey together from school P = 360

Number of students playing carom and hockey together from school Q = 520

Percentage = $\dfrac{360}{520} = 69\dfrac{3}{13}\%$

119. Number of students after 15% increase
$$= 1.15 \times 740 = 851$$

Number of students after 5% decrease
$$= 0.95 \times 680 = 646$$

Difference = 205

120. Total sum = 0.40 × 180 + 0.35 × 320
$$+ \, 0.45 \times 240 = 292$$

121. Total number of students playing hockey from all the schools together = 1060

Total number of students playing cricket from all the schools together = 1340

Percentage = 79.10% ≈ 79%

122. Total number of students selected for national level from school
$$\text{P} = 25\% \text{ of } 40\% \text{ of } 220 = 22$$

Total number of students selected for national level from school
$$\text{T} = \dfrac{2}{3} \text{ of } 45\% \text{ of } 280 = 84$$

Sum = 84+22 = 106

123. Total urban population of Maharashtra and

Odisha $= \left(\dfrac{17}{45} \times 2250000\right) + \left(\dfrac{5}{16} + 1136000\right)$
$$= 850000 + 355000 = 1205000$$

Total population of Maharashtra and Odisha
$$= 2250000 + 1136000 = 3386000$$

Percentage = $\dfrac{1205000}{3386000} \times 100 \approx 35.59$

124. Urban Population of Maharashtra = 850000

Rural Population of Maharashtra = 1400000

Difference = 550000

Percentage = $\dfrac{550000}{1400000} \times 100 \approx 39\%$

Alternate solution:

Required percentage = $\dfrac{28-17}{28} \times 100 \approx 39\%$

125. Total illiterate population of West Bengal, Odisha and Madhya Pradesh
$$= 880000 + 355000 + 410500 = 1645500$$

Total population of West Bengal, Odisha and Madhya Pradesh = 5258000

Percentage = $\dfrac{1645500}{5258000} \times 100 = 31.2\%$

126. Total number of graduates in Madhya Pradesh
$$= \dfrac{35}{100} \times \dfrac{3}{4} \times 1642000 = 431025$$

Total number of graduates in Uttaranchal
$$= \dfrac{44}{100} \times \dfrac{3}{4} \times 248000 = 81840$$

Difference = 349185

127. Total number of literates in Odisha = 781000

Total number of literates in West Bengal
$$= 1600000$$

Total number of literates in Maharashtra
$$= 1406250$$

Total number of graduates in Odisha
$$= 296780$$

Total number of graduates in West Bengal
$$= 672000$$

Total number of graduates in Maharashtra
$$= 675000$$

Total graduates = 1643780

128. Total female population of Tamil Nadu and Jharkhand = 432000 + 984000 = 1416000

Total male population of Tamil Nadu and Jharkhand = 1066000 + 528000 = 1594000

Ratio = $\dfrac{1416000}{1594000} = 708 : 797$

(Q. 129 – 135) :

Language	dentistry		homoeopathy	
	boys	girls	boys	girls
English	18	54	64	84
Hindi	45	27	48	84
Bengali	72	27	16	28
English + Hindi	108	54	48	112
Bengali + Hindi	63	27	32	84
Bengali + English	90	54	80	112
bengali+ Hindi + English	54	27	32	56
Total	450	270	320	560

129. Total number of students studying Dentistry who know only either English or Hindi
$$= 108 + 54 = 162$$

130. Total number of students in the college who knows all the three languages = 169

131. Total number of girls who know bengali in the college = 415

Percentage = $\dfrac{415}{560 + 270} = 50$

132. Total number of students studying homeopathy who do not know English
$$= 48 + 16 + 32 + 84 + 28 + 84 = 292$$

133. Total number of girls who know hindi = 336

Total number of girls who know English = 224

$$\text{Ratio} = \frac{224}{336} = \frac{2}{3}$$

134. Total number of studying dentistry who know at least two languages

= 108 + 63 + 90 + 54 + 27 + 27 + 54 + 54 = 477

$$\text{Percentage} = \frac{477}{720} \times 100 = 66\frac{1}{4}\%$$

135. Total number of girls in the college who do not know Hindi

= 54 + 27 + 54 + 84 + 28 + 112 = 359

$$\text{Percentage} = \frac{359}{830} \times 100 = 43.2 \approx 43\%$$

136. Total number of watches sold by F and H = 17% of 56000 = 9520

Total number of watches sold by C and H = 23% of 56000 = 12880

Total number of sports watches sold by C and H = 19% of 32000 = 6080

Total number of luxury watches sold by C and H = 12880 – 6080 = 6800

$$\text{Percentage less} = \frac{9520 - 6800}{9520} \times 100 = 28\frac{4}{7}\%$$

137. Total watches sold by D = 15% of 56000 = 8400

Total number of sports watches sold by C, F and G = 21% of 32000 = 6720

Difference = 1680

$$\text{Percentage} = \frac{1680}{6720} \times 100 = 25\%$$

138. Total number of watches sold by Store D = 32% of 32000 = 10240

Total number of watches sold by Store C, F and G = 22% of 56000 = 12320

Ratio = 64 : 77

139. Total number of watches sold by A, D, E, F and H = 70% of 56000 = 39200

Total number of sports watches sold by A, D, E, F and H = 71% of 32000 = 22720

Total number of luxury watches sold by A, D, E, F and H = 39200 – 22720 = 16480

$$\text{Average} = \frac{16480}{5} = 3296$$

140. Number of luxury watches sold by A after increase

= 1.1 × (18% of 56000 – 16% of 32000) = 5456

Number of luxury watches sold by D after increase

= 1.35 × (15% of 56000 – 13% of 32000) = 5724

Number of luxury watches sold by E after increase

= 1.15 × (20% of 56000 – 22% of 32000) = 4784

Number of watches sold by A, D and E after increase = 15964

141. Central angle = 11% of 360° = 39.6°

142. Total number of sports watches sold by E and F = 30% of 32000 = 9600

Total number of watches sold by E = 20% of 56000 = 11200

$$\text{Percent} = 85\frac{5}{7}$$

143. Average no. of sports watches sold by store B, C, G and H

$$= \left(\frac{16 + 7 + 6 + 12}{100}\right) \times \frac{32000}{4}$$

$$= \frac{13120}{4} = 3280$$

Average no. of (luxury + sports) watches sold by store B, C, G and H

$$= \left(\frac{11 + 14 + 5 + 9}{100}\right) \times \frac{56000}{4} = 5260$$

No. of luxury watches sold

= 5260 – 3280 = 1980

Required difference

= 3280 – 1980 = 1300

144. Difference between the investments

$$= 84000\left(\frac{54 - 46}{100}\right) = 6720$$

Difference in interest in 4 years = 4436.520

$$= \frac{6720 \times 4 \times r}{100} = 4436.520$$

$$\Rightarrow r = 16.5\%$$

145. Total investment of both together;

In scheme O = 32000

In scheme Q = 64000

Gautam's Investment in Scheme O

$$= \frac{40}{100} \times 32000 = 12800$$

$\therefore$ Rudra's Investment in Scheme O

= 32000 – 12800 = 19200

Gautam's investment in Scheme Q

$$= \frac{42}{100} \times 64000 = 26800$$

$\therefore$ Rudra's Investment = 64000 – 26880 = 37120

Gautam's total investment in Scheme O & Q

= 39680

Rudra's total investment in Scheme O & Q

= 56320

$$\therefore \text{Required ratio} = \frac{39680}{56320} = \frac{31}{44}$$

146. Interest earned

$$= 60000\left[1 + \frac{8}{100}\right]^2 - 60000 = ₹\,9984$$

147. Interest earned by Gautam in scheme O

$$= \left[\frac{40}{100} \times 32000\left[1+\frac{12}{100}\right]^2\right] - \frac{40}{100} \times 32000$$

$$= 3256.32$$

Interest earned by Rudra in scheme O

$$= \left[\frac{60}{100} \times 32000\left[1+\frac{12}{100}\right]^2\right] - \frac{60}{100} \times 32000$$

$$= 4884.48$$

Difference = ₹1628.16

148. Average amount invested by Gautam in schemes M, N, O, P & Q together is,

$$= \left(\frac{\begin{array}{c}84 \times 0.54 + 72 \times 0.60 + 32 \times 0.40\\ + 60 \times 0.30 + 64 \times 0.42\end{array}}{5}\right) \times 1000$$

$$= \left(\frac{45.36 + 43.20 + 12.50 + 18 + 26.88}{5}\right) \times 1000$$

$$= 29.298 \times 1000 = ₹29248$$

149. Amount invested by Rudra

$$= \frac{36}{100} \times 96000 = ₹34560$$

Simple interest accrued $= \dfrac{34560 \times 7 \times 2}{100} = 4838.40$

Total Amount = 39398.40

Amount after 2 years at 10% compound interest = 47672.06

Interest = 47672.064 − 34560 = ₹13,112.06

$$\simeq ₹13,112$$

150. Investment of Gautam in scheme N = 72000

⇒ Investment of Gautam in scheme S = 72000

Difference between CI and SI for 2 years

$$= P\left(\frac{r}{100}\right)^2 = 349.92$$

$$\Rightarrow \quad r = \sqrt{\frac{349.92 \times 10000}{72000}} \approx 7\%$$

(Q.151–154):

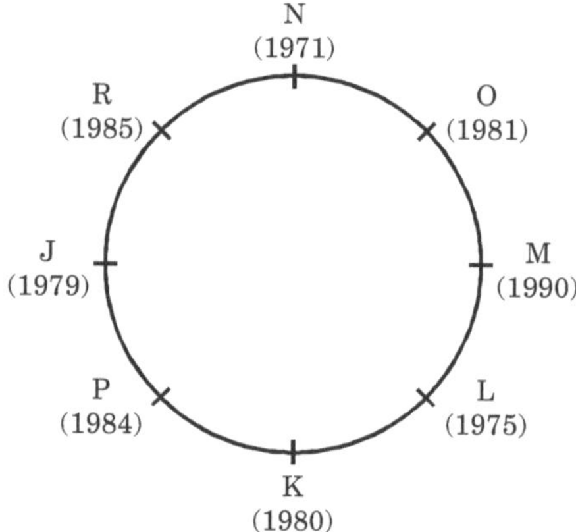

N > L > J > K > O > P > R > M

(Q.155–156):

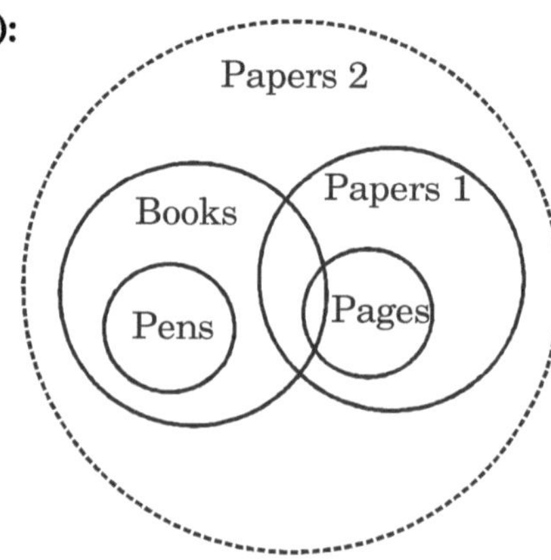

155. As shown in the Venn diagram, none of the conclusions follow. Hence, option (d) is the correct answer.

156. As shown in the Venn diagram, either of the conclusions will follow. Hence, option (c) is the correct answer.

(Q.157-158):

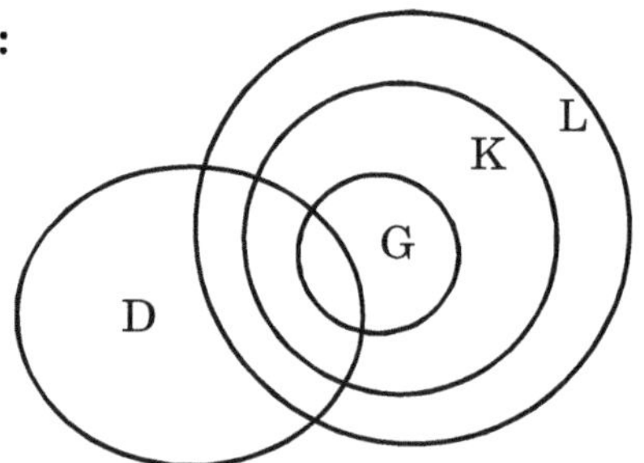

157. As shown in the Venn diagram, both the conclusions follow. Hence, option (e) is the correct answer.

158. As shown in the Venn diagram, only conclusion (a) follows. Hence, option (a) is the correct answer.

159.

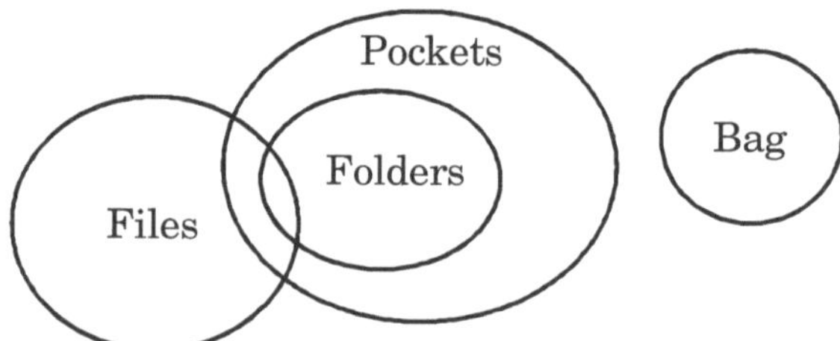

As shown in the Venn diagram, none of the conclusions follow. Hence, option (d) is the correct answer.

160. As shown in the Venn diagram, none of the conclusions follow. Hence, option (d) is the correct answer.

161. The answer sequence is P < O < N < L < M.

Here M being the tallest statue, M = 20 feet and O being the second smallest statue, O = 11 feet

Since P < O and O = 11 feet, then the value of P must be less than 11 feet, which is 9 feet.

162. The third tallest statue is N. Its value should lie between 20 feet and 11 feet. The answer 19 feet or 13 feet could be the answer. But as per the given information, L is only smaller to M, then the height of third tallest statue is 13 feet.

(Q.165–169) :

hope	to	see	you	please	come	the party
so	di	na	re	ke	ge	figo

(Q.170–173):

170. $A \geq B = C$ ....(i)

$B < D \leq E$ ....(ii)

From (i) and (ii) $A > B = C < D \leq E$, A & D cannot be compared whereas E > C is true.

Hence, conclusion I is not true and conclusion II is true.

171. $L > U \geq K$ ...(i)

$Z < U < R$ ....(ii)

From (i) and (ii), L > Z and K < R could be established. Hence both conclusions are true.

172. $Y < J = P \geq R > I$ ...(i)

From (i), Y & R cannot be compared whereas J > I could be established. Hence conclusion I is true.

173. $V \geq K > M = N$ ...(i)

$M > S$ ...(ii)

$T < K$ ...(iii)

From (i) and (ii),

$V \geq K > M = N > S$

So, V = S is not true.

From (i) and (iii),

$T < K > M = N$

So, T and N can't be compared. Hence neither conclusion I nor II is true.

174. From statement I, the gender of J is not clear. Hence it is not sufficient.

From statement II, the gender of J is male. Hence J is nephew of P. Thus statement II alone is sufficient.

175. From statement I, since only second and fourth floor is occupied, and G does not stay on second floor, then G must be staying on fourth floor. Hence statement I alone is sufficient to answer the question

From statement II, the answer cannot be determined. Hence statement II alone is not sufficient to answer the question.

176. From statement I, Raju worked for more than 3 days but less than 9 days whereas from statement II, Raju worked for more than 7 days but less than 11 days. Thus it is clear that Raju worked for 8 days. Thus both the statements together are required to answer the question.

177. From Statement I:

From Statement II:

From either statement I or II, the code for the word 'GATES' could be determined, which is 'TFUBH'.

178. From both the statements, no relation between school B and school D could be established. Thus option (d) is the answer.

(Q.179 – 183):

The correct order as per the given question is,

$$\underline{C}\ \underline{F}\ \underline{G}\ \underline{D}\ \underline{H}\ \underline{E}$$

184. The statement says that the number of dropouts is increasing in government run primary schools in the state. It is the government's duty to look into the matter and find out the reason for this trend. Also, the government should make the parents of the students aware about the importance of education. Hence, option (d) is the correct answer. Shutting down schools will not solve the problem. It will only discourage those students who are willing to attend school.

185. Since most of the roads deteriorate every year during monsoon, the reason can either be that the materials used are not of good quality or the roads are not maintained. If materials are not of good quality, then heavy penalty clause should be included in the contract. If roads are not maintained, then the civic officials in charge of maintenance should be asked to give an explanation. So, both (a) and (b) valid courses of actions. Hence, option (d) is the correct answer. (c) is not a good course of action as it will not solve the problem at hand.

186. Malaria is not a contagious disease. It is transmitted by the bite of a mosquito, which means that if someone near you has malaria, those mosquitoes that bite him are carrying the disease. So, keeping the patients in isolation will not help solve the problem. Also, discharging such patients will not help as other patients might still get malarial infection. Putting a ban on admitting new patients too will not help solve the problem. In such a situation, the hospital authorities should take steps to prevent malaria through medications, mosquito elimination and the prevention of bites. This idea is not brought about in any of the given courses of action. Hence, option (d), none follows, is the correct answer.

187. Public sector companies aim to provide public services. They have been set up for the betterment of the people at large. Closing down or selling all the loss making public sector companies is not a feasible option. The government will need to analyze as to which companies it would need to close down, sell off or divest. An umbrella decision cannot be taken for all the companies. Hence, none of the given courses of action are valid.

188. Extending shops and occupying part of footpath is both ethically and legally wrong. To prevent this, the civic authority should keep a check on such encroachments and penalize those who extend their shops illegally. Hence, option (*c*), both (*b*) and (*c*), is the correct answer. (*a*) is invalid since it is too extreme a measure. The word 'immediately' suggests that those shop owners should not even be given a warning or a few days time to remove the illegally extended part of their shops.

189. Option (*b*) clearly depicts that P > F

190. Given:

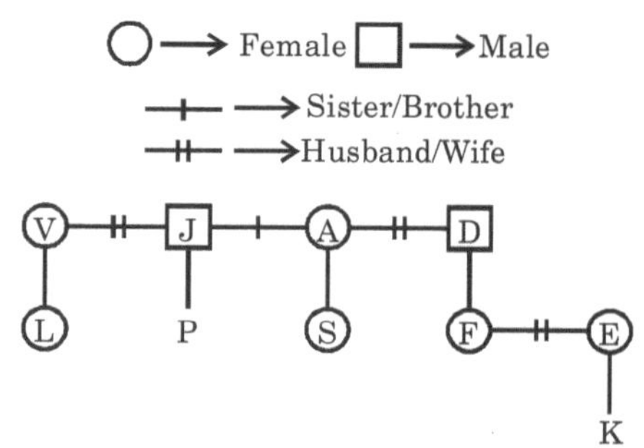

Clearly SP are first cousins.

191. Since in the given information, mother and son relation is not defined. Hence the answer cannot be determined

192. From option (*d*), it is clear that P is definitely less than M.

193. Since Kevin is seven ranks down Joseph, who is at 16th place from top, then Kevin holds 23rd rank from the top in the class of 42.
So, Kevin's rank from bottom would be $(42 - 23 + 1) = 20$.

(Q.194–200) :

In the given input, all the words are arranged in descending order from the left and the numbers are arranged in descending order from the right.
The answer sequence for the given input (I/P) is given below:

I/P	arrow	98	paint	58	lamb	38	each	78	great	18	most	48	rent	88
I	rent	arrow	paint	58	lamb	38	each	78	great	18	most	48	88	98
II	rent	paint	arrow	58	lamb	38	each	great	18	most	48	78	88	98
III	rent	paint	most	arrow	lamb	38	each	great	18	48	58	78	88	98
IV	rent	paint	most	lamb	arrow	each	great	18	38	48	58	78	88	98
V	rent	paint	most	lamb	great	arrow	each	18	38	48	58	78	88	98
VI	rent	paint	most	lamb	great	each	arrow	18	38	48	58	78	88	98

Printed by Libri Plureos GmbH in Hamburg,
Germany